# North A...

## a Lonely Planet travel survival kit

Damien Simonis
David Willett
Ann Jousiffe
Geoff Crowther
Hugh Finlay

**North Africa**

**1st edition**

**Published by**
**Lonely Planet Publications**
Head Office:    PO Box 617, Hawthorn, Vic 3122, Australia
Branches:       155 Filbert St, Suite 251, Oakland, CA 94607, USA
                10 Barley Mow Passage, Chiswick, London W4 4PH, UK
                71 bis rue du Cardinal Lemoine, 75005 Paris, France

**Printed by**
SNP Printing Pte Ltd, Singapore.

**Photographs by**

| | |
|---|---|
| Geoff Crowther (GC) | Damien Simonis (DS) |
| Hugh Finlay (HF) | Tony Wheeler (TW) |
| Ann Jousiffe (AJ) | David Willett (DW) |
| Peter Ptschelinzew (PP) | |

Front cover: Tuareg Camel Caravan,  Tom Owen Edmunds (The Image Bank)

**First Published**
April 1995

National Library of Australia Cataloguing in Publication Data

Simonis, Damien.
North Africa – a travel survival kit.

1st ed.
Includes index.
ISBN 0 86442 258 X.

1. Morocco – Guidebooks. 2. Africa, North – Guidebooks.
I. Jousiffe, Ann. II. Willett, David. III. Title.
(Series : Lonely Planet travel survival kit).

916.4045

text & maps © Lonely Planet 1995
photos © photographers as indicated 1995
climate charts compiled from information supplied by Patrick J Tyson, © Patrick J Tyson, 1995

### Damien Simonis

Damien is an Australian freelance journalist based in London. Since taking a degree in modern languages and working as a reporter and subeditor on the *Australian* in Sydney and the Melbourne *Age*, he has worked, studied and travelled extensively in Europe and the Arab world. Damien coordinated this first edition of *North Africa* and updated the introductory chapters and Morocco. He also wrote the text for the Arts & Crafts chapter. In addition to this guide, he has updated the *Jordan & Syria*, *Egypt & the Sudan* and *Morocco* travel survival kits, as well as contributing to shoestring guides such as *The Middle East*, *Africa* and *Mediterranean Europe*. When not travelling and writing for Lonely Planet, Damien has worked for the *Guardian*, the *Independent* and the *Sunday Times* in London, and written for publications in Australia, the UK and North America.

### David Willett

David is a freelance journalist based on the mid-north coast of New South Wales, Australia. He grew up in Hampshire, England, and wound up in Australia in 1980 after stints working on newspapers in Iran (1975-78) and Bahrain. He spent two years working as a subeditor on the Melbourne *Sun* before opting to live somewhere warmer. Between jobs, he has travelled extensively in Europe, the Middle East and Asia. David updated Tunisia and adapted Algeria for this book. He has also contributed to the *Mediterranean Europe* and *Africa* shoestrings.

### Ann Jousiffe

After spending 10 years working as an advertising photographer in London, Ann decided to abandon the sweet life and head for the wilder shores of freelance photojournalism. A love of deserts and ruined cities led her to specialise in the Middle East and North Africa, and Libya in particular. During the last six years, she has worked on assignments including Jordan, Syria, Turkey, Oman and, of course, Libya for UK and international magazines and newspapers. She has recently been involved in a campaign for the rights of abducted children and was co-organiser of a mass access visit for British mothers to visit their children in Libya. This trip was the subject of a Channel 4 *Cutting Edge* documentary. Ann wrote the section on Libya for this book, which is Ann's first Lonely Planet guide.

### Geoff Crowther

Born in Yorkshire, England, Geoff took to his heels early on in search of the miraculous, taking a break from a degree in biochemistry. The lure of the unknown took him to Kabul, Kathmandu and Lamu in the days before the overland bus companies began digging up the dirt along the tracks of Africa. In 1977, he wrote his first guide for Lonely Planet – *Africa on the cheap*. He has also written *South America on a shoestring*, travel survival kits to *Korea & Taiwan*, *Korea* and *East Africa* and has co-authored guides to *India* and *Malaysia, Singapore & Brunei*. Geoff was the co-author of *Morocco, Algeria & Tunisia*.

### Hugh Finlay

After an unsuccessful foray into academia in Melbourne, Hugh first hit the road in 1976, on a trail which eventually led him to Africa via Asia, Europe and the Middle East in the early 1980s. Since joining Lonely Planet in 1985, Hugh has co-authored with Geoff Crowther the LP travel survival kits to Kenya and East Africa. Other LP books he is involved with include *India*, *Australia* and *Malaysia, Singapore & Brunei*. Hugh was the co-author of *Morocco, Algeria & Tunisia*.

## From the Authors

**Damien Simonis** Thanks go to *MEED* and the *Guardian* in London, which, as always, lent access to their resources. Mohammed ben Madani, also in London, was helpful in the hunt for research material and insights into Moroccan life. Thanks also to the staff at Le Tiers Mythe bookshop in Paris for their indulgence while I rummaged through their wares.

The assistance of Abdelhamid Boumediene, secretary-general of the ONMT in Rabat, was indispensable.

In Tangier, Mohammed Abdel Aoui kindly showed me around some of the nooks and crannies of the kasbah. Thanks also to Mme Alawi Harrauni Aziza and Safi Abd ar-Razak in Meknès for their assistance. James Turner and Elizabeth Renshaw (UK) helped me out, shared a laugh and provided some invaluable tips on tea. I am grateful to Lichir el-Houcine in Taroudannt for letting me photograph his merchandise, and likewise to Mahna Mohammed in Tiznit. Thanks also to Ouhammou Mohammed of Tafraoute for his time and help. Brahim Toudaoui, of Imlil, gave me a hand during my all too brief stay in the High Atlas. Stuart & Gill (Aus) – it was an interesting trip back to Algeciras.

I am especially indebted to Michael Sklovsky for his expertise on Moroccan arts and crafts.

Many thanks to Michèle Nayman in London for holding the fort for me while I was on the road.

Above all, I owe an immeasurable debt of thanks to my wife, Lucrezia, for her help and support, and for making many things possible that would otherwise have been well beyond my reach.

**David Willett** My thanks to my partner, Rowan, and our son, Tom, for their patience and understanding. My view of Tunisia would not have been the same without the hospitality of my friends from Sousse – Larbi, Kamel, Lamia and Anis. Last, and by no means least, thanks to all at LP (Diana Saad in particular) for their support, advice and good humour.

**Ann Jousiffe** Many thanks to my husband, Peter, who helped out with the research; Abdulrazzag Gherwash and Bashir Abugeneh of Winzrik Travel & Tourism Services for their considerable help on the ground; Abdulaatif and his wife, Fatma, for their hospitality in Gabraoun; my guide and the drivers from Ghat who saw me safely across the desert; Haj, Yahya, Musa and the others (remember a shovel next time); Mohammed from Ghat for his kind hospitality; Dr Abdulrahman Yedder for his help and encyclopedic knowledge of Ghadhames; and Mustafa al-Alem, director of information at the Foreign Ministry, for all his patience and friendship. Last but not least, thanks to all the people of Libya who took so much time and trouble to help me on my travels.

## This Book

This book was adapted from Lonely Planet's *Morocco, Algeria & Tunisia: a travel survival kit*, first published in 1989 and written by Geoff Crowther and Hugh Finlay.

## From the Publisher

This first edition of *North Africa* was edited by Janet Austin, with the help of Adrienne Costanzo and Alison White. It was proofed by Diana Saad and Samantha Carew. Margie Jung handled the mapping, with the assistance of Jacqui Schiff, Sally Woodward, Matt King and Maliza Kruh. Margie was also responsible for the layout of the book. Glenn Beanland designed the section on Moroccan arts and crafts, and Margie, Maliza and Jane Hart drew the illustrations. Valerie Tellini designed the cover and Margie drew the title pages. Thanks to Michael Sklovsky for his assistance with the arts & crafts colour section.

Thanks to all the readers whose letters helped us with this new edition. They include:

Eric Antonow (USA), Todd Bailey (USA), Miss F L Barltrop (UK), Rhonda Bell, J Blase (NL), Pieter Blom (S), Mrs Pina Bonanni (I), Pam Bowers (UK), Warren K Braucher (USA), P J Bruyniks (NL), Mark

Bukawski (UK), Richard Bullock (USA), Tyge Busk (DK), Denise Cauchi (Aus), Ugo Pica Ciammarra (I), Michelle Claydon (Aus), Mike Collins (UK), Ronald Corlette-Theuil (F), Elsa Dalmasso (UK), Martien Das (NL), Rik De Clercq (B), Maria Demsar, Alice Dijkman (NL), Jan-Willem Doornenbal (NL), Gerhilde Egghart (A), David Elliot (UK), Joshua Emmott (USA), Martin Fiems (B), Nienke Gaastra (NL), C Garnier (UK), Marios Gavalas (UK), Annabel Gaywood (UK), Michael Geist (UK), Joseph Gourneau (USA), Sally Green (UK), Paul Gregory (UK), Francisco Guix Gros (Sp), Nils Hack (D), Bob Hammond (UK), Harry Hansma (NL), Brian Harrison (UK), Richard Haverkamp (C), Michael Hawley (USA), Alex Henderson (Aus), Esther Hommes (NL), Arpad Horvath (C), Tony Howard (UK), Liz Hughes (UK), Attila Ja'ndi (NL), Robert Jeffers, Gregers Jorgensen (DK), Anne Juhl (DK), Ronald Keijzer (NL), Greg Kennedy (Aus), Shelley & George Kissil (Isr), John Kitts (UK), Timon Koulmasis (F), Peter Kuijer (NL), Peter Lawson (UK), Michael Lee (UK), Russell Leonard (USA), Ian Lund (NL), Stefan Lundstrom (S), Rachel Manolson (UK), Eric Marienfeldt (F), Runar Mathisen (N), Gillean McCluskey (UK), Richard McHugh (Aus), Darren McLean (Aus), Francesco Melillo (I), Karla Milne (UK), Roger Mimo, Chris Murphy (UK), John Oei (USA), Jose Luis Cabo Pan (Sp), Jacques Paquin (C), Frank Patris (USA), Carlos Pimenta (B), Esther Piulman (NL), Julie Redgrove (UK), David E Reibscheid (UK), Judy Reid (UK), Theresa A Richards (USA), Deborah Roper (USA), Ineke Roverts (NL), Stuart Sanders (UK), Erik Schober (D), Liliane Schwob (C), Steve Scott (UK), Maria & Eric Searle (UK), T Seiden (D), Cpt Jeff Sheehan (USA), Jonathon Shellard (UK), Amy Silverston (USA), Austin Smith (USA), Robin Smith, Uta Specht (D), Miss A Spignesi, Rebecca Stancer (UK), B M Stanton (NZ), David Steinke (D), Donald Stevenson (UK), Syan Tapp (UK), Thomas Tesch (A), Alsion Thackray (UK), Laurent Tognazzi (F), Kathleen Torkano (NL), Yumiko Uehara, Anton Van Niekerk (NL), Bas Verboom (NL), L Vernon (C), Grit Vltavsky (D), George S Vrontos, Florence Vuillet (F), Adrian Wainer (UK), Amanda Waite (UK), D Walling (C), Steven Whiffen (UK), Ronald Wijchers (NL), J P Wilson (UK) and Julie Yahiat (Aus).

A – Austria, Aus – Australia, B – Belgium, C – Canada, D – Germany, DK – Denmark, F – France, I – Italy, Isr – Israel, N – Norway, NL – Netherlands, NZ – New Zealand, S – Sweden, Sp – Spain, UK – United Kingdom, USA – United States of America.

## Warning & Request

Things change – prices go up, schedules change, good places go bad and bad places go bankrupt – nothing stays the same. So if you find things better or worse, recently opened or long since closed, please write and tell us and help make the next edition better.

Your letters will be used to help update future editions and, where possible, important changes will also be included in a Stop Press section in reprints.

We greatly appreciate all information that is sent to us by travellers. Back at Lonely Planet we employ a hard-working readers' letters team to sort through the many letters we receive. The best ones will be rewarded with a free copy of the next edition or another Lonely Planet guide if you prefer. We give away lots of books, but, unfortunately, not every letter/postcard receives one.

# Contents

## ALGERIA

## TUNISIA

## FACTS ABOUT THE COUNTRY .............................................................538

# Map Legend

## BOUNDARIES

............... International Boundary

................... Provincial Boundary

## ROUTES

.................................... Freeway

.................................... Highway

................................ Major Road

.......... Unsealed Road or Track

................................ City Road

.................................. City Street

.................................... Railway

............... Underground Railway

................................... Tram

.............. Walking Track

.......................... Walking Tour

.................................. Ferry Route

................. Cable Car or Chairlift

## AREA FEATURES

........................... Park, Gardens

........................... National Park

............................ Built-Up Area

........................ Pedestrian Mall

.................................. Market

............................ Cemetery

............................ Reef

.................... Beach or Desert

............................ Rocks

## HYDROGRAPHIC FEATURES

............................ Coastline

............................ River, Creek

.......... Intermittent River or Creek

.............. Lake, Intermittent Lake

............................ Canal

............................ Swamp

## SYMBOLS

| | | | |
|---|---|---|---|
| ✪ CAPITAL | ....................... National Capital | ⊕ ★ | ............... Hospital, Police Station |
| ◉ Capital | ...................... Provincial Capital | ✈ ✝ | .......................... Airport, Airfield |
| 🕸 CITY | ................................. Major City | ☗ ✿ | ....................... Cafe, Gardens |
| ● City | .......................................... City | ❖ 🐘 | ............... Shopping Centre, Zoo |
| ● Town | ...................................... Town | ⚘ 🌲 | ... Winery or Vineyard, Picnic Site |
| ● Village | ..................................... Village | ← A25 | One Way Street, Route Number |
| ■ | ............................. Place to Stay | ⁘ | ...... Archaeological Site or Ruins |
| ▼ | ............................. Place to Eat | 🏛 ▲ | .......... Stately Home, Monument |
| ▯ | ................................. Pub, Bar | 🛡 ■ | ............................ Castle, Tomb |
| ✉ ☎ | .............. Post Office, Telephone | ⌂ ⌂ | ................. Cave, Hut or Chalet |
| ❶ ⑤ | .......... Tourist Information, Bank | ▲ ☀ | .......... Mountain or Hill, Lookout |
| ⊖ 🅿 | .................... Transport, Parking | ⛺ ⚓ | ............. Lighthouse, Shipwreck |
| 🏛 ⌂ | .............. Museum, Youth Hostel | )( ⌐ | ............................. Pass, Spring |
| ⚑ ⛺ | Caravan Park, Camping Ground | | ................. Ancient or City Wall |
| † ⊞ † | .................. Church, Cathedral | | ............. Rapids, Waterfalls |
| ☪ ✡ | ................. Mosque, Synagogue | | ........ Cliff or Escarpment, Tunnel |
| ⚘ ⚕ | Buddhist Temple, Hindu Temple | | ............................. Railway Station |

Note: not all symbols displayed above appear in this book

# Introduction

For most people, a trip to this region focuses on one of two activities: seeing the splendours of the imperial Moroccan cities, or crossing the greatest desert of them all – the Sahara. Without doubt, these are North Africa's two principal attractions but the area offers much more for the traveller, especially if their interest extends to Roman history and Islamic architecture.

Morocco is, of course, the star attraction, overshadowing its neighbours to the east. It's a fascinating mix of African, Islamic, Arab, Berber and European influences, and this, combined with its accessibility from Europe, makes it a popular and memorable place to visit. As well as the four imperial cities – Fès, Meknès, Marrakesh and Rabat – there are the natural attractions of the Atlantic beaches

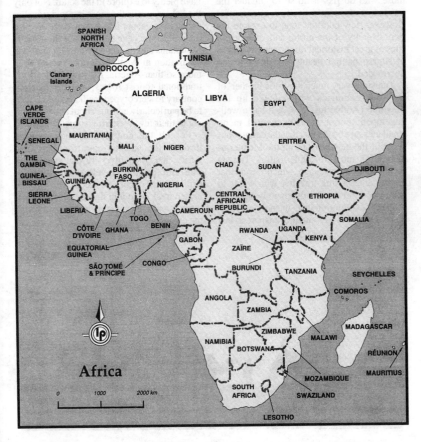

Africa

0    1000    2000 km

and the remote villages of the High Atlas and Rif mountains. The contrasts are great – poverty and opulence, hospitality and aggression – but memorable.

Algeria has for years been the lumbering socialist giant of the region, but the fundamentalist ferment that has rocked the country in the past few years could yet bring about big changes. In spite of an optimistic government campaign to encourage tourism from Europe, travellers should think carefully, and find out the latest situation, before deciding to travel to what can be a dangerous and unstable destination. The majority of those who do risk it do so to conquer the Sahara, a once-in-a-lifetime experience. However, few take the time to explore the rich diversity of the north, and, as a result, sites of great historical importance and areas of superb natural beauty are unspoilt and uncrowded.

Tunisia is very much the 'little brother' of the four countries which make up the Maghreb (Arabic for 'west'). It has a well-developed tourist industry, helped in no small measure by the fact that the country has some of the best beaches on the Mediterranean. For most foreign visitors Tunisia comes as a neat package, which means that for the enterprising traveller who wants to get away from the resorts, there is plenty of scope for exploration in an unspoilt environment. Distances are small, transport is fast and efficient, and the variety of things worth seeing would do justice to a country many times bigger – ruined Roman towns, holy Islamic cities, Berber strongholds, underground villages, desert oases, endless sands and, of course, the beaches.

Of all the North African countries, Libya is the least visited and, arguably, the most adventurous undertaking of them all. The country's attractions have been almost totally hidden from Western travellers since 1969. Roman and Greek history buffs will find plenty to satisfy them in Leptis Magna and Cyrene on the coast, while desert lovers have plenty to explore in the south. Not only the Sahara awaits the more intrepid traveller penetrating deeper into Libya; there are also the prehistoric cave paintings of the Acacus Mountains and the ruins of the Garamantian civilisation in Wadi al-Hayat. Perhaps even more so than Algeria, Libya is well off the traditional tourist routes, and the locals – contrary to stereotyped media images – tend to be particularly curious about and welcoming to their few Western visitors.

For all the common threads running through the various countries of North Africa, it is their diversity that stands out. The enterprising traveller with time to explore can choose to keep well off the beaten track or to join the occasional tourist throng, and either way is unlikely to forget the experience in a hurry.

# Facts about the Region

## HISTORY
### Prehistory

Archaeological evidence of human habitation in North Africa has been dated back as far as 200,000 BC, and some scholars believe that the presence of *Homo erectus* goes back farther still. Much of the Sahara is believed to have once been covered in forest, scrub and savanna grasses, and to have teemed with animal life. The last decent, regular rainfalls are thought to have occurred around 6000 BC, after which grasslands began to give way to arid desert.

Evidence also suggests the appearance of two distinct races in North Africa between about 15,000 and 10,000 BC: first the Oranian and then the Capsian (the former named after Oran in Algeria and the latter after Qafsah – ancient Capsa – in Tunisia), the origins of both virtually unknown. Their integration with indigenous peoples resulted in the spread of Neolithic (New Stone Age) culture and the introduction of farming techniques. Rock paintings, particularly in the Hoggar Mountains in modern Algeria and the Acacus and Mathandous areas in Libya, are the greatest source of knowledge about this period.

It is from these Neolithic peoples that the Berbers (the indigenous peoples of North Africa) are thought to be descended. Allowing for regional variations and the lack of hard clues, they appear to have been predominantly nomadic pastoralists, although continuing to hunt and occasionally farm. By the time of contact with the first of the outside civilisations to arrive from the east, the Phoenicians, these local tribes were already well established, although their existing social organisations and divisions remain unclear.

### Carthaginian Dominance

The strategically located North African coast attracted the attention of the competing sea-going powers of Phoenicia and Greece, and the area's fortunes became inextricably linked to those of its conquerors.

The Phoenicians first came cruising the North African coast around 1000 BC in search of staging posts for the lucrative trade in raw metals from Spain. These ports remained largely undeveloped and little was done to exploit the interior of the continent. From the 7th century BC settlements were established at Sabratha, Oea (modern Tripoli), Leptis Magna, Macomades-Euphranta (near modern Sirt) and Charax (Medinat Sultan) in Libya; at Utica, Carthage, Hadrumètum (Sousse) and Hippo Diarrhytus (Bizerte) in Tunisia; Hippo Regius (Annaba), Saldae (Bejaia) and Cesare (formerly Iol, now Cherchell) in Algeria; and Tamuda (near Tetouan), Lixus, Mogador (Essaouira) and Tingis (Tangier) in Morocco.

The foundation of the major settlement of Carthage is traditionally given as 814 BC. Long politically dependent on the mother culture in Tyre (in modern Lebanon), Carthage eventually emerged as an independent, commercial empire partly because Tyre came under increasing pressure from the Babylonians, but largely in reaction to Greek attacks on Carthage launched from Sicily.

The Greeks colonised North Africa to exploit its strategic location, founding the city of Cyrene in eastern Libya around 630 BC and, later, other towns in the Green Mountain region. The surrounding area came to be known as Cyrenaica and flourished until the arrival of the Romans in the 1st century BC.

By the 4th century BC, Carthage controlled the North African coast from Tripolitania (western Libya) to the Atlantic. The Carthaginians developed the hinterland, particularly the fertile Cap Bon peninsula, and did their utmost to guard the trade routes. This led to a clash with the Greeks in Sicily in 396 BC in which the Carthaginians were defeated. In 310 BC, Greek raiders led by

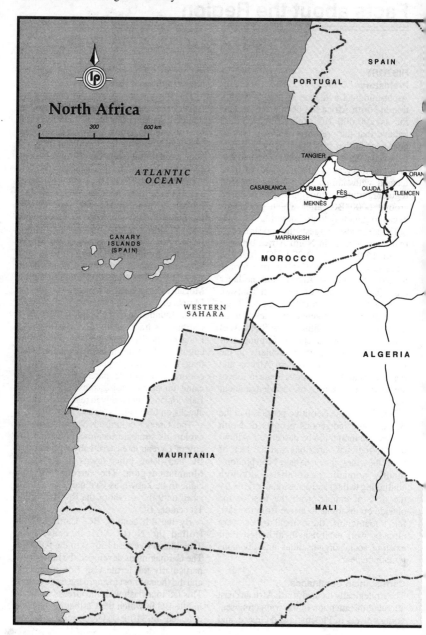

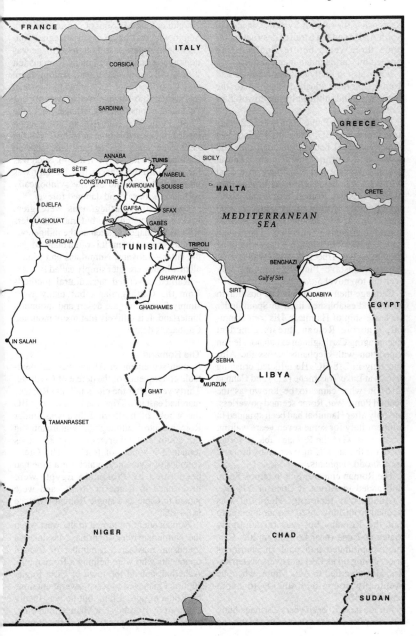

Agathocles, the ruler of Syracuse, landed in North Africa and left a trail of destruction for some three years before finally being crushed by Carthaginian mercenaries.

It was also in Sicily that Carthaginian and Roman interests clashed, leading to the Punic Wars and, ultimately, the downfall of Carthage.

The first of the Punic Wars lasted 22 years from 263 to 241 BC. The Carthaginians lost numerous naval battles, although they did defeat and capture the Roman general Regulus. Having lost their navy in a final skirmish, and being close to broke, they finally accepted Roman terms and abandoned Sicily, followed by Sardinia and Corsica in 238 BC. Trouble at home grew as unpaid mercenaries revolted. They were starved into submission in what came to be known as the Truceless War, which later inspired Gustave Flaubert's memorably over-the-top novel *Salammbô*.

Carthage then consolidated its position in Africa and established itself in Spain under the leadership of Hamilcar. His son, Hannibal, ignoring Roman threats aimed at discouraging Carthaginian expansion, led an expedition with elephants across the Alps into Italy in 218 BC. He inflicted crushing defeats at Lake Trasimene (217) and Cannae (216) in what came to be known as the Second Punic War. Rome seemed powerless, and only after Hannibal had been stranded in southern Italy for some seven years waiting for support were the Romans able to forget about the threat of being overrun by him and his 300-odd elephants.

The Roman emperor Scipio retook Spain and landed in Africa at Utica in 204 BC. Carthage was teetering; Hannibal was recalled from Italy in 203 in an attempt to halt the Romans but was resoundingly beaten at Zama (near Le Kef) in 202. Carthage capitulated and paid an enormous price, giving up its fleet and overseas territories. Hannibal fled to Asia Minor, where he eventually committed suicide to avoid capture in 182.

For the next 50 or so years Carthage hung on, despite incessant threats from the Numidian king Massinissa, a former ally of Scipio who was based at Cirta Regia (Constantine in Algeria). Although Carthage was no longer a major power, many Romans felt it was still a potential threat. Among them was Cato the Elder, an eminent statesman and writer who became well known for his vehement opposition to Carthage. So, in the Third Punic War, the Roman army again landed in Utica, this time in 149 BC. For the next three years the Romans laid siege to Carthage, and it finally fell in 146. Such was the Roman thoroughness that the city was utterly destroyed and the site symbolically sprinkled with salt and damned forever.

Overall, the Carthaginians were great traders and merchants, but ruthless rulers who had managed to alienate the indigenous peoples around them. It is often claimed that the latter – Libyans, Numidians and Mauri, all of whom were later simply called Berbers – learned advanced agricultural methods from the Carthaginians, but many were simply forced into the desert and mountain hinterland. It is unlikely that many mourned Carthage's demise.

### The Romans

Roman settlement in Africa was an inevitable consequence of the defeat of Carthage. Thirty years after the city's fall, the Romans marched east into Tripolitania, and by 64 BC the whole of northern Libya was under Roman control, although the Garamantes in the south and other more remote tribes remained a source of trouble. The Greek colonies of Cyrenaica, which for a time had been ruled by Ptolemaic Egypt, were bequeathed to Rome in 96 BC and were joined to Crete as a single Roman province in 74 BC.

Roman attention turned to the west when the Numidian ruler Jugurtha, Massinissa's grandson, massacred a number of Roman opponents who were helping a Roman ally, Adherbal, defend the town of Cirta Regia. Jugurtha managed to resist several attempts by Rome to uproot him, but he was finally betrayed by Bocchus I, a Mauretanian king, in 105 BC. The boundaries of the Roman colony were extended and settlers (mostly veterans) were given land in the area.

Over the next 50 years, a trickle of Roman settlers moved in, and, after Julius Caesar crushed the last Numidian king, Juba I, in 46 BC, more organised state expansion got underway. The new province of Africa Nova was amalgamated with the old and renamed Africa Proconsularis by the emperor Augustus, who refounded Carthage in 44 BC and installed a proconsul to govern the new colony, an indication of Africa's growing importance as the expanding empire's breadbasket.

When Bocchus II of Mauretania died in 33 BC, bequeathing his kingdom to Rome, Augustus fostered local rule by installing Juba II (a renowned scholar married to the daughter of Cleopatra and Mark Antony). After the murder of Juba's son, Ptolemy, in about 40 AD, the kingdom was split into two provinces – Mauretania Caesariensis, with its capital in Caesarea (in modern Algeria), and Mauretania Tingitana, with its capital at Tingis (Tangier).

From this time on until the decline of Rome in the 4th century AD, North Africa proved a stable and integral part of the empire. Agriculture was all important, and by the 1st century AD, Africa was supplying more than 60% of the empire's grain requirements. Animal husbandry and fishing were widely practised; from Africa too came the majority of the wild animals used in amphitheatre shows, as well as gold, olive oil, slaves, ivory, ostrich plumes and *garum* (a fish-paste delicacy).

The period of Roman rule witnessed increasing urbanisation, particularly in Tunisia, northern Algeria and some parts of Morocco. Cities as far apart as Leptis Magna in Libya and Volubilis in Morocco prospered. The coastal colonies of veterans and civilians in particular assisted the spread of urbanisation and Roman ways. Many indigenous communities also prospered and some of their members were granted Roman citizenship; indeed many upper-class Roman citizens were of African origin. The African colonies even provided an emperor,

Septimius Severus, a Libyan from Leptis Magna who took power in 193 AD and died in Yorkshire of all places. It was these wealthy citizens who donated the monumental public buildings that graced the Roman cities of the region. However, many tribes continued to challenge Rome – especially those operating out of the Moroccan mountain ranges.

By the 4th century signs that all was not well in North Africa were multiplying. Landowners rebelled against increasingly harsh economic policies and there were tribal uprisings in Mauretania Caesariensis (Mauretania Tingitana having been abandoned the previous century).

Christianity spread rapidly, especially with the conversion of the emperor Constantine in 313 AD, but any hopes that this might stabilise the situation were dashed by the Donatist controversy that emerged in Carthage. Donatus, a Carthaginian priest, split from the orthodox church and soon gained a big following for his schismatic movement. Historians regard the schism as more an expression of discontent with Rome than a truly religious impulse. In any case, following vigorous support for orthodoxy by St Augustine of Hippo Regius (Annaba, Algeria), laws were formulated at a conference in Carthage on religious unity which the Donatists were forced to obey, and the schism was healed.

## The Vandals & the Byzantines

In 429 AD, king Gaeseric (or Genseric), who had been busy marauding in southern Spain, decided to take the entire Vandal people (about 80,000 men, women and children) across to Africa, bypassing Tingis, and within a few years he had defeated the Romans and wrung hefty concessions from them. By the middle of the century his ships were in control of much of the western Mediterranean and Rome was all but a spent force.

The Vandals confiscated large amounts of property and their exploitative policies accelerated North Africa's economic decline. The Berbers became increasingly rebellious and, as the Vandals recoiled, small local kingdoms sprang up.

The Byzantine emperor Justinian, based in Constantinople (modern Istanbul), had in the meantime revived the eastern half of the Roman empire and had similar plans for the lost western territories. His general Belisarius defeated the Vandals in 533; there followed a century of fairly ineffectual Byzantine rule, which saw increasing Berber uprisings, the decay of town life and the loss of territory under Byzantine control.

## The Coming of Islam

No-one could have guessed that the tribal clashes and emergence of an obscure new religion in the distant peninsula of Arabia in the early 7th century would completely change the face of North Africa. Islam's green banner was flying over the cities of Egypt by 640 (for more details of the birth of Islam, see Religion later in this chapter), and soon after Tripoli was in Muslim hands too.

It was not until Uqba bin Nafi al-Fihri began his campaign of conquest that the full military force of Islam was brought to bear on North Africa. For three years from 669 he swept across the top of the continent, establishing Islam's first great city in the Maghreb, Kairouan (Qayrawan) in modern Tunisia. With an army of Arab cavalry and Islamised Berber infantry from Libya, he marched into the Atlas and is said to have reached the Atlantic.

Uqba went campaigning again, mostly in Morocco, in 681. In 683 he was defeated by a Berber chieftain, Qusayla, and the Muslim troops retreated back to Libya, with Qusayla occupying Kairouan.

The days of the Byzantines were numbered, and by 698 the Arabs had succeeded in evicting them from North Africa. Various Berber tribes continued to resist, including those led by the legendary princess Al-Kahina.

Under the command of Musa bin Nusayr, the conquering armies pushed decisively into Morocco, breaking down resistance by sensibly making allies rather than enemies of the Berber tribes which had converted to the new religion. By 710 Musa considered his work in Morocco done, and turned his attention to Spain. With his lieutenant Tariq, he set about conquering Spain (thus 'Gibraltar' derives from the Arabic 'jebel Tariq', or Tariq's Mountain), and by 732 he had made his deepest advance into Christian Europe, reaching Poitiers in France.

Although Islam had become well established, the Berbers, although accepting the religion, were not to be pacified. A mass rebellion, in reaction to the tyrannical behaviour of the occupying troops and inspired by the Muslim heresy of Kharijism, set out from Morocco in 740 and conquered the Umayyad armies west of Kairouan.

With the shift of the caliphate from the Umayyads in Damascus to the Abbasids in Baghdad, the Muslim west (North Africa and Spain) split from the east. Three major Islamic kingdoms finally emerged in North Africa: the Idrissids in Fès, the Rustamids in Tahart and the Aghlabids in Kairouan.

Idriss was a sherif (descendant of the Prophet through his daughter Fatima) who had fled Abbasid persecution to northern Morocco, where, with Berber support, he established the Idrissid kingdom. He and his son, Idriss II, founded Fès (present-day Fès el-Bali) – a city of diverse influences from both Andalusia and Kairouan.

In 800 the caliph of Baghdad appointed the Aghlabids to promote religious orthodoxy in the Maghreb. This they did with some success, and the dynasty founded by Ibrahim bin Aghlab lasted until 909. This period saw the construction of the Great Mosque in Kairouan (their capital) and the *ribats* (monastic forts) at Sousse and Mahdia.

The only people to embrace Islam's Shiite sect to any great extent were the Berbers of the Kabylie region of northern Algeria. Led by Obeid Allah, an Arab Shiite bent on becoming caliph, they defeated the Aghlabids and installed themselves in Kairouan. The Fatimids, as they were called, built their new capital, Mahdia, on a small, easily defended headland on the coast. Obeid

Allah then set his sights on Egypt. After several unsuccessful attempts, his successor, Amir al-Muizz, defeated the Egyptians and founded Cairo in 969.

Before leaving for Egypt, however, the Fatimids entrusted their North African territory (Ifriqiyya, or roughly modern Tunisia and parts of Algeria and Libya) to the rule of the Berber Zirids. Like the Hammadids, their neighbours to the west, they were unable to resist pressure for religious orthodoxy from within and officially returned to Sunnism in open defiance of the Fatimids in Cairo. The reply from Cairo was devastating: the Beni Hillal and Beni Sulaim tribes of upper Egypt were encouraged to invade the Maghreb, and over the following century North Africa was slowly reduced to ruins. The Zirids managed to hang on to a few coastal cities until 1148, while the Hammadids retreated to the coastal town of Bejaia.

## Berber Empires

As Idrissid power in Morocco expired, a new force emerged from the Sahara. Inspired by a Qur'anic teacher, Abdallah bin Yasin, the Sanhaja confederation of various Berber tribes began to wage wars throughout southern and central Morocco. They were known as 'the veiled ones' (al-mulathamin) because of their dress, and later for some unknown reason as the 'people of the fortress' (al-murabitin) – the Almoravids. In 1062 their leader, Youssef bin Tachfin, founded Marrakesh as his capital and led troops on a march of conquest that, at its height, saw a unified empire stretching from Senegal in Africa to Zaragoza in northern Spain.

This brilliant flash was just that, for as quickly as they had risen, they crumbled in the face of another Moroccan movement: strictly conservative Muslims known as 'those who proclaim the unity of God' (al-muwahhidin) – the Almohads. Inspired by the teachings of Mohammed ibn Tumart, which attacked the religious laxness of the Almoravids, Abd al-Mu'min began a successful campaign against them. In the 30 years to 1160, the Almohads conquered all of Almoravid Morocco as well as what are now Algeria, Tunisia and parts of Libya. In the following years, Muslim Spain also fell. This was a high point in Moroccan cultural development, and the major cities expanded rapidly. It was during this time that Europeans made their first attempt in centuries to make a comeback in North Africa, when Roger II of Norman Sicily briefly took Tripoli castle in Libya. The Almohads quickly threw him out.

But the empire grew too fast and soon began to crumble under its own weight. As it caved in, the Maghreb split into three parts: Ifriqiyya (Tunisia and parts of Libya) came under the Hafsids; Algeria under the Banu Abd al-Wad; and Morocco under the Merenids. Although borders have changed and imperial rulers have come and gone, this division remains more or less intact today.

The Hafsids managed to hang on until the middle of the 15th century, when Tunisia became the scene for rivalry between the Spanish and the Turks. In Morocco the Merenids prospered for a full century and a half before falling under the sway of the Wattasid dynasty of viziers in 1459. Under the Merenids, Morocco went through another golden age with the establishment of Fès el-Jedid (New Fès) and the building of fine mosques and medersas (a French corruption of madrassa, a religious foundation and school which was usually attached to a mosque), many of which still stand today. The Abd al-Wadids formed an alliance with Granada in an effort to survive, but fell to the greater power of the Merenids in 1352 and then to the Turks in 1555.

The Wattasids' biggest mistake was to allow Portuguese traders and raiders to settle at various points along the coast. It was ostensibly in opposition to the Portuguese that the Saadians rose from the Drâa oases in a holy war. In fact, they used the opportunity to conquer Morocco and set themselves up in Marrakesh.

The Saadian sultan, Ahmed al-Mansour, made only one major raid – against the Muslims of the southern Sahara in 1591 – in the course of which he captured Timbuktu, from where he obtained slaves and massive wealth in gold. Marrakesh became a rich and decadent city and so was ripe for overthrow.

Enter the Alawite sherifs, who took Fès in 1666 under the leadership of Moulay ar-Rashid. He was assassinated in 1672 and his brother, Moulay Ismail, became the last imperial ruler of any importance. He built a splendid new capital at Meknès and gradually established a rare degree of control over most of Morocco – admittedly thanks to an equally rare degree of cruelty. He died in 1727, and Morocco again slowly began to slide into a morass.

### The Ottoman Turks
In the early 16th century, the pirate Barbarossa (or Khair ed-Din) and his brother Aruj, sons of a Turk from the Greek island of Lesbos, were permitted to settle on the island of Jerba (Tunisia). Aruj captured Algiers from the Spanish, but they retook the city and killed Aruj in 1518. Thereupon Khair ad-Din allied himself with the Turks in order to protect his Barbary possessions. The Ottomans jumped at the chance, conferred on him the title of *beylerbey* (governor) and sent him 6000 artillery men. In 1529 he managed to boot the Spaniards out of Algiers once again and five years later was in control of Tunis as well. However, the following year saw Spain's Charles V take that city and the Hafsid ruler Moulay Hassan installed as a Spanish vassal.

There was a flurry of activity as Spaniards and Turks fought for supremacy in North Africa. In 1551, the Turkish admiral Darghut Pasha attacked and took Tripoli, which had fallen to Spain 40 years earlier and subsequently been entrusted to the Knights of Malta. Shortly thereafter Tripolitania became a province of the Ottoman empire.

Then a Turkish pirate and associate of Barbarossa settled on Jerba and controlled Kairouan; Tunis was taken for the Turks in 1569 but it fell to Don John of Austria the next year. The Turks rallied and retook Tunis in 1574 and Tunisia, like Algeria and Tripolitania, also became an Ottoman province.

The three provinces were governed by a pasha, assisted by a dey (administrative chief) and a bey (military chief). Power in fact resided more in the dey in Algeria and the bey in Tunisia, and the pashas were little more than figureheads. The dey's power declined in Algeria with the assassination of the last dey elected directly from Turkey in 1671.

In Tunisia, the beys carried on strongly until the beginning of the 19th century. Hussein bin Ali, a Greek soldier from Crete, founded the last of the Tunisian dynasties, the Husseinids, when he had himself elected bey by the Turkish janissaries (the Ottoman army elite) in 1705.

Tripolitania was run by a succession of semi-autonomous rulers until 1711, when Ahmed Karamanli founded a dynasty that lasted until 1835.

From fairly early on, Turkey's 'rule' over its North African possessions was little more than a formality. The sultan's name was used in the weekly sermons and new leaders sought confirmation of their nominations from Constantinople, but to all intents and purposes Algeria, Tunisia and Tripolitania acted independently, and frequently attacked one another.

In all three (as indeed to a large extent in Morocco too), piracy played a pivotal role in the local economies, and the Barbary pirates, operating mainly from Algiers, Tunis and Tripoli, were the scourge of Europe's Mediterranean shipping. European fleets occasionally blockaded North African ports and attacked the corsairs, but rarely with any lasting effect. The USA sent warships to Tripoli in 1804, but a plan to destroy the corsairs' fleet there failed. The Americans did, however, manage to extract a line from the occasion for the US marines' theme song ('From the Halls of Montezuma to the shores of Tripoli...'), and although this attack met with little success, the pirates' days were numbered.

### Meanwhile, Back in Morocco...
Morocco's fortunes revived somewhat under Moulay Ismail's grandson, Sidi Mohammed III (1757-90). He kicked the Portuguese out

of Mazagan (El-Jadida), their last Moroccan possession, and started trading with Europe. Chaos again followed his death, but order of a kind was restored by Moulay Suleiman, who ruled from 1792 to 1822. However, by this stage there was little left to govern and the British, French and Spanish were all looking to grab a bit of the action in North Africa.

### European Rule & Independence

The French overran Algeria in 1830. Tunisia and Morocco were made protectorates in 1881 and 1912, respectively. Tripoli and Cyrenaica (Libya) went to Italy in 1911 after a short struggle between Rome and the Ottoman Turks. The four countries' struggles for independence followed different paths, with Libya being established as an independent state in 1951, followed by Morocco and Tunisia in 1956, and Algeria (after a bitter and bloody six-year war) in 1962. The colonial era, independence and recent history to the present day are dealt with in the individual country chapters.

### SOCIETY & CONDUCT

The countries of North Africa are all Muslim and as such are conservative about dress. Although dress codes vary quite widely from the chic Moroccan and Tunisian resorts and cities to the conservative countryside, you can save yourself trouble and embarrassment by erring on the side of modesty in what you wear.

Women, in particular, are well advised to keep shoulders and upper arms covered and to opt for long skirts or trousers. Stricter Muslims consider excessive display of flesh, whether male or female, offensive. Women disregarding such considerations risk not only arousing the ire of the genuinely offended, but also the unwanted interest of the lascivious; see Women Travellers in the introductory Facts for the Visitor chapter. Men wearing shorts (away from the coast at any rate) are considered to be in their underwear and can occasionally arouse indignation too. A little common sense goes a long way. You can get away with a lot more on the beaches of Agadir or Hammamet than in a Berber village in the Atlas Mountains or your average Libyan town.

Public display of affection is much frowned upon in most parts of the region.

### RELIGION

Islam is the predominant religion of North Africa. Prior to 1948, there was a large Jewish population resident in Morocco. Algeria, Tunisia and Morocco have very small Christian and Jewish communities, generally constituting less than one per cent of the population.

### Islam

The first slivers of dawn light are flickering on the horizon, and the deep quiet of a city asleep is pierced by the cries of the muezzin exhorting the faithful to the first of the day's prayers:

Allahu akbar, Allahu akbar
Ashhadu an la Ilah ila Allah
Ashhadu an Mohammed rasul Allah
Haya ala as-sala
Haya ala as-sala

Of all the sounds that assault the ears of the first-time visitor to North Africa, it is possibly the call to prayer that leaves the most indelible impression. Five times a day, Muslims are called, if not actually to enter a mosque to pray, at least to take the time to do so where they are. The midday prayers on Friday, when the sheikh of the mosque delivers his weekly sermon, or *khutba*, are considered the most important. The mosque also serves as a kind of community centre, and often you'll find groups of children or adults receiving lessons (usually in the Qur'an), people in quiet prayer and others simply sheltering in the tranquil peace of the mosque.

Islam shares its roots with the great monotheistic faiths that sprang from the harsh land of the Middle East – Judaism and Christianity – but it is considerably younger than these religions. The holy book of Islam is the Qur'an. Its pages carry many references to the earlier prophets of both the older religions – Adam, Abraham, Noah, Moses and others are recognised as prophets – but there the similarities begin to end. Jesus is seen merely as another in a long line of prophets that ends definitively with Mohammed. What makes Mohammed different from the rest is that the Qur'an, unlike either the Torah of the Jews or the Christian Gospels, is the word of God, directly communicated to Mohammed in a series of revelations. For Muslims, Islam can only be the apogee of the monotheistic faiths from which it derives so much. Muslims traditionally attribute a place of great respect to Christians and Jews as *ahl al-kitab*, the People of the Book. However, the more strident will claim Christianity was a new and improved version of the teachings of the Torah, and that Islam was the next logical step and therefore 'superior'. Do not be surprised if you occasionally run into someone wanting you to convert!

Mohammed, born into one of the trading families of the Arabian city of Mecca (in present-day Saudi Arabia) in 570 AD, began to receive revelations in 610 AD, and after a time started imparting the content of Allah's message to the Meccans. Its essence was a call to submit to God's will (*islam* means submission), but not all Meccans were impressed.

Mohammed gathered quite a following in his campaign against Meccan idolaters, but the powerful families of the city became so hostile that he felt forced to flee to Medina in 622. Mohammed's flight from Mecca, or *hijra* (migration), marks the beginning of the Muslim calendar. In Medina he continued to preach, while increasing his power base. Soon he and his supporters began to clash with the Meccans, led by powerful elements of the Quraysh tribe, possibly over trade routes.

By 632, Mohammed had revisited Mecca and many of the tribes in the surrounding area had sworn allegiance to him and the new faith. Mecca became the symbolic centre of the faith, containing as it did the Ka'aba, which housed the black stone supposedly given to Ibrahim (Abraham) by the Angel Gabriel. Mohammed determined that Muslims should face Mecca when praying outside the city.

On his death in 632, the Arabs exploded into the Syrian desert, quickly conquering the areas which make up modern Syria, Iraq, Lebanon, Israel and Palestine. This was accomplished under Mohammed's successors, the caliphs (or Companions of Mohammed), of whom there were four. They in turn were succeeded by the Umayyad (661-750) dynasty in Damascus, followed by the Abbasid line (749-1258) in the newly built city of Baghdad.

Islam quickly spread west, first taking in Egypt and then fanning out across North Africa. By the end of the 7th century, the Muslims had reached the Atlantic and thought themselves sufficiently in control of the Gezirat al-Maghreb ('Island of the West', or North Africa beyond Egypt) to consider marching on Spain in 710.

Islam is now the religion of almost all the inhabitants of the Maghreb. In order to live out a devout life, the Muslim is expected at least to carry out the Five Pillars of Islam:

*shahada* – this is the profession of faith, Islam's basic tenet: 'There is no god but Allah, and Mohammed is His Prophet'. It is a phrase commonly heard, as part of the call to prayer and at many other events, such as births and deaths. The first part has virtually become an exclamation good for any time of life or situation. People can often be heard muttering it to themselves, as if seeking a little strength to get through the trials of the day.

*sala* – sometimes written 'salat', this is the obligation of prayer, ideally five times a day, when muezzins call the faithful to pray. Although Muslims can pray anywhere, it is considered more laudable to do so together in a mosque (masjid or *jami'*). The important midday prayers on Friday (the loose equivalent of Sunday Mass for Catholics) are usually held in the jami', which is the main district mosque.

*zakat* – the giving of alms to the poor was from the start an essential part of the social teaching of Islam, and was later developed in some parts of the Muslim world into various forms of tax to redistribute funds to the needy. The moral obligation towards one's poorer neighbours continues to be emphasised at a personal level, and there are often exhortations to give posted up outside mosques.

*sawm* – Ramadan, the ninth month of the Muslim calendar, commemorates the revelation of the Qur'an to Mohammed. In a demonstration of the Muslims' renewal of faith, they are asked to abstain from sex and from letting *anything* pass their lips from dawn to dusk every day of the month. For more information on the month of fasting, see Islamic Holidays later in this chapter.

*hajj* – the pinnacle of a devout Muslim's life is the pilgrimage to the holy sites in and around Mecca. Ideally, the pilgrim should go to Mecca in the last month of the year, Zuul Hijja, to join Muslims from all over the world in the pilgrimage and the subsequent feast. The returned pilgrim can be addressed as 'hajji', and in simpler villages at least, it is still quite common to see the word 'al-hajj' and simple scenes painted on the walls of houses showing that its inhabitants have made the pilgrimage. For more details see Islamic Holidays later in this chapter.

## Sunnis & Shiites

The power struggle between Ali, the last of the four caliphs of Mohammed and his son-in-law, and the emerging Umayyad dynasty in Damascus caused a great schism at the heart of the new religion. The succession to the caliphate had been marked by considerable intrigue and bloodshed. Ali, the father of Mohammed's sole male heirs, lost his struggle, and the Umayyad leader was recognised as the legitimate successor to the caliphate.

Those who favoured the Umayyad caliph became known as the Sunnis. The majority of Muslims are Sunnis, considered to be the orthodox mainstream of Islam. The Shiites, on the other hand, recognise only the successors of Ali.

The Sunnis have divided into four schools of religious thought, each lending varying degrees of importance to different aspects of doctrine. In Morocco, where the population is virtually entirely Sunni, it is the Maliki school that predominates. The Malikis, along with the Hanafi school, are somewhat less rigid in their application and interpretation of the Qur'an than the other schools. This trend had already emerged by the 15th century, when qadis (community judges) are recorded as having applied *shari'a* (Qur'anic law) in accordance with local custom rather than to the letter.

## Saints & Mysticism

From an early point in the life of Islam, certain practitioners sought to move closer to God through individual effort and spiritual devotion, rather than simply living by God's laws. These people came to be known as Sufis (from *suf*, meaning wool and referring to the simple cord they tended to wear as a belt for their garments), and various orders emerged throughout the lands where Islam held sway.

Orthodox Muslims have always regarded such manifestations with suspicion, particularly as the orders tend to gather in the name of a holy man (or *wali*, a term which has come to be loosely translated as 'saint', although saints in the Christian sense play no role in Islam). Public gatherings take many forms, from the dances of the 'whirling dervishes' to more ecstatic and extreme demonstrations of self-mutilation (participants may, for instance, push skewers into their cheeks, apparently without feeling any pain).

The orders generally gather at the mosque or tomb of their 'saint' and follow a particular *tariqa* (path), or way of worshipping. Various orders have acquired permanence over the centuries, and 'membership' can run through generations of the same families, tracing their lineage back to the original saint or spiritual master and through him to the Prophet (the veracity of such links is of secondary importance).

For orthodox Muslims, veneration of the saint is tantamount to worship of an idol, although Sufis would not see it that way. The wali is a 'friend' (the more literal meaning of the word) of God and so an intermediary, and all marabouts (or holy men) are regarded in a similar fashion. The great *moussems* or pilgrimages to the tombs of such saints are as much a celebration of the triumph of the spirit as an act of worship of a particular saint.

In North Africa, Morocco proved the most fertile ground for this kind of mysticism – see the Religion section of the Morocco Facts about the Country chapter for more details.

**Islamic Architecture** The earliest construction efforts undertaken by Muslims were more often than not mosques, which inherited a great deal from Christian and Greco-Roman models. However, various styles soon developed and, increasingly, they owed less to their architectural forebears. This was particularly so in Morocco and in the Maghreb in general, where monumental prototypes left behind by other civilisations were scarcer than in Egypt, Syria and Iraq to the east.

Indeed, a sweep from west to east across the Muslim world reveals a remarkable diversity in design obvious even to the untrained eye. The angular, austere Moroccan style, for example, contrasts with the opulent mosques of the Ottoman Turks,

Wall ornamentation

characterised by their great cupolas and pencil-thin minarets, and again with the Persian-influenced, onion-shaped domes found in Iraq and farther east.

## Islam & the West

Ignorance abounds in the West about the nature of Islam and Muslims, associated all too readily with a fearful image of unpredictable and unreasonable, gun-toting terrorists. Ever since the Crusades, this sort of image has tended to stick in the Western subconscious, and has been fuelled by the intractable conflict in the Middle East between Israel and its Arab neighbours and the demonisation of Arab leaders who are considered a menace to Western interests. Muslims would be justified in pointing to conflicts in the heart of the West, such as the horrors perpetrated in Northern Ireland, and rhetorically asking whether they make everyone living in Ireland and the UK blood-thirsty extremists.

It also has to be said that people in the Arab world, Muslims or otherwise, sometimes have a startlingly contorted picture of the West and what makes it tick. A grudging respect for and envy of its wealth and technological advantages, combined occasionally with disdain for its perceived moral decadence, colour the way many Muslims deal with Westerners. Western TV's soap-opera drivel does little to change this view.

For all of this, visitors to North Africa generally find that the reality could not be further from the truth. That a gulf separates East and West in terms of mentality and world view few would dispute, but the warmth accorded to outsiders by the average Muslim belies any stereotypes. Of course, there are bad eggs – you get them anywhere – but Islam demands of its faithful a sense of community and hospitality to strangers.

Much is made of religious fundamentalism in Muslim countries. Again, the picture in the West is of bearded fanatics with a slightly crazed look in the eye, happy to kill or die for a rigid Islamic state and turn the clock back centuries. There are elements of truth in the caricature, but care should be taken. Islam is not just a religion that can be separated from daily life and government, as is now the case with the Christian churches in the West. Islam is, for want of a better word, more holistic – it provides a framework for both secular and spiritual life. Calls for an Islamic state therefore do not sound as strange to Muslim ears as to Westerners. Having said that, it is probably fair to observe that the majority of ordinary Muslims do not favour such a development, and that the popular following of fundamentalist groups is not as great as some imagine. Much of the success they do have is less a result of religious fervour than a reflection of the frustrated hopes of many classes in countries grappling with severe economic difficulties. Nowhere has this become clearer in recent years than in Algeria, but the issue bubbles below the surface in the rest of North Africa too. ■

Mosques are generally built around an open courtyard, off which lie one or more covered halls *(liwans)*. The liwan facing Mecca is the focal point of prayer. All mosques feature a vaulted niche in the wall, the mihrab, which indicates the direction of Mecca (the *qibla)*, which Muslims must face when they pray. The khutba (sermon) is given from the *minbar*, or pulpit, which is raised above a narrow staircase and sometimes ornately decorated.

The minaret (from *menara*, meaning lighthouse) most often consists of a square base leading to more slender cylindrical or hexagonal stages. Most have internal staircases for the muezzins to climb to the top, from where they call the faithful to prayer (the advent of the microphone now saves them that effort).

In the Maghreb and Spain, however, the dominant style of minaret is square-based all the way to the top – the single most distinguishing characteristic of what is often referred to as Andalusian (Muslim Spain was known as Al-Andalus) religious architecture (the comparison between such minarets and bell towers in many Spanish churches is revealing). Only one rather small and comparatively modern minaret in the sacred town of Moulay Idriss, near Meknès in Morocco, departs from the standard – it's cylindrical.

The decoration of mosques (Maghreb and Andalusian religious buildings tend to be fairly austere on the outside) and many other public buildings is an exercise in geometric virtuosity. As Islam frowns on the artistic representation of living beings, the art of carving out complex arabesques of vines, palms and other flora in various deceptive designs merged with a growing tradition of intricate, decorative calligraphy. Much of the decoration consists of more or less stylised verses from the Qur'an. The phrase 'la illah illa Allah' (there is no god but Allah) appears in a seemingly unlimited variety of designs as an integral part of decoration, fusing religious precept and the very reference to God with the art that exhalts Him.

In the Maghreb and Muslim Spain, this art form was taken to particular lengths in the delicate stucco and plaster carvings, the majority of which are found inside buildings. The carved woodwork ceilings in some liwans reveal painstaking and graceful geometric decoration.

**Islamic Customs** When a baby is born, the first words uttered to it are the call to prayer. A week later this is followed by a ceremony in which the baby's head is shaved and an animal is sacrificed.

The major event of a boy's childhood is circumcision, which normally takes place sometime between the ages of seven and 12.

Marriage ceremonies are colourful and noisy affairs which usually take place in summer. One custom is for all the males to get in their cars and drive around the streets in a convoy making as much noise as possible. The vows are made some time prior to the ceremony, which usually takes place in the home of the bride or groom. The partying goes on until the early hours of the morning, often until sunrise.

The death ceremony is simple: a burial service is held at the mosque and the body is then buried with the feet facing Mecca.

Wedding ceremony

When Muslims pray, they must follow certain rituals. First they must wash their hands, arms, feet, head and neck in running water before praying; all mosques have an area set aside for this purpose. If they are not in a mosque and there is no water available, clean sand suffices; and where there is no sand, they must just go through the motions of washing.

Then they must face Mecca (all mosques are oriented so that the mihrab, or prayer niche, faces the right direction) and follow a set pattern of gestures – photos of rows of Muslims kneeling in the direction of Mecca with their heads touching the ground are legion. You regularly see Muslims praying by the side of the road or in the street as well as in mosques.

In everyday life, Muslims are prohibited from drinking alcohol and eating pork (considered unclean), and must refrain from gambling, fraud, usury and slander.

**Islamic Holidays** The principal religious holidays in Muslim countries are tied to the lunar Hijra calendar. The word 'hijra' refers to the flight of the Prophet Mohammed from Mecca to Medina in 622 AD, which marks the first year of the calendar (the year 622 AD is the year 1 AH). The calendar is about 11 days shorter than the Gregorian (Western) calendar, meaning that in Western terms the holidays fall at different times of the year.

**Ras as-Sana** This means New Year's day, and is celebrated on the first day of the Hijra calendar year, 1 Moharram.

**Achoura** This is a day of public mourning observed by Shiites on 10 Moharram. It commemorates the assassination of Hussain ibn Ali, grandson of the Prophet Mohammed and pretender to the caliphate, which led to the schism between Sunnis and Shiites.

**Mawlid an-Nabi** This is a lesser feast celebrating the birth of the Prophet Mohammed on 12 Rabi' al-Awal. For a long time it was not celebrated at all in the Islamic world. In the Maghreb this is generally known as Mouloud.

**Ramadan & 'Eid al-Fitr** Most Muslims, albeit not all with equal rigour, take part in the fasting that characterises the month of Ramadan, a time when the faithful are called upon as a community to renew their relationship with God. Ramadan is the month in which the Qur'an was first revealed. From dawn until dusk, the Muslim is expected to refrain from eating, drinking, smoking and sex. This can be a difficult discipline, and only people in good health are asked to participate. Those engaged in exacting physical work or travelling are considered exempt. In a sense, every evening during Ramadan is a celebration. *Iftar* or *ftur*, the breaking of the day's fast, is a time of animated activity, when the people of the local community come together not only to eat and drink and so break the day's fasting, but also to pray.

| Table of Islamic Holidays | | | | | |
|---|---|---|---|---|---|
| Hijra Year | New Year | Prophet's Birthday | Ramadan Begins | 'Eid al-Fitr | 'Eid al-Adha |
| 1415 | 10.06.94 | 19.08.94 | 01.02.95 | 04.03.95 | 10.05.95 |
| 1416 | 31.05.95 | 09.08.95 | 22.01.96 | 22.02.96 | 29.04.96 |
| 1417 | 19.05.96 | 28.07.96 | 10.01.97 | 10.02.97 | 18.04.97 |
| 1418 | 09.05.97 | 18.07.97 | 31.12.98 | 31.01.98 | 08.04.98 |
| 1419 | 28.04.98 | 07.07.98 | 20.12.99 | 20.01.99 | 28.03.99 |
| 1420 | 17.04.99 | 26.06.99 | – | – | – |

Non-Muslims are not expected to participate, even if more pious Muslims suggest you do. Restaurants and cafés that are open during the day may be harder to come by, and at any rate you should try to avoid openly flouting the fast – there's nothing worse for the strung-out and hungry smoker than seeing outsiders cheerfully wandering about, cigarettes in hand and munching away.

The end of Ramadan, or more accurately the first days of the following month of Shawwal, mark the 'Eid al-Fitr, the Feast of the Breaking of the Fast (also known as 'Eid as-Sagheer, the Small Feast), which generally lasts four or five days, during which time just about everything grinds to a halt. This is not a good time to travel, but can be a great experience if you are invited to share in some of the festivities with a family. It is a very family-oriented feast, much in the way Christmas is to Christians.

***Hajj & 'Eid al-Adha*** The fifth pillar of Islam, a sacred duty of all who can afford it, is to make the pilgrimage to Mecca – the hajj. It can be done at any time, but at least once should be accomplished in Zuul Hijja, the 12th month of the Muslim year. At this time, thousands of Muslims from all over the world converge on Islam's most holy city.

The high point is the visit to the Ka'aba, the construction housing the stone of Ibrahim in the centre of the *haram*, the sacred area into which non-Muslims are forbidden to enter. The faithful, dressed only in a white robe, circle the Ka'aba seven times and kiss the black stone. This is one of a series of acts of devotion carried out by pilgrims.

The hajj culminates in the ritual slaughter of a lamb (in commemoration of Ibrahim's sacrifice) at Mina. This marks the end of the pilgrimage and the beginning of the *'Eid al-Adha*, or Feast of the Sacrifice (aka the Grand Feast, or *'Eid al-Kabeer*). Throughout the Muslim world the act of sacrifice is repeated, and the streets of towns and cities seem to run with the blood of slaughtered

sheep. The holiday runs from 10 to 13 Zuul-Hijja.

## LANGUAGE

The official language throughout North Africa is Arabic, but what you will hear in Libya differs greatly from the Moroccan version (Darija). In Morocco, Algeria and Tunisia French is still very widely spoken. Local languages, such as Berber, are at their strongest in more remote areas, particularly in Morocco, where at least three main dialects are widely used.

In Libya, some people in the cities understand English, and older people still speak some Italian, but a knowledge of Arabic would go a long way – particularly as all public and road signs are in Arabic script only. Spanish can come in handy in northern Morocco. Otherwise, you can generally get by with French throughout the former French territories of North Africa. In the heavily touristed centres you'll find people who speak English and German – the Moroccans seem to have a special gift for languages.

### Arabic

Moroccan Arabic is a dialect of the standard language, but it's so different in many respects as to be virtually like another tongue. It is the everyday language that differs most from that of other Arabic-speaking peoples. More specialised or educated language tends to be much the same across the Arab world, although pronunciation varies considerably.

The spread of radio and television have increased all Arabs' exposure to and understanding of what is commonly known as Modern Standard Arabic (MSA). MSA, which has grown from the classical language of the Qur'an and poetry, is the written and spoken lingua franca of the Arab world, and in fact is not so far removed from the daily language of the Arab countries of the Levant (such as Syria, Jordan and Lebanon). It is the language of radio and television presenters and the press, and also of the great majority of modern Arabic literature. Of the four countries covered in this book, Libya's Arabic is closest to the standard; basically, the farther west you head, the greater the differences become.

Foreign students of the language constantly face the dilemma of whether first to learn MSA (which could mean waiting a while before being able to talk with shopkeepers) and then a chosen dialect, or simply to acquire spoken competence in the latter. Dialects supposedly have no written form (the argument goes it would be like writing in Cockney or Strine), although there is no reason why they could not avail themselves of the same script used for the standard language. If this leaves you with a headache, you will have some idea of why so few non-Arabs or non-Muslims embark on the study of this complex tongue.

Nevertheless, if you take the time to learn even a few words and phrases, you will discover and experience much more while travelling through the region – this is particularly the case in Libya, where European languages are not widely understood.

**Pronunciation** Pronunciation of Arabic can be tongue-tying for someone unfamiliar with the intonation and combination of sounds. Pronounce the transliterated words and phrases slowly and clearly.

The following guide should help, but it isn't complete because the rules governing pronunciation and vowel use are too extensive to be covered here.

For a more comprehensive guide to the Arabic spoken in the Maghreb, get hold of Lonely Planet's *Moroccan Arabic Phrasebook*, by Dan Bacon with Abdennabi Benchehda & Bichr Andjar. Libyan Arabic is closer to that spoken in Egypt than the Moroccan version – if you've picked up any Egyptian colloquial Arabic, you should be able to make yourself understood among the Libyans.

**Vowels** In spoken Arabic, there are at least five basic vowel sounds that can be distinguished:

**a**  like the 'a' in 'had' (sometimes very short)
**e**  like the 'e' in 'bet' (sometimes very short)
**i**  like the 'i' in 'hit'
**o**  like the 'o' in 'hot'
**u**  like the 'oo' in 'book'

The ¯ symbol over a vowel gives it a long sound.

**ā**  like the 'a' in 'father'
**ē**  like the 'e' in 'ten', but lengthened
**ī**  like the 'e' in 'ear', only softer, often written as 'ee'
**ō**  like the 'o' in 'for'
**ū**  like the 'oo' in 'food'

Long vowels are also informally transliterated as double vowels, eg aa (ā), ee (ī), oo (ū).

**Combinations** Certain combinations of vowels with vowels or consonants form other vowel sounds (diphthongs):

**aw**  like the 'ow' in 'how'
**ai**  like the 'i' in 'high'
**ei & ay**  like the 'a' in 'cake'

These last two are tricky, as one can slide into the other in certain words, depending on who is pronouncing them. Remember these rules are an outline, and far from exhaustive.

**Consonants** Most of the consonants used in this section are the same as in English. However, a few of the consonant sounds must be explained in greater detail.

Three of the most common are the glottal stop ('), the 'ayn' sound ('), and the 'rayn' (**gh**). These are difficult sounds, especially for a non-native speaker, so don't be discouraged if you aren't being understood, just keep trying.

The glottal stop is the sound you hear between the vowels in the expression 'oh oh!', or the Cockney pronunciation of 'water' (wa'er). It is actually a closing of the glottis at the back of the throat so that the passage of air is momentarily halted. It can occur anywhere in the word – at the beginning, middle or end.

The ('), or 'ayn', and the (**gh**), or 'rayn', are two of the most difficult sounds in Arabic. Both can be produced by tightening your throat and sort of growling, but the ('gh') requires a slight 'r' sound at the beginning – it is like the French 'r'. When the (') occurs before a vowel, the vowel is 'growled' from the back of the throat. If it is before a consonant or at the end of a word, it sounds like a glottal stop. The best way to learn these sounds is to listen to a native speaker pronounce their written equivalents.

Other common consonant sounds include the following:

**j**   more or less like the 'j' in 'John'
**g**   for those who read some Arabic, it is worth noting that the Moroccans have added a letter for the hard 'g' (as in Agadir) – a kaf (letter 'k') with three dots above it
**H**   a strongly whispered 'h', almost like a sigh of relief
**q**   a strong guttural 'k' sound. Often transcribed as 'k', although there is another letter in the Arabic alphabet which *is* the equivalent of 'k'
**kh**  a slightly gurgling sound, like the 'ch' in Scottish 'loch'
**r**   a rolled 'r', as in the Spanish 'para'
**s**   pronounced as in English 'sit', never as in 'wisdom'
**sh**  like the 'sh' in 'shelf'
**ż**   like the 's' in pleasure

**Double Consonants** In Arabic, double consonants are both pronounced. For example the word *istanna*, which means 'wait', is pronounced 'istan-na'.

**Transliteration** What you read and hear will as often as not be two or three entirely different things. No really satisfactory system

of transcribing the 'squiggles' of Arabic into Latin script has ever been devised, not for want of attempts.

Since most modern maps, books and the like dealing with Morocco, Algeria and Tunisia tend to reflect French (rather than English) conventions, this guide generally goes along with such conventions. The exception is Libya, where the Arabisation drive has been such that the question of transliteration out of the Arabic script hardly arises.

There is only one word for 'the' in Arabic – *al*. It modifies before certain consonants: ie in Arabic, Saladin's name is Salah ad-Din ('righteousness of the faith') – 'al' has been modified to 'ad' before the 'd' of Din. Also, in Morocco *el* is more commonly used. In Moroccan Arabic, the pronunciation is such that the initial 'a' or 'e' is hardly heard at all, and many language guides simply prefix words with 'l' to indicate this.

It may be useful, especially to travellers who have been elsewhere in the Arab world and become accustomed to certain transliterations, to consult the following list of common sounds and words often found in former French possessions and their 'standardised' equivalents:

**ou**  as in oued; it is the French equivalent of **w** in wadi (a usually dry, seasonal river bed). You may see references to the Alaouites (the dynasty of Hassan II) or, alternatively, to the Alawites. The name Daoud can also be written Dawud.
**dj**  as in djebel; it is the French equivalent of simple **j** in jebel – mountain.
**k**   often corresponds to the Arabic letter qaf, or the English **q**. Ksar versus qasr (castle) is an example.
**e**   often appears where some would prefer to see an **a**. Vowels in Arabic are not as important as in other languages. Vowel and consonant order are sometimes at variance. The common word for school, which also refers to older religious learning institutions, is madrassa, which most commonly appears as medersa.

**Arabic Greetings**
When Arabic speakers meet, they often exchange more extensive and formalised greetings than Westerners are used to. How and when they are used varies from country to country, and often according to the social status of the people concerned. Even an attempt to use a couple of them (whether correctly or not) will not go astray. As in all the Arabic vocabulary in this section, some expressions are more specifically Moroccan (indicated 'M'), but most will be understood throughout North Africa. Occasionally both MSA and Moroccan versions are given.

When addressing a man or woman in Morocco, the polite terms more or less equivalent to Mr and Mrs or Ms are *Si* or *Sidi* and *Lalla*, followed by the first name. Elsewhere in the Arab world more common versions are *Sayyid* and *Sayyida*. You may notice yourself being addressed as 'Mr John' or 'Mrs Anne'. ■

**Useful Words & Phrases** The following words and phrases should help you communicate on a basic level in Arabic.

### Greetings & Civilities

| | |
|---|---|
| Hello (literally, 'peace upon you'). | *as-salaam 'alaykum* |
| Hello (in response – 'and upon you be peace'). | *wa 'alaykum as-salaam* |
| Goodbye ('go in safety'). | *ma' as-salaama* |
| Good morning. | *sabaH al-khēr* |
| Good morning (in response). | *sabaH an-nūr* |
| Good evening. | *masa' al-khēr* |
| Good evening (in response). | *masa' an-nūr* |
| Please. | *'afak/'afik/'afakum* (to m/f/pl) |
| Thank you (very much). | *shukran (jazilan)* |
| You're welcome. | *la shukran 'ala wajib* |
| Yes. | *eeyeh/na'am* |
| Yes, OK. | *wakha* (M) |
| No. | *la* |
| No, thank you. | *la, shukran* |
| Excuse me. | *smeH leeya* |
| How are you? | *kayf Haalek? la bas?* (M) |
| Fine, thank you. | *la bas, barak Allah feek* (M) |
| Fine, thanks be to God. | *bikhēr, al-Hamdu lillah* |

**Essentials** Here are some nuts and bolts to get you through the simple encounters:

### Essentials

| | |
|---|---|
| I | *ana* |
| you | *inta/inti/intum* (m/f/pl) |
| he/she | *huwa/heeya* |
| we | *eHna* |
| they | *huma* |
| Why? | *laysh?* |
| now | *allaan/daba* (M) |
| Is there...? | *wash kayn...?* (M) |
| big/small | *kabeer/sagheer* |
| open | *meHlool* |
| Do you speak English? | *tatakallem ingleezee?* *wash kt'aref ngleezeeya?* (M) |
| Who is that? | *meen hadha?* *shkoon had?* (M) |
| I understand. | *fhemt* |
| I don't understand. | *ma fhemtesh* |
| Go ahead, move it, come on! | *zid!* (M) |

### Emergencies

| | |
|---|---|
| Call the police! | *'eyyet al-bolis!* |
| Call a doctor! | *'eyyet at-tabeeb!* |
| Help me please! | *'awenee 'afak!* |
| Thief! | *sheffar!* |
| They robbed me! | *sheffaroonee!* |

### Small Talk

| | |
|---|---|
| What's your name? | *asmeetak?* |
| My name is... | *ismee...* *smeetee...*(M) |
| How old are you? | *shaHak fi 'amrak?* |

| | |
|---|---|
| I'm 25. | *'aandee khamsa wa 'ashreen* |
| Where are you from? | *min een inta/inti/intum? (m/f/pl)* |
| I/We are from... | *ana/eHna min...* |
| America | *amreeka* |
| Australia | *ustralya* |
| Canada | *kanada* |
| England | *inglaterra* |
| France | *fransa* |
| Germany | *almanya* |
| Italy | *itaaliyya* |
| Japan | *al-yaban* |
| Netherlands | *holanda* |
| Spain | *isbanya* |
| Sweden | *as-sweed* |
| Switzerland | *sweesra* |

| | |
|---|---|
| I am... | *ana...* |
| American | *amreekanee* (m) |
| | *amreekaniyya* (f) |
| Australian | *ustralee* (m) |
| | *ustraliyya* (f) |
| British | *britaanee* (m) |
| | *britaaniyya* (f) |
| French | *fransee* (m) |
| | *fransiyya* (f) |
| Swedish | *sweedee* (m) |
| | *sweediyya* (f) |

**Getting Around**

I want to go to...
   *ureed/bgheet amshee ila...*
What is the fare to...?
   *bshaHal at-tazkara ila...?*
When does the...leave/arrive?
   *emta qiyam/wusuul...?*

| | |
|---|---|
| bus | *al-otobīs* |
| | *al-otobīsat* (pl) |
| intercity bus | *al-kar* (M) |
| | *al-keeran* (pl) |
| train | *al-qitar* |
| | *al-masheena* (M) |
| boat | *as-safeena* |
| | *al-baboor* (M) |

| | |
|---|---|
| Where is (the)...? | *fein...?* |
| bus station for... | *maHattat al-otobīs li...* |

| | |
|---|---|
| train station | *maHattat al-masheena/ al-qitar* |
| ticket office | *maktab al-werqa/ at-tazkara* |
| street | *az-zanqa* |
| city | *al-medīna* |
| village | *al-qarya* |
| bus stop | *mawqif al-otobīs* |
| station | *al-maHatta* |

Which bus goes to...?
   *ey kar yamshee ila...?*
Does this bus go to...?
   *yamshee had al-kar ila...?*
How many buses per day go to...?
   *fi/kayn kam kar kul yūm ila...?*
Please tell me when we arrive...
   *qulnee emta nassil...*
Stop here, please.
   *qif hena, 'afak*
Please wait for me.
   *intazarnee 'afak*
May I/we sit here?
   *(wash) yimkin ajlis/najlis hena?*
Where can I rent a bicycle?
   *fein yimkin ana akra beshkleeta?*

| | |
|---|---|
| address | *'anwān* |
| air-conditioning | *kleemateezaseeyon* |
| airport | *matār* |
| camel | *jamal* |
| car | *tomobeel, sayara* |
| crowded | *zHam* |
| daily | *kull yūm* |
| donkey | *Humār* |
| horse | *Husān* |
| number | *raqm* |
| ticket | *werqa, tazkara* |
| Wait! | *tsanna!* |

**Directions**

| | |
|---|---|
| How far is...? | *kam kilo li...?* |
| left/right | *yasar/yameen* |
| | *leeser/leemen* (M) |
| here/there | *huna/hunak* |
| next to | *bi-janib* |
| opposite | *muqabbal* |
| behind | *khalf/mor* (M) |
| Which? | *ash men?* |

| Where? | fein? |
|---|---|
| north | shamal |
| south | janoob |
| east | sharq |
| west | gharb |

### Around Town

| Where is (the)...? | fein...? |
|---|---|
| bank | al-banka |
| barber | al-Hallaq |
| beach | ash-shaatta' al-plāẑ (M) |
| embassy | as-sifāra |
| market | as-sūq |
| mosque | al-jāmi' |
| museum | al-matHaf |
| old city | al-medīna |
| palace | al-qasr |
| pharmacy | farmasyan |
| police station | al-bolīs |
| post office | al-bōsta/maktab al-barīd |
| restaurant | al-mat'am |
| university | al-jami'a |
| zoo | Hadīqat al-Haywān |

| I want to change... | ureed/bgheet asrif... |
|---|---|
| money | fulūs |
| US$ | dolār amreekānī |
| UK | jinay sterlīnī |
| A$ | dolār ustrālī |
| DM | mārk almānī |
| travellers' cheques | shīkāt siyaHiyya |

### Accommodation

Where is the hotel?
  *fein (kayn) al-otēl?*
Can I see the room?
  *(wash) yimkin lee nshūf al-bayt?*
How much is this room per night?
  *bshaHal al-bayt lilayl?*
Do you have any cheaper rooms?
  *wash kayn bayt rakhees 'ala had?*
That's too expensive.
  *ghaalee bazyaf*
This is fine.
  *had mezyan*

| bed | namooseeya |
|---|---|
| blanket | bataneeya |
| camp site | mukhaym |
| full | 'amer |
| hot water | ma skhūn |
| key | saroot |
| roof | staah |
| room | bayt |
| sheet | eezar |
| shower | doosh |
| toilet | bayt al-ma, mirHad |
| youth hostel | oberẑ, dar shabbab |

### Shopping

| Where can I buy...? | |
|---|---|
| *fein yimkin ashteree...?* | |
| How much? | bi-kam? |
| | bish-hal? (M) |
| too much | ghalee |
| Do you have...? | wash 'andkum...? |
| stamps | tawaaba |
| | tanber (M) |
| newspaper | al-jarida |

### Time

| When? | emta? |
|---|---|
| today | al-yūm |
| tomorrow | ghaddan |
| yesterday | al-bareh |
| morning | fis-sabaH |
| afternoon | fish-sheeya |
| evening | masa' |
| day/night | nahar/layl |
| week/month/year | usbu'/shahr/'am |

| What is the time? | sa'a kam? |
|---|---|
| | shahal fessa'a? (M) |
| At what time? | fī sa'a kam? |
| | fooqtash? (M) |
| after | min ba'd |
| on time | fil-waqt |
| early | bakrī |
| late | mu'attal |
| quickly | dgheeya |
| slowly | bishwayya |

### Days of the Week

| Monday | (nhar) al-itnēn |
|---|---|
| Tuesday | (nhar) at-talata |
| Wednesday | (nhar) al-arba' |

| Thursday | *(nhar) al-khamīs* |
| Friday | *(nhar) al-juma'* |
| Saturday | *(nhar) as-sabt* |
| Sunday | *(nhar) al-ahad* |

**Months of the Year** The Islamic year has 12 lunar months and is 11 days shorter than the Gregorian calendar, so important Muslim dates fall about 10 days earlier each (Western) year. It is impossible to predict exactly when they will fall, as this depends on when the new moon is sighted. The Islamic, or Hijra (referring to the year of Mohammed's flight from Mecca in 622 AD), calendar months are:

| 1st | *Moharram* |
| 2nd | *Safar* |
| 3rd | *Rabi' al-Awal* |
| 4th | *Rabi' al-Akhir* or |
| | *Rabi' at-Tani* |
| 5th | *Jumada al-Awal* |
| 6th | *Jumada al-Akhir* or |
| | *Jumada at-Taniyya* |
| 7th | *Rajab* |
| 8th | *Sha'aban* |
| 9th | *Ramadan* |
| 10th | *Shawwal* |
| 11th | *Zuul Qe'da* |
| 12th | *Zuul Hijja* |

In the Levant, in addition to the Hijra calendar, there is also another set of names for the Gregorian calendar. Luckily, in Morocco, the names of the months are virtually the same as their European counterparts and easily recognisable:

| January | *yanāyir* |
| February | *fibrāyir* |
| March | *maaris* |
| April | *abrīl* |
| May | *māyu* |
| June | *yunyu* |
| July | *yulyu* |
| August | *aghustus/ghusht* |
| September | *sibtimbir/* |
| | *shebtenber* |
| October | *uktoobir* |

| November | *nufimbir/nu'enbir* |
| December | *disimbir/dijenbir* |

**Arabic Numbers** Arabic numerals are simple enough to learn and, unlike the written language, run from left to right. Often you won't need to recognise the Arabic figures, as the European ones are commonly used in Morocco.

| 0 | • | *sifr* |
| 1 | ١ | *wāHid* |
| 2 | ٢ | *itneen/jooj* (M) |
| 3 | ٣ | *talata* |
| 4 | ٤ | *arba'a* |
| 5 | ٥ | *khamsa* |
| 6 | ٦ | *sitta* |
| 7 | ٧ | *saba'a* |
| 8 | ٨ | *tamanya* |
| 9 | ٩ | *tissa'* |
| 10 | ١٠ | *'ashara* |
| 11 | | *wāHidash* |
| 12 | | *itna'ash* |
| 13 | | *talattash* |
| 14 | | *arba'atash* |
| 15 | | *khamastash* |
| 16 | | *sitt'ash* |
| 17 | | *saba'atash* |
| 18 | | *tamantash* |
| 19 | | *tissa'atash* |
| 20 | | *'ashreen* |
| 21 | | *wāHid wa 'ashreen* |
| 22 | | *itneen wa 'ashreen* |
| 30 | | *talateen* |
| 40 | | *arba'een* |
| 50 | | *khamseen* |
| 60 | | *sitteen* |
| 70 | | *saba'een* |
| 80 | | *tamaneen* |
| 90 | | *tissa'een* |
| 100 | | *miyya* |
| 101 | | *miyya wa wāHid* |
| 125 | | *miyya wa khamsa wa 'ashreen* |
| 200 | | *miyyateen* |
| 300 | | *talata mia* |
| 400 | | *arba'a mia* |
| 1000 | | *alf* |
| 2000 | | *alfeen* |
| 3000 | | *talat alāf* |
| 4000 | | *arba'at alāf* |

### Ordinal Numbers

| | |
|---|---|
| first | *'awwal* |
| second | *tānī* |
| third | *tālit* |
| fourth | *rābi'* |
| fifth | *khāmis* |

### French

The most commonly spoken European language in North Africa (except Libya) is French, so if the thought of getting your mind around Arabic is too much, it would be a good investment to learn some French.

**Useful Words & Phrases** The following words and phrases should help you communicate on a basic level in French:

### Greetings & Civilities

| | |
|---|---|
| Hello/Good morning/ Good day. | *Bonjour.* |
| Goodbye. | *Au revoir/Salut.* |
| Good evening. | *Bonsoir.* |
| (Have a) good evening. | *Bonne soirée.* |
| Good night. | *Bonne nuit.* |
| Please. | *S'il vous plaît.* |
| Thank you. | *Merci.* |
| You're welcome. | *De rien/Je vous en prie.* |
| Yes. | *Oui.* |
| No. | *Non.* |
| No, thank you. | *Non, merci.* |
| Excuse me. | *Excusez-moi/ Pardon.* |
| How are you? | *Comment allez-vous/Ça va?* |
| Well, thanks. | *Bien, merci.* |

### Essentials

| | |
|---|---|
| I | *je* |
| you | *vous* |
| he/she | *il/elle* |
| we | *nous* |
| they | *ils/elles* (m/f) |
| Why? | *Pourquoi?* |
| now | *maintenant* |
| Is/Are there...? | *(Est-ce qu')il y a...?* |
| big/small | *grand/petit* |
| open/closed | *ouvert/fermé* |

| | |
|---|---|
| Do you speak English? | *Parlez-vous anglais?* |
| Who is that? | *C'est qui, celui-là/ celle-là?* (m/f) |
| I understand. | *Je comprends.* |
| I don't understand. | *Je ne comprends pas.* |

### Emergencies

| | |
|---|---|
| Call the police! | *Appelez la police!* |
| Call a doctor! | *Appelez un médecin!* |
| Help me please! | *Au secours/Aidez-moi!* |
| Thief! | *(Au) voleur!* |

### Small Talk

| | |
|---|---|
| What's your name? | *Comment vous appelez-vous?* |
| My name is... | *Je m'appelle...* |
| How old are you? | *Quel âge avez-vous?* |
| I'm 25. | *J'ai vingt-cinq ans.* |
| Where are you from? | *D'où êtes-vous?* |

| | |
|---|---|
| I/We are from... | *Je viens/Nous venons...* |
| America | *de l'Amérique* |
| Australia | *de l'Australie* |
| Canada | *du Canada* |
| England | *de l'Angleterre* |
| Germany | *de l'Allemagne* |
| Italy | *de l'Italie* |
| Japan | *du Japon* |
| Netherlands | *des Pays Bas* |
| Spain | *de l'Espagne* |
| Sweden | *du Suède* |
| Switzerland | *de la Suisse* |

| | |
|---|---|
| I am... | *Je suis...* |
| American | *américain/e* (m/f) |
| Australian | *australien/ne* (m/f) |
| British | *britannique* (m/f) |
| Swedish | *suédois/e* (m/f) |

### Getting Around

| | |
|---|---|
| I want to go to... | *Je veux aller à...* |
| What is the fare to...? | *Combien coûte le billet pour...?* |

When does (the)... | À quelle heure part/arrive...?
bus | l'autobus
intercity bus/ coach | le car
train | le train
boat | le bateau
ferry | le bac

Where is (the)...? | Où est...?
bus station for... | la gare routière pour...
train station | la gare
ticket office | la billeterie/le guichet
street | la rue
city | la ville
village | le village
bus stop | l'arrêt d'autobus

Which bus goes to...? | Quel autobus/car part pour...?
Does this bus go to...? | Ce car-là va-t-il à...?
How many buses per day go to...? | Il y a combien de cars chaque jour pour...?
Please tell me when we arrive... | Dîtes-moi s'il vous plaît à quelle heure on arrive...
Stop here, please. | Arrêtez ici, s'il vous plaît.
Please wait for me. | Attendez-moi ici, s'il vous plaît.
May I sit here? | Puis-je m'asseoir ici?
Where can I rent a bicycle? | Où est-ce que je peux louer une bicyclette?

address | adresse
air-conditioning | climatisation
airport | aéroport
camel | chameau
car | voiture
crowded | beaucoup de monde
daily | chaque jour
donkey | âne
horse | cheval
number | numéro

ticket | billet
Wait! | Attendez!

## Directions

How far is...? | À combien de kilomètres est...?
left/right | gauche/droite
here/there | ici/là
next to | à côté de
opposite | en face
behind | derrière
Which? | Quel?
Where? | Où?
north | nord
south | sud
east | est
west | ouest

## Around Town

Where is the...? | Où est...?
bank | la banque
barber | le coiffeur
beach | la plage
embassy | l'ambassade
market | le marché
mosque | la mosquée
museum | le musée
old city | le centre historique
palace | le palais
pharmacy | la pharmacie
police station | la police
post office | la poste
restaurant | le restaurant
university | l'université
zoo | le zoo

I want to change... | Je voudrais changer...
money | de l'argent
US$ | des dollars américains
UK | des livres sterling
A$ | des dollars australiens
DM | des marks allemands
travellers' cheques | des chèques de voyage

## Accommodation

| | |
|---|---|
| Where is the hotel? | *Où est l'hôtel?* |
| Can I see the room? | *Peux-je voir la chambre?* |
| How much is this room per night? | *Combien est cette chambre pour une nuit?* |
| Do you have any cheaper rooms? | *Avez-vous des chambres moins chères?* |
| That's too expensive. | *C'est trop cher.* |
| This is fine. | *Ça va bien.* |
| | |
| bed | *lit* |
| blanket | *couverture* |
| camp site | *camping* |
| full | *complet* |
| hot water | *eau chaude* |
| key | *clef or clé* |
| roof | *terrasse* |
| room | *chambre* |
| sheet | *drap* |
| shower | *douche* |
| toilet | *les toilettes* |
| washbasin | *lavabo* |
| youth hostel | *auberge de jeunesse* |

## Shopping

| | |
|---|---|
| Where can I buy...? | *Où est-ce que je peux acheter...?* |
| How much? | *Combien?* |
| How much does it cost? | *Ça coûte combien?* |
| more/less | *plus/moins* |
| too much | *trop cher* |
| Do you have...? | *Avez-vous...?* |
| stamps | *des timbres* |
| newspaper | *un journal* |

## Time

| | |
|---|---|
| When? | *Quand?* |
| today | *aujourd'hui* |
| tomorrow | *demain* |
| yesterday | *hier* |
| morning | *matin* |
| afternoon | *après-midi* |
| evening | *soir* |
| day/night | *jour/nuit* |
| week/month/year | *semaine/mois/an* |

| | |
|---|---|
| What is the time? | *Quelle heure est-il?* |
| At what time? | *À quelle heure?* |
| after | *après* |
| on time | *à l'heure* |
| early | *tôt* |
| late | *tard* |
| quickly | *vite* |
| slowly | *lentement* |

## Days of the Week

| | |
|---|---|
| Monday | *lundi* |
| Tuesday | *mardi* |
| Wednesday | *mercredi* |
| Thursday | *jeudi* |
| Friday | *vendredi* |
| Saturday | *samedi* |
| Sunday | *dimanche* |

## Months of the Year

| | |
|---|---|
| January | *janvier* |
| February | *février* |
| March | *mars* |
| April | *avril* |
| May | *mai* |
| June | *juin* |
| July | *juillet* |
| August | *août* |
| September | *septembre* |
| October | *octobre* |
| November | *novembre* |
| December | *décembre* |

## Numbers

| | |
|---|---|
| 0 | *zéro* |
| 1 | *un* |
| 2 | *deux* |
| 3 | *trois* |
| 4 | *quatre* |
| 5 | *cinq* |
| 6 | *six* |
| 7 | *sept* |
| 8 | *huit* |
| 9 | *neuf* |
| 10 | *dix* |
| 11 | *onze* |
| 12 | *douze* |
| 13 | *treize* |
| 14 | *quatorze* |
| 15 | *quinze* |

| | | | | |
|---|---|---|---|---|
| 16 | *seize* | 125 | *cent vingt-cinq* |
| 17 | *dix-sept* | 200 | *deux cents* |
| 18 | *dix-huit* | 300 | *trois cents* |
| 19 | *dix-neuf* | 400 | *quatre cents* |
| 20 | *vingt* | 1000 | *mille* |
| 21 | *vingt-et-un* | 2000 | *deux milles* |
| 22 | *vingt-deux* | 3000 | *trois milles* |
| 30 | *trente* | 4000 | *quatre milles* |
| 40 | *quarante* | | |
| 50 | *cinquante* | | |
| 60 | *soixante* | **Ordinal Numbers** | |
| 70 | *soixante-dix* | first | *premier* |
| 80 | *quatre-vingts* | second | *deuxième* |
| 90 | *quatre-vingt-dix* | third | *troisième* |
| 100 | *cent* | fourth | *quatrième* |
| 101 | *cent un* | fifth | *cinquième* |

# Facts for the Visitor

## MONEY

What currencies you take and how you carry them will vary a little from country to country; see the Money section in each country's Facts for the Visitor chapter.

Currencies can be exchanged most easily and flexibly in Morocco and Tunisia. It is not recommended to bring 'obscure' currencies such as Australian and NZ dollars or the Irish punt. Cash or travellers' cheques in major currencies are perfectly acceptable, and most banks are fast and efficient. American Express travellers' cheques are recommended in Morocco, as the company has offices there.

Major credit cards can be used in many hotels, shops and restaurants in both Morocco and Tunisia. Some cards can also be used to get cash advances. In Morocco you can use some automatic telling machines (ATMs) with Visa or MasterCard. In both Morocco and Tunisia you will need a minimum of about US$15 a day to survive in fairly basic style.

Algeria and Libya present more of a problem. In both countries, credit cards are useless. Black markets thrive, with rates up to three times higher than the official rate in Algeria and six times higher in Libya. Changing money on the black market will make the difference between an expensive or cheap travelling experience, but it can be dangerous (for further details see the Money section in Algeria's Facts for the Visitor chapter). In Libya, US dollars are the best currency to carry, and French francs are recommended for Algeria.

In all four countries the export of local currency is prohibited. Re-exchanging local currency on departure is fairly easy in Morocco, but becomes increasingly difficult as you travel through Tunisia, Algeria and Libya. Make sure you keep all your exchange receipts, as banks re-exchanging local currency need to see proof that the initial exchange occurred locally and not abroad. For more details, see the Money sections in each country's Facts for the Visitor chapter.

## WHEN TO GO

Deciding on the ideal time of year to travel depends on where you want to go and for how long. Spring (mid-March to mid-June) is the best time to be in North Africa. Autumn (mid-September to mid-December) is OK too, but the skies can be very hazy for much of the time. Although summer (mid-June to mid-September) counts as high season in these countries (mostly because that's when Europe goes on holiday), it can be viciously hot, whether you're in Tunis or Casablanca, the peaks of the High Atlas or the Sahara. In the Sahara especially you'll be unwilling or even unable to move for the searing heat. There are variations. While winter (mid-December to mid-March) on the Mediterranean coast can be wet and dreary, and the mountains can become snowbound, it can be very pleasant in the desert or on the south Moroccan coast. Note that the temperature drops dramatically at night in the desert, and in the higher mountains.

## WHAT TO BRING

Bring the minimum. When you have gathered all the stuff you think you're going to need, throw half of it out and you'll probably be close to a sensible amount. There is nothing worse than having to lug loads of excess stuff around, so, unless it's essential, *leave it at home*!

A rucksack is far more practical than an overnight bag and more likely to stand up to the rigours of African travel. It is worth paying for a good one. Buckles and straps soon start falling off cheap rucksacks and before long all you have is a worthless bit of junk.

What type of pack you take is a matter of personal preference. Berghaus, Lowe and Karrimor are three recommended brands,

40

and one of the best stockists in London is the YHA Adventure Centre, 14 Southampton St, London WC2.

Because of the extremes of temperature experienced in desert countries, you may need to pack for all climates. Also bear in mind the clothing guidelines outlined under Society & Conduct in the Facts about the Region chapter. For most of the year, a hat, sunglasses and sunscreen are useful, and they become indispensable in the desert. It gets chilly in the mountains even in summer, so bring a warm jacket. In winter it can get quite wet, so rainproof clothing is a good idea. You can also get waterproof covers for your rucksack.

Hikers will need decent boots, and travellers considering trekking Morocco's High Atlas should note that trekking above the snow level in winter requires specialised equipment. For more details, see the section on High Atlas Trekking in the Morocco chapter.

In out of the way places, a water bottle and purification tablets or tincture of iodine are worth their weight in gold. You could well have to sleep out, so a sleeping bag and groundsheet are worth considering. Some people take a stove and tent. If you are heading farther south this is worth considering, but for North Africa alone the extra weight and inconvenience aren't justifiable.

Other handy items include a Swiss army knife, compass (especially in the desert and mountains), a universal sink plug (a tennis ball cut in half will often do the trick), a torch (flashlight), a few metres of nylon cord, earplugs (for successful sleeping in the noisier cheapies), a small sewing kit and a medical kit (see the Health section in this chapter for details).

Most toiletries – soap, shampoo, toothpaste, toilet paper, washing powder – are available all over Tunisia and Morocco, although tampons can usually only be found in supermarkets. In Algeria, toilet paper is not hard to find, but other supplies can be difficult to obtain and of dubious quality, so it's best to bring your own. In Libya, even toilet paper is hard to come by outside the big cities, so all toiletries should be brought with you.

Although you can get contraceptives in the main centres in Morocco, the general rule across North Africa applies here too: bring your own. The same goes for any special medication you may need.

In Libya, bring a supply of passport photos in case you need to get permits for travel or other papers sorted out.

## WEIGHTS & MEASURES
The countries of North Africa use the metric system. There is a standard conversion table at the back of this book.

## RESPONSIBLE TOURISM
There are a few common-sense rules to keep in mind when traipsing around North Africa. Although some of the locals seem to care little about littering natural beauty spots, there is no need to add to the muck.

At ancient sites like Volubilis in Morocco or Carthage in Tunisia, take care not to trample over the ruins needlessly – you'll only contribute to their decay.

## BOOKS
For more specific books on each country, refer to the Books entries in each country's Facts for the Visitor chapter. What follows is some suggested reading on the Arab world, Islam and North Africa.

### History & Society
For those wanting to become generally acquainted with the wider Arabic-speaking world, there are several books to recommend. Philip Hitti's highly readable *History of the Arabs* (Macmillan paperback) is regarded as a classic.

A more recent but equally acclaimed work is Albert Hourani's *A History of the Arab Peoples* (Faber, 1991). It is as much an attempt to convey a feel for evolving Muslim Arab societies as it is a straight history, with an extensive, if largely generalised, treatment of various aspects of social, cultural and religious life.

*The Arabs* by Peter Mansfield (Penguin)

offers an excellent insight into the Arab psyche and is one of the most accessible texts for newcomers to the topic.

If you want a more comprehensive reference on the whole Muslim world (although it's weak on more recent history), you could try delving into the two hardback or four paperback volumes of *A Cambridge History of Islam*. Volume 2A has a section devoted to North African history.

*The Qur'an* may seem like a strange recommendation, but it makes interesting reading for those who want to know more about the foundations on which Islam is based.

If you are interested in recent events, *The Islamic Threat: myth or reality?* by American academic John L Esposito (Oxford University Press, 1992) provides a lucid assessment of Islamic politics over the past 25 years.

*Maghreb: histoire et société* (SNED, 1974) is one of a number of studies by Jacques Berque, regarded as one of the better historians of the region working in the French language. His book covers Morocco, Algeria and Tunisia.

In an attempt to get away from a French interpretation of Maghreb history, Abdallah Laroui wrote *The History of the Maghreb* (translated from the French by Ralph Manheim, Princeton University Press, 1970). He asserts an indigenous view and is regarded by some Moroccans as the best there is. Unfortunately, it's out of print and hard to track down. Its analysis of how historians have dealt with Maghreb history makes it less useful as an introduction to events, and it does not cover Libya.

For a completely different perspective, *L'Afrique du Nord au Féminin* by Gabriel Camps (Perrin, 1992) presents stories of heroines of the Maghreb and the Sahara from 6000 BC to the present. Camps has written several works dealing with various aspects of Maghreb history.

*Africa in History* by Basil Davidson (Paladin, 1974) is a very readable account of the history of the whole continent by one of the most knowledgeable experts on Africa.

**Travel Guides**
For complete coverage of the African continent, Lonely Planet's *Africa on a shoestring* is the definitive guide. People planning any desert driving across the Sahara should consider the *Sahara Handbook* by Simon Glen (Roger Lascelles, 1990), which has detailed advice on how to plan such adventures. It has descriptions of all the navigable routes in the Sahara. Lascelles has also published a similar book called *Africa Overland*.

Other good books on similar lines are the Hachette (French) and Polyglott (German) guides.

**Periodicals**
The *Africa Review* and *Middle East Review* are published annually in the UK by World of Information, 21 Gold St, Saffron Waldon, Essex CB10 1EJ. They are a useful source of information about recent developments within the individual countries of the region, and they include a business guide and directory of useful addresses for each country. It may be worth consulting an issue before setting off.

**Arts & Architecture**
*Islamic Architecture: North Africa* by Antony Hutt (Scorpio Publications, 1977) is a pictorial overview of the great buildings of the Maghreb.

**MAPS**
Few decent maps of North Africa are available in the countries themselves, so you should get one before leaving home.

There are several reasonable maps covering all of North-West Africa, taking in parts of Egypt and the Sudan in the east. Kümmerley & Frey publishes one called *Africa, North & West* on a scale of 1:4,000,000. It costs UK£6.95. At the same price comes another by VWK, with the same title and virtually the same quality. Michelin map number 953 covers much the same area and costs UK£4.45.

See the Maps entries in each country's Facts for the Visitor chapter for information on individual country maps.

## PHOTOGRAPHY

For most daylight outdoor shooting, 100 ASA is quite sufficient. Generally, it is best to shoot in the early morning and late afternoon, as the harsh North African noonday light can give your pictures a glary, washed-out look.

Dust is a hazard to cameras, particularly if you are travelling to the desert regions. To minimise damage always keep a UV filter on your lenses and keep your camera wrapped in a plastic bag when not in use. Also try not to change lenses or films when you are out in the open. Apart from mechanical damage, tiny particles can easily leave a scratch down an entire film.

North Africa is full of photo opportunities, but there are two important cautions. Don't point your camera at anything vaguely 'strategic'. This includes airports, bridges, government buildings and members of the police or armed forces. In Libya especially, you may attract the attention of security people, although you'd be unlucky to have your films confiscated.

The second point is to be careful whom you aim your lens at. Some people, women especially, intensely dislike it, and their wishes should be respected. It is always best to ask first.

The other side of this coin is the growing tendency in the main tourist centres, mainly in Morocco, for people to demand payment for photos. Moroccan water sellers make more money from tourists taking photos of them than they could ever hope to from merely selling water. Tourists can find themselves being pursued up the street by people, demanding money for having their mugs immortalised.

## HEALTH

Travel health depends on your predeparture preparations, your day-to-day health care while travelling and how you handle any medical problem or emergency that may develop. While the list of potential dangers can seem quite frightening, with a little luck, some basic precautions and adequate information, few travellers experience more than upset stomachs.

Don't forget that you should always see your doctor for medical advice before heading off for a trip overseas.

### Travel Health Guides

There are a number of books on travel health. *Staying Healthy in Asia, Africa & Latin America* (Volunteers in Asia) is probably the best all-round guide to carry, as it's compact but very detailed and well organised.

*Travellers' Health* by Dr Richard Dawood (Oxford University Press, 1992) is comprehensive, easy to read and authoritative, although it's rather large to lug around.

*The Traveller's Health Guide* by Dr Anthony C Turner (Lascelles, 1991) is also recommended.

*Travel with Children* by Maureen Wheeler (Lonely Planet Publications) includes basic advice on travel health for younger children.

### Pre-Departure Preparations

**Health Insurance** Get some! You may never need it, but if you do you'll be very glad you got it. There are many different travel-insurance policies which cover medical costs for illness or injury, the cost of getting home for medical treatment, life insurance and baggage insurance. Some protect you against cancellation penalties on advance-purchase tickets should you have to change travel plans because of illness.

Check out what your insurers consider to be a 'dangerous activity', and whether or not they will cover it. Trekking and many sports fall under this heading.

It is worth getting cover for ambulances and emergency repatriation in the case of serious illness.

Some policies will only reimburse claimants when they have returned home, or at any rate after expenses have been incurred. Keep all proof for making claims, including doctors' certificates, bills and police statements that may be relevant.

Increasingly, policies are backed by an international medical assistance organisation (many of them are based in France for some reason). You will be given a telephone number in the country where you bought the policy, or for example in the UK, which you should call (if possible by reverse charge) if you strike trouble. They will then try to assess your needs or get in touch with registered medical practitioners in the country where you're travelling.

Most travel and insurance agents should be able to recommend a policy, but check the fine print before you decide which one to take out.

**Medical Kit** It is always a good idea to travel with a small first-aid kit. Some items to include are: Band-aids, a sterilised gauze bandage, Elastoplast, cotton wool, a thermometer, tweezers, scissors, antibiotic cream or ointment, an antiseptic agent (Dettol or Betadine), burn cream (Caladryl is good for sunburn, minor burns and itchy bites), insect repellent and multivitamins. Don't forget water sterilisation tablets or iodine, antimalarial tablets (if you feel the need for them), any medication you're already taking and contraceptives, if necessary.

Recommended traveller's medications include diarrhoea tablets (such as Lomotil, but note that some experts warn against this one, or Imodium), a rehydration mixture, antihistamines, paracetamol or aspirin for pain and fever, and a course of antibiotics (check with your doctor). Erythromycin is recommended for respiratory, teeth and skin infections and is a safe alternative to penicillin. Metronidazole (Flagyl) is recommended for amoebic dysentery and giardiasis. Again, check with your doctor before leaving home.

Many of these or similar items, other than water-sterilisation tablets and insect repellent, are available in Moroccan pharmacies at lower prices than in the West. Condoms are also available but are not good quality. Contraceptive pills are still hard to get, and securing your preferred strength will be difficult indeed.

**General Precautions** Make sure your teeth are in good shape before you leave home.

If you wear eyeglasses, carry a second pair or at least a copy of your prescription in case of loss or breakage.

Public toilets are bad news: fly-infested, dirty and stinky. Some toilets are still of the squat-over-a-hole-in-a-little-room variety. Always carry a roll of toilet paper with you; it's easy to buy throughout most of North Africa, but can be problematic in Libya.

**Vaccinations**
These should be obtained before you arrive in North Africa.

The recommended vaccinations are polio, typhoid and tetanus. These injections last for differing periods of time and boosters are highly recommended to maintain immunity. Keep a record of all your shots on an International Certificate of Vaccination, which you can get from your doctor or health department. You might consider gamma globulin for protection against infectious hepatitis (a hepatitis A prophylactic is officially recommended for Libya). Check out the new hepatitis A vaccine, Havrix. It's not cheap, but if you travel a lot in dodgy places, three shots over a year give you 10 years' protection. You should check with your doctor for up-to-date details.

You'll need to have evidence of Yellow Fever shots when entering Algeria or Libya from the south. Algeria also requires you to produce proof of cholera shots – if you don't have one, they may insist you have one on the spot.

Although cholera shots are generally frowned upon as being of extremely little use, the disease has been a problem in the Meknès area of Morocco since 1971. In 1990, 214 people reportedly died out of a total 2500 who had contracted the disease in Meknès, Fès, Taza and the Sebou river valley. There have been several smaller outbreaks since.

Officially at least, cholera shots are recommended for Libya – but check this with an expert first.

In London, there are several places where you can get advice and vaccinations. Trailfinders (see under Air in the Getting

There & Away chapter) has an inoculation centre, as does British Airways at its Victoria Station office. The Travel Clinic of the Hospital for Tropical Diseases (☎ 0171-637 9899) at Queen's House, 180-182 Tottenham Court Rd, is open from 9 am to 5 pm for consultations and shots. It also runs a recorded info line on specific destinations (☎ 01839-337733).

The problem with all these options is that some of the shots can be quite expensive. If you are resident in the UK and on the National Health Service, ask your GP what shots he/she can do for you – many will either be free or cost UK£3 or UK£4 for the prescription. Compared with, say, UK£25 for a shot of Havrix, the saving is obvious.

If you are in Melbourne, Australia, the Travellers' Medical & Vaccination Centre (☎ 03-602 5788) can help.

People planning extended stays, particularly in more remote areas, are advised to consider taking a pre-exposure rabies vaccine, along with cover for tuberculosis or hepatitis B.

Malaria is not a significant problem in North Africa, but again, if you are contemplating a long stay, especially in out-of-the-way places, you will want to consult your doctor about prophylactics. If you are heading on into West Africa, you will need antimalarials, and may as well start taking them while still in North Africa.

### Food & Water

Tap water in North African cities is generally chlorinated and safe to drink. The chlorination doesn't always agree with people, so if the tap water makes you feel sick it is possible to buy bottled water. Make sure the seals on the bottles have not been tampered with, as it is not unheard of to be handed a bottle refilled with tap water.

In the countryside the water is not so safe. You should only drink tap water that has been boiled for at least 10 minutes. Simple filtering won't remove all dangerous organisms, so if you can't boil water it should be treated chemically. Chlorine tablets (Puritabs, Steritabs or other brands) will kill many but not all pathogens. Iodine is very effective for purifying water and is available in tablet form (such as Potable Aqua), but follow the directions carefully and remember that too much iodine can be harmful.

If you can't find tablets, tincture of iodine (2%) or iodine crystals can be used. Two drops of tincture of iodine per litre of clear water is the recommended dosage; the water should then be left to stand for 30 minutes. Iodine crystals require a more complicated process, as you have to first prepare a saturated iodine solution. Iodine loses its effectiveness if exposed to air or damp, so keep it in a tightly sealed container. Flavoured powder will disguise the taste of treated water and is a good idea if you are travelling with children.

Avoid milk that hasn't at least been boiled; the same goes for cream. You can buy pasteurised milk in cartons in Morocco. It is usually OK, but if it tastes at all funny, give it a miss.

There are a few common-sense precautions to take with food in North Africa. You should always wash and peel fruit and vegetables and preferably avoid salads, as food isn't always well washed before it reaches your plate. Steering clear of salads is easier said than done, and many travellers eat them without ill-effects – it is a mixture of judging each case on its merits and plain luck.

Meat and fish are safe as long as they have been thoroughly cooked, but they are perishable and potentially a nice home for worms and other nasties if only half-cooked. Take particular care with shellfish and the like.

Contaminated food or water can cause dysentery, giardiasis, hepatitis A, cholera, polio and typhoid – all of which are best avoided! In any case of doubt, the UK Travel Clinic's advice, and it is sound, is 'cook it, peel it or leave it'.

North Africa is hardly a vegetarian's delight, and sticking to a limited range of food could result in vitamin deficiencies. Even those not so handicapped may find they are not eating as well as they could, and in both cases a course of multivitamins is worth considering to supplement local diet.

**Climatic & Geographical Considerations**
**Coping with the Heat** Protect yourself against the heat of the sun in North Africa. In some parts of the region, especially in the south, it can be difficult to gauge how quickly you are losing body water, because the climate is so dry. Headaches, dizziness and nausea are signs that you have lost too much water and might have heat exhaustion. To prevent this, take a bit of extra salt with your food, drink plenty of fluids (don't wait till you are thirsty) and wear a hat and sunglasses. The salt helps prevent dehydration. Incidentally, the caffeine in coffee and tea also contributes to dehydration.

**Sunburn** Sunscreen will prevent the sun from frying your skin. Wearing trousers and long sleeves is cooler than shorts and short sleeves because your body moisture stays closer to your skin. Lastly, remember that when you're on the beach or in the water you will burn quite quickly, so wear a shirt while snorkelling or swimming.

**Prickly Heat** Prickly heat is an itchy rash caused by excessive perspiration trapped under the skin. It usually strikes people who have just arrived in a hot climate because their pores have not yet opened sufficiently to cope with greater sweating. Keeping cool and bathing often, using a mild talcum powder or even resorting to air-conditioning may help until you acclimatise.

**Heat Exhaustion** Dehydration or salt deficiency can cause heat exhaustion. Take time to acclimatise to high temperatures and make sure you get sufficient liquids. Vomiting or diarrhoea can also deplete your liquid and salt levels. Salt deficiency is characterised by fatigué, lethargy, headaches, giddiness and muscle cramps, and salt tablets may help.

Anhydrotic heat exhaustion, caused by an inability to sweat, is quite rare. Unlike the other forms of heat exhaustion, it is likely to strike people who have been in a hot climate for some time rather than newcomers. You will stay cooler by covering up with light, cotton clothes that trap perspiration against your skin, rather than by wearing brief clothes.

**Heat Stroke** This serious, sometimes fatal, condition can occur if the body's heat-regulating mechanism breaks down and the body temperature rises to dangerous levels. Long, continuous periods of exposure to high temperatures can leave you vulnerable to heat stroke. You should avoid excessive alcohol intake or strenuous activity when you first arrive in a hot climate.

The symptoms are feeling unwell, little or no sweating and a high body temperature (39°C to 41°C). Where sweating has ceased, the skin becomes flushed and red. Severe, throbbing headaches and lack of coordination will also occur, and the sufferer may be confused or aggressive. Eventually ,the victim will become delirious or convulse. Hospitalisation is essential, but meanwhile get patients out of the sun, remove their clothing, cover them with a wet sheet or towel and fan continually.

**Fungal Infections** Hot-weather fungal infections are most likely to occur on the scalp, between the toes or fingers (athlete's foot), in the groin (jock itch or crotch rot) and on the body (ringworm). You get ringworm (a fungal infection, not a worm) from infected animals or by walking on damp areas, like shower floors.

To prevent fungal infections wear loose, comfortable clothes, avoid artificial fibres, wash frequently and dry carefully. If you do get an infection, wash the infected area daily with a disinfectant or medicated soap and water, and rinse and dry well. Apply an antifungal powder like Tinaderm. Try to expose the infected area to air or sunlight as much as possible and wash all towels and underwear in hot water, as well as changing them often.

**Cold** Too much cold is just as dangerous as too much heat, particularly if it leads to hypothermia. Although not generally a problem in North Africa, take care when trekking high up in Morocco's Atlas Mountains (especially in winter) or indeed when taking an overnight bus through the mountains.

Hypothermia occurs when the body loses heat faster than it can produce it and the core temperature of the body falls. It is surprisingly easy to progress from very cold to dangerously cold due to a combination of wind, wet clothing, fatigue and hunger, even if the air temperature is above freezing. It is best to dress in layers; silk, wool and some of the new artificial fibres are all good insulating materials. A hat is important, as a lot of heat is lost through the head. A strong, waterproof outer layer is essential, as keeping dry is vital. Carry basic supplies, including food containing simple sugars to generate heat quickly and lots of fluid to drink.

Symptoms of hypothermia are exhaustion, numb skin (particularly toes and fingers), shivering, slurred speech, irrational or violent behaviour, lethargy, stumbling, dizzy spells, muscle cramps and violent bursts of energy. Irrationality may take the form of sufferers claiming they are warm and trying to take off their clothes.

To treat hypothermia, first get the patient out of the wind and/or rain, remove their clothing if it's wet and replace it with dry, warm clothing. Give them hot liquids – not alcohol – and some high-kilojoule, easily digestible food. This should be enough for the early stages of hypothermia, but if it has gone further it may be necessary to place victims in warm sleeping bags and get in with them. Do not rub patients, place them near a fire or remove their wet clothes in the wind. If possible, place a sufferer in a warm (not hot) bath.

**Altitude Sickness** Acute Mountain Sickness, or AMS, occurs at high altitude and can be fatal. The lack of oxygen at high altitudes affects most people to some extent. Take it easy at first, increase your liquid intake and eat well. Even with acclimatisation you may still have trouble adjusting – headaches, nausea, dizziness, a dry cough, insomnia, breathlessness and loss of appetite are all signs to heed. If you reach a high altitude by

trekking, acclimatisation takes place gradually and you are less likely to be affected.

Mild altitude problems will generally abate after a day or so, but if the symptoms persist or become worse the only treatment is to descend – even 500 metres can help. Breathlessness, a dry, irritative cough (which may progress to the production of pink, frothy sputum), severe headache, loss of appetite, nausea and sometimes vomiting are all danger signs. Increasing tiredness, confusion and lack of coordination and balance are real danger signs. Any of these symptoms individually, even just a persistent headache, can be a warning.

There is no hard and fast rule as to how high is too high: AMS has been fatal at altitudes of 3000 metres, although 3500 to 4500 metres is the usual range. Jebel Toubkal, in the High Atlas Mountains, is the highest peak in North Africa, at 4165 metres. It is always wise to sleep at a lower altitude than the greatest height reached during the day.

**Motion Sickness** Eating lightly before and during a trip will reduce the chances of motion sickness. If you are prone to motion sickness try to find a place that minimises disturbance – near the wing on aircraft, close to midships on boats, near the centre on buses. Fresh air usually helps, reading or cigarette smoke doesn't. Commercial anti-motion-sickness preparations, which can cause drowsiness, have to be taken before the trip commences; when you're feeling sick it's too late. Ginger is a natural preventative and is available in capsule form.

### Diseases of Insanitation

**Diarrhoea** Most travellers are sooner or later hit by a bout of diarrhoea. There is usually nothing you can do to prevent the onslaught; it is simply your system trying to adjust to a different environment. It can happen anywhere. There is no 'cure', but following certain regimens will eventually eliminate or suppress the problem. Avoid taking drugs if possible, as it is much better to let it run its course.

The procedure to follow is fairly basic: drink plenty of fluids to prevent dehydration, but not milk, coffee, strong tea, soft drinks or cocoa. Avoid eating anything other than dried toast or, perhaps, fresh yoghurt, and stick to a bland diet as you recover.

If you are travelling, it may be difficult to follow these guidelines. That is when Lomotil, Imodium, codeine phosphate tablets, a liquid derivative of opium prescribed by a doctor or a medicine with pectin (like kaopectate) can be useful. Lomotil is convenient because the pills are tiny, but it tends to clam your system up so that nothing, including the nasties causing the problem, can get out. If you are still ailing after all of this, then you might have dysentery. See a doctor.

**Giardiasis** The parasite causing this intestinal disorder is present in contaminated water. The symptoms are stomach cramps, nausea, a bloated stomach, watery, foul-smelling diarrhoea and frequent gas. Giardiasis can appear several weeks after you have been exposed to the parasite. The symptoms may disappear for a few days and then return; this can go on for several weeks. Tinidazole, known as Fasigyn, or metronidazole are the recommended drugs for treatment. Either can be used in a single treatment dose. Antibiotics are of no use.

**Dysentery** Unfortunately, this illness is quite common among travellers. It is characterised by diarrhoea containing blood and lots of mucus; seek medical assistance if you have these symptoms.

There are two types of dysentery. Bacillary dysentery, the most common variety, is highly contagious, short, sharp and nasty but rarely persistent. It hits suddenly and lays you out with fever, nausea, cramps and diarrhoea, but, as it's caused by bacteria, it responds well to antibiotics.

Amoebic dysentery, which, as its name suggests, is caused by amoebic parasites, is much more difficult to treat, often persistent and more dangerous. It builds up more slowly, cannot be starved out and if untreated will get worse and permanently damage your intestines. Metronidazole is the recommended drug for the treatment of amoebic dysentery; it should be taken under medical supervision only.

**Hepatitis** Hepatitis A is a very common problem amongst travellers to areas with poor sanitation. Protection is through the new vaccine Havrix (two shots give protection for a year, and a third shot within six months to a year takes it to 10 years) or the antibody gamma globulin (said to provide protection for three to six months, but its effectiveness is debatable).

The disease is spread by contaminated food or water. The symptoms are fever, chills, headache, fatigue, feelings of weakness and aches and pains, followed by loss of appetite, nausea, vomiting, abdominal pain, dark urine, light-coloured faeces and jaundiced skin and eyes. You should seek medical advice, but in general there is not much you can do apart from rest, drink lots of fluids, eat lightly and avoid fatty foods. You should be over the worst in about 10 days but continue to take it easy after that. Do *not* take antibiotics. People who have had hepatitis must forego alcohol for six months after the illness, as hepatitis attacks the liver and it needs that amount of time to recover.

Hepatitis B, which used to be called serum hepatitis, is spread through contact with infected blood or bodily fluids, for example through sexual contact, unsterilised needles or blood transfusions. Other risk situations include having a shave or tattoo in a local shop, or having your ears pierced. The symptoms of type B are much the same as type A except that they are more severe and may lead to irreparable liver damage or even liver cancer; symptoms appear 15 to 50 days after infection (generally around 25 days). Although there is no treatment for hepatitis B, an effective prophylactic vaccine is readily available in most countries. The immunisation schedule requires two injections at least a month apart followed by a third dose five months after the second.

Hepatitis Non-A Non-B is a blanket term

formerly used for several different strains of hepatitis, which have now been separately identified. Hepatitis C is similar to B but is less common. Hepatitis D (the 'delta particle') is also similar to B and always occurs in concert with it; its occurrence is currently limited to IV drug users. Hepatitis E, however, is similar to A and is spread in the same manner, by water or food contamination.

Tests are available for these strands but they are very expensive. Travellers shouldn't be too paranoid about this apparent proliferation of hepatitis strains; they are fairly rare (so far) and following the same precautions as for A and B should be all that's necessary to avoid them.

**Cholera** This disease can be extremely dangerous, as it is very contagious and usually occurs in epidemics. The symptoms are: very bad but painless watery diarrhoea (commonly known as 'rice-water shits'), vomiting, quick and shallow breathing, fast but faint heart beat, wrinkled skin, stomach cramps and severe dehydration.

Do not attempt to treat cholera yourself – see a doctor immediately. Vaccinations are valid for six months and if you're revaccinated before the expiry date it is immediately valid. The vaccine doesn't give 100% protection but if you take the usual precautions about food and water you should be safe.

As noted previously, cholera can be a minor problem in parts of Morocco, particularly in the Meknès region.

**Polio** This is another disease spread by unsanitary conditions and found more frequently in hot climates. There is an oral vaccine against polio – three doses of drops taken at four to eight-week intervals. If you were vaccinated as a child you may only need a booster. Once again, take care with food and drink while travelling.

**Typhoid** Typhoid fever is a dangerous infection that starts in the gut and spreads to the whole body. It can be caught from contaminated food, water or milk and, as its name suggests, the main symptom is a high temperature. Another characteristic is rose-coloured spots on the chest and abdomen, which may appear after about a week. Two vaccinations, a month apart, provide protection against typhoid for three years. Seek medical assistance if you think you've been infected.

**Diseases Spread by Animals & Humans**
**Bilharzia** Bilharzia, also called schistosomiasis, is said to be present in river valleys and the oases of southern Morocco. The bilharzia parasite and the microscopic snail that carries them prefer warm, stagnant pools of water. Do not drink, wash, swim, paddle or even stand in water that may be infected. The parasites, which are minute worms, enter humans by burrowing through the skin. They inhabit and breed in the blood vessels of the abdomen, pelvis and sometimes the lungs and liver. The disease is painful and causes persistent and cumulative damage by repeated deposits of eggs.

The main symptom is blood in the urine, and sometimes in the faeces. The victim may suffer weakness, loss of appetite, sweating at night and afternoon fevers. If you have contracted bilharzia, you will begin noticing these symptoms anywhere from one to four weeks after contact. Treatment is possible, so see a specialist in tropical medicine as quickly as possible.

**Rabies** If you are bitten, scratched or even licked by a rabid animal and do not start treatment within a few days, you may die. Rabies affects the central nervous system and is certainly an unpleasant way to go. Typical signs of a rabid animal are: mad or uncontrolled behaviour, inability to eat, biting at anything and frothing at the mouth. If you are bitten by an animal, react as if it has rabies – there are no second chances. Get to a doctor and begin the course of injections that will prevent the disease from developing. Remember that a pre-exposure rabies vaccine is now available.

**Tetanus** Tetanus is a killer disease, but it can

easily be prevented by immunisation. It is caught through cuts and breaks in the skin caused by rusty or dirty objects, animal bites or contaminated wounds. Even if you have been vaccinated, wash the wound thoroughly.

**Worms** These parasites can be present on unwashed vegetables or in undercooked meat and you can pick them up through your skin by walking in bare feet. Infestations may not show up for some time, and although they are generally not serious, if left untreated they can cause severe health problems. A stool test is necessary to pinpoint the problem and medication is often available over the counter.

**Sexually Transmitted Diseases** Sexual contact with an infected person spreads these diseases. While abstinence is the only 100% preventative, use of a condom is also effective. Gonorrhoea and syphilis are the most common of these diseases, and sores, blisters or rashes around the genitals, discharges or pain when urinating are common symptoms. Symptoms may be less marked or not observed at all in women. The symptoms of syphilis eventually disappear completely but the disease continues and can cause severe problems in later years. Treatment of gonorrhoea and syphilis is by antibiotics.

There are numerous other sexually transmitted diseases, for most of which effective treatment is available. However, there is no cure for herpes or AIDS. Using condoms is the most effective preventative.

**HIV/AIDS** HIV, the Human Immunodeficiency Virus, may develop into AIDS, Acquired Immune Deficiency Syndrome. HIV is a major problem in many countries. Any exposure to blood, blood products or bodily fluids may put the individual at risk. In many developing countries transmission is predominantly through sexual activity between heterosexuals. This is quite different from industrialised countries, where transmission is mostly through contact between homosexual or bisexual males or the use of contaminated needles by IV drug users. Apart from abstinence, the most effective preventative is always to practise safe sex using condoms, and if you do need an injection, buy a new syringe. It is impossible to detect the HIV-positive status of an otherwise healthy-looking person without a blood test.

Vaccinations, acupuncture and tattooing can potentially be as dangerous as intravenous drug use if the equipment is not clean. However, fear of HIV infection should never preclude treatment for serious medical conditions. Although there may be a risk of infection, it is very small indeed.

### Insect-Borne Diseases

**Malaria** Malaria is spread by mosquitoes. The disease has a nasty habit of coming back in later years – and it can be fatal. Malaria is a minimal problem in North Africa, and many travellers do not bother with precautions at all. However, if you're in remote regions during the summer months, especially in the south, it boils down to a case of being better safe than sorry.

Sleeping near a fan (mosquitoes hate fast-moving air) and using insect repellent are usually adequate. Chloroquine is considered to be effective protection in North Africa and tablets are usually taken once or twice a week. It does not actually prevent the disease, but suppresses its symptoms. People travelling on into West Africa will need to take appropriate measures anyway, and so they may as well start while in the Sahara.

Mosquitoes appear after dusk. Avoiding bites by covering bare skin will further reduce the risk of catching malaria. Insect screens on windows and mosquito nets on beds offer protection, as does burning a mosquito coil. Mosquitoes can be attracted by perfume, aftershave or certain colours.

**Yellow Fever** This viral disease is endemic in many African countries between 15° north and 15° south. It is transmitted by mosquitoes, and the initial symptoms are fever, headache, abdominal pain and vomiting. There may appear to be a brief recovery before the disease progresses to more severe complications, including liver failure. There is no medical treatment apart from keeping the fever down and avoiding dehydration, but vaccination gives good protection for 10 years.

## Bugs, Bites & Cuts

Cuts of any kind can easily become infected, especially in the hot months, and should be treated with an antiseptic solution. Trekkers should wear good boots, socks and long trousers, especially in high grass. Creatures to look out for include scorpions, which often shelter in shoes and the like and pack a powerful sting, and snakes. Snake bites are a definite possibility, although there are anti-venenes for most. Wrap the bitten limb tightly, immobilise it with a splint and seek medical help (if possible bringing the dead snake for identification). Tourniquets and sucking out the poison are now comprehensively discredited.

**Bedbugs & Lice** Bedbugs live in various places, but particularly in dirty mattresses and bedding. Spots of blood on bedclothes or on the wall around the bed can be read as a suggestion to find another hotel. Bedbugs leave itchy bites in neat rows. Calamine lotion may help.

All lice cause itching and discomfort. They make themselves at home in your hair (head lice), your clothing (body lice) or in your pubic hair (crabs). You catch lice through direct contact with infected people or by sharing combs, clothing and the like. Powder or shampoo treatment will kill the lice and infected clothing should then be washed in very hot water.

## Women's Health

**Gynaecological Problems** Poor diet, lowered resistance due to the use of antibiotics for stomach upsets and even contraceptive pills can lead to vaginal infections when travelling in hot climates. Keeping the genital area clean, and wearing cotton underwear and skirts or loose-fitting trousers will help to prevent infections.

Yeast infections, characterised by a rash, itch and discharge, can be treated with a vinegar or even lemon-juice douche or with yoghurt. Nystatin suppositories are the usual medical prescription. Trichomonas is a more serious infection; symptoms are a discharge and a burning sensation when urinating. Male sexual partners must also be treated and if a vinegar douche is not effective, medical attention should be sought. Flagyl is the prescribed drug.

**Pregnancy** Most miscarriages occur during the first three months of pregnancy, so this is the most risky time to travel. The last three months should also be spent within reasonable distance of good medical care, as quite serious problems can develop at this time. Pregnant women should avoid all unnecessary medication, but vaccinations should still be taken where possible and if recommended by your doctor.

## WOMEN TRAVELLERS

Women travellers in North Africa face an additional problem – sexual harassment. It is constant in all the countries of North Africa, particularly Algeria. The harassment may be limited to being stared at in ways that leave little to the imagination, or it may take other forms such as being followed or touched. Such harassment is uncomfortable and annoying, but it probably won't go any further. Tunisia is probably the least painful country in this regard.

Even women travelling with a male companion are not immune: it's quite possible for an Arab man to ask the male in a Western couple if he can take liberties with his partner! It's unfortunate that Arab men (especially Muslims) have this stereotyped idea that Western women are ready to jump into bed at the drop of a hat. Western films and TV soapies only help to reinforce these ideas.

Despite all this, women can travel, alone or in pairs, throughout most North African countries and still have a great time. There are certain things you can do to minimise the friction. Modest dress is the first and most

---

**Travelling with Children**

It is quite possible to take small children (around one year old and over) to Morocco, but there are some things worth bearing in mind.

The three biggest considerations with children of this age are keeping them amused on long journeys and finding suitable food and bathroom facilities. Where your child is already eating solids, you shouldn't have too much trouble. Certain things will be out though, such as street-stall food, if you want to minimise the risks of diarrhoea and the like. Soups, tajines (stews), couscous, fried or grilled fish, omelettes/boiled eggs and fruit (washed and peeled, of course) should all be OK. For liquids, you can get powdered milk in many places and mix it with bottled mineral water. Where this isn't possible, on long journeys, for example, you may have to stick to mineral water alone.

As for nappies (diapers), it's impractical to take along more than half a dozen of the washable variety. Disposable nappies, despite their environmentally unfriendly nature, are the only practical solution. These are readily available all over Morocco but they aren't cheap (about US$5 for a packet of 10). Babidou is the only decent brand.

Keeping infants and their clothes clean is the biggest constraint. You may find that for most of the time you will have to take rooms in hotels with private showers and hot water.

The biggest plus about travelling in Morocco with a child was the attitude of the Moroccans themselves – they just love children. They have all the time in the world for them, and go out of their way to help you. Having a child with you is an instant introduction to just about any Moroccan – man or woman. Hotels do their best to give you a room with an extra bed or provide a cot, usually at no extra cost. And no-one cares what they get up to. Kids will be kids and you'll never encounter a disapproving glance or comment even when they're bawling their heads off.

You should have little trouble with children a few years older, and they attract the same goodwill. It is probably wise to steer clear of street-stall food even at this age.

Geoff Crowther ■

---

obvious thing. By tradition, Muslims are modest people when it comes to dress and Westerners who travel in a Muslim country with no regard for the local customs are asking for trouble. See Society & Conduct in the Facts about the Region chapter for hints on how to dress. Note that wearing a wedding ring will also generally increase North African perceptions of your respectability. Algeria and Libya are the most conservative countries of North Africa.

Women travelling without male companions are advised not to hitchhike, and you should think twice about travelling without a male companion in Libya, where any Westerner is a curiosity. Finally, you should avoid eye contact with a man you don't know, and ignore any rude remarks.

The best way for female travellers to meet and talk to local women is to go to a *hammam* (bathhouse). Most towns have one, and if there is not one that is exclusively for women there are times set aside each day for women and men.

## DANGERS & ANNOYANCES

Generally, travellers exercising basic common sense should have little trouble travelling in North Africa. Sure, you do hear of people getting ripped off, drugged or worse, and these things *do* happen; but they also happen in London, Melbourne and New York, and probably a lot more frequently. If you exercise caution and discretion, you shouldn't have any problems.

### Terrorism

At the time of writing, Algeria was a very hot place to be. Foreigners are dying as Muslims target them in their antigovernment campaign. For this reason Lonely Planet decided not to return there for this guide. You should keep as well informed about the situation as you can before deciding to go there.

### Hustlers, Hasslers & Touts

Morocco has the worst reputation for these annoyances. There is a long tradition of seeking to make a few bob by guiding foreigners around towns or helping them into shops for a commission. With mass tourism, the phenomenon has grown somewhat out of control. In the bigger centres, like Fès, Marrakesh and Tangier, you may well want to use guides every now and then. Official guides charge from Dr 30 to Dr 50 per half-day. Whether you deal with them or the cheaper, unofficial variety, establish very clearly from the start what you want to see. If this does not include shops, let them know.

If you don't want guides, you will have to be patient and courteous. At times you will cop abuse and be informed you're a 'racist', but if you reply with abuse, you could get into deep water. There are many subterfuges for getting your attention and leading you off for tea and a carpet-viewing, and to an extent you are going to have to develop a sense for the hustle. Don't believe a lot of common lines – like the one about the 'Berber market, today only', or 'don't you remember me...?'. Some of these people stick like glue, and if all else fails, polite mention of the word 'police' can have a loosening effect on them. Remember that the bad eggs are a small minority and the rest are unemployed and trying to scrape together a bit of a living.

## Theft

As far as theft goes, be sensible and don't leave belongings unattended except where you know they will be safe. Fools deserve to be robbed. Don't leave your gear for any length of time (even if not visible) in a locked vehicle – sooner or later you'll return to find a window smashed and your belongings gone.

The place for money and passports is in a pouch against your skin, around your waist or neck. Neither method is foolproof, but both give a good measure of security and make it much harder to lose belongings. Cotton or leather pouches are far more comfortable to have against your skin than nylon. Cameras are best kept with you or left at your hotel reception, although nine times out of 10 they'll be safe in hotel rooms.

Moroccans are, on the whole, remarkably honest people, interested in striking up conversations and generally helpful. They are persistent and superb business negotiators, but 'dishonest' they are not.

The people in Tunisia, Algeria and Libya (particularly in the latter two countries where tourists are so rare) are some of the most hospitable you'll find anywhere. Getting invited into a house for a meal is not uncommon and people will invariably go out of their way to help.

One exception to note is Sebha in Libya, where cross-border bandits have a reputation for holding up tourists and robbing them of their vehicles and goods – you're advised not to camp alone in the area, although Libyan police are trying to put a stop to such incidents.

## Physical Violence

Violence against tourists is extremely rare. It's possible in Tangier and wandering in some medinas late at night is not a great idea, but generally it's not a problem. Certain remote parts of the Rif Mountains are potentially troublesome, and in this respect it's suggested you avoid the area around Ketama.

## The Evil Weed

Morocco is famous (or infamous – depending on your point of view) for its cannabis; Ketama became a household word among dope freaks in the 1970s. However, despite the number of people who smoke it, dope is illegal in Morocco.

As a tourist, you need to be discreet about using it. Blatant public use is going to land you in a heap of trouble including possible jail. If you're a user, don't jump at the first offer. Take your time. Be especially careful in the north around Tetouan and Ketama. There's plenty of money to be made from selling you cannabis and then shopping you to the police. Many travellers have learnt this to their cost.

The quality of dope in Morocco is generally good and the cost very modest in comparison with Europe.

Ever since the northern European dealers

descended upon Ketama in the early 1970s, the Rif has acquired a reputation for hassles. If you don't want those hassles, avoid the area like the plague. Chefchaouen, however, is still sweet. Do not show the slightest interest in dope in the streets of places like Tangier. More often than not travellers end up in dark alleyways scared out of their wits by nasty characters promising to report them to the police if they don't hand over large wads of money. These situations can and should be avoided.

In Tunisia, Algeria and Libya, there is not the tradition of smoking that there is in Morocco. Penalties are stiffer and the law is enforced with much less flexibility. If you bring any dope with you from Morocco and get caught, the consequences could be disastrous. Algerian officials at the Moroccan border are looking specifically for two things – drugs and dinar. If they find the latter, it will be confiscated, if they find the former, you are in deep shit.

## FOOD

North Africa ought to be an area of gastronomic delights, given the peoples and civilisations that have come and gone over the centuries. It's true, it is a foodie's paradise but, with some notable exceptions, only if you're prepared to pay over the odds for a meal. You can eat well and cheaply but the lack of variety at this level can become tedious. The places with the biggest variety and the best quality are those with the most tourists, so in parts of Tunisia and Morocco the choices are good.

The most basic local eateries barely warrant being called restaurants. They usually have just one or two dishes, and will often run out by early evening. As might be expected, the farther south you go, the more basic the restaurants become and the less variety they have. Vegetables become rarer and the emphasis is on meat and starch, so soups and salads disappear and basically all you get is meat and couscous, spaghetti or bread.

In the larger towns there are restaurants with set menus, which will get you soup, salad, main course and dessert, although in southern Algeria such places are often out of the range of the budget traveller.

If you're on a strict budget and get tired of eating in basic restaurants, you may well have to splurge occasionally and go to a decent restaurant. This won't always guarantee you a better or more tasty meal but you might welcome the change. In Morocco and Tunisia, for example, there are quite a few such places to splash out, although you'll be looking at around US$8 to US$10 per person in the more modest restaurants and up to US$35 to US$40 in the very best.

The French influence is noticeable in Morocco, Algeria and Tunisia, and the Italians have left some of their influence behind in Libya. 'French sticks' are the most commonly eaten bread in Morocco, Algeria and Tunisia, and every town has at least one pâtisserie selling all manner of sticky cakes. You can get traditionally baked bread in Morocco and Tunisia (*tabouna*, 300 mills a loaf), too.

Menus in the three former French territories, where they are supplied, are always in French and/or Arabic. In Libya they tend to be in Arabic only. Croissants or the equivalent are available everywhere and, with a cup of coffee, make a reasonable breakfast.

The food is fairly uniform throughout North Africa, but there are a few specialities which are served in one country only.

### Snacks

**Morocco** One of the biggest growth industries is kebab and *kefta* (grilled ground meat) fast-food outlets. What you get is a serving of barbecued kebab or kefta wrapped in bread with or without salad, and a dose of hot sauce plus chips. They're popular, essentially a meal in themselves, and cost as little as Dr 10 (about US$1). There are quite a few variations on this theme, and a growing array of Western-style hamburger places. Some of these are not bad at all, although you'll be looking at more like Dr 20 or more for a meal.

McDonald's opened its first Moroccan restaurant near the lighthouse in Casablanca in 1992, and plans a network of at least 12 franchises around the country – so if you're hankering for a Big Mac, head for Casablanca!

**Algeria** *Bourek*, a battered and fried mix of meat, egg and onion, is one of Algiers' specialities. Other snacks include *méchoui* (roast meat) and spicy sausages called *merguez*.

**Tunisia** The great invention here is the *casse-croûte*. It consists of a large hunk of French bread which is stuffed with any or all of the following: olives, tuna, egg, sausage, chips and oil. Just about all snacks and meals include a generous slathering of *harissa*, a spicy chilli sauce which varies in strength but is often hot enough to bring tears to your eyes and have you reaching for a drink. Many pâtisseries, particularly in Tunis, serve individual pizzas (sold by weight, about TD 6 a kg) and savoury pastries. These are very rich and filling and can be a meal in themselves. Pasta dishes are available for about TD 1.500 and burgers for about 900 mills a go.

### Soups & Starters

Soups (*chorba*, or *harira* in Morocco) are usually tasty and filling. They are based on a meat stock, with macaroni and vegetables as their main ingredients. Any flavours these might impart are often cunningly concealed by a hefty dose of pepper or chilli. Moroccan lentil-based harira is far and away the best; with a chunk of bread it makes a pretty good meal in itself. It's usually only available in the late afternoon/early evening.

Salad is a great catch-all that can include anything from a limp piece of lettuce and a tired tomato right through to a tasty mix of chopped vegetables and herbs, olives, anchovies, tuna and spicy dressing. Unfortunately it's the former that you are most likely to encounter in cheap restaurants. Coriander leaves and parsley are the most common herbal ingredients. It is generally unwise to eat salads if you have just arrived from Europe, as the ingredients are unlikely to have been washed thoroughly, if at all. After a while, when your stomach has had a chance to acclimatise, you should be able to handle them without any problem.

**Algeria** The soup of this region is chorba, a spicy stew of meat and vegetables.

**Tunisia** One speciality (peculiarity?) here is the *briq à l'œuf*. This is a strange creature: it consists of a thin, crisp pastry envelope containing a range of fillings that always include egg. Not winding up with egg on your face is something of an art, and using a knife and fork is considered cheating. The bad ones are awful, but a good one is very tasty.

**Libya** The soup you get with most meals in Libya is a spicy version of Italian minestrone – full of vegetables, lamb and pasta.

### Main Courses
Most of the dishes are starch based, which usually means couscous, spaghetti or rice.

Couscous is the staple food of the region: an enormous bowl of steamed semolina topped with a meat and vegetable sauce. It is available virtually everywhere and varies tremendously according to the sauce, which can make the difference between a good meal and a plate of dry couscous not unlike sawdust. Fortunately there is enough variety most of the time for you not to have to live off it. Having said that, almost every Moroccan will assure you, in no uncertain terms, that the couscous prepared in private homes is a totally different species from that served in restaurants and that it's absolutely delicious. This may well be true and it's what you will be offered if you're invited for dinner.

Regarding couscous ordered at a restaurant, if you want to cut costs and aren't too bothered about not eating meat, ask how much the dishes are without meat (*sans viande*), as you still get the rest of the sauce and the price drops significantly.

Chicken has taken off in a big way right across North Africa and is often the only meat available. It is usually roasted and served with chips, which, unless you ask specifically, are often cold. There's something about cold chips which really make you feel as though you've hit rock bottom.

Brochettes are one of the most basic meals and are available just about everywhere. They're essentially kebabs (as they are known in Libya) – pieces of meat on a skewer barbecued over hot coals. A chilli sauce is often provided.

Seafood is big in the coastal regions of Tunisia and Morocco and there are many restaurants which specialise in it. Some do nothing else. At the better restaurants in Tunisia, a tray of fresh fish is usually brought to your table and you select what you want. Elsewhere you take your chances, but it is rare to get one that doesn't taste fine.

In Moroccan coastal towns, you can be sure that the seafood is fresh; also, the culinary traditions of Portugal and Spain have long been assimilated into the art of preparing dishes so you're looking at something far more exotic than just plain fish and chips (you can get that too if you want it). Fish is also good in Libyan coastal towns.

**Morocco** Other than couscous, the big dish here is *tajine*. This is basically a meat and vegetable stew cooked very slowly in an earthenware dish over hot coals. The meat used is usually lamb, goat or chicken, but you can also find beef or rabbit.

The vegetables usually cooked with the meat are potatoes, onions, carrot and squash, but it's not unusual for fruits such as prunes, apricots and raisins to be included, and you would definitely expect them in a better class restaurant. Tajines vary, depending on the restaurant, from being absolutely delicious to almost tasteless.

The other dish worth trying, although not widely available, is *pastilla* (*bastaila* in Arabic). It is a delicious and incredibly rich pigeon pie, which is made in layered *ouarka* pastry (like filo pastry) with nuts and spices and is then coated with sugar and baked. It is common in Fès, where you just get a chunk from a stall, but it is also served in some restaurants in other cities.

**Tunisia** Tajine in Tunisia bears no relation to its Moroccan namesake. The Tunisian version is like a quiche, and is normally served cold with chips and salad.

Another delight in Tunisia (and to a certain extent in Algeria and Libya) is *shakshuka*. This is rather like a thick vegetable stew and consists of onions, peppers, tomatoes and egg all fried up in a spicy tomato sauce; it's usually excellent. Alas for vegetarians, it's usually made with a meat stock. *Ojja*, often misleadingly described as Tunisian scrambled eggs, is not dissimilar to shakshuka, except that an egg is mixed in at the end.

*Lablabi* is a chickpea broth doled out on a bed of broken bread and spiced up with various additions. It costs about 700 mills and is found at only the most basic local restaurants.

*Kammounia* is a meat stew made with lots of cummin. One to look for is *mloukhia*. It's similar to kammounia, except that it's made with a blend of dried herbs. Cuts of lamb or beef are simmered for hours until they almost disappear into the rich green sauce.

Other dishes include *salade tunisienne*, made of finely diced salad vegetables mixed with a dressing of lemon juice and olive oil, and *salade mechouia*. This is a spicy mixture of roast vegetables in which eggplant normally features prominently. It is often served as an accompaniment with roast chicken and other plain meals.

**Libya** Couscous in Libya tends to be spicier than elsewhere in North Africa and is made with a stock to give it a bright orange colour.

Pasta of a vaguely Italian nature appears on most menus, but it is highly seasoned with cinnamon, chilli, coriander and parsley to appeal to local palates.

In the desert you may encounter *f'taat*, layers of thin pancakes in a hot sauce with meat and hard-boiled eggs. *M'baton*, vegetables stuffed with a savoury meat mixture and deep-fried, are a southern speciality. Another speciality is *rishtit kas kas* – thin, home-made pasta ribbons with a spicy chickpea sauce.

### Desserts & Pastries

Desserts and sweets are more often available from pâtisseries than from restaurants, but dishes such as crème au caramel, cakes and fruit are served in the better restaurants. European-style pastries compete for space with local and Middle Eastern sweets – in Morocco, European sweets are more prevalent, but the farther east you go the stronger the local and Middle Eastern influences become. The *corne de gazelle*, a pastry horn filled with chopped nuts and drowned in honey, is a good representative of the latter and a universal favourite throughout the former French Maghreb territories.

In Kairouan, Tunisia, one dish to look for is *makhroud*, made from semolina and dates. *Doigt du nègre* (negro's finger) probably wouldn't be an acceptable name for an almond biscuit dipped in chocolate in most Western countries, but that's what it's called in Tunisia. Another is *œil de chat* (cat's eye), a ball of almond paste with colourful icing and a chocolate button.

In Morocco, a great local version of the Spanish *churro* (for want of a better comparison) is a light, deep-fried doughnut called a *sfinj*. They cost practically nothing, are not sweet and go perfectly with coffee.

### Fruit

In season there's a great variety of fruit available, particularly in the north of Tunisia, including apples, pears, peaches, grapes, melons, watermelons, figs, dates, cactus fruit and pomegranates. In Morocco, the usual fruits are mandarins, grapes, dates, oranges, bananas (in the south) and watermelons.

| English | Arabic | French |
|---|---|---|
| **Soup** | | |
| soup | *chorba* | *potage* |
| spicy lentil soup | *harira* | |

### Salads & Vegetables

| English | Arabic | French |
|---|---|---|
| carrots | *kheezoo/ gazar* | *carottes* |
| chips | *ships* | *frites* |
| cucumber | *khiyaar* | *concombre* |
| green beans | *loobeeya* | *haricots verts* |
| haricot beans | *fasooliya* | *haricots blancs* |
| lentils | *'aads* | *lentilles* |
| lettuce | *khess* | *laitue* |
| mixed salad | – | *salade marocaine/tunisienne* |
| olives | *zeetoun* | *olives* |
| onion | *besla* | *oignon* |
| peas | *zelbana/ bisila* | *petits pois* |

| potatoes | batatas | pommes de terre |
| tomato | mataisha/ tamatim | tomate |

**Meat**

| camel | lehem jemil | chameau |
| chicken | farooj/dujaj | poulet |
| kidneys | kelawwi | rognons |
| lamb | lehem ghenmee | agneau |
| liver | kebda | foie |
| meat | lehem | viande |

**Fruit**

| apple | teffah | pomme |
| apricot | mesh-mash | abricot |
| banana | banan/moz | banane |
| dates | tmer | dattes |
| figs | kermoos | figues |
| fruit | fakiya | fruits |
| grapes | 'eineb | raisins |
| orange | leemoon | orange |
| pomegranate | remman | grenade |
| watermelon | dellah | pastèque |

**Miscellaneous**

| bread | khubz | pain |
| butter | zebda | beurre |
| cheese | fromaj | fromage |
| eggs | bayd | oeufs |
| oil | zit | huile |
| pepper | filfil/lebzaar | poivre |
| salt | melha | sel |
| sugar | sukur | sucre |
| yoghurt | zabadee/ laban/danoon | yaourt |

## DRINKS
### Tea & Coffee

Tea and coffee are the national obsessions in all four countries and are drunk in copious quantities. They are also extremely strong and, when your body is not used to them, drinking either in the evening is usually a recipe for a sleepless night.

The main pastime for men is sipping tea or coffee in a café while reading the paper, chatting or playing cards or backgammon. Every town has at least one café – they are the social centres and are a good place to meet the local men. Local women don't frequent these places but Western women can enter. Often the tables and chairs are set out on the footpath, and are a good spot to sit and watch the world go by.

Tea (shay or, in Morocco, atay) is served in glasses or pots and heavily sweetened. In Morocco it also comes complete with a substantial sprig of mint (nanaa'). Indeed, mint tea is almost synonymous with Morocco. It's what you will be served (free of charge and without any obligation to buy) whenever you get down to the serious business of negotiation in any shop in a souq (market).

Coffee in Morocco, Algeria and Tunisia is always strong and served the French way: small black or large white. Sugar is optional and served in cubes on your saucer. A glass of water is invariably served at the same time. In Libya the options are similar (with the Italian names of espresso and cappucino), but Turkish-style coffee (qahwa) is also available. It comes in small cups and is half liquid, half grounds – very strong and usually drunk sweet.

### Soft Drinks & Bottled Water

Morocco and Tunisia both have those pillars of multinationalism: Coca-Cola and Pepsi. In Morocco they generally come in bottles of 300 or 500 ml for about Dr 5. In Tunisia, cafés charge 250 mills for a small bottle and corner stores 180 mills. Large bottles cost 450 mills, and you have to pay a deposit for the bottle.

Algeria makes its own and, for the most part, these are quite OK, although it depends on water quality. In places like In Salah, where the ground water is salty, the drinks are unpalatable.

Libyans drink Pepsi Cola and an orange fizzy drink called Miranda. They have a weird one called Bitter Soda that looks and tastes just like Campari.

There are several brands of bottled water in Morocco (Sidi Harazem is one). The bigger bottles contain 1.5 litres and cost Dr 4 to Dr 5. Smaller bottles costs Dr 2.50.

In Tunisia, Safia (winner of a gold medal

at the 1990 Luxembourg Show!) is the most common brand. You'll pay between 270 and 400 mills for a 90 cl bottle. Bottled water is also available in Algeria and Libya.

### Juices

Fresh fruit juices are commonly available across North Africa. They are usually cheap and are great thirst quenchers.

### Alcohol

Drinking alcohol is frowned upon in Islam, but that doesn't stop quite a lot of North Africans from indulging in the odd tipple. Libya is the big exception, as it is 'dry' (ex-pats brew their own, as do some locals; their *ez-az* is lethal). All that's on offer is some nonalcoholic beer.

Morocco is easily the most liberal of the four countries in this respect. Only some of the better (or at least more expensive) restaurants are licensed. The cheapest places are rarely licensed, unless they have a bar attached. There are, however, more bars around than is at first obvious. They tend not to advertise themselves and most are pretty basic, temporary places. The bigger cities have the odd liquor store, where you can get hold of beer, wine and spirits for considerably less than they cost in the bars or restaurants. The other option is discos and nightclubs, where entry will cost you at least Dr 50 (including a drink) and subsequent drinks the same.

In Tunisia, the situation is much the same, except with fewer bars. Most foreigners will feel more comfortable in hotel bars. This is even more the case in Algeria. The best place to buy alcohol in Tunisia is at the Monoprix chain of supermarkets. Alcohol is sold only after noon, and not at all on Fridays.

**Beer** The two main locally produced beers in Morocco, Flag Spéciale (brewed in Tangier) and Stork (Fès and Casablanca) are quite drinkable but nothing to write home about. Smallish bottles cost between Dr 6 and Dr 8 in liquor stores, and Dr 12 to Dr 15 in bars and restaurants. Amstel and Heineken are also produced in Morocco under licence,

and you can come across the odd imported brand, such as US Budweiser, in the liquor stores.

Celtia is the only beer in Tunisia. It sells for TD 1.200 per bottle in Tunis, or as little as 900 mills outside the capital.

Algerian beer comes in an anonymous bottle and is similar to what you get in Tunisia. The biggest problem is that about one in four bottles are dead flat, and the usual custom is to drink it nevertheless.

**Wine** Some quite reasonable drops of wine are produced in Morocco. In the past, most wine production was carried out by the Jewish population, but following their departure for Israel since 1948 the business is now controlled by the Arabs. Sincomar, based in Casablanca, produces quite a few labels, including Rabbi Jacob and Toulal (reds), Coquillage (white) and various others.

Les Celliers de Meknès is another reasonable company, and in fact the plains around Meknès are good grape and wine country. Guerrouane Rouge is not bad. Another good Meknès red is Aït Souala, which sells for Dr 35 in liquor stores. For those with a more expensive palate, a recommended red is Beau Vallon (Dr 80).

Tunisia produces a wide range of wines, most of which sell for under TD 3. The top of the range is Vieille Magon, a very passable full-bodied red that sells for TD 5.600. Gris de Hammamet rosé is good value at TD 2.900.

**Spirits** Various spirits can be purchased in Morocco, although they are hardly cheap. There is a French emphasis, especially in the northern half of the country. If you like the aniseed-based pastis, one of the better known brands, 51, sells in Morocco for Dr 120.

The only local Tunisian spirit is a fiery number called *boukha*, generally consumed with a mixer. If you are curious, a ⅛ bottle costs TD 2.300. Whisky drinkers are advised to include some as part of their duty-free allowance – a bottle costs at least TD 60 locally.

# Getting There & Away

However you're travelling, it's worth taking out travel insurance. Work out what you need. You may not want to insure that grotty old army-surplus backpack – but everyone should be covered for the worst possible case: an accident, for example, that will require hospital treatment and a flight home. It's a good idea to make a copy of your policy, in case the original is lost. If you are planning to travel for a long time, the insurance may seem expensive – but if you can't afford it, you certainly won't be able to afford to deal with a medical emergency overseas. Check out the details. In most cases you need to pay extra to cover you for 'dangerous sports' such as skiing or trekking. Also, you often need to pay a surcharge for expensive camera equipment and the like.

North Africa's proximity to Europe makes it a popular travel destination. There are regular air connections between many European and North African cities, and ferries from Spain, France, Italy and Malta serve up to a dozen North African ports as well.

Note that at the time of writing a UN air travel embargo on Libya was still in place. About the easiest and cheapest way to get there is to fly to Tunisia or Egypt and then head overland.

Many travellers visit the region as part of a longer journey through Africa, often with a vehicle, and take ferries which are generally cheaper than flying.

## AIR
### To/From Europe

The cheapest way to fly to Morocco or Tunisia can be by charter flight from various European cities. These flights are generally booked up with package tourists, but if you are lucky you may get a return ticket for less than UK£100 from London for example. At that price, you could afford to simply throw away the return half of the ticket. Good travel agents should be able to help

you. There's nothing in this line to Algeria or Libya.

Advance purchase excursion (Apex) tickets are cheaper than standard return fares, but they impose limits on period of stay and often involve a forfeit if you want to change dates. Scheduled fares to any of the Maghreb countries tend to hover around UK£200, although you can find cheaper ones. Hunt around the bucket shops of London, Amsterdam and Paris for discounted fares.

From northern Europe and the UK, an alternative is to hunt for cheap flights to southern Spain, France or Italy, and to then catch a ferry from there.

Flying *from* North Africa, there is virtually no discounting, and fares to Europe tend to be very expensive.

In London, check out the travel-page ads of the Sunday newspapers, *Time Out*, *TNT*, *City Limits* and *Exchange & Mart*. A good source of information on cheap fares is the magazine *Business Traveller*.

Most British travel agents are registered with ABTA (Association of British Travel Agents). If you have paid for your flight with an ABTA-registered agent who then goes out of business, ABTA will guarantee a refund or an alternative. Unregistered bucket shops are riskier but sometimes cheaper.

The Globetrotters Club (BCM Roving, London WC1N 3XX) publishes a newsletter called *Globe* that covers obscure destinations and can help in finding travelling companions.

One of the most reliable London agents is STA Travel (☎ 0171-937 9962) at 86 Old Brompton Rd, London SW7; 117 Euston Rd, London NW1; and 38 Store St, London WC1. Another is Trailfinders (☎ 0171-938 3366/3939), 42-50 Earl's Court Rd, London W8 (with another office around the corner at 194 Kensington High St). The latter offers an inoculation service and a research library for customers. The US agent Council Travel

(☎ 0171-287 3337) has an office at 28a Poland St, London W1V 3DB.

The Africa Travel Shop (☎ 0171-387 1211), at 4 Medway Court, Leigh St, London WC1, caters to the growing number of travellers interested in Africa. It is ABTA bonded, has a free video library and can organise overland safaris and most other travel requirements.

### To/From North America

The *New York Times*, the *LA Times*, the *Chicago Tribune* and the *San Francisco Examiner* produce weekly travel sections in which you'll find any number of travel agents' ads. Council Travel and STA Travel have offices in major cities nationwide.

The magazine *Travel Unlimited* (PO Box 1058, Allston, Mass 02134) publishes details of cheap airfares.

In Canada, Travel CUTS has offices in all major cities. The *Toronto Globe & Mail* and the *Vancouver Sun* carry travel agents' ads. The magazine *Great Expeditions* (PO Box 8000-411, Abbotsford BC V2S 6H1) is useful.

The cheapest way to get to North Africa from North America is to buy a cheap return flight to Europe and proceed from there.

### To/From Australasia

There are no direct connections between North Africa and Australia or New Zealand. Again, the most convenient way is to go to, say, London and hunt around there for a cheap flight; otherwise go overland through Europe.

STA is one of the more reliable travel agents and has branches around Australia. Flight Centres International is another reasonable place to check out.

### To/From Asia

Hong Kong and Bangkok are the two main centres for cheap air tickets in South-East Asia, although there's not a huge market for flights to North African destinations. If you can't find anything direct, try for a cheap ticket to Europe and head down from there.

### Buying a Plane Ticket

The plane ticket will probably be the single most expensive item in your budget, and buying it can be an intimidating business. It is worth putting aside a few hours to research the state of the market and check around the many travel agents hoping to separate you from your money. Start early: some of the cheapest tickets have to be bought months in advance, and some popular flights sell out early. Talk to other recent travellers – they may be able to stop you making some of the same old mistakes. Look at the ads in newspapers and magazines, consult reference books and watch for special offers. Then phone round travel agents for bargains. (Airlines can supply information on routes and timetables; however, except at times of inter-airline war they do not supply the cheapest tickets.) Find out the fare, the route, the duration of the journey and any restrictions on the ticket. (See restrictions in the Air Travel Glossary.) Then sit back and decide which is best for you.

You may discover that those impossibly cheap flights are 'fully booked, but we have another one that costs a bit more...'. Or the flight is on an airline notorious for its poor safety standards and leaves you in the world's least favourite airport in mid-journey for 14 hours. Or they claim only to have the last two seats available for that country for the whole of July, which they will hold for you for a maximum of two hours. Don't panic – keep ringing around.

Use the fares quoted in this book as a guide only. They are approximate and based on the rates advertised by travel agents at the time of going to press. Quoted airfares do not necessarily constitute a recommendation for the carrier.

If you are travelling from the UK or the USA, you will probably find that the cheapest flights are being advertised by obscure bucket shops whose names haven't yet reached the telephone directory. They sell airline tickets at up to a 50% discount where

**Air Travel Glossary**

**Apex** Apex, or 'advance purchase excursion' is a discounted ticket which must be paid for in advance. There are penalties if you wish to change it.

**Baggage Allowance** This will be written on your ticket: usually one 20 kg item to go in the hold, plus one item of hand luggage.

**Bucket Shop** An unbonded travel agency specialising in discounted airline tickets.

**Budget Fare** These can be booked at least three weeks in advance but the actual travel date is not confirmed until seven days prior to travel.

**Bumped** Just because you have a confirmed seat doesn't mean you're going to get on the plane – see Overbooking.

**Cancellation Penalties** If you have to cancel or change an Apex ticket there are often heavy penalties involved; insurance can sometimes be taken out against these penalties. Some airlines impose penalties on regular tickets as well, particularly against 'no show' passengers.

**Check In** Airlines ask you to check in a certain time ahead of the flight departure (usually one to two hours on international flights). If you fail to check in on time and the flight is overbooked, the airline can cancel your booking and give your seat to somebody else.

**Confirmation** Having a ticket written out with the flight and date you want doesn't mean you have a seat until the agent has checked with the airline that your status is 'OK' or confirmed. Meanwhile you could just be 'on request'.

**Discounted Tickets** There are two types of discounted fares – officially discounted (see Promotional Fares) and unofficially discounted. The lowest prices often impose drawbacks like flying with unpopular airlines, inconvenient schedules, or unpleasant routes and connections. A discounted ticket can save you other things than money – you may be able to pay Apex prices without the associated Apex advance booking and other requirements. Discounted tickets only exist where there is fierce competition.

**Full Fares** Airlines traditionally offer first class (coded F), business class (coded J) and economy class (coded Y) tickets. These days there are so many promotional and discounted fares available that few economy-class passengers pay the full fare.

**ITX** An 'independent inclusive tour excursion' (ITX) is often available on tickets to popular holiday destinations. Officially it's a package deal combined with hotel accommodation, but many agents will sell you one of these for the flight only. They'll give you phoney hotel vouchers in the unlikely event that you're challenged at the airport.

**Lost Tickets** If you lose your airline ticket an airline will usually treat it like a travellers' cheque and, after enquiries, issue you with another one. Legally, however, an airline is entitled to treat it like cash and if you lose it then it's gone forever. Take good care of your tickets.

**MCO** A 'miscellaneous charge order' (MCO) is a voucher that looks like an airline ticket but carries no destination or date. It is exchangeable with any IATA airline for a ticket on a specific flight. Its principal use for travellers is as an alternative to an onward ticket in those countries that demand one, and it's more flexible than an ordinary ticket if you're not sure of your route.

**No Shows** No shows are passengers who fail to show up for their flight, sometimes due to unexpected delays or disasters, sometimes due to simply forgetting, sometimes because they made more than one booking and didn't bother to cancel the one they didn't want. Full-fare passengers who fail to turn up are sometimes entitled to travel on a later flight. The rest of us are penalised (see Cancellation Penalties).

**On Request** An unconfirmed booking for a flight; see Confirmation.

places have not been filled, and although airlines may protest to the contrary, many of them release tickets to selected bucket shops – it's better to sell tickets at a huge discount than not at all. Many such firms are honest and solvent, but there are a few rogues who will take your money and disappear, to reopen elsewhere a month or two later under a new name. If you feel suspicious about a

firm, don't give them all the money at once – leave a deposit of 20% or so and pay the balance when you get the ticket. If they insist on cash in advance, go somewhere else. And once you have the ticket, ring the airline to confirm that you are actually booked onto the flight.

You may decide to pay more than the rock-bottom fare by opting for the safety of

**Open Jaws** A return ticket where you fly out to one place but return from another. If available, this can save you backtracking to your arrival point.

**Overbooking** Airlines hate to fly empty seats and since every flight has some passengers who fail to show up (see No Shows), airlines often book more passengers than they have seats. Usually the excess passengers balance those who fail to show up but occasionally somebody gets bumped. If this happens, guess who it is most likely to be? The passengers who check in late.

**Point-to-Point** This is a discount ticket that can be bought on some routes in return for passengers waiving their rights to stop over.

**Promotional Fares** Officially discounted fares like Apex fares, available from travel agents or direct from the airline.

**Reconfirmation** At least 72 hours prior to departure time of an onward or return flight, you must contact the airline and 'reconfirm' that you intend to be on the flight. If you don't do this the airline can delete your name from the passenger list and you could lose your seat. You don't have to reconfirm the first flight on your itinerary or if your stopover is less than 72 hours. It doesn't hurt to reconfirm more than once.

**Restrictions** Discounted tickets often have various restrictions on them – advance purchase is the most usual one (see Apex). Others are restrictions on the minimum and maximum period you must be away, such as a minimum of 14 days or a maximum of one year. See Cancellation Penalties.

**Round-the-World** An RTW ticket is just that. You have a limited period in which to circumnavigate the globe and you can go anywhere the carrying airlines go, as long as you don't backtrack. These tickets are usually valid for one year, the number of stopovers or total number of separate flights is worked out before you set off and they often don't cost much more than a basic return flight.

**Stand-by** A discounted ticket where you only fly if there is a seat free at the last moment. Stand-by fares are usually only available on domestic routes.

**Tickets Out** An entry requirement for many countries is that you have an onward or return ticket, in other words, a ticket out of the country. If you're not sure what you intend to do next, the easiest solution is to buy the cheapest onward ticket to a neighbouring country or a ticket from a reliable airline which can later be refunded if you do not use it. Also, see MCO.

**Transferred Tickets** Airline tickets cannot be transferred from one person to another. Travellers sometimes try to sell the return half of their ticket, but officials can ask you to prove that you are the person named on the ticket. This is unlikely to happen on domestic flights; on an international flight tickets may be compared with passports.

**Travel Agencies** Travel agencies vary widely and you should ensure you use one that suits your needs. Some simply handle tours while full-service agencies handle everything from tours and tickets to car rental and hotel bookings. A good one will do all these things and can save you a lot of money but if all you want is a ticket at the lowest possible price, then you really need an agency specialising in discounted tickets. A discounted ticket agency, however, may not be useful for other things, like hotel bookings.

**Travel Periods** Some officially discounted fares, Apex fares in particular, vary with the time of year. There is often a low (off-peak) season and a high (peak) season. Sometimes there's an intermediate or shoulder season as well. At peak times, when everyone wants to fly, not only will the officially discounted fares be higher but so will unofficially discounted fares, or there may simply be no discounted tickets available. Usually the fare depends on your outward flight – if you depart in the high season and return in the low season, you pay the high-season fare. ■

a better known travel agent. Firms such as STA, who have offices worldwide, Council Travel in the USA or Travel CUTS in Canada are not going to disappear overnight, leaving you clutching a receipt for a nonexistent ticket, but they do offer good prices to most destinations.

Once you have your ticket, write its number down, together with the flight number and other details, and keep the information somewhere separate. If the ticket is lost or stolen, this will help you get a replacement.

It's sensible to buy travel insurance as early as possible. If you buy it the week before you fly, you may find, for example, that you're not covered for delays to your flight caused by industrial action.

## Air Travellers with Special Needs

If you have special needs of any sort – you've broken a leg, you're vegetarian, travelling in a wheelchair, taking the baby, terrified of flying – you should let the airline know as soon as possible so that they can make arrangements accordingly. You should remind them when you reconfirm your booking (at least 72 hours before departure) and again when you check in at the airport. It may also be worth ringing round the airlines before you make your booking to find out how they can handle your particular needs.

Airports and airlines can be surprisingly helpful, but they do need advance warning. Most international airports will provide escorts from check-in desk to plane where needed, and there should be ramps, lifts, accessible toilets and reachable phones. Aircraft toilets, on the other hand, are likely to present a problem; travellers should discuss this with the airline at an early stage and, if necessary, with their doctor.

Guide dogs for the blind will often have to travel in a specially pressurised baggage compartment with other animals, away from their owner; though smaller guide dogs may be admitted to the cabin. All guide dogs will be subject to the same quarantine laws (six months in isolation etc) as any other animal when entering or returning to countries currently free of rabies, such as Britain or Australia.

Deaf travellers can ask for airport and in-flight announcements to be written down for them.

Children under the age of two travel for 10% of the standard fare (or free, on some airlines), as long as they don't occupy a seat. They don't get a baggage allowance either. 'Skycots' should be provided by the airline if requested in advance; these will take a child weighing up to about 10 kg. Children aged between two and 12 can usually occupy a seat for half to two-thirds of the full fare, and they get a baggage allowance. Push chairs can often be taken as hand luggage.

## LAND

### To/From West Africa

If you are coming north from West Africa, the only way to enter North Africa is to go from either Mali or Niger to Algeria. The crossing points are at In Guezzam on the route from Niger, and at Borj Mokhtar if coming from Mali.

The western route between Morocco and Mauritania is now at least a technical possibility. See the Morocco and Algeria Getting There & Away chapters for more details.

### To/From Egypt

The Egyptian frontier with Libya has been open for a few years now, and you can get daily buses from Cairo and Alexandria to Libya. There are even occasional buses as far as Morocco from Cairo with the Hebton company, which has offices just east of Midan Opera. Alternatively, you can take local transport to the border and move on once on the other side.

### Taking Your Own Vehicle

**Carnet** A *carnet de passage en douane* is not required for Morocco, Algeria, Tunisia or Libya, but if you are heading through to West Africa and beyond it is mandatory. You also don't need to prearrange them for most West African countries (Nigeria is an exception); documentation can be arranged at the Niger or Mali borders. At the Niger border they'll issue documents that should cover you for all CFA *(Communauté Financière Africaine)* countries.

The purpose of a carnet is to allow you to take a vehicle into a country without paying the duties which would normally apply. It guarantees that if a vehicle is taken into a country but not exported, the issuing organisation will accept responsibility for payment of import duties. Carnets can only be issued by national motoring organisations. The UK Automobile Association (and most other such organisations) requires a financial guarantee for the carnet, which acts as an import duty waiver, as it could be liable for customs and other taxes if the vehicle's exit is not registered within a year.

| | | **Fuel Costs** | | |
|---|---|---|---|---|
| | *Morocco* | *Algeria* | *Tunisia* | *Libya* |
| Regular | N/A | N/A | 530 mills | 105 dirhams |
| Super | Dr 6.98 | N/A | 570 mills | 140 dirhams |
| Lead-free | Dr 6.98 | N/A | N/A | N/A |
| Diesel | Dr 3.99 | N/A | 310 mills | N/A |
| N/A = not applicable or not available | | | | |

The kind of deposit they are looking at can be well in excess of US$1000. The carnet costs UK£57.50 to UK£67.50 in the UK, depending on the number of countries you want to cover (up to 25). It is essential to ensure that the carnet is filled out properly at each border crossing, or you could be up for a lot of money. The carnet may also need to have listed any expensive spares you plan to carry, such as a gearbox.

Full details regarding carnets and related matters can be found in the Lonely Planet guides to the relevant areas, such as *Africa on a shoestring*.

It is important to note that, although you don't need a carnet to take a foreign-registered vehicle into Algeria, if you have to abandon it in the desert, you'll be up for import duties. And they won't let you out of the country until you pay. You might think this is unfair, since you haven't sold the car – you've simply been forced to abandon it. Tough luck! As far as the customs officials are concerned, you've sold it and they are not prepared to go out into the desert to confirm that it had to be abandoned. Your only option for getting around paying the import duties is either to get the vehicle going again or have it towed in. The latter would cost a fortune.

The amount of import duty can vary considerably but, generally speaking, it's between one and 1½ times the new value of the vehicle. There are exceptions to this where duty can be as high as three times the new value.

The road between Tamanrasset and the Algeria-Niger border is littered with abandoned cars, so you won't be the first. The moral of the story is simple: make sure your vehicle is in top mechanical condition before you set off, carry sufficient spare parts and be able to fix it if anything goes wrong.

**Insurance** You need a Green Card proving that you have third-party insurance in all North African countries. If your insurer won't issue one covering any of the countries you intend to drive in, you'll have to arrange insurance on the border.

The liability limits on these policies are often absurdly low by Western standards and if you have any bad accidents you could be in deep water. Also, you can only guess whether or not the premium is simply pocketed by the person collecting it or is actually passed on to the company, although this is more of a problem farther south than in the Maghreb.

It may be advisable to arrange more comprehensive and reliable cover before you leave. If you're starting from the UK, a company often recommended for insurance policies and for detailed information on carnets is Campbell Irvine (☎ 0171-937 9903), 48 Earl's Court Rd, London W8 6EJ.

Note that in Libya you'll be issued a local plate for 60 LD (refundable if you leave by the same border post, but probably not if you choose a different exit point).

**Books** In addition to Simon Glen's *Sahara Handbook*, Lascelles also publishes *Overland & Beyond* by Jon & Theresa Hewatt, which covers driving in the Sahara and beyond. If you understand German, a good book is *Dürch Afrika* by K & E Darr (Touring Club Suisse, 1977).

## SEA

Which ferry you take depends on where you want to travel and how much you want to pay. The Spain-Morocco ferries are the cheapest, followed by those from Sicily to Tunis, although drivers heading to Tunisia might find it better value to get a ferry from Genoa and save themselves the trip through Italy.

The most expensive of the ferries are those linking France and Algeria. The least reliable are those to Libya. There should be daily services from Malta, and very occasional ones to Egypt, Turkey and Morocco.

*All* routes are heavily subscribed in summer. If you plan to take a vehicle across you must try to book in advance, especially for the Tunisian and Algerian crossings. The

situation is not as bad for Morocco, as there are more crossings.

For full details of routes, schedules and operators, check the Getting There & Away chapters for each country.

## TOURS

Organised tours are only really an option in Morocco and Tunisia. They generally cost more than doing things under your own steam but, depending on what you're after, they can take some of the hassle out of your trip. They can be useful for certain activities, such as trekking and exploring remote regions. See each country's Getting There & Away and Getting Around chapters for more details.

# Morocco

# Facts about the Country

## HISTORY SINCE 1830
### European Interference (to 1912)

Following the death of Moulay Ismail in 1727, Morocco entered a period of slow decline. Moulays Abd ar-Rahman (1822-59) and Mohammed bin Abd ar-Rahman (1859-73), grappling with internal problems, had to face the unpleasant fact that powerful European powers were taking a growing interest in the whole of North Africa. France's occupation of neighbouring Algeria in 1830 was the most obvious manifestation of this development, and the sultanate's powerlessness to do anything about it was further cause for worry.

As Europe's big players moved to secure advantages over each other, the competition for influence in Morocco grew. In 1856, Britain extracted a treaty guaranteeing free trade. French and Spanish influence also grew, although it temporarily waned after 1870. Moulay al-Hassan (1873-94) began some economic, administrative and military reforms and managed to keep Europe at arm's length, but he could not prevent attempts by Spain and Britain to get a foothold along the coast (Río de Oro, Ifni and Cap Juby). Europeans stepped up trade and set up industries in Morocco, but the benefit to Moroccans was minimal.

Al-Hassan's successor, Moulay Abd al-Aziz, came to the throne ill-prepared to cope with the problems in store for him. An attempt at tax reform and repeated French military intervention caused uproar. France virtually bought off Italy (which was given a free hand in Libya), Spain (with the promise of a northern sphere of interest in Morocco) and Britain (which was given a free hand in Egypt and the Sudan). As a result, in 1905 France hoped to pull off the establishment of a protectorate with a so-called 'plan of reforms'.

Germany, which had been left out of the international wheeling and dealing, put paid to this and called for an international confer-

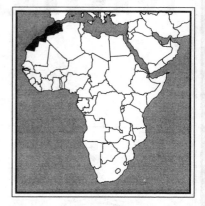

ence, achieving little more than to delay the inevitable. Moulay Abd al-Hafiz became sultan in 1909, but the situation had already slipped beyond the Moroccans' control. In 1911 Germany was pacified by the other European powers with concessions in the Congo (after sending a gunboat to Agadir and so pushing Germany and France to the brink of war), leaving the way free for France to move in. Spain had already sent troops to the northern zone allocated to it by agreement in 1904.

### French Protectorate (1912-56)

The treaty of Fès was signed on 30 March 1912, and although the sultan was to maintain the appearance of power, effective control rested with the governor, or resident-general, General (later Marshal) Lyautey and his successors. Spain controlled the northern part of the country and Tangier was made an international zone in 1923.

Moroccans were none too pleased and, in the mountains especially, remained beyond colonial control. After WW I, Abd el-Krim led a revolt in the Rif and Middle Atlas mountains, and for five years had the

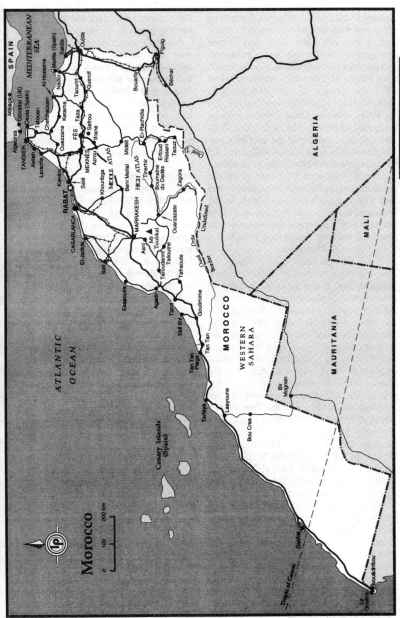

MOROCCO

Spaniards and French on the run. Spain came close to a massive and embarrassing defeat and it was not until 1934 that France managed to end effective Berber resistance.

The process of colonisation in the French zone was rapid. From a few thousand before 1912, the number of foreigners living in Morocco rose to a peak of more than 100,000 by 1929, when the Great Depression put a dampener on growth. The French built roads and railways, developed the port of Casablanca virtually from scratch and moved the political capital to Rabat. In the French zone, *villes nouvelles* were built next to the old medinas (largely the result of an enlightened policy on Lyautey's part – in Algeria he had witnessed the wholesale destruction of many old cities by his French compatriots). The Spaniards followed suit in their zone, but on a much more modest scale.

WW II brought a new wave of Europeans into Morocco, virtually doubling their numbers, but it also brought hardship as prices rose and industry came to a standstill. After Franco came to power in Spain in 1939 and Hitler overran France in 1940, Spanish Morocco became a seat of Nazi propaganda, tending oddly enough to foment nationalist aspirations in the rest of the country. Various opposition groups were formed, but the French administration ignored pleas for reform. The Allied landings in 1943 further muddied the waters, but the Free French forces, in spite of US President Roosevelt's sympathy to the nationalists' cause, were adamant that nothing in Morocco should change. In January 1944 the Istiqlal (Independence) party led by Allal al-Fasi, one of Morocco's most intractable nationalists, demanded full independence.

When the war ended, nationalist feeling grew and French reaction became increasingly inflexible. Moroccans boycotted French goods and terrorist acts against the administration multiplied. The sultan, Mohammed V, sympathised with the nationalists, so much so that the French authorities in Rabat had him deposed in 1953 – an act that served only to make him a hero in the people's eyes and turn up the heat. In 1955,

Paris allowed his return and talks began on handing power to the Moroccans.

Madrid's administration of the Spanish zone after the war was considerably less heavy-handed than that of the French, and in fact it became something of a haven for Moroccan nationalists. Spain had not been consulted on the expulsion of the sultan, and had continued to recognise him during the period of his removal from power. As a result, there was virtually no cooperation at all between the two zones.

### Independence

Mohammed V returned to Morocco in November 1955 to a tumultuous welcome. Within five months, as the French protectorate formally came to an end, he was able to appoint Morocco's first independent government. The country's independence was formally proclaimed on 3 March 1956. Shortly afterwards, Spain pulled out of its zone in the north, but hung on to the enclaves of Ceuta, Melilla and Ifni. It abandoned the latter in 1970, but Madrid has shown no desire to give up its last two areas of influence.

The sultan resumed virtually autocratic rule and, when the Istiqlal Party split into two groups in 1959 (Istiqlal and the more left-wing Union Nationale des Forces Populaires), he posed as mediator, above the mucky business of party politics. He did not have to fulfil this role for long, as he died in 1961. He was succeeded by his son, Hassan II.

In 1972 the new king introduced a constitution, having been delayed by an attempted coup in 1971. However, another coup attempt that same year led him to suspend much of it. When elections were finally held in 1977, supporters of the king won a big majority. Both halves of the Istiqlal had by now moved to the opposition.

### Western Sahara

Hassan II owes some of his popularity to the apparent *baraka* (good grace) he has displayed in surviving two attempts to get rid of him. He owes most of his popularity, however, to his organisation of the Green March into what was the Spanish Sahara in November 1975. After various about-faces, Madrid had decided to abandon the phosphate-rich territory in 1974, and finally pulled the last of its troops out shortly after 350,000 Moroccan civilians walked in. Mauritania dropped its claims to any of the territory in 1979 in exchange for Rabat renouncing any plans to absorb Mauritania, to which it had claimed historical rights.

From the late 1960s, however, it had become clear that the 130,000 or so inhabitants of the territory wanted independence. The Popular Front for the Liberation of Saguia al-Hamra and Río de Oro (Polisario), set up to harass the Spaniards, did not take kindly to Moroccan intervention and embarked on a long guerilla war against Rabat.

Backed by Libya and Algeria, Polisario scored occasional successes against the far superior Moroccan forces but, as the latter completed a ragged defensive wall inside the territory's Mauritanian and Algerian frontiers, Polisario's room to move became extremely limited. In 1984, Morocco and Libya proclaimed a 'union' in Oujda that came to nothing but resulted in the latter withdrawing its support for Polisario. As Algeria's internal problems grew in the late 1980s and early 1990s, it too abandoned its Saharan protégés.

In 1991, the UN brokered a cease-fire that has more or less held since that time, on the understanding that a referendum on the territory's future would be held. The two sides have been unable to agree on who should vote. Polisario wants only those registered as citizens prior to the Green March to participate, while Rabat naturally wants to include many of those who have since moved into Western Sahara, claiming many of them are originally from the territory. At the time of writing, it looked as though Hassan II would eventually get his way. The UN, preoccupied with other problems, seemed little disposed to devoting too much time to what it appeared to regard as a backwater, and the referendum had been indefinitely postponed.

There were signs too that European governments were losing interest in the issue and coming around to Rabat's point of view that the territory was historically a part of Morocco. Algeria, Polisario's main backer, had its own problems and, in a sign of *rapprochement* with Rabat, signed an accord

---

## Relations with Israel

Morocco has maintained a unique position in the Arab-Israeli conflict. Although at the time of writing the two nations still did not have diplomatic relations, Morocco had hosted Israeli guests, often in secret, long before Egypt's President Anwar Sadat went to Israel in 1977. Various senior politicians have travelled to Rabat incognito, and Shimon Peres, the foreign minister at the time of writing, made several open visits, including one to Ifrane in 1987. After signing a peace accord with the PLO in Washington in September 1993, Yitzak Rabin, the Israeli prime minister, stopped at Rabat on his way home to thank Hassan II for his behind-the-scenes work as intermediary.

There could be several reasons for Morocco's rather independent stance on Israel. After the Jewish state was established in 1948, the bulk of Morocco's Jewish population decided to move. The Israeli intelligence organisation, Mossad, organised the transfer with the connivance of Franco's Spain, while Rabat turned a blind eye to an operation it could have blocked. More than 80,000 of Morocco's Jews left via Ceuta and Melilla, heading to France through Spain, and then on to Israel. Mossad officials have since claimed that without Franco's help it could never have been done, and that Spain had asked nothing in return. This is now seen as a gesture of reconciliation after the horrors inflicted on the Jews in WW II by the fascist states, with which Franco's Spain had been closely identified. Morocco's motivation for cooperating seems less clear, but Moroccan Jews have long been allowed to holiday in Morocco and, officially at least, there is little bad blood between Jews and the rest of the Moroccan population. ∎

with Morocco in 1993 on defining the border between the two countries. The nitty-gritty of this agreement was still to be implemented.

## Morocco Today

The 1980s in Morocco were marked above all by economic stagnation and hardship. This boiled over into open rioting over bread price rises in Fès in 1984, during which at least 100 people died.

Hassan II has friends in useful places, however, and the rulers of Saudi Arabia and the Gulf States are among them. Accorded most-favoured nation trading status, they sometimes reciprocate when things are particularly bad – in 1985, US$250 million turned up in the central bank at a time when Morocco was practically bereft of foreign exchange reserves. Hassan's pro-Allied position during the Gulf War in 1990-91 has done him no harm either. Although popular sentiment tended to side with Iraq's Saddam Hussein, Hassan managed to keep in with the West and the Gulf States in a low-profile fashion that aroused little rancour among his subjects.

Although things have improved in some sectors recently, unrest has bubbled below the surface and it occasionally bursts through. Strikes and riots over low wages and poor social conditions saw unions clashing with the authorities in the early 1990s. In one such event, at least 33 people died and hundreds were jailed. In early 1994, the trade unions were heading for renewed clashes with the authorities over pay and social policy, calling for mass protests and strikes.

In spite of constitutional reforms and more open recent elections (see the Government section later in this chapter), Hassan is still an absolute ruler. On the economic front, the pressures of a rapidly expanding population, a top-heavy public sector and disappointing progress in most industries remain considerable obstacles, but the news is not all black, particularly if Morocco secures a free-trade deal with the European Union (EU) (see the Economy section later in this chapter).

Despite the wave of fundamentalist trouble crashing over neighbouring Algeria and the very real problems confronting Hassan II and his people, it appears his baraka will hold for a while yet.

## GEOGRAPHY

Morocco presents by far the most varied geological smorgasbord in all North Africa, and some of the most beautiful country throughout the continent. With its long Atlantic and Mediterranean coasts it has remained to some degree shielded from the rest of the continent by the Atlas Mountains to the east and the Sahara desert to the south.

Including the Western Sahara, occupied by Morocco since the Green March of 1975, the kingdom covers 710,850 sq km, more than a third of it in the disputed territory.

There are four distinct mountain ranges or massifs in Morocco. They are considered geologically to be unstable and leave Morocco subject to earthquakes, such as the one that devastated Agadir in 1960. In the north, the Rif (sometimes confusingly known as the Rif Atlas) forms an arc of largely impenetrable limestone and sandstone mountain territory, shooting steeply back from the Mediterranean to heights of

about 2200 metres and populated largely by Berbers – many engaged in the cultivation of kif (the local name for marijuana).

Running north-east to south-west from the Rif is the Middle Atlas range (Moyen Atlas), which rises to a maximum altitude of 3290 metres. It is separated from the Rif by the only real access route linking Atlantic Morocco with the rest of North Africa – the Taza Gap.

The low hills east of Agadir rise to form the highest of the mountain ranges, the High Atlas, which more or less runs parallel to the south of the Middle Atlas. Its tallest peak, Jebel Toubkal, is 4165 metres high and, like much of the surrounding heights, is covered in a mantle of snow through the winter and into spring.

Farther south again, the lower slopes of the Anti-Atlas drop down into the arid wastes of the Sahara.

The river valleys (known as *oued*, from the Arabic *wadi)* are mostly torrential and, depending on seasonal rainfall and melting snows, can flow quite strongly at certain times of the year. The valleys of the Drâa, Ziz and the Dadès, among others, drain off into the Sahara, although occasionally the Drâa completes its course all the way to the Atlantic coast north of Tan Tan. Among other rivers draining into the Atlantic are the Sebou, which rises south of Fès and empties into the ocean at Mehdiya, about 40 km north of Rabat, and the Oum er-Rbia, which has its source in the Middle Atlas, north-east of Khénifra, and reaches the Atlantic at Azemmour, just north of El-Jadida.

Between each of the mountain ranges and the Atlantic lie the plains and plateaux, generally well watered and in places quite fertile.

South of the Anti-Atlas, the dry slopes, riven by gorges, trail off into the often stony desert of the Western Sahara, which is also the name the rebels of the former Spanish Sahara have given to the territory they want to see independent of Morocco. This is a sparsely populated and unforgiving region bounded to the east and south by Algeria and Mauritania.

## CLIMATE

The geological variety of Morocco also gives it a wide range of climatic conditions.

Weather in the coastal regions is generally mild but it can become a little cool and wet, particularly in the north. Average temperatures in Tangier and Casablanca range from about 12°C (54°F) in winter to 25°C (77°F) in summer, although the daytime temperatures can easily go higher. Rainfall is greatest in the Rif and northern Middle Atlas, where only the summer months bring dry conditions.

While the interior of the country can become stiflingly hot in summer, particularly when the desert winds from the Sahara (known as the sirocco or *chergui*, from the Arabic *ash-sharqi*, meaning 'the easterly') are blowing, the Atlantic coast is kept comparatively agreeable by sea breezes. Nevertheless, the southern Atlantic coast is more arid. Rainfall here drops off and renders the cultivation of crops less tenable.

The rainy season is from November to January, but can go on as late as April. From 1991 to late 1993, however, drought dried the country out and cut cereal production by around 60%. There was a sigh of relief when heavy rains struck in November 1993, replenishing reservoirs for drinking water, power stations and irrigation.

The lowlands can be quite hot during the day even in winter, with the mercury hitting as high as 30°C (86°F), but temperatures drop quickly in the evening. In the mountains, it can get as cold as -20°C (-4°F), and that is without taking the wind-chill factor into account. As snow can often block mountain passes, it is important to remember to have enough warm clothing to cope with an unwelcome night stuck in an unheated bus. In summer, the opposite is true during the day, particularly when the chergui is up, with temperatures easily exceeding 40°C (104°F). This goes for Marrakesh too.

In the desert, temperatures can swing wildly from day to night. This is due to the

MOROCCO

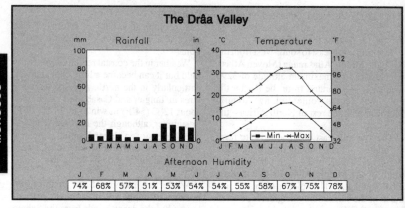

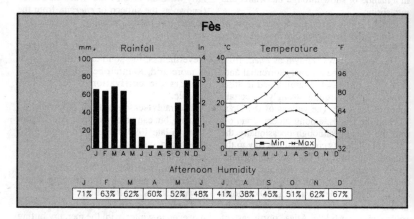

dryness of the atmosphere, with humidity almost nonexistent.

The chergui, which sometimes blows laden with dust, can occur at any time of the year, but is most common in spring.

### FLORA

Until the first century or so of the Christian era, sweeping savanna and good pastures covered much of the Maghreb. But the increasing desert conditions gradually forced the mainly Berber population to seek refuge in the mountains of the Atlas, a process which had been developing over thousands of years.

Nevertheless, the first-time visitor may be surprised at the amount of green encountered in a country more popularly associated with vast stretches of desert. Travellers arriving in northern Morocco after crossing the arid *meseta* of central and southern Spain are often struck by the comparative lushness they find across the Strait of Gibraltar.

Although many areas have suffered from deforestation, in the higher altitudes you can still find yourself in thick woodland and even what could be loosely described as forest.

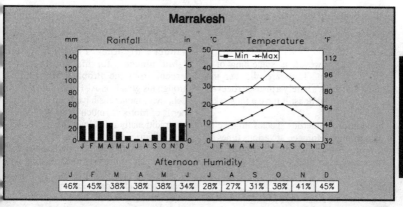

Marrakesh

| J | F | M | A | M | J | J | A | S | O | N | D |
|---|---|---|---|---|---|---|---|---|---|---|---|
| 46% | 45% | 38% | 38% | 38% | 34% | 28% | 27% | 31% | 38% | 41% | 45% |

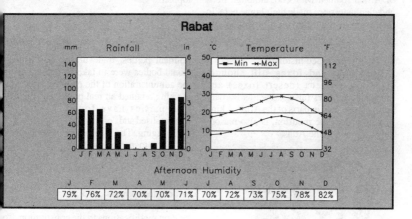

Rabat

| J | F | M | A | M | J | J | A | S | O | N | D |
|---|---|---|---|---|---|---|---|---|---|---|---|
| 79% | 76% | 72% | 70% | 70% | 71% | 70% | 72% | 73% | 75% | 78% | 82% |

The lower plains are generally either cultivated or covered by the coarse grasses and scrub that has adapted to handle the extremes of climate and, particularly, the ravages of summer-time cherguis.

Where areas have managed to remain comparatively arboreous, in spite of human handiwork, various species of oak (including cork and evergreen shrubs) and cedar are among the more common native trees. Eucalyptus and the so-called Barbary fig are imports. In addition, you will see occasional stands of fir and juniper trees.

A tree peculiar to the south of the country is the argan, which bears a fruit not unlike the olive, from which oil is also extracted.

You will come across date palms in various places, but they are really only native to the desert fringes.

The best time to be walking in the mountains is the spring, when the slopes and even parts of near-desert areas are brightly decorated by a variety of wildflowers.

## FAUNA
### Bird Life

Morocco does not boast a huge range of native resident species. There are various kinds of eagle and falcon but smaller species are more common, including several types of lark and finch and others peculiar to the desert.

The stork, however, is something of a national emblem. They are all over the country, and there's barely a disused (or even used) minaret that doesn't have a fat stork's nest on top of it.

In addition, numerous species migrate to or pass through Morocco at various times of the year. These include flamingos and various species of ducks and gulls.

### Animals

It is a long time since any of the great beasts of Africa roamed Morocco, although lions and elephants once made their home here. In fact, most of the time you'll be unlikely to see much more than mules, donkeys, goats, sheep, horses and camels, introduced into the area before recorded history.

Wild boar and foxes still abound. Gazelles, fennecs (desert foxes) and macaque monkeys (also known as Barbary apes) can be seen in parts of the Atlas. A kind of wild sheep, the mouflon, is also reasonably common in the Atlas.

Barbary ape

### GOVERNMENT

For all its trappings of parliamentary democracy, Morocco remains essentially an absolute monarchy. In power since 1961, Hassan II is the latest in a long dynastic line, the Alawites, who have been at the helm, at least in name, since the 17th century. One of the titles the king takes for himself is Commander of the Faithful (Amir al-Mu'mineen), for his family claims descent from the Prophet Mohammed, through his grandson Al-Hassan bin Ali. As such, these monarchs have been considered sherifs of Morocco, much in the way Mecca was traditionally ruled by a sherif. The religious significance of Hassan II's claim to legitimacy should not be underestimated, and goes part of the way to explaining how he has managed to stay in power for so long, when other traditional rulers in the Arab and wider Muslim world have tended to be toppled.

### Constitution

Under a constitution established in 1972, political parties, trade unions and professional bodies were to take an active part in the administration of the country. However, the king retained all real power and opposition parties have found themselves marginalised and continually complaining of vote-rigging. The king reserved for himself the right to name his prime minister and ministers, control of the armed forces, the right to dissolve the Chamber of Representatives *(majlis an-nuwab* – parliament) and a raft of other powers.

In September 1992, a referendum was held on modifications to the constitution. To the dismay of many, the vote was an all-too resounding 'yes' – the usual 99%. Hassan II is playing a delicate game, trying to present an image of slow but definite democratisation to the West, and particularly to his European neighbours with whom he wants closer economic links, yet still conserving his control over the political life of the country. The opposition deemed the reform insufficient. Under it, the king renounced the right to appoint ministers, but retained his right to appoint the prime minister. On 11 January 1994, to signal their dissatisfaction with the changes, the opposition used the 50th anniversary of the Istiqlal Party's demand for independence in 1944 to call for greater democracy in modern Morocco.

## Elections & Political Parties

Elections to the 333-seat parliament are held in two stages. The first 222 seats are thrown open to a popular vote. The last of these took place in June 1993 (the first general polls since 1984), and were a considerable success for the four-party opposition, Bloc Démocratique, which won 99 seats. However, the vote for the remaining 111 seats is carried out among trade unions and professional bodies, and traditionally favours loyalist groups. In September 1993, loyalists took 79 of these seats.

In the following months, the opposition refused to bend to the king's request that it join a government of national coalition. Nevertheless, the comparatively low (some would say realistic) turnout of voters – 63% – and the result will be a feather in his democratic cap abroad. Another pleasant surprise was the election of two women to seats in parliament – a first in Morocco.

The opposition parties forming the Bloc Démocratique are a ragbag of groups, including Istiqlal, the Union Socialiste des Forces Populaires, the former communist Parti du Progrès du Socialisme and the smaller Organisation de l'Action Démocratique et Populaire. Ranged against them, particularly as they have refused to participate in the government formed in the wake of the 1993 elections, is a centre-right alliance of five promonarchy parties. The Mouvement Populaire, the biggest of them, attracts most of its support from the rural Berber population. Others include the liberal Union Constitutionelle and the Rassemblement National des Indépendants.

## Tiers of Government

For administrative purposes, the country is divided into 40 provinces (*wilayas*), four of which make up the territory of the Western Sahara. The provinces are subdivided into préfectures (Casablanca is made up of five), and further into *qaidates*. *Qaids* (or *caids*) have similar powers to those of pashas, who are responsible for administering urban municipalities. Other local-government officials go by the name of *moqadams*.

## Outlook

In spite of several assassination attempts, and a relatively small Islamist movement operating in the country, the king's position as head of the government seems secure. Although disturbed by the troubles plaguing Algeria next door, few believe Morocco will experience the same problems. This does not make it an impossibility. Various radical Islamists are in jail, and Abdessalam Yassine, the leader of Al-Adl wal-Ihsan (Justice & Charity), the most important of such groups in Morocco, has long been under house arrest in Salé.

Amnesty International claims that, despite several releases of prisoners in recent years, more than 600 people remain incarcerated because of their political activities. Dissident Moroccans outside the country hope economic difficulties and Hassan's desire for greater integration into the Western economies will lead him to make concessions along the path to more open government. The Morocco of today has often been compared to Franco's Spain of the 1950s and '60s. If Hassan II has a full innings, the thinking goes, he might even be succeeded by a full parliamentary democracy.

## ECONOMY

After years of mishaps and harsh austerity measures, there are signs that Morocco has turned a difficult corner. As a privatisation drive gets up steam and Morocco returns to international finance markets after 10 years of tough slimming measures imposed by the International Monetary Fund, analysts see hope of continued improvement. Along the way, maximum tariffs have come down from 400% to 35%, the dirham has moved close to full convertibility and Morocco has become a member of the General Agreement on Tariffs and Trade – in fact Marrakesh was chosen as the site for the signing of the final accord which ended the long-contested Uruguay round of talks in April 1994. As if to add to the cheer, heavy rains in November 1993 broke a two-year drought that had decimated agriculture.

Inflation has been brought down as low as 5% from highs above 12% in the mid-1980s, but unemployment remains at least at 20%, if not higher. Official estimates say the number of people living below the poverty line has dropped by a third to 13% since 1985. In that same period, it is claimed per capita income has nearly doubled to US$1100.

If the news remains good, it will bring relief to a government anxiously watching the growing frustration of the country's underemployed young, but among the hopeful signals are plenty of worrying indicators of an uneven economy.

Foreign debt, at US$21.5 billion, remains a heavy burden, although Saudi Arabia's decision to forgo US$3 billion in loans in the wake of the Gulf War eased the load. Morocco is still a heavy borrower. The World Bank reports that Morocco is the biggest recipient of its aid throughout North Africa and the Middle East.

Morocco's growing youth unemployment problem moved the government to set up a special job-creation fund of US$100,000 in 1994.

## European Connection

King Hassan II pins great hopes to anchoring Morocco as firmly as possible in the EU's orbit. To this end, both sides are negotiating a deal to create a free-trade zone by 1996 between the kingdom and the EU, or European Community (EC) as it was until the Treaty of Maastricht went into effect in November 1993. In 1987, Morocco applied for membership of the then EC but was knocked back, and Mediterranean EU members fear a flood of cheap Moroccan agricultural produce could provide unwelcome competition. As it is, the trade balance between the EU and Morocco only moderately favours Europe. However, there are some quid pro quos to be made, and the EU is well aware of the fact.

The government has moved to dampen illegal immigration to Europe and drug smuggling. In return, Western countries have promised US$1 billion to help persuade farmers in the Rif Mountains currently planting kif (cannabis) to take up other crops. European police chiefs fear Morocco could become a major route for South American hard drugs coming into Europe. The stakes are high, and the drugs issue gives Rabat some leverage when bargaining with the EU.

## Resources

Agriculture still employs about 40% of the population, and although Morocco doesn't produce enough grain and cereals to meet its own needs, food exports (mainly fruit and vegetables) make up about 30% of the total. Occasional drought makes it impossible to predict what contribution the farm sector will make to the economy in any one year.

Top of its mineral assets are phosphates, of which Morocco is said to have between two-thirds and three-quarters of the world's reserves (including those in the Western Sahara). It is the world's third-biggest exporter of the mineral, after the USA and Russia. With world prices well down, it is not the money-spinner the government might have hoped for. Phosphate mining is controlled by the Office Cherifien des Phosphates, a state monopoly.

Other mineral exports include fluorite, barite, manganese, iron ore, lead, zinc, cobalt, copper and antimony, but with phosphates accounting for 90% of mineral exports, these are relatively insignificant.

Although Morocco's search for oil has turned up nothing, there are two refineries for processing imported oil at Mohammedia and Sidi Kacem.

Remittances from the 1.6 million Moroccans living abroad (mostly in Europe and half of them in France) are the biggest source of foreign income. In 1992, they brought in Dr 19 million.

Tourism, hard hit by the effects of the Gulf War in 1990-91, is picking up again and is the second-largest hard currency earner. About 3½ million visitors arrived in Morocco in 1992, a little over a third of them

Europeans, and a big proportion of them French. More were expected in 1993 (the statistics take a while to come out). Tourism is thought to provide jobs, formal and not so formal, to half the working population of cities like Marrakesh. 'Informal' is a polite way of saying black, and this 'sector' of the economy is reckoned conservatively to make up 30% of GDP.

In addition to the ill-reputed US$2 billion hashish trade (Morocco is said to supply at least 30% of Europe's dope), there is a flourishing smuggling business in all sorts of consumer items via the Spanish enclaves in the north of the country.

A new link tying Europe to the Maghreb is the gas pipeline under construction between Algeria and Spain. The Moroccan stretch will be 525 km long and will cost US$1300 million. Spain is paying for the construction and gas is due to start flowing by 1996. This comes after a friendship treaty signed between Rabat and Madrid in June 1991. Since the signing, Spanish investment in Morocco has grown by leaps and bounds, at a time when French investment is levelling off.

The ties to Europe have a down side. Morocco still exports too much to too few countries (France takes a third of the total), making it vulnerable to recession in Europe.

Privatisations, lifting of subsidies, government spending cuts and other measures may be helping the economy into gear, but many are suffering. Government figures put the number of poor by World Bank definitions at around four million, but the opposition claims the real figures are worse (the average farm or factory worker's wage does not rise above Dr 1000 a month, and is often less), and that the gap between wealthy and poor is widening. Sound familiar?

## POPULATION

The population of Morocco is estimated at between 27 and 28 million. About half the total is under 20 years of age and, with a growth rate of 2.2%, the population threatens to become a destabilising factor in a country where a great rift separates the well-off

minority and the growing legions of unemployed youth.

As the rural flight to the cities continues, the urban population continues to expand, and more than two-thirds of the populace is estimated to live in the cities. By far the most populous city is the Atlantic port and commercial centre of Casablanca, with 2.9 million people. The capital, Rabat, counts 1.23 million if Salé is included. Marrakesh has about 1.4 million inhabitants, and Fès is pushing close to a million. Meknès, Oujda and Agadir are not far behind.

## PEOPLE
### Arabs, Berbers & Moors

The bulk of the population is made up of Berbers or Arabs, although the distinction is not always easily made. The numbers of ethnic Arabs who came to Morocco with the first Islamic invasion of the 7th century, or 400 years later with the Beni Hillal, were comparatively small. Bigger contributions came from Spain as the Catholics evicted the Muslims in the course of the Reconquista. They have to a large degree mixed with Berbers, who in turn have in great measure been Arabised. When one talks of the people of the northern coastal areas and big cities as being largely Arab, what is usually meant is Arabic-speaking. Probably less than a quarter of the population is now monolingual in Berber, and bilingualism has increased thanks to modern communications and transport.

Little is known of the racial origins of the Berbers. The word itself comes from an Arabic word possibly borrowed from the Latin (and ultimately ancient Greek) *barbari*, signifying the non-Latin speaking peoples of the Maghreb. (The antiquated name for this area of North Africa, Barbary, has the same origins.)

The Berbers inhabit the mountain regions and parts of the desert, and are generally considered to be roughly divided into three groups identified by dialect and located in the Rif, Middle Atlas and High Atlas areas. See the Language section later in this chapter for more details.

MOROCCO

Europeans have long talked of the 'Moors' as a generic description of the whole populace of the Maghreb, and even for the whole Muslim world. The name probably more justly refers to a group of people living in the south of Morocco, but also spread out across Mauritania (*Mauros* was a Greek word to describe these people, from which Moor was probably derived), Algeria and Mali. Only a small proportion of these groups, also known as the 'blue people' because of the colour of their attire and the fact that the dye lends a bluish hue to their skin, live on Moroccan soil. For simplicity's sake they can be roughly lumped together with the Tuaregs of southern Algeria. In spite of tourist hype, few if any actual Tuaregs live in Morocco.

### Jews

Morocco once hosted as many as 160,000 Jews, roughly divided into those of obscure Berber origin and those, Arabic-speaking, who found themselves compelled to leave Andalusian Spain in the face of the Reconquista. By the end of the 1960s this population had dropped to 30,000, as most Jews opted to migrate to the state of Israel from 1948. The *mellah*, or Jewish quarter, of many Moroccan towns can still often be identified, but few Jews remain in the country.

### Other Ethnic Groups

Growing commercial links with the interior of Africa over the centuries has attracted a population of Negroes from various parts of sub-Saharan Africa into the south of Morocco, particularly into the southern oases and desert settlements. Many came as slaves.

Morocco once played host to half a million foreigners but, since the end of the French protectorate in 1956, the number has dropped considerably. Among those absorbed into the general populace are Iberians who came to Morocco as the Muslims were forced out of Spain. They were joined in later times by Spanish traders and workers, many of whom have also melted into the Moroccan populace.

### EDUCATION

Morocco spends a lot on educating its young – as much as 27% of the state budget according to some claims – but it still has a long way to go. In spite of boasting enrolments of nearly four million children in schools and some 230,000 students in the country's 11 universities, around half the adult male population is still estimated by UNESCO to be illiterate. The figure among women is higher still, possibly as much as 70%.

The gulf between the urban and rural populations is also highlighted by literacy figures. As few as 23% of people living in the country can read, whereas 64% of city dwellers are literate.

National service, which applies to males, lasts up to 18 months.

### ARTS
#### Music

Invasion and cultural cross-fertilisation have bequeathed several musical traditions to Morocco. If you are seriously interested in buying recordings of various types of Moroccan music, you should try Le Comptoir Marocain de Distribution de Disques (☎ 02-269538) at 26 Ave Lalla Yacout in Casablanca. It has a wide range of material on LP, cassette and CD. Popular cassettes can be had for a dollar or two at music stands throughout the country.

**Arab-Andalusian** In addition to the more 'standard' musical inheritance from Arab lands farther to the east, Morocco knows a classical tradition that actually developed in Muslim Spain under the guidance of a man called Ziryeb, a musician who settled in Granada in the 9th century.

He developed a suite system known as the *nawba*, which played on the alternate use of rhythmic and nonrhythmic, and vocal and instrumental passages. In all, there are 24 tightly structured *nawbat*, corresponding to the 24 harmonic modes of Andalusian music and each purportedly in tune with an hour of the day.

Another musical system that emerged under the guidance of the same man aligned music with the Ptolemaic system of viewing medicine and human health as determined by humours, the four chief fluids of the body (blood, phlegm, choler and melancholy).

As the Muslims were forced out of Spain by the end of the 15th century, the music moved and took root in Morocco. The palaces of Rabat and Oujda, among others, became havens for the preservation of the Andalusian tradition.

Sheikh Salah was one of the best modern exponents of the art, and it is possible to pick up cassettes of his orchestra in Morocco, and even the odd CD is available in Europe.

**Berber Music** Long before the Arabs even knew of the existence of Morocco, the Berber tribes had been developing their own music, later enhanced by the arrival of various Arab instruments and styles.

Music is not just entertainment – it has also been the medium for storytelling and the passing on of oral culture from generation to generation. It can still be heard at moussems (religious pilgrimages), wedding ceremonies, public gatherings and festivals, as well as during private celebrations. The music of any tribe is often a reflection of the musicality of the local dialect. Instrumental pieces can be heard, but often the music is accompanied by song and dancing – the latter can involve men *and* women, something that occasionally raises the hackles of some city (generally orthodox Arab) Muslims.

Storytelling is a big part of the musical repertoire of the Berbers. The *heddaoua*, wandering minstrels, move from one small town to another and recite poetry and the like, often in a hazy, allusive style usually attributable to the benefits of kif. Often they provide musical accompaniment, but dance is not necessarily part of the deal. They, like many manifestations of Berber and Arab traditional culture, are gradually giving way to the universal hypnotism of television.

**Contemporary Music** Various Moroccan musicians have experimented with moves to

---

### Moroccan Musical Instruments
Some of the instruments you may encounter include:

#### Wind
*andir* – a long narrow trumpet, most often used for celebrations during Ramadan
*ghaita* – a reed oboe, in wide use throughout Morocco
*nira or lira* – a generic Arabic term for various types of reed flute
*zmar* – an odd-looking double clarinet

#### String
*amzhad* – a single-chord violin, made of wood with a goatskin cover and played with a horsehair bow. It is a specifically Berber instrument.
*guimbri* – a long lute with two or three strings
*kanza* – very loosely like a guitar, a three-stringed instrument with a rectangular base
*kemenja* – a typical Arab instrument, not unlike the Western viola

#### Percussion
*bendir* – other Berber names for this single-headed oriental drum are *tagnza* and *allun*
*darbuka* – a generic term for a form of drum typical throughout the Arab world. They are usually made of terracotta in the form of a jug, with a goatskin cover on one side.
*guedra* – another kind of drum most commonly used by the so-called 'blue people' to accompany a dance performed solely by women. The dance is one you're less and less likely to see, except perhaps in a watered-down hotel floor-show version.
*qarqba*, plural *qaraqib* – large, metal castanets
*tbel* or *tabala* – a cylindrical wooden drum hung around the neck or held under the arm ■

combine aspects of their heritage and Western influences. Hassan Erraji, a blind oud (Arabic lute) player who moved to Belgium and studied European as well as Arabic classical music, has released several albums, including those entitled *Marhaba*, *Ia Dounia* and *Nikriz*. Although the Arabic roots of his music prevail, he introduces other elements into some of his pieces that are well removed from the Oriental tradition, such as saxophone.

Aisha Kandisha goes several steps further, taking traditional sound and infusing what might seem to some an overwhelming stratum of modern Western music – hence perhaps the title of one CD is *Jarring Effects*.

**Raï** Although identified more with Algeria, raï ('opinion') is fast gaining popularity in Morocco, and the voices of its leading exponents, such as Cheb Khaled, can be heard in cassette stores as far east as Egypt and Jordan. Despite its distinctly Arab-African rhythms (it owes much to Bedouin music), it is probably the most thoroughly West-ernised, combining a variety of modern electrical instruments to create an often hypnotic effect using North Africa's rich traditional musical heritage. Morocco itself has given rise to several less well-known raï performers.

### Dance
Talk of dance in the Orient, and the first thing to pop into most Western minds is the belly dance, something you can see (for a price) at plenty of the more expensive tourist hotels (and occasionally in quite sleazy 'night clubs' in the bigger cities, especially Casablanca), although it is not essentially a Moroccan art. You may also see so-called folk dancing in hotels, which is usually a poor imitation of the real thing out in the Berber hinterland.

A cross-section of some of the kinds of dance you may be lucky enough to encounter outside the hotels include the following:

*ahidous*
>This is a complex circle dance seen in the Middle Atlas. Usually associated with harvest rites, it is an occasion for the whole community to pitch in. Alternating circles of men and women dance and sing antiphonally around musicians, usually playing bendirs only, but sometimes with other instruments.

*ahouach*
>This is linked to the Ahidous of the Atlas Mountains, but performed in the kasbahs of the south. The dancing this time is done by women alone, again in a circle around musicians.

*gnaoua*
>The term refers mainly to Blacks (often descendants of slaves brought to Morocco from central and West Africa) who perform as musicians and acrobats in southern Morocco. They were once a not uncommon sight in the Djemaa el-Fna in Marrakesh, but have become a rarity.

### Architecture
**Islamic Architecture** The jewels of medieval Moroccan urban architecture are to be found in the medinas of the imperial cities, and especially in Fès and Marrakesh.

Although Spain's Muslim heritage has bequeathed more spectacular sites (such as the Alhambra in Granada), Morocco still offers a rich trove of monuments. The great

Kairaouine (Qayrawin) Mosque in Fès is the most impressive monument to Almoravid and Almohad power, with the elaborate interior decoration and vaulting which was developed over the centuries as an essential element of specifically Moroccan architecture. It is a shame that non-Muslims are denied access to such treasures. The present ban on non-Muslims entering mosques and other functioning religious institutions is said to date back to an edict by France's first resident-general in Morocco, General Lyautey.

In compensation, there are many medersas open to view that reward a visit, the best of them built by the Merenid dynasty. Like many other classic buildings throughout Moroccan cities, they bear the hallmarks of Andalusian influence in their green-tiled roofs (when you look out over a city like Fès, you can easily identify where the major monuments are by their roofs) and their intricate interior stucco and woodwork. Zellij tiles were often used to decorate the lower strip of the inner walls, and the designers left hardly a square centimetre empty of artwork.

Most buildings in Morocco share a distinctive feature, be they mosques, medersas or private residences. They are built around an internal courtyard, with the bulk of the windows looking over the courtyard and far fewer onto the streets and outside world. The reasoning combines practicality with custom, for such an organisation maximises protection against the heat and maintains a premium on privacy.

**Berber Architecture** Throughout the centuries, the Berbers of southern Morocco have adhered to a spare building style in their more important centres, unmoved by contact with other traditions (most notably that of Islam and the Arabs).

Three basic types of building are encountered: the agadir (Berber for granary); the kasbah, usually the abode of a local potentate around which would nestle the simple homes of his subjects; and the ksar (from the Arabic qasr – castle or palace), a kind of fortified village that predominates in the Todra, Drâa and Ziz valleys. The kasbahs and ksour (plural of ksar), can often look quite similar. The lower half of the defensive walls are earthen and the upper halves are made of baked brick. The towers taper somewhat towards the top and there is little decoration – none at all in the lower half. Slit windows let light in and missiles out.

The most unfortunate thing about these ochre-coloured, starkly impressive constructions is their fragility – they were not built to last. Within 50 years a magnificent new kasbah can be reduced by the elements to a ruinous pile of mud and rubble.

**Western Influences** Thanks to an unusually enlightened policy of leaving the old indigenous cities intact and building new administrative zones alongside them, the French protectorate authorities saved much of Morocco's ancient legacy and at the same time created a kind of time warp – the villes nouvelles built outside the old medinas are, to a greater or lesser extent, replicas of southern European cities of about the 1930s. For most people they are of little architectural interest, but Casablanca, which boomed as a modern port under the French, is home to a plethora of Art Deco buildings that can make a walk around the city centre a pleasant excursion of discovery for the European-architecture buff.

### Literature

Far from the heart of Muslim Arab civilisation and great seats of power and learning like Cairo, Damascus, Baghdad and Jerusalem, Morocco has never really been at the forefront of Arab letters, although several greats spent time in Morocco.

They include Ibn Khaldun and Ibn Rushd (or Averroes as he was known in the West). The former, who lived in the 14th century, is considered to be the foremost Arab historian. Born in Algeria, he spent some time in Fès, but his travels took him on to Spain, Cairo and Syria. Averroes was known for his medical treatises and commentaries on Aris-

**MOROCCO**

## Morocco on Film

As far back as 1930, Hollywood's eyes turned to the Maghreb, when Marlene Dietrich starred in the not overly demanding Paramount picture, *Morocco*. Dietrich was nominated for an Academy Award for her role as a cabaret singer finally trapped by true love – Gary Cooper of course. Not a second of what was Dietrich's American debut was filmed on location.

The same can be said of probably *the* Moroccan movie, *Casablanca*. Shot in 1942, the Humphrey Bogart classic had almost nothing to do with Casablanca, but was based on the activities of wartime Tangier, which maintained its international zone status during WW II. Rick's Café probably has more in common with that city's Dean's Bar, and visitors to Casablanca in search of traces of Ingrid Bergman and Claude Rains will be sorely disappointed by the paltry offerings – a few movie posters in the Hyatt Hotel's Bar Casablanca. In one of his more memorable exchanges, Bogart (Rick) says to Rains (Captain Louis Renault): 'I came to Casablanca for the waters.' 'What waters?' comes the reply. 'We're in the desert.' 'I was misinformed.' Nice line, but a little inaccurate. Believe it or not, Ronald Reagan was originally slated for the lead role.

Ten years later, a picture of a totally different calibre won the award for best film at the Cannes film festival. Orson Welles's epic recreation of Shakespeare's *Othello* won little box-office acclaim at the time of its release, but it has since gained a cult following – a restored copy was doing the cinematic rounds again in 1994. Welles shot some of the scenes in Essaouira and the Citerne Portugaise of El-Jadida. A small square in Essaouira has been named in his honour.

Another cinema classic filmed in Morocco was *Lawrence of Arabia*, for which the kasbah of Aït Benhaddou, south of Marrakesh, was chosen as a set. Peter O'Toole was not the only one to leave his cinematic mark here. At least 20 films have been partly shot in the kasbah, including *Jesus of Nazareth*. The Sean Connery and Michael Caine classic, *The Man Who Would Be King*, was partly shot at the kasbah of Aït Benhaddou, a few km from Tamdaght.

Another misplaced film is Bernardo Bertolucci's *The Sheltering Sky*. Although Paul Bowles had Oran (Algeria) in mind as the introductory setting for this very personal story, Bertolucci found Tangier a much better option. He chose various locations, including the Hôtel Continental in the medina, from which to launch the American couple Port (John Malkovich) and Kit (Debra Winger) on their bizarre and self-destructive adventure into the desert. Bowles, himself a longtime resident of what some know as Sodom-on-Sea, made a cameo appearance in the film. ∎

totle. Born in Córdoba, in Muslim Spain, he spent his last years in Marrakesh.

In terms of modern literature, Algeria has tended to dominate the field, especially that in French, but this does not mean Moroccans have been inactive. The bulk of it, however, is not known beyond the Maghreb and France.

Among some of the better known writers are Tahar ben Jelloun, Abdel Krim Ghallab, Ahmed Sefrioui and Driss Chraïbi. For more details and a reading selection, turn to the Books entry in the Morocco Facts for the Visitor chapter.

### Crafts

Morocco has a rich and varied tradition of handicraft production, and the better souqs are crawling with items to keep the avid souvenir hunter well occupied. See the Arts & Crafts colour section which follows the Morocco Facts for the Visitor chapter.

## SOCIETY & CONDUCT
### Traditional Lifestyle

First-time visitors to Muslim countries and experienced travellers alike find that Morocco's curious mix of conservatism and Westernised 'liberalism' never ceases to confuse. In general, men take the leading public role in Moroccan society, with the women left very much in the background. As a result, the bulk of travellers' contacts with Moroccans are with men.

As a rule, a high degree of modesty (in dress and behaviour) is demanded of both sexes. Even among the older and/or more traditionally minded, there are distinctions. While women of Arab descent are generally discouraged from, say, selling fruit and vegetables in shops and markets, Berber women have no trouble with this. Arab women are, theoretically, not supposed to dance, especially not in public. However, it is not uncommon for Berber women to participate in communal dances with men.

None of the rules are adhered to uniformly, and in the bigger cities, especially Casablanca, the veil and *hijab* (head covering) are more the exception than the rule. Younger women walk around in often stylish Western clothes and even the odd miniskirt can be seen. Possibly the most worrying fashion development in Morocco is the reappearance of bell-bottomed jeans! In addition, women work in a wide range of jobs – most of the bus conductors in Rabat and Casablanca are women, something virtually unheard of in, say, Cairo or Damascus.

The strict segregation of the sexes in public life that is a characteristic of Muslim societies is far from uniform in Morocco, and predictably enough it is in the big cities where the most mixing goes on – although the average bars and cafés remain largely a male preserve.

### Taboos

Unfortunately, mosques in active use, including some of the most impressive, are off limits to non-Muslims. You may be able to get the odd glimpse through the doors, but don't push it if people make it known that your curiosity is not appreciated. The same applies to most other religious monuments still in use.

### Sport

**Football** Among the Western imports that have really stuck in Morocco, as indeed in many African countries, football (soccer to some) is the most prominent sport. Moroccans are avid fans, and it is not unusual to see crowds of men glued to TV sets showing games between teams that have nothing to do with Morocco. The national team was good enough to qualify for the World Cup staged in the USA in 1994.

## RELIGION
### Mysticism & Marabouts

Sufism and Islamic mysticism are touched on in the Religion section of this book's introductory Facts about the Region chapter.

This mystic tendency found particularly fertile ground in the traditions and superstitions of the Berbers. There is little doubt that the cults that prosper in Morocco do so mostly in rural Berber areas. The focal point of gatherings of such groups is generally a *zawiyya*, which can be anything from a small meeting place or a big complex grouping mosque, school and hostels around the tomb of the saint, or marabout. (Marabout, from the Arabic *muraabit*, is a word used more by French scholars than the locals, and has come to designate the saint *and* the tomb.)

In Morocco, possibly the best known of these saints is Moulay Idriss, whose tomb stands in the town of the same name outside Meknès. He died in 791 AD, and is one of a number of equally venerated figures across the Muslim world, who include Ahmed al-Badawi in Tanta, Egypt, and Abdal Qadir in Baghdad.

In Morocco as elsewhere, such cults and their individualistic approaches to Islam were considered by the mainly city-dwelling orthodox Muslims as deviant, and by their leaders as politically dangerous.

Since the days of the Almoravids, armed with imprecations against heresy, various attempts have been made to put an end to the phenomenon in Morocco. In more recent times, concerted efforts were made again in the 1930s, but there are two obstacles to such campaigns. The territory of the rural Berbers is difficult to control, and the people who follow the cults make up a big chunk of the total populace – you cannot simply get rid of them all!

## LANGUAGE
### Berber

In addition to Arabic and French, the mother tongue of many Moroccans is Berber. Most Berber speakers also speak at least some Arabic and/or French.

There are three main dialects commonly delineated among the speakers of Berber, which in a certain sense also serve as loose lines of ethnic demarcation. In the north, centred on the Rif, the locals speak a dialect which has been called Riffian and is spoken as far south as Figuig on the Algerian frontier.

The dialect that predominates in the Middle and High Atlas and the valleys leading into the Sahara goes by various names, including Braber or Amazigh. More settled tribes of the High Atlas, Anti-Atlas, Souss Valley and south-western oases generally speak Chelha, or Tashelhit.

# Facts for the Visitor

## VISAS & EMBASSIES

Most visitors to Morocco do not require a visa and are granted leave to remain in Morocco for 90 days on entry. Exceptions to this rule include nationals of the Benelux countries (Holland, Belgium and Luxembourg) and South Africa, who can apply for a one-month single-entry visa (UK£4.20) or a three-month double-entry visa (UK£7). The rates vary with exchange-rate fluctuations between the Moroccan dirham and the currency of the country where you get the visa. Holders of British Visitors passports should note that the Moroccan authorities do *not* accept them.

People requiring a visa who are contemplating travelling to and fro between Morocco and, say, Spain or Algeria, should consider getting a double-entry visa to avoid the hassle of applying for new visas. If you have to get a visa, you will need to fill in up to four forms and provide four photos. In Europe it generally takes one to two days to issue the visas.

In Spain, visas are available at consulates in Madrid, Barcelona, Málaga and Las Palmas de Gran Canaria. A visa valid for one month in Morocco costs about 900 ptas (Dr 60) and can be issued in 24 hours.

In Algeria, it is possible to get a Moroccan visa at the consulates in Algiers or Oran.

Children under the age of 12 must have their photo attached to their parents' passports if they do not carry their own.

Nationals of the following European countries on *organised* tours to Morocco need only their national identity cards to enter: Austria, Denmark, Finland, France, Germany, Iceland, Norway, Spain, Sweden and Switzerland.

The position of Israelis is, to say the least, anomalous. If the momentum towards a comprehensive peace between Israel and the Arab countries continues, all could soon change, and in late 1993 Israeli tour operators visited Morocco to check out the possibilities for doing business there. For the moment, the Moroccan consulate in Málaga, southern Spain, seems to handle many of the visas requested by Israelis (about 5000 a year), generally of Moroccan origin. The process can be complicated, and the visa costs US$50. Despite the official position denying entry to those with Israeli stamps in their passports, the reality seems lax in this regard.

South Africans should encounter no difficulties entering Morocco.

### Moroccan Embassies

Moroccan embassies and consulates abroad include:

Algeria
    Embassy: 8 Rue des Cèdres, Parc de la Reine, Algiers (☎ 607737, 607408)
    Consulates: 5 Ave de l'ANP, Sidi Bel Abbès, Algiers (☎ 243470)
    26 Rue Cheikh Larbi Tebessi, Oran (☎ 333684)
Australia
    Suite 2, 11 West St, North Sydney, NSW 2060 (☎ 957 6717)
Austria
    Unter Donaustr 13/15-6, 1020 Vienna (☎ 214 2568/2393)
Belgium
    Embassy: Blvd Saint Michel 29, 1040 Brussels (☎ 736 11 00/1/2/3)
    Consulates: 52 Rue Paul Emile Janson, 1050 Brussels (☎ 649 60 10/9)
    54 Quai Saint-Léonard, 4000 Liège (☎ 27 41 59/24)
Canada
    Embassy: 38 Range Rd, Ottawa, Ontario KIN 8J4 (☎ 236 7391/2)
    Consulate: 1010 Rue Sherbrooke West, Suite 1510, Montreal H3A 2R7 (☎ 288 8750/6951)
Denmark
    Oregaards Alle 19, 2900 Hellerup, Copenhagen (☎ 62 45 11, 62 40 80)
Egypt
    10 Sharia Salah ad-Din, Zamalek, Cairo (☎ 340 9677/9849)
France
    Embassy: 5 Rue Le Tasse, 75016 Paris (☎ 45.20.69.35)
    Consulates: 19 Rue Sauliner, 75009 Paris (☎ 45.23.37.40)

**MOROCCO**

RN 193 Casatorra, 20600 Bastia, Corsica (☎ 95.33.70.40)

22/24 Rue Anatole France, 59800 Lille (☎ 20.55.18.30)

8 Rue Tête d'Or, 69006 Lyons (☎ 78.93.18.02)

22 Allées Léon Gambetta, 13001 Marseilles (☎ 91.50.02.96)

7 Rue Erckmann-Chatrian, 67000 Strasbourg (☎ 88.35.23.09)

**Germany**
Embassy: Gotenstr 7-9, 5300 Bonn, Bad Godesberg (☎ 35 50 44/5/6)

Consulates: Cecilienallee 14, 4000 Düsseldorf 30 (☎ 45 10 41)

Wiesenhuttenplatz 26, 6000 Frankfurt/Main (☎ 23 17 37)

**Italy**
Enbassy: Via Lazzaro Spallanzani 8-10, 00161 Rome (☎ 884 86 53, 440 25 87)

Consulate: Via Boscovich 31, 20124 Milan (☎ 669 45 21)

**Libya**
Embassy: Blvd Ben Achour, BP 908, Tripoli (☎ 600110, 601102)

Consulate: Madinat al-Hadaiq, Sharia Bashir al-Ibrahimi, Tripoli (☎ 34239, 41346)

**Netherlands**
Embassy: Oranjestraat 9, 2514 JB The Hague (☎ 346 69 17)

Consulates: Oranje Nassaulan 1, 1075 AH Amsterdam (☎ 73 62 15/6)

Calendastraat 11, 3016 CA Rotterdam (☎ 436 61 77/60 40)

**Spain**
Embassy: Calle Serrano 179, 2 Madrid (☎ 563 1090/150)

Consulates: Calle Leizaran 31, 28002 Madrid (☎ 561 2145)

Rambla de Cataluña 78, 08008 Barcelona (☎ 215 3470/4)

Ave de Andalucia 15, 29002 Málaga (☎ 329 950/62)

Ave Jose Mesa Y Lopez 8, Las Palmas de Gran Canaria (☎ 262 859, 268 850)

**Sweden**
Kungsholmstorg 16, 11221 Stockholm (☎ 54 43 88/97 88)

**Switzerland**
Helvetiastr 42, 3005 Bern (☎ 43 03 62/3)

18A Chemin François-Lehmann, 1218 Grand Saconnex, Geneva (☎ 798 15 35/6)

**Tunisia**
Embassy: 39 Rue du 1er Juin, Mutuelleville, Tunis (☎ 782775)

Consulate: 26 Rue Ibn Mandhour, Notre Dame, Mutuelleville, Tunis (☎ 283492)

**UK**
Embassy: 49 Queen's Gate Gardens, London SW7 5NE (☎ 0171-581 5001)

Consulate (visas): 97-99 Praed St, Paddington, London SW2 (☎ 0171-724 0719)

**USA**
Embassy: 1601 21st St NW, Washington DC 20009 (☎ 462 7979)

Consulates: 767 Third Ave, 30th floor, New York, NY 10017 (☎ 421 1580)

437 Fifth Ave, New York, NY 10016 (☎ 758 2625)

## Visa Extensions

Should the usual 90 days be insufficient, it is possible to apply for an extension or even for residence, although the latter process is far from straightforward.

It is probably easiest to simply leave the country and attempt to re-enter after a few days. Your chances improve if you enter by a different route the second time around.

People on visas may, however, prefer to try for the extension. Go to the office of the Sûreté Nationale in Rabat (off Ave Mohammed V), taking with you your passport, a photo, a form (which you'll need to pick up beforehand at the same office) and a letter from your embassy requesting a visa extension on your behalf. The entrance is around the back and you'll have to queue at a tiny booth just inside. With luck, it should take a maximum of three days to process.

Should this fail, or if you want to get residence for any other reason, you will have to go to the local Bureau des Etrangers of the police headquarters (Préfecture de Police), and in some cases you may well have to go to Rabat. The process is long and involves opening bank accounts, producing proof of your capacity to support yourself and reasons for staying – good luck.

## Foreign Embassies in Morocco

Foreign embassies are concentrated in the capital, Rabat. In some cases the embassies do not deal with consular activities, or have separate consular offices elsewhere in the city. In addition, many countries have consulates and vice-consulates in other parts of the country (particularly Casablanca, and to a lesser extent in Tangier, Agadir, Oujda, Fès and Marrakesh). All are listed under the appropriate city or town entry. Visa information for various countries appears in the

Rabat section of this book (with the exception of Senegal, details for which are in the section on Casablanca).

## Ceuta & Melilla

These two enclaves are Spanish territory, so anyone requiring a visa to enter Spain will also need one to enter the enclaves. For more details of visa requirements, turn to the information on embassies in the Rabat chapter.

## DOCUMENTS
### Driving Licences

Although technically you need an International Driving Permit to drive in Morocco, most national licences are recognised. If bringing your own car, bring all the appropriate documentation, including a Green Card of third-party insurance (for details see this book's introductory Getting There & Away chapter).

### Hostel & Student Cards

You can stay at most hostels without a membership card, usually for a couple of dirham extra. International student cards do not seem to open many magic doors (museums and the like) in Morocco, although they could be useful for purchasing flight tickets out.

## CUSTOMS

The import or export of Moroccan currency is prohibited, but any amount of foreign currency (cash or cheques) may be brought into the country. Hang on to any exchange receipts as you will need them to re-exchange leftover dirhams on the way out of Morocco. Reconversion of currency *is* possible (and with the receipts should be straightforward), in spite of what some Bank al-Maghrib employees may tell you (see Re-exchange below).

Visitors are permitted to import up to 200 cigarettes and one litre of spirits. The latter could work out profitably if you buy duty-free alcohol in Ceuta, Melilla or Gibraltar and sell it on in Morocco.

A pamphlet, *Customs Guide for Tourists*, is supposedly, but not always, available from tourist offices and consulates.

## MONEY
### Currency

The Moroccan dirham (Dr) is divided into 100 centimes. You will find notes in denominations of Dr 5, 10, 50 and 100 and coins of 1, 2, 5 (these are becoming a little on the rare side), 10, 20 and 50 centimes, as well as Dr 1.

This is quite straightforward, but when dealing with shopkeepers you may come up against some local usages that could throw you. You will almost never hear the word 'centime', as more often than not prices are quoted in francs, an anachronism from the days of the French protectorate. One thousand francs is actually Dr 10 – so if you are quoted what sounds an outrageous amount for a bag of fruit, it might be an idea to ask if they mean francs, although often enough shopkeepers will 'convert' their price to dirhams for confused foreigners. Another unit sometimes used is the rial. It is especially common in the south, where 200 rials equals Dr 1. Elsewhere, a rial can refer to 20 or even 50 centimes.

### Exchange Rates

| Algeria | AD 1 | = | Dr 0.21 |
|---|---|---|---|
| Australia | A$1 | = | Dr 6.70 |
| Canada | C$1 | = | Dr 6.45 |
| France | FFr1 | = | Dr 1.65 |
| Germany | DM1 | = | Dr 5.67 |
| Japan | ¥100 | = | Dr 8.98 |
| Libya | 1 LD | = | Dr 24.81 |
| New Zealand | NZ$1 | = | Dr 5.51 |
| Spain | 100 pta | = | Dr 6.82 |
| Tunisia | TD 1 | = | Dr 9.05 |
| UK | UK£1 | = | Dr 13.84 |
| USA | US$1 | = | Dr 8.85 |

### Carrying Money

Don't put all your eggs in one basket. A combination of cash and travellers' cheques (in major currencies) and credit cards (particularly Visa and MasterCard) will give you several options and reduce the risk of being left stuck should you lose one or the other.

In out-of-way places, particularly if you intend to spend a lot of time trekking in remote reaches of the Atlas Mountains, you should keep a reasonable supply of cash

MOROCCO

MOROCCO

(local and a major currency) to cover you until you reach a decent-sized town again.

In addition to Visa and MasterCard, Access, Eurocard and a couple of others are accepted by many of the bigger hotels, restaurants and shops for payment of bills and purchases. Keep your eyes open, as some shopkeepers in particular like to whack on commissions of up to 5% they claim are imposed on them by banks. If you are relying on cards, withdraw money on them and spend cash.

### Changing Money

**Banks** You have a choice of banks where you can change money in Morocco, and generally it is a quick and efficient process. The currency, although not yet fully convertible, operates in a largely free market, virtually eliminating any black market. Rates vary little from bank to bank, but it can't hurt to look around. Remember to carry your passport, as you will need it to change travellers' cheques and get cash advances, and some banks will even want to see it when you change cash.

Probably the best of the banks is the Banque Marocaine du Commerce Extérieur (BMCE). In the bigger cities, it usually has one branch with an out-of-office-hours exchange office where you can change cash or cheques or get a cash advance on Visa or MasterCard. These offices are usually open daily from 10 am to 2 pm and again from 4 to 8 pm. In addition, the BMCE has the most widespread and reliable network of ATMs (or *guichets automatiques*), which allow international transactions on Visa and MasterCard. Most banks do not charge a commission for changing cheques but, unfortunately, the BMCE does. It asks Dr 4.20 per cheque, which is deadly for small-denomination cheques – try another bank if you want this service.

Other reasonable banks include the Banque Marocaine pour le Commerce et l'Industrie (BMCI), Banque Populaire (often the only bank to be found in southern towns), Uniban and Interbank. Main branches of these banks can make cash advances on Visa

and MasterCard, and computerisation ensures this is a relatively quick operation.

Cash advances on credit cards and ATM transactions generally carry a handling charge of about 1.5%, deducted from your account in addition to the amount you request. Any limits on cash advances generally depend on the conditions attached to your particular card, although Dr 6000 seems to be the ceiling. The daily ATM limit on most cards is Dr 4000.

**Travellers' Cheques** Travellers' cheques are not always accepted by banks advertising exchange facilities, although generally there is no problem. Those already listed are joined by the Banque Marocaine pour l'Afrique et l'Orient, the Banque Crédit du Maroc and the Société Générale Marocaine de Banques. Some of these ask you to show your travellers' cheque receipts, which of course you are supposed to keep separate from cheques in case of loss. This argument seems lost on those bank employees who ask to see them, so go elsewhere if you strike this gratuitous irritation.

The best travellers' cheques to carry are American Express, if only because they have four branches in Morocco. They are represented by Voyages Schwartz at:

Agadir
  c/- Mopatours, 87 Place du Marché (☎ 08-841082; fax 08-841066)
Casablanca
  112 Ave Prince Moulay Abdallah (☎ 02-222946/7)
Marrakesh
  Immeuble Moutaouakil, 1 Rue Mauritania (☎ 04-436600/3)
Tangier
  54 Blvd Pasteur (☎ 09-933459/71)

Thomas Cook has just the one office in Morocco, care of KTI Voyages (☎ 02-398572/3/4; fax 02-398567), 4 Rue des Hirondelles, Casablanca.

**Changing on Arrival** Nobody has anything good to say about changing money at airports. Even at the main Mohammed V gateway outside Casablanca, the two BMCE branches are notoriously slow and sometimes closed. They have ATMs too, but you can't always rely on them (this goes for ATMs all over the country).

Arriving from or heading for the enclaves of Ceuta and Melilla, the Moroccan banks on the border change cash only. The same goes for Algeria. It is difficult to obtain Moroccan currency in mainland Spain and it's not worth the effort. The banks in Melilla and Ceuta, however, deal in dirham at inferior rates (if you want to cash in dirham) to those in Morocco. Another option in the enclaves and on the borders is the black market – check the bank rates first, which are usually just as good.

Coming from Algeria, there is a bank in Figuig and plenty of banks and black marketeers in Oujda.

**Re-Exchange** As it is illegal to take Moroccan currency in or out of the country (although it's unlikely anyone will bother you if you take out a little as a souvenir), the best thing is to wind down to nothing as you approach the end of your trip, and avoid the question of re-exchange.

Should you find yourself stuck with unseemly amounts of the stuff when you're about to leave, you can change it for hard currency at most Moroccan banks (including at borders and airports) if you can present bank receipts proving exchange in Morocco – so hang on to these as you go. Credit card cash-advance slips should be sufficient, but you may have trouble with receipts issued by ATMs.

### Black Market

The near convertibility of the dirham leaves little room for a black market, but you will find people asking you if you want to exchange money, especially in Tangier and Casablanca. There is no monetary benefit to be had from such transactions and, unless you are desperate for cash when the banks are closed, it is wiser to avoid these characters.

There is also a frontier black market. You will find plenty of Moroccans dealing in dirhams and hard currencies on the Ceuta

frontier and inside the Melilla enclave. In Ceuta itself there seems to be less activity; likewise on the actual Melilla border.

In the Moroccan frontier towns of Oujda and Figuig it is possible to buy and sell Algerian dinar for dirhams or, in Oujda, hard currency.

When dealing in Algerian dinar, shop around in Oujda before concluding an exchange. You can get dinar in Figuig and Melilla too, although the rates available in Melilla are unlikely to be as good as in the two Moroccan frontier towns.

### Costs

Although not the cheapest of all possible destinations, travellers coming to Morocco from, say, Spain will be pleasantly surprised. If they are willing to stick to the very bottom rung of hotels, a fairly monotonous diet and local transport, those hoping to push their money furthest should be able to get by on the equivalent of about US$15 to US$20 a day. For a few comforts, the odd taxi and a more varied diet, reckon on $US30 to US$40.

To give some idea of what to expect, a bed in the cheapest pensions starts at about Dr 30. Fairly decent sandwiches and stall food can provide filling meals for as little as Dr 10, although a full sit-down meal in the lower-end restaurants will normally come to more like Dr 50. A kg of apples can cost anything from Dr 6 to Dr 13, and a kg of bananas about Dr 10.

A pot of tea in a normal *salon de thé* (tea shop or café) costs between Dr 2 and Dr 3. In similar places at the heart of tourist centres like the Djemaa el-Fna in Marrakesh, you're more likely to be looking at Dr 4 for a glass of mint tea so weak it's doubtful they put any tea in at all! Coffee tends to be a little more expensive, and one litre of bottled water is about Dr 4. A 500 ml bottle of Coca Cola will set you back around Dr 5. Juice stands can be good value – a big, freshly squeezed orange juice can go for as little as Dr 3.

Beer is not cheap. The two main local brands, Flag Spéciale and Stork, cost about Dr 12 and Dr 15, respectively, in restaurants and bars. They are cheaper in liquor stores (about Dr 6 to Dr 8). Local wines, too, are much cheaper in liquor stores, where you'll pay from Dr 28 to Dr 35 for a decent drop that could easily cost you Dr 80 in a restaurant.

A packet of American contraband cigarettes will go for Dr 18 to Dr 22. You can, as many locals do, buy them one at a time for Dr 1. Local brands, such as Marquise, cost Dr 10 for 20.

Although you can buy many foreign newspapers and magazines in the bigger cities, they are not cheap, often starting at more than Dr 20 for papers. The exception is the French press, which costs pretty much what it does in France and generally arrives on the same day. *Le Monde* costs Dr 8 (oddly, the Spanish press is usually days old and quite expensive, despite the country's proximity).

Practically all museums and monuments charge a standard Dr 10 entry charge (at about US$1, quite reasonable really).

If your shoes are on the dusty side, there is no shortage of shoeshine boys and men. They charge about Dr 2.

### Tipping

Restaurant waiters generally expect a tip (baksheesh) – 10% is an unwritten rule in the swisher spots, although a dirham or two will do in smaller places such as cafés. If it's just a tea or coffee you've had, you're hardly going to cause a scandal if you leave nothing at all.

A whole range of other services, some of which you may not consider as such or even want, are also performed with the object of getting a tip. Hotel porters, museum guides and, of course, the hosts of hustlers hoping to guide you to shops, hotels, restaurants and bus stops also expect compensation.

You should not feel obliged to part with your change at the drop of a hat, but it is worth judging each situation on its merits. Bear in mind that this is how a lot of people make a living, and the exchange of small amounts of money to oil human affairs is a long-established tradition. On the other hand, aggressive hustling should not, if it can be helped, be rewarded. Parting with money

left and right will probably ease your way, but it's this very attitude that has allowed the hustling scene to become such a rampant phenomenon. For more on that subject, see Dangers & Annoyances in the introductory Facts for the Visitor chapter.

### Bargaining

Some people love it, others hate it, but whatever your view, bargaining is an integral part of Morocco's commercial culture. Those who have travelled elsewhere in the Arab world will be little surprised by this and, of course, the sparring is at its toughest in the heavily touristed cities, and mainly in the souqs. Fixed prices generally apply to hotels, restaurants and transport (taxis can be an exception to the rule).

Just about everyone has a personal modus operandi for dealing with the merchants. The best advice is to enter into the spirit of the thing. By not bargaining, you almost seem to rob the vendor of one of the pleasures of the trade (and yourself of cash).

When on the hunt for souvenirs and the like, take it easy. Look around, indulge in the banter over prices and get a feel for what people are asking – there's never an obligation to buy, despite the sometimes overbearing tactics of some less scrupulous shopkeepers. Let the vendors name their price, and then offer as little as 10%. Feign only mild interest in the item and be prepared to walk off as you haggle. If that fails, and you don't want to meet the vendor's offer, you'll probably find more of what you want around the corner. It can be a time-consuming process, but that is part of its charm – it's not a trip to your local department store. Taking the many cups of tea proffered during the process in no way puts you under an obligation to buy.

Do not allow yourself to be intimidated into buying anything you don't want at a price you don't like. Whatever they tell you, no one can *make* you buy.

You may not have to part with any money at all. A lot of Western goods, such as decent jeans and printed T-shirts, can easily be traded for local products. It'll be up to you to decide how much worth you attach to whatever you're trading and haggle accordingly.

## Guides & Hustlers

More will be said about these fellows later in this chapter, but on the subject of money, official guides will generally charge between Dr 30 and Dr 50 for a 'half-day'. It is as well to plan carefully where you want these people to take you and make sure they know their wage is dependent on their fulfilling their half of the bargain. The unofficial guides will often do the same for less, and can be OK. The same rules apply, but unfortunately you will sometimes get a bad 'un. A few Dr will suffice for being guided to one specific location (like a medina exit). Whatever you give, you'll sometimes get the you-can't-possibly-be-serious look. The best reply is the I've-just-paid-you-well-over-the-odds look.

## Begging

Whatever advances Morocco may be making economically, great chunks of the population are still being left behind, and social security is an empty phrase here.

Although it is noticeable that well-heeled Moroccans are not always so willing to part with donations, it is hard to find a reason for not giving the elderly and infirm something. It is difficult to recommend giving children money though, however pathetic they look. Their conditions may well be straitened, but if they find begging the most lucrative way of making a crust now, they'll have little incentive to stop later on. That won't benefit anyone in the long run.

## TOURIST OFFICES
## Local Tourist Offices

The Moroccans rely heavily on tourism as a source of national income, and the Office National Marocain du Tourisme (ONMT) has a network of offices throughout the country. These usually go by the name of Délégation Régionale du Tourisme. You will also occasionally find a *syndicat d'initiative* office in some towns, although it appears these parallel offices are being wound down.

The offices are sometimes quite helpful, but more often they simply stock standard colour brochures and little else. ONMT branches in Morocco include:

Agadir
    Immeuble A, off Ave Prince Héritier Sidi Mohammed (☎ 08-822894, 841367)
Al-Hoceima
    Calle Tariq ibn Zayid (☎ 982830)
Azilal
    Ave Hassan II (☎ 458334)
Beni Mellal
    Ave Hassan II, IB Chichaoui, 1st floor (☎ 483981)
Casablanca
    55 Rue Omar Slaoui (☎ 02-271177, 279533)
Dakhla
    1 Rue Tiris (☎ 898228)
El-Jadida
    Chambre de Commerce, Rue Ibn Khaldoun (☎ 342724, 342704)
Er-Rachidia
    Ave Moulay Ali Cherif (☎ 572733)
Fès
    Place de la Résistance, Immeuble Bennani (☎ 06-623460, 626279)
Goulimime
    3 Résidence Sahara, Blvd d'Agadir (☎ 872545)
Ifrane
    Hôtel Michlifene (☎ 566038)
Khenifra
    Immeuble Lefraoui, Hay Hamou Hassan (☎ 07-586038)
Laayoune
    Ave de l'Islam (☎ 892233/75)
Marrakesh
    Place Abdel Moumen ben Ali (☎ 04-448889; fax 04-448906)
Meknès
    Place Administrative (☎ 05-524426)
Mohammedia
    14 Rue El-Jahid (☎ 324199)
Nador
    80 Blvd Ibn Rochd (☎ 606518)
Ouarzazate
    Blvd Mohammed V (☎ 882485)
Oujda
    Place du 16 Août (☎ 689089, 684329)
Rabat
    Rue al-Abtal (☎ 07-775171)
Safi
    Rue Imam Malek (☎ 04-464553)
Tangier
    29 Blvd Pasteur (☎ 09-938239)
Tetouan
    30 Calle Mohammed V (☎ 964407, 967009)

MOROCCO

## Overseas Reps

The ONMT also maintains offices abroad. They generally stock brochures, tourist maps and lists of tour operators, and they might also have a free copy of *Maroc: guide et histoire*. Although hopelessly out of date, it is full of interesting bits and pieces. Copies in French and English are sporadically available in Moroccan bookshops for Dr 150 or more.

Australia
    c/-Moroccan Consulate, Suite 2, 11 West St, North Sydney, NSW 2060 (☎ 957 6717, 922 4999)
Belgium
    66 Rue du Marché aux Herbes, 1000 Brussels (☎ 512 21 82)
Canada
    2001 Rue Université, Suite 1460, Montreal H3A 2A6 (☎ 842 8111)
France
    161 Rue Saint Honoré, Place du Théâtre Français, 70075 Paris (☎ 42.60.63.50/47.24)
Germany
    Graf Adolfstrasse 59, 4000 Düsseldorf 1 (☎ 37 05 51/2)
Italy
    Via Larga 23, 20122 Milan (☎ 583 03 633/756)
Netherlands
    150 Rokin 1er, 1012 Amsterdam (☎ 24 00 25, 23 90 89)
Portugal
    Rua Artilharia Un 79, 85 Lisbon (☎ 685871)
Spain
    Calle Quintana 2, 28008 Madrid (☎ 542 7431, 541 2995; fax 247 0466)
Sweden
    Sturegatan 16, 11436 Stockholm (☎ 660 99 13)
Switzerland
    Schifflande 5, 8001 Zürich (☎ 252 7752)
UK
    205 Regent St, London W1R 7DE (☎ 0171-437 0073)
USA
    420 East 46th St, Suite 1201, New York, NY 10017 (☎ 949 8184; fax 949 8148)

## USEFUL ORGANISATIONS

The following organisations in Morocco may prove useful:

Club Alpin Français
    BP 6178, Casablanca 01 (☎ 02-270090; fax 02-297292). Useful if you want to book refuges in the High Atlas Mountains for trekking.

Division de la Cartographie
    This section of the Conservation & Topography Department (☎ 07-705311; fax 07-705885), located at 31 Ave Moulay Hassan in Rabat, sells detailed survey maps of interest to people doing serious hiking or travelling well off the beaten track. Maps of the most popular areas of the High Atlas can be obtained on the spot (Dr 30 a sheet); for other areas you may need your passport and an official request – this can take days.
Fédération Royale Marocaine de Ski et Montagne
    Parc de la Ligue Arabe, BP 15899, Casablanca 01 (☎ 02-203798)
Fédération Royale Marocaine des Auberges de Jeunes
    The head office of the Moroccan hostel organisation (☎ 05-524698) is on Blvd Oqba ben Nafii in Meknès. There is another office in Casablanca (☎ 02-970952) on the Parc de la Ligue Arabe.

## BUSINESS HOURS

Although a Muslim country, Morocco adheres, for business purposes, to the Western Monday-to-Friday working week (in Muslim countries, Friday is the equivalent of Sunday for Christians, and hence usually the main day off during the week). During Ramadan office hours are reduced.

### Banks

In the bigger centres at least, banks tend to be open from 8.30 to 11.30 am and again from 2.30 to 4.30 pm, Monday to Thursday. On Friday, the midday break generally runs from 11.15 am to 3 pm because of the Friday prayers. These hours can vary slightly from bank to bank, but usually not more than by a quarter of an hour or so either way. See the Money section for details of BMCE's out-of-hours exchange service.

### Offices

Government offices are generally open from 8.30 am to noon and 2 to 6.30 pm from Monday to Thursday. On Friday, the midday break lasts from about 11.30 am to 3 pm. As with the banks, these times are generally adhered to in the main centres, but should be taken with a pinch of a salt.

### Museums & Monuments

It is difficult to pin down hard and fast rules on the monuments, but most museums are closed on Tuesday and otherwise loosely follow office hours, meaning they are generally closed from about 11.30 am to 3 pm. Not all of the sights follow this rule. Some of the medersas have the irritating habit of closing at noon on Friday and not opening again at all in the afternoon.

### Shops & Souqs

Shops tend to open from about 8 am to 6 pm, often closing for a couple of hours in the middle of the day, but there are no strict rules about this. Most shops, apart from grocery stores and the like, tend to close over the weekend. Medina souqs and produce markets in the villes nouvelles of the bigger cities tend to wind down on Thursday afternoon and are usually dead on a Friday but, again, there is no fixed procedure.

### Ramadan

Typically, the office working day runs from about 9 am to 3 pm during Ramadan but, again, this can vary.

### HOLIDAYS

For the main Islamic holidays, refer to the entry in the introductory Facts about the Region chapter.

### Secular Holidays

There are five national secular holidays:

*New Year's Day* – 1 January
*Feast of the Throne* – 3 March
*Labour Day* – 1 May
*Anniversary of the Green March* – 6 November
*Independence Day* – 18 November

### CULTURAL EVENTS

Festivals are often held in honour of local saints or marabouts. Sometimes no more than an unusually lively market day, quite a few have taken on regional and even national importance. These festivals are common among the Berbers and are usually held during the summer months.

This is one of those religious frontiers where orthodoxy and local custom have met and compromised. The veneration of saints

is frowned upon by orthodox Sunni Muslims but Islam, no less than Christianity, is made up of many sects (see Religion in Facts about the Region and the Facts about the Country chapter for Morocco), and such festivals, which take some of their inspiration from a mix of pre-Islamic Berber tradition and Sufi mystic thought, continue.

Nevertheless, some of the more excessive manifestations – such as self-mutilation while in an ecstatic trance, once not an unusual sight at such gatherings – have all but disappeared in the face of official disapproval of such 'barbarism'.

It's worth making enquiries to determine when moussems and other festivals are due to happen, especially since many do not take place at any rigidly fixed date in the Western calendar. The most important events are:

**March**
    *Moussem of Moulay Aissa ben Driss*, Beni Mellal
**May**
    *Moussem of Moulay Abdallah ben Brahim*, Ouezzane
    *Fête des Roses* (rose festival), Kélâa des M'Gouna in the Dadès Valley – held late in the month
    *Moussem of Sidi Bou Selham*, south of Larache – sometimes takes place in June
    *Moussem of Sidi Mohammed M'a al-'Ainin*, Tan Tan – an occasion to see the so-called 'blue people', Moors from the Sahara, which also acts as a commercial gathering of tribes; usually held at the end of May or in early June
**June**
    *National Folklore Festival*, Marrakesh – runs for 10 days and is held around the end of May or in early June. Essentially a tourist event (although it attracts many Moroccans), it nevertheless is colourful and well worth attending, since groups of dancers, musicians and other entertainers are invited from all over the country.
    *Moussem*, Goulimine – with its big camel market, this is as much a trade affair as a religious get-together
    *Fête des Cerises* (cherry festival), Sefrou
**July**
    *Moussem*, Mdiq, north-west of Tetouan – takes place early in the month
**August**
    *Moussem of Moulay Idriss*, Zerhoun, north of Meknès
    *Moussem of Moulay Abdallah*, south of El-Jadida – takes place late in the month

*Moussem of Sidi Ahmed*, Anti-Tiznit – this celebration of prayer is held towards the end of the month
*Moussem of Setti Fatma*, Ourika Valley, south of Marrakesh
*International Arts Festival*, Asilah
September
    *Fête des Fiancés*, Imilchil – held late in the month
    *Moussem of Sidi Moussa* or *Quarquour*, near El-Kelas du Straghna, north of Marrakesh
    *Moussem of Moulay Idriss*, Fès – sometimes held in early October
    *Moussem of Sidi-Allal*, in Arbaoua, north of Meknès
October
    *Fête du Cheval* (horse festival), Tissa, north-east of Fès – takes place in early October
    *Fête des Dattes* (date festival), Erfoud – takes place in late October

## SUGGESTED ITINERARIES

For those with limited time and/or resources, it is quite possible to map out itineraries which take in a selection of sights, tailored to your interests. What follows are two suggested routes, but obviously there are plenty of possible combinations.

### Imperial Cities

For the history buff and urban creature, a tour of the four imperial cities – Fès, Meknès, Marrakesh and Rabat – can be accomplished in pretty quick time if necessary, although you should set aside about two weeks to do them any justice. Equally, you could spend several weeks exploring these four great capitals of Morocco and some of the surrounding country.

If you arrive in Morocco by air, you could easily begin in **Marrakesh** (there are quite a few direct charter flights from European capitals; alternatively, this southernmost of the imperial cities is about four to five hours from Casablanca by bus or train). From here you can travel by bus north to **Fès** (the longest stretch on such a circuit – you are looking at up to 10 hours on the road). From Fès it is a short hop (less than an hour by train) to Morocco's 'Versailles' (a slightly hyperbolic description, but a common enough one) – **Meknès**. While you're here, a recommended day trip would be to the best

preserved site of Roman occupation in Morocco – **Volubilis**, which lies only about 33 km to the north.

To complete the circuit, and to wind down from some of the inevitable pressures of being in the main tourist hives, you can push on to the Atlantic capital of **Rabat** (some three to four hours by rail or road) and neighbouring **Salé**, where you can savour the pleasure of exploring a handful of monuments and modest medinas with virtually no hassle whatsoever. From Rabat you can travel directly to the Mohammed V international airport south of Casablanca by shuttle bus or train, or head north to Tangier and on across the Strait of Gibraltar to Spain.

For those coming down from Spain, the obvious tack is to start with Meknès, and then loop around to Marrakesh via Fès, before making the trip back north via Rabat (the entire train journey time from Marrakesh to Tangier is 10 to 12 hours, so a couple of days in Rabat along the way would break it up nicely).

It is also common for travellers coming down from Spain to either skip Rabat, or head there after Meknès and Fès, and pop into Casablanca briefly before heading on to Marrakesh. For those with a little more time, this has the advantage of allowing you to then head south-west down the valleys towards the Sahara and/or finish up with a visit to Agadir or Essaouira to wind down on the Atlantic beaches.

### Atlantic Coast & Southern Morocco

Starting in Tangier, those wanting to bypass the interior and keep close to the sea can quite easily make their way down the Atlantic coast, stopping in places that appeal and skipping those that don't. Although quite feasible with public transport, such a trip especially lends itself to those with their own vehicles. First up from Tangier is the small town of **Asilah**, a pretty and comparatively prosperous spot with a small, largely Portuguese-built medina set on a broad sweep of ocean beach.

Another 40 km farther south is **Larache**, a more derelict looking place, but with a tumbledown medina that invites exploration. The nearby attractions, about five km north, are the windswept and overgrown Roman bastion of **Lixus** and the local beaches.

The next stop of interest would be **Rabat**, followed by **Casablanca**. The latter has some reasonable beaches in its southern suburbs. South of Casablanca is **El-Jadida** which, then known as Mazagan, was the last of the Portuguese redoubts in Morocco. A day trip from El-Jadida is another fortress town built by the Portuguese, the little visited **Azemmour**.

To proceed on to **Safi**, about 160 km farther south, you either take the inland road or preferably, if you have your own transport, follow the coast. The next main stop, **Essaouira** (another former Portuguese base), is one of the most popular Atlantic coast stops, with good beaches and surf, and a reasonably laid-back feel to it. From there it is another 170 km to **Agadir**, which may be a little too much like Europe's Mediterranean resorts for some. There is nothing to stop you pushing south away from the madding crowds to places like **Sidi Ifni, Tan Tan** and beyond into the wastes of what was the Spanish Sahara until 1975. The last big city on this route is **Laayoune**, after which it's a long and lonely 550 km to **Dakhla**, which is great for fishing but not much else – you shouldn't have too much competition from other travellers this far south!

Alternatively you could head inland from Essaouira or Agadir to **Taroudannt** and over the remarkable Tizi n'Test Pass to **Marrakesh**. Although this second-largest city in Morocco may put some off with its swarms of hustlers and 'guides', few travellers will want to miss the chance to at least give the red city a glance. From there, the obvious route would take you south-west down the **Drâa Valley** and to the edge of the **Sahara** via **Ouarzazate** and **Zagora**. From Ouarzazate you can also head west along the 'Route des Kasbahs', so-called because of the sheer number of these fortified villages along the way. The **Dadès** and **Todra gorges** are highlights along the way to **Erfoud**. Heading north from Erfoud towards **Midelt** would complete the experience with a tour along the **Ziz Valley**.

To head out, you would then be best off making your way back to Marrakesh or even Fès and then on to your point of exit (unless of course Algeria is your next stop, in which case you'd be better off heading farther west to the pretty border post of **Figuig**).

## POST & TELECOMMUNICATIONS

There are only a few Moroccan towns which lack a post office (PTT or Postes, Télégraphes et Téléphones). A colourful new logo has recently been introduced – La Poste (*al-barid* in Arabic). All services are housed in the one or adjacent buildings.

### Post

Although the postal system is fairly reliable, it is not necessarily very fast. It can take about a week for letters to get to their European destinations (it also depends a little on the efficiency of individual European postal services), and two weeks or so to get to Australia or the USA. Occasionally you get lucky and mail moves faster. Mail takes about the same amount of time to arrive in Morocco.

**Postal Rates** Standard letters and postcards to Europe cost from Dr 4.40 (France) to Dr 4.80 (UK). Postcards to Australia or the USA cost Dr 6 and standard letters are Dr 11. In the main tourist centres it is not unheard of to be charged above the standard rates.

You can buy stamps at some tabacs, the small tobacco and newspaper kiosks you see scattered about the main city centres. This is useful, as post-office counters are often besieged.

**Parcel Post** The parcel office (*colis postaux*) is generally in a separate part of the post office building. Take your parcel unwrapped for customs inspection. It's best to take your own wrapping materials, as more often than not the parcel office won't provide them. There is a 20 kg limit and parcels should not be longer than 1.5 metres on any side.

A 10-kg parcel to Australia will cost Dr 780 by surface mail and Dr 1500 by air. The same parcel to the UK is Dr 270 by surface mail and Dr 352.80 by air.

**Express Mail** Usually in the same office as parcel post is an Express Mail Service (EMS), or Poste Rapide. You can send up to 500 grams to France, Spain or Portugal for Dr 160, to the rest of Europe for Dr 200, to the Americas for Dr 300 or to Australia for Dr 400. The idea is that your letter or package should arrive within 24 hours in Europe and within two to three days elsewhere, although you should not depend on such speed.

**Receiving Mail** Having mail addressed to 'Poste Restante, La Poste Principale' of any big town should not be a problem. There is generally a small charge for picking up any items you receive. Note, however, that some offices don't hang on to parcels for more than a couple of weeks before returning them to sender. Remember to take your passport as proof of identity. No other document will be accepted.

Possibly a more reliable method for receiving mail is via American Express, which has four branches in Morocco (see Money for addresses). To qualify for the client mail service, you are supposed to have American Express travellers' cheques or an American Express card. In practice, you are usually asked only to produce a passport for identification. There is no charge for any letters you receive.

### Telephone

The business of making a phone call is getting easier in Morocco and hundreds of millions of dollars are being poured into the system. Although the number of lines has more than doubled in the past 10 years, fewer Moroccans have phones than in practically any other Middle Eastern or North African state. According to one report, only 43% of local calls get through, and less than 30% of international calls, although this seems to be an overly pessimistic assessment. The defects of the system are actually most obvious to the user making local calls, where lines are frequently so bad that you can't hear the person on the other end.

Most cities and towns have at least one phone office (increasingly known by its Arabic title – Itissalat al-Maghrib), and in the main centres they are open round the clock and seven days a week.

Phone boxes are not hard to find around the bigger cities, but they become scarcer in more out-of-the-way locations. Card phones are becoming increasingly common, and they are generally the easiest way to make a call, especially abroad.

**Costs** To make a local call from a coin-operated phone, you must initially insert a minimum of Dr 1.50. Costs are worked out in terms of units (one unit equals 80 centimes), and your initial Dr 1.50 gets you about 12 minutes. You can phone from hotels, but they generally charge about Dr 5 for a local call!

For long-distance calls within Morocco, one unit gets you from two minutes (35 km or under) to 12 seconds (300 km or more). Calls are half-price from midnight to 7 am, and 40% off at any other time on Sunday and holidays as well as from 12.30 pm to midnight on Saturday and from 8.30 pm to midnight on other days. There is also a reduction of 10% on calls made between 12.30 and 2 pm on weekdays.

International calls are *expensive*. The cheap rate (40% off) operates all day Sunday and holidays, all day Saturday except from 7 am to 12.30 pm and from midnight to 7 am on weekdays. From 10 pm to midnight on weekdays the rate is 20% off.

There are six international zones for telephone purposes, and rates range from Dr 8.20 a minute in Zone 1 to Dr 32 in Zone 6 (respectively just under US$1 and just over US$3). France, for instance, lies in Zone 2 (Dr 13.70 a minute), as do most other Western European countries. Australia and New Zealand, naturally, are in Zone 6, while the USA and Canada lie in Zone 5 (Dr 27.40 a minute).

It makes no difference whether you use a

phonecard or place a call through a telephone office. There is, thankfully, no three-minute minimum, but in the telephone offices you'll pay for every minute or part thereof.

**Card Phones** You can buy cards from phone offices and occasionally newspaper kiosks and tabacs. *Télécartes* sell for Dr 68.50 (50 units), Dr 93.50 (70 units) and Dr 156 (120 units – this one seems to be a rarity). When your card runs out during a call, you are technically supposed to be able insert another without losing the call – in practice this does not always work.

You will notice enterprising lads trying to sell you cards outside phone offices. Or rather, they are trying to sell units on cards. This 'service' may suit some locals unable to afford to buy a full card and wanting only to make short calls, but for outsiders it is a perfect way to get done. If you can't afford a new card, you'll barely be able to afford to make an international call either.

**Reverse Charges** It is possible to make reverse-charge (collect) calls from Morocco, but it can involve painfully long waits in phone offices. If you want to do this, ask to 'téléphoner en PCV' (pronounced peh-seh-veh) – the French expression for this service.

An increasingly popular international service known as 'home direct' is barely acknowledged as yet in Morocco but, before you leave home, it might be worth investigating whether such a link exists between your country and Morocco. It involves calling a toll-free number that connects you with an operator in your home country, through whom you can then request reverse-charge calls and the like. You can do this direct from any phone. The only country that appeared to have such a link with Morocco at the time of writing was Spain, for which you dial ☎ 002 802828, but more countries are bound to be linked up in good time.

**Telephone Directories** There is one standard phone book for all Morocco in French – the *Annuaire des Abonnés au Téléphone*. Most phone offices have a copy lying around. Since 1993 a slimmer volume along the same lines containing just fax numbers has also been available.

A kind of Yellow Pages, *Télécontact*, is sporadically available in some bookshops – try the Librairie Farairre in Casablanca.

If your French is OK, you could try dialling information *(renseignements)* on ☎ 16.

**Area Codes** When calling overseas from Morocco, dial 00, your country code and then the city code and number.

When calling Morocco from overseas, the international direct-dialling code is 212.

For telecommunications purposes, Morocco is divided up into the following regions:

| Code | Region |
| --- | --- |
| 02 | Casablanca & immediate vicinity |
| 03 | El-Jadida & Beni Mellal |
| 04 | Marrakesh, Essaouira, Safi & Ouarzazate |
| 05 | Fès, Meknès, Taza & Er-Rachidia |
| 06 | Nador, Oujda, Bouarfa & Figuig |
| 07 | Rabat, Kenitra & Ouezzane |
| 08 | The rest of the country south of a line running roughly east to west and including Agadir, Taroudannt, Tata & all of the Western Sahara |
| 09 | Tangier, Tetouan, Al-Hoceima, Larache & Asilah |

### Fax, Telex & Telegraph

Only the main post offices have telex and telegraph services. They can be sent from special counters in the post (not phone) office. Few if any post offices offer fax services – the central post and phone offices in Rabat flatly denied that the Moroccan post and telecommunications system offered any such service, although one or two phone offices in the country claim they *can* send a fax for you. The bigger hotels usually offer international phone and fax services, but remember that it can easily cost you double.

### Ceuta & Melilla

Although situated in North Africa, the two enclaves of Ceuta and Melilla are Spanish territory and so their post and phone services are part of the Spanish system.

**Post** Post offices are called Correos y Telégrafos. Don't expect a super-fast service. Post can take a good week or more to arrive from just about anywhere – distance seems to make little difference.

Postcards and letters up to 20 grams cost 45 pta to EU countries and 65 pta elsewhere. Within Spain the same letters would cost 17 pta within the same town and 28 pta to the rest of the country. Aerograms are 65 pta.

**Parcel Post** Parcels can also be sent from the post office, up to a maximum weight of 20 kg. Surface mail for a two-kg parcel abroad costs 440 pta. Charges for larger packages vary considerably.

**Express Mail** Express Mail Service also goes by the name of *postal expres*. You can send up to one kg for 3200 pta to Europe, Turkey and the countries of the Maghreb. The same parcel would cost 5300 pta to the Americas and most Middle Eastern countries, and 6000 pta to the rest of the world. Each extra 500 grams up to a maximum of 20 kg costs 650, 1300 and 1550 pta, respectively.

**Receiving Mail** Poste restante is in the main post office of each of the enclaves. Ask for the *lista de correos*.

**Telephone** The Telefónica is a separate organisation from the Correos y Telégrafos. Phoning is generally no problem. Telefónica either has its own phone office, or has contracted the service out to bureaux known as *locutorios*, which are generally open from 10 am to 10 pm, with a three-hour afternoon break from 2 pm.

You can buy phonecards from post offices and selected newsstands and kiosks, and they cost 1000 and 2000 pta. Most phones accept both cards and coins.

There is nothing cheap about the phone system in Spain (and hence its enclaves). The standard day rate for international calls will make that clear: five minutes to other EU countries costs 657 pta; 792 pta to the rest of Europe and the Maghreb; 1163 pta to the Americas; and 2286 pta to the rest of the world. There is no minimum call time, but you pay for every minute or part thereof. The cheap rate (about 30% to 40% off) for international calls is from 10 pm to 8 am.

For calls within Spain, there are three different bands – urban, provincial and interprovincial – and three rates – morning, evening and night. The latter is the cheapest and runs from 10 pm to 8 am on weekdays, and from 2 pm on Saturday until 8 am on Monday.

Calling reverse charges is possible from phone offices, but a growing number of countries are linked with Spain in the home direct or *país directo* service. The numbers are listed on the newer telephones.

To call outside Spain dial 07 first, and then the country code and number. Spain's international dialling code is 34. Ceuta's area code is 056 (same as Algeciras) and that of Melilla 05 (the same as Málaga). If calling from within Spain, dial 09 first.

**Fax, Telex & Telegraph** All these services are in the post office. Ordinary telegrams to the rest of Europe and the Mediterranean basin cost 42 pta per word (with a fixed minimum charge of 1300 pta), and elsewhere it's 135 pta a word. Urgent telegrams cost about double that rate. Telexes cost 60 pta a minute to Europe and the Maghreb, 300 pta to the USA and 370 pta to more distant destinations.

Faxes cost from 750 to 1650 pta for the first page, depending on where you are sending it, and slightly less for each subsequent page. Receiving incoming faxes from abroad will cost 350 pta for the first page and 205 pta for each following one.

## TIME

Morocco is on GMT/UTC throughout the year. So (not taking account of summer time) when it's noon in Morocco it's the same in London, 1 pm in Western Europe, 7 am in New York, 4 am in Los Angeles, 8 pm in Perth and Hong Kong, 10 pm in Sydney and midnight in Auckland. If you're travelling between Morocco and Spain, remember that the latter is two hours ahead in summer, which can affect plans for catching ferries and the like.

On the subject of time, Moroccans are not in nearly as much of a hurry to get things done as Westerners. Rather than letting yourself be frustrated by this, it pays to learn to go with the flow a little (although not necessarily to surrender altogether).

## ELECTRICITY
Throughout most of the country, electricity supply is 220 V, 50 AC, although in some places you'll still find 110 V. Sockets are of the European two-pin variety.

## LAUNDRY
Straightforward laundries are hard to find, and you will inevitably be directed to drycleaners, which are rather expensive. Even hotels don't seem to know the difference half the time. So, unless you have lots of money to waste on dry-cleaning bills, the simplest option is to do it yourself in your room! If you do send your washing out to be done, remember to leave yourself time – it always takes a few days.

## BOOKS
Because of Morocco's colonial heritage under the French, and the continued importance of the French language in Moroccan society, the following selection of suggested reading material includes French-language titles. Some Moroccan writers choose to write in French rather than Arabic, one sign of how deep a mark the French protectorate left on the country.

### People & Society
Peter Mayne's highly readable *A Year in Marrakesh* (Eland, 1991) is his account of time spent living among the people of the city and observations on their lives, first published in 1953.

*The House of Si Abdallah: the oral history of a Moroccan family* (recorded, translated and edited by Henry Munson Jr, Yale University Press, 1984) is a unique insight into the daily life and thoughts of Moroccans, mainly through the eyes of a traditional pedlar in Tangier and his Westernised cousin, a woman living in the USA.

A fascinating look at the lives of women in the Maghreb is Leonora Peets's *Women of Marrakesh* (C Hunt & Co, 1988). Peets, married to an Estonian doctor, got about as close as a non-Muslim can to the lives of Moroccan women, as she lived there for 40 years from 1930. The book has been translated from the Estonian.

For a comparatively recent study of the Berber population of Morocco, you could do worse than consult *Les Berbères* by Gabriel Camps (Editions Errance, 1987).

Another account is Salem Chaker's *Berbères Aujourd'hui* (L'Harmattan, 1989).

### Moroccan History
Histoire du Maroc by Bernard Lugan (Critérion, 1992) is a reasonable potted history of the country.

*Les Almoravides* by Vincent Lagardare (L'Harmattan, 1988) traces the history of this great Berber dynasty from 1062 to 1145.

*The Conquest of the Sahara* by Douglas Porch (Jonathon Cape, 1985) describes France's attempts to gain control of the Sahara and subdue the Tuaregs. His *The Conquest of Morocco* (Papermac, 1987) examines the takeover of Morocco by Paris, leading to the establishment of the protectorate.

*A Country with a Government & a Flag* by C R Pennell (Menas, 1986) is an account of the anticolonial struggle in the Rif from 1921 to 1926 that threatened French and Spanish control over their respective protectorates.

In *Lords of the Atlas* (Arrow Books, 1991), Gavin Maxwell recounts the story of Thami el-Glaoui, the Pasha of Marrakesh. Subtitled *The Rise & Fall of the House of Glaoua 1893-1956*, it relates some of the more extraordinary events linked with this local despot who, even after WW II, ordered the heads of his enemies be mounted on the city gates.

A contentious issue remains the Western Sahara, which Morocco claims and to all intents and purposes now controls. There are a few books on this in English and French. It

MOROCCO

has been an important feature of the government's policy and if you want to read its side of the story you could try *Hassan II Présente la Marche Verte* (Plon, 1990). The title refers to the Green March, when Moroccan troops and civilians moved in to take control of the territory in 1975 as Spain pulled out.

*The Western Saharans*, by Virginia Thompson & Richard Adloff (Croom Helm, 1980), takes a less government-friendly view of the conflict.

On contemporary Morocco, the French writer Gilles Perrault caused a diplomatic storm with his none-too complimentary *Notre Ami le Roi* (Gallimard). Don't be seen carrying this one around with you in Morocco!

## Moroccan Fiction

Literary genres such as the novel and drama, long taken for granted as an integral part of Western culture, are a comparatively recent development in the Arab world, where the bulk of literature until the late 19th century consisted of traditional veins of poetry, much of it in imitation of older classics. For a full treatment of literature past and present in the Arab world, you may like to consult the three-volume *Cambridge History of Arabic Literature* (Cambridge University Press, 1992).

Egypt has tended to lead the way in the past 100 years, but Morocco too has seen a growth of modern talent. Output in neighbouring Algeria, however, is considerably greater. Many Moroccan authors still write in French, although more and more are turning to their native tongue, even at the risk of not getting wider recognition for want of translation into French or other European languages. Little Moroccan writing has gone into English.

*Year of the Elephant*, by Leila Abouzeid (1989), has been published by the Center for Middle Eastern Studies of the University of Texas at Austin, which has embarked on a program of translation of Middle Eastern and Arabic literature. The stories recount the life of Zahra, a Moroccan woman who in the face of an unsympathetic society carves out a degree of independence for herself, without abandoning the pillars of her upbringing, including the Islamic faith.

In *Si Yussef* (Quartet, 1992), Anouar Majid evokes Moroccan life through the eyes of a man who looks back on his life in Tangier – a book-keeper for years, his apprenticeship in survival began, like the bulk of the port city's urchins, as a guide for foreigners.

One of Morocco's better known authors (and winner of the 1994 Prix Méditerranée) is Tahar ben Jelloun, resident in France since 1971. At least two of his works, which he writes in French, have appeared in English. *Solitaire* (Quartet, 1988) explores the seemingly insurmountable difficulties encountered by a Moroccan migrant in France. In *Silent Day in Tangier* (Quartet, 1991), an elderly and bedridden man ruminates over his past. Although largely a personal exploration, the allusions to Tangier and Morocco's history from about the time of the Rif war and on are rich and unobtrusively woven into the observations of an old and angry man.

Abdel Krim Ghallab, the editor-in-chief of *Al-'Alam* newspaper and considered among the finer modern writers in Morocco, works in Arabic, but some of his works, including *Le Passé Enterré*, have been translated into French.

Ahmed Sefrioui, a writer of Berber origin who grew up in Fès, describes the lives of ordinary Moroccans through the eyes of his characters, such as little Mohammed in *La Boîte à Merveilles* (Seuil, 1978). Here is all the hubbub and local colour of the Fès of half a century ago.

An important representative of Moroccan émigré literature is Driss Chraïbi, born in El-Jadida and now living in France. A prolific author whose novels tend to be politicised in a way that sets him at odds with Sefrioui (who prefers to deal with what he sees as more essential human issues), his works include *Le Passé Simple* and *Mort au Canada*. The English translation, *Heirs to the Past* (Heinemann, 1986) has also been published. A couple of other novels have been translated, but they are hard to come by.

Mohammed Khaïr-eddine, who writes in French and Arabic, is one of Morocco's ground-breaking authors. His poems, novels and other writings express a desire for revolt and change, not only in the context of Moroccan society and traditions, but in his own methods of writing. One of his better known anthologies is *Ce Maroc!* (Seuil, 1975).

For something closer to the pulse of traditional society there's *Contes Berbères de l'Atlas de Marrakech*, a series of Berber tales edited by Alphonse Lequil (L'Harmattan, 1988).

## Foreign Writers

Of the foreigners who have written in and/or on Morocco, Paul Bowles is probably the best known. *The Sheltering Sky* (Paladin, 1990), made into a film by Bernardo Bertolucci in 1990 (in which Bowles makes a cameo appearance), tells the story of an American couple who arrive in North Africa shortly after WW II trying to put their relationship back together. The early stages of the film were shot in Morocco, although in the author's mind the action took place in Oran (Algeria).

The film served to propel the author, who still lives in Tangier, back to public prominence. His other books include *The Spider's House* and *Let It Come Down*, the latter set in Tangier. *Their Heads are Green* (Abacus, 1990) is a collection of travel tales set in several countries, and it includes some interesting insights into Morocco.

Bowles has also translated a series of oral tales from the Moroccan Arabic by Mohammed Mrabet, Mohammed Choukri and Larbi Layachi (whose work was published under the pseudonym Driss ben Hamed Charhadi). Among Mrabet's works are *Love with a Few Hairs* and *M'Hashish*. His is an uncompromising account of life for Tanjawi street lads, and the sometimes irksome activities poverty led them to take on to earn a crust.

Choukri's main work is *For Bread Alone: an autobiography*, in which he describes the almost unbearable saga of his own family, one of many forced by drought in the Rif during the early 1940s to seek opportunities

in Tangier and largely crushed by its indifference.

Layachi's best known work is *A Life Full of Holes*. Layachi, also of humble origins, is said to have wanted to use a pseudonym because he didn't want anyone to know who he was jobless and living in 'a rotten country in rotten times'.

Iain Finlayson's *Tangier: city of the dream* (Flamingo, 1993) is an intriguing look at some of the Western literati who found a new home in Morocco at one time or another. The single biggest entry deals with Paul and Jane Bowles and those around them, but there is interesting material on William Burroughs & the Beats, Truman Capote, Joe Orton, and others. It is a highly readable account of the life of this 'seedy, salacious, decadent, degenerate' city.

Elias Canetti, a foremost novelist in the German language, ended up in Marrakesh in 1954 in the company of a film team and penned his recollections in a slim but moving volume of short and elegantly simple stories called *Die Stimmen von Marrakesch* (Fischer, 1989). It has appeared in English as *The Voices of Marrakesh* (Marion Borays/ Farrar Straus & Giroux).

From the 1890s to the early 1930s, the *Times*' correspondent Walter Harris lived through the period that saw Morocco fall under the growing influence of France. His whimsical and highly amusing, if not always totally believable, *Morocco That Was* (Eland, 1983) first appeared in 1921.

At the beginning of the century, Budgett Meakin put on paper one of the first serious attempts by a Westerner at an overall appraisal of Moroccan society and history. First published in 1901, Darf Publishers in London thought *The Land of the Moors* interesting enough to republish in 1986.

Equally interesting, but potentially very irritating for modern readers, is Frances Macnab's *A Ride in Morocco* (Darf, 1987) – a British woman's rather strident account of her adventures on horseback from Tangier to Marrakesh at the turn of the century.

If writings on Morocco from this period appeal, another title of casual interest,

MOROCCO

mainly for its reflection on the ideas of the more zealous of Westerners living in the Orient, could be Donald Mackenzie's *The Khalifate of the West* (Darf, 1987; first published in 1911).

## Travel Guides

Michelin's *Guide de Tourisme: Maroc* is a detailed and excellent route guide through Morocco. The bad news is it's only available in French. If this is not an obstacle, you can find it in some London bookshops outside the Francophone world, including Stanford's in London (see Bookshops later in this section).

For English speakers there is a fairly thin *Blue Guide* on Morocco, which lays the emphasis on historical and urban cultural detail, with only limited information on natural beauty spots.

Quite a number of travel guide publishers have books on Morocco, including Frommer, Fodor (not for the budget traveller), Cadogan and Insight (more of a glossy, essay-style guide, which is attractive and well written but not too hot on practicalities).

*Morocco: the traveller's companion*, by Margaret & Robin Bidwell (I B Tauris, 1992), is a compilation of excerpts from the writings of Westerners who in one way or another have come into contact with Morocco. The line-up ranges from the likes of Leo Africanus to Samuel Pepys and George Orwell.

One of the first attempts at a travel guide to the country was undertaken by Edith Wharton, who arrived in 1917 and three years later published *In Morocco*. Century brought it out again in 1984.

An entertaining account of a Westerner's travails in Morocco more than a century ago is *Morocco: its people & places* by Edmondo de Amicis (translated by C Rollin-Tilton and published by Darf in 1985), which first appeared in 1882.

## Arts & Architecture

*A Practical Guide to Islamic Monuments in Morocco* by Richard Parker (Baraka Press, 1981) is exactly what its title suggests and is

full of town maps, pictures and ground plans of important monuments.

Titus Burckhardt's *Fès: city of Islam* (Cambridge University Press, 1992) is a pictorial treasure, including many of the art historian's own B&W shots of the city from his visits in the 1930s.

*Zillij: the art of Moroccan ceramics* by John Hedgecoe & Salma Sanar Damluji (Garnet, 1992) is a decent study of an important aspect of Moroccan decoration, also often known as zellij.

*Les Tapis* (Solar, 1993) contains all you ever wanted to know (in French) about carpets and rugs from Morocco.

*Living in Morocco* by Lisl & Landt Dennis (Thames & Hudson, 1992) is a sumptuous coffee-table affair which includes a lot of material on Moroccan arts and crafts.

For an aerial approach, try *Maroc Vu d'en Haut* by Anne & Yann Arthus-Bertrand (Editions de la Martinière).

## Culture

If traditional Moroccan dancing fascinates you, a look at *Danses du Maghreb* by Viviane Lièvre (Karthala, 1987) will give you a deeper insight into its meaning and history.

*Musique du Maroc* by Ahmed Aydoun (Eddif, 1992) seems to be almost the only serious book dealing with Moroccan music. Unfortunately, it is hard to find outside Morocco.

## Food

*The Taste of Morocco* by Robert Carrier (Century, 1987) is an excellent illustrated guide to Moroccan cuisine.

Another good title is *Good Food From Morocco* by Paula Wolfert (John Murray, 1989). She loves the food, but says there are only half a dozen good Moroccan restaurants in Morocco. The best way to learn the joys of the cuisine, she writes, is to try home-cooking or get invited to a banquet.

If there are not enough recipes in her book, another possibility is *240 Recettes de Cuisine Marocaine* by Ahmed Laarri (Jacques Grancher, 1982).

## Phrasebooks

For an introduction to the complexities of Moroccan Arabic, pick up a copy of Lonely Planet's *Moroccan Arabic Phrasebook* by Dan Bacon.

## Bookshops

**In Morocco** Morocco is not exactly bursting with good bookshops, and you will certainly be much better served if you are up to reading French, as the better stores have a far wider choice of French-language titles covering both Morocco and general subjects. Branches of the American Language Center (ALC) in Rabat, Marrakesh and Casablanca have small bookshops dedicated mainly to English literature and learning English. In addition, there is an English bookshop in Rabat and Fès. Rabat has about the best general bookshops (mostly works in French, although you'll find the occasional book on Morocco in English), and there are one or two in Casablanca, Tangier, Fès and Marrakesh. For details, see the relevant chapters.

**Outside Morocco** The bulk of the French-language books are not readily available outside France, although one exception is the small Maghreb Bookshop (☎ 0171-388 1840) at 45 Burton St, London WC1H 9AL, which leans towards the academic side.

For a good range of travel guides and literature, and a wide selection of maps, Stanford's (☎ 0171-836 1915) at 12-14 Long Acre, London WC2E 9LP, is one of the best shops of its kind in the UK. Some of the bigger mainstream bookshops also have a range of material on Morocco.

Another good source of travel literature is the Travellers' Bookshop (☎ 0171-836 9132) at 25 Cecil Court, London WC2N 4EZ.

If you are interested in literature on Moroccan history and politics, or a wide range of subjects pertinent to Islam and the Muslim world including fiction, travel and the like, Al-Hoda (☎ 0171-240 8381; fax 0171-497 0180) at 76-78 Charing Cross Rd is a useful resource.

A couple of specialist shops in Paris are worth investigating if you have more than a passing interest in things North African. L'Harmattan (☎ 46.34.13.71), at 21 rue des Écoles in the Latin Quarter is probably the best. It publishes a great deal of Maghreb literature in French. Another shop worth trying in the same part of town is Le Tiers Mythe (☎ 43.26.72.70) at 21 rue Cujas.

## MAPS

Few decent maps of Morocco are available in the country itself, so you are advised to get one before leaving home if you require any degree of detail and accuracy.

There are several possibilities for maps of Morocco, and the choice depends partly on what you want from the map. Michelin No 959 (UK£4.45) is the best. In addition to the 1:4,000,000 scale map of Morocco, including the disputed territory of Western Sahara, there is a 1:1,000,000 enlargement of Morocco proper and further 1:600,000 enlargements of Marrakesh, Casablanca, Rabat, the Middle Atlas and Meknès.

If you want six small city maps included, you could try Kümmerley & Frey's *Morocco* (UK£5.45). However, its 1:1,000,000 scale main map does not cover all of the Western Sahara.

GEOprojects, based in Beirut, produces *Maroc* (UK£6), a very basic map of the country with a half dozen fairly detailed city plans and some information about the cities and background to the country. The 1:2,000,000 scale main map and the 1:500,000 area enlargements are thin on detail.

Hallwag's *Morocco* (UK£3.95), aside from being cheap, is distinguished by its comparatively detailed maps of the Canary Islands. The main map is on a scale of 1:1,000,000.

## Survey Maps & Air Charts

The Ministère de l'Agriculture et de la Réforme Agraire in Rabat produces highly detailed survey maps on a scale of 1:100,000, but only a series of 15 from the centre of the country around Marrakesh and stretching to Zagora in the south-east are made available outside Morocco, and even

MOROCCO

MOROCCO

then can be difficult to obtain. You can get these and other maps from the office in Rabat, but most are too detailed to be of interest to travellers. See the Rabat section for more details.

Operational Navigation Charts on a scale of 1:1,000,000 cost UK£7.50 each. Charts G-1, H-1, H-2 and J-1 cover all Morocco. They each subdivide into four Tactical Pilotage Charts at 1:500,000, again for UK£7.50 each. While of topographical interest and of obvious use to fliers, they will not be of much use to most travellers.

## MEDIA
### Local Newspapers & Magazines
Morocco possesses a diverse press in Arabic and French and it is fair to say there is parallel coverage in the two languages. The bulk of the daily papers owe their allegiance to one or other political party or grouping. Although overt censorship does not exist, none of the papers rock the boat much. Even those run by opposition parties rarely, if ever, say anything that could be construed as being antimonarchist. It is quite all right for the parties to attack one another, and for the opposition to criticise the government, but the country's real power – the royal family – is another kettle of fish.

None of the papers makes riveting reading, and none have a huge circulation. The government's French-language daily, *Le Matin du Sahara et du Maghreb* (an extremely turgid read which also appears in Arabic and Spanish), sometimes manages a print run of 100,000, but most papers put out under 50,000 copies.

Among the French papers (most of which have their Arabic equivalent), the Casablanca-based *l'Opinion*, attached to the opposition Istiqlal Party, is perhaps the most interesting for getting an idea of points of contention in Moroccan society.

*Libération*, the Union Socialiste des Forces Populaires' daily, produced in Rabat, is similar if less punchy. *Al Bayane*, another opposition daily, is not too bad for foreign news. All have listings pages for Casablanca or Rabat cinemas, airport shuttle timetables,

Royal Air Maroc arrivals and departures and a list of late-night pharmacies (which work on a rotating roster).

There is a plethora of sports papers and magazines, fashion rags and the like, and a surprising number of weeklies dedicated purely to economics.

For readers of French who happen to be trying to learn Arabic, the monthly *La Tribune du Maroc* is worth tracking down. It culls the local Arabic and French-language press to cover the main events of the month, and runs pieces in both languages.

There is virtually nothing produced locally in English. A tiny monthly published in Fès, the *Messenger of Morocco* (Dr 3), is of minimal interest.

### Foreign Press
In the main centres, a reasonable range of foreign papers is available at central newsstands and in some of the big hotels. News magazines like *Newsweek* and *Time* are usually fairly easy to find, as is the *International Herald Tribune*. A range of UK papers and their European equivalents can also usually be found. The French press is about as easy to obtain and current as in France itself, and by far the cheapest – there seems to be virtually no added charge for import costs.

### Tourist Publications
A useful booklet loaded with practical information, listings and the like is called *La Quinzaine du Maroc*, which appears every fortnight. Unfortunately, it is hard to find outside Casablanca, although it is supposed to be available in the bigger hotels around the country. It costs from nothing to Dr 15, depending on where you stumble across it.

### Radio
Local radio is an odd mix. There is only a handful of local AM and FM stations, the bulk of which broadcast in Arabic and French. At least one of the FM stations plays quite reasonable contemporary music. The frequencies change from one part of the country to another.

Throughout northern Morocco and along

MOROCCO

much of the Atlantic coast you can pick up a host of Spanish stations, especially on the AM band. In fact, you can usually tune into Spanish radio just about anywhere in Morocco, although reception can be patchy.

None of this is much use if you don't understand Spanish, but it may give you a choice in music terms.

On the north coast around Tangier and across to Ceuta, you can often pick up English-language broadcasts from Gibraltar.

The Voice of America (VOA) has long had a presence just outside Tangier, and in September 1993 it opened its biggest transmitter outside the USA, at a cost of US$225 million. You can tune into VOA on various short-wave frequencies.

The other short-wave option in English is the BBC World Service. It broadcasts into the area on MHz 15.070, 12.095 and 9410, and several other frequencies. The bulk of the programs are broadcast from about 8 am to 11 pm.

## TV
As with radio, Moroccans in the north of the country can pick up the full gamut of Spanish stations – and the more risqué stations like Tele 5 are extremely popular. It is a rare thing to see Moroccan TV on the screens in Tangier cafés.

In the rest of the country, the choice is fairly limited. There are basically two government-run stations – RTM-1 (also known as TVM, and the more staid of the two) and 2M. Both broadcast in Arabic and French, and RTM-1 also has the news in Spanish at 7 pm. The third choice is basically a European satellite import from the Francophone world – TV5. It is an all-French station with programs from France, Belgium, Canada and Switzerland.

Should it be of interest, you can see Algerian TV in the east of the country.

## FILM & PHOTOGRAPHY
Most of the common brands of film are readily available in the big cities and towns, including slide film. It costs about as much as it would in Europe, so you won't save anything by not bringing your own. If you

do buy it in Morocco, be sure to check expiry dates. A 36-frame roll of Kodak 100 ASA print film will cost around Dr 45 to Dr 50. A 36-frame roll of Kodak Ektachrome slide film (100 ASA) goes for about Dr 70. There are quite a few processing shops in the cities and larger towns. It costs about Dr 82 to have a 36-frame roll of colour prints developed, and as little as Dr 55 to have slides (unmounted) processed.

## DANGERS & ANNOYANCES
When driving into hot spots such as Fès and Marrakesh, you are likely to be accosted by hustlers on motorbikes. They will try to direct you to hotels and the like and are every bit as persistent as their colleagues on foot – worse, dodging around these guys can be downright dangerous.

There have recently been reports of hitch-hike hustlers. If you pick them up, they try to lead you to their 'home' – often a carpet factory or the like. The road south from Ouarzazate is particularly bad, as is the road from Asni to Imlil in the High Atlas.

In the Rif Mountains around Ketama, stories abound of tourists being stopped and having large wedges of hash foisted on them by particularly unpleasant characters, only to land in trouble farther on when they reach the police roadblock they've been shopped to.

## WORK
Morocco is not the most fruitful ground for digging up work opportunities. A good command of French is usually a prerequisite, and a knowledge of Arabic would certainly not go astray. If you do secure a position, your employer will have to help you get a work permit and arrange residency, which can be an involved process. There is some very limited scope for teaching English and for voluntary work.

### Teaching English
It is technically possible to get this kind of work here, but the openings are limited. The British Council has only one branch in Morocco, in Rabat, but as a rule it recruits all its staff directly from London. You could try

them for supply work and they might have suggestions on smaller local outfits.

The only really credible alternatives are the ALC and the much smaller International Language Centre. The ALC has schools in Rabat, Casablanca, Fès, Marrakesh, Tangier, Tetouan and Kenitra; their addresses are listed under the cities' entries. Don't get your hopes up though. These are all fairly small operations and the chances of just walking into a job are not high. Obviously, qualified teachers of English as a foreign language (TEFL) will have a better chance. The minimum qualification is generally the RSA Certificate. The best time to try is around September and October (the beginning of the academic year) and to a lesser extent in early January. Casablanca has about half a dozen outfits and so is the best hunting ground.

ALC rates (about the highest) in 1994 ranged from Dr 82 per teaching hour for someone with a Bachelor of Arts degree and no prior experience to Dr 123 for a teacher with 12 years' experience and at least an MA in a relevant field.

### Voluntary Work

There are several organisations in Morocco that organise voluntary work on regional development projects. They generally pay nothing, sometimes not even lodging, and are aimed at young people looking for something different to do for a few weeks over the summer period. If this sort of thing interests you, a couple of possible sources of information in Morocco may be:

Chantiers Jeunesse Maroc
  BP 1351, 31 rue du Liban, Rabat
Chantiers Sociaux Marocains
  BP 456, Rabat (☎ 07-791370)
Les Amis des Chantiers Internationaux de Meknès
  BP 8, Meknès

### ACTIVITIES
### Trekking

Morocco is becoming increasingly popular as a trekking destination, and while the possibilities are not as breathtaking as in Nepal, there is some good walking to be done in the High and Middle Atlas mountains. Various tour companies outside of Morocco organise trips, or you can do things more haphazardly and organise something on the ground in Morocco. You can do relatively easy walks, such as the two-day trek up Jebel Toubkal in the High Atlas, or get together guides, porters and mules for longer adventures through the mountains. For more detailed information and some suggested reading, see the High Atlas Trekking section.

### Skiing

Although no match for Europe's Alpine offerings, skiing is a viable option in winter. The higher slopes and peaks usually have decent cover from December to March. Oukaimeden, about 70 km from Marrakesh, is a popular ski station and boasts the highest ski lift in Africa. A day lift pass costs Dr 80 and full equipment hire is usually around Dr 100 a day, although it's not always of the greatest quality. There are a couple of other spots dotted around the Middle Atlas equipped for snow sport, the best known and equipped being Mischliffen and Ifrane (18 km apart from one another).

Skiing is possible in the Rif, but the business has all but died because of the increased problem of dope dealers. Jebel Tidirhine, near Ketama, is one such spot. Another possibility is Bou Iblane, north of Taza, but not much is organised here either.

### White-Water Rafting

Morocco will never be one of the world's great rafting centres, but some specialist adventure companies do organise this kind of activity, particularly on some of the rivers in the High Atlas near the Bin el-Ouidane lake, in the area around Azilal and Afourer. People raft here as much for the setting as for the sport itself.

### Surfing

With thousands of km of ocean coastline, Morocco is not a bad place to take your board. Surfing has had little or no attention in Morocco, but you would not be the first to abandon the chill of the European Atlantic or something a little warmer. Essaouira has een singled out by some surfers, partly for ne town's attractions, but there is no reason ot to explore further afield. One Californian urfer found the beaches around Kenitra a afe and enjoyable bet. It has to be said that n a lot of places the wind makes a mess of he waves.

## Windsurfing

he winds off Essaouira are even better for vindsurfers than their wax-and-board col-eagues. Although probably quite a number f beaches up and down the Atlantic coast vould make equally good spots, this has efinitely been singled out as *the* place to vindsurf. It is possible to hire equipment on he beach there.

## Golf

Believe it or not, golf is high on the list of Morocco's advertised attractions, and it eems quite a few holiday-makers are not verse to a round or two. The oldest course, aid out in 1917, is the Royal Country Club f Tangier (☎ 09-938925), an 18-hole course hat one golfing writer described as adventurous'. The Royal Dar es-Salam ☎ 07-754692/3), 10 km out of central Rabat, is the most modern course and was he scene of the Moroccan Open in 1987. There are other courses in Casablanca (the Royal Golf d'Anfa, ☎ 02-251026), Marrakesh ☎ 04-444341), Ben Slimane, Mohammedia nd Agadir (12 km out of town).

## Fishing

Surfcasting in the area around Dakhla, in the outh, has been particularly recommended. Some of the creeks around Marrakesh are not ·ad, but the artificial lake created by the Moulay Youssef dam, purposely stocked vith fish such as black bass, is better. Fishing s permitted in most rivers, lakes and on the :oast, but only from sunrise to sunset. You need a licence, which must be organised hrough the Service des Eaux et Forêts.

## Language Courses

The business of learning Arabic is quite undeveloped in Morocco, and the possibilities for doing so are strictly limited. Apart from possible summer courses at the university in Rabat, your best bet would be to head for the Arabic Language Institute (☎ 06-624850) in Fès at 2 Rue Ahmed Hiba. The institute has been going since 1983 and is attached to the ALC. Until now, classes have been quite small, so each student can expect a reasonable amount of individual attention. The institute offers three levels of MSA and the Moroccan dialect Darija. It has a series of intensive courses that run over six weeks and cost Dr 5900 per course.

The institute can also help with accommodation, either in hotels or on a home-stay basis with Moroccan families.

Some branches of the Centre Culturel Français, such as that in Tangier, run Arabic courses.

## HIGHLIGHTS

In all of Africa, Morocco offers possibly the greatest variety of attractions. The four imperial cities are the biggest attraction, and each of them is distinctly different from the other. The medina of **Fès**, brooding in the foothills of the Middle Atlas, will swallow you up into its countless winding and twisting alleyways, taking you past exquisite monuments and labyrinths of souqs selling everything from edible delicacies through to the entire range of souvenir items that Morocco's artisans can offer. Nearby **Meknès**, once briefly the capital, presents a more open aspect, and its ambitious dimensions have often been compared to those of Versailles.

The red city of **Marrakesh**, nuzzling the snowcapped High Atlas Mountains, is another world again, and while the stamp of France's protectorate is clearly evident in the villes nouvelles of the northern capitals, Marrakesh offers an altogether different and somehow wilder picture. The city walls and rambling medina, basking in the bright sun and clean air (the climate is reputedly perfect for anyone with respiratory problems or even a simple cold) and dominated by the minaret of the great Koutoubia Mosque, has long been one of North Africa's most popular destinations. The focal point is its main square, the Djemaa el-Fna, one of the last redoubts of a more traditional Moroccan nightlife, thronged with storytellers, snake charmers, food stalls and herbalists selling all sorts of charms and cures.

The fourth of the imperial cities, **Rabat**, and its sister town of Salé, once home to the Corsairs (pirates who struck fear into the merchant seamen of Europe), is a curious mix of remnants of its long past and the new. Along with the modern, booming economic capital of Casablanca to the south, Rabat presents Morocco's most modern and go-ahead face.

With thousands of km of Atlantic coast, Morocco is blessed with dozens of good spots for a beach holiday. While **Agadir** is an up-market resort for Europeans tired of the European Mediterranean resorts, **Essaouira** to the north is a laid-back place favoured by windsurfers and backpackers.

Inland, trekkers can find plenty of satisfying challenges in the **High Atlas Mountains**, and those haunted by desert fantasies can head south-east of Marrakesh through the extraordinary landscape of kasbahs and oases to reach the edge of the **Sahara**, which stretches on into the vast expanses of Algeria to the east.

## ACCOMMODATION
### Camping
Provided you have the site owner's permission, you can camp practically anywhere in Morocco. There are also quite a few official camp sites dotted around the country. Most of the bigger cities have one, often located well out of town and of more use to people with their own transport. Some of them are brilliantly located and worth the extra effort to get to them, but many offer little shade and are hardly worth what you have to pay. Most have water, electricity, a small restaurant and grocery store. Where there is hot water, you will pay at least Dr 5 for a hot shower.

As a rule, you'll be up for Dr 10 per person, plus a charge for pitching your tent (also often around Dr 10), along with charges

for cars, motorbikes and caravans. Hot water and electricity also cost extra. For two people travelling by car, the total costs can easily come to nearly Dr 30 a head, so there are times when it will be better to spend a little more for a hotel.

### Hostels
Hostelling International (HI) recognises 10 hostels in the country, located in Asni, Azrou, Casablanca, Chefchaouen, Fès, Marrakesh, Meknès, Rabat and Tangier. The head office of the Fédération Royale Marocaine des Auberges des Jeunes (☎ 05-524698) is on the Blvd Oqba ben Nafii in Meknès. The organisation has another office in Casablanca (☎ 02-970952) on the Parc de la Ligue Arabe. A bed usually costs from Dr 20 to Dr 30 (a little more without membership card). Generally they are not too bad – those in Marrakesh, Meknès and Casablanca are among the better ones.

### Hotels
About the cheapest hotel rooms you're likely to find anywhere will cost you about Dr 30 for a single and Dr 50 for a double. As a rule you get what you pay for, and the bulk of these unclassified hotels tend to be clustered in certain parts of the medinas of the bigger cities. For a little more, you can often find other unclassified hotels, or one-star jobs, outside the medinas that are better. This is especially the case in the high season, when the unclassified hotels tend to crank prices up as high as they think possible.

It is always worth looking around, but most of these places are clean if basic. In some cases, the single biggest objection is the size of the room – they can be pretty tiny. Hot water is either not available or involves a Dr 5 charge per gas-heated shower. Where there is no hot water at all, hotel staff can point you to a local public shower (douche) or baths (hammam). You should not get too excited by claims of hot water in the cheapies either – sometimes it amounts to little more than a warm trickle.

If you have a little flexibility on the money front, you can dig up some very good hotels in the one and two-star range, although clearly there are other places that should be condemned. In the better cases, you are looking at good, clean rooms with comfortable beds, and with a bit of luck a halfway decent shower. Hot water tends to be available only at certain times.

In the three and four-star bracket you will sometimes come up with a gem of an older place left over from more elegant days and, with luck, tastefully renovated. In the upper bracket you're more likely to be confronted with more modern and sterile places.

At the top end of the scale are the five-star places. Many of the worldwide chains are represented, and prices and amenities are on a par with what you would expect of such places.

Although many unclassified places put up their prices in the high season in the most popular locations, it is fair to say that cities like Marrakesh offer a reasonable choice of places to stay. Not-so-popular destinations like Tetouan offer little and the quality of the offerings is low.

If you are resident in Morocco, you are entitled to a 25% discount on the classified hotel rates in some establishments. Always ask.

You will almost always be asked to leave your passport with reception so they can fill in their hotel register. There is no reason for not asking to have it back when they're done, although this occasionally sparks requests for advance payment.

The Classified Accommodation Costs table gives an idea of prices in the classified hotels. There has been some suggestion that hotels are no longer required to stick to these maximum room rates, but there is little evidence of any hotels overstepping their set rates. Some charge a little less, and some clearly don't deserve their rating. Five-star hotels are not governed by this regime and can charge what they like.

A third bed costs from Dr 43 (one star) to Dr 98 (four star). Breakfast is also extra, from Dr 19 a person (one star) to Dr 40 (four star). An additional tourist tax ranges from Dr 3 to Dr 8 per person.

## Classified Accommodation Costs

| Category | Room | Shower (Dr) | Shower & Toilet (Dr) |
|---|---|---|---|
| 1 star B | Sing/Doub | 75/90 | 87/111 |
| 1 star A | Sing/Doub | 86/110 | 110/127 |
| 2 star B | Sing/Doub | 97/119 | 119/144 |
| 2 star A | Sing/Doub | 121/142 | 153/179 |
| 3 star B | Sing/Doub | 153/195 | 195/240 |
| 3 star A | Sing/Doub | 179/225 | 226/273 |
| 4 star B | Sing/Doub | 247/303 | 302/377 |
| 4 star A | Sing/Doub | 297/387 | 362/460 |

## ENTERTAINMENT

Morocco is not the last word in nightlife. In fact your choices are fairly limited. The bigger centres have cinemas, and some of them are quite good. Bars are scarce in small towns but, again, the big cities have enough to keep you going. Beyond that it's discos and nightclubs, mostly of little interest, and the odd folkloric show, which can be interesting first time around.

### Cinemas

The best cinemas are in Rabat and Casablanca. It's pretty cheap entertainment, with seats costing from Dr 7 to Dr 12, depending on where you sit. The better cinemas get some quite up-to-date films, but where they are not French films, they are almost invariably dubbed into French. It is interesting to note that half the time they don't seem to bother with Arabic, not even subtitles. Draw what conclusions you will from that.

Every town has at least one cinema specialising in kung fu-style movies, often with a sprinkling of the Indian equivalent of the genre. If you can believe the posters, there is a sprinkling of cinemas showing porn films – another surprise in a Muslim country.

### Bars

There are basically two kind of bars. The majority are pretty basic, and tend to be discreet about their existence. Many have a Flag Spéciale sign outside – push the door open and there you are. In Casablanca, some go by the name of *drogueries*. The local punters will probably be surprised to see you.

MOROCCO

MOROCCO

Note that most of these bars close pretty early.

The other version is the expensive hotel bar. These stay open a little later, and are considerably more expensive and not terribly interesting.

### Discos & Nightclubs

Discos are discos, and the difference between them and nightclubs is not always clear. Generally you'll have to pay at least Dr 50 to get in (this usually includes a drink) and subsequent drinks cost an average of Dr 50. Many discos are decidedly overpopulated with local lads. A couple of the more chic jobs in the Casablanca suburbs are better, but very dear.

Some of the sleazier nightclubs, particularly in central Casablanca, put on a cabaret or floor show, usually of the belly-dancing variety, but rarely terribly captivating. They can be a curious experience though. Some of these places are clearly the hunting ground of prostitutes.

### Folkloric Shows

Some of the big hotels and tourist restaurants put on folkloric performances. The ones in the restaurants are probably preferable, since the settings are often quite sumptuous. The shows themselves can be a mixed bag, but entertaining enough if reasonable musicians have been engaged to play traditional Andalusian or Berber music. The dancing is more often than not Egyptian-style belly-dancing (it's not really a Moroccan genre). A few of the top hotels opt for Western cabarets.

### THINGS TO BUY

The souvenir hunter could spend weeks, if not longer, burrowing through the souqs of Morocco turning over all sorts of things. From leather goods through copper and brassware to the myriad collections of rugs and carpets, there is an enormous choice. Obviously a lot of rubbish is produced alongside the higher-quality objects, and it pays to take your time before buying. For a better idea of what to look for, see the Art & Crafts colour section at the end of this chapter.

For some people the big attractions are the herbs and spices. Besides the cumin, saffron, ginger and so on that are usually displayed in huge colourful mounds, there are occasionally stands selling all sorts of obscure things for medicinal purposes. The Djemaa el-Fna in Marrakesh is a good place for this. If you've got a cough, cold or other ailment point to the part that hurts and you'll soon have a small plastic bag with the wonder herb in your hand. Directions for use vary, so try to get an explanation of how to take your herbal remedy. The locals swear by these *'ashaab*.

### Markets

In common with most African and Middle Eastern countries, Moroccan towns and villages have a special weekly market day (sometimes twice a week) when people from the surrounding area come to sell their wares and buy goods they cannot produce for themselves.

These markets differ from the permanent covered markets you'll find in most towns and usually provide a lively opportunity to observe the distinctive customs and clothing of local tribespeople. Some of the most interesting include:

| Town | Market Days |
| --- | --- |
| Agadir | Saturday & Sunday |
| Figuig | Saturday |
| Ifrane | Sunday |
| Khenifra | Sunday |
| Larache | Sunday |
| M'Hamid | Monday |
| Midelt | Sunday |
| Moulay Idriss | Saturday |
| Ouarzazate | Sunday |
| Ouezzane | Thursday |
| Oujda | Wednesday & Sunday |
| Sefrou | Thursday |
| Tafraoute | Wednesday |
| Taroudannt | Friday |
| Tinerhir | Monday |
| Tinzouline | Monday |
| Zagora | Wednesday & Sunday |

# Moroccan Arts & Crafts

Since the 16th century, merchant ships have been leaving Moroccan shores laden with exotic goods bound for Europe. *Maroquinerie* (leatherware) was the single most prized item in those days, and the word became synonymous with quality leather goods throughout the fashionable courts and houses of Europe.

That tradition lives on, accompanied by a rich heritage in the production of all sorts of goods – from carpets to fine pottery, heavy silver jewellery to elegant woodwork.

The traditional crafts of Morocco are the living embodiment of its preindustrial manufacturing industry. Although much of what is made today is aimed at tourists and is for decorative use, it all has its roots in the satisfaction of the everyday needs of people – from the humblest person to the most elevated.

The government goes to some lengths to keep these arts alive because they are as important to the economy as phosphates and agriculture. As far back as 1918, the then resident-general of the French protectorate over Morocco, General Lyautey, set up the Office des Industries d'Art Indigène to promote craft sales abroad. No doubt some of what is produced today is garbage – quick, cheap souvenirs that end up in the hands of tourists too impatient to look around for quality – but there is plenty of decent stuff to be found.

Moroccan tourism took a battering during the Gulf War, and although the number of visitors is back to prewar levels, craft sales in 1993 were still only a quarter of what they had been in 1990. It sounds a little selfish, but this can be good news for the patient bargainer, as shopkeepers are more anxious than ever to make a sale.

Many of the products that attract visitors, such as rugs and chased brass and copperware, owe at least some of their visual appeal to a meeting of religious precept and traditional tribal design.

Considering the depiction of all living beings an affront to God, Islam imposed strictures on the artist. There was no question of art imitating life (let alone life imitating art). Consequently, public art had little choice but to follow an abstract and decorative path which inspired the serene contemplation of seemingly endlessly repeated and interlaced motifs.

Alongside variations on floral designs, geometry developed as a prime tool of the artist. In Morocco and throughout the Islamic world, artisans have, over the centuries, perfected the creation of

*Detail of rug, Tangier (DS)*

*Top: Quartier des Potiers, Safi (DS)*

*Bottom: Detail of mausoleum in the garden of the Saadian tombs, Marrakesh (DS)*

intricate geometrical patterns, many of which are elaborations or tribal themes long known in Morocco.

Added to this came calligraphy, which made of the Arabic language, and particularly the sacred words of the Qur'an, an artistic medium in itself. For although it was sacrilegious to portray the image of God, it was praiseworthy to have His words on display for all the world to see. The calligraphy you see in great religious buildings in Morocco is generally composed of extracts from the Qur'an or such ritual declarations as *la illah illa Allah* ('There is no god but Allah').

An artistic peak was reached in the 13th century under the Merenids. This dynasty seemed to specialise in sponsoring the construction of theological colleges (medersas) in all the great cities, and they are the most richly decorated of all of Morocco's historical buildings. Visiting these, you will soon notice that not a centimetre of the interior wall surfaces is left bare. The base of the walls is covered in zellij tiles – fragments of ceramic tiles in hues

*Bab Bou Jeloud,*
*Fès (DS)*

of green, blue and yellow interspersed with black on a white background. Above these tiles, the stylised decoration is continued in lacework stucco, topped finally by carved wood (often cedar) panels, which are continued on the ceiling.

Geometric finesse and harmony in design (much of it introduced by Arabs from Muslim Spain) spread through all levels of artisanal handicrafts, although the origins of many Berber designs, especially in textiles and jewellery, predate the emergence of Islam. Carpets and rugs almost always feature some geometric decoration; of course today you will find items depicting animals and the like, but they have nothing to do with traditional artistic norms. More often than not the popular copper and brass trays boast flurries of calligraphic virtuosity. The beauty of the most intricate of jewellery is in the sum of its many simply shaped parts.

Although much craftwork is now aimed at tourists, little of it has been specifically designed *for* them. Rugs and trays, silver jewellery and swords were being made for local use long before tourism became a phenomenon. There are exceptions. Much of the leatherware is more inspired by an attempt to imitate popular

*Tuareg bags,*
*Taroudannt (DS)*

European tastes than it is by tradition. The same can be said of most woollen products, such as caps, multicoloured coats, sweaters and the like – you'll be lucky to see a Moroccan wearing any of these items. A lot of woodwork, especially thuya-wood carvings from the Essaouira region, is a reaction to the influx of tourists hungry for original souvenirs.

## IN THE SOUQ

The most useful tool when hunting for crafts is patience. Morocco is crawling with craft souqs, and tourists often find themselves subjected to heavy sales pressure. Before you even get to the shops in many cities you will have to deal with 'guides' and touts of various types. Once inside the shops, you will, in the best circumstances, be caught up in the age-old mint tea ritual, in which gentle but persistent pressure is applied to you to purchase something. Less scrupulous (or more desperate) shopkeepers tend to go for more strong-arm tactics, and badger unsuspecting visitors into buying things they barely even wanted to look at – this species is a minority and mainly inhabits the bigger tourist cities like Marrakesh. Most shopkeepers are perfectly all right, although some can put on childish long faces if you leave with your hands empty and wallet full.

Before buying anything, you should look around. You may be taken with the first items you see, but if you buy them you may well be disenchanted with them by the time you leave. Every big city has an Ensemble Artisanal. These are government-run 'supermarkets'. Prices are generally higher than those you would pay if you bargained in the souqs, but here you can check out the goods in peace and get an idea of what good-quality items are like. It might also be an idea to visit some of the various Moroccan traditional arts museums, where you can admire classical pieces of work, be they rugs or rings.

## WEAVING & TEXTILES
### Carpets & Rugs

Carpet shops. The words themselves evoke for many the sum total of their Moroccan experience. All the touts in Morocco seem to assume the first (and only) thing the tourist wants is a carpet.

The selling of carpets is exclusively men's business and the same can be said for practically all arts and crafts. The big difference between carpets and other crafts is that making them is virtually a women's preserve. Good rugs and carpets can take months to make, and the women see little cash for their labours.

The heavy woollen carpets and throw rugs vary greatly in design and colouring from region to region. Rabat is reputed to be one of the best centres and maintains a tradition inspired by the carpet-makers of the Middle East. Carpets here come in rich blends of blues, reds, greens and yellows. They generally feature a central motif and an intricate border – the wider and more complicated the work in the border, the more the carpet is worth.

Outside Rabat, most of the carpets and rugs are the work of Berber tribes, each of which (when the work is at its best) pass down certain designs and colour combinations. If browns dominate in the Middle Atlas, the famous carpets of Chichaoua (on the

*Inside Raissouli Palace, Asilah (DS)*

*Top, Middle & Bottom: Detail of cushion, Meknès (GB)*

road from Marrakesh to Essaouira) are almost always a stunning red to dark-red wine colour. Unlike the highly prized Rabat carpets, most of those made by the Berbers do not have a frame around the edges.

The value of a carpet is based not only on the intricacy of design, but also on its age, the number of knots and, perhaps most importantly, the strength of the wool. The tougher and more wiry the wool, the longer the rug is likely to last – many Moroccan soft-wool carpets will not stand up well to much foot traffic.

A handmade carpet can become something of an antique if it's well made, and those done by masters are much sought after by connoisseurs and are hard to come by. A square metre of carpet contains tens of thousands of knots and it's basically a case of the more the better, as they indicate a product is more likely to last. Top-class examples will have some 150,000 knots per square metre. These are comparatively rare, and glib claims that the item in front of you has several hundred thousand knots per square metre can, as a rule, be confidently discounted.

For decades, chemical colours have been used instead of vegetable dyes, but despite what you may be told, they tend to fade too, sometimes quite dramatically. Vegetable dyes are still used, and tend to fade more slowly. A wide range of products are used to create different colours, including almond leaves, bark, iron sulphate and cow urine.

For the locals, carpets are utilitarian as much as works of art, and the brilliant colours of a new rug are not expected to retain their intensity. If you find a genuinely old piece (of 40 or so years), you can be fairly confident that it *won't* change colour significantly.

### Kilims

More suitable as wall-hangings or bedspreads than carpets are the flat-weave kilims. What sets kilims apart from other rugs is the fact that they are woven rather than knotted. While knotted woollen rugs tend to have great splashes of colour, kilims are characterised by a finer design. One or two colours may dominate, but they are always interwoven in delicate, rectilinear patterns. As with knotted carpets, there are any number of variations in design, motif and choice of colour, depending on the region or tribe that produces them.

*Detail of Berber rug, Erfoud (GB)*

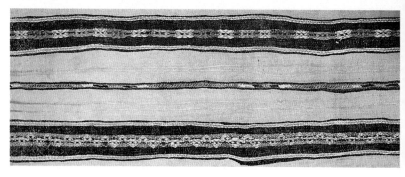

## Buying Carpets

You will hear many absurd asking prices while bargaining in Morocco. A high but not insane starting price for good wool carpets is Dr 100 per square metre. If you hold out and the item is not of great quality, the price will soon come down. Kilims require more work and are generally more expensive. Dr 500 for two square metres is a not unreasonable price, but insistent bargaining would bring it down to Dr 300 or perhaps less. Again, much depends on the quality of the handiwork and the eagerness of the shopkeeper to sell.

*Kilim, Tangier (DS)*

### Other Wool Products

There are plenty of other good woollen purchases to be made. Chefchaouen and Ouezzane are in flourishing wool country, and in the former especially all manner of garments can be found. Perhaps the best are thick sweaters, which tend to cost from Dr 50 up, depending on quality and thickness. Jackets, head gear and woven bags are further items. Inspect the goods closely. The most attractive coats made of superb wool can look great, but if they're of poor quality, you'll find them unravelling within weeks. Another item popular with some visitors are the heavy, hooded cloaks (burnouses), worn by Berbers from all over the country. They are practical in the cold mountain weather, but Westerners look a little silly in them.

### Textiles

Although Morocco does not have Egypt's reputation for producing cotton, many visitors are tempted by jellabas, the full-length cotton garments worn by men, and similar clothing items worn by women, which are very comfortable in hot climes.

Various materials are used to produce a whole range of what for Berber households are useful floor covers and the like. Depending on the designs, they can be as attractive a buy as the carpets.

Fès is reputedly Morocco's great silk and brocade centre, but both these artforms are apparently heading for extinction and so are increasingly hard to find.

### LEATHERWORK

The bulk of contemporary leatherware is aimed solely at tourists. The tanneries of Fès provide raw material for about half the country's total production in leather goods, but several other big cities maintain their own tanneries.

The most 'authentic' of these items are *babouches*, slippers that

*Above: Kilim, Tangier (DS)*

*Right: Detail of leatherwork on bag, Marrakesh (GB)*

are still the most common footwear among Moroccans of both sexes. Men wear yellow or white ones, while all the bright colours or more ornate styles are reserved for women.

A whole range of products designed for Westerners in search of leather goods more affordable than in the designer stores at home can be found in Fès, Marrakesh, Rabat and Tetouan. They include jackets, bags of all descriptions, wallets, belts and poufs. The latter are a genuinely traditional item and are made of goat leather. If camel saddles are your thing, try Marrakesh. Some of the best shoulder bags are made in the Rif and find their way into the markets of Tetouan and Chefchaouen. Tiny bags designed to carry around personal minicopies of the Qur'an form popular souvenir items.

The leather is often of a high quality, and to this extent the fame of maroquinerie remains justified. Unfortunately, the artisanship of many items leaves a lot to be desired – check the links, stitching and so on of anything you're interested in.

## POTTERY & CERAMICS

The potteries of Safi have long been touted as the main centre of ceramic production in Morocco, but smaller cooperatives are springing up in other parts of the country, and the cities of Fès and Meknès have a centuries-old heritage of ceramics production. A lot of it is prosaic, such as the ubiquitous green roof tiles that are largely made in these two Middle Atlas cities and to some extent in Safi.

Safi's pottery makers have taken their inspiration from the ceramics once produced in Málaga (southern Spain), which are

*Detail of large decorative bowl, Safi (GB)*

*Top: Tajine bowls and vase, Safi (GB)*

*Middle: Potters' souq, Safi (DS)*

*Bottom: Cache-pots (flowerpot holders) and candlestick, Safi (GB)*

dentified by a characteristic metallic sheen. The arrival of many potters from Fès has led to an increasing mixture of that city's traditional designs, which were mostly handed down by artisans exiled from Al-Andalus.

Fès's ceramics are dominated by browns, blues or yellow and green on a white background. You can see fine examples of jars, pots and other household items (for well-to-do households!) in most of the museums of Moroccan art in the big cities. Meknès inherited much of its skills from Fès, and its pottery industry really only began to flourish in the 18th century.

Among the handiest commercially available souvenirs are decorative ceramic plates or coffee and tea sets. The rougher examples can sell for as little as Dr 50, but expect to pay several hundred for a decently made plate.

A uniquely Moroccan item is the *tajine*, the casserole dish with the conical cover used to cook the meal of the same name (and indeed other meals, too). You can get a classy decorative tajine, or settle for the locally used product. One of the latter can cost as little as Dr 10 or Dr 20.

One way to tell the difference between something of value or production-line tourist trash is the gaudiness of colour and brightness of finish. The more precious pottery tends to be muted in colour, decoration and finish. This doesn't make the other stuff intrinsically bad, but it *does* mean you should not pay an arm and a leg for it.

In contrast to the largely urban and sophisticated pottery are the rougher, rustic products of the Berbers. Although simpler, they have their own charm, and are characteristic of the regions in which they are made. In the High Atlas south of Marrakesh, ochre is the dominant colour, the exception being down by Zagora, where you can find pots, jars and cups with a green finish. Water vessels are often decorated with a mysterious black substance that is said to purify the water.

## BRASS & COPPERWARE

One of the best things about brass and copperware is that it is

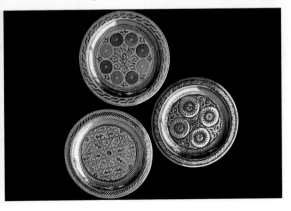

*Bottom: Brass plates, Fès (GB)*

comparatively hard to cheat on quality. Probably the most commonly bought items are plates and trays of chased copper and sometimes brass. You can start at about Dr 10 for saucer-sized decorative plates of low quality to several hundred for large, heavy trays. The latter are lavishly decorated and can be used to make a coffee table or hung on the wall as decoration.

There are plenty of other souvenirs. Candlesticks and lamp bases come in all shapes and sizes, and are best looked for in Marrakesh, Fès and Tetouan. Tetouan can be quite a good place to pick up these products, provided you are not accompanied by guides and hangers-on. Also worth buying are brass mirror frames,

*Top left: Copper utensils (AC)*

*Top right: Copper jug (GB)*

*Bottom: Brass plate detail, Fès (GB)*

often sporting patterns and designs reminiscent of what you will see in the best of Moroccan Islamic architecture.

For hammered rather than chased copper items, Taroudannt is about the best place.

## JEWELLERY

Much of the jewellery around is not what it is claimed to be. Gold and silver are more often than not plated, and amber is plastic (put a lighted match to it and smell). Unless you are sure of your stuff, you should be cautious about what you buy and be prepared for disappointment.

This is not to say that genuinely good jewellery cannot be found, but you have to look for it. The making of jewellery in Morocco was once the preserve of the country's Jewish population, and it is said that Muslims at one stage had a superstitious aversion to metal-work. Whatever the truth of that, the Jews have left and Muslims have been fashioning jewellery for centuries.

Silver jewellery,
Tiznit (DS)

## Gold

Fès is traditionally *the* place to buy gold jewellery, as much because of the sophisticated, urban and well-off clientele as anything else. Some of the city's artisans started a minor migratory wave to Essaouira a century ago, making the Atlantic town a secondary centre for the production of gold. Gold markets are to be found in various other big cities too – the one in Meknès, which is not overwhelmed by gold-hunting tourists, is worth investigating.

Classic jewellery made in Fès and Tangier remains largely faithful to Andalusian recherché lines, and is often ostentatious and

*Top & bottom: Silverware and jewellery, Taroudannt (DS)*

beyond the means of most. The Meknès products are generally more modest.

Essaouira, apart from the contribution made by the jewellers from Fès, boasts a local style dominated by floral designs and enamel work, although little of the jewellery produced has any gold content.

## Silver

You can find cheap silver-plated jewellery just about anywhere. If you're looking for slightly more valuable and characteristically Moroccan items, you should head south to Tiznit, Rissani, Tan Tan or Taroudannt. Silver has long been highly prized by Berber women – a look in some of the museums of Moroccan art will soon convince you of that. The reason for this is that few peasant families, however powerful in their own stamping ground, could afford the luxury of gold.

Silver necklaces, bracelets, rings and earrings are invariably quite chunky, and often enlivened with pieces of amber or comparatively cheap precious stones. A particular item you will see in jewellery souqs is the hand of Fatima. The open palm is supposed to protect its wearer from ill fortune.

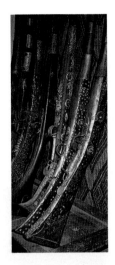

## OTHER METALWORK

While down around Tiznit and Taroudannt, you might be interested in other silverwork. Specialities in both towns are silver-encrusted

*Top: Guns, Taroudannt (DS)*

*Bottom: Tin box to carry the Qur'an (GB)*

sabres and muskets. You can also come across silver daggers and silver (or silver-plated) scabbards.

For wrought iron, the place to hunt around is the ironsmiths' souq in Marrakesh. Here you can find heavy frames for mirrors, fire screens, lanterns and the like. There is little of this sort of work outside Marrakesh, and it is generally classed among the artisanal arts originally imported from Muslim Spain.

## WOODWORK

The artisans of Tetouan, Salé and Meknès continue to produce veritable works of art in wood. Painted and sculpted panels for interior decoration are commonplace, and the infinitely more intricate work required to produce the stalactite-like decoration that graces the interior of various medersas and other religious build-

*Top: Berber painted wooden box, Rabat (GB)*

*Bottom: Thuya wood table, Essaouira (DS)*

ings and private houses of the rich also survives. Nor has the *mashrabiyya* (sometimes also spelled *mousharabiyya*) been consigned to history. These screens were and are designed to allow women to observe the goings-on in the street without being seen themselves. Fès and Meknès are the main centres of production.

While these items don't make likely candidates for souvenirs, they do serve to show that Moroccan crafts are not completely dependent on floods of tourists.

Pleasantly perfumed cedar is used for most woodwork, and in some of the better workshops you will find beautiful bowls, candlesticks, painted cribs, chests, jewellery boxes and the like. Fès is particularly good for this sort of work. Tetouan produces some interesting pieces too.

For marquetry, inlaid chessboards, caskets and all sorts of trinkets, you should wait until you get to Essaouira. The artisans here mainly use thuya wood *(Tris articuta)*, the most common tree in Essaouira's hinterland, but virtually unknown outside Morocco. The wood is so coveted that it is valued like a precious metal. From little jewellery boxes right through to enormous wooden statues, the range of thuya products is almost unlimited. The remarkable natural patterns that show up in the grain of better-quality items are found in the roots of the thuya tree.

## STONE & PRECIOUS STONES

In Taroudannt you can pick up lamps, paperweights and boxes made of stone. Various kinds of softer stone are also sculpted into all sorts of shapes and sold for a pittance.

Throughout the Middle and High Atlas you'll pass roadside

*Top: Stone statue,
Er-Rachidia (GB)*

*Bottom: Stone masks,
Er-Rachidia (GB)*

stands with people offering clumps of all sorts of semiprecious stones such as quartz and amethyst.

In the desert around Erfoud are black marble quarries that furnish the base element for that town's souvenir industry. There are several stores there selling everything from statues to paperweights in black marble, as well as plenty of kids trying to unload more modest trinkets.

Fossils in rock, especially ammonite, are occasionally offered alongside the semiprecious stones. Morocco is full of fossils, and more enterprising souvenir merchants convert them into all sorts of things, including bowls and superb table-top sections.

## MUSICAL INSTRUMENTS

It is possible to pick up traditional Moroccan instruments in a few places. One of the best places to look around is in the Bab el-Jedid area of the Meknès medina, where you'll find various string, wind and percussion instruments. For more information on Moroccan music and instruments see Music in the Arts section of the Facts about the Country chapter.

## BASKETWARE

Throughout Morocco you will come across basketware, a wide term that covers everything from the Rif-style straw hats of the north to baskets with cone-shaped covers used by Berbers to carry dates and other merchandise. They make cheap souvenirs and are obviously not made to last forever.

*Wooden tambourine and ceramic darbukas (drums) with goatskin heads, Safi (GB)*

# Getting There & Away

## AIR

Morocco is well served by air from Europe, the Middle East and West Africa. Mohammed V Airport, the country's main international airport, is 30 km south of Casablanca, but there are also flights from some European cities to Tangier, Agadir and Marrakesh. In the high season most of these are charters. Although there is a small airport 10 km north-east of Rabat, the capital is increasingly served by Mohammed V, to which it is directly linked by train and bus shuttles.

Oujda is linked to Paris and several other French cities, as well as Amsterdam, Brussels, Düsseldorf, Frankfurt, Munich and Stockholm. There are connections from the USA to Casablanca, and you can get direct flights to Marrakesh from various European cities, including Paris, Geneva, London, Rome and Munich. Direct flights to Fès are less frequent. There are direct flights between Paris and Ouarzazate, and most Middle Eastern capitals can be reached from Casablanca.

Laayoune, the capital of the disputed territory of Western Sahara, is linked to the Canary Islands, Abidjan (Côte d'Ivoire) and Libreville (Gabon) by the national carrier, Royal Air Maroc (RAM).

RAM and Air France take the lion's share of the flights, but other airlines operating to Morocco include Air Algérie, Alitalia, British Airways, EgyptAir, GB Airways, Iberia, KLM, Lufthansa, Royal Jordanian, Sabena, Swissair, TAT European Airlines and Tunis Air. RAM has had some rather unflattering reports from travellers, particularly on the subject of lost luggage.

The northern summer months, Christmas to New Year and the weeks around Easter are high-season periods.

### To/From Europe

**UK** RAM's cheapest return Superpex low-season fares from London to Tangier are UK£190 for one month and UK£234 for two.

RAM also has direct flights from London to Casablanca, Marrakesh and Agadir. The airline offers various other fares, including a special youth ticket.

A quick ring around a few bucket shops soon reveals some big price differences, so it is worth shopping around. Many use GB Airways, which flies from London and Manchester via Gibraltar to Tangier, Casablanca and Marrakesh. Return tickets to any of the three destinations, valid for one month, cost between UK£120 and UK£180. GB Airways has four flights a week to Casablanca from Manchester and London Heathrow via Gibraltar. There are two weekly flights to Tangier and two others from London Gatwick to Marrakesh.

Air France and KLM have tickets valid for three months return to Casablanca for about UK£230, and it is possible to fly British Airways return to Casablanca for UK£173 in the low season.

Some agents also have charter flights, usually requiring that you return within one or two weeks, and costing anywhere from UK£100 return up. If you can get one in the bottom range, it's generally cheaper to throw away the return half than buy a regular one-way ticket.

If you only want to go for a short time, consider taking a hotel or fly-drive package. Three nights in, say, Marrakesh in a reasonable hotel near the medina, with half-board, optional escorted tours, flights and transfers, can cost well under UK£300. See also the Tours section in this chapter.

If you are not in too much of a hurry and are counting pennies, the most efficient way to get to Morocco is to fly to Málaga in southern Spain and either get a boat from there to the Spanish enclave of Melilla or a bus round to Algeciras and from there a boat across to Ceuta or Tangier (see the Sea section later in this chapter). It is feasible to get a one-way ticket to Málaga for around UK£60 or even less. Return fares generally start at about UK£100, but deals on charters and the like abound, so look around.

Sometimes charter tickets for either Morocco or Spain are tied to specific accommodation, but some agents are prepared to give you bogus vouchers for the accommodation, enabling you to benefit from the cheap flight.

**France** There is no shortage of flights from Paris (and many other French cities) direct to Casablanca, Agadir, Rabat, Tangier, Fès, Marrakesh, Oujda and Ouarzazate. Most travel agents can do deals, and often fly-drive arrangements are an attractive option. Given the sheer volume of traffic from France, the deals are often more attractive than from the traditional bucket-shop paradises of London and, to a lesser extent, Amsterdam. RAM alone has four to five flights a day from Paris to Casablanca. Air France boasts some 50 weekly connections between a range of Moroccan and French destinations.

Various agencies often offer charter flights at very low prices, and it is possible to get one-way flights or deals including accommodation. Some of the cheapest return charter flights from Paris include Marrakesh for FFr1100 and Agadir for FFr1200, with a maximum stay of four weeks. You could try asking at Sélection Informations Vacances (☎ 42.60.83.40) at 9 Rue de l'Echelle, 75001 Paris, or Nouvelles Frontières (☎ 41.41.58.58) at 87 Blvd de Grenelle, 75015 Paris.

If you are looking for something more organised or for a desert expedition, you could try Explorator (☎ 42.66.66.24), 16 Place de la Madeleine, 75008 Paris, or Déserts (☎ 46.04.88.40), 6 et 8 Rue Quincampoix, 75004 Paris.

The possibilities are much more limited from Morocco. Despite the plethora of travel agents in central Casablanca, there seems to be little discounting. A standard one-way fare to Paris is hardly a bargain at Dr 4305.

**Spain** Despite its proximity, Spain is not the ideal place from which to fly to Morocco,

unless you are in a hurry and want to take an organised tour (see the section on Tours later in this chapter).

Cheap tickets from Madrid include 30,000 pta return to Tangier with a maximum stay of six months, or 44,800 pta return to Marrakesh. Such prices are not always easy to find, and flights can easily cost 20,000 pta more. However, it is possible to find package deals that come in a lot cheaper, such as a return flight and one night's stay in Morocco for 19,500 pta. In the high season there also are flights from numerous Spanish cities direct to Agadir.

Travel agents in Madrid tend to be clustered in the vicinity of the Gran Vía. Budget travellers should try Unijoven at Calle San Bernardo 98 or Mundojoven at Calle Hortaleza 8.

The options *from* Morocco are more limited still. A one-way ticket to Madrid from Casablanca, regardless of the airline, comes to about Dr 2750. Spain's national carrier, Iberia, has four weekly flights between Casablanca and Madrid and two between Tangier and Madrid.

About the only scheduled flights possibly worth a serious look are those between the Spanish enclave of Melilla and Málaga. A one-way ticket costs 8800 pta, and there are quite a few daily flights.

**Gibraltar** Few travellers will want to fork out large sums of money to fly from 'the Rock' across the strait to Morocco, but it can be done. GB Airways has four weekly direct flights to Casablanca and two each to Tangier and Marrakesh. The one-way flight to Tangier costs from UK£49 to UK£69. To Marrakesh, the range is UK£143 to UK£180 (return UK£270). There are plenty of travel agents in Gibraltar (and in Algeciras) through which you can book tickets. For reservations with the airline in Gibraltar, call ☎ 79300.

GB Airways has various agents in Morocco (noted under the city entries). A one-way fare from Tangier costs Dr 520. The full return fare from Tangier costs Dr 1225, although there is a one-day excursion fare for Dr 620.

**Netherlands** Amsterdam is a popular departure point. Some of the best fares are offered by the student travel agency NBBS Reiswinkels (☎ 620 5071). It has seven branches throughout the city, and its fares are comparable to those of London bucket shops. NBBS Reiswinkels also has branches in Brussels (Belgium).

## To/From Algeria & Tunisia

Air Algérie and RAM have flights to Algiers, but there is not much in the line of discounts. One-way and return tickets go for Dr 1560 and Dr 2170, respectively. The trip to Tunis with Tunis Air costs Dr 2465/3445 one-way/return. It also offers an excursion fare of Dr 2740.

## To/From Mauritania

At the time of writing, the only way you could get a visa for Mauritania was to arm yourself with a return air ticket on Air Mauritanie for Dr 4745.

## To/From North America

The cheapest way from the USA or Canada to Morocco and North Africa is usually a return flight to London or Paris and a bucket-shop deal from there.

RAM flies from New York to Casablanca. It also has flights from Montreal in Canada to Casablanca, via New York. The standard one-way fare from New York is US$839, or US$1678 return. Youth fares are 25% off, and an excursion fare valid for six months costs US$918 return. From Montreal the standard economy fares are C$1386 one way and C$2772 return, while the excursion fare is exactly the same price as the economy one-way ticket.

## To/From Australasia

There are no direct flights between Australia or New Zealand and Morocco. The best bet is to get a flight to Europe and make your way to Morocco from there.

## To/From South Africa

As a sign of South Africa's increasing acceptability in Africa, RAM is considering options for direct flights to Johannesburg.

## LAND

Taking your own vehicle to Morocco is straightforward. In addition to such obvious papers as vehicle registration and preferably an International Driving Permit (although many foreign licences are acceptable), an insurance Green Card is required from the car's insurer. You can get this in Algeciras (Spain) before crossing to Morocco or at the border. See also the introductory Getting There & Away chapter.

## To/From Europe

**Bus** It is possible to get a bus ticket to destinations in Morocco from as far away as London.

*UK* A one-way ticket with Eurolines, in conjunction with the Moroccan national line, Compagnie de Transports Marocains (CTM), to Tangier or Marrakesh costs UK£128 or UK£208 return. The service leaves Victoria coach station (☎ 0171-730 0202), 164 Buckingham Palace Rd, London SW1, four to six days a week, depending on the season (summer is high season) at 10 pm and arrives at the bus station (*gare routière*) in Paris the next day at 7 am. There you change buses and leave at 10.30 am or noon, depending on the service you have been booked onto. The Eurolines office in London (☎ 0171-730 8235) is at 52 Grosvenor Gardens, London SW1W 0AU, and in Paris (☎ 49.72.51.51) at 3-5 Ave Porte de la Villette, 75019 Paris.

The bus travels via Tours and Bordeaux and arrives in Algeciras in southern Spain the next evening for the crossing to Tangier, where you supposedly should land by 9.30 pm.

It is possible to book a ticket right through to one of about 30 destinations, although the timetable for some of these is limited (as few as one a week) and it would seem better to stick to the main centres such as Tangier, Rabat, Marrakesh and the like. Indeed, after

MOROCCO

so much time spent on buses, you may want to get off at the earliest possible moment (Tangier), have a rest and proceed by train or local bus.

**France** From Paris, the fares vary according to final destination and season. One-way tickets to Tangier, Kenitra, Rabat and Casablanca cost FFr730 and FFr880 in the high season (15 May to 7 August). The return fares are FFr1250 and FFr1400, respectively.

To Marrakesh, Agadir, Taroudannt, Tiznit and other destinations in between, one-way and return fares are FFr880/1500 (low season) and FFr1030/1650 (high season). Children between the ages of four and 12 travel for half-price.

Whether starting in Paris or coming from elsewhere (such as London), you must pay a FFr30 embarkation tax. Passengers are allowed to carry 30 kg of luggage free. Each extra kg is another FFr10.

CTM operates buses from Casablanca and most other main cities and towns to France (including Paris, Toulouse, Marseilles and Lyons), Belgium (Brussels and one or two other stops) and northern Italy (Milan, Turin and a couple of other intermediate stops).

Most of the services originate in Casablanca and pass through various other Moroccan cities before crossing the Strait of Gibraltar. You must book at least a week in advance to get a seat. Frequency varies depending on your starting point, but on average there are four or five runs to Paris every week. The runs to Belgium and Italy leave once a week.

Fares vary little, regardless of your point of departure. To most of France (including Paris) and Italy you pay about Dr 1200. To Belgium and northernmost France it's Dr 1440.

**Spain** From Madrid, you can take a bus from the Estación Autobuses Sur (☎ 527 9927), which is not too far from the Atocha railway station. The bus, with Enatcar (Empresa Nacional de Transporte de Viajeros por Carretera), goes to the major ferry port of Algeciras, via Málaga, Torremolinos,

Fuengirola, Marbella and Estepona and takes about 10 hours. There are departures from Madrid at 9.30 am and 11 pm.

From Algeciras, buses doing the reverse route leave at 6 and 9 pm; the 6 pm bus also stops in Granada. The one-way fare is 3385 pta. Enatcar has long-distance buses from Algeciras to Paris (16,900 pta one way) and London (18,500 pta one way) departing Tuesday (and Friday in summer). For information, call ☎ 527 9927 in Madrid or ☎ 665067 in Algeciras.

**Train** It is possible to travel by train from a number of European locations to various jumping-off points for Morocco.

**UK** From London's Victoria station you can get a train ticket to take you all the way through to a number of Moroccan destinations. It is more expensive than the bus, but the tickets are good for two months, which means you could make Morocco part of wider trip through France and Spain. A one-way ticket to Algeciras costs UK£137, and return is UK£225. This trip, leaving at 9.25 am, takes about 48 hours all up, including a 12-hour wait to change trains in Madrid. To Tangier the fares are UK£164 and UK£278.

People under the age of 26 can get 30% off with a Wasteels or BIJ *(billet de jeunesse)* ticket. Such tickets have to include travel across at least one frontier, and you can't make stops until you have left the country of purchase. At Victoria station the Wasteels (☎ 0171-834 7066) office is near platform two. You can also buy these tickets in Morocco for travel into Spain and beyond.

Wasteels offers Eurodomino passes, which entitle the holder to three, five or 10 days' travel on a specific country's network within a one-month period. The fares for 1st-class passes for use in Morocco are UK£35, UK£52 and UK£103, respectively, and UK£25, UK£38 and UK£75 in 2nd class. The tickets cannot be purchased in Morocco itself, and are best for 2nd-class travel and if you are sure you'll want to do a lot of train travel in a short time.

Morocco is part of the Inter-Rail network.

For UK£249, travellers under the age of 26 can purchase an Inter-Rail ticket entitling them to a month of free 2nd-class travel on trains in up to 26 countries in Europe (including Morocco). To do this, they have to be able to prove they have been resident in a European country for at least six months. In practice this rule is often interpreted leniently. In the unlikely event you will want, or be able, to get an Inter-Rail ticket in Morocco, they cost Dr 3150.

Train travel is not that expensive in Morocco, so buying an Inter-Rail ticket just for Morocco would be of dubious value. (People over the age of 26 can now also buy Inter-Rail passes, but they are not valid in Morocco.)

**France** From Paris, the best bet is probably to take the TGV *(train à grande vitesse)* from Gare Montparnasse, changing at Irun for Madrid and on to Algeciras. If you want to do it in one hit, take the 6.55 am train. The trip takes at least 25 hours and the standard adult fare is FFr715 (one way) and FFr1430 (return). There is also a train from Gare Austerlitz at 10.15 pm every day. This journey takes about 33 hours and is more expensive.

**Spain** From Madrid, there is a daily train (the Estrella del Estrecho) from Chamartín station to Algeciras, leaving at 10 pm and arriving at about 9 am the following day. The one-way 2nd-class fare is 5300 pta. Alternatively, you could go from Atocha station at 3.25 pm, changing at Bobadilla and arriving in Algeciras at 10.25 pm. The fare, including a 1000 pta supplement, is 6900 pta. From Algeciras you can connect for the ferry to Ceuta or Tangier. Travelling the other way, the direct train to Chamartín leaves at 9 pm and arrives in Madrid at around 8.45 am. The Estrella Media Luna also leaves at 9 pm for Hendaye on the Spanish-French border. There are a couple of morning trains to Bobadilla, from where you can connect to other destinations.

Alternatively, you could head for Málaga or Almería and take the boat from there to Melilla. There are four trains a day from Chamartín to Málaga, taking from seven to nine hours and costing 4600 pta. The luxury Talgo 200 train runs three times daily between Madrid and Málaga, taking just four hours and forty minutes. The fare is 6000 pta to 9700 pta, depending on what class you choose and when you travel.

There are two trains a day between Almería and Madrid's Atocha station. The faster train is the Talgo, which takes about seven hours to complete the journey and costs 5700 pta. The slower train leaves from Chamartín in Madrid, takes 10 hours and costs 4000 pta. From Almería, there are three trains a day to Granada (1065 pta).

Again, those under the age of 26 could invest in a Wasteels ticket. The trip from Madrid to Marrakesh, including the Algeciras ferry crossing, is 8710 pta one way and 16,030 pta return.

### To/From North Africa

**Bus** CTM has a weekly bus to Tripoli (Libya) from Casablanca on Saturday for Dr 1000, travelling via Algeria and Tunisia. At least one private company, Rostoum, offers a similar run for Dr 750.

From Oujda there are local buses and *grands taxis* to the border, and several daily buses (US$1.50) and taxis to and from Tlemcen on the Algerian side – the latter take about an hour.

**Train** The rail link between Morocco and Algeria (and on to Tunisia), long suspended, has now been up and running for several years.

The Al-Maghreb al-Arabi, as it is known, leaves Casablanca (Casa-Port) every night at 8.35 pm. The journey to Algiers takes about 24 hours, and it's another 20 hours on to Tunis. You have to change trains at the Algerian border and again in Algiers (the latter stop takes about half an hour). Going the other way, the train leaves Tunis at 10.20 am (Tunisian time), arriving at 6.55 am (Algerian time) in Algiers the following day and Casablanca at 8.20 am (Moroccan time) the day after (there's a 3½-hour wait at

Oujda on this leg). Note that these times can vary because of seasonal changes. Algeria and Tunisia both have daylight-saving time; Morocco does not. For the rest of the year, Algeria is on GMT (as is Morocco) and Tunisia is an hour ahead.

The train, also known as the Trans Maghreb Express, runs via Rabat and Fès to Oujda, where Moroccan passport control and customs are carried out. It is also possible to hook up with the train coming from Tangier (this involves a three-hour wait at Fès). Going the other way, you have a four-hour wait at the intermediate station of Sidi Slimane.

From Rabat to Oran (Algeria), the 2nd and 1st-class fares are Dr 222.50/299.50. To Algiers the fares are Dr 273.50/368.50 and to Constantine they're Dr 336.50/452.50. Second and 1st-class fares from Rabat to Tunis (Tunisia) are Dr 446.50/600.50; to Sousse they're Dr 474.50/640.50. For the run to Oujda you can get a couchette for an extra Dr 46.50 (2nd class) or Dr 56 (1st class), which is a worthwhile investment. It is also possible to pay for the more expensive *voiture lit*, or sleeper.

**Car** There are two crossing points between Morocco and Algeria: between Oujda and Tlemcen in the north near the coast and between Figuig and Beni Ounif some 300 km farther south.

In the past, it was necessary for people bringing their own vehicle into Morocco from Algeria to have a telex from their embassy in Rabat guaranteeing that they would take the vehicle out of the country. This may now have lapsed but it's worth checking well in advance, as getting such a telex can take up to a couple of weeks.

### To/From Mauritania

Although a UN cease-fire has kept the Western Sahara quiet since September 1991, it is still difficult to cross the border into Mauritania. Since early 1994, the Moroccans have been issuing travel permits in Dakhla and escorting civilian convoys to the border. However, the Mauritanian embassy in Rabat

will not issue visas for overland travel, which would seem to cast doubt on the feasibility of such plans (French citizens do not need visas, and so probably can get through). It is worth checking the latest situation with the Mauritanian embassy, and it may also be worth trying to get an overland visa at a Mauritanian embassy outside Morocco.

## SEA
### To/From France
**Sète-Tangier** This car-ferry service, considerably more luxurious than those linking Spain and Morocco (with a swimming pool and a nightclub of sorts on board), and commensurately more expensive, is operated by the Compagnie Marocaine de Navigation (Comanav). The crossing is made between six and seven times per month, usually once every four to five days. As a rule, the ferry, which can carry 634 passengers and 220 vehicles, leaves Sète at 7 pm and Tangier at 6 pm (local time).

The trip takes 36 to 38 hours and the fare, depending on class, is between FFr1250 and FFr2100 (or FFr2130 and FFr3570 return) in shared cabins of two to four people. If you want to have a cabin to yourself, you'll be up for about another FFr1000. There are sometimes supplements to be paid on top of the fare. Children between the ages of two and 11 travel for half-price. Cars under four metres long cost FFr1540.

There are special reduced fares per passenger and vehicle for students and people aged under 26. A berth in a cabin of four costs FFr880 to FFr950.

You can book tickets for this ferry service at Southern Ferries (☎ 0171-491 4968; fax 0171-491 3502), 179 Piccadilly, London W1V 9DB, or in France at SNCM Ferryterranée (☎ 49.24.24.24; fax 91.56.36.66), 12 Rue Godot de Mauroy, 75009 Paris. The Sète (☎ 67.74.96.96; fax 67.74.93.05) office is at 4 Quai d'Alger, 34202 Sète. There are also agents in Germany, Italy, Belgium, Holland and Switzerland.

In Morocco, Comanav's (☎ 302412; fax 300790) main office is in Casablanca, at 7 Blvd de la Résistance. In Tangier, Comanav's

(☎ 932649; fax 943570) office is at 43 Ave Abou al-Alaa al-Maari.

**Sète-Nador** The same company runs a similar service at much the same rates between Sète and Nador in the high season (mid-June to mid-September).

**To/From Spain**

A variety of car ferries are operated by companies such as Compañía Trasmediterranea, Islena de Navigación SA, Comarit, Limadet and Transtour. Jetfoils also make the crossing from Algeciras to Tangier and Ceuta. The most popular service is the Algeciras-Tangier route, although for car owners the service to Ceuta might be more worthwhile because of the availability of tax-free petrol in the enclave. The others are Tarifa-Tangier, Almería-Melilla and Málaga-Melilla. The majority are car ferries of the drive-on and drive-off variety.

On most routes, more boats are put on in the high season, from 15 June until 15 September.

If you want the latest information on Trasmediterranea's services prior to turning up at one of the ports, you could contact Southern Ferries (☎ 0171-491 4968) at 179 Piccadilly, London W1V 9DB, or the Trasmediterranea offices in Madrid (☎ 431 0700) at Calle Pedro Muñoz Seca 2 and in Barcelona (☎ 412 2524) at the Estación Marítima, Muelle Barcelona 1.

There are various reductions available on some of the services. Pensioners from EU nations and people under 26 should enquire about them before buying tickets.

**Algeciras-Tangier** Trasmediterranea, the government-run company, runs at least nine car ferries daily between Algeciras and Tangier in tandem with Islena de Navigación, Comarit and Limadet. Depending on demand, the number of boats can rise to about 20. It doesn't matter whose boat you end up on, as the fares remain the same, although there are a few variations: on Comarit's boats children up to the age of four go for free, whereas the limit is two years old

on Trasmediterranea's boats (in both cases children up to the age of 12 pay half-price). In addition to each line's official outlet at the Estación Marítima in Algeciras, there is a plethora of other ticket offices at the port and along the waterfront.

The crossing takes 2½ hours. The one-way adult fare is 2700 pta, and the fee for cars is between 8500 pta and 14,000 pta, depending on the dimensions of the car. If you happen to be considered a Moroccan resident, the fares are reduced. Motorbikes and bicycles cost 2400 pta. You can usually pay for your ticket with a credit card on the Spanish side.

Holders of Eurail and Inter-Rail passes are entitled to a 20% discount on ferry tickets between Algeciras and Tangier and should make a point of asking for it. This can prove more problematic on the Moroccan side.

Trasmediterranea's jetfoil service is a quicker (some would say more nauseating) deal if you don't have a vehicle. It leaves Algeciras daily at 9.30 am and Tangier at 3.30 pm. In the high season there is usually a second service in the afternoon. The run takes an hour and the fares are the same as on the ferry.

The fare per person from Tangier on both ferry and jetfoil is Dr 196. Cars up to six metres long cost Dr 618, and Dr 290 more for every metre extra. Bikes and motorbikes attract a charge of Dr 175.

Spanish passport control is quite straightforward leaving Algeciras, but customs can be slow coming from Morocco. Leaving Tangier, you must fill in an exit form before getting your passport stamped and boarding. You should be given one when you buy your ticket. There are hordes of people pretending to be officials of one sort or another (most of them *écrivains publics* – public scribes!) who will try to get one last dirham out of you before you leave. One of their services is to give you an exit form and lend you a pen to fill it out. If you approach the port at Tangier on foot, there'll usually be a few of them around trying to create a sense of urgency and bustling you about, or guiding you to a boat (not all boats dock at the main port). All these people want money, so if you're not feeling overly generous, watch out for them.

You can buy tickets in the main port building, although the booths are not always open (this is when the 'public scribes' come into their own, producing tickets as if from nowhere). You must pay for the ticket in cash. There are a few banks represented just outside the terminal, and you'll have to change a bit more of your hard-earned money if you don't have enough Dr to buy a ticket. They should open by 7 am (before the first departure), but this rarely happens.

Tangier is swamped with agencies where you can buy tickets but, as a rule, you are best advised to go to the port early and get a ticket on the spot.

**Algeciras-Ceuta** There are at least six ferry and six jetfoil crossings daily on this route in either direction, except on Sunday, when there are only four. Around Easter and Christmas the number of services can rise to 10 each way.

The ferry trip takes 1½ hours and the fare is 1625 pta (1700 pta in the high season; children between two and 11 pay half-price). Vehicles between 2.5 and six metres long cost from 7500 pta to 13,650 pta, depending on dimensions. Motorbikes cost from 1700 pta to 2550 pta, depending on engine size.

The jetfoil costs adults 2650 pta one way (2700 pta in the high season) and double that fare for a return. The trip takes about 30 minutes.

**Tarifa-Tangier** There is a daily ferry from Tarifa to Tangier (one hour; 2700 pta/Dr 196 per person) at 10 am (9 am on Friday). It sets off from Tangier at 4 pm from Monday to Thursday and at 7 am and 4 pm on Saturday. Costs for cars are identical to those for the Algeciras-Tangier ferries. In Tarifa, you can buy your tickets on the morning at the dock or from Viajes Marruecotur (☎ 681821; fax 680256), Calle Batalla del Salado 57.

Should you land in Tarifa from Morocco, the bus station is Calle Batalla del Salado. There are occasional departures for Seville, Cádiz, Huelva, Jerez and La Linea (Gibral-

tar), and regular runs to Algeciras (14 km to the west; 195 pta).

**Almería-Melilla** The timetable for services between Almería and the Spanish enclave of Melilla is not quite so straightforward. In the low season there is generally a ferry from Almería at 1 pm daily except Sunday and Monday, and at 11.30 pm on Sunday. There is no boat on Monday. Going the other way, there is a departure every day except Sunday at 11.30 pm.

In the high season (from mid-June to mid-September), the timetable operates on a system of alternating weeks, under which there are two ferries four days a week (Monday, Wednesday, Friday and Sunday) at 2 am and 6 pm and one at 10 am on the other days one week, and the reverse every other week.

The trip takes 6½ to eight hours. The cheapest fare *(butaca turista* or deck) is 3050 pta (3150 pta in the high season) each way. You can also get beds in cabins of four or two, some with toilets. Prices range from 5000 pta a head for four to 8500 pta for single occupation of a twin-berth cabin. Fares are a little higher in the high season. Children from two to 12 years of age travel for half-price (infants go free). A car can cost from 7550 pta to 22,650 pta in the low season, depending on the vehicle's dimensions. You also pay to take across motorbikes. You can buy tickets at the Estación Marítima (about a 10 to 15-minute walk from the rail and bus stations) or from travel agents in the centre of town. They accept credit cards.

If you arrive in Almería from Morocco, you can push on into Spain by train or bus. The train station is about 10 minutes' walk off to the right from the port. The bus station is five minutes' walk farther down the road in front of the railway station. Trains to Granada leave at 6 am and 1 and 5 pm. The Talgo to Madrid leaves at 2.15 pm and the slower train leaves at 10.05 pm. For fare details see the previous Train section. There are six buses a day to Granada, and a handful of connections to Seville, Córdoba and Cádiz.

**Málaga-Melilla** Also operated by Trasmediterranea, these ferries leave Málaga daily but Sunday in the low season at 1 pm and Melilla at 11 pm (occasionally an exceptional Sunday service is put on). In the high season the Sunday service is permanent. The journey time is 7½ to 10 hours and fares are the same as for the Almería-Melilla ferry. As in Almería, you can buy tickets most easily at the Estación Marítima, more or less directly south from the town centre.

### To/From Gibraltar

**Gibraltar-Tangier** Twice a week, the *Idriss I* ferry links Gibraltar with Tangier. The voyage costs UK£16 one way and UK£27 return. The ferry can carry up to 30 cars (the charge is UK£30) and runs all year, leaving Gibraltar at 8.30 am on Monday and 6.30 pm on Friday. From Tangier, it leaves at 9 am on Friday and 5 pm on Sunday. The Gibraltar agent is Tourafrica (☎ 79140; fax 76754), 2a Main St. The ferry departs from the nearby North Mole. Several Tangier travel agents can sell you tickets for the Gibraltar ferry. They cost Dr 220 per person and Dr 480 for a car up to 4.5 metres long. On Friday, you can pay the one-way fare for a same-day return excursion. The trip takes about two hours.

**Gibraltar-Tetouan** Jasmine Lines sometimes runs a catamaran to Restinga Smir (a little north of Tetouan), usually in the summer, but inclement weather often leads to cancellations. When the going is good (in summer), it runs four or five times a week, costing UK£16.50 one way and UK£27.70 return. The agent is Parodytur (☎ 76070; fax 70563), in the Cazes Arcade, 143 Main St.

### TOURS

A growing number of operators are dedicating more effort to organised trips to Morocco. More than 40 agencies operate out of the UK alone, and although the ONMT in London keeps a list of them, the Paris equivalent does not. Before diving into something, it pays to do a bit of research. The ONMT in your country is a good place to begin. Possibilities range from the more traditional style of tour of the imperial cities through beach holidays, golf trips, trekking, bird-watching and desert safaris.

The following information is only intended as a guide to the options, and not as a recommendation of the operators. It should be remembered that the programs on such trips are usually tight, leaving little room for roaming around on your own. But they do take much of the hassle away. Shop around and check itinerary and ticketing details, accommodation, documentation services, insurance and tour conditions carefully.

### From the UK

**Morocco Specialists** In the UK, Best of Morocco (☎ 01380-828533; fax 01380-828630), at Seend Park, Seend, Wiltshire SN12 6NZ, is one of the better established tour operators. It offers horse-trekking tours, Land Rover safaris in the Sahara and a host of other possibilities. Its seven-day tour of the imperial cities costs about UK£700, depending on the season, including flights, transfers, four-star hotels (which should be treated with a pinch of salt) and meals. Two days of white-water rafting in the Middle Atlas can cost as little UK£300, depending on numbers.

The Moroccan-run Moroccan Sun (☎ 0171-437 3968; fax 0171-287 9127) and Morocco Bound (☎ 0171-734 5307; fax 0171-287 9127), both at Triumph House, 189 Regent St, London W1R 7WB, organise classic itineraries such as circuits of the imperial cities. They also offer activity holidays ranging from golf trips to bird-watching and trekking. Morocco Bound has a series of possible short-break trips for people who want a quick escape from the UK and a taste of Morocco.

**Adventure Tours** Quite a few adventure-travel specialists do tours to Morocco, as well as organising long trips which cross the length and breadth of Africa and travel through Morocco along the way. These trips usually involve a group of people travelling in a communal fashion on board an overland truck. You share tents, food and time. Considering that some of these trips can last as long as 30 weeks, there is a certain amount of risk involved that it won't be quite what you were hoping for. If you don't get on with your fellow travellers (or they don't get on with you!), or you simply want to branch off on your own, you have to forfeit your money. On the other hand, such trips can remove much of the bureaucratic hassle of traipsing through Africa, and you benefit from the experience of tour leaders who have (usually) been around before and can anticipate problems.

You could try the Africa Travel Shop in London and perusing the free *TNT* magazine will turn up a selection of operators to Africa. Encounter Overland (☎ 0171-370 6951; fax 0171-244 9373), at 267 Old Brompton Rd, London SW5 9JA, is one such operator. Other names worth looking out for are Africa Explored and Dragoman.

Guerba Expeditions (☎ 01373-826689; fax 01373-858351) runs shorter (usually about two weeks) trips for trekking in the Atlas Mountains or slightly longer Saharan 'experiences'. Its tours start at about UK£500.

**Other Tours** For a more exclusively cultural holiday, you could do worse than check out what British Museum Tours (☎ 0171-323 8895; fax 0171-436 7315), 46 Bloomsbury St, London WC1B 3QQ, has to offer. Tours of the imperial cities are the speciality, accompanied by expert lecturers. You'd be looking at more than UK£1000 for 11 days.

Ramblers Holidays (☎ 01707-331133; fax 01707-333276), Box 43, Welwyn Garden, Hertfordshire AL8 6PQ, is one of several UK tour operators that organises walking holidays in the Atlas.

### From France

As already noted, there are any number of agencies and tour operators to turn to in France.

In addition to those noted in the previous Air section, a number specialise in trekking tours to Morocco. Terres d'Aventure (☎ 43.29.94.50), 16 Rue Saint-Victor, 75005 Paris, has been running walking trips to various parts of Morocco, including the High Atlas and the southern oases, since 1976. Allibert (☎ 48.06.16.61), 39 Rue du Chemin Vert, 75011 Paris, is another such operator.

### From Spain

If you're in Spain, the best way to experience Morocco is simply to head down independently through southern Spain. However, if your time is limited, it might be worth considering a package tour, of which there are plenty on offer (particularly through the summer).

Solafrica, for instance, has four-day long weekends in Marrakesh from about 60,000 pta, depending on the quality of the hotel.

Juliatours offers a range of eight-day and 15-day tours ranging from 60,000 to 90,000 pta, including flights, accommodation and tour.

Mundo Joven and Akali Joven are among the operators offering bus trips for younger people into Morocco from Madrid and other Spanish cities. These tours typically start at about 35,000 pta for about a week, with tours of about two weeks costing about 60,000 pta. Some of them concentrate on less challenging elements like the beaches, while others follow what are becoming fairly well-trodden routes around the imperial cities, Atlas Mountains or Sahara.

### LEAVING MOROCCO

There is no departure tax on leaving Morocco, and departure formalities are straightforward. You must fill in an exit card and have your passport stamped before exiting.

# Getting Around

## AIR

If your time is limited, it's worth considering the occasional internal flights offered by RAM or its subsidiary, Royal Air Inter.

Several reductions are available. If you buy a return ticket for internal flights, you get 25% off the normal one-way fares. If you're under the age of 22 or a student aged under 31, you are entitled to 25% off all fares. There are group reductions and children aged between two to 12 travel at half-price. Generally these reductions can only be had through RAM offices and not through travel agents. Beware of the 'Discover Morocco' vouchers which are sometimes offered by the airline's overseas offices. They are supposed to give you a set number of discounted internal flights, but travellers have reported that airline staff in Morocco simply won't accept them.

For an idea of what you'll pay, the standard one-way fare from Casablanca to Fès is Dr 405 (about US$45), and Fès to Agadir one way is Dr 810 (US$90). Casablanca to Marrakesh one way is Dr 340 (US$38).

Internal airports serviced by RAM are Agadir, Al-Hoceima, Casablanca, Dakhla, Er-Rachidia, Fès, Goulimine, Kenitra, Laayoune, Marrakesh, Ouarzazate, Oujda, Rabat, Smara, Tan Tan, Tangier and Tetouan. About the longest flight you could take is the weekly Dakhla-Tangier run via Casablanca, which takes six hours and 50 minutes the return flight is shorter because there's no stop in Marrakesh en route. Most internal flights involve a connection in Casablanca.

Among the direct flights, there are at least two daily runs between Marrakesh and Casablanca (35 minutes). Four times a week there is a direct flight from Marrakesh to Agadir (45 minutes), and once a week to Fès (1¼ hours). Agadir is also connected by two weekly direct flights to Laayoune and Dakhla, and one to Tan Tan. Up to three flights connect Tangier with Casablanca (55

minutes). You can pick up a free timetable from most RAM offices.

## BUS

A dense network of buses operates throughout Morocco, and many private companies compete for business alongside the main national carrier, CTM. The latter is the only firm to have a truly national service. In most cities or towns there is a single central bus station, but CTM occasionally maintains a separate terminal, and there are sometimes other stations for a limited number of fairly local destinations. CTM tends to be a little more expensive than the other lines, but often there is only a few Dr in it. Bus fares work out to about Dr 1 for every four or five km, and are comparable to 2nd-class fares on normal trains.

Supratours runs a subsidiary bus service in conjunction with the railways (see Train later in this chapter).

### Compagnie de Transports Marocains
The best and most secure bus company in Morocco, CTM serves most destinations of interest to travellers. As part of Morocco's program of economic reform, CTM was privatised in May 1994.

CTM offers different classes (*mumtaz* – 'excellent' – and 1st and 2nd class), but the distinction seems to be made mostly on longer routes away from the big centres. Always ask about different fares, but where there is only one quoted, the official line is usually that you are getting a mumtaz bus. Children four years old and older pay full fare.

Where possible, especially if services are infrequent or do not originate in the place you want to leave, it is not a bad idea to book ahead. Unfortunately, it is not always possible to do so. Of the more popular places travellers get to, Chefchaouen can be one of the most painful to get out of again.

CTM buses are fairly modern and comfortable. Mumtaz buses have videos (a mixed blessing) and heating in winter (they sometimes overdo this). The first 20 seats are theoretically reserved for nonsmokers.

Sample mumtaz fares are as follows:

| From | To | Fare | Hours |
|------|-----|------|-------|
| Casablanca | Agadir | Dr 117.50 | 10 hours |
| | Marrakesh | Dr 57.50 | 4½ hours |
| Fès | Casablanca | Dr 69 | 5 hours |
| | Oujda | Dr 60 | 6 hours |
| | Tangier | Dr 77.50 | 6 hours |
| Marrakesh | Agadir | Dr 63 | 4 hours |
| | Fès | Dr 115 | 9 hours |
| | Ouarzazate | Dr 49 | 3 hours |
| Tangier | Agadir | Dr 205.50 | 15 hours |
| | Casablanca | Dr 88 | 7 hours |
| | Marrakesh | Dr 146 | 11 hours |

There is an official charge for baggage on CTM buses. Once you have bought your ticket you get a baggage tag (hang on to this; you'll need it when you arrive). The charge for your average backpack is about Dr 3 to Dr 4.

### Other Companies

The other bus companies are all privately owned and only operate regionally. The biggest of them is SATAS, which operates from Casablanca south and is every bit as good as CTM. Some of the others are two-bit operations with one or two well-worn buses, so the degree of comfort can be a matter of pot luck. Some of the stations seem like mad houses, and touts run about screaming out any number of destinations for buses about to depart. Occasionally you'll find would-be guides, anxious to help you to the right ticket booth – for a small consideration of course.

Some companies offer 1st and 2nd class, although the difference in fare and comfort is rarely great. On the secondary runs you can often buy your tickets on the bus, but if you do you'll probably have to stand. They also tend to stop an awful lot. More often than not you'll be charged for baggage, especially if it's going on top of the bus. You should not pay more than Dr 2, but foreigners frequently find themselves quite forcefully obliged to hand over Dr 5 per item.

These buses rarely have heating in winter, even when crossing the High Atlas, so have plenty of warm clothing with you. Occasionally buses are held up by snow drifts in mountain passes; then you'll really feel the cold. The Marrakesh-Ouarzazate road is prone to this.

### TRAIN

Morocco's Office National des Chemins de Fer (ONCF) operates one of the most modern rail systems in Africa, linking most of the main centres. The trains, mostly Belgian-made, are generally comfortable and fast, and are preferable to buses. Lines go as far south as Marrakesh, and a new one is planned from there to Agadir and on to Laayoune.

Timetables for the whole system are posted in French at most stations. It is occasionally possible to get hold of a handy pocket-sized timetable called the *Indicateur des Horaires*.

### Classes

There are two types of train and two classes on each (1st and 2nd), giving four possible fares for any given trip. The main difference between the normal trains and the *rapides* is not, as the name suggests, speed (there is rarely any difference), but comfort and air-conditioning. Second class is more than adequate on any journey, and on normal trains 2nd-class fares are commensurate with bus fares.

**Sleepers** You can get couchettes on the overnight trains from Marrakesh to Tangier and from Casablanca to Oujda. They are worth the extra money and cost Dr 46.50 in 2nd class or Dr 56 in 1st class.

On the Al-Maghreb al-Arabi train from Casablanca to Oujda and on to Algeria you can also get a proper sleeper (single or twin). The full fare per person to Oujda is Dr 359 in the twin and Dr 406 in the single.

### Reservations

You are advised to buy tickets at the station, as a supplement is charged for doing so on

|   |   |
|---|---|
| A | B |
| C | D |
| E | F |

A Boys at wedding, Libya (AJ)  B Bread baked in campfire, Douz, Tunisia (DW)
C Shepherds, Morocco (DS)  D Old Libyan men, Sirtic Desert, Libya (AJ)
E Revolutionary Guards, Libya (AJ)  F Moroccan boys on Tafraoute-Agadir road (DS)

|     |     |
|-----|-----|
| A   | B   |
| C   | D   |
| E   | F   |

A Turkish fountain, Tripoli Castle, Libya (AJ)  B Doorway, Marrakesh, Morocco (DS
C Serpent Fountain, Tripoli Castle, Libya (AJ)  D Garamantes Chariot, Acacus, Liby
E Leptis Magna, Libya (AJ)  F Gazelle Fountain, Tripoli, Libya (A

the train. Although you can buy a ticket up to six days in advance, there are no reserved seats, so it seems a little pointless. A ticket is technically valid for five days, so that you can use it to get off at intermediate stops before reaching your final destination. You need to ask for a *bulletin d'arrêt* at the intermediate stop. Always hang on to tickets, as inspectors check them on the trains and they are collected at the station on arrival.

### Costs

Children under four travel free. Those up to 12 years old get a reduction of between 10% to 50%, depending on the service.

Sample 2nd-class fares in normal and rapide trains include:

| From | To | Fare | Hours |
| --- | --- | --- | --- |
| Casablanca | Marrakesh | Dr 52.50/ 66.50 | 4 hours |
| | Oujda | Dr 142/ 179.50 | 11 hours |
| Rabat | Fès | Dr 59.50/ 62.50 | 3½ hours |
| | Marrakesh | Dr 71/90 | 4½ hours |
| | Tangier | Dr 62.50/79 | 5 hours |
| Tangier | Casablanca | Dr 81.50/ 103 | 6 hours |
| | Fès | Dr 66/84 | 6 hours |
| | Marrakesh | Dr 134/169 | 10 hours |

### Shuttles

In addition to the normal and rapide trains, there are express shuttles (TNR) running frequently between Kenitra, Rabat, Casablanca and Mohammed V Airport. From Rabat to Casablanca you pay Dr 19 in 2nd class (normal) and Dr 24 in 2nd class (rapide and TNR). The 1st-class fares are Dr 28 (normal), Dr 34 (rapide) and Dr 43 (TNR). For more on airport connections, see the Getting Around sections for Casablanca and Rabat.

### Supratours Buses

The ONCF runs buses through Supratours to widen its network. Thus Nador, near Melilla on the Mediterranean coast, is linked to the Oujda-Casablanca lines by a special bus to Taourirt station. Tetouan is linked to the main line from Tangier by bus to Tnine Sidi Lyamani. Rail passengers heading farther south than Marrakesh can link up with buses for Essaouira, Agadir, Smara, Laayoune and Dakhla.

## TAXI

### Grands Taxis

Shared taxis (grands taxis or *taxiat kebira* in Arabic) link towns to their nearest neighbours in a kind of leapfrogging system. Usually ageing Mercedes imported from Europe, they take six passengers and leave when full. There are fixed-rate fares, generally a little higher than on the buses, but attempts to extract more from foreigners are not uncommon – try to see what other passengers are paying. When asking about fares, make it clear you want to pay for a *plasa* ('place', presumably a corruption of the Spanish *plaza*) in a *taxi collectif*. Another expression that helps explain you don't want to hire a taxi for yourself is that you wish to travel *ma'a an-nas* ('with other people').

As a rule, they are faster on shorter runs than the buses because they don't make as many stops. There are, however, certain disadvantages. Six people is a tight fit, and longer trips can be quite uncomfortable.

Worse, the bigger cities are littered with grand taxi stops, but there are several subspecies of this particular beast, which are impossible for the outsider to differentiate. They either do set routes within a town or more or less behave like normal urban taxis (*petits taxis* – see Local Transport later in this chapter).

Now, if it were just a matter of asking and being told, 'No, this is not where to get the interurban grands taxis to such-and-such a destination', it would not be so bad. The fact is, you will almost always be told that they are prepared to take you wherever you want to go – for a price. And they won't tell you where the interurban grand taxi stand is for the destination you want. To hire a grand taxi (these special rides are called *corsa*, presumably because many city taxis have Italian meters displaying the *prezzo della corsa* – the 'price of the trip', or fare) in this way can be a reasonable idea if you have six people –

you can organise to have the driver stop along the way for photo opportunities. Otherwise it's no help at all. The Ziz and Drâa valleys and the Tizi n'Test Pass particularly lend themselves to shared taxis, and there are many other scenic routes.

Appropriate grand taxi stops have been marked on maps and fares mentioned in individual city entries.

### Pick-Up & Land Rover

In some of the more remote parts of the country, especially in the Atlas Mountains, about the only way you can get around from village to village is by local Berber market pick-up trucks, which is how the locals do it. This is a bumpy but adventurous way to get to know the country and its people a little better, but can mean waiting even days at a time for the next lift. Land Rover taxis also operate on the more remote piste routes that would destroy normal taxis.

### CAR & MOTORBIKE

The roads connecting the main centres are pretty good in most of Morocco, and plenty of people bring their own cars and motorbikes into the country. There are many places you simply cannot reach without private transport, so a vehicle can be a definite advantage.

### Road Rules

In Morocco you drive on the right, as in continental Europe.

Daylight driving is generally no problem, and even in the bigger cities it is not too stress-laden in the modern villes nouvelles. You'd need to have your head examined if you wanted to drive into the medinas. When in towns, note that you should give way to traffic entering a roundabout from the right when you're already on one (quite a departure from prevailing rules in Europe). Speed limits in built-up areas range from 40 to 60 km/h.

Outside the towns there is a national speed limit of 100 km/h, rising to 120 km/h on the only stretch of motorway, between Rabat and Casablanca. A new motorway is being built between Rabat and Tangier. The Rabat-Casablanca run is actually a toll road – you pay Dr 10 about halfway along.

Many minor roads are too narrow for normal vehicles to pass without going onto the shoulder. You'll find yourself hitting the dirt a lot in this way. Stones thrown up by on-coming vehicles present a danger for windscreens – locals (drivers or front-seat passengers) press their hands against the inside of the windscreens to reduce the chances of debris shattering the glass. This also makes driving at night a pretty fraught experience.

Be aware that driving across the mountain ranges in winter can easily involve negotiating a passage through snow and ice. This kind of driving is obviously dangerous. If a strong chergui wind is blowing and carrying a lot of dust, you should wait until it eases to prevent doing considerable damage to your car.

### Roadblocks

Morocco's roads are festooned with police and customs roadblocks. Be sure to stop at all of them and put on your sunniest smile – with luck you should be waved through about half of them. For the rest, you'll have to show your passport and answer lots of silly questions (not knowing how to speak French or Arabic may well speed up the process!). Some of these blocks come with tyre-eating traps, so keep your eyes peeled.

### Parking Attendants

In most towns there are parking zones watched by *gardiens*. The going rate is a few Dr for a few hours and Dr 10 overnight. The parking attendants are not a guarantee of safety, but they do provide some peace of mind.

### Fuel

Petrol is readily available just about everywhere. Super and lead-free petrol *(sans plomb* – found only sporadically) cost Dr 6.98 a litre, and diesel is Dr 3.99 a litre. Normal petrol *(essence)* is not so commonly available. Costs rise the farther you get from the north-west of the country. Super costs up to Dr 7.11 south of Marrakesh and towards Oujda in the east. The big exception is the territory of Western Sahara. Petrol here is sold by the Atlas Sahara service station chain and is tax free. It costs about a third less than in the rest of Morocco. Heading south, the first of these stations is just outside Tarfaya, on the road to Laayoune. If heading north, stock up as much as you can here.

The same situation applies in the Spanish enclaves of Ceuta and Melilla, so drivers heading to Morocco and mainland Spain via the enclaves should do their best to arrive there with a near-empty tank.

### Mechanics & Repairs

Moroccan mechanics are generally pretty good, but it's best to try to find a well-disposed local to help with buying parts, such as replacement tyres, in order to keep the price closer to local levels.

### Car Rental

Most of the major car-rental companies have representatives throughout Morocco, including Hertz, Avis, Budget and Europcar/InterRent. There are also many local agencies. Renting a car in Morocco is not cheap, but you can strike bargains with some of the smaller dealers, and with four people it becomes affordable. The competition is greatest in Casablanca, and there are many agencies in Marrakesh, Tangier and Fès. The cheapest cars are the Renault 4 and Fiat Uno.

Cars rented from a major company are not necessarily better than those from a local company; what differs is the degree of service or help you can get in the event of a breakdown. Major companies will replace a car from their nearest depot if there are problems; local companies often don't have branch offices so there isn't much they can do. In any event, make an effort to get a look at the car yourself before you sign up.

In many cases you can hire in one place and leave the car elsewhere, although this usually involves a fee if you want to leave it in a city where the company has no branch.

Always haggle for a discount when renting a car, especially if it's for an extended period. Most companies offer excellent discounts for rentals over one month. Without even trying, many will automatically offer 25% off their quoted rates on longer rentals.

Compare the prices shown in the Car Rental table. The table is intended as a general guide only; for example, some of the models are put into different categories by different companies. Most of the savings are on rentals for seven days or more.

The rates in the table do not include a government tax of 19% that you must pay on all rentals. It's also advisable to take out Collision Damage Waiver insurance (around Dr 40 to Dr 100 per day, depending on the make of car and the company), as otherwise you'll be liable for the first Dr 3000 to Dr 5000 (depending on the company) in the event of an accident. You may also want to take out personal insurance (around Dr 30 per day).

Most companies demand a (returnable) deposit of Dr 3000 to Dr 5000 in cash when you hire the car, unless you're paying by credit card, in which case it's waived. The minimum age for drivers is 21 years, with at least one year's driving experience. An international driving licence is technically required, but most agencies will accept your national licence.

All companies charge from Dr 35 to more than Dr 100 (depending on make) per hour that you go over time on the return date. After the first two or three hours this becomes a full extra day's rent.

Virtually all cars take super petrol. Keep receipts for oil changes and, should they be necessary, mechanical repairs – these costs should be reimbursed.

Few companies seem to offer motorbike hire. In Agadir you'll find plenty of booths in among the big hotels that hire out scooters – you're looking at about Dr 80 per day.

Addresses of the international companies and a couple of local ones appear under individual city entries but, in Casablanca especially, it is worth doing some legwork.

MOROCCO

## CAR RENTAL

### Major Companies

| category | model | cost with km... | | unlimited km | |
|----------|-------|-----------------|----------|--------------|-----------|
| | | per day | per km | 3 days | 7 days + |
| A | Renault 4 | Dr 250 | Dr 2.50 | Dr 1962 | Dr 3437 |
| B | Fiat Uno | Dr 280 | Dr 2.80 | Dr 2400 | Dr 4200 |
| C | Peugeot 205 | Dr 330 | Dr 3.30 | Dr 2826 | Dr 4949 |
| D | Peugeot 309 | Dr 440 | Dr 4.40 | Dr 3768 | Dr 6594 |
| E | Renault 19 | Dr 525 | Dr 5.25 | Dr 4500 | Dr 7875 |
| F | Peugeot 405 | Dr 600 | Dr 6.00 | Dr 5139 | Dr 8995 |

### Local Companies

| category | model | cost with km... | | unlimited km | |
|----------|-------|-----------------|----------|--------------|-----------|
| | | per day | per km | 3 days | 7 days + |
| A | Renault 4 | Dr 170 | Dr 1.70 | Dr 1270 | Dr 2265 |
| B | Fiat Uno | Dr 210 | Dr 2.10 | Dr 1670 | Dr 2985 |
| C | Peugeot 205 | Dr 250 | Dr 2.50 | Dr 1985 | Dr 3450 |
| D | Peugeot 309 | Dr 320 | Dr 3.20 | Dr 2290 | Dr 3950 |

## BICYCLE

There's no reason not to take a bicycle into Morocco – there is no better way to see some of the beautiful countryside. However, you need to be pretty fit to cover a lot of the territory. The biggest problem on secondary roads is that they tend to be narrow and dusty, and the traffic none too forgiving. It is possible to transport bikes on trains and buses, although on the latter they may well take a beating.

On the whole, bicycles are not much help in cities like Marrakesh and Fès, which are best explored on foot.

Remember to take decent supplies (lots of drinking water) and a good repair kit whenever you are on the road. When you are in more remote parts of the country in particular, you will need to be almost self-sufficient.

Mountain biking is another possibility. There are plenty of trails away from the well-worn tourist paths to explore. If you don't want to take your own, some hotels in Marrakesh organise mountain-bike trips into the High Atlas.

## HITCHING

Hitching is never entirely safe in any country in the world, and we don't recommend it. Travellers who decide to hitch should understand that they are taking a small but potentially serious risk. However, many people do choose to hitch, and the advice that follows should help to make their journeys as fast and safe as possible.

Hitching in Morocco demands a thick skin and considerable diplomatic expertise in the north due to aggressive hustlers. They simply won't take 'no' for an answer and feign outrage if you express lack of interest in whatever they're trying to sell you – usually drugs. It's particularly bad on the road between Tetouan and Tangier. Giving lifts to people in these areas is similarly a bad idea.

It goes without saying that people, especially women, attempting to hitch are placing themselves at risk.

More often than not drivers expect some money for picking you up, so it as well to offer a little – it may be refused, but more likely not. Keep in mind what public transport fares would be so that, should you strike someone trying to extort silly amounts from you, you'll know what *not* to give.

## WALKING

There is plenty of good walking and trekking

in the Middle and High Atlas. See the section on High Atlas Trekking.

## LOCAL TRANSPORT

### Bus

The bigger cities, such as Casablanca, Rabat, Marrakesh, Fès and Meknès, have public bus services. They are especially good for crossing from the ville nouvelle of a city to the medina, and there are a few other useful runs. Tickets usually cost around the Dr 2 to Dr 3 mark.

### Taxi

Cities and bigger towns have local petits taxis, a different colour for every city. They are licensed to carry up to three passengers and are often metered. They are not permitted to go beyond the city limits. Where they are not metered (or don't use the meter), you'll have to set a price in advance. It's like everything else; many of the drivers are perfectly honest and some are rotten. As already noted, many grands taxis will also do city runs. They certainly do not have meters and

you'll have to set a price or, if you're sure of yourself, simply pay what you think is right. Multiple hire is the rule rather than the exception, so you can get half-full cabs if they are going your way. From 8 pm, there is a 50% surcharge.

## TOURS

There are plenty of travel and tour agents scattered around the big cities, but most seem quite surprised by individuals walking in off the street asking about tours. If you want an organised tour around Morocco, do it from home (see Tours in the Getting There & Away chapter).

One exception to the rule is Marrakesh, from where you can organise trips down to Ouarzazate and Zagora and the like through agencies and hotels. They also put together walking, mountain-bike and other excursions into the High Atlas. Agadir is another centre for package excursions. For more information, refer to the Marrakesh and Agadir entries.

# The Mediterranean Coast & the Rif

From those two bastions of Spanish tenacity, the enclaves of Ceuta and Melilla, to the cosmopolitan hustle and hassle of Tangier and the contrasting laid-back ambience of Chefchaouen in the Rif Mountains, northern Morocco offers a diverse range of experiences for the independent traveller.

East of Chefchaouen, the Rif presents a spectacular mountain crest trip through the unfortunately dodgy Ketama area – the heartland of kif cultivation. Those who brave the hustlers will be rewarded by the views, and a couple of modest Mediterranean resorts where the Rif makes a rare concession and gives way to beaches – Al-Hoceima and Saidia.

## Tangier

For more than 2500 years people have inhabited this strategic point on the straits separating Europe from Africa. And just about every race or power that ever had any interests in this corner of the Mediterranean has left its mark. The world-weary port has seen them all come and go: Phoenicians, Romans, Visigoths, Arabs, Portuguese, British and Spaniards among others. For some 40 years under the dubious control of an international council, Tangier (Tanja to the locals) today is like an ageing libertarian – propped up languidly at a bar, he has seen it all.

In the days of what William Burroughs called Interzone, every kind of questionable activity was carried on. Smugglers, money-launderers, currency speculators, gun-runners, prostitutes and pimps formed a good part of the Moroccan and foreign population. And in its way, Tangier (often erroneously referred to as Tangiers) flourished.

Since its incorporation into the rest of independent Morocco, the city has lost much of its attraction. But the odd cruise ship still calls in and new activities are always to be

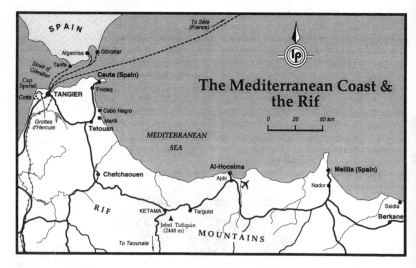

discovered. Alongside the exploding business of drug-running (including a growing contribution from South American cocaine barons), there is the commerce in people, many of whom come from sub-Saharan Africa. Moroccan and Spanish boat captains charge them as a much as US$1000 a person to smuggle them into Spain. Often the boats are so small and overcrowded that they don't make it – bodies of those who have risked and lost all frequently wash up on the Spanish and Moroccan coasts. The Socco Chico (also known as the Zoco Chico or Petit Socco) in the heart of Tangier, long *the* place for transactions of the greatest diversity, is one of the centres for organising this nasty trade.

King Hassan II has his own plans for the port, and has poured money into infrastructure programs and set the city up as an international offshore banking zone. His hope is that it will compete for international funds with Gibraltar, Tunis and Cyprus. Only the big banks need apply, for, as the king said: 'We don't want banks that create scandals. We do not want banks that come here to launder drug money'.

Little of this may be obvious to travellers passing through, but they are soon aware of what makes the place tick – money. From shoeshine boys up, everyone is on the make, and for the small-time hustlers the main trade is in tourists, especially those newly arrived from Europe. In Tangier, a city of half a million, it was always so but today a veritable army of multilingual hustlers prey on unsuspecting newcomers and can be quite implacable. You may have them in your taxi, 'finding' you a hotel, or accompanying you on foot. Many will want to be your 'guide' or have something to sell, more often than not dope. Most visitors cannot wait to get out, which is a pity, because it is a unique city – hardly truly Moroccan, and not really belonging anywhere else. After the first few days you are generally left alone; you can finally breathe easier and absorb the faded atmosphere of this mongrel creation.

There are days when all of the hassle can seem just that much more irritating – when the chergui (east wind) is blowing. Tahar ben Jelloun, a leading Moroccan writer who grew up in Tangier, claims that if the chergui arrives on a Friday during the midday prayers, it will keep blowing for seven days and nights.

## History

Tangier has been coveted for millennia as a strategic site commanding the Strait of Gibraltar. The area was settled by the ancient Greeks and Phoenicians, for whom it was a trading port, and its early days are shrouded in myth. Paradise on earth, the Garden of the Hesperides, supposedly lay nearby, and it was here that Hercules slew the giant Antaeus and fathered a child, Sophax, by the giant's widow, Tinge – no prizes for guessing where the city's original name, Tingis, comes from. The name has changed little since, and also gave rise to the name of the citrus fruit tangerine, although the tree was imported by either the Romans or Arabs at a later date.

Since those early days, the port has been one of the most contested in the Mediterranean. During the Roman period, Diocletian made it the capital of the province of Mauretania Tingitana, garrisoned by British (ie Celtic) cavalry. Not long after, it became part of the Christian episcopal see of Spain, and in fact may have been the seat of the bishops.

Following the break-up of the Roman empire, the Vandals arrived from Spain in 429 AD. Whether they ever took Tangier is uncertain. The Byzantines took an erratic interest in the port, but for the most part they contented themselves with their strongly fortified outpost at Ceuta. Apart from them and scant reports suggesting the Visigoths from Spain occupied it for a time in the 7th century, little was recorded about the area until the arrival of the Arabs in 705 AD. This may have been partly due to a smallpox epidemic that wrought havoc throughout Europe and North Africa not long after the Byzantines left the scene; continual warfare between the indigenous Berber tribes and the conquering Arabs may not have helped.

MOROCCO

Once Arab supremacy had been established, however, Tangier became a bone of contention between the Umayyads of Spain and the Idrissids of Morocco, and was even occupied by the Fatimids of Tunis in 958. A little over 100 years later, it was taken by the Almoravids as they swept across Morocco from their Mauretanian desert strongholds; it eventually passed to the Almohads in 1149. As the Almohad regime gradually reached its nadir, the city elected to be ruled by the Hafsids of Tunis, but passed to Merenid control shortly afterwards in 1274.

Following the victories of the Christian armies in the Iberian peninsula, the Portuguese attempted to take Tangier in 1437. Unsuccessful at first, they finally made it in 1471. The city passed to Philip II of Spain in 1580 when Spain and Portugal were united. It reverted to Portugal when that country regained its independence, only to be passed to England in 1661 as part of Catherine of Braganza's dowry to Charles II.

The English were not to remain long. Tangier was besieged by Moulay Ismail in 1679 and the English abandoned the city seven years later (after destroying the port and most of the city), following a dispute between parliament and the king in which the former refused to fund the reinforcement of the garrison in Tangier.

The Moroccans were left in control until the mid-19th century, when Tangier became the object of intense rivalry between the French, Spanish, Italians, British and Germans. The situation was partially resolved by the Treaty of Algeciras in 1906, whereby the British were bought off with Egypt and the Italians with Libya, leaving the remaining three European powers intriguing for the spoils. The status of the city was finally resolved only in 1923, when Tangier and the surrounding countryside was declared an 'international zone' controlled by the resident diplomatic agents of France, Spain, Britain, Portugal, Sweden, Holland, Belgium, Italy and the USA. Even the Moroccan sultan was represented by an agent, although the latter was appointed by the French resident-general (by this time

France and Spain had divided Morocco into protectorates). In fact, much of the administration of Tangier had been in European and American hands since the late 19th century, and their hold had been progressively tightened by the Treaties of Madrid (1880) and Algeciras.

Tangier was to remain an international zone until a few months after Morocco became independent, when it was reunited with the rest of the country (although it was some years before all its economic and financial privileges were removed). In the meantime it became one of the most fashionable Mediterranean resorts, and a haven for freebooters, artists, writers, refugees, exiles and bankers; it was also renowned for its high profile gay and paedophile scene. Each of the countries represented in Tangier maintained its own banks, post offices and currency, and took a share in the policing of the city. Banks, in particular, made fortunes out of manipulating the currency markets. All this came to an end in 1956, but the legend of notoriety lingers on.

## Orientation

The square known as the Grand Socco (officially renamed Place du 9 Avril 1947) is the centre of things and the link between the medina and the new city. The small and rather hilly medina lies to the north. Rue Semmarine leads off the Grand Socco almost immediately into Rue as-Siaghin, which quickly takes you to the modest central square inside the medina – the Petit Socco (also known as the Zoco Chico, and officially Place Souq ad-Dakhil). The kasbah occupies the north-west corner of the medina and is built in a dominating position on top of the cliff.

East of the medina lie the port and ferry terminal. A little to the south of the port are the main train station and the CTM bus station.

The ville nouvelle spreads out west, south and south-east of the medina, but the heart of it, Blvd Pasteur, Blvd Mohammed V and the immediately surrounding area, is compact and close to the medina. It contains the main post office, banks, some of the consulates, many of the restaurants and bars and the bulk of the middle and top-end accommodation.

Farther south is the bus station (gare routière) and grand taxi stand. They are on Place Jamia el-Arabia, at the end of Ave Louis van Beethoven. It's a good half-hour walk to the Grand Socco and the bulk of the cheap hotels.

Farther out, to the north-west, is the Marshan, a modestly elevated plateau where the rich once maintained (and in some cases still maintain) their palatial villas. Dominated by 'the Mountain', it has a prominent place in the legends and myths surrounding the colourful band of expatriates that has passed through here.

### Information

**Tourist Office** The Délégation Régionale du Tourisme (☎ 938239), at 29 Blvd Pasteur, has the usual limited range of maps and brochures. The staff speak several languages (you can usually rely on English, French, German and Spanish), but they seem not to want to make more use of them than necessary. The office is open Monday to Friday from 8.30 am to noon and 2.30 to 6 pm. As if sensing you're unlikely to get much joy from the office, there is usually at least one chap waiting outside with a solicitous air, enquiring 'did you find it?' or some such nonsense. Of course, it's another 'faux guide' – a brisk pace and a display of healthy disinterest are usually enough to shake these fellows, who seem a little less energetic than their harbourside colleagues.

**Money** There are plenty of banks along Blvd Pasteur and Blvd Mohammed V as well as a quick and efficient BMCE branch on the bottom side of the Grand Socco at the junction of Rue d'Italie. Mid-range hotels can also change money at much the same rate as the banks.

The BMCE head office is on Blvd Pasteur and has ATMs. It also has an exchange booth where you can change cash or cheques and get cash advances on Visa and MasterCard.

The booth is open seven days a week from 10 am to 2 pm and 4 to 8 pm.

The agent for American Express is Voyages Schwartz (☎ 933459/71), 54 Blvd Pasteur. It's open from 9 am to 12.30 pm and 3 to 7 pm.

**Post & Telecommunications** The main post office is on Blvd Mohammed V, 15 to 20 minutes' walk from the Grand Socco. Go to the right end of the counter for poste restante. The office is open from 8.30 am to 12.15 pm and 2.30 to 6.45 pm.

The phone and fax office is around the corner to the right of the main post office entrance and appears to be open much the same hours. A less helpful crew of people it would be hard to find. If you have a phonecard, there are card phones outside both the phone and post offices. There are a few late-night phone offices dotted about the new city. One, on the corner of Blvd Pasteur and Rue du Prince Moulay Abdallah, is open daily from 7.30 am to 10.30 pm. They don't have card phones, but you can book overseas phone calls. They also have telex and fax services.

**Foreign Consulates** Quite a few countries have diplomatic representation in Tangier, including the following:

Belgium
    Consulate: Immeuble Jawara (apartment 5a), 83 Place al-Medina (☎ 943234; fax 935211)
    Visa office: 97 Blvd Sidi Mohammed Abdallah (☎ 933163)
France
    Place de France (☎ 932039/40)
Germany
    47 Ave Hassan II (☎ 938700)
Italy
    35 Rue Assad ibn al-Farrat (☎ 931064). The consulate is open Monday to Friday from 9.30 am to noon.
Netherlands
    Immeuble Miramonte, 42 Ave Hassan II (☎ 931248)
Spain
    85 Ave Président Habib Bourghiba (☎ 935625, 937000; fax 932381)
UK
    4 Ave Mohammed V (☎ 941563)

MOROCCO

**Cultural Centres** The Centre Culturel Français (☎ 942589; fax 940937), 41 Rue Hassan el-Ouezzane, puts on a rich variety of films, exhibitions and the like, as well as classes in Arabic. They use the Galerie Delacroix on Rue de la Liberté for art exhibitions.

The Spanish are well represented in Tangier, too, which is hardly surprising. The Instituto Cervantes and its Biblioteca Española (☎ 931340; fax 947630) are at 9 Rue de Belgique. The library was founded in 1941. The complex is open Monday to Friday from 10 am to 1 pm and 4 to 7 pm and in the morning only on Saturdays. The library has a varied collection of material on Tangier (some in English) as well as Moroccan, Spanish and Gibraltarian phone books.

**Language Schools** The American Language Center (☎ 933616) is at 1 Rue M'sallah. You might be able to pick up work here teaching English.

If you want to learn Arabic, see Cultural Centres.

**Bookshops & Books** The *Rogue's Guide to Tangier* is (or was) a humorous alternative

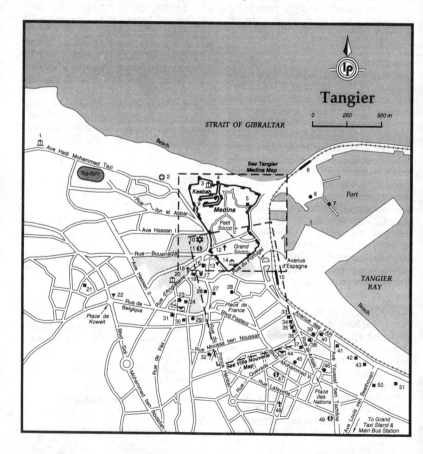

guide to the city. At best it was only ever sporadically available from some of the larger hotels, and now seems to have disappeared altogether.

A much easier guidebook to obtain is the thoroughly enjoyable and well-written *Tangier: city of the dream* by Iain Finlayson, which dwells on some of the 'luminaries' that have graced Tangier since 1923.

By far the best bookshop in Tangier is the Librairie des Colonnes (☎ 936955), on Blvd Pasteur. It has material on the city itself, including Finlayson's book, although it concentrates more on Francophone literature. The shop was founded in the interwar years and taken over by the prestigious French publisher Gallimard. It was run for a long time by a couple of august French women, Yvonne and Isabelle Gerofi, who played host to pretty well all the high and low-life of European Tangier – most found their way into the bookshop at one time or another.

**Emergencies** The police can be contacted in an emergency on ☎ 19 and the fire brigade on ☎ 15.

For an all-night chemist, or information on where to find one, ring ☎ 932619. Alternatively, buy a copy of the local rag in French, *Le Journal de Tanger*, which usually lists the day's 'pharmacies de garde', which are open late, if not all night. The pharmacies in Morocco operate a rotating roster for late-night service.

**Film & Photography** There are plenty of places along Blvd Pasteur where you can buy films or have them developed.

**Ensemble Artisanal** This government-backed arts and crafts centre on Rue de Belgique is not a bad place to browse and get an idea of what crafts you might like to buy in the souqs. On the whole, Tangier is not a great place for souvenir hunting, as the quality is not too hot and prices are inflated. Still, you can get an idea of top end of the price scale at the Ensemble and do so in relative peace.

**Street Names** As in many other Moroccan cities, street names are being changed in

MOROCCO

| PLACES TO STAY | PLACES TO EAT | OTHER | |
|---|---|---|---|
| 5 Hôtel Continental | 13 Cafés & Snack Stands | 14 Old American Legation Museum | |
| 21 Hôtel Inter Continental | 22 Guitta's Restaurant | 15 Main Railway Station | |
| 24 Pension Holland | | 16 Cinéma Rif | |
| 26 Pension Gibraltar | **OTHER** | 17 Dean's Bar | |
| 27 Hôtel El Minzah | | 18 St Andrew's Church | |
| 30 Pension Safari | 1 Forbes Museum of Military Miniatures | 19 Local Bus Terminal | |
| 33 Hôtel Marco Polo | 2 Hôpital al-Kortobi | 20 Musée d'Art Contemporain | |
| 34 Hôtel El Djenina | 3 Dar el-Makhzen | 23 American Language Center | |
| 35 Hostel | 4 Bab el-Raha | 25 Post Office | |
| 36 Hôtel Bristol | 6 Tanger Port (railway station) | 28 Gran Teatro de Cervantes | |
| 37 Pension Omar Khayam | 7 Hydrofoil Dock | 29 Instituto Cervantes | |
| 38 Hôtel El Farabi | 8 Ferry Terminal | 31 Ensemble Artisanal | |
| 39 Hôtel Charf | 9 Banque Populaire (exchange) | 32 Club Regina | |
| 40 Hôtel Rif | 10 Mendoubia Gardens | 44 Post Office (PTT) | |
| 41 Hôtel Miramar | 11 BMCE (ATMs) | 45 UK Consulate | |
| 42 Hôtel Shéhérazade | 12 Spanish Church | 46 Europcar | |
| 43 Hôtel Les Almohades | | 47 Bank al-Maghrib | |
| 50 Hôtel El Oumnia | | 48 Church | |
| 51 Hôtel Solazur | | 49 BMCI (ATMs) | |

Tangier, largely to replace foreign with home-grown names. Not all of these have caught on with equal success, and the process seems somewhat haphazard. You may well come across more than one name for the same street.

## Grand Socco

The Grand Socco was once as full of life as the Djemaa el-Fna in Marrakesh, with make-shift shops, snake charmers, musicians, storytellers and food stalls filling the night air with cacophonous activity. It is still a busy place, and on Thursday and Sunday, when Riffian peasants come to market, the area comes alive.

## Medina

You enter the medina from the Grand Socco by Rue Semmarine and quickly veer right onto **Rue as-Siaghin**. This was once Tangier's principal gold market (some jewellery stores remain), located on the northern flank of what was once the Jewish quarter, or mellah. On your right you soon pass the Spanish **Church of the Immaculate Conception** (closed), which was built in 1880, at a time when Spaniards made up one-fifth of the city's population. A few doors down is what used to be the residence of the sultan's agent *(naib)*, who was the point of contact between the Moroccan leader and European legations until 1923. From you here you emerge on to the **Petit Socco**.

Gone are the days when William Bur-roughs could cheerfully write of the endless stream of louche offers from young boys and men around the Petit Socco, but it is still a buzzy little square and a great place to sit over a mint tea, watch the world go by and contemplate its colourful past. And just in case you feel disappointed about the passing of Tangier's sleazy era, there's enough still going on to give you a taste of what it was like. Whispers of 'something special, my friend' are still a feature of the area, and one of the cheap pensions overlooking the square, the Fuentes, is a brothel. It is perhaps difficult to imagine now, but the Fuentes was one of Tangier's luxury hotels at the end of the 19th century. At that time there was little more to the town than the medina and, as the Europeans became more influential, the city's administration was established here, including the Spanish postal service and the main banks.

If you head down Ave Mokhtar Ahardan (formerly Rue de la Poste), you will probably find it equally hard to believe that some of the little pensions here were classy hotels squeezed in among such important offices as the Spanish Legation and French post office. (From here you can descend a series of stair-ways and walk down to the railway station and port.) This era came to an end as the new city was built and the administration was transferred out of the medina in the early 20th century.

At the end of Rue Jemaa el-Kebir (ex-Rue de la Marine) you come to a small belvedere overlooking the port. You could easily miss the **Grand Mosque** on the corner. The build-

---

## Evil Eye

The Evil Eye, whether you happen to believe in it or not, is a potent force in the minds of many Moroccans. A common symbolic means of warding it off is to show the open palm of the hand, fingers pointing upwards. You may well notice hand prints on the walls of houses. Often applied on the occasion of some festivity, such as a wedding, it is one way of trying to avert misfortune from befalling the inhabitants.

There are more dubious methods of dealing with the Evil Eye, and you may come across one of them in the herb and spice markets – the chameleon *(al-boua)*. This highly adaptable little creature is great to have in the home for eating flies and mosquitoes. It is also used in a cure involving an oven – a no-win situation for the chameleon and a 'cure' to be avoided. ■

ing itself is of little interest, but it is said to have been the site of a Roman temple and at one time housed a church built by the Portuguese.

From the Petit Socco Rue des Almohades (formerly Rue des Chrétiens) takes you north past some very determined shopkeepers and a hammam to the kasbah.

**Kasbah** The kasbah is on the highest point of the city and isolated from the rest of the medina by its walls; you enter from Bab el-Assa (one of four gates) at the end of Rue Ben Raissouli in the medina. The gate gives onto a large open courtyard, to the right of which once stood the fort's stables. Around to the right of them is Bab Haha, which leads back into the medina. Directly in front of you is Bab ar-Raha (Gate of Rest), which leads onto to a windswept viewpoint across to Spain.

Off to the left is the Dar el-Makhzen, the former sultan's palace and now a good museum devoted to Moroccan arts. There is also a small archaeological collection, most of the exhibits of which come from Volubilis. You can see a modest pavilion that served as the Beit al-Mal (the Treasury).

The museum is open from 9 am to noon and 3 to 6 pm in winter and 9 am to 3.30 pm in summer (closed Tuesday). Entry is Dr 10.

The palace was built by Moulay Ismail in the 17th century and enlarged by later sultans. The interior has some beautifully carved wooden ceilings and a marble courtyard. Parts of the palace are being restored by Rif craftsmen and will eventually host an artisanal gallery and rooftop café.

The future café may provide some competition for the Café Détroit on the 2nd floor in the walls, which you can reach if you leave the present museum by the gardens. It was set up by Brion Gysin, the 1960s writer and friend of the Rolling Stones, and was called The Thousand & One Nights. It became famous for the trance musicians who played here in the 1960s and released a record produced by Brian Jones.

Musicians still play here, but it's a tourist trap. The tour groups are all brought here,

and after the obligatory mint tea they file out to the tune of songs like 'Roll Out the Barrel'. The views are good, but the tea is expensive.

Quite a few of the houses inside the kasbah are owned by wealthy foreigners, only some of whom live here for much of the time. Just outside the kasbah is the Calle Amrah, where Paul Bowles bought himself a small house in 1947. Not far away was the Sidi Hosni palace where Barbara Hutton, the Woolworth heiress, lived and gave some of her grandest parties. It is said that when things were going well, she had an annual income of US$3 million, but by the time she died in 1979 in Los Angeles, she had less than US$4000 in the bank.

**Old American Legation Museum** An intriguing relic of the international zone is the former US legation, now a museum funded by the Americans. The three-storey building was donated to the USA in 1820 by Sultan Moulay Suleyman. The Americans had sent a representative there late in the previous century, as Morocco was the first nation to recognise the new country. The museum houses archives and interesting material on the history of Tangier, and it was here that American and British agents did much of the local planning for the Allied landings in North Africa in 1942.

The easiest way to find it is to turn into Rue du Portugal from Rue Salah ed-Din el-Ayoubi and enter the medina at the first gate on your left. The museum is a little way down the lane, after the dogleg turn. Getting in might prove harder. It is supposedly open on Monday, Wednesday and Thursday from 10 am to 1 pm and 3 to 5 pm, or by appointment (☎ 935317). It may not be open even at the advertised times, but knock on the door to be sure. Entrance is free.

**Musée d'Art Contemporain**
Housed in the former British Consulate on Rue d'Angleterre, this art gallery is devoted to modern Moroccan art, some of which leaves a little to be desired. Nevertheless, the place itself is pleasant and occasionally they

MOROCCO

have good exhibitions. It's open from 8.30 am to noon and 2 to 6.30 pm (closed Tuesday). Entry is Dr 10.

### Forbes Museum of Military Miniatures

A half-hour walk from the Grand Socco, heading north-west from town along the coast is the villa (a former palace of the Mendoub, or sultan's representative in Tangier) owned by the family of the American tycoon Malcolm Forbes (of Forbes Magazine), who died in 1990. The villa, still occasionally used by Forbes's family, now houses a military miniatures museum, with an 'army' of 120,000 miniatures and dioramas depicting all sorts of unrelated conflicts, from the Battle of the Three Kings (1578) to the Green March (1975), with stops in the Sudan, various WW I battlefields and several

sea engagements along the way. You can also wander around the gardens outside, but the swimming pool is out of bounds.

It's open from 10 am to 5 pm and entry is free, although the Spanish-speaking attendant may want a tip. Apparently the Forbes family gets to see the visitors' book – so maybe you should sign it so that they don't shut the place down for want of visitors.

### Ville Nouvelle

The core of the new city, largely unchanged since its heyday in the 1930s, is worth a wander. The area around Place de France and Blvd Pasteur, with its cafés and pâtisseries, still retains something of its glamour. There is a lively **market** along a lane down from Rue de la Liberté near the Hôtel El Minzah. It is not a tourist market, but rather concen-

---

### Literary Tangier

Ever since Paul Bowles first landed in Tangier in 1931, the port city has exercised a fascination on the minds of many writers. For some it was an exotic break, for others a more lasting refuge. Not that Bowles was the first – as far back as the 17th century, Samuel Pepys was complaining of the sleaziness and debauchery of the then British possession, and Mark Twain visited in 1867.

Bowles returned to stay in 1947 with his wife Jane. Both travelled a great deal, but while Paul and his writing flourished, Jane suffered and eventually died in a Málaga hospital in 1973.

Bowles, now in his eighties, gets a lot of unsolicited visitors and has become something of an unofficial tourist attraction. He was first encouraged to come to Tangier by the American writer Gertrude Stein, whom he met in Paris after she herself had a made a trip to Tangier in the 1920s. In those days, Bowles was a composer, and although he would later turn his focus to writing books, he never abandoned music. One of his services to Moroccan culture was a job he undertook to research and record the gamut of traditional Berber music. His account of the assignment appears in *Their Heads are Green*.

Music was Bowles's link with the American playwright Tennessee Williams, for whom he previously wrote scores and whom he managed to entice to Tangier for a time. A somewhat more outrageous character, Truman Capote, could not resist the temptation and visited Tangier for several months in 1949.

Not long afterwards, the first of the Beat writers arrived on the scene. William Burroughs, who spent much of his early days in Tangier pushing himself as close to the edge as he could, ended up becoming one of the port's longer-term literary residents. As he wrote to his friend and mentor, Allen Ginsberg, he found Bowles a rather tricky character, but did not let this stop him from developing an uneasy rapport with the old hand. Ginsberg himself visited Burroughs several times in Tangier, on one occasion bringing Jack Kerouac along, but neither liked it sufficiently to stay.

One of England's more iconoclastic modern playwrights, Joe Orton, spent the summer of 1966-67 just outside Tangier with his lover, Kenneth Halliwell. Orton's growing success irked Halliwell, who showed his displeasure by killing Orton and himself in London after their second trip. A French contemporary of Orton's, the much tormented Jean Genet, had a similar affection for Tangier and visited the city frequently.

Samuel Beckett also spent a lot of time here with his wife, apparently leading a considerably quieter and more introspective existence than some of his colleagues.

All of them came and went, but Bowles has remained, seeming more and more like Tangier's patron saint of authors. ■

trates on food, household products and all sorts of bits and bobs.

A remnant of the days when Spaniards formed the largest non-Moroccan community in Tangier is the **Gran Teatro de Cervantes**, in a side street off Rue Salah ed-Din el-Ayoubi (also known as Rue de la Plage). Opened in 1913, the theatre enjoyed its heyday in the interwar years. You can't miss the dazzling Art Deco façade. The building has long been in decline but is now being restored with Spanish funding.

Ever since Tangier passed to British control for about 20 years in 1661, Britons have had a special relationship with the city, immortalised by some of the literary figures who have graced the city with their presence. There was a small English church in Tangier as far back as the 1660s. The present church, **St Andrew's**, on Rue d'Angleterre, was consecrated in 1905 on ground donated by the Sultan Moulay al-Hassan in the 1880s. The caretaker, Mustapha Chergui, will be pleased to show you around the building, which was largely constructed in the Moroccan style, with the Lord's Prayer in Arabic atop the chancel. At the western end of the church is a plaque to the memory of Emily Kean, an English woman who married the sherif of Ouezzane and spent many years of her life introducing vaccination to the people of northern Morocco. Others buried here include Walter Harris, the British journalist who chronicled the goings-on here from the late 19th century, and 'Caid' Maclean, a military adviser to the sultans who, like Harris, was at one time imprisoned and held to ransom by the Rif bandit Raissouli.

Virtually across the road stands the closed **Grand Hôtel Villa de France**. The French impressionist painter Henri Matisse stayed here in the early years of this century, his imagination captured and his brush driven by the African light. He had been preceded in 1831 by Delacroix, although the latter mainly produced sketches during his time in Tangier.

There is a story that the **mosque** on Place de Koweit was built after a rich Arab Gulf sheikh sailed by Tangier and noticed that the modern cathedral's spire overshadowed all the minarets of Tangier. Shocked, he paid for the mosque and now the spire plays second fiddle to the new minaret.

The **beaches** of Tangier, although not too bad, are hardly the best in Morocco. Women will not feel at ease sunning themselves here. The much reduced European gay population still frequents certain of the beachside bars, some of which can be fun in summer. The beach is not a good place to be in the evening, however.

### Places to Stay – bottom end

**Camping** Campers have a choice. The most convenient of the two sites is *Camping Miramonte* (☎ 937133), or *Camping Marshan* as it's also known. It lies three km west of the centre of town, facing the Mountain near Jews' Bay. It's a good site, close to the beach, and there's a reasonable restaurant. To get there, take bus Nos 12, 21 or the combined 12/21 (Dr 2) from the bus terminal near the Grand Socco and get off at the Café Fleur de la Montagne. Don't leave valuables unattended here – things disappear. It costs Dr 15 a person plus Dr 10 to pitch a tent and Dr 8 for a car. There is hot water, and they have some low-quality rooms for Dr 100/150.

The other site is *Caravaning Tingis*, about six km east of the town centre. It is much more expensive but includes a tennis court and swimming pool. To get there, take bus No 15 from the Grand Socco.

**Hostel** The hostel (☎ 940127) is on Rue al-Antaki, just up past the hotels Marco Polo and El Djenina. Beds cost Dr 20 with ID card and Dr 22.50 without. Dr 5 will get you a hot shower. The dorms are almost an open-plan arrangement, meaning minimal privacy. The hostel is open from 8 to 10 am, noon to 3 pm and 6 to 10.30 pm.

**Hotels** Most of the traditional Moroccan-style hostelries are in the medina around the Petit Socco and on Ave Mokhtar Ahardan, which connects the Petit Socco and the port area. They run the gamut from flophouses to two-star hotels.

If you arrive by ferry, walk out of the port until you reach the main railway station on your left. Then take the road on the extreme right-hand side, which goes uphill until you get to a set of steps just past the junction with Rue du Portugal. Go up the steps and you'll find yourself at the bottom of Ave Mokhtar Ahardan.

Alternatively, once out of the port gates, carry on past the railway station and take the first street on your right, Rue Salah ed-Din el-Ayoubi, which has a string of cheapies. Better are some of the unclassified, one and two-star, hotels farther along or just back from the waterfront, as well as up the narrow Rue Magellan in the ville nouvelle.

Some unclassified places simply charge per head, and singles often mean getting a small double to yourself. People travelling in pairs who want a bit of extra space might want to try turning up separately in one of these places and each asking for a single rather than paying the same price to share a room. Of course the risk is that one of you will get a room and the other might find there are none left!

**Hotels – medina** There are plenty of cheap

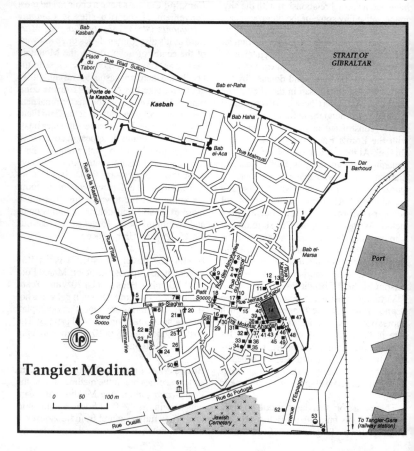

Tangier Medina

pensions to choose from here. Most are basic and you won't get much more than a bed and shared bathroom facilities, although some have hot water (for a small extra charge). Prices vary slightly and you're looking at Dr 30 to Dr 40 for singles and Dr 50 to Dr 80 for doubles. Some are grubby, whereas others are well maintained.

One of the better places on the Petit Socco (on Rue as-Siaghin) is the *Pension Mauritania* (☎ 934677). The best rooms look out on to the Socco. Clean rooms with washbasin and bidet cost Dr 50/70. Toilets are shared and there are only cold showers. The entrance is just off the Socco.

A little farther along Rue des Almohades is the *Pension Ifrikia* (☎ 933821). This is a good example of a place to avoid. They charge Dr 40 a head and claim to have hot water, but the grubby little rooms are like prison cells. A little better, and just around the corner up a lane, is the *Pension Agadir* (☎ 938084). They also charge Dr 40 a person and hot water is Dr 5 extra.

Back on the square, the *Pension Fuentes* (☎ 934669) is basically a knock-up shop. If this doesn't bother you, you can get an ad-

equate room for Dr 40 a head. There is a lively café on the 1st floor. A little way up a lane off the square behind the Fuentes are the pensions *Essaada* and *Al-Massira*.

Others scattered about inside what was once the mellah (in the western part of the medina) include the pensions *Marisa, Lillian, Regina, Marrakesh* and, on Rue as-Siaghin, the *Touahine*.

Across the Petit Socco from the Fuentes is the *Pension Becerra* (☎ 932369). The rooms are a little better than in the Fuentes, and cost the same.

Down Rue Jemaa el-Kebir (formerly Rue de la Marine) and in a side alley are a few others: the *Hôtel Larache*, *Pension Amar* and the *Pension el-Wedad*. The *Pension Lixus* is a little farther on to the left on Rue Kammal.

The main street for accommodation, however, is Ave Mokhtar Ahardan. In the lower range, two of the best options are the *Pension Palace* (☎ 936128), at No 2, and the *Hôtel Olid* (☎ 931310), at No 12. They both charge Dr 40/80 for singles/doubles. The Palace's rooms are small but otherwise reasonable, and many of them front on to a quiet, verdant courtyard. There are shared toilets and hot

**MOROCCO**

---

**PLACES TO STAY**

| | |
|---|---|
| 1 | Hôtel Continental |
| 6 | Pension Touahine |
| 7 | Pension Monaco |
| 8 | Pension Agadir |
| 9 | Pension Ifrikia |
| 10 | Hôtel Larache |
| 11 | Pension Amar |
| 12 | Pension el-Wedad |
| 13 | Pension Lixus |
| 16 | Pension Essaada |
| 17 | Pension Becerra |
| 18 | Pension Mauritania |
| 21 | Pension Monaco |
| 22 | Pension Marrakech |
| 23 | Pension Regina |
| 24 | Pension Lillian |
| 26 | Pension Marisa |
| 28 | Pension Al-Massira |
| 29 | Pension Fuentes |
| 31 | Pension Palace |
| 32 | Pension Aziz |
| 33 | Pension Bahja |
| 35 | Pension Colon |
| 36 | Pension Touzoni |
| 38 | Pension Amal |
| 39 | Pension Maarifa |
| 40 | Hôtel Mamora |
| 41 | Pension Karlton |
| 43 | Hôtel Olid |
| 44 | Pension Tan Tan |
| 45 | Pension Fès |
| 46 | Pension Victoria |
| 47 | Pension Nahda |
| 49 | Pension Américain |
| 52 | Pension Avenida |

**PLACES TO EAT**

| | |
|---|---|
| 3 | Grèce Restaurant |
| 4 | Restaurant Andalus |
| 5 | Restaurant Mamounia |
| 15 | Cheap Snack Bar |
| 19 | Café Central |
| 37 | Restaurant Ahlan |
| 42 | Restaurant Moderne |
| 48 | Restaurant Granada |

**OTHER**

| | |
|---|---|
| 2 | Hammam |
| 14 | Grand Mosque |
| 20 | Spanish Church |
| 25 | Spanish Church |
| 27 | Place Takadoum |
| 30 | Café |
| 34 | Hammam |
| 50 | Hammam |
| 51 | Old American Legation Museum |
| 53 | CTM Bus Station |
| 54 | Port Entrance |

showers for Dr 5. The Olid has seen better days, but the rooms come with private shower, from which you can occasionally coax out some hot water. The *Pension Amal* is a pokey place that has the gall to ask Dr 50 a head and Dr 5 extra for hot water.

Others along this street, few with anything more to recommend them than the Amal, include the pensions *Fès, Karlton, Maarifa, Tan Tan, Victoria* and *Américain*.

In a side street running south of Ave Mokhtar Ahardan next to the Restaurant Ahlan you will find four others of the flop-house variety: the pensions *Bahja, Colon, Touzoni* and *Aziz*.

There is also a hammam here, which may come in handy given the scarcity of hot water in many of the pensions. A few other cheapies with nothing in particular going for them are noted on the map.

Also worth checking out is the *Hôtel du Grand Socco*, just outside the medina in the square of the same name, which has basic singles/doubles with shared bathroom facilities for Dr 42/55. They have no phone and no shower.

The absence of showers is not a huge problem, as there's a hammam opposite the entrance, which is in a backstreet behind the Grand Socco. There is another hammam at 80 Rue des Almohades. It costs Dr 5 for a shower, and is open from 8 am to 8 pm.

**Hotels – ville nouvelle** First up are the unclassified hotels and pensions along Rue Salah ed-Din el-Ayoubi, but most are no better than the cheapies in the medina and some are decidedly characterless. Most offer basic accommodation with shared bathroom and toilet facilities for Dr 30 to Dr 40 for singles and Dr 50 to Dr 60 for doubles. Some have hot water.

Heading up from the waterfront you strike four in a row on the left-hand side – they seem to improve as you climb. The first of them, the *Royale*, is cheap and basic. Rooms go for Dr 30/60 and they have no shower. Next is the slightly better *Madrid*, which charges Dr 40 a head but does have hot water (Dr 5 a shower). *Le Détroit* (☎ 934838)

offers clean, simple rooms for Dr 40/60 and hot showers for Dr 5 extra. The *Miami* (☎ 932900) offers much the same deal. Around the corner is the *Pension Chams*, a slightly grubbier place with beds for Dr 30. The last place on the left side of Rue Salah ed-Din el-Ayoubi is the *Pension Talavera* (☎ 931474). Its rates are Dr 40 per person plus Dr 5 for a hot shower.

Of the three places on the right side of the street, the *Pension Atou* possibly has the most going for it. Some of its 150 (!) rooms are not bad, and as it is fairly high up, the sundeck has sweeping views of the city. Singles/doubles/triples cost Dr 30/60/90. There's a public shower, *Douche Cléopatra*, just by the Hôtel Valencia. A shower here costs Dr 5.

If none of these appeals, or you just want to be a bit farther away from the medina walls, you could try some of the places along Ave d'Espagne. Among the cheapest are the *Pension Majestic*, the *Pension Mendez* and the *Hôtel L'Marsa* (☎ 932339). The latter is the most expensive of the three at Dr 60/100. The rooms are quite clean and comfortable, but some look straight on to a café – there's something irksome about a bunch of noisy people sitting virtually next to your bed through the day and night. Of the other two, the Majestic is extremely basic and not recommended. The rooms are bearable, but there's no shower at all – at Dr 40/70 there are better deals around. The Mendez is little better at Dr 50/80.

If you have a little more dosh, one that is considerably better is the *Hôtel Biarritz* (☎ 932473), 102-104 Ave d'Espagne. For Dr 70/133 you can get comfortable, spacious old rooms overlooking the sea. Slightly better are the front rooms with balcony in the *Hôtel Cecil* (☎ 931087), at 112 Ave d'Espagne. Most of them are big and self-contained and also have a phone. They charge Dr 83 per person, but this appears to be negotiable.

The little lane heading uphill between these last two is Rue Magellan. There are a couple of good places here. The first two you come across, the *Hôtel Family* and *Pension*

*Excelsior* are nothing special. The latter has rooms for Dr 50/90, and although they are roomy, with big beds, the loos stink. Keep winding up the hill until you reach the *Hôtel L'Amor* and the *Hôtel Magellan* (☎ 938726). They have big, clean, carpeted rooms for Dr 40/80. The latter has a hot trickle pretty much whenever you ask, though it's difficult to describe it as a shower. The staff are friendly, and if you can get a front room, it's a good deal.

Head farther up around to the left and you strike two more places opposite each other. Both the *Hôtel Ibn Batouta* (☎ 937170) and the British-run *Hôtel El Muniria* have spotless rooms. The latter is probably a better bet, although on the expensive side for the budget wallet at Dr 100/120. This is where William Burroughs wrote *The Naked Lunch*. The Tanger-Inn downstairs is a popular haunt for a beer, particularly for Anglo-Saxons, and one of the last remnants of the Tangier of yesteryear.

Close by and with wonderful views over the harbour (assuming you get a front room) is the one-star *Hôtel Panoramic Massilia* (☎ 935015), on the corner of Rue Ibn Joubair and Rue Targha. The staff here are friendly and singles/doubles with private shower, toilet and hot water (in the morning) cost Dr 80/130. This is definitely one of the better deals in Tangier.

Heading back down the price scale, there are a number of other cheap pensions scattered about the ville nouvelle, but they are not overly convenient. The *Pension Omar Khayam* is past the hostel heading south up Rue al-Antaki from Ave d'Espagne. The *Pension Holland* is simple but OK and in a pleasant shady spot in a backstreet behind the French Consulate. Unfortunately, the manager seems to speak only Moroccan Arabic and a Berber dialect. Another slightly out-of-the-way place is the *Pension Safari*, on Rue de Hollande.

A little more accessible, but less pleasant, are the pensions *Atlal* and *Al Hoceima* on Rue al-Moutanabi and the *Pension Gibraltar* on Rue de la Liberté, virtually opposite the El Minzah. For the truly desperate, there are

a few more south of Rue Moussa ben Noussair, but you shouldn't need them.

## Places to Stay – middle

**Medina Area** If you prefer a modicum of luxury but still want to stay in the medina area then one place to stay is the two-star *Hôtel Mamora* (☎ 934105), 19 Ave Mokhtar Ahardan, which offers spotlessly clean singles/doubles with shower for Dr 110/127 in the low season and Dr 135/152 in the high season. There's hot water in the mornings. Some of the rooms overlook the Grand Mosque, which means an early morning wake-up call unless you're a sound sleeper.

The pick of the crop and a good choice by any standards is the *Hôtel Continental* (☎ 931024; fax 931143). Used for some scenes in the film version of Paul Bowles's *The Sheltering Sky*, it is full of character, even if it is ragged around the edges. Some of the long-term residents are a little ragged themselves, but what stories they could tell. The best of the 56 rooms are those overlooking the port. Singles/doubles cost Dr 150/200. It's popular with tour groups and film crews, so book ahead if possible. The entrance is off Dar Barhoud, and the best way to get there from the port is to head *up* the street past the Pension Avenida and continue along past the Grand Mosque, veering right at the fork (don't take the covered lane). The entrance is about 100 metres up on the right, shortly after *Jimmy's* perfume shop – 'patronised by film stars and the jet set'.

**Ville Nouvelle** There are a few possibilities at the lower end of this scale (where a single will cost a little more than Dr 100). One of the better ones is the *Hôtel de Paris* (☎ 931877), virtually opposite the tourist office at 42 Blvd Pasteur. Good, comfortable rooms with private shower and breakfast thrown in cost Dr 107/130. A few rooms have toilets too and cost somewhat more.

Back along the waterfront, you could stay at the popular *Hôtel Valencia* (☎ 930770), 72 Ave d'Espagne. It's not the most salubrious location, but a reasonable place and close to

MOROCCO

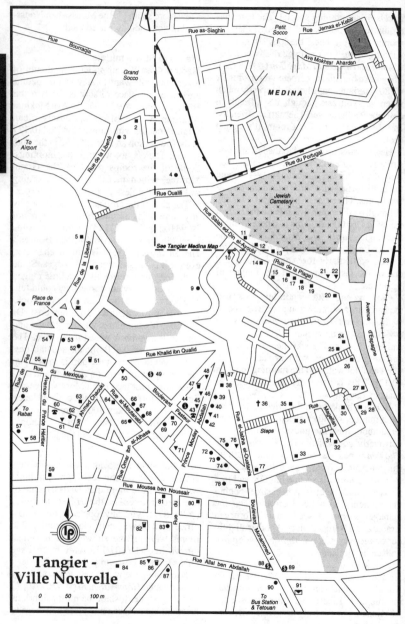

Rue Bourraqia

Rue as-Siaghin

Petit Socco

Rue Jemaa el-Kebir

Ave Mokhtar Ahardan

1

Grand Socco

MEDINA

2

To Airport

3

Rue de la Liberté

Rue du Portugal

4

Rue Oualili

Jewish Cemetery

Rue Salah ed-Din el-Ayoubi

5

See Tangier Medina Map

11

12

13

23

6

10

14

(Rue de la Plage)

15  21  22

16  17

9

18  19

20

Rue de la Liberté

7

Place de France

8

Avenue d'Espagne

54  53

52

24

Rue Khalid ibn Oualid

25

51

26

Rue du Mexique

50

49

48  37

27

55

Boulevard

47

38

Fès

Rue de Fès

56

63

64

66  67

45  46

39

36  35

Rue Magellan

30

29  28

Avenue du Prince Héritier

60  62

65

68

69

70

44  43

40

41

42

Rue el-Jabha el-Ouatania

34

To Rabat

61

57

58

71

75  76

Steps

31  32

59

72

73  74

33

77

Rue Moussa ben Noussair

78  79

81

80

Rue du

82  83

Rue Omar ibn al-Alhass

Boulevard Mohammed V

Tangier – Ville Nouvelle

84  85  86

87

Rue Allal ben Abdallah

88

89

90  91

To Bus Station & Tetouan

0   50   100 m

ransport. It's often booked solid. Singles/ doubles cost Dr 122/150.

At the junction of Ave des FAR and Ave Youssef ben Tachfine, the *Hôtel Miramar* (☎ 941715) is not bad for what you pay, but definitely on the tatty side. Singles/doubles with private shower are Dr 102/144, including the obligatory breakfast. Rooms with private toilet cost Dr 106/149. The prices can go up quite a lot in summer in this undeservedly three-star hotel.

Where Rue al-Antaki heads up from Ave d'Espagne (and where Ave d'Espagne becomes Ave des FAR) is the spotless German-run *Hôtel Marco Polo* (☎ 938213, 941124). It has quite impeccable rooms as well as a restaurant and bar service. It charges Dr 157/187/244 for singles/doubles/ triples.

Next door is the two-star *Hôtel El Djenina* (☎ 942244), 8 Rue al-Antaki. It also has decent rooms, which at Dr 106/131 are a

**MOROCCO**

| PLACES TO STAY | | |
|---|---|---|
| 2 | Hôtel du Grand Socco | |
| 5 | Pension Gibraltar | |
| 6 | Hôtel El Minzah | |
| 11 | Pension Atou | |
| 12 | Pension Playa | |
| 13 | Pension Azzeraf | |
| 14 | Pension Talavera | |
| 15 | Pension Chams | |
| 16 | Pension Miami | |
| 17 | Pension Le Détroit | |
| 18 | Pension Madrid | |
| 19 | Pension Royale | |
| 20 | Hôtel Valencia | |
| 24 | Pension Mendez | |
| 25 | Pension Majestic | |
| 26 | Hôtel L'Marsa | |
| 27 | Hôtel Biarritz | |
| 28 | Hôtel Cecil | |
| 29 | Hôtel Family | |
| 30 | Pension Excelsior | |
| 31 | Hôtel Magellan | |
| 32 | Hôtel L'Amor | |
| 33 | Hôtel Panoramic Massilia | |
| 34 | Hôtel Ibn Batouta | |
| 35 | Hôtel El Muniria & Tanger-Inn | |
| 38 | Hôtel Bar Restaurant Maroc | |
| 39 | Hôtel Lutetia | |
| 59 | Hôtel Atlas | |
| 63 | Hôtel Astoria | |
| 64 | Pensions Atlal & Al Hoceima | |
| 70 | Hôtel de Paris | |
| 77 | Hôtel Rembrandt | |
| 79 | Hôtel Tanjah-Flandria | |
| 80 | Hôtel Africa | |
| 81 | Hôtel Ritz | |

| 84 | Hôtel Chellah |
|---|---|

| PLACES TO EAT | |
|---|---|
| 8 | Café de Paris |
| 10 | Restaurant Le Bon Goût |
| 21 | Restaurants Africa & Hassi Baida |
| 22 | Restaurant/Bar La Paix |
| 24 | Restaurant Mendez |
| 26 | Restaurant L'Marsa |
| 41 | Morocco Palace |
| 45 | Romero's Restaurant |
| 46 | Restaurant Damascus |
| 48 | Restaurant Les Ambassadeurs |
| 50 | Big Mac |
| 54 | Café de France |
| 55 | Restaurant Negresco & English Bar |
| 58 | Restaurant Andalou |
| 61 | La Pagode |
| 71 | Eric's Hamburger Shop |
| 76 | Restaurant La Grenouille |
| 85 | Lee Wong |

| OTHER | |
|---|---|
| 1 | Grand Mosque |
| 3 | Covered Market |
| 4 | Glacier Liberté |
| 7 | French Consulate |
| 9 | Gran Teatro de Cervantes |
| 23 | Tanger-Gare (railway station) |

| 36 | Church |
|---|---|
| 37 | Bar |
| 40 | Budget |
| 42 | Limadet Boat Ticket Office |
| 43 | Telephone & Fax Office |
| 44 | Tourist Office |
| 47 | Bar |
| 49 | BMCE (Late Bank & ATMs) |
| 51 | Bar Lisba |
| 52 | Discothèque Monocle |
| 53 | Royal Air Maroc |
| 56 | Cinéma Le Paris |
| 57 | Club Troya |
| 60 | Telephone & Fax Office |
| 62 | Laundry |
| 65 | Scott's Nightclub |
| 66 | Koutoubia Palace Nightclub |
| 67 | Churchill's Nightclub |
| 68 | Gospel Nightclub |
| 69 | The Ranch Club |
| 72 | Librairie des Colonnes |
| 73 | Avis |
| 74 | Voyages Schwartz (American Express agent) |
| 75 | Iberia |
| 78 | Cinéma Flandria |
| 82 | The Pub |
| 83 | Cinéma Goya |
| 86 | Bar |
| 87 | Cinéma Roxy |
| 88 | Banque Populaire |
| 89 | Wafabank |
| 90 | Hertz |
| 91 | Main Post Office |

little cheaper than next door, along with a restaurant and bar. A couple of doors up is the two-star *Hôtel Bristol* (☎ 931070), 14 Rue al-Antaki. It has 33 rooms with shower, and some with toilet. Doubles with shower or shower and toilet are Dr 144/149, which includes an obligatory breakfast. The hotel has a restaurant and bar.

Across from the Bristol, a side street runs off Rue al-Antaki leading to another good deal, the *Hôtel El Farabi* (☎ 943473), 8 Rue Saidia. Singles/doubles are Dr 90/120 and some rooms have sea views. Across the intersection is the pricey two-star *Hôtel Charf* (☎ 943340). If you can afford it, the self-contained rooms are very good and have magnificent views, as does the 4th-floor restaurant. Singles/doubles are Dr 166/185.

In the heart of the ville nouvelle are some more expensive alternatives to the Hôtel de Paris. The *Hôtel Astoria* (☎ 937201), 10 Rue Ahmed Chaouki, has been renovated and offers 27 attractively furnished, mostly self-contained rooms for Dr 113/133 in the low season.

On Rue du Prince Moulay Abdallah is the fairly popular *Hôtel Lutetia* (☎ 931866). Rooms with shower and toilet cost Dr 144/194, including breakfast. There are cheaper rooms with toilet and some without shower or toilet. The hotel has parking facilities.

The *Hôtel Atlas* (☎ 936435; fax 933095), 50 Rue Moussa ben Noussair, is a little out of the way, but not bad in its class. Singles/doubles with shower cost Dr 161/207 while rooms with complete bathroom are Dr 202/249.

Heading into what most people would consider the top range is the inconveniently located and depressing *Hôtel Chellah* (☎ 943388; fax 945536), 47-49 Rue Allal ben Abdallah. They have characterless but perfectly comfortable rooms for Dr 326/373, or Dr 100 less in the low season.

### Places to Stay – top end

With a tourist trade the size of Tangier's, there is a good choice of top-range hotels.

In the four-star category with some character is the ageing *Hôtel Rif* (☎ 935908/09/10) on Ave des FAR. Singles/ doubles cost Dr 402/ 477.

A cheaper option is the *Hôtel Rembrandt* (☎ 937870), at the junction where Blvd Pasteur becomes Blvd Mohammed V. They charge Dr 360/470. Across the road, the *Hôtel Tanjah-Flandria* (☎ 933279) offers all the mod-cons for Dr 411/495.

Another four-star joint is the *Solazur* (☎ 940264), down on Ave des FAR. Not far away are a couple of also-rans relegated to the three-star division, the *El Oumnia* (☎ 940366), Ave Louis van Beethoven, and the *Shéhérazade* (☎ 940500), on Ave des FAR, next to the four-star *Hôtel Les Almohades* (☎ 940026; fax 946371). Also in the four-star category is the *Hôtel InterContinental* (☎ 936053; fax 937945), Park Brooks.

The only five-star hotel in Tangier that deserves this ranking is the *El Minzah* (☎ 935885; fax 934546), 85 Rue de la Liberté. A well-maintained reminder of the 1930s, when it was anyone in the transient and not-so-transient European community, the hotel is beautifully conceived along the lines of a Moroccan palace. In 1931 the US business-man Ion Perdicaris, who at one point spent an uncomfortable spell as a prisoner of the Rif bandit Er-Raissouli, converted what had been the Palmarium casino into a hotel. The building was once the mansion of a certain Lord Bute. During WW II, as Tangier turned into a vipers' nest of spies and mercenaries of all types, the hotel hosted a mainly American clientele. It has all the amenities you would expect of a hotel in this category, including a swimming pool, bars and a couple of rather expensive restaurants.

### Places to Eat

**Medina Area** There are several cheap eating possibilities in and around the Petit Socco, in between the cafés. There's a good takeaway snack bar just where Rue Jemaa el-Kebir begins. Huge rolls filled with meat, salad and pickles cost about Dr 10. Heading north of the Socco on Rue du Commerce there are two small sit-down places, the *Restaurant Andalus* and the *Grèce Restaurant*, which offer the standard fare – a meal won't cost more than Dr 30. The *Restaurant Ahlan* on Ave Mokhtar Ahardan offers a filling meal of brochettes, salad and a drink for Dr 25. Virtually across the road is the *Restaurant Moderne*, which is similar. Down the first flight of stairs towards the port is an oddly louche place, the *Restaurant Granada*. You can get meals of indifferent quality for about Dr 50, but few of the locals seem interested in the food. There are good views over the port, and the Moroccan men and women who find their way in here bring plenty of local colour.

There are a few food stalls at the bottom of the steps at the end of Ave Mokhtar Ahardan. They serve up fried fish and one or two other things for a few dirham.

More expensive is the *Restaurant Mamounia* on Rue as-Siaghin, which offers full Moroccan feasts in more sumptuous surroundings than any of the other medina eateries.

**Ville Nouvelle** A good place for snacks is the *Restaurant Le Bon Goût* on Rue Salah ed-Din el-Ayoubi. Farther down this street, towards Ave d'Espagne, are two reasonably priced sit-down restaurants, the *Africa* (No 83) and, next door, the *Hassi Baida*. Both offer set meals for around Dr 40 or main courses of fairly generous proportions for Dr 25 to Dr 35. The *Restaurant/Bar La Paix*, right on the corner of Ave d'Espagne is more a bar than restaurant.

The *Restaurant Mendez*, in front of the pension of the same name on Ave d'Espagne, serves mediocre fish and is a little expensive at Dr 50 for a set menu. You can do better for this price in the centre of town.

If you feel like Western-style fast food, you could do worse than *Big Mac*, which is on the corner of Blvd Pasteur and Rue Ahmed Chaouki. They do good hotdogs for Dr 20. Also in this line is the unlikely-sounding *Eric's Hamburger Shop*, which claims to be open 24 hours a day. It's in the arcade between Blvd Pasteur and Rue al-Moutanabi. For as little as Dr 10 you can get a decent imitation of a basic burger.

The stretch of Rue du Prince Moulay Abdallah around the corner from the tourist office is laden with eating possibilities. *Les Ambassadeurs* and the *Restaurant Damascus* are good for Moroccan food, whereas *Romero's* concentrates on fairly pricey Spanish cuisine. *Brenda's Tea Shoppe*, between the Hôtel Lutetia and the Hôtel Bar/Restaurant Maroc, serves good old baked beans, but at the time of writing looked like shutting down. Next door is a tiny pizza place. The *Morocco Palace* is the best choice in town for a full Moroccan spread and show featuring Moroccan music and belly-dancing. You'll be looking at well over Dr 100 a head for the whole evening. A few prostitutes operate here.

The *Restaurant Negresco*, on Rue du Mexique, is a posh place serving French and Moroccan cuisine. A full meal will come close to Dr 100 per person.

The *Carrousel* caters for homesick Brits hungry for pub grub (at about Dr 40 for mains) and a beer. It's more or less opposite the expensive *La Pagode* Chinese restaurant, just off Rue du Prince Héritier.

On the subject of Asian food, you could also try *Lee Wong* for Vietnamese food, near the Hôtel Chellah on Rue Allal ben Abdallah. Mains are about Dr 60.

*Restaurant La Grenouille*, on Rue el-Jabha el-Ouatania, serves up quite a decent French set meal for Dr 80.

A bit of a walk from Blvd Pasteur is another leftover from the days of the international zone, *Guitta's*, on Place de Koweit. They do no-nonsense food, with main courses starting at about Dr 50.

The *Restaurant Andalou*, in a side street between Rue de Fès and Rue du Prince Héritier, has Spanish *tapas*.

For ice cream, you should try the Glacier Liberté on Rue de la Liberté.

### Entertainment
**Cafés & Bars** In the heart of the medina, the *Café Central* on the Petit Socco was a favourite hang-out for William Burroughs and others and today is a good place to have a glass of tea, watch the world go by or catch

up on Spanish TV. There are a couple of other cafés on the square, including upstairs in the Pension Fuentes.

There are several cafés on the Grand Socco where you can while away the time, or you could take a walk up to Blvd Pasteur, which is lined with elegant, European-style cafés, their tables spilling out onto the footpaths. Of these the pick of the crop has to be the *Café de Paris*, an ageing grande dame of Tangier coffee society. Take a seat inside and you're likely to have an odd assortment of characters for company – remnants of the Spanish population, genteel Moroccans and the odd ageing northern European – all in all an atmosphere redolent of bygone days. Your Dr 4 coffee will be served by the most correct of waiters, making it well worth the little extra. There are plenty of others to try for variety along the rest of the street. A coffee and cake or croissant from one of the pâtisseries make a great start to the day.

There are numerous bars around the ville nouvelle. *Restaurant/Bar La Paix* on Ave d'Espagne has been mentioned – it seems to be a preferred rest stop for some of the city's 'working girls', but is quite all right. A couple of local spit-and-sawdust bars are located near each other on Rue du Prince Moulay Abdallah and Rue Omar ibn al-Alhass. Another of the species, the *Bar Lisba* is on a side street between Blvd Pasteur and Rue du Mexique. There is also one near the Hôtel Chellah.

Anyone who has done any reading about Tangier will have come across *Dean's Bar*, on Rue Amérique du Sud. Hardly a Westerner of any repute (or ill-repute) did not prop up this bar at some time. It's not all that interesting now, but may be worth a drink if you've steeped yourself in Tangier mythology. Others of the same ilk, such as the Parade Bar (a favourite haunt of Jane Bowles), have long since disappeared.

For something a little more up-market, you could try the *English Bar*, next to the Restaurant Negresco. Apart from the not-so-cheap pint glasses, there's nothing very English about the place. A pint of Flag Spéciale with Spanish-style bar snacks will set you back Dr 36. Another similar place, but slightly more English, is the *Pub*, also known as *Le Pub*.

A place well worth investigating is the *Tanger-Inn*, next to the Hôtel El Muniria. It's open from 9 pm to about 1 am; knock on the heavy grill door to get in. It's a tiny place where the clientele can give you a taste of Interzone.

Many of the middle and top-range hotels have bars. The *Caid's Bar* in the Hôtel El Minzah is good for an expensive tipple.

**Cinema**  There are a few cinemas around town, a couple of which have been marked on the maps. The *Cinéma Rif* on the Grand Socco serves up a rigid diet of kung fu-style movies.

**Discos & Nightclubs**  There is a quite a collection of late-night places in the ville nouvelle, although they are not necessarily to be recommended. Rue al-Moutanabi has a cluster of them; *Scott's*, *Gospel* and *Churchill's* (with the London Underground sign) can be vaguely interesting. The first of them has a reputation as a gay bar. Also here is the *Koutoubia Palace*, where you can see some tacky Egyptian belly-dancing into the wee hours. The *Morocco Palace* puts on a better version with a full meal. Some other discos and clubs are marked on the maps, but most are mainstream local hang-outs that generally have little promise, and can be unpleasant for unaccompanied women. They include the *Discothèque Monocle*, *Club Troya* the *Ranch Club* and the *Club Regina*.

### Getting There & Away

**Air**  RAM (☎ 935505) has an office on Place de France. With the exception of two weekly flights to Al-Hoceima, all RAM's internal flights from Tangier go via Casablanca. The one-way fare to Casablanca is Dr 430. To Marrakesh it's Dr 705 and Dr 940 to Agadir.

RAM has connections to several European destinations, as do the following airlines:

Air France
    7 Rue du Mexique (☎ 936477)

British Airways
Rue de la Liberté (☎ 935211)

GB Airways
83 Rue de la Liberté (☎ 935877). GB Airways has flights to Gibraltar leaving at 11.05 am on Saturday and Sunday mornings. They go on to London Heathrow. The one-way fare is Dr 520. They also have a same-day return fare for Dr 620.

Iberia
35 Blvd Pasteur (☎ 936177/8/9). Iberia has two flights a week from Tangier to Madrid.

KLM
7 Rue du Mexique (☎ 938926)

Lufthansa
7 Rue du Mexique (☎ 931327)

**Bus – CTM** The CTM office is near the port entrance, opposite the Tanger Gare railway station, although it runs some buses from the main bus station (gare routière), which is on Place Jamia el-Arabia, a good half-hour walk from the Grand Socco. There are six departures for Casablanca from 11 am to midnight (Dr 88; seven hours). They stop at Rabat (Dr 57; 5½ hours) and Kenitra (Dr 57). At 6 pm there is a bus to Meknès (Dr 63) and Fès (Dr 77.50; six hours). The CTM booth at the main station advertises a bus to Fès for only Dr 66 at 12.30 pm. At 4.30 pm a bus sets off for Marrakesh (Dr 146), Agadir (Dr 205.50) and Tiznit (Dr 228.50).

CTM has 13 buses a day to Tetouan (Dr 13) from the main bus station. Four buses also leave for Larache (Dr 22; about 2½ hours), three going via Asilah (Dr 10, one hour). They leave at 10 am, noon, 5.15 and 7 pm. The last is direct to Larache, but there is a fourth bus to Asilah at 7.45 pm. At 12.30 pm a bus leaves for Chefchaouen (Dr 27) and Ouezzane (Dr 39).

**Bus – others** The other companies run buses from the main bus station. They have departures for Casablanca, Rabat, Fès, Meknès, Tetouan, Larache and Asilah. Some put on 'de luxe' buses for a few extra dirham. Fares vary but tend to be lower than the CTM fares in some cases as much as Dr 20 lower, as with the fare to Casablanca).

Transports L'Étoile du Nord offers buses to Ketama (Dr 49) that go on to Al-Hoceima (Dr 74) and Nador (Dr 106). Transports Bradley runs buses to the Ceuta border (Dr 19).

**Train** There are two railway stations – Tanger Gare and Tanger Port. Most trains leave from the Gare station, although more seem to proceed to the Port station on arrival from elsewhere. All trains leaving from the port stop at Tanger Gare on the way out.

There are two direct trains to Marrakesh. The morning service departs from Tanger Gare at 8.10 am (about 9½ hours) and the night run from Tanger Port at 11.30 pm (about 10½ hours).

Both stop in Rabat and Casablanca. Three other trains head for Casablanca and Rabat too, departing at 9.45 am, 1.40 pm (Tanger Gare only) and 4.05 pm. You have to change at Sidi Kacem on the first two of these (a wait of about 40 minutes). The trip to Casablanca takes about six hours on the direct trains.

There are five daily trains to Fès via Meknès. They depart at 12.55, 8.10 and 9.45 am, and 1.40 and 4.05 pm. Only the last of these starts at Tanger Port. You have to change on three of these runs, with a wait not exceeding 40 minutes. The direct train takes about six hours to Fès. All but the 4.05 pm train go on to Oujda (about 12 hours).

The 2nd-class fares to Casablanca are Dr 81.50 in the normal trains and Dr 103 in the rapide; to Fès (Dr 63.50/84); Marrakesh (Dr 134/169); Rabat (Dr 62.50/79); and Oujda (Dr 142/179.50). All trains from Tangier stop at Asilah (Dr 10/12.50).

**Taxi** Grands taxis leave from a lot next to the main bus station. The main destinations are Tetouan (Dr 20) and Asilah (Dr 19). You may have to wait a while for Asilah-bound taxis to fill up. The bus is a better bet given that it's half the price.

**Car Rental** Car-rental agencies in Tangier include:

Avis
54, Blvd Pasteur (☎ 938960)
Airport (☎ 933031)

Budget
7 Ave Prince Moulay Abdallah (☎ 937994)

Europcar
87 Blvd Mohammed V (☎ 941938)

Goldcar
   Hôtel Solazur, Ave des FAR (☎ 940164, 946568)
Hertz
   36, Blvd Mohammed V (☎ 709227, 707366)

**Sea** If you're heading to Spain or Gibraltar by boat you can buy tickets from the company offices down at the dock (closed weekends), in the terminal building (unreliable on weekends), or from virtually any travel agency around town. The Wasteel agency by the port entrance is a popular one. The prices are always the same (if someone tries to add on extras, go elsewhere). For more details see the Getting There & Away chapter.

There are ferries to Algeciras and Tarifa (Spain), Gibraltar and Sète (France). When the weather is calm, hydrofoils also make the run to Algeciras.

### Getting Around

**To/From the Airport** Tangier's rather tiny Boukhalef Airport is 15 km from the town centre. From here you must arrange taxis into town, as there is no direct bus service.

**Bus** The local bus terminal is just up from the Grand Socco on Rue d'Angleterre.

**Petits Taxis** The price for a standard petit taxi journey around town is about Dr 5. Remember that fares go up by 50% after 8 pm.

### AROUND TANGIER
### Cap Spartel

A 14-km drive west of Tangier (there is no public transport) lies Cap Spartel, the north-western extremity of Africa's Atlantic coast, marked by a lighthouse and fish restaurant. If you're driving, take Rue de Belgique, cross Place de Koweit and head west for La Montagne. The road beyond this to Cap Spartel is heavily wooded. Below it, **Robinson Plage** stretches off to the south. Four km away are the so-called **Grottes d'Hercule** (about 100 metres from the Robinson Plage Village de Vacances), which have been something of a tourist trap since the 1920s. You may be heavied into paying a few

dirham to get into this hole in the rock that looks onto the ocean. For a long time locals quarried stone here, but tourists are more profitable business. Early morning is the best time to arrive, as the hasslers are still in bed. There are several overpriced cafés around the entrance to the grotto which overlook the Atlantic.

About one km inland are the remains of a tiny Roman settlement, **Cotta**. Like the more important town of Lixus farther south, it was a centre for producing garum – a kind of fish-paste delicacy. Walk about 200 metres down the road (which continues seven km south-east to the main Tangier-Rabat highway) past the camp site on the left and you'll find a track with a barrier. Ignore the latter and proceed down the track – the sparse ruins are about 800 metres in front of you.

You can stay at the *Robinson Plage Village de Vacances* (☎ 938765) near the caves or *Camping Robinson*. The former is pleasant enough but pricey at Dr 156/212/268 in the low season (and quite a bit more in the high season). They have no hot water and the restaurant is a rip-off. The camp site is spartan and has no showers. Despite this it costs Dr 15 per person, Dr 20 to pitch a tent and Dr 12 for a car. If it's open the *Restaurant/Bar Mirage* by the grotto might be a better alternative.

### Road to Ceuta

If you have your own transport, the drive along the wild and hilly 'coast' road to Fnideq and Ceuta is an attractive alternative route if you are thinking of heading to Tetouan and Chefchaouen from Tangier, although it will add a couple of hours to the trip.

# Spanish Morocco

For hundreds of years, Spain has controlled the two North African enclaves of Ceuta and Melilla. It has also controlled five islets that have served as military bases and prisons: the three Jaafariya Islands off the Cap de l'Eau about 25 km west of Saidia; the Peñon de Alhucemas, just off the coast near Al-Hoceima; and the Peñon de Velez de la Gomera, some 50 km west of the same town. Moroccan independence in 1956 brought no change, as Spain claims a historical right to the enclaves. Curiously, it does not recognise any such historical British right to control Gibraltar. Morocco has made several half-hearted attempts to have the enclaves returned. Rabat is not keen to rock the boat, however, as Spain is an increasingly important trading partner.

By the end of 1993, a process of granting Spain's regions a large degree of political autonomy was complete, except in the enclaves, which were still waiting to have their statutes approved. In mid-1994, however, it appeared that Melilla would accept a limited self-government agreement without legislative powers by the end of the year.

Moroccans fear that autonomy would mean Rabat could no longer negotiate the enclaves' future with Madrid, but would have to talk directly to the enclaves' political leaders, who will have no interest in restoring Moroccan rule. Indeed, many of the enclaves' Muslim inhabitants, mostly of Rif Berber origin, would themselves regard such a transfer with mixed feelings.

Because of its distance from Ceuta, Melilla has been included in the East Coast section later in this chapter.

## CEUTA (SEBTA)

With a population of 75,000, about a third of which is made up of Muslims (to all intents and purposes Berbers, but officially 'Spanish Muslims'), the island is devoted to the military (almost half of its 19 sq km is owned by the army), duty-free shopping and a lot of shadier cross-border commerce. Although Spanish citizens get huge tax breaks for residing in Ceuta (and Melilla), the enclave's uncertain future has led some to migrate to the Spanish mainland.

Ceuta has an Andalusian feel to it, but the presence of so many Muslims (clearly treated as second-class citizens) gives it an other-wordly air. Just as it is odd to hear the bobbies of Gibraltar speaking English *and* Spanish, so it strikes you to hear the bus drivers of Ceuta speaking Spanish and Arabic.

Although Ceuta is pinning hopes on its tourist potential, there is not an awful lot here. If you're driving, stock up on duty-free petrol before leaving. The duty-free liquor is also worth a look before heading on to Morocco.

Many people enter Morocco via Ceuta to avoid the touts who hang around in Tangier, and you can easily push straight on from Ceuta to Tetouan (and on to Chefchaouen) in the same day.

### History

Ceuta's Arabic name, Sebta, stems from the Latin Septem. Two heroes of Greek mythology, Hercules and Ulysses, are both supposed to have passed through here, but more certainly it served as one of the Roman empire's coastal bases. The city later passed into the control of the Byzantine empire and, in 931, was taken by the Arab Umayyad rulers of Muslim Spain. In 1083 it fell to the Almoravids and remained under direct Moroccan control until 1309, when James II of Aragon took it. In 1415 Portugal grabbed Ceuta and, when Portugal and Spain united under one crown in 1580, it passed by default to Spain. When the two countries split in 1640, Ceuta remained Spanish, as it has ever since.

### Orientation & Information

Ceuta is a peninsula jutting into the Mediterranean. Most of the hotels, restaurants and offices of interest are gathered around the narrow spit of land linking the peninsula to the mainland. The port is a short walk to the west.

**Tourist Office** There are two tourist offices: the main one in the middle of town by the local bus terminus, and the other by the ferry terminal (☎ 509275). They have a decent brochure, a tiny map and an out-of-date accommodation list. The town office is open

MOROCCO

MOROCCO

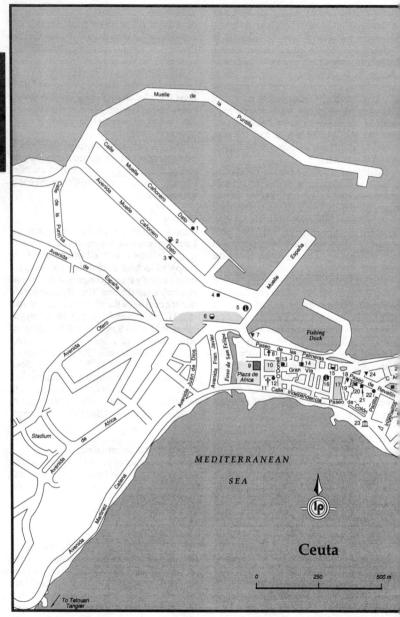

Ceuta

0    250    500 m

MEDITERRANEAN

SEA

To Tetouan
Tangier

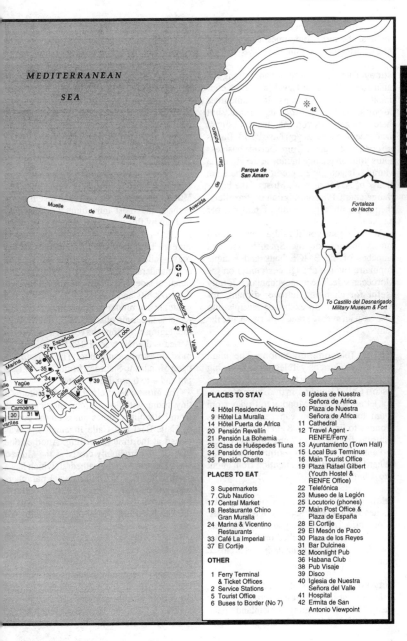

**PLACES TO STAY**

4 Hôtel Residencia Africa
9 Hôtel La Muralla
14 Hôtel Puerta de Africa
20 Pensión Revellín
21 Pensión La Bohemia
26 Casa de Huéspedes Tiuna
34 Pensión Oriente
35 Pensión Charito

**PLACES TO EAT**

3 Supermarkets
7 Club Nautico
17 Central Market
18 Restaurante Chino
   Gran Muralla
24 Marina & Vicentino
   Restaurants
33 Café La Imperial
37 El Cortije

**OTHER**

1 Ferry Terminal
  & Ticket Offices
2 Service Stations
5 Tourist Office
6 Buses to Border (No 7)

8 Iglesia de Nuestra
  Señora de Africa
10 Plaza de Nuestra
   Señora de Africa
11 Cathedral
12 Travel Agent -
   RENFE/Ferry
13 Ayuntamiento (Town Hall)
15 Local Bus Terminus
16 Main Tourist Office
19 Plaza Rafael Gilbert
   (Youth Hostel &
   RENFE Office)
22 Telefónica
23 Museo de la Legión
25 Locutorio (phones)
27 Main Post Office &
   Plaza de España
28 El Cortije
29 El Mesón de Paco
30 Plaza de los Reyes
31 Bar Dulcinea
32 Moonlight Pub
36 Habana Club
38 Pub Visaje
39 Disco
40 Iglesia de Nuestra
   Señora del Valle
41 Hospital
42 Ermita de San
   Antonio Viewpoint

Monday to Friday from 8 am to 3 pm, but the one near the ferry sometimes also opens in the late afternoon and on Saturday.

**Money** There are plenty of banks along the main street, Paseo de Revellín, and its continuation, Calle Camoens. It's sometimes possible to buy Moroccan dirham, but there's no need, as you can change easily at the border (so long as you have *cash*). Banks are open from 8 am to 2 pm. Outside business hours you can change money at the Hotel La Muralla. If you have a credit card, there are plenty of ATMs around. Most of the banks charge about 1% commission on travellers' cheques, with a minimum of 650 pta per transaction.

At the border you'll find a few informal moneychangers on the Spanish side and branches of the BMCE bank and Banque Populaire (which change *cash only*) on the Moroccan side. The moneychangers are only useful for changing leftover dirhams for which you have no exchange receipts into pesetas at an average rate. Otherwise, use the banks.

**Post & Telecommunications** The main post office (Correos y Telégrafos) is the big yellow building on Plaza de España, a square just off Calle Camoens, in the centre of town. For letters it's open Monday to Friday from 9 am to 8 pm. You can send telegrams Monday to Friday from 8 am to 9 pm and on Saturday from 9 am to 7 pm. Spanish public servants take the siesta seriously, so it may be hard to get anyone's attention from about 2 to 4 pm.

**Telephone** There are plenty of blue public phones around. They accept coins and cards. A locutorio, from where you can book overseas calls, has been marked on the map. It's open from 10 am to 10 pm daily, but is closed from 2 to 5 pm.

**Duty-Free** Ceuta is a duty-free zone, although nothing seems extravagantly cheap. If you are heading to mainland Spain, duty of 10% to 14% may be slapped on items

worth more than 6840 pta. Going to Morocco, the main attraction is petrol. Normal and diesel cost 45 pta a litre, super 64 pta and unleaded 60 pta. If you want to stock up on goodies, there are a couple of supermarkets on Calle Muelle Cañonero Dato (Dumaya and Eurospar) which are worth a browse. Liquor is the best deal. A couple of service stations are on the same street.

### Museums

There are a few museums in Ceuta, although none are worth too much of your time. The **Museo de la Legión**, on Paseo de Colón, is perhaps the most intriguing. Dedicated to and run by this army unit, which was set up in 1920 as Spain's answer to the French Foreign Legion, it is full of medals of the brave fallen and memorabilia of various commanders. These guys are a little on the fanatical side, and the reverence with which Franco's bits and pieces are treated (by the guide) is a reminder of how strong the Right remains in certain quarters of Spain. Most of the legion's actions have been in North Africa – the Rif war of 1921-26 being the most disastrous campaign. The museum is open Monday to Saturday from 11 am to 1.30 pm and 4 to 6 pm. Entry is free.

The **Museo Municipal**, which contains a tiny room with local archaeological finds from Palaeolithic times on, is on the corner of Calle Real and Calle Ingenieros. It was closed at the time of writing. Another one that seems perpetually closed is the **Museo de la Catedral**, in the cathedral, which has a small collection of ecclesiastical paraphernalia and paintings. There is a small **military museum** at the Castillo del Desnarigado on the south-eastern tip of the peninsula. It's only open at weekends.

### Peninsula

If you have a couple of hours to spare, it's easy to walk around the peninsula (the No 4 bus goes part of the way), which is capped by Monte Hacho, said by some to be the southern Pillar of Hercules (Jebel Musa, west of Ceuta along the coast towards

Tangier, is the other contender. Gibraltar is the northern pillar). From the **Convent of the Ermita de San Antonio** there is an excellent view towards Gibraltar.

The convent, originally built in the 17th century and reconstructed in the 1960s, is the venue for a large festival held annually on 13 June to mark Saint Anthony's Day.

Monte Hacho is crowned by the **Fortaleza de Hacho**, a fort first built by the Byzantines and added to since by the Moroccans, Portuguese and Spanish.

The **Castillo del Desnarigado** on the south-eastern end of the peninsula was built as a coastal battery in the 19th century, but there are remnants of earlier Spanish and Portuguese fortifications.

### City Walls

The most impressive leftovers of the city walls and the navigable **Foso de San Felipe** date back to Almohad times, although they were largely reconstructed by the Spaniards at the end of the 17th century.

### Places to Stay – bottom end

**Camping** Camping Ceuta (☎ 503840) is a good four km west of the town centre, and hardly worth the effort if you don't have your own transport.

**Hostel** The Residencia de la Juventud is not an HI hostel and, at 1663 pta a bed, is hardly cheap. It is nevertheless often full. Tucked away on Plaza Rafael Gilbert, it opens in the early morning and late afternoon (no precise time). Turn up the stairs off Paseo de Revellín by the Restaurante China Gran Muralla. The hostel is on your right as you enter the square.

**Hotels** There is no shortage of fondas and casas de huéspedes, easily identifiable by the large blue-and-white 'F' or 'CH' on the entrances. The cheapest of these is the small Pensión Charito (☎ 513982), on the 1st floor at 5 Calle Arrabal, about 15 minutes' walk along the waterfront from the ferry terminal. The only indication that it is a guesthouse is the 'Chambres' sign, and the 'CH' sign on

the wall. Basic singles/doubles cost 800/1400 pta. There are no hot showers. Just up the hill a little is the Pensión Oriente (☎ 511115). It has five rooms and was closed at the time of writing. They normally charge 1200/2000 pta. There are quite a few others in this category. If you're having trouble, pick up a list from the tourist office.

Conveniently situated in the centre, the Pensión Revellín (☎ 516762) is on the 2nd floor at 2 Paseo de Revellín. The doorway is right in the middle of the busy shopping street and, again, can be identified by the 'CH' sign. It is opposite the Banco Popular Español. Singles/doubles cost 1200/2200 pta, and hot showers are available in the morning. It's OK but the manager is none too friendly.

If you can afford a little more, the two best deals in town are the Casa de Huéspedes Tiuna (☎ 517756), at 3 Plaza Teniente Ruiz, and the Pensión La Bohemia (☎ 510615), 16 Paseo de Revellín. They both charge 2000/3000 pta for good singles/doubles, but the Bohemia (look for the small sign in the shopping arcade) is definitely the better of the two. It has piping-hot showers in spotless shared bathrooms.

Should you be stuck, the Pensión Real (☎ 511449), 1 Calle Real, offers singles/doubles for 2500/3000 pta.

### Places to Stay – middle

A conveniently located place just near the ferry terminal is the Hotel Residencia Africa (☎ 514140), on Calle Muelle Cañonero Dato. In the low season it has singles/doubles for 3900/7000 pta (breakfast 500 pta), but in summer prices go up to 5500/8500 pta.

### Places to Stay – top end

The premier establishment is the entirely characterless four-star Hotel La Muralla (☎ 514940; fax 514947), at 15 Plaza de Africa. It'll set you back 10,000/12,500 pta for singles/doubles with private bath. It has a restaurant, bar, parking and swimming pool.

**MOROCCO**

Just east of the square a new place is being built, the *Hotel Puerta de Africa*. Another four-star joint is the *Hotel Ulises* (514540), 5 Calle Camoens. They charge marginally less than La Muralla.

## Places to Eat

You won't find food as cheap here as in neighbouring Morocco. There are plenty of cafés that serve snacks, such as bocadillos and *pulgas*, which are basically rolls with one or two fillings in them. They are simple and reasonably good but hardly constitute a proper meal.

*Café La Imperial* at 27 Calle Real has set menus (*platos combinados*) – standard Spanish fare, comprising meat, chips and salad or cooked vegetables, for 750 pta. It closes at 10 pm. Farther east along the same street are a few cheap tapas bars. Closer to the centre, the *Marina* and *Vicentino* restaurants have pricey mains for 1300 to 1500 pta. They are in a side street connecting the Paseo de Revellín and Marina Española.

The *Club Nautico* (☎ 514440), Paseo de las Palmeras, is a simple place overlooking the fishing port and offers solid fish meals for about 1300 pta.

The *Restaurante Chino Gran Muralla* is Ceuta's only Asian food place. It's on the Paseo de Revellín, just off Plaza de la Constitución.

## Entertainment

**Cafés & Bars** The *Marina* and *Vicentino* restaurants are good places for a coffee and tostada (toasted sandwich) for breakfast.

In the evening, *El Cortije* and *El Mesón de Paco* are a couple of bright, lively, slightly up-market places for a coffee or beer. Slightly more posh is *Bar Dulcinea* on Calle Sargento Coriat. A caña (small glass of beer) costs an expensive 200 pta.

**Nightclubs** If you want a late night, the *Moonlight Pub* on Calle Camoens has a kind of beer garden-cum-disco out the back. Other places you might try include the *Habana Club* on Calle Arabal or the *Pub Visaje*, which has a disco next door.

## Getting There & Away

**To/From Morocco** Buses to the border run every 15 minutes or so from Plaza de la Constitución. The No 7 bus costs 60 pta and takes 20 minutes.

If you arrive by ferry and want to head straight for the border, there is a bus stop for the No 7 just past the tourist booth and off to the right opposite the ramparts.

You walk across the border. The Spaniards barely take any notice of you going out, but are more meticulous if you're going the other way. On the Moroccan side you must fill in a white or yellow entry card. If you have a car you must also fill out a green one; keep the green customs slip they give you as you'll need it on the way out again. Just beyond the banks there are plenty of grands taxis to Tetouan. A seat costs Dr 15. The whole trip from Ceuta to Tetouan should take no more than two hours and it often takes a good deal less.

Occasional buses run from various towns, such as Chefchaouen, to the Ceuta border, but it's a matter of luck whether any happen to be there when you arrive. You're best off taking a taxi and arranging further transport from Tetouan. If you set off early enough, you could conceivably make it to Fès or Meknès, and certainly to Chefchaouen, in the one day.

**To/From Mainland Spain** The Estación Marítima (ferry terminal) is west of the town centre on Calle Muelle Cañonero Dato, and there are frequent ferry and jetfoil departures to Algeciras. See the Getting There & Away chapter for details. You can purchase through train tickets to European destinations at the RENFE office on Plaza Rafael Gilbert, or at one of the travel agencies dotted about town. The bus between the ferry terminal and the centre is marked 'Puerto-Centro'. Be aware that Tetouan touts send a small advance guard to Ceuta – you're bound to meet some of them on debarkation.

Top: Volubilis, Morocco (HF)
Middle Left: Basilica, Volubilis, Morocco (DS)
Middle Right: Cyrene, Libya (AJ)
Bottom: Leptis Magna, Libya (AJ)

Morocco skylines
Top (GC), Middle (DS), Bottom (GC)

# The Rif Mountains

## TETOUAN

For more than 40 years the capital of the Spanish protectorate established in 1912, Tetouan is unique for its mixed Hispanic-Moroccan look and feel. The medina, a conglomeration of cheerfully whitewashed and tiled houses, shops and religious buildings set against the brooding Rif Mountains, shows off its Andalusian heritage. The Spaniards added the new part of town, where even now you can buy a bocadillo and more people speak Spanish than any other foreign language.

Unfortunately for travellers and Tetouan's shopkeepers, the town remains a painful introduction to Morocco (most visitors come from Ceuta). Although not as bad as it once was, Tetouan is an active hive of touts, false guides and hustlers. Wandering around the medina at night is a definite no-no – you can stumble across some decidedly inhospitable individuals. Many visitors simply stop here to change buses and push on, which is a shame, because the medina is interesting and even the modern part of the city, although neglected, is worth a quick look.

## History

Tetouan's ancient predecessor was Tamuda, a Mauretanian city founded in the 3rd century BC. Destroyed in the 1st century AD after a local revolt, the Romans built a fortified camp in its place, remnants of which are visible about five km from the modern town.

In the 14th century, the Merenids created the new city of Tetouan as a base from which to control rebellious Rif tribes, but the city was destroyed by Henry III of Castile in 1399.

Reoccupied in the 16th century by Muslim and Jewish refugees from Granada, Tetouan prospered, and was the last of the Muslim kingdoms in Spain to fall to the Christians. Part of that prosperity was due to piracy, to which the Spanish put an end by blockading Tetouan's port at Martil. They succeeded in stopping the piracy, but legitimate trade suffered too.

Moulay Ismail built Tetouan's defensive walls in the 17th century, and the town's trade links with Spain improved and developed on and off until 1859, when Spanish forces occupied it for three years during a punitive campaign against Rif tribes aimed, it was said, at protecting Ceuta. In 1913 the Spanish made it the capital of their protectorate, which they only abandoned in 1956, when Morocco regained independence.

## Orientation & Information

The medina makes up about two-thirds of the city, while the modern town is tucked into the south-western corner. It is in the latter that you'll find the hotels, banks, most of the restaurants and cafés, bus station and taxi stands. Many streets, called 'calles', still advertise the town's Spanish heritage, but this is changing as, alongside Arabic, French takes over as Morocco's semiofficial second language.

**Tourist Office** The Délégation Régionale du Tourisme (☎ 964407, 967009) is at 30 Calle Mohammed V, just near the corner of Rue Youssef ben Tachfine. The guy here is helpful and speaks quite a bit of English. Don't be talked into hiring a guide (unless, of course, you want one), as the medina is manageable on your own. If you get lost, it's never far to the walls or a gate. The office is open from 8.30 am to noon and 2.30 to 6.30 pm Monday to Thursday; on Friday it's open the same hours but closes from 11.30 am to 3 pm.

**Money** There are plenty of banks along Calle Mohammed V. The most useful is the BMCE, which has a branch with ATMs on Place Moulay el-Mehdi, in the new city.

**Post & Telecommunications** The post office is also on Place Moulay el-Mehdi, and open from 8.30 am to 12.15 pm and 2.30 to 6.45 pm. The telegram section is open from 7 am to 9 pm.

The main telephone office is around the

MOROCCO

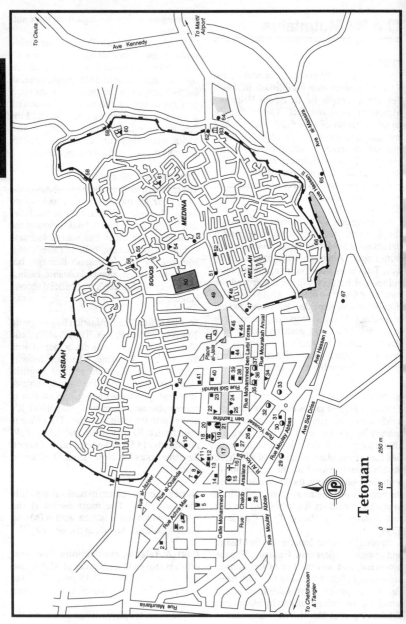

Tetouan

corner from the main entrance to the post office, on Rue al-Ouahda.

**Foreign Consulates** Spain has a consulate in Tetouan at Avenida al-Massira (☎ 973941/2; fax 973946) and a visa office at Carretera Martil, km 3 (☎ 971325; fax 971326). They are open Monday to Friday from 9 am to noon.

**Language School** The American Language Center has a branch at 1 Rue Maerakate Zelaka.

**Ensemble Artisanal** On Ave Hassan II south of the town walls is a large government-sponsored emporium of Moroccan arts and crafts. It is not a bad place to get an idea of the upper range of prices of Moroccan crafts without the pressure of souq sales

tactics. It is open Monday to Friday from 9 am to 12.30 pm and 3.30 to 6.30 pm.

**Medical Services & Emergencies** There is a night pharmacy (☎ 966777) on Rue al-Ouahda. The police can be called on ☎ 19 and the fire brigade on ☎ 15.

**Film & Photography** There is a Kodak store on Rue Youssef ben Tachfine, just up from the El Yesfi Snack bar.

### Medina & Around
Place Hassan II, which links the medina to the new city, is the heart of the city. It has traditionally been a meeting place, and there are a couple of cafés where you can sit and watch the world go by. Heading west, Calle Mohammed V is a pedestrian zone right up

**MOROCCO**

---

**PLACES TO STAY**

2  Hôtel Oumaima
12  Pension Rio Jana
14  Pensions Fès, Bienvenida & Florida
23  Hôtel Regina
26  Hôtel Príncipe
27  Pension Iberia
28  Hôtel Paris
31  Hôtel Trebol
38  Hôtel Nacional
40  Pension Cosmopolita
41  Hôtel Persa
44  Hôtel Bilbao

**PLACES TO EAT**

8  Picinic Snack Bar
11  Bakery
22  El Yesfi Snack
24  Restaurant Restinga
34  Sandwich Ali Baba
36  Restaurant Zarhoun
45  Restaurant Granada
46  Restaurant Saigon
54  El Yesfi Snack

**OTHER**

1  Bab Noider
3  Café
4  Café & Cinema Avenida
5  Bar Ideal
6  Café/Pâtisserie
7  Drycleaners
9  Grands Taxis to Tangier & Chefchaouen
10  Modern Hammam (Duchas y Sauna)
13  Café
15  Wafabank
16  Cathedral
17  Place Moulay el-Mehdi
18  Telephone Office
19  Post Office
20  Men's Hammam
21  Tourist Office
25  Voyages Hispamaroc
29  Bus to Martil
30  Taxis to Tangier
32  Taxis to Ceuta
33  Bus Station
35  Grands Taxis to Ceuta

37  Grands Taxis to Martil
39  Café Détroit
42  Bab Tout
43  Museum
47  Cinema Español
48  Cafés
49  Place Hassan II
50  Royal Palace
51  Bab er-Rouah
52  Gold Souqs
53  Dyers
55  Leather
56  Carpentry
57  Bab M'Kabar (Bab Sebta)
58  Bab Sfli
59  Bab as Saida
60  Saidi Mosque
61  Great Mosque
62  Bab el-Okla
63  Musée Marocain
64  Artisanat School
65  Spanish Consulate
66  Bab Remouz
67  Ensemble Artisanal (Artefact Emporium)

to Place Moulay el-Mehdi, and is lined with shops, cafés, restaurants and the odd hotel.

The main entrance into the medina is Bab er-Rouah ('Gate of the Winds'), to the right of the former Spanish consulate. The medina is a bustling place, great for just wandering at random. It is quite unlike the great medinas farther south, in that the Spaniards had a hand in some of the building in the 19th century. In any case, most of its inhabitants from the 16th century on were refugees from what had been Muslim Spain. There are some 20 **mosques** within the medina, of which the Great and Saidi mosques stand out a little more than the others. As is usual in Morocco, non-Muslims may not enter.

The north-eastern area of the medina, north of Bab el-Okla, was the up-market end of town. Some of the fine houses built by the city's residents in the last century still stand here and several have been turned into carpet showrooms and extravagant tearooms. You'll probably stumble across them yourself, but there are plenty of touts around who will gladly take you to one, particularly the carpet shops.

Although the shopkeepers don't do a roaring tourist trade here, wood and leatherwork are two local artisanal specialities. It might be worth wandering up towards Bab M'Kabar (or Bab Sebta) for a look. You'll also come across other shops dedicated to the tourist trade, selling copper and brassware, babouches and a limited selection of souvenirs. If you're interested in Tetouan carpets, go first to the Artisanat school to get an idea of what to look for.

**Musée Marocain** Also known as the Museum of Moroccan Art, this collection of traditional clothing, instruments, carpets, arms and household implements is a pleasing and peaceful stop built in a bastion in the town wall, just south of Bab el-Okla – cannon are still in place in the garden. Unfortunately, most of the labelling is in Arabic. The chap following you around to turn lights on and off will expect a small tip when you've finished.

It is open Monday to Friday from 8.30 am to noon and 2.30 to 6 pm. The entry fee is Dr 10.

**Artisanat School** Just opposite Bab el-Okla is the artisan school, where you can see children being taught traditional crafts such as carpet-weaving, leatherwork, woodwork and the making of enamel zellij tiles. Their work is on display but not for sale. The building itself is worth a visit. The school is open from 8.30 am to noon and 2.30 to 5.30 pm (closed weekends). Entry is Dr 10.

**Archaeology Museum** There is a small archaeology museum opposite the end of Rue Prince Sidi Mohammed but it is only for the dedicated. It has a few prehistoric stones, some Roman coins and a number of small mosaics and other artefacts from Lixus. It is open Monday to Saturday from 8.30 am to noon and 2.30 to 5.30 pm; closed weekends. Entry costs Dr 10 but the enclosed gardens in front of the museum, where many of the larger exhibits have been set up, are free.

### Places to Stay – bottom end

**Camping** The nearest camp site is by the beach at Martil, about eight km away (see the Around Tetouan section). There's also a site not far from Club Med, about halfway between Tetouan and the (Ceuta) border.

**Hotels** There are plenty of cheap, very basic pensions available in Tetouan, most of which charge from Dr 50 for a single. Little store seems to be set by quality. Few have hot water, and even at the upper end of the price scale, most of the staff at these places seem to be exceptionally ill-humoured.

Some of the pensions could be straight out of Spain, with their wrought-iron balconies overlooking the street. Others are flophouses or straight-out brothels. The pensions *Fès, Bienvenida, Florida* and *Rio Jana* all fall into this category, and want about Dr 50/80 (they may ask for more) for singles/doubles. The Florida has small but clean and comfortable rooms. The Rio Jana is a brothel, but they'll let you have a room if you really want one.

One pension that can be recommended is

the *Pension Iberia* (☎ 963679), on the 3rd floor above the BMCE on Place Moulay el-Mehdi. Although there are only a few rooms, it has a homey atmosphere and some rooms have great views over the square. They cost Dr 60/70 for singles/doubles with shared bathroom. They don't seem to have hot showers.

The *Hotel Bilbao* (☎ 967939), 7 Calle Mohammed V, is a good cheap alternative to the pensions and has a lot of character, especially if you can get one of the front rooms. It costs Dr 52 for a room, regardless of whether one or two people occupy it, with shared bathroom and cold showers.

If you're looking for something a little better, but not too expensive, try the one-star *Hotel Trebol* (☎ 962018), which is close to the bus station. It has singles/doubles without private shower for Dr 50/80 or Dr 70/103 with shower. There is hot water in the morning and a dry-cleaner's next door.

Another possibility is the undeservedly two-star *Hotel Príncipe* (☎ 962795) at 20 Rue Youssef ben Tachfine. Clean singles/doubles/triples are Dr 59/98/145. They only have cold water and are basic. Since the prices don't reflect the star-rating, however, it's not bad value.

**Hammams** Given that so few of the cheaper hotels offer hot water, the public baths may well come in handy. The hammam off Rue al-Jazeer is pretty new. The sign says 'Duchas y Sauna', and men and women can go from 6 am to 9.15 pm, seven days a week. A shower costs Dr 5, a sauna is Dr 30 and a massage and sauna cost Dr 60. There is a second public shower (men only) on Rue Youssef ben Tachfine across the road from the El Yesfi Snack bar, and another behind the post office.

### Places to Stay – middle

The *Hotel Persa* (☎ 964215) is a dusty old place with a cavernous café on the ground floor. It offers ill-lit doubles with private shower, toilet and sagging beds for Dr 84.

Better is the *Hotel Nacional* (☎ 963290), 8 Rue Mohammed ben Larbi Torres, which has singles/doubles with private shower and toilet for Dr 71/108 including taxes. The rooms are a little gloomy, but are otherwise quite good.

A particularly unhelpful crew run the *Hotel Regina* (☎ 962113), 8 Rue Sidi Mandri. Doubles with private shower and toilet here cost Dr 109 and there's hot water in the morning. The rooms themselves are on a par with those in the Nacional.

Better, but considerably more expensive (especially for lone travellers) and devoid of character, is the *Hotel Paris* (☎ 966750), 11 Rue Chakib Arsalane, where singles/doubles with private shower, toilet and hot water are Dr 151/171 including taxes. The management is friendly but you'll need to hassle for soap and toilet paper.

The pick of the bunch in Tetouan itself is the *Hotel Oumaima* (☎ 963473), Rue Achra Mai. It has rooms for Dr 151/190/241, and they are considerably better than those at the Paris. The staff even turn on the central heating in winter – sometimes.

### Places to Stay – top end

The four-star *Hotel Safir* (☎ 970144/77), Ave Kennedy, is the only top-range hotel in Tetouan. It has 98 rooms, a swimming pool, tennis courts and a nightclub, but is a long way out of the centre of town.

### Places to Eat

The best place to get a cheap, filling and nutritious meal is *El Yesfi Snack*. They do great baguette sandwiches with various meats, potato salad, chips and salad for Dr 10.

The *Picnic* snack bar, on Rue Achra Mai, does an average version of a hamburger. Another reasonable and cheap snack place is *Sandwich Ali Baba* on Rue Mourakah Anual. Despite the name, they also have chicken, chips, soups and tajines. It's popular and you practically have to fight through the crowd at the front to get to the seating area in the back.

A good-value restaurant is the *Restaurant Saigon* on Rue Mohammed ben Larbi Torres, although there's nothing Vietnamese about

**MOROCCO**

it. You can get a huge serve of tasty couscous or brochettes for Dr 20, preceded by a big bowl of chunky soup for Dr 4. It's justifiably popular.

Close by, down a lane opposite the Cinema Español, is the *Restaurante Moderno*. It's a bit more down to earth, but the prices are much the same. Locals recommend it, and there are a couple of lively cafés in the same spot.

Not so good is the *Restaurant Restinga*, which you get to through a small alley off Calle Mohammed V. You can eat inside or in a partly open courtyard. The staff are friendly and the menu is about the same as at the Saigon, though many items are not available. The big plus, however, is that they serve beer. A bottle of Amstel costs Dr 13.

The *Restaurante Granada*, on Calle Mohammed V at Place al-Jala, is clean and cheap and serves the usual tajines, couscous and soups.

The best restaurant in Tetouan by far is the *Restaurant Zarhoun*, on Rue Mohammed ben Larbi Torres. They do a great pastilla (pigeon pie). At Dr 55, it's pricey but good. The rest of the limited menu features the usual couscous, tajine and brochettes for about Dr 45 a serve. You can get beer and wine, and some locals clearly use it as an up-market bar. The interior is like something from *A Thousand & One Nights*.

### Entertainment

**Cafés & Bars** There appears to be only one bar, the *Ideal* – look for the Flag Spéciale sign off Rue Achra Mai. It's a spit-and-sawdust place. The *Zarhoun* and *Restinga* restaurants are about the only other places where you can get a drink.

On the other hand, Spanish-style cafés (without alcohol) abound, and the coffee and tea are good. There are a lot along the Calle Mohammed V pedestrian zone and Rue Achra Mai. On the latter, the *Avenida* and another café closer to Place Moulay el-Mehdi are slightly chic and very pleasant. The *Café Détroit* on Calle Mohammed V is another rather European-style spot that does a good cup. The cafés on Place Hassan II are more down to earth and Moroccan in flavour. There are plenty of others to choose from, and quite a selection of cake shops too.

**Cinema** The *Cinema Avenida*, on Rue Achra Mai, is the main movie house in Tetouan and offers four sessions a day.

### Getting There & Away

**Bus** The bus station is at the junction of Rue Sidi Mandri and Rue Moulay Abbas. It is a dark and gloomy place with the ticket windows upstairs, buses downstairs and touts all over.

CTM has six buses to Chefchaouen a day, starting at 5 am and finishing at 10 pm. They cost Dr 16.50. Buses for Tangier leave at 5.30 am and 2.30, 4.15 and 6.15 pm, take about an hour and cost Dr 13.

At 10.30 pm there is a bus to Casablanca (Dr 91.50) via Rabat. The trip takes about seven hours. There is a second bus nonstop to Casablanca at 11 pm. There is one bus to Fès at 11.30 am, which stops in Ouezzane on the way. It takes about five hours and tickets cost Dr 55.

Four buses a day head for Al-Hoceima (about seven hours), and two of them go on to Nador (close to 10 hours).

If you can't get on a CTM bus, there are plenty of other private lines. These buses are often not in such great shape, but the competition means you have quite a few choices. There are regular departures for Chefchaouen and Tangier, and some of these companies cover destinations CTM doesn't. Transports AMA, for instance, goes to Oujda for Dr 117.65. It also has a bus every three hours to Cabo Negro for Dr 3.

A local bus to Martil (Dr 2) leaves from Rue Moulay Abbas, not far from the bus station.

**Train** There is no train station at Tetouan but the ONCF runs two Supratours buses to Tnine Sidi Lyamani at 7.30 am and 3.30 pm to link up with trains to and from Tangier. The Supratours office is on Rue Achra Mai, near the Cinema Avenida.

**Taxi** Grands taxis for the Spanish enclave of Ceuta leave frequently from the corner of Rue Mourakah Anual and Rue Sidi Mandri, just up from the bus station. A seat costs Dr 15 for the 20-minute trip to Fnideq on the Moroccan side. Although the border is open 24 hours a day, transport dries up from about 7 pm to 5 am.

On the Spanish side of the border, the No 7 public bus runs every half-hour or so to the centre for 60 pta.

Local grands taxis to the beach at Martil leave from farther up Rue Mourakah Anual and cost Dr 3.

Grands taxis to Chefchaouen leave frequently from a rank on Rue al-Jazeer (Dr 20). There are less frequent departures from the same rank for Tangier (Dr 30).

**Car Rental** Zeit (☎ & fax 961664) is at Immeuble Yacoub el-Mansour.

### Getting Around

**Taxi** It's unlikely you'll need one, but a petit taxi ride around town should not be more than about Dr 6. If you need to get to or from the airport (also fairly unlikely), you'll pay Dr 15 for the four-km run.

## AROUND TETOUAN
### Martil & Cabo Negro
About eight km east of Tetouan is the beach town of Martil. Once Tetouan's port and home to pirates, there is little to it now but a reasonable beach and a couple of waterfront cafés. Farther north up the coast is Cabo Negro (or Ras Aswad in Arabic), a headland jutting out into the Mediterranean clearly visible from Martil beach.

**Places to Stay & Eat** *Camping Martil* is the closest camping ground to Tetouan, but it's a sparse affair. It costs Dr 6 a person, Dr 6 for a car and Dr 10 for pitching a big tent. There are cold showers and electricity costs an extra Dr 2. *Camping Ch'bar*, on the road from Martil up to Cabo Negro, is a little better.

As Martil is so close to Tetouan, there is hardly any need to stay here, but you could

try the *Charaf Pension*. In summer they charge a hefty Dr 70/90/120/160 for a room with beds and basin. Another place is the *Pension Badia*, near the bus stop.

An up-market place is the *Hotel Estrella del Mar* (☎ 979276), which has modern rooms for Dr 157.50/204/273 including breakfast. In summer they impose half-board, which takes a double to Dr 340. Apart from the hotel restaurant, there are a few nondescript cafés and small eateries scattered about.

**Getting There & Away** The local bus to Tetouan leaves from a dirt patch near the camping ground, but it'll stop for you on the main road back to Tetouan.

### Road to Ceuta
The stretch of coast between Cabo Negro and Fnideq (the border with Ceuta) is littered with expensive chalets, small-scale beach resorts and a Club Med. Just near Restinga Smir (where, by the way, a catamaran occasionally lands from Gibraltar during summer) is the *Camping Fraja*.

## CHEFCHAOUEN
Also called Chaouen, Chechaouen and Xauen, this delightful town in the Rif Mountains is a favourite with travellers for obvious reasons: the air is cool and clear, the people are noticeably more relaxed than in Tangier or Tetouan, there's more kif than you can poke a stick at, and the town is small and manageable. All this makes it a great place to hang out for a few days.

Founded by Moulay Ali ben Rachid in 1471 as a base from which to attack the Portuguese in Ceuta, the town prospered and grew considerably with the arrival of Muslim refugees from Spain. It was these refugees who built the whitewashed houses with blue painted doors and window frames, tiny balconies, tiled roofs and patios with a citrus tree planted in the centre that give the town its distinctive Hispanic flavour. The obvious intention was to re-create at the base of Jebel al-Qala'a (1616 metres) what they had been forced to leave behind in Spain.

The town remained isolated, and almost xenophobic, until occupied by Spanish troops in 1920, and the inhabitants continued to speak a variant of medieval Castilian. In fact, Christians were forbidden entry to the town and only did so on pain of death. Two managed to do so in disguise: the French adventurer Charles Foucauld in 1883 and, five years later, the British wanderer and journalist Walter Harris (disguised as a Jew).

The Spanish were briefly thrown out of Chefchaouen by Abd el-Krim between 1924 and 1926 during the Riffian rebellion but returned to stay until independence in 1956.

Despite being firmly on the tourist circuit, Chefchaouen (Chaouen means 'peaks', referring to the Rif heights around the town, and Chefchaouen 'look at the peaks') is remarkably easy-going, with only a few touts around. The new bus station is a 20-minute hike south-west of the town centre, which is downhill when you leave but a rather steep incline on arrival. The main street in the new town is Avenida Hassan II. At Bab al-'Ain it swings south and follows the medina wall around towards Oued Laou.

## Information

**Tourist Office** There is a syndicat d'initiative in a lane just north of Plaza Mohammed V, open Monday to Friday from 9 am to noon and 3 to 6 pm, but it is of limited use. They have a sketch map of the town with hotel phone numbers, but that's it.

**Post & Telecommunications** The post office (PTT) is on Avenida Hassan II, about 50 metres west of the Bab al-'Ain entrance to the medina. It's open from 8.30 am to 12.15 pm and 2.30 to 6.45 pm Monday to Saturday (on Friday it is closed for noon prayers from 11.30 am to 3 pm). You can make international phone calls from here but there are no card phones.

**Money** The BMCE and the Banque Populaire are both on Avenida Hassan II. You can change cash and travellers' cheques and get cash advances on Visa and MasterCard at both. There are no ATMs.

**Newspapers** There is a reasonable newsstand between the Banque Populaire and the Pâtisserie Magou on Avenida Hassan II. It has the odd publication in French, English, Spanish and German.

## Market

The market (see map) is much the centre of things on Mondays and Thursdays, when merchants come from all over the Rif to trade. The emphasis is on food and second-hand clothes, although there are sometimes a few interesting souvenirs.

## Medina

The old medina is small, uncrowded and easy to find your way around in. For the most part, the houses and buildings are a blinding blue-white and, on the northern side especially, you'll find many with tiny ground-floor rooms crowded with weaving looms. These are a legacy of the days when silkworms were introduced by Andalusian refugees and weaving became the principal activity of families living here. Most of the weaving done now is of wool, which is one of the biggest products of the area. The people working these looms are friendly and, to break the monotony of their work, they may well invite you in for a smoke and a chat.

There is also a fair smattering of tourist shops, particularly around Plaza de Makhzen and Plaza Uta el-Hammam – the focal points of the old city.

## Plaza Uta el-Hammam & Kasbah The

shady, cobbled Plaza Uta el-Hammam, with the kasbah along one side, is at its busiest in the early evening, when everyone starts to get out and about after the inactivity of the afternoon. It's a great time to sit in one of the cafés opposite the kasbah and relax. The atmosphere is sedate and almost medieval, except for the cars and, unfortunately, the tour buses.

The red-hued ruins of the 17th-century kasbah dominate the square and its walls enclose a beautiful garden. It was built by Moulay Ismail to defend the town against unruly Berber tribes as well as outsiders such as the Spaniards. For a time it was Abd el-Krim's headquarters, but, in one of those twists of history, he ended up being imprisoned here by the Spaniards.

To the right of the entrance to the kasbah are the cells, complete with neck chains at floor level, where Abd el-Krim was imprisoned in 1926. To the left is a small museum containing a collection of traditional arms, instruments, textiles and some old photos of the town. It also houses a small Andalusian studies centre. You can climb up a couple of storeys onto the roof for some good views of the town.

The kasbah is open from 9 am to 1 pm and 3 to 6.30 pm, and entry costs Dr 10.

**Great Mosque** Next door to the kasbah is Chefchaouen's Great Mosque, built in the 15th century by the town's founder, Ali ben Rachid. Non-Muslims may not enter.

**Plaza de Makhzen** The Plaza de Makhzen is the lesser of the two town squares; it has a large old gum tree in the centre. Instead of cafés, it has mostly tourist shops. However, on market days you still get people squatting under the tree selling bundles of mint and vegetables grown in the surrounding area.

If you take the lane heading north-east from the square you'll eventually come out at Bab al-Ansar; after this comes the river, Oued Laou, with a couple of agreeable shady cafés on its banks. Off to the left is Ras al-Ma', the spring at the source of the Oued Laou's clear, fresh water. This is also where women come to do the washing while the men busy themselves drinking tea.

### Activities
**Hiking** The hills around Chefchaouen offer some good hiking possibilities. If you want to do anything ambitious, you should probably consider engaging a guide – ask at your hotel. It is supposedly possible to organise small hikes in the hills on donkey-back, if you like that sort of thing. Again, the best place to start making enquiries is at your hotel.

**Music Festival** Chefchaouen occasionally hosts a modest festival of traditional Andalusian music in August.

### Places to Stay – bottom end
**Camping & Hostel** Right up on the side of the hill behind the Hotel Asma is the camp site and hostel (☎ 986031). They are only really worth considering if you have your own vehicle, as it's quite a hike to get to them. It's a steep 30-minute walk by the road (follow the signs to the Hotel Asma), or a 15-minute scramble up the hill through the cemetery; you shouldn't attempt the latter on a Friday, as the locals don't take kindly to it.

The camping area is shady and costs Dr 5 per person, Dr 10 per vehicle and Dr 10 to Dr 15 to pitch a tent, depending on how big it is. Showers are Dr 5. The hostel is extremely basic and poor value at Dr 20 per person.

**Hotels** If you've come from Tetouan, you'll find the standard of accommodation considerably better and cheaper here. There are plenty of places around, but in peak periods especially they can all fill up quickly. In winter (when it can be very cold) the main problem is that, with a couple of exceptions, no-one has considered the idea of heating.

The cheapest places are the pensions in the medina. For the most part they are OK, if a little gloomy and claustrophobic at times. It all depends on what you are offered, but some of them are very popular with budget travellers so, if you want a good room, get there early in the day.

The *Pension Castilliano*, just off the western end of Plaza Uta el-Hammam, is a popular travellers' hang-out, with beds for Dr 20 a person and hot showers for Dr 5 more. At that price, some of the other places are definitely better. One of these is the *Hotel Andaluz*, which costs Dr 30 a double; there are no singles. The rooms all face an internal courtyard and while those on the upper floor are light and airy, the ones on the ground floor are dark and gloomy. Hot showers are available for Dr 5.

Another place travellers zero in on is the *Pension Mauritania*, Zankat al-Qadi, which

MOROCCO

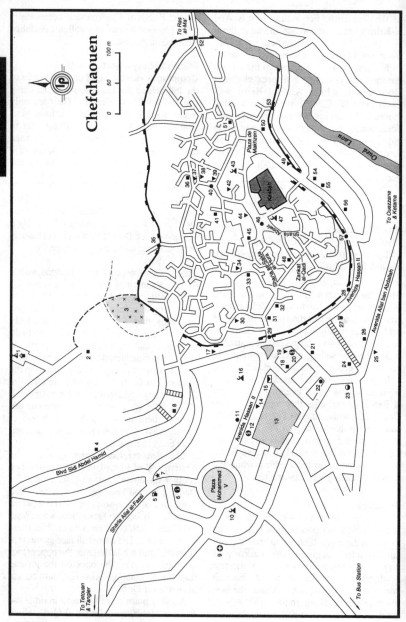

Chefchaouen

offers singles/doubles for Dr 25/50 including a good breakfast. The staff are friendly and there's a beautiful traditional lounge area. Also good value is the *Pension Znika*, north of the kasbah, which is spotlessly clean, light and airy and costs Dr 20 a person. Hot showers are available on the ground floor.

Up in the higher reaches of the medina, with good views and the chance of a breeze, is the *Pension Valencia*. The doubles and triples are clean, simple and good value at Dr 35/50, but the singles are glorified cupboards. The communal showers and toilets are well maintained. To find the Valencia, take the lane off to the north from Plaza Uta el-Hammam; it twists back and forth up the hill but after a few minutes you come to the Restaurant Granada. From there take the left fork and follow it around to the right.

Just inside the Bab al-'Ain on the right is the *Hotel Bab El Ain* (☎ 986935), which is a little expensive at Dr 50 a head, but is clean and comfortable with occasional hot water. A little farther up is the *Hotel Abie Khanda*

(☎ 986879). The rooms are clean and bright and there is a roof terrace and hot water some of the time. The beds are a little on the rock-hard side, but it's not a bad deal at Dr 30 a person.

Outside the medina area below (south of) the Bab al-'Ain is the *Hotel Sahra*, which also has singles/doubles for Dr 20/30. It's a little gloomy and doesn't have the atmosphere of the pensions in the medina. Farther south is the noisily located *Hotel Ketama*, which doesn't have a whole lot to recommend it either, especially at Dr 30/40 – the medina places are better.

North-east of Plaza de Makhzen is the *Pension al-Hamra* (☎ 986362). It's a quiet place away from the bulk of the tourist trade and is OK at Dr 30/60. Hot showers are Dr 5. A bit farther along towards Bab al-Ansar is the *Hostal Gernika* (☎ 987434), which is run by two Spanish women. It has 10 rooms, some with private shower. They have hot water and prices range from Dr 60 for a single to Dr 120 for a double.

**MOROCCO**

---

| PLACES TO STAY | | PLACES TO EAT | | | |
|---|---|---|---|---|---|
| 1 | Camping Ground & Youth Hostel | 14 | Café | 9 | Hospital |
| 2 | Hôtel Asma | 17 | Restaurants Zouar & Moulay Ali ben Rachid | 10 | Mosque |
| 4 | Residencia La Estrella | | | 11 | Newsstand |
| 8 | Auberge Granada | 19 | Pâtisserie Magou | 12 | BMCE Bank |
| 18 | Hôtel Magou | 25 | Café Ahlan | 13 | Market |
| 21 | Hôtel Sahra | 30 | Restaurant Assaada | 15 | Post Office (PTT) |
| 24 | Hôtel Ketama | 34 | Restaurant El Baraka | 16 | Sidi Ali ben Rachid Mosque |
| 26 | Hôtel Sevilla | 37 | Restaurant Granada | 20 | Banque Populaire |
| 28 | Hôtel Rif | 38 | Restaurant Chez Fouad | 22 | Kodak Shop |
| 31 | Hôtel Bab El Ain | 39 | Restaurant Maravilia | 23 | Grands Taxis to Ouezzane |
| 32 | Hôtel Abie Khanda | 42 | Restaurant Tissemlal | 27 | Bar |
| 33 | Hôtel Andaluz | 44 | Cafés & Restaurants | 29 | Bab al-'Ain |
| 36 | Pension Valencia | 49 | Restaurant Chefchaouen | 35 | Bab Djenan |
| 41 | Pension Znika | | | 40 | Fountain |
| 45 | Pension Castilliano | **OTHER** | | 43 | Mosque |
| 48 | Pension Mauritania | | | 46 | Plaza Uta el-Hammam |
| 50 | Hôtel Parador | 3 | Cemetery | 47 | Great Mosque |
| 51 | Pension al-Hamra | 5 | Mobil Service Station | 52 | Bab al-Ansar |
| 54 | Hôtel Marrakech | 6 | Syndicat d'Initiative | 53 | Bab al-Muqaddam |
| 55 | Hôtel Salam | 7 | Police | 57 | Bab Hammar |
| 56 | Hôtel Madrid | | | | |

Outside the medina again is the *Hotel Salam* (☎ 986239) on Avenida Hassan II. At Dr 40/58, it is a pretty good deal. It has hot water most of the time and its own restaurant. If you're lucky, you'll get a room with a decent view over the valley to the south, or you can get the same view from the terrace.

The *Hôtel Marrakech* (☎ 987113) opened virtually next door in 1992 and provides tough competition for the Salam. Rooms without private shower go for Dr 50/100 and with shower for Dr 60/120. They are a little small, but modern, clean and comfortable. Breakfast costs an extra Dr 15.

Off to the north-west of the town centre on the long and winding road to the Hotel Asma is the *Residencia La Estrella* (☎ 986526) on Blvd Sidi Abdel Hamid. It's some way out and doesn't have a lot of character, but the rooms, at Dr 60 a head, are quite comfortable and the place has a homey atmosphere. It's equipped with a kitchen, so those wanting to do their own cooking could find it ideal.

### Places to Stay – middle
The *Hotel Sevilla* (☎ 986911) on Avenida Allal ben Abdallah is a good choice if you can pay just a little extra. Rooms are basically Dr 70 per person, but in the low season management can be persuaded to lower the price. The rooms are modern and comfortable, and reasonably spacious. Some have private toilet and others have a shower as well. The main problem seems to be hot water – they promise it all day, but it never happens. The tearoom downstairs has an extremely low ceiling and satellite TV.

A long-time favourite with travellers has been the *Hotel Rif* (☎ 986207), just below the city walls on Avenida Hassan II. They've jacked their prices up considerably, so it's not the good value it once was. Rooms, some with a valley view, cost Dr 100/150/235 with hot water and the obligatory breakfast.

For a little more you can go to the *Hotel Magou* (☎ 986275), near the market at 23 Calle Moulay Idriss. In the low season it charges Dr 117/145/205 for decent rooms that sometimes have central heating; there is

hot water in the mornings. Prices go up considerably in summer.

Another recent addition to Avenida Hassan II's hotel population is the *Hotel Madrid* (☎ 987498). The rooms are spotless and have heaters in winter. You pay Dr 120/184/246.

### Places to Stay – top end
The cheapest of the top-end hotels is the three-star *Hotel Asma* (☎ 986002, 986265), a huge concrete structure overlooking the town, above the cemetery. It has 94 very pleasant, self-contained rooms, a bar and restaurant, though meals in the restaurant are very pricey at a minimum of Dr 100. The rooms are Dr 226/273. The disadvantage of staying here is the distance from town. The advantage is the views – especially at night. Avoid having laundry done here, however, as the rates are extortionate.

The most expensive hotel in Chefchaouen is the four-star *Hotel Parador* (☎ 986324, 986136), on Place de Makhzen, which costs Dr 302/377 for singles/doubles. The hotel has its own bar and restaurant and all the usual facilities you would expect of a hotel at this price.

### Places to Eat
Among the cafés on Plaza Uta el-Hammam are a number of small restaurants that serve good local food. You are looking at about Dr 20 for a full meal with soft drink.

Up near the Pension Valencia, the *Restaurant Granada* is run by a cheery character who cooks a variety of dishes at reasonable prices. A block back down is a reasonable place recommended by locals, the *Restaurant Chez Fouad*. Prices are roughly the same as in the Granada and the food is equally good. Another one worth checking out if you're in the area is the *Maravilia*, opposite the fountain on the tiny square.

The *Restaurant Assaada*, just inside the Bab al-'Ain to the left, serves decent food at modest prices.

Outside the medina, just up the hill from the Bab al-'Ain, are Chefchaouen's best eateries: the *Restaurant Moulay Ali ben*

*Rachid* and the *Restaurant Zouar* – take your pick. They are simple and very good – and usually full of Spaniards down for a short holiday. The Zouar has a filling set menu for Dr 25, and both offer good mains for around Dr 15. Even if the food were bad, it would be hard to argue with the price.

For something of a splurge, try the *Restaurant Chefchaouen* on the street leading up to Plaza de Makhzen. It's pleasantly designed in traditional style, but don't come here for breakfast as it will take forever to arrive. A full meal (soup, tajine/couscous and fruit) for lunch or dinner costs Dr 50.

More expensive is the *Restaurant Tissemlal*, 22 Rue Targui, just up from Plaza Uta el-Hammam and off to the right. Like the Chefchaouen, this restaurant has been beautifully conceived and even has an upstairs balcony running the whole way around. The service is quick but the food, unfortunately, is only average. You're looking at Dr 70 for a full lunch.

A cheerfully enough decorated but overpriced (for what you get) restaurant is the *El Baraka*, near the Hotel Andaluz. At Dr 70, the rather ordinary set menu is hardly breathtaking.

The hotels *Rif*, *Salam*, *Marrakech* and *Madrid* all have decent restaurants, although the Madrid is pricier than the rest. For those with fatter wallets, there are also the top-end hotels.

Drinkers have few choices. Aside from the bar on Avenida Hassan II, you are virtually obliged to try the two big hotels.

The *Pâtisserie Magou* on Avenida Hassan II has good pastries and fresh bread.

Most of the cafés on Plaza Uta el-Hammam have seedy rooms upstairs where the hard smoking goes on – you can just about cut the air with a knife in some of them – and there are certainly worse ways to pass a few hours than to sit around playing dominoes with the locals.

### Getting There & Away

**Bus** The new bus station is about a 20-minute walk south-west of the town centre. CTM and all other buses leave from here but

be warned: many of them are through services from elsewhere and are often full on arrival. Since it is not always possible to book, you could easily be in for a long wait.

CTM has a bus to Casablanca (Dr 79) via Ouezzane (Dr 16.50), Souq Arba'a, Kenitra and Rabat at 6.30 am. There are buses to Fès (Dr 42; 4½ hours) via Ouezzane at 1.15 and 3.30 pm. You can book in advance for the first but not the second service. They come from Tetouan, and CTM only has six seats reserved in advance from Chefchaouen.

The easiest place to get to is Tetouan (departures at 7.30 and 8.45 am, and noon, 3, 4 and 7 pm). The fare is Dr 16.50. There is a bus at 3 pm to Tangier.

Three buses a day head to Ketama and Al-Hoceima; two of them continue on to Nador. There is one bus to Taza.

Other companies are represented at three other windows. The timetables are posted and it's all quite easy to follow. However, you can't *book* to, say, Fès (the most popular destination), for which all services are through buses from Tetouan.

At window No 2 they sell tickets for Fès buses at 9.30 and 11.45 am and 1.15 pm. Since you can't book and they often arrive from Tetouan full (in spite of what they will tell you at the window), you could be in trouble. If this happens and you decide only then that you want one of the above CTM buses, you will have to fight with everyone else to get one of the six seats on the 1.15 pm bus or just wait and hope for the 3.30 pm bus. It is easy to see how you could end up stuck at the station for the day trying to get to Fès!

At window No 2 they also have eight runs to Tetouan (Dr 15); three to Fnideq (Ceuta) at 6 and 11.15 am and 12.30 pm (Dr 22); and two to Tangier via Tetouan (Dr 26) at 9.30 am and 2.45 pm. Window No 4 has another six buses to Tangier via Tetouan.

Window No 3 has seven runs to Ouezzane (Dr 15; 1½ hours) and five to Tetouan. At 7.30 am they have a bus to Casablanca (Dr 62) via Souq Arba'a, Kenitra and Rabat.

There are three buses to Meknès, at 6 am, noon and 4 pm (Dr 45; four hours). The first and last of these stop at Moulay Idriss. These buses are far less likely to be full than the Fès buses, and a lot of locals catch them and link up with the frequent transport to Fès from Meknès. This is not a bad tip if the morning bus to Fès comes and goes without you on it and you're staring at a day spent fruitlessly at Chefchaouen bus station.

If you get the feeling the Fès *and* Meknès buses are all going to be full, catch a bus (or grand taxi in the morning) to Ouezzane and try again from there.

**Taxi** Grands taxis go to Tetouan (Dr 20) and Ouezzane only (from near the old CTM offices, about 50 metres west of the Hotel Sevilla). To Ouezzane they cost about Dr 25 per person. They don't go all that often, so be there early. For any other destinations you'll have to bargain for a special deal. Ouezzane is a bit of a transport hub, so it could be worth the trip there just to pick up something going farther your way (Fès or Rabat for instance).

## OUEZZANE

Lying in the plains at the southern edge of the Rif, Ouezzane is another town to which Andalusian refugees, many of them Jews, fled in the 15th century. Muslims regard it as a holy city, with a zawiyya dedicated to the memory of Moulay Abdallah ben Brahim, one of several contenders for supremacy in the chaotic Morocco of the early 18th century. His moussem is celebrated in late March. Jews too make an annual pilgrimage (around May) to visit the tomb of Rabbi Amrane ben Diwan, an Andalusian 'miracle worker' who died in about 1780 and whose tomb lies nine km north-west of Ouezzane off the road to Rabat, in the Jewish cemetery of Azjem.

The bus and grand taxi lot is a huge dirt patch to the north-west of the central Place de l'Indépendance. The small medina, the southern half of which forms the old Jewish quarter (the mellah), lies to the south-east. North of the medina are the **Moulay Abdallah Sherif Mosque** and the **Mosque of the Zawiyya**, which is also known as the Green Mosque. If you enter the Bab ash-

Shurfa, the main gate in the south-eastern corner of the square, you'll find yourself walking through the metalworkers' market and soon after across into the woodworkers' market. There are a few places where rugs and the like can be bought, and you're bound to meet one of the town's two or three guides pretty soon. With so few travellers coming through, you could well strike a good bargain for a carpet.

### Information

There is a bank and post office on the main road leading north off Place de l'Indépendance.

### Places to Stay & Eat

Of the three hotels on the southern end of Place de l'Indépendance, the *Hôtel El Alam* is possibly the best. It has clean rooms around an open courtyard on the top floor and shared cold showers and toilets for Dr 30/50/70. The *Grand Hôtel* is also OK but *L'Horloge*, at Dr 30 for awful rooms, is to be avoided.

There are a few cafés and snack stands on the square. For a classy view of the northern plains, head through Bab ash-Shurfa and after a couple of hundred metres you'll come to the *Café Bellevue* on your right.

### Getting There & Away

**Bus** The station is a mucky old affair, and confusion seems to reign. There are buses from Ouezzane to Casablanca, Rabat, Fès, Meknès, Chefchaouen (Dr 15 to Dr 16.50), Tetouan and Tangier.

Ouezzane is a bit of a crossroads and if you are losing hope of getting out of Chefchaouen to head south, it might be worth trying your luck here. There is no guarantee, and the earlier you start the better. There are virtually no buses after 5 pm.

**Taxis** Grands taxis run from the bus station to Fès (Dr 60), Rabat (Dr 50) and Chefchaouen (Dr 25). They are not that frequent, but if you get there in the morning you should be able to pick up something, as most people just pass through Ouezzane.

1. Bus & Grand Taxi Station
2. Bank
3. Post Office
4. Hôtel l'Horloge
5. Hôtel El Alam
6. Grand Hôtel
7. Bab ash-Shurfa
8. Mosque of the Zawiyya
9. Café Bellevue
10. Moulay Abdallah Sherif Mosque

## KETAMA

Instead of heading south out of the Rif from Chefchaouen towards Ouezzane and on to the coast or the Middle Atlas, you could turn east instead and plunge into the heart of the Rif and on to a couple of minor Mediterranean resorts. Buses head right across to Al-Hoceima and Nador via Ketama, and the ride along what is virtually the backbone of the Rif is among the most breathtaking trips in the country. The first stop might be Ketama, but there is little reason for getting off here, and you could be inviting hassles. This is the centre of kif country, and it will be assumed you've come to buy a load, which might have unpleasant consequences

(see Dangers & Annoyances in the Facts for the Visitor chapter).

## AL-HOCEIMA

Set on a bay at one of the rare points along the coast where the Rif drops away and makes a little room for beaches, Al-Hoceima is a relaxed and largely modern town. Founded in 1920 by a Spanish officer, General Sanjuro, it was known initially as Villa Sanjuro. The fact that the Rif rebel Abd el-Krim had, from 1921 to 1926, one of his main bases only 10 km away at Ajdir shows how tenuous was Spain's hold over this part of its protectorate after 1912.

### Orientation

Al-Hoceima only began to grow after Spain pulled out in the wake of Morocco's accession to independence in 1956, and now numbers about 60,000 inhabitants. The Spanish influence remains – all the streets seem to be 'calles' here – but all new construction is resolutely cheap North African style. The main attraction is the couple of small beaches, making Al-Hoceima a pleasant stop while en route east or west through the Rif. In high summer it fills up with Moroccan holiday-makers and European charter tourists. What attracts the latter is hard to guess (boastful tourist-office pamphlets?), for while it is a pleasant enough place to rest up while touring the country, it's hardly one of the Mediterranean's great package resorts.

Most of the banks, better hotels and restaurants are on or near Calle Mohammed V, the main road in from Nador. Just east of this road, as you enter the town proper, is the old village centre, with the budget hotels and eateries, as well as all transport. Apart from the town beach, Plage Quemado, there are a couple of quieter ones a few km out of town on the Nador road. From some vantage points you can see the Spanish-controlled islet of Peñón de Alhucemas off the coast. It may look pretty, but it has served mainly as a prison and military base.

MOROCCO

MOROCCO

## Information

**Tourist Office** The Délégation Régionale du Tourisme (☎ 982830) is on Calle Tariq ibn Ziad, and is open Monday to Thursday from 8.30 am to noon and 2.30 to 6.30 pm, and Friday from 8.30 to 11 am and 3 to 6.30 pm. They have colourful brochures but little else.

**Money** There are plenty of banks along Calle Mohammed V, where you can change cash and travellers' cheques. You can get cash advances on Visa and MasterCard at the BMCE and BMCI.

**Post & Telecommunications** The post and telephone office is on Calle Moulay Idriss Alkbar, a few blocks west of Calle Mohammed V.

## Beaches

The town beach, Plage Quemado, is OK but with the large ugly hotel of the same name forming the main backdrop, it is a little off-putting. Better are the small beaches at **Cala Bonita** (where there is a camp site), before the southern entry into town, and **Plage Sebadella**, about a two-km walk to the north-west. **Plage Espalmadero**, four km

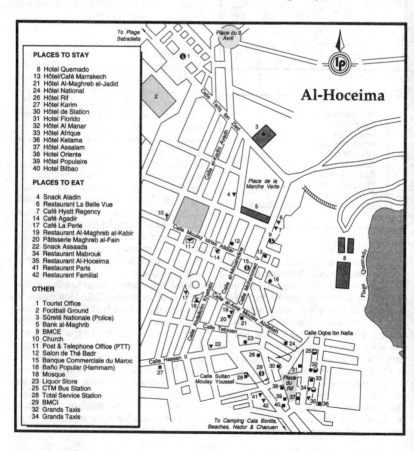

**PLACES TO STAY**

8  Hotel Quemado
13  Hôtel/Café Marrakech
21  Hôtel Al-Maghreb el-Jadid
24  Hôtel National
26  Hôtel Rif
27  Hôtel Karim
30  Hôtel de Station
31  Hotel Florido
32  Hôtel Al Manar
33  Hôtel Afrique
36  Hôtel Ketama
37  Hôtel Assalam
38  Hotel Oriente
39  Hôtel Populaire
40  Hotel Bilbao

**PLACES TO EAT**

4  Snack Aladin
6  Restaurant La Belle Vue
7  Café Hyatt Regency
14  Café Agadir
17  Café La Perle
19  Restaurant Al-Maghreb al-Kabir
20  Pâtisserie Maghreb al-Fain
22  Snack Assaada
34  Restaurant Mabrouk
35  Restaurant Al-Hoceima
41  Restaurant Paris
42  Restaurant Familial

**OTHER**

1  Tourist Office
2  Football Ground
3  Sûreté Nationale (Police)
5  Bank al-Maghrib
9  BMCE
10  Church
11  Post & Telephone Office (PTT)
12  Salon de Thé Badr
15  Banque Commerciale du Maroc
16  Baño Popular (Hammam)
18  Mosque
23  Liquor Store
25  CTM Bus Station
28  Total Service Station
29  BMCI
32  Grands Taxis
34  Grands Taxis

**Al-Hoceima**

To Plage Sebadella

Place du 9 Avril

Place de la Marche Verte

Place du Rif

Plage Quemado

Calle Tariq ibn Ziad

Calle al-Kathi Aiyadh

Calle Moulay Idriss Alkbar

Calle al-Mahakama

Calle Mohammed V

Calle Abderrahim Khatabi

Calle el-Amir Moulay Abdallah

Calle Tetouan

Calle Hassan II

Calle Sultan Moulay Youssef

Calle Oqba ibn Nafia

To Camping Cala Bonita, Beaches, Nador & Chaouen

from the centre of town along the road to Nador, and **Plage Asfiha**, five km farther on, are usually fairly quiet, especially in late spring. Local buses to Ajdir run by the turn-offs for both. Neither will win beautiful beach prizes, but they're OK.

## Places to Stay – bottom end

**Camping** The *Camping Cala Bonita* is right on what is probably the prettiest little beach in Al-Hoceima (the name is Spanish for 'pretty cove'). Unlike at other camp sites in the country, there is a simple flat fee of Dr 45 for a place. This includes tent space, car and amenities. About a km from the town centre on the road to Ajdir, it is a nice spot.

**Hotels** There is no shortage of budget hotels in the area immediately around Place du Rif, but things can still get crowded in midsummer. The *Hôtel Populaire* is about as cheap as they come at Dr 20 a person, but that's all you can really say about the place.

A fairly decent choice is the *Hôtel Rif* (☎ 982268) on Calle Sultan Moulay Youssef, which is away from the chaos of the square. Simple rooms with a washbasin cost Dr 30/40. There are cold communal showers.

On the square itself is a curious Art Deco building called the *Hotel Florido* (☎ 982 235). The better rooms look on to the square, and it was getting a paint job at the time of writing. Rooms cost Dr 30 a head and there are cold showers along the corridor.

Although the beds are a tad hard, the nearby *Hôtel Afrique* (☎ 983065) can be recommended. The rooms are clean and bright and cost Dr 31/42. Again, it has only cold showers. Not so great is the *Hôtel Assalam*, which has singles/doubles for Dr 40/60. Others to choose from around here are the *Hotel Oriente*, *Hôtel de Station*, *Hôtel al-Manar*, *Hôtel Ketama* (dive) and *Hotel Bilbao*.

## Places to Stay – middle

About the cheapest of the mid-range hotels and good value is the *Hôtel Marrakech* (☎ 983025) on Calle Mohammed V. Rooms with comfortable beds, sea glimpses and en

suite bathroom (hot water 24 hours a day) cost Dr 110/127.

For a little more (Dr 123/152), the *Hôtel Karim* (☎ 982184; fax 984340), 27 Calle Hassan II, is also a decent investment in comfort. Rooms have en suite bathrooms and phone and the staff are obliging.

The *Hôtel National* (☎ 982681), closer to public transport, is perfectly all right, with singles/doubles/triples costing Dr 157/187/299.

Not spectacularly better than the others, but considerably pricier, is the *Hôtel Al-Maghreb el-Jadid* (☎ 982504) on Calle Mohammed V. It has self-contained rooms for Dr 196/237 in the low season and Dr 226/273 in the high season. All prices are exclusive of taxes. The hotel has a bar on the 4th floor.

If you want to pay that much, you may as well head for the *Hotel Quemado* (☎ 983315) on the beach, where the rooms are not quite as good but you do wake up next to the Mediterranean.

## Places to Stay – top end

There is a *Club Med* about 11 km south-east of town near Ajdir.

## Places to Eat

For breakfast and a spot of people-watching, you could do worse than the *Pâtisserie Maghreb al-Fain* on Calle Mohammed V. Several other cafés and salons de thé are scattered about the town.

There are numerous little restaurants serving up the usual fare for about Dr 25 to Dr 30 on or near Place du Rif. Two that are reasonable are the *Restaurant Familial* and *Restaurant Paris* on Calle Mohammed V. *Snack Assaada* on Calle Hassan II serves various meats by weight. A filling meal with salad, chips and a soft drink will cost about Dr 25.

A generous meal of brochettes on a bed of rice, with chips, costs about Dr 35 in the *Restaurant Al-Maghreb Al-Kabir* next door to the pâtisserie. The *Restaurant La Belle Vue*, also on Calle Mohammed V, is another option, or you could try one of the better

MOROCCO

hotels. One of the few bars around is in the *Hôtel Al-Maghreb el-Jadid*. There's also a liquor store around the corner from the Hôtel Rif on Calle Hassan II.

### Getting There & Away

**Air** RAM has one or two weekly flights from Al-Hoceima to Tangier, Tetouan and Casablanca. There is also a weekly flight to Amsterdam (why?). In summer the airport, 17 km to the south-east, plays host to charter flights, mainly from France.

**Bus** All the bus companies have their offices on or near Place du Rif. CTM has buses to Nador at 5.30 am and 12.30 pm (Dr 35.50; 3½ hours). Its services to Tetouan (Dr 102.50; eight hours) via Chefchaouen (Dr 49; about five hours) leave at 9 and 10 pm. At 8 pm a CTM bus leaves for Casablanca (Dr 140.50; 11 hours) via Fès, Meknès and Rabat.

There are three or four other small companies. As always, it's best to turn up in the morning and check out what's going. Nador is the most frequently served destination, with at least six departures apart from the CTM ones. Fares range from Dr 29 to Dr 32. Buses to Fès (Dr 63.50) via Ketama (Dr 30) and Taounate (Dr 46) along the Route de l'Unité highway (a spectacular drive over the Rif) leave at 3.15 and 9.45 am; obviously, the first of these is not much good for enjoying the scenery. There is a bus for Oujda at 11 am (Dr 55; about six hours). Alternatively, go to Nador and pick up further transport there. Buses to Tetouan via Chefchaouen leave at 7 and 8 am and 7 pm. Another goes through to Tangier at 8 am (Dr 74; about 11 hours). Buses to Targuist leave four times a day and cost Dr 16.50.

**Taxi** The best time to try to get a grand taxi is the morning, but you may find yourself hanging about for one to fill up. They line up on the street in front of the Hôtel al-Manar and Restaurant Mabrouk. The fare to Taza and Nador is Dr 50.

# The East Coast

## MELILLA

Melilla is marginally smaller than its Spanish sister enclave to the west, Ceuta, with about 70,000 inhabitants, a third of whom are Muslims of Rif Berber origin. The presence of 10,000 troops provides a boost to the local economy, but Melilla lives mainly from contraband trade. Anything up to 80% of the goods that arrive in the enclave end up not only in Morocco, but in countries throughout north-west Africa. Some people within Melilla's business community worry that a free-trade agreement between the EU and Morocco could kill this business, leaving Melilla in deep trouble – it already has an unemployment rate higher than any city in the EU.

Relations between the Muslim population, worst hit by the unemployment, and the rest of the enclave's inhabitants are strained. The ill-feeling bubbled over into violent protests in the 1980s when new citizenship laws threatened to leave many Muslims without proper papers in limbo.

Spaniards in the enclave also worry that the Muslims will one day push for the enclave to be handed over to Morocco. Most of the Muslims say this is rubbish, that as Rif Berbers they owe no allegiance to the Moroccan king and that in any case they would prefer to be under Spanish rule. Other Spaniards fear that, with their big families, the Muslims will eventually outnumber the Christians and gain power. Melilla, like Ceuta, lives under a cloud of uncertainty.

The city also leaves the visitor with equally ambiguous impressions. Uncompromisingly Spanish in look and feel, and not a little run-down, the presence of so many Muslims (some of them Moroccans who have slipped across the border), most of whom are underemployed or jobless, lends it an atmosphere quite unlike that of any city on the peninsula.

## History

The port and peninsula of Melilla have been inhabited for more than 2000 years. The Phoenicians and Romans both counted it among their network of Mediterranean coastal bases – it was then known as Russadir. After the departure of the Romans, the city fell into obscurity until it was captured by Abd ar-Rahman III of Cordova. In 1496 it was taken by a Spanish raiding party and has remained in Spain's hands ever since. Abd el-Krim's rebels came close to taking the town during the Rif war in 1921, and it was from here that Franco launched the Spanish Civil War in 1936.

Its excellently preserved medieval fortress gives the city a lingering fascination. Right up until the end of the 19th century virtually all of Melilla was contained within these massive defensive walls. This old part of town has a distinctly Castilian flavour, with its narrow, twisting streets, squares, gates and drawbridges, and the area has been declared a national monument.

## Orientation

Plaza de España is the heart of the new part of town, which was largely designed by Don Enrique Nieto, a contemporary of Gaudí. Most of the hotels are in the grid of streets leading north-west of the plaza. In the same area you'll find banks and other offices, and most of the restaurants and bars. East of Melilla la Vieja (the old town) lies the ferry port; the frontier with Morocco is a 20-minute bus ride south, over the trickle of effluent inappropriately known as the Río de Oro.

## Information

**Tourist Office** The tourist office (☎ 684013) is at the junction of Calle de Querol and Avenida General Aizpuru, close to Plaza de Toros (the bullring). It's well stocked and the staff are helpful. Opening hours are roughly 9 am to 2 pm Monday to Friday, and to noon on Saturday.

**Money** You'll find several banks along or near Avenida de Juan Carlos I Rey, starting with the Central Hispano on Plaza de España, which is as good as any. They buy and sell dirham at a slightly inferior rate to that found in Morocco, but as good as anything you'll get from the Moroccan dealers in the streets. The latter hang about Plaza de España and deal in Algerian dinar as well. Don't believe their stories about the atrocious bank rates – check them first. This will of course be difficult with Algerian dinar, but for these you are better off waiting until you get to Oujda or even Figuig.

**Post & Telecommunications** The main post office (Correos y Telégrafos), on Calle Pablo Vallescá, is open Monday to Friday from 9 am to 8 pm for ordinary mail, and a little longer for telegrams. It is also open on Saturday mornings.

The main public phone offices are on Calle Sotomayor, on the western side of the Parque Hernández (open daily from 9 am to 2 pm and 6 to 9 pm), and the Teléfonica is just north of the Río de Oro. There are plenty of public phones that accept coins and cards, and from which you can also use the home direct service to make reverse-charge calls.

**Petrol & Supplies** Remember that Melilla is a duty-free zone. If you are driving it is worth waiting to fill up here, as the petrol is about a third cheaper than in Morocco or the rest of Spain. The EcoAhorro supermarket on the road to the border post of Beni-Enzar is open from 10 am to 10 pm and might be worth checking out for supplies on your way south.

## Melilla la Vieja

Under normal conditions, Old Melilla (or, according to some guides, the Medina Sidonia) is well worth exploring for a half-day or so. Perched over the Mediterranean, it is a good example of the kind of 16th and 17th-century fortress stronghold the Portuguese (and in this case the Spaniards) built along the Moroccan littoral. At the time of writing, however, it looked like the Moroccans had just launched an attack to retake the place. Virtually all of the old town is buried in scaffolding and rattles to the sounds of the reconstruction and maintenance work being

MOROCCO

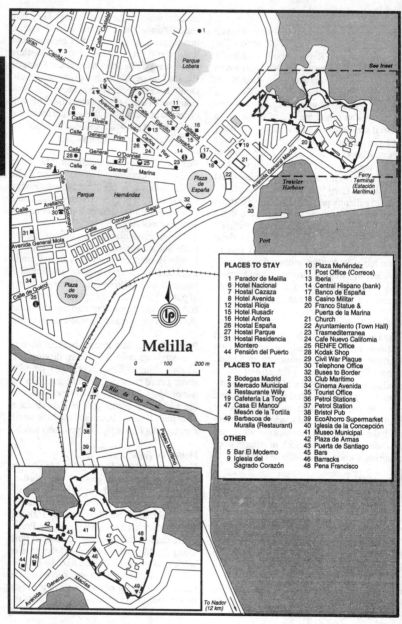

**PLACES TO STAY**

1 Parador de Melilla
6 Hotel Nacional
7 Hostal Cazaza
8 Hotel Avenida
12 Hostal Rioja
15 Hotel Rusadir
16 Hotel Anfora
26 Hostal España
27 Hostal Parque
31 Hostal Residencia Montero
44 Pensión del Puerto

**PLACES TO EAT**

2 Bodegas Madrid
3 Mercado Municipal
4 Restaurante Willy
19 Cafetería La Toga
47 Casa El Manco/ Mesón de la Tortilla
49 Barbacoa de Muralla (Restaurant)

**OTHER**

5 Bar El Moderno
9 Iglesia del Sagrado Corazón
10 Plaza Meñéndez
11 Post Office (Correos)
13 Iberia
14 Central Hispano (bank)
17 Banco de España
18 Casino Militar
20 Franco Statue & Puerta de la Marina
21 Church
22 Ayuntamiento (Town Hall)
23 Trasmediterranea
24 Cafe Nuevo California
25 RENFE Office
28 Kodak Shop
29 Civil War Plaque
30 Telephone Office
32 Buses to Border
33 Club Marítimo
34 Cinema Avenida
35 Tourist Office
36 Petrol Stations
37 Petrol Station
38 Bristol Pub
39 EcoAhorro Supermarket
40 Iglesia de la Concepción
41 Museo Municipal
42 Plaza de Armas
43 Puerta de Santiago
45 Bars
46 Barracks
48 Pena Francisco

Melilla

0          100          200 m

one. When they've finished, it will probably be a very pleasant, if sanitised, little spot.

Worth a look are the **Iglesia de la Concepción**, with its gilded reredos and shrine to Nuestra Señora la Virgen de la Victoria (the patroness of the city), and the **Museo Municipal** (open Monday to Saturday from 10 am to 1 pm and 5 to 7 pm; entry free), which has a good collection of historical documents and Phoenician and Roman ceramics and coins. The former was closed for restoration in 1994 and the latter had been moved to a new building.

The main entrance to the **fortress** is through the Puerta de la Marina on the Paseo de General Macías (you'll also see a monument to Franco here). After your visit, you could leave by the **Puerta de Santiago**, which takes you west over a couple of drawbridges and the Plaza de Armas and out by the Foso de Hornabeque.

## New Town

Construction of the new part of town, to the west of the fortress, was begun at the end of the 19th century. It was laid out by Don Enrique Nieto, who, following Gaudí's lead, is considered by some to have made of Melilla Spain's 'second modernist city' after Barcelona – a somewhat inflated boast. A combination of shiny duty-free shopfronts and general decay has failed to rob the area entirely of its charm, and travellers arriving from Morocco (especially the likes of Nador) will hardly fail to notice the difference.

A walk around can be instructive in the city's more recent past. A statue on Avenida de Juan Carlos I Rey and a plaque you can see opposite the Parque Hernández on Calle de General Marina celebrate 7 July 1936, the day Franco began the campaign against the government in Madrid, with the cry of 'Viva España'.

## Beaches

For the desperate, there is a string of beaches south of the Río de Oro to the border. They are hardly special – you would be better off heading for mainland Spain or continuing on into Morocco.

## Places to Stay – bottom end

If you're coming from Morocco, you'll know you've arrived in Europe when you look for a place to stay. Hotels at all levels charge a little more in the high season (summer and Easter week). The cheapest option is the *Pensión del Puerto*, a largely Moroccan establishment just back from Paseo de General Macías. A bed should cost less than 1000 pta, but it's a little rough and seems to serve as a brothel too.

Easily the best place for the tight budget is the *Hostal Rioja* (☎ 682709), at 6 Calle Ejército Español. It has decent singles/doubles for 2000/3000 pta outside the high season, with communal hot showers. It's a friendly place with a homey atmosphere.

Another decent alternative for about the same money is the *Hostal Parque* (☎ 682 143), which fronts the Parque Hernández and is often full. Not such good value, but acceptable, is the *Hostal Cazaza* (☎ 684648) on Calle Rivera. Gloomy doubles with basin only are 3850 pta. Those with shower cost 4500 pta. A block west and a little better, depending on which rooms you end up with, is the *Hotel Nacional* (☎ 684540/1) on Calle Rivera. Pokey singles start at 2200 pta, and comfortable doubles with en suite bathrooms and balconies range from 4500 to 5700 pta, depending on the season. The *Hotel España*, on Avenida de Juan Carlos I Rey, seems to be closed.

## Places to Stay – middle

Heading up the price scale is the *Hotel Avenida* (☎ 684949), on Avenida de Juan Carlos I Rey. It has singles/doubles for 3970/6930 pta. In a similar bracket is the *Hotel Anfora* (☎ 683340), on Calle Pablo Vallescá. Across the road is the still more expensive *Hotel Rusadir* (☎ 681240).

## Places to Stay – top end

The *Parador of Melilla* (☎ 684940; fax 683486), one of a series of top-class hotels around Spain, is the top of the tree here, with a pool and views over the Mediterranean, but with an uninspired concrete exterior. Singles

MOROCCO

MOROCCO

(without a sea view) start at 6900 pta and doubles go up to 12,000 pta.

## Places to Eat

Any of the bars is decent for a morning coffee and pastry, but if you want churros and hot chocolate, head for *Cafetería La Toga* on Plaza de Don Pedro de Estopiñán.

The best area to search for good cheap bocadillos and the like is along Calle Castelar, not far from the Mercado Municipal (food market). The *Bodegas Madrid*, with its old wine casks for tables, is easily the most popular spot here for a beer and a bite.

For mostly seafood snacks, the *Bar El Moderno* is open until midnight, when most of the rest are firmly shut. Across the road is a pretty decent pizza place, the *Restaurante Willy*, where a filling small pizza will cost from 450 to 550 pta.

There are countless other bars and the odd restaurant where you can get a meal in the streets around Avenida de Juan Carlos I Rey.

In Melilla la Vieja, search out the *Casa El Manco/Mesón de la Tortilla*. Like the whole area, it was closed for refurbishment at the time of writing, but it's worth tracking down when open.

For a splurge, you can't beat the *Barbacoa de Muralla*, in the southernmost corner of Melilla la Vieja.

## Entertainment

Apart from exploring the many bars and cafés around the centre of town and joining in the evening *paseo* (promenade), you could try a folk-music club such as the *Peña Francisco* (or *Peña Flamenca*) inside the fortress (see map). The *Bristol* is a popular drinking hole on the road to the border. Of the various discos and disco-pubs (a Spanish speciality), *Logüeno*, on the Carretera de Alfonso XIII, and *El Paraíso*, on Calle de General Polavieja, are locally recommended.

The *Casino Militar*, on Plaza de España, has a Centro Cultural de los Ejércitos, which occasionally stages little art exhibits.

## Getting There & Away

**Air** Iberia, the Spanish national carrier, has an office on Avenida de Juan Carlos I Rey. The one-way fare to Málaga is 8800 pta, and there are numerous daily flights (except in bad weather) on 46-seat Fokkers. There's a flight a day to Almería (8500 pta). To Madrid there are up to six daily flights, and tickets cost 23,000 pta one way.

**Bus & Taxi** Local buses (catch the one marked for 'Aforos') run between Plaza de España and the Beni-Enzar border post from about 7.30 am to late evening. From where the buses stop, it's about 150 metres to Spanish customs and another 200 metres to Moroccan customs. Spanish checks seem largely cursory both ways, but the Moroccans can hold things up for quite a while. Remember that some nationalities require visas to enter Spain (see Foreign Embassies in the Rabat section). If they don't stop you here, they will when you try to move on to the mainland.

Don't give in to Moroccan customs officers suggesting that you'd like to give them a few hundred of your excess dirham 'for a coffee'. Just change it at the bank (if you have an exchange receipt) or deny having any and change it to pesetas in Melilla. You can buy dirham in Melilla or at the Moroccan side of the border (the latter accepts *cash only*).

From Beni-Enzar there are Moroccan local buses (No 19; Dr 2) and grands taxis (Dr 4) to Nador, from where you can catch other buses and grands taxis to a host of destinations farther inside the country (see the following section). If driving in, remember to retain the green customs slip, which you must present when you (and your vehicle) leave Morocco.

**Sea** Trasmediterranea ferries leave Melilla every night but Sunday for Málaga and Almería. For details, see the Getting There & Away chapter. You can buy tickets at the Trasmediterranea office on Plaza de España (open Monday to Friday from 9 am to 1 pm and 5 to 7 pm, and 9 am to noon Saturday), or direct at the port (Estación Marítima). You can also buy rail tickets for mainland Spain nd beyond at the RENFE office on Calle de General O'Donnell. Ferries are sometimes cancelled because of bad weather.

There are fairly thorough passport and customs checks at Melilla (although technically you're travelling inside Spain). Cars are all searched, and the process can delay departure considerably. Similar but less rigorous checks are carried out on arrival in Málaga and Almería.

## NADOR

Only the traveller with plenty of time and a love of unloved places would want to do more than catch the first bus or grand taxi out of Nador, a sprawling town set on a lagoon 13 km south of Melilla and earmarked, officially at least, for development as a business centre. Luckily, most of the transport is located in the one place, which makes arriving and leaving comparatively painless asks. Should you get stuck and have to stay overnight, there is no shortage of hotels of all classes, and quite a few of them are near the bus and grand taxi lots.

### Information

The tourist office (☎ 606518) is at 80 Blvd Ibn Rochd. Spain has a consulate in Nador at 12 Rue Mohammed Zerktouni (☎ 606136; fax 606152).

### Getting There & Away

**Bus** The bus station (gare routière) is down by the lagoon, south of the city centre. CTM and other lines run from here. Heading westwards, there are bus services to Al-Hoceima at 7 and 9.30 am, and noon, 2.45, 4.45 and 5 pm. The trip takes about 3½ hours. Beyond Al-Hoceima, there are buses to Tetouan via Ketama and Chefchaouen at 5.30 and 8 am, and 6, 7 and 9.30 pm. Even if you're only going to Chefchaouen this is a long trip, and breaking it up with a stop in Al-Hoceima is worth thinking about.

Buses to Taza leave at 1 and 1.40 pm. For those who are in a hurry, there are through services to Fès (6.30 and 8 am, noon, 4 pm and midnight), Meknès (5, 9 and 10.30 am), Rabat (2, 7 and 8 pm), Casablanca (4, 5, 8

and 8.30 pm) and Tangier (4.15 am and 4, 5 and 9.30 pm). There are at least 10 runs a day to Oujda (about 2½ hours) between 6 am and 5 pm.

CTM's fares include Al-Hoceima (Dr 35.50), Oujda (Dr 23.50), Chefchaouen (Dr 84), Rabat (Dr 131) and Casablanca (Dr 152.50).

**Train** It is possible to get a Supratours bus to Taourirt to catch connecting trains going west to Fès and beyond or east to Oujda. The bus leaves Nador at 7.30 pm and you buy a ticket for the bus and train to the destination you want. The same trip can be done in the other direction (leaving Taourirt at 5 am). As a rule, it's easier to use buses and grands taxis.

**Taxi** The main grand taxi lot is across the road from the bus station. Taxis cost Dr 100 per person to Fès, Dr 50 to Taza and Al-Hoceima, and Dr 35 to Oujda. There are usually taxis available to most of these and other destinations until about 8 pm.

**To/From Melilla** The local bus lot is next to the main bus station. The No 19 regularly makes the 20-minute run to Beni-Enzar for Melilla, but stops operating by about 8 pm. Unfortunately, the grands taxis to the border (Dr 4 for a place) use a lot that is a fair distance from the main grand taxi station. The best way to get between the two is by petit taxi.

## SAIDIA

A couple of km short of the Algerian border (you can't cross here) is the charming little seaside town of Saidia. In summer it is often packed with Moroccans, especially during the August traditional music festival, but out of season it's empty and offers a fine sandy beach and crystal-clear water.

There are a few hotels in the town, but they only open for the summer season from mid-June. Saidia's distance from the main Moroccan cities thankfully makes it a spot unlikely to become a huge resort.

MOROCCO

**PLACES TO STAY**

1 Hôtel Select
3 Hôtel Hannour

**PLACES TO EAT**

2 Café
4 Restaurant Coq Magique
5 Café/Restaurant Langouste
8 Café La Corniche
9 Restaurant En-Nassim
10 Restaurant de la Paix
11 Restaurant Plus

**OTHER**

6 Bar Atlas
7 Bar Bleu
12 Sûreté Nationale
13 Gendarmerie Royale
14 Bus office - Oujda
15 Grands Taxis - Oujda
16 Douche El-Witak
17 Camping International
18 Municipalité (local council)

Saidia

To Oujda & Nador

0    50    100 m
Approximate Scale

## Places to Stay & Eat

There are two one-star hotels: the *Hôtel Select* (☎ 623120) and *Hôtel Al-Kalaa* (☎ 625123). If you have a little more money, the *Hôtel Hannour* (☎ 625115), in the centre of town, is probably a better bet, although you're looking at about Dr 100 a head.

There are quite a few little restaurants in the centre of town. The *Restaurant Coq Magique*, which specialises in seafood, and the *Restaurant En-Nassim*, which serves pizzas and crêpes, are both on Blvd Hassan.

You can get a drink in a couple of bars, and such nightlife as there is in summer seems to revolve around the Hôtel Hannour and the *Kiss* disco, which is about a km west along the beach.

## Getting There & Away

Without your own transport, the easiest access to Saidia is from Oujda by bus (Dr 11; at least four a day throughout the year) or grand taxi (Dr 15). See also the Oujda section.

A visit to the Middle Atlas can take in such diverse activities as snow skiing in the exclusive mountain resort of Ifrane, visiting Morocco's best preserved Roman ruins at Volubilis, trekking or simply relaxing in Azrou in the mountains, wandering through the labyrinthine medina of Fès, and visiting Moulay Ismail's huge palace complex at Meknès. From Fès, a natural route leads via Taza and Oujda on the border to Algeria. The road south from Oujda is the easiest way to get to the frontier oasis town of Figuig, reputedly the hottest place in Morocco, and an alternative gateway to Algeria.

## Meknès

Although Meknès is thought of by some as the Versailles of Morocco, you could be forgiven for thinking that it hardly warrants that kind of hyperbole. Had the enormous building projects of the Alawite sultan, Moulay Ismail, survived the ravages of time, the comparison might not seem so outlandish today. Although for most people Meknès runs third behind its more illustrious sisters, Marrakesh and Fès, it was the heart of the Moroccan sultanate for a short time and is worth at least a couple of days' exploration. Moreover, it is a convenient base for visiting Volubilis, and the intriguing village of Moulay Idriss, a holy site that contains the tomb of the founder of Morocco's first imperial dynasty.

Surrounded by the rich plains that precede the Middle Atlas Mountains, Meknès is blessed with a hinterland that provides abundant cereal crops, olives, wine, citrus and other agricultural products that have long been the city's economic backbone. The comparative prosperity of the city and the surrounding countryside continues to fuel its population – at last count 735,000 inhabitants and growing.

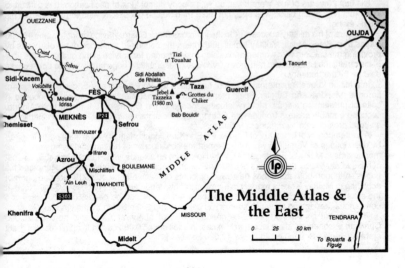

The Middle Atlas & the East

0    25    50 km

To Bouarfa & Figuig

MOROCCO

## History

Meknès is a good thousand years old. The Berber tribe of the Meknassis (hence the city's name) first settled here in the 10th century. Under the Almohads and Merenids, the medina was expanded and defensive walls and some of the city's oldest remaining monuments were built. The fall of the Merenids brought a hiatus in the city's fortunes.

It was the accession to power of Moulay Ismail in 1672 on the death of his brother and founder of the Alawite dynasty, Moulay ar-Rashid, that yanked Meknès back from obscurity. He reigned for 55 years and selected Meknès as his capital, which he endowed with an enormous palace complex (which was never finished) and 25 km o imposing walls pierced by monumenta gates. That he was able to devote so muc energy to construction was partly due to hi uncommon success in subduing all opposition in Morocco and keeping foreig meddlers well at bay.

His death in 1727 also struck the death knell for Meknès, as his grandson Mo hammed III (1757-90) moved back t Marrakesh. Meknès again became a back water, and its monuments were, as so ofte happened in the course of Moroccan history stripped for materials to build elsewher The 1755 earthquake that devastated Lisbo had already dealt Meknès a heavy blow.

The arrival of the protectorate in 191

### Moulay Ismail

Moulay Ismail, the second sultan of the Alawite dynasty (which still rules today), marked his ascent to power at the age of 25 in 1672 in an unforgettable manner. As a warning to unruly tribes, he sent the heads of 10,000 slain enemies to adorn the walls of the two great imperial capitals, Fès and Marrakesh. He had presumably collected these earlier during battles against insurgents in the north of Morocco.

It was the beginning of a particularly gruesome period of rule, even by Moroccan standards, but Moulay Ismail is one of the few Moroccan sultans ever to get the whole country under his control. His cruelty was legendary, and the cheerful ease with which he would lop off the heads of unfortunate servants who displeased him or labourers not working hard enough probably contributed much to his hold over the country.

His first 20 years of rule were taken up with bloody campaigns of pacification. It is difficult to know just how much blood was spilt, but more than 30,000 people are said to have died at his hands alone.

The core of his military success lay in the infamous Black Guard. Having brought some 16,000 slaves from Black Africa, Moulay Ismail guaranteed the continued existence of his elite units by providing the soldiers with women and raising their offspring for service in the guard. By the time of his death, the Black Guard had grown tenfold and resembled a huge family whose upkeep was paid for by the treasury.

In addition to quelling internal rebellion, he chased the Portuguese and English out of Asilah, Larache, Mehdiya and Tangier. Spain managed to hang on to Ceuta, Melilla and Al-Hoceima in spite of unrelenting sieges. Moulay Ismail disposed of the Ottoman Turk threat from Algeria, securing a stable eastern frontier with a string of fortifications centred on Taza, and established a virtual protectorate over modern Mauritania.

A contemporary of Louis XIV of France, the Sun King, Moulay Ismail was at least partly inspired by descriptions of Versailles when he planned the construction of his imperial palace and other monuments in Meknès. For decades he tried to secure an alliance with France against Spain, but continued attacks by the corsairs of Salé on French merchant shipping effectively scuppered his hopes. Although both monarchs bestowed presents on each other, Louis XIV stopped short of acceding to Moulay Ismail's request to marry one of his daughters, the Princess of Conti. Not that the sultan was in need of more female company – it is reckoned he had 360 to 500 wives and concubines (depending on which source you believe) and 800 children by the time he died.

To carry out his building plans, he needed plenty of labour, and it is said he used 25,000 Christian prisoners as slave labour in Meknès, in addition to 30,000 common criminals. His great stables (Heri as-Souani) could house 12,000 horses. ∎

ave the town a fillip, as the French made it
heir military headquarters. The army was
ccompanied by a corps of French farmers,
ttracted by the good land around the city.
Most of their properties were taken over by
he Moroccan government after indepen-
ence in 1956 and leased out to local
armers.

It is only in the past few decades, as the
ourist potential of the city has become
bvious, that any serious attempts at restora-
on have taken place.

## Orientation

The old medina and the French-built ville
ouvelle are neatly divided by the valley of
he Oued Bou Fekrane. The (usually dry)
iverbed also marks an administrative
oundary. The Wilayat Ismailia covers the
edina side and the Wilayat al-Menzah the
odern side.

Train and CTM bus connections are in the
ew city, as are most offices and banks. All
he more expensive hotels and most of the
etter restaurants are also in the new city.

All the private bus lines and the main
tercity grands taxis use a station on the
est side of the medina. The cheap hotels,
amping ground and sights are in the old city.
's a 20-minute walk between the old and
ew cities, but there are regular (and very
rowded) local buses as well as petits taxis.

## Information

**Tourist Office** The Délégation Régionale du
ourisme (☎ 524426) is next to the main
ost office facing Place de France (or Place
dministrative) in front of the Hôtel de Ville.
has the usual brochures, and staff will try
answer any questions you may have. Inter-
stingly enough, it has a police list of hustlers
aux guides) operating in the medina, but it
eems there is little anyone can or wants to
o to haul them into line. It's open Monday
Friday from 8.30 am to noon and 2.30 to
.30 pm; on Friday it's closed from 11.30 am
3 pm. The syndicat d'initiative seems to
e closed for good.

**Money** The banks are concentrated in the
new city, mainly on Ave Hassan II, Ave
Mohammed V and Blvd Allal ben Abdallah.
As usual, the BMCE, on Rue Rouamzine
near the Hôtel de Paris, is the best bet. Its
main branch operates an out-of-hours
change office on Ave des FAR, opposite the
Hôtel Excelsior, open daily from 10 am to 2
pm and 4 to 8 pm. It also has a couple of
ATMs.

The Banque Populaire has a branch on
Rue Dar Smen in the old city and the Crédit
du Maroc has a branch on the medina side of
Ave Moulay Ismail.

**Post & Telecommunications** The main
post office is in the new city on Place de
France. It's open from 8.30 am to 12.15 pm
and 2.30 to 6.45 pm. The phone office is in
the same building and is open daily from
8.30 am to 9 pm. The parcel post and EMS
department is around the corner to the left.

There is another large post office in the
medina, on Rue Dar Smen, near the corner
of Rue Rouamzine.

**French Consulate & Cultural Centre** The
Centre Culturel Français is on the corner of
Ave Moulay Ismail and Rue Farhat Hachad.
It has a program of films and lectures and a
small library. It's open Monday to Saturday
from 9 am to noon and 3 to 7 pm. The
consulate (☎ 522227) does *not* issue visas –
you'll have to go to Fès.

**Bookshops & Newsstands** If you don't
read French or Arabic, there's not much
around in terms of books. The Librairie La
Ville Nouvelle on Ave Hassan II is one of the
better French-language bookshops. There
are several newsstands where you can get
hold of English-language press, as well as
the usual full range of French press. One that
is OK is virtually across the road from the
Hôtel Majestic on Ave Mohammed V.

**Medical Services & Emergencies** There
are two hospitals in Meknès: the Hôpital
Mohammed V (☎ 521134) and the Hôpital
Moulay Ismail (☎ 522805). A reasonable

MOROCCO

**PLACES TO STAY**

1   Hôtel Transatlantique
2   Hostel
15  Hôtel de Nice
22  Hôtel Majestic
27  Hôtel Toubkal
28  Hôtel Volubilis
29  Hôtel Excelsior

**PLACES TO EAT**

9   Rôtisserie Karam
12  Restaurant La Coupole
23  Pizzeria Le Four

25  Montana Bar &
    Restaurant

**OTHER**

3   French Consulate &
    Centre Culturel Français
4   Syndicat d'Initiative
5   Police
6   Unban
7   Unban Office
8   Librairie La Ville Nouvelle
10  Market
11  Bar
13  Wagons-Lits
14  Cinéma Camera
16  Bars
17  Post Office (PTT)
18  Palais de Justice
19  Hôtel de Ville
20  Liquor Store
21  Stopcar Car Rental
24  El-Amir Abdelkader
    Train Station
26  Mobil Service Station
    (24 Hours)
27  CTM Bus Terminal
30  BMCE Late Bank
31  Hospital
32  Royal Palace

Meknès

pharmacy is the Pharmacie El Kadi Soussi on Ave Hassan II.

**Film & Photography** There are several places around the ville nouvelle where you can have film developed. There's a Kodak place next door to the Hôtel Majestic.

**Travel Agencies** Wagons-Lits (☎ 521995) has an office at 1 Zankat Ghana. Wasteels (☎ 523062) is at 45 Ave Mohammed V.

### Old City

From the ville nouvelle, you get to the old city by crossing Oued Bou Fekrane along Ave Moulay Ismail.

On the other side, you follow the street up into a little square as it veers to the right. This is Rue Rouamzine, which you take until you get to the post office, at which point you turn left into Rue Dar Smen. Follow this until a great square opens up on your right, Place el-Hedim. The heart of the old medina lies to the north (with the old Jewish quarter, the mellah, to the west). On your left (to the south) Moulay Ismail's imperial city opens up through one of the most impressive monumental gateways in all Morocco, the Bab el-Mansour. Although not as bad as, say, Fès, there are 'guides' in Meknès. If they're going to get you it will most likely be around Rue Dar Smen and Place el-Hedim. Once inside the medina itself, they are few and far between.

### Medina

**Dar Jamaï Museum** Bab el-Mansour opens onto Place el-Hedim. On the far north side of this square is the Dar Jamaï, a palace built in 1882 by the powerful Jamaï family. Two of their number were viziers to Sultan Moulay al-Hassan I in the late 19th century. When the sultan died in 1894, the Jamaï family fell into disgrace, as so often happened in the fickle political atmosphere of the Moroccan court. They lost everything, including their Meknès palace, which went to Al-Maidani al-Glaoui. The French turned it into a military hospital in 1912 and since 1920 it has housed the Administration des Beaux Arts.

The building, which boasts a peaceful Andalusian garden and courtyard, is as interesting as the exhibits. The latter consist largely of Fès ceramics, jewellery (note the silver *sebsi*, for smoking kif), rugs, textiles and woodwork. The domed reception room upstairs is furnished in the style of a well-to-do salon, complete with plush rugs and cushions. It is open daily, except Tuesdays and holidays, from 9 am to noon and 3 to 6.30 pm. Entry costs Dr 10.

**Medina Souqs** Before plunging into the heart of the old medina from Place el-Hedim, you might want to take a look at the food market west of the square (behind the rows of barber shops), which borders on the old mellah. If you like olives, you'll think you've died and gone to heaven.

The easiest route into the medina proper is through the arch to the left of the Dar Jamaï. If you plunge in here, you will quickly find yourself in among the **carpet shops**. As you walk along the streets, you will occasionally notice covered market areas (or qissariat) off to your right or left. A couple of these are devoted to carpets, and the hard sell is not as hard here as elsewhere. Keeping more or less to the lane you started on, you will emerge at Rue Najarine. Here the carpets give way to textiles and to quite a few shops specialising in babouches. If you follow the street west and veer with it left into Rue Sekkakine, you will find yourself at an exit in the west wall of the medina leading onto the mellah. Virtually opposite it is the **Qissariat ad-Dahab**, the gold and jewellery market.

If you take the exit and follow the lane north hugging the city wall on the outside, you'll go past the colourful nuts and spices souq, a flea market and, a bit farther to the west, Meknès's tanneries. Enter the city again at Bab el-Jedid, and as you pass inside the gate you'll find yourself in a small **musical instruments souq**. Turning left up Rue el-Hanaya, the local-produce markets open up in front of you – this is a cheap place to do your grocery shopping. Eventually, if you continue north, you will arrive at the

Berdaine Mosque and, just beyond it, the city's northernmost gate, **Bab Berdaine**. Outside is a Muslim cemetery, in which is located the tomb and **koubba** (sanctary) of Sidi ben Aissa, who gave rise to one of the more extreme religious fraternities in Morocco. At his moussem, entranced followers would cheerfully digest anything from glass to snakes, but nowadays such practices have been all but suppressed.

You could then proceed straight back down Rue Zaouia Nasseria (which becomes Rue Souika) to get to the Great Mosque and the nearby Medersa Bou Inania.

**Medersa Bou Inania** The Great Mosque is, of course, closed to non-Muslims, but you can enter the medersa, which was built in the 14th century during the reign of the Merenids. Completed in 1358 by Bou Inan (after whom a more lavish medersa in Fès is also named), the Meknès version of the Qur'anic school is typical of the exquisite interior design that distinguishes Merenid monuments from those of other periods. For some general ideas on the use and layout of the medersa, see the Arts entry in the Facts about the Country chapter. The standard zellij-tile base, stucco middle and carved olive-wood top of the interior walls (only the ceiling is made of cedar) is repeated here in all its elegance. Students aged eight to 10 once lived two to a cell on the ground floor, while older students and teachers lived on the 1st floor. You can climb on to the roof and see the green-tiled roof and minaret of the Great Mosque next door.

The medersa is open daily from 9 am to noon and 3 to 6 pm. Entry is Dr 10. A guide will probably want to show you around for a fee. It's a quick walk back to Place el-Hedim.

### Imperial City
**Bab el-Mansour** The focus of the old city is the massive gate of Bab el-Mansour, the main entrance to Moulay Ismail's 17th-century imperial city that stands opposite Place el-Hedim. The gate is well preserved and lavishly decorated, with (faded) zellij tiles and inscriptions that run right across the

top. The gate was completed by Moulay Ismail's son, Moulay Abdallah.

**Koubbat as-Sufara'** After passing through Bab el-Mansour and along the *mechouar* (parade ground), where Moulay Ismail reviewed his famed Black regiments, the road runs straight ahead and then round to the right. On the right is an open grass area with a small building, the Koubbat as-Sufara', which was once the reception hall for foreign ambassadors. It's very plain and hardly worth visiting, but beside it is the entrance to an enormous underground granary complete with vents that open onto the surface of the lawn. The popular story has this as a huge prison in which thousands of Christians (most captured by corsairs operating out of Salé) were held captive as slave labour on Moulay Ismail's building schemes. This story has largely been discredited, but it dies hard. Entry to the vaults and the reception hall, open daily from 9 am to noon and 3 to 6 pm, costs Dr 10. Almost directly opposite are royal gardens, which form part of what was Moulay Ismail's imperial city complex. It's off limits.

**Mausoleum of Moulay Ismail** To the left of the gardens is a more imposing gateway, through which you proceed to the resting place of the man who elevated Meknès to capital in the 17th century. He is generally considered one of the greatest figures in Moroccan history, and perhaps because of this non-Muslims are allowed in to the sanctuary, although only Muslims can visit the tomb itself. The mausoleum, except for the inner sanctuary, is modestly decorated. Entry is free but it's customary to tip the guardian. The mausoleum is open from 9 am to noon and 3 to 6 pm. It's closed on Friday. On the opposite side of the road are a number of craft and carpet shops belonging to a cooperative of artisans. It's worth having a look in these shops because there's an excellent selection of Meknassi specialities and little pressure to buy.

**Heri es-Souani & Agdal Basin** If you turn

eft on leaving the mausoleum and pass
ınder the Bab er-Rih (Gate of the Wind), you
ıave about a 20-minute walk around what
emains to this day an official royal residence
no visitors). The complex was known as the
)ar el-Makhzen ('the House of the
Government'). Follow the street to the end
ınd turn right (you have no choice) and head
traight down past the main entrance of the
Royal Palace (on the right) and on past the
amping ground (on the left). Virtually in
ront of you are the Heri es-Souani granaries
ınd vaults. The storerooms are impressive in
ize, and wells for drawing water can still be
een. The first few vaults have been restored,
ut the stables, which once housed 12,000
ıorses, stand in partial ruin with no roof,
eemingly stretching forever. Such is the
ıtmosphere here that the place vies with Aït
Benhaddou (near Ouarzazate) as one of the
ountry's favourite film sets. It is open daily
rom 9 am to noon and 3 to 6 pm. Entry costs
Dr 10.

Another doorway farther around to the
Agdal Basin leads upstairs to a charming
ooftop café, from where you have sweeping
riews back towards the Royal Palace and of
he Agdal Basin below.

The basin is an enormous stone-lined lake
ıbout four metres deep that was once fed by
he Oued Bou Fekrane and served as both a
eservoir for the sultan's gardens and a plea-
ure lake.

## ²laces to Stay – bottom end

**ʒamping** There is a good, shady camping
ground near the Agdal Basin on the south
ide of the imperial city. It's a long walk to
ʒamping Agdal, and a taxi from the train,
ʒTM or private bus stations will cost about
Dr 12. The camping ground is a little expen-
ive. It costs Dr 17 per person (Dr 12 for
hildren), Dr 10 to pitch a tent, Dr 17 for a
ar (Dr 20 camper van), Dr 7 for a hot shower
ınd Dr 10 for electricity.

**Hostel** The hostel (☎ 524698) is close to the
large Hôtel Transatlantique in the ville nouvelle, about one km from the centre. It's open
from 8 to 10 am, noon to 3 pm, and 6 to 10.30
pm except on Sundays, when it's open from
6 to 10 pm only. A dormitory bed costs Dr
20. They also have family rooms for three
and four people, which come to Dr 25 per
person. Hot water is available.

**Hotels – medina** Most of the cheapest
places are clustered together in the old city
along Rue Dar Smen and Rue Rouamzine.
The best of the lot and excellent value for
money is the *Hôtel Maroc* (☎ 530075), on
Rue Rouamzine. It's quiet, clean, pleasantly
furnished (all rooms with a washbasin) and
most rooms face a well-kept courtyard. The
(cold) showers and toilets are clean and well-
maintained. It's a bargain at Dr 30/60/70 for
singles/doubles/triples. Not as good, but
acceptable, is the *Hôtel de Paris*, also on Rue
Rouamzine. This is an older hotel with large
airy singles/doubles, with a table, chair and
washbasin, for Dr 30/50. There are no
showers and the loo is decidedly stinky.

The rest of the cheapies are nothing
special, and many don't have showers. The
*Hôtel Agadir*, Rue Dar Smen, is clean but the
rooms are tiny and there are no showers.
Rooms cost Dr 30/50. Slightly better but
rather gloomy is the nearby *Hôtel Regina*, a
cavernous edifice with the air of a Dickensian workhouse. Rooms are overpriced at Dr
40/70, and the bed linen could do with more
regular changing. The ground-floor rooms
are even darker and danker than those
upstairs. Again, there are no showers. The
*Hôtel de Meknès*, a few doors away from the
Regina, is similar, and charges Dr 30/60. The
*Hôtel Nouveau*, opposite the Banque Populaire, is little better and charges Dr 30/50.

You'll be pleased to know the local
hammam is close by. It's down an alley
between the Hôtel de Paris and the BMCE
bank. Look for the yellow signs marked
'Douche' and 'Bain'. The showers are for
men only (7 am to 7 pm); they cost Dr 4 and
there are small towels and soap if you forget
your own. The actual baths are open from
noon to 8 pm for women and 8.30 pm to 2
am for men. Another hammam for men only
is at the northern end of Rue Ben el-Maacer.

MOROCCO

MOROCCO

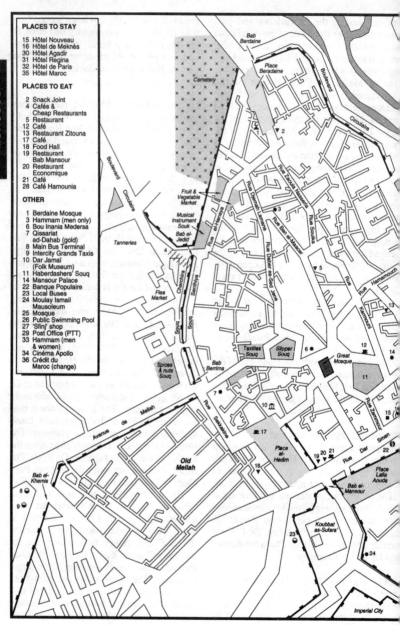

**PLACES TO STAY**

15  Hôtel Nouveau
16  Hôtel de Meknès
30  Hôtel Agadir
31  Hôtel Regina
32  Hôtel de Paris
35  Hôtel Maroc

**PLACES TO EAT**

2   Snack Joint
4   Cafés &
    Cheap Restaurants
5   Restaurant
12  Café
13  Restaurant Zitouna
17  Café
18  Food Hall
19  Restaurant
    Bab Mansour
20  Restaurant
    Economique
21  Café
28  Café Hamounia

**OTHER**

1   Berdaine Mosque
3   Hammam (men only)
6   Bou Inania Medersa
7   Qissariat
    ad-Dahab (gold)
8   Main Bus Terminal
9   Intercity Grands Taxis
10  Dar Jamaï
    (Folk Museum)
11  Haberdashers' Souq
14  Mansour Palace
22  Banque Populaire
23  Local Buses
24  Moulay Ismail
    Mausoleum
25  Mosque
26  Public Swimming Pool
27  'Sfinj' shop
29  Post Office (PTT)
33  Hammam (men
    & women)
34  Cinéma Apollo
36  Crédit du
    Maroc (change)

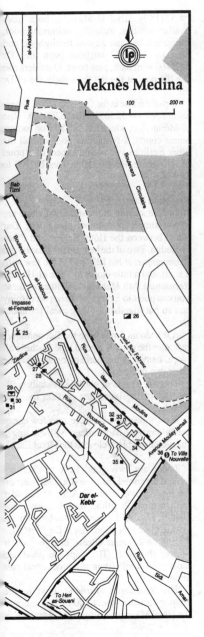

**Meknès Medina**

**Hotels – ville nouvelle** One of the cheapest places to stay is the *Hôtel Central*, 35 Ave Mohammed V, close to the CTM bus station and El-Amir Abdelkader train station. Inside, the place is quite attractively arranged around a central courtyard and has reasonable rooms for Dr 40/70/85/125. The mattresses are thin, the showers cold and the toilets basic. It has been said that the place is used as a brothel and the sheets aren't always changed.

In the same price range is the *Hôtel du Marché* on Ave Hassan II. At Dr 40/80 you can't expect too much, but some of the rooms are crumbling away. Others are better and have balconies. The bed linen is dubious and there are only cold showers.

Considerably better, but a little dearer, is the *Hôtel Toubkal* (☎ 522218), back on Ave Mohammed V. The rooms have big beds, the showers and toilets are clean and occasionally there is hot water. The staff are a friendly lot. It costs Dr 60 per person in a single or double.

There's also the *Hôtel Guillaume Tell*, down an alleyway next to the Hôtel Volubilis. However it rarely gets Western guests and seemed unwilling to name a price for the rather basic rooms.

The one-star *Hôtel Touring* (☎ 522951), 34 Blvd Allal ben Abdallah, is quite adequate and reasonably good value at Dr 79/98, although the 'hot' water in the showers is only ever lukewarm. The rooms are a decent size and some have private showers, but the beds are on the saggy side.

Virtually overlooking the railway is the *Hôtel Excelsior* (☎ 521900), 57 Ave des FAR. It's in the same category as the Continental but somewhat better. Rooms without shower cost Dr 86/110, while those with bathroom are Dr 110/127. Add a few dirhams in taxes.

An altogether better deal is the *Hôtel Majestic* (☎ 522035), 14 Ave Mohammed V. It has a bit of character, and although the beds are rather narrow the rooms with washbasin, bidet and sometimes balcony are fine. Rooms without private shower cost Dr 86/111 for singles/doubles, Dr 169 for triples, plus taxes. The shared showers are clean and the water piping hot. They even have central heating which sometimes works in winter. There are some rooms with private shower and toilets for more.

Quite reasonable (except for the lack of hot water) is the more modern *Hôtel Panorama* (☎ 522737), just off Ave des FAR. For a big room with a private shower and very comfortable beds you pay Dr 114/135.

### Places to Stay – middle

At the lower end of this category is the two-star *Hôtel Moderne* (☎ 524228), 54 Ave Allal ben Abdallah, which has singles/doubles with shower and shared toilet for Dr 157/187.

Farther up the line and not bad value in its class is the *Hôtel Palace* (☎ 525777), 11 Zankat Ghana, which has rooms with private bathroom for Dr 195/240 or Dr 153/195 without.

Those looking for guaranteed creature comforts and a full range of private facilities couldn't do better than the popular *Hôtel de Nice* (☎ 520318), 10 Zankat Accra, a three-star hotel with singles/doubles/triples for Dr 201/252/344.

There are three three-star hotels within a stone's throw of each other around Ave des FAR and Ave Mohammed V. The *Hôtel Bab Mansour* (☎ 525239; fax 510741), 38 Rue El-Amir Abdelkader, has clean and modern, if somewhat sterile, rooms with carpet and phone. Those with bath cost Dr 226/273, while those without are Dr 179/225. A bit older and not so good is the *Hôtel Volubilis* (☎ 525082), 45 Ave des FAR, which has rooms at the same prices (including triples for Dr 377). Unfortunately, it is on a noisy intersection.

Quieter and newer is the *Hôtel Akouas* (☎ 596768; fax 515994). It has some excellent self-contained rooms, and others that are not nearly so good, so ask to see a few. They charge Dr 232/285/377.

### Places to Stay – top end

The four-star *Rif Hôtel* (☎ 522591; fax 524428), Zankat Accra, and the *Hôtel Zaki*

(☎ 521140), Blvd al-Massira, both have similar facilities, including swimming pool, restaurant, bar and air-con throughout, and cost Dr 297/387 without bath and Dr 362/460 with bath, plus taxes. Outsiders can use the pool at the Rif for a daily fee of Dr 50.

Top of the line is the five-star *Hôtel Transatlantique* (☎ 525051; fax 520057), Rue el-Mériniyine, which has 120 air-con rooms, tennis courts, a swimming pool and all the other facilities you would expect of a hotel of this nature. Rooms range from Dr 700 to Dr 900.

### Places to Eat

If you are staying in the old town, there are a few simple restaurants along Rue Dar Smen between the Hôtel Regina and Place el-Hedim. Two of the best are the *Restaurant Economique*, at No 123 (one of the few with a sign), and a little closer to Place el-Hedim, *Restaurant Bab Mansour*. In either of these you can point to a range of dishes on display and so put together a filling meal for about Dr 25.

A few doors down from the Economique, just after the café, is a good hole-in-the-wall place, nameless but perhaps better than the other two mentioned.

There is a mass of cheap-eats stalls spilling out in the lanes just outside the Bab el-Jedid.

In the ville nouvelle, there are a few cheap eats along Ave Mohammed V, including a roast-chicken place close to the Hôtel Excelsior.

There are two good little restaurants around the corner from the Hôtel Majestic on the road leading to the El-Amir Abdelkader train station. A filling meal of, say, brochettes, salad and a drink costs about Dr 30.

One place that stands out is the *Rôtisserie Karam*, at 2 Zankat Ghana, near the corner of Ave Hassan II. The chips are good and most main meals (typically brochettes) cost about Dr 20.

The *Restaurant Marhaba*, next to the Empire Cinema (about 100 metres south of the Hôtel Majestic) on Ave Mohammed V, is a modestly touristy restaurant, with somewhat kitsch décor but reasonable food. You'll leave about Dr 60 lighter, but the fact that it advertises itself as recommended in guide books is hardly a good sign for the future.

For Western-style fast food, try *Free Time* on Ave Hassan II, where a small hamburger plus chips goes for Dr 18.

*La Coupole*, also on Ave Hassan II, is a popular local restaurant with set menus for Dr 70 and comparatively cheap main meals à la carte. There is also a bar and, at night, a rather noisy and tacky nightclub.

Many travellers go to the *Restaurant Metropole Annexe*, 11 Rue Charif Idrissi, around the corner from the junction of Ave Hassan II and Ave Mohammed V. A three-course, Moroccan-style set meal costs about Dr 80. The food is excellent, the service quick and beer and wine are available. Next door on the corner is the *Restaurant Gambrinus*, which offers a set menu for Dr 50.

*Pizzeria Le Four* is a favourite meeting place for chic Meknassis, and you can get surprisingly good pizza for Dr 30 to Dr 40. Wine and beer are also available. Watch out for the 19% taxes. Across the road is the *Montana*, which is a bar downstairs and a Moroccan restaurant upstairs – a good meal will cost Dr 40 to Dr 60. Another place for pizza is the *Pizzeria La Mama*, around the corner from the Hôtel de Nice.

If you are desperate for Asian food, you could do worse than the licensed *Restaurant Tangerois-Hai Phong* (☎ 515091) in Zankat Beyrouth. A main meal will cost you at least Dr 60 plus taxes. Across the road is a rather good bakery, pâtisserie and café.

For a splurge in traditional Moroccan surroundings, check out the *Restaurant Zitouna* (☎ 532083), 44 Jamaa Zitouna, in the medina. This is a veritable palace of a restaurant with an atmosphere as enjoyable as its Moroccan specialities. Meknès is full of places like this, but despite its definite tourist orientation, it can make a pleasant once-off. There's a set menu for Dr 100 or à la carte mains, which makes it quite cheap compared

with its Fès counterparts. Alcoholic drinks are not available. There's a similar place just south of where Rue Souika and Rue Ben el-Maacer meet.

If you want to really lash out, there's the formal *Palais Terrab* (☎ 521456), 18 Ave Zerktouni, in the ville nouvelle east of the El-Amir Abdelkader train station. A full meal here costs around Dr 350 per person.

### Entertainment

**Cafés & Bars** There are cafés all over the old city and the ville nouvelle. *La Comtesse* café under the Hôtel de Paris on Rue Rouamzine is a new, lively place; it has ice cream in summer. Just by the Restaurant Economique on Rue Dar Smen is a lovely old café with an interior décor of smoky wooden beams. The cafés on Place el-Hedim are good for people-watching. The *Café Hamounia* on Rue Rouamine is also not bad, and just down from it is a hole-in-the-wall selling freshly fried sfinj – a kind of light, deep-fried doughy doughnut great for dunking in coffee. You buy a few at a time and they are tied together with a strand of palm frond.

The ville nouvelle, especially on and around Ave Mohammed V, is full of French-style cafés good for a relaxing coffee or tea and cake.

There are a few basic bars around the Ave Mohammed V end of Blvd Allal ben Abdallah. There's nothing particular to recommend them, and you may want to try the highly discreet liquor store farther up Blvd Allal ben Abdallah for some take-home alcohol. As noted, some of the restaurants in the ville nouvelle are licensed. There is a bar in the Restaurant Montana and the bigger hotels all have bars.

**Discos & Cinemas** The *Rif Hôtel* has a disco in which it stages an 'Oriental show'. Otherwise, there are a couple of dubious nightclubs about, including one in the Hôtel Volubilis and one a bit farther east along Ave des FAR, the *Café de France Club de Nuit*. Entrance to these places starts at Dr 50,

MOROCCO

including your first drink, but subsequent tipples are in the order of Dr 50 a go.

There are a few cinemas around town.

### Getting There & Away

**Air** RAM has several representatives, including Wasteels and Wagons-Lits, mentioned in the earlier Information section. It also has an office (☎ 520963) at 7 Ave Mohammed V. There is a small airstrip just outside Meknès, but no regular flights.

**Bus – CTM** The CTM terminal is on Ave Mohammed V near the junction with Ave des FAR. There are nine departures daily to Casablanca (Dr 55) and Rabat (Dr 33), the first at 5.30 am and the last at 8 pm; seven a day to Fès (Dr 14.50), the first at 11 am and the last at 11 pm; two daily to Er-Rachidia (at 10 and 11.30 pm – the first continues on to Rissani); two daily to Ifrane and Azrou, at 4 and 8 pm; one daily to Tangier (Dr 63) at 7 pm; and one daily to Taza (Dr 45), at 5 pm.

CTM also operates international buses to Paris and Brussels – for details see the Getting There & Away chapter.

**Bus – others** The main bus terminal for all other companies is just outside Bab el-Khemis on the northern side of the new mellah along Ave du Mellah. There is a left-luggage office, a café and phone office. The various companies are represented at nine windows, but almost all the information posted up is in Arabic. At Window 9 you can get tickets for a 6.30 am bus to Marrakesh (Dr 96). For Moulay Idriss, go to Window 8 (Dr 7). There are fairly regular buses to Kenitra, Rabat and Casablanca – tickets can be bought at Window 5.

Window 6 has tickets for Tetouan (Dr 56) and Chefchaouen (Dr 45), which leave at 5 am and noon, with a third service to Chefchaouen only at 6 am. Buses for Ouezzane leave at 5, 6, 7, 8, 11 am and noon (Dr 30). Finally, you can also get tickets for Tangier (Dr 50) at this counter. The Tangier buses leave at 6.45, 8, 10 am, noon and 3 pm. The trip takes about six hours.

Fès bus tickets (Dr 12) can be purchased

at Window 7. Buses leave every hour or so until 4 pm, after which there are a few more at uncertain times in transit from Rabat.

From the same window, you can also get tickets for Taza (Dr 35; 6.30 and 8.30 am); Sefrou (Dr 48; 7 am); Oujda (Dr 84.50; 5.30 am) and Nador (Dr 78 to Dr 82; 4.30, 8.30 and 9.30 am).

**Train** The main train station is some way from the centre of the new city, on Ave du Sénégal. It's much more convenient to use the El-Amir Abdelkader station, one block down from and parallel to Ave Mohammed V, as all trains stop here. All trains to or from Fès also stop in Meknès.

A total of 11 trains go to Fès (one hour), six of which go on to Oujda (6½ hours), and at least nine to Casablanca (4¼ hours) via Rabat. There are seven services to Marrakesh, three of them direct (7½ hours).

Second-class fares on normal and rapide services include: Fès (Dr 12/15); Tangier (Dr 55.50/70); Casablanca (Dr 56.50/72.50) and Marrakesh (Dr 109/137.50).

**Taxi** All the grands taxis leave from a dirt lot between Bab el-Khemis and the main bus station. You can't miss it. There are regular departures to Fès (Dr 15), Rabat (Dr 38), Moulay Idriss (for Volubilis, Dr 7), Sidi Kacem and Beni Slimane. As always, it's best to arrive in the morning.

**Car Rental** Zeit (☎ & fax 525918) has an office at 4 Rue Anserabi. Stopcar (☎ 525061) is at 5 Rue de la Voûte.

### Getting Around

**Bus** There are local buses between the medina and the new city, but they are invariably crowded and hard to get on at times.

Useful routes include the No 2 (Bab el-Mansour to Blvd Allal ben Abdallah, returning to the medina along Ave Mohammed V) and No 7 (Bab el-Mansour to the CTM bus station).

**Taxi** A useful urban grand taxi route, which connects the new and old cities, starts in the new city from Zankat Ghana near the corner of Ave Hassan II, directly opposite the Rôtisserie Karam. The grands taxis are silver Mercedes with black roofs. The fare is Dr 5 per person. Pale-blue petits taxis covering the same distance would cost about Dr 10. A petit taxi ride from the main bus station to El-Amir Abdelkader train station is Dr 12.

## AROUND MEKNÈS

### Volubilis

About 33 km from Meknès is the site of the largest and best preserved Roman ruins in Morocco. Volubilis dates largely from the 2nd and 3rd centuries AD, although excavations have revealed that the site was originally settled by Carthaginian traders in the 3rd century BC.

Volubilis (Oualili in Arabic) was one of the Roman empire's most remote outposts. Direct Roman rule lasted for only 240 years after the area was annexed in about 40 AD. According to some historians, Rome imposed strict controls on what could or could not be produced in its North African possessions, according to the needs of the empire. One result was massive deforestation and the large-scale planting of wheat. The sweep of largely treeless plains around Volubilis certainly makes such a thesis plausible.

Volubilis' population of Berbers, Greeks, Jews and Syrians continued to speak Latin and practise Christianity right up until the coming of Islam. Unlike Lixus, to the northwest, which was abandoned shortly after the fall of the Roman empire, Volubilis continued to be inhabited until the 18th century, when its marble was plundered for the building of Moulay Ismail's palaces in Meknès.

If you like ancient ruins, Volubilis is worth a visit. It is an easy day trip from Meknès, and you can also take in the nearby town of Moulay Idriss.

The whole site has been well excavated. Its most attractive feature is the stunning mosaics, made even more so by the fact that they have been left *in situ*. A few officious men in blue coats with whistles patrol the site, making sure you don't do what you shouldn't (ie walk on the mosaics); this is good to see, but they tend to take themselves a bit too seriously at times. The site is open daily from sunrise to sunset and entry is Dr 20. A couple of guides will offer their services at the entrance, but they don't try very hard.

The major points of interest are in the northern part of the site, although it's more convenient to start in the south. Once over the Oued Fertassa, the path from the entrance takes you through an unremarkable residential quarter. The **House of Orpheus**, a little higher up and identifiable by the three pine trees growing in the corner, was a sumptuous mansion for one of the city's wealthier residents. Its two mosaics, one representing the Orpheus myth and the other the chariot of Amphitrite, are still in place.

The basilica, capitol and forum are, typically, built on a high point. The **capitol** dates back to 217 AD; the **basilica** lies to the north of it.

On the left, just before the Triumphal Arch, are a couple of roped-off **mosaics**. One depicts an athlete being presented with a trophy for winning a *desultor* race, a competition in which the rider had to dismount and jump back on his horse as it raced along. Opposite these mosaics are the remains of an aqueduct and fountain.

The **Triumphal Arch** on the major thoroughfare, the *decumanus maximus*, built in 217 AD in honour of Emperor Caracalla and his mother, Julia Domna, used to be topped with a bronze chariot. The arch was reconstructed in the 1930s, and the mistakes made then were rectified in the 1960s.

The **decumanus maximus** stretches up the slope to the north-east. The houses lining either side of the road contain the best mosaics on the site. The first house on the far side of the arch is known as the House of the Ephebus and contains a fine mosaic of Bacchus in a chariot drawn by panthers. Next along is the House of Columns (so named because of its columned façade), and adjacent to this is the Knight's House, with its incomplete mosaic of Bacchus and Ariadne.

Behind these houses you can still see the trolley tracks laid to cart away excavated

MOROCCO

material. The size of the pile of waste moved to uncover the site is astonishing – there's a sizable artificial hill out there.

In the next couple of houses are excellent mosaics entitled the *Labours of Hercules* and *Nymphs Bathing*. The best collection on the whole site, however, is in the House of the Cortege of Venus, one block farther up and one block to the right. Although some of the house is roped off, there is a viewing platform built along the southern wall that gives you a good vantage point over the two best mosaics – the *Abduction of Hylas by the Nymphs* and *Diana Bathing*.

The decumanus maximus continues up the hill to the Tangier Gate, past the uninteresting Gordien Palace, which used to be the residence of the city's administrators.

**Places to Stay & Eat** The only nearby hotel is the four-star *Hôtel Volubilis*, about half a km farther on from the site coming from Meknès. There is also a camping ground 11 km back on the road towards Meknès. Apart from the hotel restaurant, there is a good café at the entrance to the site where you can rehydrate and nourish yourself – at a price (a glass of tea costs Dr 5).

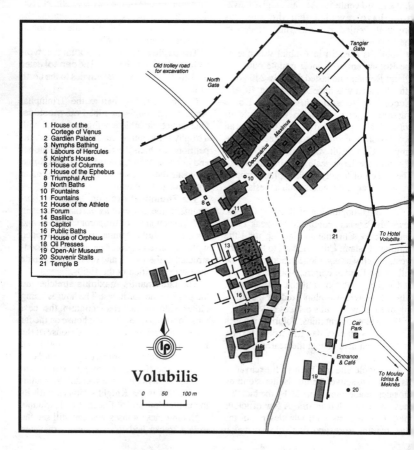

1 House of the Cortege of Venus
2 Gardien Palace
3 Nymphs Bathing
4 Labours of Hercules
5 Knight's House
6 House of Columns
7 House of the Ephebus
8 Triumphal Arch
9 North Baths
10 Fountains
11 Fountains
12 House of the Athlete
13 Forum
14 Basilica
15 Capitol
16 Public Baths
17 House of Orpheus
18 Oil Presses
19 Open-Air Museum
20 Souvenir Stalls
21 Temple B

Volubilis

0    50    100 m

**Getting There & Away** To get to Volubilis from Meknès, take one of the infrequent buses or more frequent grands taxis to Moulay Idriss from the bus station outside Bab el-Khemis. Get off at the turn-off to Moulay Idriss. From there it's about a 30-minute walk – extremely pleasant when it's not too hot – and follow the turn-off to the left for Oualili.

Getting back can be a little more problematic, but if you don't fancy hitching, your best bet will be to walk up to Moulay Idriss (a good hour away) and wait for a bus or grand taxi back. Do so early in the day, as transport dries up in the mid-afternoon. The last option is to get a group together and a hire a grand taxi for half a day, which will probably come to about Dr 150.

## Moulay Idriss

The other main place of interest outside Meknès is Moulay Idriss, about 4.5 km from Volubilis. The town is named after Morocco's most revered saint, a great-grandson of the Prophet and the founder of the country's first real dynasty. Moulay Idriss fled Mecca in the late 8th century AD in the face of persecution at the hands of the then recently installed Abbassid Caliphate, which was based in Baghdad. Idriss settled at Volubilis, where he managed to convert the locals to Islam and made himself their leader. From there he went on to establish Morocco's first imperial dynasty.

Moulay Idriss is an attractive town from a distance, nestled in a cradle of verdant mountains, and for Moroccans it's a place of pilgrimage. Non-Muslims may well get the feeling that they are only grudgingly tolerated (it has been open to them only for the past 70 years or so). You cannot visit any of the mosques or shrines and you are not allowed to stay overnight.

**Things to See** Although the twin hilltown is a veritable maze of narrow lanes and dead ends, it is not hard to get around to the few points of interest.

First to the **Mausoleum of Moulay Idriss**, the object of veneration and the reason for the country's greatest annual moussem in late August. From the main square (where buses and grands taxis arrive), walk up the street that starts to the left of the bus ticket booths. This brings you into the main street, which is lined on both sides by cafés and cheap food stands; those on the right overlook the square from which you have just emerged. Proceed straight down this street and under the arch – the increasing number of quite unnecessary guides and package-tourist groups should reassure you that you're getting warm. About 50 metres on to your left you'll see a three-arched gateway. Go through and straight ahead – you'll soon come up against the barrier that marks the point beyond which non-Muslims may not pass. The mausoleum that stands here today was built by Moulay Ismail, and various additions have since been made.

You can now head left into the maze of streets and try to find your way to a couple of vantage points that give you a **panoramic view** of the mausoleum and the town – plenty of guides will offer to help.

If you don't feel like being guided, there is an alternative. Head back to the beginning of the main street, which you reached coming up from the bus station square. Looking again in the direction of mausoleum, you'll notice a side street heading uphill to your left and signposted 'Municipalité'. Follow it, and just before the Agfa photo shop on the left take the cobbled street to the right. As you climb up you'll notice the only **cylindrical minaret** in Morocco. The green tile décor spells out in stylised script the standard Muslim refrain, *la illah illa Allah* – 'There is no god but Allah'.

Proceed another couple of hundred metres and you're close. This is where you have to ask a local for the 'grande' or 'petite terrasse' – this should produce no problem. The terraces are nothing of the sort, but are simply vantage points high above the mausoleum and a good part of the town.

Saturday is market day and so a more lively time to be in Moulay Idriss; it's also easier to get there on a Saturday.

**Places to Eat** There is nowhere to stay in Moulay Idriss. The main battery of cheap restaurants and cafés is in the main street above the bus station. There are a few cafés on the square and its approaches too.

**Getting There & Away** Occasional buses and more frequent grands taxis run from the bus station outside Bab el-Khemis in Meknès. The ride costs Dr 7. Note that it can be extremely difficult getting out of Moulay Idriss after about 3 pm. There are few services and often a lot of customers. The occasional bus stops here en route to or from such places as Casablanca.

# Fès

The oldest of the imperial cities, Fès is arguably the symbolic heart of Morocco. Founded shortly after the Arabs swept across North Africa and Spain, it quickly became the religious and cultural centre of Morocco. Even in those periods when it was not the official capital of the whole country, Fès could not be ignored and never really ceased to be considered the northern capital.

All the great dynasties left their mark on the city, but it owes much of its magnificence to the people who from the start made up its cosmopolitan population. In the early days, thousands of families from Muslim Spain came, followed by Arabs from farther east along the North African littoral. Despite the arrival over the centuries of some Berbers from the interior, Fès has retained a distinctly Arab identity.

It has also long considered itself the centre of Islamic orthodoxy, and its allegiance, or at least submission, has always been essential to Morocco's rulers. With such symbolic importance attached to their city, Fassis (the people of Fès) have always been conscious of the power they wield. The city has, up to the present day, acted as a barometer of popular sentiment. Morocco's independence movement was born in Fès, and when there

are strikes or protests, they are always at their most vociferous here.

The medina of Fès el-Bali (Old Fès) is one of the largest living medieval cities in the world and the most interesting in Morocco. With the exception of Marrakesh, Cairo and Damascus, there is nothing remotely comparable anywhere else in the Arab world.

Its narrow winding alleys and covered bazaars are crammed with every conceivable sort of craft workshop, restaurant, meat, fruit and vegetable market, mosque and medersa, as well as extensive dye pits and tanneries – a veritable assault on the senses as you squeeze past recalcitrant donkeys and submit to the sounds and smells of this jostling city.

The gates and walls that surround the whole are magnificent, all the more so because, unlike many other medieval walled cities, Fès el-Bali has not burst its banks. The expanding population instead has filled out the ville nouvelle to the south-west and spread to the hillsides in an arc stretching principally north and south of the new city.

But Fès is a city in trouble. Its million or so inhabitants are straining it to the utmost, and the old city especially, some experts have warned, is slowly falling apart. UNESCO has done a lot to stop this deterioration, and is working on a cultural heritage plan for the city, but in the long term it will need huge investment if its unique beauty is to be preserved.

For now, it still represents an experience you are unlikely to forget. You could easily spend a week wandering through this labyrinth and still not be ready to leave. In spite of the hordes of tourists that pile through, Fès gives the impression of living largely in the centuries-old traditions that have shaped it.

The ville nouvelle and its chic, café-lined avenues provide a jarring contrast – the modern flipside to the ancient city. Sipping coffee and watching the passers-by along Blvd Mohammed V, you could just about be forgiven for thinking you're in a southern French city.

Young Fassis, like young Moroccans in the other big cities, appear to have cast aside the trappings of their parents' lives, instead adopting fashions and lifestyles more readily identified with the West. The downside is that many are without work. The smart, clean centre of the ville nouvelle disguises the sad lot of the poorer people living on the periphery. This aspect of the city's life will be most evident to travellers in the touts, hustlers and beggars who will undoubtedly be encountered. Most of them operate in the area stretching from the centre of the ville nouvelle to the old city gates. Once inside Fès el-Bali you will largely be left alone.

## History

There is some dispute over who founded Fès. Some say that Idriss I, who founded Morocco's first imperial dynasty, decided Oualili (Volubilis) was too small for the role of capital and began work on a new one here in 789 AD. Others claim his son, Idriss II, was responsible. In any event, a town was well established here by 809. The town's name is believed to come from the Arabic word for 'axe', and one tale relates that a golden pickaxe was unearthed at the beginning of construction around Oued Fès.

The city started off modestly enough as a predominantly Berber town, but its complexion changed with the arrival on the east bank of 8000 families fleeing Al-Andalus. They were later joined by Arab families from Kairouan (or Qayrawan – in modern Tunisia), who set up home on the west bank – the quarter of the Kairaouine (people from Kairouan). They brought with them the religious, cultural and architectural heritage of two great Muslim centres, thereby forming a solid foundation for future greatness. As his father is venerated still in the village of Moulay Idriss, so the memory of Idriss II is perpetuated in his zawiyya in the heart of Fès el-Bali.

Idriss II's heirs split the kingdom up, but for a while Fès continued to enjoy peace and prosperity. In the 10th century, Berber tribes descended on the city, which was torn by a bitter civil war and was also experiencing a famine.

The chaos continued until the arrival of the Almoravids in 1070. For 80 years they ruled the city, which was second in importance only to Marrakesh, the chosen capital of their greatest leader, Youssef bin Tachfin. The Almoravid stay was short, however, for a still more ascetic movement arose to take their place – that of the Almohads.

In their conquest of Fès in about 1154, the Almohads destroyed the walls of the city and only replaced them when they were assured of the inhabitants' loyalty. Large sections of the walls of Fès date from this period. Although Marrakesh remained the imperial capital, Fès continued to be a crucial crossroads and, with the importance of the Kairaouine mosque and university already well established, it became *the* centre of learning and culture in an empire that stretched from Spain to Senegal.

Fès recovered its political status only much later, with the arrival of the Merenid dynasty. They took the city around 1250, but it took them another 20 years to wrest control of Marrakesh from the Almohads and so definitively remove their predecessors from power.

Never sure of his subjects' loyalty, the second Merenid sultan, Abu Youssef Yacoub (1258-86), built a self-contained walled city outside the old one – Fès el-Jdid (New Fès) – and there stationed loyal troops, most of whom were Syrian and Christian mercenaries.

In the 14th century, the Jewish community was relocated from Fès el-Bali to the new city. In this way the first Jewish ghetto, or *mellah*, was created in Morocco. Although regarded as second-class citizens, the Jews were important economically in the life of the nation and were to become increasingly so. The records suggest that the move was partly inspired by a desire to offer the Jews greater protection from pogroms. Whatever the truth of this, they enjoyed the protection of the sultan, and could be relied upon to side with him in the event of an insurrection.

Few Jewish families remain in Fès. Most left for Israel during the 1950s and '60s, and their synagogues have been converted into carpet warehouses and the like.

The Merenids' single greatest gift to posterity, in Fès as in several other cities, is the exquisite medersas they built.

As the Merenids in their turn collapsed, two dynasties vied for power, the Saadians in the south and the Fès-based Wattasids in the north. Although the latter won, they did not last long. Saadian rule was short-lived too, and the Alawites arrived on the scene in 1664. The second of their sultans, Moulay Ismail, shifted the capital to Meknès in 1672; however, his successors chose to move back to Marrakesh. Fès never really lost its importance, however, and successive sultans made a point of residing there at intervals in order to maintain some control over the north.

As central power crumbled and European interference increased over the 19th century, the distinction between Marrakesh and Fès diminished – they effectively both served as capitals of a fragmented country. If anything, Fès retained its status as the 'moral' capital and it was here that the treaty introducing the French and Spanish protectorates over Morocco was signed on 30 March 1912. On 17 April, three days of rioting and virtual revolt against the country's new French masters proved a reminder of the city's volatile history.

Largely because of the insurrection, France moved the political capital to Rabat, where it has remained ever since, but Fès is still a constituency to be reckoned with. The Istiqlal (Independence) Party of Allal al-Fassi was established here, and many of the impulses towards ejecting the French came from Fès. Fès was also the scene of violent strikes and riots in the 1980s, showing that Morocco's rulers, wherever they make their capital, must still reckon with Fès.

In 1916, following the establishment of the protectorate, the French began construction of the ville nouvelle on the plateau to the south-west of the two ancient cities. That Fès, in common with most Moroccan cities, did not experience the wholesale destruction and rebuilding that characterised colonial practice in Algeria is largely due to General (later Marshal) Lyautey.

## Orientation

Fès is comprised of three distinct parts: Fès el-Bali, Fès el-Jdid and the ville nouvelle. The first two form the medina, while the last is the administrative area built by the French.

### The 1912 Insurrection

The insurrection of 17-19 April 1912, caught the French somewhat by surprise, although in the wake of the violence it appeared a fairly predictable reaction to the signing of the Treaty of Fès, which ushered in the protectorate. Several French journalists were in Fès at the time. *L'Illustration* reported:

The Mellah, the Jewish quarter, was the first to be sacked – still a Moroccan tradition. How many corpses have been swallowed up in its ruins?

There were only some 1400 to 1500 troops to bring the situation under control, colonial infantry and sharpshooters camped at Dar Debibagh, some of whom were still engaged in operations around Sefrou.

Throughout the afternoon the struggle between the rebels and our soldiers continued in the streets. By nightfall, all the Europeans who had escaped the insurgents' assaults were safe. Our officers and noncommissioned officers had many an occasion to display their courage and sangfroid...

The following day, however, the rebels dared attack Dar Debibagh. They were pushed back, but Captain Bourdonneau was mortally wounded.

It was only on the 18th that the uprising was brought under control; General Dalbiez's troops, called in from Meknès, arrived and quickly overcame the last sparks of resistance...By the time General Moinier had arrived at a forced march beneath the ramparts of Fès, it was all over.

Losses among the rebels have been estimated at 800 dead. For our part, we can only deplore the deaths of nine civilians...Among the military, it has been a bloodbath. ■

Fès el-Bali is the original medina and the area of most interest to visitors. Its walls encircle an incredible maze of twisting alleys, blind turns and souqs. Finding your way around, at least at first, can be difficult but this is no problem: you can either take a guide or, if you do get lost, pay an eager kid a couple of dirham to guide you at least as far as a familiar landmark. In spite of what you'll hear, it is not at all necessary to take a guide to find your way around if you don't want to.

The wall has a number of gates, of which the most spectacular are Bab Bou Jeloud, Bab el-Mahrouk and Bab Guissa. Bab Bou Jeloud, in the south-west corner of the old part of the city, is the main entrance to the medina. You will probably pass through it many times during your stay, and there is a cluster of cheap pensions in the area. For a good view over the medina, walk up to the Merenid tombs on the hill north of the Bab.

Next to Fès el-Bali is the less interesting Merenid city of Fès el-Jdid, which houses the old Jewish quarter. There are a couple of hotels here, where you can stay if you want to be close to the medina and the hotels around Bab Bou Jeloud are full.

The new city lies south-west of Fès el-Jdid and is laid out in typical French colonial style with wide, tree-lined boulevards, squares and parks. Here you'll find the majority of restaurants and hotels, as well as the post office, banks and most transport connections. It lacks the atmosphere of the medina, but pulses to the rhythm of modern Morocco and is where you'll stay if you're looking for something other than a medina cheapie. There are local buses connecting the ville nouvelle with various parts of the old city. They run regularly and don't take long, so there's no great disadvantage in staying here. It is also quite possible to walk between the two – set aside about half an hour to go from Place de Florence in the ville nouvelle to Bab Bou Jeloud.

## Information
**Tourist Offices** The ONMT office (☎ 623460, 626279) is on Place de la Résistance (Immeuble Bennani) in the new city. It has little of interest other than the usual brochures, although if pressed can be helpful with specific local information. You can supposedly hire official guides to the medina at about Dr 35 for a half-day here. The problem is they will tell you to arrange it at the syndicat d'initiative on Place Mohammed V, which appears to be permanently closed. You don't absolutely need a guide, but if you want an official one and get no joy at the tourist offices, try one of the big hotels.

The ONMT is open Monday to Friday from 8.30 am to noon and 2.30 to 6.30 pm, and in the morning on Saturday.

**Money** Most of the banks are in the new city on Blvd Mohammed V. The BMCE branch on the corner of Blvd Mohammed V and Ave Mohammed es-Slaoui has ATMs. Several other banks have branches in the ville nouvelle and the medina. The RAM office has a booth where you can change cash and cheques. The Restaurant Mounia and several of the bigger hotels will also change money.

**Post & Telecommunications** The main post office is in the new city on the corner of Ave Hassan II and Blvd Mohammed V. It is open Monday to Friday from 8.30 am to 6.45 pm, and on Saturday from 8 to 11 am. Poste restante is at window No 9. The parcels office entrance is on Ave Hassan II.

The telephone office next to the post office on Blvd Mohammed V is open daily from 8.30 am to 9 pm.

There is another post office in the medina near the Dar Batha.

**Guides** In addition to the official guides, a host of unofficial guides are waiting for your business. They tend to hang about some of the hotels, and at various strategic points approaching Fès el-Jdid and Bab Bou Jeloud. On a good day, you'll hardly notice any, and once inside the medina you are generally OK. Drivers should note a Fès speciality; motorised hustlers and guides on the approach roads to the city.

MOROCCO

MOROCCO

To Rabat &
Meknès

Oued Fès

Route Principale No 1

To Meknès

See Fès - Ville Nouvelle Map

Avenue des Almohades

FÈS
EL-JDID

Boulevard des Saâdiens

Boulevard des Alaouites

Avenue des FAR

Avenue Mohammed el-Hayani

Rue Chergui

Avenue des Sports

Boulevard Moulay Youssef

Place
des
Alaouites

21 22
Rue des Mérinides

Boulevard ben Jerrah

Boulevard Tariq Ibn Zied

Ave de France

Avenue M. el-Korri

Mellah

Rue Arabie

Saôudite

Place de la
Résistance

Place de
L'Florence

Avenue de la Liberté

Avenue Hassan II

Avenue Mohammed V

Boulevard Abdallah Chefchaouri

Avenue Mohammed
Youssef ben Tachfine

Rue Moulay Slimane

Boulevard
es-Slaoui

27

28

Boulevard Dhar Mahres

Avenue Hussein de Jordanie

Avenue de Sefrou

Avenue Ibn el-Khatib

Avenue Sidi Brahim

To Ifrane, Airport &
Camping Diamant Vert

Fès

0        250        500 m

To Sefrou

MOROCCO

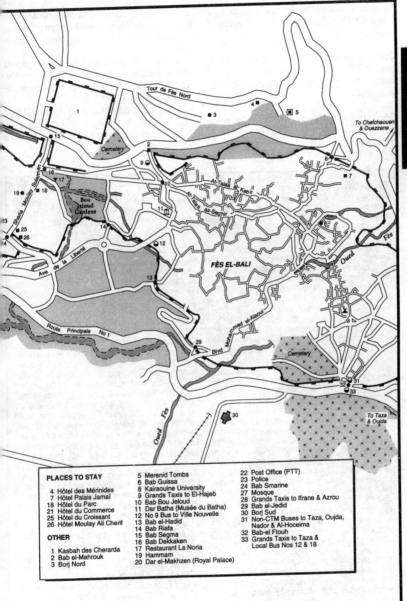

**PLACES TO STAY**

4 Hôtel des Mérinides
7 Hôtel Palais Jamaï
18 Hôtel du Parc
21 Hôtel du Commerce
25 Hôtel du Croissant
26 Hôtel Moulay Ali Cherif

**OTHER**

1 Kasbah des Cherarda
2 Bab el-Mahrouk
3 Borj Nord

5 Merenid Tombs
6 Bab Guissa
8 Kairaouine University
9 Grands Taxis to El-Hajeb
10 Bab Bou Jeloud
11 Dar Batha (Musée du Batha)
12 No 9 Bus to Ville Nouvelle
13 Bab el-Hadid
14 Bab Riata
15 Bab Segma
16 Bab Dekkaken
17 Restaurant La Noria
19 Hammam
20 Dar el-Makhzen (Royal Palace)

22 Post Office (PTT)
23 Police
24 Bab Smarine
27 Mosque
28 Grands Taxis to Ifrane & Azrou
29 Bab el-Jedid
30 Borj Sud
31 Non-CTM Buses to Taza, Oujda, Nador & Al-Hoceima
32 Bab-el Ftouh
33 Grands Taxis to Taza & Local Bus Nos 12 & 18

**Foreign Consulates** France maintains a consulate (☎ 625547) in Fès at Ave Obaid Bnou el-Jarrah.

**Cultural Centre** The Centre Culturel Français (☎ 623921) at 33 Rue Loukiki puts on films, lectures and sometimes offers classes in Arabic.

**Bookshops** The English Bookshop, at 68 Ave Hassan II, close to Place de la Résistance, has a wide range of textbooks and novels. It has some books on Morocco in English and French, but its main market is students of English. The shop closes at lunch times.

The best place to find foreign newspapers and magazines is along Blvd Mohammed V. The stand virtually across the road from the police building is not bad.

There are a few decent bookshops if you read French. One of the best is the Librairie Papeterie du Centre (☎ 622569), at 134 Blvd Mohammed V.

---

### Fès in the 19th Century

Entering Fès el-Bali today is like stepping into a time warp back to the Middle Ages, not so different from the city discovered by Edmondo De Amicis on a diplomatic visit from Italy in the 1880s. He described his experiences in *Morocco: its people & places* (Darf Publishers, 1985), and had this to say about Fès:

The first impression is that of an immense city fallen into decrepitude and slowly decaying. Tall houses, which seemed formed of houses piled one upon the other, all falling to pieces, cracked from roof to base, propped up on every side, with no opening save some loophole in the shape of a cross; long stretches of street, flanked by two high bare walls like the walls of a fortress; streets running uphill and down, encumbered with stones and the ruins of fallen buildings, twisting and turning at every thirty paces; every now and then a long covered passage, dark as a cellar, where you have to feel your way; blind alleys, recesses, dens full of bones, dead animals, and heaps of putrid matter; the whole steeped in a dim and melancholy twilight. In some places the ground is so broken, the dust so thick, the smell so horrible, the flies so numerous, that we have to stop to take breath. In half an hour we have made so many turns that if our road could be drawn it would form an arabesque as intricate as any in the Alhambra. Here and there we hear the noise of a mill, a murmur of water, the click of a weaver's loom, a chanting of nasal voices, which we are told come from a school of children, but we see nothing...We approach the centre of the city; people become more numerous; the men stop to let us pass, and stare astonished; the women turn back, or hide themselves; the children scream and run; the larger boys growl and shake their fists at a distance...We see fountains richly ornamented with mosaics, arabesque doors, arched courts...We come to one of the principal streets, about six feet wide, and full of people who crowd about us...There are a thousand eyes upon us; we can scarcely breathe in the press and heat, and move slowly on, stopping every moment to give passage to a Moor on horseback, or a veiled lady on a camel, or an ass with a load of bleeding sheep's heads. To the right and left are crowded bazaars; inn courtyards encumbered with merchandise; doors of mosques through which we catch a glimpse of arcades and figures prostrate in prayer...The air is impregnated with an acute and mingled odour of aloes, spices, incense and kif; we seem to be walking in an immense drug-shop. Groups of boys go by with scarred and scabby heads; horrible old women, perfectly bald and with naked breasts, making their way by dint of furious imprecations against us; naked, or almost naked, madmen, crowned with flowers and feathers, bearing a branch in their hands, laughing and singing...We go into the bazaar. The crowd is everywhere. The shops, as in Tangier, are mere dens opened in the wall...We cross, jostled by the crowd, the cloth bazaar, that of slippers, that of earthenware, that of metal ornaments, which altogether form a labyrinth of alleys roofed with canes and branches of trees...

Essentially, the only way in which Fès has changed since then is that the moderate affluence Fassis now enjoy has enabled them to restore many of the buildings and clean up the streets. However, that hasn't radically altered the atmosphere; Fès is still worlds apart from anything you will find north of the Strait of Gibraltar. ■

**Language Schools** The American Language Center (☎ 624850) and its affiliated Arabic Language Institute are at 2 Rue Ahmed Hiba in the ville nouvelle, near the hostel. This is one of the few places in Morocco set up for the systematic teaching of Arabic to foreigners. For more details, refer to Activities in the Facts for the Visitor chapter. If you're interested in teaching English, you could look up the International Language Centre rep, Mme Bassou (☎ 641408), at 15 Blvd el-Joulan.

**Medical Services & Emergency** There is a night pharmacy (☎ 623380) on Ave Abdelkrim el-Khattabi.

For the police, call ☎ 19. The fire brigade is on ☎ 15.

**Film & Photography** There are quite a few places around the ville nouvelle and the well-trodden parts of the medina where you can buy film. For developing films you could try the Kodak store on Blvd Mohammed V, a block in from Ave Hassan II.

### Fès el-Bali

According to one count, about 9400 streets and lanes twist and turn their way through the original old medina of Fès el-Bali (Old Fès). Because there are many cemeteries outside the walls, and also as a result of the enlightened policies of General Lyautey in siting the ville nouvelle well away from the old city, nothing has been built immediately outside the walls.

Finding your way around can be confusing but a delightful way to get lost and found. Although it is easy to become quickly disoriented, one 'rule' is worth bearing mind while navigating. Through the labyrinth are threaded a few main streets that will bring you to a gate or landmark sooner or later. It is not always evident whether you are on one of these, but the density of crowds moving up and down them is a clue. The easiest stretch is from Bab Bou Jeloud down At-Talaa al-Kebir or At-Talaa as-Seghir to the Kairaouine Mosque area – it is virtually downhill all the way. Heading back there-

fore, you'll know you aren't far wrong if you follow the crowds and head uphill. Similarly, if you want to get towards the Hôtel Palais Jamaï and the northern gates, keep heading *up*. If this fails, you can always ask shopkeepers for directions or pay someone a few dirham to lead you to where you want to go.

It will take you at least a couple of days to get around and appreciate the city's sights to any degree. And, even though notable buildings such as mosques and medersas are interesting, they form only part of the essence of Fès. You're much more likely to find the real Fès by letting your senses lead you slowly through the crowded bazaars, pausing wherever the mood takes you to watch something of interest, rummage through the articles for sale, or simply sit down over a glass of tea and take it all in.

Like any Moroccan medina, Fès el-Bali is divided into areas representing different craft guilds and souqs interspersed with houses. It is replete with fascinating old

Woodworker in the medina

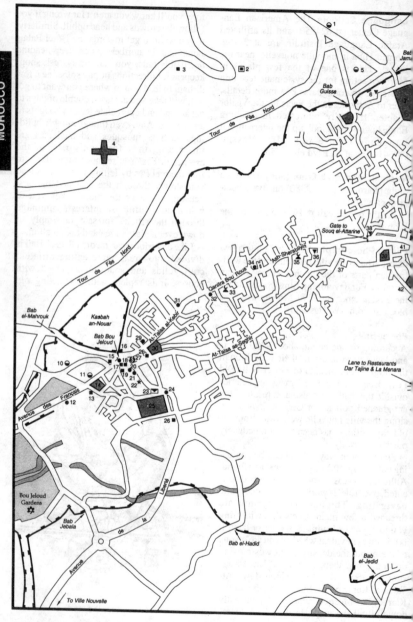

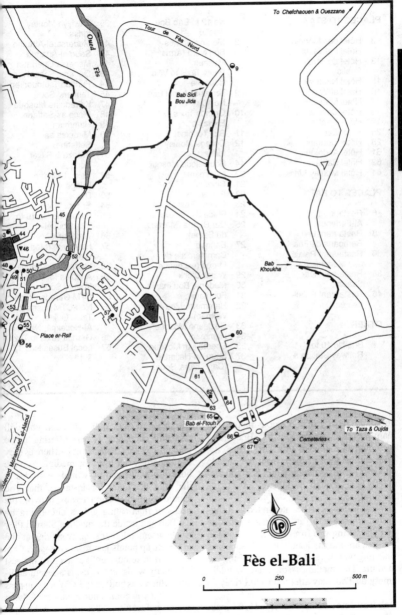

MOROCCO

To Chefchaouen & Ouezzane

Oued Fès

Tour de Fès Nord

9

Bab Sidi
Bou Jida

45

3
44
46
48
50
49
51
52
53
55
56

Place er-Rsif

Boulevard Mohammed el-Alaoui

57
58
59

Bab
Khoukha

60

61

62
63
64
65
Bab el-Ftouh
66
67

To Taza & Oujda

Cemeteries

Fès el-Bali

0        250        500 m

MOROCCO

## PLACES TO STAY

| | |
|---|---|
| 3 | Hôtel des Mérinides |
| 7 | Hôtel Palais Jamaï |
| 13 | Hôtel du Jardin Public |
| 15 | Hôtel National |
| 16 | Hôtel al-Watani |
| 17 | Hôtel Mauritania |
| 18 | Hôtel Cascade |
| 19 | Hôtel Erraha |
| 26 | Hôtel Batha |
| 28 | Hôtel Lamrani |
| 61 | Hôtel Andalous |
| 62 | Hôtel Bahia |
| 64 | Hôtel Moulay Idriss |

## PLACES TO EAT

| | |
|---|---|
| 6 | Restaurant Al-Firdaous |
| 8 | Restaurant Les Remparts de Fès |
| 36 | Restaurant Palais des Mérinides |
| 38 | Restaurant Dar Saada |
| 46 | Restaurant Palais de Fès |

## OTHER

| | |
|---|---|
| 1 | Bus No 10 to Railway Station & No 12 to Bab Bou Jeloud |
| 2 | Merenid Tombs |
| 4 | Borj Nord (Arms Museum) |
| 5 | Petits Taxis to Ville Nouvelle |
| 9 | Terminal, Local Bus No 10 |
| 10 | Grands Taxis to El-Hajeb |
| 11 | Bus Terminal |
| 12 | College Moulay Idriss |
| 14 | Bou Jeloud Mosque |
| 20 | Hammam |
| 21 | Cinema |
| 22 | Police |
| 23 | Branch Post Office |
| 24 | Place de l'Istiqlal |
| 25 | Dar Bartha (Musée du Batha) |
| 27 | Banque Commerciale du Maroc (exchange) |
| 29 | Water Clock |
| 30 | Medersa Bou Inania |
| 31 | Fountain |
| 32 | Hammam (Men & Women) |
| 33 | Gazleane Mosque |
| 34 | Hammam |
| 35 | Sherabliyin Mosque |
| 37 | Souq an-Nejjarine (Carpenters' Souq) |
| 39 | Zawiyya Moulay Idriss |
| 40 | Medersa el-Attarine |
| 41 | Souq el-Attarine |
| 42 | Medersa Cherratia |
| 43 | Qur'anic School |
| 44 | Funduq Tsetouanien |
| 45 | Tanners' Souq |
| 47 | Kairaouine Mosque |
| 48 | Place as-Seffarine |
| 49 | Hammam |
| 50 | Medersa as-Seffarine |
| 51 | Bronze & Silver Souq |
| 52 | Bein al-Mudun Bridge |
| 53 | Dyers' Souq |
| 54 | Er-Rsif Mosque |
| 55 | Local Bus No 19 to Ville Nouvelle |
| 56 | Wafabank |
| 57 | Hammam (Men & Women) |
| 58 | Medersa es-Sahriji |
| 59 | Andalus Mosque |
| 60 | Pottery Souq |
| 63 | CTM Garage Office |
| 65 | Non-CTM buses to Taza, Oujda, Al-Hoceima, Nador |
| 66 | Grands Taxis to Taza |
| 67 | Local Buses Nos 12 & 18 |

buildings, mostly of a religious nature, but many are closed to non-Muslims. Because of the compact nature of this part of the city, little can be seen of them from the outside either. No-one particularly minds if you discreetly peer through the doorways, but that's the limit.

What follows can be interpreted as a suggested itinerary for an excursion into the medina, taking you from Bab Bou Jeloud to the area around the Kairaouine Mosque and finishing with several options for exiting the medina. The medina's souqs are virtually empty on Thursday afternoon and Friday.

**Bab Bou Jeloud** Bab Bou Jeloud is the main entrance to Fès el-Bali. Although you will probably encounter people offering to be guides, they are not nearly as bad here as they can be farther out from the medina. You are bound to be warned by would-be guides in the ville nouvelle, for instance, that you should accept their services now to avoid the packs of man-eating guides circulating by the Bab and inside the medina. Should they be persistent, tell them you're staying at one of the cheap hotels just inside the gate.

Bab Bou Jeloud, unlike much of the rest of the city walls and gates, is a recent addition, which was built in 1913. When you pass through it you come upon a cluster of cheap hotels and cafés – this area is a hive of activity and a great place to sit and watch people's comings and goings.

**Medersa Bou Inania** Not far from the Bab Bou Jeloud is the Medersa Bou Inania, built by the Merenid sultan Bou Inan between 1350 and 1357, and said to be the finest of the theological colleges built by the Merenids. The entrance is on At-Talaa al-Kebir. You can't really miss it, as the minaret is visible from the moment you enter the city by Bab Bou Jeloud.

The medersa has been restored in recent years with a degree of skill proving that Moroccans have lost none of the talents for which they are justly famous. The carved woodwork and stucco are magnificent. There are excellent views over Fès from the roof (closed at the time of writing for further restoration work).

This medersa differs in a number of ways from others you may have seen already; most of those that can be visited in Morocco were built under the Merenids and all betray a common artistic inspiration. A comparison with its namesake in Meknès is sufficient to get the point across. All medersas come equipped with what we might call a prayer hall, but what Muslims would still call a mosque (masjid) – of admittedly modest dimensions and containing a simple mihrab. Here, opposite the entrance, the 'mosque' is more elaborate, and the outstanding feature is its minaret. This distinguishes it from other medersas, as they rarely come equipped with minarets.

One explanation is that the medersa required something approaching a full-scale mosque of its own because of the absence of a nearby mosque at the time it was built. As this little mosque is still in use, non-Muslims may not pass the barrier marked by a tiny tributary of the Oued Fès.

Opposite the entrance to the medersa, to your left, is a water clock designed by a clockmaker who was said to be a part-time magician. Unfortunately, it, too, was covered up for restoration at the time of writing.

The medersa is open between 8 am and 5 pm (except at prayer times), and closed on Friday mornings. Entry costs Dr 10.

**Towards the Zawiyya Moulay Idriss II** Turn right out of the medersa and head down At-Talaa al-Kebir. About 150 metres down the street on a bend you will pass a **fountain** on your left and a little farther on a **hammam**, which precedes one of the medina's 300 or so mosques, the **Gazleane Mosque**. At-Talaa al-Kebir continues right down to the Medersa el-Attarine, but changes its name along the way. At the Gazleane Mosque it is known as the Qanitra Bou Rous. About 100 metres farther down, at an unmistakable dogleg (there is another **hammam** on the left just after it), it becomes Ash-Sherabliyin ('the slippermakers'); the **mosque** you pass on the right another 200 or so metres farther down has taken the same name. Note on the right also, a little way past the mosque, one of the numerous 'traditional' Moroccan restaurants that Fès boasts, the Restaurant Palais des Mérinides (see Places to Eat).

Another 100 metres on, At-Talaa as-Seghir (the parallel artery from Bab Bou Jeloud) joins this street and takes you on to an unassuming gate, beyond which it makes a slight incline into the Souq el-Attarine (the spice market). Just past the gate on the left is another restaurant and café worth noting, the **Dar Saada**. It doubles as a carpet warehouse, and is a useful landmark. Virtually across the road and down a short narrow alley is the **henna souq**, where you can buy, well, henna. It is used as a hair dye and, more importantly, to paint complicated tattoo-like designs on women's hands and feet. Certain designs are associated with particular events, such as weddings.

In the jumble of back lanes and small squares just south of where At-Talaa as-Seghir and Ash-Sherabliyin meet is the **Souq an-Nejjarine** (carpenters' souq), through which you will come across a pretty little square, **Place an-Nejjarine**, dominated by one of the city's most beautiful fountains and an impressive *funduq* – a former caravanserai for travelling merchants who would

MOROCCO

MOROCCO

store and sell their goods below and take lodgings on the floors above.

**Zawiyya Moulay Idriss II** Son of the founder of Morocco's first dynasty, Moulay Idriss II is often credited with having founded the city of Fès. In fact it is probable that his father took that decision, but there is no doubt that Moulay Idriss II brought the city to life. He is almost as highly revered as his father, and his zawiyya is an object of pilgrimage. You can get to two gates leading into the sanctuary. From Place an-Nejjarine, a lane leads off the south-east corner to the women-only gateway into sanctuary. Alternatively, from the Dar Saada (see the previous section) you can continue a few metres east into the Souq el-Attarine and take the first alley to the right – this leads to the main entrance. Both usually have bars across them marking the point beyond which non-Muslims may not pass. With discretion, you can go up to the gates and get a look inside. Next to the Kairaouine mosque and university, it is one of the main monuments in the heart of Fès. From vantage points overlooking the city, its green-tiled roof stands out with those of the Kairaouine against the white-grey backdrop of the surrounding houses and buildings.

**Medersa el-Attarine** The street that leads through the Souq el-Attarine continues another 200 metres or so (past a qissaria, or covered market, on the right) until it ends in a T-junction. Right in front of you is the Medersa el-Attarine. It was built by Abu Said in 1325 and follows the traditional pattern of Merenid artisanship. The central courtyard is flanked by halls for teaching and the modest masjid. The zellij tile base, intermediate stucco work and cedar wood completion at the top of the walls and the ceiling cede nothing in elegance to the artistry of the Medersa Bou Inania. It's open from 9 am to noon and 2 to 6 pm (closed Friday mornings and often Thursday afternoons, too). Entry costs Dr 10. There are good views of the courtyard of the Kairaouine Mosque from the roof, if you're allowed up there.

**Kairaouine Mosque** Emerging again from the medersa, turn left. You'll see Rue Bou Touil on the left with a few snack stalls. The walls of the great Kairaouine (or Qayrawin) mosque and university stretch down this street and ahead of you on the left-hand side (the qissaria opens up on your right).

The mosque is said to be capable of holding 20,000 people, and the university, one of the oldest in the world, has for centuries been one of the most highly regarded centres of Muslim religious learning, sur-

---

**Ibn Khaldoun**

Although Fès cannot count him as one of its own, Ibn Khaldoun, one of the Arab world's greatest thinkers, was one of many luminaries attracted to Morocco's centre of learning, where he studied in the Kairaouine University for some years.

Considered the greatest of Arab historians, Ibn Khaldoun developed the first philosophy of history not based on religion. Called the *Muqaddimah* (Introduction to History), his book is regarded as a classic. The 20th-century historian Toynbee has called it 'a philosophy of history which is undoubtedly the greatest work of its kind that has ever yet been created by any mind in any time or place'. Ibn Khaldoun also wrote a definitive history of Muslim North Africa.

He was born in Tunisia in 1332 and spent the early years of his life there, but by the age of 23, after completing his studies at the Kairaouine, he had become a secretary to the sultan of Fès. After having been imprisoned for two years on suspicion of being involved in a palace rebellion, Ibn Khaldoun moved to Granada, then Bejaia, Tlemcen, Biskra and Fès before ending up back in Granada.

In 1375 he gave up the world of business and politics and retired to the village of Frenda in Algeria where, under the protection of the local emir, he spent four years writing the *Muqaddimah*.

He spent the later years of his life teaching at the Kairaouine's eastern counterpart, the Al-Azhar in Cairo. He died in 1406. ■

passed in reputation only by the Al-Azhar in Cairo.

It was built between 859 and 862 by Fatma bint Mohammed ben Feheri for her fellow refugees from Tunisia. It was enlarged in 956 and brought to its present size by the Almoravid sultan Ali ben Youssef. The Almohads and Saadians also contributed to its detail. The buildings include one of the finest libraries in the Muslim world, and there are usually 300 students in residence in the university. Unfortunately, non-Muslims may not enter, and it's so hemmed in by other buildings that little can be seen of it from the outside.

You can follow the walls right around it and occasionally get a look inside.

**Around the Kairaouine** If you head down Rue Bou Touil, following the university walls, you will be obliged to make a right turn. Just on your left is the 14th-century **Funduq Tsetouanien** (Tetouan Funduq). For centuries it served as a hotel and warehouse for travelling merchants; the name suggests that it was originally the preserve of businessmen from Tetouan. Mohammed Bouzoubaa, who runs a carpet factory in the former funduq, will be happy to tell you a bit about the place, but may be a little disappointed if you don't stay a while for some tea and a look at his wares.

A little way down and still on the left is a wonderful 14th-century merchant's mansion that has been converted into a carpet shop and restaurant, the **Palais de Fès**. The rooftop café has superb views over the Kairaouine University. Proceeding along the university walls, you emerge on another small square, Place as-Seffarine (Brassmakers' Square). With the university walls still on your right (the entrance to its library opens on to this square), there is a small and not particularly captivating **medersa**, named after the square, on your left – look for the heavy studded cedar door. Built in 1280, it is the oldest in Fès, but is in an advanced state of disrepair. Across the main street leading east off the square (away from the Kairaouine) is a **hammam**.

**Itinerary Options** You could now continue to follow the walls of the Kairaouine back to where you started and head back to Bab Bou Jeloud, ideally taking At-Talaa as Seghir and perhaps winding up the day's visit with a look at the Dar Batha museum. On the way, if you're interested, you could get off the beaten track south of the Kairaouine University to have a quick look at the **Medersa Cherratin**, which was built in 1670 under Moulay ar-Rashid, the first of the Alawites. It is far less interesting than its Merenid precursors.

There are other options from Place as-Seffarine. You can head off north-east to see Fès's famous tanneries (from where you could push on over the Oued Fès towards the Andalus quarter, south to the Bab el-Ftouh and buses to the ville nouvelle) and then return to the square before setting off for the dyers' souq, Er-Rsif mosque and an alternative bus stop for rides back into the ville nouvelle.

Yet another possibility would be to return to the gateway into the Souq el-Attarine for an excursion north towards Bab Guissa, the Hôtel Palais Jamaï and perhaps beyond to the Merenid tombs (see that entry). You can also pick up a bus to the ville nouvelle from Bab Guissa.

**Tanneries** From Place as-Seffarine, take the lane just north of the medersa on the square. Take the left fork after about 50 metres and follow your nose – or the directions locals are bound to give you. You will probably be led to a platform overlooking the tanners' pits through a leather shop. It's also fairly likely that someone will ask you for a donation (Dr 10) for a 'workers' fund'. They can be quite insistent about this, although it's all rather dubious.

The tanneries are best visited in the morning, when the pits are awash with the colours used in the tanning and dyeing process. It doesn't smell good, but is not quite as bad as you might be led to believe.

**Dyers' Souq & Er-Rsif Mosque** From Place as-Seffarine, take the main lane heading east away from the Kairaouine, and south of the medersa on the square, and you will quickly find yourself in the Dyers' Souq by the Oued Fès. There are two small bridges over the fairly filthy-looking stream, whose water is used in the dyeing of textiles. If you cross either one and head off to the right you will emerge on to a wide square by the Er-Rsif Mosque. From here you can get the No 19 bus back to the ville nouvelle.

**Andalus Quarter** The only real attractions here are the Andalus Mosque and the Medersa es-Sahriji next door. To get there from Place as-Seffarine, take the lane for the tanneries, but turn right instead of left at the fork and you will reach the Bein al-Mudun ('Between the Cities') bridge over the Oued Fès. It will not be immediately obvious how to proceed from here, and you may want to enlist someone's help. There are at least two ways to choose from. The first is as follows. As soon as you cross the bridge, turn right and then take the first left (which starts out as a covered street). At the T-junction turn right and then take the first left; about 100 metres up on your right is a hammam for men and women. As you head up to an archway over the street, you pass a small square on the left and a mosque on the right. Once through the arch (you emerge on a small square), turn left. Dead ahead is the women's entrance to the Andalus Mosque and, shortly before on the right, the entrance to the medersa. The main entrance to the mosque is around the corner to the left of the women's entrance.

The **medersa** was built in 1321. The basic structure of this college is simple, but the inside is richly decorated and there are good views from the roof. Much of the structure lay in ruins until fairly recently, but restoration work is still continuing. It is open daily from 8.30 am to 5 pm, usually with a break from noon to 3 pm. It is closed on Friday morning. Entry is Dr 10.

The **mosque** was founded as a small local place of worship in the 9th century and was expanded by the Almohads in the 13th century, not long before the arrival of the

Merenids, who also added to the decoration and installed a library.

If you want to leave the medina at this point, you can return to the small square, turn left and follow the wide street heading south off the square. It leads right down to Bab el-Ftouh, where you can catch local buses to the ville nouvelle.

**Northern Medina** The best way to reach Bab Guissa and the Hôtel Palais Jamaï in the north of the medina is to start off at the gateway to Souq el-Attarine. Take the street just on the west side of the gate. If you stick to the wider streets and keep going *up*, you really can't go wrong. You'll know you're on the right track if you pass by a little square with a cinema on its northern side. From there you will probably arrive at Bab Guissa, from which you can easily see the Hôtel Palais Jamaï to the east. What is now a luxury hotel was built in the late 19th century by the Grand Vizier to Moulay al-Hassan I, Sidi Mohammed ben Arib al-Jamaï. (He and his brother also had a palace built in Meknès, on Place el-Hedim, which now houses a museum.) The Jamaï brothers fell from grace at the rise of Sultan Abd al-Aziz, and lost all their properties. Set in lush gardens, the palace is a wonderful place to have a refreshment – if you can afford Dr 20 for a cup of coffee!

Across the road from Bab Guissa you can pick up local buses back into the ville nouvelle. There are also petits taxis.

**Fès el-Jdid**
Fès el-Jdid was built next to Fès el-Bali by the Merenids in the 13th century. It has some spectacular buildings and the old Jewish quarter and, although less interesting than the older city, is much easier to explore. No-one will hassle you for guide services (except perhaps to suggest that you engage a guide here to take you into Fès el-Bali).

The entrance to the Dar el-Makhzen (Royal Palace) on Place des Alaouites is a stunning example of modern restoration. The grounds cover some 200 acres and house palaces, pavilions, medersas, mosques and pleasure gardens; the complex has been used to host an Arab League conference. It used to be possible to visit the palace with prior permission from the tourist office, but this is no longer the case unless you have political or cultural elbow.

At the northern end of the main street, Sharia Moulay Suleiman (formerly Grande Rue de Fès el-Jdid), is the **Petit Mechouar**, a parade ground for the sultan's troops, and the enormous Merenid gate of **Bab Dek-kaken**, once the main entrance to the royal palace. Between it and Bab Bou Jeloud are the well-maintained and relaxing **Bou Jeloud Gardens** (or Jnan Sebil), though the partially dried-up lake is used as a rubbish dump. Through the gardens flows the Oued Fès, still the city's main source of water. North of the gate is the **Grand Mechouar**, leading up to Bab Segma. Behind the western wall of the Grand Mechouar was the royal arms factory, established in 1886 by Moulay al-Hassan. It now serves as a carpet factory.

Sharia Moulay Suleiman is lined with shops and a few hotels and cafés, but lacks the atmosphere of the main streets in Fès el-Bali. South of it is the old **mellah**, the Jewish quarter. Few Jews live here now, but their houses, with windows and balconies looking into the streets, are in marked contrast to the usual Muslim practice of having windows opening on to an internal courtyard. They were transferred from the centre of the old city by the Merenids. Some say they were moved for their own protection, others maintain that it made it easier to keep an eye on their activities, and others believe it was to provide the Merenids with a loyal bulwark against possible rebellions from Fassis of the old city, whose loyalty they were unsure of.

### Dar Batha

One place on the border of Fès el-Jdid and Fès el-Bali that you should not miss is the Dar Batha, now the Musée du Batha (also known as the Museum of Moroccan Arts). It is on Place de l'Istiqlal, about five minutes' walk from Bab Bou Jeloud. Built as a palace

---

**Mellah**

The word 'mellah' (from the Arabic for salt) appears to have referred to the area of Fès el-Jdid to which the city's Jewish population was transferred under the Merenids. Some say it was watered by a salty tributary of the Oued Fès, whereas others describe something more along the lines of a salty swamp. The word 'mellah' eventually took on the same meaning in Morocco as 'ghetto' in Europe – the Jewish quarter. According to a more colourful explanation, the area in which the Jews lived derived its name from a job some were assigned by the Muslim city authorities – salting the heads of criminals, rebels and the like before they were hung up to adorn the city's gates and walls. ■

---

about 100 years ago by Moulays al-Hassan and Abd al-Aziz, it houses historical and artistic artefacts from ruined or decaying medersas, fine Fassi embroidery, tribal carpets and ceramics dating from the 14th century to the present. As usual, the explanations are in Arabic and French. It's open from 8.30 am to noon and 2.30 to 6.30 pm (closed Tuesday). Entry costs Dr 10.

### Outskirts

For a spectacular overview of Fès, head through the Grand Mechouar and Bab Segma, cross the highway (Route Principale No 1), veer off to the left and walk around the old Kasbah des Cherarda (which now houses secondary schools, a university and hospital), following the road behind the cemetery to the Borj Nord. The borj (like its counterpart on the southern side of the city) was built by the Saadian sultan Ahmed al-Mansour in the late 16th century to keep a watch on the potentially disloyal populace of Fès.

It now houses a military museum, which consists mainly of endless rows of muskets, rifles and cannon, many of them taken from Riffian rebels in 1958. Opening hours are the same as for the Dar Batha and entry is Dr 10.

### Merenid Tombs

Farther along here, a short way past the Hôtel des Mérinides, are the Merenid tombs. These date from the time when the Merenids abandoned Chellah in Rabat as their necropolis. Unfortunately, they're in an advanced state of ruin and little remains of the fine original decoration. There are good views over Fès from here, but watch out for stone-throwing kids.

## Places to Stay

Fès is a large city, so where you stay on arrival will depend largely on the season and the time of day you arrive. In summer, when many of the smaller hotels tend to fill up quickly, there's little point in heading for Fès el-Bali if it's getting late. Take something close to where you are for the first night and have a look around the following morning. In summer many of the cheapies in Fès el-Jdid and Fès el-Bali hike up their prices, and you end up paying the same as you would for better accommodation in the ville nouvelle. At this time, too, single rooms in the cheapies are almost impossible to find, as hoteliers make more money by letting them out to two or three people at corresponding double and triple prices.

## Places to Stay – bottom end

**Camping** Camping isn't really feasible unless you have your own transport, as the nearest site is at 'Ain Chkef, some six km out of town off the Ifrane road. It's known as *Camping Diamant Vert* and sits at the bottom of a valley through which a clean stream runs. There's plenty of shade. Facilities include a swimming pool and disco. Camping costs Dr 15 per person (Dr 5 for children), Dr 10 for a car, Dr 15 for a caravan and Dr 10 to pitch a tent. Motorised 'guides' tend to hang about here. Bus No 218 will get you here from Fès. Bus No 17 to 'Ain Chkef will also get you close to the camp site. You can pick it up in the ville nouvelle on Blvd Tariq ibn Ziad, near the mosque.

There are other camp sites in the region, in Sefrou for instance, but they are hardly practical for Fès.

**Hostel** The cheapest place in the new city is the hostel (☎ 624085), 18 Rue Mohammed el-Hansali. It costs Dr 15 per person in dormitory accommodation (Dr 17 without membership card) and there are cold showers. It's a fairly new building, and you can sleep on the roof if there are no beds left. They are planning to add family rooms and a communal kitchen. The hostel is open from 8 to 9 am, noon to 3 pm and 6 to 10 pm.

**Hotels – Fès el-Bali (Bab Bou Jeloud)** The most colourful places to stay are the bunch of cheapies clustered around Bab Bou Jeloud. They're basic and the shower situation is grim, but there are hammams all over the city. The cheapest are the hotels *Erraha* and *Al-Watani* (Arabic for 'hotel') opposite each other just outside Bab Bou Jeloud. Singles/doubles cost Dr 30/50 and the Al-Watani claims to have hot water. Better is the *Hôtel du Jardin Publique*, which is in a quiet location and has rooms for the same price. There are a couple of rooms on the 3rd floor with windows in the outside wall. These are preferable to the more claustrophobic lower rooms which face the internal courtyard, although the upper ones are hotter in summer. There is no hot water.

Just inside the Bab is the *Hôtel Cascade*. It has simple but clean rooms for Dr 50/80, and occasionally there is hot water. Next door is the *Hôtel Mauritania*, which charges Dr 40 per person and Dr 10 for a hot, shared shower.

Closer to the Medersa Bou Inania is the *Hôtel Lamrani*, a friendly place with acceptable rooms but still higher prices at Dr 60/80 (or Dr 50 for singles on the roof).

Various hammams have been marked on the Fès el-Bali map, and there are others to be discovered. Ask at your hotel.

**Hotels – Fès el-Bali (Bab el-Ftouh)** If you want to be near the buses that leave from Bab el-Ftouh, or happen to be desperate for a cheapie, you could look at the handful of hotels down here.

The *Hôtel Moulay Idriss*, with rooms for Dr 20/40, is about as cheap as you'll find. It's simple but clean. Farther up the road, the *Hôtel Andalous* is also basic and quiet, with cold showers. They charge Dr 30/50. Another nearby possibility is the *Hôtel Bahia*.

**Hotels – Fès el-Jdid** There are at least four cheap hotels spread out in this area, if you have no luck around Bab Bou Jeloud or don't want to be quite so close to the action. The *Hôtel du Parc*, nearest the Bab, is a clean, cheap deal at Dr 20 a head on Sharia Moulay Suleiman. Down near Bab Smarine (Semmarin), also on Sharia Moulay Suleiman, the *Hôtel du Croissant* has beds for the same price, cold showers and somewhat smelly loos. The rooms are on several floors gathered around a sunny courtyard behind a café. Virtually around the corner is the *Hôtel Moulay Ali Charif*, which is much the same, but a bit noisier.

Practically in the ville nouvelle is the *Hôtel du Commerce* on Place des Alaouites. It's nothing special, but OK at Dr 60 for two people.

If showers prove a problem, there is a hammam on Sharia Moulay Suleiman.

**Hotels – ville nouvelle** The cheapest hotels here are the *Hôtel Moghreb* (also called *Hôtel du Maghreb*), 25 Ave Mohammed es-Slaoui, the *Hôtel Regina*, 25 Rue Moulay Slimane, and the *Hôtel Renaissance*. The Moghreb and the Regina are basic but clean and the latter has cold, shared showers. They cost Dr 40 to Dr 60 for a single, Dr 80/100 for a double/triple. The Renaissance is an old, cavernous place with an lobby resembling a decrepit art gallery. It's friendly and clean, has no showers and costs the same as the two other hotels.

Slightly better are the *Hôtel Volubilis*, Blvd Abdallah Chefchaouni, and, just round the corner, the *Hôtel Savoy* (☎ 620608). Both have good, clean, airy rooms with washbasins and there are communal showers (cold water). Singles/doubles/triples cost around Dr 30/70/90.

There are several hammams and public showers (douches) around the ville nouvelle if hot water is a problem. In the lane behind the CTM bus station is a modern place called *Douche el-Fath*. You pay Dr 4.50 for 30 minutes. Men can go from 6 am to 8.30 pm and women from 8 am to 8 pm. Soap and towels are available.

### Places to Stay – middle

The ville nouvelle has plenty of one and two-star hotels. Among the cheapest is the *Hôtel CTM* (☎ 622811). It offers singles/doubles with communal shower for Dr 72/86, or rooms with private shower for Dr 83/100 plus taxes. The rooms are OK, but the beds are a little dodgy. They occasionally come up with hot water.

Not far away is the *Hôtel Central* (☎ 622333), 50 Rue du Nador, at the junction with Blvd Mohammed V. It's friendly, very clean and secure. Rooms with private shower (hot water in the mornings and evenings), bidet and washbasin cost Dr 72/86/130 plus taxes. Baggage can be safely left in reception if you're catching a late bus or train. Unfortunately, guides hang about outside the front door in the mornings.

The *Hôtel Excelsior* (☎ 625602), on Blvd Mohammed V, is not bad either. Singles/doubles cost Dr 76/94 with shower, toilet and a little furniture in the room. Hot water is sporadically available and they have a TV lounge on the first floor.

Closer to the railway station and particularly good value in comparison with most other places in this range is the *Hôtel Kairouan* (☎ 623596), 84 Rue du Soudan. It has spacious rooms with big clean beds, basin and bidet for Dr 70/111. Rooms with private shower cost Dr 107/129. Not bad at all is the nearby two-star *Hôtel Royal* (☎ 624656), 32 Rue du Soudan, although it is more expensive at Dr 117/146 for rooms with private shower.

Also in the two-star range is the *Hôtel Lamdaghri* (☎ 620310), 10 Kabbour el-Mangad. It is a friendly place with good singles and twins (no double beds) for Dr 120/146. There are showers in the rooms and shared toilets. The hotel also has a pleasant dining area on the first floor. Although it was not obvious at the time of researching, travellers have written in to say it is used as a brothel.

MOROCCO

**Fès - Ville Nouvelle**

0    100    200 m

Place de la Gare

Avenue des Almohades

Boulevard des Alaouites

Boulevard Moulay Youssef

Avenue des Sports

Avenue de la Liberté

Avenue Mohammed el-Hayani

Rue Chenguit

Avenue Mohammed el-Korri

Place de la Résistance

Ave de France

Rue Arabie Saoudite

Place de Florence

Boulevard ben Jerrah

Boulevard Tariq Ibn Ziad

Avenue des FAR

Avenue Hassan II

Boulevard Mohammed V

Boulevard Abdallah Chefchaouni

Rue A el-Khattabi

Avenue Mohammed es-Slaoui

Avenue Youssef ben Tachfine

Rue Moulay Slimane

Not as good is the *Hôtel Amor* (☎ 623304), 31 Rue Arabie Saoudite. It has rooms for the same prices and hot water in the evenings, but cockroaches are a bit of a problem.

Going up in price again and reasonable without being spectacular is the *Hôtel Olympic* (☎ 624529), around the corner from the covered market on Blvd Mohammed V. Singles/doubles/triples go for Dr 150/179/233 and the clean rooms come with private bathroom and toilet. There is hot water for a few hours in the evening.

Moving up to the three-star range, a good choice is the *Hôtel Zalagh* (☎ 625531), on Rue Mohammed Diouri, not far from the hostel. Many of the big rooms have wonderful views across to Fès el-Bali. Singles/doubles with toilet but shared shower cost Dr 171/215 plus tax or Dr 216/256 with shower and toilet. In winter they have heating. If you have a bit of money to spend, this is a good deal.

The *Grand Hôtel* (☎ 625511; fax 653 847), on Blvd Abdallah Chefchaouni, is an older place with a little character. It has rooms with shower and toilet for Dr 202/250

**MOROCCO**

## PLACES TO STAY

| | |
|---|---|
| 3 | Hôtel Moussafir |
| 10 | Hôtel Sofia (closed for repairs) |
| 12 | Hôtel Amor |
| 16 | Hôtel Royal |
| 17 | Hôtel Kairouan |
| 23 | Hôtel de la Paix |
| 30 | Hôtel Olympic |
| 32 | Hôtels Savoy & Volubilis |
| 33 | Hôtel Zalagh |
| 34 | Hostel |
| 38 | Hôtel Excelsior |
| 39 | Hôtel Lamdaghri |
| 42 | Grand Hôtel |
| 46 | Hôtel Renaissance |
| 48 | Hôtel Splendid |
| 49 | Hôtel Palais de Fès |
| 50 | Fès Motel |
| 51 | Hôtel Regina |
| 52 | Hôtel Central |
| 61 | Hôtel CTM |
| 62 | Hôtel Jnan Palace |

## PLACES TO EAT

| | |
|---|---|
| 7 | Restaurant La Cheminée |
| 11 | Cracos & Venisia |
| 36 | Central Market |
| 37 | Pizzeria Oliverdi |
| 41 | Restaurant Chamonix |
| 43 | Restaurant du Centre |
| 47 | Restaurant Mounia |
| 56 | Restaurant Oued La Bière |
| 58 | Restaurant Golding Palm |

## OTHER

| | |
|---|---|
| 1 | Railway Station |
| 2 | Grands Taxis to Meknès |
| 4 | Swimming Pool |
| 5 | Café |
| 6 | Café |
| 8 | Mosque |
| 9 | Hertz |
| 13 | Bar Lala Iris |
| 14 | Bank al-Maghrib |
| 15 | BMAO (Exchange) |
| 18 | Centre Culturel Français |
| 19 | Budget |
| 20 | ONMT Office |
| 21 | English Bookshop |
| 22 | ABM Bank (Visa & Eurocheques) |
| 24 | Uniban (Exchange) |
| 25 | Europcar |
| 26 | Main Post & Telephone Office (PTT) |
| 27 | Police |
| 28 | Newsstand |
| 29 | Kodak Shop |
| 31 | Bar |
| 35 | American Language Center |
| 40 | Goldcar |
| 44 | BMCE (ATMs) |
| 45 | Bar |
| 53 | Place Mohammed V |
| 54 | French Consul's Residence |
| 55 | Church |
| 57 | Bar |
| 59 | Grands Taxis to Rabat & Casablanca |
| 60 | Douche el-Fath |
| 61 | CTM Bus Station |

It is a reasonable place and has a basement parking lot.

More modern, with large carpeted, comfortable rooms and en suite bathrooms is the *Hôtel Splendid* (☎ 622148) at 9 Rue Abdelkrim el-Khattabi. Prices are Dr 216/261/342 plus taxes. The hotel also has a small swimming pool.

The *Hôtel Mounia* (☎ 62 4838), 60 Rue Azilah, is not so hot, but a little cheaper and handy for the CTM bus station. They have their own bar and hammam. Rooms cost Dr 192/241/328.

The *Hôtel de la Paix* (☎ 625072; fax 626880), 44 Ave Hassan II, near the Place de la Résistance, has slightly more expensive

rooms at Dr 222/273/360. The rooms are self-contained, quiet and comfortable.

Right by the railway station is the *Hôtel Moussafir* (☎ 651902; fax 651909). It is part of a chain of modern hotels located at railway stations and rooms come with all the modcons. The big plus is its proximity to the trains. Singles/doubles cost Dr 216/261 plus taxes.

### Places to Stay – top end

An excellent location within quick strolling distance of the medina is the four-star *Hôtel Batha* (☎ 636441) on Place de l'Istiqlal (or Place Batha, depending on whom you talk to). It is not the cheapest hotel in this category but has good, modern rooms for Dr 380/420.

A little cheaper but located in the ville nouvelle at the opposite end of town, not really within quick strolling distance of anything, is the *Fès Motel*, formerly known as *Hôtel Volubilis* (☎ 621126; fax 621125) on Ave Hassan II. It has singles/doubles/triples for Dr 355/460/565.

At the five-star end of the spectrum, there are two places near the Fès Motel in the ville nouvelle. On the corner of the Ave Hassan II and Ave des FAR, the *Hôtel Palais de Fès* (☎ 623006; fax 620486) has rooms ranging from Dr 525 to Dr 1600 plus taxes. Farther out still is the extremely posh *Hôtel Jnan Palace* (☎ 653965; fax 651917), on Rue Moulay Slimane, where rooms start at Dr 1300/1500.

More interesting is the recently rebuilt *Hôtel des Mérinides* (☎ 645226; fax 645 225), with its sweeping views of the old medina from near the Merenid tombs. It has a swimming pool and two restaurants, and rooms start at Dr 820/1040.

If you had the money, the most interesting place to stay in Fès would without doubt be the *Hôtel Palais Jamaï* (☎ 634331; fax 635096), once the pleasure dome of a late 19th-century grand vizier to the sultan. Set in a lush Andalusian garden, its rooms start at Dr 900 and head for the sky. Along with the Mamounia in Marrakesh, it is a jewel of another epoch.

### Places to Eat

**Medina** The restaurants around Bab Bou Jeloud in Fès el-Bali remain among the most popular places to hang out in the medina. Although the quality-price relationship is not always as good as it might once have been, enough Moroccans eat here to reassure the wary diner.

The *Restaurant Bouayad*, which has been going since 1939, is definitely one of the better ones, although not the cheapest place in Morocco to get a meal. Pastilla (pigeon pie), when they have it, costs Dr 50. On the other end of the scale, you can get a steaming bowl of harira for just Dr 2; ordering just

harira does not always endear you to the owners, but this shouldn't deter you. Most of the other mains cost about Dr 40. Watch out if you start ordering side dishes and extras from the display – they don't appear on the menu and prices can be inflated.

The *Restaurant des Jeunes*, closer to the gate, also has good set meals but it has been reported that they have two menus and give you the one they think you can afford, even though the food is the same!

There are some great-value snack stands interspersed among the restaurants and cafés. For Dr 10 you can get a huge sandwich stuffed with meat, sausage, chips, salad and various other condiments – easily a satisfying lunch.

There are similar restaurants along Sharia Moulay Suleiman, close to Bab Smarine. For something better check out *La Noria*, in the Bou Jeloud Gardens. This is popular with young Moroccans, but you can expect to pay more for a meal here (a glass of tea alone costs Dr 4).

If you get hungry down around the Kairaouine Mosque, there is a small huddle of cheap food stands and an ice-cream stall between the Kairaouine and the Medersa el-Attarine.

**Ville Nouvelle** There are a few cheap eats on or just off Blvd Mohammed V, especially around the municipal market. They are mixed in with pâtisseries, cafés and the like. A couple of these food places are on the same side street off Blvd Mohammed V as the Hôtel Olympic. Watch the prices.

The *Restaurant Chamonix*, in a side street a block south, offers a limited range of good food, including a tasty set menu for Dr 42.50. Across the street is the *Pizzeria Oliverdi* (☎ 620231), a pizza place that does home delivery. Most of the pizzas are around Dr 35 and they also do some pasta dishes.

If you want a drink with your meal, you could do worse than the *Restaurant du Centre*, not far from the Chamonix but directly on Blvd Mohammed V (there's a Crédit du Maroc bank opposite). They prepare good, simple French fare which washes down nicely with some wine or beer.

Farther south and just opposite the Hôtel Central is another restaurant in a similar vein, the *Oued La Bière*. Despite its name, it doesn't serve beer, but there's a bar next door. A lively bar/restaurant, the *Golding Palm*, is a little farther south on Blvd Mohammed V, just short of the CTM station. It's popular with Moroccans, but mostly for drinking, as the meals start at about Dr 50.

By comparison, the *Restaurant Mounia* (☎ 626661), at 11 Blvd Mohammed Zerktouni, is a class act. It offers good serves of Moroccan food for Dr 50 to Dr 70 (main course only). They have a decent wine list and the waiters even wear bow ties. If you're skint or sick of couscous, you could try the spaghetti for Dr 15. You can even change money here and they accept credit cards for payment.

*La Mamia* on Place de Florence does eat-in and takeaway pizzas and hamburgers. The pizzas cost from Dr 30 to Dr 50 and are not bad at all.

Around the corner to the left of the Hôtel Amor on Ave de France, among the cafés and shops, are a couple of hamburger joints, *Cracos* and the *Venisia*. They are similar, although you get a better serve of chips at the Cracos. A decent hamburger will set you back about Dr 15. There are a few other such places scattered about the ville nouvelle, particularly in the side streets off Blvd Mohammed V.

**Splurges** Fès is dotted with a good half-dozen restaurants housed in old mansions and the like offering expensive Moroccan meals in grand 'traditional' surroundings. Many of these also stage shows, including Moroccan music and Oriental dancing. The idea is to create something of the atmosphere of a Thousand and One Nights, and although it is a bit artificial, one extravagant evening along these lines can be good fun. You'll be looking at about Dr 200 per person. These places are at their best in the evening and when reasonably well patronised. If it's just

you, the expensive menu and some desultory singing, they can be rather depressing.

There are two such restaurants in Fès el-Bali near the Hôtel Palais Jamaï: *Al-Firdaous* (☎ 634343) and *Les Remparts de Fès*. The latter offers set menus ranging from Dr 170 to Dr 220 and puts on a nightly music and dance show.

In the winding lanes near the Er-Rsif Mosque are another couple of the genre. *La Menara* and the *Dar Tajine* (☎ 634167), 15 Ross Rhi, are signposted from the main road – the latter is much easier to find. They are both in a part of town you would otherwise have little cause to visit. They are open only for dinner, and if business is slow may not be open at all.

The *Dar Saada* (☎ 633343), down in the Souq el-Attarine in the heart of the medina, has already been mentioned (see Fès el-Bali). They offer set menus up to Dr 220 and à la carte. The *Restaurant Palais des Mérinides* (☎ 634028), near the Ash-Sherabliyin Mosque, has somewhat cheaper menus.

Possibly the pick of the crop is the *Palais de Fès*, a gracious 14th-century mansion housing a restaurant and roof terrace café. The coffee costs Dr 5 a shot, but is worth it for the views. It is open for lunch.

You could also head for the *Hôtel Palais Jamaï*, which has a terrace overlooking the medina. The food is excellent and there's a choice of French or Moroccan cuisine, but you'll be up for about Dr 200 per person for food alone.

### Entertainment

**Cafés & Bars** There is no shortage of cafés and salons de thé. There are a few inside Bab Bou Jeloud, and an innumerable collection of them along the main streets of the ville nouvelle, particularly on Blvd Mohammed V. Take your pick. You could buy yourself some croissants or cakes in one of the pâtisseries and then settle down for breakfast at one of the outdoor tables and watch the morning slide by.

There are a few bars scattered around the ville nouvelle. Some have already been mentioned, as they are part of or just next door to restaurants. They are generally spit and sawdust places and some of the clientele can get a bit rowdy towards the end of a night's drinking. In addition to those already referred to, there's one next to the Hôtel Olympic and another next to the BMCE. The *Lala Iris*, on Ave Hassan II, is another well-patronised bar. Apart from these, which have little enough going for them, especially for women, there are bars in the middle and top-range hotels. Again, however, the company is more often than not all male.

Some of the bigger hotels have nightclubs or discos. Entry generally costs at least Dr 50, drinks are expensive and decent dress is expected. After going to all that effort, you often find they are little more than a glorified version of some of the bars with mirror balls. Among these is the *Salam Nightclub* in the Hôtel Zalagh.

The expensive 'traditional' Moroccan restaurants listed earlier sometimes put on a show with music and dance. *Al-Firdaous* does this every night (see Places to Eat).

### Getting There & Away

**Air** The airport serving Fès is at Saiss, 15 km to the south. There are five flights a week to Casablanca, five a week to Marrakesh (all but one via Casablanca), nine a week to Agadir (all but one via Casablanca), three to Tangier (all via Casablanca) and a weekly direct flight to Er-Rachidia. There are also a couple of weekly direct flights to Paris.

RAM (☎ 625516) is at 54 Ave Hassan II. The one-way fare to Casablanca is Dr 405. To Marrakesh (direct flight on Tuesday), it costs Dr 590 one way. The same flight goes on to Agadir. The one-way fare is Dr 810. The office is open Monday to Friday from 8.30 am to 12.15 pm and 2.30 to 7 pm; on Saturday mornings from 8.30 am to noon and 3 to 6 pm; and on holidays from 9 am to noon and 3 to 6 pm. You can only use credit cards to purchase air tickets.

**Bus – CTM** The CTM station is in the ville nouvelle on Blvd Mohammed V. Demand is high, especially on the Fès-Tangier and Fès-Marrakesh runs, so where possible you should buy tickets in advance.

There are eight daily departures to Casablanca, starting at 7 am and finishing at 7 pm (Dr 69; five hours). All but the 7 am bus call at Rabat (Dr 47.50; 3½ hours). They also call at Meknès (Dr 14.50; one hour), except for the 9.30 am service. There is an additional Meknès run at 6 pm.

Two buses a day depart for Marrakesh, at 6.30 am and 9 pm (Dr 115; nine hours), and for Tangier, at 11 am and 6 pm (Dr 77.50; six hours). There are two daily buses for Tetouan, which leave at 8 and 11 am (Dr 55; five hours).

Once a day a bus leaves for Oujda (Dr 62; six hours) at 12.30 pm via Taza (Dr 30.50; two hours). Another one heads for Taza at 6.30 pm.

There are international departures at 8 pm on various days of the week for Paris and Brussels as well as other French and Belgian destinations. For more details, see the Bus section of the Getting There & Away chapter.

**Bus – others** The bulk of the non-CTM departures are from a station at Place Baghdadi, near Bab Bou Jeloud. There are various companies doing regular runs to such destinations as Meknès (about Dr 13), Rabat (about Dr 39) and Casablanca (Dr 55). There are at least four daily departures to Tangier for Dr 60 and two to Marrakesh for Dr 92. It's all very higgledy-piggledy, so the best thing to do is get there as early as you can and get yourself shepherded to the right window and on to the right bus.

Three CTM buses leave from here: one to Meknès at 3.30 pm, one to Ouezzane at 7.30 am (via ville nouvelle station) and another to Taza at noon (via the ville nouvelle and Bab el-Ftouh).

Buses for Oujda (about Dr 60), Chefchaouen, Al-Hoceima and Taza (Dr 23 to Dr 30.50) leave from the station at Bab el-Ftouh, the south-eastern gate. Get here early, as the runs are quite irregular.

It appeared in early 1994 that a new bus station was being built at the foot of the cemetery next to the kasbah. How long this will take to complete is anyone's guess.

**Train** The railway station is in the ville nouvelle, 10 minutes' walk from Place de Florence. Trains are the best bet if you are headed for Casablanca, Marrakesh, Meknès, Oujda, Rabat or Tangier.

There are at least nine daily departures to Casablanca (five hours), all of which stop at Rabat (four hours) and Meknès (one hour) en route. There are two direct runs to Marrakesh (7.20 and 9.40 am; about 8¼ hours) and four other services requiring changes at Casa-Voyageurs or Kenitra. The longest wait is about 50 minutes. There are two direct trains (coming from Oujda) for Tangier (1.10 and 4.10 pm; 6½ hours). Three other trains (heading south) require changes at Sidi Kacem or Sidi Slimane. They all stop at Meknès and Asilah. Direct trains for Oujda (6½ hours) via Taza (2½ hours) leave six times a day.

Examples of 2nd-class fares (normal and rapide) include: Casablanca (Dr 69/87); Marrakesh (Dr 121.50/153.50); Meknès (Dr 12/15); Oujda (Dr 74/93.50); Rabat (Dr 49.50/62.50) and Tangier (Dr 63.50/84).

**Taxi** Grands taxis on fixed-price routes leave for Rabat (Dr 50) and Casablanca (Dr 80) from a rank near the CTM bus station. Taxis for Meknès (Dr 15) leave from Ave des Almohades in front of the railway station.

Others for Taza (Dr 30) leave from just outside Bab el-Ftouh.

Local ones run to places like El-Hajeb from a rank near the Place Baghdadi bus station and if you want to get to Ifrane (Dr 16) or Azrou (Dr 21), there is a rank behind the mosque on Blvd Dhar Mahres in the ville nouvelle.

For any other destination you will have to negotiate a corsa (special) fare.

**Car** Car-rental agencies located in Fès include:

Avis
    50 Blvd Chefchaouni (☎ 626746)

Budget
    On the corner of Ave Hassan II and Rue Bahrein (☎ 620919)
    Hôtel Palais Jamaï, Bab Guissa (☎ 634331)
Europcar
    41 Ave Hassan II (☎ 626545)
Goldcar
    Rue Abdelkrim el-Khattabi (☎ 620495)
Hertz
    Blvd Lalla Maryam (☎ 622812)
    Airport (☎ 651823)
Zeit
    35 Ave Mohammed es-Slaoui (☎ & fax 654063)

### Getting Around

**To/From the Airport** There is a regular bus service between the airport and the railway station. Look for No 16. The fare is about Dr 3. Otherwise you'll have to get a grand taxi, which will cost Dr 70.

**Bus** Fès has a fairly good local bus service, although the buses are like sardine cans at certain times of the day. The route number is usually displayed on the side of the bus, near the back door, or at the front. You get on the back and off at the front door. There's a conductor sitting at the back. Fares hover around the Dr 1.70 mark.

Useful routes include:

No 2
    Bab Smarine – Ave Hassan II – Hay Hussein
No 9
    Place de l'Atlas – Ave Hassan II – Dar Batha
No 10
    Railway station – Bab Guissa – Sidi Bou Jidda
No 12
    Bab Bou Jeloud – Bab Guissa – Bab el-Ftouh
No 16
    Railway station – Airport
No 17
    Blvd Tariq ibn Ziad – 'Ain Chkef
No 18
    Bab el-Ftouh – Dar Batha
No 19 & 29
    Ave Hassan II – Bab el-Jedid – Bab er-Rsif
No 47
    Railway station – Bab Bou Jeloud
No 50
    Bab Smarine – Ave Hassan II – Soukarin

**Taxi** The red petits taxis are cheap and plentiful. The drivers generally use the meters without any fuss. Expect to pay about Dr 10 to go from the CTM station to Bab Bou Jeloud. Only grands taxis will go out to the airport and although it's only 15 km they're virtually impossible to beat down to less than Dr 70.

## SOUTH OF FÈS

For travellers heading south, there are two main options from Fès. You can take highway P24 towards Marrakesh, stopping in at the odd alpine village of Ifrane and then Azrou on the way. A detour from Beni Mellal on this route would also allow you to take in the impressive Cascades d'Ouzoud (see the Around Marrakesh section for more on this) before finally reaching the southern imperial capital.

Alternatively, you could make a stop at Sefrou on your way along highway P20 to the southern valleys, including a tour through the Ziz Gorges before reaching Er-Rachidia. From there you could head east to Figuig, south to Erfoud or west to Ouarzazate via the still more impressive Todra and Dadès valleys.

### Ifrane

Just 17 km short of Azrou on highway P24 from Fès is Ifrane (altitude 1650 metres), where you would be hard-pressed not to do a double-take and wonder whether you hadn't just left Morocco. Built by the French in the 1930s as an Alpine resort, the red-tiled roofs of this highly un-Moroccan looking place are a bit of a shock when they come into view. The place is popular with Moroccans though, and more villas are being jerry-built in much the same style. Outside the uncertain winter ski season and high summer weekends, when the better-off flock to their holiday homes to escape the heat of the big cities, the place is a bit of a ghost town. Many of the grander villas are actually company hotels – the post office, Banque Populaire and CTM are among those that have 'hotels' here for staff holidays.

Ifrane could make a reasonable base for those with their own vehicles to explore the surrounding gentle countryside, and for walkers too, although a better option would

probably be the somewhat more lively Azrou to the south-west. If you have a decent car, pleasant **lakes** circuit starts at a turn-off 1 km north of Ifrane ('Tour Touristique de Lacs'). First up is Dayet Aoua, after which the road deteriorates badly. At the far end o the lake turn off away from it, or you'll end up doing a circle and finish up where you started.

**Information** The tourist office (☎ 566038 is in the Hôtel Michlifen (see the nex section).

**Places to Stay & Eat** Other than the camp site on Blvd Mohammed V, which is not bad at all, there is no budget accommodation in Ifrane. The camp site, west of the bus station costs Dr 5 a person and the same each for car tent place and electricity. It's a pleasant, leafy spot.

The surly individuals at the *Hôtel/Restaurant Chamonix* (☎ 566028), on Ave de l Marche Verte in what could be described a the centre of town should be enough to put you off taking a room here. The rooms cost Dr 150 and there are no showers! You can also rent antediluvian ski equipment here.

1 Hôtel Michlifen
2 Hôtel/Restaurant Chamonix
3 Post Office (PTT)
4 Grand Hôtel
5 Bus & Grand Taxi Station

To Meknès
To Camping Ground
Blvd Mohammed V
Route de – la Source
Avenue de – l'Atlas
Vittel
Rue des Catalpas
Avenue de la Poste
Avenue Prince Moulay Abdallah
Avenue Mosquée du Niger
Rue des Cèdres
Rue des Rossignols

**Ifrane**

To Azrou (17 km)

0    100    200 m

Inside the *Grand Hôtel* (☎ 566203; fax 566407), Ave de la Poste, you would swear you were in the Alps. Built in 1941, it's the most characterful of Ifrane's hotels and has its own bar and restaurant. Singles/doubles are Dr 226/273 – you'd need to book ahead in winter.

The top of the range is the *Hôtel Michlifen* (☎ 566607; fax 566623), north of the town centre. It overlooks and dominates the town, and its five-star prices will do much the same to your wallet.

Outside the hotels, the eating choices are limited. There are a few small restaurant cafés in the centre of town near the Chamonix.

**Getting There & Away** The main bus and grand taxi station is on Blvd Mohammed V, west of the town centre. Occasional buses between Fès and Marrakesh stop here, and there are two CTM runs a day from Meknès but otherwise bus activity is slow.

Grands taxis are a better bet. They run to Azrou (Dr 6), Sefrou (Dr 17.50), Fès (ville nouvelle) for Dr 16 and Meknès for the same amount.

**Mischliffen**

This is the premier ski playground of the Middle Atlas, but apart from a couple of lifts, café and nice views, there's precious little to be seen here. Both Ifrane (17 km to the north) and Azrou (24 km west) make decent bases. The uneven season – snow is not always reliable – runs more or less from December to March. You can hire antiquated gear in Ifrane.

**Azrou**

The green-tiled rooftops of central Azrou are in total contrast to Ifrane, and this primarily Berber town is a cheerful, hassle-free little place – and full of life in a way that Ifrane is not. Surrounded by pine and cedar forests, which are ideal for exploring either on foot or by car, the cool mountain air helps make this a good location to relax after the pressure-cooker of Fès. The Tuesday market is a lively affair, and the centre of the town busy

enough to hold your interest, but there's not much to do in Azrou, which is part of its charm. The cheaper hotels and most of the little restaurants are on or near Place Mohammed V or just south of it in the narrow lanes of the old town. The banks and post office are also on Place Mohammed V. The bus and taxi stations are five minutes' walk to the north, beyond the big new mosque that seems destined to remain forever 'under construction'.

Azrou means 'rock', and the clump of stone that gives the town its name, below which the weekly market takes place, lies near Blvd Mohammed, to the west of the town centre.

**Information** You can change money at the BMCE or Banque Populaire on Place Mohammed V. The post office is next to the Banque Populaire, just east of the square.

**Places to Stay – bottom end** The cheapest place to stay, and probably the least convenient, is the *hostel* (☎ 562496). It's a couple of km from the bus station, east of the town centre on the Midelt road. Cardholders pay Dr 15 and nonmembers Dr 20. The showers are cold and there's no kitchen.

Of the little places around Place Moulay Hachem ben Salah, the cheapest is *Hôtel Beau Séjour*, at Dr 20 a person. Cold showers are available. Try for a room overlooking the square. The *Hôtel Atlas* next door was closed at the time of writing. The *Hôtel Ziz* (☎ 562362) has rooms ranging from Dr 20 to Dr 50. A big bed in a windowless cell costs Dr 25. The same room with a tiny window is Dr 30. The *Hôtel Salam* (☎ 562562) is the best of the cheapies. A small but decent single is Dr 30. Bigger rooms range up to Dr 70. Some of the rooms smell a little too lived in, and again showers are cold.

In winter, none of these places would be much chop – blankets are always in short supply and you can forget about heating.

**Places to Stay – middle** By far the best value for money (and often full), is the one-star *Hôtel des Cèdres* (☎ 562326), Place Mohammed V, which has large, airy, comfortable and spotlessly clean rooms for Dr 90/112/149. Rooms have a basin, table and chairs and a balcony overlooking the square.

The bathroom has a big tub, and when the water is steaming makes for a wonderful hot bath (yes, there's a plug!).

There's also the one-star *Hôtel Azrou* (☎ 562116), Route de Khenifra, which costs

## PLACES TO STAY

18  Hôtel des Cèdres
23  Hôtel Salam
28  Hôtel Ziz
30  Hôtels Beau Séjour & Atlas
33  Hôtel Panorama

## PLACES TO EAT

3   Food Market
4   Juice Stands & Pâtisseries
8   Restaurant Atlas
9   Restaurant Echaab

10  Cheap Restaurants
11  Café
14  Café Rex
15  Café Atlas
17  Restaurant Relais Forestier
22  Café Salam
24  Cheap Eats
26  Cheap Eats
27  Cheap Eats

## OTHER

1   Grands Taxis (Main Station)
2   Bus Station

5   Hôtel de Ville
6   The Rock ('Azrou')
7   Grands Taxis for 'Ain Leuh
12  Place Hassan II
13  Salon de Thé Azrou
16  BMCE
19  Place Mohammed V
20  Banque Populaire
21  Post Office (PTT)
25  Great Mosque
29  Place Moulay Hachem ben Salah
31  Small Bar
32  Ensemble Artisanal

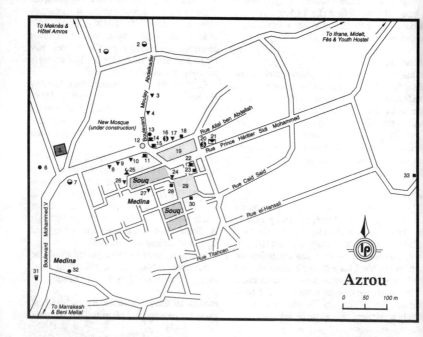

Azrou

the same as the Cèdres but is quite a way from the centre of town and not so easy to find.

Further up the scale, and a long walk or olive green petit-taxi ride from the bus station is the pricier *Hôtel Panorama* (☎ 562010). The 40 rooms (heated in winter) cost Dr 153/195 without shower (but with private loo) and Dr 193/240 with en suite, plus taxes. The hotel has a restaurant and bar.

**Places to Stay – top end** About five km out on the road to Meknès is the four-star *Hôtel Amros* (☎ 563663; fax 563680). It has all the amenities you would expect of a top-class hotel, including a pool, tennis courts and a nightclub. Singles/doubles cost Dr 362/460, plus taxes.

**Places to Eat** There is no shortage of cheap eats in Azrou – a couple are scattered through the old town and there is a string of at least 10 of them across the road from the big unfinished mosque. Of these, the *Restaurant Echaab* is pretty decent value. They sometimes have a huge pot of steaming harira by the entrance in the evenings – a bowl of this is just what the doctor ordered on a cool evening. A big meal of harira, brochettes, chips, salad and a drink comes to Dr 26. Pricier but with good food is the *Restaurant Relais Forestier* on Place Mohammed V.

The numerous cafés around here are great for breakfast – the one opposite the Hôtel des Cèdres does bread, jam and tea for Dr 6. There are a few juice stands and pâtisseries on Blvd Moulay Abdelkader.

**Things to Buy** A visit to the Ensemble Artisanal on the right-hand side on the road to Khenifra (signposted) is worthwhile. Here you can find work in cedar and iron, as well as Berber carpets typical of the Middle Atlas.

**Getting There & Away** Azrou is a crossroads, with one axis heading north-west to south-east from Meknès to Er-Rachidia and the other north-east from Fès to Marrakesh in the south-west. The bus station (gare

routière) and taxi station are located just north of the mosque construction site.

*Bus* CTM has departures to Fès at 2.30 pm (Dr 22); Casablanca (Dr 76) via Rabat at 4 and 7.30 am, Marrakesh (Dr 82) at 8.30 am; Meknès (Dr 16) at 7.30 and 9 am; and Midelt and Beni Mellal at 8 am. The other lines have buses to these destinations at other times and for a dirham or two less. All up, there are plenty of departures for Fès and Meknès, but for places like Marrakesh you'd want to book ahead. There is at least one bus to Er-Rachidia (Dr 62) at 3.30 pm; otherwise you would be better off getting one of the more frequent Midelt buses and hooking up with transport there.

*Taxi* Grands taxis leave the lot behind the bus station regularly for Fès (Dr 21), Meknès (Dr 16), Ifrane (Dr 6), Immouzer (change for Sefrou), Midelt and Khenifra. From the last two you could arrange further transport on to Er-Rachidia and Beni Mellal (or even Marrakesh), respectively.

### Around Azrou
If you have your own transport, a good drive takes you through some of the best of the Middle Atlas greenery along a forest lane to the Berber village of 'Ain Leuh. Leave Azrou by the Midelt road and take the first right (the S3398). Once in the village, you could continue south into the heart of the Middle Atlas along the S303 – be warned that some of the tracks here are difficult and impassable in or after foul weather. This route would eventually take you to Khenifra, from where you could continue south towards Marrakesh, or you could simply follow the S303 north from 'Ain Leuh to head back to Azrou.

### Sefrou
At 28 km from Fès, Sefrou is much easier to contemplate as a day trip than either Ifrane or Azrou, and with virtually no accommodation at the time of writing, a dubious choice for an overnight stop on the way south to the Ziz Valley and Er-Rachidia.

MOROCCO

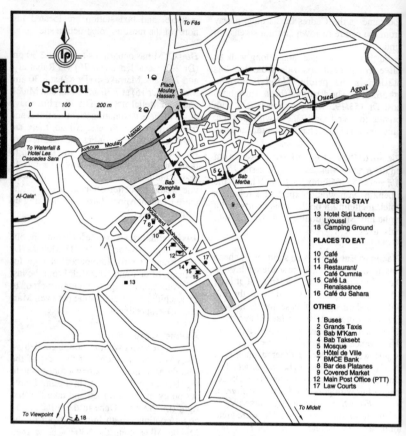

**Sefrou**

0    100    200 m

PLACES TO STAY

13  Hotel Sidi Lahcen
    Lyoussi
18  Camping Ground

PLACES TO EAT

10  Café
11  Café
14  Restaurant/
    Café Oumnia
15  Café La
    Renaissance
16  Café du Sahara

OTHER

1   Buses
2   Grands Taxis
3   Bab M'Kam
4   Bab Taksebt
5   Mosque
6   Hôtel de Ville
7   BMCE Bank
8   Bar des Platanes
9   Covered Market
12  Main Post Office (PTT)
17  Law Courts

About the size of Chefchaouen, this pic-turesque Berber town is well worth the effort. With the exception of the odd Fès-trained 'guide' hanging about the gates near the bus station, you will be left in complete peace to wander the compact medina. Sefrou once had one of the largest Jewish communities of any Moroccan city and it was here, in a nearby ksar (fortified stronghold), that Moulay Idriss II lived while he planned the development of Fès.

The walled medina and mellah lie on either side of the garbage-strewn Oued Aggaï, across which there are a number of bridges. The best points of entry/exit are the Bab Taksebt, Bab Zemghila and the Bab Merba. The town walls that stand today were built in the 19th century.

Once you've visited the walled town, walk up the gorge of the river to the waterfall about 1.5 km from town. To get there, follow the Ave Moulay Hassan over the bridge which spans the river and turn left at the first turn-off (signposted 'Cascades'). Follow this road around to the right (north side) of Al-Qala' (a sort of semiwalled ksar) and follow the dirt road alongside the river until you get to the waterfall.

**Information** The main post office and a branch of the BMCE bank are along Blvd Mohammed V.

**Places to Stay** Somebody doesn't want anyone to stay in Sefrou. About the only option is the *camp site* on the hill overlooking the town. It's a long, steep walk (take a taxi), but a pleasant spot. There are toilets and cold showers; it costs Dr 5 per person, Dr 5 to pitch a tent and Dr 5 for a car. The guy who runs it is a laid-back sort of a chap. If you continue a little farther up the hill, you'll find a magnificent viewpoint over Sefrou and the plains below.

The unclassified *Hôtel les Cerises*, on Blvd Mohammed V, has been firmly shut since 1991. The two-star *Hôtel Sidi Lahcen Lyoussi* (☎ 660497) was also shut at the time of writing. Another one, the *Hôtel Sara Les Cascades*, right by the waterfall, was not a bad little place in a peaceful location. Even if it ever re-opens, though, you may not want to stay. The authorities shut it in 1993 after the bodies of a couple of young local girls were discovered there, apparently after a night's revelry with off-duty soldiers turned nasty.

**Places to Eat** There's a good choice of small, cheap restaurants on either side of the covered market and at the entrance to the Bab Merba. Otherwise, pickings are slim. You could try the *Restaurant Café Oumnia* up near Blvd Mohammed V in the new part of town. There's a string of cafés and a bar on the same street, all near the post office.

**Getting There & Away** There are regular buses between Fès and Sefrou (Dr 5) which drop you off at Place Moulay Hassan in front of Bab M'Kam and Bab Taksebt. Grands taxis (Dr 7) can also be found here. Grands taxis go to Immouzer (Dr 10), from where you can pick up others for Azrou. A few taxis heading south leave from the law courts on Blvd Mohammed V.

# The East

## TAZA

Despite its tempestuous history, Taza is a relatively quiet city these days. Nevertheless, it is worth a visit if you are passing through the area going to or coming from Algeria, if only for the views and the crumbling fortifications. And, if you have your own transport, the drive around Jebel Tazzeka with a visit to the Gouffre du Friouato – one of the most incredible open caverns in the world – is superb.

Since it was an important French military and administrative centre during the protectorate, Taza too has a ville nouvelle which, as usual, is separate from the old town. However, the two are quite some distance from each other – three km in fact – although urbanisation is rapidly closing the gap.

### History

The fortified citadel of Taza, built on the edge of an escarpment overlooking the only feasible pass between the Rif Mountains and the Middle Atlas, has been important throughout Morocco's history as a garrison town from which to exert control over the eastern extremities of the country. The Taza Gap, as it is known, has provided the traditional invasion route for armies moving west from Tunisia and Algeria. The Romans and the Arabs entered Morocco via this pass, and the town itself was the base from which the Almohads, Merenids and Alawites swept down on Fès to conquer lowland Morocco and establish their respective dynasties.

All the various Moroccan sultans had a hand in fortifying Taza. Nevertheless, their control over the area was always tenuous, since the fiercely independent and rebellious local tribes were always willing to exploit any weakness in the central power in order to overrun the city.

Never was this more the case than in the first years of the 20th century, when 'El-Rogui' (the pretender to the sultan's throne), Bou Hamra, held sway over Taza (although

MOROCCO

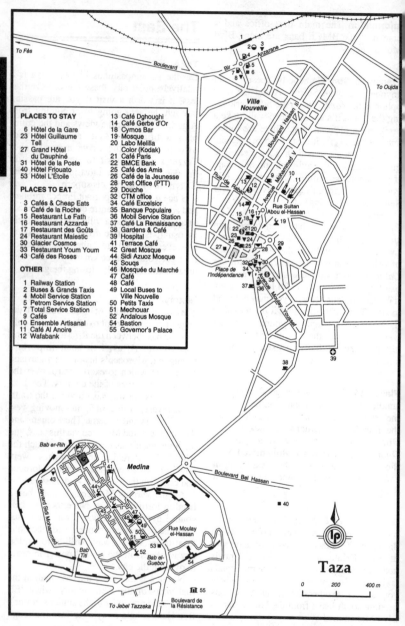

PLACES TO STAY

6 Hôtel de la Gare
23 Hôtel Guillaume
   Tell
27 Grand Hôtel
   du Dauphiné
31 Hôtel de la Poste
40 Hôtel Friouato
53 Hôtel L'Étoile

PLACES TO EAT

3 Cafés & Cheap Eats
8 Café de la Roche
15 Restaurant Le Fath
16 Restaurant Azzarda
17 Restaurant des Goûts
24 Restaurant Maiestic
30 Glacier Cosmos
33 Restaurant Youm Youm
43 Café des Roses

OTHER

1 Railway Station
2 Buses & Grands Taxis
4 Mobil Service Station
5 Petrom Service Station
7 Total Service Station
9 Cafés
10 Ensemble Artisanal
11 Café Al Anoire
12 Wafabank

13 Café Dghoughi
14 Café Gerbe d'Or
18 Cymos Bar
19 Mosque
20 Labo Melilla
   Color (Kodak)
21 Café Paris
22 BNCE Bank
25 Café des Amis
26 Café de la Jeunesse
28 Post Office (PTT)
29 Douche
32 CTM office
34 Café Excelsior
35 Banque Populaire
36 Mobil Service Station
37 Café La Renaissance
38 Gardens & Café
39 Hospital
41 Terrace Café
42 Great Mosque
44 Sidi Azuoz Mosque
45 Souqs
46 Mosquée du Marché
47 Café
48 Café
49 Local Buses to
   Ville Nouvelle
50 Petits Taxis
51 Mechouar
52 Andalous Mosque
54 Bastion
55 Governor's Palace

**Taza**

0    200    400 m

he was based largely in Selouan, 24 km south of Melilla) and most of north-eastern Morocco. After some early successes, his claims to the throne were revealed to be a sham and he met a colourfully grizzly end at the hands of Sultan Moulay Abd al-Hafiz.

The French occupied Taza in 1914 and thereafter made it the main base from which they fought the prolonged rebellion against their rule by the tribes of the Rif and Middle Atlas.

### Orientation

Arriving by bus (except CTM) or train, you'll find yourself on the main Fès-Oujda road, which might appear to be in the centre of town but is actually quite some distance away.

Place de l'Indépendance is the heart of the ville nouvelle. On it or nearby are the banks, post office and most of the hotels and restaurants. If you arrive by CTM bus, you're in luck because the terminal is right on this square. The old town is another three km to the south. Local buses and petits taxis run regularly between the two parts of the town.

### Information

**Tourist Office** The tourist office (☎ 672737) is in the Immeuble des Habous, Ave Hassan II, but seems to be defunct.

**Post & Telecommunications** The post and telephone offices are on the south-eastern corner of Place de l'Indépendance. Both are open during normal office hours only.

**Money** There are a couple of banks in Taza, including the BMCE on Ave Mohammed V and the Banque Populaire on Ave Moulay Youssef, on the way from the ville nouvelle to the medina.

**Film & Photography** Across the road from the Restaurant Majestic is Labo Melilla Color, where you can stock up on film (check the dates).

### City Walls

Most of the city walls, which are about three km in circumference, date from the time of the Almohads (12th century). Having withstood so many sieges, they are ruined in parts. There's also a bastion built by the Saadians in the 16th century in a part of the walls that juts out to the east of the medina.

The most interesting section of a trip around the walls is the **Bab er-Rih** (Gate of the Wind), with its superb views over the surrounding countryside. On the extreme left you can see the wooded slopes of Jebel Tazzeka and before that, across the Oued

---

### Bou Hamra

Bou Hamra (the 'Man on the She-Ass'), or Jilali ben Driss as he came into the world, was one of a host of colourful and violent characters who strode across the Moroccan stage at the turn of the century as central power evaporated and the European powers prepared to take greater control.

Born in 1868 in the Jebel Zerhoun area, he became a minor government official in Fès. In 1894, he was jailed for forgery, but managed to escape to Algeria six years later.

In for a penny, in for a pound, Bou Hamra decided on a more ambitious fraud – claiming with conviction to be Sultan Abd al-Aziz's elder brother Mohammed. He acquired his name by dint of his custom of travelling around on a she-donkey and staked a claim in eastern Morocco as the legitimate pretender to the throne – 'El-Rogui'. As the British journalist Walter Harris wrote, he had learned 'a few conjuring tricks' – but surely the best was having himself proclaimed sultan in Taza in 1902.

Another character of a different style, Er-Raissouli, who at this time held sway in the Tangier area of northern Morocco, placed an each-way bet by signing a deal with Bou Hamra recognising him as sultan. In the end he needn't have worried, for in 1908 the real Mohammed stood up and the Rif tribes that had backed Bou Hamra turned on him. He soon fell into the hands of the new sultan, Moulay Abd al-Hafiz. Bou Hamra was paraded around the country for a month in a one-metre-high cage on the back of a camel before being thrown to the lions of the sultan's menagerie in Fès in March 1909. ∎

Taza, the terraced gardens and dry ravines of the foothills of the Rif. On the right, below the park, is the ville nouvelle, with the Rif Mountains in the distance.

## Great Mosque

Not far from Bab er-Rih is the Great Mosque, which was begun by the Almohads in 1135 and added to by the Merenids in the 13th century. Non-Muslims are not allowed to enter, and it is difficult to get much of an impression of the outside of the building. Stretching from here down to the far end of the old town is the main thoroughfare (Rue Kettanine/Rue Nejjarine/Rue Koubet/Rue Sidi Ali Derrar). This is perhaps the most interesting part of town: there are many examples of richly decorated doorways and, occasionally, windows high up in the walls guarded by old, carved cedar screens.

## Souqs

The souqs are about halfway down the street, around the Mosquée du Marché. Although some of the shops offer mats and carpets woven by the Beni Ouarain tribe in the surrounding mountains, the souqs are virtually bereft of tourist shops. The place is devoid of 'guides' and the like, meaning you can wander around the souqs observing the workings of a normal Berber market without looking constantly over your shoulder or being distracted by one irritant after another.

Most of the shops cater for household necessities and foodstuffs, as do the ones in the nearby qissaria (the commercial centre of the medina). While in this part of the city, don't miss the minaret of the **Mosquée du Marché**, which is perhaps unique in Morocco in that its upper part is wider than its base.

## Andalous Mosque

Right at the end of the main street, close to the mechouar, is the Andalous Mosque, constructed in the 12th century. Nearby is a ruined house once occupied by Bou Hamra, and the Merenid Bou Abu al-Hassan Medersa. It may be possible to gain entry to the latter if you ask around and enlist the help of a guide.

## Places to Stay – bottom end

**Medina** In the medina itself about the only choice is the fairly basic *Hôtel de l'Étoile*, inside Bab el-Guebor on the left along Rue Moulay el-Hassan. It costs Dr 35 and has no shower (the manager suggests that the only hotel in town with a shower is the up-market Hôtel Friouato, a slight exaggeration).

**Ville Nouvelle** Down by the traffic lights on the main Fès-Oujda road, more or less in front of the railway station, is the *Hôtel de la Gare* (☎ 672443). It has cheap and not overly inviting rooms (some of them decidedly on the nose) without shower for Dr 42/60, and substantially better rooms with en suite shower for Dr 70/85. It's convenient for the transport but not for the centre of the new town or the medina.

The remaining moderately priced hotels are around Place de l'Indépendance. About the cheapest and most reasonable is the *Hôtel Guillaume Tell* (☎ 672347), which offers big, simple rooms with double beds for Dr 41/62. Some have cold showers in the room, otherwise there is a shared shower which is just as cold.

Just off Ave Moulay Youssef is the *Hôtel de la Poste* (☎ 672589), which has small but clean and comfortable rooms for Dr 48/64 but no shower at all and somewhat smelly loos. If you need a shower, there's a public one for men and women not far away (Dr 4.80 a go). Ask the hotel employees for directions.

## Places to Stay – middle

The *Grand Hôtel du Dauphiné* (☎ 673567) is a two-star hotel, to the left of Place de l'Indépendance, housed in an attractive colonial-style building. It is the best place to stay if you have the money, as it's comfortable and old-fashioned, with period bathrooms, and balconies overlooking the square. You can get rooms without bathroom for Dr 70/92 and others with private shower for Dr 96/120. There's hot water in the evenings only. Downstairs there's a lively bar and a sedate dining hall with a limited choice of food. Meals here are fairly expensive.

## Places to Stay – top end
The only top-end hotel in Taza is the *Hôtel Friouato* (☎ 672593/8), set in its own well-maintained grounds between Place de l'Indépendance and the old town. It's part of the Salam chain and, although quite an ugly concrete building and awkwardly located, it is a quiet and pleasant enough place. Self-contained singles/doubles·go for Dr 194/245. The hotel has a bar, restaurant, swimming pool and tennis courts.

## Places to Eat
**Medina** A pleasant place to have breakfast is the *Café des Roses* on Rue Riad Azmag in the medina.

While wandering around the medina, there are numerous small stands where you can pick up a snack, and some of the cafés sometimes do food as well.

**Ville Nouvelle** There is a series of cafés and cheap eateries by the grand taxi lot on Blvd Bir Anzarane (the Fès-Oujda road).

Probably the best choice for a meal remains the *Restaurant Majestic*, on Ave Mohammed V. Here you can get a filling dish of chicken and chips, with a plate of beans and another side dish of a sort of pea salad for Dr 30.

Around the corner from the Hôtel de la Poste is the *Restaurant Youm Youm*, a reasonable alternative. Apart from these places, you could also try the more expensive hotel restaurants.

For dessert you could do worse than head to *Glacier Cosmos* for an ice cream.

## Entertainment
**Cafés & Bars** There is no shortage of cafés and salons de thé in both the ville nouvelle and the medina, but probably the best is the nameless terrace café on the eastern side of the medina. From here you have sweeping views of the new town and the countryside.

In addition to the hotel bars, you could try the locals' *Cyrnos Bar*, on Ave d'Oujda in the ville nouvelle.

## Getting There & Away
**Bus** The CTM bus terminal is on Place de l'Indépendance, but it offers only a few services. At 7 am there are two buses: one to Casablanca (Dr 99.50, 7½ hours) via Fès, Meknès and Rabat; the other is a mumtaz run to Fès for Dr 30.50. At 2.30 pm there is another bus to Fès for Dr 23, and half an hour later a service to Oujda for Dr 39.

All other buses gather near or pass by the grand taxi lot on the main Fès-Oujda road. There are quite a few to Oujda (Dr 35 to Dr 40) and Fès (mostly to Bab el-Ftouh; you'll need to take a local bus or petit taxi from there to Bab Bou Jeloud or the ville nouvelle – see the Fès Getting Around section). Many of the buses on these runs just pass through Taza, so getting a seat is sometimes problematic.

There are three buses a day to Nador, at 11.30 am and 2.30 and 5.30 pm; they cost Dr 40. At 1 pm (more or less), a bus leaves for Al-Hoceima (Dr 35). As there is no organised bus station as such, it can be a bit chaotic. The best bet is to turn up as early as you can and choose between the buses and grands taxis – taking whichever leaves first.

**Train** Going east or west, the train is a more reliable and comfortable option. There are daily trains to Fès and Meknès at 12.52, 1.47 (summer only) and 10.51 am and 1.20, 5.08 and 11.08 pm. The 12.52 am and the pm trains go through to Casablanca; the others turn north to Tangier. To Oujda there are daily trains at 3.37, 6.07 and 8.55 am (this last one in summer only) and 5, 6.19 and 10.07 pm. The 2nd-class fares in standard/rapide trains are: Dr 49.50/62.50 to Oujda; Dr 25/31.50 to Fès and Dr 93/119 to Casablanca. There are no through trains to Marrakesh from Taza.

Trains to Oujda pass through Taourirt, from where there is a once-daily Supratours connection to Nador, but this is really doing it the hard way – buses and grands taxis are simpler.

**Taxi** Grands taxis all leave from a lot near the railway station on the main Fès-Oujda road. They depart fairly regularly for Fès (Dr 30; they take you to Bab el-Ftouh – see the preceding Bus section) and Oujda (Dr 50) throughout the day, but the morning is best. Less regular taxis go to Nador and Al-Hoceima for Dr 50 a person.

## AROUND TAZA
### Jebel Tazzeka Circuit

If you have your own transport (hitching isn't really feasible), you can make a fascinating day trip around Jebel Tazzeka, which takes in the Cascades de Ras el-Oued (waterfalls), the Gouffre du Friouato (cavern), Daïa Chiker (a lake) and the gorges of the Oued Zireg. There's a good sealed road the whole way. If you don't have your own transport it would be worthwhile getting a small group together and hiring a taxi for the day.

Having negotiated the long, winding road up from Taza onto the plateau, you'll find yourself in a different world. It's almost eerie in its apparent emptiness, with small patches of farmland, a few scattered houses and, closer to Jebel Tazzeka itself, dense coniferous forests. There are superb views from many points, including the semiderelict hamlet of Bab Bouidir (this hamlet must have been a beautiful retreat at one time, with its tiled Alpine-style houses, but it appears to have been largely abandoned – weekend picnickers notwithstanding).

The **waterfalls** are the first stop. Shortly before you reach the Daïa Chiker plateau, you'll see a sign on your left for Ras el-Ma ('headwater'). The waterfalls are here, but they are really only worth a stop after the winter rains. By the summer they have usually slowed to a trickle.

A little farther on, where the road flattens out, you take a right fork and have the odd depression of the **Daïa Chiker** on your left. The lake bed is usually pretty dry, but the earth is good and is used for grazing and

crops. Daïa Chiker is a geological curiosity associated with fault lines in the calciferous rock structure. It is connected to a subterranean reservoir, the water of which is highly charged with carbon dioxide. Depending on the season and the state of affairs in the subterranean reservoir, the surface of the lake can change dramatically. The nearby **Grottes du Chiker** (caves) at the northern end of the lake have been explored and are said to give access to a five-km-long underground river, but they are not open to casual visitors.

A little farther along the road, the **Gouffre du Friouato** is signposted off to the right. You can drive up or take a steep, 20-minute walk to the entrance. It is the main attraction of this circuit and a must at any time of the year.

This vast cavern is said to be the deepest and possibly the most extensive in the whole of North Africa and has only been partially explored to date. The main part plummets vertically some 100 metres to a floor below, from where various chambers break off and snake away to who knows where. Several flights of precipitous steps with handrails lead you to the floor of the main cavern, and since there's a large hole in the roof of the cavern letting in light, you can get this far with ease. At the bottom of the steps is a hole through which you can drop to start exploring the more interesting chambers below. Here you will need your own light. Some of the stalactite formations are extraordinary. Speleologists have made explorations to a depth of 300 metres, and it is believed a fossil river runs another 500 metres below.

There is usually a guardian at the cavern entrance who will expect to be paid. He may ask for all sorts of sums, but Dr 10 a head will be enough (and seems reasonable as it's the same as the official monument entry price throughout the country). If it's locked, wait around, as someone will soon appear to open it up for you. You may be offered guide services too, but if you have your own light you should be OK.

As you leave the Daïa Chiker behind, the road begins to climb again into coniferous forests past Bab Bouidir. Along the way you can catch good views of the snowcapped Atlas. About eight km past Bab Bouidir, a poor piste branches nine km off to the right (north). If you can get your car up the incline, you'll find the TV relay station at the top of Jebel Tazzeka (1980 metres) and wonderful views all around, to the Rif in the north and the Atlas in the south.

The main road continues around for another 38 km back to the main Fès-Taza road at Sidi Abdallah de Rhiata. On the way you will wind your way around hairpin bends through some dense woodland and then down through the pretty **gorges** of the Oued Zireg.

From the intersection at Sidi Abdallah de Rhiata, you can take the main highway back east to Taza, pausing at Tizi n'Touahar on the way for some more views. If you're coming from Fès, take the *left* turn signposted for Bab Bouidir. This road curves round and

under the main highway to head south. There is often a police checkpoint here.

## OUJDA

This is the last town before the Algerian border. If you have just come from Algeria, make the most of the relaxed atmosphere – there is no hassling, apart from the occasional offers to change money.

The town boasts a busy but small medina surrounded by the undistinguished sprawl of a modern city. Essentially, Oujda has little to interest travellers, but it is not a bad place to just hang about in for a day or two. An added attraction is the fact that the Mediterranean beach town of Saidia (see the chapter on the Mediterranean Coast & the Rif) is only 58 km from Oujda and relatively accessible.

Oujda has a bustling atmosphere, mostly fuelled by the Algerians who come to buy products unavailable at home for resale. For this reason, although it is full of hotels,

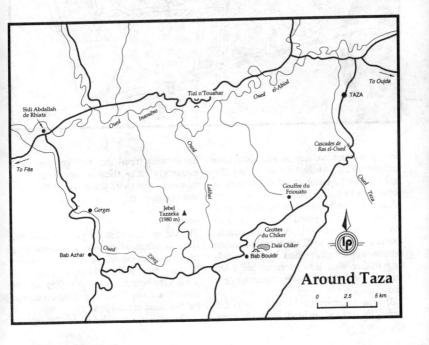

**Around Taza**

0    2.5    5 km

MOROCCO

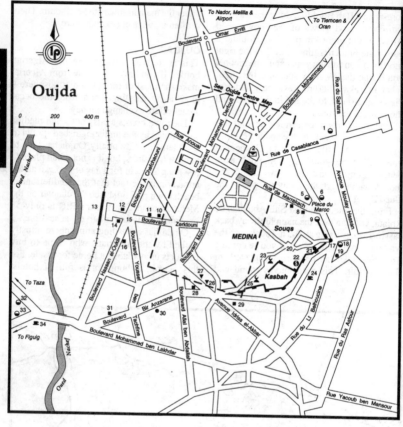

Oujda

0      200      400 m

finding a place to stay is not always so straightforward. At the time of writing, the problems in Algeria had led the Moroccan authorities to tighten controls on incoming Algerians, slowing the usual steady stream – even hotels are supposed to keep an eye on the activities of their Algerian guests. Oujda's proximity to Algeria has long had an influence on its affairs, and Oujdans travelling farther west into Morocco are often mistaken for Algerians by their western cousins.

If you arrive from Tlemcen (Algeria) during the day and are heading for Fès, there are evening trains that will get you there extremely early (before dawn) the next morning – otherwise you could try the buses and grands taxis.

### History

The site of Oujda has long been important, lying as it does on the main axis connecting Morocco with the rest of North Africa (the Romans built a road through here). Like Taza, it has been a key in controlling the east and often a step towards seizing control of the heartland around Fès.

The town was founded in the 10th century

MOROCCO

## PLACES TO STAY

7 Hôtel Nouvel
8 Hôtel el Menzeh
10 Hôtel Rofaïda
11 Hôtel Al-Manar
12 Hôtel Moussafir
14 Hôtel Terminus
16 Hôtel Lutetia
28 Hôtel Riad
29 Hôtel Al Massira
31 Hôtel Chafik

## PLACES TO EAT

26 Restaurant Quick Food
27 Iris Sandwich

## OTHER

1 Buses to Algerian Border
2 Main Post Office (PTT)
3 Town Hall & Clock Tower
4 Place du 16 Août 1953
5 Petits Taxis
6 Grands Taxis to Algerian Border & Saidia
9 Grands Taxis to Nador
13 Railway Station
15 Place de l'Unité Africaine
17 Bab el-Ouahab
18 Local Buses
19 Douche (Men Only)
20 Place el-Attarine
21 Qissaria
22 BMCE
23 Great Mosque
24 Café El Maghrib El Arabi
25 Mosque
30 Algerian Consulate
32 Grands Taxis to Taza & Fès
33 Bus Station
34 Café de la Foire

by the Meghraoua tribe, and it remained independent until the Almohads overran it in the 11th century. All the subsequent dynasties left their mark on its fate. Under the Merenids, however, Algerian rulers based in Tlemcen took the town on several occasions, and in the 17th century it fell under the sway of the Ottoman administration set up in Algiers. Moulay Ismail put an end to this in 1687, and Oujda remained in Moroccan hands until 1907, when French forces in Algeria crossed the frontier in one of a series of 'incidents' and occupied the town. The protectorate was still five years away, but the sultan was powerless to oppose the move.

The French soon expanded the town, which has since swelled in size as provincial capital and in its role as the main gateway for commerce with Algeria. Its industrial role rests on mining, particularly zinc, which is carried out farther to the south.

## Orientation

Although quite large, only the centre of Oujda is of any interest to travellers. The main street is Blvd Mohammed V, along or near which you'll find banks, the post and

tourist offices, and many of the better budget and mid-range hotels and restaurants. About a five-minute walk to the west along Blvd Zerktouni is the railway station. A farther 15 minutes to the south-west, across Oued Nachef, is the main bus station (gare routière). Also here, on the Taza exit road, are grands taxis for Taza and Fès. Buses and taxis to the Algerian border leave from Place du Maroc, just outside the medina.

## Information

**Tourist Office** The tourist office (☎ 689089, 684329) is on Place du 16 Août 1953 at the junction with Blvd Mohammed V. It has the usual brochures and the staff try to help out.

**Money** Most Moroccan banks have branches in Oujda. The BMCE and BMCI on Blvd Mohammed V have ATMs and give cash advances. The Banque Populaire on Blvd Mohammed Derfoufi should also be good for cash advances and most banks will change cash and cheques.

There is no shortage of people lurking around Place du Maroc and Blvd Mohammed V offering to change money. They will buy and sell dirham or Algerian dinar. Don't go looking for them – they'll soon find you. Take your time about changing, and compare offers. At the time of writing, it appeared you could get about eight dinar for each dirham, but this is bound to change. Ideally, if you come across travellers coming from Algeria ask them what the minimum should be. Equally, people coming from Algeria should get an idea of dirham and hard-currency rates in the banks before unloading unwanted dinar. The street dealers also buy and sell hard currency, which might is only useful if you want to dispose of dinar.

**Post & Telecommunications** The main post office is in the centre of the ville nouvelle on Blvd Mohammed V. It's open from 8.30 am to 12.15 pm and again from 2.30 to 6 pm. The phone office, next door to the right of the main entrance to the post office, is open seven days a week from 8.30 am to 9 pm. There are card phones outside.

**Foreign Consulates** The following countries have foreign consulates in Oujda:

Algeria
11 Blvd Bir Anzarane (also known as Blvd de Taza; ☎ 683740/1). Nonresidents of Oujda can apply for visas here (UK citizens must apply in Rabat), but even when things are going well you can easily wait a month for a response. You may be able to get a 10-day visa more easily, but don't count on it. There have been reports that visas are issued on the spot for Dr 100; you will need three passport photos. The consulate is open from 8 am to 3 pm Monday to Thursday and from 8 am to noon on Friday. You may well meet an enterprising chap outside who claims to have a friend working on the inside. For a consideration (and some business on the money-changing front), he says he can help you get a visa within 10 days. You obtain and fill in all the papers and then leave it to him. Who knows whether or not this works?
France
16 Rue Imam Lechaf (☎ 682705)
Sweden
Ave Allal al-Fassi, B23 Apt 2 (☎ 685753)

**Film & Photography** There's a place where you can have film developed just by the Hôtel L'Oasis on Blvd Mohammed V.

**Swimming Pools** There is a municipal pool in the south of the city, or you could try the Hôtel Al Massira, which will let you into its pool for a daily fee of Dr 30.

**Emergencies** There is an all-night chemist (☎ 683490) on Rue de Marrakech.

### Medina
Although hardly the most fascinating of medinas, Oujda's old centre warrants a bit of stroll at least. The most animated part is the area inside and outside the eastern gate, **Bab el-Ouahab**. Also known as the Gate of Heads – local pashas had a habit of having the heads of criminals and renegades hung here – it is full of food stalls, beggars, shoppers and all the noise and bustle of a typical North African market. Plunging deeper into the medina you'll find mainly clothes shops and a few hotels. The **Great Mosque**, built in the 14th century by the Merenids, is in bad shape and in any case is closed to non-Muslims.

### Places to Stay – bottom end
Oujda is armed to the teeth with hotels. Although many of them may be full of visiting Algerians when you arrive, you would be unlucky not to find a room sooner or later.

**Medina & Around** The medina has a few fairly simple places, but there are so many hotels just outside it that it hardly seems worth the effort of searching them out. For the die-hard lovers of medina living, they include the *Ifriquia* (☎ 682095), *En-Nasr* (☎ 683932), *Rissani*, *Du Peuple* and *Al-Kasbah*. As a rule of thumb, rooms in these places cost about Dr 30/60, usually with shared cold showers. They are adequate without being exciting.

Closer to the centre, on and around Rue de Marrakech, is another bunch of similar places, the main difference being that they are easier to find. Among the better ones here is the *Hôtel du 16 Août* (☎ 684197), on Rue de Figuig. Rooms cost Dr 30/60 and hot showers are supposedly included in the price. Farther down the street at No 10 is the rather grand sounding *Hôtel-Résidence Gharnata* (☎ 681541). It is a little depressing. Rooms cost Dr 40/70; the shared cold showers are the combined shower/squat loo arrangements, which are sensible but unpleasant. At the same price, the *Hôtel Marrakech* (☎ 681556) is better but unspectacular (hot showers cost an extra Dr 5). The rooms could do with a bit more fresh air. Other similar places here include the *Hôtel el Menzeh* and the *Hôtel Nouvel* (nothing new about it at all).

Slightly pricier, but the best of this lot, is the *Hôtel Al-Hanna* (☎ 686003) at 132 Rue de Marrakech. Singles/doubles with basin (shared shower) cost Dr 48/64. Clean rooms with private shower are Dr 64/77. Try to get one of the rooms upstairs, as the lower floors are a little gloomy.

**Ville Nouvelle** A better hunting ground for cheap hotels is the pedestrian zone off Blvd Mohammed V and the area nearby.

A popular, cheap but showerless place is the *Hôtel Majestic* (☎ 682948). The rooms are big and have a basin, and cost Dr 30/60. Around the corner, the *Hôtel El-Andalous* (☎ 684491) also has quite decent rooms, and again is without a shower. Rooms cost Dr 35/50.

Right on Blvd Mohammed V is the *Hôtel Victoria* (☎ 685020). At Dr 40/60/90 it is fairly cheap too, and it does have cold communal showers. It is often full.

A pretty good deal is the *Hôtel Isly* (☎ 683928) at 24 Rue Ramdane el-Gadhi, which has rooms a cut above the budget average for Dr 45/70/90. The hot water in the showers is hit and miss, however. A place to avoid is the *Hôtel de Nice*, which charges Dr 35/60 for crummy, crumbly rooms. It has no shower.

A little more money will get you a considerably better deal. The *Hôtel Simon* (☎ 686304), 1 Rue Tarik ibn Ziad, for example, has rooms with private shower, bidet, basin and (some of them) wrought iron balcony for Dr 60/93. This hotel, with its restaurant/café, has a busy, friendly air.

Better still is the *Hôtel Afrah* (☎ 686533), 15 Rue de Tafna. Rooms for Dr 60/120 are small but comfortable and contain spotless en suite bathrooms and the promise of hot water.

Others you can try in the area include the *Hôtel Zegzel*, *Hôtel d'Alger* (a dump), *Hôtel En-Nazaha*, *Hôtel Bahia*, *Hôtel Tlemcen* and the *Hôtel Chic* (I kid you not).

Two places on the other side of Blvd Mohammed V are really only for hard-luck situations. The *Hôtel Ziri* in particular is pretty awful value, even at Dr 30/50/75. The beds are falling apart, as are the en suite showers (cold only).

The *Hôtel L'Oasis* (☎ 683114) is not much better but often full nonetheless. Rooms cost Dr 40/60. There is a cramped restaurant and bar opposite, and the hotel does have limited parking.

Not far away, at 13 Blvd Zerktouni, is one of the best lower-end deals in Oujda. The one-star *Hôtel Royal* (☎ 682284) is excellent value at Dr 60/90 for rooms without shower and Dr 105/121 with private shower and toilet (hot water more or less all day). The hotel has limited guarded garage parking (Dr 12 a night).

If you have shower problems, the Douche Moderne in the pedestrian area is an alternative.

**Places to Stay – middle**
There's a small group of hotels to the north-west of the post office. The *Grand Hotel* (☎ 680508/9) on Rue Beni Merine is not as grand as it might once have been, but it's not too bad at Dr 75.50/92.50. It's a big place and unlikely to be full. A block farther north is the more expensive *Hôtel/Restaurant Mamounia* (☎ 690072; fax 690073). It has perfectly comfortable, carpeted rooms with phone for Dr 95/147, which is probably straining most wallets on a tight budget. A couple of other hotels around here include the *Iris* and the *Ghilane*.

Another very good deal in its range is the *Hôtel Lutetia* (☎ 683365), 44 Blvd Hassan el-Oukili. It is directly opposite the railway station, and has comfortable, carpeted rooms with phone. They even put towels in the bathrooms without your having to ask. Rooms with shower but shared toilet are Dr 85/111 and rooms with full bathroom are Dr 109/129.

New hotels are going up all over Oujda. One that claims to have opened in 1993 but looks like it's been around for quite some time is the *Hôtel Rofaïda* (☎ 703768), at 44 Blvd Zerktouni. The taciturn manager offers mediocre rooms with showers and stinking squat loos for Dr 100/120. Avoid this place.

On the other end of the new hotel scale there's the *Hôtel Al Fajr* (☎ 702293), just off Blvd Mohammed Derfoufi. This place opened in early 1994 and it has 48 sparklingly clean and modern rooms with central heating, en suite bathroom and telephone. At the time of writing they were inexplicably operating as a one-star hotel and charging Dr 109/129. The prices will probably rise, but it might be worth checking out if you have a slightly more generous budget.

Back in the pedestrian precinct is the overpriced *Hôtel Angad* (☎ 681452). Apart from the cockroaches, there is nothing intrinsically wrong with the place, and they will probably bargain down quickly from their stated room rates of Dr 140/170.

Better value but a bit farther away and heading up the price scale is the *Hôtel Riad* (☎ 688353), on Ave Idriss el-Akbar. It's another new place and it appears that the bar doubles as a pick-up joint. The rooms on the higher floors are quite good though, with phone and en suite bathroom. They cost Dr 146/171 plus taxes.

Older and crustier is the *Hôtel La Concorde* (☎ 682328), on Blvd Mohammed V. Rooms with private bathroom and phone cost Dr 140/200 and, although a bit ragged around the edges, the place has a bit of character. The bar especially has the grittiness of typical local drinking houses but with just a slight edge in atmosphere.

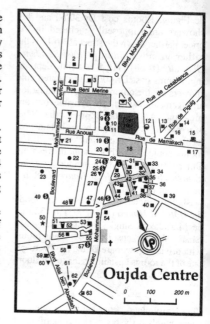

Oujda Centre

### Places to Stay – top end

There are a few hotels in the three-star bracket and up. Right near the railway station, the *Hôtel Moussafir* chain (☎ 688202; fax 688208) has one of its standard and fairly reliable hotels for people who want to be near railway stations. Rooms, as usual, are modern and well kept at the standard Dr 216/261 plus taxes.

The *Hôtel Terminus* across the square is closed.

A little way up Blvd Zerktouni is yet another brand-new place, with staff eager to please. The *Hôtel Al-Manar* (☎ 697037; fax 681670) has air-con rooms with en suite bathrooms, direct-line phones and satellite TV for Dr 186/229. Parking is also available.

Older and not as gleaming is the *Hôtel des Lilas* (☎ 680840), at Rue Jamal ed-Din el-Afghani. It has 38 rooms and 10 suites. The rooms are good, with private bathroom and TV, and cost Dr 216/261. Parking is available.

MOROCCO

The two top hotels are the *Hôtel Oujda* (☎ 684093; fax 685064), on Blvd Mohammed V, and the *Hôtel Al Massira* (☎ 685300/1), off Ave Idriss el-Akbar. They both charge Dr 222/273 and have their own restaurants and bars. The latter has been taken over by the government, and it now has something of the air of an Intourist establishment of the Cold War era.

### Places to Eat

Probably the cheapest place to eat snack food is at the stalls set up inside Bab el-Ouahab, providing you have a taste for broiled sheep heads, deep-fried intestines and very large bags of snails. Fortunately, you can also find slightly more standard meals along the lines of cooked potatoes and omelettes.

Otherwise, there's not an oversupply of cheap eating places in Oujda. *Iris Sandwich* is a good snack-food place on Ave Idriss el-Akbar. You can get a baguette stuffed with meat, salad and chips for Dr 12 to Dr 16. Virtually next door is the *Restaurant Quick Food*, which offers a common Middle Eastern dish, shawarma (lamb's meat cooked on a huge, upright rotisserie) – something of a rarity in these parts.

There are other cheap places in the pedestrian area off Blvd Mohammed V which are OK. The *Café Holiday*, for instance, does an unexciting tajine for Dr 25. There are also a few nondescript places along Rue de Marrakech.

A good place is *Sandwich Taroudannt*, on Blvd Allal ben Abdallah, just around the corner from the Hôtel Royal. It serves generous portions of the usual dishes, although it's not the cheapest place to eat – Dr 45 to

Dr 50 will get plenty of meat, chips and salad.

A little farther afield, the *Restaurant aux Délices*, on Blvd Mohammed Derfoufi and close to the Grand and Mamounia hotels, offers hamburgers, brochettes, salads and pizzas, all priced at around Dr 20.

For a splurge in air-conditioned comfort, with black-suited waiters and starched white linen, try the *Brasserie Restaurant de France*, on Blvd Mohammed V. The food here is of uneven quality and can cost you about Dr 100 a head with wine, but on a good night it's good. The extensive menu includes a rather watery spaghetti bolognese (Dr 42), pizza and a range of fish dishes. A small bottle of beer costs Dr 17 or more, depending on your poison.

Not far behind this place in price, but with equally good food on a good night, is the *Restaurant Marius*, just off Blvd Mohammed Derfoufi. A full meal will cost about Dr 80 a head. The *Restaurant du Palais*, a block south, has a noisy all-male bar next door. The Palais is nothing special.

### Entertainment

**Cafés & Bars** There is no shortage of cafés all over the ville nouvelle and in the area around the medina. Some have been marked on the maps, but it is hard to particularly recommend one over the other. A couple of those on Blvd Mohammed V have a definitely more swish air about them. *Le Trésor* is one.

The few bars marked on the maps are of the usual discreet spit-and-sawdust variety. The bigger hotels have bars and some of these double as dubious discos.

### Getting There & Away

**Air** The airport serving Oujda is 15 km from the town centre (about a Dr 50 petit taxi ride). RAM (☎ 683909), which has an office below the Hôtel Oujda, has six flights a week to Casablanca (Dr 715 one way; one hour 40 minutes). There is also a weekly direct flight to Rabat/Salé (Dr 625) and a flight to Agadir via Casablanca (Dr 1290). There is one direct

flight a week to Paris (Dr 4115 one way) on Saturday at 8 am. Air France also has a weekly flight to Paris, departing on Sunday at 3.55 pm.

**Bus** CTM has a small office behind the town hall. There are only two departures from here: Casablanca (Dr 158.50) via Rabat (Dr 131) at 8 pm and a mumtaz run to Fès (Dr 83.50) at 8.30 pm. The SAT bus company has an office across the road for its Casablanca and Rabat runs at 6 and 8 pm.

All other buses, including CTM's other services, leave from the bus station (gare routière) across Oued Nachef on the southwestern edge of town, about 15 minutes' walk from the railway station. Advance booking is available on the main runs.

Several companies operate buses to most destinations, including Fès at 5, 8.30 and 11 am (Dr 60; six hours); Meknès at 2.30 pm; Taza at least five times daily (Dr 39); Figuig at 4.30, 6, 7 and 10 am and 3 pm (Dr 66.50 – check departure times carefully in advance as the information seems unreliable at best); Bouarfa at the same times (Dr 47.50); Nador up to 13 times daily (Dr 23.50); Al-Hoceima via Nador at 2 pm; and Saidia four or five times a day (Dr 11).

CTM has daily departures to Taza and Fès at 5 and 11 am, and to Taza and Nador at 7 and 10 am and 1 and 3.30 pm. Ligne du Sahara has departures to Figuig (via Bouarfa) at 6 am and 1.30 pm (Dr 61.60; seven hours). Transports des Hauts Plateaux has departures to Figuig at 10 am and 3 pm and to Bouarfa at 7 am. Ligne de Casablanca has departures to Fès at 2.30 pm and to Casablanca/Rabat at 6 am and 5, 6, 7.30 and 8.30 pm.

**Train** The railway station is fairly close to the centre of town, at the western end of Blvd Zerktouni. There are departures for the west of the country at 7.05 and 9.55 am and 1.15, 7.30, 9.25 and 10.20 pm (the last of these services runs in summer only). All these trains call at Taza (four hours), Fès (6½ hours) and Meknès (7½ hours). The 7.05 am and 10.20 pm trains continue on to Tangier, while the others continue on to Rabat and Casablanca. First and 2nd-class sleepers are available on the evening trains.

Second-class fares on normal/rapide services include: Taza (Dr 49.50/62.50); Fès (Dr 74/93.50); Casablanca (Dr 142/182.50); Tangier (Dr 142/179.50); and Marrakesh (Dr 194.50/246, no direct trains).

There's a weekly train to Bouarfa. See below for details.

Supratours has an office at the station, should you want to book rail/coach tickets to destinations south of Marrakesh.

**Taxi** Grands taxis to Taza and Fès leave fairly regularly from outside the main bus station. The fares per person are Dr 50 and Dr 80, respectively. Taxis to Fès take you to Bab al-Ftouh (see the Getting Around section for Fès).

Grands taxis to Nador leave from Place du Maroc (Dr 35). Others travelling to Saidia on the Mediterranean coast leave from the other side of the square, but they are infrequent outside summer (Dr 15). Taxis from here also serve other regional towns.

**To/From Algeria** There are buses to the Algerian border (13 km) every half-hour throughout the day from near Place du Maroc; the cost is Dr 3.

The train to Algeria and on to Tunisia leaves Oujda at 8.30 am. The Moroccan section of the journey is a short ride to the border, where you must change to an Algerian train. One-way fares include Tlemcen (Dr 33), Oran (Dr 47), Algiers (Dr 81) and Tunis (Dr 217). You can get off at the border and change for a taxi if you want to, but you still pay a minimum of the Tlemcen fare.

Grands taxis to the Algerian border leave from Place du Maroc and cost Dr 7 (day rate) and Dr 10 (night rate).

There are plenty of taxis at the border. Allow two hours for border formalities.

**Car Rental** The following agencies can be found in Oujda:

Avis
  (Maroc Voyages), 110 Blvd Allal ben Abdallah
  (☎ 683993)
Budget
  Immeuble Kada, Blvd Mohammed V
  (☎ 682437)
Europcar
  (Wagons-Lits), Place Mohammed V (☎ 682520)
Hertz
  Blvd Mohammed V (☎ 683802)

## AROUND OUJDA
### Sidi Yahia Oasis
About seven km east of Oujda is the fairly unexciting oasis village of Sidi Yahia. If you happen to be in Oujda in September, however, it might be worth enquiring about the annual moussem held there. It is one of the bigger celebrations of this type in the country.

## BOUARFA
There is an argument for skipping the Oujda crossing to Algeria and heading first to the oasis of Figuig, 376 km to the south, especially for those who see the desert routes through the Sahara as the main attraction of Maghreb travel. Figuig itself warrants a visit, but the towns on the way down from Oujda do not. Bouarfa is no exception, and the only thing that separates it from the others is the fact that it is a minor transport hub.

### Places to Stay & Eat
Should you get stuck here, or want to stay for some perverse reason, the best accommodation bet is the *Hôtel Tamlalte*, on the town's main street and about 100 metres from the bus lot. Rooms are clean but basic and cost Dr 30/60. The *Hôtel des Hauts Plateaux* is better known, more expensive and poorer value. It's located at the Oujda exit of town. Neither of these places has showers, but they do have basins. There is supposedly a third hotel lost in the warren of streets to the west of the bus lot. A few cafés and snack stands are scattered around town.

MOROCCO

## Getting There & Away

**Bus** Buses to Oujda cost Dr 47.50, and leave at 6.30, 7, 7.30 and 10 am and 2 and 4 pm. Departures to Figuig are at 10.30 am and 3, 5.30 and 7 pm. The fare is Dr 19. Heading west to Er-Rachidia there is a bus for Dr 50 at 12.45 pm.

**Train** Believe it or not there is a weekly passenger train between Bouarfa and Oujda. It leaves Oujda on Saturday night at 10.42 pm and takes about eight hours. It then turns around at 9.20 am on Sunday to return to Oujda.

**Taxi** Few grands taxis run these routes, but you might get lucky if you need one. Grands taxis leapfrog the towns north to Oujda, but you should be covered by the through buses if you need a connection.

## FIGUIG

Some 100,000 palm trees are fed by artesian wells in this oasis on the edge of the Sahara. Figuig was once the last stop before crossing the Sahara for Moroccan pilgrims heading to Mecca, and as the second border post with Algeria after Oujda, it retains the feel of a frontier town. There are several ksour of varying interest throughout the palmeraies (palm groves), and from some vantage points you can get great views across the extent of the oasis.

Figuig's greatest charm is as a place to simply unwind. It would be hard to find a more laid-back place, although in summer this is due more than anything to the oppressive heat. The main road from Bouarfa goes right through the oasis and on to Beni Ounif, on the Algerian side of the frontier. The hotels, along with such cafés and eating places as there are, are all along this road.

## Information

There is a Banque Populaire here, especially handy for those entering the country from Algeria. There is a mild black market in Algerian dinar and Moroccan dirham in the oasis – ask about discreetly. There is also a post and phone office set back off the main

road. Note the police post (Sûreté Nationale) where the street makes a dogleg, shortly before the Hôtel Diamant Vert on the way to the frontier. People leaving and arriving must stop here to have their passports stamped.

## Places to Stay & Eat

The *Hôtel Diamant Vert* is the best option – it's a good 20 minutes' walk from the roundabout where the buses usually stop on the road to the border. You can camp here for Dr 10 a head, or take a room for Dr 30/40. There are cold showers and a pool.

The *Hôtel Sahara*, about 50 metres on from where the buses stop, has basic rooms for Dr 25 a head. There is a hammam opposite (Dr 5 a go; women during the day and men in the evening). The worst place is the *Hôtel El-Meliasse* at the Shell service station, which you'll see on the right entering the town from Bouarfa. Rooms are Dr 30/60.

For food there's a small, nameless place by the roundabout where the buses stop where you can eat brochettes for about Dr 4 each. The *Café Fath* and *Café Oasis* (the latter just short of Moroccan customs on the border) are other possibilities.

## Getting There & Away

**Bus** There are buses to Oujda at 6 and 8 am

very day, and occasionally at 2 pm. They all stop at Bouarfa (in case you want to link up with the Er-Rachidia bus there at 12.45 pm). The fare is Dr 66.50 to Oujda.

**To/From Algeria** It's a three-km walk to Moroccan customs, another km to Algerian customs and three more km to the first Alge-rian town, Beni Ounif. With luck you might get a lift part of the way. Coming or going, be sure to have your passport stamped by the Moroccan police in Figuig, on the right just before the Hôtel Diamant Vert on the way to the border. Be prepared for long waits on the Algerian side, and thorough searches.

# The North Atlantic Coast

From Tangier to the Mauritanian border, Morocco boasts an Atlantic seaboard of some 2500 km (including the still-disputed territory of the Western Sahara, which is under Rabat's control). If Tangier is a unique mix of Moroccan and European influences, the cities and towns of the coast, too, present a different face from those of the interior. Most were occupied, or even founded, by European powers over the centuries, and this is reflected in their appearance and feel. Long used to the sight of foreigners among them, the people of the coastal cities have been handed down a legacy quite different from that of the long-xenophobic interior.

Rabat and Casablanca, the political and economic capitals since the French installed their protectorate in 1912, are cosmopolitan centres at the heart of modern Morocco. They are flanked up and down the coast by towns that at one time or another served as bridgeheads for European merchant empires. Such was the case in Asilah and Larache, which changed hands several times

before ending up as part of Spain's zone in the protectorate. What remains is a curious combination of European and Moroccan fortifications and medinas. In between lie hundreds of km of beaches, many of them crowded in summer. Foreigners tend to head still farther south, to Essaouira and Agadir.

## North Coast

### ASILAH

A 46-km drive south of Tangier through soft verdant country along a stretch of Atlantic beaches lies the small port of Asilah. Small it may be, but, over two millennia, it has had a tumultuous history far out of proportion to its size.

The first settlers were the Carthaginians, who named the port Zilis. Next were the Romans. Forced to deal with a population that had backed the wrong side during the Punic Wars, Rome decided to move the inhabitants to Spain and replace them with Iberians.

Asilah featured again in the 10th century when it held Norman raiders from Sicily at bay. In the following century it became the last refuge of the Idrissids. The town's most turbulent period, however, followed the Christian victories over the forces of Islam on the Iberian peninsula in the 14th and 15th centuries. In 1471 it was captured by the Portuguese, and the walls around the city date from this period, although they have been repaired from time to time.

In 1578 King Dom Sebastian of Portugal chose Asilah as the base for an ill-fated crusade, which resulted in his death and the subsequent passing of Portugal (and its Moroccan possessions) into the hands of Spain.

Asilah was captured by the Moroccans in 1589, lost again to the Spanish, and then was recaptured by Moulay Ismail in 1691. In the

The North
Atlantic
Coast

0   25   50 km

TANGIER

ASILAH
M'Soura
Lixus
LARACHE
KSAR-EL-
KEBIR
OUAZZANE

SOUK
EL-ARBA
DU-RHARB

ATLANTIC
OCEAN

Oued

Sebou

Kenitra

SALÉ
RABAT
SIDI-KACEM

Meknès

MOHAMMEDIA
CASABLANCA

● BEN
SLIMANE

9th century, as a result of pirate attacks on its shipping, Spain sent in the navy to bombard the town.

Early this century, Asilah was used as a base by one of the most colourful bandits ever produced by the wild Rif mountains – Er-Raissouli (see the aside below). Shortly after the end of WW I he was forced to abandon Asilah, and within a few years had lost everything.

Asilah has found its niche in the late 20th century as a bijou resort town. Money has been poured into gentrifying the houses within the city walls by both affluent Moroccans and Europeans. Consequently, the streets gleam with fresh whitewash, ornate wrought-iron work adorns windows, and chic craft shops have sprouted along virtually every alley. A new harbour is under construction and should soon be providing berths for pleasure yachts and the small local fishing fleet. A little farther north along the beaches, camping resorts have mushroomed, catering to European summer holiday-makers.

Despite the changes mass tourism has brought (including the arrival of a handful of touts and guides), it is worth staying in Asilah for a while, especially in the low season, when there are hardly any tourists around.

### Information

**Money** Both the BMCE and Banque Populaire will change cash and travellers' cheques and issue cash advances on credit cards. There are no ATMs.

**Post & Telecommunications** The post and telephone office is on the east side of town, just in off the Tangier-Rabat road. It is open during regular office hours. There are a couple of card-operated telephones outside the office.

---

### Er-Raissouli

Moulay Ahmed ben Mohammed er-Raissouli (or Raisuni) began his career in the late 1800s as a petty mountain bandit but soon progressed to murder on such a scale that the whole countryside around Tangier and Tetouan lived in fear of him. At this time, however, he had been made pasha of Asilah, which was to become his main residence and base. In 1899, when Er-Raissouli was 23 years old, the sultan lost patience (or summoned up the nerve to act against the 'pasha') and had him arrested and jailed in Mogador (modern Essaouira) for several years.

When he was released home, but was soon at it again. His most profitable game proved to be the kidnapping of Westerners. He and his band held various luminaries to ransom, including US businessman Ion Perdicaris, who was ransomed in 1904 for US$70,000. In return for promising good conduct, Er-Raissouli was made governor of the Tangier region. His conduct, however, was anything but good, and by 1907 the European powers were sufficiently worried by his antics that they compelled the Moroccan government to attack him. It did, but failed to capture him.

Things were looking grim for Er-Raissouli, but in 1909 Moulay Abd al-Hafiz became sultan, and Er-Raissouli – whose influence over the Rif tribes was still great – proclaimed his allegiance to the new sultan immediately. In return he was made governor of most of north-west Morocco except Tangier.

Spain, which took control of the north under the deal that cut Morocco up into protectorates in 1912, tried to make use of Er-Raissouli to keep order among the Rif tribes. Madrid invested considerable money and military hardware in the effort, but in vain. Er-Raissouli as often as not used the arms against the Spanish, inflicting several stinging defeats.

Having obtained promises from Germany that he would be made sultan after WW I, he found himself at loggerheads with everyone when Germany lost the war in 1918. The Spaniards forced him to flee Asilah, but for the following few years he continued to wreak havoc in the Rif hinterland.

The final irony was his arrest and imprisonment at the beginning of 1925 by a Rif rebel with a slightly broader political outlook, Abd el-Krim. Er-Raissouli, who had submitted to the medical attention of a Spaniard, stood accused of being too closely linked to the Spanish! He died on 10 April 1925. ■

MOROCCO

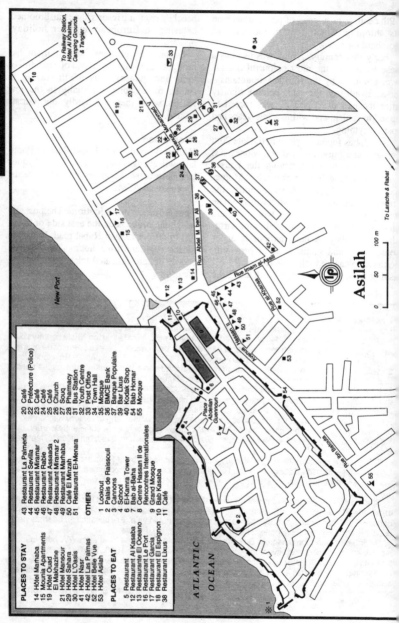

**PLACES TO STAY**

14 Hôtel Marhaba
15 Mounia Apartments
19 Hôtel Ouad
El Makhazine
21 Hôtel Mansour
29 Hôtel Sahara
30 Hôtel L'Oasis
41 Hôtel Nasr
42 Hôtel Las Palmas
52 Hôtel Belle Vue
53 Hôtel Asilah

**PLACES TO EAT**

5 Restaurant
12 Restaurant Al Kasaba
13 Restaurante El Oceano
16 Restaurant Le Port
17 Restaurant Garcia
18 Restaurant El Espignon
38 Restaurant Lixus

43 Restaurant La Palmeria
44 Restaurant Sevilla
45 Restaurant Miramar
46 Restaurant Rabie
47 Restaurant Assaada
48 Restaurant Miramar 2
49 Restaurant Marhaba
50 Café El Minzah
51 Restaurant El-Menara

**OTHER**

1 Lookout
2 Palais de Raissouli
3 Cannons
4 School
6 El-Kamra Tower
7 Bab al-Baha
8 Centre Hassan II de
Rencontres Internationales
9 Grand Mosque
10 Bab Kasaba
11 Café

20 Café
22 Prefecture (Police)
23 Café
25 Café
26 Church
27 Souq
28 Pharmacy
31 Bus Station
32 Youth Centre
33 Post Office
34 Town Hall
35 Mosque
36 BMCE Bank
37 Banque Populaire
39 Bar Lixus
40 Kodak Shop
54 Bab Homar
55 Mosque

New Port

ATLANTIC
OCEAN

To Railway Station,
Hôtel Al Khaima,
Camping Grounds
& Tangier

Avenue Hassan II

Rue Abdel M ben Ali

Rue Imam al-Aselii

Avenue Hassan II

Rue Ibn Batouta

To Larache & Rabat

Place
Abdellah
Guennoun

Asilah

0    50    100 m

**edical Services** Asilah has several pharmacies. The easiest one to find is just down om the bus station.

**amparts & Medina**
he impressive 15th-century Portuguese mparts are largely intact, partly a result of odern restoration work. Access is limited, nce many private houses abut them. The vo prongs that jut out into the ocean, owever, can be visited at any time and these fford the best views. It's reminiscent of the ld towns enclosed behind the walls of El-dida and Essaouira and there are plenty of hotographic opportunities.

The bright medina is worth a wander round. You'll notice a lot of cheery **murals** n many of the houses. Of more historical ote is the **Bab Homar** (also known as Bab -Jebel or, to the Spaniards, Puerta de la ierra), topped by the much-eroded Portuuese royal coat of arms. On Place Abdellah uennoun is an interesting-looking **tower** nown as the El-Kamra. There are a few old nnons left just inside the seaward wall, though you can only see them from a disnce – access has been cut off by another ment wall.

**alais de Raissouli (Raissouli Palace)**
ndoubtedly one of the town's most intersting sights, this beautifully preserved ree-storey building was constructed in 909 and includes a main reception room ith a glass-fronted terrace overlooking the a. It was from this terrace that Er-Raissouli rced convicted murderers to jump to their eaths onto the rocks 30 metres below. nfortunately, all the furniture has been moved, so it's hard to get an idea of the mptuousness of Er-Raissouli's life at the eight of his power. Access is through a door st inside the seaward wall; a guardian will pen it up, for a small tip. Entry is free. The alace is the venue for an international arts stival held in August each year.

**eaches**
ther than the medina, the beaches to the orth of town are the main attraction. During the summer months they are awash with tourists from Europe. A whole service industry has grown up to cater for the needs of these people, including camp sites, restaurants, discos and the like. It's a smaller-scale version of Agadir at this time of year, and you can meet people from as far afield as Brisbane and Bremen.

**Places to Stay – bottom end**
**Camping** For campers, there are a number of resorts/sites along the beach, all of them north of town. The first two you come across walking out of town are *Camping As-Saada* (Dr 12 per person and Dr 10 for a car) and *Camping Echrigui*. They are much of a muchness, and both have small grocery shops and claim to have hot water. Just beyond the Hôtel El Khaima and about one km inland is *Camping El Minzah* – its location makes it a rather unlikely candidate for most popular camp site in Asilah.

Closer to the Mohammed V Bridge, which lies about 10 km north of Asilah, are at least three more Atlantic coast camps, *L'Océan*, the *Atlas* and the *Sahara*. They tend to be pretty full in summer and at Easter, as they are often block-booked by tour groups from Europe. At other times of the year, you'll virtually have the place to yourself. They all have guarded camping facilities, shower and toilet blocks, and restaurants and bars.

**Hotels** About the cheapest place is said to be the *Hôtel Nasr*, which offers small, basic rooms. However, it was closed at the time of writing. Next up is the *Hôtel Marhaba* (☎ 917144), which overlooks Place Zelaka, in front of the main entrance (Bab Kasaba) to the old town, and is quite adequate for most travellers. It costs Dr 70 for a single or double. Each room has a double bed with clean sheets and a washbasin, but you share the bathroom. Hot showers are Dr 5 extra. Try for a room at the front, as some of the ones farther back are a bit pokey. The *Hôtel Asilah* was another reasonably cheap place, but it was closed for refurbishment at the time of writing.

Another similarly priced hotel is the *Hôtel*

MOROCCO

*Sahara* (☎ 917185), 9 Rue Tarfaya, which is on a par with the Marhaba, although a little more expensive at Dr 80/100. Showers are Dr 5 extra. Nearby is yet another closed hotel, *L'Oasis*.

### Places to Stay – middle

There are a few mid-range options in Asilah. The *Hôtel Belle Vue* (☎ 917747), Rue al-Khansa, offers comfortable, clean rooms with shared shower and toilet and plenty of hot water. Rooms cost Dr 100/120, although you can be fairly sure they'll ask more in summer. It also has self-contained apartments with lounge, kitchen and refrigerator (Dr 300), or larger ones which can accommodate up to six people (Dr 400).

A rather characterless place with spacious, comfortable rooms is the *Hôtel Ouad El Makhazine* (☎ 917090; fax 917500), on Ave Melilla. The rooms have carpet, showers, toilets and phones and cost Dr 115/137.

The *Hôtel Mansour* (☎ 917390) is a cosy little place with sparklingly clean rooms, all with shower and toilet. The small dining area is almost reminiscent of an English tea room. Rooms cost Dr 153/181 and the staff are helpful.

Another mid-range place, *Las Palmas*, was closed at the time of researching.

### Places to Stay – top end

The three-star *Hôtel El Khaima* (☎ 917428; fax 917566) is beside the road heading north, just out of town on the right-hand side. Singles/doubles here cost Dr 266/273 (plus taxes). Breakfast costs Dr 34. The hotel has 110 rooms, a restaurant, a pool and a disco.

Out near the camp sites by the Mohammed V Bridge are a couple of other hotels, the *Club Solitaire* and the *Atlantis*, which are more important for the pools, restaurants and discos they offer campers than for their accommodation.

### Long-Term House Rentals

Because many people have bought houses in the old town and converted them into holiday homes, it is possible to find long-term rentals outside the high season. Ask around and the

grapevine will do the rest. What you pay f[or] these houses will depend on the standard [of] accommodation offered, but they won't b[e] cheap. References or a substantial deposit f[or] wear and tear or breakages would be norma[l]

### Places to Eat

You'll find a string of restaurants and café[s] on Ave Hassan II, and around the corner o[n] Rue Imam al-Assili. A main course in any [of] them will cost around Dr 30. There is a sma[ll] restaurant inside the medina near the E[l] Kamra tower. It's nothing special either, b[ut] is a change of location if nothing else.

There are two slightly more expensiv[e] restaurants across from Bab Kasab[a,] *Restaurante El Oceano* and *Restaurant [El] Kasaba*. Both specialise in fish (which [is] quite good), and a full meal at either will co[st] around Dr 70. Heading north along th[e] waterfront (the views are not so hot, as th[e] esplanade is wide and construction work [is] underway) are three more restaurants, aga[in] offering fish as a speciality. A little cheap[er] is the more straightforward *Restaurant [El] Noujoum*, under the Hôtel Marhaba. It serve[s] standard Moroccan fare.

The *Restaurant Le Port* and the *Resta[u]rant Garcia* are right next to each othe[r,] while the *Restaurant El Espigon* is at the en[d] of the street. All three are a little more exper[n]sive than the two by the city gates.

There are a couple of other nondescri[pt] places around, and several cafés near th[e] grand taxi stand.

If it's a drink you're after, try the local *Bar Lixus* or head out to the Hôtel [El] Khaima. There is also a small liquor sto[re] next to the Hôtel Marhaba.

### Getting There & Away

**Bus** Your best bet for getting to and fro[m] Asilah is the bus. All buses leave from th[e] same lot, with just the one ticket windo[w.] There are lots of buses to Tangier (Dr 10[)] and about eight a day that stop in Larac[he] (Dr 10), although there is nothing betwee[n] 12.45 and 6 pm. Pay on the bus. The tr[ip] either way takes just under an hour.

There are two buses a day to Meknès an[d]

wo to Rabat (Dr 40 to Dr 50, depending on the company), although the more numerous uns to Casablanca (about Dr 80) usually top there too. There are about six buses to ès (Dr 52 or more, depending on the company).

**Train** This is the painful way to get to Asilah, as the station is 2.5 km north of town. Rapide/2nd-class ordinary fares are Dr 67/53 o Rabat, Dr 91/72 to Casablanca and Dr 2.50/10 to Tangier.

**Taxi** Grands taxis to Tangier cost Dr 19, and you might be able to get one to Larache for Dr 10 a person, although they seem to be a rarity.

## AROUND ASILAH

### Monoliths of M'Soura

An ancient and little-understood stone circle stands on a desolate patch of ground some 25 km (by road) south-east of Asilah. The stones range from 50 cm to six metres in height, and some historians believe they surround the tomb of a noble, perhaps dating back to Punic times. To get to it you must first reach the village of Souq Tnine de Sidi el-Yamani, off highway P37, which branches east off the main Tangier-Rabat road. From here, six km of bad piste lead north to the site. You need a good vehicle, and a local guide would help.

## LARACHE

Most people come to Larache to visit the Roman ruins of Lixus, four to five km out of town to the north, but it's worth staying a night or two just for its own sake. Bigger and scruffier than Asilah and with a more substantial fishing port, Larache is a tranquil town where you'll have few hassles.

The old town was once walled, but the casbah and ramparts are now in almost total ruin. What remains intact are the old medina, a fortress known as the Casbah de la Cigogne and a pocket-sized, Spanish-built citadel that houses the archaeological museum. The medina, a tumbledown affair, is worth walking around to get a feel for a typical,

living Moroccan town without any of the tourist trappings and hassle. The heart of the new town is Place de la Libération (formerly the Plaza de España), a typical example of Spanish colonial urban planning. The whitewashed town, inside the medina and out, is dominated by one other colour – the blue used on doors and window frames.

One thing that makes Larache interesting is the nightlife. Although it's a long time since the Spanish left, the social institution of the evening stroll lives on in the warmer months. Between the hours of 5.30 and 9 pm, everyone emerges from the woodwork to promenade, drink coffee or beer, play cards and talk about the day's events. Not so Spanish, however, is the fact that by 10.pm the streets are virtually empty. Naturally, there's some good seafood available in the restaurants.

### Information

**Money** Across the road from the post office is a cluster of banks, all of which accept cash and travellers' cheques. There are no ATMs.

**Post & Telecommunications** The post and telephone office is on Blvd Mohammed V and is open normal office hours. There are some card-operated phones outside.

**Foreign Consulates** Spain has a consulate at 1 Rue Casablanca (☎ 913302). It's open from 8 am to 1 pm Monday to Friday and from 10 am to 12.30 pm on Saturday.

### Musée Archéologique

The tiny archaeological museum contains a small collection of artefacts, mostly from nearby Lixus, including coins, ceramics, utensils and the like from Phoenician and Roman times. The display is on two floors but is so small that, if you are on a tight budget and want to save yourself the tenner, you could probably skip it. The explanations are in Arabic and French only. The building itself is a former Spanish citadel and bears the arms of Charles V above the main door. It's open daily from 9 am to 12.30 pm and 3 to 6 pm (closed Tuesday). Entry costs Dr 10.

MOROCCO

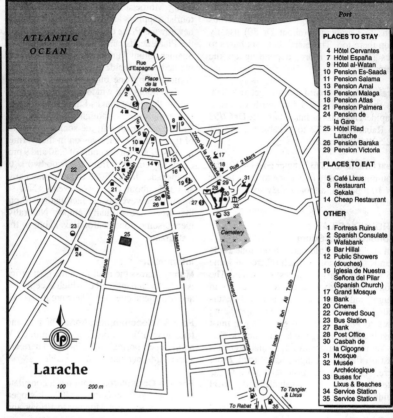

**Larache**

0    100    200 m

PLACES TO STAY

4   Hôtel Cervantes
7   Hôtel España
9   Hôtel al-Watan
10  Pension Es-Saada
11  Pension Salama
13  Pension Amal
15  Pension Malaga
18  Pension Atlas
21  Pension Palmera
24  Pension de
    la Gare
25  Hôtel Riad
    Larache
26  Pension Baraka
29  Pension Victoria

PLACES TO EAT

5   Café Lixus
8   Restaurant
    Sekala
14  Cheap Restaurant

OTHER

1   Fortress Ruins
2   Spanish Consulate
3   Wafabank
6   Bar Hillal
12  Public Showers
    (douches)
16  Iglesia de Nuestra
    Señora del Pilar
    (Spanish Church)
17  Grand Mosque
19  Bank
20  Cinema
22  Covered Souq
23  Bus Station
27  Bank
28  Post Office
30  Casbah de
    la Cigogne
31  Mosque
32  Musée
    Archéologique
33  Buses for
    Lixus & Beaches
34  Service Station
35  Service Station

## The Old Town

The only intact fortification here is the **Casbah de la Cigogne**, which was built by the Spaniards under Phillip III in the 17th century. However, it is out of bounds to visitors. The old city walls and ruined kasbah (the *Qebibat*, or cupolas) constructed by the Portuguese in the 16th century, while not out of bounds, are made dangerous by the possibility of falling masonry.

The old cobbled **medina**, on the other hand, is alive and well, and, although it may not be comparable with the medinas of the imperial cities, it is worth exploring. No-one will hassle you about guide services and there are excellent photographic possibilities.

As you enter by the large, unmistakable Mauresque arch on Place de la Libération (the Bab al-Khemis), you come immediately into a colonnaded market square, the **Zoco de la Alcaiceria**, built by the Spaniard during their first occupation of Larache in the 17th century. It is the busiest part of the medina, full of vendors displaying their wares.

You can also get into the heart of the medina through a similar arch opposite the

MOROCCO

Woman wearing ceremonial headdress

archaeological museum. If you want to go down to the port, head for the eastern corner of the Zoco and turn past the Pension Atlas down Rue 2 Mars, which will take you through, among other things, the woodworkers' market.

### Beaches

The nearest beaches are north of Larache, across the other side of the Loukkos estuary. To get there, you can take a small boat across the estuary from the port, or go by the more circuitous road route (seven km), using the No 4 bus, which you can also pick up from the main bus stop opposite the Casbah de la Cicogne. The buses run approximately every hour throughout the day.

There are a number of simple restaurants at the beach, offering the usual range of seafoods.

### Places to Stay – bottom end

There's a good choice of budget accommodation to be found in Larache. Inside the medina there are at least three extremely basic places: the *Pension Atlas, Pension Victoria* and *Hôtel al-Watan*. They are all close to the Zoco, but you're really better off staying in one of the places in the new part of town.

If you want to be right near the bus station, you could try the *Pension de la Gare*, which has singles/doubles for the pretty much standard Dr 30/50, but no hot water.

The bulk of the other cheapies are on or near Ave Mohammed ben Abdallah. The three best, all with hot water, are the *Pension Baraka* (☎ 913127), which has clean and comfortable rooms for Dr 40/60; the *Pension Malaga* (☎ 911868), which is virtually the same, although doubles cost a little more at Dr 70; and the *Pension Amal* (☎ 912788), which has good rooms for Dr 30/60 and hot showers for Dr 5.

Not so good is the *Pension Es-Saada*, which is closest to Place de la Libération. The cramped rooms (Dr 30/50) have only cold water and, on the ground floor, are very noisy. Better, but still without hot water, are the *Pension Palmera* (☎ 911220) and the *Pension Salama*, both of which charge Dr 30/60.

For Dr 60/90 you could try the *Hôtel Cervantes*, possibly once a decent Spanish hotel but now quite frankly a dump. They claim to have hot water in the shared showers, and some of the rooms do have ocean glimpses.

If you have problems with showers, you could try the public showers (Dr 5) on Ave Mohammed ben Abdallah.

### Places to Stay – middle

Once *the* place to stay during Spanish colonial times, the two-star *Hôtel España* (☎ 913195), which fronts onto Place de la Libération, still exudes an air of grandness. It has 50 rooms, some with private bathroom and balcony. The cost is Dr 130/150 for singles/doubles with private bathroom and Dr 80/130 without. It is a reliable, clean place and the rooms have phones.

A few km south of Larache on the road to Rabat, the *Hostal Flora* is of little use to anyone without a car.

## Places to Stay – top end

The only top-end hotel in town is the three-star *Hôtel Riad Larache* (☎ 912626; fax 912629), Ave Mohammed ben Abdallah, apparently once the private home of some French nobles, and now part of the Kasbah Tours Hotels chain. Set in its own somewhat neglected grounds with swimming pool and tennis courts, the hotel offers spacious, self-contained rooms at Dr 270/450 plus taxes. As well as a beer garden, there's an internal bar and restaurant that offers expensive meals. Breakfast, by the way, is included in the room price.

## Places to Eat & Drink

There are a number of small eateries around Place de la Libération and the Zoco, inside the medina, where you can get cheap Spanish-style meals. The best of them by far, the *Restaurant Sekala*, is on your left just before you enter the Zoco through Bab al-Khemis. For Dr 25 you get a big serve of paella-style rice, chicken, fish, salad and a soft drink.

There are a few eateries among the cafés along Ave Hassan II as you head away from Place de la Libération. One block up from the Hotel España is a good, cheap brochette and sandwich joint.

Apart from the cafés around Place de la Libération and along Ave Hassan II and Blvd Mohammed V, the only other kind of drinking institution is the *Bar Hillal*, for a soothing beer with the locals. You could also try the bar and beer garden at the Hôtel Riad.

## Getting There & Away

**Bus** Larache is most easily reached by bus. CTM and several private lines run buses through here. Since booking is not always possible, the best bet is to turn up in the morning and get the first service you can.

CTM has a daily bus to Fès (Dr 55.50), at 7.30 am; four to Tangier (Dr 22), at 11.15 am and 4.30, 7.30 and 11 pm; and six to Casablanca (Dr 67) via Rabat, at 12.30, 4, 6 and 11.45 pm and 12.45 and 1.30 am. There is also a daily bus to Tiznit at 6 pm.

Other buses also cover these destinations, and a few others besides, including Tetouan and Fnideq (for the Ceuta frontier).

**Taxi** Grands taxis run from just outside the bus station. The main standard run is to Ksar el-Kebir, which will be of little interest to most travellers. Otherwise they seem cagey about whether anything will go anywhere except as a special corsa (ride). Should enough people want to go (the mornings are always best), you should pay no more than Dr 10 to Asilah and Dr 50 to Dr 60 to Rabat.

## Getting Around

The main local bus stop is just outside the Casbah de la Cicogne. The blue and red buses could do with an overhaul, but they do work. The average ride costs Dr 2.50. Bus Nos 4 and 5 go to Lixus, and bus No 4 goes on to the beaches north of Larache, but many buses are unnumbered, so it is as well to ask. For the beach try *ash-shaata'* (Arabic), *le plage* (French) or *la playa* (Spanish).

## AROUND LARACHE
### Lixus

Four to five km north of Larache on a hillock overlooking the Loukkos estuary and the Tangier-Larache highway are the Roman ruins of Lixus. Although not as substantial or as well excavated as those at Volubilis, they are definitely worth a visit. An hour or so is sufficient for most people to explore these ruins. To get there, take bus No 4 or 5 (or simply ask for Lixus, as many of the local red and blue buses have no number at all) and ask to be dropped at the turn-off. There's no entry fee and the site is not enclosed, so you're at liberty to wander around on your own. If you exercise some discretion about where you enter the ruins (head down the side road a way before entering), no-one will hassle to be your guide. Otherwise, there'll be the inevitable unemployed youth offering his services.

The site was originally occupied by a pre-historic sun-worshipping people about whom little is known, except that they left a number of stones in the vicinity of the citadel. The positioning of the stones sug-

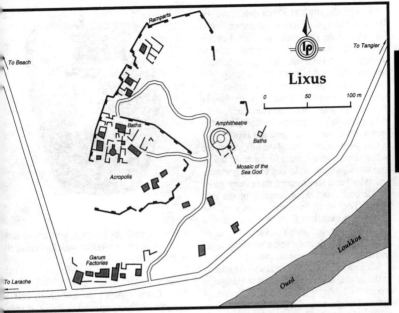

Lixus

To Beach

To Tangier

Ramparts

Baths

Acropolis

Amphitheatre

Baths

Mosaic of the
Sea God

Garum
Factories

To Larache

Loukkos

Oued

0    50    100 m

gests these people were in touch with developments in astronomy and mathematics that ...ed to the building of stone circles in places as far apart as The Gambia and Scotland during the megalithic period.

The Phoenicians set up a colony here, known as Liks, around 1000 BC or even earlier – at about the same time they settled Cádiz (Gades or Gadera, as it was known to them) in Spain. Trade here, and through the later-established colonies of Tingis (Tangier), Tamuda (Tetouan), Russadir (Melilla) and Chella (Rabat), was principally in gold, ivory and slaves.

Nevertheless, the Atlantic colonies were never very important to the Phoenicians until the destruction of the mother city of Tyre by Nebuchadnezzar in the 6th century BC and the subsequent rise of the city-state of Carthage.

As a result of explorations as far south as the mouth of the Niger River about this time by the Carthaginian Hanno, Carthage is said to have been able to monopolise the trade in gold from West Africa and to keep its source a secret. There is some dispute as to whether or not Hanno or any other Carthaginians really did find gold. Liks was, at any rate, a key trading base, and, even when Carthage fell to the Romans in 146 BC, it continued to exert a civilising influence on this area until the establishment in 25 BC of the Roman vassal state of the Berber king Juba II.

Direct Roman rule over this part of the world came in AD 42 under Emperor Claudius, and Lixus now entered its second period of importance. Its main exports during Roman times were salt, olives, garum (an aromatic anchovy paste), and wild animals for the various amphitheatres of the empire.

Lixus rapidly declined following the Roman withdrawal north under Diocletian, but was not finally abandoned until some time in the 5th century AD, when the Roman empire fell apart.

Most of the ruins at Lixus date from the Roman period, and include the garum factories alongside the highway. Just beyond these (at the end of a line of green-painted railings), a gravel track leads up the hillside past a number of minor ruins to the public baths and amphitheatre. Restoration has been done on these, and they're undoubtedly the most impressive of the ruins here. Also to be found is a mosaic of the Sea God – the only such mosaic to be seen at Lixus.

Carrying on to the top of the hill, you come to the citadel where most of the civic buildings were located, including the main temple and associated sanctuaries, an oratory, more public baths and what remains of the city walls. The view over the estuary of the Loukkos is excellent from here, but most of the antiquities are in an advanced state of decay and there's been some woefully amateurish restoration done on them.

It's a pity Lixus has been allowed to decay to the degree that it has. Were it in Europe, it would no doubt be regarded as an important national monument. On the other hand, there is something exhilarating about finding this place in its overgrown state, largely unprettified by human hands – nature is reclaiming the site. In winter, your only companions will be the wind and the odd goat.

To get back to Larache, you could walk (one hour), try to hitch or wait for one of the infrequent buses.

### Ksar el-Kebir

The 'Great Castle', 36 km south-east of Larache on the main road to Rabat, is today a quite uninteresting town. In Almoravid and Almohad times it was a comparatively important base, but nothing much remains as a reminder of its past. It was near here that the Battle of the Three Kings was fought in

---

### The Battle of Three Kings

Dynasties wouldn't be true to their nature without dynastic quarrels, but the one that began in 1574 in Morocco was destined for quite a Shakespearian end. When Mohammed al-Mutawwakil took the reins of Saadian power in 1574, on the death of his father, he contravened the family rule that the eldest *male* in the family should succeed, not the eldest *son*. Al-Mutawwakil's uncle, Abdel Malik, then in Algiers and an ally of the Ottoman Turks, decided to rectify the situation, and after two victories with the help of Turkish troops in 1576, he succeeded in evicting his nephew.

Al-Mutawwakil fled and asked Philip II of Spain to help him regain power. Philip declined in what turned out to be a very astute move, and sent Al-Mutawwakil to King Dom Sebastian of Portugal. Promised a virtual protectorate over Morocco in exchange for his help, Dom Sebastian could not resist. Abdel Malik went to considerable lengths to dissuade Dom Sebastian, offering Portugal a Moroccan port of its choice, but to no avail.

When, in 1578, the Portuguese army of some 20,000 landed in northern Morocco, Abdel Malik gathered a force of 50,000 to meet it. On 4 August, caught in marshy territory near Ksar el-Kebir, Dom Sebastian was routed. He and Al-Mutawwakil drowned trying to flee across the Oued Makhazin (hence the Arab name of the battle) and Abdel Malik died of an illness that had long plagued him, although some say it was a heart attack.

Ahmed al-Mansour succeeded in Morocco, but in Portugal there was no heir. Philip II of Spain became the biggest winner of all, swallowing Portugal into his empire. ■

1578, costing the lives of the king of Portugal and two Moroccan sultans.

## KENITRA

About 40 km north of Rabat lies the French-built town of Kenitra (population about 100,000), the country's sixth-largest port, known until 1958 as Port Lyautey. There is nothing in the town to attract anyone, but the nearby Plage Mehdiya and nature reserve of Lac de Sidi Bourhaba are worth a stop, for those with time.

### Information

A couple of banks and the post office (PTT) are all at the junction of Blvd Mohammed V and Ave Hassan II.

### Places to Stay

There are a couple of basic hotels around. The *Hôtel Marignan*, near the train station, has simple rooms for Dr 60/100, as does the *Hôtel du Commerce* (☎ 371503), near the town hall.

More expensive is the *Hôtel La Rotonde* (☎ 371401/2), at 60 Ave Mohammed Diouri (Dr 146/171 plus taxes). The *Hôtel Ambassy* (☎ 362926), at 20 Ave Hassan II, is in the same league. Back near the town hall is the fancier *Hôtel Mamora* (☎ 371775), with rooms for Dr 231/262. Top of the tree is the four-star *Hôtel Safir* (☎ 371921), near the town hall, on Place Administrative.

An alternative is the three-star *Hôtel Atlantique*, on Mehdiya beach.

### Places to Eat

You'll find a few simple eateries and cafés in the town centre, especially along Ave Mohammed Diouri, but the best place is the *Restaurant L'Embouchure*, on the corner of Ave Mohammed Diouri and Rue Mohammed el-Fetouaki. They have respectable pizza imitations for Dr 35, and ice cream for dessert.

### Entertainment

There seem to be a disproportionate number of bars and purported nightclubs in Kenitra.

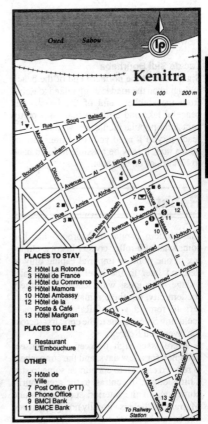

PLACES TO STAY
2  Hôtel La Rotonde
3  Hôtel de France
4  Hôtel du Commerce
6  Hôtel Mamora
10 Hôtel Ambassy
12 Hôtel de la
   Poste & Café
13 Hôtel Marignan

PLACES TO EAT
1  Restaurant
   L'Embouchure

OTHER
5  Hôtel de
   Ville
7  Post Office (PTT)
8  Phone Office
9  BMCI Bank
11 BMCE Bank

### Getting There & Away

There are regular trains and buses to Rabat, 40 km to the south. Going by train is probably the easiest bet. The one-way 2nd-class fare is Dr 10 (Dr 12.50 rapide).

## AROUND KENITRA

### Mehdiya

Local bus No 15 and the orange grands taxis from Ave Mohammed Diouri make the seven-km run to Mehdiya from Kenitra. Apart from the beach, which is popular with locals and not bad (though hardly Morocco's best), there are also the ruins (which you pass on the way in from Kenitra) of a **kasbah** built by Moulay Ismail. There are some good views of the Oued Sebou estuary from here.

### Lac de Sidi Bourhaba

Signposted at the northern end of the beach and again on the road leading inland to Rabat from the southern end of the beach, this peaceful lake and bird sanctuary is a pretty spot and a popular picnic area with locals. To reach it, you'll need your own transport, or take a taxi. It may be possible to hitch back to Kenitra or on to Rabat.

# Rabat

The modern capital of Morocco has had somewhat of a roller-coaster history, climbing at one point to imperial capital only to descend later to the level of a backwater village. The great walls enclose a largely modern city, but there remain several quarters to remind you of Rabat's rich past, including Salé – home to the corsairs – across the river Bou Regreg.

There is enough to keep the sightseer occupied for a few days, and the atmosphere is relaxed enough to encourage some to stay a little longer. In contrast to the great tourist attractions of the interior, such as Fès and Marrakesh, there is virtually no sign of hustle and hassle here, not even in the souqs.

The new city is comparatively quiet, and although its people appear as cosmopolitan as their counterparts down the coast in Casablanca, Rabat lacks the gritty big-city edge of its economic big brother.

### History

Apart from two brief spells as imperial capital, Rabat has been the capital of Morocco only since the days of the French protectorate. However, as far back as the 8th century BC, indigenous people had a settlement in the area of the necropolis of Chellah. They were followed by the Phoenicians and the Romans, who successively patrolled the coast and set up outposts of the empire.

The Roman settlement, known as Sala Colonia, was built along the river of the same name (today's Bou Regreg, which has since altered its course). Like Volubilis, it lasted long beyond the break-up of the Roman empire and eventually became the seat of an independent Berber kingdom.

The settlement's fate is obscure enough to have given rise to varying stories about what happened next. It appears the people of Sala Colonia embraced Islam on the arrival of the Arabs in the late 7th century, but with unorthodox modifications. The first Moroccan dynasties, the Idrissids and Almoravids, largely neglected Sala Colonia and, as its river port silted up, the town declined. By the 10th century, the new town of Salé had sprung up on the north bank of the river. Its inhabitants, of the Zenata tribe (although some sources attribute the rise of the new town to the people of the old), built a *ribat* (fortress-convent) on the present site of Rabat's kasbah, as a base for fighting a rival and heretic tribe south of the river. Whether Sala Colonia had already been emptied of its population by then or whether the process was accelerated by the fighting is unclear.

Things changed with the arrival of the Almohads in the 12th century. They put an end to the fighting and built the kasbah on the site of the ribat. Their intention was to make it the jumping-off point for campaigns against the Christian Reconquista in Spain.

It was under Yacoub al-Mansour ('the Victorious') that Rabat enjoyed a brief peak of glory. After successful campaigns in Spain, Ribat al-Fatah ('Victory Fortress') was to become a great capital. Al-Mansour had extensive walls built, added the Oudaia gate to the kasbah and began work on what was intended to be the greatest mosque in all of the Muslim west, if not in all Islam. His death, in 1199, brought an end to these grandiose schemes. The great Hassan Mosque was never completed – all that remains today are the impressive, squat (and incomplete) minaret (the Tour Hassan), and some columns that have since been re-erected on the site. The city lost all significance quickly thereafter.

Its fortunes began to change in the 17th century with the arrival of Muslim refugees from Christian Spain. At the same time, the population of the sister cities of Rabat and Salé received a colourful injection of Christian renegades, Moorish pirates, freebooters and adventurers of many nationalities. The two cities flourished as what English chroniclers called the Sallee Rovers (or corsairs) set about intercepting merchant ships and men-of-war, especially those returning to Spain and Portugal from the Americas. They brought such a rich booty in gold, Christian slave labour and other goods that the cities briefly formed the independent Republic of Bou Regreg, in the first half of the 17th century.

Although the first Alawite sultans curtailed their activities, no sultan ever really exercised control over the corsairs, who continued plundering European shipping until well into the 19th century, by which time Europe's wishes were becoming writ in Morocco. Sultan Mohammed ben Abdallah briefly made Rabat his capital at the end of the 18th century, but with little appreciable effect on its destiny.

France decided to shift the capital of its protectorate, established in 1912, from Fès to Rabat. The new capital was on the coast (and therefore easily supplied and defended), far from the hornet's nest of political intrigue and potential unrest of Fès or Marrakesh, long the two traditional choices for capital. Since independence (in 1956), Rabat has remained the seat of government and home to the king.

## Orientation

Rabat is best approached by rail, since the central railway station lies on the city's main thoroughfare, the wide, tree-lined Ave Mohammed V.

Arrival by bus is inconvenient, as the bus station lies a good four or five km outside the centre and you will need to take a local bus (No 30) or taxi into the centre – not always an easy task because of the competition. If you do arrive by bus from northern destinations, it is easier to get off at Salé and take a local bus or grand taxi into central Rabat. That way you'll be looking for a hotel before the bus you were on has even made it to Rabat's main bus terminal.

All the main administrative buildings and many of the hotels lie on or just off Ave Mohammed V, although there are others farther afield. Most of the embassies are scattered around the streets to the east, between Ave Mohammed V and Place Abraham Lincoln.

The medina is divided from the ville nouvelle by the wide and busy Blvd Hassan II, which follows the line of the medina walls to Oued Bou Regreg.

Rabat is an easy and pleasant city to walk around, and you will probably need public transport only to visit the twin city of Salé.

## Information

**Tourist Office** The extraordinarily inconvenient location of the ONMT office (☎ 775171), on Rue al-Abtal in the west of the city, renders a visit there a total waste of time unless you desperately want a fistful of the usual handouts and brochures. It's open Monday to Friday from 8.30 am to noon and 2.30 to 6 pm (closed from 11.30 am to 3 pm on Fridays). There is a tourist office on Ave al-Jazaïr, but it's an administrative centre for the ministry only (they sometimes have an odd brochure lying around). The syndicat d'initiative on Rue Lumumba is open but empty.

**Money** The banks are concentrated along Ave Mohammed V. The BMCE is open from 8 am to 8 pm Monday to Friday; on weekends it's open from 10 am to 2 pm and 4 to 8 pm. There are plenty of banks dotted around the ville nouvelle.

**Post & Telecommunications** The post office is open from 8.30 am to 6.30 pm Monday to Friday. The phone office is open 24 hours a day, seven days a week. Poste restante is not in the main post office building but in the telephone office across the

MOROCCO

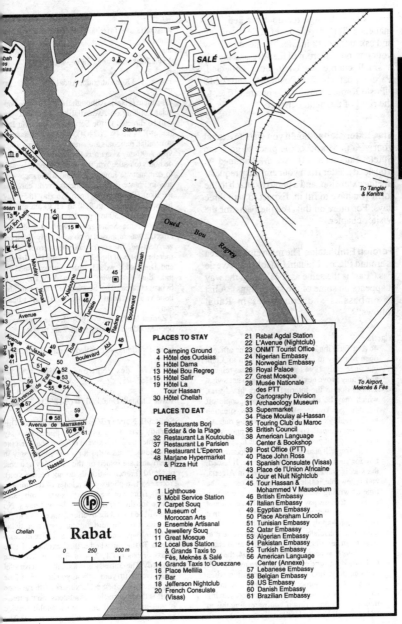

**SALÉ**

Stadium

*Oued Bou Regreg*

To Tangier
& Kenitra

To Airport,
Meknès & Fès

Chellah

**Rabat**

0        250        500 m

**PLACES TO STAY**

3  Camping Ground
4  Hôtel des Oudaias
5  Hôtel Darna
13  Hôtel Bou Regreg
15  Hôtel Safir
19  Hôtel La
   Tour Hassan
30  Hôtel Chellah

**PLACES TO EAT**

2  Restaurants Borj
   Eddar & de la Plage
32  Restaurant La Koutoubia
37  Restaurant Le Parisien
42  Restaurant L'Eperon
48  Marjane Hypermarket
   & Pizza Hut

**OTHER**

1  Lighthouse
6  Mobil Service Station
7  Carpet Souq
8  Museum of
   Moroccan Arts
9  Ensemble Artisanal
10  Jewellery Souq
11  Great Mosque
12  Local Bus Station
   & Grands Taxis to
   Fès, Meknès & Salé
14  Grands Taxis to Ouezzane
16  Place Mellilia
17  Bar
18  Jefferson Nightclub
20  French Consulate
   (Visas)
21  Rabat Agdal Station
22  L'Avenue (Nightclub)
23  ONMT Tourist Office
24  Nigerian Embassy
25  Norwegian Embassy
26  Royal Palace
27  Great Mosque
28  Musée Nationale
   des PTT
29  Cartography Division
31  Archaeology Museum
33  Supermarket
34  Place Moulay al-Hassan
35  Touring Club du Maroc
36  British Council
38  American Language
   Center & Bookshop
39  Post Office (PTT)
40  Place John Ross
41  Spanish Consulate (Visas)
43  Place de l'Union Africaine
44  Jour et Nuit Nightclub
45  Tour Hassan &
   Mohammed V Mausoleum
46  British Embassy
47  Italian Embassy
49  Egyptian Embassy
50  Place Abraham Lincoln
51  Tunisian Embassy
52  Qatar Embassy
53  Algerian Embassy
54  Pakistan Embassy
55  Turkish Embassy
56  American Language
   Center (Annexe)
57  Lebanese Embassy
58  Belgian Embassy
59  US Embassy
60  Danish Embassy
61  Brazilian Embassy

road. Go in through the door marked 'Permanence Télégraphique et Téléphonique' and ask at the desk inside. You need to show your passport as proof of identity, and there's a small charge for each letter collected. Parcel post ('Colis Postaux') and EMS ('Poste Rapide') are in a separate office, to the right of the main entrance.

**Visa Extensions** Should you want to extend your visa in Morocco, the place to go is the Sûreté Nationale, off Ave Mohammed V. You need a letter from your embassy requesting the extension, and a photo to attach to the form you have to fill in. Expect to wait three days. For more on this, see the Facts for the Visitor chapter.

**Foreign Embassies** The main embassy area is around Place Abraham Lincoln and Ave de Fas ('Fas' is the same as 'Fès' and is the way it appears on some of the street signs). A list of embassies and consulates in Rabat follows:

Algeria
    46 Ave Tariq ibn Zayid (☎ 767668). The office is open Monday to Friday from 8.30 am to 3 pm, but since early 1994 total confusion has reigned and it may prove next to impossible to get a visa. This is due to the internal troubles in Algeria, which may be enough to put most people off trying to go. You should check out the situation as thoroughly as you can before setting out. All things being equal, you will need four photos and a photocopy of your passport details to apply for a visa. You will also have to provide documentation for your car if you intend to drive. If issued, the visa is valid for a month's travel in Algeria, and renewable inside the country. Costs at the time of writing were as uncertain as everything else. Australians pay nothing, US citizens about Dr 150 and Britons about Dr 350. Note that Britons must apply in person in Rabat, and not at the Oujda consulate. All applications are sent to Algiers. In late 1993, they were taking an average of 10 days to process, but by early 1994, the wait had turned into one of weeks or even months. All you can do is find out the latest position when you get there. Some travellers have found it easier to pick up the Algerian visa before leaving their home country (but if you're reading this in Rabat, it will be a bit late!).

Australia
    Australia's affairs are handled by the UK embassy.
Canada
    13 bis Zankat Jaafar as-Sadiq, Agdal (☎ 772880)
France
    Embassy: 3 Rue Fahnoun, Agdal (☎ 777222; fax 777752)
    Consulate (visas): Although there is a large consular building on Ave Allal ben Abdallah, you will be directed to the Service de Visas on Rue Ibn al-Khattib (☎ 702404), off Blvd Hassan II Australian nationals are among those requiring a visa. A 90-day visa costs Dr 328 and takes about 48 hours to issue. You'll probably need to be able to demonstrate how you intend to finance your stay in France (bank statements, credit card and the like). The office is open Monday to Friday for applications from 8.30 to 11.30 am and for pick-up from 1.30 to 3 pm. Note that all this may change if the Schengen agreement goes into effect; it was supposed to do so in early 1994, but was delayed. The agreement, which covers all the member states of the EU (except the UK, Ireland and Denmark), would replace visas issued by individual states with one issued for the whole Schengen area. The Service de Visas can also issue visas for Togo, Djibouti and Burkina-Faso.
Germany
    7 Zankat Madnine (☎ 709662). The embassy is open Monday to Friday from 9 am to noon.
Ireland
    Ireland's affairs are handled by the UK embassy.
Japan
    70 Ave des Nations Unies, Agdal (☎ 674163/4/5).
Libya
    1 Rue Chouaib Doukkali (☎ 731888).
Mauritania
    Souissi II, Number 266, OLM (☎ 656678). This recently moved and awkwardly placed embassy has some equally awkward information. First the good news. Visas valid for a one-month stay in Mauritania are issued on the same day at a cost of Dr 70 (French nationals do not need a visa). You need two photos and a letter of recommendation from your embassy; some embassies charge for this service. Now the bad news. No visa will be issued for overland travel, and to get any visa at all you must present a *return* air ticket with Air Mauritanie, which has an office in Casablanca. To find out whether this has changed, take a taxi or bus No 1, 2, 4 or 8 down Ave John Kennedy. The embassy is in a small street parallel to the avenue (to your right as you head out of the city centre). The nearest landmark on the avenue itself is the Pharmacie al-Andalous, on the left – if you pass a Shell and then a Mobil service station (also on the left), you've gone too far. The

embassy is open from 8.30 am to 3 pm Monday to Thursday and until noon on Friday.

**New Zealand**
New Zealand's affairs are handled by the UK embassy.

**Netherlands**
40 Rue de Tunis (☎ 733512).

**Niger**
Niger has no diplomatic representation in Morocco.

**Senegal**
Rue Qadi Amadi (☎ 730636). The embassy here will direct you to the consulate in Casablanca for visas.

**Spain**
Embassy: 3-5 Zankat Madnine (☎ 707600, 707980; fax 707964)
Consulate: 57 Ave du Chellah (☎ 704147/8; fax 704694). Nationals of various countries require visas to enter Spain (this means Ceuta and Melilla, too), including Australians, South Africans, Israelis and Malaysians. You can ask for 30-day visas with two entries (Dr 208) or 90-day visas with three entries (Dr 320). The latter can be harder to obtain. You need to fill in three forms and attach three photos. In addition, you may be asked for photocopies of passport details, credit cards and/or bank statements. The Spaniards prefer you to apply for a visa in your country of residence – an awkward requirement, so be prepared for some diplomatic haggling. If they go along with your request, it takes at least 24 hours to issue. Apply between 9 am and noon and pick up the following day (1 to 2 pm). The consulate is open Monday to Friday. Note the observations on the Schengen agreement above, under the France entry.

**Tunisia**
6 Ave de Fès (☎ 730576, 730636/7; fax 727866). EU, US and Japanese citizens are among those who do not require a visa for Tunisia. Australians are among those who do (although for a one-month stay, you technically shouldn't). A visa costs Dr 56, is valid for one to three months (seemingly depending on your luck) and could take as long as a week to issue. You need two photos.

**UK**
17 Blvd de la Tour Hassan (☎ 731403; fax 720906). The embassy is open Monday to Friday from 8.30 am to 12.30 pm and 2 to 5 pm.

**USA**
2 Ave de Marrakech (☎ 762265; fax 765661). The embassy is open Monday to Friday from 8.30 am to 12.30 pm and 2.30 to 6.30 pm.

**Cultural Centres** Apart from those listed below as language schools, the Centre Culturel Français (☎ 701138) has a branch at 2 Zankat al-Yanboua. They put on films, theatrical performances and lectures, and have a library open Tuesday to Saturday from 10 am to noon and 2.30 to 7 pm.

The German Goethe Institute (☎ 706544) is at 10 Rue Djebli.

Spain maintains a Centro Cultural Español (☎ 708738) by its embassy, at 5 Zankat Madnine. The Istituto Italiano di Cultura (☎ 720852) is at 2 Zankat al-Aghouat, near Place de l'Union Africaine. Its library is open Monday, Wednesday and Friday from 9 am to noon.

**Language Schools** The British Council (☎ 760836) is at 34 Rue Tanger (or Zankat Tanja). As well as a library, which holds a stock of some 14,000 books and periodicals, they have a program of feature films and occasional lectures. The library is open from 2 to 7 pm on Monday, 9.30 am to 7 pm Tuesday to Friday and 9.30 am to 1.45 pm on Saturday.

You could try to wangle some part-time work as an English teacher here, but you need to be qualified. The chances of full-time work are low, as teachers are usually recruited in London.

Another possible source of work as an English teacher is the American Language Center (☎ 766121), at 4 Rue Tanger.

You also try your luck at the International Language Centre (☎ 709718) at 2 Rue Tihama.

**Bookshops & Newsstands** The English Bookshop (☎ 706593) is at 7 Zankat Alyamama and is run by Mohammed Belhaj. He's a friendly person and stocks a good selection of mainly second-hand English and American novels, guides, language books, dictionaries, etc. Books taken back in under two weeks can usually be swapped for another (for a small service charge). The American Bookstore, part of the American Language Center at 4 Rue Tanger, has a smaller collection of new books.

Rabat has the best bookshops in Morocco for Francophone readers. There are several along Ave Mohammed V and Ave Allal ben Abdallah. One of the best is the Librairie Libre Service (☎ 724495), at 46 Ave Allal ben Abdallah.

All the French press is available at newsstands scattered around the ville nouvelle. For other foreign press, there a few places – the shop inside the Rabat Ville railway station is as good as any.

**Maps** It is possible to get a range of maps of Morocco and some of its towns and cities from the Cartography Division of the Conservation & Topography Department (☎ 705311; fax 705885), 31 Ave Moulay Hassan. The survey maps are extremely detailed, and for the most part only of interest to hikers planning serious mountain treks. Maps of the most popular areas of the High Atlas can usually be obtained on the spot; for other areas you may need your passport and an official request. Maps cost Dr 40 a sheet. The office is open on weekdays from 8.30 to 11 am and 2.30 to 5.30 pm. These maps, if at all obtainable in places like Imlil, cost at least twice as much there as in Rabat.

**Medical Services & Emergencies** As throughout Morocco, the emergency police phone number is ☎ 19. For the fire brigade or ambulance call ☎ 15. To keep up to date on where there are late-night chemists, pick up one of the local French-language papers, such as *Le Riverain*. They usually have a listings page with the day's rostered 'pharmacies de garde' on it.

**Film & Photography** There are plenty of places along Ave Mohammed V that sell photographic supplies and develop film.

**Medina**
The walled medina is far less interesting than those in Fès, Meknès and Marrakesh, and dates only from the 17th century. Nevertheless, it's worth a stroll, and there is no hustling to worry about. About the most interesting medina street is Rue Souika. Starting out from Rue Sidi Fatah and heading east, you will find mainly food, spice and general stores until you reach the area around the Great Mosque. From here to the Rue des Consuls, you are in the Souq as-Sebbat, where jewellery is the main item for sale. If you continue past the Rue des Consuls (so called because foreign diplomats lived here until 1912), you end up in a flea market before emerging at the river. Most of the stuff is junk, but you never know what a rummage might turn up.

If you head north along the Rue des Consuls on the way to the kasbah, you will find yourself surrounded on all sides by carpet and rug shops, along with the occasional leatherwork, babouche or copperwork place. The street ends in a fairly broad, open area that leads up the hill to the kasbah. In the days of the Sallee Rovers, this was the site of slave auctions.

**Kasbah des Oudaias**
The Kasbah des Oudaias, built on the bluff overlooking the estuary and the Atlantic Ocean, dominates the surrounding area and can be seen from some distance. It is unfortunate that a much-used city circular road runs right past the entrance. Apart from the obvious aesthetic displeasure, you can only guess at the long-term damage done to the buildings by the passing traffic.

The main entry point is the enormous Almohad gate of **Bab Oudaia**, built in 1195. This is one of the few places in Rabat where you will encounter 'guides'. It's totally unnecessary to take one – once through the gate, there's only one main street, Rue Jamaa, so you can't get lost. Most of the houses here were built by Muslim refugees from Spain. There are great views over the estuary and across to Salé from what is known as the *'plateforme du sémaphore'*, at the end of Rue Jamaa. On your left as you head towards the viewpoint is the oldest **mosque** in Rabat, built in the 12th century and restored in the 18th.

From just inside Bab Oudaia you can turn to your right (south) and walk down to a passage running more or less parallel to Rue Jamaa. Turn into this and on your right is a 17th-century palace built by Moulay Ismail.

It now serves as part of the **Museum of Moroccan Arts**, or Musée des Oudaia. To get the tickets, however, you have to proceed a little farther south into the Andalusian Gardens (actually laid out by the French during the colonial period). Built into the walls of the kasbah here are two small galleries that form part of the museum. The northernmost of these contains a small display of traditional musical instruments and the ticket desk for the whole museum, while the second gallery houses a display of traditional costumes. Back up in Moulay Ismail's palace (which later became a medersa), two of the four galleries are devoted to Fès ceramics and one to jewellery. The last has been decked out as a classic high-class Moroccan dining and reception room. Tickets cost Dr 10, and the rooms are open from 9 am to noon and 3 to 5 pm (6 pm in summer). The gardens stay open later.

The *Café Maure*, on the far side of the gardens and overlooking the river, is a pleasant place to relax. It serves soft drinks and snacks at reasonable prices. A coffee will cost you Dr 3.50.

### Tour Hassan

Rabat's most famous landmark is the Tour Hassan, which overlooks the bridge across the Oued Bou Regreg to Salé. Construction of this enormous minaret – intended to be the largest and highest in the Muslim world – was begun by the Almohad sultan Yacoub al-Mansour in 1195, but abandoned on his death some four years later. Meant to reach a height of more than 60 metres, it only made it to 44 metres. The tower still stands, but little remains of the adjacent mosque, which was all but destroyed by an earthquake in 1755. Only the re-erected but shattered pillars testify to the grand plans of Al-Mansour.

On the same site is the **Mausoleum of Mohammed V**, the present king's father. Built in traditional Moroccan style and richly decorated, the tomb of the king is located below ground in an open chamber. Above, visitors enter a gallery from which they can see the tomb below. Entry is free, but you must be dressed in a respectful manner.

### Chellah

Beyond the city walls, at the end of Ave Yacoub el-Mansour at the junction with Blvd ad-Doustour, are the remains of the ancient Roman city of Sala Colonia, enclosed within the walls of the necropolis of Chellah, built here by the Merenids in the 13th century. The city of Rabat had by this time fallen on hard times, and this pretty spot south of the city gates was as close as the Merenids came to taking an interest in it.

The construction has a defensive air about it, and this is no coincidence. The sultan who completed it, Abu al-Hassan Ali, was intent on protecting his dynasty from possible attack or interference.

After entering through the main gate, you are pretty much obliged to follow a path heading diagonally away from the gate. You can see what little remains of the Roman city,

Guard at Mausoleum of Mohammed V

but it is all fenced off. Around you, fig, olive and banana trees and all sorts of other vegetation prosper, almost wild, amid the tombs and koubbas. At the bottom of this short walk are the remains of a mosque. A couple of fairly half-hearted would-be guides hang about here – you're in no way obliged to take up their offers. Penetrate into the mosque: behind it a chunk of wall is still standing and in front of it are a couple of tombs. Here lie Abu al-Hassan Ali and his wife.

You will have already noticed a minaret topped by a stork's nest (hardly anything in here *isn't* topped by a stork's nest). At one point this was a small medersa that functioned as an endowment of Abu al-Hassan Ali. You can make out where the students' cells were on either side of the building, as well as the mihrab (prayer niche) at the end opposite the minaret.

This peaceful, half-overgrown monument is open daily from 8.30 am until sunset. Entry costs Dr 10.

### Archaeology Museum
The best museum in Morocco, at least among those dealing with the country's ancient past, is Rabat's modern Archaeology Museum, almost opposite the Hôtel Chellah on Rue al-Brihi, off Ave Moulay Hassan. The ground floor is given over to displays of implements and other finds from the oldest known civilisations in Morocco. Some of the material dates back 350,000 years to the Pebble Culture period. In a courtyard to the right are some prehistoric rock carvings. On the 2nd floor you can see finds from various periods in Moroccan history, from the Roman era to the Middle Ages. There are some more in-depth studies on several towns, but the explanations are all in French. In a separate building (ask to have it opened) is the Salle des Bronzes. Most of the ceramics, statuary and implements in bronze and other metals date from the period of Roman occupation and were found at Volubilis, Lixus and Chellah. There are various bronze plates with Latin texts, including a 'military diploma' awarded by the emperor to a local worthy.

The museum is open daily (except Tuesday) from 8.30 am to noon and 2.30 to 6 pm (9 am to noon and 3 to 5.30 pm in winter). Entry costs Dr 10.

### Royal Palace
Of the four remaining Almohad gates in Rabat's city walls, by far the most impressive is Bab ar-Rouah (Gate of the Winds), which forms the north-west corner of the walls around the Royal Palace complex.

You can get into the palace grounds by several entrances. The main one is off Ave Moulay Hassan, a little way inside Bab ar-Rouah. It takes you south towards the mechouar (parade ground), on the east side of which is the Ahl al-Fas (People of Fès) Mosque. If you're lucky, you might catch the king making a grand entry for the Friday prayers around noon. All the palace buildings, which were built in the last century, are off-limits, so you're not likely to be tempted to hang around here for long. It makes a pleasant enough walk on the way from the centre of town out towards Chellah.

### Musée Nationale des PTT
There is a small and much-ignored postal museum on Ave Mohammed V whose collection of stamps and first-day covers goes back to preprotectorate days. Entry is free, and the museum is open during office hours.

### Places to Stay – bottom end
**Camping** The nearest camp site is the *Camping de la Plage* (☎ 782368), back in from the beach at Salé; it's well signposted from the Salé end of the bridge over the Oued Bou Regreg. It's open all year and costs Dr 10 per person, plus Dr 5 for a car, Dr 10 for a power line and Dr 5 for water (for two people). There's very little shade – just a few small trees – but the snack bar can provide food if you order in advance. The facilities include showers and toilets.

There are several more camp sites on the road south towards Casablanca. The first of them is the *Palmeraie*, about 15 km south of Rabat, on the beach at Temara. Another 10 km south, near Ech-Chiahna beach, are two others: *Camping Gambusias* (☎ 749142) and *Camping Rose Marie* (☎ 749251). Both are OK, and the location is pleasant enough.

**Hostel** The hostel (☎ 725769) is on Ave de l'Egypte, opposite the walls of the medina. It's a pleasant place to stay, costing Dr 25 per night in dormitory accommodation, including a small, obligatory breakfast. There are cold showers but no cooking facilities. The hostel is open from 8 to 10 am, noon to 3 pm and 6 to 10 pm. You need a membership card.

**Hotels – medina** There are several basic budget hotels on or just off the continuation of Ave Mohammed V as it enters the medina. Few make any concessions to creature comforts and some don't even have showers, cold or otherwise. An extra dollar or two will buy you better accommodation outside the medina.

The best by a mile is the *Hôtel Dorhmi* (☎ 723898), at 313 Ave Mohammed V. The hotel, which has been completely renovated, is in a good location and has rooms for Dr 70/100. Hot showers are Dr 7 more.

As for the rest, there's not an awful lot in it. The *Hôtel de Marrakech*, on Rue Sebbahi just off Ave Mohammed V, costs Dr 40/70 for singles/doubles and is OK. The *Hôtel des Voyageurs*, just off Ave Mohammed V, is similar and costs Dr 40/60 but there are no showers and it's often full. Beds at the *Hôtel du Marché* are overpriced at Dr 40 a head. They claim to have hot showers for Dr 5. The *Hôtel France* costs Dr 30 or Dr 35 for a single, depending on whether you want a double bed. Doubles/triples cost Dr 50/60, which is certainly cheap. The *Hôtel d'Alger* (☎ 724829) has a pleasant courtyard but no shower. Singles/doubles/triples/quads cost Dr 35/60/90/110. The *Hôtel Chaab* (☎ 731 351), in the first lane inside the medina wall between Ave Mohammed V and Rue Sidi Fatah, is nothing special but is cheap (Dr 25/40).

The *Hôtel du Centre*, on the right just as you enter the medina, also costs Dr 60 for a double (there are no singles). The rooms are clean, with table, chair and washbasin, but there are no showers.

Others in this area include the hotels *Al Alam, Regina, Magreb al-Jadid, Du Midi, National* and *Renaissance*, and the *Hôtel Nouvel*, which is anything but new.

If you end up in one of these places and need a good hot wash, there is a public douche next door to the Hôtel National and a couple more with a hammam (for men and women) in the lane one block north of Rue Sebbahi.

Right up at the kasbah end of the medina is a quiet little place, the *Hôtel des Oudaias* (☎ 732371), at 132 Blvd al-Alou (it's in a bit of a laneway just parallel to the main street). It's not top value for money, at Dr 60/100 for basic rooms and Dr 10 for hot showers, but it is in a pleasant location. They have a nice little tea room downstairs.

A little more expensive is the *Hôtel Darna* (☎ 736787), 24 Blvd al-Alou. The rooms come with shower or full bathroom and cost Dr 100/120. Reception is in the busy café downstairs.

**Hotels – ville nouvelle** West of Bab al-Had, there is a small clutch of hotels on and around Blvd Hassan II. The area is nothing special, but close enough to the action to consider if you are having trouble elsewhere.

The best of the cheapest is the *Hôtel d'Alsace* (☎ 721671), a quiet place in a back lane just off Blvd Hassan II. Most of the rooms, which cost Dr 36/60, look onto a peaceful internal courtyard. Hot showers cost Dr 5.

The *Hôtel Afrique*, on Ave al-Maghrib al-Arabi, is basic, but quite acceptable at Dr 40/70. Hot showers are Dr 5. On the intersection facing Bab al-Had is the *Hôtel Paris*, and in a lane just behind it another cheapie, the *Hôtel Rif*.

Heading into the middle range, the most expensive of this little pocket of places is the spotlessly clean *Hôtel Dakar* (☎ 721671), on the street of the same name. Rooms with shower cost Dr 108/127.

Back inside the city walls, a couple of

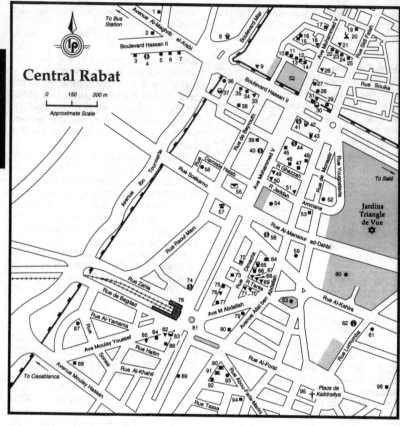

MOROCCO

**Central Rabat**

places along Blvd Hassan are worth considering. The *Hôtel Petit Vatel* (☎ 723095) is modest, but the rooms are not bad. Singles/doubles go for Dr 50/70 (or Dr 80 with two double beds) and showers are Dr 5. Virtually next door is the *Hôtel Majestic* (☎ 722997), 121 Blvd Hassan II. Through the dust, you can almost see that it might once have been majestic, but it's still not a bad deal at Dr 86/98 for rooms with private shower, Dr 76/88 without. Try for one at the front.

A block south of these is a quiet, reasonable place to stay. The *Hôtel Mamounia* (☎ 724479), 10 Rue de la Mamounia, is clean and offers bright rooms for Dr 50/72. Hot showers are Dr 5 extra.

Long a popular place and still one of the best budget deals, the *Hôtel Central* (☎ 707356), 2 Zankat al-Basra, has spacious rooms with basin, bidet, wardrobe, table and chairs for Dr 63/103. The (shared) showers are not cheap at Dr 9 but they are steaming hot (mornings only).

A little more expensive for single rooms but a definite rival for value in doubles is the *Hôtel Velleda* (☎ 769531), 106 Ave Allal ben Abdallah. Generous rooms with private

MOROCCO

## PLACES TO STAY

1 Hôtel Dakar
2 Hôtel Afrique
3 Hôtel Touring
6 Hôtel d'Alsace
7 Hôtel Paris
8 Hostel
10 Hôtel de France
11 Hôtel d'Alger
12 Hôtel Essaada
13 Hôtel du Marché
14 Hôtel des Voyageurs
15 Hôtel National
17 Hôtel du Midi
19 Hôtel Renaissance
22 Hôtel Maghreb al-Jadid
23 Hôtel al-Alam
24 Hôtel de Marrakech
25 Hôtel Regina
27 Hôtel Dorhmi
28 Hôtel du Centre
29 Hôtel Chaab
34 Hôtel Petit Vatel
35 Hôtel Majestic
38 Hôtel Mamounia
39 Hôtel Gaulois
45 Hôtel Berlin
46 Hôtel Splendid
47 Hôtel de la Paix
48 Hôtel Capitol
53 Hôtel Royal
72 Hôtel Central
73 Hôtel Balima
80 Hôtel Velleda
84 Hôtel d'Orsay
86 Hôtel Terminus
88 Hôtel Bélère
94 Hôtel Les Oudayas
96 Grand Hôtel

## PLACES TO EAT

9 Seafood Restaurants
18 Restaurant de l'Union & Restaurant de la Libération
21 Restaurant Taghazout
26 Café de la Jeunesse
29 Juice Stand
31 Restaurant El Bahia
33 Fax Food
45 Restaurant Hong Kong
48 Restaurant Capitol
49 Restaurant Tagardit (Hamburgers)
50 Restaurant La Comédie
51 Café L'Empire
67 La Bidoche (Hamburgers)
68 Dolce Vita (Ice Cream)
69 Pizza La Mamma
70 Restaurant La Bamba
71 Pizza Hot
76 Restaurant Le Fouquet's
82 Café de la Paix
85 Restaurant/Brassrie Français
96 Café Restaurant Chantilly

## OTHER

4 BMCI Bank (ATM)
5 Hammam
16 Douche (Public Showers)
20 Mosque
30 Petit Taxi Stand
32 Municipal Market
36 Douche al-Mamouniya
37 Bus Nos 30 (to Bus Station) & 17 (to Temara via Zoo)
40 BMCE Bank (ATM)
41 Wafabank
42 Total Service Station
43 Bar Le Grillon
44 BMCE Bank (ATMs)
52 Royal Cinema
54 Ministry of Information
55 Post Office (PTT)
56 Sûreté Nationale (Immigration Office)
57 Telephone Office
58 Banque du Maroc
59 Bagdad Nightclub
60 Théâtre Mohammed V
61 Europcar
62 Syndicat d'Initiative
63 German & Spanish Embassies & Centro Cultural Espaõul
64 Café/Bar La France
65 Bar Le Rêve
66 Bar de Tanger
74 BMCI Bank (ATM)
75 International Language Centre
77 Royal Air Maroc
78 Rabat Ville Railway Station
79 Wagons-Lits Office
81 Place des Alaouites
83 Airport Shuttle Bus & Café Terminus
87 English Bookshop
89 Hertz
90 Café Lina
91 Café Krypton
92 French Consulate
93 Avis
95 St Pierre

shower cost Dr 87/109 (Dr 106/131 with toilet as well). Hot water is normally available from 9 pm to 9 am, but it's more warm than hot in the morning.

Staff at the *Hôtel Berlin* (☎ 703435), 261 Ave Mohammed V, are friendly enough, and the rooms, though quite tiny, are clean and secure. The hotel is on the 2nd floor, above a Vietnamese restaurant. Rates are Dr 71/92, plus Dr 5 for a hot shower. The Central and Velleda are better value for money.

The *Hôtel Gaulois* (☎ 730573, 723022), 1 Rue Hims, has a deceptively grand entrance, but for all the disappointment on stepping inside, it's not a bad place to stay. A single without shower costs Dr 63 and a double with shower and toilet Dr 116, which is no bargain compared with a few of the hotels listed earlier. A bit of renovation would go a long way. The one-star *Hôtel Capitol* (☎ 731216), on Ave Allal ben Abdallah, has singles/doubles with shared shower for Dr 77/101 (Dr 98/116 with private shower).

Doubles in the *Hôtel Splendid* (☎ 723 283), 8 Rue Ghazza, are overpriced at Dr 130 without shower and Dr 161 with private shower and toilet. The singles without shower are more reasonable in comparison with the competition, at Dr 80; Dr 136 for those with full bathroom is a bit much. Showers cost extra. The hotel boasts a pleasant internal courtyard.

Those with bath trouble could head for the *Douche al-Mamouniya*, just off Blvd Hassan II, near the Majestic Hôtel, or the already-noted public showers and hammam inside the medina.

### Places to Stay – middle

For those in search of a tad more comfort, there are a few decent two-star possibilities. The *Hôtel Royal* (☎ 721171/2), 1 Rue Amman, has 67 comfortable and reasonably furnished rooms with telephone and bathroom. Singles are Dr 116 with private shower, or Dr 149 with shower and toilet. Doubles cost about Dr 30 more. There is piping hot water all day. Try to get a room with views over the park.

Pretty much as good is the *Hôtel de la Paix* (☎ 722926), on Rue Ghazza. It offers attractively furnished rooms with private toilet, shower and telephone for Dr 136/171.

Going up in price, there are two three-star hotels near the railway station at the junction of Ave Mohammed V and Ave Moulay Youssef. The cheaper of the two is the *Hôtel d'Orsay* (☎ 701319), 11 Ave Moulay Youssef. This small hotel (only 30 rooms) charges Dr 175/220 with private shower and toilet. They have cheaper rooms without toilet, too. Round the corner, the *Hôtel Terminus* (☎ 700616, 709895; fax 701926), 384 Ave Mohammed V, has singles/doubles with

private shower and toilet for Dr 222/272. Both these hotels are a good choice in this category.

Farther along Ave Mohammed V is the huge *Hôtel Balima* (☎ 707755, 708625; fax 707450), with self-contained singles/doubles for Dr 221/299, but it's a poor choice, with sagging beds. Avoid the overpriced breakfasts. The hotel does have a nightclub, though.

Better value, but farther afield and not really offering anything more than the better two-star hotels, is the *Grand Hôtel* (☎ 727285), 19 Rue Patrice Lumumba. It has self-contained singles/doubles for Dr 168/195 (including breakfast), a restaurant and the somewhat seedy Bar Manhattan.

Better is the *Hôtel Bou Regreg* (☎ 724110), Rue an-Nador, near the main city bus terminal, on the corner of Blvd Hassan II. The location is a little noisy, but handy for the medina and buses to Salé. Very clean, self-contained rooms with phone cost Dr 149/172. The hotel has a restaurant and a café.

Heading off into four-star territory is the *Hôtel Les Oudayas* (☎ & fax 707820, 709130), 4 Rue Tobrouk. Self-contained singles/doubles cost Dr 251/331.

### Places to Stay – top end

The two high-grade four-star hotels in Rabat are the *Hôtel Bélère* (☎ 709801), 33 Ave Moulay Youssef, and the *Hôtel Chellah* (☎ 701051; fax 706354), 2 Rue d'Ifni (near the Archaeological Museum). The Bélère is a little cheaper, at Dr 358/488 including breakfast. The Chellah charges Dr 380/484 plus taxes.

There are three five-star hotels. The *Hyatt Regency* (☎ 771234; fax 772492) is out in the swish Rabat suburb of Souissi. The *Hôtel La Tour Hassan* (☎ 733815/6; fax 725408), 26 Ave Abderrahman Annegai, is a little less characterless. Finally, the best placed of them is the *Hôtel Safir* (☎ 726431; fax 722155), on Place Sidi Makhlouf. It offers all you would expect from such places and charges Dr 1100/1250 a night plus taxes.

## Places to Eat

If you want to eat in Rabat, don't leave it too late, as most restaurants are firmly shut by about 9 pm, and a lot of the cafés die about then, too. The exception is during Ramadan, since people don't come out to play until well after sunset during the month of fasting.

**Medina** Perhaps cheapest of all is the collection of small restaurants under a common roofed area directly opposite the Hôtel Majestic, on the medina side of Blvd Hassan II. In some of them you can get fried fish along with the usual chips and salad, though you will probably be offered more standard red-meat dishes. For a full meal, you are looking at around Dr 20.

Equally cheap are the restaurants close to the market on Ave Mohammed V. One that has been popular with travellers for years is the *Café de la Jeunesse*, where you can get a more-than-sufficient meal of meat, chips, rice and olives, plus a soft drink, for Dr 19. It gets quite packed with locals in the early evening. You can eat upstairs or get takeaway food downstairs.

Virtually across the road are a couple of similar places, the *Restaurant de l'Union* and the *Restaurant de la Libération*, where meals cost a fraction more than at the Jeunesse. On Rue Sebbahi is the *Restaurant Taghazout*, again in much the same vein.

Built into the medina walls on Blvd Hassan II is the *Restaurant El Bahia*. You can sit in the Moroccan-style interior section upstairs, in a shaded patio or outdoors on the footpath. Tajine with a drink costs about Dr 30, but the serves are a little stingy. Service is awful, and asking for the advertised set menu appears not to register with the waiters, whose main concern seems to be chatting with pals. If you can ignore this, it is still a pleasant spot to eat.

The place to splurge in the medina is *Dinarjat* (☎ 704239), 6 Rue Belgnaoui, off Blvd al-Alou. It's built in an old mansion and is *the* place in Rabat for a lavish 'Moroccan experience'.

**Ville Nouvelle** A rather good choice is the nameless snack bar and restaurant directly opposite the train station on Ave Mohammed V, next to Henry's Bar (who's Henry?). Proceed through the snack bar (about Dr 10 for a filling roll) into the cavernous and rather gloomy oval-shaped dining area. A decent sit-down meal here, with a beer thrown in, costs about Dr 25. Many locals just use it as a bar.

Another good place is the *Restaurant La Comédie*, on the corner of Ave Mohammed V, opposite the Ministry of Information. A lively café downstairs, the restaurant upstairs offers solid set menus for around Dr 30. It's popular with the locals.

The *Restaurant/Café Majestic*, next to the Librairie Libre Service on Ave Allal ben Abdallah, is one of several places in the city centre that function mostly as bars but offer food to the hungry drinker. There's nothing special about the standard fare, but it won't cost an arm and a leg and you'll obviously have no trouble ordering a cleansing ale with your food. The *Restaurant/Brasserie Français*, on Ave Moulay Youssef, and the nearby *Café de la Paix* also fall into this class.

The *Restaurant La Koutoubia*, at 10 Rue Pierre Parent, is a rather colourful place, with a fragile-looking mock Andalusian extrusion onto the footpath. The house speciality, tajine, is not especially cheap (around Dr 50), but it is good. The waiter seems in a hurry to clear the table, though, so keep an eye out or you'll find your half-eaten meal disappearing. Around the corner to the right is the *Pizzeria Napoli*.

Farther afield, near the Grand Hôtel, try the *Café Restaurant Chantilly*, which offers plats du jour and fish specialities. It's a minor splurge. They sometimes have live traditional Moroccan music.

A block behind the Hôtel Balima is a cluster of restaurants. *La Bamba* offers largely Moroccan food, including two set menus (Dr 55 and Dr 95). To justify the Spanish name, they promise paella every night. Next door and across the road are two pizza joints, *Pizza Hot* and *La Mamma*. The latter is the more expensive, but does a fine pizza with (if you want it) real ham. Also here is the *Restaurant Baghdad*, which specialises in shish kebabs (brochettes) and has a bar, *La Bidoche* (a hamburger joint) and *Dolce Vita* (for ice cream). Another pizza place is *Pizza America*, near the American Language Center. It's not particularly cheap, but attracts a chic Rabat crowd seemingly drawn by the country and western music in the background.

On the subject of hamburger places, there is a surprising number of Western-style fast-food restaurants, where you can generally eat a filling meal for Dr 20 to Dr 30. These include the *Tagardit*, on Ave Mohammed V next to the Restaurant La Comédie, and *Fax Food*, on Blvd Hassan II.

For Chinese and Vietnamese food, try the *Hong Kong* (☎ 723594), on Ave Mohammed V, below the Hôtel Berlin. Main courses start at Dr 50 and are OK.

The *Restaurant de la Plage* and the *Borj Eddar* serve mediocre food down by the Rabat beach – to get to them, just follow Tariq al-Marsa past the kasbah. They are generally closed in winter, although the first of the two keeps a café open all year.

If you feel like something more up-market, *Le Fouquet's* is a charming and understated little French restaurant with not-so-understated prices (count on Dr 100 plus per head). It's on Ave Mohammed V, just across from the BMCI bank. A couple of similar restaurants include *L'Eperon* (☎ 725901), on Ave al-Jazaïr, and the *Restaurant Le Parisien*, around the block from the British Council.

Plenty of the more expensive hotels have restaurants. The Hôtel Balima is among them. The Hôtel Chellah has a classy French restaurant, *Le Bistrot*.

Outside town, along the coastal road to Casablanca, is a highly recommended seafood restaurant, the *Sable d'Or*. A meal here, with wine, will cost you a good Dr 200 per person.

### Entertainment

**Cafés & Bars** Rabat is crawling with largely European-style cafés, which are great places for a morning croissant and coffee. Some of them double as bars (alcohol can be consumed inside only), and there are a few simple drinking holes around, too. Not many cafés or bars are open after about 9.30 pm.

Unfortunately, juice stands are not as commonplace in Morocco as elsewhere in North Africa. However, there is a good one by the Hôtel Petit Vatel, on Blvd Hassan II.

Many of the cafés remain predominantly male preserves, although Western women can usually drink in them without any fuss. A couple that attract a more mixed crowd are the *Café Krypton* and the *Café Lina*. The latter has a better balance of men and women. The *Café Terminus* is not a bad spot to wait for trains or airport shuttles.

Some restaurants and other eateries that also have bars have been mentioned in Places to Eat. Among the straightforward bars, you could do worse than the *Bar de Tanger* or the *Bar Le Rêve*. They are 20 metres up from the Hôtel Central on Rue Dimachk.

A rougher place is the *Café/Bar La France*. A couple of others have been marked on the map, without particular recommendation: the *Bar Le Grillon* and a bar on Place Mellilia.

If you prefer to drink at home (or in your hotel room), there is a liquor store between Café Terminus and Café de la Paix. You can also buy booze at the supermarket on the corner opposite the Restaurant La Koutoubia.

**Nightclubs** There's a good choice of nightclubs in Rabat, some of which are attached to the more expensive hotels, and they're all popular with well-heeled young people. The music is standard international disco fare. The normal entry fee, Dr 50, includes the first drink. Before ordering, make sure you know the prices of subsequent drinks, as they can be as high as Dr 50! Some of the best nightclubs are *Jefferson*, *Jour et Nuit* and *L'Avenue*, and the disco at the *Hôtel Bélère*. You need to be suitably dressed to get into any of these places. At the Jefferson and L'Avenue, men may not be allowed in without a member of the opposite sex. Discos close around 3 am.

**Cinema** Rabat has a wide choice of cinemas, although only a few are of any serious interest. The *Salle 7ème Art* is the closest Morocco comes to an art-house cinema, with a program that tends to change every few days. The *Royal*, near the hotel of the same name, usually screens doubles – the first of Jackie Chan variety but often with something more cerebral to follow. The French-language newspapers advertise what's on around town. Films, if they are not French, tend to be dubbed into that language.

**Theatre** The *Théâtre Mohammed V* puts on a wide variety of performances, ranging from classical music recitals to dance or the occasional play. The theatre is centrally located, on Rue Moulay Rachid.

## Getting There & Away

**Air** RAM (☎ 709766, 769710 for bookings), Air France (☎ 707066) and Iberia are all on Ave Mohammed V. It's unlikely that you'll fly into Rabat's local airport, which is near Salé, 10 km north-east of town. RAM does have a few direct international flights from here, as well as daily flights to Casablanca – in other words, the Mohammed V International Airport. Most of the internal flights from Rabat-Salé go via Mohammed V, so it makes more sense to go there directly, by express train or shuttle bus.

**Bus** The intercity bus station (gare routière) is inconveniently situated about five km south-west of the city centre on the road to Casablanca. Fortunately, there are local buses (No 30 is the most convenient) and petits taxis (about Dr 12) into the centre. There is a left-luggage service at the station.

All the various bus companies have their offices in this cylindrical building, but *everything* is in Arabic, except for the CTM ticket office.

There are 13 ticket windows, stretching around to the left of the main entrance to the CTM window (interrupted by a café on the way). You may notice the white boards above the windows, with destinations in Arabic – the number written on each indicates the window number.

Window Nos 1 to 6 deal mainly with destinations north and east of Rabat, while Nos 7 to 13 are for southern destinations. Next to Window 13 is the CTM booth. Tickets for various destinations can be bought at the following ticket windows.

Window No 1
    Tangier, Tetouan and Ouezzane
Window No 2
    Fès, Meknès, Er-Rachidia, Kenitra, Sidi Kacem and Moulay Idriss
Window No 3
    Fès, Meknès, Er-Rachidia, Khenifra, Al-Hoceima, Sefrou, Nador and Oujda
Window No 4
    Tangier, Tetouan, Chefchaouen, Sefrou, Er-Rachidia, Nador and Oujda
Window Nos 5 & 6
    Minor destinations
Window No 7
    Mohammedia and El-Jadida
Window No 8
    El-Jadida, Safi and Essaouira
Window No 9
    Not in use
Window No 10
    Agadir (eight departures a day), Taroudannt and Ouarzazate
Window No 11
    Marrakesh (departures every hour or so) and Casablanca
Window Nos 12 & 13
    Casablanca

Some sample fares include Casablanca (Dr 18; 1½ hours), Marrakesh (Dr 58.50; 5½ hours), Essaouira (Dr 79; about eight hours), Agadir (Dr 112.50; about 10 hours), Taroudannt (Dr 127.50), Ouarzazate (Dr 106), Safi (Dr 61.40) and El-Jadida (Dr 35).

CTM has buses to Casablanca (Dr 22; six times daily), Fès (Dr 47.50, 3½ hours; seven times daily), Tangier (Dr 67; 5½ hours; six times daily), Er-Rachidia, Oujda, Tetouan and Tiznit (via Agadir).

If you arrive from the north, you're better off alighting at Salé and catching a local bus or grand taxi from there into central Rabat.

**MOROCCO**

**Train** This is the best way to arrive in Rabat, as the Rabat Ville station is in the centre of town, on Ave Mohammed V at Place des Alaouites. (Don't get off at Rabat Agdal.)

There are 17 shuttle trains (Train Navette Rapide – TNR) to Casablanca. The first leaves at 5.10 am and the last at 6.45 pm, and they take 50 minutes. Twelve go to the more convenient Casa-Port station and the rest to Casa-Voyageurs. This is in addition to other, slower trains passing through Rabat on the way to Casablanca and making intermediate stops.

For Fès and Meknès, there are departures at 7.23, 9.10, 10.35 and 11.59 am and 1.33, 3.15, 6.22, 9.41 and 11.23 pm. They take about three hours and 40 minutes to Fès.

There are four daily trains to Tangier, leaving at 12.27 and 8.13 am and 1.33 (change at Side Kacem) and 7.48 pm. The trip takes about 5½ hours.

To Marrakesh, there are nine trains a day via Casablanca. The 5.39 am and 3.47 and 11.42 pm services involve changes at Casablanca. The others are direct, taking a little less than six hours. There is a daily train to El-Jadida at 7.25 pm.

Some 2nd-class ordinary and *rapide* fares are: Casablanca (Dr 19/24), Fès (Dr 49.50/62.50), Marrakesh (Dr 71/90) and Tangier (Dr 62.50/79).

**Taxi** Grands taxis leave for Casablanca from just outside the intercity bus station. They cost Dr 22. There are other grands taxis from a lot between the main city bus station and the Hôtel Bou Regreg on Blvd Hassan II. They leave for Fès (Dr 50), Meknès (Dr 35) and Salé. You can't take petits taxis between Rabat and Salé, because they come under separate city jurisdictions.

**Car Rental** The following are among the car-rental agencies located in Rabat:

Avis
    7 Rue Abou Faris al-Marini (☎ 769759)
Budget
    Train station, Ave Mohammed V (767689)

Europcar
    25 bis Rue Patrice Lumumba (☎ 722328 724141)
Hertz
    46 Ave Mohammed V (☎ 709227)

## Getting Around

**To/From the Airport** Buses between Rabat and Mohammed V International Airport leave from outside the Hôtel Terminus, on Ave Mohammed V, at 5, 6.30, 8.30 and 10 am and 12.30, 3.30 and 6.30 pm. From the airport they leave for Rabat at 6.45, 8.15 and 10.45 am and 1.30, 4.30, 7.30 and 9.30 pm. The fare is Dr 50 and the journey takes 1½ hours.

There are now five direct shuttle trains (TNR) between Rabat and the airport via Casablanca. They leave Rabat Ville station at 5.10, 6.25, 9.50 and 10.10 am and 3 pm. Departures the other way are at 11.10 am and 1.15, 4.30, 7 and 9.35 pm. The 1¼-hour trip costs Dr 67/50 in 1st/2nd class.

The local Rabat/Salé airport is 10 km north-east of town, but it's unlikely that you'll need to use it unless you catch an internal flight to Rabat.

For more information on airport transport and services, refer to the Getting There & Away chapter and the Casablanca Getting Around section.

**Bus** The main city bus terminal is on Blvd Hassan II. From here, bus No 16 goes to Salé (get off at the Salé intercity bus station). Bus Nos 2 and 4 go to Bab Zaer for Chellah.

Bus Nos 30 and 17 run past Rabat's intercity bus station; they leave from a bus stop around the corner from the Hôtel Majestic, just off Blvd Hassan II, inside Bab al-Had. No 17 goes on past the zoo to Temara. Bus Nos 37 and 52 also go from the intercity bus station into central Rabat. Tickets cost Dr 2.30 to Dr 2.70 (hold onto them for inspectors).

**Taxi** Grands taxis to Salé leave when full from just near the Hôtel Bou Regreg, on Blvd Hassan II, and cost Dr 2 a head.

A ride around town in the blue petits taxis

will cost Dr 8 to Dr 10, depending on where you want to go. It's about Dr 12 to the intercity bus station.

## SALÉ

Although just across the estuary from Rabat, the white city of Salé has a distinct character. Little within the city walls seems to have changed over the centuries, and it is difficult to escape the feeling that Salé has been left by the wayside as Rabat forges ahead.

With a long history of action independent from central authorities, Salé is also a strongly traditional enclave amid the comparative liberalism of its sister city. The two elements are best symbolised by the presence here of Abdessalam Yassine, who heads the Al-Adl wal-Ihsan (Justice & Charity) religious movement and is here under house arrest. He has long been considered a threat to the king and the central government, and never more so than with the fundamentalist ferment gripping, to some extent, the rest of North Africa.

Although it's hardly the most interesting of Moroccan medinas, Salé's is pretty much free of touts, and a good introduction to medina navigation. If you've already been to places like Fès, it makes a tranquil change. Few tourists get around in here.

### History

The origins of the town are little known, but Salé rose as Sala Colonia, south of the Oued Bou Regreg, sank into obscurity. The Almohads took control of the area in the 12th century, putting an end to local warring and establishing neighbouring Rabat as a base for expeditions to Spain. Salé's walls were not built until the following century, by the Merenids (who otherwise took little interest in either Salé or Rabat), after a raid in 1260 by Spanish freebooters. A canal was dug from the river to Bab Mrisa to allow safe access for shipping.

Salé subsequently entered its most prosperous period, establishing trade links with Venice, Genoa, England and the Netherlands. It was this position as a trading city on the coast that led to Salé and Rabat becoming home to the Sallee Rovers (see the Rabat History section) in the 16th century. Both cities prospered from the pirates' activities, and an influx of Muslim refugees from Spain in the 17th century only improved matters.

The end of pirating, in the 19th century, and Rabat's promotion to capital under the French left Salé to turn in on itself.

### Orientation

The town's sights can be seen in half a day. The main point of access into the city is Bab Bou Haja, which opens onto Place Bab Khebaz. From here it's a short walk to the souqs, although getting from these to the Great Mosque through the somewhat complicated system of narrow alleyways and arches can be tricky. You may need to ask the local people for directions. Alternatively, you can approach the Great Mosque via the road that follows the line of the city walls past Bab el-Jedid and Bab Malka.

### Information

If you need to get money or post a letter, various banks and a post office are marked on the map.

### Great Mosque & Medersa

These are two of the most interesting buildings in Salé. The Great Mosque, built during Almohad times, is out of bounds to non-Muslims. The medersa, on the other hand, no longer functions as such and is open to visitors. Constructed in 1333 by the sultan Abu al-Hassan Ali, it's a superb example of Merenid artistry and, although smaller, certainly the equal of the Medersa Bou Inania in Fès. It follows what will be a familiar formula to those who have already seen Merenid medersas: all the walls display a zellij-tile base, followed by intricately carved stucco and topped by equally elegant cedarwood work.

Students once occupied the small cells around the gallery. A narrow flight of stairs leads onto a flat roof above the cells, from which there are excellent views of Salé and

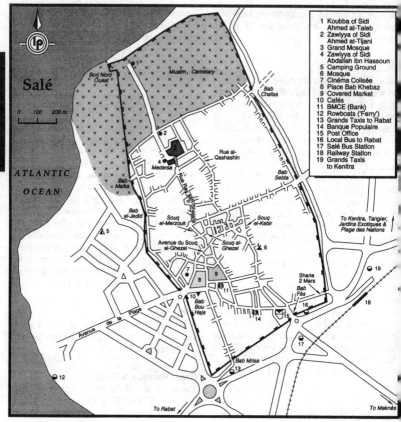

**Salé**

ATLANTIC OCEAN

1 Koubba of Sidi Ahmed at-Taleb
2 Zawiyya of Sidi Ahmed at-Tijani
3 Grand Mosque
4 Zawiyya of Sidi Abdallah ibn Hassoun
5 Camping Ground
6 Mosque
7 Cinéma Colisée
8 Place Bab Khebaz
9 Covered Market
10 Cafés
11 BMCE (Bank)
12 Rowboats ('Ferry')
13 Grands Taxis to Rabat
14 Banque Populaire
15 Post Office
16 Local Bus to Rabat
17 Salé Bus Station
18 Railway Station
19 Grands Taxis to Kenitra

across to Rabat. Entry to the medersa costs Dr 10, and the guardian who shows you around will expect a small tip (they don't get many visitors, so their income is limited). Photography is allowed inside the building and from the roof.

At the back of the Great is the Zawiyya of Sidi Abdallah ibn Hassoun, the patron saint of Salé. Revered by many Moroccan travellers in much the same way as St Christopher is among Christians, this respected Sufi, who died in 1604, is the object of an annual pilgrimage and procession through the streets of Salé on the eve of Mouloud, the Prophet's birthday. On this day, local fishers dress in period costume, and others carrying decorated candles parade through the streets ending up at the marabout's shrine, one of three shrines in Salé. In the lane between the mosque and medersa is the Zawiyya Sidi Ahmed at-Tijani, and the white koubba of Sidi Ahmed at-Taleb ('the doctor') is in the cemetery north-west of the mosque.

**Souqs**

The souqs are connected to the Great Mosque via Rue Ras ash-Shajara (also known as Rue de la Grande Mosquée), along which rich merchants in previous times constructed their houses. There are three souqs in all, but perhaps the most interesting of them is the Souq el-Ghezel, the wool market. Here under the shade of trees you can watch wool being bought and sold with the aid of scales suspended from a large tripod, as it has been for centuries. Close by is the Souq el-Merzouk, where textiles, basketwork and jewellery are made and sold. A little farther out is the Souq el-Kebir, featuring second-hand clothing and household items.

There are plenty of hole-in-the-wall cafés in the souqs and in the surrounding streets where refreshments and good, cheap meals can be found. It's worth calling into one or more of them to soak up the unhurried atmosphere of this timeless place.

### Getting There & Away
**Bus** Bus No 16 passes the intercity bus station on its way to Rabat's urban bus terminal. Bus No 28 stops at the same bus station on its way north towards Bouknadel and the Plages des Nations.

**Train** You could get the train to Rabat if you really felt like it.

**Taxi** There are grands taxis to Blvd Hassan II in Rabat from Bab Mrisa (Dr 2). Note that Salé's beige petits taxis are not permitted to cross into Rabat. Grands taxis for Kenitra leave from a lot just north of the railway station.

**Boat** Small boats run across the Oued Bou Regreg from just below the mellah in Rabat to Salé and back. They operate all day, leaving when full. On the far side, simply follow the rest of the people up the rise to Bab Bou Haja. It costs locals half a dirham, but you'll probably find yourself paying more.

### AROUND RABAT-SALÉ
### Jardins Exotiques & Plage des Nations
About 13 km north of Rabat on the road to Kenitra, the Jardins Exotiques are as much a monument to one man's persistent eccentricity as anything else. Created in 1951 by one M François, a horticulturalist, the gardens contain a sampling of flora from all over the world, and although they appear disappointing when you first enter, they are quite interesting once you're farther inside. François spent a lot of time roaming the forests of Africa. His conclusion on his own efforts was that 'it is poetry that recreates lost paradises; science and technology alone are not enough'. The gardens are open from 9 am to 5.30 pm and entry costs Dr 5. Have the exact change ready, as the fellow in the ticket booth does not have any. You can get there on the No 28 bus from the bus station in Salé – ask to be let off; there's a sign to the gardens on the left-hand side of the road.

The same bus will take you part of the way farther on to the Plage des Nations, which is six km north of the gardens. A track leading from the end of the bus line will get you to the beach, which is also known as Sidi Bouknadel. There are a few cafés and a hotel here, and it's a much more pleasant place to swim than the city beaches in Rabat or Salé.

### National Zoo
The Parc Zoologique National, nine km south of Rabat on the road to Temara, is a surprisingly well-kept place. Most of the animals – and there's a wide range of them – have more space to move around than those in many European zoos. There are snack stands and games for the kids. It's open Monday to Saturday from 10 am to 6 pm, and Sunday and holidays from 9 am to 6 pm; entry is Dr 5.

There are several buses on this route. No 17 leaves from a side street off Blvd Hassan II, just inside Bab al-Had. Ask to be let off at the zoo. From the main road, you have to walk a few hundred metres off to the left (east), as the entrance is at the back. You'll notice the rather depressing sight of a growing shantytown opposite the zoo entrance.

MOROCCO

# Casablanca

With a population of 2.9 million, Casablanca is by far Morocco's largest city, industrial centre and port. This growth is a fairly recent phenomenon, however, dating from the early days of the French protectorate, when Casa was chosen to become the economic heart of the country. The dimensions of the modest medina give some idea of just how small the place was when the French embarked on a massive building program, laying out a new city in grand style, with wide boulevards, public parks and fountains, and imposing Mauresque civic buildings.

The port handles almost 60% of Morocco's total sea traffic, the lion's share being phosphate exports. Some 20 million tonnes of goods are processed here each year. As this is not a natural haven, ships docked here are protected from the Atlantic by a 3180-metre-long jetty.

With all this economic activity, Casa became, and to an extent remains, the place to which Moroccans aspiring to fame, fortune or simply a better living tend to gravitate.

The influx of hopefuls from the countryside in search of a job has fuelled the creation of *bidonvilles* (slums), as in any other huge conurbation, although the problem has been brought under control in the past 20 years. Many of those who arrived hopeful have ended up broken – the parade of well-heeled Casablancans who have made it stands in stark contrast to the beggars, prostitutes and other less fortunate residents.

Amid the striking white medium-rise 1930s architecture – and there are many jewels, Art Deco and otherwise, of this period to be found – it is, above all, the people who strike you. You hardly ever see the veil, and it is hard to imagine the miniskirt anywhere else in the Muslim world. Men and women mix more easily here than in other Moroccan cities, especially those of the interior. On the ocean beaches and in the clubs, the bright young things strut their stuff much like the beautiful youth of many Western countries.

Casablanca has all the hallmarks of a brash Western metropolis, with a hint of the decadent languor that marks many of the southern European cities it so closely resembles. But rubbing shoulders with the natty suits, designer sunglasses and high heels are the old jellabas and hooded burnouses of traditional Morocco. True, the latter almost seems out of place here, but the mix of the population serves to remind you of where you are. And if you were in any doubt, laying eyes upon one of the marvels of modern religious architecture – the enormous Hassan II Mosque – should set you straight.

The mosque itself is just one element of an ambitious urban redevelopment plan that will ultimately see a lot of changes to road layout, the creation of a cultural centre in the former Sacré Cœur cathedral and the construction of a huge US$100 million marina.

Despite the pressures of urban living, it's relatively easy to strike up conversations with Casablancans, another reminder that you're not in one of the frenzied financial powerhouses of the West.

## History

Settlement of the Casablanca area has a long history. Prior to the Arab conquest, what is now the western suburb of Anfa was the capital of a Berber state set up by the Barghawata tribe. The Almoravids failed to bring this state into their orbit, and it was not until 1188, during the time of the Almohads, that it was finally conquered. Some 70 years later, Anfa was taken by the Merenids, but when that dynasty became weak, the inhabitants of the area reasserted their independence, taking to piracy, and trading directly with England and Portugal.

By the second half of the 15th century, the Anfa pirates had become a serious threat to the Portuguese. A military expedition, consisting of some 10,000 men and 50 ships, was launched from Lisbon. Anfa was sacked and left in ruins. It wasn't long before the pirates were active again, however, and in 1515 the Portuguese were forced to repeat he operation. Sixty years later they arrived to stay, renaming the port Casa Branca and erecting fortifications.

Although harried by the tribes of the interior, the Portuguese stayed until 1755, when the colony was abandoned following a devastating earthquake (which also destroyed Lisbon). Sultan Sidi Mohammed ben Abdallah subsequently had the area resettled and fortified. However, its importance declined rapidly, and by 1830 it was little more than a village, with some 600 inhabitants.

It was about this time, however, that the industrialised nations of Europe began casting their nets abroad for ever-increasing quantities of grain and wool – two of the main products of the Chaouia hinterland. To secure these commodities, European agents established themselves in Casablanca (Dar el-Baïda in Arabic). Prosperity began to return, but the activities and influence of the Europeans caused much resentment among the indigenous population. In 1907, this spilled over into violence and European workers on a quarry railway that crossed a Muslim cemetery in the town were killed.

This was the pretext for intervention that the procolonialist faction in the French Chamber of Deputies had been waiting for. A French warship, along with a company of marines, was dispatched to Casablanca and proceeded to bombard the town. Accounts of what followed vary wildly, but it appears that French troops, pillaging tribes from the interior and locals collapsed into an orgy of violence. The Jews of the mellah, in particular, suffered, and many of the town's 20,000 inhabitants died in the upheaval.

The incident led to a campaign to subdue the Chaouia hinterland, and eventually to the dethronement of the sultan, Abd al-Aziz, his replacement by Abd al-Hafid, and the declaration of the French protectorate in 1912. General Lyautey, previously the French commander of Oran, was appointed the first French resident-general. He pursued a program aimed at expanding Casablanca as the main port and economic nerve-centre of the new protectorate, and it was largely his ideas on public works and the layout of the new city that made Casablanca what it is today.

### Orientation
Casablanca is a huge, modern metropolis.

---

**The Bombing of Casablanca**
Walter Harris, the London *Times'* man in Morocco at the turn of the century, was quickly on the spot after the French bombarded Casablanca. His account appears in *Morocco that Was* (now published by Eland):

A French warship arrived on the scene, and an armed party landed for the protection of the European population of the town. The forts and native quarters were at the same time bombarded. Scenes of the wildest confusion ensued, for not only was the town under the fire of the cannon of the warship, but the tribes from the interior had taken advantage of the panic to invade and pillage the place. Every sort of atrocity and horror was perpetrated, and Casablanca was a prey to loot and every kind of crime. The European force was sufficient to protect the Consulates, and the greater part of the Christian population escaped murder. When order was restored, the town presented a pitiful aspect. I saw it a very few days after the bombardment, and the scene was indescribable – a confusion of dead people and horses, while the contents of almost every house seemed to have been hurled into the streets and destroyed...Many of the houses had been burned and gutted. Out of dark cellars, Moors and Jews, hidden since the first day of the bombardment, many of them wounded, were creeping, pale and terrified...Blood was everywhere. In what had once been the poorer quarter of the town...I only met one living soul, a mad woman – dishevelled, dirty but smiling – who kept calling, 'Ayesha, my little daughter; my little son Ahmed, where are you: I am calling you.'
...It was the beginning of the French occupation of Morocco. ■

MOROCCO

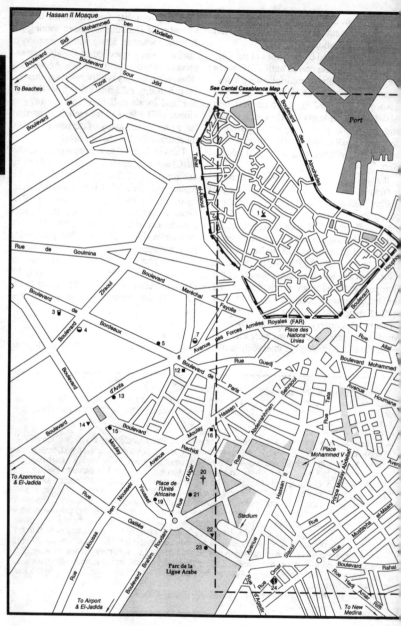

Hassan II Mosque

See Cental Casablanca Map

Port

To Beaches

Boulevard Sidi Mohammed ben Abdallah

Boulevard

Boulevard de Tiznit

Sour Jdid

Boulevard

Talaa el-Aloui

Boulevard des Almohades

Rue de Goulmina

Boulevard Zirkoul

Boulevard de Bordeaux

Boulevard Maréchal

Fayolle

Avenue des Forces Armées Royales (FAR)

Place des Nations Unies

Rue Allal

Boulevard Mohammed

Avenue Houmane

Rue Guedj

Boulevard de Paris

Rue

Hassan I

Rue Abderrahman

Rue Tata

Rue Sebrioui

d'Anfa

Boulevard

Moulay

Boulevard

Rachidi

Rue Hassan II

Place Mohammed V

To Azemmour & El-Jadida

Avenue Moulay Youssef

Rue ben Nousseir

Rue Moussa

Rue Galilée

Place de l'Unité Africaine

Rue d'Alger

Avenue Prince Moulay Abdallah

Stadium

Boulevard Brahim Roudani

Parc de la Ligue Arabe

To Airport & El-Jadida

Rue Omar

Rue el Gadir

To New Medina

Boulevard Rahal

Rue Haqj Amar Riffi

Avenue

Rue Mustapha el Maani

Rue Spriou

Avenue Hassan II

**PLACES TO STAY**

12 Hôtel Windsor
16 Hôtel Les Almoravides
18 Hôtel Métropole

**PLACES TO EAT**

14 Pizza Hut
22 Cafés

**OTHER**

1 Great Mosque
2 Gare du Port
  (Casa-Port
  Railway Station)
3 Red Fez bar
4 No 30 Bus Terminus
5 Cinéma
  Le Verdun
6 Place Oued
  al-Makhazine
7 Local Bus Terminus
8 CTM Bus Station
9 Grands Taxis
  to Rabat
10 Central Market
11 Syndicat
  d'Initiative
  & Post Office (PTT)
13 UK & Swiss
  Consulates
15 American Language
  Center & Bookshop
17 Place Paquet
19 US Consulate
20 Cathédrale du
  Sacré Cœur
21 Spanish Consulate
  & Centro
  Cultural Español
23 Yasmina
  Amusement Park
24 Tourist Office
25 Bus Station (non-CTM)

Casablanca

0     150     300 m

MOROCCO

MOROCCO

With few of the complications posed by the arcane medinas of the cities of the interior, however, it is easy enough to find your way around.

The heart of the city is Place des Nations Unies (formerly Place Mohammed V). From this large traffic roundabout at the southern end of the medina, the city's main streets branch out – Ave des Forces Armées Royales (FAR), Ave Moulay Hassan I, Ave Hassan II and Blvd Mohammed V.

Casa-Port railway station lies about 200 metres north of this main square, at the end of Blvd Houphouet Boigny. The CTM bus station is about 300 metres east of the square, on Rue Léon Africain. The city's main administrative buildings are clustered around Place Mohammed V. Just to the south-west are the carefully maintained lungs of the city centre – the Parc de la Ligue Arabe. West of the gardens lies the exclusive suburb of Anfa, the site of the original medieval Berber town.

The main bus station is a few km southeast of Place des Nations Unies, off Rue Strasbourg, while the principal railway station, Casa-Voyageurs, is about four km east of the town centre.

Most of Casablanca's budget and midrange hotels are in the area bounded by Ave des FAR, Ave Hassan II, Ave Lalla Yacout (named after the mother of King Mohammed V, Hassan II's predecessor) and Blvd Hassan Seghir.

An unaccustomed sight in Muslim countries is open prostitution on the streets, but Casablanca offers this dubious attraction. The 'red light' district is concentrated in the streets and lanes around Blvd Hassan Seghir and Rue Mohammed Smiha, between Ave des FAR and Place du 20 Août. There seems to be a pimp for every *fille de joie*, and the atmosphere at night is decidedly seedy. Occasional attempts by the police to clear the area appear to have made little impression.

**Street Names** Casablanca is undergoing a name-change nightmare, and it is not uncommon to strike three versions for the one street. It is largely a matter of Arabisa-

tion, but there are a few other spanners in the works. The two main squares – Place de Nations Unies and Place Mohammed V – have had their names swapped around by royal decree. Worse, what is now known a Place des Nations Unies sometimes seems to take the name of the street linking it to Casa Port railway station (Houphouet Boigny) itself a recent change.

Where possible, the latest names (or wha seem to be the latest names) appear on th maps – but be aware of the problem if yo buy local street directories.

### Information

**Tourist Offices** The Délégation Régional du Tourisme (☎ 271177, 279533) is at 5 Rue Omar Slaoui and the syndica d'initiative is at 98 Blvd Mohammed V Neither will overwhelm you with usefu information, but the syndicat has the advan tage of being open on weekends. The ONM is open from 8.30 am to noon and 3 to 6.3 pm Monday to Friday. The syndicat has th same hours Monday to Saturday, and is als open from 9 am to noon on Sunday.

**Money** There are plenty of banks in Casa blanca, so changing money should pose n problems. A few are marked on the maps including BMCE branches on Ave Lall Yacout and Ave des FAR. They have ATMs

American Express is represented b Voyages Schwartz (☎ 222946/7), 112 Ru Prince Moulay Abdallah. Thomas Cook i represented by KTI Voyages (☎ 398572/3/4 fax 398567), 4 Rue des Hirondelles.

**Post & Telecommunications** The centra post office is on Place Mohammed V. Thi building can be confusing because the fror entrance is closed. It's open from 8 am t 6.30 pm Monday to Friday and until noon o Saturday.

The poste restante counter, however, is i the same section as the international tele phones. The entrance is the third door alon Blvd de Paris. The telephone service is ope 24 hours a day and sells phonecards. The don't have phone books, though, whic seems strange considering Casablanca accounts for more than 60% of all Morocco's phone numbers! The number for telephone information is ☎ 16.

The parcel post office is farther west along Blvd de Paris, opposite the music conservatorium. The telex office is around the corner to the left.

The main building, erected in 1918, merits a look as part of the impressive array of Mauresque administrative edifices that face onto the square. Marshal Lyautey opened the post office in June 1919 – the commemorative plaque is inside, to the right of the entrance.

**Touring Club de Maroc** This is at 3 Ave des FAR. It's open Monday to Friday from 9 am to noon and 3 to 6.30 pm, and on Saturday from 9 am to noon.

**Foreign Consulates** The main consulates are in the area to the south-west of Place Mohammed V:

Austria
45 Ave Hassan II (☎ 266904; fax 221083)
Belgium
Consulate General: 13 Blvd Rachidi (☎ 223049; fax 220722)
Benelux visa office: 136 Ave Moulay Hassan I
France
Rue Prince Moulay Abdallah (☎ 265355). Hours are Monday to Friday from 8.45 to 11.45 am and 2.45 to 4.45 pm.
Germany
42 Ave des FAR (☎ 314872). It's open Monday to Friday from 8 to 11.30 am.
Italy
21 Ave Hassan Souktani (☎ 277558)
Netherlands
26 Rue Nationale (☎ 221820)
Norway
c/- Scandinavian Shipholders SA, Villas Paquet, 45 Rue Mohammed Smiha (☎ 305961).
Portugal
104 Blvd de Paris (☎ 220214)
Senegal
5 Rue Rouget de l'Isle (☎ 201511/2). The consulate is in a side street by the Hôtel des Almohades, and is open from 9.30 am to 3 pm Monday to Friday. EU and US citizens do not need a visa for a stay of up to three months in Senegal. Others must pay Dr 102 for a visa

allowing a stay of up to one month, or Dr 236 for up to three months. You need three passport photos. Visas are generally issued on the same day.

Spain
31 Rue d'Alger (☎ 220752, 276379; fax 205048); the consulate is open Monday to Friday, 8 am to 1 pm.
Sweden
c/- Saida Star Auto, 88 Blvd Lalla Yacout (☎ 319003)
Switzerland
43 Blvd d'Anfa (☎ 205856; fax 205855); the office is open Monday to Friday, 8 to 10 am.
UK
43 Blvd d'Anfa (☎ 203316; fax 265779); the consulate is open Monday to Friday, 8 to 11 am.
USA
8 Blvd Moulay Youssef (☎ 264550; fax 204127); the consulate is open Monday to Friday, 8 am to 1.30 pm.

**Cultural Centres** Several countries maintain cultural centres in Casablanca. The Centre Culturel Français (☎ 259078) is at 123 Blvd Mohammed Zerktouni. They organise films, lectures and other events, and also have a library. The German version, the Goethe Institut (☎ 200445), right on Place du 16 Novembre, is a more modest affair. They conduct German classes and also put on the occasional film. The Centro Culturale Italiano (☎ 260145) is at 22 Rue Hassan Souktani. The Centro Cultural Español (☎ 267337) is next door to the Spanish consulate, at 31 Rue d'Alger. Its library is open on weekdays from 10 am to 1 pm and 4 to 6 pm.

**Language Schools** The American Language Center (☎ 277765, 275270), 1 Place de la Fraternité, just down from the US consulate, might be your best hope for finding work teaching English in Casablanca.

Failing this, you could try the Centre International d'Études de Langues (☎ 441989; fax 441960), Place de la Victoire, Dar Mabrouka, 4th floor. The tiny British Centre is marked on the Central Casablanca map. It was not open at the time of writing, but could be a place to seek work or suggestions on other places to check out.

MOROCCO

MOROCCO

**Bookshops & Newsstands** Casablanca is a little disappointing for the bibliophile. For books in English, the best bet is the American Language Center bookshop. Otherwise, try the Librairie Farairre, on the corner of Blvd Mohammed V and Rue Araibi Jilali.

There are a number of reasonable newsstands around Place des Nations Unies, at Casa-Port and Casa-Voyageurs train stations, and in the big hotels. The one across the road from the Excelsior Hôtel is as good as any.

A small weekly magazine worth picking up is *7 Jours à Casa*. It has some useful local listings (not all totally reliable) and the odd interesting article (provided you read French). You can't lose anyway, as it's free. The tourist offices should have copies, and it is often lying around in hotels and more expensive restaurants. Casablanca is also the easiest place to encounter *La Quinzaine du Maroc*, a more comprehensive listings booklet covering the main centres throughout Morocco.

**Music** For anyone with more than a passing interest in Moroccan music, a good place to go for LPs, cassettes and CDs is Le Comptoire Marocain de Distribution de Disques (☎ 369153), 26 Ave Lalla Yacout, just west of the Hôtel Champlain. They have, or can get, a pretty substantial range of recordings of most types of traditional music.

**Medical Services & Emergencies** There are several decent hospitals in Casablanca. Among them is the CHU Averroès (Ibn Rochd; ☎ 224109), on Ave du Médecin Général Braun, and the nearby Hôpital du 20 Août (☎ 271459).

For medical emergencies, you could try SOS Médecins Maroc (☎ 989898). The doctors operate around the clock and can come to your hotel. A late-night pharmacy (☎ 269491) is open on Place Mohammed V. To be sure, look for the list of pharmacies de garde in any of the local French-language newspapers.

**Film & Photography** There are quite a few places where you can buy film or have it developed. A couple of them are in Centre 2000, by Casa-Port train station.

**Medina**
The medina, although comparatively small, is definitely worth a little time. The busiest shopping areas are along Rue Chakab Arsalane and Rue de Fès. Such craft stalls as there are to see are mostly outside the city walls (along Blvd Houphouet Boigny), and just inside, on Rue Mohammed al-Hansali (which quickly changes its name to Rue de Fès). The medina is a pleasant, bright place to stroll around, and if you want to get to the Chleuh Mosque, the old city's main Friday mosque, just follow Rue Chakab Arsalane and its continuation.

If you want a new watch, this is the place to get it. Along with dope, watches seem to be the main illegal product on offer, and you're bound to be offered a good many 'Rolexes' during even a cursory visit. A pleasant spot for a cup of coffee is down on Place de l'Amiral Philibert, where the hostel is.

And if you're feeling bouts of wistful nostalgia for the guides of Fès and Marrakesh, you might just get the odd one or two people offering to guide you to the Hassan II Mosque.

**Hassan II Mosque**
Rising up on a point above the Atlantic north of the medina, the Hassan II Mosque is one of the biggest in the world. Completed in August 1993, it is well worth a visit, even though you can only get within a couple of hundred metres of it at the moment. The whole area and the access roads around it are due to be reconstructed, but whether average visitors will be able to get any closer to the mosque when everything is finished is a moot point.

The easiest way to it is along Blvd des Almohades and its extension, Blvd Sidi Mohammed ben Abdallah, from near the Casa-Port railway station. It's about a 20-minute walk. You may run into the occasional irritating kid on the way – an nfortunate by-product of the completion ot only of a new place of worship but of a ew tourist attraction.

## Ville Nouvelle

### Place Mohammed V

Formerly known as Place des Nations Unies, this animated square is flanked by what are probably the country's most impressive examples of Mauresque architecture. The French approximation of Arabo-Andalusian design produced a not-unhappy result. The main buildings of interest are the post office (on the west side), the law courts (on the east side and a little farther south) and the préfecture police headquarters), closing off the south side of the square. What is now the fenced-off rear of the French consulate lies between the last two buildings and contains a statue of General Lyautey.

### Parc de la Ligue Arabe

The biggest park in the city, the Parc de la Ligue Arabe has an essentially French layout, although the flora is more faithful to its location in Africa. It is an extremely pleasant place to walk, take a leisurely coffee or enjoy the diversions of the Yasmina amusement park, entry to which costs Dr 1.

### Cathédrale Sacré Cœur

Built in 1930, the somewhat neglected former cathedral is an unexpected sight in the heart of a Muslim city, and symbolic of modern Casablanca's essentially European genesis. Sitting on the edge of the Parc de la Ligue Arabe, it reflects the best of the more adventurous architectural products of the Art Deco era. Deconsecrated some time ago and converted into a school, it is now destined to become a cultural centre. The first stage of this transformation will see the creation of an 800-seat theatre.

### Beaches

Casablanca's beaches are west of town along Blvd de la Corniche, at the end of which (where it becomes Blvd de Biarritz) begins the affluent beachside suburb of 'Ain Diab. It's a trendy area, lined with four-star hotels, up-market restaurants, bars, coffee shops and nightclubs, and you may feel a little out of place unless you dress accordingly and have a wallet to match.

In high summer the beaches are generally covered wall-to-wall with chic Casablancans, but for the rest of the year you can usually find some space pretty much to yourself at the southern end of 'Ain Diab. When

---

### The Hassan II Mosque

More than 30,000 craftspeople laboured for six years to create the most remarkable homage to Allah (and perhaps also to the monarch who ordered it to be built) in recent history. The Hassan II Mosque, which was opened in grand style in August 1993, can accommodate up to 100,000 people, 25,000 of them in its main central hall. There is some dispute over whether its dimensions make it the biggest mosque in the world, but there is no doubt that it has the tallest minaret (210 metres). In the weeks after it was opened, a green laser light pierced the night sky from the top of the minaret, pointing in the direction of Mecca.

The mosque is built over the water's edge in such a way that well-placed worshippers can see the Atlantic below. Above them, a 1100-tonne central section of the roof is sliced down the middle – it can slide open, superbowl fashion, to turn the central hall into an open-air prayer stadium. The cavernous interior reveals a floor of green and gold-coloured marble, with pink granite columns rising to the ceiling. When the sliding roof is shut, 50 one-tonne chandeliers of frosted Venetian glass provide the lighting. The interior decoration is faithful to the best traditions of Moroccan-Andalusian sculpted and painted wood and stucco work.

In all, US$800 million went into the project, and from 1988 all Moroccans could feel like they had a direct part in it – a levy was imposed on them to help finance the construction. Whatever one's thoughts on the sum spent, Hassan II has achieved what the Almohad Sultan Yacoub al-Mansour set out to do in Rabat in the 12th century – building the greatest mosque in the western Muslim world. Indeed, the modern minaret is more than three times higher than Rabat's incomplete Tour de Hassan was designed to be. ∎

MOROCCO

it's not crowded, the beaches are perfectly all right, although they are better suited to a lazy afternoon than a 'beach holiday'. For the latter, you are better off heading farther south-west towards Essaouira.

Bus No 9 takes you along the southern end of the beaches at 'Ain Diab from the big bus terminal at Place Oued al-Makhazine.

### Sidi Abderrahman
A few km south of the 'Ain Diab beaches, atop a tiny rocky outcrop jutting into the Atlantic, is the small marabout and settlement of Sidi Abderrahman. At high tide, it is cut off from the mainland, but otherwise you can stumble across the rocks. Non-Muslims are not allowed into the shrine itself, but you can walk past the handful of houses and sit down to look out over the ocean. It's about a half-hour walk along the beach south of the No 9 bus terminal at 'Ain Diab.

### Places to Stay – bottom end
**Camping** Campers should head for *Camping de l'Oasis* (☎ 253367), Ave Mermoz (the main road to El-Jadida). It's a long way from the centre, so unless you have your own transport, it's hardly worth it, though bus No 31 runs past it. If you do have your own transport, you might want to get out of the big smoke altogether. About 16 km along the road to Azemmour (which starts off in town as Blvd d'Anfa) are two other camp sites: *Camping Desserte des Plages* and *Camping Tamaris*.

**Hostel** The hostel (☎ 226551), 6 Place de l'Amiral Philibert, faces a small, leafy square just inside the medina, off Blvd des Almohades. It's a fairly large hostel, comfortable and clean, and costs Dr 30 (or Dr 32.50 without a membership card) per person, including breakfast. They also have family rooms (Dr 5 extra per person). It's open from noon to 11 pm. A notice board features local information, including transport timetables. From Casa-Port railway station, walk out to the first major intersection and then turn right along Blvd des Almohades. Turn left when you get to the

second opening in the medina wall. Go throug[h] it and you'll see the hostel on the right.

**Hotels – medina** All the hotels in the medin[a] are unclassified, cheap and quite basic. A fe[w] of them are not bad and are possibly wort[h] considering, but in general they are n[ot] overly inviting. For a little more money, yo[u] can find something better in the centre [of] town. Prices are in the vicinity of Dr 30 t[o] Dr 40 per person. A reasonable one amon[g] this lot is the *Hôtel Central*, on Place d[e] l'Amiral Philibert. It's near the hostel, and [if] you prefer not to be in a dormitory, this is [a] viable alternative, especially if you can get [a] room overlooking the square. Rooms ar[e] clean but have only cold showers. Th[is] shouldn't pose big problems, as there is [a] hammam for men and women on the sam[e] square. Singles/doubles are Dr 35/70.

Equally, if you're not overly fussy abou[t] the rooms, the hotels clustered around th[e] little square between Rue Centrale (or Ru[e] al-Markiziya) and Rue de Fès are in an inte[r]esting bit of the medina. Places like the *Hôte[l] Marrakech* are typical of the area's specie[s] with rooms at Dr 30/60 and no shower[s.] Other hotels to choose from include th[e] *Genève, Helvetia, Al-Nasr Widad, Brési[l] Soussi, Gibraltar, Des Amis, De Medine Candice, London, Chichaoua, Kaawaki Moghreb* and *De la Reine*.

In addition to the hammam on Place d[e] l'Amiral Philibert, there are a couple of othe[r] public showers (douches) and hammam[s] dotted about the medina.

The most convenient approach to th[e] hotels in the medina is from the entrance o[n] Place des Nations Unies.

**Hotels – central Casablanca** At any tim[e] of the year a lot of the lower-end hotels ar[e] full, so it is best to arrive in the morning.

The *Hôtel du Palais* (☎ 276191) offer[s] about the best value for money you will find[.] Located at 68 Rue Farhat Hachad, near th[e] French Consulate, it has clean and spaciou[s] rooms, some with balconies. When the ho[t] water is working you pay a little extra, but a[t] Dr 51/72 without shower it's hard to bea[t] his place is popular and (it goes without saying) often full.

Close by is the *Hôtel Welkom* (☎ 276191), a dive with cells for Dr 52 a person.

If price is the main concern, you could try the *Hôtel Gallia* (☎ 221055), 19 Rue Ibn Batouta. It has basic singles/doubles for Dr 46/70, including (so they say) hot showers.

A couple of blocks south is the still cheaper *Hôtel de Mamora* (☎ 311511), 52 Rue Ibn Batouta. At Dr 38/52/90, it's cheap, although no better than any of the medina places. A few steps away is the *Hôtel Volubilis* (☎ 207789), 20-22 Rue Abdel Karim Diouri. Rooms, which come with a table, washbasin and bidet, are OK, if a little on the musty side, and cost Dr 60/90. If you continue south on Ave Lalla Yacout, you can't miss the *Hôtel Champlain*. It looks rather imposing from the outside, but the dingy rooms are disappointing. They cost Dr 40 per person.

Another collection of cheapies is to be found on and around Rue Allal ben Abdallah.

Virtually across the road from one another are the *Hôtel Kon Tiki* (☎ 314927) and the *Hôtel Touring* (☎ 310010). The former is pretty ordinary, with rooms at Dr 60/80 (Dr 5 extra for a hot shower). The latter is not too bad, though doubles cost Dr 5 more than in the Kon Tiki. The rooms are clean and the beds big. For others, head east and turn left into Rue Chaoui (ex-Rue Colbert). The *Hôtel Mon Rêve* (☎ 311439) is no dream, but cheap at Dr 46/62 (plus Dr 4 for a hot trickle). Like many of the cheapies, it is often full. Around the corner is the even less inspiring *Hôtel Miramar*, with rooms at similar prices.

Back on Rue Chaoui, retrace your steps and proceed south of Rue Allal ben Abdallah. On your right, at No 38, the pleasant *Hôtel Colbert* (☎ 314241) offers singles/doubles/triples without shower or toilet from Dr 47/84/99. Those with shower only are Dr 66/77/112, while others with full bathroom go for Dr 73/95/130. It may not look like much from the outside but, as one of the better-value places around, is often booked out.

Two hotels that have long been popular with travellers are the unclassified *Hôtel du Périgord* (☎ 221085), 56 Rue Araibi Jilali (ex-Rue Foucauld), and virtually next door, the *Hôtel de Foucauld* (☎ 222666), at No 52. The first has rooms for Dr 49/68/104. The singles are pretty cramped, and the place has cold showers only, but it's OK for the money. The Foucauld has singles without private shower (Dr 70) and doubles with shower (Dr 130). Again, it's reasonable without being a breathtakingly good deal.

Farther south, at 36 Rue Nationale, the *Hôtel du Louvre* (☎ 273747) is not a bad place, although some rooms are definitely better than others. Singles/doubles start at Dr 50/68; rooms with private shower cost Dr 65/78, and those with private shower and toilet cost Dr 75/90. This would all be quite good if they didn't throw in a compulsory breakfast (brought to your room at about 8 am, regardless of whether you like it). This and the taxes add about Dr 16 to the price.

Up on Blvd de Paris is the *Hôtel Moumen* (☎ 220798), which has undergone a name change (from Hôtel Lafayette), but little other visible improvement. Rooms are Dr 70/100.

A handy place if you arrive late or intend to leave early from Casa-Voyageurs railway station is the *Hôtel Terminus* (☎ 240025). It's nothing special, but at Dr 38/52/80 you can't really argue. Around the corner are a bar and a couple of decent places to eat.

### Places to Stay – middle

The jump from one-star to two-star quality is quite startling. If you're prepared to pay about Dr 130/170, you can choose from a number of places and end up with a very comfortable deal.

Possibly one of the first hotels you'll notice if you're walking up from Casa-Port train station is the *Hôtel Excelsior* (☎ 200263, 262281), just off Place des Nations Unies, at 2 Rue el-Amraoui Brahim (ex-Nolly). It's OK, but is cashing in on its fast-fading status as one of Casablanca's former premier hotels. Rooms come with phone, and breakfast is included, but for the price you can find better. Singles/doubles with shower cost Dr 140/220. Those with full bathroom are Dr 170/295.

MOROCCO

MOROCCO

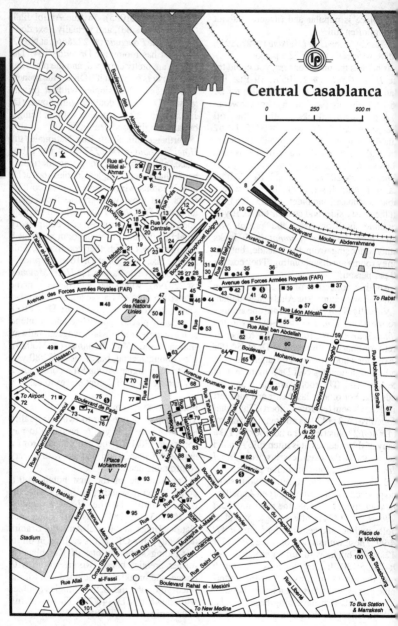

# Central Casablanca

0      250      500 m

**MOROCCO**

## PLACES TO STAY

2 Hostel
5 Hôtel Central
13 Hôtel Helvetia
14 Hôtel al-Nasr
15 Hôtels des Amis,
   de Medine & Gibraltar
16 Hôtel Marrakech
17 Hôtel Chichaoua
18 Hôtel Candice
19 Hôtel Soussi
20 Hôtel/Café London
21 Hôtel Kaawakib Moghreb
23 Hôtel de Widad
24 Hôtel Genève
29 Hôtel Plaza
31 Hôtel du Centre
32 Hôtel Toubkal
33 Hôtel Royal Mansour
36 Hôtel Marhaba
37 Hôtel Safir
39 Hôtel Sheraton
45 Hôtel de Foucauld
46 Hôtel du Périgord
47 Hôtel Excelsior
48 Hyatt Regency Hotel
49 Hôtel Basma
54 Hôtel Touring
55 Hôtel Mon Rêve
56 Hôtel Miramar
61 Hôtel Colbert
62 Hôtel Kon Tiki
66 Hôtel Gallia
67 Hôtel Métropole
71 Hôtel al Mounia
77 Hôtel Lausanne
78 Hôtel du Louvre
79 Hôtel Guynemer
80 Hôtel Volubilis
81 Hôtel de Mamora
82 Hôtel Majestic
84 Hôtel de Paris
86 Hôtel Moumen
89 Hôtel de Noailles
90 Hôtel Champlain
92 Hôtel Astrid
96 Hôtel du Palais
97 Hôtel Welcom
100 Hôtel de Sully

## PLACES TO EAT

6 Café Central
11 Taverne du Dauphin
64 Restaurant Au Petit Poucet

68 Pizza Hot
69 Restaurant Le Tonkin
70 Casablanca Lights
85 Snack Bohayra
98 Restauant La Pagode
99 L'Entrecôte

## OTHER

1 Chleuh Mosque
3 Post Office (PTT)
4 Hammam
7 Men's Hammam
8 Centre 2000
9 Gare du Port (Casa-Port Railway
   Station)
10 Buses for Mohammedia
12 Hassan II Mosque
22 Mosque
25 Clock Tower
26 Le Don Quichotte Nightclub
27 Touring Club du Maroc
28 Air France
30 Iberia Airlines
34 Avis
35 Comanav
38 Europcar
40 BMCI Bank (ATMs)
41 Budget
42 Royal Air Maroc
43 German Consulate
44 Hertz
50 L'Arizona Nightclub
51 Air Algérie
52 Wagons-Lits
53 Librairie Farairre
57 Wasteels Travel Agent
58 CTM Bus Terminal
59 Grands Taxis for Rabat
60 Central Market
63 Goethe Institut
65 PTT & Syndicat d'Initiative
72 Senegalese Consulate
73 Telex Office
74 Parcel Post
75 Citibank
76 Main Post Office (PTT)
83 BMCE Bank (ATMs)
87 Voyages Schwartz (American
   Express)
88 Café National
91 BMCI Bank
93 Law Courts
94 Préfecture (Police Headquarters)
95 French Consulate
101 Tourist Office

MOROCCO

The *Hôtel du Centre* (☎ 312448), just off Ave des FAR, offers better value than the Excelsior. It's been done up, and has clean, modern rooms with bathroom and phone for Dr 126/158.

If you prefer a bit more atmosphere, you should have a look at the *Hôtel Majestic* (☎ 446285), 55 Ave Lalla Yacout, whose foyer is decorated after the fashion of the Merenid era. The comfortable rooms, with shower, toilet, phone and even TV, cost Dr 150/170 plus taxes and breakfast.

Another very good place, along much the same lines as the Hôtel du Centre, is the *Hôtel de Lausanne* (☎ 268083), 24 Rue Tata (ex-Rue Poincaré). Its 31 spotless rooms with full bathroom, carpeting and phone cost Dr 138/170.

There are a couple of surprise packets away from the centre. The comparatively new *Hôtel Astrid* (☎ 277803), 12 Rue Ledru-Rollin, off Rue Prince Moulay Abdallah, has good, clean rooms with en suite bathroom for Dr 150/180. The paint job on the doors is a little on the garish side, though.

In the west of the city centre, on Place Oued al-Makhazine (near the main local bus terminal), is the *Hôtel Windsor* (☎ 200352). Though a little inconveniently located, it's good value at Dr 158/206 with private shower, or Dr 198/246 with shower and toilet. Some places claim to have central heating in winter, but this hotel actually turns it on!

Should you want to be near the main bus station (not the CTM station), you could stay at the *Hôtel de Sully* (☎ 309535), on Place de la Victoire. It's a noisy, polluted location, but could be a useful first stop if you arrive late at night. Rooms go for Dr 138/165 and are quite adequate.

Moving into the three-star bracket, there is the excellent and well-situated *Hôtel de Paris* (☎ 298069), in the pedestrian zone off Rue Prince Moulay Abdallah. The rooms have heating, phones and plenty of hot water. They cost Dr 198/246. Not so hot, but a stone's throw from Casa-Port train station is the *Hôtel Plaza*, with singles/doubles for the same price.

At 22 Blvd du 11 Janvier, there is the somewhat more expensive *Hôtel de Noailles* (☎ 202554; fax 220589). It has spotless, elegant rooms for Dr 228/276, and the tearoom on the 1st floor is a very civilised affair indeed.

The *Hôtel Metropole* (☎ 301213; fax 305801), 89 Rue Mohammed Smiha, is a reasonable alternative to the above if you are having problems finding a room. It costs Dr 220/260 plus taxes.

As usual, the *Moussafir Hôtel* (☎ 401984; fax 400799) chain has a representative, which is just outside Casa-Voyageurs train station. Its modern, comfortable rooms go for Dr 242/286 plus taxes.

The *Hôtel Guynemer*, at 2 Rue Pergoud, used to be a good deal, but at the time of writing was being refurbished for upgrading to a three-star rating.

### Places to Stay – top end

Most of Casablanca's top-end hotels are on Ave des FAR. They include the *Hôtel Sheraton* (☎ 317878), *Hôtel Safir* (☎ 311212), *Hôtel Royal Mansour* (☎ 313011) and *Hôtel Marhaba*. All are five-star hotels. Nearby is the four-star *Hôtel Toubkal* (☎ 311414). Right on Place des Nations Unies is the five-star *Hyatt Regency Hotel* (☎ 261234), and a couple of blocks south you'll find the four-star *Hôtel Basma* (☎ 223323). Still farther south along Ave Moulay Hassan I is the *Hôtel Les Almoravides* (☎ 220505). The four-star *Hôtel al Mounia* (☎ 203211) is at 24 Blvd de Paris, close to the main post office.

Most other top-end hotels overlook the beaches along Blvd de la Corniche. They include the four-star *Hôtel Tropicana* (☎ 367595), *Hôtel Tarik* (☎ 391373), *Hôtel de la Corniche* (☎ 363011) and *Hôtel Suisse* (☎ 360202) and the five-star *Hôtel Riad Salam* (☎ 392244).

### Places to Eat

Casablanca is full of places to eat; what follows is little more than a taste of what's available (a more comprehensive list appears in *La Quinzaine du Maroc*). If your budget is tight, you'll be largely restricted to the

Moroccan version of fast-food joints, where you can get good sandwiches with meat, chips, salad and so on for around Dr 10, or sit-down meals for around Dr 30 to Dr 40. For anything else, you're looking at a minimum of Dr 60 for a main meal.

**Central Casablanca** There are a few cheap restaurants around the Place des Nations Unies entrance to the medina. No particular place stands out, but one that is clean, bright and good is the *Restaurant Widad*, attached to the hotel of the same name. They serve generous helpings of good Moroccan food. A big steaming bowl of soup costs Dr 3.50.

For those staying anywhere near the pedestrian mall (Rue Prince Moulay Abdallah), Ave Lalla Yacout has quite a number of Moroccan fast-food cafés that are popular with the locals at lunchtime and in the early evening. One is *Kwiki Sandwich*, where you can get a kefta sandwich with salad and chips for Dr 10.

A slightly more up-market version is *Snack Bohayra*, at 62 Rue Nationale, where you can get filled sandwiches for about Dr 15 or filling sit-down meals of kefta, chips, salad and a soft drink for Dr 30 to Dr 35.

For something a little better, *Las Delicias*, at 168 Blvd Mohammed V, has a good range of tajines (such as chicken with prunes and onions or beef with raisins). Watch out for the service charge and taxes here. Also good in this area is the *Restaurant Le Cardinal*, close to Place des Nations Unies.

Another place that is highly recommended by some travellers is the *Restaurant Nesma*, just off Blvd Mohammed V, at 21 Rue Ghali Ahmed. A meal of several courses costs about Dr 30.

*Casablanca Lights*, on Ave Hassan II, is a particularly bright and popular snack bar. When you've finished eating, you can go downstairs for a game of pool. A popular new 'self-service' restaurant, *Welcome*, is a couple of blocks in from Place des Nations Unies.

Another good place in the new city is the *Restaurant de l'Étoile Marocaine*, at 107

Rue Allal ben Abdallah, not far from the Hôtel Touring. It's a friendly place where you can eat good Moroccan food in traditional surroundings. They occasionally serves of delicious pastilla (pigeon pie) for Dr 40.

If you're hankering after south-east Asian food, you could head for the *Restaurant Le Tonkin*, on the pedestrian mall, or *La Pagode*, which is close to the Hôtel du Palais. A decent meal at either will cost you Dr 70 or more. Alternatively, you could try the Korean restaurant, *Le Marignan*, on the corner of Blvd Mohammed V and Rue Mohammed Smiha.

For much the same money, you could have a reasonable and intimate French meal at *L'Entrecôte*, on Ave Mers Sultan, next to the RAM office.

For good but not-too-generous servings of Indian food, you could do a lot worse than the *Natraj*, at 13 Rue Chenier, just off the east side of Place des Nations Unies. They have a decent set menu for Dr 75.

A couple of blocks south-east of the Hôtel Noailles on Blvd du 11 Janvier is the *Restaurant Tout Va Bien*, which occasionally serves up a Spanish-style paella. *Pizza Hot*, on Ave Houmane el-Fetouaki, does a reasonable imitation of the real thing.

For seafood, go straight to the *Taverne du Dauphin*, on Blvd Houphouet Boigny. It may not look too inviting, but the food is pretty good and not overly expensive.

If you have at least Dr 60 handy for a main meal, there is a selection of restaurants to choose from in the Centre 2000, next to the Casa-Port railway station. They include *Le Mékong* (Vietnamese), *La Marée* (mostly French), *Le Chalutier* (Spanish seafood), *Le Tajine* (Moroccan), *Retro 1900* (expensive French nouvelle cuisine) and a couple of others.

In the laneway running east off Rue Prince Moulay Abdallah opposite the Restaurant Le Tonkin is *Gelatino* – a good place for an after-dinner ice cream.

**'Ain Diab** For a totally different atmosphere, you could head out to the beaches and 'Ain

Diab. You'll need a fairly fat wallet for the three up-market restaurants, *Le Cabestan, La Mer* and *La Petite Roche*, which are gathered around the El-Hank lighthouse.

If you head farther out along Blvd de Biarritz, you will find many more places to choose from. Overlooking the sea is the *Sijilmassa*, which serves the usual Moroccan fare. For a welcome variation on a theme, try the Lebanese *Restaurant Baalbek* across the road. A few metres along the boulevard heading back towards central Casablanca, *La Mama* has good pizzas for Dr 40.

The splurge of the city would have to be *A Ma Bretagne*, a few hundred metres south of Sidi Abderrahman along the coastal road. It is run by a French maître cuisinier (master chef), André Halbert, who concentrates on seafood specialities.

**Western Fast Food** Not far from the lighthouse is the first of the 12 *McDonald's* franchises that have been planned for Morocco. So, if it's a while since you've swallowed a Big Mac, that's the place to go. For the *Pizza Hut*, go to Place de la Fraternité, near the American Language Center.

**Entertainment**

**Cafés & Bars** There are few cafés in the medina, perhaps the most pleasantly located being the *Central*, on Place de l'Amiral Philibert.

The city centre is filled with French-style cafés, and there is little doubt that an important occupation for much of the city's male population is coffee-sipping and people-watching – and who can blame them? Although cafés are still largely the preserve of men, the sight of Western women sitting down for a coffee, especially at the outdoor tables, is unlikely to arouse much attention. On the inside, some of these places are interesting Art Deco leftovers.

Speaking of interiors, quite a few of the cafés and bars serve alcohol inside (until about 9 pm). There is a bit of a misconception that Casablanca doesn't have many bars. Nothing could be further from the truth.

Those with a taste for Flag Spéciale (or something a little stronger) will find that the city centre is riddled with drinking establishments, going by the name of cafés, bars, brasseries or drugstores. Some have been marked on the maps, but there are plenty of others. Most are pretty much spit and sawdust places, and the clientele can be a little rough around the edges (this is a port after all).

There are three in a row just east of the Restaurant de l'Étoile Marocaine. The *Red Fez*, on Blvd de Bordeaux, is nothing special, but the name appeals.

For something more genteel, the only fallback is the bars in the expensive hotels, which tend to stay open later. *Bar Casablanca*, in the Hyatt, has a happy hour from 6.30 to 7.30 pm, and is plastered with posters and other references to the Humphrey Bogart classic, *Casablanca*. The title was somewhat of a misnomer, as it was filmed entirely in Hollywood and based more on Tangier, which maintained its international status throughout WW II and was a hive of activity, crawling with spies, refugees en route from occupied Europe, and smugglers. The Hyatt bar, posters aside, is no more reminiscent of the film and wartime Tangier, or Casablanca for that matter, than the hotel itself. Still, it might be worth going to hear what the pianist plays...

**Nightclubs** As the bars shut down around 9 to 10 pm, the choices for kicking on are restricted to discos and nightclubs. The more up-market places are concentrated out in 'Ain Diab, but they are expensive (at least Dr 50 to get in and as much for a drink) and most expect snappy dress sense. In addition, unaccompanied women are unlikely to enjoy themselves if they just want a drink.

In the city centre, it's a man's world. The so-called nightclubs (which charge about the same as the discos, one way or another) are largely sleazy joints where you get a bit of Cairo-style belly dancing and cabaret entertainment. Quite a few hostesses and prostitutes work these places. *La Fontaine*, on Blvd Houphouet Boigny, is an unashamedly slimy hostess bar – you buy a drink for yourself and another for your company, and so on...There are a couple of slightly less tacky places opposite the Hôtel de Paris, in the pedestrian zone. Other cabaret bars include *Le Don Quichotte*, on Place des Nations Unies (Ave des FAR), and *L'Arizona*, near the Hôtel Excelsior. There are plenty of others.

If you have wads of money, and like cabarets (but not at this level), you could try the big hotels – the Hyatt and Sheraton both put on Western-style cabarets.

**Cinema** There are about half a dozen cinemas around the city centre, but the best of them are the twin *Dawliz* cinemas off Ave des FAR, a little way east of Place des Nations Unies on Rue Léon Africain. You can quite often catch films only recently released in the West, although there are no guarantees about what is cut out. Those films that are not French are generally dubbed into that language.

**Getting There & Away**

Innumerable travel agencies are squeezed into the same area as the bulk of the hotels. The Wagons-Lits representative is marked on the map. Trasmediterrranea and Intercona (☎ 221737) have a representative on Place 16 du Novembre. Wasteels (for cheap intercontinental rail tickets) has an agency by the CTM bus station. Comanav (☎ 312050), for boats from Tangier to France, is at 43 Ave des FAR. Supratours (☎ 277160), the ONCF's bus service, is in the Centre 2000.

**Air** From Casa's Mohammed V Airport (30 km south-east of the city), there are regular connections to most of the countries of Western Europe, as well as to West Africa, Algeria, Tunisia, Egypt and the Middle East.

Internally, the vast majority of RAM's flights go via Casablanca. Consequently, you can get to any destination direct from Casablanca. For instance, there are three to five daily flights to Agadir (Dr 585, one hour), five weekly flights to Fès (Dr 405, 50 minutes), at least two daily flights to Marra-

kesh (Dr 340, 50 minutes) and at least one flight a day to Tanger (Dr 430, one hour).

For detailed information on airport services and transport, see the Getting There & Away chapter and the Casablanca and Rabat Getting Around sections.

Airlines flying into and out of Mohammed V International Airport include:

Aeroflot
  47 Blvd Moulay Youssef (☎ 206410)
Air Afrique
  Tour des Habous (☎ 318379)
Air Algérie
  1 Rue el-Amraoui Brahim (☎ 266995)
Air France
  15 Ave des FAR (☎ 294040)
Alitalia
  Tour des Habous (☎ 314181)
British Airways/GB Airways
  Place Zellaqa (☎ 307629)
Iberia
  17 Ave des FAR (☎ 279600)
KLM
  6 Blvd Houphouet Boigny (☎ 203222)
Lufthansa
  Tour des Habous (☎ 312371)
RAM
  44 Ave des FAR (☎ 311122)
Royal Jordanian
  Place Zellaqa (☎ 306273)
Sabena
  41 Ave des FAR (☎ 313991)
Swissair
  Tour des Habous (☎ 313280)
Tunis Air
  10 Ave des FAR (☎ 293452)

**Bus – CTM** The CTM bus terminal is on Rue Léon Africain, at the back of the Hôtel Safir (which is on Ave des FAR). They have a left-luggage counter.

There are regular CTM departures to Agadir (six times daily from 5.30 am to 11 pm), Essaouira (twice daily, at 5.30 am and 5 pm), Fès/Meknès (nine times daily), Marrakesh (five times daily from 7.30 am to 9 pm), Oujda (twice daily), Rabat (19 times daily), Safi (six times daily from 5.30 am to 7 pm), Tangier (six times daily), Taza (at 1 pm) and Tetouan (three times every morning). At the time of writing, CTM's services to El-Jadida had been suspended. What's weird is that buses the other way were still running! The bus to Safi does *not* go via El-Jadida.

Fares are Dr 117.50 to Agadir (10 hours), Dr 69 to Fès (five hours), Dr 57.50 to Marrakesh (4½ hours), Dr 22 to Rabat (1½ hours), Dr 60 to Safi (four hours) and Dr 88 to Tangier (seven hours).

CTM also operates international buses to France, Belgium and Italy from Casablanca. See the Getting There & Away chapter for further details.

**Bus – others** The station for the other lines is just off Rue Strasbourg, two blocks down from Place de la Victoire, some way from the centre of the city. There are a couple of urban buses to Place de la Victoire and down Rue Strasbourg (see Getting Around), or you could get a taxi.

Rue Strasbourg must be one of the noisiest and most air-polluted streets in North Africa, and the chaos of buses and touts could just about put you off trying to leave Casablanca. In fact, the touts are good news – they'll find you long before you find the bus you want. Nevertheless, it might be an idea to squirm your way to the ticket windows – a lot of them have prices posted, which will give you an idea of what you should pay. Some of these companies offer 1st and 2nd-class fares. The difference is usually a matter of a few Dr.

There are buses to Agadir (Dr 96), Er-Rachidia (Dr 123/114 in 1st/2nd class), Fès (Dr 55), Marrakesh (Dr 42), Midelt (Dr 80), Ouarzazate (Dr 88.50), Oujda (Dr 119/111 in 1st/2nd class), Rabat (Dr 18/16 in 1st/2nd class), Sefrou (Dr 61), Tangier (Dr 66/60 in 1st/2nd class), Tinerhir (Dr 125) and Tiznit (Dr 137).

There's a petit taxi stand next to the station – the fare into central Casablanca should not be more than Dr 10.

The No 900 bus to Mohammedia leaves regularly from a stop near Casa-Port train station. The ticket costs Dr 5.50.

**Train** Casablanca has five railway stations. The main one is Casa-Voyageurs, four km east of the city centre. The Casa-Port station is a few hundred metres north of Places des Nations Unies, right where you want to be. The other stations, 'Ain Sebaa, Nouvelle Medina and Mers Sultan, are of no interest to travellers.

Most departures are from Casa-Voyageurs station, which is a Dr 15 taxi ride from the centre. There are also plenty of buses between the station and the centre – it's about an hour's walk, which is silly if you're carrying luggage.

Departures include:

El-Jadida (8.50 am, 8.30 pm; 1½ hours); these trains may also go on to Azemmour
Fès (10.52 am and 12.30, 5.20 and 10.17 pm; five hours)
Marrakesh (1.30, 6.23, 7.40 and 9.48 am and 12.11 2.05, 3.06, 5.55 and 7.28 pm; three hours 50 minutes)
Oujda (9.32 am and 1.55 and 10.17 pm; 10½ hours)
Tangier (12.30, 6.50 and 11.20 pm; 6½ hours)

Departures from the Gare du Port ('Casa-Port' on the platform signs) include Fès (8.05 am and 8.35 pm; five hours), Oujda (8.35 pm, 10½ hours) and Tangier (7.10 am; six hours).

All trains to Fès call at Meknès. Trains to Oujda call at Meknès and Fès.

All trains heading north call at Rabat. The trip takes about 1¼ hours. However, the shuttle trains between the two cities are faster. There are 17 a day (from 6.50 am to 9.59 pm): 12 from Casa-Port and the others from Casa-Voyageurs. They take 50 minutes.

Some 2nd-class normal/rapide fares include El-Jadida (Dr 24.50/31), Fès (Dr 69/87), Marrakesh (Dr 52.50/66.50), Oujda (Dr 142/182.50), Rabat (Dr 19/24) and Tangier (Dr 81.50/103).

**Taxi** Grands taxis to Rabat leave from Blvd Hassan Seghir, near the CTM bus station. The fare is Dr 22.

**Car Rental** The following are among the car-rental agencies in Casablanca, but a plethora of smaller agencies is concentrated around Ave des Far and Blvd Mohammed V

They often employ runners to bring in business – follow some of them and you could end up with a much better deal:

Avis
    19 Ave des FAR (☎ 312424, 311135)
    Mohammed V International Airport (☎ 339072)
Budget
    Tour des Habous, Ave des FAR (☎ 313945)
    Mohammed V Airport (☎ 339157)
Europcar
    Complexe des Habous, Ave des FAR (☎ 313737)
    144 Ave des FAR (☎ 314069)
    Mohammed V International Airport (☎ 339161;
    fax 339517)
Goldcar
    5 Ave des FAR (☎ & fax 202510, 260109)
    81 Ave Hassan II Intermarket (☎ 202509,
    220950)
Hertz
    25 Rue de Foucauld (☎ 312223)
    Mohammed V International Airport (☎ 339181)

If you do rent a car, you should be aware of Casablanca's horrendous parking problems. It is virtually impossible to find a park in the centre between 8 am and 6 pm. During these hours, cars will be parked nose to tail in every conceivable spot. How they disentangle themselves at the end of the day is anyone's guess.

### Getting Around
**To/From the Airport** You can get from Mohammed V Airport to Casablanca or Rabat direct by shuttle bus or train (TNR).

The trains leave from below the ground floor of the terminal building, with 12 services day from 8 am to 9.35 pm to Casablanca's main station, Casa-Voyageurs; they take 24 minutes and are comfortable and reliable.. Seven continue to the more convenient Casa-Port station. The other five go on to Rabat (1¼ hours) instead. The system is being expanded, and some of these fast shuttles go on to Kenitra. The first run from Casa-Voyageurs is at 6.01 am. The 2nd-class fare to Casablanca is Dr 25 and the totally unnecessary 1st-class fare (2nd is quite good enough) Dr 37.50.

There are CTM shuttle buses to Casablanca almost every hour from 5.30 am to 11 pm. They cost Dr 20 and take about half an hour.

If none of this suits you, the fare for a taxi into central Casablanca is Dr 150, or Dr 200 after 8 pm (don't let the drivers tell you anything else).

**Bus** The main terminal for Casablanca's city buses is on Place Oued al-Makhazine. There is even a faded route map posted up here. Some useful city routes are:

No 4
    Along Rue Strasbourg and down Ave Lalla
    Yacout to Blvd de Paris
No 5
    From the terminal to Place de la Victoire
No 9
    From the terminal to 'Ain Diab and the beaches
No 30
    From Blvd Ziraoui to Casa-Voyageurs train
    station via Ave des FAR and Blvd Mohammed V

In addition, bus No 2 regularly runs along Blvd Mohammed V to Casa-Voyageurs and beyond. Coming from the train station, you could walk up to Place al-Yassir, from where you have a greater choice of lines serving the city centre.

**Taxi** There's no shortage of petits taxis in Casablanca, but you'll usually find drivers unwilling to use the meters, so negotiate the fare before getting in, especially if you're going a long way. Expect to pay Dr 10 for a ride in or around the city centre.

### AROUND CASABLANCA
#### Mohammedia
About 30 km north of Casablanca lies the local resort town of Mohammedia, which also doubles as the centre of Morocco's petrol industry. The two might seem incompatible, but Mohammedia, which until the 1960s was little more than a decaying fishing village (then known as Fedala), manages to keep the two activities apart. Site of the SAMIR oil refinery, it is one of the country's busiest ports, the traffic being almost entirely devoted to petroleum products. At the height of summer, the place tends

MOROCCO

**PLACES TO STAY**

12 Hôtel Miramar
13 Sabah Hotel (in construction)
14 Hôtel Samir
15 Hôtel Argana
18 Hôtel Ennasr
22 Hôtel Castel

**PLACES TO EAT**

1 Restaurant des Sports
2 Restaurant La Friture
3 Restaurant Sans Pareil
4 Diner Grill
7 Restaurant du Parc
23 Café de Paris

**OTHER**

5 Total Service Station
6 Centre Culturel Français
8 Ranch Club
9 Church
10 Post Office (PTT)
11 BMCE Bank
16 Mosque
17 Royal Air Maroc
19 Douche Publique
20 BMCI Bank
21 Petrom Service Station
24 Buses to Casablanca
25 Train Station

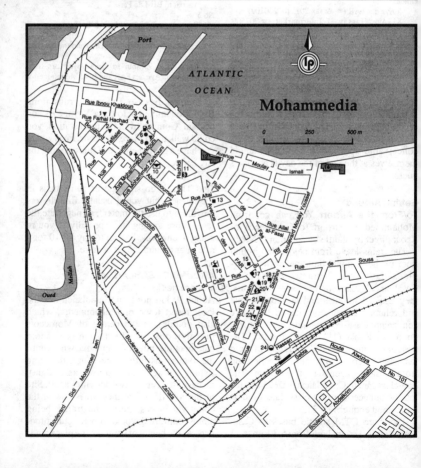

to fill to bursting with Casablancans, but out of season it makes a pleasant place to stop off for a day or two. The walls of an old kasbah still stand, but there is nothing much to see.

It's an easy day trip from Casablanca and not hard to find your way around. When you arrive by train or bus, head down the street leading north-west directly away from the station and you arrive on Ave Abderrahmane Sarghini. Turn right and you can continue right down to the beach. Ave des FAR runs off a roundabout (note the BMCI bank) about 100 metres down Ave Abderrahmane Sarghini to the main restaurant area, the Hôtel Miramar and the western end of the beach.

**Information** The tourist office (☎ 324199) is at 14 Rue El-Jahid. The main post office (PTT) is on Ave Mohammed Zerktouni, a couple of blocks in from the beach. Several banks have branches in Mohammedia. BMCI is closest to the train station, just opposite the kasbah on Ave des FAR. There are no ATMs. If the banks are closed, you can change money in the Hôtel Miramar. There's even a small Centre Culturel Français, in an arcade off Rue de Fès.

**Places to Stay** There are three cheapies. Hôtel Castel (☎ 322584) and Hôtel Ennasr (☎ 322373), close to one another on Ave Abderrahmane Sarghini, are similar and offer only cold showers. Doubles are Dr 70; singles are Dr 40 in the Castel and Dr 60 in the Ennasr. The Hôtel Argana, down a side street off Ave des FAR and two blocks west of the abovementioned roundabout, is much the same. There are douches for men and women a block back towards the roundabout.

Otherwise, there's the Hôtel Samir (☎ 310

770; fax 323330), with singles/ doubles for Dr 300/370, or the town's premier establishment, the Hôtel Miramar (☎ 322021; fax 324613), with rooms for Dr 620/740. Another four-star hotel, the Sabah, is being built on Ave des FAR.

**Places to Eat** The waterfront is lined with cafés, and there are a few standard hole-in-the-wall places on Ave des FAR and in the area around the train station. There is also a collection of decent restaurants around Rue de Fès and its continuation, Rue Farhai Hachad, west of the Miramar. Not surprisingly, fish is the theme.

The Restaurant La Friture, on Rue Ibn Tumert, offers fish and salad or tajine for as little as Dr 20. Virtually across the road is the Restaurant des Sports, a classier and very pleasant place. Farther east down the Rue Farhai Hachad is the popular Restaurant Sans Pareil, which serves a variety of food, with main courses starting at about Dr 50. The Diner Grill, a little farther on, is a more modest place, but the food is OK.

Overlooking the park at Ave Mohammed Zerktouni is the Restaurant du Parc. For a little nightlife, try the Ranch Club next door.

**Getting There & Away** Bus No 900 is virtually a suburban bus, running regularly between a stop by Casa-Port train station and the square in front of Mohammedia's train station. It costs Dr 5.50. The 2nd-class (normal) train fare is Dr 10.

**Getting Around** You're highly unlikely to need them, but there are lime-green petits taxis should you be in a hurry to get somewhere. A couple of buses run down to the beach from the square in front of the train station.

# The Atlantic – South of Casablanca

From Casablanca, the Atlantic coast stretches some 350 km towards Essaouira in the south-west, where it then rounds off at Cap Sim and drops south to Agadir, before again pursuing a more south-westerly course, to the tiny coastal town of Tarfaya, just north of the Western Sahara desert.

Along the way down the coast from Casa, you're reminded of Europe's long history of interference on the Moroccan seaboard. Azemmour, El-Jadida, Safi, Essaouira and Agadir were all at one time European (mostly Portuguese) military and commercial bridgeheads, and all but Agadir retain the architectural evidence of this. Agadir, the country's premier beach resort, is where modern Europeans, in the guise of package tourists, choose to invade the country. In between these towns are plenty of beaches and some stunning, wild coastal scenery. From Agadir, you can make several excursions, such as to Taroudannt, a 'real' Moroccan city with no ville nouvelle. From there you could head on into the High Atlas and Marrakesh.

# Central Coast

## EL-JADIDA

Situated 96 km south of Casablanca, El-Jadida is one of history's could-have-beens. The port town, established by the Portuguese, was destined by French protectorate authorities to be made into Morocco's main port, but the foreign Casablanca merchant lobby put paid to these plans, and El-Jadida was relegated to the second division. Its principal activities revolve around maintaining sardine fishing fleets. The historic centre of this quiet, relaxed town of 150,000 is one of the best preserved examples of Portuguese military architecture in the country. Like other Atlantic towns, El-Jadida is a hassle-free and pleasant place to spend a couple of days.

### History

The Portuguese founded Mazagan, as El-Jadida used to be known, in 1513, on the site of an old Almohad fortress, in the days when Portugal was building up a maritime trading empire that would stretch as far as China and Japan. Mazagan was to become their main Atlantic entrepôt in Morocco, and they held on to it until 1769, when, following a siege by Sultan Sidi Mohammed bin Abdallah, the Portuguese were forced to evacuate the fortress. Although they left with little more than the clothes they stood in, the ramparts were mined and, at the last moment, blown to smithereens, taking with them a good part of the besieging army.

The walls of the fortress lay in ruins until 1820, when they were rebuilt by Sultan Moulay Abd ar-Rahman. The Moroccans who took over the town after the Portuguese withdrawal preferred to settle outside the walls of the fortress. The medina inside the walls was largely neglected until the mid-19th century, when it was recolonised by European merchants following the establishment of a series of 'open ports' along the Moroccan coast.

A large and influential Jewish community became established at this time. The Jews controlled trade with the interior and particularly with Marrakesh. And, contrary to common Moroccan practice, the Jews of El-Jadida were not confined to their own separate quarter (the mellah).

Tourism and a prosperous agricultural hinterland have made the modern town an animated and growing commercial centre, and this is reflected in its clean look and busy atmosphere.

### Orientation

El-Jadida faces north-east onto the Atlantic, and the protection this affords partly accounts for the town's suitability as a port. Coming from Casablanca, the Cité Portugaise (the old Portuguese fortress) is at the north-western end of town. The focal point of the town is the pedestrianised Place Hansali, and you'll find the post office, banks, tourist office and some of the hotels in the cluster of streets just to the south of it. The bus and grand taxi stations are a good km south-east of the town centre, and the railway station so far out as to make it useless.

## Information

**Tourist Office** The Délégation Provinciale du Tourisme (☎ 342724, 342704) is in the Chambre de Commerce, Rue Ibn Khaldoun, and is open from 8.30 am to noon and 2.30 to 6.30 pm Monday to Friday. They have a few useful handouts, including hotel and restaurant lists – why can't more of the offices in Morocco do this? There is what appears to be a very closed syndicat d'initiative opposite the Municipal Theatre.

**Money** Several banks have branches here, including the BMCE and BMCI. You can change cash and cheques in the Bank al-Maghrib, but the process takes forever.

**Post & Telecommunications** The post and phone offices are together, on the block bounded by Ave Mohammed V and Ave Jamia al-Arabia. They are open Monday to Friday from 8.30 am to noon and 2.30 to 6 pm. There are card phones outside the office, on Ave Jamia al-Arabia.

**Medical Services** There's a night pharmacy (☎ 343928) at 59 Place Abdelkrim al-Khattabi.

## Cité Portugaise

The Cité Portugaise is the main point of interest. Although its enclosed medina has suffered from neglect, it's still inhabited and well worth exploring. There are two entrance gates to the fortress; the southernmost one, which is more convenient, opens onto the main street through the medina. The street

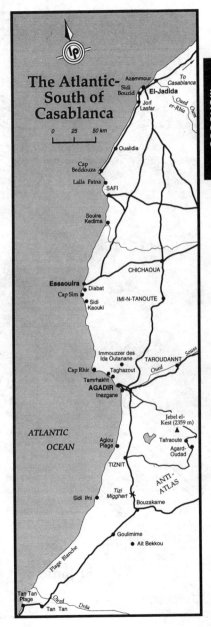

MOROCCO

MOROCCO

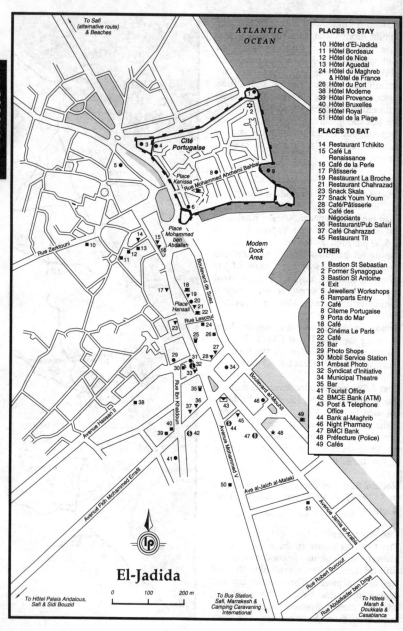

ATLANTIC OCEAN

Cité Portugaise

Place Kanissa

Place Mohammed Ahchemi Bahbai

Rue Lescoul

Modern Dock Area

Place Mohammed ben Abdallah

Rue Zerktouni

Boulevard de Suez

Place Hansali

Rue Lescoul

Boulevard al-Mouhit

Avenue Hassan II

Rue Ibn Khaldoun

Avenue Mohammed V

Avenue Jama al-Arabia

Ave al-Jaich al-Malaki

To Safi
(alternative route)
& Beaches

To Hôtel Palais Andalous,
Safi & Sidi Bouzid

To Bus Station,
Safi, Marrakesh &
Camping Caravaning
International

To Hôtels
Marah &
Doukkala &
Casablanca

Avenue Ftéh Mohammed Errafii

Rue Robert Surcouf

Rue Abdelkader ben Driga

0      100      200 m

**El-Jadida**

### PLACES TO STAY

10  Hôtel d'El-Jadida
11  Hôtel Bordeaux
12  Hôtel de Nice
13  Hôtel Aguedal
24  Hôtel du Maghreb
    & Hôtel de France
26  Hôtel du Port
38  Hôtel Moderne
39  Hôtel Provence
40  Hôtel Bruxelles
50  Hôtel Royal
51  Hôtel de la Plage

### PLACES TO EAT

14  Restaurant Tchikito
15  Café La
    Renaissance
16  Café de la Perle
17  Pâtisserie
19  Restaurant La Broche
21  Restaurant Chahrazad
23  Snack Skala
27  Snack Youm Youm
28  Café/Pâtisserie
33  Café des
    Négociants
36  Restaurant/Pub Safari
37  Café Chahrazad
45  Restaurant Tit

### OTHER

1   Bastion St Sebastian
2   Former Synagogue
3   Bastion St Antoine
4   Exit
5   Jewellers' Workshops
6   Ramparts Entry
7   Café
8   Citerne Portugaise
9   Porta do Mar
18  Café
20  Cinéma Le Paris
22  Café
25  Bar
29  Photo Shops
30  Mobil Service Station
31  Ambsat Photo
32  Syndicat d'Initiative
34  Municipal Theatre
35  Bar
41  Tourist Office
42  BMCE Bank (ATM)
43  Post & Telephone
    Office
44  Bank al-Maghrib
46  Night Pharmacy
47  BMCI Bank
48  Préfecture (Police)
49  Cafés

ends at the Porta do Mar, which is where, in the Portuguese era, ships used to discharge their cargo.

**Citerne Portugaise** About halfway down the main street of the Cité Portugaise is the famous Citerne Portugaise (Portuguese Cistern). Although the Romans built water-collection and storage cisterns similar to this, it remains a remarkable piece of architecture and engineering that has stood the test of time and is still functional. The reflection of the roof and 25 arched pillars in the water covering the floor creates a dramatic and beautiful effect. This hasn't escaped the attention of various film directors, who have staged scenes for several movies here. Perhaps best known of all is Orson Welles' *Othello*, some of whose most stunning scenes were done in the cistern. It's open seven days a week from 8.30 am to noon and 2.30 to 6 pm (sometimes later). Entry costs Dr 10. If you want, you can pay a little extra for a guide.

**Medina** The Portuguese built a number of churches within the medina, but unfortunately, they're all closed. You see the principal one, the **Church of the Assumption**, as soon as you enter the main gateway of the medina. Even if it were possible to visit them, however, you'd see little of their original features, since they were taken over and used for secular purposes long ago. Even the **Great Mosque**, adjacent to the Church of the Assumption, used to be a lighthouse. Just inside the Bastion of St Sebastian, on the extreme northern seaward side, you can enter a one-time synagogue; again, there is precious little to see inside nowadays.

**Ramparts** Entry to the ramparts, which you can walk all the way around, is through the large door at the end of the tiny cul-de-sac which is first on the right after entering the fortress. The man with the key for this is usually hanging around; if not, he won't be far away. There's no charge, but he'll expect a tip either when you enter or when he lets you out at the far side (more often than not,

the gates are open at both ends, but if the exit door is shut, you may have to hammer for several minutes before the guardian arrives).

### Beaches
There are beaches to the north and south of town, although the ones to the north occasionally get polluted by oil. They're pleasant enough out of season but can get very crowded during July and August. Possibly the best of them is Sidi Bouzid (see below), about 10 km out of El-Jadida.

### Places to Stay – bottom end
**Camping** *Camping Caravaning International* (☎ 342755), on Ave des Nations Unies, is well outside the town centre, about a 15-minute walk south-east of the bus station. It's a shame, because this is one of the better, shadier Moroccan camp sites. It costs Dr 12 a person, Dr 6.50 per car, Dr 10 to pitch a tent, Dr 5 for a hot shower and Dr 11 for electricity.

**Hotels** Because this is a seaside resort, you will have to be prepared to pay much higher prices in the summer months in some of the hotels – it's called market forces. The hotels also fill up quickly then, so finding a decent, cheap room will not be easy.

There is a trio of cheapies in some lanes a couple of hundred metres from the fortress. The cheapest of them is the *Hôtel Aguedal*, a very basic locanda-style place offering beds in little rooms around a courtyard for Dr 15 a head. The *Hôtel de Nice* (☎ 352272), 15 Rue Mohammed Smiha, has tidy but tiny rooms for Dr 52/80, and very much has the air of a brothel. The best of the three is the *Hôtel Bordeaux* (☎ 342356), 47 Rue Moulay Ahmed Tahiri, whose pleasant if smallish rooms are gathered around a covered courtyard. There is a hot shower on the 1st floor (Dr 5). Singles/doubles/triples cost Dr 40/60/80.

In the much busier local market area, the *Hôtel d'El Jadida* (☎ 340178), on Rue Zerktouni, offers simple rooms, with washbasins, bidets and big beds but no showers. You pay Dr 41/62/83.

There are two very cheap places just off Place Hansali, the *Hôtel du Maghreb* and *Hôtel de France* (☎ 342181), owned by the same guy. Some of the big rooms, with heavy wooden ceilings, look out to sea. They cost Dr 25/40, and a hot shower is Dr 4. All up, it's one of the better budget deals. Not so hot is the *Hôtel du Port* (☎ 342701), on Blvd de Suez. It's seedy and grubby and costs Dr 26/38.

Quite adequate but unspectacular is the *Hôtel Moderne* (☎ 343133), 21 Ave Hassan II. Rooms with basin and bidet cost Dr 52/78, but some are rather small and the whole place could do with a spring clean. Hot showers are Dr 6.

Handy for the bus station and reasonable value is the newly spruced-up *Hôtel Royal* (☎ 341100). It has some big, bright rooms, and some even have old-fashioned bathtubs. The only problem is that there is only cold water to put in them. Out-of-season prices are Dr 50/78, but they cheerfully admit to jacking them up a lot in summer. They have a bar and restaurant in a pleasant open courtyard.

The friendly *Hôtel de la Plage* (☎ 342 648), Ave Jamia al-Arabia, has more modest pretensionsis and is also handy for the bus station. It has clean, perfectly good rooms for Dr 45/60/85. There is hot water in the bath on the corridor (Dr 5).

Going up in price are two one-star places, both of them perfectly OK. At 40 Rue Ibn Khaldoun, the *Hôtel Bruxelles* (☎ 342072) is the easier of the two to find, and offers clean if somewhat spartan rooms with private bathroom for Dr 70/100 plus taxes.

The friendly but more expensive *Hôtel Suisse* (☎ 342816), 147 Rue Zerktouni, has singles/doubles without shower or toilet for Dr 85/110 and rooms with both for Dr 105/130. It's rather awkwardly placed, about a 10-minute walk south-west of the Cité Portugaise fortress, well away from the bus station.

### Places to Stay – middle

If you have the money, El-Jadida's only two-star hotel, the *Hôtel Provence* (☎ 342347; fax 352115), 42 Ave Fkih Mohammed Errafil, is still one of the most pleasant places in town. It costs Dr 121/149/204/269 (plus taxes) for rooms with private shower and toilet. Some of the rooms are definitely better than others. The hot water is very hot, and there is access to covered parking (Dr 10 a day). The Provence has a popular licensed restaurant that serves delicious food, with a choice of Moroccan, French and seafood specialities. A full meal with wine would cost about Dr 100 a head. Visa cards are accepted and English is spoken (the owner, Geoffrey Hurdidge, is English).

### Places to Stay – top end

If you can afford a touch of exotic – even florid – luxury, then the three-star *Hôtel Palais Andalous* (☎ 343745), Blvd Docteur de la Lanouy, is the hotel of choice. The place was converted in 1980 into a spacious (56-bed) hotel from a local pasha's residence. There are hectares of polished marble, stunning plasterwork, comfortable salons and a bar and restaurant. The rooms, a more modest version of the same thing, cost Dr 256/332/448 plus tax – excellent value. A garage is available if you have your own transport. The hotel is a little out of the way and can be awkward to find. Follow the orange 'hotel' signs up Ave Hassan II from the city centre and you will eventually stumble across it.

Going up in price, the most expensive hotel in El-Jadida is the *Hôtel Doukkala* (☎ 343737), Ave Jamia al-Arabia. This rather grim concrete bunker of a hotel has all the amenities you would expect of a four-star establishment, including a swimming pool and tennis courts. Singles/doubles cost Dr 312/394 plus taxes. Just nearby is the *Marah Hôtel* (☎ 344170), which is cheaper but of a poorer standard. Rooms cost Dr 178/226 with shower, Dr 228/276 with full bathroom.

### Places to Eat

The tourist office has a list of the more up-market restaurants in town.

Along the seafront on Blvd al-Mouhit is a whole line of cafés, which make good places to eat breakfast (coffee and pastries) for reasonable prices. There are a lot of cafés on Place Hansali, and also near Hôtel d'El-Jadida, on Rue Zerktouni.

For cheap eats, *Snack Youm Youm*, across the road from the Municipal Theatre, is a deservedly popular little place. A plate of meat (your choice of brochettes, sausages and several other items), rice, chips and tomato sauce costs Dr 13.

Fish enthusiasts should investigate the *Restaurant Tchikito*, in a side lane a short walk north-west of Place Hansali. A filling meal of fresh fried fish can cost as little as Dr 20.

*Restaurant La Broche*, on Place Hansali, is a homely, family-run little place that seems popular with expatriates in the area. The fish is poor but the brochettes are exceptionally good. A bowl of harira costs Dr 5 and a full meal will set you back about Dr 50.

On the other side of the cinema is the *Restaurant Chahrazad*. It's cheaper than the La Broche and the food is just as good. The only problem is that most of the items on the menu aren't available.

Don't forget the restaurant at the *Hôtel Provence* for a splurge in intimate surroundings. Another place worth investigating if you have some money to burn is the *Restaurant Tit*, just behind the post office.

### Entertainment

The *Royal*, *Provence* and *Palais Andalous* hotels all have bars; the most comfortable and 'barry' of them is the one in the Provence. There is a rough sort of bar next door to the Hôtel de la Plage, or try the *Pub Safari*, just down from the Provence. For movies, there's the *Cinéma Le Paris*, on Place Hansali.

### Getting There & Away

**Bus** The bus terminal (gare routière) is south-east of town on Rue Abdelmoumen el-Mouahidi, close to the junction with Ave Mohammed V. It's a 15-minute walk along Ave Mohammed V from the fortress.

There are buses to Casablanca, Rabat and Kenitra (window No 2), Azemmour (window No 5), Oualidia and Safi (window No 7) and Marrakesh (window No 8).

CTM has three runs to Casablanca: at 8.45 am (Dr 17; 2nd class), 11.15 am (Dr 23; 1st class) and 4.30 pm (mumtaz; Dr 27). There are at least 11 runs to Marrakesh (Dr 35; about 3½ to four hours). The fare to Azemmour is Dr 3. There is one bus to Safi at 6.30 am (Dr 30), and a couple more leave later in the day.

**Train** The train station is about three km out of town along the Marrakesh road. It's all highly impractical. You can get a train to Oujda at 8.10 am via Azemmour, Casablanca and all subsequent main stops. At 6.10 pm, there is a train to Casa-Voyageurs. There is a free bus service from the train station to the town centre; otherwise you can take a petit taxi.

**Taxi** Grands taxis gather along the side street next to the bus station. A place in a taxi to Azemmour is Dr 5.

### AROUND EL-JADIDA
#### Azemmour

While in El-Jadida, it's worth making a half-day excursion to this little-visited fortress town 15 km to the north. Here you'll find another monument to those energetic seafaring and fortress-building people, the Portuguese. Although they only stayed in Azemmour for a short while, from 1513 to 1541, it was sufficient time for them to build this fortress alongside the banks of the wide Oum er-Rbia. One of Morocco's largest rivers, the Oum er-Rbia rises in the Middle Atlas and empties into the sea about one km downriver from Azemmour. The best views of this fortress and its crumbling, whitewashed medina are from the bridge across the river.

Azemmour once had a thriving Jewish community, but since their exodus to Israel, their houses have fallen into ruin, with only the façades remaining in many cases. However, there is still a synagogue here, in

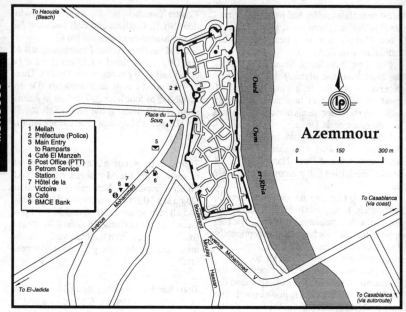

1 Mellah
2 Préfecture (Police)
3 Main Entry to Ramparts
4 Café El Manzeh
5 Post Office (PTT)
6 Petrom Service Station
7 Hôtel de la Victoire
8 Café
9 BMCE Bank

Place du Souq

Oued Oum er-Rbia

To Haouzia (Beach)

Azemmour

0    150    300 m

To Casablanca (via coast)

To El-Jadida

To Casablanca (via autoroute)

reasonable shape, with lettering in Hebrew and English above the door saying 'Rabbi Abraham Moul Niss'.

The ramparts are open to visitors – the main entry is on the inside to the left after you enter the fortress town from Place du Souq. You could also enter by a door on the open square at the extreme north-eastern tip of the fort, but you might have to wait for the guardian to arrive with the keys. In all probability you'll have been waylaid by kids before he gets to you, and they will take over as your guides. Whether you get them or the official guardian/guide, you'll have to pay – no more than Dr 10.

Once up on the ramparts, the guide rattles off a plethora of dates, facts and not a little fantasy and carefully steers you under a live, high-tension electricity cable that loops across the walls at waist height at one point. After that, he walks you through the medina and brings you back to where you entered. The kids steer you under the same cable, but

in terms of explanation tend to stick to the obvious ('this, cannon').

There's nothing much of interest in the new part of town outside the ramparts, but if you get here early in the day and aren't in a hurry to get back to El-Jadida, you might like to visit the **beach** (Haouzia), which is about half an hour's walk from Place du Souq (signposted). When the wind's not howling, this is a pretty good beach.

**Information** The post office, a branch of the BMCE bank, a hotel and some cafés are located on Ave Mohammed V, the main road in from El-Jadida.

**Places to Stay & Eat** There are at least two basic hotels in Azemmour, the *Hôtel de la Victoire* (☎ 347157), 308 Ave Mohammed V and the *Hôtel Moulay Bouchaib*.

The *Café El Manzeh*, on Place du Souq, is the most pleasant of a series of cafés along the main road. In summer you could try *La*

*Perle*, a moderately priced restaurant on the beach (it's closed out of season).

**Getting There & Away** Local buses connect Azemmour with El-Jadida (Dr 3), but grands taxis (Dr 5 a head) are probably an easier bet as there are plenty of them. The bus station is located east of Ave Mohammed V, near the town centre. Some of the trains that go from Casablanca to El-Jadida also stop at Azemmour.

### Sidi Bouzid

About 10 km south of El-Jadida is one of the area's better beaches, Sidi Bouzid. You can get local bus No 2 there from Place Mohammed ben Abdallah, near the Portuguese fortress. There is a rather expensive place to stay, the *Motel Club Hacienda* (☎ 348311), which has a pool, a tennis court and its own restaurant. Doubles cost Dr 281.

### OUALIDIA

Seventy-six km down the coast from El-Jadida lies the slow but pleasant seaside fishing village of Oualidia. The drive (there are occasional buses) is a pleasant one, at least once you get past the Jorf Lasfar (formerly Cap Blanc) phosphate port. Your first impression of Oualidia as you arrive along the highway is of just another dusty roadside town. You have to take one of the turn-offs that lead quickly down to the village proper, situated between the sea and a lagoon. There's not much to do here, and out of the summer season it's quite dead. The village's main claim to fame is the oysters grown in the lagoon.

#### Places to Stay & Eat

The cheapest place to stay is *Camping Oualidiya* (Dr 3 a person, Dr 2 per car and Dr 30 per tent). There is no hot water.

Up on the main road is the *Hôtel La Lagune* (☎ 366477), which offers double rooms with half-board for Dr 350. The *Hôtel Shems* (☎ 366478), back in the village proper, costs Dr 400 for the same arrangement.

About 40 km north of Oualidia is a well-located unclassified hotel looking out over the Atlantic, the *Hôtel La Brise*.

The hotel restaurants and two others, *L'Araignée* and *Les Roches*, offer seafood menus – or you could just buy some from any of the fishers getting around town with the day's catch and cook it up yourself.

### SAFI (ASFI)

Largely a modern fishing port and industrial centre, Safi sits on the Atlantic coast in a steep crevasse formed by the Oued (river) Chabah. Its industrial side is pretty obvious if you arrive from the north. A lot of Morocco's raw phosphate rock and fertilisers pass through here, the latter produced in chemical plants south of the town.

The sardine fleet is one of the world's biggest, although the canning industry has declined from the peaks it reached under the French protectorate – the majority of the canneries on the southern side of the city seem to have been closed for a long time.

The city centre has a lively and charming walled medina and souq, with battlements dating from the brief Portuguese period of occupation. Safi is also well known for its traditional potteries, and even if you are not interested in buying any souvenirs, it is worth walking around the potteries to see how they work.

#### History

Safi's natural harbour was known to the Phoenicians, and was probably used by the Romans later on. Involvement with Europeans didn't really begin until the Portuguese arrived on the scene, in 1508. By then, an important religious and cultural centre had already been in place since its foundation in the 12th century by the Almohads. The Portuguese built a fortress, using Essaouira as their base, but despite its monumental proportions (as with all Portuguese military installations), they didn't stay at Safi long, abandoning it in 1541.

This event didn't herald the end of European contact. In the late 17th century the French established a consulate at the port and were responsible for signing trading treaties

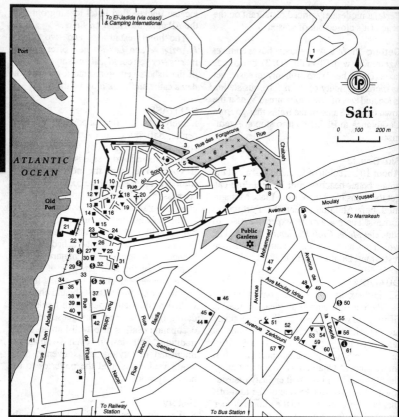

with the indigenous rulers. By the 19th century, however, the port had faded into insignificance. Its revival came in the 20th century, with the expansion of the sardine fishing fleet and the construction of a huge industrial complex for the manufacture fertilisers and sulphuric and phosphoric acids using local pyrites and phosphate ores.

## Orientation

The bus and train stations are a few km to the south of the town centre – a long walk or a bus or taxi ride. The post office and the bulk of the cheaper hotels, restaurants and banks

are on or near Place de l'Indépendance and just inside the medina walls. More expensive hotels, cafés, the main post office and the syndicat d'initiative are up the hill in the area around Place Mohammed V.

## Information

**Tourist Office** The syndicat d'initiative (☎ 464553) is on a lane a little way off Place Mohammed V. Rachid, the man who staffs it, is friendly and keen to help out, although he can't offer you anything very concrete in terms of maps and the like. The office is open from 9 am to noon and 3 to 6.30 pm.

## PLACES TO STAY

11 Hôtel Sabah
13 Hôtel & Café L'Avenir
14 Hôtel de Paris
15 Hôtel Majestic
16 Hôtel Essaouira
17 Nameless Hotel
34 Hôtel Sevillana
39 Hôtel L'Océan
42 Hôtel Novelty
43 Hôtel Anis
44 Hôtel Atlantide
46 Hôtel Safir
56 Hôtel Assif

## PLACES TO EAT

1 Café La Chope
3 Restaurant Les Potiers
10 Juice Stand
12 Café
19 Cheap Fish Restaurants
22 Café/Pâtisserie M'Zoughen

25 Restaurant Gegene
26 Café/Bar de la Poste
27 Restaurant de Safi
35 Café Restaurant El Bahira
38 Cheap Café
40 Cheap Café
41 Café Safina
53 Café Triomphe
54 Glacier Jour et Nuit
55 Café La Cascade
57 Café al-Marjan
58 Café Oukaïmeden
59 Café Samif

## OTHER

2 Arches of Bab Khouas
4 Pottery Souq
5 Bab Chabah
6 Cemetery
7 Kechla
8 Musée National de Céramique
9 Mobil Service Station

18 Great Mosque
20 Chapelle Portugaise
21 Qasr al-Bahr
23 Post Office
24 Local Buses (No 4 to Sidi Bouzid)
28 BMCE Bank
29 BMCI Bank
30 Zanzi Bar
31 Shell Service Station
32 Bank al-Maghrib
33 Place de l'Indépendance
36 Crédit du Maroc
37 Cinema
45 Cinéma Atlantide
47 Préfecture (Police)
48 Hôtel de Ville
49 Place Mohammed V
50 Banque Populaire
51 Souna Mosque
52 Post Office (PTT)
60 Studio Samif (Kodak)
61 Syndicat d'Initiative

**Money** The BMCE and BMCI have branches on Place de l'Indépendance. The Banque Populaire is on Place Mohammed V.

**Post & Telecommunications** The phone section of the main post office (PTT), near Place Mohammed V, is open seven days a week from 8 am to 9.45 pm.

**Film & Photography** There is a Kodak processing shop called Studio Samif, on Ave Zerktouni.

### Qasr al-Bahr

Overlooking the Atlantic and in impressively good shape is the main fortress erected by the Portuguese to enforce their short-lived control here. Built not only to protect the port but also to house the town governor, the 'Castle on the Sea' was restored in 1963.

There are good views from the south-west bastion, as well as a number of old Spanish and Dutch cannons dating from the early 17th century. Notably, two of the cannons were manufactured in Rotterdam in 1619 and two in the Hague in 1621.

Just to the right of the entrance is the prison tower. The prisoners went to the bottom, but you can climb to the top for some pretty views across the medina. Visiting hours are 8.30 am to noon and 2.30 to 6 pm and entry costs Dr 10. You can ask for a guide if you want.

### Medina

Across the street from the Qasr al-Bahr lies the walled medina. Dominating the medina at its eastern end is the **Kechla**, a massive defensive structure with ramps, gunnery platforms and living quarters. It houses the **Musée National de Céramique**, a moderately interesting display of Safi pottery (although to be honest, a good walk around the potteries themselves is more interesting). The views over the medina and the Qasr al-Bahr, however, make a visit worthwhile.

Inside the medina are the remains of the so-called **Chapelle Portugaise**, which would have become Safi's cathedral had the Portuguese remained; as it turned out, they stayed only long enough to complete the choir. To get to it, head up Rue du Souq (the main thoroughfare through the medina) from Blvd Front de la Mer and turn right just after the **Great Mosque**. It's about 100 metres down the alley. Long used as a hammam, it's not in great condition. Shortly before Rue du Souq leads out of the medina, you'll notice, off to your left, a colourful **pottery souq**. The shopkeepers in here are pretty low-key, and little inclined to bargain. If you are intent on buying a few pieces, take the time to look at the different shops and establish some prices – then head on out to the potteries themselves and see if you can't strike a better deal. If not, you can always come back down to the market.

### Potteries

Rue du Souq passes out of the medina by Bab Chabah. Outside this gate and to the left, you'll see an enormous series of arches; they look as though they were an aqueduct at one time but in fact were probably associated with the defensive walls of the medina. Straight ahead, on the hill opposite Bab Chabah, are Safi's famous potteries.

Opinions vary wildly on the quality of the ceramics produced here. Some of the many cooperatives devote themselves to the rather mundane production of tiles (the green variety you see on many important buildings throughout the country), but many manufacture a wide range of jars, vases, decorative plates, candlesticks and other objects. It is well worth taking a walk around and getting a look inside the workshops. Apart from the kilns, you can see potters moulding the clay for tiles and utensils, enamelling and glazing. If you're collared by a guide (possibly an asset here for the uninitiated), buying a small item or two from 'his' cooperative will save you forking out the usual guide's tip (not that there's anything to stop you paying a tip as well).

### Places to Stay – bottom end

**Camping** About three km north of town, just into the coast road to El-Jadida, is the *Camping International*. It's a reasonable site, and much cooler than the town below in the hot summer months. They charge Dr 10 per person, Dr 9 per car, Dr 7 to pitch a tent, Dr 10 for a hot shower and Dr 20 to use the pool. You'll need to get a petit taxi up here from the centre or the bus station.

**Hotels** There's a fair choice of budget hotels in Safi, most of them clustered around the port end of Rue du Souq and along Rue de R'bat.

Inside the medina itself, the *Hôtel Essaouira* (☎ 464809) has comparatively small and gloomy rooms for Dr 30/50/60. Hot showers are Dr 5. It's adequate. Much the same is the *Hôtel de Paris*, where rooms with big saggy beds cost Dr 30 to Dr 70. Hot showers are Dr 5. A little farther in is a hotel with no name. It's cramped, but quite clean and costs Dr 30/50, including cold showers. At the same price (but a desperate choice) is the *Hôtel Sabah*, a grim place with no shower at all.

Best value is the *Hôtel Majestic*, right next to the medina wall, at the junction of Ave Moulay Youssef and Place de l'Indépendance. It offers very clean, pleasant rooms with washbasin and bidet for Dr 30/60/90; shared showers with hot water are Dr 5 extra. The best rooms look out onto the Qasr al Bahr and the ocean. The staff are friendly and one of the managers speaks French, Spanish and some English.

Another good place is the *Hôtel L'Avenir*, which charges the same as the Majestic. The rooms have toilets and some have cold showers. The drawback is the café and small eatery inside, which can make it a bit noisy. There are good views from the roof.

On the south side of Place de l'Indépendance you can get yourself a tiny room for Dr 30/60 in the *Hôtel Sevillana*, Impasse Ben Hassan. The old guy who runs it claims there are hot showers for Dr 7. This place is not an attractive option.

Considerably better, but not up to the

Majestic's standard, is the *Hôtel L'Océan*
(☎ 464207). The rooms are quite OK, and
there is a shower (Dr 5 for a hot one) on each
floor. Rooms again cost Dr 30/60. The *Hôtel
Novelty* (☎ 422999) is unused to foreign
guests. Its rooms (Dr 30/50) seem a little
grim, but they are kept clean and the beds are
fine. There are no showers, but there is a
hammam nearby.

### Places to Stay – middle

The only mid-range hotel down in the centre
is the two-star *Hôtel Anis* (☎ 463078), Rue
de R'bat, where you can get a comfortable
room with private shower and toilet for Dr
118/141. They have a restaurant and café,
too, and limited parking.

The other mid-range hotels are higher up
in the city, around Place Mohammed V.
Rooms at the *Hôtel Assif* (☎ 622311; fax
621862), Ave de la Liberté, are well decked-
out, with heating, telephone and en suite
bathrooms (Dr 157/187). The *Hôtel Les
Mimosas* (☎ 463208), Rue Ibn Zeidoun, can
be a little confusing to find; follow Ave de la
Liberté off the map and the hotel is on the
second block down a small street off to the
right (coming from Place Mohammed V). It
charges the same as the Assif, for rooms that
are a little the worse for wear. The hotel has

its own restaurant and bar, and across the
road is the *Golden Fish* nightclub.

### Places to Stay – top end

There are two four-star hotels in Safi, the
cheaper of the two being the *Hôtel Atlantide*
(☎ 462160/1), Rue Chaouki, at Dr 226/273
for singles/doubles. It has a little more character than its more expensive cousin up the
road, the *Hôtel Safir* (☎ 464299), Ave
Zerktouni. This one charges Dr 362/420 plus
taxes.

### Places to Eat

There are several cafés (and a good juice
stand) along Rue du Souq, and at the port end
a few snack stalls are generally set up at
night, but the real treat in Safi is sampling the
pokey little fish eateries. Several of them are
clustered behind the Great Mosque, and it's
worth making the effort to find them. A meal
of superbly fresh fish with chips, salads and
soft drinks will cost about Dr 20 per person.

Near the main port installations at the
northern end of town is a bunch of similar
places, run by somewhat more aggressive
people. Driving through here, you'll probably encounter fishers rushing out in front of
you waving half-cooked fish.

The *Café Restaurant El Bahia*, which

Fruitsellers in Rue du Souq, Safi

takes up the whole top side of Place de l'Indépendance, is a tourist trap. You get the same unexceptional food in the sit-down part as at the takeaway bar downstairs, and pay a lot more for the pleasure. The *Restaurant de Safi* and the *Restaurant Gegene*, on the same square, are much the same story. The *Restaurant Les Potiers*, outside Bab Chabah, looks promising from a distance but is little more than an unappetising café.

The only real alternative to these places are the restaurants in the bigger hotels.

There is an extremely pleasant fish restaurant a few km north of Safi on the coast road to Sidi Bouzid, *Le Refuge* (☎ 464354). It's closed on Mondays and is a little pricey, but is possibly *the* choice restaurant in the area. You'll need your own car or a petit taxi to get there.

There is no shortage of cafés along Place de l'Indépendance and Rue de R'bat. Up around Place Mohammed V, there is a wide selection of slightly fancier places, the most interesting being the cavernous *Al-Marjan*. You can pick up an ice cream at the *Glacier Jour et Nuit*.

### Entertainment

You can get a soothing ale is the *Café/Bar de la Poste*, on Place de l'Indépendance, and a couple of the other cafés here may well serve alcohol inside. Otherwise, you're obliged to try the bars in the bigger hotels.

### Getting There & Away

**Bus** Most of the CTM buses stopping in Safi originate elsewhere, so it might be a good idea to book in advance. Generally, though, you shouldn't have much trouble on the main runs. CTM has six buses a day to Casablanca, starting from 4.30 am. Its Marrakesh departure is at 8 pm and costs Dr 28.50. A bus to El-Jadida leaves at 8.30 am (Dr 37; 1st class) and another at 2.30 pm (Dr 24.50; 2nd class).

SATAS, the biggest bus company operating in southern Morocco, has a 7 am departure for Tan Tan, calling at Essaouira, Agadir and Tiznit on the way. It also has connections for Taroudannt and Tafraoute.

The Transit bus company has a bus to

Essaouira at 9 pm (Dr 32.50), and another for Agadir and Tiznit at 10 am.

To the right of the CTM window is a booth advertising five runs a day to Essaouira and two early morning buses to El-Jadida.

Transport Chekkouri has nine buses a day to the main bus station in Casablanca. The same company offers six runs a day to Marrakesh and four to Agadir.

**Train** There are two trains daily from Safi. The first, at 6 am, can get you to Oujda via Casablanca or Marrakesh – for either destination, you must change at Benguerir. The second goes to Rabat via Casablanca at 5 pm. Again, you must change at Benguerir.

### Getting Around

Both the bus terminal (Ave Président Kennedy) and the railway station (Rue de R'bat) are quite some way from the centre of town, so it would be a good idea to either take a bus (No 7 from the bus station) or share a taxi from these places to the centre (Place de l'Indépendance). A bypass (Blvd Hassan II) circles the main part of town, so buses don't go through the centre.

## AROUND SAFI
### Beaches

The beaches in the immediate vicinity of Safi are not much chop, so you need to go a little farther afield. To the north you have the choice of **Lalla Fatna** (nine km) and **Cap Beddouza** (20 km). In summer there are local buses to both from Place de l'Indépendance. Otherwise, you'll have to rent a grand taxi if you don't have your own transport. The coast road along the first 40 km or so north of Safi is particularly breathtaking in parts.

About 30 km to the south is **Souira Kedima**. This place is not special, whatever anyone in Safi may tell you; however shortly before it, after you've cleared the Maroc Phosphore plant, there are a couple of wild and woolly Atlantic beaches that beg to be stopped at – if the wind dies down.

# Essaouira

Essaouira is the most popular of the coastal towns with independent travellers, and only rarely do you see package tourists here. The town has a magnificent beach that curves for miles to the south, and its atmosphere is in complete contrast to that of the souq cities of Marrakesh, Fès, Meknès and Tangier. It can be summed up in one word: relaxation. It is also Morocco's best-known windsurfing centre, and increasingly promotes itself as 'Wind City, Afrika'. Indeed, the Atlantic winds can be powerful, which is good news for windsurfers, but for much of the year bad news for sunbathers!

The fortifications of the old city are a mixture of Portuguese, French and Berber military architecture, and their massiveness lends a powerful mystique to the town. Inside them it's all light and charm. You'll find narrow lanes, whitewashed houses with blue painted doors, tranquil squares, artisans in tiny workshops beavering away at fragrant thuya wood, friendly cafés, and barely a hustler in sight. Here, for a refreshing change, you aren't made to feel like a walking wallet.

The bad news is that Essaouira's reputation is spreading, and its tranquillity can be stretched to breaking point in summer. Rooms can be difficult to find even outside the summer months.

## History

As far back as the 7th century BC, Phoenician sailors had discovered this part of the Moroccan coast, and it is believed the Romans followed in their footsteps. The main evidence for this comes from the little offshore islands, which were celebrated in ancient times for being the site of manufacture of purple dyes (much used by the Romans). It is from this activity that the islets derived their name: the Purple Isles (Îles Purpuraires).

It was the Portuguese who established a commercial and military bridgehead here towards the end of the 15th century, which they named Mogador. They lost it in 1541, however, and the coastal town fell into decline.

Most of what stands today is the result of a curious experiment. In 1765, Sultan Sidi Mohammed bin Abdallah hired a French architect, Théodore Cornut, to design a city suitable for foreign traders. Known from then on as Essaouira, it became an open commercial link with Europe until the French protectorate was established, in 1912, at which time it was rebaptised Mogador and lost much of its importance. With independence, in 1956, it again became Essaouira.

## Orientation

Essaouira is a pretty compact place. Most of the cheaper hotels, restaurants, cafés, banks and shops are concentrated in or near the western third of the old town. The bus station and grands taxis are about one km to the north-east of the walled town, in a particularly depressing part of Essaouira's small-scale version of urban sprawl.

## Information

Despite the signs, there is no functioning tourist office. There are three banks around Place Prince Moulay Hassan. All are good for exchange, and the BMCE should do credit-card cash advances.

The post office is a 10-minute walk from Place Prince Moulay Hassan. The phone office, two doors down on the left, is open Monday to Saturday but only during normal working hours. An alternative for making phone calls and sending faxes is Jack's Kiosk, on Place Prince Moulay Hassan.

## Ramparts

You can walk along most of the ramparts on the seaward part of town and visit the two main forts (skalas) during daylight hours. The **Skala du Port** (closed at lunchtimes) has an entry charge of Dr 10. This bastion was designed to protect the town's sea trade, and today affords picturesque views over the busy fishing port and of the Île de Mogador.

MOROCCO

MOROCCO

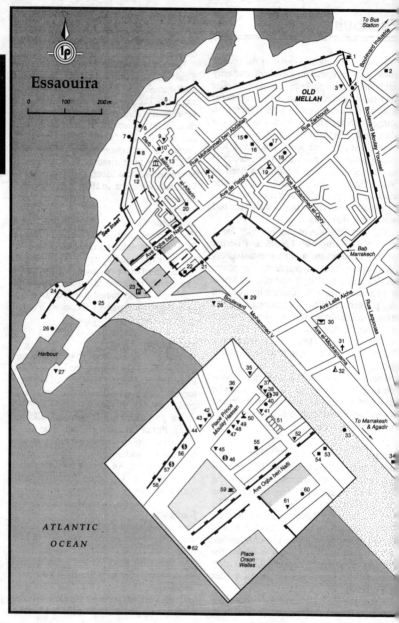

# Essaouira

0    100    200m

*To Bus Station*

*Boulevard Industrie*

1
2
3

OLD MELLAH

*Boulevard Moulay Youssef*

5

6

7

Derb

9
10
Kasbah
13
11
al-Attarin
8
12

*Rue Mohammed ben Abdallah*

15
16

17

18

19

14

20

*Ave de l'Istiqlal*

*Rue Zerktouni*

*Rue Mohammed el-Qory*

Bab Marrakech

Sea Inset

*Ave Oqba ben Nafi*

22    21

23

24

25

26

Harbour

27

29

28

*Boulevard Mohammed V*

*Ave Lalla Aicha*

*Rue Laayoune*

30

31

32

*Ave el Mouahidin*

To Marrakesh & Agadir

33

34

35

36
37
38
39
40
41

42
43
44

Place Prince Moulay Hassan

50
48  49
47

51

52

45  46

55

56
57

58

59

53
54

60

61

ATLANTIC OCEAN

62

Place Orson Welles

## PLACES TO STAY

| | |
|---|---|
| 2 | Hôtel Argana |
| 8 | Hôtel Smara |
| 10 | Hôtel Majestic |
| 12 | Hôtel des Remparts |
| 14 | Hôtel Chakib |
| 16 | Hôtel des Amis |
| 20 | Hôtel Tafraout |
| 22 | Hôtel du Tourisme |
| 29 | Hôtel des Iles |
| 32 | Camping International |
| 34 | Hôtel Tafoukt |
| 42 | Hôtel Beau Rivage |
| 53 | Hôtel Mechouar |
| 54 | Hôtel Sahara |
| 55 | Hôtel Villa Maroc |

## PLACES TO EAT

| | |
|---|---|
| 3 | Cheap Eats |
| 9 | Restaurant Riad |
| 13 | Restaurant El Khaima |
| 27 | Chez Sam Restaurant |
| 28 | Restaurant Chalet de la Plage |
| 35 | Sam's Fast Food |
| 36 | Café/Pâtisserie L'Opéra |
| 37 | Café de la Place |
| 38 | Driss Pâtisserie |
| 41 | Chez Toufik |
| 43 | Café de France |
| 44 | Café Marrakech |
| 45 | Restaurant Essalam |
| 48 | Snack Stand |
| 49 | Jack's Kiosk |
| 52 | Restaurant l'Horloge |
| 58 | Restaurant Bab Laachour |
| 61 | Restaurant El Minzah |

## OTHER

| | |
|---|---|
| 1 | Café |
| 4 | Bab Doukkala |
| 5 | Bab al-Bahr |
| 6 | Entry to Ramparts |
| 7 | Skala de la Ville |
| 11 | Museum |
| 15 | Spice, Herbs & Cures Shop |
| 17 | Souqs |
| 18 | Souqs |
| 19 | Mosque |
| 21 | Bab es-Sebaa |
| 23 | Car Parking |
| 24 | Skala du Port |
| 25 | Customs & Fish Market |
| 26 | Shipyards |
| 30 | Post Office (PTT) |
| 31 | Church |
| 33 | Fanatic Fun Center & Café |
| 39 | BMCE Bank |
| 40 | Carpet & Curio Shops |
| 46 | Crédit du Maroc |
| 47 | Afalkai Art |
| 50 | Mosque |
| 51 | Carpet & Curio Shops |
| 56 | Banque Populaire |
| 57 | Banque Commerciale du Maroc |
| 59 | Café |
| 60 | Galerie d'Art |
| 62 | Bab al-Minzah |

Orson Welles spent some time here, too, again working on his film *Othello*. A rather dreary little square was named in his honour in 1992.

The **Skala de la Ville** is more impressive still, with its collection of 18th and 19th-century brass cannon from various European countries, particularly Spain and Holland. There's no entry charge to this part.

Just off the coast to the south-west is the Ile de Mogador, on which there's another massive fortification. It's actually two islands and several tiny islets, the famed Purple Isles of antiquity. There is a disused prison on the biggest of the islands. These days, the islands are a sanctuary for Eleanore's falcon – a rare breed – and other birds. Visits are normally prohibited.

### Museum

The museum, on Darb Laalouj al-Attarin, has displays of jewellery, costumes and weapons. Given the history of this town, it could be better. It has, in any case, been closed for refurbishment since 1992. Maybe it'll look better if and when it reopens. If you're determined to get in, you may be able to convince someone to open it up. There is nothing to distinguish the museum from the surrounding buildings, so you'll have to ask one of the local shopkeepers to show you which one it is.

### Art Expositions

Essaouira plays host to a number of European artists, some of whom have bought houses and apartments in the old town. One of them is Frederic Damgaard, who runs a Galerie d'Art on Ave Oqba ben Nafii, where he and some of the others sometimes display their work.

### Beach & Watersports

The beach stretches some 10 km down the

coast to the sand dunes of Cap Sim. On the way you'll pass the ruins of an old fortress and pavilion partially covered in sand, as well as the wreck of a ship. As Essaouira gains in popularity, it is becoming one of the classic windsurfing destinations. Along the beach, shortly before the Hôtel Tafoukt, you'll find at least two places renting windsurfing equipment. Fanatic Fun Centre, a German-run place, charges Dr 100 per hour for full gear. Next door is a more recently established Moroccan equivalent which, when it gets properly up and running, should have competitive prices. Both organise horse-riding excursions along the beach towards Cap Sim (not cheap, and usually only possible in summer). Fanatic Fun Centre can organise more ambitious horse riding excursions farther into the interior, lasting up to a couple of weeks. Out of season, contact Ludmilla de Wendau (☎ 1-42.51.81.59), 6 Rue Garreau, 75018 Paris.

### Places to Stay – bottom end
**Camping** The best camp site is the one near Diabat (see the Diabat section).

*Camping International*, along Blvd Mohammed V in Essaouira, is nothing but a patch of dirt with no shade whatsoever. You'd have to be hard-up to stay here. In case you are, it costs Dr 7 per person, Dr 8 per car, Dr 10 for electricity and up to Dr 20 to pitch a tent. Hot showers are available.

**Hotels** The three places traditionally most popular with travellers continue to lead the way among the budget hotels. If you arrive later in the day, don't be surprised to find them full. The first (and probably the most attractive, because of the sea views) is the *Smara Hôtel* (☎ 472655), Rue de la Skala, which is quiet, clean and friendly and offers singles/doubles/triples for Dr 42/65/80. The rooms with sea views are much sought after, so you may have to wait a day or so before you can get one. The same views can be had from the roof – which is not a bad place to catch some sun protected from the wind. Showers cost an extra Dr 2, and breakfast is available for Dr 15.

The second place is the *Hôtel Beau Rivag* (☎ 472925), overlooking Place Prince Mou lay Hassan. It is decent value, clean an friendly. Hot water is available most of th time, but it has to be said that the prices ar beginning to outstrip the quality of the place Rooms with two beds and no shower cost D 70. The same with private shower is Dr 12C The manager is friendly enough, and sell films and other odds and ends at his receptio desk. A good pâtisserie and café next doo mean that one of the best spots on the squar for breakfast is just outside the front door.

The third place is the *Hôtel des Remparts* a big building on three floors with a vast roo terrace. Unfortunately, few of the room have sea views, and some of them could de with a bit of sea air. Singles/doubles cost D 60/90, including use of a shared shower (hc water), and some rooms are equipped with bath (cold water only). It's clearly not a good as the Smara, especially at the prices but it's quite acceptable.

A decent place, though not as popula (perhaps because it's a few more minute from the main square), the *Hôtel du Tou risme*, Rue Mohammed ben Massaoud offers clean, quiet singles/doubles for D 36/47. Hot showers are available for Dr 5 They also have bigger rooms that sleep up to four, and some rooms with views towards the port and beach.

The *Hôtel des Amis* (☎ 473188) is a huge sprawling place, but pretty poor. The room are uninviting, to say the least, the shower are cold and the sheets are decidedly unclean.

The *Hôtel Majestic*, 40 Darb Laalouj al Attarin, is old and just as basic. Rooms cos Dr 50/80 – well over the top for what's or offer. The only shower (cold) is right by reception.

Farther afield is the fairly modern *Hôte Chakib*, which charges Dr 35/70/80 fo singles/doubles/triples with shared bath room (cold water only). It's ordinary but acceptable.

Another fairly modern-looking place is the *Hôtel Argana*. Rooms here are OK for Dr 41/55/85, but the awful, dusty, shantytowr location makes it a last choice for the desperate.

Going up in price, the one-star *Hôtel Tafraout* (☎ 472120), 7 Rue de Marrakech off Rue Mohammed ben Abdållah), is clean, comfortable and friendly. Singles/doubles without private bathroom cost Dr 60/80, while those with bathroom cost Dr 70/100. There's hot water in the showers. The 'double' rooms contain a double and a single bed.

### Places to Stay – middle

The two-star *Hôtel Sahara* (☎ 472292), Ave Oqba ben Nafii, has a mixed bag of rooms, so if you can get a look at a few before deciding, so much the better. Singles/doubles without shower or toilet cost Dr 105/133 plus tax. Those with shower and toilet are Dr 123/155 plus taxes. There is hot water in the evenings.

Next door is the *Hôtel Mechouar* (☎ 472018), something of a strange place at which few people seem to stay (which is good news if everything else is full). It looks rather like a London Tube tunnel, at the end of which is a noisy bar. As for the rooms, you have the choice of singles/doubles without shower (Dr 74/95) or rooms with cold shower (Dr 95/110). The only hot water is in a shared shower and is unreliable.

Going up in price, there's the three-star *Hôtel Tafoukt* (☎ 784504/5; fax 784416) at 98 Blvd Mohammed V, which has 40 self-contained singles/doubles for Dr 232/285. For the price, the rooms are hardly special, although they're clean, comfortable and have phones. There is a restaurant and bar, and the hotel is virtually on the beach, although a bit of a walk from where things are happening.

### Places to Stay – top end

The four-star *Hôtel des Îles* (☎ 472329; fax 472472), Blvd Mohammed V, is closer to the old town than the Tafoukt, but although equipped with pool, bar, nightclub and the conveniences you would expect from such a hotel, it is hardly exciting. Its 70 rooms start at Dr 398/506 for basic singles/doubles and rise to Dr 2000 for the main suite. All prices are exclusive of taxes.

The *Villa Maroc* (☎ 473147; fax 472806), located just inside the city walls, at 10 Rue Abdallah ben Yassin, is one of those rare top-grade establishments well worth paying for. Consisting of two renovated 18th-century houses, the villa contains only a dozen or so rooms, so booking well ahead is essential – they can be full up for months. Singles/doubles cost Dr 415/515 plus taxes. Guests (only) can eat in the restaurant or in one of the several salons – a meal costs Dr 130.

### Places to Eat

**Breakfast** About the most popular and relaxing place for a slow breakfast is Place Prince Moulay Hassan. The *Driss Pâtisserie* has a good range of croissants and other pastries to get the day going. Equally good is the *Café/Patisserie L'Opéra*, which spills out in front of the Hôtel Beau Rivage. The *Café de France* is popular with locals right through the day, as is the *Café Marrakech*. The *Café de la Place* is not hot on pastries but is a decent spot for coffee. The food is otherwise mediocre (about Dr 30 for a main course and an outrageous Dr 10 to Dr 15 for soups). Some people spend the better part of a day on the square, slowly shifting from café to café with the moving sunlight.

**Restaurants** For simple snacks and cheap hole-in-the-wall-type food, there are a few little places along Rue Mohammed ben Abdallah, Rue Zerktouni and in the old mellah just inside Bab Doukkala.

On Place Prince Moulay Hassan, you'll find two great snack stands for excellent baguettes stuffed with meat, salad and just about anything else you want. These cost Dr 10 to Dr 15. There's a reasonable food stall next to the Hôtel Chakib too.

The *Restaurant L'Horloge*, tucked away on a shady little square close to the inner walls of the old town, is a popular place with travellers, either for a mint tea or a moderately priced Moroccan meal (the cheapest menu features an omelette as its main dish

MOROCCO

and costs Dr 25). Just near here is the *Restaurant Chez Toufik*, which has been done up as a traditional Berber salon. It's more expensive, and open only in the evenings – you come more for the setting than the food, which is nothing amazing.

Deservedly popular is the *Restaurant Essalam*, on Place Prince Moulay Hassan, where you can pick up an excellent meal for around Dr 35. The tajine is exceptionally good. The restaurant is generally packed with foreigners, with good reason. They take credit cards here.

A good little place to hunt out for seafood can be the *Restaurant Riad*, at the end of an alley off Rue Mohammed ben Abdallah. If they hit you with stories about bad fishing conditions, they'll only have the usual couscous (Dr 49) and tajine (Dr 60) fixed menus, which are unexciting at best.

Another place with a slight twist is the *Restaurant Dar Baba*, which attempts to do a small range of Italian dishes. It's just by the Hôtel Tafraout.

The *Restaurant El Minzah*, Ave Oqba ben Nafii, has set menus for about Dr 60, and is a perfectly adequate if uninspiring choice.

A step up in the price scale, with a more formal atmosphere, the *Restaurant E Khaima* is set back on a small square of Darb Laalouj al-Attarin. You can eat on the patio or upstairs and inside. Main courses generally cost about Dr 60, and they offer two fixed menus: a cheapie at Dr 70, and a seafood splashout at Dr 160.

A long-standing institution famous throughout Morocco is *Chez Sam Restaurant*, at the far end of the port area, past the boat builders. It looks like it's been transported from some windswept cove on the coast of Cornwall or Brittany, and has a delightfully eccentric atmosphere. Chez Sam specialises in seafood. The cuisine is excellent. You can either eat à la carte (reckon on about Dr 100 a head, including wine) or take one of the two set menus (Dr 60 or Dr 140). Ask for recommendations on the best fish of the day. The restaurant is licensed (beer and wine), takes most major credit cards and is open daily for lunch and dinner. Don't leave Essaouira without having a meal here.

Back on Place Prince Moulay Hassan, the licensed *Restaurant Bab Laachour* also

Breadmaker at work

pecialises in seafood. It's probably as good
s Chez Sam and the salads are excellent.
ou're looking at Dr 70 for a full meal.

The *Restaurant Chalet de la Plage* is right
n the beach, just outside the city walls. It
ffers four-course meals for Dr 80 (extra for
heese, tea and coffee). Main courses á la
arte range from Dr 40 to Dr 70, and wine is
ossibly more expensive here than in any of
e other restaurants. It's open for dinner
nly.

## Entertainment
Apart from drinking in the licensed restau-
ants, Essaouira doesn't have many night-
ime alternatives. Local drinkers gather in
he bar under the Hôtel Mechouar. More
p-market tipplers can head to the bar at the
*Hôtel des Îles* – which also has a nightclub.

## Things to Buy
Essaouira is the main centre for thuya carv-
ng, and the quality of the work is superb.
Many of the carvers have workshops under
he Skala de la Ville, and they're very accom-
modating, so you can walk around and look
t what they are doing without any pressure
o buy (but because there's no hard sell, don't
xpect to be able to reduce their stated prices
y much).

A quality store where you can inspect a
whole range of thuya wood products, from
ables to bizarre life-size statues, is Afalkai,
n Place Prince Moulay Hassan. Not the
heapest place around, it will nevertheless
ive you a good feel for prices and for what's
available.

There are also quite a few craft shops in
he immediate vicinity, with an equally
mpressive range of goods. Interesting chess
ieces are the only thing you won't find here;
lthough they are made in Essaouira, most
re very plain indeed.

Carpet and rug shops, as well as bric-a-
rac, jewellery and brassware shops, are
lustered together in the narrow street, and
n the small square between Place Prince
Moulay Hassan and the ramparts that flank
he Ave Oqba ben Nafii.

Thuya wood statue, Essaouira

## Getting There & Away
**Bus** The bus station is about one km to the
north-east of the old town centre. It's not
signposted and is in a pretty awful area.

CTM is at window No 7. There is a bus at
10 am to Safi for Dr 21.50. Another at the
same time goes to Casablanca (Dr 56; 6½
hours) via El-Jadida (Dr 40.50). The fast
midnight bus to Casa costs Dr 85.50 (five
hours). The 12.30 pm bus to Agadir costs Dr
37 (about three hours).

SATAS has a more extensive network in
the south than CTM. It, too, runs a 10 am bus
to Casablanca via El-Jadida, for about the
same price. Buses to Agadir and on to Tiznit
leave at 5.30, 9 and 11.30 am and 9.30 pm.
There is a 9.30 am departure to Tan Tan, and
two buses to Safi, at 1 and 6 pm. The daily
bus to Marrakesh leaves at 7 pm.

You can also get tickets on smaller lines
to Safi (window No 3; up to 10 services a

MOROCCO

day) and Marrakesh (window No 9; up to seven runs a day). The Marrakesh bus costs Dr 29 and takes about 3½ hours.

Several other private-line buses also do the run to Casablanca, for about Dr 60. Other destinations include Rabat, Taroudannt and Tafraoute.

**Train** Supratours, which has an office in the Hôtel des Îles, runs buses to connect with trains. The Supratours bus to Marrakesh train station leaves at 6.30 pm and takes 2½ hours; it's more expensive than a normal bus. You can buy a through ticket from here to any destination served by train.

**Taxi** The grand taxi lot is next to the bus station. The fare to Agadir (or nearby Inezgane) is Dr 50.

### Getting Around

The blue petits taxis are a good idea for getting to and from the bus station. You can also take a ride around town in one of the horse-drawn calèches that gather just outside Bab Doukkala.

### AROUND ESSAOUIRA
#### Diabat

Close to Cap Sim and inland about a km through sand dunes and scrub is the Berber village of Diabat, which became a legend among hippies in the 1960s after a visit by Jimi Hendrix. It subsequently became a freak colony similar to those on the beaches of Goa (in India), but was cleared by the police in the mid-1970s following the murder of several freaks by local junkies. These days it has returned to its own tranquil self, but there seems little reason to visit.

Less than one km farther up the rocky track from Diabat is the long-established *Auberge Tangaro* (☎ 785735). Once a rather basic and cheap place to stay, it has been done up by its Italian owner and costs Dr 450 a double with half-board. Driving from Essaouira, take the coast road for Agadir, and turn up the track just after the bridge about five km out of town. The track is lousy. You

can camp next door – this a better place to d so than at the camping ground in Essaouira

#### Sidi Kaouki

About eight km farther south is anothe windsurfing spot that is fast growing in pop ularity. About the only way to get here is wit your own car, which you'd need anyway t carry all the windsurfing gear.

# Agadir

Agadir was destroyed by an earthquake i 1960. Although since rebuilt, it can no longe be described as a typical Moroccan city Most of the activity centres on catering fo the short-stay package tourists from Europe who arrive daily by the planeload in searc of sun, sand and a sanitised version of th mysteries of the Barbary Coast. Agadir' high tourist profile often leads people t forget its growing importance as a commer cial and fishing port – a big chunk o Morocco's sardine catch now comes throug Agadir, and the driver arriving in Agadi from the north can hardly fail to notice th ugly, sprawling port facilities.

The reek of Ambre Soleil and the rustle o *Paris Match*, *Der Spiegel* and the airmai *Sunday Times* fill the air. Not that it' unpleasant – it's just that it could be an resort town on the northern Mediterranea coast. Modern Agadir, not the most attractiv of towns (cheap North African architectura 'styles' predominate), is also one of the mor expensive cities in Morocco. However, it i a take-off point for visits east and farthe south, so you'll probably find yoursel staying here at least overnight.

### History

Little is known of Agadir's distant past, bu in 1505 an enterprising Portuguese marine decided to build himself a fort, Santa Cru de Cap de Gué, a few km north of the moder city. Sold to the Portuguese governmen eight years later, it became a busy centre o commerce, visited by Portuguese, Genoese nd French merchants. Retaken by the Moroccans in 1541 and subsequently used as the main outlet for products (especially sugar ane) from the Souss region, it slowly began to decline, and was finally eclipsed by the se of Essaouira in the late 18th century. A entury later, only a dozen houses were left tanding.

It was here that the Germans took gunboat iplomacy to the limit with France in 1911, ending the warship *Panther* to make noises ff the Agadir coast. They managed to avoid oing to war on this occasion, but only for aree years.

The earthquake that struck on 29 February 960 flattened the town and killed 15,000 eople. Agadir has since been completely ebuilt, and continues to grow as Morocco's op beach resort.

## Orientation

Agadir's bus station and most of the budget otels are in a small area in the north-east of he town. From here it's about a 20-minute valk down to the beach, lined with cafés, estaurants and expensive hotels. Most of the anks and the main post office are located etween the beach and Ave du Prince Moulay Abdallah.

## Information

Tourist Office The Délégation du Tourisme (☎ 822894, 841367) is in the central market rea, just off Ave Prince Héritier Sidi Mohammed (Immeuble A). It's open standard weekday office hours, and has the usual rochures but not a lot else.

More useful is the syndicat d'initiative ☎ 840307) on Blvd Mohammed V at the unction with Ave du Général Kettani. Here, ou can buy a small *Guide d'Agadir*, which ontains some useful information (such as sts of doctors and the like) for Dr 10. They lso have a notice board with bus timetables nd details of market days in surrounding owns. It's open from 9 am to noon and 3 to 4.30 pm Monday to Saturday, and on Sunday mornings.

Money Most banks have branches in Agadir.

The BMCE and BMCI, both at the beach end of Ave du Général Kettani, have ATMs, and the BMCE has a bureau de change. If you need money on the weekend and the ATMs fail you, about your only chance will be the big hotels, such as the Beach Club – they change only cash and cheques.

The American Express representative is Voyages Schwartz (☎ 841082; fax 841066), 87 Place du Marché Municipal, Ave Hassan II. They are in the Mopatours office.

**Post & Telecommunications** The main post office, on Ave du Prince Moulay Abdallah near the Hôtel de Ville (town hall), is open daily from 8.30 am to 6.45 pm. There is another post office (La Poste), on Rue du 29 Février, in the budget hotel area.

The phone office is in the central post office. It's open seven days a week from 8 am to 9 pm. There are also a couple of *Téléboutiques*, one of them about 50 metres up from the *Hôtel Talborjt*. They generally stay open until 10 pm.

**Foreign Consulates** Foreign consulates in Agadir include:

Belgium
    Consulate: Impasse d'Amman (☎ 842573)
    Visas: Immeuble Rachdi, Ave Hassan II (☎ 844080)
France
    Blvd Mohammed Saadi (☎ 840826)
Italy
    Rue du Souvenir (☎ 823013)
Netherlands
    Visa office for Moroccan citizens only (see under Belgium)
Norway
    c\- Institution al-Hanane, Cité Anouar Souss (☎ 821987)
Spain
    49 Rue Ibn Batouta, Secteur Mixte (☎ 845681; fax 845843)
Sweden
    Rue de l'Entraide (☎ 823048)
UK
    Hôtel Sud Bahia, Rue des Administrations Publiques (☎ 823741)

**Language Schools** The American Language Center (☎ 821589) has a branch at 6

MOROCCO

MOROCCO

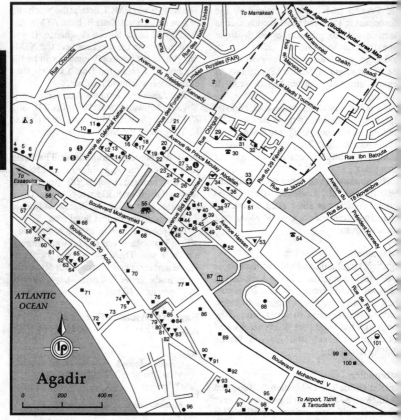

Impasse de Baghdad. The Moroccan Institute of Management (☎ 823356), on Ave Hassan II, operates as a representative for the International Language Centre.

**Newsstands** There are several decent newsstands with a fair selection of European and international press (usually a day or two late). The one on the corner of Ave Hassan II and Ave des FAR is as good as any.

**Laundry** There is a coin-operated laundry (the only one in Morocco?) at the Hôtel al-Madina Palace.

**Film & Photography** You can buy film and have it developed in several places around town. New Labcolor, on Ave du Prince Moulay Hassan, is one of the nearest to the budget hotel area.

**Medical Services & Emergencies** The Clinique Al-Massira, on Ave du Prince Moulay Abdallah, is as good as any. The *Guide d'Agadir* contains lists of doctors, dentists, clinics and pharmacies. The main tourist office also posts a list of doctors. An all-night chemist (☎ 820349) is located near the Hôtel de Ville.

MOROCCO

## PLACES TO STAY

3 Camping Ground
7 Résidence Tilila
10 Hôtel Petite Suède
14 Hôtel Sud Bahia
29 Hôtel Talborjt
31 Hôtel Itrane
32 Hôtel Ayour
38 Atlantic Hôtel
41 Hôtel Kamal
44 Hôtel Les Palmiers
45 Résidence Sacha
46 Hôtel Aladin
49 Résidence Yasmina
66 Sheraton
68 Hôtel Ali Baba
69 Hôtel Anezi
70 Hôtel Europa Safir
71 Hôtel Tafoukt
76 Hôtel Al Medina Palace
77 Hôtel Salam
85 Hôtel Tagadirt
86 Hôtel Transatlantique
89 Hôtel Adrar
92 Hôtel Mabrouk
94 Résidence Club La Kasbah
97 Agadir Hôtel
99 Hôtel Solman
100 Hôtel Les Cinq Parties du Monde

## PLACES TO EAT

6 Restaurant Marine Heim (bei Hilde)
12 Restaurant Darkoum
13 Restaurant La Tour de Paris
19 Cafés
23 Restaurant La Dolce Vita
24 Restaurant Le Dôme
25 Restaurant Via Veneto
36 Restaurant Chahoua
40 Restaurant Scampi
44 Restaurante Les Palmiers
47 Restaurant La Tonkinoise
48 Steak House
53 Café Tafarnout
58 Restaurant Le Côte d'Or
59 Restaurant Don Vito
60 Café Le Kermesse
61 Restaurant Le Nil Bleu
62 Restaurant Le Vendôme
63 Hollywood Fast Food
64 The Palace Bar/Café
72 Restaurant La Perla del Mare
73 Restaurants
74 Restaurant Golden Gate
75 Pizzeria & Gelato
78 Café Le Central & Disco
79 Restaurant Imin
80 Restaurant Jockey
81 Restaurant Pizza Pino
82 Restaurant Le Petit Dôme
83 Restaurant La Mamma
90 Restaurant El Marrakchi
91 Restaurant Grill du Soleil
93 Restaurant Jazz
97 Restaurant Complex
98 Kim Hoa Vietnamese Restaurant

## OTHER

1 American Language Center
2 Jardin de Olhâo
4 Budget
5 Hertz
8 BMCE Bank (ATM & Bureau de Change)
9 BMCI Bank (ATM)
11 Royal Air Maroc
15 Tour Agents
16 Banque Populaire
17 Newsstand
18 Supratours
20 Cinéma Rialto
21 Bar Crystal
22 Voyages Schwartz (American Express)
26 Uniprix
27 Central Market
28 Tourist Office
30 Téléboutique (Phones)
33 Clinique Al Massira
34 Post Office
35 Hôtel de Ville
37 Liquor Store
39 Car/Motorbike Hire
42 Place de l'Espérance
43 Air France
50 Travel Agents (Local Excursions & Charter Flights)
51 New Labcolor (Kodak)
52 Royal Tennis Club of Agadir
54 Téléboutique (Phones)
55 Vallée des Oiseaux (Zoo)
56 Syndicat d'Initiative
57 Public Swimming Pool
65 Banque Populaire & Clinic
67 Vallée des Oiseaux
73 Shopping Mall
84 Newsstand
87 Musée Municipal
88 Stadium
95 Cabaret Al Hambra
96 Newsstand
101 Place Taxis et Bus (Local Buses & Taghezout Grands Taxis)

The Moroccan Red Cross (☎ 821472) might be a useful emergency contact.

## Musée Municipal

This modest museum contains displays of southern Moroccan folk art provided by Dutch art lecturer and long-time resident of Marrakesh Bert Flint (he has opened up the Maison Tiskiwin in Marrakesh with further displays). It's open Monday to Saturday from 9.30 am to 1 pm and 2.30 to 6 pm.

## Vallée des Oiseaux

This tiny 'zoo', for want of a better word, runs along a narrow strip between Ave Hassan II and under Blvd Mohammed V, with an entrance on both sides. It costs Dr 5 to get in (Dr 3 for children). The zoo is closed in the middle of the day.

## Kasbah

A good hour's walk to the north-east of the town is what's left of the old kasbah. A Dutch inscription from 1746 still adorns the gateway, exhorting visitors to 'fear God and honour your king'. The fort was originally built in 1540, overlooking the former Portuguese emplacement, and was restored and regarrisoned in 1752, lest Portugal decide to make a comeback. The ramparts were partially restored after the 1960 earthquake, but nothing remains within. Thousands of people lie where they died when the quake hit.

## Jardim de Olhão

These rather odd-looking gardens mark the twinning of Agadir with the Portuguese town of Olhão, and commemorate the 'historical ties' that have so often had Morocco and Portugal at loggerheads. The gardens are open from 2.30 to 6.30 pm only.

## Beach & Watersports

The main reason for being in Agadir is to go to the beach. When the Atlantic winds are blustering elsewhere along the coast, Agadir's beach usually remains unruffled. In front of the main beach hotels, you are supposed to pay a fee for use of the beach, deckchairs, umbrellas and the like. In practice you can generally plonk your towel down somewhere without any hassle.

In the area down in front of the Hôtel Beach Club, you can rent various implements to enhance your enjoyment of the water, including pedalos, jetskis, surfboards and surfskis (surf is not one of Agadir's strengths). It ain't cheap – an hour on a surfski (which usually means paddling around) costs Dr 150. A surfboard will set you back Dr 100 an hour, and a wetsuit will be another Dr 30 an hour.

Farther south down the beach you'll find people with horses, camels and dune trikes for hire. Prices, again, are high.

Most of the larger hotels organise all sorts of activities for their guests. Those interested in fishing may want to enquire about the possibilities. Otherwise, try Sports Évasion Maroc (☎ 846122), next to the Hôtel Sud Bahia, which claims to organise ocean fishing trips, including shark fishing. They also offer horse riding.

## Organised Tours

Agadir is a thriving centre for locally organised tours, most aimed at charter flight tourists who are in Morocco for a week or two and are anxious to do more than lounge around on the sand. There is any number of agents, many of them branch offices of European package-tour companies. You'll find a bunch of them clustered around the intersection of Ave Hassan II and Ave des FAR. There are more around Ave Sidi Mohammed.

Principal destinations include Marrakesh, Taroudannt, Tafraoute and Immouzzer des Ida Outanane. Of these, only the latter can be a little difficult (but hardly impossible) to do under your own steam – which is by far the better way to approach them, especially as none of the organised trips is cheap. They range from Dr 200 for a day at Immouzzer to Dr 1400 for a day trundling about in a Land Rover.

## Places to Stay – bottom end

**Camping** Agadir's camp site (☎ 846683) is not the worst of Moroccan camping grounds,

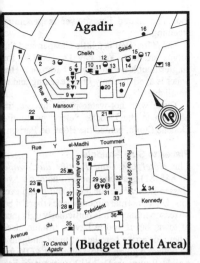

**Agadir**

**(Budget Hotel Area)**

To Central Agadir

<table>
<tr><td colspan="2">PLACES TO STAY</td></tr>
<tr><td>1</td><td>Hôtel Excelsior</td></tr>
<tr><td>2</td><td>Hôtel Aït Laayoune</td></tr>
<tr><td>5</td><td>Hôtel Sindibad</td></tr>
<tr><td>11</td><td>Hôtel Massa</td></tr>
<tr><td>13</td><td>Hôtel Canaria</td></tr>
<tr><td>15</td><td>Hôtel Amenou</td></tr>
<tr><td>21</td><td>Hôtel El Bahia</td></tr>
<tr><td>22</td><td>Hôtel Moderne</td></tr>
<tr><td>23</td><td>Hôtel Select</td></tr>
<tr><td>26</td><td>Hôtel Diaf</td></tr>
<tr><td>28</td><td>Hôtel de la Baie</td></tr>
<tr><td>32</td><td>Hôtel La Tour Eiffel</td></tr>
<tr><td>33</td><td>Hôtel de Paris</td></tr>
</table>

**PLACES TO EAT**

4 Ice-Cream Place
6 Restaurant Ibtissam
7 Café Restaurant Coq d'Or
8 Restaurant Chahab
9 Restaurant Mille et Une Nuits
27 Restaurant Select
30 Restaurant Tamouate

**OTHER**

3 CTM (Buses)
10 Café Fairouz
12 SATAS (Buses)
14 Bus Company
16 Ensemble Artisanal
17 Bus Company
18 Post Office
19 American Language Center
20 Cinema Sahara
24 Douche Select
25 Café/Pâtisserie Oufella
29 BMCE Bank
31 Banque Populaire
34 Mohammed V Mosque
35 Café Les Arcades
36 Café La Terrasse

but the ground is pretty stony and camper-vans predominate. It costs Dr 10 per person, Dr 10 for a car, Dr 10 to Dr 15 to pitch a tent (depending on its size), Dr 12 for electricity and Dr 7.50 for a hot shower. All this plus 14% tax. There's also a general grocery store.

**Hotels** Most of the budget hotels and a few of the mid-range hotels are concentrated in a small area around the bus terminal and Rue Allal ben Abdallah. In the high seasons, you must get into Agadir early in the day if you want to be sure of a room. If you arrive late, you may have to sleep out, or pay through the nose at an expensive hotel. Disappointed backpackers wandering around with no-where to stay are a common sight by 8 pm. By standards elsewhere in the country, you pay more for less in Agadir.

The two cheapest places here are also among the worst. The *Hôtel Canaria* (☎ 822291) costs Dr 30/40/62 for basic rooms, with a cold shared shower. You'll be lucky to get a room here anyway, as it's mainly in the brothel business. Whether or not the same can be said of the *Hôtel Massa* is hard to say, but it's a rather unfriendly

place. The basic but clean rooms cost Dr 30/40/60, and there's a cold shower.

With a little more money, the choices widen somewhat. Although the rooms are little better (and the locks are a joke), the *Hôtel Select*, down a lane off Rue Allal ben Abdallah, is a quieter, more pleasant place to stay than the above two. Rooms cost Dr 45/60. The hotel has no shower, but runs a public shower next door (Dr 4.50), which is guaranteed to be hot.

A trio of hotels charge Dr 70/90 for singles/doubles and are a definite improvement on the above: the *Hôtel La Tour Eiffel* (☎ 823712), *Hôtel Amenou* (☎ 823026) and *Hôtel Aït Laayoune* (☎ 824375). Despite the toilets, the Amenou is marginally better than the Tour Eiffel, and hot water seems a surer thing here. It's right by the bus offices (a mixed blessing) on Rue Yacoub el-Mansour. The pick of them, however, is the Aït Laayoune. Problem is, it's often full.

Just across the road, and another place that is often full, the *Hôtel Excelsior* (☎ 821028) has rooms without shower for Dr 66/90 (a hot shared shower costs Dr 5), and with shower for Dr 100/130. It's quite OK, without being spectacular.

The *Hôtel de la Baie* (☎ 823014), on the corner of Rue Allal ben Abdallah and Ave du Président Kennedy, is a mixed bag. The rooms without shower for Dr 49/66 (a hot, shared shower is Dr 5) are adequate, but certainly no better than those at the previous two hotels. The rooms with shower (Dr 75/96) are not too bad, although for a dollar or two more you could dramatically improve your quality of life elsewhere.

The *Hôtel Moderne* (☎ 823373), Rue Mehdi ibn Toummert, is in a quieter spot and offers parking space. Singles/doubles without shower are overpriced (Dr 90/110), but those with shower are quite acceptable (Dr 100/130). The receptionist is one of the grumpiest people in Agadir.

You need a little money for two of the best places in this area, both of which, you may as well know, act as brothels as well. The activity is usually pretty discreet, though, and shouldn't deter you from staying at them.

The better of the two is the *Hôtel de Paris* (☎ 822694), on Ave du Président Kennedy. It has clean and very comfortable little rooms (with washbasin and wardrobe) for Dr 80/100 without private bathroom, or Dr 136/166 with. The rooms are gathered around a peaceful courtyard dominated by a majestic old tree. You can sit up on the roof,

too. The shared hot shower is generally steaming.

The *Hôtel Diaf* is a little cheaper, and the rooms are fine. You pay Dr 100/150 for singles/doubles with private bathroom. Hot water is available only in the evening and is unreliable.

Those with hot-water problems can, in addition to the Douche Select, go to the Douche Étoile, behind the Hôtel de Paris.

### Places to Stay – middle

The *Hôtel Les Cinq Parties du Monde* (☎ 845481) is a good, modern hotel on Ave Hassan II, near the local bus and grand taxi lots. Under normal circumstances there'd be no reason to stay in this particularly ugly part of town, but if you're having trouble elsewhere, or arrive here late at night and can't be bothered going farther afield, it's OK for a night. Rooms are Dr 70/120 without private bathroom, Dr 129/170 with bathroom.

If you want to get out of the budget hotel area, there is a fairly tranquil little place just off Ave du Général Kettani, the *Hôtel Petite Suède* (☎ 840779). Don't let them talk you into taking rooms with breakfast (you can get the same breakfast a lot cheaper in any café), but for Dr 140/173, the comfortable rooms with en suite bathroom are not a bad deal at all.

There are three hotels on Rue de l'Entraide, just on the beach side of Ave du Président Kennedy. The cheapest is the *Hôtel Itrane* (☎ 821407), which charges Dr 99/117 for reasonable singles/doubles but is often full.

The two-star *Hôtel Ayour* (☎ 824976), at No 4, is a modern establishment that even boasts a solarium. It has decent-sized rooms with private bathroom for Dr 164/194.

More expensive still, but very good, the *Hôtel Talborjt* (☎ 841832) offers pleasant, carpeted rooms, some overlooking lush gardens. They cost Dr 215/264 in the low season, Dr 222/275 in the high season, plus taxes.

Back up in the heart of the budget hotel area and near the buses are two slightly fancier hotels than the surrounding ones. The

Hôtel Sindibad (☎ 823477; fax 842474) has pleasant rooms with own phone. They also have a restaurant, and *glacier* for ice creams. Yes, the odd lady of the night has her base here, too (obviously a thriving business in Agadir).

Another comfortable place, and one of the better hotels in this range, is the *Hôtel el Bahia* (☎ 822724; fax 824515). Again, rooms have a phone, and in winter are centrally heated. The cheapest rooms cost Dr 98/130 (a hot shared shower is Dr 6). Rooms with shower only cost Dr 134/158, while those with full bathroom are Dr 170/200. The staff are helpful.

One often overlooked is the *Hôtel/Restaurant Les Palmiers* (☎ 843719), on Ave Sidi Mohammed. This friendly place is reasonably well located, near several restaurants and not too far from the beach. It has decent rooms priced at Dr 164/194.

A little more expensive but a fine two-star place to stay is the *Atlantic Hôtel* (☎ 843661/2), on Ave Hassan II. It's clean and comfortable, and has boiling hot water 24 hours a day. Rooms cost Dr 202/257. Breakfast is available in the pleasant, leafy courtyard. Better still, and with its own small pool, is the *Hôtel Aladin* (☎ 843228; fax 846071), Rue de la Jeunesse. They charge a trifle more than the Atlantic in the low season (Dr 215/264 plus taxes) and Dr 223/275 plus taxes in the high season.

From here on, prices start to climb well beyond the reach of many pockets. The *Hôtel Kamal* (☎ 842817; fax 843940), Ave Hassan II, is a perfectly acceptable place to stay, but breakfast is obligatory, so rooms cost Dr 272/357.

### Places to Stay – top end

You will find no shortage of expensive hotels in Agadir. The bulk of them are inhabited by block-booked charter groups, which generally get a considerable discount on the normal individual prices.

At the lower end of the scale, and not in the most appealing position compared to some of its beachside counterparts, the *Hôtel Sud Bahia* (☎ 840782; fax 840863), off Ave du Général Kettani, charges Dr 365/493, including breakfast. The rooms are modern and in reasonable shape, with bathroom and phone, and there are 246 of them, so the place is unlikely to be full. There's a heated swimming pool out the back.

You'd be much better off, however, if you want this kind of hotel, hunting around the beachside places and seeing what kind of deal you can come up with. One of the newer, swankier hotels is the *Transatlantique* (☎ 842110; fax 842076). Their low-season rates start at Dr 362/460, plus taxes, and it's a much better place to stay than the Sud Bahia.

Places like the *Résidence Club La Kasbah* (☎ 823636) cost more like Dr 850/1360.

There are numerous such places up and down Agadir's beachfront, particularly along Blvd Mohammed V and Blvd du 20 Août and on the beach itself (you can get a full list from the tourist offices and in the *Guide d'Agadir*). They usually have swimming pools, restaurants, bars and other amenities. La Kasbah even has tennis courts.

### Places to Eat

Agadir is crawling with restaurants and cafés – many, but by no means all, are a little on the expensive side. In addition to the following, a few more are marked on the map – the best idea, especially if you do have a bit of money to throw around, is to wander about and see what takes your fancy. The *Guide d'Agadir* also has a list of the more pricey places. Don't leave it too late – Moroccan foodies are no night owls, so a lot of places close their doors by 10 pm.

**Breakfast** There are plenty of cafés where you can ease into the day with breakfast. A particularly good one with fairly decent pastries is the *Café/Patisserie Oufella*, just across the road from the Hôtel Diaf, on Rue Allal ben Abdallah.

Another pleasant place for breakfast or a beer is the café by the municipal swimming pool, on the beachfront. A little farther south there is a string of cafés and restaurants up to a large open square.

**Budget Restaurants** A number of cheap restaurants and sandwich bars are on the same street as the bus terminals, and they're reasonable value, serving almost anything from seafood to kebab sandwiches.

Just at the back of the bus terminal street is a small plaza, four restaurants next to each other are very popular with travellers and night strollers from the tourist district in search of a change. They are the *Restaurant Chabab*, the *Restaurant Mille et Une Nuits*, the *Café Restaurant Coq d'Or* and the *Restaurant Ibtissam* (the latter means 'smile'). They might look expensive but they're not, and the food is very good. All offer you a choice of sitting inside or at tables in the open air. Typical prices are: couscous or tajine (about Dr 20), omelette (about Dr 10) and salads (up to Dr 10).

The *Restaurant Select*, just by the hotel of the same name, does a solid range of old favourites, and you can eat well for about Dr 20. Do *not* order the crêpes – they are awful. Similar in style but a few dirham more expensive is the *Restaurant Tamouate*, next to the BMCE branch on Ave du Président Kennedy.

Getting a little flasher, and commensurately more expensive, *Restaurant Les Palmiers* is under the hotel of the same name. It does similar food to the others, with little appreciable difference in quality. Main courses cost Dr 20 to Dr 40.

Just where Ave Sidi Mohammed runs into Blvd Mohammed V, you'll find a Vietnamese restaurant, *La Tonkinoise* and the incredibly tacky *Steak House*. The latter seems to attract a lot of people, but surely it can't be because of the Julio Iglesias-style duo playing in the gardens!

For a bizarre experience, try the *Restaurant Chahoua*, down a small street behind the post office. There's a liquor store across the road from this Korean restaurant, which seems purpose-built for the small community of Korean workers here. The place is simple and the food very authentic, and for a while you'll forget you're in Morocco as all the family and friends gather about the main table and dig in. The staff speak Korean and English, and maybe a little French. If it's been a while since you last read a Korean pulp novel or magazine, this is the place to come (videos too)! It's not really a budget traveller's haven – you could easily spend close to Dr 100 for a full meal – but it's worth it, and better value than the rather bland standard Vietnamese alternatives.

**Expensive Restaurants** The *Restaurant La Tour de Paris* is a luxury restaurant at the Ave du Général Kettani end of Ave Hassan II. The mainly French menu is tempting and the food of a reasonably high standard, but it costs a minimum of Dr 150 per person.

No Moroccan tourist city would be complete without at least one 'Moroccan experience'-style restaurant, where you can eat in lavish Moorish surroundings, be entertained with traditional music and be served by waiters in impeccably white robes and red fezzes. In Agadir, the *Restaurant Darkoum* is that place. It's on Ave du Général Kettani near the Hôtel Sud Bahia, and it will set you back about Dr 150. If you're travelling through Morocco and want to do this sort of thing, wait for Fès, where most of the restaurants of this ilk are at least set in genuine old nobles' palaces.

One place that seems rather popular with Finns and locals is the *Restaurant Scampi*, Ave Hassan II, opposite the Hôtel Atlantic. They have an excellent range of dishes and the food is good. It isn't cheap, at around Dr 250 for two people (including wine), but at least it doesn't involve a long walk from the budget hotel zone.

Set right on the beach, near the Hôtel Tafoukt, is the classy *La Perla del Mare* (☎ 840065). It's not only classy, it's pricey.

Along Blvd du 20 Août, in among some of the swish hotels and tourist boutiques, is any number of expensive restaurants to choose from. *Restaurant Pizza Pino* and *La Mamma*, predictably enough, do Italian food. The *Jazz* and *El Marrakchi* are pricey Moroccan joints – expect to pay in excess of Dr 150 each for a full meal.

The Agador Hôtel complex contains several restaurants, including *Le Cap*, *Pub*

*L'Oasis* and the *Asmas Restaurant*. The latter puts on evening performances of Moroccan music during meals.

For Vietnamese food (about Dr 70 for a main meal), try the *Restaurant Kim Hoa*. It's a bit of a hike, down past La Kasbah hotel.

## Entertainment

**Bars & Nightclubs** A lively little bar that's popular with the locals is located just by the southern entrance to the Vallée des Oiseaux. You can also get a beer at quite a lot of the beachfront restaurants and cafés, including the one by the swimming pool. Otherwise, there are many bars to choose from in the bigger hotels, if you want to rub shoulders with hordes of short-term visitors from every conceivable part of Europe.

For takeaways, you could try the liquor store opposite the Restaurant Chahoua, the Uniprix supermarket on Ave Hassan II or one of a couple of similar markets dotted about Agadir. Between them, there's a good choice of local and imported beers, wines and spirits.

Most of the bigger hotels have nightclubs. For a comprehensive list, consult the *Guide d'Agadir*. Remember that entry usually costs from Dr 50 up (a drink included), and subsequent drinks can cost as much again. The average backpacker doesn't drag around the kind of glad rags required to be allowed into most these places. If you like cabarets, maybe the *Alhambra Cabaret*, near the Hôtel Sahara on Blvd du 20 Août, is for you.

**Theatre & Cinema** The *Alliance Franco-Marocaine* (☎ 841313), 5 Rue Yahchech, puts on films, theatre and lectures. You can usually pick up their program in the syndicat d'initiative. Most of the performances are in French.

There are also a few cinemas scattered about town.

## Things to Buy

Agadir is not a great place to pick up souvenirs. Most of what's on offer is trucked in from other parts of the country, and the steady stream of package tourists unaware of what's on offer elsewhere in the country keep prices up on low-quality goods. If you still want to look around, the Central Market is full of kitsch souvenir shops.

## Getting There & Away

**Air** The new Al-Massira airport lies 28 km south of Agadir. Take the Tafraoute road if you're driving out there. The airport bank (cash and travellers' cheques only) is not always open, but there are restaurants and a tourist information counter. The bulk of the traffic through here consists of European charter flights.

RAM (☎ 840145) has an office on Ave du Général Kettani. Most of its flights, internal and abroad, go via Casablanca. There are several flights a day to Casa (Dr 585 one way; 50 minutes) and a few each week to Marrakesh (35 minutes). In addition, there are flights to Laayoune on Monday (via Tan Tan) and Tuesday (Dr 735 one way; 1½ hours direct). Two flights a week connect Agadir with Dakhla, too. RAM has a few direct international flights, including to Las Palmas (Canary Islands) for Dr 2575 one way.

**Bus** Although a good number of buses and grands taxis serve Agadir (and they should be adequate for the purposes of leaving), there is a huge bus and taxi station in the nearby town of Inezgane. It is quite possible that you'll be dropped here when you arrive. There are grands taxis and local buses between Agadir and Inezgane (see the following Taxi section and Getting There & Away under Inezgane).

In Agadir, all the bus companies have their terminals along Rue Yacoub el-Mansour, in the budget hotel area.

CTM has buses to Casablanca at 7.30 am and 9.30, 10 and 10.30 pm (Dr 117.50; 10 hours). The 10.30 pm bus goes on to Rabat (Dr 139) and Tangier (Dr 205.50; 14 hours).

A bus for Essaouira (Dr 36.50) leaves at 7.30 pm, and goes on to Safi and El-Jadida. There are buses for Tiznit at 6.30 am (Dr 16) and 3.30 pm (Dr 24 mumtaz). At 8.30 pm there's a service to Laayoune (Dr 194.50), going on to Smara. The Dakhla bus leaves at 8 pm, and a bus for Taroudannt at 5.30 am (Dr 18.50).

You can also get on to buses bound for France and Belgium here. You need to book a week in advance. See the Getting There & Away chapter for more details.

SATAS is the other main company operating out of Agadir. It has several buses to Essaouira (Dr 38), Marrakesh (Dr 55; four hours), Casablanca (Dr 115 via Marrakesh, Dr 95 via Essaouira), Tiznit (Dr 18), Taroudannt, Tafraoute (one a day, at 1.30 pm), Goulimime and Tan Tan (at 6 am and 2 pm), Safi and El-Jadida.

About 10 other smaller companies have buses to most of these destinations as well.

**Train** Supratours (☎ 841207), which runs buses in connection with the train network, has an office at 10 Rue des Orangiers. Services to Marrakesh (about four hours) leave at 4.45 and 9.30 am and 1.45 pm, and you are dropped at the train station.

You can get a through ticket from Agadir to any rail destination.

**Taxi** Grands taxis to Tiznit (Dr 17.50) leave from a lot about one km south-east of the centre of town. Grands taxis also go to Inezgane (Dr 2.50) from here.

Grands taxis for Taghazout (Dr 8) leave from near the local bus station at Place Taxis et Bus.

**Car Rental** There are at least 40 car-rental outlets to choose from in Agadir, many of them on Ave Hassan II, so it is worth shopping around before settling on a deal. Some of the main agencies are:

Avis
    Ave Hassan II (☎ 841755)
    Airport (☎ 840345)
Budget
    Bungalow Marhaba, Blvd Mohammed V (☎ 844600)
    Airport (☎ 839071)
Europcar
    Bungalow Marhaba, Blvd Mohammed V (☎ 840203)
    Airport (☎ 839066)
Hertz
    Bungalow Marhaba, Blvd Mohammed V (☎ 840939)

**Motorbike** A walk around the big hotels will soon reveal a series of booths that rent out motorbikes and scooters. Again, it is important to hunt around. Dr 80 a day or Dr 350 a week seems to be an average charge for a scooter.

Of greater interest could be some of the 4WD and camel excursions into the desert, but again, they aren't cheap.

## Getting Around

**To/From the Airport** Airport transport is just a little complicated. Local bus No 22 runs from the airport car park to Inezgane every 40 minutes or so (Dr 3) until about 9 pm. From Inezgane you can change to bus Nos 5 and 6 for Agadir, or take a grand taxi (Dr 2.50).

Petits taxis between the airport and Agadir should not cost more than Dr 100.

Otherwise, plenty of travellers have stories of simply walking onto tour and hotel buses with other passengers, since most of them are generally in package tours and it's unlikely any questions will be asked. Don't *ask* for a lift on one of these buses – they may give you one but they'll also charge you the earth.

**Bus** The main local bus station is a block in from Ave Hassan II, at Place Taxis et Bus, in the southern end of town. Bus Nos 5 and 6 go to Inezgane. The green-and-white No 12 goes to Taghazout.

**Taxi** Unless you have to get to the airport in a hurry, you're unlikely to use the orange petits taxis.

**Bicycle** There are several stands set up around the big hotels near the beach renting out bicycles for Dr 20 an hour.

## AROUND AGADIR

### Immouzzer des Ida Outanane

A pleasant little side excursion, but one that could mean an overnight stay if you rely on public transport and have no luck hitching, takes you about 60 km north of Agadir to the village of Immouzzer des Ida Outanane. The village itself is nothing special, but the trip up is pretty. The waterfalls (cascades) for which the village is known can be a disappointment – often little more than a dribble.

One local bus a day leaves for Inezgane from near the Agadir bus terminals. Ask around the day before, as its departure times (about 4 am at the time of writing) seem to change. You may have to wait until the fol-

lowing day for the bus back, although hitching isn't too difficult. Otherwise, there's a pleasant but fairly expensive hotel at Immouzzer. The best time to get up there would be Thursday, which is market day.

### Northern Beaches

If you're looking for less-crowded beaches than those at Agadir, and for fellow independent travellers (most with their own transport), then head north of Agadir. There are beautiful sandy coves every few km.

Most of the beaches closer to Agadir have been colonised by Europeans who have built their winter villas here. Farther north, this gives way to a sea of camper vans, but by the time you are 20 to 25 km north of Agadir, you might find something resembling space and even peace and quiet.

The first village of any size you pass is Tamrhakht, about 14 km north of Agadir, and six km farther on is Taghazout. The latter hosts a large and fairly ugly camping ground at the southern end of the town. It's usually crammed with camper vans. There are a couple of eateries and cafés, too, but it's really not a very appealing place. The beaches are OK but the ambience is hardly the best. Europeans have built villas along parts of the coast between Taghazout and Agadir, and the stream of foreigners has attracted banana sellers onto the roadsides – you could buy a lot of bananas on your way north from Agadir.

For peaceful and largely unspoilt beaches, you need to go still farther north. Those around Aghrod, 27 km north of Agadir, are more like it. You can find a few other attractive spots just south and north of Cap Rhir (easily identified by its shipwreck), before the road turns inland again to Tamri.

There are local buses from Agadir (Place Taxis et Bus) to Taghazout, but beyond that you'll have to rely on your thumb.

### Inezgane

Inezgane is a completely uninteresting and very noisy town 13 km south of Agadir. It also happens to be one of the biggest transport hubs for the whole region, and you could easily end up here, although, if you're lucky, no longer than it takes to change buses or get a taxi. Should you get stuck, there is no shortage of cheap hotels in the bus station area. A big market is held in the town on Tuesdays.

**Getting There & Away** There are plenty of buses to most major destinations from here, if you have no luck in Agadir. The bus station (gare routière) is just off the Agadir-Tiznit road. Even at 6 pm, you'll find touts trying to fill places on buses to Marrakesh, Casablanca, Essaouira and other cities. There are also loads of grands taxis to Essaouira (Dr 50), Tiznit (Dr 16) and Taroudannt (Dr 15). Less regular taxis leave for Goulimime (Dr 40) and Tan Tan (Dr 70). Local buses to Agadir and the airport also leave from around here.

### Sidi R'bat

About 80 km south of Agadir, off a side track from the main P30 highway, is a tiny little coastal village called Sidi R'bat. There's nothing much here, but two interesting claims are attached to the village. According to one story, this is where the biblical Jonah is supposed to have been spewed up by the whale. And Uqba bin Nafi, the first Arab commander to penetrate Morocco, in the 7th century, supposedly rode his horse triumphantly into the sea here. Believe it or not.

---

# Taroudannt

Just 85 km inland from Agadir, Taroudannt, with its magnificent and well-preserved red mud walls, stands out as a Moroccan city more Moroccan than the rest. The French never tacked on a ville nouvelle here, and although there is not an awful lot to see, it gives the impression of not having changed much in the past hundred or so years. A fairly easy day trip from Agadir (the squadrons of tour buses are proof of that), it is well worth spending a couple of days here. Taroudannt

also makes a good intermediate stop between Agadir and Marrakesh.

Busloads of day-trippers pour into Taroudannt from Agadir, and have given rise to a small-scale irritant in the form of touts. If you hang about for a day or two, they'll soon leave you alone. The central souq, where most of the souvenirs are sold, is so small that guides are completely superfluous. The tout problems overcome, Taroudannt is a relaxed and pleasant place to stay, with a strongly southern Moroccan feel to it.

### History

As far back as 1056, Taroudannt was overrun by the Almoravids at the beginning of their conquest of Morocco. It played only a peripheral role in the following years until, in the 16th century, the newly emerging Saadians made it their capital for about 20 years. This dynasty was responsible for the construction of the old part of town and the kasbah; most of the rest dates from the 18th century.

The Saadians eventually moved on to Marrakesh, but not before the fertile Souss valley in which the city stands had been developed into the country's most important producer of sugar cane, cotton, rice and indigo – valuable items of trade along the trans-Saharan caravan routes.

The city narrowly escaped destruction in 1687 at the hands of Moulay Ismail, after it became the centre of a rebellion opposing his rule. Instead, Moulay Ismail contented himself with a massacre of its inhabitants. It regained some of its former prominence when one of Moulay Abdallah's sons was proclaimed sultan here at the end of the following century, but his reign during this, one of the more turbulent periods in Moroccan history, was brief.

Taroudannt was to remain a centre of intrigue and sedition against the central government well into the 20th century, and indeed played host to the Idrissid El-Hiba, a southern chief who attempted to rebel after the Treaty of Fès (introducing French protectorate rule) was signed in 1912.

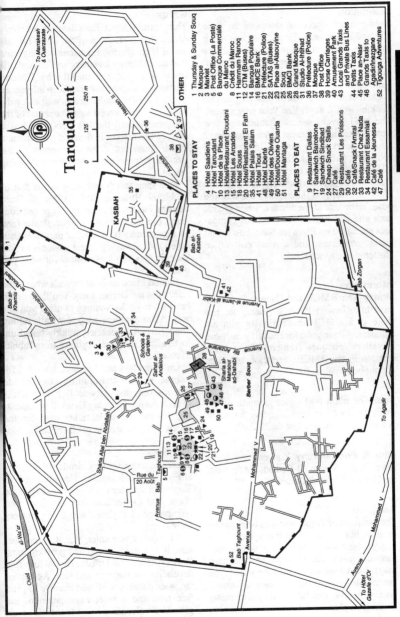

# Taroudannt

0  125  250 m

To Marrakesh & Ouarzazate

KASBAH

Bab el-Kasbah

Bab el-Khemis

Bab Ighiln

Schools & Gardens

Sahat al-Andalous

Berber Souq

Bab Zorgan

Sharia Allal ben Abdallah

Bab Taghount

Rue du 20 Août

Avenue Bab Taghount

Avenue Mohammed V

To Agadir

To Hotel Gazelle d'Or

Oued al-Wa'ar

Avenue Hassan II

Sharia al-Mansour

Sharia ad-Dahabi

Avenue al-Jama al-Kabir

Avenue Bir Anzarane

**PLACES TO STAY**
4   Hôtel Saadiens
7   Hôtel Taroudant
10  Hôtel de la Place
13  Hôtel/Restaurant Roudani
15  Hôtel Les Arcades
18  Hôtel Souss
20  Hôtel/Restaurant El Fath
35  Hôtel Palais Salam
41  Hôtel Ilout
48  Hôtel Liberté
49  Hôtel des Oliviers
50  Hôtel/Douche Ouarda
51  Hôtel Mantaga

**PLACES TO EAT**
9   Restaurant Dallas
17  Sandwich Barcelone
19  Sandwich Sindibad
24  Cheap Snack Stalls
27  Café
29  Restaurant Les Poissons
32  Café/Snack l'Amiral
33  Restaurant Chez Nada
34  Restaurant Essamlali
42  Café de la Jeunesse
47  Café

**OTHER**
1   Thursday & Sunday Souq
2   Mosque
3   Market
5   Post Office (La Poste)
6   Banque Commerciale du Maroc
8   Crédit du Maroc
11  Hammam Ranoq
12  CTM (Buses)
14  Banque Populaire
16  BMCE Bank
21  Préfecture (Police)
22  SATAS (Buses)
23  Place al-Alaouyine
25  Souq
26  BMCI Bank
28  Grand Mosque
31  Studio Al-Ihtihad
36  Préfecture (Police)
37  Mosque
38  Post Office
39  Horse Carriages
40  Amusement Park
43  Local Grands Taxis and Private Bus Lines
44  Petits Taxis
45  Place an-Nasr
46  Grands Taxis to Agadir/Inezgane
52  Tigouga Adventures

MOROCCO

MOROCCO

## Orientation

Unlike many Moroccan towns of the same size and importance, Taroudannt was never chosen as a French administrative or military centre. Consequently, there is no 'European' quarter of wide boulevards and modern buildings.

On first arriving, you could be forgiven for thinking you'll never find your way around. The road layout seems chaotic, and few street signs are in French, so you just plunge into the heart of the medina. In fact, you'll soon sort yourself out. The cheaper hotels are all located on or near the two central squares: Place al-Alaouyine (formerly Assarag) and Place an-Nasr (ex-Talmoqlate). Most of the buses terminate at the former, while grands taxis and some smaller private bus companies are based on Place an-Nasr. You'll find banks, restaurants and a small post office clustered in this area.

## Information

**Money** The BMCE and Banque Populaire have branches on Place al-Alaouyine, and there is a BMCI on Sharia Ibrahim ar-Roudani. All are good for changing cash and travellers' cheques (remember the commission in the BMCE), and cash advances should be possible, too.

**Post** The main post office is south of the main Agadir-Marrakesh highway, but there is a smaller office on Rue du 20 Août.

**Film & Photography** You can get films developed at Studio Al-Ihtihad, not far from the Hôpital Mokhtar Soussi.

## Ramparts

The ramparts of Taroudannt can be explored on foot, but it is better to hire a bicycle, or engage one of the horse-and-cart drivers who hang out just inside the main entrance (see map). It's a long way round the walls! You can climb up onto the ramparts at various points, but be careful, as they are pretty crumbly in places.

## Souqs

The central souq at Taroudannt is relatively small. However, some of the items for sale are of high quality; limestone carvings and traditional Berber jewellery are featured (the town is populated mainly by Chleuh Berbers). This jewellery has been influenced by the tribes of the Sahara as well as by the Jews; the latter were a significant part of the community until the late 1960s. Only the core of the market is devoted to crafts and kitsch souvenirs – the rest serves as the Roudanis' (people of Taroudannt) shopping centre.

One shop worth searching out is that of Lichir el Houcine (☎ 852145), 36 Souq Semata. He has an extensive range and considers himself a serious antiques dealer (and as a result may be a tougher bargainer than others). As always, the best advice is to take your time as you look around for what you want.

Behind Place an-Nasr extends what some refer to as the Berber souq. You'll no doubt have a few guides wanting to usher you this way. Although there are a few stalls selling crafts here, it is generally a fairly humdrum local affair, selling everything from rabbits to rope.

On Thursdays and Sundays, a market for people in the surrounding countryside spreads out just outside Bab al-Khemis (which means Thursday Gate). It is interesting for the spectacle rather than for the goods, but you need to get there early.

## Tanneries

There are tanneries here similar to the ones at Fès, but much smaller. Head out of Bab Targhount and turn left, then continue for about 100 metres and take the first right (signposted). Let your nose guide you from there.

As soon as you enter, you'll be encouraged to buy lamb, sheep and goatskin rugs. Prices start at about Dr 70 to Dr 100 for a rug, depending on the type and size. As part of the sales patter, you should manage to get a free tour and a brief explanation of the process involved in getting to the rug stage, which is interesting, and less likely to happen in Fès.

Also interesting is a small room on the right as you enter, where various animal skins are hung up. The locals don't fall over themselves to show you these, perhaps aware of Western sensitivities on the subject of wildlife extermination.

### Kasbah

The walls around the kasbah date mainly from the time of Saadian rule in Taroudannt, and the area is worth a little stroll, though there are no sights as such inside its walls. Walled off as it is from the rest of the city (you can't get to the Hôtel Palais Salam this way either), it seems almost like a separate little town.

### Swimming

It can get mighty hot in Taroudannt during the summer. You can use the pool at the Hôtel Palais Salam for Dr 30 a day, if the hotel is not full of guests.

### Organised Tours

Tigouga Adventures (☎ 853122) specialises in trekking expeditions in the Western High Atlas. Run by Tali Abd al-Aziz, the agency is located just inside Bab Targhount and deals mainly with English speakers. Tali can organise short local walks, multiday treks or ski treks on the Tichka Plateau, as well as excursions farther afield, such as to Jebel Sirwa. For more information, write to BP 132, Taroudannt Ville, Morocco.

### Places to Stay – bottom end

Most travellers like to stay as close to the centre of activity as possible, and in Taroudannt you can do this without paying a lot of money. There are many hotels around or close to Place al-Alaouyine, and there's not a huge difference in quality or price.

There are four budget places right on the square. One of the cheapest is the Hôtel de la Place, which is pleasant enough and has a variety of rooms. Tiny cell-like singles cost Dr 30, and something more roomy with views over the square can be had for Dr 40.

Doubles are Dr 50. The shared shower is bracingly cold.

On the other side of the lane is the Hôtel/ Restaurant Roudani. There are good views from the upper terrace but, unlike the rooms on the lower floor, the rooms up here don't have private showers. This hotel is clean and the staff friendly. Singles/doubles, regardless of whether they have a private shower, cost Dr 30/60. Hot water is available in the evenings, but the tank is small, so don't leave it too late. The Hôtel Les Arcades, virtually next door, costs the same and is on a par with the Hôtel de la Place.

The Hôtel Riad is somewhat sloppier than the others, and should be left until last when looking for a room. Those dying for a hot shower or bath can try the Hammam Ranoq, just behind the square.

Just off the square, heading towards Place an-Nasr, you'll find the Hôtel Souss. It's dirt cheap (Dr 20 a bed) but not terribly inviting.

Closer to Place an-Nasr is the Hôtel des Oliviers (☎ 852021). It's not bad, with clean beds for Dr 40/60. The showers are cold. A pretty reasonable deal for the money is the Hôtel Mantaga, which has clean rooms with big beds for Dr 25/50. It's on a little lane off Place an-Nasr. On the square itself, the Hôtel Liberté is a little grottier than the Mantaga (there's not a lot in it, though) and has beds for the same prices. On the same lane as the Mantaga is another similarly priced hotel, the Hôtel Ouarda. There's a public (read 'hot') douche (shower) in the same building.

There are two alternatives for people on tightish budgets seeking a little more comfort. The Hôtel Tiout (☎ 850341), on Ave al-Jama' al-Kabir, is a modern sort of place with decent, clean rooms and comfortable beds. Ask for the upstairs rooms with balcony. All rooms, which cost Dr 80/120, have private bathroom.

While perfectly acceptable, the Tiout has none of the charm of one of this city's institutions – the Hôtel Taroudant (☎ 852416). Although fading, this French-run hotel has a unique flavour to it, from the tree-filled courtyard around which the rooms are located to the creaky old dining room, where you can get simple but homely French cooking. Singles/doubles/triples cost Dr 50/68/105 without bathroom, Dr 74/95/132 with private shower, and Dr 95/110/147 with shower and toilet. The water is boiling hot, the hotel has one of the few bars in town and the food in the restaurant is good and moderately priced. This is easily the best deal in Taroudannt.

### Places to Stay – middle
The only mid-range hotel in Taroudannt is the two-star *Hôtel Saadiens* (☎ 852589; fax 852118), Borj Oumansour, which offers B&B for Dr 155/199. Used by some adventure travel groups, the hotel is clean, comfortable and functional, but unremarkable. They have a rooftop restaurant (no alcohol), a swimming pool and access to locked parking, but overall, it's nothing great.

### Places to Stay – top end
The four-star *Hôtel Palais Salam* (☎ 852 312) is right inside the ramparts, by the town's main roundabout and Agadir-Marrakesh road. One of the best of the Salam chain, the building started life as a pasha's residence in the 19th century. Set in luxuriant gardens, with swimming pool, tennis courts, bar and restaurant and guarded parking, it offers singles/doubles/triples for Dr 430/585/740.

Quite possibly the snootiest, most conceited establishment in all Africa is the *Hôtel La Gazelle d'Or* (☎ 852039; fax 852537). Built in 1961 by a French baron, it has 40 bungalows set in extensive gardens, with all the amenities you would expect of a five-star hotel, including a swimming pool, tennis courts and even horse riding. Advance booking is compulsory (anyone simply turning up at the gate will be turned away by a rather silly-looking security chap in a red fez) and the bungalows cost a fortune. The hotel is a couple of km out of town, but well signposted.

### Places to Eat
There are quite a few small cheap eateries

along Sharia Wali al-'Ahd Sidi Mohammed, near the Hôtel Souss, where you can get traditional food like tajine, salads and soups. Some offer quite good fish for very little money at all.

Also good are the restaurants on the ground floors of the hotels on Place al-Alaouyine. The one at the *Hôtel Roudani* is particularly good, with generous helpings of brochettes, chips and salad for Dr 29. Tour groups very often commandeer this place for some lunch-time tea. No matter, the others are about as good.

At *Sandwich Sindibad*, you can buy yourself a very good, fat baguette stuffed with kefta, chips and salad for Dr 17.

The *Restaurant Les Poissons* is exactly what its name suggests: a fish restaurant. It's a pokey little place, but don't let that deter you – you can get a filling plate of the stuff for about Dr 20. It's on Sahat al-Andalous, a little square off Sharia Ibrahim ar-Roudani.

If you want a break from the centre of town, two popular places with locals, and just a little nattier than your run-of-the-mill hole in the wall, are the *Restaurant Essamlali* and *Restaurant Chez Nada*, both on the main street that leads towards Bab al-Kasbah.

In the evening, head for the restaurant and bar at the *Hôtel Taroudant*. The menu here includes the old Moroccan stalwarts, but people looking for a change may want to opt for one of the various French dishes – they don't do a bad steak. Most main courses cost about Dr 40 to Dr 50, and a beer Dr 13 to Dr 15. They also have two set menus (Dr 60 and Dr 70).

There is no end to the cafés scattered throughout Taroudannt's winding streets. A good one with an upstairs terrace can be found on Place an-Nasr, if you're sick of people-watching in the cafés on Place al-Alaouyine and would like to do some elsewhere.

### Getting There & Away
**Bus** The main bus companies have terminals on Place al-Alaouyine. CTM, next door to the Hôtel Les Arcades, has a 9 pm bus to Casablanca (Dr 136.50) via Agadir (Dr

18.50). This bus supposedly goes via Marrakesh (Dr 79) as well, avoiding the Tizi n'Test. Another bus goes to Ouarzazate (Dr 68) en route from Agadir, passing through at about noon.

Across the square is the SATAS station, more useful in this part of Morocco. There are two early morning buses to Marrakesh: one at 4.30 pm via the Tizi n'Test (Dr 55.50, seven hours) and the other at 5 am via Agadir (Dr 70, five hours).

There are three other departures for Agadir, at 5.30 and 11 am and 2.30 pm. A bus to Igherm and Tata (Dr 40.50) leaves at 8 am.

Several other small companies operate buses from the same square and Place an-Nasr, the main destination being Agadir.

**Taxi** The grands taxis gather at Place an-Nasr. Apart from small towns in the area around Taroudannt, the main regular destination is Inezgane (for Agadir), and some times Agadir itself. Either way, the fare is Dr 2015.

### Getting Around

It's highly unlikely that you'll need one of the brown petits taxis, but if you do, they gather at Place an-Nasr.

You can hire bicycles (Dr 5 an hour or Dr 35 a day) from a workshop on Place al-Alaouyine.

You could also tour around town in a *calèche* (horse-drawn carriage). They gather just inside Bab al-Kasbah, near the small amusement park.

### AROUND TAROUDANNT
#### Tioute

Some 37 km to the south-east of Taroudannt lie the impressive ruins of the kasbah of Tioute. Part of the kasbah has been turned into an expensive restaurant, but there's nothing to stop you simply enjoying the views over the palmeraies and village below. Scenes for *Ali Baba & the Forty Thieves*, starring Yul Brynner, were shot here in 1952.

Without your own transport, you'll have to organise a taxi to take you out there from

Taroudannt. If driving, take the P32 towards Marrakesh for about eight km, turn right and cross the oued just before the village and ruined kasbah of **Freija**. From here it's another 15 km down the S7025 towards Igherm before you hit a turn-off to the right. After five km, this reverts to a two-km stretch of piste. At the point where the bitumen ends, you're bound to be befriended by someone wanting to guide you up to the kasbah and restaurant.

# South Coast & Anti-Atlas

From Agadir, the main route south heads inland, maintaining a respectful distance from the coast until it hits Tan Tan Plage, 240 km to the south-west. The terrain rapidly becomes harsher, and by the time you leave Goulimime – the last town on anything approaching the 'tourist circuit' – the stony desert takes over. Few travellers get beyond this point, and it has to be said that there is not an awful lot to see or do down here. It *is* refreshing to get away from the tourist buses, however, and the journey is potentially useful now that convoys are getting through from Dakhla (in Western Sahara) to Mauritania.

The jewel of the area, however, lies 107 km inland from the 19th-century fortress town of Tiznit, in the heart of the Anti-Atlas range. The village of Tafraoute, which lies within this area, is not particularly stunning, but the surrounding mountains, valleys and Berber villages together make up one of the prettiest and most relaxing pieces of walking country in Morocco.

### TIZNIT

In an arid corner of the Souss Valley at the very end of the Anti-Atlas range, Tiznit has the appearance of an old town, with its six km of encircling red mud walls. In fact, the town is a fairly recent creation, but still worth a short stay if you've come this far south. It's

MOROCCO

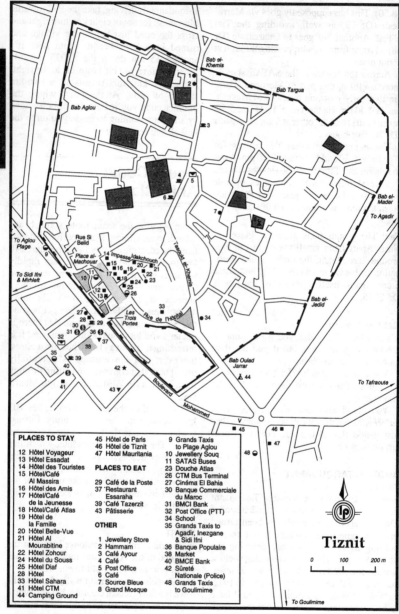

**PLACES TO STAY**

12 Hôtel Voyageur
13 Hôtel Essadat
14 Hôtel des Touristes
15 Hôtel/Café
   Al Massira
16 Hôtel des Amis
17 Hôtel/Café
   de la Jeunesse
18 Hôtel/Café Atlas
19 Hôtel de
   la Famille
20 Hôtel Belle-Vue
21 Hôtel Al
   Mourabitine
22 Hôtel Zohour
24 Hôtel du Souss
25 Hôtel Diaf
28 Hôtel
33 Hôtel Sahara
41 Hôtel CTM
44 Camping Ground

45 Hôtel de Paris
46 Hôtel de Tiznit
47 Hôtel Mauritania

**PLACES TO EAT**

29 Café de la Poste
37 Restaurant
   Essaraha
39 Café Tazerzit
43 Pâtisserie

**OTHER**

1 Jewellery Store
2 Hammam
3 Café Ayour
4 Café
5 Post Office
6 Café
7 Source Bleue
8 Grand Mosque

9 Grands Taxis
   to Plage Aglou
10 Jewellery Souq
11 SATAS Buses
23 Douche Atlas
26 CTM Bus Terminal
27 Cinéma El Bahia
30 Banque Commerciale
   du Maroc
31 BMCI Bank
32 Post Office (PTT)
34 School
35 Grands Taxis to
   Agadir, Inezgane
   & Sidi Ifni
36 Banque Populaire
38 Market
40 BMCE Bank
42 Sûreté
   Nationale (Police)
48 Grands Taxis
   to Goulimime

**Tiznit**

0     100     200 m

also not a bad staging point for a couple of other destinations – the quirky former Spanish town of Sidi Ifni, on the coast, and Tafraoute, to the east.

The best time to be in Tiznit is when the package-tour buses from Agadir have left (mid to late afternoon). It then reverts to normality and is a pleasant place to hang around and explore. This is also the best time to have a look at the silver jewellery, reputedly some of the best in the south – indeed, in all Morocco.

## History

Although there was a settlement of sorts here previously, the town dates substantially from 1881. In that year it was chosen by Sultan Moulay al-Hassan as a base from which to assert his authority over the semiautonomous and rebellious Berber tribes of the Souss and Anti-Atlas. He was only partly successful in this quest; it wasn't until the 1930s – 20 years after Spain and France had divided Morocco between themselves – that the tribes were finally 'pacified'.

In the first decade of the 20th century, Tiznit became a focal point of the resistance against the 1912 treaty that turned Morocco into a French and Spanish protectorate. The resistance was led by El-Hiba, an Idrissid chief from Mauritania who was regarded as a saint and credited with performing miracles. In 1912 he had himself proclaimed sultan at the mosque in Tiznit, and he succeeded in uniting the tribes of the Anti-Atlas and the Tuareg in what proved to be a vain effort to dislodge the French. Ejected from Tiznit and at one point forced to move to Taroudannt, he pursued the campaign of resistance until his death, in 1919.

## Orientation

The main drag, Blvd Mohammed V, runs just outside the south-west wall of the city. At the main set of gates, known as Les Trois Portes (Three Gates), a road leads away from Blvd Mohammed V to the main grand taxi lot. The post office, a couple of banks, restaurants and a food market are on this street. Entering the town through the gates, you end up on

Place al-Machouar, a square on or near which you'll find the jewellery souq and most of the buses and cheap hotels.

## Information

The banks in Tiznit include the BMCE, BMCI and Banque Populaire. The post office is open during normal office hours only.

## Things to See & Do

Apart from wandering around the sleepy interior of the town or hunting for bargains in the just-as-sleepy **jewellery souq**, there's little to see. Of note is the minaret at the **Grand Mosque**. Souls of the dearly departed supposedly rest on the perches sticking out of its mud walls – not a standard element of orthodox Islam!

Nearby is a pretty mucky spring – a popular bathing spot with local kids. Known as the **Source Bleue**, legend has it that a certain Lalla Zninia, a woman of ill repute, turned up at this spot, repented her wicked ways and gave her name to the village that preceded Moulay al-Hassan's 19th-century fortress town.

It's possible to climb onto sections of the city walls, at Bab Targua for instance. Things liven up a little on Thursday, which is market day.

## Places to Stay – bottom end

**Camping** You'll find a fairly uninspiring camp site about halfway between the main roundabout and Bab Oulad Jarrar. Devoid of shade, it's really only of use to people with camper vans. It costs Dr 5 per person and the same per car (Dr 10 per caravan). Water costs Dr 2 and electricity Dr 15.

**Hotels** Travellers prefer to stay at the hotels right on Place al-Machouar, the main square within the city walls. Many have rooftop terraces where you can escape the tourist hordes during the middle of the day. They're all much the same price and offer similar facilities, so where you stay will largely depend on what you take a fancy to and which hotel has a room.

One of the best is off the square, on Impasse Idakchouch. The *Hôtel Belle-Vue* (☎ 862109) is a cheerfully done-up place with clean rooms. Singles/doubles cost Dr 35/60 and a hot shower is Dr 5. That this place has a shower at all distinguishes it from a lot of the competition.

Many travellers stay at the *Hôtel Atlas*, which has a lively restaurant. Singles/doubles cost Dr 30/50, but frankly it's no better than the others. Some of the front rooms have good views of the square, but that's about it. There are cold communal showers. Similar are the *Hôtel des Amis*, *Hôtel de la Jeunesse*, *Hôtel/Café Al Massira*, *Hôtel des Touristes* and *Hôtel Voyageur*. The latter costs Dr 30/50 for singles/doubles with shared bathroom (cold water only), but for some reason is often full. There's a tiny place just behind it, down an alley: the *Hôtel Essadat*.

In addition to the Belle-Vue, there are half a dozen or so other cheapies along Impasse Idakchouch. *Hôtel Al Mourabitine*, at the end of the street, is not bad. Smaller rooms cost Dr 30/50, but they have a bigger and more pleasant room at the front for Dr 50/70 (single/double occupation). The hotel is up on the first floor with a little café. There is no shower.

Opposite the Belle-Vue is the *Hôtel Zohour*. It's Dr 25 for a bed, they have no sheets and it's basically a dump.

A bit closer to the square, the *Hôtel de la Famille* has acceptable rooms for Dr 25/40. Again, they have no showers. Across the road are two more hotels. Rooms in the *Hôtel du Souss* cost Dr 25/30. The rooms are basic, but some are quite big, and the doubles are about as cheap as you'll find anywhere in Morocco. There's no shower and the loos stink to high heaven. Next door, the *Hôtel Diaf* offers OK rooms for Dr 25 per person.

A little farther away from Place al-Machouar is the dark and gloomy *Hôtel Sahara* (☎ 862498), which charges Dr 20 per person. The rooms have clean double beds and little else.

All those with shower problems in this area can head for the *Douche Atlas*, down a side alley off Impasse Idakchouch. It costs Dr 4.50 and there are separate showers for men and women. Another men's and women's hammam is located just inside Bab el-Khemis.

There's a cheapie near the grand taxi lot the *Hôtel CTM* (☎ 862211) – CTM used to have its office here. Cells cost Dr 30/50, but they're clean enough. Hot showers are Dr 5 extra. There's also a little hotel with no name next to the Cinéma El Bahia, on Blvd Mohammed V.

Going up in price, the one-star *Hôtel Mauritania* (☎ 863632), which is on the road to Goulimime, has singles/doubles with private shower and toilet for Dr 110/127. A big room with a kind of alcove at the front of the hotel can sleep three (Dr 150). The hotel, which has its own bar and restaurant, is a very clean and friendly place – a good deal.

## Places to Stay – middle

The only mid-range hotel in town is the two-star *Hôtel de Paris* (☎ 862863), on Ave Hassan II, by the big roundabout. Rooms here are comfortable and clean. Singles/doubles/triples with showers and toilets cost Dr 138/165/215. There is hot water and the hotel has its own restaurant.

## Places to Stay – top end

Tiznit's top-range hotel is the three-star *Hôtel de Tiznit* (☎ 862411/21), Rue Bir Inzaran, also close to the main roundabout. Self-contained singles/doubles with hot water cost Dr 244/301. The hotel has its own bar, restaurant, swimming pool and guarded parking.

## Places to Eat

One of the best restaurants in Tiznit is the *Restaurant Essaraha*, on the corner just across Blvd Mohammed V from Les Trois Portes. Dr 20 will get you a 'petit tajine', which is quite enough for most appetites. The food is good and the service quick. There are a couple of other café/restaurants around here where you can get a bite to eat.

In the evening, a decent place is the restaurant at the *Hôtel Atlas*. Mind you, most of the hotels on the square have cafés offering food, and the difference in quality is not marked.

Those wanting to put together their own meals should go to the covered market, just over Blvd Mohammed V from Les Trois Portes, which offers an excellent selection of meat, vegetables, fruit (fresh and dried) and many other foodstuffs.

There are quite a few cafés dotted about the town, some of them marked on the map. Those with a sweet tooth will find a good pâtisserie in a street off Blvd Mohammed V, just around from the Sûreté Nationale.

### Getting There & Away

**Bus** CTM has two daily buses from its terminal on Place al-Machouar. At 5.30 am there is one to Casablanca (Dr 98.50) via Agadir (Dr 15.50), Essaouira (Dr 43), Safi (Dr 64.50) and El-Jadida (Dr 83.50). At 9 am a mumtaz bus leaves for Tangier (Dr 228.50, 16 hours) via Agadir (Dr 24.50; 1¼ hours), Marrakesh (Dr 85, 5¾ hours), Casablanca (Dr 140.50, nine hours) and Rabat (Dr 162, 10½ hours). You may be able to get on a southbound bus to Goulimime and beyond, but these buses come from Agadir (or farther north), so they often leave already full or don't stop in Tiznit at all.

SATAS, whose office is on the same square has buses to Casablanca (8 am), Marrakesh (9.45 pm) and Agadir (9.30 and 9.45 am, noon and 7.30 pm). A bus to Tafraoute leaves at 3.45 pm (Dr 20), and three go to Goulimime (Dr 23), at 8 and 11 am and 4 pm. A bus to Akka and Tata departs at 9.30 am.

Several small companies run a few services from here, too. There is at least one bus to Sidi Ifni, at about 4 pm.

**Taxi** Grands taxis to Sidi Ifni (Dr 16, about two hours) and Inezgane (for Agadir – Dr 16) leave from the main grand taxi lot. Some taxis go right into Agadir (Dr 17.50). The occasional taxi goes to Tafraoute (Dr 28), but this depends on demand. For Goulimime, there are grands taxis from a rank opposite the Hôtel Mauritania (Dr 25 per person). You

may be able to get one through to Tan Tan, too. Taxis to Aglou Plage leave from another rank, on Blvd Mohammed V by the city walls. They cost Dr 5 a head.

## AROUND TIZNIT
### Aglou Plage

About 15 km from Tiznit lies Aglou Plage, which has a reasonable beach and good surf, though you'll come across the occasional glass and plastic bottle as well as other rubbish. Most of the time it's deserted and, when Atlantic winds start blustering, it's a wild and woolly sort of place.

**Places to Stay** There's a walled *camp site* at the entrance to the village, but it's stony and has no shade whatsoever. Camping at the site (open only in summer) costs next to nothing.

You may well be met there by someone trying to drum up some business. A rocky track off to the left just before the camp site leads up to his house, and to what he has established as a very basic hotel out the back. A bare room with a bed costs Dr 30 and there's a cold shower. You're so far away from everything here that you'll need to cook your own food (no facilities), unless you get lucky with the family.

Forget it and just head down to the beach to the *Motel Aglou*, which has 15 basic cabins (Dr 45) with a sea view. Bathrooms (cold showers) are shared. There's a restaurant – they cook up good meals for Dr 30. It would be 100% better if someone did some work on it, but who cares? – you're only going to sleep there and the beach is all yours. Sherif, the manager, is an obliging guy.

**Getting There & Away** Grands taxis run to Tiznit fairly regularly during the day (Dr 5 per person).

## TAFRAOUTE

Nestled in behind the enchanting Ameln Valley is the village of Tafraoute, itself unspectacular but extremely relaxed – the

MOROCCO

## Berber Houses

Traditional building methods throughout the Atlas Mountain villages had, until recently, changed little over the centuries. Prosperous mountain Berbers now use more modern techniques, but many subsistence farmers and their families continue to employ age-old methods.

The typical house is flat-roofed and made of pisé, a French term referring to the combination of clay, stone and sun or kiln-dried brick. A decent house has three or four floors, and argan-wood beams and palm fronds are typically used for the ceilings between each floor. The bottom floor is basically for the animals. Cows and the like are kept in a dark area, to reduce the number of flies. Scraps are dropped through a hole in the ceiling, from the kitchen above – a natural form of waste disposal. Farming tools are also kept on this floor, along with utensils for making flour and for grinding coffee and argan nuts for oil. If there is a toilet, it's down here.

A better house has a stairway or ladder up to the next floor, both inside and out. Visitors thus have no reason to see the bottom floor. The kitchen might occupy the main floorspace on this level. Gathered around it are what amount to corridors. One (the biggest) is the family dining room, while the rest serve as bedrooms. Occasionally, these rooms host women on festive occasions (there is traditionally, although not always, strict segregation of the sexes if men from outside the immediate family are visiting, whatever the reason).

A ramp leads up to the next floor, most of which is occupied by the most sumptuous room in the house, where the men usually eat with guests or take tea. Here you take your shoes off before walking on the mats, and all the silver teaware is brought out. On the same floor or above it would be the inevitable open terrace – especially important in the summer, when it can be far too hot to sleep inside.

The models vary (sometimes the second and top floors are reversed), but the basic formula remains pretty much the same.

Some of these houses have been standing for hundreds of years, but only in a very loose sense. Habitation of villages has historically been cyclic. Berber villages were, until early this century, regularly exposed to epidemics and subject to raids by enemy tribes, and as a result were often abandoned, sometimes for generations. Where the population was severely reduced, the excess houses stood empty and slowly began to crumble. In better days, these same old houses would be reoccupied, the top floors rebuilt and so the cycle begun again. ∎

perfect base for days of hiking in the hills and Berber villages around it. The more ambitious might consider scaling Jebel al-Kest or taking on guides to follow palm-filled gorges leading towards the bald expanses of the southern Anti-Atlas. Stay here a few days, go on some hikes around the countryside and you'll find it hard to leave.

The village can be reached on roads from Tiznit (107 km) or Agadir (198 km); ideally, a circuit taking in both would be the most satisfying way of doing the trip. It is one where you'd definitely appreciate having your own transport.

From Tiznit, the road starts off in an ordinary enough fashion across gentle farming country, until it reaches Oued Assaka. From here it winds up into the mountains, which in the late afternoon light take on every hue imaginable – greens, reds and golden browns. Sprinkled about the hills are precari-

ous Berber pisé (mud brick) villages (most of the Berbers in this region are Souss Chleuh), surrounded by the cultivated terraces that are worked all through the day – mostly by the women. At 1100 metres you cross the stunning Col de Kerdous (there is a four-star hotel up here), and from here you hardly lose altitude for the remainder of the run into Tafraoute.

The route to Agadir is just as fascinating. Leaving Tafraoute, the road passes through the eastern half of the Ameln Valley and over the Tizi Mlil Pass before doubling back on itself for the trip north-west to Agadir. The land is generally much gentler and more heavily cultivated on this run, but the road passes through plenty of villages – often little agglomerations of houses bunched together, sometimes in the most unlikely places. The most remarkable along the way is **Ida-ou-Gnidif**, perched on a solitary hilltop back from the highway, about 40 km south of Aït Baha. From Aït Baha the road flattens out, and the final stretch up to Agadir is of no interest.

Tourism is on the increase in Tafraoute, which may well be good news for many locals. The region has a long history of emigration. Apart from almond, argan and palm trees (it is said that, where there's a palmeraie there's a natural spring and where there are almond or argan trees is a mere well), along with limited wheat and barley cultivation, there's not much to the local economy. For centuries, this strikingly beautiful area has allowed its inhabitants to eke out only the barest of livings.

The down side is the Agadir tour buses that inevitably make an appearance in the late morning. Still, they're all gone by the afternoon and, so far at least, have had no noticeable effect on the townspeople.

### Information
There are two banks in Tafraoute, the BMCE and the Banque Populaire. The post office (PTT) is on the main square, Sahat Mohammed al-Khamis.

### The Painted Rocks & Napoleon's Hat
Tafraoute is famous for its painted rocks – the work of Belgian artist Jean Veran. (He has done similarly bizarre things in places like the Sinai in Egypt.) In this case he had a collection of the smooth, rounded boulders peculiar to this patch of the mountains spray-painted in living colour, predominantly blue, in 1984. It could be argued that this was a silly thing to do, but no great harm was done by it either.

To get to the rocks, take the road heading north-east to the village of Agard-Oudad (the opposite way to the Agadir exit). It's about three km out. On the way you'll notice a distinctive rock formation on the right, known as **Le Chapeau de Napoléon** (Napoleon's Hat). At the sign indicating a fork (about two km), take the right branch and go through the village to the square, where there's a mosque. From here, turn right and then left to get around the mosque,

and head out into the countryside for a farther two to three km. You'll come to some pale-blue rocks on the left-hand side, but keep going and follow the track bearing left to another set, which includes a large blue boulder with a purple rock on top. Go around this and to your right and you'll come to the best display of painted rocks. The walk is worthwhile even without the painted rocks.

If you're driving, head past Oulad Argad and follow the signs to a turn-off about five km beyond the village. Follow the couple of km of piste and leave the car where the track peters out. About 100 metres on you arrive at a good viewpoint over the rocks. You can climb down to get a closer look.

### The Carved Gazelle
To get to this beautiful and supposedly very old carving, take the road for Tazka past the Hôtel Les Amandiers and head for the village on your right. The road climbs up a hill from here; you need to get in behind this hill and leave it to your left. You'll see a crude drawing of an animal on a rock on the hill. Walk up to it. The carving is on the top side of a fallen rock right in front of this one. The walk from Tafraoute should take about 20 minutes.

### Organised Tours
A couple of local people are setting themselves up as guides to the region around Tafraoute. A friendly and reliable guy seems to be Mohammed Sahnoun Ouhammou. He lives in the village of Tiouadou in the Afella-Ighir oasis south of Tafraoute, and can be contacted through the Hôtel Reddouane or on ☎ 800180. He speaks English and French and specialises in hikes and mountain bike trips through the valleys and oases around his village. When you have fixed a price, he will generally put you up in his home, where you can dump your heavier luggage before setting off.

### Places to Stay – bottom end
**Camping** *Camping Les Trois Palmiers* is set in a small stony compound – all the palm trees are outside the walls – but it's still not

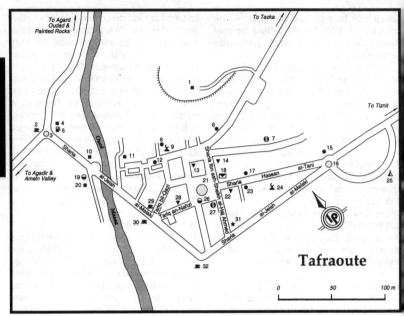

a bad little place. It costs Dr 6 per person, the same to pitch a tent, Dr 7.50 for a car and Dr 207 for a hot shower. The people running it are very laid-back.

**Hotels** The two cheapest places in Tafraoute are just opposite each other towards the Agadir exit end of town. Of these, the *Hôtel Tanger* (☎ 800033) is the most basic, offering singles/doubles for Dr 20/40 – and a possibly hot shared shower (Dr 7), but don't bank on it. Better is the *Hôtel Reddouane* (☎ 800066), where rooms cost Dr 35/55 and a potentially hot shower is included. There is a sun terrace, and the restaurant downstairs is a popular hang-out.

Should you need one, there is a hammam by the old mosque, near the craft shops.

With a little more money you could make a quantum leap to the *Hôtel Tafraout* (☎ 800061, 800121), Place Moulay Rachid. The guy in the fez is the manager, Ibrahim Arkarkour, and he's an affable chap. The

rooms are simple but modern and clean (Dr 2060/100). Some of them overlook the square below and all are comfortable. The shared showers are included in the price and are steaming hot.

**Places to Stay – middle**
The *Hôtel Salam* is on the rebound after 'blowing up' years ago. It is due to reopen as a mid-range 60-room hotel in mid-1995, so by the time you read this, it may be open. They plan to have a sun terrace and a tea room.

**Places to Stay – top end**
The only remaining choice in Tafraoute is the four-star *Hôtel Les Amandiers* (☎ 800033), an amateur architect's travesty of a kasbah, which sits on the crest of the hill overlooking the town. Self-contained singles/doubles cost Dr 315/393 plus taxes. The hotel has its own bar, restaurant, swimming pool and

MOROCCO

guarded parking. They also put on the occasional folkloric dancing and singing show.

For those with a car and a yen for four-star hotels, there is an infinitely better choice 47 km west of Tafraoute on the road to Tiznit. The *Hôtel Kerdous* (☎ 862053; fax 862835), open since 1992, is perched in a former kasbah right on the pass of the same name. There are extraordinary views on all sides, but especially towards Tiznit. The hotel has 39 rooms, two restaurants, a bar and a swimming pool (not heated). Rooms cost Dr 312/377 plus taxes. It's worth stopping here for a drink en route to or from Tafraoute, just for the outlook.

### Places to Eat

Both the cheap hotels have their own reasonably priced restaurants, and it's really a toss-up between the two. You can eat your fill for about Dr 25. Another option along similar lines is the *Restaurant Marrakech*, off the main square.

The *Restaurant L'Étoile d'Agadir*, just up from the post office, has undergone several name changes. They do a filling breakfast of orange juice, bread, butter, cheese and jam, finished off with tea or coffee. It's a little expensive though, at Dr 20.

The best restaurant, if you have a bit of money to spare, is the *Restaurant L'Étoile du Sud*, opposite the post office on Sharia Hassan at-Tani. The Dr 70 menu, although not offering much of a choice of main courses, is tasty. The interior is done up as a traditional Moroccan salon, and the atmosphere is laid back. You can also eat under the tent outside.

For an ice cream you could try the crémerie near the Restaurant L'Étoile d'Agadir.

### Getting There & Away

**Bus** SATAS has a daily bus from Agadir to Tafraoute at 1.30 pm daily, and one from Tiznit at 3.45 pm (Dr 20). Going the other way, the SATAS Tiznit bus leaves at 6.30 am from near the Hôtel Tanger, and goes on to Casablanca. The Agadir run seemed in doubt at the time of writing. There are up to five other buses (with other companies) from various spots along Sharia al-Jeish al-Malaki. They all seem to go to Tiznit.

**Taxi** The occasional grand taxi goes to Tiznit in the morning (Dr 28). Otherwise, Land Rover taxis do the rounds of various villages in the area around Tafraoute. There is no rhyme or reason to their movements, except demand – which mostly means doing business on market days. If there are any to be had, they hang around Sahat Mohammed al-Khamis or on Sharia al-Jeish al-Malaki.

## AROUND TAFRAOUTE
### Ameln Valley

Tafraoute lies in a basin, largely surrounded by craggy rocks and cliffs. To the north-west lies one such ridge, on the other side of which runs the Ameln Valley (Ameln is the name given to the local tribe of Chleuh Berbers). North again of this valley is a mountain range dominated by Jebel al-Kest.

The Agadir road takes you to the valley, which is lined by a string of picturesque Berber villages, some of them only partly inhabited. Four km out of Tafraoute, the road forks, the right branch turning off to take you eastwards out of the valley and on to Agadir. The other proceeds ahead, west down the valley. You could take either way and then head off down a track to any of the villages. It is possible to hike for days, going directly from village to village through barley fields or following narrow goat tracks and irrigation channels.

One of the most visited of the villages is **Oumesnat**, a few km farther down the Agadir road after the fork and off to the left along a short piste. The main attraction here is the **Maison Traditionelle**. Si Abdessalam decided to open up his three-storey house to visitors years ago as a way of drumming up a bit of income. Blinded as a young man in Tangier, he is a gentle host and gives you a tour of every nook and cranny of his place, followed by a glass of tea. He expects a small consideration for his efforts, and is worth every dirham. If you go unguided, just ask about for him and the house – it's poorly signposted and you need to follow a string of water channels into the heart of Oumesnat to find the house. A guide may well be useful, as Si Abdessalam speaks only Arabic and French.

Another village popular with foreigners is **Anameur**, although the only thing that sets it apart from the others is a natural spring. It's about 10 km west of Oumesnat.

**Taghdichte**, between Oumesnat and Anameur, is used by several adventure-travel groups (mainly English and German) as a base for ascents of Jebel al-Kest (which locals maintain is no easy undertaking). You can hire taxis to get you to some of these villages.

### Afella-Ighir

The Tafraoute area offers plenty of hiking possibilities for people who want to hang around for a while. Among these are a couple of routes taking you south to the oasis of Afella-Ighir. You could cover most of it in a 4WD, but it's preferable to drive part of the way, then leave the car and do a circuit on foot or mountain bike. The road south of Agard-Oudad takes you some 15 km over a mountain pass (sometimes snowed over in winter) to Tlata Tasrite. From here it is possible to take several pistes that drop into lush palm-filled valleys, and do a loop of about 30 to 40 km through to the Afella-Ighir oasis and back up to Tlata Tasrite. A new road is being built to Souq al-Had, in Afella-Ighir, which will ease things for ordinary cars but detract from the charms of a long hike. About nine km south of Souq al-Had is Oussaka, where there are ancient animal carvings. More can be seen eight km farther on at Tasselbte. It would be best to talk to a guide (see Organised Tours under Tafraoute) about the latter part of this hike. Land Rover taxis will sometimes do the run to various villages of this area on market days (Wednesday in Tafraoute itself).

## SIDI IFNI

Known to some simply as Ifni, Sidi Ifni is the town at the heart of the former Spanish enclave of Ifni. Shrouded for much of the year in an Atlantic mist, this haunting and short-lived coastal outpost of Spanish imperial ambitions has a neglected but somehow fascinating air. The town dates largely from the 1930s and features an eclectic mix of Spanish Art Deco and traditional Moroccan styles. The church just off the main plaza and the building (in the form of a ship) on the edge of the cliff next to the Hotel Suerte Loca shouldn't be missed. The old balustraded esplanade is crumbling, the still-unrenamed calles are half-empty and the town clearly suffers from not being served by a main coastal road. This may change, as there are plans to build a highway down the coast from Agadir and on to Tan Tan, and hotel-chain scouts have looked the place over for potential.

But that all seems far away now, and the town of 15,000 lives mainly from small-scale fishing; most of the catch is sold in Agadir. It is a curious place to visit, and attracts a surprising number of travellers. There's not a great deal to do or see, and you certainly won't have any problems with touts. The town beaches are deserted but unfortunately not the best, as a lot of rubbish tends to be dumped on them.

### History

After the Spanish-Moroccan war of 1859, which Morocco lost (just 14 years after being defeated at the hands of a French army from Algeria), Spain obtained the enclave of Ifni by treaty. Quite what they were going to do with it seems to have been a question in a lot of Spanish minds, because they didn't take full possession until 1934. By the 1950s, some 60% of the town's population was Spanish, but under pressure from the UN, Spain agreed to cede the enclave back to Morocco in 1969. Morocco had sealed off its land borders three years before. Only three Spanish families now remain.

### Information

There are two banks on the main street, Ave Mohammed V (away from the heart of the former Spanish town), where you can change cash and cheques. The post office is also on Ave Mohammed V (the letter box outside is still marked 'Correos').

### Things to See & Do

Apart from wandering round the old Spanish part of town, the heart of which is Place Hassan II (formerly Plaza de España), there's precious little to do in the town, except perhaps search for an acceptable stretch of beach. There's a fairly decent market (Marché Municipal) that takes up the block where Ave Mohammed V runs into Ave Hassan II. There are a few grocery shops along Ave Mohammed V too.

The area is not a bad one for excursions into the countryside, too (the drive from Tiznit, particularly where the road runs through the hills just in from the coast, is itself worthwhile, as is the 58-km run to Goulimime). One possibility would be to hike along the coastal piste to **Sidi Ouarsik**, a fishing village with a good beach 18 km south of Sidi Ifni. The trip to Mesti, a Berber village 25 km out of Sidi Ifni, off the road to Goulimime, is also a pleasant diversion. The Hotel Suerte Loca can organise guides and mountain bikes for such trips.

### Places to Stay – bottom end

**Camping** Just south of the hospital, a cheap but basic patch of ground has been set aside for campers, but it's really only any good for people with camper vans.

**Hotels** The justifiably most popular hotel is the *Hotel Suerte Loca* (☎ 875350), which is run by a friendly old man (who speaks Spanish and French) and his family (two of the sons speak English). The hotel is divided into two wings, one of them considerably newer than the other. The older rooms are perfectly comfortable, and some have balconies. They cost Dr 45/75 (hot showers along the corridor are Dr 5 extra). The clean, cosy rooms in the new wing (Dr 85/125) have en suite bathrooms and balconies. The hotel has a small collection of novels and the like to lend to guests, a good restaurant (excellent breakfast and crêpes), a terrace for sunbathing and mountain bikes for hire.

If the Hotel Suerte Loca is full (which is quite possible), there are a few standard Moroccan cheapies scattered around Ave Mohammed V. The *Hôtel Ifni* is as good as any, with very basic rooms for Dr 20 a head. They have cold showers. Two others in the same class are marked on the map.

If you want a hot shower, there is a public douche just up the road from the Hotel Suerte Loca. There are separate times for men and women.

MOROCCO

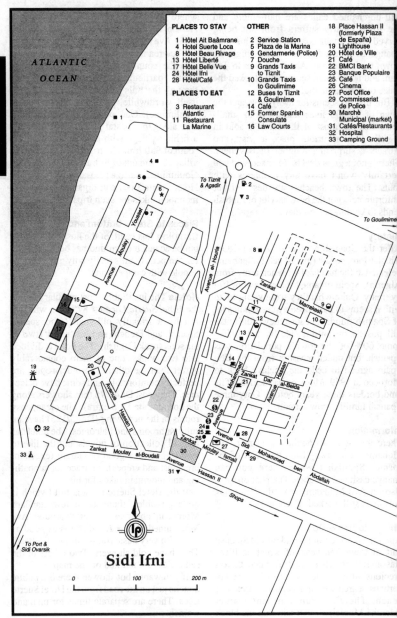

**PLACES TO STAY**
1  Hôtel Ait Baâmrane
4  Hôtel Suerte Loca
8  Hôtel Beau Rivage
13  Hôtel Liberté
17  Hôtel Belle Vue
24  Hôtel Ifni
28  Hôtel/Café

**PLACES TO EAT**
3  Restaurant Atlantic
11  Restaurant La Marine

**OTHER**
2  Service Station
5  Plaza de la Marina
6  Gendarmerie (Police)
7  Douche
9  Grands Taxis to Tiznit
10  Grands Taxis to Goulimime
12  Buses to Tiznit & Goulimime
14  Café
15  Former Spanish Consulate
16  Law Courts
18  Place Hassan II (formerly Plaza de España)
19  Lighthouse
20  Hôtel de Ville
21  Café
22  BMCI Bank
23  Banque Populaire
25  Café
26  Cinema
27  Post Office
29  Commissariat de Police
30  Marché Municipal (market)
31  Cafés/Restaurants
32  Hospital
33  Camping Ground

ATLANTIC OCEAN

To Tiznit & Agadir

To Goulimime

To Port & Sidi Ovarsik

Sidi Ifni

0    100    200 m

MOROCCO

The *Hôtel Beau Rivage* is shut (so ignore the signs).

## Places to Stay – middle

There are two one-star places in Sidi Ifni, but they are no better than the new wing of the Suerte Loca. They are the *Hôtel Belle Vue* (☎ 875072), 9 Place Hassan II, and the *Hôtel Ait Baâmrane* (☎ 875267), on the beach. Rooms at both have private shower (hot water promised in both cases) and cost Dr 110/127. Those in the Belle Vue are more comfortable; some have sea views while others look onto the plaza. The hotel has a restaurant and bar, and the terrace overlooking the square is a good place for a tea. The slow-moving staff understand more Spanish than anything else.

Rooms in the Ait Baâmrane are tattier but some look right onto the ocean. There is a restaurant and bar, and the English-speaking staff offer a discount if you stay for more than one night.

## Places to Eat

Apart from a few small café/restaurants on Ave Hassan II and dotted about the town, the only choices are really the hotel restaurants. The one at the *Hotel Suerte Loca* is particularly good value. Another possibility is the *Restaurant Atlantic*, down by the petrol station at the main town exit.

## Getting There & Away

**Bus** There are one or two buses between Sidi Ifni and both Tiznit and Goulimime. Virtually all the buses leave Sidi Ifni from along Ave Mohammed V, early in the morning.

**Taxi** By far the easiest way to get to and from Sidi Ifni is by grand taxi. Taxis leave from a couple of dirt lots around the corner from the northern end of Ave Hassan I and cost Dr 16 a head to either Tiznit (about 1½ hours) or Goulimime (one hour).

## GOULIMIME

Several things are striking about Goulimime, the dusty little town that proclaims itself the Gateway to the Sahara. The first is the bold crimson colour of almost all the buildings. The second is the disproportionate number of touts – enough people are still drawn here for the legendary Saturday camel market to have created a pool of aggressive and nasty little hustlers. Be careful what stories you believe – the one about the Berber market in the oasis of Aït Bekkou (today only!), and 'could you possibly give me a lift there' (this to people with their own transport) is a good one.

Once upon a time, 'blue men' came in from the desert every week to buy and sell camels at a souq just outside town. In the evenings, the women would perform the

MOROCCO

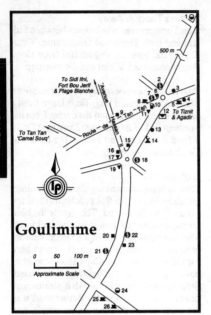

### PLACES TO STAY

9   Hôtel Salam
15  Hôtel Oued Dahab
16  Hôtel Bir Anazarane
20  Hôtel La Jeunesse
23  Hôtel L'Ere Nouvelle

### PLACES TO EAT

6   Café de la Poste
11  Café Le Diamant Bleu
17  Rotisserie Al-Jawda
19  Rotisserie El Menara

### OTHER

1   Buses & Grands Taxis
2   BMCI Bank
3   Studio Color (Film)
4   CTM Office & Café
5   Café
7   Crédit du Maroc
8   Café
10  Petrom Service Station
12  Post Office (PTT)
13  Hammam
14  Mosque
18  Banque Populaire
21  BMCE Bank
22  Banque Commerciale du Maroc
24  Grands Taxis to Asrir
25  Café Ali Baba
26  Café Paloma

mesmerising *guedra* dance to the beat of drums of the same name. This is what the flocks of package tourists pile into Goulimime for on Friday night and Saturday, but they must leave sorely disappointed. The market is now more of a butchers' convention for goat meat, with busloads of foreigners in search of the one or two camels dragged in here specially for them. Forget the tourist literature; about the only good thing to come out of Goulimime are the roads to Tiznit and Sidi Ifni. The former offers a couple of pretty stretches, particularly about halfway along, when crossing the **Tizi Mighert Pass**.

### Information

The tourist office (☎ 872545) is at 3 Résidence Sahara, Blvd d'Agadir. Should you find yourself stuck here for any reason, four banks have branches in Goulimime, so changing money should be no problem. The post office is near the mosque between the two main roundabouts.

### Camel Souq

If you feel you must contribute to the myth of the camel market, it takes place a couple of km outside town along the Route de Tan Tan (take a taxi) on Saturday mornings. Unless you get there just after sunrise, you won't be able to see the camels for the tourists.

### Places to Stay – bottom end

**Camping** There is a camp site at Fort Bou Jerif, 40 km from Goulimime. It is an oasis of civilisation in the desert, meals are available and getting there is well worth the effort.

ake the Plage Blanche turn-off just out of Goulimime on the road to Sidi Ifni. Be aware that some of the road is piste.

You could also try *Camping Abainou*, at a village of the same name about 12 km out of Goulimime (take the Sidi Ifni road, turn right after four km and follow the signs). The *Auberge Abainou* also advertises 'free caravanning', which presumably means you can park your camper van there and just pay for use of facilities.

**Hotels** There are four cheap hotels from which to choose, but none of them is all that enticing. In the centre, the *Hôtel Bir Anzarane* is one of the cheapest, at Dr 20/30 for singles/doubles. The rooms are little cell-tyle arrangements, and the hotel has no shower at all. Worse still is the *Hôtel Oued Dahab*, on the other side of the roundabout, which is very primitive. They do have a cold shower, and rooms cost the same as at the Bir Anzarane.

Farther down Ave Hassan II, away from the centre, are the other places, across the road from each other and near the BMCE Bank. Of these, the *Hôtel L'Ere Nouvelle* is marginally better than the *Hôtel La Jeunesse*, and distinguishes itself from all the others by promising a hot shower (Dr 5).

**Places to Stay – middle**
The only hotel in this range is the two-star *Hôtel Salam* (☎ 872057), which has its own bar and restaurant and costs 136/165 for rooms with private shower and toilet, plus taxes. They also have cheaper rooms without toilet. It is advisable to book ahead here if you want to turn up for the camel charade.

**Places to Eat**
There are a couple of good little rotisseries near the Hôtel Bir Anzarane – it's a toss-up between *Al-Jawda* and *El Menara*. You can get a filling meal of chicken, chips and salad for around Dr 20.

Something more like a restaurant, with the usual Moroccan fare, is the *Café de la Poste*, on the BMCI bank end of the Route de Tan Tan. A full meal here will cost about Dr 40.

Similar food is on offer at the *Café Le Diamant Bleu*, and occasionally at the café near the CTM office on the Agadir road. About the only other option is the bar and restaurant at the *Hôtel Salam*.

The most pleasant cafés are the *Café Ali Baba* and the *Café Paloma*, about half a km south of the main roundabout, opposite the Asrir grand taxi lot.

**Getting There & Away**
**Bus** The main bus and grand taxi terminals are about one km north of the town centre, although CTM also has a small office on the Agadir road. CTM has buses to Agadir (Dr 48) via Tiznit, leaving at 3.30 and 4 am (!) and one to Casablanca via both, at 8 pm. Buses to Marrakesh leave at 9 pm, midnight and 12.30 am. Others head for Laayoune (Dr 141), at 12.30 am and 2 and 6.30 pm. The first of these goes on to Dakhla, and you can change in Laayoune for Smara. At 6.30 am, a bus leaves for Tan Tan (Dr 26).

SATAS also operates out of this station, along with several smaller local companies, so you have a reasonable choice.

**Taxi** If bus departure times look inconvenient, you're probably better off with a grand taxi. They leave from behind the bus station. You can get a taxi to Sidi Ifni (Dr 16), Tiznit (Dr 25), Tan Tan (Dr 28), Inezgane (for Agadir; Dr 40) and Laayoune (Dr 100).

**AROUND GOULIMIME**
**Plage Blanche**
About 65 km out of Goulimime (take the Sidi Ifni exit and turn left at the signposted road), the Plage Blanche is, as yet, a little visited and unspoilt stretch of Atlantic beach. The road turns to piste after about 20 km, so you want a solid vehicle to get out here. Apart from the beach, there is virtually nothing around, but that is bound to change if schemes to construct a coastal highway south from Agadir ever take off.

**Aït Bekkou**
About 17 km south-east of Goulimime, Aït Bekkou is a pleasant oasis village – you'll

MOROCCO

probably see more camels here than in Goulimime on a Saturday, but don't fall for the old 'Berber market, today only' story. You can get grands taxis as far as Asrir, but you may well have to hitch the remaining seven km of piste to Aït Bekkou. Alternatively, hire a taxi for the day.

## TAN TAN

Taking the road south from Goulimime, you soon get the feeling you're heading well into the unknown – few travellers bother to go this far. The 125 km of desert highway is impressive in parts, but is harsh hammada (stony desert) rather than the soft, sandy dune variety. Breaking up the monotony, the road also crosses several oueds, including the Oued Drâa, which is usually dry this far away from its sources. Something else that creates mild interest are the police roadblocks, which become more frequent as you head south; you may or may not have to hang about at these while bored gendarmes check your passport and ask idiotic questions.

You could drive through the main street of Tan Tan (population 50,000) and not realise you had missed most of the town, which spreads south of the highway (known as Ave

Hassan II within the town boundaries). If you're on a bus or grand taxi, however, there's no danger of this. Tan Tan is situated in what was once part of Spanish-occupied Morocco, an area known under the Spaniards as Tarfaya which stretched south to the border with the so-called Spanish Sahara, a colony Spain abandoned only in 1975. The Tarfaya zone was handed over in 1958, two years after independence.

There's nothing much to do in Tan Tan although it has quite a busy air about it. If you are heading south, it makes a more interesting overnight stop than Tarfaya (to the south).

### PLACES TO STAY

| | |
|---|---|
| 1 | Hôtel Bir Anzarane |
| 4 | Hôtel Aoubour |
| 5 | Hôtel Royal |
| 18 | Hôtel/Restaurant du Sud |
| 19 | Hôtel/Café Chahrazad |
| 20 | Hôtel/Café Sahara |
| 21 | Hôtel/Café Essaada |
| 22 | Hôtel/Café Dakar |
| 25 | Hôtel Atlas |
| 26 | Hôtel El Ansar |
| 27 | Hôtel Rahma |

### PLACES TO EAT

| | |
|---|---|
| 16 | Snack Stand |

### OTHER

| | |
|---|---|
| 2 | Shell Service Station |
| 3 | BMCE Bank |
| 6 | Petrol Station |
| 7 | Cinema |
| 8 | Banque Populaire |
| 9 | Grands Taxis to Tarfaya & Laayoune |
| 10 | Café |
| 11 | Market |
| 12 | Mosque |
| 13 | Kodak Shop |
| 14 | Salon La Jeunesse |
| 15 | Telephone Office |
| 17 | Petits Taxis |
| 23 | Grands Taxis to Goulimime, Tiznit & Agadir |
| 24 | Bus Station (Gare Routière) |

To Tan Tan Plage & Laayoune

Avenue

Avenue Mohammed V →

Hassan II

To Goulimime

Boulevard el-Amir Moulay Abdallah

800 m

**Tan Tan**

0    200    400 m

## Information

BMCE has a branch next to the Shell station where Ave Mohammed V runs into Ave Hassan II. There is a Banque Populaire on the first square heading down Ave Mohammed V away from Ave Hassan II. There's a telephone office on the main square.

## Places to Stay & Eat

Tan Tan is crawling with cheap hotels, so you'll have no trouble finding a bed. The best of the lot around the bus station square is the *Hôtel Dakar*, although it's hardly great. Rooms with a double bed cost Dr 60 or Dr 80 with private shower (there's a gas heater, so you might even get hot water). The others here and the multitude in side lanes heading north along Ave Mohammed V are generally basic places costing about Dr 30 to Dr 40 per person. Most offer cold showers at best, but can direct you to a hammam (there's one near the bus station).

There are several more such hotels on the main square. Here you can try the *Hôtel/Restaurant du Sud*, *Hôtel/Café Chahrazad*, *Hôtel Sahara* or *Hôtel Essaada*. They all have cafés or restaurants downstairs. The *Hôtel Aoubour*, on Ave Hassan II, is more convenient for people with their own transport, but it's no great shakes.

The best hotel by far, but a bit of a hike from the bus station, is the *Hôtel Bir Anzarane* (☎ 877834). It costs Dr 50 per person in clean, carpeted rooms. The shared showers are clean, and have hot water in the evenings.

## Getting There & Away

**Bus** All the buses leave from the bus station (gare routière), about one km south of the main central square. CTM and SATAS are the best companies operating buses from here, although a lot of the services are through runs from other towns.

**Taxi** Grands taxis to Laayoune (Dr 70) and, occasionally, Tarfaya leave from a small square off Blvd el-Amir Moulay Abdallah. Others, for Goulimime (Dr 28), Tiznit and Inezgane (for Agadir – Dr 70), leave from a lot by the bus station.

**Car** Much cheaper petrol is available in the Western Sahara, which begins just south of Tarfaya. The first of the Atlas Sahara petrol stations is just outside Tarfaya and about 240 km south of Tan Tan – try to get there with a tank as close to empty as possible!

## AROUND TAN TAN
### Tan Tan Plage

About 27 km west of Tan Tan is the beach of the same name. It's a rather uninspiring little spot, with a few cafés in among the scruffy housing and public buildings. With the main business being fish exports, the port area does nothing to improve the atmosphere on the beach.

# The High Atlas

MOROCCO

The ochre-coloured city of Marrakesh is possibly Morocco's biggest drawcard. Founded almost 1000 years ago, it basks in a clear African light that gives it an entirely different feel from the cities farther north. From the ad hoc, fairground atmosphere of the Djemaa el-Fna to the busy hum of the souqs, there is more than enough to keep the newcomer's senses fully occupied.

If the big city becomes too much, there are several escape routes into the majestic High Atlas mountain range that hovers snowcapped in the background. You can trek with the crowds on some of the more well-trodden routes, or, if you're fit and experienced, embark on more ambitious wanderings that could easily last weeks and take you into territory penetrated by only a handful of outsiders.

Valleys cut through the range and spill ou south and east towards the Sahara. Dotte with kasbahs and palm groves, the spectac ular natural settings are endowed with largely mediocre towns. These valleys an passes truly exemplify the bastardise maxim that 'it is better to travel than t arrive'.

## Marrakesh

There can be few people who have not hear of Marrakesh. During the 1960s and '70s i was a magnet for travellers, along with Istan bul, Kabul and Kathmandu – and rightly so The hippies have since been replaced b hordes of package tourists with more mone

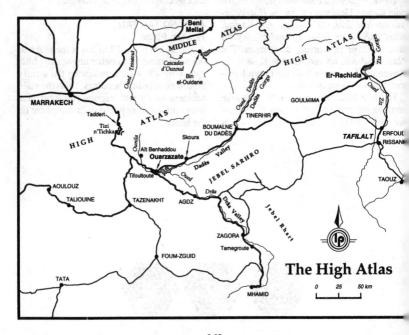

The High Atlas

0      25      50 km

and considerably less time than their more laid-back predecessors. The unfortunate side-effect of this onslaught has been the rise and rise of the unpleasant phenomenon of hustlers. However, although an undoubted irritant, it would take a lot more to detract from the fascination of this place.

Marrakesh is Morocco's second-largest city, with a population of about 1,400,000, although to walk around the centre it would not seem so. The red walls of the old city contain a busy, humming core, but you rarely get the sense of being suffocated by over-population. Perhaps the extensive gardens that spread out around the old city contribute to this – in any event they provide a welcome and tranquil refuge from the bustle of the souqs. Red, by the way, is supposedly the city's 'official' colour, just as it is blue for Fès, green for Meknès and white for Rabat.

Sitting against the backdrop of Morocco's highest mountains, which are snowcapped for much of the year, the city has a scenic setting that is hard to surpass.

## History

Once one of the most important artistic and cultural centres in the Islamic world, Marrakesh was founded in 1062 AD by the Almoravid sultan Youssef bin Tachfin. It experienced its heyday under Youssef's son, Ali, who was born to a Christian slave mother. It was Ali who had the extensive underground irrigation canals (khettara) built that still supply the city's gardens with water.

As the Almoravids proceeded with their conquest of Spain, much of the wealth that flowed to the kingdom was lavished on extending and beautifying the city. When Youssef bin Tachfin died in 1106, he could do so content in the knowledge that he had not only consolidated his dynasty's control of Morocco and Spain (in 1085 he had defeated the Christians after they had seized the city of Toledo), but he had also bequeathed an urban jewel to his successors. Inside the city's red stone and earthen ramparts, characteristic of Berber defensive architecture, artisans from Muslim Spain

erected the first of the refined, Andalusian-style buildings that were to grace the city.

These buildings were largely razed to the ground by the Almohads in 1147, although the walls and the gateway to Ali's huge palace were spared. The city was rebuilt shortly afterwards, and, again, it was artisans from Andalusia who were responsible for the greater part of its construction. Marrakesh remained the capital of the Almohad empire until its collapse in 1269, when the Merenids moved the capital north to Fès, which then became the focus of Moroccan brilliance in the arts.

With the rise to power of the Saadians in the 16th century, Marrakesh again became the capital, following a brief period when the city of Taroudannt enjoyed that particular honour. The city had experienced hard times prior to the Saadian takeover. Even the Portuguese had tried to capture Marrakesh in 1515, and in the following years famines had crippled activity in the city and surrounding countryside.

Saadian control brought prosperity once again. During their reign the Portuguese were forced to abandon the bulk of their coastal enclaves. The mellah, the huge Mouassine Mosque and the Ali ben Youssef Medersa were built in these times. The Saadians also set up a customs house for the Christian colony that had been established in Marrakesh. Ahmed al-Mansour was one of the more outstanding of the Saadian sultans, and was known as 'the Golden One' because of his riches, largely accumulated in his 'conquest' of Timbuktu. His legacy included the exquisite Andalusian El-Badi Palace and the long-hidden necropolis of his dynasty, now known simply as the Saadian tombs.

As so often in Morocco's turbulent history, the golden days were soon followed by chaos and decadence. The Saadians' successors, the Alawites, moved the capital to Meknès.

Marrakesh could not be ignored, however. Although Moulay Ismail was responsible for tearing apart the El-Badi Palace for its building materials, his successor, Sidi Mohammed bin Abdallah, poured resources

MOROCCO

**PLACES TO STAY**

5  Hostel
6  Camping Ground
7  Hôtel de la Ménara
23 Hôtel Islane
27 Hôtel La Mamounia

**OTHER**

1  Hospital
2  Tourist Office
3  Post Office (PTT)
4  Train Station
8  Bab Larissa
9  Bab Doukkala
10 Bus Station
11 Zawiyya of Sidi ben Slimane
12 Zawiyya of Sidi Bel Abbes
13 Bab el-Khemis
14 Bab Kechich
15 Bab Debbagh
16 Tanneries

17 Ali ben Youssef Medersa
18 Ali ben Youssef Mosque
19 Bab Doukkala Mosque
20 Hôtel de Ville
21 Ensemble Artisanal
22 Public Swimming Pool
24 Koutoubia
25 French Consulate
26 Bab el-Jedid
28 Dar Si Said (Museum of Moroccan Arts)
29 Palais de la Bahia
30 Bab Allen
31 Bab Ghemat
32 Place des Ferblantiers
33 Palais el-Badi
34 Saadian Tombs
35 Kasbah Mosque
36 Bab Agnaou
37 Bab er-Rob
38 Bab Ksiba
39 Royal Palace
40 Mechouar
41 Bab al-Ahmar

# Marrakesh

To Ouarzazate,
Meknès & Fès

0          250          500 m

Route principale No 24

Rue Assouel

Rue de Bab Tarnzout

Rue el-Gza

Rue de Bab Khémis

Route des Remparts

See Marrakesh
Medina Map

Rue de Bab Debbagh

Rue de Bab Doukkala

Rue Issebtyne

Rue Dar el-Glaoui

Rue Souk es-Smarine

Rue Azbezt

Rue de Bab Ailen

Rue Fatima Zohra

Rue Sidi el-Yamani

Rue Mouassine

Rue Dabach

Rue Abbes Sebti

Rue el-Kouloubia

Place Djemaa
el-Fna

Rue Graoui

Rue Ba Ahmad

Avenue Mohammed

See Marrakesh
(Budget Hotel Area)

Avenue
el-Mouahidine

Rue Riad Zitoun el-Jdid

Ave Houmane el-Fetouaki

Rue Zitoun el-Qedim

Ave Houmane el-Fetouaki

Rue de Bab Agnaou

Rue Sidi Mimoun

Mellah

Boulevard es-Yarmouk

To Ouarzazate

Kasbah

Rue de la Kasbah

Jardin
Agdal

Airport

To Asni &
Taroudannt

into rebuilding or restoring the walls, kasbah, palaces, mosques and mechouars of the city, as well as creating new gardens (such as the Jardin Ménara).

By the 19th century, Marrakesh was again on the decline, although it did regain some of its former prestige when Moulay al-Hassan I was crowned there in 1873. Its most recent return to good fortune is largely the result of French activities during the protectorate period, when the ville nouvelle was built, the medina was revitalised and resettled, and the Place de Foucauld was created below the Djemaa el-Fna. Increasing tourism in Marrakesh since then has ensured its continued prosperity. The importance attached to the city by Morocco itself was symbolised in April 1994, when it was chosen as the location for the final signing of the international GATT agreements on world trade.

### Orientation

As in Fès and Meknès, the old city and the ville nouvelle of Marrakesh are about the same size. It's about a half-hour walk from the centre of activity in the ville nouvelle to the Djemaa el-Fna, the main square in the heart of the old city, so you'll find it convenient to use public transport to get from one to the other. The two main areas of the ville nouvelle are Gueliz and Hivernage. The latter contains little more of interest than some middle and top-range hotels, and it borders on the Ménara Gardens.

Gueliz forms the working centre of the ville nouvelle, and the bulk of the city's offices, restaurants, cafés and shops and a collection of hotels are all clustered on or near the city's main thoroughfare, Ave Mohammed V, mostly west of Place du 16 Novembre. The railway station lies southwest of Ave Mohammed V along Ave Hassan II, which joins the former at Place du 16 Novembre. The main bus station is near Bab Doukkala, about a 10-minute walk northeast of the same square, and about 20 minutes on foot from the Djemaa el-Fna.

The walls around the medina enclose a far more open area than that found behind the walls of Fès and Meknès. It is not until you have penetrated to the heart of the old city, the Djemaa el-Fna, that you reach the familiar maze of souqs and twisting alleys.

The Djemaa el-Fna itself is a large, irregularly shaped square dominated from a distance by the city's most prominent landmark, the Koutoubia Mosque. The area is in many ways rather nondescript. There are no grand monuments overlooking the jumble of people, food stalls, tourists, hustlers and snake charmers who lend it its life, but you will soon be beguiled by its atmosphere. For centuries, traders, farmers, thieves, slaves and just about every other possible species have milled around here.

Most of the budget hotels are clustered in the narrow streets branching off the eastern and south-eastern sides of the square. The souqs and principal religious buildings lie to the north of the Djemaa el-Fna, and the palaces are to the south.

### Information

**Tourist Office** The ONMT office (☎ 448 889; fax 448906) is on Place Abdel Moumen ben Ali, at the junction of Ave Mohammed V and Rue de Yougoslavie (or Ave du Président Kennedy, depending on which map you believe). It has the usual range of glossy leaflets and a list (without prices) of the classified hotels in Marrakesh, but precious little else. If you're lucky, it will have a couple of copies of the free booklet *Welcome to Marrakesh*. It may be able to put you in touch with guides in Asni for treks in the High Atlas, but then so can some of the hotels. The office is open Monday to Friday from 8.30 am to noon and again from 3.30 to 6.30 pm.

**Money** You should have no trouble changing money. As usual, your best bet is the BMCE. The branch across from the tourist office in Gueliz has an ATM as well as a change office, open daily from 10 am to 2 pm and 4 to 8 pm. You can change cash or travellers' cheques or get a cash advance on Visa or MasterCard. The BMCE branch on Rûe de Moulay Ismail, just south of the Djemaa el-Fna, offers the same services. The Bank al-Maghrib (Banque du Maroc) on the Djemaa el-Fna will change cash and travellers' cheques.

American Express is represented by Voyages Schwartz (☎ 436600/3), Immeuble Moutaouakil, 1 Rue Mauritania. Although it's a little hard to believe, the operators claim to have someone manning the office from 6 am to 11 pm, Monday to Friday.

**Post & Telecommunications** The main post office is on Place du 16 Novembre in the ville nouvelle. There is a branch office on the Djemaa el-Fna. The main office is open from 8.30 am to 6.45 pm from Monday to Friday, and on Saturday morning. Poste restante is at Window 6. The rather small phone office is to the left of the main entrance and is open seven days a week from 8.30 am to 9 pm. If you want to send a package, there is a separate office around the corner from the PTT on Ave Hassan II. Your parcel can be wrapped for a small fee after customs inspection.

**Foreign Consulates** Foreign consulates in Marrakesh include:

France
  Rue Ibn Khaldoun (or Dar Moulay Ali, just by the Koutoubia) (☎ 444006)
Sweden
  Immeuble As-Saada, angle Rue Moulay Ali et Rue de Yougoslavie (☎ 449660)

**Cultural Centres** The Centre Culturel Français (☎ 443196) is quite a small affair just off the Djemaa el-Fna on Rue de Moulay Ismail. Apart from French classes, it organises a range of films, lectures and the like that might provide an interesting diversion for Francophiles.

The American Language Center (ALC; ☎ 447259) has a branch in Gueliz at 3 Impasse du Moulin. The ALC's main activity is its English classes for Marrakshis – and if you're looking for work you might want to drop by on the off chance that there is a

vacancy. Otherwise, they put on the occasional film and lecture.

The International Language Centre is represented by Radi Ahmed (☎ 309237).

**Guides** You can arrange an official guide for Dr 30 to Dr 50 for a half-day at the tourist office or in the bigger hotels. The benefits of a guide, especially if you don't have a lot of time, are twofold: they can save you from taking wrong turns, and they immediately stop you being pestered by other would-be guides, which considerably reduces your blood pressure.

**Travel Agencies** The bulk of the travel agents (including RAM's office – see Getting There & Away) are located around Ave Mohammed V, west of Place du 16 Novembre. They include Wagons-Lits and Menara Tours (☎ 446654; fax 446107). The latter, at 41 Rue de Yougoslavie, represents GB Airways, which has a couple of flights a week linking the UK to Marrakesh via Gibraltar. Some of these agencies can organise trips into the High Atlas and also tours down the Drâa Valley. However, they are generally quite expensive and you'd be better off going it alone.

**Bookshops** For books in English, head straight for the ALC bookshop. It has a range of English literature and quite a few titles on Morocco, but it is open from 3 to 7 pm only.

Otherwise, there are a couple of reasonable bookshops for readers of French and Arabic along Ave Mohammed V, west of Place du 16 Novembre.

**Medical Services & Emergency** There is an all-night chemist (☎ 430415) on Rue Khalid ben el-Oualid. Private ambulances can be reached on ☎ 443724.

**Film & Photography** There are several places along Ave Mohammed V where you can buy film and get rolls developed. One reasonable place is Photo Magic.

MOROCCO

**Ensemble Artisanal** As in most of the major Moroccan cities, the Ensemble Artisanal is a sensible first stop to get an idea of *maximum* prices to offer for souvenirs once you are rummaging around in the souqs. It's better for sampling the quality of merchandise than for purchasing.

An awful lot of shops have notices posted in their windows inviting you to call one of several numbers if you feel you've been unfairly treated in a purchase, either on price or quality of the goods. What exactly can be done and what would constitute a rip-off in these circumstances is difficult to imagine. However, if you want to have a chat with the head of the Price Control Service, call ☎ 308430 (ext 360).

### Djemaa el-Fna

The focal point of Marrakesh is the Djemaa el-Fna, a huge square in the old part of town where many of the budget hotels are located. According to Paul Bowles, without it, Marrakesh would become just another Moroccan city. Other than the souqs, this is where everything happens; visitors are destined to spend a lot of time here.

Although it's a lively place at any time of day, it comes into its own in the evening, as the curtain goes up on one of the world's most fascinating spectacles. Rows and rows of open-air food stalls are set up and mouthwatering aromas fill the square. Jugglers, storytellers, snake charmers, magicians, acrobats and benign lunatics take over the rest of the space, each surrounded by an audience of jostling spectators who listen and watch intently, or fall about laughing and move on to another act starting up nearby. Before they can get away, assistants hassle them for contributions.

If you are feeling poorly, you might want to try some herbal cures, which the Marrakshis swear by. No matter what your ailment, the vendors of herbs and potions can prescribe something for the common cold or something a little stronger to administer to your worst enemy! In between the groups of spectators, diners, shoppers and tourists weave hustlers, thieves, knick-knack sellers and the occasional glue-sniffing kid. On the outer edges, kerosene lanterns ablaze, are the fruit and juice stalls.

It is a scene that, to one extent or another, was previously played out in the great squares of many Moroccan cities. Unfortunately, TV has killed much of it off. It is often claimed that the activity in the Djemaa el-Fna survives mostly because of the tourists. In the case of the water sellers and snake charmers this may well be the case, but how do you explain the crowds around the storytellers? Precious few outsiders know what marvels or lunacies they are recounting to the obvious delight of the locals.

Around the edge of the square you can take a balcony seat in one of a number of rooftop cafés and restaurants and take in the whole spectacle at a respectful and more relaxing distance. Down below, the medieval pageant presents its nightly cornucopia of delights; Bruegel would have had a field day here!

Snake charmer

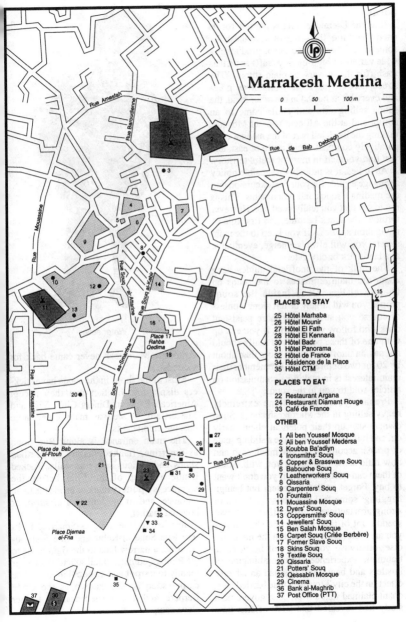

MOROCCO

# Marrakesh Medina

0    50    100 m

### PLACES TO STAY

25  Hôtel Marhaba
26  Hôtel Mounir
27  Hôtel El Fath
28  Hôtel El Kennaria
30  Hôtel Badr
31  Hôtel Panorama
32  Hôtel de France
34  Résidence de la Place
35  Hôtel CTM

### PLACES TO EAT

22  Restaurant Argana
24  Restaurant Diamant Rouge
33  Café de France

### OTHER

1   Ali ben Youssef Mosque
2   Ali ben Youssef Medersa
3   Koubba Ba'adiyn
4   Ironsmiths' Souq
5   Copper & Brassware Souq
6   Babouche Souq
7   Leatherworkers' Souq
8   Qissaria
9   Carpenters' Souq
10  Fountain
11  Mouassine Mosque
12  Dyers' Souq
13  Coppersmiths' Souq
14  Jewellers' Souq
15  Ben Salah Mosque
16  Carpet Souq (Criée Berbère)
17  Former Slave Souq
18  Skins Souq
19  Textile Souq
20  Qissaria
21  Potters' Souq
23  Qessabin Mosque
29  Cinema
36  Bank al-Maghrib
37  Post Office (PTT)

MOROCCO

## Souqs

Just as the Djemaa el-Fna is famous for its energy and life, the souqs of Marrakesh are some of the best in Morocco, producing a wide variety of high-quality crafts as well as trash (for the unwary or plain stupid). The streets here are just as labyrinthine as in Fès and every bit as busy. On the other hand, the shops selling arts and crafts come to an abrupt end at the Ali ben Youssef Mosque, making the hard-sell part of the medina comparatively compact. Head north or east, and you find yourself in more peaceful territory.

As in Fès, it is probably a sensible policy to engage a guide for your first excursion into the medina's souqs and monuments. This is not to say that you really need one. However tortuous the lanes become, the first rule of navigation applies – if you keep to the main streets, you will always emerge, eventually, at a landmark or city gate.

The bulk of the unofficial guides hang about the main entrances to the souqs on Djemaa el-Fna. Once inside the souqs proper, you will largely be left alone – unless of course you strike some more persistent ones who follow you right in. If you end up with one of these people (you really should not pay an unofficial guide more than about Dr 20 for two or three hours), remember their main interest is in making a commission on articles sold to you in the souqs.

Prepare yourself for some extremely heavy selling in the Marrakesh souqs. Shop owners size up their potential clients early on, and it is claimed they have a sliding scale of prices, according to how much cash and how little sense they credit you with. Some of them can get quite nasty if you don't want to buy. Forget endlessly patient but benign haggling; some feel that abuse and a bit of strong-arm tactics are just as effective. Never spend a lot of time in any one shop unless you are seriously interested in the merchandise, otherwise you may well be in for a traumatic experience. The combination of hustlers and heavy sell has had an adverse effect on the city's tourism. One harried merchant claimed that a Moroccan government study had revealed that 94% of first-time

Water seller

visitors to Marrakesh never came back for seconds!

Most of the shops in the souqs have stickers displaying the fact that they accept American Express, Diners Club, Visa and MasterCard, as well as many other more obscure credit cards.

The main entrance is along Rue Souq as-Smarrine, flanked mainly by **textiles** shops and various souvenir stalls. Tucked inside a group of buildings before the entrance is a **pottery** market. Inside the main entrance, and to the left, is a *qissaria*, or covered market.

Just before Rue Souq as-Smarrine forks into Rue Souq al-Kebir and Rue Souq al-Attarine, a narrow lane to the right leads to the Rahba Qedima, a small square given over mainly to **carpet** and **sheepskin** sales. The carpet souq is also known as the Criée Berbère, and it is situated near the former slave souq.

Back on the Rue Souq as-Smarrine, you could take either fork. Both more or less lead to the Ali ben Youssef mosque and medersa. If you take the left fork and veer off to the west, you will find yourself among **dyers**, **carpenters** and **coppersmiths**. Much of their work is not really aimed at tourists, and the atmosphere is a little more relaxed. Closer to the mosque all gives way to the clamour of the iron forges that dominate here. With a little luck, you'll emerge at either the mosque or the Koubba Ba'adiyn. Along the right fork, you'll encounter **jewellers**, whose stores then give way to **leatherwork** and **babouche** shops.

## Mosques & Medersas

Like their counterparts elsewhere in Morocco, the mosques and working medersas in Marrakesh are generally closed to non-Muslims, and those inside the medina are so hemmed in by other buildings that little can be seen from the outside.

**Koutoubia** The only mosque with a perspective you can really appreciate, and the one you are most likely to encounter first, is the Koutoubia, across the other side of Place de Foucauld, south-west of the Djemaa el-Fna. It is also the tallest (70 metres) and most famous landmark in Marrakesh, visible for miles in any direction.

Constructed by the Almohads in the late 12th century, it features the oldest and best preserved of their three most famous minarets – the other two being the Tour Hassan in Rabat and the Giralda in Seville (Spain). The name (from *koutoub* or *kutub*, Arabic for

---

### Souq Survival

Bargaining in the souqs is essential, although when souvenir-hunting some Western visitors may sometimes get the impression it is a game reserved for them. Nothing could be further from the truth, as the following extract from *La Boîte à Merveilles*, by the Fès author Ahmed Sefrioui, demonstrates. Some of the merchant's lines may ring a bell, and the purchaser's replies are a neat introduction to basic souq-survival tactics:

...The shopkeeper asked: 'So you like this vest, Madame?'

'That depends entirely on how much it costs', my mother replied.

'Ah well, in that case I'll start wrapping it up right away. I'm always happy to give serious customers a discount. Now this vest usually sells for five rials, but I'll let you have it for just four.'

'Let's cut out all the chitchat – I'll give you two rials.'

'You're offering less than what it cost me to buy it in the first place, I swear. I can't possibly let you have it for that price – I'd have to go begging in the streets tonight to feed my children.'

The shopkeeper had finished carefully folding up the vest and was looking for a sheet of paper to wrap it in.

'Listen,' said my mother, 'I've got kids and things to do at home; I haven't got time to hang around here bargaining with you. Would you let me have the vest for two and a quarter rials? I'm ready to make a sacrifice for my son, who would like so much to wear this on the day of Achoura.'

'I like the lad, so I'll make every effort for his sake – give me three and a half rials.' The shopkeeper held out his hand for the money, but my mother turned around, took me by the hand and started to walk off.

'Come on', she said. 'There are plenty of vests in the *qissaria*. We'll soon find a shopkeeper who talks sense.'

The shopkeeper cried out: 'Come back Madame! Do come back! Your son likes this vest...take it...pay me what you think is fair...'

She pulled out two and a half rials, which she handed to the shopkeeper without a word. Not waiting long enough to hear his protests, she seized the package and dragged me off.

**From the French by Damien Simonis**
**Copyright Editions du Seuil (1978)** ∎

books) comes from a booksellers' market that once existed around the mosque.

The Koutoubia minaret is a classic of Moroccan-Andalusian architecture; its features are mirrored in many other minarets throughout the country, but nowhere else has its sheer size been attempted.

When first built, the Koutoubia was covered with painted plaster and brilliantly coloured zellij tiles, but this decoration has all disappeared. What can still be seen, however, are the decorative panels, which are different on each face and practically constitute a textbook of contemporary design. The views from the summit would be incredible, if non-Muslims were allowed to climb up there. Unfortunately, at the time of writing, the minaret was to some extent hidden by a thick web of sky-blue scaffolding.

**Koubba Ba'adiyn** After a stroll up through the souqs, the first monument open to non-Muslims that you'll probably come across is the most modest Marrakesh has to offer, and (restoration aside) about the oldest. Most of Almoravid Marrakesh was destroyed by the zealous Almohads who succeeded them, but the Koubba is a rare exception. Built in the early 12th century, it is a small but elegant display of Muslim decorative invention. Signposted on a small square in front of the Ali ben Youssef Mosque, entrance is Dr 10 and the guardian will want to show you around. He'll probably dig up a friend to 'guide' you to the Ali ben Youssef Medersa too, although it's just around the corner.

**Ali ben Youssef Mosque** The largest of the mosques inside the medina is the Ali ben Youssef Mosque, first built in the second half of the 12th century by the Almoravid sultan of the same name. It's the oldest surviving mosque in Marrakesh. However, the building itself is of fairly recent date, as it was almost completely rebuilt in the 19th century in the Merenid style in response to popular demand. When first constructed it was about twice its present size but it was severely damaged when the Almoravids were over-

thrown by the Almohads. It was later restored by both the Almohads and the Saadians. The mosque is closed to non-Muslims.

**Ali ben Youssef Medersa** Next to the Ali ben Youssef Mosque is the medersa of the same name. It is the largest theological college in the Maghreb, and was built by the Saadians in 1565 (and much restored in the 1960s). Heading east from the Koubba, simply follow the mosque walls around to the left, and you'll come to the entrance of the medersa on your right.

Although all Moroccan medersas at least loosely follow a similar ground plan (see Architecture in the Arts section of the Facts about the Country chapter), the Ali ben Youssef is not only bigger but also quite a bit different in layout.

You walk down a corridor and turn right onto the central courtyard, entering which you find yourself facing the *masjid*. Like virtually every other great medersa on view to non-Muslims, this was built under the Merenids, and it betrays the taste of those times for intricate stucco decoration combined with a zellij tile base and crowned by carved cedar.

Go back to the corridor and take the entrance opposite the courtyard. Two sets of stairs lead up to students' cells. As usual, they are small and bare. It's hard to imagine how, as is claimed, they crammed as many as 900 people into these rooms! The big difference between their arrangement here and that in other medersas is that many of them are clustered around seven small 'mini-courtyards'. Moreover, a few look out on to the street – somewhat of an exception to the general rule of Moroccan and Andalusian architecture.

Believe it or not, it is worth giving the lavatories a look. This is where they have always been, and it seems that little has changed. Not the most inviting place to relieve yourself.

**Mouassine Mosque** The other large mosque in the medina is the Mouassine

Mosque, built in the 16th century by the Saadians on land formerly occupied by the Jewish community. Its most notable features are the three huge doorways and the intricately carved cedar ceilings. The fountain attached to this mosque still survives and is quite elaborate, with three sections – two for animals and one for humans. The mosque is closed to non-Muslims.

**Ben Salah Mosque** Of the other mosques in the medina, the Ben Salah Mosque (also known as the Ben Salah Zawiyya) is the most prominent; its brilliant green-tiled minaret can be seen from many places. It was built by the Merenid sultan Abu Said Uthman between 1318 and 1321. Again, it's closed to non-Muslims.

**Zawiyyas** In the north-western zone of the medina are two zawiyyas dedicated to two of the seven saints claimed by Marrakesh (pilgrimage to the tombs of all seven is, in the popular mind at any rate, the equivalent of a pilgrimage to Mecca – a considerably more arduous undertaking for Moroccans). North of the Sidi ben Slimane Zawiyya is that of Sidi Bel Abbes, the most important of the seven saints. Entry to the sanctuaries is forbidden to non-Muslims.

### Palaces & Environs
**Palais el-Badi** The most famous of the palaces of Marrakesh was the El-Badi Palace, built by Ahmed al-Mansour between 1578 and 1602. At the time of its construction it was reputed to be one of the most beautiful in the world (and was known as 'the Incomparable'); it included marble from Italy and other precious building materials from as far away as India. The enormous cost of building the palace was met largely from the ransom the Portuguese were forced to pay out following their disastrous defeat at the hands of the Saadians in 1578 in the Battle of the Three Kings. Unfortunately, the palace is now largely a ruin, having been torn apart by Moulay Ismail in 1696 for its building materials, which were used to build his new capital at Meknès.

What remains is essentially a huge square surrounded by devastated walls enclosing a sunken orange grove and a number of modern concrete pools. When you're inside by the orange grove, you'll notice a large structure to the west. This is the Koubba al-Khamsiniyya, which was used as a great reception hall on state occasions and was named after its 50 marble columns.

Proceed south towards the walls of the Royal Palace (which is closed to visitors) and you'll find yourself in a confusing maze of underground corridors, storerooms and dungeons. Which were which is a little hard to tell. For lovers of dark places, there's a bit of potential exploring to do – bring a torch (flashlight).

The El-Badi is open to the public daily, except on certain religious holidays, between 8.30 am and noon and 2.30 and 6 pm. Entry costs Dr 10. You're free to wander around on your own, although guides will initially hassle you to engage their services. The palace is also the venue for the annual Folklore Festival, usually held in June.

The easiest way to get to the palace is to take Ave Houmane el-Fetouaki down from the Koutoubia to Place des Ferblantiers, where the ramparts begin, and you'll see a large gateway. Go through this and turn to the right. The entrance and ticket booth are ahead of you.

**Palais de la Bahia** The Palais de la Bahia was built towards the end of the 19th century, over a period of 14 years, as the residence of Si' Ahmed ben Musa (also known as Bou Ahmed), the Grand Vizier of Sultan Moulay al-Hassan I. On Bou Ahmed's death it was ransacked, but much has since been restored.

It's a rambling structure with fountains, living quarters, pleasure gardens and numerous secluded, shady courtyards, but it lacks architectural cohesion. This in no way detracts from the visual pleasure of the place, and, as your guide will no doubt point out, the difference between the peace, quiet and coolness inside the palace and the heat, noise and chaos in the streets outside is noticeable. It exemplifies the privacy-conscious priori-

MOROCCO

ties behind Muslim architecture. In fact, and this may not have been so deliberate, you will often find that the multiple doorways linking various parts of the palace are so placed that you often can't see much past the open doorway, creating the impression of a series of separate and unconnected zones within the whole.

You can only visit part of the palace, as some of it is still used by the royal family and to house maintenance staff. You will be taken through a series of rooms, among them the vizier's sleeping quarters (he had separate ones for snoozing during the day and evening) and various courtyards set aside for his wives and concubines. The four wives each had a room arranged around a courtyard. The sleeping quarters for the rather more numerous harem were also gathered around a (separate) courtyard.

The palace is open daily from 8.30 am to 1 pm (11.45 am in winter) and 4 to 7 pm (2.30 to 6 pm in winter). Entry is free, but you must take and pay a guide. To get there (orientation is easiest from the Palais el-Badi), go back to the Place des Ferblantiers, and keep following Ave Houmane el-Fetouaki away from the budget hotel area and around to the left (north). You'll soon come to the entrance, set in a garden, on your right.

**Dar Si Said** Farther on from the Palais de la Bahia and again off to the right (it's signposted), the Dar Si Said, which now houses the **Museum of Moroccan Arts**, is well worth a visit.

Sidi Said, Bou Ahmed's brother, built what became his town house at about the same time as the grand vizier's palace was constructed. Today, the museum houses one of the finest collections in the country, including jewellery from the High Atlas, the Anti-Atlas and the extreme south; carpets from the Haouz and the High Atlas; oil lamps from Taroudannt; blue pottery from Safi and green pottery from Tamegroute; and leatherwork from Marrakesh.

As you enter, you will see a series of doors typical of the richer High Atlas and Anti-Atlas houses. At the end of this corridor is

the oldest exhibit in the museum: an old marble basin dating back to about 1000 AD, brought to Marrakesh from Spain by Ali ben Youssef.

Next up are some delightful medieval precursors of the Ferris wheel for tiny tots.

The central garden and courtyard is flanked by rooms housing displays of heavy, southern jewellery in silver, traditional women's garments, household goods, old muskets and daggers.

On the next floor is a magnificently decorated room, its characteristic stucco and zellij tiles capped by a stunning carved and painted cedar ceiling. From here, the signs lead you upstairs again and then down through various rooms dominated by rug and carpet displays. All the explanations are, unfortunately, in Arabic and French only.

It's open from 9 am to noon and 4 to 7 pm (2.30 to 6 pm in winter); closed Tuesday. On Friday it's closed from 11.30 am to 3 pm. Entry costs Dr 10.

**Maison Tiskiwin** Virtually next door to the Dar Si Said is the house of Bert Flint, a Dutch art lecturer and long-time resident of Morocco. It has been opened to the public as a small museum, and principally contains carpets and traditional textile work. The Maison Tiskiwin (☎ 443335) is only open in the morning.

**Mellah** The old Jewish quarter, established in the 16th century, is just south of the Palais de la Bahia. Much neglected and now populated mainly by Muslims, it still has quite a different look to it from the rest of the city. The main entrance is off Place des Ferblantiers, and if you want to visit any of the small synagogues (one is still in use) you'll need a local guide.

**Saadian Tombs** Next to the Kasbah Mosque is the necropolis, which was initiated by the Saadian sultan Ahmed al-Mansour in the late 1500s. Unlike the Palais el-Badi, another of Al-Mansour's projects, the tombs escaped Moulay Ismail's depredations – possibly because he was superstitious about plundering the dead. Instead he sealed the tombs and, as a result, they still convey some of the opulence and superb artistry that must also have been lavished on the palace. Sixty-six of the Saadians, including Al-Mansour, his successors and their closest family members, lie buried under the two main structures, and there are over a hundred more buried outside the buildings.

Although the mad sultan Moulay Yazid was laid to rest here in 1792, the tombs essentially remained sealed following Moulay Ismail's reign. They were not 'rediscovered' until 1917, when General Lyautey, his curiosity awakened by an aerial survey of the area, ordered the construction of a passageway down. They have since been restored.

To get to the tombs, take Rue de Bab Agnaou to Bab Agnaou itself (the only surviving Almohad gateway in Marrakesh), which is on the left and almost adjacent to Bab er-Rob. Go through Bab Agnaou and walk straight past a row of shops until you come to the Kasbah Mosque. Turn right down Rue de la Kasbah and, when you get to the end of the mosque, you'll see a narrow alleyway on the left. Go down it, and the entrance to the tombs is at the end.

After buying your ticket, you follow a very narrow passage that opens onto the main mausoleum, which is divided into three small halls. Those at either end contain tombs of children. The central one, the Hall of the Twelve Columns, is considered to be one of the finest examples of Moroccan-Andalusian decorative art. Among the columns of Italian marble are the tombs of Ahmed al-Mansour, his son and grandson.

The elegant little mausoleum set farther in amid the gardens of the necropolis houses the tomb of Al-Mansour's mother.

The tombs are open to the public every day, except Friday morning, from 8 am to noon and 2.30 to 7 pm (6 pm in winter). Entry costs Dr 10 and you're allowed to wander around at will. If you prefer, a guardian will accompany you and explain what you are looking at. You will be expected to offer a tip at the end.

### Tanneries

If you didn't *do* the tanneries in Fès, or feel you need another dose of them, you can give those at Marrakesh a whirl. They are out by Bab Debbagh, at the north-eastern end of the medina and a reasonably straightforward walk from the Ali ben Youssef Mosque. If you have trouble finding them, just ask for the road to the gate or take up the offer of one of the young lads hanging around the entrance to the medersa to guide you there.

### Gardens

A slightly more pleasant olfactory experience is provided by the several beautiful gardens which are laid out around the city.

**Jardin Ménara** About a four-km walk west of the Koutoubia, the Jardin Ménara is the most easily reached of Marrakesh's green spaces. Although it is quite popular with Marrakshis, it is generally a peaceful place to unload some of the stress and escape the summer heat of the city. The centrepiece of what is basically a more organised continuation of the olive groves immediately to the east is a large, still pool backed by a pavilion built in 1866. What is now open to the public was once the exclusive preserve of sultans and high ministers.

**Jardin Agdal** Stretching for several km south from the Royal Palace, the vegetation is more varied here than in the Jardin Ménara and there are several pavilions. To get there (a bicycle would be ideal), take the path that runs south from the south-western corner of the mechouar (parade ground) in front of the Royal Palace. It appears the gardens are often closed, so having a bicycle should take some of the sting out of the potential disappointment.

**Jardin Majorelle** Now owned by Yves Saint-Laurent, these exquisite gardens were laid out by the French painter Jacques Majorelle, who lived here from 1922 to 1962. In amongst the floral smorgasbord is what was Majorelle's deep-blue villa, which now houses a modest museum of Islamic art.

MOROCCO

The gardens are in the ville nouvelle, north of Ave Yacoub el-Mansour.

**Hôtel La Mamounia** For the price of a very expensive coffee, you could get in to what in this century has become something of a monument itself. La Mamounia (see Places to Stay) was Winston Churchill's favourite hotel, and it is blessed with lush and sedate gardens that do as much good for the frazzled as any of the public gardens.

### Église des Saints-Martyrs
Of mild interest is the Catholic church (built in 1926) in Gueliz, south of Ave Yacoub al-Mrini. It was built in keeping with its environment and is a nice example of the European interpretation of Mauresque architecture. Mass is celebrated every day.

### Festivals
If you're in Marrakesh in June (the dates seem rather fluid), enquire about the Festival of Folklore which is held in the Palais el-Badi at that time. It's a folk-dancing and singing extravaganza, performed by some of the best troupes from throughout Morocco. In July there's the famous Fantasia, a charge of Berber horsemen that takes place outside the ramparts. You often see pictures of it in the tourist literature.

It's not quite a festival, but if you enjoy watching a bit of athletics you might want to be around at the end of January for the annual Grand Prix de Hassan II Marathon.

### Places to Stay – bottom end
**Camping** The camp site (☎ 435570) is close to the hostel, just off the Ave de France. There's little shade and the ground is stony. Camping costs Dr 10 per person, Dr 11 to put up a big tent, Dr 8 for a car (Dr 7 for motorbikes) and Dr 14 for electricity. It's hardly worth it.

**Hostel** The hostel (☎ 447713) is close to the railway station and can be a good first stop on arrival. Indeed, some people prefer to spend their whole stay in Marrakesh here, because it's well hidden from the hustle and

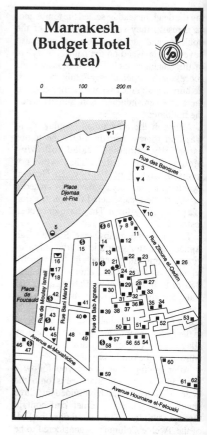

bustle of the big city. On the other hand, it is a bit far from where things are going on. It costs Dr 20 for a bed, and Dr 5 extra for a decent hot shower. You need your membership card and it's open from 8 to 9 am, noon to 2 pm and 6 to 10 pm.

**Hotels – medina** Most of the cheapest accommodation deals can be found in the area immediately south of the Djemaa el-Fna and east of Rue de Bab Agnaou, where there are scores of reasonably priced hotels. There's not a lot to choose between most of them, other than whether they offer hot

## PLACES TO STAY

| | |
|---|---|
| 8 | Hôtel CTM |
| 11 | Hôtel des Amis |
| 12 | Hôtel Cecil |
| 13 | Hôtels Jeunesse & Echamal |
| 17 | Hôtel Ali |
| 22 | Atlas & Menzah Hôtels |
| 23 | Hôtel du Sud |
| 24 | Hôtel Elazhar |
| 25 | Hôtel Nouzha |
| 26 | Hôtel de France |
| 27 | Hôtel Mauritania |
| 28 | Hôtel Provence |
| 29 | Hôtel de la Paix |
| 30 | Hôtel Central |
| 31 | Hôtel Afriquia |
| 32 | Hôtel Eddakhla |
| 33 | Hôtel Zagora |
| 34 | Hôtel Medina |
| 35 | Hôtel Essaouira |
| 36 | Hôtel Sahara |
| 37 | Hôtel Central Annexe |
| 38 | Hôtel El Ward |
| 39 | Hôtel Mabrouk |
| 41 | Hôtel Ichbilia |
| 46 | Hôtel de Foucauld |
| 48 | Hôtel La Gazelle |
| 49 | Hôtel du Tourisme |
| 50 | Hôtel El Atlal |
| 51 | Hôtel Gallia |
| 52 | Hôtel Arabia |
| 53 | Hôtel Chellah |
| 54 | Hôtel Souria |
| 55 | Hôtel Hillal |
| 56 | Hôtel El Farak |
| 59 | Grand Hôtel du Tazi |
| 60 | Hôtel Le Minaret |
| 61 | Hôtel El Bouchra |
| 62 | Hôtel Kawakib |

## PLACES TO EAT

| | |
|---|---|
| 1 | Café/Restaurant El Fath |
| 2 | Restaurant Le Marrakechi |
| 3 | Café de France |
| 4 | Café de la Place |
| 7 | Le Grand Balcon |
| 10 | Pâtisserie Toubkal |
| 14 | Restaurant Étoile |
| 18 | Restaurant Ali |
| 45 | Iceberg Restaurant |

## OTHER

| | |
|---|---|
| 5 | Grands Taxis |
| 6 | Banque Populaire |
| 9 | Old CTM & SATAS Terminals |
| 15 | Bank al-Maghrib |
| 16 | Post Office (PTT) |
| 19 | Crédit du Maroc |
| 20 | Women's Hammam |
| 21 | Men's Hammam |
| 40 | Cinema Mabrouka |
| 42 | Wafabank |
| 43 | BMCE (ATM) |
| 44 | Centre Culturel Français |
| 47 | BMCI Bank (ATM) |
| 57 | Men's Hammam |
| 58 | Banque Populaire |

showers or not (not important in summer but definitely so in winter) and how clean they are. Some places have no showers at all, in which case you could try one of the hammams.

Most of the cheapies will charge extra for hot showers (Dr 5 to Dr 10) and some even charge for cold showers (Dr 2). Prices in most vary little and start at Dr 30 a single, Dr 50 a double and Dr 70 to Dr 75 a triple. Some of the better ones charge more, and in summer most of them hike up their prices according to demand, so you could end up paying more here than you would for a better room in a classified hotel.

A short way down from the Djemaa el-Fna, between Rue Zitoune el-Qedim and Rue de Bab Agnaou, is the *Hôtel Souria*. It is one of the better ones, and charges Dr 50/70 for singles/doubles (or Dr 80 for two big beds) and a slightly over-the-top Dr 10 for a hot shower. Slightly cheaper (Dr 35 for singles) is the adjacent *Hôtel El Atlal*, which has bright and clean (if small) rooms upstairs. It also charges Dr 10 for a hot shower.

Possibly the biggest joke in all Marrakesh is the *Hôtel Le Minaret*. At Dr 100/150 for a basic single/double with private toilet and shower, it's hard to imagine anyone wanting to stay there. How does it make any money?

Along to the north is the *Hôtel Essaouira* (☎ 443805). Its well-placed terrace and tiny café makes it a cut above some of its neighbours, although most of the rooms are very small. You pay from Dr 30 to Dr 40 each, and a hot shower is Dr 5.

Others that appear marginally better than the rest include the *Panorama* (☎ 445047), *Cecil*, *Afriquia* and *Chellah* (☎ 442977). The Chellah charges Dr 60/90 and Dr 10 for a hot shower, making it a bit borderline.

Be careful not to confuse the *Hôtel de France* (☎ 443067) on Rue Zitoune el-Qedim, which charges Dr 30 per head, with its namesake (attached to the Café de France) on the Djemaa el-Fna. Although the latter (☎ 442319) is nothing special, its rooms, at

MOROCCO

Dr 40/60/80 for doubles/triple/quadruples, are not the worst you'll find and the rooftop café is a good vantage point overlooking the square.

In the centre of the budget hotel area, the *Hôtel de la Paix* must be one of the cheapest places going, at Dr 25/40/50/60. The rooms are cell-like but clean, but it has no showers (and is not alone in this regard).

The *Hôtel Charaf* (☎ 427089), a bit farther south of the Djemaa el-Fna, charges about Dr 30 a person for OK rooms, but there is little to recommend its location and it has no showers.

Of the rest, the *Arabia* (☎ 441920), *Sahara, Zagora, Mauritania, El Ward* (☎ 423354), *Hillal* and *El Farak* distinguish themselves mainly by their firm declarations of having only cold showers.

The only other advice that can be given is to wander around a bit for something that suits. All these places are in pretty short walking distance of one another.

Three hotels that are a little more expensive but can be recommended are within a stone's throw of the Djemaa el-Fna, and offer more comfort than the run-of-the-mill cheapies. The *Hôtel Ichbilia* (☎ 434947) is just off Rue Bani Marine, and it has singles/doubles for Dr 60/95. The showers are outside and are hot in the mornings. Try to get a room upstairs, as the street can be noisy. Farther north, the *Hôtel Ali* (☎ 444979) has decent rooms for Dr 70/90/125, or you can sleep on the terrace for about Dr 30 and lock your things up in a storage room. This is a good place to get information on High Atlas trekking possibilities and guides. Back on Rue Bani Marine, the *Hôtel La Gazelle* (☎ 441112) is a good place which offers rooms for Dr 60/100 on the first night and Dr 50/90 on subsequent nights.

On the Djemaa el-Fna itself you could try the *Hôtel CTM* (☎ 442325). The bus company of the same name used to be here and so there is parking space. Singles/doubles with private shower and toilet are Dr 78/103. The rooms are OK, although the beds are on the saggy side. You may be able to get cheaper rooms without shower and toilet, but they don't seem keen to advertise them. With its terrace café, it's the location that really makes the place.

Finally, there are a few cheapies on the north-eastern side of the Djemaa el-Fna which are not so often used by travellers. They are no more exciting than the main group of unclassified hotels, but the position, virtually by the souqs, might appeal to some. They include the *Marhaba, Mounir, El Fath, El Kennaria* and *Badr*.

**Hotels – Gueliz** There are no unclassified pensions and not too many cheap hotels in the ville nouvelle. You'll find the few there are around Ave Mohammed V, west of Place du 16 Novembre. The cheapest is the one-star *Hôtel Franco-Belge* (☎ 448472), 62 Blvd Mohammed Zerktouni, close to the tourist office. It has a pleasant courtyard and rooms cost Dr 60/80 without shower and Dr 80/104 with shower and toilet.

A few doors down towards Ave Mohammed V is the one-star *Hôtel des Voyageurs* (☎ 431235), at 40 Blvd Mohammed Zerktouni. Singles without a shower or toilet cost Dr 60, while singles and doubles with shower and toilet cost Dr 100/130. The Franco-Belge is preferable.

Another possibility is the *Hôtel Oasis* (☎ 447179), at 50 Ave Mohammed V, which has singles/doubles with private shower and shared toilet for Dr 78/103.

**Places to Stay – middle**
**Medina** The two-star *Hôtel Gallia* (☎ 445913 or 444853), 30 Rue de la Recette, is with little doubt about the most pleasant hotel in the medina area. Singles/doubles with toilet cost Dr 82/101 and those with shower as well Dr 123/182. They have hot, steaming showers and central heating in winter. This place is often booked out, especially during holidays and on weekends.

The *Grand Hôtel du Tazi* (☎ 442787; fax 442152), on the corner of Ave El-Mouahidine and Rue de Bab Agnaou, is a much larger and more expensive hotel, at Dr 154/250 for rooms with shower and toilet. The rooms are quite adequate and also have hones, and the hotel boasts a small pool, a ▶ar and a restaurant (20% off meals for ▶eople staying in the hotel).

A little farther away, on Ave El-Mouahi-▲ine, is the cavernous *Hôtel de Foucauld* ☎ 445499). Although some of the rooms :an be noisy and a tad small, they are clean ▲nd comfortable, and not bad value at Dr ▲86/110 with shower or Dr 110/127 with :hower and toilet. The hotel has a restaurant ▲nd a tiny pool, and the staff can help orga-▲ise mountain-bike excursions, 4WD trips ▲nd cross-country skiing.

Back on the Djemaa el-Fna, another pos-sibility is the *Résidence de la Place* (☎ 445174). The main attraction is, as usual, the terrace café overlooking the square. Singles/doubles cost Dr 100/150, but the rate could come down as the staff seem eager to please. The rooms are OK, especially if you can get one overlooking the Djemaa (although light sleepers may well prefer something on the courtyard out the back).

Along Ave Mohammed V, heading west towards Bab Larissa and the ville nouvelle, is a good two-star place, the *Hôtel Islane*

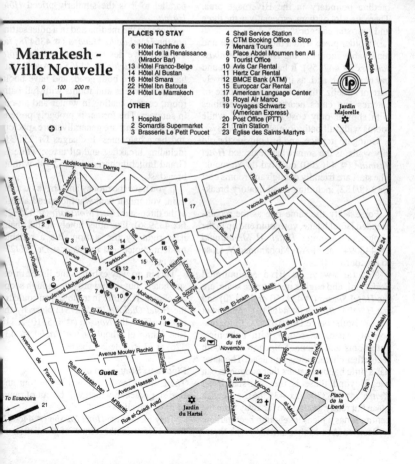

**PLACES TO STAY**
6  Hôtel Tachfine &
   Hôtel de la Renaissance
   (Mirador Bar)
13 Hôtel Franco-Belge
14 Hôtel Al Bustan
16 Hôtel Smara
22 Hôtel Ibn Batouta
24 Hôtel Le Marrakech

**OTHER**
1  Hospital
2  Somardis Supermarket
3  Brasserie Le Petit Poucet

4  Shell Service Station
5  CTM Booking Office & Stop
7  Menara Tours
8  Place Abdel Moumen ben Ali
9  Tourist Office
10 Avis Car Rental
11 Hertz Car Rental
12 BMCE Bank (ATM)
15 Europcar Car Rental
17 American Language Center
18 Royal Air Maroc
19 Voyages Schwartz
   (American Express)
20 Post Office (PTT)
21 Train Station
23 Église des Saints-Martyrs

**Marrakesh -
Ville Nouvelle**

0    100    200 m

Avenue el-Jadida

Jardin
Majorelle

Rue Abdelouahab — Derraq

Avenue Mohammed Abdelkrim el-Khattabi

Rue Ibn Zaiboun

Boulevard de Safi

Rue

Yacoub el-Mansour

Rue Ibn Aïcha

Rue

Rue Khalid

17

Avenue

Rue

Rue
2
3
14
4
13
16

Avenue

Rue

Rue Tariq

Zerktouni

Rue
El-Hourria

Loudaya

12
15
8
6
7  9
10
5  11

Boulevard Mohammed

Boulevard Mohammed

Rue Mohammed V

Rue ben Scurya

Rue Toummerz

Rue ben Zajd

Rue el-Ouald

Malik

Rue el-Imam

El-Mansour
Eddahabi

19
18

Yougoslavie

Avenue Moulay Rachid

Avenue des Nations Unies

Place
du 16
Novembre

20

Rue

Rue

Rue Oum Emba

Avenue de France

Rue El-Hassan ben

M'Barek

Avenue Hassan II

*Gueliz*

Mauritanie

Rue Oued el-Makhazine

Ave
Yacoub
el-Mrini

22

23

24

Place
de la
Liberté

Mohammed el-Mallakh

Route Principale No 24

To Essaouira

21

Jardin
du Hartsi

MOROCCO

(☎ 440081/3; fax 440085). The rooms are modern and comfortable, and some have balconies with views across to the Koutoubia. This hotel boasts a pleasant rooftop restaurant and café, and the rooms have toilet, shower and phone. Including the obligatory breakfast, singles/doubles go for Dr 177/227. It has parking, and cheerfully accepts credit-card payment – as indeed do most Marrakshi hotels in this class and up.

**Gueliz & Hivernage**  The bulk of the mid-range hotels are located outside the medina, mostly in Gueliz, with a couple closer to the medina boundary in the Hivernage area. There are a lot of them, especially in the three and four-star category.

An older place with a bit of character and reasonable rooms is the *Hôtel des Ambassadeurs* (☎ 447159). It has a restaurant and bar next door, and, as it's in the more lively part of Gueliz, there is a good choice of eateries and cafés nearby. Singles/doubles with shower only cost Dr 129/163, while rooms with full bathroom are Dr 157/187.

Going up in price, and just outside the old city walls, is the somewhat neglected *Hôtel Yasmine* (☎ 446200) on Blvd de Yarmouk. The staff are friendly enough and rooms cost Dr 138/182, including an obligatory breakfast.

For exactly the same rate as the recommended Hôtel Islane, you could end up in the altogether gloomier *Hôtel Al Mouatamid* (☎ 448094), at 94 Ave Mohammed V, close to the tourist office.

Not far away, on Blvd Mohammed Zerktouni, and edging up the price scale, are the *Hôtel Smara* (☎ 434150 or 434170) and the *Hôtel Al Bustan* (☎ 446810), adjacent at No 68. Both charge Dr 201/252/338 for reasonably spacious rooms with balconies, bathrooms and phone. Somehow they both feel rather characterless and dead. The latter has a little bar downstairs that nonguests can use. Beyond these is the four-star *Hôtel Kenza* (☎ 448330; fax 435386), a newish place but really getting too far away from the centre. It has a pleasant enough beer garden.

Back on Ave Mohammed V is the three-star *Hôtel Amalay* (☎ 449023; fax 431554) and around the corner past the former Hôtel de la Renaissance is the *Hôtel Tachfine* (☎ 447188; fax 472089), both of which charge Dr 232/285. They both have bars, and the Amalay has a restaurant.

Heading back down Ave Mohammed V towards the medina is the *Hôtel Ibn Batoute* (☎ 434145; fax 434062), which has 40 air conditioned rooms with full bathroom and phone. They cost Dr 226/273/373 plus taxes. Breakfast is Dr 30 per person. It is a good place in its class and also has a number of suites with colour TV thrown in. Virtually parallel to it is the similarly priced *Hôtel Hasna*.

Closer to the medina and in a quiet setting are the *Hôtel de la Ménara* (☎ 436478; fax 436478), Ave des Remparts, and the *Hôtel Le Grand Imilchil* (☎ 447653), Ave Echouhada. They are both good, and have pools, pleasant gardens and rooms with full bathroom, central heating in winter and air-con in summer. The former is probably preferable, as its rooms are generally more spacious and have balconies. It charges Dr 231/312 including breakfast and all taxes, while Le Grand Imilchil charges Dr 252/306 without breakfast.

If you have the money and arrive on a late train, you might well want to spend a night at the three-star *Hôtel Moussafir* (☎ 435929 fax 435936); like other hotels in this chain it is right by the station. It's a reliable modern choice and rooms cost Dr 226/273 plus taxes.

This in no way exhausts the list of three-star hotels, but should provide enough scope for choice. If you're in trouble, you could try the *Hôtel Oudaya* (☎ 448751) close by the tourist office, the *Nouzha* (☎ 435510) at 116 Rue Camp el-Ghoul or the *Pacha* (☎ 431 326) at 33 Rue de la Liberté.

**Places to Stay – top end**
There are at least 26 hotels in the four and five-star bracket, which will be out of range of most travellers.

They include the *Hôtel Nassim* (☎ 446401 fax 447458) in the centre of the action in

Gueliz on Ave Mohammed V, the *Hôtel Le Marrakech* (☎ 434351; fax 434980) on Place de la Liberté and the *Hôtel Agdal* ☎ 433670; fax 434980) on Blvd Mohammed Zerktouni.

For an idea of what you'll be up for in the four-star range, singles/doubles in the *Hôtel Les Almoravides* (☎ 445142; fax 443133) come in at Dr 332/415 plus taxes, and an obligatory breakfast costs Dr 44. Most of these places have pools, which are usually closed to outsiders.

Other hotels in the four and five-star categories are on the Ave de France and farther out of town on the road to Casablanca and the Semlalia part of town.

On Ave Houmane el-Fetouaki, just inside Bab el-Jedid, is the jewel in the crown of Marrakesh's hotels – the *La Mamounia* ☎ 448981; fax 444660), although at five-tar 'luxe', you'd want to be on an expense account to stay there. The hotel was built between 1925 and 1929 for the (French-controlled) Moroccan railways, and it was the favoured destination of well-heeled Europeans, many of them taking a break from the decadence of Tangier. Guests as diverse as Winston Churchill, who came for the climate and to indulge in his hobby of painting, and Eric von Stroheim have passed through. Renovated in 1986, it has lost some of its charm, but jet-setters still patronise it. With doubles starting at Dr 1500 and finishing in the vicinity of Dr 20,000, who else could afford to stay there?

**Holiday Residences**
Apart from the Club Med on the Djemaa el-Fna, there are a couple of residences offering long-term lets of self-contained flats. They would possibly suit families intending to spend some weeks in the area, and must usually be booked at least a month ahead. To give you an idea of what these places are about, the Résidence Al Bahja (☎ 448119; fax 346063) in Gueliz offers apartments capable of sleeping up to eight people for anything from a week up. If business is slow, you could stay for a day or two. The single rate is Dr 250 a day, or Dr 600 a day for a

family with up to three children; for a family, it costs Dr 12,000 for 30 days.

**Places to Eat**
**Medina** About the liveliest and cheapest place to eat in the evening is right on the Djemaa el-Fna. By the time the sun sets, a good portion of the square is taken over by innumerable food stands, each specialising in certain types of food. At some you can pick up kebabs with salad, while at others it's fish and chips Moroccan style. You point to the kind of fish you want, and before you know it, it's in front of you with chips, salad and whatever else might be on offer. At others, you can just sit down to munch on bread rolls stuffed with potato. It is easy to eat your fill for Dr 20 or even less. Wash it down with a Dr 4 orange juice from one of the many juice stands.

If you feel a bit iffy about eating here (the food is cooked quite publicly, so there's little to worry about), try the small restaurants on Rue Bani Marine and Rue de Bab Agnaou. The *Etoile*, for example, offers a filling set menu for Dr 30.

If your purse strings are a little less tight, a place that is deservedly popular with travellers is the self-service restaurant below the *Hôtel Ali*. For Dr 60, you can load up your plate from various pots of typical Moroccan fare, along with a selection of cooked vegetables and/or salad. There's usually a musician to provide that 'authentic' touch. It might sound a little touristy, and it is, but it has a lively atmosphere and the food is good.

Back on the Djemaa itself, most of the rooftop cafés have restaurants attached to them. Some are better than others. The *Argana* (you can't miss the bright neon sign at night) is directly opposite the Bank al-Maghrib. Its set menu is Dr 61. The food is fine, but the crêpes for dessert are better.

The *Restaurant Diamant Rouge* is a pleasant enough place with meals for similar prices, but it's set back a bit off the square.

A short walk south down a narrow lane from the Djemaa, just to the east of the budget hotel area, is the *Restaurant Dar Essalam* (☎ 443520). This belongs to a

MOROCCO

certain genre of restaurant geared to well-heeled tourists already described in the Fès chapter. For about Dr 200 you get a full traditional meal with music and dance in opulent (if a little kitsch) surroundings. The food is no better than you'll find in cheaper places – you're paying for the 'experience'. If you want this kind of thing, you'd be better off choosing one of the good places in Fès. The show here starts at about 8 pm.

A similar place is to be found farther inside the medina – the *Restaurant Dar Fez* (☎ 310150) at 8 Rue Boussouni.

Both the *Grand Hôtel du Tazi* and *Hôtel de Foucauld* have restaurants (the former on their roof terrace), where a full meal will come to around Dr 80. They're OK, but they lack the visual feast of the terrace restaurants on the Djemaa and the atmosphere of some of the others listed above. On the other hand, you can get a beer at these places. For at least Dr 100 a head, you could eat in the rooftop restaurant at the *Hôtel Islane*, which is very pleasantly located.

**Gueliz** There are any number of places to eat in the ville nouvelle; a good collection of them are concentrated in or around Ave Mohammed V and Blvd Mohammed Zerktouni.

For bottom-rung local food, you'll find a small group of small, hole-in-the-wall places on Rue Ibn Aicha, where a solid meal such as brochettes, chips and salad will cost about Dr 25.

For a reasonable imitation of a hamburger you could try *Body Food* near the Shell service station, and then top it off with an ice cream from *Boule de Neige* across the road.

Otherwise, meals start getting a little costly, and it'll be hard to find anything for under about Dr 60 a head.

The *Restaurant La Poêle d'Or*, one of a lot of places concentrating on French cuisine, serves up a main meal for about Dr 60 or a set menu for Dr 70, including soft drinks. It's closed on Sunday and service can be slow.

*Restaurant al-Fassia* (☎ 434060), across Ave Mohammed V from the Hôtel Hasna, is a fairly expensive place specialising in Moroccan cuisine, where a set menu will cost about Dr 120. It's open for lunch from noon to 2.30 pm and for dinner from 7.30 to 11 pm.

Across the road from the Hôtel Tachfine is the *Restaurant La Taverne* (☎ 446126), which offers a mix of Moroccan and French cuisine, mostly the latter. A set menu will relieve you of Dr 75 per person.

The *Restaurant Chez Jack'Line*, across Ave Mohammed V from the Hôtel Al Mouatamid, also does mainly French cuisine, with mains for about Dr 70 and pizzas for about Dr 40. Another in this line, which has had good reports, is the *Restaurant Le Jacaranda*.

If you feel like something Asian, head for the *Dragon d'Or*, a Vietnamese restaurant on Blvd Mohammed Zerktouni. Various other types of foreign cuisine are represented, including Spanish at the *Puerto Banus* (☎ 446534) on Rue Ibn Hanbal and Italian at the *Vivaldi* (☎ 435968) on Rue Al-Mouatamid ben Abbad.

Virtually all the bigger hotels have at least one restaurant. La Mamounia has five rather expensive places. Meals are sometimes accompanied by a show of one sort or another. The *Dar Mounia* (☎ 431241) is a well-established upper-end Moroccan restaurant, for which you must book tables in advance.

**Self-Catering** The *Somardis* supermarket on Rue Ibn Aicha in the ville nouvelle is a reasonable place to stock up on supplies you might find hard to get elsewhere – like Corn Flakes. It also sells alcohol. There is also a liquor store next to the Hôtel Nassim.

### Entertainment
**Cafés & Bars** As in any Moroccan city, Marrakesh is crawling with cafés and salons de thé. The more interesting of them are gathered around the Djemaa el-Fna – but don't be surprised to be charged Dr 5 for coffee or weak tea. Ave Mohammed V in Gueliz is the other part of town that usually

attracts a people-watching crowd of tea-sippers.

The *Café Verdi*, on Rue Ibn Aicha in the ville nouvelle, is a bright place for breakfast and there's a mouth-watering chocolate shop across the road. Next to the cinema by the Hôtel Tachfine is the *Café Siroua*, another good place for breakfast.

Possibly the most popular bar in town is at the top of the former Hôtel de la Renaissance, the *Mirador*. The bar on the ground floor of the same building is a great Art Deco relic and a good place for a beer (inside) or coffee (outside).

The *Brasserie Le Petit Poucet* on Ave Mohammed V is a pretty down-to-earth place to get a drink. Even more so is the bar next door to the Restaurant La Taverne. The *Bar L'Escale* is another one you could pop into, although there's nothing special about it. Some of the restaurants in Gueliz also have an alcohol licence.

**Discos** If you want to party on, many of the hotels in the ville nouvelle have nightclubs. There are several others independent of hotels. As elsewhere in Morocco, the usual entry fee varies between Dr 50 and Dr 100, which includes the first drink. Each drink thereafter costs (usually) at least Dr 50. Most offer the predictable standard fare of Western disco music and cliques who appear to avoid eye contact like the plague, but there are a few exceptions.

One of them is a nightclub in the street at the back of the Hôtel de la Renaissance that caters to Moroccans. It kicks off around 11 pm with two hours of the best folk music you'll hear, after which it's contemporary Moroccan pop music mixed with normal disco music.

As far as regular discos go, two of the most popular are the *Diamant Noir* in the Hôtel Le Marrakech, on Place de la Liberté, and the *Temple de la Musique* in the Hôtel N'Fis, at the junction of Ave de France and Ave de la Ménara. Another is the *Cotton Club*, in the Hôtel Tropicana on the road to Casablanca.

**Folkloric Shows** As already noted, there are several up-market restaurants, some in the bigger hotels, that put on distractions involving local tribal singing and dancing. Enquire at the tourist office or have a flip through the *Welcome to Marrakesh* booklet.

### Getting There & Away

**Air** RAM (☎ 446444) has an office on Ave Mohammed V. There are at least two flights a day to and from Casablanca and four a week to Agadir and Ouarzazate. The one-way fare to Casablanca is Dr 340, and it's Dr 235 for the 30-minute flight to Ouarzazate. The airport is five km south-west of town.

**Bus** The main bus station from which all buses (regardless of the company) leave is just outside the city walls by Bab Doukkala. This is a 20-minute walk or a Dr 8 taxi ride from the Djemaa el-Fna.

The main building is a big place with a good many booths covering all sorts of local and long-distance destinations. Window No 10 is the CTM booking desk. CTM has buses to Fès at 6.45 am and 9 pm (Dr 115; nine hours), and buses for Agadir leave at 8 am and 6.30 pm (Dr 43; 3½ hours). CTM also has four daily buses for Casablanca (Dr 57.50; 4½ hours) and Ouarzazate (Dr 49 and Dr 34.50 depending on the service; four hours). There are also buses for Safi, Er-Rachidia, M'Hamid (via Zagora at 7.30 am), Laayoune (7 pm) and Tan Tan (10 pm).

You can get tickets for other bus lines at the other windows. Tickets to Beni Mellal (Dr 34.75) are sold at window No 1, and at window No 2 tickets are sold for nine daily buses to Rabat (Dr 58.50) via Casablanca (Dr 41.80). Note the unusually big difference between this and the CTM Casablanca price.

You can buy tickets to Asni (for Jebel Toubkal) at window No 3 (Dr 10.90). Window No 4 is the Safi line, with six daily departures and tickets for Dr 25.60 (normal) and Dr 27.50 (mumtaz). Next door at window No 5 is the El-Jadida line, with 10 buses a day for Dr 35.10. For buses to Ouarzazate, queue at window No 6 (Dr 47). There are also a couple of runs to Agadir and Taroudannt.

For Essaouira, you want window 7 (Dr

29). These buses go via Chichaoua (Dr 13.50), which is famous for its rugs but has little else of interest. There are two buses a day to Azilal, at 8.30 am and 3.30 pm, and they cost Dr 40.

CTM also has a booking office on Blvd Mohammed Zerktouni, and some of the buses departing from Marrakesh stop outside it on their way out of the city.

Local buses to the villages on the north side of Jebel Toubkal, including Ourika and Asni, leave when full from a dirt patch on the southern side of the medina outside Bab er-Rob. The buses to Asni cost Dr 10.

**Train** The railway station is on Ave Hassan II and is a long way from the Djemaa el-Fna. Take a taxi or No 8 bus into the centre.

There are direct trains from Marrakesh to Fès via Casablanca, Rabat and Meknès at 7.20 and 9.10 am and 2 pm. They take 8¼ hours. You could take the 5.20 or 6.20 pm trains to Casa-Voyageurs and pick up the 10.17 pm train to Fès, but you wouldn't arrive until 3 am.

Trains to Tangier (via Casablanca and Rabat) depart at 9.10 am (change at Sidi Kacem – a brief wait), 3.30 pm (direct) and 7.45 pm (direct). The 3.30 pm direct train is a bad choice as it arrives in Tangier at about 12.45 am. On the later run the journey takes 10½ hours, and should make it to Tangier in time for the first boat of the day to Algeciras. You can book a couchette on this trip.

To get to Oujda, you have to take the 3.30 pm train to Casablanca and then pick up one of two night trains from there.

All up, there are nine trains to Casablanca and eight on to Rabat. There are four trains to Safi (change at Ben Guerir).

Second-class normal/rapide fares include: Casablanca, Dr 52.50/66.50; Fès, Dr 121.50/153.50; Oujda, Dr 194.50/246; Rabat, Dr 71/90; and Tangier, Dr 134/169.

**Supratours** The ONCF organises buses through Supratours to take rail passengers from Marrakesh to destinations such as Agadir, Essaouira, Tiznit, Tan Tan, Laayoune, Smara and Dakhla. You might be able

to get onto one if you can catch a Supratours representative in the train station café *(buvette)*.

**Taxi** Standard grands taxis to Ourika, Asni (Dr 13; about one hour) and other nearby High Atlas destinations depart from outside Bab er-Rob.

**Car Rental** There are at least 25 car-rental agencies in Marrakesh (for a more complete list, pick up the free booklet *Welcome to Marrakesh*). One local company to avoid is Sister's Car, which has had bad reports from travellers. The addresses of the main companies are as follows:

Avis
    137 Ave Mohammed V (☎ 433727; fax 449485)
Budget
    583 Ave Mohammed V (☎ 434604)
Europcar
    63 Blvd Mohammed Zerktouni (☎ 431228; fax 432769)
Goldcar
    Hôtel Semiramis Méridien, Route de Casablanca (☎ 431377)
Hertz
    154 Ave Mohammed V (☎ & fax 434680)
Zeit
    Apt 17, 129 Ave Mohammed al-Bakkal (☎ 431888; fax 431701)

### Getting Around

**To/From the Airport** A petit taxi from Marrakesh to the airport should be Dr 50 but you'll rarely get it for that price. Bus No 11 runs irregularly to Djemaa el-Fna.

**Bus & Taxi** The creamy-beige petits taxis around town cost about Dr 8 per journey, but if you give them a Dr 10 note don't expect any change. From the railway station to the Djemaa el-Fna the official fare is Dr 10 but you'll rarely get away with less than Dr 15.

Local bus No 8 runs from the Djemaa el-Fna area, passing close by the Bab Doukkala bus station and then going on to the main post office and train station. Nos 1 and 20 run right up Ave Mohammed V from near the Djemaa el-Fna into Gueliz. No 11 runs between the airport and the Djemaa el-Fna. The No 3 bus goes to the Bab Doukkala bus station from the Djemaa el-Fna and then on to the main post office.

**Horse-Drawn Carriages** Horse-drawn carriages (calèches) are a feature of Marrakesh you won't find in many other Moroccan cities, and they can be a pleasant way to get around – if you establish the right price. Theoretically, this should present no difficulties. Posted up inside the carriage are the official fares: Dr 9 for a straightforward trip from A to B 'intramuros' (within the medina walls) and Dr 12 for the same 'extramuros' (outside the medina walls). Otherwise, it's Dr 60 an hour for pottering around the sights. This may seem steep – it isn't cheap – but at least you know where you stand. If you're interested, they're based at the south-western side of the Djemaa el-Fna.

**Tours** It is quite possible to organise tours down the Drâa Valley and to the Atlantic coast through agents in Marrakesh. FRAM Orange tours has one-day excursions (!) to Essaouira for Dr 300 a head and to Ouarzazate for Dr 350.

Adra Aventure (☎ 435663), 43 Rue Mauritanie, organises High Atlas treks in spring, cross-country skiing in winter and 4WD trips.

Marocaquad (☎ 448139), based on Ave Mohammed V, runs trips out of Ouarzazate for up to six days on that odd vehicle, the four-wheeled bike (quad). Six days costs Dr 5250. You could ask at the Hôtel de Foucauld, which also organises mountain bike trips.

For information on High Atlas trekking and the phone numbers of guides in Asni and Imlil, you could do worse than go to the Hôtel Ali, inspect their notice board and make some enquiries.

## AROUND MARRAKESH – NORTH
### Cascades d'Ouzoud
About 167 km north-east of Marrakesh are the best waterfalls you'll see in Morocco; they're well worth the effort of getting there. If you have a car, it's an easy enough propo-

sition as a day trip; otherwise, you might have to be prepared to stay overnight in the area – not a bad option.

The falls (*ouzoud* is Berber for olives and refers to the cultivation of olive trees in the area) drop about 100 metres into the river below, forming natural pools that are great for a swim. It is possible to walk along the course of the river to the **Gorges of Oued el-Abid**, and indeed the whole area is good hiking territory as it is cool even in summer. An increasingly popular destination is the so-called **Mexican village** – there's nothing Latin American about the place at all as it's just another Berber village. Plenty of locals and foreign tourists come here, and the souvenir stalls are proof of its popularity, but as yet it is all on a modest scale. The drive between Ouzoud and Afourer, which brings you to the main Marrakesh-Beni Mellal road, is a treat in itself, especially the views of the lake formed by the **Bin el-Ouidane Dam**.

**Places to Stay & Eat** Around the falls there are several camp sites, all much of a muchness. It is a beautiful place to pitch a tent, and generally you'd be looking at about Dr 7 per person and Dr 5 to pitch a tent. There are a few snack stands in among the souvenir stalls.

In **Azilal**, a nearby town you'll almost have to visit, there is an unclassified hotel, the *Funduq Ouzoud*, which has very basic singles/doubles for Dr 28/50. The sign is in Arabic only and it's close to the buses' departure point. A few km farther on, at the Beni Mellal exit, is the *Hôtel Tanoute* (☎ 488281), next to the Shell service station. It's a pleasant two-star place. Singles/doubles with shower cost Dr 121/142, while those with full en suite bathroom are Dr 153/179, plus taxes. The town, by the way, is itself of no interest – it's hard to imagine what its tourist office employees find to tell people.

There are two other accommodation possibilities in this area. About 27 km from Azilal, just north of Bin el-Ouidane, is the *Hôtel du Lac*. It's well signposted and in an idyllic position. You can camp there too. In the town of Afourer, 62 winding km from

MOROCCO

Azilal, there is the four-star *Hôtel Tazarkount*.

**Getting There & Away** Coming from Marrakesh, it would be preferable to get transport direct to Azilal. Two buses a day run from the Bab Doukkala bus station (at 8.30 am and 3.30 pm) and cost Dr 40. From Azilal, they leave at 7 am and 2 pm. There are also occasional grands taxis to Marrakesh for Dr 60 per head, so it stands to reason that you can get them going the other way (try Bab er-Rob).

Some suggest that it's better to go first to Beni Mellal from Marrakesh (Dr 34.75), and get transport to Azilal from there, although with only one bus a day running between Beni Mellal and Azilal, this hardly seems a promising solution. If you do want to head north from Azilal, the Beni Mellal bus leaves at 2 pm and costs Dr 20. There is also a bus south from Azilal to Demnate at 3 pm, from where you may well be able to pick another bus or grand taxi the rest of the way to Marrakesh.

Getting between Azilal and Ouzoud is fairly straightforward, with local grands taxis doing the 38-km run fairly regularly for Dr 10 a head. When you arrive at Ouzoud, follow the dirt track lined with snack and souvenir stalls to get to the waterfalls.

## AROUND MARRAKESH – SOUTH

Several roads lead south from Marrakesh. The principal one leads south to Ouarzazate over the **Tizi n'Tichka**, a popular route with tourists exhausted by Marrakesh and eager to taste the oasis valleys of the south. For more on the Marrakesh-Ouarzazate road, see the section on that town.

Two other minor roads wind south of Marrakesh into the High Atlas, one down the **Ourika Valley** to the ski resort of Oukaïmeden, the other over the **Tizi n'Test** towards Taroudannt and on to Agadir. This latter road takes you to Asni, from where the bulk of trekkers take off into the High Atlas, usually with **Jebel Toubkal** as their goal. For more on Asni and trekking, see the High Atlas Trekking section.

### Ourika Valley

Skiers and trekkers alike could skip the Asni-Imlil area (see the High Atlas Trekking section) and instead head down the Ourika Valley, to the east of Jebel Toubkal. The main options as bases are the ski resort of Oukaïmeden (which is virtually deserted outside the November-March snow season) or the village of **Setti Fatma** farther south. Druing spring Oukaïmeden is beautiful, and in addition to long treks, you can investigate the immediate vicinity in search of rock carvings (see the GTAM book *Gravures Rupestres du Haut Atlas* by Susan Searight & Danièle Hourbette). In winter, if snow cover is decent enough, lift passes cost about Dr 80 a day and equipment hire (there are several outlets in the town) is about Dr 100 a day. Oukaïmeden boasts the highest lift in Africa.

Setti Fatma, 24 km farther south along a poor road, is the site of an important moussem in August and another starting point for treks.

For more details on trekking see the High Atlas Trekking section.

**Places to Stay & Eat** On the way to Oukaïmeden there are two fairly expensive hotels about 42 km out of Marrakesh. The more expensive of the two is the *Hôtel Ourika* (☎ 117531), with singles/doubles at Dr 262/327. Just beyond it is the more modest *Le Temps de Vivre*.

The only place open to all comers throughout the year in Oukaïmeden is the *Hôtel L'Angour – Chez Ju Ju* (☎ 319005; fax 448378). During the ski season it charges Dr 250 a person for rooms with full board – very nice if you can afford it. Out of season they drop it to half-board if you want (but try to find somewhere else to eat around here!) The CAF refuge here is open exclusively to CAF members. Another hotel open only in winter is the *Hôtel Imlil*.

In Setti Fatma, the best place is the *Hôtel Tafoukt*, with singles/doubles for Dr 90/127. The *Hôtel Azrou* is an unpleasant, unclassified dump with rooms for about Dr 40/60.

**Getting There & Away** Out of season there

little or no transport to Oukaïmeden from Marrakesh, although you should be able to arrange a grand taxi, for a price. Otherwise you could take a bus or grand taxi as far as Aghbalou and try hitching up the mountain. Buses to Setti Fatma from Bab er-Rob in Marrakesh cost Dr 10 and are not overly fast.

### Imilchil

Although it is stretching the idea to describe his remote High Atlas village as 'around Marrakesh', it is from Marrakesh that the bulk of the tours to Imilchil depart. Some 363 km distant, Imilchil has become known for its September moussem, a kind of tribal marriage market where the women do the choosing, and it is in danger of losing all genuineness as more foreigners turn up to gawk.

You can get to Imilchil under your own steam, but it requires some patience. The easy bit is heading north-east by bus or a series of grands taxis to Kasba Tadla. From here you need to get another grand taxi to El-Ksiba. Here you may have to wait to get something for Aghbala. The turn-off for Imilchil is near Tizi n'Isly, before Aghbala. From there 61 km of piste lead south to Imilchil. Around here you will have to rely on souq lorries or the occasional passing private vehicle.

### To the Tizi n'Test

**Ouirgane** Ouirgane is a pretty spot about 15 km south of Asni (see the High Atlas Trekking section), and it makes an attractive place to stop for a night or two if you're in no particular hurry. The cheapest place to stay is the cosy, French-run *Au Sanglier Qui Fume* (☎ 117447). You pay Dr 133 a person for good rooms. It has a swimming pool and the rooms are heated in winter. Camping is possible in the grounds for Dr 20 a person. A little farther back along the road to Marrakesh is the beautiful and expensive *Résidence de la Roseraie* (☎ 432094; fax 32095 – booking numbers in Marrakesh), where you're looking at Dr 500 a person. It has a pool and hammam, and can organise expensive horse rides. The hotel also

organises a shuttle to and from Marrakesh for guests.

**Tin Mal Mosque** Heading south to Tin Mal, along the pretty Oued Nfiss and just past a couple of **kasbahs** (you can't miss the one on the left, perched up on a rocky outcrop), travellers with their own transport should take the time to stop at the only mosque in Morocco which non-Muslims can enter. Built in 1156 by the Almohads in honour of Mohammed ibn Tumart, the dynasty's 'founding father' and spiritual inspiration, it is now in the process of restoration. Work began in 1991 and is expected to continue until the end of the century. The first of three stages is complete, and the next was due to begin in June 1994 and take two years, which means it may well be closed when you read this. You can still see the outside of it and it's worth the detour in case it is open. The guardian will expect a tip.

**Tizi n'Test** Over the next 30 km, the road winds its way rapidly up to the pass known as Tizi n'Test – at 2092 metres, one of the highest in the country. The views are breathtaking from numerous points along the way, but if you are driving note that heavy cloud and mist often cuts vision to near zero at the top of the pass and during the descent on the Taroudannt side. In winter it is quite possible that you'll find the road blocked by snow, so be prepared. If you're going the other way, SATAS has a bus from Taroudannt to Marrakesh at 4.30 am that approaches the pass at about daybreak. The road from Taroudannt heads straight on to Agadir on the coast.

# High Atlas Trekking

If you have good shoes or boots, plenty of warm clothes and a sleeping bag, trekking to the summit of Jebel (Mt) Toubkal (4165 metres), Morocco's highest mountain, is worth considering. It's a beautiful area and on clear days there are incredible views in all directions, but especially south over the Sahara.

You don't need mountaineering skills to get to the top so long as you're going up the normal route from Imlil, although there are one or two semi-dangerous patches of loose scree along the trail. You can stay at the Toubkal (still commonly known by its old name, Neltner) Hut (*refuge* in French) for the night. This trek can be done in two days – up to the Toubkal Hut the first day, then up to the summit and back down on the second.

The best time to go is during April and May after most of the snow has melted and before it gets unbearably hot. In October the weather can be very unpredictable, even if there is no snow. You will not get to the summit of Toubkal after snow has fallen unless you have *full alpine gear*. Of course, unofficial guides will agree to take you, knowing full well that it's impossible (or, at best, extremely dangerous).

Don't take these considerations lightly. Snow, the sudden appearance of dense cloud and fog and high winds can all turn an enjoyable hike into a memorable fright – or worse. An American who was said to be experienced, went up in winter in 1994 with an unofficial guide and never came back. Fearing the damage to Moroccan tourism, a huge hullabaloo went up as official guides and police carried out a 21-day search until they found his body.

The usual starting point for the trek is the village of Imlil, 17 km south of Asni on the Tizi n'Test road from Marrakesh to Agadir. Other possible starting points are the villages of Setti Fatma and Oukaïmeden in the Ourika Valley, but you're looking at a longer trek if you start from these places.

Trekkers intending to go to the summit of Jebel Toubkal should be familiar with the symptoms of altitude sickness (AMS) and hypothermia. Both are dangers at this altitude.

### Information

**Guides** You don't need a guide if you're just doing the normal two-day trek, but if you're going farther afield or for a longer period,

then you're going to want to engage one. You may also need a mule to cart your gear – make sure it's a mule you hire and not donkey – there's a big difference.

All this should be arranged in Imlil. The guide business is gradually being made little more professional. There is a small an rather empty Bureau des Guides et Accompagnateurs. This is staffed most of the day and they have a list of official guides and even mugshots up on the wall. Depending o whom you strike, you should be able to as for a little free advice on short local hikes an the basic Toubkal trek without having to for out money for a guide. It has to be said though, that even a couple of the official guides feel they should be paid just to tak you around the corner.

Some of the official guides specialise i canyoning, climbing or ski-trekking. The latter, known to French trekkers as *ski-mule* involves a combination of walking with mules to carry your equipment and the skiing downhill or on cross-country runs.

The French have played a big role i recent years in training these official guides. The Centre Régionale des Enseignement Touristiques (CRET) had a contract unt 1993 to lift standards, and a number o guides even did some of their training outside Morocco. In 1992 all the guide joined up to form a national association aimed at laying the groundwork fo common rules and keeping standards up t scratch.

It is important, especially in times o uncertain weather, to have an official guide with you rather than any old clown who ca probably lead you up the path, but won have a clue how to deal with any difficu situation, let alone an emergency.

About 50 official guides are based in th Toubkal area. All carry cards to prove the training. Have a good look at the cards, and check any potential guide's credentials wit the Bureau des Guides et Accompagnateurs.

Those starting off from the **Ourika Valle** could ask for Lahcen Izahan at the Caf Azagya, about two km before the village o Setti Fatma. He knows the Atlas like h

MOROCCO

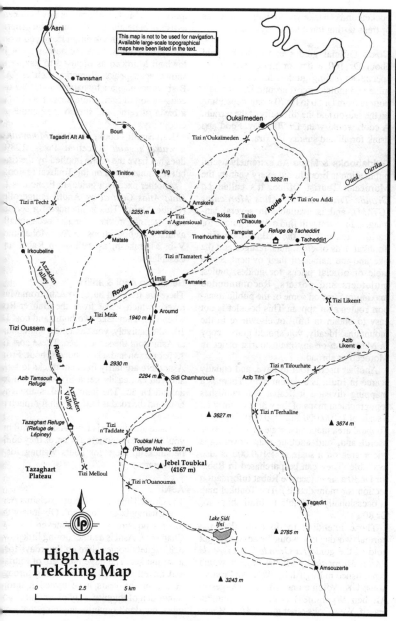

Asni

Tannsrhart

Tagadirt Aït Ali

Bouri

Tinitine

Arg

Tizi n'Techt

2255 m

Amskere

Oukaïmeden

Tizi n'Oukaïmeden

Oued Ourika

Route 2

Tizi n'ou Addi

Ikkiss

Talate n'Chaoute

Tizi n'Aguersioual

Aguersioual

Tinerhourhine

Tamguist

Refuge de Tacheddirt

Tacheddirt

Matate

Irkoubeline

Tizi n'Tamatert

Route 1

Azzaden Valley

Imlil

Tamatert

Tizi Mzik

Aroumd

1940 m

Tizi Likemt

Tizi Oussem

2930 m

2284 m

Sidi Chamharouch

Azib Tamsoult Refuge

Azzaden Valley

Azib Likemt

Tizi n'Tifourhate

Azib Tifni

Tizi n'Terhaline

3627 m

3674 m

Tazaghart Refuge (Refuge de Lépiney)

Tizi n'Taddate

Toubkal Hut (Refuge Neltner; 3207 m)

Tazaghart Plateau

Tizi Melloul

Jebel Toubkal (4167 m)

Tizi n'Ouanoumss

Tagadirt

Lake Sidi Ifni

2785 m

Amsouzerte

3243 m

**High Atlas Trekking Map**

0      2.5      5 km

MOROCCO

pockets and can take you for half-hour walks or treks lasting three to 10 days (or more).

**Costs** Official guides expect to be paid about Dr 160 a day or more if they are specialists (skiing guides, for example). A mule and muleteer cost around Dr 80 a day, porters from Dr 50 to Dr 70 a day, depending on the season and the difficulty of the terrain. A cook would want Dr 70 a day. Food and drink for all and sundry is extra.

**Guidebooks & Maps** An extremely useful publication is brought out every year by the Moroccan Tourist Office. It's called *La Grande Traversée des Atlas Marocains (GTAM)*, and is available in several languages. In it you will find a list of guides for various regions in the Atlas, including Toubkal; lists of *gîtes*, huts, refuges and the like and the names of their owners; and a table of official prices for guides, mules, muleteers and porters. Recommended maximum fares on some of the public transport routes also appear. This booklet is not easy to obtain in Imlil or elsewhere in the mountains. Ideally, you should grab a copy in Marrakesh or any main tourist office in Morocco or abroad.

Another useful tool to have, and equally scarce in Imlil, is a decent map. There is a mapping division in Rabat that publishes topographical maps of the whole country on a scale of 1:100,000 and 1:50,000. The Jebel Toubkal area map, on a scale of 1:50,000, is useful and, and another map covering a wider area on a scale of 1:100,000 is also available. They can be purchased in Rabat for Dr 30 a sheet (see the Rabat Information section for more details). The Toubkal map is occasionally available in Imlil shops for Dr 80.

Those intending to do more than the normal two-day trek would be advised to get hold of the guide *La Grande Traversée de l'Atlas Marocain* by Michel Peyron, which is published in English by West Col Productions, UK. Volume one (Moussa Gorges to Aït ben Wgemmez) covers the Toubkal massif. West Col's other guide, *Atlas Moun-*

*tains* by Robin G Collomb, is nowhere nea[r] as useful or detailed, and some of the genera[l] comments in the book might leave you won[-] dering how much time the author spent i[n] lowland Morocco as opposed to gazing a[t] snowcapped peaks. Remarks such as 'A[ll] Berbers are beggars by nature' and, '...cous[-] cous – a sort of Lancashire hot pot cooked i[n] a basin of semolina' stretch the bounds o[f] credibility.

Karl Smith's book, *The Atlas Mountains[,] a walker's guide* (Cicerone Press, 1989[)] does not have the scope implied by the title[,] but it's quite sound on the Toubkal region.

Another excellent guide, in French, is *L[e] Haut Atlas Central* by André Fougerolle[s] (Guide Alpin). This is intended for seriou[s] alpinists, not trekkers, and is occasionall[y] available in bookshops on Ave Mohamme[d] V in Marrakesh, as well as in Rabat an[d] Casablanca.

### Getting to Asni & Imlil

There are frequent buses to Asni from Ma[r-]rakesh which leave from the Bab er-Ro[b] when full. They take two hours and cost D[r] 10. Alternatively, you can take a shared tax[i] to Asni from the same place. These cost D[r] 13 per person and take about one hour. Fro[m] Asni there are fairly frequent trucks to Imli[l] and you can easily get a lift with them fo[r] around Dr 15. The journey takes about a[n] hour and the road is fairly rough for much o[f] the way.

There are also taxis from Asni to Imlil bu[t] you'll have to negotiate a price, as they coul[d] be stuck up there for hours waiting for [a] return fare.

### ASNI

The Grand Hôtel du Toubkal proclaims Asn[i] 'the Chamonix of Morocco'. Obviously th[e] joker who wrote this has never been t[o] Chamonix. Asni is a rather boring little tow[n] that vaguely comes alive on Saturdays for [a] local market. The large numbers of touris[ts] and travellers of all types coming throug[h] here over the years have turned it into [a] minor den of iniquity. Stay overnight if yo[u] must, but don't organise anything that eve[n] ounds like a trek. It may have been OK nce, but there are some very cheeky people ipping serious amounts of money off inno-ent travellers.

The road to Imlil is lined with professional itchhikers – you know the ones: in return or your Samaritan deed they feel obliged to nvite you to the 'family home' for some tea, nd there you are browbeaten into buying ome worthless trinket. The hitchhiker, neanwhile, is back on the road looking for a ide the other way...

If you want to stay the night at Asni there s a *hostel*, which is decrepit but clean and riendly and costs Dr 20 a night. The only ther place to stay is the *Grand Hôtel du ʿoubkal* (☎ 3 via the operator; or 442222 in Marrakesh), a three-star hotel with ingles/doubles/triples for Dr 169/208/282 lus taxes. The hotel has its own bar, restau-ant, swimming pool and guarded parking.

Buses and taxis leave here for Bab er-Rob n Marrakesh. You can also pick up the odd us heading the other way to Ouirgane and joukak.

## MLIL

Most trekkers sensibly give Asni a miss and stay in this fairly relaxed and attractive Berber village for the first night. The area is est known for its walnut trees, but in recent imes there has been some diversification, with apples, cherries and other trees being nore systematically planted as well.

### Places to Stay

A good place to stay is the *CAF (Club Alpin Français) Refuge* on the village square. It ffers dormitory-style accommodation for Dr 16 (members), Dr 24 (HI members) and Dr 32 (nonmembers). It also has a common oom with an open fireplace, cooking facili-ies (Dr 5 for use of gas), cutlery and rockery. Bookings for refuges (huts) farther up can no longer be made from here, but nstead must go through the CAF (☎ 270090), 1 Rue 6e Henri, BP 6178, Casa-lanca-Bourgoune, or through CAF, BP 888, Marrakesh. This could be awkward in summer without lots of forward planning, so

you might have to be prepared to sleep out. However, guides and local people are often more than willing to put you up for about what you would pay in the refuges. The Toubkal, Tacheddirt and Tazaghart (Lépi-ney) refuges cost Dr 22 (CAF members), Dr 33 (HI members) and Dr 44 (nonmembers). You need your own bedding. Note that the CAF refuge at Oukaïmeden is open to CAF members only.

Back in Imlil, there are several other accommodation options. The best deal is probably the *Hôtel el Aine*, which charges Dr 25 per person in quite comfortable and bright rooms. It's the first place you pass on your right as you enter the village, and has a pleasant tearoom stacked with coffee-table books about Morocco. Some of the rooms are set back a little around a small garden, and you can sit up on the roof for some private sunbathing. Cold water is the norm.

Next up, also on the right and virtually opposite the CAF is the *Café Aksoual*, which lets out fairly basic rooms for Dr 25. There are no sheets and the showers are cold.

On the little square is the *Café Soleil*. It has fairly simple rooms with three beds for Dr 60, even for lone guests. There's also a family room for Dr 80 that can sleep five. Their claims of being able to provide you with a hot shower should be taken with a pinch of salt. Plans are afoot to expand the place, and it already has a restaurant (the service is mind-bogglingly slow – you could grow the mint for your tea faster than they boil the water).

The 'luxury' place to stay at is the *Hôtel Étoile du Toubkal* (☎ 499767, 434387). You pay Dr 70/100/140/190 for clean singles/doubles/triple/quads with private shower in the low season and Dr 10 more in the high season. If they are not having power prob-lems, hot water comes out of the showers. They can also change money and have a restaurant offering a set menu for Dr 70 and main courses of standard Moroccan fare for Dr 40 to Dr 50.

Some of the guides in Imlil will be happy to put you up in their family homes in the surrounding villages, but set a price for

MOROCCO

accommodation and food in advance to avoid misunderstandings afterwards.

### Places to Eat

Apart from the *Hôtel Étoile du Toubkal* restaurant, about the only choices are *Café Soleil* and *Café Aksoual*, where simple meals will set you back about Dr 30.

There's also a wide range of foodstuffs available in the shops in Imlil, including canned and packaged goods, mineral water, soft drinks, cigarettes, etc, but no beer. There's also a bakery. Stock up here before starting the trek as there's nothing for sale farther up the mountain.

### TWO-DAY TREK

On the first day of the trek you walk from Imlil to the Toubkal Hut (3207 metres) via the villages of Aroumd and Sidi Chamharouch. This takes about five hours. Bottled drinks are usually available at both these villages.

The *Toubkal Hut* is a stone cottage built in 1938 and has beds for 29 people in two dormitories, but you have to provide your own sheets and blankets or a sleeping bag. There's also a kitchen with a gas stove and a range of cooking utensils; hot water is available. The charge is Dr 44 per person for non-CAF members, plus an extra charge if you use the cooking facilities or need hot water. The resident warden will let you in. You must bring all your own food with you, as there's none for sale here. The warden may, if you give him plenty of notice, prepare meals for you. Don't turn up at this hut without a booking in the high season or you may find it full.

The ascent from the Toubkal Hut to the summit should take you about four hours and the descent about two hours. It's best to take water with you in summer, but this isn't generally necessary in winter. Any water you take out of the streams on the mountainside should be boiled, otherwise there's a fair chance you'll pick up giardiasis. It can be bitterly cold at the top even in summer, so bring plenty of warm clothing with you.

### OTHER TREKS

If you prefer a longer trek (about five hour one way) than that to Tacheddirt from Imli is recommended. The walk takes you over a pass at 3000 metres above the snow line, the down the other side and up again. There's good CAF refuge here with panoramic view where you can stay for Dr 44 plus Dr 5 if yo want to use the gas for cooking. The warde is helpful and can supply bread and eggs. H may also be willing to cook you a meal in hi own home for around Dr 30. It's a beautifu place and very relaxing. Many other treks ar possible from Tacheddirt, including a seven hour trek at military pace back down to Asni

There's another CAF refuge at Tazaghar and the key for it can be found at the village of Tizi Oussem to the north. All CAF refuge are open throughout the year.

Those starting out from the Ourika Valle should head first for the village of Set Fatma (for transport and accommodatio details, see the Around Marrakesh section)

An old hand in the High Atlas, Rick Crus suggests the following treks for those wit three to seven days to spare.

### Route 1

From Imlil, take mules over the Tizi Mzik t the village of Tizi Oussem. Stay the night a the guesthouse run by Si Mohammed o Omar. This place is much more relaxed tha the CAF refuges at Imlil or Toubkal. Price are not fixed, but expect to pay about th same as at the CAF refuges. If you're happy with your muleteers keep them; if not, ask S Mohammed ou Omar if he can provide yo with mules for the next stage. The following day, ascend the Azzaden Valley to th Tazaghart Refuge, which is very peacefu Options for the next day include scrambling on foot up to Tizi Melloul or the Tazaghar Plateau. Be sure to leave early in the day s you can get back to Lépiney before dark. Yo will need a guide for this.

You could also cross over to Toubkal vi the Tizi n'Taddate – this is hard going bu worth it. Again, a guide is essential. The trac is too steep for mules but they can be sen ack the long way round via Imlil and will probably arrive at about the same time.

After the above, you can climb Toubkal itself but it won't be as good as what you've already done. From there you can follow the valleys back down to Imlil via Sidi Chamarouch and Aroumd.

### Route 2

Find transport to Oukaïmeden (see the Around Marrakesh section). There are no mules to be hired here but it should be possible to arrange mules beforehand: ask at the CAF refuge or Hôtel L'Angour-Chez Ju Ju. Better still, plan on a night at the latter and call them a few days in advance from Marrakesh to get mules organised for when you arrive. You will need to bring all your own supplies with you from Marrakesh as there are no food shops at Oukaïmeden. Should you have to wait in Oukaïmeden a few days, there's no harm done as plenty of good walking awaits you in the area (see the Around Marrakesh section).

When your mules arrive you have two possibilities: you can descend to Imlil via Tacheddirt (one day), or you can descend the upper Ourika Valley either directly or via Tacheddirt, stopping at Timichchi and ending at Setti Fatma (two to three days).

### TEN-DAY TREK

Local guides suggest several routes that would keep you marching for 10 days or more.

### Route 3

One such route would take you in the first two days to the Toubkal summit as per the standard route. On returning to the refuge you then push south-east over Tizi n'Ouanoumss to Lake Sidi Ifni. The third day would see you heading on westwards and a little farther south to the Berber village of Amsouzerte. From there, a two-day hike northwards would get you to the Tacheddirt CAF refuge, spending the intervening night with locals in Azib Likemt.

You have a few options from there, one of them being to pursue a northerly course up to Oukaïmeden. A couple of tracks and passes lead you out of there to the southwest, and on this circuit you would go via the Tizi n'Oukaïmeden (the Oukaïmeden pass) down as far as the village of Amskere. From there you could easily finish off the walk on the eighth day by heading to Imlil either via Ikkiss and the Tizi n'Tamatert or south-west to the main Imlil-Asni road over the Tizi n'Aguersioual.

If you wanted to prolong the walk by a few days, you could either proceed from Aguersioual to Matate and drop south to the Tizi Mzik and follow Route 1 to Tizi Oussem, or do the same from Imlil. Rather than going south, as in Route 1, you could turn north for Irkoubeline (day nine). The final day could be spent retracing your steps to Imlil, proceeding to Tinitine (Imlil-Asni road) via the Tizi n'Techt and then down to Imlil. You could also add a couple of days to explore the Tazaghart area as described in Route 1.

### ORGANISED TREKS

Group treks can be organised for you before you arrive in Morocco by writing (in French) to the brothers Imar and Mohammed Imzilen, Guides de Montagne, Imlil, BP 8, Asni, Région de Marrakech, Morocco, and asking for their leaflet. You can also contact them via the Hôtel Étoile du Toubkal in Imlil. They run a modest ski equipment hire shop in Imlil.

Treks ranging from seven to 14 days from May to October are available on many circuits, including Jebel Toubkal, Jebel M'Goun (to the north-east), Jebel Sarhro (to the east), Jebel Siroua (south-east) and the Plateau de Yagour. The price is approximately Dr 350 per person a day, which includes guides, mules, food and accommodation either in tents, refuges or with local people.

Another guide, Brahim Toudaoui, organises similar treks and 4WD tours, or a combination of both. You can write to him at BP 60,500, Asni, Région de Marrakech, Morocco. He speaks French and English.

# The South

If you had to choose one occasion on which to hire a car in Morocco, a visit to the great desert valleys south and south-east of Marrakesh would be the ideal candidate. The towns along the Drâa, Dadès and Ziz valleys are generally drab places, offering the traveller a chance to rest up but little else. The beauty of the region is on the road, and having your own wheels is the best way to experience it.

## Marrakesh to Ouarzazate

From Marrakesh, the P31 starts off in gentle enough and unremarkable countryside. After about 50 km (south-east) the road crosses the Oued Zat (*Le Coq Hardi*, a restaurant and hotel of long standing, sits by the bridge).

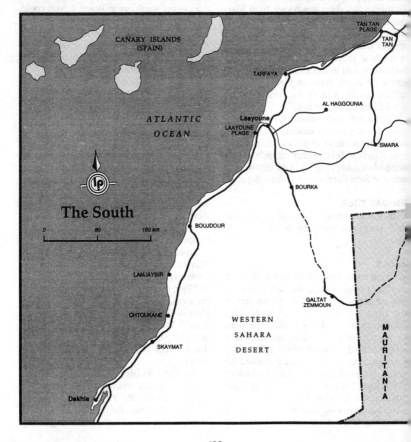

CANARY ISLANDS
(SPAIN)

ATLANTIC OCEAN

The South

0        80        160 km

TAN TAN PLAGE
TAN TAN
TARFAYA
AL HAGGOUNIA
Laayoune
LAAYOUNE PLAGE
SMARA
BOURKA
BOUJDOUR
LAMJAYBIR
CHTOUKANE
GALTAT ZEMMOUN
SKAYMAT
WESTERN SAHARA DESERT
Dakhla
MAURITANIA

Left: Oulad Driss, near M'Hamid, Morocco (DS)
Right: Kasbah, Tamdaght, Morocco (DS)
Bottom: Qasr al-Bahr, Safi, Morocco (DS)

|   |   |
|---|---|
| A | B |
| C | D |
| E | F |

A 'Aït Souka village, near Imlil, Morocco (DS)
C Sand dunes at In Salah, Algeria (HF)
E High Atlas area near Imlil, Morocco (DS)

B Grain store, Jebel Nafusa, Libya
D Old house, Birkit, Libya (AJ)
F Heri es-Souani, Meknès, Morocco

Soon after the road begins to climb towards the village of Taddert. Around here, especially in winter and spring, you could easily think you were in rural France – oaks are the predominant trees. After Taddert, the road quickly climbs and the landscape strips itself of its green mantle. The Tizi n'Tichka Pass is higher than the Tizi n'Test (2260 metres) to the west, but perhaps less spectacular. When you get over the last bends, however, a remarkable scene unveils itself: the lunar landscape of the Anti-Atlas and the desert beyond, obliterating memories of the dense woods and green fields behind you.

## TELOUET

A recommended turn-off if you have a car is to the village of Telouet (you'll see the turn-off to the left a few km after crossing the pass), 21 km east off the highway. Watch out in winter, as the narrow road can be snowbound. The village is a lively little place and

the drive itself is worth the effort. Telouet is dominated by a kasbah that once served as a palatial residence and headquarters of the powerful Glaoui tribe. Until independence in 1956, the Glaouis were virtually given a free hand in southern Morocco by the French, in return for support for the protectorate.

There is a small hotel here. Without your own transport it is a little difficult to get to, as the closest major town is Ouarzazate. Getting a bus or grand taxi to drop you off at the turn-off is easy enough, after which you would have little choice but to stick out your thumb for the last 21 km.

## OUARZAZATE

Ouarzazate was created by the French in 1928 as a garrison and regional administrative centre. Before that, all there was around here was the Glaoui kasbah of Taourirt at the eastern end of the modern town on the road to Tinerhir. It's something of a boom town

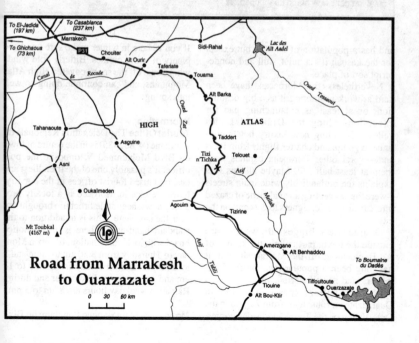

### Road from Marrakesh to Ouarzazate

0    30    60 km

MOROCCO

---

### The Glaoui Tribe

A minor tribe until the 19th century, the Glaouis (or Glaoua) did not come into their own until 1859, when Si Hammou Glaoui, whose wealth came from salt-mine exploitation, was made Qaïd of Telouet by the sultan. From that time, developments were to move fast. The big promotion came when Al-Maidani, Si Hammou's son and successor, proclaimed his support for Sultan Moulay al-Hassan I in 1893 and in return was put in command of the whole High Atlas region and appointed Qaïd of the Tafilalt. After the death of the sultan the following year, it appeared the Glaoui star might fall as quickly as it had risen, as Al-Maidani gradually fell out of favour with Sultan Moulay Abd al-Aziz. The Glaoui clans threw in their lot with Abd al-Aziz's brother, Moulay Abd al-Hafiz, who had himself proclaimed sultan and defeated his brother in 1908. Al-Maidani was then made minister of war, but things started to go sour once again when the sultan dismissed him in 1911.

By this time, however, the sultan's power and prestige were all but exhausted, and Al-Maidani could see a new horse to back in the form of the French. When the protectorate was proclaimed in 1912, the Glaouis threw in their lot with Paris. In return for keeping all southern Morocco in order and loyal to the protectorate, France gave the Glaoui clan carte blanche. Paris was not interested in the means, only in the result.

Al-Maidani died in 1918 and was succeeded by his brother, Thami. During his brother's lifetime, Thami had been made pasha of Marrakesh, and was still hanging the heads of tribal enemies on the city gates as late as the 1940s. He continued the family policy of loyalty to the French, and the latter continued to leave him free rein, something he used to become one of the wealthiest men in Morocco by the 1930s.

Things began to go awry after WW II, when he clashed with the future independent king, Mohammed V, over independence. The sultan backed the movement, but Thami, worried that the departure of the French might end the good life, sided solidly with Paris. He was instrumental in having Mohammed V deposed as sultan in 1953, but two years later saw the writing on the wall and begged the sultan's forgiveness. He got it, but didn't live long enough to see any results, dying of cancer in January 1956. With his demise, the Glaoui tribe seemed to disintegrate, and all their great kasbahs now stand abandoned. ∎

---

and has a population of 30,000, but except for the kasbah it's a quiet, dull and nondescript sort of place.

Nevertheless, the Moroccans have been hard at work promoting it as a big destination, or at least as a launching pad for excursions along the Drâa and Dadès valleys. Sparkling new luxury hotels continue to go up, and charter flights from Paris and several other European capitals keep them at least half-full. Maybe all this fuss explains the outlandishly wide main streets – were they expecting an avalanche of crazed hire-car-driving foreigners to descend on the city?

Ouarzazate's biggest drawcards are outside the town, particularly the kasbah of Aït Benhaddou, off the Marrakesh road. It has long been a popular location for filmmakers, and is well worth a visit.

Most travellers spend the night in Ouarzazate en route to or from Zagora in the Drâa Valley or the Todra and Dadès gorges.

If you're here in winter make sure you have plenty of warm clothes. Bitterly cold winds whip down off the snow-covered High Atlas Mountains, and can continue doing so well into spring.

### Information

**Tourist Office** The Délégation Régionale du Tourisme (☎ 882485) is in the centre of town on Blvd Mohammed V, opposite the post office. It's possibly one of the friendliest and best organised tourist offices in the country. Nowhere else in Morocco is a locally produced newssheet-style brochure brought out as is the case here. This is in addition to the standard hand-outs. There is also a notice board with local information. It's open Monday to Thursday from 8.30 am to noon and 2 to 6.30 pm, and on Friday from 8.30 to 11 am and 3 to 6.30 pm. In summer and during Ramadan weekday hours are 8 am to 3 pm.

**Money** The main Banque Populaire on Blvd

Mohammed V (just west of the post office) is open for changing money Monday to Friday from 8.15 to 11.30 am and 2.30 to 5 pm. On Saturday it's open from 3 to 6 pm and Sunday from 9 am to 1 pm.

For credit-card cash advances, you need to go to the Crédit du Maroc, at the western end of town on Blvd Mohammed V, on the corner of Ave Bir Anzaran. It's open only during standard banking hours.

**Post & Telecommunications** Both the post and phone offices, on Rue de la Poste, are open normal working hours only. There are a few card phones outside.

**Medical Services** There is a night pharmacy on Ave Al-Mouahidine. There is also supposed to be one on Blvd Mohammed V (☎ 882708).

**Supermarket** The Supermarché on Blvd Mohammed V carries an excellent range of goods, including alcoholic drinks (beer and wine) and even nappies (diapers).

**Swimming** A soothing swim in one of the big hotels' swimming pools will cost from Dr 30 to Dr 50.

### Festivals
The moussem of Sidi Daoud is held in Ouarzazate in August.

### Kasbah & Around
The only place worth visiting in Ouarzazate itself is the Taourirt Kasbah at the eastern end of town, off Blvd Mohammed V. During the 1930s, in the heyday of the Glaoui chiefs, this was one of the largest kasbahs in the area. It then housed numerous members of the Glaoui dynasty, along with hundreds of their servants and workers. UNESCO is now restoring parts of it, so the general feeling of neglect that the narrow alleyways exude may in future be balanced by this welcome cultural spring-clean.

The 'palace' that the Glaouis occupied consists of courtyards, living quarters, reception rooms and the like, and is open from 8

am to noon and 3 to 6.30 pm seven days a week. Entry costs Dr 10. You can take on a guide for extra if you want to know what each of the now empty rooms was used for. It's worth a visit, but you'll only be shown a part of the complex. There are some good views over the rest of the kasbah and the Oued Ouarzazate, which, like the Oued Dadès, spills into the Al-Mansour ed-Dahabi dam to the immediate south to become the Oued Drâa. The rest of the kasbah can be visited at any time.

Opposite the entrance to the kasbah is another building in the same style, which houses the Ensemble Artisanal. Here you can find stone carvings, pottery and woollen carpets woven by the region's Ouzguita Berbers. It's open Monday to Friday from 8.30 am to noon and 1 to 6 pm, and on Saturday from 8.30 am to noon. There are plenty of other craft shops around here too, but don't expect any bargains – Club Med is virtually next door and there are direct flights to Ouarzazate from Paris!

### Places to Stay – bottom end
**Camping** There's a camping ground (signposted) next to the so-called Tourist Complex off the main road out of town towards Tinerhir, about two km from the bus station. There is some shade, and the camp site is right by Oued Ouarzazate. It also has a grocery store and restaurant. It costs Dr 7 per person, Dr 5 per car, Dr 6 to pitch a tent and Dr 10 for electricity.

**Hotels** There are effectively only five bottom-end hotels in Ouarzazate (two of them awkwardly placed if you arrive on local transport), so if you arrive late you may have to pay for something more expensive if they're all full (which does happen).

About the best and one of the cheapest places is the *Hôtel Royal* (☎ 882258), 24 Blvd Mohammed V (entrance in the side street). Belkaziz, the owner, has all sorts of rooms for all sorts of prices. Small singles start at Dr 26. Doubles without shower are Dr 63 and those with private shower are Dr 84. A quad made up of two adjoining rooms

MOROCCO

MOROCCO

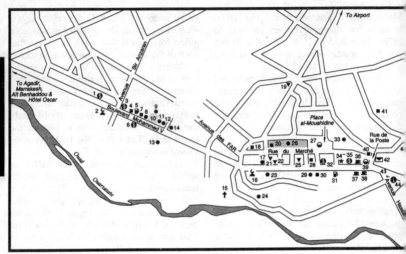

goes for Dr 154. The beds are comfortable, the linen is super clean and the showers have hot water.

Also on Blvd Mohammed V is the *Hôtel Es-Salam* (☎ 882512). It is perfectly good and has reasonable singles/doubles for Dr 52/80. The showers are shared but there is hot water (Dr 5 a go). It can be a bit noisy.

Another decent cheapie is the *Hôtel Atlas* (☎ 882307), 13 Rue du Marché. Clean singles/doubles/triples without shower cost Dr 30/45/65. Doubles and triples with private shower are Dr 55/80. There is hot water in the evening (Dr 5 in the communal shower for those in rooms without shower). It's fine but not as good as the Royal.

About two km out of town on the Zagora road is an excellent deal. The *Hôtel La Vallée* (☎ 882668) is right beside the road and is a friendly, buzzy place. There's a palmeraie just across the way. Pleasant rooms with one big bed and a small bed (no singles) cost Dr 80. There's even a TV in some rooms. The showers are shared and hot water is available. The hotel has its own restaurant.

About 100 metres farther on is the *Hôtel Saghro* on the right, but it's not as good or well located as La Vallée.

If you have a little more money to dispose of, there are two one-star hotels to choose from, too. Of these, the *Hôtel Amlal* (☎ 884030; fax 884600), a block in from Blvd Mohammed V, is newer and streets ahead. The rooms are clean and comfortable, with en suite bathroom (hot water in the evening) and wardrobe, and there is guarded parking out the front. Prices are Dr 108/130/170/210. The *Hôtel Es-Saada* (☎ 883231), 12 Rue de la Poste, also offers singles and doubles for Dr 108/130, but they are gloomy and could do with a paint job.

### Places to Stay – middle
Before heading into the higher bracket of hotel options, there are two that cost moderately more than the Amlal. The *Hôtel Résidence Al Warda* (☎ 882349), just by Place du 3 Mars on Blvd Mohammed V, offers a potentially tempting deal. The rooms are basically mini-apartments with up to five beds, bathroom and kitchen. Hot water is promised, as are reductions on longer stays. The asking rates are Dr 124/148 for singles/doubles.

The well-established *Hôtel La Gazelle* (☎ 882151), also on Blvd Mohammed V, is

MOROCCO

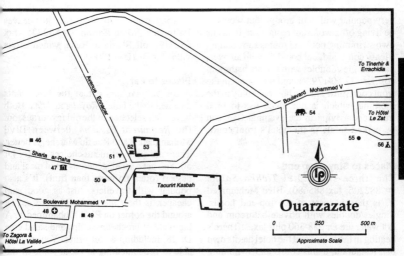

## Ouarzazate

0     250     500 m

Approximate Scale

**PLACES TO STAY**

- 4  Hôtel La Gazelle
- 7  Hôtel Résidence Al-Warda
- 18  Hôtel Amlal
- 20  Hôtel Atlas
- 28  Hôtel Royal
- 30  Hôtel Es-Salam
- 40  Hôtel Es-Saada
- 41  Le Berbère Palace
- 45  Hôtel PLM Azghor
- 46  Hôtel Karam
- 49  Hôtels Tichka Salam & Riad Salam

**PLACES TO EAT**

- 19  Restaurant Al Waha
- 21  Restaurant Essalam
- 22  Café de la Résistance
- 25  Chez Dimitri
- 51  Restaurant L'Étoile du Sud

**OTHER**

- 1  BMCI Bank
- 2  Mosque
- 3  Crédit du Maroc
- 5  Shell Service Station
- 6  Banque Populaire (branch)
- 8  Budget
- 9  Palais de la Culture et des Congrès
- 10  Place du 3 Mars (Car Rental & Tour Agencies)
- 11  Glacier du 3 Mars
- 12  Europcar
- 13  Barracks
- 14  Avis
- 15  Church
- 16  Mosque
- 17  Royal Air Maroc
- 23  Hertz
- 24  Barracks
- 26  Market
- 27  Bus Station & Grand Taxi Lot

- 29  Supermarché
- 31  Shell Service Station
- 32  BMCE Bank
- 33  Water Tower
- 34  Police
- 35  Banque Populaire
- 36  Café du Sud & Café des Voyageurs
- 37  Café Mounia
- 38  Café Errachidia
- 39  CTM Bus Station
- 40  Cinema Atlas
- 42  Post Office (PTT)
- 43  Place Mohammed V
- 44  Tourist Office
- 47  Palace
- 48  Hospital
- 50  Club Med
- 52  Café La Kasba
- 53  Ensemble Artisanal
- 54  Zoo
- 55  Tourist Complex
- 56  Camping Ground

very popular with tour groups, but seems to be living off a worn-out reputation. It has its own swimming pool and rooms surrounding a leafy courtyard, but could do with an overhaul. Singles/doubles with private bathroom cost Dr 127.50/179 – avoid the rooms in the front courtyard. There's hot water only in the morning, which is not much use to tired travellers arriving in the evening. Cars can be parked safely in the hotel's front courtyard.

### Places to Stay – top end

The three-star *Hôtel Tichka Salam* (☎ 882206; fax 885680), Blvd Mohammed V, is the cheapest of the top-end hotels. Singles/doubles with private bathroom and hot water are Dr 288/360 plus taxes. There's heating in the rooms and the hotel has its own bar, restaurant, tennis courts and swimming pool.

There are plenty of options in the four and five-star brackets. The two cheapest are the *Hôtel PLM Azghor* (☎ 885555), on Sharia ar-Raha, and the *Motel Zat* (☎ 882558; fax 885394), a couple of km out of the town centre and off the road to Tinerhir. They both cost Dr 314/400 plus taxes. The latter has a modest swimming pool.

The *Hôtel Bélère* (☎ 882303; fax 883145) is one of the best deals at this end of the scale, with rooms costing Dr 385/495. The hotel has a pool.

Heading up the line is the Salam chain's second representative here, the *Hôtel Riad* (☎ 883610; fax 882766), off Blvd Mohammed V. The rooms are modern and the hotel boasts two restaurants (one of them usually the stage for folkloric music performances and the like), a sauna and a tennis court. Singles/doubles/triples cost Dr 600/700/800 plus taxes. In much the same league is the recently opened *Hôtel Oscar*, another Salam member, just outside the town's Marrakesh exit.

Slightly more expensive again is the new *Le Berbère Palace* (☎ 883077; fax 883071), a rather sumptuous place with pool, bars, hammam and boutiques. Singles/doubles are Dr 700/850.

Apart from Club Med, that just leaves Pullman's *Hôtel Karam* (☎ 882225; fax 882319), off Sharia ar-Raha, which offers villas for Dr 1000/1200.

### Places to Eat

A lot of travellers eat at the restaurants attached to the hotels *Royal* and *Atlas*. Both have a fair selection of the old favourites, but the *Restaurant Essalam*, between Blvd Mohammed V and Rue du Marché, is better. There are eight set-menu choices, all for Dr 50. You get a salad, generous main meal and dessert (often no more than fruit). It's also popular with travellers. Just as good, and cheaper, is the *Café de la Résistance*, just around the corner on Blvd Mohammed V. A big plate of brochettes, chips and salad cost Dr 28, including a soft drink. You may be able to get something to eat at some of the cafés down near the CTM bus station.

Whatever you are told, do *not* go to the *Restaurant Al Waha*. It's a long walk for absolutely nothing. You too can sit in empty, cavernous surroundings and be served a stingy tajine (a clump of fatty meat decorated with a few prunes) for Dr 40 or a bland couscous for Dr 60. Don't waste your time.

If you *do* want to splash out a little, forget the big hotel restaurants and head for *Chez Dimitri*, between Blvd Mohammed V and Rue du Marché. Founded at the same time as the town, it once served as petrol station, general store, dance hall, telegraph office and just about everything else besides. A good meal from the surprisingly extensive menu of Moroccan and French cuisine will set you back Dr 70 to Dr 100 and be well worth it. It is very popular and is often packed to the hilt with tourists. Try the lemon tart. The restaurant also has one of the best stocked bars in southern Morocco.

The restaurant at the *Hôtel La Gazelle* also has a bar, but the food and service are not a patch on Chez Dimitri.

### Getting There & Away

**Air** RAM has an office (☎ 885102) on Blvd Mohammed V. There are flights to Casablanca (Dr 445; at least five times weekly),

Marrakesh (Dr 235; four times weekly) and possibly Agadir, although at the time of writing it appeared this weekly flight had been suspended. There are direct flights to Paris.

**Bus** CTM has its own terminal on Blvd Mohammed V, close to the post office. CTM has a bus to Zagora (Dr 35; four hours) and on to M'Hamid (Dr 52.50; seven hours) at 12.30 pm. Another bus for Agadir (Dr 86; seven hours) leaves at noon. There are four departures for Marrakesh. Those at 8.30 am and 9 pm are mumtaz services and cost Dr 49. The others are 1st-class buses; they leave at 11.30 am and 12.30 pm and cost Dr 34.50. The trip takes about four hours. The 9 pm bus to Casablanca is a mumtaz run and costs Dr 106.50. At 10.30 am there's a bus to Er-Rachidia for Dr 65.50. It goes via Boumalne du Dadès (Dr 24.50) and Tinerhir and takes about nine hours.

SATAS and several other smaller bus lines all operate from Place al-Mouahidine. SATAS has at least one departure a day to Marrakesh (Dr 46.50) at 8.30 am, and to Agadir (Dr 80) at 9.30 pm. The latter stops at Taroudannt on the way (Dr 65). A bus leaves for Zagora and M'Hamid at about 6.30 am and another for Er-Rachidia at 8 pm. The other lines between them have several runs to Agadir, Taroudannt and Zagora.

**Taxi** Grands taxis also leave from Place al-Mouahidine. A place in a taxi to Marrakesh costs Dr 70. To Zagora the fare is Dr 40. The fares to Agdz, Skoura and Boumalne du Dadès are Dr 20, Dr 10 and Dr 25, respectively.

**Car** Since the Drâa Valley route down to Zagora and beyond to M'Hamid is such a spectacular and interesting journey, it's worth considering car rental before you leave Ouarzazate. With your own vehicle, you'll be able to stop wherever you like to explore the ksour (fortified strongholds) or take photographs. In a bus or shared taxi you'll simply speed through all these places, catch only fleeting glimpses and probably

arrive in Zagora feeling disappointed. It's far better to get a group together and hire a vehicle in Ouarzazate, as there are no car-rental places in Zagora. Some of the agencies include:

Avis
    On the corner of Blvd Mohammed V and Rue A Sehraoui (☎ 884870)
Budget
    Résidence Al-Warda, Blvd Mohammed V (☎ 882892)
Europcar
    Bureau 4, Place du 3 Mars (☎ 882035)
Hertz
    33 Blvd Mohammed V (☎ 882084)

**Tours** The big hotels organise 4WD trips and the like to destinations such as Telouet, Skoura, the Todra Gorge and Zagora. They are not cheap.

## AROUND OUARZAZATE
### Tifoultoute

About nine km north-west of Ouarzazate is another Glaoui kasbah now converted into a hotel and restaurant, where you can watch evening performances of traditional dance and music. Although the kasbah is quite impressive from a distance, it's a disappointment when you get up close. When you pass the first gateway, you can wander up the first lane on the right through all the litter to have a look at the innards of a kasbah in an advanced state of disrepair. When you then try to pass through the inner gateway, they want to charge you Dr 5! Basically, all you have access to once inside is the restaurant, hotel and roof – the views from the roof are OK, but hardly worth Dr 5. Just tell them you want to go to the restaurant.

The kasbah was first used as a hotel in the 1960s, when the cast of *Lawrence of Arabia* was put up here, and it has since become somewhat kitsch. Package-tour groups are ferried in here regularly for the dinner and show. Rooms cost Dr 140 for a double and are somewhat basic. As for the restaurant, it has set menus for Dr 75 and Dr 110. It would probably be worth it if you had a car to get out there and were not accompanied by busloads of tourists.

The best way to get there is to take the road to Marrakesh and turn off at the sign for Tifoultoute. Without your own car, you'll need to negotiate for a taxi.

## Aït Benhaddou

In the same direction, again off the road to Marrakesh, and 32 km from Ouarzazate, is the village of Aït Benhaddou. Here is one of the most exotic and best preserved kasbahs in the whole Atlas region. This is hardly surprising, since it has had money poured into it as a result of being used for scenes in as many as 20 films, notably *Lawrence of Arabia* and *Jesus of Nazareth*. Much of the village was rebuilt for the filming of the latter. Its fame lives on, but the population has dwindled.

When you arrive, walk in off the road past the Auberge Al Baraka and you'll see the kasbah on the other side of the Ounila riverbed. Head down past the souvenir stalls and across the river, which is usually no more than a trickle with a ramp and stepping stones to cross, although it can flow more strongly in early spring. The main entrance to the kasbah complex is a little way upstream (you'll know you've found it when you see more souvenir stalls).

One of the locals may half-heartedly hassle you to engage him as a guide but this is totally unnecessary. There are magnificent views from the upper reaches of the kasbah of the surrounding palmeraie and, beyond, the unforgiving hammada.

You can go on camel treks here, too, if you have a lot of money. The going rate appears to be an absurd Dr 700 for a measly three hours!

**Places to Stay & Eat** There are three places to stay, and there is a lot to be said for doing so rather than bedding down in Ouarzazate.

The first you'll come across is the least appealing. The roadside *Auberge Al Baraka* (☎ 5 through the operator) has extremely primitive rooms for Dr 100 whether there's one or two of you. Skip it if you can.

The *Auberge El Ouidane* has better (but not spectacular) rooms for Dr 50/100. They only have cold showers. The compensation is that the views across to the kasbah from the adjoining restaurant and some of the rooms are wonderful.

Next door, the *Hôtel Restaurant La Kasbah* (☎ 2 through the operator) offers double rooms for Dr 140 with compulsory half-board. That's not such a bad deal really – where else are you going to eat anyway?

**Getting There & Away** To get there, take the main road to Marrakesh and turn off after 22 km when you see the signpost for the village; Aït Benhaddou is another nine km down a good bitumen road (stop at the signs for the hotels). Occasionally, local buses travel to Aït Benhaddou from Ouarzazate, but it's a lot easier to get there by sharing a taxi. Otherwise, ask around among tourists in the restaurants or at Hôtel La Gazelle. Hitching is difficult.

## Tamdaght

Five km north-east of Aït Benhaddou, the road ends abruptly where it hits the river Ounila. On the other side it continues on for a while before turning into a poor piste leading north to Telouet (an increasingly popular 4WD, mountain-bike and hiking route).

About 1.5 km north-east of where the river cuts the road stands yet another Glaoui kasbah, that of Tamdaght. It is not as spectacular as the Aït Benhaddou complex, but comparatively little visited. You can get sturdy vehicles with a high chassis over the stream, but don't try it if you are unsure. Instead, leave your vehicle at the little café (watch their prices) and wade across. If you're lucky, Larbi Embarak might be hanging around. He's quite a local character and will insist on giving you a piggy-back across to keep your tootsies dry. He will also want to act as your guide and show you a tattered photo of himself as an extra for one of the several films which have been shot here. *The Man Who Would Be King*, with

Sean Connery and Michael Caine, is one of them.

# Drâa Valley

From Ouarzazate you have the choice of following two scenic routes. One leads you south through the Drâa Valley, a natural delight that will take you through what can sometimes seem like a tunnel of kasbahs and palmeraies. The other takes you north-east along the Dadès Valley and the Dadès and Todra gorges, also known as the Route des Mille Kasbahs (Road of 1000 Kasbahs). You can then push on to Er-Rachidia and the Ziz Valley or even farther to Erfoud and the oases of the Tafilalt.

If you want to try out both, it makes sense to go down the Drâa Valley first, as, unless you have a 4WD, you have no choice but to come back up the same way when you've reached the end. Heading out along the Dadès Valley, you could proceed all the way to Figuig on the Algerian frontier, or turn up north and either circle slowly back towards

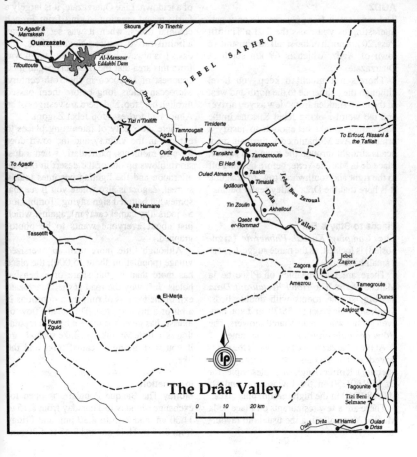

The Drâa Valley

Marrakesh via Midelt or keep going north to Fès or Meknès via Azrou.

Although you can get to the main centres by bus, there is no doubt that the freedom of having your own transport is a decided advantage in this part of the country. If you do have a car, beware of the false hitchhiker syndrome. A few less-than-honest Moroccans work the Ouarzazate-Zagora road looking for suckers to take home in 'gratitude' for the lift, only to start the hard carpet sell.

## AGDZ

The road south from Ouarzazate only gets interesting as you cross the Tizi n'Tinififft Pass, 20 km north of the small administrative town of Agdz, which is 69 km south of Ouarzazate.

There's not much to keep you here, although the palmeraie to the north and west of the town (hidden from view as you arrive) and the weird-looking Jebel Kissane in the background might be enough to justify a brief stop. Ave Mohammed V, the main road, heads straight through the town to a square, Place de la Marche Verte, before heading off to the right and southwards towards Zagora. It is here that the Drâa Valley really begins.

### Places to Stay & Eat

The *Camping Kasbah-Palmeraie* (signposted) is located, as the name suggests, near a small kasbah.

There are two cheapies on Place de la Marche Verte. The *Hôtel Restaurant Draa* has big, simple rooms with double beds. Singles/doubles cost Dr 35/70, and you may even get hot water in the shared showers. The *Hôtel des Palmeraies* is much the same.

At the Ouarzazate exit of town is the overpriced *Hôtel Kissane* (☎ 44 through the operator). It offers singles/doubles/triples for Dr 90/160/250 in the low season and Dr 100/180/260 in the high season, plus taxes.

There are a few restaurants on Place de la Marche Verte offering the usual old favourites.

### Getting There & Away

CTM, SATAS and several other buses stop here en route between Ouarzazate and Zagora. Sometimes you can get on, sometimes you can't. Otherwise, occasional grands taxis go to Ouarzazate and Zagora – Dr 20 either way.

## ZAGORA

The road from Agdz to Zagora, featuring 95 km of heavily cultivated oases lining the Drâa and some 50 ksour, is the richest stretch of the Drâa.

Arriving in Zagora, however, can be a bit of a letdown. Like Ouarzazate, it is largely a fairly recent creation, dating from French colonial times, when it was set up as an administrative centre. Nevertheless, the oasis has always been inhabited, and it was from this area that the Saadians began their conquest of Morocco in the 16th century. Moroccan rulers long before them passed through here too, and there are vestiges of an Almoravid fortress atop Jebel Zagora.

There are plenty of interesting places to explore in the vicinity and the town does have its moments, particularly when a dust storm blows up out of the desert in the late afternoon and the lighting becomes totally surreal. Zagora is also where you'll see that somewhat battered sign saying 'Tombuktoo 52 jours' (by camel caravan), against which just about everyone wants to be photographed.

Although little more than an oversized village (population about 15,000), the place has more than its fair share of expensive hotels. Just why the road at the Ouarzazate exit of the town is of runway proportions is a bit of a mystery, too. The steady flow of tourists has given the place a bit of a reputation as a 'little Marrakesh'. Take special care if you start arranging camel treks and the like.

### Information

**Money** The Banque Populaire is open for exchange Monday to Thursday from 8.15 to 11.30 am and 2.15 to 4.30 pm, and Friday from 8.15 to 11.15 am and 2.45 to 4.30 pm.

**Market** Market days are Wednesday and Sunday. Fruit and vegetables, herbs, hardware, handicrafts, sheep, goats and donkeys are brought in to be bought and sold.

### Things to See & Do
The spectacular **Jebel Zagora**, which rises up across the other side of the river, is worth climbing for the views – if you have the stamina and you set off early in the morning. The town is smack in the middle of extensive **palmeraies**, some of them out around the hotels and camp sites at the southern end of town. They are peaceful and beautiful and enough to make you forget the dreary nature of the town centre.

If you are here over the period of Mouloud (check the Table of Holidays in the Facts about the Region chapter), you may well coincide with the moussem of Moulay Abdelkader, which brings the town to life.

It is possible to arrange **camel treks** of up to a week or so. You could try calling Yassin Ali on ☎ 847497, or enquire at the two camp sites near the Hôtel La Fibule or at the hotel itself. It should cost about Dr 200 to Dr 250 a day (including an overnight stay in the desert).

### Places to Stay – bottom end
**Camping** Campers have a choice of three sites. About the most popular is *Camping d'Amezrou*, about 200 metres past the Hôtel La Fibule along the dirt track that runs alongside the irrigation channel. It costs Dr 7.50 a person, Dr 5 for a car, Dr 5 to pitch a tent and Dr 7 for electricity. Hot showers are supposedly free. The setting is attractive and close to the restaurants of the hotels La Fibule and Kasbah Asmaa.

Also over this side of town is *Camping de la Montagne*, at the foot of the mountain. You get to it by crossing the bridge over the irrigation channel immediately past La

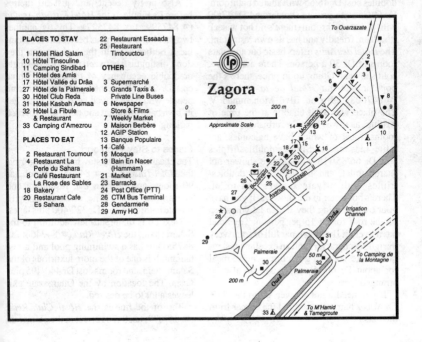

**PLACES TO STAY**
1  Hôtel Riad Salam
10  Hôtel Tinsouline
11  Camping Sindibad
15  Hôtel des Amis
17  Hôtel Vallée du Drâa
27  Hôtel de la Palmeraie
30  Hôtel Club Reda
31  Hôtel Kasbah Asmaa
32  Hôtel La Fibule
    & Restaurant
33  Camping d'Amezrou

**PLACES TO EAT**
2  Restaurant Toumour
4  Restaurant La
   Perle du Sahara
8  Café Restaurant
   La Rose des Sables
18  Bakery
20  Restaurant Cafe
   Es Sahara

22  Restaurant Essaada
25  Restaurant
    Timbouctou

**OTHER**
3  Supermarché
5  Grands Taxis &
   Private Line Buses
6  Newspaper
   Store & Films
7  Weekly Market
9  Maison Berbère
12  AGIP Station
13  Banque Populaire
14  Café
16  Mosque
19  Bain En Nacer
   (Hammam)
21  Market
23  Barracks
24  Post Office (PTT)
26  CTM Bus Terminal
28  Gendarmerie
29  Army HQ

Zagora

To Ouarzazate

To Camping de la Montagne

To M'Hamid & Tamegroute

Fibule, and then following the signpost off to the left. It's about two km down the dirt track from here. There are toilets and plenty of shade. Cold drinks are available, but you're advised to bring your own food. It costs Dr 8 per person and the same for a car. Pitching a tent costs Dr 4.

The third site is *Camping Sindibad*, off Ave Hassan II, where there are toilets, hot showers and a café. It's a perfectly decent camp site surrounded by palm trees, but most travellers choose to stay at the other two. The people here find that a little irksome, but they do their cause little good with the prices they charge. It costs Dr 7 per person, Dr 10 for a car, Dr 10 to pitch a tent, Dr 10 for electricity and Dr 5 for a hot shower.

**Hotels** There are two unclassified hotels next to each other on the main street, Blvd Mohammed V. The better of the two, if you can get a front room, is the *Hôtel Vallée du Drâa*, or *Oued Drâa* (☎ 847210). Singles/doubles cost Dr 46/65 with shared bathroom, Dr 69/85 with private shower and Dr 77/90 with private bathroom (there's no hot water). It's clean, friendly and has its own restaurant. The *Hôtel des Amis* offers basic but adequate rooms at Dr 30 a person. There are shared, cold showers. Going up in price, there's the popular one-star *Hôtel de la Palmeraie* (☎ 847008), also on Blvd Mohammed V. The place was a bit chaotic at the time of writing, as it was being refurbished, but the rooms, most of which have balconies, are quite reasonable. Singles/doubles/triples cost Dr 66/85/118 with private shower but shared toilet, and Dr 98/131 for doubles/triples with private shower and toilet. There's hot water in the showers. If you have your own bedding they'll also let you sleep on the roof for Dr 15 per person. The hotel has a lively if fly-blown bar full of some very intriguing characters and an excellent restaurant where you can get a three-course meal for about Dr 60. Camel treks can also be arranged here.

If you need a hot shower, go to the *Bain En Nacer* hammam, around the corner from the bakery.

**Places to Stay – middle**
It can be worth your while booking ahead in the high season for the following places, which are often full. On the other hand, you may well be able to get hefty reductions on room rates in the low season.

If you can afford it, the best value and most relaxing place to stay in Zagora is the two-star *Hôtel La Fibule* (☎ 847318; fax 847271), on the southern side of the Oued Drâa, about one km from the centre. The hotel is set in the palmeraie, with its own shady garden, restaurant, bar and swimming pool, and the rooms have been built and furnished in the traditional Berber style, with the addition of showers (hot water from 7 to 11 am daily) and toilets. Doubles cost Dr 145 with private shower but shared toilet (few of these) and Dr 290 with private shower and toilet. Excellent meals are available in the restaurant. Camel treks can be organised here for about the same price as at the camp sites.

Also pretty decent, and just 50 metres before La Fibule, is the *Hôtel Kasbah Asmaa* (☎ 847599; fax 847527). This is another two-star hotel which has been built to resemble a Berber ksar. In the high season they don't distinguish between the price of single or double occupancy of the rooms, which cost Dr 250. We've had good reports from people who have stayed here. The hotel has its own bar, restaurant and pool, and guarded parking

**Places to Stay – top end**
The cheapest place to stay in this category is the *Hôtel Tinsouline* (☎ 847252), which has 90 rooms and its own bar, restaurant and swimming pool. Singles/doubles with private bathroom cost Dr 320/400 plus taxes.

Next up is the brand-new addition to the Salam chain, the *Hôtel Riad* (☎ 847400; fax 847551). It has a swimming pool and a restaurant. It is one of the more luxurious of the Salam chain, and rooms cost Dr 440/495 plus taxes. The location by the Ouarzazate exit leaves a lot to be desired.

Top of the line is the *Hôtel Club Reda* (☎ 847079; fax 847012), set in the palmeraie next to the Oued Drâa. Singles/doubles with private bathroom cost a rather steep Dr 600/700. The hotel has all the amenities you would expect, including bar, restaurant, swimming pool and tennis courts, and has had favourable reports from travellers.

## Places to Eat

All the hotels have their own restaurants, and it's probably true to say that they all try hard to produce tasty Moroccan-style dishes – soups, tajine, salad, etc – although the quality does vary from day to day at the cheaper places.

The *Hôtel des Amis* offers cheap meals at Dr 25, but the service can be excruciatingly slow and the tajine is of minimal size. In a similar vein and of uneven quality are the *Restaurant Café Es Sahara* (soup and tajine for Dr 20), *Restaurant Essaada*, *Restaurant Toumour* and *Restaurant La Perle du Sahara*. The *Restaurant Timbouctou* is more reliable and offers dishes at about the standard Dr 25 to Dr 30. Another possibility is the *Café Restaurant La Rose des Sables*, next to the Maison Berbère carpet and souvenir shop.

It's often better to eat at either the *Hôtel Vallée du Drâa* for Dr 40 or the *Hôtel de la Palmeraie* for Dr 60, since the service is quicker and the servings more substantial. The latter stocks beer and wine, but obviously is a little expensive.

Even if you are not staying at *La Fibule* you should try to make it there for a meal. The food is excellent and the surroundings are very relaxing. If you want, the bar will sell you cans of beer over the counter to take away.

## Getting There & Away

Buses and shared taxis will give you no chance to stop and take photographs of the many fascinating villages and ksour between Ouarzazate and Zagora, let alone give you time to explore them. So, if there's any chance of you considering car rental and the freedom this will give you, think seriously about it. You will have to do so in Ouarzazate as there are no car-rental agencies in Zagora.

**Bus** The CTM bus terminal is at the south-western end of Blvd Mohammed V, and the main bus and grand taxi lot is at the northern end of Blvd Mohammed V. There's a CTM bus once daily to Ouarzazate at 7 am. This bus starts out at M'Hamid and comes past La Fibule at about 6.30 am so, if you're staying there or at the nearby camp sites, you can flag it down right outside the door. The fare to Ouarzazate is Dr 35, and the bus continues on right through to Marrakesh. The bus coming the other way leaves for M'Hamid at 4.30 pm and also costs Dr 35.

Otherwise, you could try your luck at the bus lot. The best time is in the morning.

**Taxi** If buses are scarce, a better bet might be a grand taxi. Again the best time to try is the morning. A place costs Dr 40 to Ouarzazate, Dr 20 to Agdz and Dr 22 to M'Hamid.

If you want to try out the direct desert route across to Rissani in the Tafilalt, you may be able to get a ride in a taxi as far as Tazzarine. From there you'll have to arrange further transport, such as a Land Rover taxi as far as Alnif and another taxi from there to Rissani. Be prepared to get stuck overnight on this route. The best time to try is market days.

## SOUTH OF ZAGORA
### Amezrou

Across the other side of the Oued Drâa, about three km south of Zagora, is the village of Amezrou. It has an interesting old Jewish mellah, which is still a centre for the casting of silver jewellery. Jews lived here for centuries and formerly controlled the silver trade, but they all took off for Israel after 1948, leaving the Berbers to carry on the tradition. If you look like you might buy something, the locals will be willing to show you the whole process. Because the village is so close to Zagora, local children will leap on you offering to be guides, but it's fairly low-key hassle.

Elsewhere in the palmeraie life goes on much as it always has. It's well worth spending a day wandering through the shady groves along the many tracks that dissect it.

The dates grown here are reputed to be the best in Morocco, but times have been getting harder because of a disease that attacks and kills the palms.

## Tamegroute

Farther south, about 18 km from Zagora, is Tamegroute. For many centuries, right up until recent times, the town was an important religious and educational centre whose influence was felt throughout the Drâa region and into the desert beyond. Tamegroute consists of a series of interconnected ksour, at the centre of which is the zawiyya and its famous library.

The **library** (signposted on the main road as 'Librairie Coranique') houses a magnificent collection of illustrated religious texts, dictionaries and astrological works, some of them on gazelle hides. The oldest texts date back to around the 13th century. Most of them are kept on shelves behind glass doors but others are displayed in glass cases of the type used in museums. They're beautifully illustrated but perhaps of limited interest to anyone other than an Arabic scholar. Visitors are allowed into the outer sanctuary and the library in the morning and late afternoon (it's generally closed from noon to 3 pm). You'll be expected to leave a donation for the upkeep of the place – Dr 5 to Dr 10 should suffice. There is no shortage of local people willing to act as guides but you don't need one.

Also in Tamegroute is a small potters' souq.

**Places to Stay & Eat** The town's only hotel and best restaurant is the *Hôtel Riad Nacir*, on the left-hand side as you enter town from Zagora.

## Tinfou & the Dunes

About five km south of Tamegroute you can get your first glimpse of the Sahara desert. Off the road to the left are a number of isolated sand dunes. If you've never seen sandy desert and do not intend to head to Merzouga or on into Algeria, these might be

worth a visit. Otherwise, it's hardly worth the effort.

**Places to Stay & Eat** Tinfou is supposed to be a village, but there's really nothing here but a couple of accommodation options. The first is well worth considering as an alternative to staying in Zagora. The *Auberge Repos du Sable* is a tumbledown kasbah-style building with simple rooms costing Dr 50/70. There is cold water in the shared showers. The atmosphere is relaxed and the food, although it can take a while to arrive, is very good (about Dr 30). It even has a swimming pool, although it's not always in use. The hotel is run by Majid el-Farouj, whose parents, Hassan and Fatima, are artists. Their work (which is for sale) covers the walls of the main courtyard, and the artists themselves occasionally grace the hotel with a visit. You can organise 4WD trips into the desert (Dr 1500 to Dr 2000 a day, up to eight people) and camel treks for a week or so.

A little farther on is a recent and worrying addition to the landscape, the German-run *Bivouac*, where Dr 20 will get you a mattress in a tent inside a soulless compound. This place caters mainly to tour groups from the big Zagora hotels, staging desert soirées where nomads happen to emerge from the sands to indulge in a glass of tea and chat with the guests. It also detracts a little from the peaceful isolation that the Auberge enjoyed until recently.

## M'Hamid

Most people who come to Zagora try to make it to the end of the road at M'Hamid, about 95 km to the south. The attraction of this trip is the journey itself. The road south of Tinfou soon crosses the Drâa and leaves it behind to cross a vast tract of implacable hammada desert. After crossing a low pass you hit the village of Tagounite, which has a couple of cafés, including the *Es-Saada* and *Sahara*.

A few more km take you over the dramatic Tizi Beni Selmane Pass, from which the oases of the Drâa again come into view. The village and kasbah of Oulad Driss make a

picturesque stop before the final run into M'Hamid.

With a population of about 2000, M'Hamid is nothing special, and the handful of touts can be a pain. There's little to do here except sweat and poke around a few souvenir and craft shops. Alternatively, the hotels can organise donkey and camel treks. Otherwise, they can simply guide you on treks in your own vehicle (which would want to be good and preferably a 4WD) into the dunes and sandy desert that start up 10 km to the south.

**Places to Stay & Eat** About six km back out along the road is the *Camping des Caravanes*, which was opened in 1993 and is a little better equipped. It costs Dr 10 a person and Dr 5 for a car. There are also claustrophobic rooms for Dr 30 a head. You can have a meal cooked if you ask in advance. Not far away is the *Camping Touareg*.

The *Hôtel Restaurant Sahara* has simple but adequate facilities, and charges Dr 35 per person. There are as yet no showers and the food is overpriced, so it might be an idea to

bring some with you. The town is waiting to have electricity put on, and the hotel will install showers if this ever happens. Otherwise you can tramp out about 500 metres to a palmeraie and stay at the *Auberge Al Khaima*. The few rooms, shut in by old, heavy doors with medieval key locks, are primitive and not very clean (Dr 20 a person). You can also pitch a tent here, but there's no water for washing.

**Getting There & Away** There's a daily CTM bus from Zagora (originating in Marrakesh and passing through Ouarzazate) to M'Hamid around 4.30 pm, and it returns the next day between 4 and 5 am. The fare is Dr 35. If you're lucky, you may be able to get a lift with other tourists or in one of the rare grands taxis.

If you just want to make a day trip from Zagora, it comes down to hiring a taxi. The usual charge is up to Dr 400 for the day, although this is negotiable to a degree. Taxis take up to six people, so it's a good idea to get a group together to share the cost. This is the best way to see the area, as the driver will stop wherever you like.

# Dadès Valley & the Gorges

Heading roughly east of Ouarzazate, the Dadès Valley threads its course between the mountains of the High Atlas to the north and the Jebel Sarhro range to the south. If leaving from Ouarzazate, about the first thing you notice is the lake formed by the waters of the Al-Mansour ed-Dahabi dam. Shortly after, you enter the biggest oases on the Dadès route – those preceding the town of Skoura.

## SKOURA

Skoura lies about 42 km east of Ouarzazate and makes an easy day excursion if you don't simply want to make a stop before heading farther east. The oases here contain a collection of impressive kasbahs. One of the most easily accessible is the **Kasbah ben Moro**. About 150 years old, it's just off the main road on the right, a couple of km before you reach the town. The owners, who live next door, use it mainly for animals and storage space now, but Mohammed will open it up for a small fee. There's not an awful lot to see inside, but from the top there are great views of the palmeraie and another kasbah, **Amerdihl**, which is owned by a wealthy Casablanca family and cannot be visited.

### Places to Stay & Eat

The *Hôtel Nakhil*, in the centre of town, is a basic place with rooms for Dr 30. Apart from a few cafés and snack stands, there's not much in the line of restaurants here.

### Getting There & Away

The odd bus passes through from Ouarzazate and Tinerhir, but an easier bet is a grand taxi from Ouarzazate (Dr 10). If you want to get out on the same day, you'll have to be early,

as there's not much happening in terms of transport from the late afternoon on.

## EL-KELAÂ M'GOUNA

Another 50 km north-east up the valley, the town of El-Kelaâ M'Gouna is really of precious little interest to the traveller. Its main claim to fame is as a centre of rose-water production, which is made abundantly clear long before you reach the town by the hordes of kids trying to sell you strings of rose petals on the roadside. There's one cheap hotel and another four-star job if you feel the urge to stay.

## BOUMALNE DU DADÈS & THE DADÈS GORGE

Another 23 km north-east brings you to a fork in the road. The left branch takes you up the stunning Dadès Gorge, while the main road veers off right over the river to the hilltop town of Boumalne du Dadès, where you may end up staying the night if you

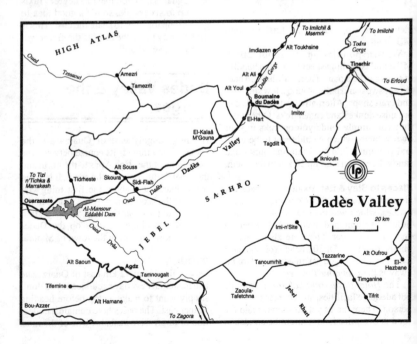

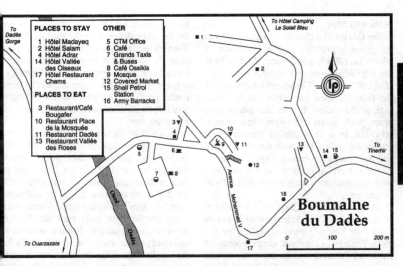

PLACES TO STAY
1 Hôtel Madayeq
2 Hôtel Salam
4 Hôtel Adrar
14 Hôtel Vallée des Oiseaux
17 Hôtel Restaurant Chems

PLACES TO EAT
3 Restaurant/Café Bougafer
10 Restaurant Place de la Mosquée
11 Restaurant Dadès
13 Restaurant Vallée des Roses

OTHER
5 CTM Office
6 Café
7 Grands Taxis & Buses
8 Café Ossikis
9 Mosque
12 Covered Market
15 Shell Petrol Station
16 Army Barracks

To Dadès Gorge

To Hôtel Camping Le Soleil Bleu

To Tinerhir

To Ouarzazate

Oued Dadès

Avenue Mohammed V

**Boumalne du Dadès**

0    100    200 m

arrive late in the day. If you have a choice, staying in the gorge is a much more attractive option.

The somewhat potholed road snakes up in a leisurely fashion inside the wide walls of the gorge for about 25 km to Aït Oudinar. On the way you will see plenty of greenery, mostly figs, interspersed with an array of kasbahs and ksour. Some of the rock formations are truly bizarre, resembling globules of molten wax dribbling down the side of a candle. By the time you reach Aït Oudinar, the river Dadès is right next to the road, and, in spring especially, flows strongly. The gorge narrows here quite abruptly, and climbs a couple of km to a cluster of cheap new hotels. Beyond them the bitumen gives way to piste as the trail winds up inside the main canyon in a series of hairpin bends. After a few km of this, the road flattens out as you leave the best of the scenery behind you. You can probably make it as far as Msemrir in an ordinary car, but beyond (say to Imilchil) you will definitely need a 4WD. In any case the driving is very slow, and this is a great place for a puncture. There are some wild and largely untouched stretches of mountain scenery to be enjoyed here, but

be aware that many of the pistes are impassable in winter or after wet weather.

If you decide to stay in the gorge, the natural splendour doesn't stop here. There are some challenging walks up into some of the smaller mountain passes west and east of the Oued Dadès. You can ask at the hotels for advice on where to go, or even take on a guide.

Without your own transport you will have to rely on an uncertain combination of hitching and walking or hire a taxi in Boumalne. Hiring a taxi for a few hours, including photo stops and the like, should cost in the region of Dr 100 to Dr 150. If you're staying at the Hôtel Adrar in the town, the staff will help you negotiate this.

**Treks**
In addition to the gorges north of Boumalne, Jebel Sarhro stretches out to the south. There is some good trekking to be done in this area, which has been left relatively untouched by tourism. The Hôtel Adrar can organise 4WD and mule treks into the region. The latter would cost between Dr 300 and Dr 400 a day for mule, muleteer, guide and their food.

## Places to Stay

**In the Gorge** The choice of places to stay in the gorge is growing rapidly, and most of what's on offer is good value. At Km 14 is the *Café Mirguirne* and, another km on, the *Hôtel Restaurant Kasba*, which overlooks the fantastic rock formations on the other side of the valley. It's an interesting little place with small balconies, and is constructed in a mixture of modern and traditional styles. The beds are comfortable and hot water is promised. Expect to pay Dr 25 per person. Anywhere else it would be a well-recommended stop, but choices abound farther up.

At Km 25 is the village of Aït Oudinar, where you'll find the *Auberge des Gorges du Dadès* (☎ 830762) perched right over the river. You have a choice of simple rooms for Dr 40/60 (shared hot showers) or classier self-contained rooms for Dr 100/140. Most of the rooms, especially the more expensive ones, overlook the river; breakfast is included in the price. There is also room for camping and you can sleep on couches in the salon for just Dr 10 a head.

There is a group of places even farther up the valley at Km 27. A common phenomenon among these places seems to be the quantum leap in quality from rooms without shower to those with.

The *Hôtel Restaurant Camping du Peuplier*, owned by Mohammed Echaouiche, was the first of what has now become a crowd of hotels. It is one of the more primitive of them and singles/doubles cost Dr 20/25, or Dr 30/40 with private bathroom. Hot water is unlikely. You can also camp right by the stream for Dr 3 a person – you can't get much cheaper than that.

Of the next three hotels, the *Hôtel Tisadrine* is the cheapest and simplest. It costs Dr 30 for a room with two beds. The shared shower is cold (very).

Of the remaining two, the *Hôtel La Kasbah de la Vallée* is probably the best. It is fairly new and has comfortable rooms for Dr 35/60 and better ones with en suite shower and toilet for Dr 60/130. Options include sleeping in the hotel's 'nomad' tent

by the stream for Dr 20, pitching your own for Dr 10 or sleeping on the roof for Dr 15. There is heating in winter, and while you eat your Dr 60 menu dinner the hotel puts on some live fireside music. The hotel management say they can organise **4WD trips** farther north and that **white-water rafting** is possible on a limited scale about 15 km north along the river.

Newer but perhaps not quite as good (though there's little in it) is the *Hôtel La Gazelle du Dadès* next door, which started business in late 1993. It's a little hard to believe the manager's advertised room rates, but if they are accurate, this place automatically becomes deal of the week. Rooms with three comfortable beds cost Dr 30, for however many people. Rooms with three beds and private shower are Dr 50, again for the whole room. They are clean and there is hot water. Sleeping on cushions in the salon or on the roof costs just Dr 5 each.

Five km farther on is one more simple place, the *Hôtel Taghia*.

**Boumalne du Dadès** If you arrive late or choose not to stay up in the gorge (it's hard to see why you'd make such a choice), there are several accommodation options in Boumalne du Dadès, which lies on the road from Ouarzazate to Er-Rachidia. Most of the hotels in the town are more expensive than those in the gorge.

About the first place you come across in the lower end of the town is also about the best budget deal, the *Hôtel Adrar* (☎ 830355). This is a popular place with travellers (read the comments book if you're unconvinced) and offers singles/doubles for Dr 40/60. The hotel has a good restaurant and can organise treks into Jebel Sarhro. The staff will also help organise share taxis into the gorge.

A long walk up the hill from the bus station is the *Hôtel Salam* (☎ 830762). It's not too bad at Dr 60 for a room (single or double occupancy) and the price includes hot showers. The hotel has its own restaurant and is unlikely to be full if other places are.

Another more or less budget option is a

little farther on still – if you've walked this far, it won't make much difference to you now. It's the *Hôtel Camping Le Soleil Bleu* (☎ 830163). You can pitch a tent for Dr 15 per person, or sleep on the roof for Dr 20. Otherwise, singles/doubles/triples without shower cost Dr 55/75/115, or Dr 75/110/145 with private shower. The rooms without shower also happen to be without sheets and are very small – not good value at all.

Much better but popular and often full is the new *Hôtel Restaurant Chems* (☎ 830 041) on Ave Mohammed V. It has doubles with shower for Dr 110 or slightly less for single occupancy. The hotel has its own restaurant and is in a great position overlooking the valley below.

Not so brilliant is the *Hôtel Vallée des Oiseaux* (☎ 830764). Singles/doubles without shower cost Dr 80/110 or Dr 120/150 with private shower and toilet. The hot water is great, but the beds in some rooms are collapsing and great swathes of paint are peeling off the walls.

The only top-end hotel is the *Hôtel Madayeq* (☎ 830763). It's a weird-looking building – you can see it well before entering the town from the Ouarzazate road. Rooms will set you back Dr 288/360 plus taxes. The restaurant is rather expensive.

## Places to Eat

Most of the hotels in the gorges have their own restaurants, and there's nothing to stop you trying the food in a hotel where you're not staying if you want some variety of décor.

The options in Boumalne aren't much wider. The restaurant below the *Hôtel Adrar* serves a filling meal of tajine or brochettes with salad and a drink for Dr 30. Three other little restaurants compete for business nearby. The *Restaurant/Café Bougafer*, just up from the Adrar, is OK but serves less generous meals for about the same price. The other two are next to each other near the mosque: the *Restaurant Place de la Mosquée* and the *Restaurant Dadès*. Up near the Hôtel Vallée des Oiseaux is the somewhat more posh *Restaurant Vallée des Roses*, where a full meal will cost about Dr 60.

Apart from this, there are a couple of cafés, the best of which is the *Café Ossikis* on the square where the grands taxis and buses gather.

### Getting There & Away

**Bus** CTM has a bus to Ouarzazate and on to Marrakesh at 9 am. Going the other way, a bus passes through on its way to Tinerhir and Er-Rachidia at about 12.30 pm. The CTM office on Ave Mohammed V seems to be closed most of the time. A couple of other buses pass through here, including one to Agadir (via Ouarzazate) at 4 pm and another to Rabat (via Ouarzazate) at 7.30 pm.

**Taxis** As is usual in smaller places like this, grands taxis are probably a better bet. The fare is Dr 25 to Ouarzazate, Dr 12.50 to Tinerhir and about Dr 10 to Aït Oudinar (these last ones up the gorge are not terribly frequent).

More than likely you will have to hire a taxi, especially for the trip up the gorge, and tailor it to your needs. You can hire one by the hour or for a simple one-way trip if you intend to stay there. A straightforward ride to Aït Oudinar should cost no more than Dr 60, but you'll have to employ all your bargaining skills. It will cost more if you want to make photo stops or carry on to the hotels beyond Aït Oudinar.

## TINERHIR & THE TODRA GORGE

Some 15 km from Tinerhir (Tineghir on some maps), at the end of a lush valley full of palmeraies and mud-brick villages hemmed in by barren, craggy mountains, is one of Morocco's most magnificent natural sights. This is the Todra Gorge: some 300 metres high but only 10 metres wide at its narrowest point, and with a crystal-clear river running through it. It's at its best in the morning, when the sun penetrates to the bottom of the gorge. In the afternoon it gets very dark and, in winter, bitterly cold.

Although the main gorge can be explored in half a day, those with more time might like

MOROCCO

to explore farther up the gorge or walk through the palmeraies on the way to Tinerhir; the people here are very friendly. There are numerous ruined kasbahs flanking the palmeraies and plenty of photographic opportunities.

The more ambitious might consider making their way farther up into the Atlas. A combination of souq lorries, Land Rover taxis and hiking could take you north to Aït Hani, from where you could push on over the Tizi Tirherhouzine towards Imilchil, or do a loop south through the Dadès Gorge that would bring you back to the main highway linking Ouarzazate and Er-Rachidia. A network of difficult pistes links the sporadic villages here in the High and Middle Atlas, many of which are snowbound in winter. You could spend weeks exploring them, but you should bear in mind that you'll be far away from banks, post offices and even basic health services most of the time. Come prepared.

Climbing is also becoming increasingly popular on the vertical rock face of the gorge; it is not uncommon to see tiny human figures clinging to various parts of Todra's sheer stone walls as you wander through.

There's little of interest in Tinerhir itself, although it certainly looks pretty from the hill above town. An enormous amount of building is going on, which has completely smothered the small core of the original town. The highway is known as Ave Mohammed V as it passes through the town on the way to Er-Rachidia. Most of the hotels and restaurants are on or near Ave Hassan II, a block in to the south. Although hardly amazing, the little backstreets and markets behind Ave Hassan II warrant a bit of a wander. Some of the town's cheapest food is to be had in this zone, too. Money is no problem, as there are several banks around the centre of town. The post office is in the centre of town on Ave Hassan II.

### Places to Stay

**Camping – in the gorge** Six km back down along the road from the gorge towards Tinerhir are three good camp sites. They're all next to each other in the palmeraies and are all equipped with showers and toilets There's a small shop that sells basic supplies across the road from the first of them.

The first you come upon on the way up from Tinerhir is the *Auberge de l'Atlas*. It's very good but marginally more expensive than the other two. It costs Dr 8 per person Dr 9 for a car, Dr 15 to pitch your tent and Dr 10 for electricity. It has well-overpriced rooms for Dr 80/90. They are for the desperate only. The *Camping Le Lac (Garden of Eden)* and *Camping Auberge* are equally good and a wee bit cheaper. Take your pick

**Camping – Tinerhir** About 2.5 km west of the Tinerhir town centre is *Camping Ourfi.* It's awkwardly located and pretty spartan. It costs Dr 8 per person, Dr 5 to pitch a tent, Dr 7 for a car, Dr 5 for a hot shower and Dr 10 for electricity. If the pool is in use, it costs another Dr 10. There are squalid little 'bungalow' rooms for Dr 35 a person. It is difficult to imagine why anyone would want to stay here given the alternatives in the gorge. The same goes for *Camping Almo,* about one km south-east of the town centre. It's a hassle to get to and not worth the effort.

**Hotels – in the gorge** Just inside the gorge are the two ideal places to stay. The *Hôtel Restaurant Yasmina* (☎ 833013) is the more expensive of them, with good rooms costing Dr 90/160 (less in winter), including breakfast. In summer they'll let you sleep on the roof for about Dr 15 a head.

The *Hôtel Restaurant Les Roches* (☎ 834814) offers rooms with two beds for Dr 60 or a place in a big tent for Dr 20.

You can get reasonable food in both places, which in summer serve meals in big 'Berber' tents out the front by the stream. This is great in summer, but you won't be eating in winter! Neither of the hotels up here sells alcohol, so bring your own. Often they put on wood fires in winter.

If these two are full, the *Hôtel Le Mansour*, a km or so back downstream (15 km from Tinerhir) and just outside the entrance of the gorge proper, has uninspiring singles/doubles for Dr 50/60. It does have a pleasant café and restaurant.

None of these hotels would have been built in a country where environmental impact studies are required before construction. What is more, while they keep a clean image around their doorsteps, they treat the rest of the upper gorge as their private garbage tip.

**Hotels – Tinerhir** If you decide not to stay at the gorge itself or need somewhere to stay in Tinerhir, there is a reasonable choice of hotels. Four of the budget ones are virtually in a row on Ave Hassan II.

The *Hôtel Salam*, next to the CTM office, has rooms with one big bed and another small one for Dr 40 and others with two big beds and one small bed for Dr 60. If you have the people to fill these, it's not a bad deal, although the place is basic and a little dreary. The *Hôtel Raha* next door is about the same price but not terribly good. Next up on the same street is the *Hôtel El Fath*, at No 56. It has clean and acceptable rooms with single beds for Dr 35/60. Rooms with a single bed and a double bed cost Dr 75. They promise hot water in the shared shower.

The *Hôtel Al-Qods*, at the end of the block, has bright, simple rooms for Dr 30/60/90.

Another reasonable, if unexciting, option is the *Hôtel L'Oasis* on Ave Mohammed V, the main road through town. It's next to the Total service station and has its own restaurant. The rooms are perfectly clean and comfortable, contain two beds and cost Dr 70 whether one or two people occupy them. There's a shared (hot) shower on the ground floor.

There are two pricier options. The *Hôtel Todra* (☎ 834249), on Ave Hassan II, has plenty of dark-wood panelling and a decayed elegance about it, but the rooms aren't exactly marvellous. The hotel has a restaurant (main meals about Dr 50) and a bar. Rooms without shower cost Dr 84/103 plus taxes. Those with shower go for Dr 103/125 plus taxes.

Back behind Ave Hassan II near the central market area is the popular Spanish-run *Hôtel de l'Avenir* (☎ 834604; fax 834 599). The rooms are good if a little pricey at Dr 85/140, but this includes breakfast. The manager, Roger Mimó, can help organise treks in Jebel Sarhro and mountain-bike trips in the area.

The *Hôtel Bougafer* (☎ 833280; fax 833282) is a three-star hotel on the road to Ouarzazate, opposite the Camping Ourfi. The location is awful, but the rooms are not bad and cost Dr 360/420.

Top of the line is the four-star *Hôtel Sargho* (☎ 834181; fax 834352), which is up on top of the hill overlooking the town. The views are superb and the hotel has an enormous swimming pool as well as a bar and restaurant. However, the rooms are small and tatty, the 'tourist menu' is outrageously expensive and there are always hustlers up here. Singles/doubles cost Dr 320/400 plus taxes. Visa cards are accepted.

### Places to Eat

In the gorges you'll probably be eating at your hotel or organising your own food, but in town the best place to look for cheap Moroccan food is in the little market area south of Ave Hassan II. There are loads of simple little stalls here. For meat eaters, they point you to the butchers, where you buy some fresh meat and take it back to the 'restaurant'. If you don't want to play this game, the right gesticulations will get the message across that you'd prefer it if they took care of it for you. There are quite a few busy little cafés around here, too.

Otherwise, there are a few restaurants along Ave Hassan II and Ave Mohammed V. The one at the *Café Centrale* is all right, as is the *Restaurant Essaada*. Better are the *Restaurant La Kasbah* on Ave Mohammed V and the restaurant attached to the *Hôtel L'Oasis*, both of which offer three-course meals for around Dr 60.

At about Dr 50 for a main dish, the *Hôtel Todra* restaurant is overpriced for the bland fare you get. Much better, and a definite change, is the paella available at the *Hôtel de l'Avenir*.

MOROCCO

### Getting There & Away

**Bus** CTM has a couple of buses that pass through Tinerhir on their way east and west. Only 10 seats are set aside for passengers boarding at Tinerhir. At noon and 1.30 pm buses go to Er-Rachidia. The first costs Dr 28 and the second Dr 30. At 8 am a mumtaz bus passes through on its way to Marrakesh (Dr 80) via Ouarzazate (Dr 35.50). Another bus leaves for Ouarzazate at 2.30 pm and costs Dr 30.

Otherwise, several private buses also leave from the nearby square, by the park.

**Taxi** Grands taxis to Ouarzazate (Dr 40) and Er-Rachidia (Dr 20) leave from the eastern end of the same gardens, near the Hôtel Al-Qods. This is also the place to hunt for occasional transport (taxis, lorries or pick-up trucks) up the Todra Gorge and beyond – perhaps as far as Imilchil, although it's unlikely you'd get one vehicle going the whole way.

As a rule, if there is no standard taxi leaving for the gorge (stress that you want to pay for a place in a normal shared taxi), you may need to bargain to hire one specially to take you up.

## Ziz Valley & the Tafilalt

### ER-RACHIDIA

At the crossroads of important north-south and east-west routes across Morocco, Er-Rachidia (named after the first Alawite leader, Moulay ar-Rashid) was originally built by the French as an administrative centre and was once known as Ksar es-Souq. It is a modern place, laid out in barracks-style grid form, and offers the traveller little to do but rest. Depending on where you are coming from, it can be a very relaxing place to hole up for a day or two just to enjoy being left to your own devices.

The main highlight is outside the town – the **Ziz Gorges** to the north, which link Er-Rachidia to the small town of Rich and on to Fès and Meknès via Midelt. More pre-

cisely, this magnificent route past palm-fringed towns and ksour begins (or ends depending on which way you are going) with the French-built Tunnel du Légionnaire 20 km south of Rich and stretches to the dam just north of Er-Rachidia. If you take this road, make sure you get a daytime bus or grand taxi.

### Information

**Tourist Office** There is a small local syndicat d'initiative (☎ 572733) in the square opposite the covered market on Ave Moulay

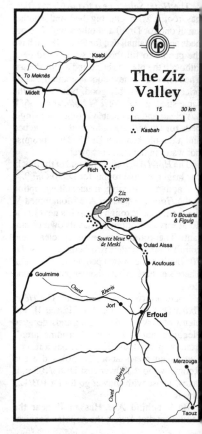

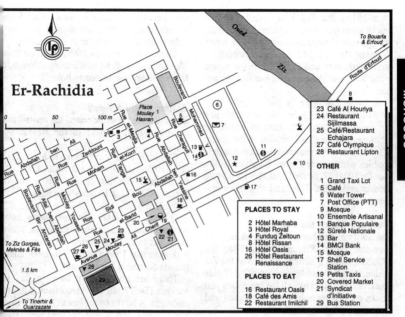

**MOROCCO**

Er-Rachidia

0    50    100 m

To Bouarfa
& Erfoud

To Ziz Gorges,
Meknès & Fès

1.5 km

To Tinerhir &
Ouarzazate

| | |
|---|---|
| 23 | Café Al Houriya |
| 24 | Restaurant Sijilmassa |
| 25 | Café/Restaurant Echajara |
| 27 | Café Olympique |
| 28 | Restaurant Lipton |

**OTHER**

| | |
|---|---|
| 1 | Grand Taxi Lot |
| 5 | Café |
| 6 | Water Tower |
| 7 | Post Office (PTT) |
| 9 | Mosque |
| 10 | Ensemble Artisanal |
| 11 | Banque Populaire |
| 12 | Sûreté Nationale |
| 13 | Bar |
| 14 | BMCI Bank |
| 15 | Mosque |
| 17 | Shell Service Station |
| 19 | Petits Taxis |
| 20 | Covered Market |
| 21 | Syndicat d'Initiative |
| 29 | Bus Station |

**PLACES TO STAY**

| | |
|---|---|
| 2 | Hôtel Marhaba |
| 3 | Hôtel Royal |
| 4 | Funduq Zeïtoun |
| 8 | Hôtel Rissan |
| 16 | Hôtel Oasis |
| 26 | Hôtel Restaurant Renaissance |

**PLACES TO EAT**

| | |
|---|---|
| 16 | Restaurant Oasis |
| 18 | Café des Amis |
| 22 | Restaurant Imilchil |

Ali Cherif, the main road through town. It's rarely open.

**Money** There are at least two banks: a Banque Populaire and a BMCI branch. The latter is diagonally opposite the post office on Blvd Mohammed V and the former is on the main street heading out to Erfoud.

**Post & Telecommunications** The phone office is to the left of the main post building (on Blvd Mohammed V), and is open daily from 8.30 am to 9 pm. There are a few card phones outside.

**Places to Stay – bottom end**

**Camping** The closest camping ground is *Camping Source Bleue de Meski* (see that section).

**Hotels** The three cheapest places are all pretty basic and located just off Place Moulay Hassan. At the western end of the

square in a small side street are the *Hôtel Royal* and the *Hôtel Marhaba*. Singles/doubles/triples in both are Dr 30/50/75. There's isn't much to distinguish them, but the Marhaba is perhaps the skuzziest. The woman who runs the Royal speaks only Arabic but you shouldn't have any problems communicating. There are cold communal showers. Perhaps slightly better is the *Funduq Zeitoun* (sign in Arabic only), on Rue Abdallah ben Yassine.

Considerably more comfortable is the *Hôtel Restaurant Renaissance* (☎ 572533), Rue Moulay Youssef, which is where most travellers choose to stay. The showers actually have hot water, but at the time of writing guests were being charged Dr 80 a head for compulsory half-board. The staff speak French and English.

**Places to Stay – middle**

If you have the money it's worth thinking about staying at the two-star *Hôtel Oasis*

(☎ 572519), Rue Sidi Bou Abdallah, which has 46 attractive warm carpeted rooms, most with private shower and toilet and hot water. It costs Dr 121/142 for singles/doubles without shower and Dr 153/179 for rooms with. The hotel has its own bar and restaurant.

A little cheaper is the *Hôtel Meski* (☎ 572065), Ave Moulay Ali Cherif. It's just far enough towards the road to Fès to be inconvenient for those arriving in the centre of town, but offers reasonable value. Singles/doubles with private shower but shared toilet cost Dr 101/127, or Dr 123/152 with private shower and toilet. The hotel also has a restaurant.

### Places to Stay – top end

The only top-end hotel in Er-Rachidia is the four-star *Hôtel Rissani* (☎ 572186; fax 572585), Route d'Erfoud, just across the Ziz bridge. Singles/doubles cost Dr 302/377 plus taxes, and the hotel has all the amenities you would expect, including bar, restaurant and swimming pool.

### Places to Eat

One of the most popular places to eat is the *Restaurant Sijilmassa*, on the main street – look out for the sign 'All food is here' in English, French, Spanish and Italian! It has the usual standard Moroccan dishes and a full meal will cost you about Dr 35. Eat inside or at the outdoor tables.

Also good is the *Restaurant Imilchil*, which is opposite the covered market. It, too, has a sign in French, saying 'Look no farther, all food here'.

In much the same league is the *Restaurant Lipton*, more or less across the main road from the Hôtel Restaurant Renaissance. The restaurant part is round the back and can feel a bit cut off from the activity in the street, but they do a decent plate of chicken, chips and salad for Dr 37. The staff almost fall over themselves to be friendly.

For a splurge, try a meal at the licensed *Restaurant Oasis*, which is attached to the hotel of the same name.

Those wishing to put their own meals together should have a look around the covered market, where a wide variety of very reasonably priced food is available.

There is a bar near the BMCI bank on Blvd Mohammed V. It is, predictably enough, a fairly uninspiring watering hole.

### Getting There & Away

**Bus** All buses operate out of the central bus station, which is next to the Restaurant Lipton.

CTM has a daily departure to Marrakesh (Dr 110.50) at 5.45 am via Ouarzazate (Dr 65.50) and Tinerhir. It also has a bus to Meknès (Dr 87) at 10 pm and to Rissani (via Erfoud) at 5 am.

Quite a few other bus companies have services running through Er-Rachidia. There are buses to Fès (via Azrou and Ifrane) at 1 and 9 am and 1 pm (Dr 78.50). Two others run via Sefrou at 2 and 11 am.

There are about seven buses a day to Meknès (Dr 77.50) via Azrou from 6 am to midnight. A bus to Casablanca (Dr 120) runs via Meknès and Rabat at 5.30 pm. Two others go via Azrou and Kasbah Tadla at 8 and 10.30 pm (Dr 113).

There are five daily departures to Rissani via Erfoud and a couple of others to Erfoud via Aoufous or Tinejdad (the long route).

Buses to Ouarzazate (Dr 60) via Tinerhir and Boumalne leave at 11.30 am and 1 pm. There is a bus for Tinerhir only at 6.30 am.

At 3 pm a bus leaves for Bouarfa (Dr 50; five hours), which is unlikely to make it to Bouarfa in time to link up with anything going north or south – very useful.

**Taxi** Most of the grands taxis leave from Place Moulay Hassan. The fare per person to Erfoud is Dr 20. Heading north, the fare to Azrou is Dr 70, while a seat for Fès or Meknès goes for Dr 100. There are also plenty of taxis heading south for Aoufous, which you could take to get dropped off at the Meski turn-off for the Source Bleue. It may be possible (but don't count on it) to get a taxi east to Bouarfa for Figuig. Try early in the morning.

## AROUND ER-RACHIDIA

### Source Bleue de Meski

The Source Bleue de Meski, about 23 km south of Er-Rachidia, is a wonderful natural spring and swimming pool that is understandably popular with the locals. On spring and summer weekends heat-plagued Er-Rachidians flock here in droves, but for the rest of the time it's pretty quiet. For the hot and sweaty traveller heading north or south between Er-Rachidia and Erfoud it is a recommended stop.

You can stay at the *Camping Source Bleue de Meski* for Dr 7 a person, Dr 10 for a tent place and Dr 10 per car. The spring is signposted and is about one km west of the main road. Any buses or grands taxis going south to Erfoud or Aoufous from Er-Rachidia will be able to drop you off at the turn-off. When leaving, you should be able to flag down a grand taxi or hitch a ride to Er-Rachidia or even Erfoud from the main road.

## ERFOUD

The oasis region of the Tafilalt was one of the last to succumb to French control under the protectorate, its tribes putting up sporadic resistance until 1932. Two years later, Morocco was officially considered 'pacified'. To make sure this state of affairs did not change, Erfoud was built as an administrative and garrison town to keep a watchful eye on the Tafilalt tribes.

With a population of about 7000, Erfoud is a comparatively uninteresting little town, but a useful staging point from which to head farther into the desert. Sunrise excursions to the Erg Chebbi dunes near Merzouga to the south are becoming part of the standard menu for passing travellers. Unfortunately, Erfoud is going the way of Rissani (see that section), and newcomers must expect to be resolutely hassled by hotel touts and the like on arrival. Once ensconced in a hotel, however, and all sales pitches exhausted, the welcome committees seem to vanish as quickly as they materialised.

Hotels, restaurants, the post office and so on are located on the town's main street, Ave Mohammed V, and to a lesser extent on Ave Moulay Ismail, which intersects Ave Mohammed V at the post office and links Erfoud to the Er-Rachidia, Rissani and Tinerhir highways.

### Information

The post and phone offices (PTT) are on the corner of Ave Mohammed V and Ave Moulay Ismail. They are open normal office hours only. The Banque Populaire is diagonally across the intersection. You can change money at the Hôtel Salam, too, but watch out for inferior rates and commission charges.

### Dunes

Most of the bottom-end hotels will do their best to dig up a clattering old Land Rover taxi to take visitors to the Erg Chebbi (see the Merzouga section). Quite a few cheap hotels have sprung up along the line of the dunes and in the village of Merzouga, about halfway down its length. For many, though, a drive out in time to watch the sunrise is sufficient. The taxi will pick you up at about 4 am and have you back in Erfoud by 10 am. Hire of the taxi costs about Dr 250 to Dr 300 (for up to seven people). Finding other travellers to make up numbers shouldn't be too difficult.

### Places to Stay – bottom end

**Camping** *Camping Erfoud*, located next to the river, is no great shakes. You pay Dr 10 per person whether you choose a patch of dirt to pitch a tent on (another Dr 10 for the place) or one of the little bedless, concrete cells. You pay the same charge for everything else too, including car, electricity and shower – all of which makes it a dubious expense.

**Hotels** The cheapest and scummiest place to stay is the *Hôtel L'Atlas*, on the road to Rissani. Basic rooms cost Dr 30/60. You should not put too much faith in the boasts about hot water.

The *Hôtel Marzouga* (☎ 576532) on Ave Mohammed V is a better bet, although travellers staying here have denied claims of hot water being available.

In a similar bracket and on the same street

MOROCCO

is the *Hôtel des Palmeraies*, which has singles/doubles for Dr 65/86. The *Hôtel Essaada*, Ave Moulay Ismail, is much the same.

Better than all the above and definitely in possession of a boiler for hot water is the friendly *Hôtel La Gazelle* (☎ 576028) across from the post office. When the water starts flowing though, the plumbing rattles so hard it threatens to come flying off the

**PLACES TO STAY**

- 1 Hôtel Farah Zouar
- 2 Hôtel Salam
- 3 Hôtel Lahmada
- 4 Hôtel L'Atlas
- 9 Hôtel La Gazelle
- 11 Hôtel Essaada
- 12 Hôtel Taifilalet
- 14 Hôtel Sable d'Or
- 17 Hôtel Marzouga
- 24 Hôtel des Palmera-
    ies
- 25 Hôtel Ziz
- 27 Camping Erfoud

**PLACES TO EAT**

- 6 Restaurant
    Sijilmassa
- 16 Restaurant des
    Fleurs
- 18 Restaurant L'Oasis
- 21 Restaurant de la
    Jeunesse
- 23 Restaurant/Café
    du Sud

**OTHER**

- 5 Hospital

- 7 Gendarmerie
    Royale
- 8 Post Office (PTT)
- 10 Mosque
- 13 Banque Populaire
- 15 Hammam (men
    only)
- 19 Hôtel de Ville
- 20 CTM Bus Terminal
- 22 Mosque
- 26 Non-CTM Bus Ter-
    minals
- 28 Law Courts
- 29 Grands Taxis
- 30 Sûreté Nationale

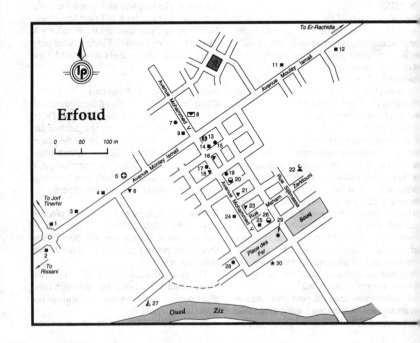

Erfoud

wall. The rooms have private showers and cost Dr 60/95. The hotel has a decent restaurant downstairs.

## Places to Stay – middle

The cheapest place in this category is the one-star *Hôtel Sable d'Or* (☎ 576348), Ave Mohammed V. It's clean and comfortable (though the pictures of Jesus seem a little out of place), all the rooms have private shower, toilet, table and chair, and there's hot water 24 hours a day. The management are friendly and there's a rooftop terrace with great views over town. Rooms cost Dr 110/127. The hotel has its own restaurant.

A new spot on the road heading to Rissani is the *Hôtel Lahmada* (☎ 576097). The rooms are spotless and have private bathrooms. At these prices, however, this place is not great value. Singles/doubles/triples cost Dr 150/200/250. The hotel has a restaurant.

Once a gungy cheapie, the *Hôtel Ziz* (☎ 576154; fax 576811), 3 Ave Mohammed V, now has refurbished rooms with en suite bathroom for Dr 150/180/200 plus taxes; however, the air-conditioning doesn't seem to work. The rooms also have phones and the restaurant has one of the few bars in town – it's a better deal than the Lahmada.

For this money, the *Hôtel Farah Zouar* (☎ 576146; fax 576230) is worth considering. It's on the corner of the Rissani and Tinerhir roads. If the prices remain as low as they are, this is possibly the best deal in town. Some of the rooms could do with some replastering, but overall they compare favourably with those of the Ziz and Lahmada, and cost Dr 150/200 (or Dr 250 for a rather comfortable suite). Like most hotels, it comes with its own restaurant.

## Places to Stay – top end

The least expensive place to stay in this category is the three-star *Hôtel Tafilalet* (☎ 576535; fax 576036) on Ave Moulay Ismail. The newer rooms on the far side of the swimming pool are superb and feature a large, sunny balcony, a comfortable bedroom and a separate dining area, all floored with local earthen tiles. The old rooms are nowhere near as attractive. Self-contained singles/doubles with hot water cost Dr 233/287. Apart from the swimming pool, the hotel has its own bar and restaurant (breakfast is Dr 30). Visits to Rissani, Taouz and Merzouga by Land Rover, including a night under tents in the desert, can be organised from here, but they're not cheap. The hotel runs a cheap place just south of Merzouga village.

Top of the line is the *Hôtel Salam* (☎ 576665), virtually across the road from the Hôtel Farah Zouar. Rooms here start at Dr 398 and rise to Dr 770 plus taxes. There are two wings, and the rooms in the new one are much better (and more expensive) than the others. The new wing also has a bar, pool and sauna.

## Places to Eat

The extremely friendly *Restaurant de la Jeunesse*, Ave Mohammed V, is the place to head for in the evening. The food is excellent and very reasonably priced.

Otherwise, the restaurant at the *Hôtel La Gazelle* has a comfortable Moroccan-style dining room where you can get a three-course evening meal for about Dr 40. There's a visitors' book here containing effusive praise from the four corners of the earth – worth a read.

The *Restaurant L'Oasis* on Ave Mohammed V offers reasonable food for a similar price. Across the road, the *Restaurant des Fleurs* is all right for breakfast, but service can be awesomely slow.

The restaurant at the *Hôtel des Palmeraies* is also rated highly by many travellers, and the restaurant at the *Hôtel Sable d'Or* is worth trying if you have about Dr 60 to spare for a square meal.

The *Restaurant Sijilmassa* on Ave Moulay Ismail is not a bad place and quite popular with locals. The food is nothing special, but it's definitely a pleasant place for tea or coffee at least.

## Things to Buy

The main item here is black marble (there are

quarries in the desert), and you can find souvenirs in several shops in Erfoud. Kids will also try to sell you little trinkets of the same substance.

### Getting There & Away

**Bus** All public transport leaves from Place des FAR, except the one CTM bus to Meknès via Er-Rachidia (Dr 21) at 8.30 pm, which leaves from outside the CTM terminal.

There are several other private bus lines, but departure times seem a little uncertain. One bus leaves at about 11 am to go to Er-Rachidia. Other buses to Meknès leave at 2.30 am and 7.30 pm. At noon a bus runs to Tinejdad (Dr 18), from where you can get other transport to Tinerhir.

A bus to Rissani (Dr 5) leaves at 4.30 pm. Several minibuses also shuttle between Erfoud and Rissani.

**Taxi** Grands taxis are, as a rule, a much more reliable bet. They run regularly to Rissani (Dr 6) and Er-Rachidia (Dr 20).

## MERZOUGA

About 50 km south of Erfoud, the village of Merzouga, with a population of about 1500, offers virtually nothing of interest to anyone. Nearby, however, is the **Erg Chebbi**, Morocco's only genuine Saharan erg – one of those huge, drifting expanses of sand dunes that typify much of the Algerian Sahara. You can pretty easily arrange a sunrise trip out here (see the Erfoud section), drive down yourself or stay for longer.

The pistes can be rough, but a Renault 4 can make it down, winding across rough, black hammada. Opinions vary on taking your own vehicle. The lousy bitumen road soon gives way to any number of pistes. If you follow the line of telegraph poles you can't really go wrong, but the pistes are hardly smooth and your car will definitely take a bit of a beating in the process.

In spring, a seasonal lake appears to the north-west of Merzouga, attracting flocks of pink flamingos and other bird life. Those

doing the 'sunrise tour' from Erfoud should ask to have this included if the lake hasn't dried out.

### Places to Stay

All up, you'll find a good dozen or so basic hotel-cafés dotted along the western side of Erg Chebbi and in the village of Merzouga itself. Most are basic and cost about Dr 30/60. Those along the erg include the *Camping La Vallée*, *Camping Hamada Dunes*, *Auberge Soleil Bleu*, *Café du Sud*, *Auberge Sable d'Or*, *Café Yasmine*, *Auberge Erg Chebbi* and *Café Oasis*. Most of these places allow you to sleep on the roof for about Dr 20 per person – watch your belongings, as theft is a problem. The Café du Sud has been recommended.

Those in the village include the *Café des Dunes*, *Auberge des Amis* and *Camping El Kheima* (in a palmeraie). Just south of the village is the *Auberge Merzouga*, run by the Hôtel Tafilalet in Erfoud. It has basic rooms but as good as those you'll find at any of the above places and for the same price. There are also cold showers; these are not to be relied on in the others. There is a group of 'Berber tents' out the back, where groups from the hotel in Erfoud often spend a night with food and musical accompaniment. When things are quiet you can sleep there for Dr 25. There is a kitchen, so the guy running the place can cook you up a meal if you ask in advance.

You can arrange camel rides into the erg and around from most of these hotels, but some of the asking prices are absurd – up to Dr 1000 a day!

### Getting There & Away

Apart from the 'sunrise tours' from Erfoud there are Land Rover taxis between Merzouga and Rissani on market days (Sunday, Tuesday and Thursday). There's obviously no timetable as such and demand for them can vary enormously. The fare per person is about Dr 20. If you're driving your own car, you are advised to engage a local guide.

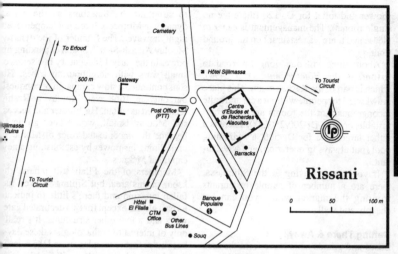

## RISSANI (ER-RISSANI)

Rissani may once have been a superb place to experience the charm and mystique of a southern Moroccan oasis unsullied by tourism, but these days it's the hustlers that you will remember this hot, dusty place by. They outdo even those in Marrakesh. From the moment you arrive, the hustlers materialise on motorbikes, thrusting cards into your hand inviting you to buy 'Tuareg handicrafts'. Even the one guy in town who claims to be an official guide and pulls out a card to prove it will run rings around you on his moped, haranguing you on the need to have a guide and pulling a very long face indeed if all his efforts remain unrewarded (as they should).

If you still think it's worth coming and want to survive the onslaught, you'll have to contemplate hanging about for more than a day. Arriving on market day (Sunday, Tuesday or Thursday) is inviting problems with hustlers, as it will be assumed you're one of the many package tourists who crowd into Rissani by the busload on market days in search of 'Moroccan experiences', and in so doing help to ruin them.

The town, in the heart of the Tafilalt oases, sits on the edge of the desert. In a sense, this is the end of the road, where the Ziz Valley peters out into the hot nothingness of stone and sand that stretches out to the south.

### Information

The centre of town is quite small. There is a post and phone office open during normal office hours. There is also a Banque Populaire, where you can change cash or travellers' cheques. A branch of the BMCE was being built at the time of writing.

### Places to Stay & Eat

The cheapest place to stay is the *Hôtel El Filalia* (☎ 575096), which is basic but adequate. This hotel is where the buses drop off and pick up passengers. It has rooms with two single beds for Dr 60 and others with one double and one single bed for Dr 75. They claim to have hot water and will organise excursions if you want. The owners also claim to be planning a 'tourist village' in a nearby palmeraie – heaven forbid!

Better is the new *Hôtel Sijilmassa* (☎ 575042), on Place al-Massira al-Khadra (Green March), which is clean, comfortable and offers spacious rooms with private shower and toilet for Dr 120 (there are no single rooms). The management is eager to please and there's a restaurant on the ground floor.

About three km out along the road to Erfoud is the *Hôtel Asmaa* (☎ 575494), which is part of the Kasbah chain. This place is awkward for people without a car and quite incongruous, but the rooms are very comfortable, costing Dr 200/250/300. There is a rather large suite for Dr 500, a swimming pool (not always in operation) and a restaurant.

If you're not staying at the Sijilmassa, there are a number of simple restaurants fronting the market where you can eat cheaply and well.

### Getting There & Away

Buses and grands taxis leave from the area in front of the Hôtel El Filalia. CTM has a bus to Meknès via Erfoud and Er-Rachidia at 7.30 pm. Other companies put on three departures to Fès via Erfoud at 6 and 10 am and 10 and 11.30 pm (this last one via Sefrou). A bus also leaves for Casablanca via Erfoud at 8.30 pm. The fare to Erfoud is generally Dr 5, and minibuses make the trip regularly on market days. Grands taxis (Dr 6) are probably the best bet though. Land Rover taxis run between Rissani and Merzouga on market days, and cost about Dr 20 per person. Departures are uncertain and depend on demand.

### AROUND RISSANI
### Sijilmassa Ruins

Just outside Rissani to the west lie the ruins of the fabled city of Sijilmassa, once the capital of a virtually independent Islamic principality adhering to the Shiite 'heresy' in the early days of the Arab conquest of North Africa. Uncertainty reigns over exactly when it was founded, but by the end of the 8th century it was playing a key role on the trans-Saharan trade routes. Internal feuding led to its collapse some time in the 14th century.

Centuries later, the Filali (from whom the Alawite dynasty is descended) swept north to supplant the Saadians as the ruling dynasty in Morocco. It did not happen over night, however. The founder of the dynasty, Moulay Ali ash-Sharif, began expanding his power in the early 17th century in a series of small wars with neighbouring tribes. His sons continued a slow campaign of conquest but only in 1668 was Moulay ar-Rashid recognised as sultan. His brother and successor, Moulay Ismail, would later go on to become the uncontested ruler of Morocco, underlining his power by establishing a new capital at Meknès.

Members of the Filali still inhabit the ksour in this area, but Sijilmassa itself has fallen into ruin and there's little to indicate its past glories except for two decorated gateways and a few other structures. It's really only of interest to archaeologists these days, but you're free to wander around the ruins if the whim so takes you. You will find the ruins off to the right-hand side of the 'Circui Touristique' (Tourist Circuit) as you enter Rissani from the north.

### Circuit Touristique

The so-called Circuit Touristique makes a 21-km loop around the palmeraies south of Rissani, often along appalling stretches of road. It takes you through most of the villages in the palmeraies but is of mild interest only. The exceptions are the beautiful gateway at Oulad Abdelhalim, built by the sultan's elder brother in 1900, and the zawiyya (closed to non-Muslims) of Moulay Ali ash-Sharif, founder of the Alawite dynasty.

The road is extremely dusty (or muddy when wet) and is only really feasible with your own (decent) transport or by hired taxi

# Western Sahara Desert

What the Moroccan tourist brochures refer to as the Saharan provinces largely comprise the still-disputed territory of Western Sahara. Evacuated by Spain in 1975, Morocco and Mauritania both raised claims to the sparsely

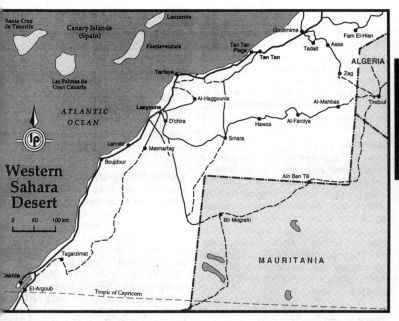

Western
Sahara
Desert

0    50    100 km

populated desert territory, but the latter soon bailed out, leaving Rabat to fight the rebel group, Polisario, which had contributed to Madrid's decision to abandon the phosphate-rich possessions in the first place. In November 1975, King Hassan II orchestrated the Green March – 350,000 Moroccans, largely unarmed civilians, marched in to stake Morocco's historical claims to the Western Sahara. The border of what had been Spanish Sahara ran just south of Tarfaya. In the following years, as many as 100,000 troops were poured in to stamp out resistance. As Polisario lost Algerian and Libyan backing, and the Moroccans erected a 1600-km-long sand wall to hamper the rebels' movements, it became increasingly clear that Rabat had the upper hand.

The UN organised a ceasefire in 1991, raising the prospect of a referendum to settle the issue of the Western Sahara region's status. The ceasefire has largely held, but the referendum is yet to materialise. In the mean-

time, Morocco has strengthened its hold on the territory, pouring money into infrastructure projects and expanding the city of Laayoune. Work-hungry Moroccans from the north have been enticed to move down by the prospect of employment and tax-free living (hence the cheap petrol). To all intents and purposes, Morocco appears to have succeeded, with the world community too preoccupied by crises elsewhere and foreign diplomats questioning the legitimacy and practicality of Polisario's independence demands.

Apart from the endless police roadblocks and checks, going south to Dakhla is now a routine affair, and it has been possible to cross into Mauritania in convoy (with some exceptions) since the running of the 1994 Paris-Dakar rally.

## Information

As part of a drive to attract Moroccans into Western Sahara, many items are tax free.

This includes petrol, which costs Dr 4.72 per litre of super and Dr 2.72 per litre of diesel. The first Atlas Sahara service station you'll hit coming from the north is just out of Tarfaya on the road to Laayoune. Remember to stock up, especially if you're heading north, where super will cost you more than Dr 7 a litre. If you are heading to Mauritania, the same applies.

## TARFAYA

Some 235 km west of Tan Tan across a comparatively monotonous stretch of desert highway, the little coastal town of Tarfaya is unlikely to hold anyone's attention for long. Located near Cap Juby, it was the second-largest town in the Spanish-controlled zone of the same name, but in fact started life late in the 19th century as a minor British trading post. The population of the surrounding area is largely nomadic, and the town itself boasts a small fishing industry. Plans are in place to build fish canneries.

### Things to See

Possibly the most interesting thing about the town is the unusual building stuck well out from the beach amid the Atlantic breakers. Known as **Casamar** (from 'casa del mar', or house in the sea), it was once a British trading house. Otherwise, there is a monument to the French pilot and writer Antoine de Saint-Exupéry (perhaps best known for his children's story *The Little Prince*), one of several aviators who, in the interwar years, used the town as a stopover on the French airmail service between Toulouse and Dakar.

The **beaches** aren't bad, particularly a few km out of town to the north, where you can also inspect a series of shipwrecks (which are clearly visible from the road). A problem can be the Atlantic winds that whip the coast for much of the year.

### Places to Stay & Eat

The *Hôtel Tarfaya* appears to be the only place to stay in Tarfaya, and it was closed at the time of researching. There are a few simple cafés around where you can get a plate of beans or an omelette – no culinary miracles in this town.

### Getting There & Away

There are occasional buses and grands taxi linking Tarfaya to Tan Tan and Laayoune but they are infrequent. Note that there is a Atlas Sahara petrol station just outside Tarfaya on the road to Laayoune (and the only one until you reach that city), where you can stock up on cheap petrol.

## LAAYOUNE (AL-'UYUN)

Laayoune, once a neglected Spanish administrative town, has been transformed out of all recognition since the Moroccans took it back in 1975. Although you'll still see the odd street name posted as a 'calle', little evidence of the Spanish presence here remains. With a population of about 120,000, mostly outsiders, it is Rabat's showpiece in the Western Sahara.

The 115-km road south from Tarfaya is unexciting, cut by the occasional dry river bed and occasionally awash with sand. There are few beaches to speak of, with the desert simply dropping away in sheer cliffs into the ocean below. Sixty-five km north of Laayoune, in the Tah depression (55 metres below sea level), there is a monument commemorating a visit this far south by Sultan Moulay al-Hassan I back in 1885 (probably on an expedition to punish unruly tribes and extract taxes) and Hassan II's 'return' on a visit 100 years later.

There is not an awful lot to see in Laayoune itself, although the atmosphere is odd enough to make a stay of a day or two worthwhile. In any case, whether you're heading north or south, the distances involved are such that you'll almost have no choice but to sleep over for at least a night.

The place is crawling with bored Moroccan soldiers and bright-white UN vehicles. Many of the Moroccans who have come to live and work here hate the place – an ocean wind blows almost without let-up, and the water is bad (basically it's all salty bore water).

Cascades d'Ouzoud, Morocco (DS)

Left: Ghadhames, Libya (AJ)
Right: Chefchaouen, Morocco (DS)
Bottom: Old mosque, Ghat, Libya (AJ)

Morocco – Western Sahara Desert – Laayoune  433

## Orientation

Although the showpiece town focus is the shiny new Place du Mechouar (where bored Moroccan youths hang about at night drinking lethal home-made hooch), there is no really obvious centre. Most of the practical considerations, such as post and phone offices, banks and some of the hotels, are somewhere along or near Ave Hassan II. There is a collection of budget hotels at the north-west end of town in a lively market area. SATAS buses also gather there, but CTM has its office on Ave de Mecca. Grands taxis north are on a square at the north-west end of Ave Hassan II, but there are several other stations scattered about town.

## Information

**Tourist Office** The Délégation Régionale du Tourisme (☎ 892233/75) is just back from Ave de l'Islam, virtually across the road from the Hôtel Parador. It's open Monday to Friday from 8.30 to 11.30 am and 2 to 6 pm.

Apart from a couple of brochures, they have little to offer, but they are anxious to please and can tell you how to get to bus stations and the like.

**Money** The BMCE has a branch on Place Hassan II, next to the post office. There is a Banque Populaire and a couple of other banks up from the intersection of Ave Hassan II and Blvd Mohammed V. There is another Banque Populaire on Place Dchira.

**Post & Telecommunications** The post and phone offices are lumped together at the south-eastern end of Ave Hassan II, and open only from 8.30 am to noon and 2 to 6 pm.

## Things to See & Do

**Colline aux Oiseaux** Set on the hill between the tourist office and Ave de Mecca, this small aviary has a few quite spectacular parrots and other birds. Enter through the Centre Artisanal on Ave de Mecca. It's free.

MOROCCO

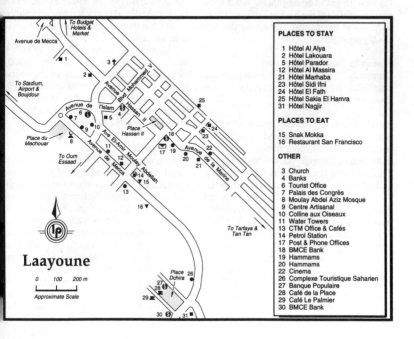

**Laayoune**

0    100    200 m

Approximate Scale

**PLACES TO STAY**

1 Hôtel Al Alya
2 Hôtel Lakouara
5 Hôtel Parador
12 Hôtel Al Massira
21 Hôtel Marhaba
23 Hôtel Sidi Ifni
24 Hôtel El Fath
25 Hôtel Sakia El Hamra
31 Hôtel Nagjir

**PLACES TO EAT**

15 Snak Mokka
16 Restaurant San Francisco

**OTHER**

3 Church
4 Banks
6 Tourist Office
7 Palais des Congrès
8 Moulay Abdel Aziz Mosque
9 Centre Artisanal
10 Colline aux Oiseaux
11 Water Towers
13 CTM Office & Cafés
14 Petrol Station
17 Post & Phone Offices
18 BMCE Bank
19 Hammams
20 Hammams
22 Cinema
26 Complexe Touristique Saharien
27 Banque Populaire
28 Café de la Place
29 Café Le Palmier
30 BMCE Bank

**MOROCCO**

**Centre Artisanal** The 22 little domed boutiques (the domes are typical of the simpler housing in Laayoune) that constitute the Centre Artisanal on Ave de Mecca are worth a quick look if you're interested in fairly standard Moroccan souvenirs. Pressure to buy is at a minimum.

**Laayoune Plage** About 25 km out along the road south to Boujdour and Dakhla is a reasonable little beach. There is a simple camp site and Club Med has organised a few rooms here for anglers. Apart from that, a few houses in the village of Foum el-Oued (which is a couple of km inland) and the nearby port, there's nothing else to it. You may need to hire a taxi to get out here, or join the hitchers at the Boujdour exit from Laayoune, near the new stadium.

**Dunes** Kilometres of dunes spread north and west of Laayoune, and are clearly visible from several vantage points in and around the city. To get in among them, you'd need to take a 4WD off the road to Tarfaya. It may be possible to organise something through the bigger hotels.

### Places to Stay – bottom end
**Camping** There is a simple camping ground with minimal facilities at Laayoune Plage (Foum el-Oued).

**Hotels** You will probably find most of the hotel guests at the budget end are soldiers – there are a lot of them about. There is a collection of cheapies on Ave Maître Salem Bida, out near the market in the north-west end of town. These include the *Hôtel La Victoire*, *Hôtel Atlas*, *Hôtel Tafilalet*, *Hôtel Inezgane* and the *Hôtel Errimal Eddahabia*. You'll pay from Dr 30 to Dr 40 for a double in any of these. They are quite basic and the best cleaning material you can hope for is a cold salty bore-water shower.

A number of similar places back near Place Hassan II include the *Hôtel Sakia El Hamra*, *Hôtel El Fath* and *Hôtel Sidi Ifni*. They all offer primitive little rooms for about Dr 15 per person.

Slightly better and popular with travellers is the *Hôtel Marhaba*, on Ave de la Marine (the continuation of Ave Hassan II). The rooms are clean and have a table, chair and wardrobe, but the mattresses are rather thin. Again the showers are cold and it's bore water only. The bathroom has a habit of flooding. Rooms cost Dr 26/36.

### Places to Stay – middle
From the Hôtel Marhaba there is a huge leap in prices. The cheapest and worst is the *Hôtel Al Alya* (☎ 894144), 1 Rue Kadi El Ghalaoui. The rooms are only marginally better than in the Marhaba and they often can't organise hot water. All this costs Dr 174/218.

Much better but block-booked by the UN observer force here is the *Hôtel Lakouara* (☎ 893378), on Ave Hassan II. Rooms cost Dr 200/250.

### Places to Stay – top end
The least expensive of the top-end places is the *Hôtel Nagjir* (☎ 894168), on Place Dchira. At Dr 310/393 for singles/doubles it's OK but there are rarely any rooms available, as most are occupied by UN staff.

The two top hotels are the *Hôtel Al Massira* and the *Hôtel Parador* (☎ 894500). Both have all the facilities of expensive hotels but for years now have been block-booked by the UN. Even the restaurant and bar in the Parador are reserved exclusively for guests (ie UN observers).

### Places to Eat
The cheapest (and probably best) place to hunt for food is around the budget hotel and market area. There are plenty of small stalls and café-restaurants selling the usual meat dishes and good local fish. Dr 20 should get you a filling meal of whatever you want.

For an adequate impersonation of a hamburger, try the *Restaurant San Francisco* on Ave de Mecca. *Snak Mokka* across the road doesn't do a bad plate of brochettes.

If you want to go a little more up-market, the *Complexe Touristique Saharien* has a restaurant specialising in fish, where a full meal will cost you about Dr 50. It's at the

Place Dchira end of Ave de Mecca, and is hard to miss.

There are numerous cafés scattered about the place, some of which are marked on the map. Getting a real drink may be difficult if the bigger hotels don't let you into their bars – your best bet is the Hôtel Nagjir.

### Getting There & Away

**Air** RAM (☎ 894071) has an office at 7 Place Bir Anzarane. It has daily flights to Casablanca for Dr 1270 one way. Every Thursday there's a flight to Dakhla (Dr 570). You can also fly to Las Palmas (Canary Islands) for Dr 1210 twice a week. The flight takes 50 minutes.

**Bus** The CTM office and terminal is on Ave de Mecca. A bus leaves for Dakhla at 8 am (Dr 140.50). There are two to Agadir, one direct at 8 pm (Dr 194.50), the other at 6 pm via Smara. The fare as far as Tan Tan is Dr 112. At 3 pm there is a bus to Marrakesh for Dr 250.

SATAS has slightly more runs, and its buses run from a dirt lot in among the budget hotels and market area.

A few other local lines run to Place Dchira.

**Train** It is possible to book a bus-train ticket to anywhere on the Moroccan rail network. The Supratours/ONCF office is on Place Oum Essaad.

**Taxi** Grands taxis to Tan Tan (Dr 70), Goulimime (Dr 100) and Inezgane (for Agadir; Dr 150) leave from a lot at the northwestern end of Ave Hassan II. You might even be able to get one right through to Marrakesh. Taxis to Boujdour, Smara and Dakhla leave from another lot (ask for the *station taxis Boujdour*) on the southern periphery of town. A red-and-white petit taxi there will cost you Dr 4.

## SMARA (AS-SMARA)

About 240 km east of Laayoune (245 km south of Tan Tan) lies what the ONMT brochure bluntly calls 'A Historic City'. The original town was established here on a Saharan caravan route a century ago. There's really very little left of the old town, except for the mosque.

There are banks and a post office and a few hotels largely full of Moroccan soldiers and UN observers. Buses and taxis run between Smara, Laayoune and Tan Tan.

## DAKHLA (AD-DAKHLA)

Established by the Spanish in 1844 and formerly called Villa Cisneros, Dakhla is just north of the Tropic of Cancer on the end of a sandy peninsula stretching out 40 km from the main coastline. It's a long, lonely 542 km drive from Laayoune through endless hammada, and only worth the effort if you are making an attempt to get into Mauritania.

The place is crawling with soldiers, but with the threat posed by Polisario receding, there is little sense of danger.

Dakhla has a bit of a name for ocean fishing, so that may be an added incentive for those travellers who like to catch and cook their own fish. It's not a bad place to take a surfboard either.

### Information

The tourist office (☎ 898228) is at 1 Rue Tiris. There is a branch of the BMCE bank on Blvd Mohammed V.

### Places to Stay

There are many cheap hotels but these are almost always full of soldiers, so just keep looking. The average price for a double room is around Dr 40. The town's top hotel is the three-star *Hôtel Doums* (☎ 898045/6), Ave al-Waha, but as long as the UN is here you can forget about it.

If you are in a vehicle you are allowed to camp overlooking the sea on the landward side of the peninsula.

### Getting There & Away

**Air** The airport is five km out of town. RAM (☎ 897050), Ave des PTT, has three flights a week to Casablanca, one of them stopping in Laayoune and the other two in Agadir.

**Bus, Train & Taxi** There's a daily CTM bus to Laayoune for Dr 140.50. SATAS also has buses between Dakhla and Laayoune. There are grands taxis and it is also possible to organise a bus-train ticket from Dakhla with Supratours to any destination on the rail network.

**To/From Mauritania** Since the beginning of 1994, the border with Mauritania has, as far as Rabat is concerned, been open. There are several exceptions. There are no buses doing this run, so you need to arrange transport (which would have to be good to cope with travelling on the Mauritanian side of the frontier). Once this is done you have to get a permit from the military. It appears this no longer poses a huge problem. Finally, you have to wait until a convoy of at least half a dozen vehicles is assembled. It is then escorted (in case of an attack by Polisario) 363 km to the frontier.

All of this supposes you have been able to get a Mauritanian visa allowing you to enter the country overland. At the time of writing this was not possible in Rabat (see the Information entry under Rabat). You may have more luck at Mauritanian consulates elsewhere; for French citizens it's irrelevant, as they do not require visas to enter Mauritania.

# Algeria

# Facts about the Country

**ALGERIA**

## HISTORY SINCE 1830
### French Colonisation

The French presence in North Africa started in earnest in 1830, when they blockaded and attacked Algiers, supposedly because the Dey of Algiers had insulted the French consul. A more likely motive, however, was the need at home for a military success to revive the flagging fortunes of Charles X.

Within three weeks of the French landing on 5 July, the government of the dey had capitulated. A couple of weeks later, Charles X himself had been overthrown; his successor, Louis Philippe, favoured colonisation.

By 1845, General Bugeaud had conquered the greater part of the country and had been proclaimed governor general of Algeria. However, it wasn't until 1847 that the west of the country, which had been the territory of the famous Abdelkader, finally came under French control.

Abdelkader was a sherif (descendant of the Prophet), who had been elected locally as the leader in the conflict with the invading European Christians. He had been recognised by the French by the Desmichels

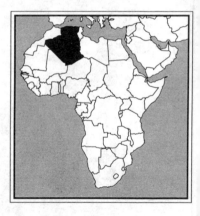

Treaty of 1834, which effectively gave him control of western and inland central Algeria. His position was further strengthened by the Treaty of Tafna in 1837. Such was his charisma and ability to rally people around him that, by late 1838, the area under his control stretched from Biskra to the Moroccan border in the south, and from the Kabylie region east of Algiers to Oran in the north. This area virtually constituted a separate state, with its own judicial and administrative system.

After a six-year struggle against the French following their breaking of the treaty in 1839, Abdelkader was forced into Morocco, where he called on the sultan, Abd ar-Rahman, for support. This was provided, but the army was trounced by the French at Isly (near Oujda) in 1844. Abdelkader finally surrendered to the French in 1846 on condition that he be allowed to live in the Middle East. Despite this, he was imprisoned in Toulon, Pau and Amboise until 1852; he was finally allowed to settle in Damascus, where he died in 1883 after 36 years of exile. He was by far the greatest figure in Algeria's nationalist movement and is a national hero today, with many streets named after him and a major statue commemorating him in central Algiers.

French domination of the entire country was complete by 1871, when the people of the mountains of the Kabylie region were finally subdued.

During the next 50 years of French occupation, land was appropriated and European settlers – mainly of French, Italian, Maltese and Spanish origin – established their domination over the local inhabitants. Local culture was actively eliminated, and the Arab medinas were replaced with streets laid out in grids. The Great Mosque of Algiers was converted to the Cathedral of Saint Philippe, complete with a cross atop its minaret.

## Towards Independence
Many Algerians worked in France, particularly in the factories supporting the war effort from 1914 to 1918, and it was among these expatriate workers that some of the first stirrings of nationalism occurred. This led to the formation of the Parti du Peuple Algérien, which was followed by the establishment of the Association of Algerian Ulama, a largely religious body, in Algeria itself.

After WW II the French president, Charles de Gaulle, offered citizenship to certain categories of Muslims. This was considered inadequate, and an uprising near Sétif saw the massacre of more than 80 Europeans. By 1947, however, all Muslims had been given full French citizenship rights and the right to live and work in France.

The Algerian war of independence began on 31 October 1954 with an outbreak of violence in Batna. This was led by young men who had formed the new National Liberation Front (FLN) – a body whose stated aim was the bringing down of the French administration by military means at home and diplomacy abroad. The bitter and bloody fight, which was to continue for the next seven years, cost at least a million Algerian lives.

By 1956, the fight for Algerian independence was being actively supported by the country's neighbours, both former French protectorates. This led to the construction by the French of a series of massive barbed-wire fences and observation posts to separate Algeria from both Morocco and Tunisia. The fence along the Moroccan border was over 1000 km long, and the remnants can still be seen today. The fences were actually some distance in from the border, and the buffer zones were patrolled day and night by Algerian forces. The idea (which turned out to be successful) was to cut off Tunisian and Moroccan support for the revolutionaries.

As Algeria was in fact a part of metropolitan France, there were over three million French settlers living there. They were obviously unwilling to see the country lose touch with France and, in an uprising in early 1958, thousands of these settlers called for continued integration with France; it was largely these people (colons) who voted de Gaulle back into power, using the slogan *Algérie Française*.

These same settlers became increasingly troubled when it became obvious that de Gaulle was thinking about granting Algeria independence. In 1961 some of them even went to the extent of forming what amounted to a settler terrorist organisation, the Organisation de l'Armée Secrète (OAS). De Gaulle was unmoved and, on 18 March 1962, agreement was reached for a referen-

ALGERIA

dum in Algeria which, if the vote went the right way, would grant the country independence. In the event, the vote was six million in favour and only 16,000 against. The trickle of French settlers returning to France turned into a flood, with only some 40,000 staying on after independence.

The cost of the war to Algeria had been tremendous – over a million Algerians had lost their lives, and a further two million had been displaced in an effort by the colonial authorities to disrupt all attempts to organise an effective nationalist movement.

### The Socialist State

Ahmed ben Bella was the first elected premier; he pledged a 'revolutionary Arab-Islamic state based on the principles of socialism and collective leadership at home and anti-imperialism abroad'. Although popular, his leadership style did not foster orderly administration and he was overthrown in 1965 by the defence minister and FLN chief of staff, Colonel Houari Boumedienne. Ben Bella spent many years in exile in Switzerland, but in 1990 he returned to lead his party, the Movement for Democracy in Algeria (MDA).

Boumedienne was a cautious pragmatist. He set about rebuilding the country's economy, which had come unstuck at the time of independence with the departure of the majority of the country's administrators and technical experts, all of whom were Europeans. Unemployment and underemployment remained serious problems and many Algerians were forced to work in France, despite the ill feeling which existed there towards them.

Large·gas and oil reserves in the Sahara were developed and, despite the fact that over 70% of the workforce was employed on the land, agriculture was neglected in favour of industry in the 1970s. As a result, agricultural production fell below levels achieved under the French.

Colonel Boumedienne died in December 1978 and, at a meeting of the FLN in Algiers, Colonel Chadli Benjedid was elected presi-

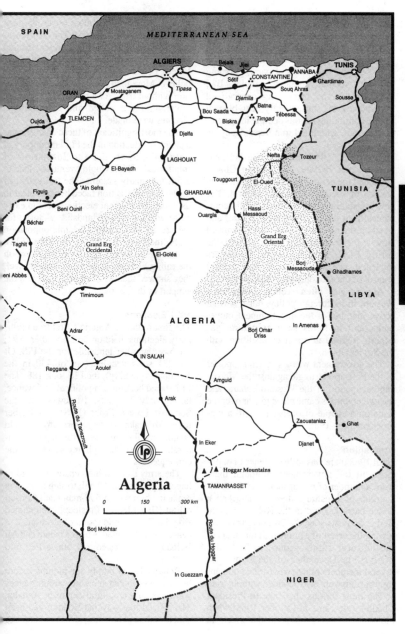

SPAIN

MEDITERRANEAN SEA

ALGIERS  Bejaia  Jijel  TUNIS

ANNABA

Mostaganem  Tipasa  Sétif  CONSTANTINE  Ghardimao

ORAN  Djemila  Souq Ahras

Oujda  Bou Saada  Batna  Sousse

TLEMCEN  Biskra  Timgad  Tébessa

Djelfa

El-Bayadh  LAGHOUAT  Touggourt  Nefta  Tozeur

Figuig  'Ain Sefra  GHARDAIA  El-Oued  TUNISIA

Beni Ounif  Ouargla

Béchar  Hassi  Messaoud

Taghit  Grand Erg  Grand Erg  Oriental

eni Abbès  Occidental  El-Goléa  Borj  Messaouda  Ghadhames

Timimoun  LIBYA

ALGERIA

Adrar  Borj Omar  In Amenas

Driss

Reggane  Aoulef  IN SALAH

Amguid

Arak

Zaouataniaz  Ghat

In Eker  Djanet

Algeria  ▲ ▲ Hoggar Mountains

TAMANRASSET

0  150  300 km

Borj Mokhtar

In Guezzam  NIGER

ALGERIA

dent. He was re-elected in 1984 and 1989, and ruled until he resigned in January 1992.

There was very little political change in Algeria under Boumedienne and Chadli. The FLN was the sole political party, pursuing basically secular, socialist policies. Bad planning by the lumbering centralised bureaucracy has subsequently been blamed for the continuing serious decline in agricultural output, which led to a dependency on food imports.

The most radical reform since independence came in late 1987 when Chadli abolished the central planning authority, the bastion of socialist economic control. The new legislation removed most public companies from direct government control and freed up the banking system. Chadli moved slowly for fear of opposition within the ruling FLN, as the party's old-timers regarded any moves away from central control of the economy with deep suspicion.

Algeria was often seen as being anti-Western in its foreign policy, but it was an active member of the nonalignment movement, and in fields such as natural gas exports it stood in direct competition with the Soviet Union.

The government was a staunch supporter of the Polisario struggle against the Moroccan occupation of the Western Sahara, and the two countries came close to war over the issue on a couple of occasions until a rapprochement in 1988.

## Opposition

Until 1988 there was little evidence of opposition to the government, although there were a number of minor incidents. In 1985, a group of Muslim extremists attacked a police barracks, and in the Kabylie region, Berber activists staged a 24-hour strike following the arrest of a number of members of the cultural rights group, Enfants des Martyrs. In December of the same year several members of a newly formed human-rights group were also detained without trial.

The most serious challenge to President Chadli's rule came in October 1988, when thousands of people took to the streets in protest against government austerity measures and food shortages. The army was called in to restore order and, in the ensuing violence, between 160 and 600 people were killed, depending on whose figures you believe. More than 3000 were held in detention without trial. As a result of the riots, a referendum was called and constitutional changes were made.

The most significant of these changes was a pledged reduction in the FLN monopoly of political power and the formation of 'platforms', which would eventually lead to a full multiparty system. The full extent of the level of opposition faced became clear in the local-government elections held in early 1990, which produced landslide victories for the previously outlawed Islamic opposition party, the Front Islamique du Salut (FIS). Although the results had no direct effect on the ruling FLN at central-government level, they showed that the FLN no longer had the support of the people.

### 1991 Elections

The first round of Algeria's first free multiparty elections, held on 26 December 1991, produced another landslide for the FIS. Of the 231 seats decided (out of 430 in the National Assembly), the FIS took 188. The FLN faced becoming a political irrelevance, taking only 15 seats, 10 fewer than the Socialist Forces Front (FFS) – a Berber party. To make matters worse for the old guard, Chadli seemed set on seeing the democratic process through regardless of the consequences.

The army stepped in to ensure this didn't happen, persuading Chadli to step down and replacing him with a five-man Haut Conseil d'Etat (HCE) led by President Mohammed Boudiaf. The second round of elections was cancelled, FIS leaders Abbas Madani and Ali Belhadj were arrested and others fled into exile.

Boudiaf lasted barely six months before he was assassinated in bizarre circumstances while opening a cultural centre in Annaba. The official line was that Boudiaf had been shot by a lone gunman, who also managed to wound 40-odd members of the audience before escaping undetected by the legions of security guards at the scene. Adding that the gunman had acted out of religious conviction didn't make the story any more plausible. There were suggestions that Boudiaf was the victim of an establishment plot hatched by people opposed to his attempts to tackle institutionalised corruption.

Whatever the truth of the matter, he was replaced by a hardliner in former FLN stalwart Ali Kafi, who remained at the helm until he was replaced by a former general, Liamine Zéroual, on 31 January 1994, with the country on the brink of civil war.

## Second War of Liberation

Early reports that Islamic leaders had rejected violence as a means of taking power from the military soon proved ill-founded. By the end of April 1994, more than 3000 people had died in what militants were calling the second war of liberation.

The death toll included a growing list of foreigners, most of them resident in the country. Among the victims were 12 Croatian engineers whose throats were slit after their attackers had confirmed that the victims were Christians. Eight others were spared after convincing their attackers that they were Bosnian Muslims. Attacks against foreigners have been justified on two grounds: firstly, to sabotage Algeria's already troubled economy – which many regard as being propped up by the West; secondly, as vengeance on the 'spies of the unbelievers in the land of Islam'. From October 1993 to July 1994, 51 foreigners had died.

The vast majority of the Algerian victims were policemen, mayors, judges and Francophile intellectuals. The attacks have been claimed by various underground groups such as the Groupes Islamiques Armés and the Mouvement Islamique Armé.

The government has responded with displays of force and the mass arrests of suspects. It has been accused of links with South American-style death squads who carry out revenge killings.

The blood-letting peaked at 300 deaths a week in early 1994, signalling the failure of a so-called commission of national dialogue to have any impact on proceedings. It also signalled the end of the road for President Kafi.

Former defence minister Liamine Zéroual was given the presidency amid talk of amnesty and reconciliation – in spite of his reputation as a hardliner following his campaign against the Islamic activists while holding the defence portfolio.

At the time of writing, there seemed little immediate hope of a change for the better.

Whoever wins will face an even bigger battle – to resurrect an economy brought to the verge of collapse by years of alleged corruption and incompetence.

## GEOGRAPHY

The greater part of the country is occupied by the Sahara, while the Tell region in the north makes up the rest.

The Tell accounts for only about 15% of the land area but has the vast majority of the population and all the arable land. It is broken up by a few mountain ranges. The first of these is the Tell Atlas, which is a continuation of the Moroccan Atlas Mountains and cuts right across the north and into Tunisia. It is not an unbroken chain: it consists of a number of separate ranges, and so doesn't constitute an impenetrable barrier. There is some fantastic mountain scenery here, particularly in the Kabylie region to the east of Algiers.

To the south of the Atlas lie the High Plateaus (Hauts Plateaux). Farther south again, the Saharan Atlas (Atlas Saharien) is the last mountain range before the Sahara takes over.

The Sahara occupies the other 85% of Algeria, as well as large slabs of half a dozen other countries. It is absolutely enormous, and statistics tend to be incomprehensible – there are just too many zeros! It covers more than nine million sq km and stretches from the Atlantic Ocean to the Red Sea.

Despite the common misconception, the Sahara is not just one big expanse of sand. Such expanses certainly do exist, but it also

ALGERIA

has mountain ranges (such as the Hoggar, which peak at about 3000 metres), dead-flat plains (where the most prominent feature for miles around is a rock the size of a tennis ball) and numerous oases, which support small numbers of people and produce some of the most delicately flavoured dates in the world.

The vegetation of the desert varies from esparto plains in the M'Zab to areas the size of England where not a thing grows. Absolutely nothing.

As might be expected, the only major river systems are in the north of the country, and many of these are seasonal. The main reservoirs for irrigation are in the mountains to the west of Algiers, while those in the north-east produce the 5% of the country's power which is generated by hydroelectricity.

### Distances

With an area of some 2.381 million sq km (about the size of Western Australia, or five times the size of California or France), Algeria is the second-largest country in Africa, smaller only than the Sudan.

Distances are great: from Algiers to Tamanrasset, for example, is more than 2000 km – greater than the distance from Algiers to Paris.

### CLIMATE

Algeria's annual rainfall ranges from 1000 mm in the Kabylie region to virtually nil in some places in the Sahara; in fact, some Saharan towns go for up to 20 years without any rainfall at all! Summer in the north is generally hot (around 32°C), with high humidity along the coast. In the Sahara the temperature is regularly 45°C, and it's not that uncommon for the mercury to climb to 50°C and above.

Winter in the north is wet and cold, with snow common on the peaks south of Algiers; in the Sahara it never really cools down that much, and daytime temperatures are about 25°C.

Tamanrasset, in the Hoggar Mountains at an elevation of over 1500 metres, has a milder summer and a colder winter. At nearby Assekrem, the temperatures drop to below freezing at night.

### GOVERNMENT

Officially known as the People's Democratic Republic of Algeria, the country approved a new constitution by referendum in 1989. Reforms included the end of FLN's position as the sole party of government, the legalisation of opposition parties and removal of references to socialism. The president of the republic is head of state, head of the armed office and head of government, and is elected by universal suffrage for a five-year term. (That's the theory – President Zéroual was appointed by the military for three years.)

The president appoints the prime minister and other ministers.

Legislative power in Algeria is vested in the 430-member National Assembly which is elected to a five-year term by universal adult suffrage.

Directly below the central government is the wilaya (province). There are 48 wilayas, each of which is headed by an elected executive council and a member of the central government, known as the *wali*. The FIS won control of 32 of these wilayas in the 1990 local-government elections.

On the bottom of the administrative ladder are the local collectives. These are financed predominantly by local taxes, although the state does intervene with funds to meet the commune's needs.

### ECONOMY

Algeria's economy has become something of a black hole, especially since demand for the country's oil and gas products was hit by the world recession that began in the late 1980s. It is burdened by a foreign debt that was estimated at US$25.3 billion as long ago as 1990.

Since independence, the emphasis has shifted away from agriculture towards industry (it was the reverse during the French colonial days).

At present, only about 5% of the land is under cultivation, and local cultivation supplies only about 40% of the country's food

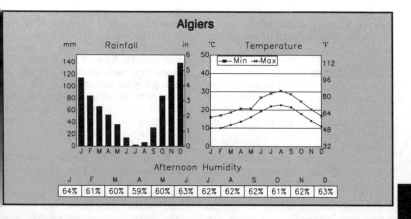

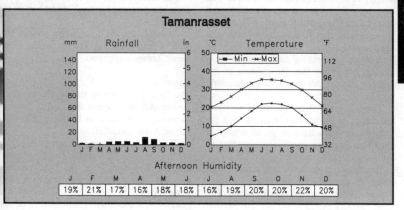

needs (as against 95% at independence). The country produces almost 300,000 TV sets a year, but no-one has yet worked out a way of eating them.

The country relies almost exclusively on oil and gas for export income. Oil production levels stood at 58 million tonnes in 1992, while gas production runs at about 50,000 million cubic metres per annum. Other natural resources include deposits of iron ore and phosphates.

The forests in the north were devastated during the war of independence, but large areas have been replanted in an effort to generate some more income; the country is one of the world's major suppliers of cork.

A tight control is kept over imports, the result being that there is very little for sale in the shops which is not produced in Algeria. There are often shortages of certain items so the demand for foreign goods is high.

The government has introduced a number of controversial measures to make Algeria more attractive to foreign investors. Foreigners are allowed to hold 100% equity in companies and to repatriate all profits. A law passed in 1992 permits foreign companies to own up to 49% of known gas and oil reserves. These conditions are unlikely to survive the transition to an Islamic government.

## Social Conditions

As usual, statistics give a somewhat false picture of conditions. The per-capita income of US$2170 (1989 figure) is one of the highest in Africa. Who gets their hands on it is another matter.

Unemployment levels stood at 22% in 1989, and by now that figure is undoubtedly much higher. Those who do have work are paid a minimum wage of AD 3500, set in July 1992.

The most striking feature of Algerian society is the *haitists* (literally, people who prop up walls) – the masses of unemployed young men who just hang out in the streets. It's estimated that 70% of the population is aged under 30, and the majority have no immediate prospect of finding work. It is among this group that the policies of the Islamic parties find their most enthusiastic support.

There is great strain on social services. Education is particularly affected and the younger children have to go to school in shifts, as there are insufficient numbers of both schools and teachers.

Health care is available free to those aged under 16 and over 60, and income earners pay according to what they can afford. The state provides pensions for the old, the disabled and war veterans.

Housing is a major problem, particularly with the movement of people out of rural areas and into the larger cities in recent years. To alleviate the problems and to encourage people to stay in the country, row upon row of massive apartment blocks have been built on the outskirts of many towns in the interior; these are available for low rent or subsidised purchase from the government.

## POPULATION & PEOPLE

The population of Algeria is about 28 million, based on statistics from the 1987 census and a government estimate of 25.36 million in 1990. It is increasing at the alarm-ing rate of more than 3% per year. More than 50% of Algerians are under the age of 18. Life expectancy is 62.5, with no separate figure available for men and women. The average population density is just over 10 people per sq km but, obviously, this figure is affected by the massive unpopulated areas of the Sahara. Ninety per cent of the population lives in only 5% of the total land area, and of this population figure, half live in urban areas.

The majority of the people are Berbers, with the main minority group being Arabs; however, there has been so much intermingling over the centuries that there is no clear ethnic boundary between the two.

The Berber language and lifestyle have been best preserved in the Kabylie region of the north.

Arabic is the main language, spoken by 83% of the population. The remaining 17% speak Berber languages.

## Tuaregs

The Tuareg people in the south are also Berber and often speak the Berber dialect Tamahaq. They live in southern Algeria, Libya, Niger and Mali.

The two main Tuareg groups in Algeria are the Kel Ahaggar from the Hoggar region and the Kel Ajjer from the Djanet area, although within each group there are various subgroups which have slightly different languages and customs. Traditional Tuareg society is rapidly breaking down, mainly due to the agrarian reform policies of the government, the influx of large numbers of Arabs from the north and a series of crippling droughts which have forced many people into the towns to search for work.

Tuareg women play a much more active role in the organisation of their society than do their Islamic counterparts. The fact that they generally go unveiled has led to some misunderstandings about their morals.

The men often wear a blue or white head cloth *(tagelmoust)*, tied in such a way that it covers most of the face; in the past, this cloth was usually dyed with indigo – these days it is imported and synthetically dyed.

## RELIGION

Sunni Islam is the predominant religion and is one of the few things which unites a number of fairly disparate groups. There are also small Christian and Jewish communities.

Algeria is very conservative. Outside of Algiers, a high proportion of women wear veils. These vary from the lacy, white handkerchief-type ones worn in the north, which cover just the lower half of the face, to the robes worn by the women of the M'Zab (the area around Ghardaia), which are held together in such a way that only one eye is visible – a bizarre sight.

It was only a few years ago that Algiers was described as a place where 'the hemlines were higher and the veils few and far between'. What to wear has become a much tougher decision after Islamic militants shot dead a schoolgirl in the street for not wearing a veil – and two veiled students were killed in retaliation as they waited for a school bus. The incidents followed threats by both sides.

'You'll die if you don't wear the veil. You'll die if you do wear the veil, too. So shut up and die', wrote poet Tahar Djaout before she herself was killed in 1993.

For a full rundown on Islam, see the Religion section in the introductory Facts about the Region chapter.

ALGERIA

# Facts for the Visitor

## VISAS & EMBASSIES

People planning to visit Algeria are advised to check the visa situation before leaving home, as the country's political situation is extremely fluid.

The story has been muddied by the country's internal problems, but people from the following countries do not require a visa for a stay of up to three months: Denmark, Finland, Italy, Norway, Sweden and Switzerland. All other nationals require visas, and they must be obtained before you show up at a border, as they are not issued on the spot.

Tourist visas vary in price from free for a lucky few, including Australians and New Zealanders, to US$90 for Germans. Americans get off quite lightly with US$10, while Britons pay US$30 (UK£20) and the French pay US$35.

Consular staff don't exactly bend over backwards to issue tourist visas, so make sure you apply with plenty of time to spare. You are very likely to be asked to come back in two weeks. Business visas, on the other hand, take only a couple of days.

At the time of writing, the process has been thrown into confusion as foreigners have increasingly become a target for Islamist gunmen. In Rabat, the Moroccan capital, waits of weeks and even months have been experienced. The situation is just as unclear in Oujda, near the Algerian border, where a wait of a month seems the rule and there are no guarantees that the wait will eventually pay off. You might be able to get 10-day transit visas more easily.

According to some officials, Britons must apply for a visa *in the UK only*. In spite of this, the Algerian embassy in Rabat seems to have no problem with UK citizens applying there. However, they can forget about doing so in Oujda.

The Algerian Embassy in Tunis is reported to be issuing visas to nonresidents of Tunisia, but don't rely on it. Nationals of South Africa and Israel are still banned from entering,

although the situation may change soon for South Africans.

### Algerian Embassies

Visas can be obtained from the following Algerian embassies and consulates:

France
50 Rue de Lisbonne, 75016 Paris (☎ 42.25.70.70)
Germany
Rheinalee 32, 5300 Bonn, Bad Godesberg (☎ 35 60 54)
Greece
Vassileos Constantinou 14, Athens 78 (☎ 751 8625)
Italy
Via Barnaba Oriani, 2600197 Rome (☎ 87 86 80)
Libya
12 Sharia al-Qayrawan, Tripoli (☎ 34631, 40025)
Morocco
46 Ave Tariq ibn Zayid (off Ave de Fas), Rabat (☎ 767668)
11 Blvd Bir Anzarane (Blvd de Taza), Oujda (☎ 683740/1)
Spain
Calle General Oraa 12, Madrid (☎ 411 6065)
Switzerland
Wallading 74, WEG 3006 Bern (☎ 44 69 61)
Tunisia
136 Ave de la Liberté, Tunis (☎ 280055) – visas for Tunisian residents only
UK
6 Hyde Park Gate, London SW8 (☎ 0171-221 7800)
USA
2118 Kalorama Rd NW, Washington SCN 20008 (☎ 32 8530)

### Visa Extensions

Tourist visas are valid for one month. Applications for extensions are handled at the Département des Étrangers, Blvd Zeroud Youssef 19a, Algiers. To get an extension, however, you need to show bank receipts to prove that you have been changing money legally and not playing the black market. If you have changed the equivalent of the necessary AD 1000 (see the Money section later

n this chapter), the receipts which prove this
are sufficient.

Visas can supposedly be extended at the
capital of any wilaya, but in practice you may
be sent to Algiers, so be prepared for this
eventuality. In addition to a processing fee
(payable only in fiscal stamps available from
he post office), visas require two photos and
ake 24 hours to issue.

You may also be asked for a certificate
from the hotel you are staying at, although
often a receipt is sufficient.

## MONEY
### Currency
The local currency is the Algerian dinar
(AD), which is divided into 100 centimes.
Coins in use are 5, 10, 20 and 50 centimes,
and 1, 5 and 10 dinars. The coins have only
Arabic writing and numbers. The 10 dinar
coin is very distinctive, as it is 10-sided and
the colour of brass. Notes in circulation are
5 (rare), 10, 20, 50, 100 and 200. Again, they
have only Arabic writing but, unlike the
coins, they have familiar numerals, so are a
bit easier to identify. There used to be an AD
500 note, but this has been taken out of
circulation in order to make it harder to
smuggle large amounts of cash in or out of
the country. If you buy dinar in Morocco or
elsewhere don't accept any AD 500 notes, as
some people will try to off-load these onto
unsuspecting foreigners.

The fact that prices are sometimes expressed
in French can be confusing. For instance, AD
20 is *deux milles* (2000 centimes).

### Exchange Rates

| | | | |
|---|---|---|---|
| Australia | A$1 | = | AD 31.79 |
| Canada | C$1 | = | AD 30.59 |
| France | FFr1 | = | AD 7.85 |
| Germany | DM1 | = | AD 26.92 |
| Japan | ¥100 | = | AD 42.63 |
| Libya | 1 LD | = | AD 117.73 |
| Morocco | Dr 1 | = | AD 4.74 |
| New Zealand | NZ$1 | = | AD 26.14 |
| Sain | 100 pta | = | AD 32.36 |
| Tunisia | TD 1 | = | AD 42.88 |
| UK | UK£1 | = | AD 65.68 |
| USA | US$1 | = | AD 41.99 |

### The AD 1000 Catch
The catch when entering Algeria is that all
foreigners must change the equivalent of AD
1000 on arrival. In theory, there are no exceptions to the rule – Algerians themselves have
to change AD 700 if they have been away. It
is also necessary to prove that you have
changed the compulsory AD 1000 if you
need to get a visa extension, buy an internal
plane ticket or an international plane or ferry
ticket.

Not only must you change AD 1000, you
must do so at the official rate. It is quite
possible that on arrival you will not be compelled to change on the spot, but will just be
told to change at the first bank. In this case,
you will not be compelled to change the
money and you could use the black market
the whole time. However, if you haven't
changed the right amount you can expect
hassles when you leave, particularly if you
cross from In Guezzam into Niger.

The likely penalty for not playing by the
rules is that you will have to change AD 1000
and then hand it straight over to the officials.
This is not always the case; some people
have got away with changing only half that
amount, but it's most unlikely that you will
get out without having to hand over some
money. You might just as well change it
officially to start with and get something for
your money, rather than see it go to a customs
official who then does who-knows-what
with it.

A couple of travellers have reported
recently that they were not obliged to buy
AD 1000 at the official rate when travelling
by train from Morocco to Tunis; they had to
change only enough at the official rate to pay
for the Algiers-Tunis leg of the journey.

### Re-Exchange
It is supposed to be possible to re-exchange
dinar back to hard currency if you have
receipts, but in practice it is extremely difficult and can only be done at the international
ports and airports, and not on the land
borders. If you have Algerian currency when
leaving the country, you can hand it in and
get an official receipt for it. It is then suppos-

ALGERIA

edly possible to get the money back if you return within 12 months.

## Currency Declaration Form

Everyone entering the country has to fill in one of these forms. On it you must list all your foreign currency in both cash and cheques, and the officials may demand to see and count it. All official transactions are then recorded on the form during your stay. On departure, the money you are carrying must tally with what you brought in, minus exchanges recorded on the form. It is important to keep this form in order and get bank receipts to back up any official transactions.

If you lose the form you are in deep shit, and can expect to spend a week or so learning the ins and outs of Algerian bureaucracy. It is possible that you may even get sent back to the point of entry at which the form was issued, so look after it!

If you can't show the right amount on leaving, expect a 'fine' which might be as much as (or more than) your shortfall.

It's also a good idea to declare any valuables, particularly cameras, and get them put on the form. In the past, travellers have had such items confiscated when leaving because they were not listed on the form. The same applies if you are bringing in a vehicle and carrying lots of big spare parts.

Exactly how thoroughly you and your form get scrutinised on leaving varies from day to day and border to border, but as long as you keep a cool head things should be OK.

## Black Market

The country's uncertain future and the demand for hard currency from foreign residents and Francophile Algerians wanting to flee the country means that the black market is thriving like never before. It operates in hard currencies and goods which are hard to obtain in Algeria. The black-market rate is reported to be about three times the official rate, although this may have changed following the latest devaluation.

By far the best currency is the French franc. You can also use US dollars and pounds sterling, but in many places people are reluctant to take anything other than francs.

Obviously, if you want to change money on the black market, it must be with money that is over and above the official amount listed on your form. Searches at some borders are thorough (particularly Figuig-Beni Ounif), so make sure that any extra money is very well hidden. Any which is found will be confiscated.

The black market is usually not that hard to find, especially in places which are on the tourist route, such as it is. Algiers is one place where it is not that easy to change money unofficially.

The best people to deal with are the owners of souvenir shops, as they are used to dealing with foreigners and are the most ready to change money. The most discreet way of bringing up the subject is to express interest in an item and then ask if they take dollars or francs. If you get no response, try another shop. It is really very straightforward and the risks are minimal, but tact and common sense are necessary. Hotel owners are also often willing to change money. The bottom line is that the risk is greater for the locals than for you.

The people not to deal with are the ones who approach you in the street. Some may be OK, but others definitely are not.

The government keeps tight control on imports, and foreign items in demand include jeans, T-shirts, sunglasses (Raybans), running shoes, instant coffee, cameras (as long as they are not on your currency form), car parts and jerry cans (metal or plastic). At the official rate it will appear that you are being offered outrageously high prices for things, but keep in mind that it is the black-market rate which reflects the true value of the dinar; the official rate is there only to get more out of you (and the locals) when entering the country.

If you are coming from Morocco, it is well worth considering buying Algerian dinar in Oujda. The rate is usually better than what you would get on the black market inside Algeria. There are plenty of money changers in Oujda, and you can even change in Figuig, although it is not as easy. It is also possible to buy Algerian dinar in the Spanish enclave of Melilla, although the rates will probably not be as good as in Morocco itself.

It is often possible to barter goods such as jeans, running shoes and cameras when buying souvenirs.

## Credit Cards
The only places in Algeria which accept credit cards are some of the expensive hotels in Algiers and the head-office branch of Air Algérie. Everywhere else you'll need to have cash or travellers' cheques.

The Banque Extérieure d'Algérie in Algiers may accept American Express cards, but don't count on it.

## Costs
Algeria is pretty expensive if you're changing money at the official rate, cheap if you're getting a good rate on the black market. Your AD 1000 won't last more than a couple of days, so you will need to learn the ropes quickly or pay the price.

## TOURIST OFFICES
The national tourist body, the Office National Algérien du Tourisme (ONAT), has offices in just about every major town. However, they are more like travel agencies for Algerians travelling overseas than offices for foreign tourists looking for info. Of more use are the local tourist offices run by the various wilayas.

## BUSINESS HOURS
To a certain extent, business hours are dictated by the climate. In summer, shops tend to close up for most of the afternoon, and a lot of businesses close altogether after about 2 pm.

The working week is from Saturday to Thursday morning. During the month of Ramadan, businesses are open for only a few hours in the morning; shops open up again late in the evening.

### Banks
Most banks are open from Saturday to Thursday from 9 am to 3 pm, although some banks shut on Saturday as well as Friday.

### Offices
These are open Saturday to Wednesday from 8 am to noon and 2 to 5.30 pm. On Thursday, they open only in the morning.

### Shops
Shops are open from approximately 8.30 am to noon and 2.30 to 6 pm, but these hours are quite flexible.

## HOLIDAYS
Most public holidays are connected with important events in the Islamic year; they are listed in the introductory Facts about the Region chapter.

There are also a number of holidays which are related to events and people important in the formation of the modern state:

*New Year's Day* – 1 January
*Labour Day* – 1 May
*Anniversary of the Overthrow of Ben Bella* – 19 June
*Independence Day* – 5 July
*Anniversary of the Revolution* – 1 November

## CULTURAL EVENTS
There are numerous fêtes and festivals held throughout the year. The main ones are:

March-April
    *Spring Festivals*, Biskra, Djanet, Ghardaia & Timimoun
March-May
    *Tomato Festival*, Adrar
    *Cherry Festival*, Tlemcen
    *Carpet Festival*, El-Oued
    *Old Ksar Festival*, El-Goléa
May
    *International Fair*, Algiers
December-January
    *Folklore Festival*, Tamanrasset

## SUGGESTED ITINERARIES
To most people, a trip to Algeria means a trip across or into the Sahara. However, there are many places in the north of the country which are well worth a visit, particularly if you are interested in Roman history.

Whether you are going south from Tunisia

ALGERIA

or Morocco to West Africa, or are doing a trans-Maghreb trip across the top of North Africa, it is easy to spend at least a month exploring Algeria.

The following itineraries are suggestions that make the most of what Algeria has to offer.

### Overland through Algeria

**Tunisia to Niger** Most people enter Algeria at El-Oued, but the more interesting crossing is up in the north between Tabarka or 'Ain Draham and Annaba. From Annaba you could go along the coast and the Corniche Kabyle, and then cut south to Sétif and the Roman ruins at Djemila.

From Sétif you could head back east to Constantine, Batna and the exceptionally well preserved Roman city at Timgad. The long trip south could take in the El-Abiod Gorges and Biskra, the desert between El-Oued, Ghardaia and In Salah, finishing further south at Tamanrasset and the Hoggar Mountains.

**Morocco to Niger** The best bet would be to cross the border in northern Morocco at Oujda, travel to Tlemcen in north-western Algeria, and then head south for Béchar. From there you could loop around the southern edge of the Grand Erg Occidental (Great Western Erg), taking in Taghit, Beni Abbès and Timimoun.

Many people use the crossing further south, between Figuig and Beni Ounif, but this route misses the fascinating city of Tlemcen in northern Algeria, and you also have to walk from Figuig to the border, and from there to Beni Ounif (about seven km).

From Timimoun you have the choice of heading south for Adrar and then across to the main route south at In Salah, or continuing around the erg to El-Goléa and possibly nipping up to Ghardaia (highly recommended), before heading south again. Both routes are served by public transport, but the latter route is more reliable if you are hitching. Either way, it's pretty inevitable that you will end up on a bus to get from In Salah to Tamanrasset.

**Morocco to Tunisia** These routes can be done easily in either direction by public transport. A good route is to head south from Tlemcen to Béchar, and travel around the Grand Erg Occidental to Ghardaia and then up to Algiers. From Algiers, you could head east through the mountains of the Kabylie region to Bejaia; from there, you could head south to Sétif and Djemila through the Kherrata Gorge (although you now don't see a lot of the best scenery in the gorge because of a new tunnel) and then to Constantine.

If you want to see more of the desert, you could head south from Constantine through Batna (and Roman Timgad) and Biskra to El-Oued, from where there are good connections to Tozeur in Tunisia. Alternatively, you could take the northern route from Constantine through Annaba to Tabarka on the north coast of Tunisia, or 'Ain Draham up in the mountains behind the coast.

### POST & TELECOMMUNICATIONS
### Post

The Algerian postal system is slow but, in the end, the mail gets through. Allow at least three weeks for letters posted from Algeria to reach their destination, and about the same for letters to arrive in Algeria from overseas.

It is far better to hang onto letters and send them from a major town, rather than from a smaller centre, where it's likely to take a week or more for the letter to reach even Algiers. There have been no reports of mail going astray if it is posted in the yellow post boxes which are all over the country, but you can expect the service to take even longer than from a post office. Post offices can be distinguished by the 'PTT' symbol.

**Parcel Post** Sending a parcel is simple enough, but is best done at one of the bigger post offices such as in Algiers, Constantine or Tlemcen.

Take your parcel to the post office for inspection before you wrap it. Parcels posted by surface mail to Australia take up to four months to arrive; they take a bit less to get to Europe.

**Receiving Mail** All post offices in the larger towns operate a poste restante service. Make it clear to people writing to you that it is important that they write your surname clearly in block letters, preferably putting only the initial for the given name to avoid confusion.

Mail is held for a period of one month before being returned to the sender (or whatever), except at Tamanrasset, where it is held for 15 days only.

American Express is not represented in Algeria, so there are no card-holder services available.

**Telephone**
The Algerian telephone system is badly overloaded but manages to cope most of the time. There are public phones all over the country and they are heavily used.

In theory, it is possible to make international calls from public phones. In the north of the country it is usually possible to get through after a dozen or so attempts; in the south you may have to try for an hour or more and so it's often easier to go through an operator at a post office or large hotel. Local and internal long-distance calls suffer similar problems.

Payphones take AD 1, AD 5 and AD 10 coins. To make a direct international call, get the dial tone, dial 00 and wait for a second dial tone, then dial the country and number you want.

All post offices have a telephone office, easily recognised by the yellow-and-red PTT symbol. These offices are often open longer hours than the regular post office. The Algiers and Constantine offices are open 24 hours a day.

**Area Codes** The area dialling codes for the main towns in Algeria are:

| Code | Region |
| --- | --- |
| 02 | Algiers |
| 04 | Batna, Biskra, Constantine & El-Oued |
| 05 | Bejaia, Jijel & Sétif |
| 06 | Oran |
| 07 | Adrar, Béchar & Tlemcen |
| 08 | Annaba |
| 09 | Ghardaia, Ouargla & Tamanrasset |

**TIME**
Time in Algeria is the same as GMT/UTC from November to April, and plus one hour from May to October.

**ELECTRICITY**
Algeria uses both the 240 and 120 V systems, so check before using any appliances.

**BOOKS**
For general reading on the region, refer to the Books entry in the Facts for the Visitor chapter at the beginning of this book.

**People & Society**
In 1846 Alexandre Dumas was asked by the Ministry of Public Instruction in France to travel around Algeria and write a book describing his experiences, so that the French could learn a bit about their country's new acquisition. The result was *Adventures in Algeria* (or *Tangier to Tunis*), and it provides a good insight into the life of both colonists and locals in the early days.

Early this century, Isabelle Eberhardt went to North Africa, became a Muslim and spent years travelling around Algeria on horseback, dressed most of the time as a man, before she drowned in a flash flood in 'Ain Sefra in 1904. She was the illegitimate daughter of a French woman and an ex-pope of the Russian Orthodox Church. Her diaries have been translated into English and are published as *The Passionate Nomad* (Virago, 1987). The book makes interesting reading, as she had a deep understanding of Arab culture and politics.

**Travel Guides**
The best overall guide to the country's attractions is the French *Algérie* (Hachette Guides Bleues, 1986). It is expensive but compact, and is well worth carrying if your French is up to it.

Neither it nor any of the guides listed in the Facts for the Visitor chapter at the beginning of this book are available in Algeria.

**MAPS**
The problem with most maps of Algeria is

ALGERIA

that they cover only the north of the country – not much use if you want to see the Sahara.

Hallwag's map of Algeria and Tunisia covers the whole of Algeria, and the level of detail is quite adequate for most people. If you require more detail, the best available for the north is Michelin No 958, which covers Algeria and Tunisia, published in 1992. It's hard to find a detailed map of the Sahara: Michelin No 953 covers the whole of West and North Africa and so doesn't have the depth of detail which some people may require.

The Lascelles map of Algeria is another that covers only the north of the country.

The state oil company, Sonatrach, published an excellent map of the country in the 1970s, but there are very few copies floating around now.

There is a National Mapping office on Rue Abane Ramdane, Algiers, not far from the Touring Club d'Algérie office. It has topographic maps covering large areas of the country, but you need to give 24 hours notice and fill in a form to get hold of any of these. It also has some good city maps, such as Oran, and these are readily available.

Finding your way around cities can present problems, as a lot of the bilingual street signs have had the names in French painted over, leaving only the Arabic – very handy.

## MEDIA
### Newspapers & Magazines
There are no English-language newspapers or magazines published in the country, nor can you find any of the international current-affairs magazines such as *Time* and *Newsweek*.

The closest you come to finding some news in English is on the inside back page of Monday's edition of the daily *Horizons* newspaper; this is printed in English, but one page once a week doesn't exactly keep you well informed.

The major French-language daily is the *El-Moudjahid*. Papers printed in Arabic include *El-Massaa*, *Al-Chaab*, *An-Nasr* and *Al-Joumhouria*.

## Radio & TV
Radio broadcasts are predominantly in French and Arabic, with some transmissions in Berber and English. TV transmissions are exclusively in Arabic and French.

## FILM & PHOTOGRAPHY
Agfa and Fuji film is sold everywhere and prices are reasonable, although the expiry date should be checked – some of it looks like it has been lying around for years.

There are facilities for getting film developed in all the major towns of the north, but this is not especially cheap and it takes a couple of days.

## HEALTH
For a full rundown of the health precautions you need to be aware of for the whole of North Africa, see the introductory Facts for the Visitor chapter.

If you are arriving from a yellow fever zone (West Africa) you will need to show a vaccination certificate.

Make sure that you have an up-to-date International Health Certificate with a valid cholera stamp. Despite the fact that the vaccination is less than 100% effective, officials will not allow anyone to enter the country from the south without a cholera jab; they may even demand that you have one on the spot.

## Water
Tap water throughout the country is safe to drink, although at times it tastes pretty awful.

The water in the southern oases comes from underground and varies from sweet (El-Goléa) to hard and saline (In Salah).

Bottled water is sporadically available for those with troublesome guts. Don't bother buying it in El-Goléa, however, because the bottles contain only local ground water. When buying bottled water, check the plastic seal to make sure it is intact; otherwise you may be paying for plain old tap water.

Mineral water is also available, mainly in Algiers where it is known by the generic name of Vichy.

## ACCOMMODATION
### Camping

There are a number of camp sites in the country, particularly along the tourist trail in the Sahara. In the north the sites are limited to a few low-key resorts along the coast.

In the south it is possible to sleep under the stars for much of the year, so if you have a sleeping mat or groundsheet this is the way to go. It's the cheapest way to travel and, if you are hitching, the camp sites are the best places to hunt around for lifts with other travellers.

Camping facilities range from primitive (Tlemcen and In Salah) to above average (Ghardaia), and cost from about US$1.50 to US$2.50 per person and a similar amount for a vehicle.

In the south of the country the best camp sites are in the middle of nowhere but, obviously, these are an option only if you have your own vehicle.

If you have your own campervan and are looking for a place to stay in towns in the north, it is usually possible to park in the corner of a Naftal service station for the night. Always ask permission and give the manager a packet of cigarettes or other small gift.

### Hostels

There is a system of hostels throughout the country and these can often be good, cheap places to stay if you don't mind dormitory accommodation. The charge is generally about US$2.50. The major drawback is that they are often inconveniently located.

There are hostels in the following towns: Annaba, Batna, Bejaia, Biskra, Constantine, El-Kala, El-Oued, Ghardaia, Ouargla, Tamanrasset, Touggourt and Zeralda.

### Hotels

In most towns there is a fair selection of hotels, particularly in the budget range. A room in a basic hotel costs about US$5 to US$8 for a double.

In the north, most of the hotel buildings date back to the colonial days and still have the original fittings and furnishings: window shutters, washbasin, bidet, wardrobe and a bed which is so old it wouldn't be out of place in a museum. Occasionally, breakfast is added to the price and, although it is tacked on as an extra, it will usually be compulsory: no breakfast – no room.

Even in the cheapest hotels the rooms are often cleaned daily, and the general standard of cleanliness is good.

For men, an option at the very bottom of the range is to stay at a hammam (bain maure in French). Although hammams are not spectacularly appointed and are usually hot and damp, they are a last resort when everything else is full. They are certainly not a realistic choice for any length of time, as you always have to vacate early in the morning and then find somewhere to put your gear all day. Just ask around in the centre of any town.

Top-end accommodation is in fairly short supply, but there is always at least one hotel in each town which offers above-average accommodation. These hotels are often government run and suffer from indifferent service and the couldn't-give-a-stuff attitude (from both management and staff) that frequently goes with state-run hotels. It often happens that these places check your currency form. The usual charge is around US$12/18 for a one-star hotel, up to US$25/30 for three-star rating.

Places fill up early in the day in summer and it's not uncommon to find a couple of places full before you strike it lucky.

## THINGS TO BUY

As usual, carpets make an excellent souvenir but, unless it's possible to buy and post in the same place, their sheer bulk make them an impractical purchase.

Ghardaia is the main centre for carpets, and there are a dozen or so shops selling them. Designs vary from region to region and many of the rugs you see displayed are actually from another region.

In Algiers there are a couple of large shops in the centre which sell nothing but carpets and, although prices are high, they have some good ones.

Tamanrasset also has a lot of stuff in the way of souvenirs, most of it of Tuareg origin. At the market across the oued there are always Tuaregs from the whole region selling jewellery, bags and other knick-knacks – much of it made purely for the tourist market.

El-Oued is another big centre for handicrafts but, again, most items are made with the tourist industry in mind and the prices asked are often ridiculous.

# Getting There & Away

You can enter Algeria by air from Europe, the Middle East and West Africa, by sea from France or Spain, or overland from Morocco, Tunisia, Niger and, if the border is open, Mali.

Regardless of where and how you enter the country, it is compulsory to declare your foreign currency on a declaration form and to change the equivalent of AD 1000. Read the Money section in the Facts for the Visitor chapter before entering Algeria.

## AIR

The main international airport is at Algiers, but there are others at Oran, Tlemcen, Constantine, Ghardaia and Annaba. Most of the flights from these other towns go only to places in France.

Airlines serving Algiers include Aeroflot, Air Algérie (the national flag carrier), Air France, Alitalia, EgyptAir, Iberia, Royal Air Maroc, Sabena and Tunis Air.

Air Algérie flies from Algiers to the following cities: Athens (weekly); Bamako, Nigeria (twice weekly); Barcelona (twice weekly); Berlin (weekly); Cairo (twice weekly); Casablanca (daily); Dakar (weekly); Frankfurt (three times weekly); London (four times weekly); Lyons (daily); Madrid (twice weekly); Marseilles (twice daily); Moscow (twice weekly); Niamey, Niger (weekly); Nouakchott, Mauritania (weekly); Ouagadougou, Burkina-Faso (weekly); Paris (twice daily); and Tunis (daily).

### To/From Europe

There are frequent connections with all the major cities in Europe but, as there is not a great volume of traffic, you will be up for the full economy fare. The one-way fare from Paris to Algiers is US$160, flying Air France.

### To/From North America

There are no direct flights from North America to Algeria. The best way would be a flight to London or Paris and then another flight from there. The full economy fare from New York to Algiers is about US$950.

### To/From Australasia

Again, there are no direct flights. The cheapest way is to fly with Aeroflot via Moscow, but you're probably better off going via London or Paris.

## LAND
### To/From Morocco

There are two crossing points between the two countries: between Oujda and Tlemcen in the north, and between Figuig and Beni Ounif, about 380 km to the south.

**Oujda-Tlemcen** From Tlemcen there are several buses a day to the border. The trip takes about an hour and costs US$1.50.

The two border posts are on either side of the fence, so there is no enormous tract of neutral territory to cross. You'll find banks on both sides of the border. From the Moroccan side there are regular buses (Dr 3) and grands taxis (Dr 7 day rate; Dr 10 night rate) to Oujda, 13 km away.

In the past, it was necessary for people bringing their own vehicle into Morocco from Algeria to have a telex from their embassy in Rabat guaranteeing that they would take the vehicle out of the country. This may now have lapsed but it's worth checking well in advance, as getting such a telex can take up to a couple of weeks. This telex, if necessary, would be in addition to a Green Card.

**Train** The Al-Maghreb al-Arabi (or Trans Maghreb Express) runs daily each way between Oujda and Tlemcen as part of the trip between Casablanca (Morocco) and Sousse (Tunisia). It leaves Oujda at 8.30 am Moroccan time, and the fare to Tlemcen is Dr 33. It arrives in Oran at 2.50 pm Algerian

ALGERIA

time. It is quicker to go by bus and cross on your own, rather than wait while hundreds of passengers get processed at the border.

**Figuig-Beni Ounif** This border crossing is straightforward enough, although you will have to walk about seven km if you can't get a lift with anyone. In summer make sure you have some water and a hat, as this is an extremely hot place.

This crossing has a reputation for the thoroughness of the Algerian officials when searching baggage for Algerian dinar and undeclared foreign currency.

Don't bother setting off from Figuig late in the afternoon, as the formalities and walking can take up to three hours. Remember to have your passport stamped by the Moroccan police in Figuig before walking to the border or on arrival from Algeria.

### To/From Tunisia
There are several crossing points between Algeria and Tunisia, the most popular being between El-Oued and Nefta in the south, and between Souq Ahras and Ghardimao in the north.

**Bus** There is a daily air-con bus from Tunis to Annaba run by the Tunisian national bus company, SNTRI. You need to book 24 hours in advance at the southern bus station in Tunis or at the Annaba bus station. The trip takes about 8½ hours (depending on the border crossing) and costs TD 17.250. Services leave Tunis and Annaba at 6 am. These buses don't stop en route to pick up passengers.

**Train** Heading west, the daily Al-Maghreb al-Arabi service leaves Tunis at 10.20 am, Ghardimao at 2.25 pm and Annaba at 8.25 pm (Algerian time). It arrives at Constantine at 11.35 pm and Algiers at 7 am. In the opposite direction, the train departs Algiers at 8.45 pm and Annaba at 6.56 am (both Algerian time), arriving in Tunis at 4.47 pm Tunisian time. For more details, see the Getting There & Away chapters for Morocco and Tunisia.

**Taxi** Regular *louages* (shared taxis) run between the medina in Tunis and Annaba (TD 18) and Constantine (TD 25).

In the south, there are louages from Nefta to the border on the Tunisian side and from El-Oued to the border on the Algerian side. There's a four-km walk between the two posts.

The Algerian post is called Bou Aroua and there is a small bank here, although it's not always open.

### To/From Niger
The border post between the two countries is between In Guezzam (Algeria) and Assamaka (Niger), a bit more than 400 km south of Tamanrasset.

When leaving Algeria, it is not necessary to clear immigration in Tamanrasset, as this is taken care of when you get to In Guezzam. However, you must check with customs before leaving Tamanrasset.

There is a weekly truck/bus from Tamanrasset to In Guezzam on Monday, returning the next day. Although it does get you 400 km further along the way it is next to useless as you still have to wait around for a lift to take you further on from In Guezzam. As any vehicle leaving Tamanrasset will be going through In Guezzam anyway, you may as well wait in relative comfort and try to get a lift right through.

The chances of hitching south from Tamanrasset depend on the amount of tourist traffic. The camp site is the best place to try

### To/From Mali
At the time of writing, the Algeria/Mali border was closed. Check with the Mali consulate in Tamanrasset or Algiers, or ask other travellers for the latest information.

There is a crossing on the Route du Tanezrouft between Algeria and Mali at a place called Borj Mokhtar. This isolated outpost 660 lonely km south of Reggane.

There are buses from Adrar to Borj Mokhtar, but you are better off trying to hitch out of Adrar, rather than catching the bus down to the border and then having to wait a week for a lift going further. If heading

orth, Gao is the place to wait for a lift, not
Bourem.

There are trucks doing the run from Adrar
o Gao, a further 800 km south of the border,
ut it may take a few days to get a lift. The
rip takes up to a week, so stock up with
upplies before setting off.

It is necessary to clear customs at Adrar,
nd you will need to check in with the police
t Reggane. Just for good measure, you will
e checked again in Borj Mokhtar. There are
o banking facilities between Adrar and Gao,
o make sure you have what you need. When
eading south (with a vehicle) there is a
harge of CFA 1000 payable at the border,
while coming north you'll be up for Algerian
nsurance (AD 250 per month for large
4WDs, AD 130 for cars and AD 60 for
notorbikes), so make sure you are carrying
ome French francs.

If you are driving, the road south is sur-
aced as far as Reggane; from there on it is
iste (tracks, often a couple of miles wide),
lthough 4WD is not necessary and the route
s in fact easier on vehicles than the Route du
Ioggar from Tamanrasset. You need to carry
nough fuel to get from Reggane to Gao;
lthough there is a station at Borj Mokhtar,
ou might have to wait for a few days for
ome fuel to arrive. Borj Mokhtar is also the
nly watering point between Reggane and
Gao.

Heading north from Borj Mokhtar, there
s a piste direct to Tamanrasset. It is a long,
onely stretch of road.

## SEA

### To/From France

The government-owned Compagnie Nation-
le Algérienne de Navigation (CNAN)
perates regular ferry services between Mar-
eilles and Oran, Algiers, Bejaia, Skikda and
Annaba, and between Sète and Oran.

In summer, these services are very heavily
ubscribed; if you intend bringing a vehicle
cross, make a reservation as far in advance
s possible.

These are the most expensive of the Med-
terranean ferries. Those to Morocco and
Tunisia are cheaper.

**Marseilles-Algiers** This is the most popular
(and therefore most crowded) route. In
summer, there are departures almost daily
but this drops to three or four per week in
winter. Basic fares from Marseilles are
FFr903 one way and FFr1631 return, plus
FFr115 extra for a couchette. Cars/caravans
cost from FFr1394. The crossing takes 19
hours.

**Marseilles-Annaba** Four ferries sail per
month in summer, and there are two sailings
per month in winter. Fares are as for Algiers.

**Marseilles-Bejaia** There are seven crossings
per month in summer, and one per week or
less in winter. Fares are as for Algiers.

**Marseilles-Oran** There are 20 sailings per
month in summer, dropping to two or three
weekly in winter. Fares are FFr1012/1824
one way/return for passengers.

**Marseilles-Skikda** There are one or two
departures per month. The journey takes 24
hours and fares are the same as for Algiers.

**Sète-Oran** There are three sailings per
month in summer.

### To/From Spain

There are regular sailings from the Spanish
port of Alicante to Oran and Algiers. The port
of Palma on the Balearic island of Majorca
is also served by ferries from Algiers.

**Alicante-Algiers** There are only two sailings per month in summer, and none in
winter.

**Alicante-Oran** There are eight sailings per
month in summer, and three in winter.

**Palma-Algiers** This is another popular
route. The boats stop in Palma and continue
on to Marseilles. There are four per month in
summer, and one per month in winter; fares
are as for Oran.

ALGERIA

## CNAN Addresses

CNAN has the following offices in France and Spain:

France
Lyons – 37 Rue Servient, 69003 Lyons (☎ 60.13.87)
Marseilles – 29 Blvd des Dames, 13002 Marseilles (☎ 91.90.64.70)
Paris – 25 Rue St Augustin, Metro Opéra (☎ 49.27.91.20)
Spain
Alicante – Agencia Romeu Jorge, Plaza 18 Julio 2 (☎ 208 333)
Madrid – Romeu y Cia SA, Cristobal Bordiu 19-21 (☎ 234 7407)
Palma – Agencia Schembri, Plaza Lonja 2-4 (PO Box 71) (☎ 221 417)

In Algeria, there are CNAN offices in all the major towns and cities along the coast; these are listed in the appropriate sections on each city.

## LEAVING ALGERIA

If you buy a ferry or plane ticket (local or international), you have to specifically change money (at the official rate) to do so. Even if you have receipts to prove that you have already changed AD 1000, these are not sufficient. When changing money for an international ticket, ask for a paper called an Attestation de Cession de Devises, which the bank will fill out in triplicate. You then give one copy to the office where you buy the ticket and you keep another to show when leaving the country, if asked. The fact that you have been issued this form is also noted on your currency declaration form.

# Getting Around

## AIR

Algeria has a well-developed internal air network with frequent flights between Algiers and other major centres. One of the main problems is that most of the flights radiate from Algiers, so although two towns might have good connections with Algiers there will be no direct flight between them.

Flying is cheap. Airfares are subsidised by the government to the extent that internal flights are looked on rather like a bus service. There are no in-flight comforts such as food or drinks; this is basic, no-frills people transport, and you'll be lucky if you even have a safety belt which works.

Refinements such as seat allocation are also unheard of, and with overbooking a common event, boarding a flight can be a real circus. This was the scenario experienced by Lonely Planet's Hugh Finlay at Algiers' Houari Boumedienne Airport for an *international* flight:

...find the correct check-in desk (unmarked), thrust arm holding passport and ticket into the tangle of other arms and passports and tickets, all trying to get the clerk's attention; receive boarding card (without seat number) and proceed to departure lounge. Jostle for a place on the shuttle bus to plane, jump out of bus, identify baggage (now placed on tarmac – wet or dry) and stow in hold of aircraft. Race around or under plane to stairs on other side, jump on and hopefully (if you haven't been dragging your heels), there'll be a spare seat.'

### Bookings

As all flights are usually heavily booked and even overbooked, you need to make a reservation as far in advance as possible. Air Algérie, which has a computerised booking system and offices in most towns, operates flights that cover almost the entire country.

## BUS

Virtually all buses in the country are operated by the national bus company. This is known by various initials, most commonly TVE, but also SNTV and TVSE. The buses are usually bright orange, although the newer ones are white.

The larger towns have a purpose-built bus station, while the smaller towns have, at the very least, an office where you can make reservations and from which the buses leave.

Bus travel is fast and comfortable throughout the north, with frequent departures connecting all the towns. In the south, things are much the same on the good roads except that there are fewer services. Points as far south as Adrar, El-Goléa and Hassi Messaoud are all served daily by regular buses.

The buses that operate on the unmade roads of the south are quite an experience. They are usually Mercedes trucks, with a passenger cabin with seats for about 20 people built on to the chassis. As you can well imagine, these are real boneshakers: 18 hours on one of them along roads which defy description leaves you feeling totally shell-shocked.

These trucks/buses operate on the route south from In Salah to Tamanrasset and In Guezzam, and from Adrar to Borj Mokhtar and across to In Salah. The incredibly tough conditions that they have to endure day after day mean that they are prone to breakdowns. The main routes are usually kept serviced, but services on the less frequented ones, such as from In Salah to Adrar, may be suspended if there aren't enough buses in one piece at any one time.

From Tamanrasset there are no buses out to the Hoggar Mountains or to Djanet, nor are there any services south of In Amenas on the route to Djanet from Touggourt.

Booking in advance is advisable, particularly in the summer. It is only possible to book 24 hours in advance (and sometimes it's as little as 12 hours); this varies from one place to the next. Bus fares are reasonably priced: US$9 from Algiers to Constantine, US$12 to Ghardaia and US$9 to Oran; there is a charge for any bag which goes in the luggage compartment.

In summer, especially, it's worth trying to work out which side the sun is going to be beating down on, as tinted windows and air-conditioning are nonexistent, and curtains are rare.

## TRAIN

There is a rail network in the north of the country and the trains are reasonably fast and efficient. The greatest advantage of travelling by train is that, on the main lines at least, they have air-conditioning (and heating). This is something of a mixed blessing, however, as there is consequently little ventilation and on long journeys the pungent cigarette smoke can become stifling. Second-class is much worse than 1st class in this respect. There are couchettes on the night journeys between Constantine and Algiers, and Oran and Algiers, which must be booked in advance; seven days is the maximum.

The main line goes clear across the north of the country, connecting Souq Ahras in the east with Tlemcen in the west. There are small feeder lines heading south from Constantine to Touggourt, Annaba to Tébessa and from Mohammadia (near Oran) south to Béchar.

Trains are generally fairly uncrowded, and there are buffet cars on the main routes. The main services are as follows:

| From | To | Frequency | Journey Time |
|------|-----|-----------|--------------|
| Algiers | Annaba (via Constantine) | three daily | 11 hours |
| | Constantine | two daily | 8 hours |
| | Oran | five daily | 6 hours |
| Constantine | Touggourt | two daily | 8 hours |
| Mohammadia | Béchar | one daily | 10 hours |
| Tlemcen | Moroccan border | three daily | |

## TAXI

Louages (large shared taxis) operate only in the northern part of the country. They go as far south as Adrar on the Route du Tan-

ezrouft, El-Goléa in the centre and Hassi Messaoud in the east.

They don't run to any schedule but just leave when full. For this reason they can be more convenient than the buses, but they are considerably more expensive. Count on about AD 40 per 100 km.

All taxis are yellow Peugeot station wagons, either the old 404 or the newer 504 or 505.

## CAR
### Car Rental

It is possible to rent cars, but the tariffs are astronomically high, especially as you have to show that you have changed money officially. The main rental company is Algérie Auto Tourisme, which has offices in Algiers, Annaba, Oran, Constantine and El-Oued.

The tariff for the smallest category (Peugeot 205) is US$50 per day, plus AD 4.6 per km, AD 96.50 per day insurance, and fuel – not cheap.

### Fuel

Fuel is fairly cheap in Algeria, particularly in comparison with neighbouring Tunisia and Morocco.

The hydrocarbons industry is wholly owned and run by the state company Sonatrach. The state's petrol and service stations are called Naftal.

Particularly in the south, it is sometime possible to pay for your fuel with goods which you don't want, especially vehicle spare parts and jerry cans.

The price of fuel is cheap by world standards – even at the official rates, and on the black market the prices are downright crazy. Diesel is much cheaper than petrol, and more widely available.

When buying petrol check whether you are getting super or regular, as there is often a shortage of super.

### Vehicle Insurance

When you are bringing your own vehicle into Algeria, insurance has to be purchased at the port or border post.

The cost of insurance varies for different

vehicles and is shown in the Insurance table below. There is also a vague tax of about US$4 that has to be paid on top of the insurance.

## Insurance

| Type | 10 Days | 20 Days | 1 Month | 2 Months |
|------|---------|---------|---------|----------|
| Motorbike | AD 40 | AD 50 | AD 60 | AD 110 |
| Car | AD 70 | AD 90 | AD 130 | AD 250 |
| Truck/4WD | AD 120 | AD 190 | AD 250 | AD 450 |

## HITCHING

Hitching is never entirely safe in any country in the world, and we don't recommend it. Travellers who decide to hitch should understand that they are taking a small but potentially serious risk. However, many people do choose to hitch, and the advice that follows should help to make their journeys as fast and safe as possible.

Hitching – for single men and couples – was once one of the best ways to see Algeria. Travellers have written to say that this is no longer the case amid the paranoia of the present fighting. Hitching has never been a good idea for single women.

Hitching in the south is largely dependent on the number of foreigners passing by. They will usually give lifts where possible, but most are so loaded to the eyeballs with gear that there is just no room for an extra body or two. A lot of the vehicles on the roads are trucks, many of which belong to the state-owned transport company (SNTR) and have a large 'D' on top of the cabin. Drivers of these trucks are forbidden to carry passengers and risk losing their jobs if they are caught with someone else in the cab. Some drivers will pick people up if they know there is no police checkpoint along the road they will be using.

### Registration Plates

The last two numbers on the licence plates of Algerian vehicles identify the wilaya that the vehicle is from. It can sometimes be useful, especially when hitching, to know whether the vehicle is local or from somewhere else and therefore likely to be travelling further. It could also help to pass the time.

The main wilaya numbers are:

| Number | Wilaya |
|--------|--------|
| 01 | Adrar |
| 05 | Batna |
| 06 | Bejaia |
| 07 | Biskra |
| 08 | Béchar |
| 11 | Tamanrasset |
| 13 | Tlemcen |
| 16 | Algiers |
| 23 | Annaba |
| 25 | Constantine |
| 30 | Ouargla |
| 31 | Oran |
| 33 | Illizi |
| 37 | Tindouf |
| 39 | El-Oued |
| 47 | Ghardaia |

## LOCAL TRANSPORT
### Bus
Most cities and towns have a local bus network but, other than in Algiers, usually only the route number is intelligible to non-Arabic speakers. You will probably need local advice on which bus to catch.

In Algiers, the system is well organised and there are route maps at all the main stops.

### Taxi
Local taxis are yellow, just the same as the long-distance ones. Fares should be negotiated in advance, although in Algiers drivers will use the meter.

### Metro
There is a metro system under construction in Algiers but it is unlikely to open in the near future.

ALGERIA

# Algiers

Known as Alger in French and El-Djazair in Arabic, Algiers is the capital of Algeria; with a population of more than two million, it is also far and away the largest city in the country.

Little remains of old Algiers – when the French arrived they pulled down most of what they found to make way for a new French-style city. There are a few magnificent mansions and palaces built by the Turks but, with a couple of exceptions, you can look at these from the outside only.

## History

Known as Icosium in Phoenician and Roman times, Algiers lived in the shadow of the region's major city, Caesarea (Cherchell), about 100 km to the west.

It fell to the Vandals in the 5th century, but its fortunes revived under the Byzantines. Icosium remained a commercial outpost until the 10th century, when the town was revived by a Berber dynasty of the Sanhaja federation under the name of El-Djazair.

Piracy became a major occupation on the Barbary coast and, in the 16th century, the famous Turkish pirate Barbarossa (Khair ed-Din) occupied the city. After he defended it against Spanish invasion, the title of beylerbey was conferred on him by the sultan of Constantinople.

During the years of Ottoman occupation the city prospered, and the large kasbah built on the hill overlooking the harbour became the residence of the provincial governor (bey).

On 14 June 1830 the French landed at Sidi Fredj, and by 5 July the last governor of Algiers capitulated to them. Algiers became the administrative and military capital of the French colony.

During WW II the city became the headquarters of the Allied forces in North Africa. During the late 1950s and early 1960s it was the focal point in the nationalist struggle against the French. In 1962 Algiers became the capital of independent Algeria.

## Orientation

The city centre is hemmed in against the bay by the mountains which rise steeply from the coast. The skyline of the city is dominated by two structures, both impossible to miss. To the south of the centre is the Martyrs Monument (Makam ech-Chahid), a 92 metre-high concrete memorial in the shape of three highly stylised palm fronds. Close to the city centre, the box shape of the four star Hôtel Aurassi is dominant.

The commercial and business centre is the area directly south of the medina. Here you'll find all the major shops, banks, hotels and the post office. The railway station and ferry terminal are only five minutes' walk north from this area, and the bus station is 15 minutes away to the south.

Everything in the centre is within walking distance, and nothing is far from the main street, Rue Larbi ben M'Hidi. This is a tree lined pedestrian precinct running north from Place Grande Poste to the medina. Place Grande Poste is a major square, where you'll find the post office and a local bus terminal.

The medina itself is fairly run-down and has become a slum area.

In the centre, the buildings along the waterfront road, Blvd Zighout Youssef provide a grand architectural sweep as they look out over the docks and the bay; the boulevard itself is popular with evening promenaders. Below this road, almost at water level, is another road running parallel to the waterfront; on this reclaimed strip of land is the railway station and ferry terminal.

Out in front of Place Port Said, a small square on Blvd Zighout Youssef, there is what looks like a water tower. It is in fact an *ascenseur* (passenger lift), which for 50 centimes will take you from one level to another – handy if you have just got off the train and have a heavy backpack to lug up the ramp.

which connect the two road levels. On the lower level, the lift is right by the railway station entrance.

The embassies are nearly all out in the suburb of Hydra, five km south of the centre, or in the suburbs of El-Biar and Bouzaréah. All these places are easily reached by taxi. Otherwise take bus No 31 from Place Audin to a large marketplace, and bus No 44 from there to Hydra; to get to Bouzaréah, take bus No 59 from Place des Martyrs.

Just to make life easier for foreigners, all the bilingual Arabic-French street-name signs have had the French painted over, leaving only the Arabic, which is of very little use to the average visitor. This is a practice which has been pursued throughout the north.

## Information

**Tourist Offices** For what it's worth, there is a branch of ONAT (☎ 02-641550) behind the Hôtel Safir, and also one at 2 Rue Didouche Mourad (☎ 02-631066). Neither of these offices has any information, but the staff do try to help.

The Touring Club d'Algérie (☎ 02-660887) has an office at 21 Rue Abane Ramdane, which runs off Place Port Said. The people staffing this office are helpful and can sometimes supply maps of the country. If you have a vehicle and need assistance, these are the people to see.

The bookshops along Rue Larbi ben M'Hidi all sell a good map of Algiers.

Also extremely helpful are the city maps on signboards which can be found on the footpaths at various places around town. Two handy ones are at Place Port Said and behind the town hall, right near the entrance to the Hôtel Safir.

**Money** There are banks all over the central part of town. If you have to get an Attestation de Cession de Devises (for a plane or boat ticket), the Banque Centrale d'Algérie at 8 Blvd Zighout Youssef, on the waterfront, issues them without too much fuss.

If you are stuck for cash outside bank hours, any of the expensive hotels should be able to help. The most convenient is the Hôtel Safir, Blvd Zighout Youssef; the entrance is on the inland side of the building.

**Post & Telecommunications** The main post office is on Place Grande Poste, at the southern end of the main street, Rue Larbi ben M'Hidi. It's an imposing neo-Moorish building, complete with arches and mosaics, and is worth a look inside even if you have no business to do there.

The poste restante counter is in the telex office, which is at the end of the small alley on the left of the main entrance to the post office. The doorway is at the top of a short flight of steps. There is a small charge for every letter collected.

The parcel-post counter is in the main hall of the post office, as is the philatelic section.

The post office is open Saturday to Wednesday from 8 am to 7 pm, and Thursday from 8 am to 1 pm; closed on Friday.

The international telephone office is by Place Grande Poste on the corner of Rue Asselah Hocine. It is open 24 hours a day and you can dial direct to most large countries.

The Algiers telephone area code is 02.

**Foreign Embassies** Countries with diplomatic representation in Algeria include:

Austria
     Les Vergers, Rue No 2, Lot 9, Bir Mourad Rais (☎ 02-562699)
Canada
     27b Rue Ali Messaoudi, Hydra (☎ 02-606190)
Denmark
     29 Blvd Zighout Youssef (☎ 02-628871)
France
     6 Ave Larbi Alik, Hydra (☎ 02-604488)
Japan
     1 Chemin al-Bakri, El-Biar (☎ 02-786200)
Libya
     15 Rue Cheikh Bachir el-Ibrahimi (☎ 02-783193, 781512)
Morocco
     8 Rue des Cèdres (☎ 02-607408)
     5 Ave de l'ANP, Sidi-Bel-Abbès, (☎ 243470)
Spain
     10 Rue Ali Azil (☎ 02-617062)
     Consulate: 7 Rue Mohammed Benabdeslem

ALGERIA

ALGERIA

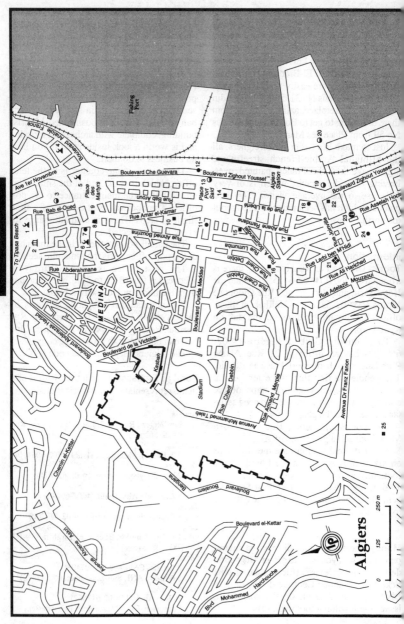

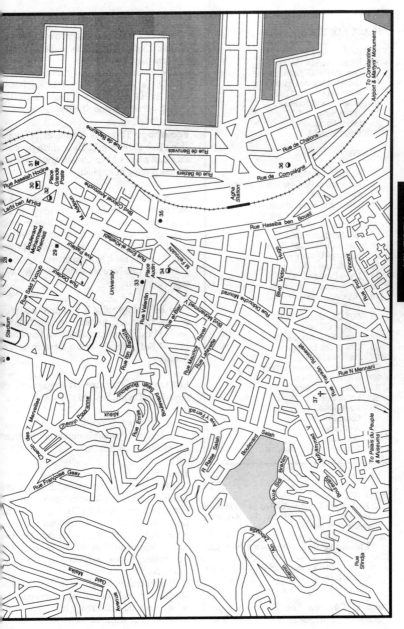

ALGERIA

ALGERIA

**PLACES TO STAY**

| | |
|---|---|
| 9 | Grand Hôtel |
| 10 | Hôtel el-Badr |
| 14 | Grand Hôtel Tipaza |
| 15 | Grand Hôtel des Étrangers |
| 16 | National Hôtel |
| 17 | Hôtel Grand Touring |
| 22 | Hôtel Safir |
| 25 | Hôtel Aurassi |
| 29 | Hôtel Albert I |

**OTHER**

| | |
|---|---|
| 1 | Ali Bichnine Mosque |
| 2 | Museum of Popular Arts & Traditions |
| 3 | Local Buses |
| 4 | Djemaa el-Kebir Mosque |
| 5 | Djemaa el-Jedid Mosque |
| 6 | Ketchaoua Mosque |
| 7 | Dar Hassan Pacha |
| 8 | Place Cheikh ben Badis |
| 11 | National Theatre |
| 12 | Passenger Lift |
| 13 | Long-Distance Taxis |
| 18 | Air Algérie |
| 19 | Airport Buses |
| 20 | Ferry Terminal |
| 21 | 501 Department Store |
| 23 | Tourist Office |
| 24 | Place Emir Abdelkader |
| 26 | Office des Étrangers |
| 27 | National Library |
| 28 | Palais du Gouvernement |
| 30 | Main Post Office |
| 31 | Telephone Office |
| 32 | Local Buses |
| 33 | Air Algérie |
| 34 | Local Buses |
| 35 | Air France |
| 36 | Bus Station |
| 37 | Sacred Heart Cathedral |

Tunisia
7 Rue Ammar Rahmani, El-Biar (☎ 02-781480)
Consulate: Route de Morsot (PO Box 280),
Tébessa (☎ 974855)
UK
7 Chemin Capt Hocine Sliman (☎ 02-605038)
USA
4 Chemin Cheikh Bachir el-Ibrahimi, El-Biar
(☎ 02-601186)

**Cultural Centres** The British Council
Library (☎ 02-605682) is at 6 Ave Boudjemaa Souidani, just above Place Addis
Ababa above the Palais du Peuple. It has live
satellite TV from the UK, as well as newspapers and magazines.

The French Cultural Centre (☎ 02-
636183) is at 7 Rue Capt Hassani Issad,
while the German Goethe Institute (☎ 02-
634683) is at 165 Rue Sfindja.

**Bookshops** There are a number of shops
along Rue Larbi ben M'Hidi which have an
excellent range of French and Arabic books,
but not a thing in English.

**Maps** There is a government mapping office
on Rue Abane Ramdane, almost opposite the
Hôtel Grand Touring, which has topographic
maps of all regions of the country. To get
copies, you need to fill in a form and then
wait 24 hours for it to be approved.

Also on sale here are some good city and
regional maps.

**Film & Photography** If you need passport
photos, there are a couple of small shops
around Place Emir Abdelkader on Rue Larbi
ben M'Hidi which can do them in a few
hours.

**Left Luggage** There are left-luggage offices
*(consignes)* at the bus and railway stations.

**Vaccinations** It is possible to get vaccinations from the Pasteur Institute, not far from
the Musée des Beaux Arts.

**Medina**
The best place to start a wander around the
medina is Place des Martyrs, at the northern
end of the corniche (Blvd Che Guevara). The
large open square is a terminus for local
buses and is busy throughout the day. The
square was created in the 1860s when the
government knocked down a large number
of old houses.

The medina is largely a tangle of narrow
streets, which still follow the ancient plan but
which are lined with French buildings; many
of these have decayed badly in the last 25

years and look like they may not last another 25. The area is definitely seedy.

**Mosques** Near the waterfront is the **Djemaa el-Jedid Mosque**, also known as the Mosquée de la Pêcherie. As the name suggests (*jedid* means new), it is a relatively new mosque, built in 1660 for the Hanefite Turks. Two blocks farther along, past the Chamber of Commerce, is the **Djemaa el-Kebir Mosque** (known as the Great Mosque). This mosque dates back to the 11th century and was built by the founder of Tlemcen, the Almoravid Youssef bin Tachfin, on the site of a Christian church from Icosium. Both these mosques are closed to non-Muslims.

Just a short way along Rue Bab el-Oued lies the **Ali Bichnine Mosque**, built in 1623 by an Italian pirate.

Rue Omar Hadj opens out at Place Cheikh ben Badis and the **Ketchaoua Mosque**. Dating originally from 1162, the mosque was completely rebuilt in 1794 by Hassan Pacha (Dey of Algiers). It was converted to a church in July 1930, and then back to a mosque after independence. No entry to non-Muslims.

**Museum of Popular Arts & Traditions** This museum is cunningly concealed in the tangle of streets up behind the Ali Bichnine Mosque. It is housed in one of the finest Turkish palaces in the city, construction of which began in 1570. After the French took Algiers in 1830 this building became the city's first town hall. To find it, follow the large orange signs from the Ketchaoua Mosque. Alternatively, take the first left up the hill beyond the Ali Bichnine Mosque, then take the first left again at a café (Rue Hadj Omar), and then turn right up the stairs of Rue Mohammed Ali Malek. The museum is 30 metres up on the right at No 9.

It has excellent displays of rugs, jewellery, costumes and pottery. The palace itself is still in good condition – the reception room on the 3rd floor has a beautiful stucco ceiling and parquet floor (the latter is in fact a French addition). It is open daily, except Saturday, from 10 am to noon and 1 to 5 pm; closed Friday morning and Saturday.

**Turkish Mansions** Back towards the centre along Rue Hadj Omar there are some more fine Turkish mansions, easily recognisable by their small windows and the way their upper floors hang over the street. At No 10 is the building known as **Dar Ahmed**, which houses the administration headquarters of the Algerian National Theatre. It was occupied by the dey Ahmed from 1805 to 1808.

Two other mansions are at Nos 12 and 17 in the same street. The relatively plain exteriors of these places belie the opulence within: faïence tiles from Europe, marble columns and doorways, stucco ceilings and mirrors.

Next door to the Ketchaoua Mosque is another Turkish palace, **Dar Hassan Pacha**; this was built in 1790 and now houses the ministry responsible for religious matters. Up a small side street, Rue Cheikh el-Kinai, is yet another mansion (at No 5); this is now home to the Wilaya Committee, and they may let you wander around. Also on this street is the **Hammam Sidna**, the oldest hammam still in use in the city. It was built in the 16th century and, for men at least, it's worth a stroll inside.

Opposite the Ketchaoua Mosque is yet another fine building, the **Dar Aziza bent el-Bey** – the Princesses' Palace. It now houses the Ministry of Tourism.

### Ville Nouvelle

From Place Cheikh ben Badis, Rue Ahmed Bouzrina leads to the market behind the National Theatre on Place Port Said, and eventually to the main street of the ville nouvelle, Rue Larbi ben M'Hidi. This street is now a pedestrian precinct and is crowded at any time of day.

About a third of the way along Rue Larbi ben M'Hidi is **Place Emir Abdelkader**, which has an enormous statue of Abdelkader on horseback. There is an expensive pavement café here. The street is lined with some

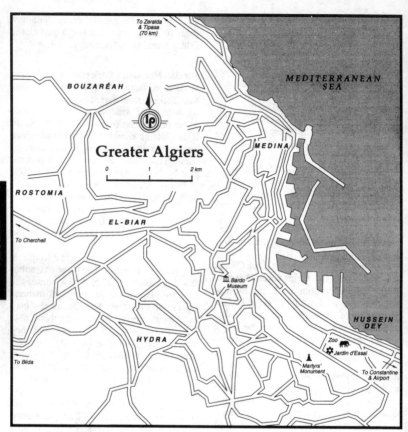

Greater Algiers

BOUZARÉAH

MEDITERRANEAN SEA

To Zeralda & Tipasa (70 km)

MEDINA

ROSTOMIA

EL-BIAR

To Cherchell

Bardo Museum

HUSSEIN DEY

HYDRA

To Blida

Zoo
Jardin d'Essai

Martyrs' Monument

To Constantine & Airport

0    1    2 km

fancy shops, one of the most amazing being the cavernous 501 department store, one block back towards the medina.

From Place Grande Poste, Rue Emir el-Khettabi leads to Rue Didouche Mourad and Place Audin – a busy intersection and another local bus terminal.

Rue Didouche Mourad, which heads up the hill to the south, is one of the main shopping streets. It also has several airline offices and some fancy restaurants. About 500 metres along, it changes to Rue Franklin Roosevelt and starts to twist and curve up the hill. Soon you will come to an absolutely

dreadful concrete church, the Sacred Heart Cathedral.

Continuing up the hill along Rue Franklin Roosevelt, before long you come to another pocket of Turkish palaces, all three of which house museums. To save your legs, take bus No 31, 32 or 33 from Place Audin, or No 35 or 40 from Place Grande Poste, and get off at the Palais du Peuple stop.

**Bardo Museum** The first museum you come to along Rue Franklin Roosevelt is the Bardo, which has a collection that's a strange combination of prehistory and ethnography.

The prehistory section has literally thousands of stone hand tools and arrow heads, and seemingly every piece of ancient bone and stone ever dug up in the country. Pride of place goes to a 20-cm-long elephant tooth and the two-metre horn of a long-extinct type of buffalo.

Upstairs, the ethnography museum has a very peaceful courtyard. The rooms around it have displays of the costumes and handicrafts of the various Algerian ethnic groups, including the Tuareg and the Kabylie. One of the most impressive displays is the collection of coral-studded jewellery.

The museum is open in summer from 9 am to noon and 2.30 to 5.30 pm, and in winter from 9 am to noon and 2 to 5 pm; it's closed on Friday morning and all day Saturday.

**National Museum of Antiquities** Farther up the hill, on the right, is the National Museum of Antiquities; it's actually in the small Parc de la Liberté, on the corner of Ave Franklin Roosevelt and Blvd Salah Bouakouir (right by the Palais du Peuple bus stop). It houses a collection of various bits and pieces from all over the country. The display of coins must be among the best anywhere, and the 5th-century Vandal manuscripts on wooden tablets are priceless. Both these displays are in the antiquities room, to the left inside the entrance. Other rooms contain Roman statuary and Islamic art. The museum is open the same hours as the Bardo, and entry is free on Friday afternoon.

**Palais du Peuple** Another 100 metres along Ave Franklin Roosevelt, on the left, are the vast, luxuriant grounds of the Palais du Peuple. This is the former residence of the Algerian head of state and, before him, of the French governor.

The palace and grounds, which hold a number of museums, were first opened to the public in 1987, but reportedly they have been closed indefinitely.

**Martyrs' Monument** From Place Audin (or Place Addis Ababa on the hill directly above the Palais du Peuple), a No 32 bus passes within a few hundred metres of the Martyrs' Monument, which is on top of the hill to the south of town. Get off at the stop where the bus goes under the overpass, right on the top of the hill.

The monument is a concrete monstrosity of truly gargantuan proportions, but somehow it works. It was built as a memorial to all those who died in the struggle for independence, and was opened in 1982 to mark the 20th anniversary of Algerian independence.

In the area beneath the three stylised palm fronds is an eternal flame guarded night and day by two armed soldiers. The views out over the city from the edge of this area are the best you'll get.

**Musée National du Jihad** Beneath the Martyrs' Monument is the Musée National du Jihad, which covers the 'holy war' – the struggle for independence from 1955 to 1962. The museum is exceptionally well set out and has excellent displays of equipment used in the war. A major drawback is that everything is labelled in Arabic. This makes it hard for most foreigners to gain a full understanding of the Algerian viewpoint, although many of the displays need no interpretation. The museum is open from 9 am to 6 pm Monday to Friday, and on Sunday from 2 to 6 pm; closed on Saturday.

**Riad el-Fet'h** Stretching away from the Martyrs' Monument is a massive concrete concourse known as Riad el-Fet'h (Victory Park). This is a major gathering point for people, especially on weekends. In the middle is a sunken courtyard, known as the Bois des Arcades, with three levels of fancy shops, boutiques and restaurants. In the centre of the courtyard is the Théâtre du Verdure – an open-air theatre.

**Army Museum** At the opposite end of Riad el-Fet'h from the Martyrs' Monument is the Army Museum. Looking more like a five-star hotel, it is another expensive reminder of the war for independence. The interior would also do justice to an international hotel – piped classical music, chandeliers, fountains, white marble floors, polished granite stairways – the works. The displays are all of a military nature and are quite interesting, although the building is so large that they tend to get lost in the open spaces. It is open the same hours as the Jihad Museum.

**Musée des Beaux Arts** At the foot of the hill below the Martyrs' Monument is the Musée des Beaux Arts (Museum of Fine Arts). It has a small collection of sculptures, and one floor of paintings including some minor works by major artists of the 19th century – Renoir, Monet, Courbet and Degas, to name a few. You may have to wake the attendants to get the lights switched on.

The museum is open Monday to Thursday from 10.30 am to 12.30 pm and 1.30 to 5.30 pm, and Friday and Sunday from 2.30 to 5.30 pm; closed on Saturday. To get there from the centre, catch a No 9 bus from Place des Martyrs; the trip takes about 20 minutes. Get off the bus directly below the Martyrs' Monument, or ask the conductor for the Musée des Beaux Arts.

**Jardin d'Essai & Zoo** Across the road from the Musée des Beaux Arts is the entrance to the somewhat overgrown botanical gardens. They must have been amazing at one stage but are sadly neglected now. At the far side, towards the sea, is a small zoo with a motley collection of animals, most of them kept in depressingly small cages. The gardens are open from 10.30 am to 6.30 pm Sunday to Friday; closed on Saturday. To get there, follow the directions for the Musée des Beaux Arts.

There is a funicular railway between the Jardin d'Essai and the Martyrs' Monument.

### Places to Stay – bottom end
**Hostel & Camping** The closest hostel and camp site is at Zeralda, on the coast 40 km west of Algiers.

**Hotels** The centre of things for cheap accommodation is Place Port Said, a fairly seedy part of town on the edge of the medina. We've heard from travellers that this area is best avoided, especially since the troubles started.

For those who want to see for themselves, the best known of the cheap hotels is the enormous *Hôtel el-Badr* (☎ 02-627102), at 31 Rue Amar el-Kamar. It is just off Place Port Said and rooms cost US$6/8 for singles/doubles with breakfast; it's extra for hot showers. Rue Amar el-Kamar is a narrow street running off the north-western corner of the square. The hotel has no sign in English, but it's about 50 metres along on the left and has a green-and-black tiled doorway.

### Places to Stay – middle
Many of the old favourites in this price bracket are also to be found around Place Port Said. On the southern side of the square is the one-star *Grand Hôtel Tipaza* (☎ 02-630040). Rooms cost US$12/16 for a single/double with bath and breakfast. The green fluorescent sign says only 'Hotel' in English; the rest of the script is in Arabic.

Just off the square and of a similar standard to the Tipaza is the *Grand Hôtel des Étrangers* (☎ 02-633245); this is a couple of doors along from the National Theatre, at 1 Rue Ali Boumandjel, the street which connects Place Port Said with Rue Larbi ben M'Hidi. Single/double rooms cost US$9/13 with breakfast and shower.

Parallel to Rue Larbi ben M'Hidi, and one block towards the waterfront, is Rue Ben Boulaid, which has two two-star hotels, the *Grand Hôtel Regina* (☎ 02-649900) at No 27 and the *Hôtel d'Angleterre* (☎ 02-636540) at No 11. The Angleterre is the cheaper of the two, with rooms at US$13/17, while rooms at the Regina are US$17/23, all with bath and breakfast.

### Places to Stay – top end
All of the top-end places listed here accept payment by Visa or American Express credit cards. Apart from the head office of Air Algérie, these are about the only places in the country that take plastic.

Right on the corniche, the four-star *Hôtel*

Safir (☎ 02-735040) actually has its entrance around the back in Rue Asselah Hocine. It is the most central of the smarter places and charges US$30/40 for singles/doubles.

The Hôtel Aurassi (☎ 02-748252), off Ave Dr Franz Fanon, is a towering great blot on the landscape. It's also the only real 'international standard' hotel in Algiers, and this is reflected in the prices: US$80/100 for singles/doubles at the back of the building, and more for rooms with a spectacular view of the whole city and harbour. You'll need to take a taxi from the centre of town, as it's a long, hard slog up the hill on foot.

Less pretentious is the three-star Hôtel Albert I (☎ 02-630020), at 5 Ave Pasteur, just 100 metres uphill from the main post office. Rooms cost US$18/26 with bath and breakfast.

The only other top-of-the-range establishment in Algiers is the Hôtel el-Djazair (☎ 02-591000), on Ave Boudjemaa Souidani, just above Place Addis Ababa. It's actually a converted palace, although it's hardly palatial these days. Rooms cost US$70/85.

## Places to Eat

**Local Food** For local Algerian food, there is a stack of places in the web of streets between Rue Larbi ben M'Hidi and Rue Abane Ramdane, which run between Place Emir Abdelkader and Place Port Said. They all sell the usual stuff – soup, brochettes (kebabs), chicken, chips and salads.

For good local food of the filling-and-unexciting kind there are a few popular restaurants in the street directly behind the Grand Hôtel Tipaza at Place Port Said.

**Fast Food** There's no escaping fast food, and Algiers boasts at least a couple of burger places in the American mould. The ones worth checking out are Royal Burger, at 23 Rue Larbi ben M'Hidi, and Fast Burger, in the Bois des Arcades at Riad el-Fet'h.

**Speciality Restaurants** The up-market restaurants are at the Martyrs' Monument in the Bois des Arcades. There is everything from the local cuisine offered by top-class Algerian speciality restaurants (El-Boustane or Dar Hizia) to seafood and Italian and Japanese cuisine.

**Seafood** There's a curious little pocket of restaurants almost beneath Place des Martyrs which specialise in seafood. To get to them, go down the stairs next to the Djemaa el-Jedid Mosque. The entrance to the stairs is through two arches which have been incorporated into the façade of the mosque and is known as the Rampe de la Pêcherie.

## Getting There & Away

**Air** Air Algérie has a number of agencies around town. The head office (☎ 02-645788) is at 1 Place Audin, near the university and about 10 minutes' walk from the post office.

The agency at 29 Blvd Zighout Youssef (☎ 02-633847) handles international bookings only. There is another agency behind this office on Rue de la Liberté, which handles internal flights only and is open seven days a week.

The following international airlines also have offices in Algiers:

Aeroflot
     7 Rue Malki Nassiba (☎ 02-605661)
Air France
     Mauritania Building, Blvd Colonel Amirouche
     (☎ 02-649010)
Alitalia
     7 Rue Hamani Arezki (☎ 02-646850)
EgyptAir
     4 Rue Didouche Mourad (☎ 02-630505)
Iberia
     11 Rue Hamani Arezki (☎ 02-633712)
Lufthansa
     49 Rue Didouche Mourad (☎ 02-642736)
Royal Air Maroc
     64 Rue Didouche Mourad (☎ 02-630458)
Sabena
     61 Rue Larbi ben M'Hidi (☎ 02-633214)
Swissair
     19 Rue Didouche Mourad (☎ 02-633367)
Tunis Air
     6 Rue Emir el-Khettabi (☎ 02-632573)

Air Algérie flies to just about every major city in the north and all the far-flung oases in the Sahara. Even at the official rate, fares are

ALGERIA

relatively cheap (US$60 to Tamanrasset, for example).

**Bus** The main bus station is down at the waterfront, south of the centre and about 15 minutes' walk from Place Grande Poste. Take the road heading towards the water from Place de Perou and then go down the road ramp to the right. There is a small bus station at the bottom but ignore this, as the main station is another 300 metres farther on.

There are buses to just about every major town in the country as far south as Béchar, Ghardaia and El-Oued. The station is well organised and all the ticket windows have the destination and departure time displayed. There is an information booth in the centre of the hall.

For most of the year there are enough departures to satisfy demand, but things get a bit hectic in the summer months. It's best to make a habit of buying tickets the day before you plan to travel – for all trips.

From Place des Martyrs, the blue-and-white city buses Nos 5, 72 and 77 go past the bus station.

The left-luggage office is on the left inside the entrance and is open from 1 am to 10 pm. It costs about US$1 per article per day.

**Train** Although the main railway station is also close to the centre, on the lower street level directly below Place Port Said, most departures are from the Agha railway station, to the south near Place de Perou.

There are departures to Annaba, Bejaia, Constantine and Oran at least twice a day.

**Taxi** The long-distance taxis leave from the ramps which connect the upper and lower street levels in front of Place Port Said. At any one time there are up to 100 taxis in the queues, and it's easy to find the one you want – just ask the drivers.

There are departures at all hours to Batna, Bejaia, Biskra, Constantine, Oran, Sétif, Tébessa, Tizi-Ouzou and many other places.

**Car Rental** Algérie Auto Tourisme has offices at 5 Rue Professeur Curtillet (☎ 02-

744855), at the Hôtel Aurassi (☎ 02-748252) and at the airport (☎ 02-751209).

**Sea** CNAN has offices at 6 Blvd Mohammed Khemisti (☎ 02-640420) and at 7 Blvd Colonel Amirouche (☎ 02-638932). There is also an office at the ferry terminal, at Quai 9, Nouvelle Gare Maritime (☎ 02-579312), and at Riad el-Fet'h (☎ 02-664232).

The passenger terminal is at the Nouvelle Gare Maritime, right in the centre of town in front of the Hôtel Safir. You can enter from either the upper or lower street levels.

CNAN operates ferries from Algiers to Marseilles and Sète in France. For details of departures, see the Algeria Getting There & Away chapter.

### Getting Around
**To/From the Airport** Blue-and-white buses leave for the 45-minute run out to the Houari Boumedienne Airport from Blvd Zighout Youssef, right across the road from the Hôtel Safir.

At the terminal building, the buses leave from an area to the right of the exit approximately every half-hour from 5 am to 11.30 pm.

**Bus** There are buses which serve all parts of the city. The four major stations for these buses are Place des Martyrs, Place Grande Poste, Place Audin and Place 1 Mai (south of the Agha railway station).

At each of the platforms (and at major stops en route) there are signboards giving the destination and the route taken. Entry is through the back door, where you pay the conductor.

From Place des Martyrs take bus No 5, 72 or 77 for the main bus station. From Place Grande Poste take bus No 35 or 40 for the Bardo and other museums. From Place Audin take No 31, 32 or 33 for the museums; No 32 goes on to the Martyrs' Monument.

**Taxi** There are taxis everywhere, and you just flag them down – there are no taxi stations. All taxis have a meter, and you should ensure that the driver uses it.

# Around Algiers

## ZERALDA

Zeralda is some 40 km along the coast to the west of Algiers. It has a reasonable beach and is about the closest you can get to the capital if you want to camp. There is a hostel here as well, but it's rumoured to be closing – ring ahead.

### Places to Stay

The *hostel* (☎ 812112), where you can also camp, is down by the beach, right behind the Complexe Touristique – just follow the signs to the latter. It's inconvenient, as it is about 20 minutes' walk from Zeralda itself and there are no restaurants in the immediate vicinity. The hostel is on the right just before the entrance to the resort. There is no sign in English, but the driveway is beside an electrical substation with the letters 'EGA' on it.

During the summer months the hostel has tents set up on frames. In winter the frames are still there, but the tents are gone. However, at this time the hostel is usually empty and you can sleep inside. If you stay here you need to bring all your own supplies.

### Getting There & Away

Buses leave from the main bus station in Algiers throughout the day, until about 6 pm. Any of the buses going to Tipasa, Bou Ismail and Cherchell go through Zeralda.

## TIPASA

The coastal village of Tipasa, about 70 km west of Algiers, is the site of a former Phoenician and Roman trading post. The ruins are right by the sea. These days they are accompanied by a couple of modern vacation resorts.

The site itself does not really compare with Djemila or Timgad, south-east of Algiers, but it is unusual in that it is right on the coast and set in quite thick bush. If you can't make it to either of the other sites or feel like a day trip out of Algiers, this is the place to come.

The streets by the entrance to the site have been made into pedestrian malls, and are lined with shady peppercorn trees and a few up-market restaurants.

### History

The ancient town prospered until the time of the Vandal invasion in 430, and the majority of the inhabitants were Christian. The invaders brought with them the heresy of Arianism, forcing the townspeople who refused to give up their orthodox Christian faith to flee to Spain.

The town revived briefly during the Byzantine occupation in the 6th century, but by the time the Arabs arrived it was derelict, hence the Arabic name, Tefassed, which translates roughly as 'badly damaged'.

### The Ruins

The entrance to the ruins is one block from the main road, towards the water. The ruins are open from 9 am to noon and 2 to 5.30 pm daily, except Saturday.

On the right as you enter is the amphitheatre, and beyond that are two **temples**. The first is known as the Anonymous Temple and the second is on the other side of the main thoroughfare, the decumanus maximus, and is known as the New Temple.

The road through here is actually the old Cherchell to Icosium (Algiers) road. It is more than 14 metres wide, and there is a stretch of about 200 metres which is not in bad condition.

From the New Temple the road continues through a residential area to the **Villa of Frescoes**, on the water's edge. This villa, which must have belonged to one of the town's wealthiest residents, was named after the decorative wall paintings which were found during the course of the excavations.

On a small rise to the right are the ruins of the **Judicial Basilica**, which dates from the 2nd century AD. Above the basilica is the well-preserved **forum** and, towards the lighthouse, you'll find a small Christian **chapel**.

Along the waterfront to the left of the Villa of Frescoes, the path leads past the ruins of

**ALGERIA**

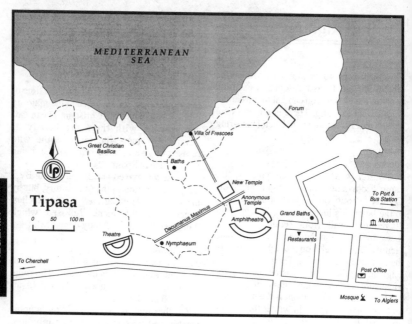

Tipasa

a garum factory (garum was a spicy, fish-based sauce), a bath complex and a cavalry station; the path eventually comes to a hemispherical well, on which the rope marks can be clearly seen.

From the well, the track heads steeply up the small cliff to what is left of the **Great Christian Basilica**; you can reach this more easily by backtracking a bit until you come to a sandy path leading up to the right. The basilica has nine naves and measures more than 40 by 50 metres. It dates back to the 4th century.

Back near the entrance, the road leads past the **Nymphaeum**, complete with marble fountain, to the theatre.

### Other Attractions

Outside the entrance to the ruins, the street leads past the ruins of another baths complex to the **museum** (on the left-hand side of the road). Although very small, the museum does have some excellent pieces, including some particularly fine glass exhibits. It is open the same hours as the ruins.

Farther along the same street is the old Punic port, which is now a small fishing harbour, and a Phoenician tomb.

### Places to Stay

**Camping** At the village of Chenoua, a couple of km along the beach to the west (or about four km by road), is a camp site which also has tents for hire. The beach here is not bad at all either. To walk to the camp site from Tipasa, get to the beach through the tourist complex and walk around from there.

**Hotels** The only hotel in Tipasa is the *Hôtel Sindbad*, on the main road near the start of town as you arrive from Algiers. There is no sign, but it is on the left and is the only building that looks remotely like a hotel. Rooms here cost US$15 for a double with breakfast.

The only alternative (apart from camping)

is one of the expensive resort hotels. The *Tipasa Plage* resort (☎ 02-461820) is 1.5 km west of town, and the enormous *Tipasa Village* (☎ 02-461761), with its 600 bungalows, is three km to the east along the Algiers road.

### Getting There & Away
Buses to Cherchell and Algiers leave regularly from the open space down by the fishing harbour.

### CHRÉA & BLIDA
The ski resort of Chréa lies 1510 metres above sea level, in the mountains 70 km south of Algiers. The resort is not too well developed, by European standards, but there are a few runs. In summer it's a popular vacation spot, and there are numerous walking trails in the area.

The ascent to the resort starts at the town of Blida, 20 km back towards Algiers, and the views are spectacular as you climb up the Atlas from the fertile Mitidja plains.

Blida, the capital of a wilaya of almost one million inhabitants, is the centre of an important agricultural region that grows oranges, lemons and olives. The town's connection with agriculture and irrigation goes back to the 16th century, when Andalusian immigrants settled there and began using the water from the Oued el-Kebir.

Today the town is of little interest to the traveller, although the Grand Mosque is impressive with its turquoise dome and four tiled minarets.

### Places to Stay
**Chréa** The only hotel in Chréa is the small, one-star *Hôtel Des Cèdres* (☎ 02-13). Rooms cost US$15 for a double with breakfast.

**Blida** It is unlikely that you would want to stay in Blida but, should the need arise, there

are a couple of possibilities. The cheapest of these is the well-appointed *hostel* (☎ 02-499601) at 39 Ave Kritli Mokhtar, about two km from the bus station. The other alternative is the *Hôtel Royal* (☎ 02-492801), which is on the main square, Place 1 Novembre.

### Getting There & Away
**Bus** The main bus station for buses to Algiers, Ghardaia and towns to the west is about 1.5 km from the centre of Blida. Local buses run from outside the gate into the centre.

Buses for Chréa leave from south of the main street in Blida; ask to be shown the departure point.

**Train** The railway station is near the bus station. There are departures for Algiers and Oran.

# North-East Algeria

The north-eastern region of the country is sadly neglected by visitors. It stands out as a tourist destination in its own right, but most people pass it by – it is the Sahara that they have come to conquer.

The mountains of the Kabylie region, in the area directly to the east of Algiers, are spectacular and the stretch of coastline between Bejaia and Jijel, known as the Corniche Kabyle, is one of the most rugged and scenic in North Africa.

Inland lie the ruins of the Roman city of Cuicul, present-day Djemila, with its beautiful setting in the mountains. A little farther on is Constantine, the seat of the ancient kings of Numidia, built right on the edge of the deep and precipitous gorges of the Rhumel.

Farther east lies Annaba, Algeria's third city, site of the ruins of the Roman city of Hippo Regius and seat of the great Christian reformer St Augustine. Today it is largely an industrial town, but it is the main northern gateway to Tunisia, as there are good transport connections all the way to Tunis.

South of Constantine are the Aurès Mountains, part of the Saharan Atlas, which run from Morocco in the west right through into Tunisia. The range roughly marks the boundary between the inhabited, arable north and the desert south. The Aurès Mountains are quite barren and spectacular, but the real drawcard is the fantastically preserved Roman city of Thamugadi (present-day Timgad). For once, the ruins are well served by public transport and there is accommodation close by.

# The Kabylie

The range of mountains known as the Grande Kabyle run from south of Algiers across to Bejaia in the east. The region is home to the country's largest Berber minority, the Kabylie. These people speak Berber first, French second and Arabic third. Over the years the government has not been at all sympathetic to their demands for a separate cultural identity, leading to serious disturbances in the area in the early 1980s.

Because of the mountainous terrain, it may be difficult to use many of the high roads for about six months of the year over winter. In spring and summer the region is cool and colourful – a blessed relief from the heat and humidity of the coast.

There is a reasonable beach at Tigzirt, which has the only accommodation along this stretch of coast.

The area around Tikjda, south of Tizi-Ouzou and in the centre of the forests of the Djurdura Mountains, is now a ski resort. During the war for independence the forests were decimated by French napalm bombs.

## TIZI-OUZOU

With a population of more than 100,000, the city of Tizi-Ouzou is the capital of the wilaya of the same name. It is not a particularly riveting place but is the best base for any exploration of the area, and the setting is pleasant.

### Places to Stay & Eat

The only budget accommodation choice is the relatively new *Hôtel Olympia*, up a side street one block north of the main street, Rue Larbi ben M'Hidi, and about 10 minutes' walk from the bus station. Rooms cost US$5/8 for a single/double with washbasin. There are no showers in the place but this is not a problem as there is a public hammam right across the street. To find the hotel from the bus station, walk uphill along the main street, turn left at the roundabout (Place Lamari Meziane) and then take the first street on the right. The hotel is on a corner about two blocks along on the left. It is above a pharmacy and has only the word 'Hotel'

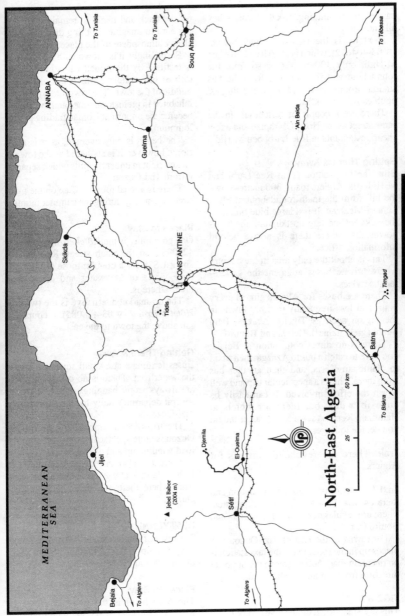

ALGERIA

painted on the building. Ask the locals – they all know it.

Next up is the two-star *Hôtel Beloua* (☎ 03-404612), which is at 16 Rue Larbi ben M'Hidi, only 100 metres or so from the roundabout and five minutes from the bus station. Rooms cost US$10/16 for singles/doubles with breakfast.

There are a couple of restaurants in the same street as the Hôtel Olympian and a few cheap restaurants in Rue Larbi ben M'Hidi.

### Getting There & Away

**Bus** The bus station is on Rue Larbi ben M'Hidi (the Algiers road), 300 metres down the hill from the main roundabout at Place Lamari Meziane. It is a large blue building; the ticket offices are upstairs and the buses downstairs, where there is also a helpful information office.

This is about the only area in the country where private buses augment the government services.

There are buses for Algiers almost every hour, and less frequently to other towns in the region such as Tigzirt, Azazga, Beni Yenni (great name!), Dellys and Bouira.

There is no direct connection to Bejaia; you have to catch a bus to Azazga, then a taxi to Hammam Keria, and then another bus from there. This is a spectacular trip and well worth the effort involved. It can easily be done in a day, but there are hotels at Hammam Keria, Adekar and Azazga should you decide to linger.

**Train** There are regular departures for Algiers.

**Taxi** Taxis also run from the bus station and there are always a few in the parking area. There are regular departures for Algiers and Bouira from here.

For towns to the east of Tizi-Ouzou and places up in the mountains, the taxi station is on the main road, 500 metres in the opposite direction from the main roundabout.

### TIGZIRT

This is a small town on the coast, very much off the track and likely to remain that way. It's hard to imagine anything disturbing the sleepy atmosphere of the place.

Surprisingly, it is a town with a history, as is testified by the ruined Christian basilica (5th or 6th century), which is right in the middle of the town. The town site was in fact inhabited in prehistoric times and eventually became the important Roman trading port of Iomnium.

The beach is only average, as it is quite stony; however, it is sheltered as the town is tucked right in under the hills which separate it from Tizi-Ouzou.

There is a local tourist office on the main street, open only during the summer months.

### Places to Stay

One possibility is the *Hôtel el-Awres* (☎ 03-428094), on the main street. Rooms cost about US$8 for a double; those at the front have views of the water and catch what breeze there is.

The up-market alternative is the two-star *Hôtel Mizrana* (☎ 03-428085), a couple of km above the town to the east.

### Getting There & Away

Buses terminate at a small square just near the waterfront. There is no office but there are always people hanging around. There are several departures daily for the short trip to Tizi-Ouzou.

The trip over the mountains from Tizi-Ouzou is quite spectacular in itself, with the road winding up and over the range.

There are also infrequent departures to Dellys, farther along the coast to the west, from where there are buses back to Tizi-Ouzou.

### BENI YENNI

The town of Beni Yenni is 760 metres above sea level, up in the mountains 50 km south of Tizi-Ouzou.

### Places to Stay

The only hotel is the two-star *Hôtel Le Bracelet D'Argent* (☎ 03-59), which charges

US$12/15 for singles/doubles with break-fast.

In summer it should be possible to camp in the area, although you would need to be pretty well self-sufficient.

### Getting There & Away

In summer there are regular buses between Beni Yenni and Tizi-Ouzou.

# Bejaia & the Corniche Kabyle

## BEJAIA

Bejaia is a port town with a population of about 140,000. It is built in a beautiful spot: it's on the flank of Jebel Gouraya, a mountain at the eastern end of the Gulf of Bejaia.

The city itself is very pleasant, although things have been spoiled to a great extent by the construction of a petrochemical complex on the edge of the town, which has resulted in pollution of both the air and water.

The centre of the town is a congested mess of very narrow streets which wind up the hillside. The view out over the harbour, the bay and the mountains from Place 1 Novembre is really something (when the pollution is not too bad, that is).

Despite its long history, there is really very little to see in the town itself. However, the beach at Tichi (17 km to the east) is one of the best in the country, and there is some good walking out to Cap Carbon and around.

### History

In Roman times the town was called Saldae. It prospered in the time of the Hammadid chief Emir En-Nasser and was renamed En-Nassria.

En-Nasser's son, El-Mansour, built a beautiful palace within the fortifications built by his father. The last Hammadid ruler, Yahia, ruled over a town which flourished on the Saharan trade and reportedly grew to more than 100,000 inhabitants.

The downfall of the Hammadid empire came in 1152, when the Almohad ruler Abd al-Mu'min invaded from Morocco. In the 13th century, the town became part of the Hafsid empire when that dynasty came to power in Tunis.

Piracy was a major occupation along the Barbary coast in the years up to the beginning of the 16th century. About this time, the activities of the pirates in Bejaia brought the town to the attention of the Spanish, who besieged it in 1509. The Spaniards were followed by the Turks in 1555 and the French in 1833, by which time the population had dwindled to a meagre 2000.

### Orientation

The centre of the town is actually up on the side of the hill but, because of the terrain, the transport connections are all at the bottom, about 20 minutes' walk from the centre.

Suburban buses run up as far as the impossibly small and busy square, Place Chérif Medjahed, which has an unusual sculpture in the centre. Around the square you'll find the post office, shipping office, Air Algérie and banks. The hotels too are close by.

Place 1 Novembre is a beautiful open terrace, 100 metres towards the water along Rue Ben M'Hidi, a small pedestrian street. It is flanked by two old colonial buildings – the Banque Centrale d'Algérie and the Hôtel de l'Étoile (the place to stay if money permits). The view from here is excellent, and a stairway near the hotel entrance leads down to a museum below.

To help you get your bearings, there is a map of the town on the wall of the cinema, on the right at the entrance to Place Chérif Medjahed as you come up from the bus station.

### Information

**Tourist Office** The ONAT (☎ 05-920261) office is on Place Chérif Medjahed. It doubles as the CNAN (☎ 05-920360) booking office for ferries to France.

**Money** The main bank is on Place 1 Novembre.

ALGERIA

**Post & Telecommunications** The post office is also on Place Chérif Medjahed. The telephone office is through the door to the left of the main entrance.

## Museum

Beneath Place 1 Novembre, the museum has an enormously varied collection, ranging from paintings by local artists to hundreds of stuffed birds in various stages of decay – a real mishmash of exhibits. The museum is closed from noon to 2 pm.

## Other Attractions

There are a few remnants from the past but they are all either run-down, closed or both. The **kasbah** (closed) is down near the waterfront, straight down from Place Chérif Medjahed, and dates from the time of the Spanish occupation.

About 10 minutes' walk up the hill behind the square, along Rue Fatima, is the small 16th-century **Sidi Soufi Mosque** with its square minaret. Farther on up the hill is the marketplace. Higher still is **Fort Moussa**, which also dates from the 16th century; it was built by the Spaniard Pedro Navarro, possibly on the site of the palace built by the Hafsids. This building is also closed.

The walk out to **Cap Carbon** takes a solid couple of hours, as it is over seven km from the centre. From the end of the road it is a further 30 minutes on foot to the lighthouse, which is near the tip of the cape.

If you are really keen, there is a road up to the Spanish fort on top of Jebel Gouraya, behind the town. To get to this, follow Rue Fatima up to Fort Moussa and then take Rue Gouraya; this goes past an Islamic institute, which was opened in 1972 and was built on the site of an Islamic university established by the saint Sidi Touati.

## Places to Stay

The best budget bet is the friendly *Hôtel Touring* (☎ 05-920383), at 6 Rue Hocine Hihat, which slopes gently uphill directly opposite the post office. Rooms cost US$6 for a double and those at the back are quieter

than the ones on the street. There are cold showers only.

Similarly priced is the *Hôtel Saada*, on the pedestrian street, Rue Ben M'Hidi, which connects the two squares.

The one-star *Hôtel l'Étoile* (☎ 05-929895), on Place 1 Novembre, has some rooms with great views from the balconies out over the bay and the coast to the east. It charges US$8/12 for a single/double with breakfast.

## Places to Eat

The cavernous *Restaurant de la Soummam*, right next to the Hôtel Touring at 4 Rue Hocine Hihat, is as convenient as any. There are a couple of other places on Rue Ben M'Hidi near the Hôtel Saada.

## Getting There & Away

**Air** The airport is three km south of town, off to the left of the road to Tichi and Jijel. Air Algérie (☎ 05-925731) has an office on the western side of Place Chérif Medjahed.

There are daily flights to Algiers, which take 50 minutes.

**Bus** The bus station is at the bottom of the hill, south of the city centre and about 20 minutes away on foot. The local buses, which depart from the terminal halfway down the hill, go past it. There is a booking office with a reasonably up-to-date timetable on display.

There are regular departures to Algiers, Bouira, Constantine, Jijel and Sétif. There are no direct buses to Tizi-Ouzou. The best you can get is a bus to Hammam Keria and then local transport on to Azazga and Tizi-Ouzou.

**Taxi** The taxis depart from the intersection of the Algiers and Jijel roads, about two km past the bus station.

**Hitching** This intersection is also the place to be for hitching, either to Algiers or Tizi-Ouzou in the west, or to Jijel and Sétif to the east. There is plenty of traffic in both directions.

## TICHI

The beach at Tichi, 17 km east of Bejaia, is quite good. The only problem is that the pollution from the oil refinery at Bejaia is sometimes so bad that the water line is dotted with dirty great globs of tar.

### Places to Stay

**Camping** It is possible to camp on the beach stretching back towards Bejaia. This area is extremely flat and exposed, with no protection from either the sun or the wind. There is a camp site, run by the *Touring Club d'Algérie*, which is open in summer only.

**Hotels** Up on the rise towards the eastern edge of the town is the *Hôtel Bar Restaurant Les Hammadites* (☎ 05-926680). The terrace has good views around the bay to Bejaia. Rooms cost about US$12 for a double with breakfast.

### Getting There & Away

Buses to and from Bejaia and Jijel stop on the road through Tichi. It's just a matter of flagging them down in the centre of the town.

## CORNICHE KABYLE

Fifteen km east of Tichi is Souq et-Tnine, and from here the roads east along the coast and south through the Kherrata Gorge to Sétif pass through some amazingly rugged country. There is quite a bit of traffic along both roads, so hitching is possible.

Between Souq et-Tnine and the fishing village of Ziama Mansouria, the mountains of the Petite Kabylie come down almost sheer to the water, and at times the road is carved out of the rock face, usually only one lane wide.

There are a few sheltered bays with sandy beaches along the coast near Grotte Merveilleuse, and it should be possible to camp here if you have your own vehicle.

Towards Jijel the mountains recede, but there is still surprisingly little development.

## Jijel

The town of Jijel is really off the beaten track, but if you spend any time on the Corniche Kabyle, you will probably end up here for at least a night. It has no specific attractions, although it does have a large, sandy beach.

**Information** The post office is on Rue 1 Novembre 1954 (the date of the start of the revolution), about 300 metres along from the town hall, the building with the clock tower on the main intersection, Place de la République.

The Air Algérie office and the banks are also on Rue 1 Novembre 1954, which is the town's main street.

**Places to Stay** There are only two cheapies. The *Hôtel du Littoral*, on Rue 1 Novembre 1954, not far from Place de la République and only about five minutes' walk from the bus station, is old and somewhat cavernous. Rooms cost US$5/7 for singles/doubles. There are no showers in the place but there are public ones right next door.

The other cheapie is the *Hôtel En-Nassre*, a couple of blocks back and inland from the Littoral.

The only other place in town is the two-star *Hôtel Tindouf* (☎ 05-962071), at 14 Rue Larbi ben M'Hidi. The rooms are arranged around a courtyard and cost US$8/10 for singles/doubles with washbasin. In one corner of the courtyard is the shower room, which is in fact a public douche – even hotel guests have to pay for a hot shower.

**Places to Eat** Slim pickings here. They include the restaurant attached to the *Hôtel En-Nassre*, and a couple of other places in the main street.

**Getting There & Away** The Air Algérie (☎ 05-965894) office is on Rue 1 Novembre 1954.

The bus station is about 100 metres from the town hall, in the opposite direction from Rue 1 Novembre 1954. There are local buses and TVE departures for Algiers, Annaba, Bejaia and Constantine.

ALGERIA

## KHERRATA GORGE

The narrow road which connects the coast with Sétif crosses the Petite Kabylie range of mountains through this narrow gorge. It is a pity, however, that the most spectacular (and dangerous) part of the gorge has been bypassed by a new tunnel which cuts right through the guts of the mountain range.

It may still be possible to use the old road but this seems unlikely, as it was chronically prone to rock falls. It would make an excellent walk but you would need to carry all your gear, as there is no accommodation between Sétif and Tichi.

The tunnel, built by an Italian company, is an impressive piece of engineering, and the approach to the northern end of it is even more so. The tunnel entrance is some 50 metres up the side of the mountain, so a bridge 1.5 km long has had to be built to gain access.

The village of Kherrata, on the inland side of the gorge, is huddled beneath Jebel Babor, which at 2004 metres is up there amongst the highest in the country. It is possible to hire guides in the village who will take you up some of the peaks in the surrounding area – technically it's not a climb, just a hard slog.

The waters of the Oued Agrioun have been dammed here by the Ighil Emda Dam to form a small lake, which is used to generate hydro-electricity.

# Sétif & Djemila

It's not the town of Sétif itself which is the attraction in this area inland from the Corniche Kabyle and west of Constantine, but the surrounding region. This is because the ruins of Roman Cuicul, present-day Djemila, are tucked away in the hills to the east.

## SÉTIF

The town of Sétif is largely a product of the French colonial era. With its tree-lined streets, fountain and theatre, it still has a very French feel to it. Until the French occupation in 1838, nothing much had happened in the town – other than the establishment of a veterans' colony by the Roman emperor Nerva, the ruins of which still are visible.

In 1945, however, the town became the focus of the emerging nationalist feeling. The raising of nationalist flags led to an uncontrolled riot in which 84 Europeans were massacred. French reprisals were both quick and indiscriminate; by French estimates, at least 2000 Muslims lost their lives – so you can be sure that the figure was a good deal higher. Similar events were reported in nearby Kherrata and Guelma; Algerian estimates put the total number of deaths at 45,000.

Today the town has a population of about 200,000 and, at 1096 metres above sea level, it's the second-highest wilaya capital in the country. Now how's *that* for trivia!

### Information

The main street, Ave 8 Mai 1945 (the date of the massacres), runs east-west through the centre of town. On it you'll find the banks, post office and airline offices.

Everything is within walking distance.

### Things to See

The town's pride and joy is the huge amusement park (**Parc d'Attraction**), a couple of blocks north of the main street. Here there are rides of all sorts, giant slides and dodgem cars, and the whole thing seems to be just a tad out of place. The park itself is enormous: it has an artificial lake and fountains, and a small zoo with animals in tiny cages. There is even a coffee shop set up in a traditional Bedouin tent.

On the western edge of the park are the ruins of a **Byzantine fortress**, while at the eastern end is the modern **museum**, accessible only from Blvd de la Palestine (outside the park). It has a collection of bits and pieces from prehistoric to Islamic times, including a couple of good mosaics. The museum is open from 9 am to noon and 2 to 6 pm; it's closed on Friday morning and all day Saturday.

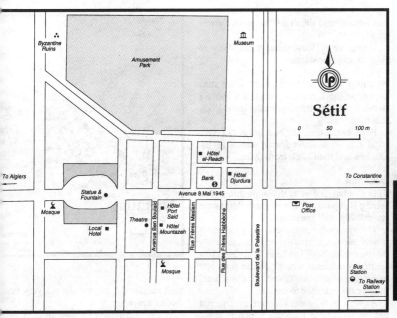

Sétif

0    50    100 m

To Algiers

To Constantine

Byzantine Ruins

Amusement Park

Museum

Hôtel el-Readh

Bank

Hôtel Djurdura

Avenue 8 Mai 1945

Statue & Fountain

Mosque

Local Hotel

Theatre

Avenue Ben Boulaid

Hôtel Port Said

Hôtel Mountazeh

Rue Frères Meslem

Rue des Frères Habbèche

Boulevard de la Palestine

Post Office

Bus Station

To Railway Station

Mosque

ALGERIA

## Places to Stay – bottom end

The *Hôtel Port Said* (☎ 05-907183), at 6 Ave Ben Boulaid, has large rooms with shower at US$4/6 for singles/doubles. The unmarked entrance is in between two restaurants.

The *Hôtel Djurdura* (☎ 05-904655) is on Rue des Frères Habbèche, the side street next to the Banque Centrale d'Algérie. Rooms cost US$6 for a double.

## Places to Stay – middle & top end

The *Hôtel el-Readh* (☎ 05-904778), on Rue Frères Meslem, is a one-star hotel that charges US$12 for a double with breakfast.

Just a couple of doors up from the Hôtel Port Said is the featureless two-star *Hôtel Mountazeh* (☎ 05-904828), at 12 Ave Ben Boulaid. Prices are the usual US$12/16 for singles/doubles.

The town's top-end place is the three-star *Hôtel el-Hidhab* (☎ 05-904043), in the north-eastern corner of the park, north of the museum.

## Places to Eat

There's a restaurant on either side of the entrance to the Hôtel Port Said. There are the usual pâtisseries all over the place, with the standard array of cakes and coffee.

## Getting There & Away

**Air** The Air Algérie (☎ 05-851818) and Air France (☎ 05-852230) offices are on Ave 8 Mai 1945.

**Bus** The bus station is south of Ave 1 Novembre 1954, 50 metres along the street which runs down beside the post office. There are daily connections to Algiers, Batna, Bejaia, Constantine and Ghardaia.

Buses for El-Ouelma, 17 km to the east, leave regularly from outside the railway station. The turn-off for Djemila is at El-Ouelma.

**Train** The railway station is another 150 metres from the bus station. Turn left past the bus station, and then take the second street on the right.

There are at least three trains daily to Algiers and Constantine.

**Hitching** The road to the north coast runs alongside the Byzantine ruins. It's about a two-km walk to the edge of the town along this road.

For Constantine, the best bet is to take a local bus from the railway station to El-Ouelma and then hitch from there.

## DJEMILA

This Roman site is really something. The setting is superb and the major buildings are remarkably well preserved.

The transport connections are good and it is easy enough to visit the ruins as a leisurely day trip, using Sétif as a base. There are a few spartan restaurants where you can get a bite to eat and a cold drink, and there is a hotel outside the entrance to the site.

As well as the ruins themselves, Djemila has an incredible museum which is absolutely overflowing with mosaics found on the site. The 10-metre-high walls are covered in them, and the effect is a bit overpowering.

The site is open daily from 7 am to 6 pm in summer, and until 5 pm in winter. The museum is open only from 9 am to noon and 2 to 5 pm; it's closed on Saturday.

### History

Ancient Cuicul was built as a military garrison on a narrow triangular plateau at the confluence of two rivers. The site was chosen largely because of the rich arable land surrounding it.

The town was built to the standard pattern of a forum at the centre with two main streets, the cardo maximus and the decumanus maximus, forming the major axes. During the reign of Caracalla in the 3rd century, however, the town's administrators pulled down some of the old ramparts and built a new forum, surrounding it with even bigger and more grandiose edifices.

The terrain so limited the building and expansion pattern that the theatre had to be

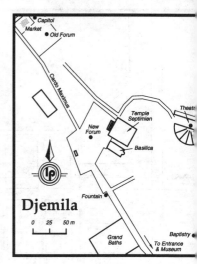

built *outside* the town walls – a very unorthodox move.

When Christianity became all the rage in the 4th century, a basilica and baptistry were built on the slope to the south of the town; they are among the major attractions of the ruins today.

### The Ruins

The **museum** is right by the entrance to the ruins. Inside, among other things, is a good model of the site; one of the attendants can point out the major features. The superb mosaics include depictions of gladiators doing battle with wild animals in an amphitheatre. There is also a very impressive collection of everyday items found during excavations. These simple artefacts, such as surgical instruments, door locks, glass and jewellery, give a much better insight into the life of these people than a hundred mosaics or marble statues ever could – fascinating stuff.

From the museum, the path down the slope is the haunt of unofficial guides and people selling bits of carved marble and other bits and pieces.

The new dome of the **baptistry** is visible

the right. The building is kept locked to ˻sure that the mosaics inside don't come to ˻y harm. It's a bit of a scramble down to the ˻ormous **Grand Baths**, which cover an ˻ea of over 2500 sq metres. The walls of ˻me rooms are still standing, and in places ˻ is possible to see the channels and pipes ˻hich carried the water and directed the ˻eam.

The road continues past a marble fountain ˻ the left to the **new forum**, officially called ˻ace Severus after the emperor Septimius ˻everus. The road to the west, spanned by ˻e highly decorative **Triumphal Arch** (built ˻ 216 AD and dedicated to the emperor ˻aracalla), was the road to Sétif. The ˻ecumanus maximus, to the north, was the ˻ad to Jijel; to the east, it led to Constantine, ˻hile the southern route was to Timgad.

The **Temple Septimien** stands on the ˻uth-eastern corner of the forum; in it were ˻und statues of Septimius Severus and his ˻yrian wife, Julia Domna.

The road leads downhill, past the town ˻rothel on the right (easily identifiable by the ˻hallic symbol carved in the stone by the ˻ntrance), to the **old forum**. There is a 3rd-˻entury altar in the centre; on the western ˻de, the bas-reliefs of the sacrificial animals ˻d a man with a mace are still amazingly ˻ear.

The **market** backs onto the forum and is ˻ntered through an arch on the cardo ˻aximus. This market is one of the delights ˻f Djemila. The tables for vendors around ˻e walls are still in position and, at about ˻oulder height in the wall which backs onto ˻e forum, there are six holes which used to ˻ld the poles for measuring scales. In front ˻f these is a small stone table with three ˻vities with holes in the bottom. These were ˻tandard measures for produce: the ˻urchaser's receptacle was placed under the ˻vity to collect the measurement of oil or ˻rain. The market was named after its ˻onator, Cosinius Primus.

Next to the market entrance on the cardo ˻aximus, under the civil basilica, is the old ˻wn prison.

The theatre, outside the original city walls, is set in the side of the valley, which is quite steep at this point.

### Places to Stay & Eat

There is a hotel right outside the entrance to the site. It charges US$10 for a double.

The township of Djemila has a few basic restaurants.

### Getting There & Away

Buses do run to Djemila but very infrequently, so you are much better off catching a taxi from El-Ouelma on the main Sétif-Constantine road. They operate frequently and cost about US$1.50 per person. Be warned that Friday is not a good day to see the ruins as there is very little traffic, especially in the afternoon. It is still possible, just a bit more difficult.

There is usually enough traffic to make hitching an option, at least on the stretch from Sétif to El-Ouelma.

From El-Ouelma, the taxis gather in a parking lot near the multistorey apartment blocks, 300 metres along the signposted road to Arbaoun and Djemila, just on the edge of town towards Sétif. The bus station is in a spare block on the other side of the apartment buildings, five minutes' walk away.

# Constantine

'An eagle's nest perched on the summit of a crag' was how Alexandre Dumas described Constantine when he travelled through here in the 19th century. A fit enough description.

The main part of the town is built on a neck of land with precipitous drops on one side to the plains below. On two other sides, the cliffs drop down into the Rhumel Gorge and rise equally sheerly on the other side, only 100 metres away.

The setting is stunning, especially with the four bridges across the gorge, all of different types. Closer inspection of the gorge, however, reveals a national disgrace – it has become little more than a massive rubbish dump. It is all too easy for residents of the medina to just chuck their rubbish over the edge; there is a Naftal service station which has its waste outlet on the edge of the cliff, so there is a dirty black stain right down one side at this point. In summer at least, the Oued Rhumel at the bottom is little more than a trickle of black water; with the higher rainfall in winter it's not so bad.

Pollution aside, this city of 600,000 inhabitants is well worth a visit, although there is little to see other than the gorge itself.

### History

The Punic town of Cirta Regia became the capital of Numidia. The Numidian king Massinissa, who reigned in the 2nd century BC, allied himself with the Romans in their battles against the Carthaginians.

Jugurtha, the grandson of the famous Massinissa, ended up doing battle with the Romans soon after the fall of Carthage and came off second best.

In the early years of the Christian era, the colonial Cirta became the capital of a confederation of cities in the region, and in the 2nd century AD it became a colony of Cuicul (Djemila) to the west. It grew to be one of the richest cities in Africa.

The town was destroyed after an uprising in 311. Its fortunes revived under the emperor Constantine and the city took on the name Constantina.

From the 8th century on, the city fell to various regional Islamic dynasties – the Fatimids, Zirids, Hammadids, Almohads and Hafsids. It was conquered again in the 16th century, by the Ottoman Turks (who were already based in Algiers), and became the important *beylik* of Qacentina.

The city finally fell to the French in 1837, on their second attempt to take it.

### Orientation

The city has two squares, Place des Martyrs and Place 1 Novembre. The latter is the main focus, and around it are the post office, theatre and banks; the hotel and restaurant area is right behind it. The square is always busy during the day but it takes on a slightly aggressive atmosphere at night, when all the

university students hang out with nothing t do and there is a strange air of expectancy.

The streets of the medina are narrow an congested and, due to the terrain, the trans port services are all some distance from th centre. The railway station is across th gorge (within easy walking distance), whil the bus station is a few km south of the city by the river.

Getting around on foot is no problem an in fact is the most interesting way to go.

### Information

**Tourist Office** There is a syndica d'initiative (☎ 04-93 2661) at 32 Rue Aban Ramdane, the street which runs uphill sout from Place des Martyrs.

**Money** There are a couple of banks on Plac 1 Novembre. The Banque National d'Algérie takes only cash. For travellers cheques, you need to go to the Banque Cen trale d'Algérie, just along Blvd Zighou Youssef.

**Post & Telecommunications** The pos office is one of the large edifices aroun Place 1 Novembre. The telephone office i adjacent to it and is open 24 hours.

**Foreign Consulates** The French consula (☎ 04-937602) is at 28 Blvd M Belouizda

**Sonacom** This national company, which i the spare-parts dealer for all foreign vehicle is at 2 Ave Bidi Louiza.

**Touring Club d'Algérie** There is an offic of the Touring Club d'Algérie (☎ 04 946129) at 6 Rue Zabaane.

**Hammam** If you need a shower there is good public douche on Rue Sidi Abdu Bouhroum, up near the Grill Room restau rant.

### City Views

For the best view of the city, walk along Blv Zighout Youssef from Place 1 Novembre This road takes you along the edge of th

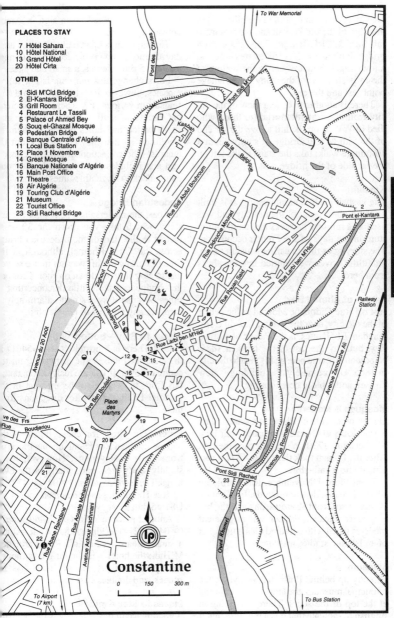

PLACES TO STAY

7  Hôtel Sahara
10  Hôtel National
13  Grand Hôtel
20  Hôtel Cirta

OTHER

1  Sidi M'Cid Bridge
2  El-Kantara Bridge
3  Grill Room
4  Restaurant Le Tassili
5  Palace of Ahmed Bey
6  Souq el-Ghazal Mosque
8  Pedestrian Bridge
9  Banque Centrale d'Algérie
11  Local Bus Station
12  Place 1 Novembre
14  Great Mosque
15  Banque Nationale d'Algérie
16  Main Post Office
17  Theatre
18  Air Algérie
19  Touring Club d'Algérie
21  Museum
22  Tourist Office
23  Sidi Rached Bridge

ALGERIA

Constantine

0    150    300 m

To War Memorial

To Airport
(7 km)

To Bus Station

Railway
Station

precipice, and winds around the cliff face to the edge of the old kasbah and the spectacular **Sidi M'Cid Bridge**. This suspension bridge, built in 1912, is 168 metres long and a towering 175 metres above the bottom of the gorge; it is one of the many good vantage points around the city.

There is another excellent view of the old city from the **war memorial** (to those who died in WW I) on the hill above the far end of the Sidi M'Cid Bridge. It's only about a 10-minute walk; take the stairs to the left on the far side of the bridge.

### Kasbah
The kasbah itself is uninteresting. It is built on the highest point of the old city and was used as a military barracks and ammunition store in the days of the French occupation. The story goes that in earlier Muslim times, unfaithful wives were hurled into the abyss from here.

### Palace of Ahmed Bey
Just off Rue Didouche Mourad in the centre of the old city, near the lively Place du Commandant El-Haouès, is the Palace of Ahmed Bey, built by the last of the beys in 1835. Napoleon III came here on his visit to the city in 1865. Unfortunately, the building is now disused and rapidly deteriorating.

### Mosques & Medersa
On the other side of Place du Commandant is the **Souq el-Ghazal Mosque**, built by a Moroccan in 1730 on the orders of the bey. After the French took the city in 1837 it was turned into a cathedral.

From Place 1 Novembre, Rue Larbi ben M'Hidi leads down towards El-Kantara Bridge. The **Great Mosque**, on the right, has a modern façade. Farther on, an ancient medersa faced with coloured tiles is now part of an Islamic studies institute.

### Museum
Directly up behind Place des Martyrs is the municipal museum, the large brown building at the top of the stairs. There is nothing in English to indicate that it is a museum, but it

has a big yellow-and-green sign in Arab above the entrance.

The museum is open daily, except Thur day afternoon and Friday, from 8 am to no and 2 to 5 pm. There is a small entry fee.

For a change this museum is not full mosaics; however, it is still jam-packed wi finds from various eras. There is an incred ble variety of stuff – there are even sna shells which had holes drilled in them b Neolithics so that they could suck out th innards! The collection of African coins vast and includes some unusual gold coin dating back to Byzantine times.

### Pedestrian Bridge
Just past the medersa is a passenger lift an stairs, which take you down the 30 or s metres to the start of the pedestrian bridg across the Oued Rhumel, although at th time of writing the lift was not in use so yo had to slog it up or down on foot. Crossin this bridge can be a little disconcerting a times because it sways quite alarmingly there are any number of people on it.

### Places to Stay – bottom end
**Hostel** There is a hostel (☎ 04-695461) i the Quartier Filali, some distance from th centre of town. If you are really keen, take bus from the centre to the mosque in th Quartier Filali, and ask for directions from there.

**Hotels** The street for cheap hotels is th narrow, cobbled Rue Hamloui, one block u from Place 1 Novembre. However, it's slightly seedy area, particularly in the eve nings. The *Hôtel National* (☎ 04-949437), 12 Rue Hamloui, has good clean rooms fo US$4/6, but no showers.

Another place to look is the *Hôtel Sahar* (☎ 04-943274) on Place Adjali Abderachid a small square leading off Rue Larbi be M'Hidi; the hotel is in the far left corner the square. This clean little hotel has n singles, and doubles cost US$6.

### Places to Stay – middle
A good place in this category is the one-sta

Grand Hôtel (☎ 04-943092) at 2 Rue Larbi en M'Hidi, right by Place 1 Novembre. It's typically French hotel, and none of the furniture or fittings look like they have been changed since independence. It's quite good value at US$7/10 for a single/double with bath and breakfast.

## Places to Stay – top end

If you can afford it, the place to stay is the grand old Hôtel Cirta (☎ 04-943033), at 1 Ave Achour Rachmani, right on the edge of Place des Martyrs. It is another remnant of the colonial era, with a grand entrance and typically overstated décor. Room rates are US$12/20 for singles/doubles with bath and breakfast.

## Places to Eat

Right at the very bottom of Rue Hamloui is small network of narrow streets, where you'll find a dozen or so snack eateries, all with their food on display. Just take a wander around and choose what you like. For something a bit more flash, try the Hôtel Cirta.

## Getting There & Away

**Air** Air Algérie (☎ 04-939211) has an enormous office at Place des Martyrs, right in the centre of town. Air France (☎ 04-936662) is at 8 Rue Abane Ramdane.

Constantine's 'Ain-el-Bey Airport is even km south of the city. There are flights to Algiers, Ghardaia, Oran, Tamanrasset and Tindouf.

**Bus** The bus station is a few km south of the centre, right by the river at the bottom of the ravine, which widens out considerably not far from the centre of town. It is known locally as sontavay, after the SNTV initials of the national bus company. The quickest way from the centre is a shared taxi from the bottom of the stairway between the Hôtel Cirta and the Touring Club d'Algérie, or on bus from the local bus station.

Because it is a major city, there are buses to just about anywhere, but the timetables are poorly displayed and the whole place is a bit of a shambles. Bookings should be made 24 hours in advance.

Destinations include Algiers, Annaba, El-Oued, Ghardaia, Jijel, Oran, Sétif and Tébessa.

**Train** It is about a 15-minute walk from the centre to the railway station, which is on the other side of the gorge. The most direct access is via the pedestrian footbridge.

Couchettes for the night train can (and should) be booked in advance; for other trains, just show up half an hour before departure.

There are five trains to Algiers every day, two to Skikda, two to Touggourt and one to Tunis (via Annaba).

**Taxi** Taxis also leave from the main bus station. There are departures for Algiers, Annaba, Sétif and Souq Ahras.

## Getting Around

**Bus** The city bus system has its main terminus just off to one side between Place des Martyrs and Place 1 Novembre.

The only buses you are likely to need are those to the bus station or the hostel.

**Taxi** Yellow taxis are everywhere and can be flagged down. Fare is by negotiation and should be established before you take off.

## AROUND CONSTANTINE
### Tiddis

Spectacularly situated some 30 km north of Constantine, the Roman site of Tiddis is well worth visiting. The only problem is that it's relatively inaccessible – you need your own vehicle, or you could charter a taxi for a half-day.

Named after the amazing red soil of the surrounding countryside, the ancient city of Tiddis is unusual in that it is located on the side of a fairly steep slope, so the Romans' usual penchant for dead-straight roads had to give way to practicality and the road here snakes up the side of the hill.

The ruins are quite extensive, the major features being the cisterns and water chan-

ALGERIA

nels. It seems that ancient Tiddis relied totally on rainwater, so almost every house and building had its own cistern for storing it.

From the car park, where a caretaker will miraculously appear and sell you a ticket, you come almost immediately to one of the more unusual sights in Tiddis, the Temple of Mithra, complete with the much-photographed carving of a large winged phallus.

It's worth taking the time to wander right through the ruins, as the unusual setting, and the red colouring of the soil, set them quite apart from anything else you'll see in North Africa. There's usually someone hanging about who will show you around the site – for a small fee. Look out for the cleft in the rock above the site which is like a walk-in sauna – hot, damp air comes up from the depths.

**Getting There & Away** The turn-off to Tiddis is signposted off to the left, 27 km north of Constantine along the Skikda road. From the main road it is seven km along a narrow bitumen road to the site. Access is not a problem at any time of year. If you don't have a vehicle, expect to pay at least US$25 return to charter a taxi from Constantine. Make it clear that you want to spend at least an hour at the ruins.

# Annaba

Set on one of Algeria's few coastal plains, Annaba is the fourth-largest city in the country, with a population of more than 500,000; it has a university and Algeria's third-largest port.

The heart of the city is the wide main street, Cours de la Révolution, and this broad avenue, with its central shady strip, is just so French it's ridiculous. It is also the focus of activity in the evenings, when the dozen or so pavement cafés and ice-cream kiosks which line the central strip come to life.

The city is ringed by hills. The skyline to the south-west is dominated by the incredi-

bly ugly Basilica of St Augustine, while th opposite direction boasts a full compleme of even uglier apartment blocks.

The city is a pleasant enough place i which to pass a day or two on the way to from Tunisia.

## History

The site of the Roman town of Hippo Regi is just to the south of town, and it was he that St Augustine was bishop for the 34 yea from 396 until his death during a Vand siege of the city in 430.

Augustine was a very influential figure early Christianity, and is now regarded one of the major writers and thinkers Christianity. His main work was *De Civita Dei* (The City of God).

Hippo Regius later became known Bona el-Hadida, and in French times this w shortened to Bône.

In the 16th century, the city was conquere by the corsair Barbarossa. It was brief occupied by the Spanish in the same centur

French troops moved into the town 1832, and the town was bombarded by th Germans during WW I. In WW II, it was a operational base for the Allied armies Britain and the USA – and was bombe heavily again during the winter of 1942-43

## Information

**Tourist Office** As the city is virtually devoi of both tourist attractions and tourists, there even less motivation to visit the tourist offic here than in other cities. If you can't hel yourself, the office is behind the Grand Hôt d'Orient on Rue Tarik ibn Zaid and is ope from 8 am to noon and 2 to 6 pm.

**Money** There are banks on Cours de Révolution and around the corner on Place Mai.

**Post Office** The main post office is on Av Zighout Youssef, the extension of Cours d la Révolution.

**Foreign Consulates** The French consula (☎ 08-826391) is at Rue Gouta Sebti; th

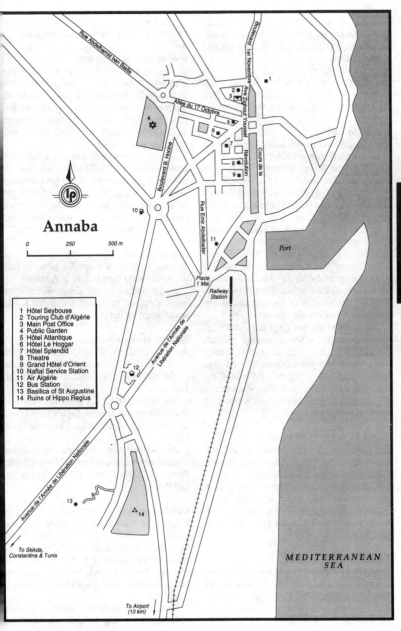

ALGERIA

## Annaba

0     250     500 m

1  Hôtel Seybouse
2  Touring Club d'Algérie
3  Main Post Office
4  Public Garden
5  Hôtel Atlantique
6  Hôtel Le Hoggar
7  Hôtel Splendid
8  Theatre
9  Grand Hôtel d'Orient
10 Naftal Service Station
11 Air Algérie
12 Bus Station
13 Basilica of St Augustine
14 Ruins of Hippo Regius

Rue Abdelhamid ben Badis

Boulevard 1er Novembre

Allée du 17 Octobre

Ave Zighout Youssef

Boulevard B. Hoche

Cours de la Révolution

Rue Emir Abdelkader

Port

Place 1 Mai

Railway Station

Avenue de l'Armée de Libération Nationale

Avenue de l'Armée de Libération Nationale

To Skikda,
Constantine & Tunis

MEDITERRANEAN
SEA

To Airport
(10 km)

Tunisian consulate (☎ 08-820666) is at 23 Rue Gouasmi Ammar and the Italian consulate (☎ 08-709707) is at 8 Rue Mohammed Tahar Rkhaya.

**Touring Club d'Algérie** The Touring Club d'Algérie (☎ 08-826461) office is at 1 Ave Zighout Youssef, right next to the post office.

### Things to See

There's very little to see, really. The **Basilica of St Augustine** is a 30-minute walk to the south, out past the bus station. It is not really a thing of beauty and is on a par with the one at Carthage in Tunisia. It was built at the turn of the century, and is open from 8.30 to 11.30 am and 2.30 to 4.30 pm.

To find your way up, take the street to the left of the factory on the far side of the roundabout by the bus station. At the far end of the factory is a street to the right and this takes you up to the top. The best part about the walk up to the basilica is not the basilica itself but the view, with the port and lovely apartment blocks in the distance.

The ruins of **Hippo Regius** (also called Hippone) are at the foot of the hill beneath the basilica. The entrance is 300 metres along from the roundabout by the bus station. The site is open on Wednesday, Thursday and Friday, and there's not really all that much to see. The museum is the white building on the small hill.

### Places to Stay – bottom end

The *Hôtel du Théâtre* is just around the corner from the Hôtel Atlantique. Rooms cost US$8 and are quite adequate.

Farther up the scale, and good value, is the one-star *Hôtel Atlantique* on Allée du 17 Octobre, 50 metres off the main street. Breakfast is included in the price of US$16 for a double.

### Places to Stay – middle

There are a couple of two-star places around a small square just off Cours de la Révolution. The *Hôtel Le Hoggar* needs to have improved out of all recognition to be worth trying.

The hotel farther up towards Allée du 17 Octobre on the same side is a better bet.

### Places to Stay – top end

On the main street is the *Grand Hôtel d'Orient* (☎ 08-822051), which is left over from colonial days and still has all the period touches like chandeliers and a grand piano in the café. It is right next to the theatre. Expect to pay about US$24 for double rooms, plus breakfast and douche.

Top of the range is the *Hôtel Seybouse International* (☎ 08-822409), on Rue 24 Février 1966 (the date of the foundation of the UGTA trade union), where you'll pay closer to US$60 for a double. The main reason you are likely to want to come here is to change money outside banking hours.

### Places to Eat

There's nothing very special here; in fact good meals are hard to find in Annaba.

In the middle of the Cours de la Révolution there are cafés and ice-cream kiosks which open up in the evenings.

### Getting There & Away

**Air** Air Algérie (☎ 08-820020) has an office at 2 Cours de la Révolution. The Air France (☎ 08-826666) office is at 8 Rue Prosper-Dubourg.

The airport is 12 km from the centre of town. There are regular flights to Algiers, Béchar, El-Oued, Ghardaia, Oran and Ouargla.

Air Algérie also operates international flights from Annaba to Lyons, Marseilles and Paris, while Air France flies to Marseilles and Paris.

**Bus** The bus station is one km along Ave de l'Armée de Libération Nationale from the centre – it's about a 20-minute walk. From the outside the station looks very modern and efficient but inside is pretty dirty and gloomy. The ticket windows are upstairs, and a timetable of arrivals and departures is displayed.

Most long-distance trips can be booked in advance, but trying to find out when the cket window is open can be an exercise in ersistence.

There is a daily departure to Tunis at 5 am or the eight-hour journey. Tickets for this ervice definitely have to be bought in dvance, particularly in summer.

Other destinations include Algiers, Con-tantine, El-Oued, Ghardaia, Ouargla, Souq Ahras and Tébessa.

**Train** The railway station is right in the centre on Place 1 Mai. It is in fact closed most of the time and only opens up when there is a train arriving or departing. If you need information, there are offices around the left-hand side of the station.

There are services to Algiers (10½ hours), Constantine (three hours) and Tébessa (five hours). The Trans Maghreb Express (aka Al-Maghreb al-Arabi) leaves for Tunis (8½ hours) at 8.20 am.

**Taxi** There are long-distance taxis to Con-stantine for US$6, leaving from a couple of blocks west of the hotel area – just ask around.

**Sea** Tickets for the ferries to Marseilles can be bought at the CNAN (☎ 08-825555) office on Cours de la Révolution, in the next block up from the theatre. The ferry port is right in the centre of town.

There are sailings about four times a month in summer to Marseilles, dropping to two per month in winter. The journey takes about 23 hours.

## EL-KALA

From Annaba the road heads inland before joining the coast again at El-Kala, a beautiful small town hemmed in against the sea by the forested mountains of the Kala National Park.

The beach here is fairly reasonable and the town is a minor summer resort for holidaying Algerians.

### Places to Stay

It may be possible to camp on the beach in the summer months at Plage de la Messida, 10 km to the east.

The town has the two-star *Hôtel el-Morjane* (☎ 08-820242), which is not especially cheap at US$16 for a double with breakfast. The *Hôtel de Post* has also been recommended.

### Getting There & Away

There are regular buses and taxis for Annaba. A shared taxi to the Tunisian border costs about US$1.

It is possible to hitch from El-Kala to Tabarka, the first town on the Tunisian Med-iterranean coast. There is less traffic along the road which heads up through the moun-tains and across the Tunisian border at Babouch. The best way to get along this road is to catch the daily Annaba-Tunis bus. It is not possible to pick the bus up en route.

### SOUQ AHRAS

This town is built in rugged country and is the last large town before the Tunisian border. There is really no reason to stop here, but if you get stuck there is the one-star *Hôtel d'Orient*.

The bus station is at the top of the hill, on the road to Annaba and about 15 minutes' walk from the centre.

The only train through here each day is the Trans Maghreb Express from Tunis to Algiers.

# Aurès Mountains

These mountains are part of the Algerian Saharan Atlas range, which is an extension of the Moroccan Atlas. The entire Atlas range runs south-west to north-east clear across Algeria into Tunisia.

The ruins of Roman Thamugadi, or Timgad, some 40 km east of the unexciting provincial capital of Batna, are the area's main attraction.

Between Batna on the northern side of the mountains and Biskra on the south, two roads wind through some spectacular country. The northern route is the faster of the two and has more transport, while the southern one is the more interesting, due mainly to the spectacular gorges of the Oued el-Abiod and the local mud-brick villages.

Biskra is an important regional centre and is really the gateway to the desert in this part of the country.

The people of the Aurès are Chaouias, a Berber tribe who, along with the Kabylies farther north, have retained their original language and culture.

## BATNA

There is not really much of interest in Batna. It's a convenient base for visiting Timgad. The setting of the town in a wide valley is pleasant, and the altitude of over 1000 metres keeps the air clear and the temperatures bearable. Batna also boasts one of the biggest collections of the ugly apartment blocks which blot the skylines of most Algerian towns.

### Information

The tourist office is on the main street, Ave de l'Indépendance.

The banks and the post office are in the compact central area, about five minutes' walk from the bus station.

There are public showers for men and women just around the corner from the Hôtel Laverdure, towards the bus station.

### Places to Stay – bottom end

There are a few cheapies here charging about US$8 for a double. The rooms are a bit on the small side at the *Hôtel Laverdure* (☎ 04-551163), which is at 3 Ave de l'Indépendance, only a couple of minutes' walk from the bus station. From the bus station, go straight on past the fountain roundabout and take the first street on the left; the hotel is on the right above a café.

The *Hôtel Es-Salaam* (☎ 04-556847), at 10 Ave de l'Indépendance, has no sign in English but it has a distinctive black-tiled entrance. There are no showers.

### Places to Stay – middle

The best bet in this category is the *Hôtel el-Hayat* (☎ 04-552601), at 18 Rue Mohammed Salah Benabbes, about five minutes' walk from the bus station. The rooms are well appointed, if a bit small, and are centrally heated in winter. To find the hotel, head down the hill along Ave de la République from the Air Algérie office and post office; the hotel is on the edge of the small square which you come across after a couple of blocks. At No 10 Ave de la République is the *Hôtel Karim* (☎ 04-558981), which has good rooms – plus bath, if you so desire. Both places charge about US$14 for a double.

### Places to Eat

For a standard local meal there's a number of places near the Hôtel el-Hayat and the market. For something a bit better, try the *Restaurant Kimel*, on Ave de l'Indépendance where it crosses the small oued in the centre of town.

### Getting There & Away

**Air** The Air Algérie (☎ 04-552665) office is near the post office, about five minutes' walk from the bus station.

**Bus** The enormous bus station is right in the centre of town in a spot where one would normally expect to find the town hall or some other public building. There is a big government supermarket opposite the station, and next to it is a large roundabout, complete with fountain.

Timetables are displayed inside the station, and tickets can be bought in advance for longer journeys. There are daily departures to Algiers, Annaba, Biskra and Constantine.

For Timgad, there are four regional buses daily which drop you off right at the entrance to the ruins. The Timgad buses leave from the small yard behind the supermarket directly opposite the bus station. The trip takes 40 minutes and costs about US$1.

**Train** The railway station is on the edge of

town, a 15-minute walk from the centre along Ave de la République. There are two trains daily to both Constantine and Biskra (with connections on to Touggourt).

**Taxi** The taxi station is a couple of blocks from the bus station, in the opposite direction to the fountain. There are departures to all surrounding towns (including Timgad) and to Algiers.

**Hitching** Batna is a difficult place to hitch out of because there is a ring road around the city and the through-traffic doesn't come anywhere near the centre of town.

From the centre, it's about a 30-minute walk to the outskirts in the direction of Constantine, and a similar distance to the south for Biskra.

## TIMGAD

The old Roman town of Thamugadi is 40 km east of Batna in rolling countryside. Even in midsummer the temperature here is mild, and walking around is a pleasure rather than an endurance test.

The ruins are unusual in that the desert sands have perfectly preserved everything up to a height of about half a metre. From there up there is little left, but the result is that the layout of the town and the buildings is exceptionally clear. Well worth a day trip from Batna.

The entrance to the site is just one block from the main road. If you come on the bus it drops you close to the gate. The site is open every day from 9 am to 5 pm, and the museum is open from 9 am to noon and 2 to 5 pm; both are closed Saturday and Wednesday morning. There is a small entry fee.

### History

The town was founded during the reign of Trajan in the 1st century AD as a place where retired legionnaires were given land.

The town prospered during the Roman era but was destroyed by Berbers during a revolt in the 6th century. It was rebuilt in part by the Byzantines, only to be destroyed again during the Arab invasion.

### The Ruins

The **museum** is just inside the entrance, on the left. The display of mosaics is not too overpowering, but the other exhibits, although good, are poorly labelled.

The exhibits include an extraordinary array of bits and pieces from everyday life, which give a very vivid idea of how the people used to live. There are items such as jewellery, geometrical and surgical instruments, coins, locks and keys, clothes pins made from bone, and an amazing glob of barely recognisable gold coins which were fused in a fire.

The town itself was small, covering an area of only about 12 hectares. On the right, past the museum and outside the town limits, are the **Grand North Baths**, an 80 by 66 metre complex which had more than 30 rooms.

Once through the north gate, with its rutted paving where the chariot wheels have worn away the stone, the cardo leads up the slope and passes the **library** on the left. This has columns and a semicircular room; the paved floor is still intact, apart from a couple of slabs which have been removed to make way for lighting (which looks like it hasn't worked for years).

The cardo meets the decumanus maximus at a T-junction. The left-hand turning leads past the east market on the right (up a few stairs). At the end of the street, on the left before the Mascula Gate, are the east baths, which were erected in 146 AD.

To the right of the T-junction, the decumanus maximus leads to the main monument, **Trajan's Arch**. It was built early in the 3rd century and marks the western extremity of Trajan's town. Once again, the stones in the roadway are deeply rutted.

Outside the gate, on the right, is a small temple (dedicated to the 'genius of the colony'); the Market of Sertius on the left is named after the official who provided the money for its construction.

Farther up to the left past the market is the **capitol**, built on a high point – again, like the baths, outside the town limits. It was built late in the 2nd century on a large platform,

ALGERIA

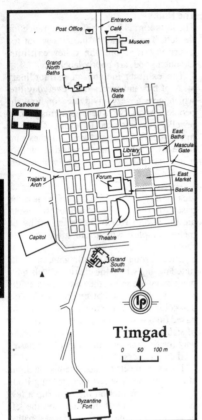

Timgad

0    50    100 m

walls are over 2.5 metres thick and enclose an area 110 metres long and 70 metres wide. Inside, the rooms and other structures are still remarkably well preserved. To the right through the entrance is a pool, and a terrace which still has the brick paving tiles in place.

The **theatre**, back in the centre of the town, could seat 3500 people. It now has modern additions for the performances held here every May.

The forum lies almost directly opposite the end of the cardo.

### Places to Stay & Eat

The two hotels right outside the entrance to the site – the *Hôtel & Restaurant Timgad* and the *Hôtel el-Kahina* are both reportedly closed due to lack of patrons. It's best to assume they're still closed and settle for a day trip from Batna.

There's a small kiosk at the site entrance which does snack meals and drinks. Otherwise there are a couple of standard local restaurants on the main street of the town.

### Getting There & Away

**Bus** Four buses make the 40-minute trip to Batna daily. They leave from the main street, 100 metres from the entrance to the ruins.

**Taxi** Taxis run most frequently from near the entrance to the town, about 10 minutes' walk from the ruins, and cost about US$1.50.

### OUED EL-ABIOD

The gorges of the Oued el-Abiod are worth seeing, either as a day trip from Batna, or en route from Batna to Biskra or vice versa. Three roads connect the two towns. The northern one (Route N3) goes through some spectacular country, including the steep gap in the ranges, the Défilé, near the village of El-Kantara. This is the route taken by the Batna-Biskra buses.

The central route (W54) is a minor road and has little of interest.

The southern route (N31) is by far the most spectacular but is not as well served by public transport. The Oued el-Abiod runs north-east to south-west alongside the road,

along the front of which is a row of small columns. The temple itself was enormous and there was a flight of 28 steps leading up to the entrance. It originally had six 14-metre-high columns, two of which have been reconstructed. The size of these columns really sinks in when you see just how big the pieces of the fallen ones are.

There's a good view over the entire site from the small hill just near the capitol. The Grand South Baths lie a bit farther over to the east. Three hundred metres south along a rough track is a large **Byzantine fort**, built in 539 during the reign of Justinian. The

and there are a few viewing points along the way. The best scenery is between **Arris** and **M'Chouneche**, and the village of **Rhoufi** is in the middle of this stretch, just off the road 90 km from Batna. The view into the gorge from here is magnificent, with the palm trees in the bottom and the old village of Rhoufi. Take the signposted 'Circuit Touristique' which takes you right out to the edge of the cliffs to the Balcon de Rhoufi – it's a couple of km walk or drive.

It's possible to visit Rhoufi as a day trip from Biskra, as there are infrequent buses and shared taxis. It's not possible from Batna, however, as the buses stop at Arris, and the route winds precariously up over an 1800-metre pass, and so takes quite a while. When coming from Batna, however, the change in the scenery and vegetation is quite dramatic – from quite heavily timbered hills in marginal agricultural land you pass through a narrow cleft and suddenly you're amongst completely barren hills and, if you're heading farther south, you won't see many more trees (apart from date palms) until the other side of the Sahara.

### Walking the Gorges

For the more adventurous types, the Oued el-Abiod gorges lend themselves perfectly to exploration on foot. If you are self-sufficient with food and sleeping gear, it is possible to trek along the gorge from Rhoufi to Biskra in four days. See the aside below for a traveller's account of a trek in the area.

### Places to Stay

There is no accommodation in either Arris or Rhoufi, the two towns on the routes, although there is the *Hôtel el-Kahina* at M'Chouneche, 37 km north of Biskra on the southern route. A double room here costs US$16 with breakfast, and this place also has a restaurant.

**ALGERIA**

---

### Walking the Gorges

We set off south from Rhoufi late one afternoon, having hitched up from Biskra the same day. The gorge is beautiful, with steep red walls, clinging to which are the ruins of old mud-brick villages which run for around 15 km. It is worth setting out around noon so you can sleep the first night in one of these villages.

We stopped in a village at dusk. It was completely deserted so we chose a house to stay in, making sure it wasn't about to collapse. We built a fire upstairs on the terrace overlooking the valley – what a view!

The next morning we walked along a path halfway up the gorge wall. The gorge itself got deeper and deeper, much like the Grand Canyon in appearance, and there were no signs of life. After around four hours' walking there was a gully which we scrambled down, and this got us to the river at the bottom. After another three hours the gorge opened out into the beautiful oasis of Baniane. There were a few more ruins at the northern end of the oasis, but the southern end is better for camping. After a night sleeping out in the oasis, we headed south again, following the riverbed, although there is also a track along the side. There are fantastic views over the plains to the south from here, and after about five hours you find yourself looking over another beautiful oasis – M'Chouneche. We lashed out on the Hôtel el-Kahina here after our two nights of roughing it.

On the fourth day, we set out on the last part of the gorge to the artificial lake on the edge of the Sahara. Again, it was a matter of walking (and wading) along the riverbed, or taking a track along the side of the gorge. After three hours the gorge ended at a small oasis, and after another hour we reached the lake shore. We hitched back to Biskra with no problems.

The walk was a highlight of my time in Algeria, and was well worth the effort. Logistically, there are supplies available in Rhoufi, Baniane and M'Chouneche; otherwise bring everything from Biskra. We drank the water from the oued after treating it. It gets cold at night but it's still possible to sleep out with just a sleeping bag. The best time to walk the gorge is September/October – in winter and spring there would be too much water in the river; in summer it's just too damned hot.

**Chris Barton, UK** ∎

## Getting There & Away

There is only one bus between Batna and Biskra along the southern road, and it leaves Biskra at 5 am! Buses from Batna go as far as Arris, but there are then buses and taxis to Biskra and the villages en route. Traffic along this road is fairly light.

## BISKRA

This is the beginning of the desert and is the first of the real oasis towns, although those farther south are much more interesting.

There is really no reason to stop here but if you want to stay the night there are a few choices. The town's most 'famous' attraction is the thermal baths, Hammam Salihine, a couple of km from the centre. This is a vast complex with baths and other activities. It's hardly worth the effort – a bath in very sulphurous hot water costs a couple of dollars.

The small local tourist office (☎ 04-713712, 712336) at 37 Ave de la République has an information booklet and map for sale.

## Places to Stay – bottom end

**Camping** The *Touring Club d'Algérie* (☎ 04-712864) runs a site south of the *palmeraie* (an oasis-like area) near the small village of Bab ed-Darb.

**Hostel** The *Biskra Hostel* (☎ 04-713222) is in an excellent location, right in the centre at 12 Ave Emir Abdelkader. The only drawback is that it is closed on Friday. A bed in a dormitory costs US$2.50.

**Hotels** Biskra has a couple of cheap places which cost around US$6/10 for singles/doubles. The best bet is the *Hôtel Chaoui*, just off the main street, Ave Emir Abdelkader, close to the fancy Hôtel Guendouz. The rooms are large and airy. The hotel has no showers, but there are two public douches very close by. There are a couple of other cheapies in the same street.

## Places to Stay – middle

The *Hôtel du Palmier* is at 23 Ave Hakim Saadane, the main street which crosses Ave Emir Abdelkader near the post office. It charges US$12/16 for a single/double with bath and breakfast. The prices are not much higher at the *Hôtel Guendouz* (☎ 04-71 5769), in the centre of town at 39 Ave Emir Abdelkader.

## Places to Eat

There are plenty of local restaurants in the small streets around the Hôtel Chaoui; a good one is the *Délices du Minaret*. The more expensive hotels also have more expensive restaurants.

## Getting There & Away

**Air** The Air Algérie (☎ 04-712371) office is on Ave Ben Badis. There is a daily flight at 3.30 pm connecting Biskra with the capital. There are also flights to Adrar, Ghardaia and Tamanrasset

**Bus** The bus station is in the north of the town, about 300 metres' walk north along the main street. It is a modern complex, complete with hotel, restaurant and separate waiting rooms for men and women.

There is a timetable displayed above the ticket windows and there are regular departures for Algiers, Batna, Constantine, El-Oued, Ghardaia, In Amenas, Ouargla and Touggourt.

**Train** There are twice-daily trains to Constantine (four hours) and Touggourt (4½ hours).

**Taxis** The large shared-taxi depot is right by the bus station. There are departures for Algiers, Batna, Bou Saada, Constantine, El-Oued and Touggourt.

For taxis to Rhoufi and Arris along the Oued el-Abiod road, the depot is at the southern end of Emir Abdelkader, about 200 metres from the post office and 100 metres before it crosses the very wide oued.

# High Plateau

The central High Plateau lies to the west of the Aurès Mountains and also forms part of the Saharan Atlas range. It's a fairly barren area as it is right on the fringe of the Sahara itself. The main towns of the region are Laghouat (pronounced 'Larouat') and Bou-Saada. The former lies on the main N1 route, about 400 km from Algiers, and is the first Saharan town you come across on the route south. Bou-Saada is set among barren hills and during colonial times was something of a weekend getaway from Algiers.

## LAGHOUAT

As mentioned, this is the first real desert town you come across on the route south. It has few attractions but there are good views of the town and surrounding oasis from the small Marabout of Sidi Mohammed ben Abdelkader and from the Great Mosque; both are on the ridge of a small hill which bisects the town.

There is a bank and post office on the main street, Ave de l'Indépendance.

The main N1 highway skirts the town to the west.

### Places to Stay

**Hostel** The hostel (☎ 09-723980) is signposted about 500 metres south of the bus station. A bed costs US$2. Sheets, like breakfast, cost more.

**Hotels** The choices here are strictly limited. The only cheapie is the *Hôtel Sayah* (☎ 09-723063), close to the Hôtel Marhaba, with singles/doubles for US$6/8. There are no showers, but there is a hammam on the ground floor.

The only other hotel is the three-star *Hôtel Marhaba* (☎ 09-724667), at the northern end of the main street. It is well set out and all rooms have a balcony overlooking the swimming pool. Your US$15/20 gets a room with bath, air-conditioning, fridge and breakfast.

### Places to Eat

Laghouat has surprisingly few restaurants. Just a short way along from the Hôtel Marhaba is the *Restaurant du Soleil Rouge*. Otherwise, the choice is limited to a couple of greasy chicken-and-chips joints on the main street, or a splash-out meal at the Hôtel Marhaba.

### Getting There & Away

**Air** The Air Algérie (☎ 09-722090) office is on Ave de l'Indépendance.

**Bus & Taxi** The bus and taxi station is right on the western edge of the town, close to the ring road. It's about one km from the centre, so you may need to catch a No 3 local bus from the roundabout at the bus station, or from opposite the Hôtel Marhaba in the town centre.

There are direct buses to Aflou, Algiers, Ghardaia and Oran, and many others call in en route to places such as Constantine.

Shared taxis run to Algiers, Djelfa, Ghardaia and Tiaret.

## BOU-SAADA

Although it's not worth a special detour, the oasis town of Bou-Saada has a spectacular setting in amongst barren hills on the edge of the Sahara. The Oued Bou Saada flows south to north along the eastern edge of the town in a deep gorge, lined along the bottom and sides with small terraces which form the basis of the oasis.

The town had its heyday during the French days, when it became popular as a weekend getaway because of the mineral springs of Moulin Ferrero, about two km south of town along the oued. All that remains of the spa centre are the ruins of the building, by a small waterfall. It's worth the wander from the town to have a look.

The focus of the town centre is the shady Place des Martyrs, and close by you'll find a bank, post office and the town's restaurants.

### Places to Stay

**Hostel** The hostel (☎ 05-544945) is about

500 metres from the centre of town near the bus station; US$2 for a bed.

**Hotels** Unfortunately, there has been no more news from the amazing *Hôtel Transat* since Lonely Planet author Hugh Finlay had this experience in 1989:

This place has to be seen to be believed! At one stage it must have been quite a comfortable hotel; these days it's a wreck. Nothing has been spent on maintenance in years and to look at the outside you'd never know the place was still functioning. The map in the lobby is a 1942 War Office publication.

Rooms still cost US$8/12 with bath, but there's cold water only and plumbing which floods the room. The toilets in the place are utterly disgusting; they're totally unusable – the worst I've seen in years of travelling on three continents. Add to this the fact that the nearby mosque gives an amazingly loud call at the usual early hour in the morning and you have the ideal place to stay!

The only other place is the *Hôtel le Caid* (☎ 05-544394), also near the bus station. This is a good three-star hotel complete with swimming pool and restaurant. Rooms cost US$20/30 with breakfast.

### Places to Eat
The best restaurants are right on Place des Martyrs.

### Getting There & Away
The bus station is 15 minutes' walk from the centre. There are regular departures for Algiers, Biskra, Constantine, El-Oued, Ghardaia, Oran and Sétif, although many of these just pass through en route and there's no guarantee of a seat.

Shared taxis leave from just up the hill from the Place des Martyrs. There are departures for Biskra, Djelfa and M'Sila.

# North-West Algeria

Apart from the city of Tlemcen (the capital of the central Maghreb for three centuries from the 12th century), the area to the west of Algiers has little to interest visitors.

The coast has some beaches but there is little accommodation, while the interior is just a collection of nondescript industrial and dormitory towns.

## Tlemcen

More so than any other city in northern Algeria, Tlemcen is a curious blend of Islamic and French-colonial architecture. The city's mosques are the country's finest, while the main tree-lined square with the town hall on one side is very European. Tlemcen's altitude of 830 metres makes it just that little bit cooler than the coastal plains.

### History

Although the area around Tlemcen was occupied from prehistoric times, it was only after the Arab invasion that things began to get interesting. Idriss I established a town here (called Agadir) late in the 8th century.

It wasn't until the 11th century that Tlemcen itself was founded by the Almoravid Youssef bin Tachfin, who named it Tagrart ('the camp'); it was under Almoravid rule that the Great Mosque was built.

The town became the capital of the central Maghreb and reached its peak under the Berber Abd al-Wadids, or Zianids, whose leader, Yaghmoracen, founded a dynasty here in 1236. The city thrived on the trans-Saharan trade and became an important link between Black Africa and Europe.

The Zianids' Berber cousins, the Merenids, ruled in Morocco and the rivalry between the two was the only threat to Tlemcen's prosperity. The Merenids fought for control of the city three times and each time occupied it briefly.

The first siege came at the end of the 13th century. It was during this siege that the Merenids built the walled city of Mansourah on the western outskirts of the city, under the leadership of Abu Yacoub. The second and third sieges took place in 1337 and 1353.

The decline in power of the Zianids in the 15th century saw the control of the city oscillate between the Merenids in the west and the Hafsids of Tunis in the east. The Spanish had settled in Oran and they too were an interested party, but it was the Turks from Algiers who, in 1555, finally were able to overrun Tlemcen.

The city went into a long decline over the next three centuries, and at the time of the French occupation of Algiers in 1830 Tlemcen was divided once again. This time the Turks and Kouloughlis (an important ethnic minority descended from Turkish men and local women) sided with the French, while the Moors and Berbers favoured union with the Alawite sultans of Morocco. The French won out, and in 1842 Tlemcen officially became part of French Algeria.

Tlemcen was an important centre in the nationalist movement. Before the French takeover, Abdelkader was very active in the area; and in 1924 the city saw the foundation by Ahmed Messali Hadj of the MTLD (Mouvement pour le Triomphe des Libertés Démocratiques), the forerunner of the FLN.

### Information

**Tourist Office** The tourist office (☎ 07-203456) is on Ave Commandant Farradj, just near the entrance to the mechouar (royal assembly place).

**Money** There are banks all over the centre, the main one being the Banque Centrale d'Algérie, next to the post office.

Outside banking hours, it may be possible

ALGERIA

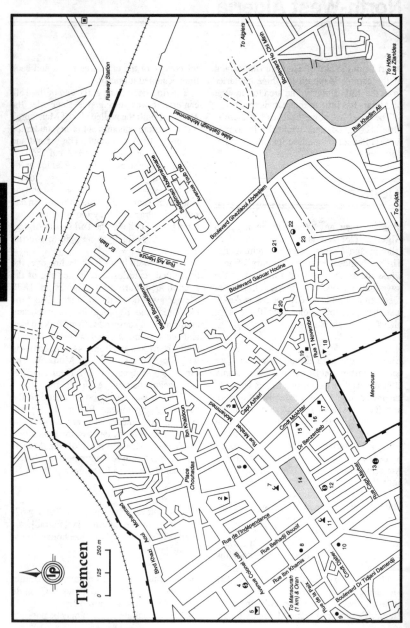

Tlemcen
0    125    250 m

## PLACES TO STAY

- 3 Hôtel el-Menzeh
- 16 Hôtel Majestic
- 17 Hôtel Maghreb
- 19 Hôtel Moderne

## PLACES TO EAT

- 2 Snack Shop
- 15 Restaurant
- 18 Restaurant du Coupole

## OTHER

- 1 Tomb of Sidi Yacoub
- 4 Banque Centrale d'Algérie
- 5 Post Office
- 6 Market
- 7 Great Mosque
- 8 Public Showers
- 9 Air Algérie
- 10 Air France
- 11 Sidi Bel Hassan Mosque
- 12 Banque Nationale d'Algérie
- 13 Tourist Office
- 14 Place Emir Abdelkader
- 20 Hammam
- 21 Local Buses
- 22 Bus Station
- 23 CNAN

to change money at the four-star Hôtel Les Zianides.

**Post & Telecommunications** The post office is in the main street, the tree-lined Ave Colonel Lotfi. It is open Saturday to Wednesday from 8 am to 6.30 pm and on Thursday from 8 am to 4 pm. The telephone office is at the rear of the building.

**Market** Tlemcen has an excellent produce market just off the central Place Emir Abdelkader.

### Place Emir Abdelkader

Place Emir Abdelkader is very much the centre of the city and is very pleasant with its fountain and cafés. On the southern side of the square is the town hall, which dates back to 1843.

### Great Mosque

The Great Mosque was built by the Almoravid Ali ben Youssef in 1135 and was later added to by the Zianid sultan Abu Ibrahim ben Yahia Yaghmoracen, who was responsible for the polychrome-tiled minaret. Tradition has it that Yaghmoracen is buried in the mosque. All the other Zianid sultans are buried in the domed *koubba* (sanctuary) in the south-western corner of the mosque, which is visible from the square.

### Sidi Bel Hassan Mosque

At the western end of Place Emir Abdelkader is the small Sidi Bel Hassan Mosque, which is now the **Museum of Antiquities**. The mosque itself was built in honour of Yaghmoracen at the end of the 13th century. It is named after a famous theologian who taught here in the early 14th century.

### Mansourah

About a km to the west of town are the ruins of ancient Mansourah. The four km of walls date from around the end of the 13th century and mark the perimeter of the walled Merenid town, which covered an area of about 100 hectares. The only ruins left inside the walls are the minaret and the mosque. Of the minaret, only three sides are left standing and even these were restored in the late 19th century. On the inside you can see where the stairs once led up to the top.

Mansourah was only used during the

Example of Merenid architecture

ALGERIA

Merenid invasions; after that time it was deserted and became a handy source of building materials for structures in Tlemcen.

### Mosque & Tomb of Sidi Bou Mediène
In the opposite direction from Mansourah, two km east of the centre of Tlemcen, is the mosque and tomb of Sidi Bou Mediène, also known as El-Eubbad. It is an important example of Merenid architecture.

Sidi Bou Mediène, a mystic born in Spain who taught in Seville, Fès and Bejaia, died here on his way from Bejaia to Marrakesh. His real name was Ibn Hussein el-Andalousi, but his surname was Bou Mediène el-Ghouts and from this came his popular name. It is no coincidence that the name is remarkably similar to that of the former president of Algeria: in 1956, Mohammed Boukharouba took on the name Houari Boumedienne in honour of the famous teacher.

The present koubba was built in 1339, but the original decoration suffered during restorations in the 18th century. With its bronze-clad cedar doors and cupola with stalactites, the monumental porch to the mosque is as fine as you'll see anywhere in the Maghreb.

To get there, walk out along the road to the left above the Hôtel Les Zianides.

### Places to Stay – bottom end
**Camping** The *Camping Municipale* is situated amongst the olive groves at Mansourah, a good 20-minute walk from the centre of town. Its facilities are extremely basic.

**Hotels** For such a large town, the accommodation is surprisingly limited. The pick of the very small bunch is the *Hôtel Majestic* (☎ 07-260766), on the shady Place Cheikh Bahir Ibrahimi, one block south-east of Place Emir Abdelkader. It is the grey building on the corner. Rooms cost US$7/11 for singles/doubles, but couples pay only for a single. There are no showers.

The *Hôtel Moderne* (☎ 07-208796), at 20 Rue 1 Novembre, is a good deal cheaper at US$4.50 for a single (no doubles), but it is a bit gloomy. The *Hôtel el-Menzeh*, near the

junction of Rue Mrabet Mohammed and Capt Azhari, also sounds promising with singles/doubles for US$7/9.

### Places to Stay – middle
The *Hôtel Agadir* (☎ 07-262149) is the best value in this bracket. The Agadir is minutes from the centre of town at 19 Rue Khedim Ali, and charges US$11/15 for singles/doubles with shower and breakfast.

The *Hôtel Maghreb* (☎ 07-263571), on Place Commandant Farradj, just along from the Hôtel Majestic, charges around US$17 for a single, although there have been reports of people being charged much more.

### Places to Stay – top end
By all accounts, the *Hôtel Les Zianides* (☎ 07-267118) is not worth the US$20/28 it wants for a single/double with breakfast. The building also happens to be a charmless monolith in an inconvenient location, 10 minutes' walk from the centre.

### Places to Eat
The *Restaurant du Coupole*, on Rue 1 Novembre, charges US$6 for a good set menu. It's opposite the *Restaurant Moderne*, attached to the hotel of the same name, where you can get soup, salad, côtelette and chips for US$4.50.

### Things to Buy
Rue Mrabet Mohammed is a good place to go looking if you want to buy a burnous, the brown full-length robes worn by Arab men in winter. Prices range from about US$12 for a rough cheapie up to about US$65 for a good camel-hair one.

### Getting There & Away
**Air** The Air Algérie (☎ 07-204518) office is on Blvd Dr Tidjani Damerdji. Tlemcen's Zenata Airport is 24 km from the centre of town, from where there are buses and taxis into the centre.

There is at least one flight daily to Algiers. Air Algérie also operates direct flights to Marseilles and Paris. Air France has weekly flights to Paris.

**Bus** The main bus station is on the basement level of the building on the corner of Rue 1 Novembre and Blvd Gaouar Hocine, about 10 minutes' walk from the centre. There are stairs down from both streets.

There is a timetable on display, and tickets are sold from numbered windows.

The main departures are to Algiers, the Moroccan border (US$1.50), Oran, Sebdou and Tiaret.

If you are staying at the camp site and are heading for the border, you can flag down the buses from the stop outside the hospital, just by the arch on the main street, 100 metres back towards town from the camp site.

**Train** The railway station is a grand white building, about 15 minutes' walk east of the town centre.

The Maghreb al-Arabi comes through Tlemcen daily each way en route between Oran and Casablanca. It leaves Oran at 1.30 pm Algerian time and arrives in Oujda about 6 pm Moroccan time. Coming the other way, it leaves Oujda at 8.30 am Moroccan time and arrives in Oran at 2.50 pm Algerian time. The one-way fare between Oujda and Tlemcen is about US$3.50. There are at least three other departures for Oran (three hours) and two to the Moroccan border.

# Oran

Oran is not the most fascinating city in the country and certainly not worth a special detour, but if you are passing through, there are enough things to do to keep you occupied for a day or so. It's also a possible entry point to the country, as there are direct ferries from Alicante (Spain) and Sète (France).

With a population of about 800,000, Oran is the second-largest city in the country. It is situated on a crescent-shaped bay, which is dominated to the west by Jebel Mudjadjo, with the 16th-century fort of Santa Cruz and the basilica clearly visible on its flanks. For a view from here, take the cable car to the top (reached by bus No 25 from the centre).

## History

Oran was founded in the 10th century by Andalusian Arab sailors. It was relatively prosperous during the Almohad and Zianid dynasties, and maintained good relations with Spain and other Mediterranean countries.

The Spanish occupied the city from early in the 15th century until 1792, a massive earthquake in 1790 influencing their decision to move on. Oran was occupied by the Turks until the French arrived in 1831.

The city's development suffered a major setback following a cholera outbreak in 1849, but after that date many people from Spain and France settled here.

After independence, as many as 200,000 Europeans were estimated to have deserted the city, and it was some time before it regained the appearance of actually being inhabited.

## Information

**Tourist Office** The local tourist office (☎ 06-395130) is at 4 Rue Mohammed Khemisti, right in the centre of the city.

**Money** The main branch of the Banque Centrale d'Algérie is on the corner of Rue des Soeurs Benslimane and Blvd de la Soummam.

Outside banking hours it may be possible to change money at the four-star Hôtel Timgad on Blvd Emir Abdelkader.

**Post Office** The post office is on Rue Mohammed Khemisti, a bit farther along and on the opposite side from the tourist office.

**Foreign Consulates** The French consulate is at 3 Square Émile Cayla (☎ 06-335300), and the Moroccan consulate is at 26 Rue Cheikh Larbi Tébessi (☎ 06-221784).

**Hammam** There is a hammam next door to the Hôtel de l'Ouest, at the bottom of Blvd Mellah Ali. For a hot shower try Douches Ghislane in the centre of town, on the edge of the cheap hotel area.

ALGERIA

ALGERIA

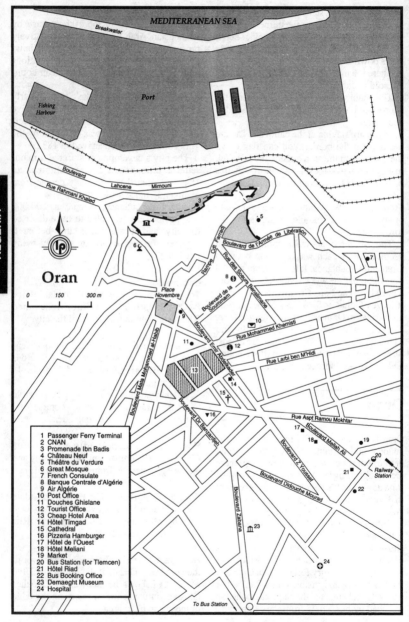

MEDITERRANEAN SEA

Breakwater

Port

Fishing
Harbour

Boulevard Lahcene Mimouni

Rue Rahmani Khaled

## Oran

0    150    300 m

Place
Novembre

Boulevard de l'Armée de Libération

Boulevard de la Soummam

Rue Mohammed Khemisti

Rue Larbi ben M'Hidi

Rue Aspt Ramou Mokhtar

Boulevard Mellah Ali

Railway
Station

Boulevard Z Youssef

Boulevard Didouche Mourad

Boulevard Dr Benzerdjeb

Boulevard Emir Abdelkader

Boulevard Meta Mohammed al-Habib

Boulevard Zabana

To Bus Station

1 Passenger Ferry Terminal
2 CNAN
3 Promenade Ibn Badis
4 Château Neuf
5 Théâtre du Verdure
6 Great Mosque
7 French Consulate
8 Banque Centrale d'Algérie
9 Air Algérie
10 Post Office
11 Douches Ghislane
12 Tourist Office
13 Cheap Hotel Area
14 Hôtel Timgad
15 Cathedral
16 Pizzeria Hamburger
17 Hôtel de l'Ouest
18 Hôtel Meliani
19 Market
20 Bus Station (for Tlemcen)
21 Hôtel Riad
22 Bus Booking Office
23 Demaeght Museum
24 Hospital

**Water** Oran's tap water is incredibly salty, so you'll have to buy bottled water (Saida) – if you can find any.

## Place 1 Novembre

The centre of the new city is Place 1 Novembre, which has the enormous town hall (1888) on one side and a rather ugly theatre (1906) on another.

## Great Mosque

The Great Mosque, or Pasha Mosque, is on Rue Boutkhil, just down the hill from the main square. It was built in 1796 by the pasha of Algiers to commemorate the expulsion of the Spanish and was heavily restored in 1900.

## Promenade Ibn Badis

Heading downhill from Place 1 Novembre, Rampe Commandant Farradj leads to the port past the open-air theatre (Théâtre du Verdure) on the right, and the Promenade Ibn Badis on the left. The promenade is a small garden and walk created in 1847 by General Létang (and still signposted as Promenade de Létang) and is planted with various exotic trees. From the top there is an excellent view out over the port and back along the promenade to the east.

## Demaeght Museum

The Demaeght Museum is on Blvd Zabana, about 15 minutes' walk from the centre. Downstairs is the prehistory section with case upon case of fossils, while the natural-history section has its full complement of stuffed animals and birds. It does give a good insight into the fauna of North Africa,

although the bizarre collection of preserved deformed animal foetuses is a bit off-putting. Upstairs is the ethnography section, with bits and pieces from Africa and Asia.

## Sacré Coeur Cathedral

The old Sacré Coeur Cathedral in the centre of town has been deconsecrated and turned into the city library. Its exterior is grotesquely decorated. At one time, churches outnumbered mosques in Oran.

## Places to Stay – bottom end

The *Hôtel Riad* (☎ 06-363846), at 46 Blvd Mellah Ali, is worth checking. It's right opposite the railway station and the bus station for Tlemcen and other western destinations. There is no sign in English, but it is next door to a driving school. Rooms with bath cost US$7/10.

Farther down the street at No 14 is the *Hôtel Meliani* (☎ 06-343845). Single/double rooms cost US$8/12 including breakfast, but there are no showers.

There is a stack of cheaper places closer to the centre of town in an area just off Blvd Emir Abdelkader, but none are fantastic value. Rue Ozanam has plenty of hotels and is easy to find, as it is the street which runs down off Blvd Hamou Boultélis directly in front of the cathedral.

## Places to Stay – middle

The *Hôtel de l'Ouest* (☎ 06-364698) at 6 Blvd Mellah Ali charges US$12/15 for a single/double with breakfast, but the rooms

have their own bathrooms, heating and air-conditioning.

## Places to Stay – top end

Top of the range is the *Hôtel Timgad* (☎ 06-394797), right in the thick of things at 22 Blvd Emir Abdelkader. It's a four-star hotel, so you can expect to pay in the range of US$40/50 for singles/doubles.

## Places to Eat

There are a couple of local restaurants around the cheap hotels on Rue Ozanam. The more up-market restaurants are on Blvd Emir Abdelkader and Rue Mohammed Khemisti.

## Getting There & Away

**Air** The Air Algérie (☎ 06-398146) office is right in the centre at 2 Blvd Emir Abdelkader. Air France (☎ 06-335944) is at 5 Place Abdelmalek Ramdane.

Oran's Es-Senia Airport is at Tafraoui, 18 km south-east of Oran. There are local buses from Place 1 Novembre.

Air Algérie has flights to Adrar, Algiers, Annaba, Béchar, Constantine, Ghardaia, Ouargla, Tamanrasset and Tindouf.

International destinations served by Air Algérie include Casablanca, Geneva, Lyons, Marseilles, Paris, Toulouse and Zürich. Air France has flights to Lyons, Marseilles, Paris and Toulouse, and Royal Air Maroc connects Oran with Casablanca and Fès.

**Bus** There are two bus stations. The one right outside the railway station is for regional buses and destinations to the west,
including Tlemcen. The booking office is on Rue Tenazet, 100 metres from the station.

The other bus station is a solid 10-minute walk south of the museum. This one is much larger (and more crowded) and handles destinations to all parts of the country not served by the smaller station.

**Train** The railway station is on Blvd Mellah Ali at the top of the hill. It is the large white building with the clock tower. There are departures to Algiers, Mohammadia (change for Béchar) and Tlemcen.

The daily Al-Maghreb al-Arabi train between Tunisia and Morocco leaves Oran at 1.30 pm heading west for Tlemcen and then Oujda in Morocco. It arrives in Oujda at about 6 pm Moroccan time and Casablanca at about 8.30 am the following day. Going the other way, it leaves Oran at 3.20 pm and arrives in Algiers about five hours later. From Algiers you have to change trains to head on to Tunisia.

**Sea** There is a CNAN (☎ 06-332767) office at 13 Blvd Abane Ramdane, near the French consulate, where you can buy tickets for ferries to Alicante and Marseilles. The ferry terminal is directly in front of the centre of town at the bottom of Rampe Commandant Farradj. There are departures for Alicante (12 hours) eight times per month in summer, falling to three per month in winter. There are also 20 departures per month to Marseilles (24 hours) in summer, fewer in winter. The French town of Sète is also served by ferries from Oran, although there are only three per month in summer. The crossing takes 29 hours.

# The Algerian Sahara

The Sahara desert, the greatest desert on earth, stretches right across the countries of northern Africa, but the lion's share lies in Algeria. A full 85% of the country is occupied by it, and yet this area accounts for only 10% of the country's population.

The Sahara offers the traveller the ultimate challenge. To get out there and cross it is one of the last great adventures left in a world which is rapidly shrinking. It is definitely not a trip for those who love their creature comforts, as transport is usually uncomfortable, conditions primitive, the climate extreme and the range of food limited.

The Saharan regions also appear to be relatively unaffected by the bloody fighting that has swept the north, probably because the Tuaregs have never embraced Islam with quite the enthusiasm of their northern cousins. There have, however, been reports of a big increase in robberies in the south, particularly on the Route du Tanezrouft near the Mali border.

The road network is fairly well developed. Without a vehicle, you can take any of the routes normally followed by the overland crowd by using a combination of public transport and hitching. However, on some of the routes transport is infrequent, so you need to be prepared to take a plane to get you out or else sit around for a week or more waiting for a lift. This applies mainly to the eastern route from Hassi Messaoud down through In Amenas and Djanet to Tamanrasset. The Route du Hoggar presents no such problems, although you may end up on a bus between In Salah and Tamanrasset.

It is essential that you are prepared for this sort of travelling, particularly if you hitch and end up for three days on the top of a truck, exposed to the elements. The two essential items to have are a decent hat with a brim, and a water bottle that will hold at least a couple of litres. Travellers do set out without these things and do survive, but why make things more uncomfortable than they need be?

## History

The prehistoric rock paintings in the Hoggar and Tassili N'Ajjer clearly show that the Sahara was a much more hospitable place 6000 years ago than it is today, appearing much like the savanna lands of East Africa today. The paintings mainly depict men hunting and women and children playing.

Before the 5th century BC, the area was inhabited by hunter-gatherers. From the 4th to the 2nd century BC, the people began herding animals and took up a more settled existence.

The horse was first seen in the desert around 1000 BC; an indication that the area was getting drier was the introduction of the camel in the early years of the Christian era.

Trans-Saharan trade became well established, and it was due to this that many of the Punic and Roman towns in the north flourished. It was the Berbers who controlled this trade, however, as they were the ones who knew the desert and were able to cross it.

With the Arab invasions in the north in the 7th century, the indigenous Berbers, keen not to be assimilated, retreated to the desert as well as the mountains of the north.

Today the towns and villages of the Algerian Sahara are populated largely by Tuaregs, who are themselves Berber. However, there have been large numbers of Arabs coming down from the north in search of work, as well as civil servants who have been sent to fill administrative posts.

The towns are relatively prosperous. Nevertheless, with the crippling droughts that have hit the Sahel (the semidesert area directly south of the true desert), they are being increasingly surrounded by slums (bidonvilles) inhabited by destitute nomadic Tuaregs who have gravitated to the population centres in the hope of finding something better.

# Grand Erg Occidental

One of the two great sand seas, the Grand Erg Occidental (Great Western Erg) occupies an enormous area south of the Saharan Atlas Mountains in the west of Algeria. Anywhere else this would constitute a sizable desert in its own right, but in the Sahara things are a bit different.

Some of the most beautiful oases in the country are on the fringes of the erg; these are all relatively accessible, as the erg is flanked on two sides by tar-sealed roads. The N6 is the main road from Oran on the north coast to Adrar, and this skirts around the western edge of the erg, passing through 'Ain Sefra, Béchar and Beni Ounif (for the Moroccan border). North of Adrar the N51 forks off to the north-east and follows the edge of the dunes to El-Goléa, which is on the eastern edge. El-Goléa is also on the main N1 road, which connects Algiers and Tamanrasset, a distance of more than 2000 km.

If you are coming from Morocco and Beni Ounif, the places to stop are Taghit and Beni Abbès; then head for Timimoun and El-Goléa if you want to hitch south. It's easy enough to get to Adrar, but the traffic from there across to the main road at In Salah is negligible. There is supposed to be a weekly bus across this route but it always seems to be the first route to be axed when there is a shortage of buses due to breakdowns, which happens quite often because of the pounding the desert buses/trucks take on the pistes of the south.

The best sand dunes are at Taghit, Beni Abbès and Kerzaz, so make sure you see at least one of these places. Timimoun is a beautiful town in itself, while El-Goléa has some good dunes but not much else.

## 'AIN SEFRA

This town in the Saharan Atlas Mountains is the gateway to the desert from the north-west.

This is about as far north as you will find sand dunes on this side of the country, and they are quite a sight blown up against the foot of the mountains.

There is little of interest in the town itself and, with the only accommodation being a flash three-star place with air-conditioning and pool, it's best to move on. The trouble is that all along the Western Erg the accommodation is not that cheap. Sleeping out in the camp sites is the best option, but these are only found in Taghit, Timimoun and El-Goléa.

Perhaps the most famous thing about 'Ain Sefra is that it was here that the young writer and adventurer Isabelle Eberhardt was drowned in a flood in 1904. She was a Russian born in Switzerland who spent most of her adult life in the Algerian Sahara. She became a Muslim, dressed as a man and spent most of her time travelling on horseback. She had a particularly good understanding of Arab culture and politics, and her diaries make interesting reading *(The Passionate Nomad*; see Books in the Facts for the Visitor chapter). She is buried in the town's Muslim cemetery.

As you come into the town from the north, the most striking feature is the modern architecture by the side of the road. These multicoloured apartment blocks must rate as some of the worst eyesores in the country.

The town has a Cultural Week from the 13th to the 19th of May, but don't plan your trip around it.

### Places to Stay

There's no choice here, as the only place in town is the *Hôtel el-Mekhter* (☎ 07-311417). Rooms cost US$17/22 for singles/doubles with breakfast and, since the hotel is more than 1.5 km out of town, you have to eat at the hotel as well.

The hotel is signposted past the military barracks, which you are advised not to photograph unless you want to take a closer look at the inside of a cell.

### Getting There & Away
**Bus** There are buses north to Algiers, Oran and Tlemcen, and south to Béchar.

**Hitching** The town lies a couple of km to the east of the main road, and there is still enough traffic as far south as Béchar to make hitching possible.

## BENI OUNIF

Still in the Saharan Atlas, this totally unremarkable little border town is the first glimpse many travellers get of Algeria. Don't worry, things get a lot more interesting before very long.

The town is small – only about half a km from one end to the other – so there is no difficulty in finding things.

There is a bank here but it is not authorised to exchange travellers' cheques; you are unlikely to want to use it anyway, as you will probably have just been made to change the equivalent of AD 1000 at the border.

The road between here and Béchar still bears some of the few remaining signs of the battle for Algerian independence. Right along this border, some distance in from the actual line, the French built a continuous barrier of barbed wire some five metres wide. The whole section was patrolled by soldiers stationed at forts, each built in sight of the next, and the line was over 1000 km long on this side of the country. The idea, largely successful, was to isolate the Algerian nationalists from any support from Morocco. Most of the forts are still there today; so is much of the barbed wire, although much of it has been rolled up into large bundles, which you see every few hundred metres.

### Places to Stay

The only hotel in town, the *Hôtel Afrique*, is reported to have closed. The closest accommodation is at Béchar, 114 km to the south.

### Getting There & Away

**Bus** There is no bus station here; all the buses just stop outside the Hôtel Afrique. You have to be lucky to get a seat at times as these buses all go through Beni Ounif in transit, and are often full.

**Train** The railway station is just near the shops in the centre of the town. There is one train daily in each direction.

**To/From Morocco** The road to Morocco leaves the main road to the south of town, just near the customs house – you can't miss it. You can see the Algerian border post about 1.5 km away in the gap in the mountains. A taxi from the town will cost about US$5.

From here, it's another few hundred metres to the Moroccan side – from where it's a further few km to Figuig. The whole crossing takes about half a day.

## BÉCHAR

This is a modern, sprawling administrative town and capital of the Saoura region (as this corner of the Sahara is known). It has nothing at all to recommend it, but you will probably find yourself stopping for a night here on the way through.

There are a couple of banks here, and it is the last major town in which you can stock up on things for the route south. The Air Algérie (☎ 07-239469) office and the tourist office are on the 'Ain Sefra side of Place de la République. The central market has a fair selection of fruit, vegetables and meat. It's next to the mosque with the large minaret on Ave Colonel Lotfi.

From Béchar, the road heads south-west for 100 km before curving around the western corner of the Grand Erg Occidental. The N50 heads west from here for the 800-km journey to Tindouf in the far west of the country. This route into Mauritania has been closed, due to the war in the Western Sahara. Tindouf is the main base for the Polisario fighters, who are actively supported by Algeria. It is out of bounds to foreigners.

### Places to Stay

The *Béchar Hostel*, signposted off the Taghit road, looks fine from the outside but is disappointing on the inside. It charges US$2.50 for a dorm bed.

A better choice is the *Grand Hôtel de la Saoura* (☎ 07-238007), at 24 Rue Kada Belahrech, just around the corner from the post office near the main square, Place de la

République. Singles/doubles are US$8/12 without breakfast.

Another option is the nearby *Hôtel de la Paix* (or *Hôtel Salaam*) with doubles for US$12.

Béchar also has a three-star place, the *Hôtel Antar* (☎ 07-237161), signposted just off the main road one km towards Beni Abbès. Rooms cost US$12/16 with breakfast, and it's quite likely that your currency form will be checked.

### Getting There & Away

**Air** The airport is seven km north of town and local buses make the trip out there.

There are flights to Adrar, Algiers, Annaba, Ghardaia, Oran and Tindouf.

**Bus** The busy bus station is in the street next to the market, on the opposite side to the mosque. Timetables are displayed, and tickets should be bought in advance whenever possible. Most of the buses heading north travel in the late afternoon and evening, as this is one of the hottest areas in the country.

The main destinations are Adrar, Algiers, Beni Abbès, Taghit, Timimoun, Tindouf and Tlemcen.

**Train** There is a daily train to Mohammadia. It takes about 16½ hours to cover the 650 km – at a lightning-fast average speed of 40 km/h.

**Taxi** Taxis to Adrar leave from outside the bus station. Taxis to Beni Ounif leave from a corner of Place de la République.

**Hitching** Béchar is the sort of town which hitchers could easily get to hate. It is extremely spread out, so getting to the edge of town is a pain. If you're heading towards Beni Abbès, there are local buses which run along the main drag the few km to the edge of town. If you're heading towards 'Ain Sefra you have to walk.

### TAGHIT

Pronounced 'Ta-rit', this small oasis village

90 km south of Béchar has some of the most spectacular dunes in the western erg. The dunes tower over the eastern edge of the town, and the view as you come over the hill is really something.

The old mud-brick part of the village is dominated by the old ksar (fortified stronghold), which is still occupied by the military. This section of the village is a real maze of winding lanes, and the architecture is typical of this part of the Sahara.

There is no bank here, but there is a post office, a fuel station and a few general stores.

A climb up the dunes is a must, as the view from the top is magnificent: the sand sea stretches endlessly to the east, while the oasis and the Oued Zousfana are spread out before you to the west. Take a lead from the local kids and have a slide down a dune on a piece of tin or cardboard.

Because of the limited transport and accommodation, if you are coming from Beni Abbès the best idea is to take the morning bus from there to Taghit, and then the afternoon bus on to Béchar.

### Places to Stay & Eat

There is a camp site on the road heading south of town, out past the shops, on the edge of the palmeraie. There are basic toilets and showers, and the nightly charge is US$2.50.

The only hotel in town is the expensive *Hôtel Taghit*. You can't miss it, as it's the only big building in the village. As far as such places go, this one is not bad; it has a nice garden and swimming pool (probably empty). Air-conditioned rooms cost US$16/20 for singles/doubles with breakfast.

Apart from the hotel, the small restaurant near the entrance of the old village is the only place to get a meal. Otherwise, it's a case of buying tinned food and bread from the bakery (near the bus stop) and putting your own food together.

### Getting There & Away

There is one bus daily to Beni Abbès and another to Béchar. There's not much traffic in either direction, although both roads have been surfaced.

Taxis go to Béchar a couple of times a day and there may be one to Beni Abbès if the demand warrants it.

## BENI ABBES

Another beautiful oasis town, Benni Abbès is built on the edge of an escarpment, so it looks down on the palmeraie and the oued. The town is backed by high dunes, and the favourite occupation of the local kids is sliding down them on pieces of tin or plastic.

### Information & Orientation

On entering the town across the oued, the track to the right just before the shops leads to the palmeraie, which has an ancient ksar and an excellent swimming pool.

To the left, the road leads to the little museum and zoo run by the Centre National de Recherches sur les Zones Arides.

The road straight ahead leads up the escarpment past a small row of shops, and then forks. Up to the right lies the market, bus station, post office and defunct Hôtel Grand Erg, while to the left is the Hôtel Rym, the bank and the dunes.

### Things to See

The track into the palmeraie leads past the old mud-brick **ksar** off to the right. This dates from the last century and is now gradually returning to the earth.

Beyond the ksar and beneath the stone water tower on the edge of the escarpment is a small swimming pool, known as **La Source**. It is a cool, green retreat from the blinding desert all around. A few trees give shade to the pool which is filled by beautifully clear spring water and is in a paved enclosure.

The other obvious sight is the **dunes**. Take a scramble up them in the late afternoon when the light is at its best.

The **museum** is about 100 metres along the track to the left along the oued, and then up the first street on the right. It has an interesting selection of desert fauna and flora, and a display with samples and descriptions of more than 70 different types of dates!

### Places to Stay

It may be possible to camp in the grounds of the former *Hôtel Grand Erg*, as well as at the small camp site on an old tennis court next to La Source.

The only hotel is the *Hôtel Rym* (☎ 07-233203), at the foot of the large dune. It was built with tour groups in mind, and charges US$17/22 for singles/doubles with bath and breakfast.

### Getting There & Away

The bus station is up by the market. There are twice-daily departures to Béchar, and buses leave once a day for Adrar and Timimoun. All these buses pass through en route from somewhere else, so seats are not guaranteed.

There is also a bus to Taghit every morning.

### ADRAR

Adrar is a major regional capital 120 km south of the road which rings the Grand Erg Occidental. Where this road branches off to the south is a café, where you can wait for a lift to Adrar if necessary.

The town has very little in the way of formal attractions, but its uniform brick-red colour is interesting. The centre of town is an absolutely enormous main square (Place des Martyrs) – you could just about land a plane on it! Around it are the main buildings: the banks, post office, Air Algérie (☎ 07-259365) and the main hotel (the Hôtel Touat). Because the square is so big, the midday sun here is blinding, and you need to follow the local example and retreat somewhere cooler. The town is virtually deserted in the afternoon.

On the way into the town from the north, keep your eyes out for signs of the *fouggaras* (underground water channels), identifiable above ground by the lines of small wells on the surface. This system of channels, now superseded by more modern methods, once stretched for more than 2000 km in this area.

If you are heading for Mali along the Route du Tanezrouft (if the border is open), make sure you check in at the customs post when leaving the town to the south. It may be that customs are now handled at the border post at Borj Mokhtar 800 km away, but you'd look pretty silly if you turned up there only to be told that formalities are taken care of in Adrar!

### Places to Stay

With only two places to choose from, the one that comes close to being affordable is the *Hôtel Timmi*, one block from the main square. Rooms cost US$12 with shower, but

treat with scepticism the claim that the room are air-conditioned.

The only other choice is the *Hôtel Toua* (☎ 07-259933) on the main square, where you have to shell out US$17/22 for an air conditioned single/double room.

### Getting There & Away

**Air** The airport is three km from the centre and, other than walking, a taxi is the only way to get out there.

Being a fairly important regional town Adrar is well served by plane. There are

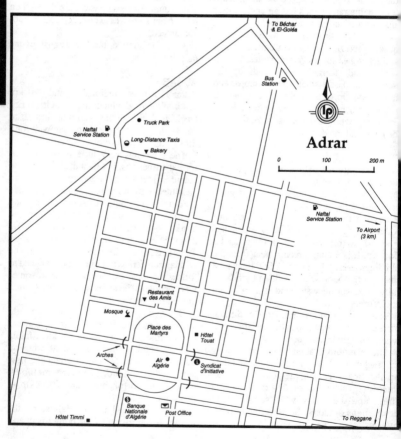

epartures to Algiers, Béchar, Borj Mokhtar, ¬hardaia, Oran and Tamanrasset.

**us** The bus station is about 500 metres ¬orth of the main square. The large depot is ¬lso the graveyard for quite a few of the ¬roken-down Mercedes trucks/buses which ¬se the pistes.

As all the departures originate here, it is ¬ossible (and advisable) to book tickets the ¬ay before you plan to leave. Main destina-¬ons include Aoulef, Béchar, Borj Mokhtar, ¬hardaia and In Salah.

If the bus to In Salah is not running, it is ¬ossible to get there by taking the daily bus ¬ Aoulef and then a 4WD taxi from there to ¬ Salah for about US$7 per person.

There is not much point catching the bus ¬ Borj Mokhtar, as you may then have to sit ¬ere for days waiting for a lift into Mali. ¬ou're better off organising a through lift in ¬drar.

**axi** Taxis run regularly to Timimoun from ¬eneath the tree close to the Naftal service ¬tation near the truck park, 10 minutes' walk ¬om the centre of town. The trip takes about ¬vo hours and costs US$7 per person.

**itching** It's about a one-km walk to the ¬orthern edge of town for the road to Béchar ¬nd Timimoun. There is an SNTR depot up ¬y the Naftal service station north-west of ¬e town centre, and it may be possible to ¬rrange a lift in a truck from here. However, ¬s always with these government trucks, you ¬eed to be discreet as it's illegal for the ¬rivers to take passengers.

## IMIMOUN

¬f you can stop at only one of the oases ¬round the Grand Erg Occidental, make it ¬imimoun. It's an enchanting place, built ¬ery much in the Sudanese red-mud style, ¬nd the residents are very friendly – it's one ¬f the best places in the Sahara.

The town is built on the edge of an escarp-¬nent, and there are fantastic views out over ¬n ancient salt lake to the sand dunes in the

distance; on a bright, moonlit night the effect is just magical.

The population of the town and the sur-rounding area is a real mix: the Haratine (non-Negroid Blacks), the Zénète Berbers, the Chaamba Arabs (originally from the east) and the Black Africans (descendants of Malian slaves). The predominant language of the region is Zénète, a Berber dialect similar to those spoken in the Kabylie and the M'Zab.

### Information
**Tourist Office** The tourist office is in the municipality building, near the roundabout on the main street. Ask about the Gourara Circuit map.

**Money** There is a branch of the Banque Nationale d'Algérie by the market square, about halfway along the main street.

**Post** The post office is also close to the roundabout, on the road that connects the main street with the main road from Adrar to El-Goléa.

### Gourara Circuit
If you have access to a vehicle, the Gourara Circuit is an absolute must. This is a 70-km loop through a few oasis villages to the north of Timimoun which takes in the finest of the desert scenery.

### Other Attractions
The town lends itself well to photography; just walking up and down the main street you'll see plenty of possibilities, with the red buildings and the koubba in the middle of the road. The Hôtel Rouge de l'Oasis is a fine old building and, although it is now only partially open, it is worth a wander around inside to see the walls, which are decorated with traditional designs.

The administrative buildings of the town are also built to a similar design but are hidden behind a high wall.

Down towards the palmeraie, along the road to the camp site, the old section of town is a maze of dusty alleys and red-mud

**ALGERIA**

houses. The **palmeraie** itself is cool and shady, and the individual plots are divided by mud-brick walls. Enter by the road which leads from the main roundabout down past the high school to the camp site and Hôtel Gourara.

### Places to Stay – bottom end

**Camping** Although you can camp in the grounds of the Hôtel Ighzer, a much better alternative is the *Camping la Palmeraie* on the edge of the escarpment.

**Hotels** The cheapest place is the *Hôtel Ighzer* on the southern end of the main street. The rooms cost US$8 and are spartan but adequate.

### Places to Stay – middle & top end

The famous *Hôtel Rouge de l'Oasis* (☎ 07-234417), one of the most colourful hotels in the whole country, is reported to have recovered from its minor collapse of a few years ago. You can expect to pay US$20/25 for singles/doubles.

The alternative is the government-run *Hôtel Gourara* (☎ 07-234451), right on the edge of the escarpment, just past the camp site. It has fantastic views over the salt lake and dunes, but rooms are not cheap at US$17/22 for singles/doubles with breakfast. Even if you are not staying here it's not a bad place to come for a cold drink on the terrace at sunset.

### Places to Eat

The choices are strictly limited here. Other than putting your own food together with bread and whatever you can find in the market, there is only one restaurant. It's just off the main street, in the road between the Hôtel Rouge de l'Oasis and the gardens opposite the municipality building.

### Things to Buy

The Artisanat du Grand Erg shop, on the road down to the camp site, has a small selection of locally made souvenirs.

### Getting There & Away

**Air** The Air Algérie (☎ 07-234555) office is on the main square.

The airport is eight km to the south-east of town. There are flights to Algiers, Béchar and Ghardaia.

**Bus** The TVE station is on the main street almost opposite the mosque. It is possible to book in advance on only some of the services, as most are just passing through and don't originate in Timimoun.

There are daily services from Timimoun to Adrar, Béchar and Ghardaia.

**Taxi** Taxis leave from just next to the bus station. The main destination is Adrar. The trip takes two hours and costs US$7 per person.

**Hitching** The town itself is only a five minute walk from the main highway connecting El-Goléa and Adrar, so getting out onto the road for hitching in either direction is easy enough.

## EL-GOLÉA

The most easterly oasis of the Grand Erg Occidental, El-Goléa is a major stop on the route south. With over 180,000 palm trees, it is one of the biggest of the south.

The town is dominated by the old ksar El-Menia, built on a rocky knoll in the east of town. It was built by Zénète Berbers in the 10th century and is now in a sad state. It's worth the scramble up to it for the views of the town and surrounding oasis.

The water here is some of the sweetest in the whole Sahara; fill up your tanks if you're driving, especially if you are heading south as the water at In Salah is absolutely foul. It is possible to buy bottled water in the supermarket here but this seems a bit pointless, as what you are getting is exactly the same as from the tap.

El-Goléa has a bank, post office and Air Algérie office. Accommodation is limited to a fancy three-star hotel, an inconveniently located budget hotel and one of the best camp sites in the country.

The oasis itself is very lush and, apart from
palms, supports a large variety of fruit trees,
including plum, peach, apricot, cherry,
orange and fig. The market here has the last
decent produce (apart from potatoes and
onions) on the southward route, so stock up.

Just near the ksar is a cemetery, where
Charles de Foucauld (who was responsible
for the hermitage in the Hoggar) was buried
in 1929.

### Places to Stay – bottom end

**Camping** There are two choices here. The
better place is the *Le Palmier* camp site
(☎ 09-833319), a couple of hundred metres
north of the town centre. It charges US$2 per
person and US$1 per tent.

The other camp site is run by the *Touring
Club d'Algérie* and is three km south of the
centre. It is not as shady or private.

**Hotels** The only reasonably priced place is
the *Hôtel Vieux Ksar* on the road to the south,
30 minutes' walk from the centre. It's good
value at US$11 for a double with breakfast,

1 Le Palmier Camp Site
2 Aswak Supermarket
3 Naftal Service Station
4 Restaurant
5 Café du Peuple
6 Bakery
7 Bus Station
8 Restaurant des Amis
9 Supermarket
10 Air Algérie
11 Police
12 Mosque
13 Market
14 Café Port Said
15 Post Office
16 Hôtel el-Boustan
17 Long-Distance Taxis
   & Local Buses

To Ghardaia

To Airport
(3 km)

To Ksar

To In Salah

El-Goléa

0     50     100 m

but its location is really against it. There are some air-conditioned rooms.

### Places to Stay – top end
The *Hôtel el-Boustan* is east of the centre, on the road to the ksar. Rooms cost US$14/17 for a single/double.

### Getting There & Away
**Air** Air Algérie (☎ 09-736100) has an office in the centre of town.

The airport is three km to the west of town. There are flights twice a week to Algiers and Tamanrasset.

**Bus** The bus station is nothing more than an office right in the centre of town.

There are daily departures for Adrar, Ghardaia and Timimoun, although you have to wait until the buses arrive to see if there are spare seats.

There is also a departure every second day at 9 pm for In Salah. The trip takes about eight hours and costs US$8.

**Taxi** The long-distance taxis leave from an area just a few minutes' walk to the south-west of the centre. The main destination is Ghardaia, but they also run to Timimoun.

**Hitching** The town stretches away about five km to the south, so if you are hitching in that direction catch a local bus from near the taxi station and take it to the end of the line; the buses go right to the very edge of town – perfect for hitching.

# Ghardaia & the M'Zab

The M'Zab is the name given to the valley occupied by the Mozabites, a puritanical Islamic sect that broke away from the mainstream in the 11th century. They are a Berber people who speak a dialect similar to that spoken by the people of the Kabylie in the north.

The 100,000 inhabitants of this deep, narrow valley live in a pentapolis – five villages which have developed indepen dently of the rest of the country. Ghardaia the main town and the others, which su round it, are Melika, Beni Isguen, Bou Nou and El-Ateuf. The Mozabites are well know for being astute merchants; many of the have migrated to Algiers and now own bus nesses there and in France. Those who hav remained in the M'Zab are still fairly conse vative, particularly the older generatio Traditions are strong here, and most of th people still wear traditional dress – bagg pants for the men, white garments of hand woven wool for the women.

One of the main reasons why the town have retained their character and traditions that the Mozabites were not involved in th fight for independence, so the French le them alone.

Each town is built on a knoll in the valle and each is crowned by a distinctiv unadorned minaret. The town centres, partic ularly Ghardaia, Melika and Beni Isguen consist of narrow, winding streets and a excellent places to explore. Beni Isguen ('th pious') is the religious town of the M'Zab foreigners can't enter unless accompanie by a guide and they cannot stay overnight.

The oasis is massive, stretching for som 10 km along the valley, and the 3000-plu wells support more than 270,000 palm tree

This is the most interesting area in th country, so be sure to put aside a few days t explore it. There is a good range of accom modation, including a very well run cam site.

### GHARDAIA
The largest and most important of the fiv towns, Ghardaia is very much the hub of th M'Zab; it's also the only one with touris facilities. As well as a number of hotels an restaurants, there are a dozen or so shop which sell souvenirs of all kinds but main rugs, which are a speciality of the area.

### Information
**Money** There are banks on the main stree You can also change money at the Hôte Rostimedes.

Ghardaia has a reputation for offering the
est black-market rates in the country.

**ost & Telecommunications** The post
ffice is also on the main street. It's open in
ummer from 7 am to noon and 4 to 7 pm
om Saturday to Wednesday, and from 7 am
1 pm on Thursday; it's closed on Friday.
inter hours are from 8 am to 6.30 pm from
aturday to Wednesday, and from 8 am to 4
m on Thursday; closed on Friday.

If you buy rugs in Ghardaia, you can post
em from here. Take them along
nwrapped, as the officials need to see the
ontents first. There is a telephone office at
e side of the post office, and you can dial
rect (with difficulty), or go through the
perator. It can be quicker to call from the
ôtel Rostimedes.

**arket** The daily market is held in the
bbled marketplace, an open square in the
iddle of the old part of the town.

**ammam** If your hotel doesn't have
owers, there is a hammam in the central
rea, to the right of the entrance to the Hôtel
-Saada. It is open for women from 8.30 am
1 pm, and the women's entrance is in the
de lane to the left. As is the custom through-
ut the country, a rag or small towel is hung
the doorway to indicate when women are
athing.

**hings to See**
he entrance to the old city is along Rue Ibn
osten, which leads to the marketplace. The
arket takes place daily, mainly in the
orning, and is a colourful affair. As well as
gricultural produce, there is all manner of
ther things for sale. Around the market
quare are a number of souvenir shops.

Off to the right of the square and leading
p to the Great Mosque is the **Souq ed-**
ellada. On Wednesday and Sunday there is
n auction; there is a similar one at Beni
guen.

The **Great Mosque** has a fortress-like
ppearance; its main feature is the un-

adorned, pyramidal minaret, typical of the
mosques of the M'Zab.

On the road up to the Hôtel Rostimedes is
a small **folklore museum**, which is open
daily from 8.30 am to noon and 3.30 to 6.30
pm. One of the best views of Ghardaia is
from the terrace of the hotel itself. Down to
the left is an old Mozabite cemetery.

**Places to Stay – bottom end**
**Camping** Ghardaia boasts one of the best
camp sites in Algeria. *Camping Bouleila* is
about one km south of the town centre on the
El-Goléa road. It is well shaded and costs
US$2 per person, US$1.50 for a tent and
US$1 for a vehicle. There are places to eat
close by.

There is a second camp site, *Camping
Oued M'Zab*, on the route out of town to the
north. It's good if you have a car, but inconvenient otherwise – especially as there are no
restaurants close by. Prices are similar to the
Bouleila.

**Hostel** There is a hostel (☎ 09-894403) on
the corner of the main street and the road that
leads up to the Hôtel Rostimedes. It is open
in the morning and late afternoon, and costs
US$2.50 for a bed. There is a three-day limit.

**Hotels** Hotel accommodation in Ghardaia is
relatively expensive. There are a few cheap
hotels, all in the same central area about five
minutes' walk from the bus station. Late in
the afternoon there may be little choice.

The *Hôtel Napht* (☎ 09-890009) is the
most popular with travellers and is in a side
street off Rue Ahmed Talbi, near the corner
of the main street. There is an air-conditioned
lounge and a reasonable restaurant downstairs. Rooms cost US$7/10 for very small
singles/doubles.

The *Hôtel Atlantide* (☎ 09-892536), on
Rue Ahmed Talbi, has larger rooms and is
better, but charges US$10 for them. In the
same area is the *Hôtel 1001 Nuits*, which is
poor value at US$6/10 and there are no
showers.

ALGERIA

ALGERIA

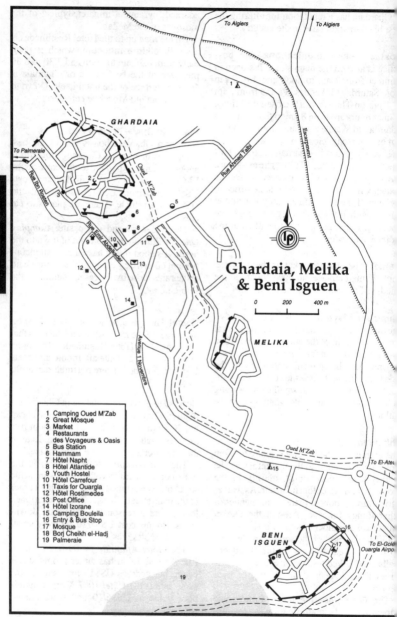

**Ghardaia, Melika & Beni Isguen**

To Algiers
To Algiers
GHARDAIA
To Palmeraie
Rue Ibn Rostem
Oued M'Zab
Rue Ahmed Talbi
Escarpment
Rue Emir Abdelkader
Avenue 1 Novembre
MELIKA
Oued M'Zab
To El-Ateu
BENI ISGUEN
To El-Gold
Ouargla Airpo

0    200    400 m

1  Camping Oued M'Zab
2  Great Mosque
3  Market
4  Restaurants
   des Voyageurs & Oasis
5  Bus Station
6  Hammam
7  Hôtel Napht
8  Hôtel Atlantide
9  Youth Hostel
10 Hôtel Carrefour
11 Taxis for Ouargla
12 Hôtel Rostimedes
13 Post Office
14 Hôtel Izorane
15 Camping Bouleila
16 Entry & Bus Stop
17 Mosque
18 Borj Cheikh el-Hadj
19 Palmeraie

## Places to Stay – middle

The *Hôtel Carrefour* (☎ 09-893179) is on Rue Emir Abdelkader, almost on the corner with Rue Ahmed Talbi. The rooms have fans and cost US$14 a double.

Up a notch is the *Hôtel Izorane* (☎ 09-91560), a good place on Ave 1 Novembre, not far from the post office. There are no singles here; doubles cost US$16 with bath and breakfast.

## Places to Stay – top end

The three-star *Hôtel Rostimedes* (☎ 09-92999) is on the hill to the west overlooking town, just a couple of minutes' walk from the centre. It has been designed to blend in with the landscape, but the result is that parts of the interior are very gloomy and dungeon-like. It costs US$19/25 for singles/doubles, including breakfast.

## Places to Eat

There is a good choice of restaurants in Ghardaia. One of the best is the *Restaurant M'Zab*, next to the Hôtel 1001 Nights on Rue Ahmed Talbi.

Near the entrance to the old city is the *Restaurant Oasis*, upstairs on the corner of the main street. It does a decent chicken and chips for US$2.50. The *Restaurant des Voyageurs*, opposite, does similar fare but is not as popular.

## Things to Buy

If you are interested in buying any of the beautifully colourful rugs here, check the quality closely as they can vary enormously. The better ones have more knots per sq cm. The greatest concentration of shops is around the market square.

You need to haggle over the prices, which may seem outrageously expensive, but when you think in real (black market) terms, are actually very reasonable. It may also be possible to do a bit of bartering with some of the shopkeepers, using any surplus goods or undeclared hard currency which you may have.

## Getting There & Away

**Air** The Air Algérie (☎ 09-893592) office is on Ave 1 Novembre. The airport is 10 km south of town on the road to El-Goléa.

As this is a major centre, it is well served by Air Algérie. There is a weekly flight direct to Paris, as well as internal flights to Adrar, Algiers, Annaba, Béchar, Constantine, Djanet, In Salah, Oran and Tamanrasset.

**Bus** The main bus station is on Rue Ahmed Talbi, just across the Oued M'Zab and only five minutes' walk from the centre. It's best to make reservations in advance. A timetable is displayed.

The main destinations are Adrar, Algiers, Biskra, Constantine, El-Goléa, El-Oued, In Salah, Laghouat, Oran, Ouargla and Timimoun.

**Taxi** Taxis for Algiers, El-Goléa and Ouargla leave from the other side of the oued. Taxis for Laghouat leave by the bridge at the bus station. As with everything in Ghardaia, there is very little activity in the afternoon.

**Hitching** For hitching south out of town, catch a local bus heading for El-Ateuf and get off at the main roundabout near Beni Isguen. The El-Goléa road heads off south up the escarpment from here.

## Getting Around

**To/From the Airport** There is a bus which goes to and from the airport to meet incoming flights. There is a timetable of departure times in the Air Algérie office, and in some of the hotels.

**Bus** The station for the local buses is just opposite the entrance to the old city. There are buses for Beni Isguen, Bou Noura and El-Ateuf.

## AROUND GHARDAIA
### Beni Isguen

This is the most important religious town in the M'Zab. The people here hang on very firmly to their traditional ways, and the amount of outside influence is kept to an absolute minimum.

The town is built on the slope of the hill, 2.5 km south of Ghardaia. The best time for a visit is in the late afternoon, when the market square comes alive with the daily auction. Here locals sell handmade cloth, rugs and other general items. It is interesting to watch: as there are no cafés in the town, it becomes the social event of the day and all the men sit out around the square. The auction takes place every day except Friday.

The town's narrow streets are entered from the main Ghardaia road. It is compulsory for all non-Muslims entering the town to have a guide, and you can pick one up at this entry point. Try to get one with whom you have a common language; many of the older men speak no English. Photography and smoking are forbidden in the town, and modest dress is compulsory (no shorts or singlets). There are signs at the entrance to remind you.

The guide will show you all the interesting bits and pieces in Beni Isguen. The highlight is the Turkish tower, **Borj Cheikh el-Hadj** (also known as Borj Boleila), in the eastern corner of the town. The view from the top of the tower is excellent. Your guide will probably leave you at the marketplace, which has a few shops nearby selling the colourful local rugs; the prices here are a bit more negotiable than in Ghardaia.

The **palmeraie** at Beni Isguen is probably the best in the M'Zab. It stretches for a couple of km behind the town. Just continue on the road, past the entrance to Beni Isguen, where it winds around to the back of the palmeraie. The gardens here are green havens, veritable Gardens of Eden. They are difficult to see properly, however, as they are mostly behind high walls. Once behind the wall, the contrast is vivid – fruit trees of all kinds battling each other for room. You'll find every kind of fruit here, from grapes and figs to bananas and dates.

**Getting There & Away** Local buses leave Ghardaia from outside the entrance to the old

city. They drop you outside the gates to Beni Isguen. Alternatively, it's a half-hour walk

### Melika

It is from Melika that you get the best overall views of the Oued M'Zab and Ghardaia itself. The town is about a km to the south east of Ghardaia, high above the oued.

The main point of interest is the curious cemetery on the northern side, although the town itself is worth a wander.

**Getting There & Away** The easiest way up to Melika is on foot from Ghardaia. It takes about 30 minutes to make the climb, and the best route is the road which leads south opposite the bus station. It is also possible to cross the oued anywhere and just scramble up the side of the hill.

### Guerara

This small oasis is 73 km east of the main road at Berriane, which in turn is 69 km north of Ghardaia. It is a good spot to rest up if you have your own transport. Check out *Restaurant Sindbad* and the camp site in the palmeraie. There's a hot spring close by which is great for swimming – there are specified times for segregated swimming.

# Grand Erg Oriental

The Grand Erg Oriental (Great Eastern Erg) is much larger than its western counterpart. From central-eastern Algeria it stretches north and east into Tunisia.

Close to its northern edge is the oasis of El-Oued, in the centre of the Souf region – a series of oases dotted throughout a small triangular area.

The people of the Souf region have developed an ingenious method of agriculture that allows dates and other fruits to be grown in one of the hottest areas of the Sahara. Great depressions are excavated with hand tools and the sand piled up on all sides; palm fronds are then stuck along the ridges to stop the sand blowing back into the dip. Palm

nd other plants are grown in the bottom of the depression, from where their roots can each the subterranean water. It is not uncommon to see just the tip of a palm tree sticking out of the top of one of these pits.

Throughout the Souf region, women wear a single robe/veil which covers everything except for one eye. If ever a garment has had a dehumanising effect, it has to be this one.

Touggourt is another oasis town, right on the western edge of the erg, south of El-Oued. The road that connects the two towns passes through some magnificent sand-dune country. It's a constant struggle to prevent the dunes from swallowing the road.

Farther south again is oil country, source of the majority of Algeria's export income. Hassi Messaoud is the town at the heart of it all, although Ouargla on the edge of the erg is as close as most people will need to go, unless they are heading for Djanet.

## EL-OUED

El-Oued has been dubbed 'the Village of a Thousand Domes' and it doesn't take long to work out why: virtually all the buildings use vaults and domes in an effort to alleviate the incredible summer heat. Temperatures as high as 60°C are not unknown here and for days on end it will hit 45°C or more. It gets so hot in this place that everything is hot to touch – even the handrails inside the buses and the door handles of the hotel rooms!

The town is also famous for its carpets, many of which bear the brown Cross of the Souf motif on a white background. There are simpler designs on the rough black rugs which have red and white lines through them. Many of the carpets sold in Ghardaia are actually made in El-Oued and, obviously, the prices at the source are better.

The dozen or so villages around El-Oued are worth a poke around, particularly Nakhla, 15 km to the south-east, and Guemar, 18 km along the Biskra road.

## Information

**Tourist Office** The tourist office and the local syndicat d'initiative (☎ 04-728248) are on Ave Taleb Larbi near the corner of Rue Mohammed Khemisti. The syndicat d'initiative has a reasonable handout map of the town and Souf area.

Because of the heat everything shuts up tight by noon, and throughout the afternoon nothing stirs until about 4 pm.

**Money** There are two banks on Ave Taleb Larbi which are open for exchange. It is also possible to change money at the Hôtel du Souf, and there is a bank at the Tunisian border, although it is not always open.

**Post & Telecommunications** The post office is just behind the tourist offices, in a small pedestrian precinct. There are direct-dial phone boxes outside.

**Water** The town's tap water tastes pretty dreadful but is safe to drink. Bottled water is not widely available.

### Things to See
The daily **market** in the old part of the town is a colourful and animated affair. It is at its busiest on Friday. Most stalls sell food and everyday items, but a few cater to the tourist trade.

The **museum** opposite the tourist offices consists of just one room. However, it has some good displays, including old aerial photos of the area, a collection of the various insects and animals of the region, some good sand roses and other geological curiosities. There are also a couple of traditional rugs, and a pair of special wool-and-camel-hair soles which are used to walk on the burning hot sand. The whole thing is a bit dusty and moth-eaten but is worth a quick look. It is open daily from 9 am to noon and 3 to 6 pm; closed on Monday.

### Places to Stay – bottom end
**Hostel & Camping** The *Camping de Crépuscule* is a few km north of town on the Tunis road, close to the Naftal service station. Facilities are limited and there is not a scrap of shade.

There is a hostel at Nakhla, 15 km to the south-east, where you can stay or camp.

ALGERIA

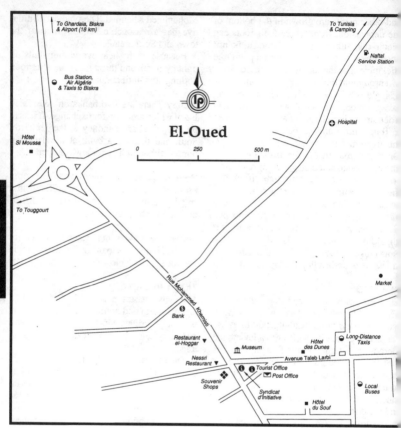

**Hotels** The most central place is the *Hôtel des Dunes*, a traditional domed building on Ave Taleb Larbi with the feel of a caravanserai. The facilities are basic and rooms cost US$4/8 for singles/doubles. Showers cost extra, water permitting.

Much more modern and comfortable is the *Hôtel Si Moussa* (☎ 04-728381). It's on Rue Mohammed Khemisti near the fancy roundabout, complete with pavilion, at the intersection of the Touggourt road. It is a 15-minute walk from the centre but is very handy to the bus station for early-morning departures. There are also local buses which

shuttle back and forth to the centre, so the location is not too bad. Rooms cost US$7/9 for a single/double with washbasin, US$9/12 with air-conditioning, and there are free showers. It is also possible to sleep on the roof here.

Another place in the centre, next to the Hôtel des Dunes, is the *Hôtel Central* (☎ 04-728825). It charges US$6/11, but there are no showers.

### Places to Stay – top end

The only other place is the *Hôtel du Souf* (☎ 04-728170), a couple of blocks south of e tourist office, complete with swimming ool and tower. Rooms here cost US$25 for single with breakfast.

## laces to Eat

ood is expensive in El-Oued. About the best lace in town is the *Restaurant el-Hoggar*, alfway along the main street. It's one of the w places that doesn't close in the afteroons and is a cool retreat from the heat utside. The *Nessri Restaurant*, 100 metres arther south on the main street, is very imilar.

## Getting There & Away

ir The Air Algérie (☎ 04-728666) office is t the bus station, 20 minutes' walk north of ne centre on the Biskra road. The airport is t Guemar, 18 km to the north, and can be eached by local bus. There are flights to lgiers and Annaba.

Bus The main bus station is about two km orth of the town centre – a 20-minute walk, r there are local minibuses which take you o or from the centre.

There are departures to Algiers, Annaba, Constantine, Ghardaia and Ouargla.

axi Yellow long-distance taxis leave when ull from just next door to the Hôtel des )unes for Touggourt (two hours, US$8 per erson), the Tunisian border (US$5), )uargla and towns in the Souf area.

Taxis for Biskra leave from next to the bus tation.

## Getting Around

ocal bus services for the surrounding towns eave from opposite the taxi station. Not nuch happens after 7 pm. Minibuses run etween here and the main bus station.

## TOUGGOURT

A totally unremarkable oasis town, Tougourt is perhaps most famous as the starting oint of the first motorised crossing of the ahara. The Citroen half-track vehicles of he Haardt and Audouin-Debreuil expedition et off from here in 1922 for Timbuktu via Tamanrasset. The event is marked by a simple pillar in the town square.

Today the town is a regional administrative centre, with a large palmeraie and a couple of old, vaguely interesting mud-brick villages to the south. There are a couple of banks, a post office and an Air Algérie office.

Market day is Friday; in winter especially, the town is full of itinerant merchants who have come for the market. The marketplace is just off the road to El-Oued, near the taxi station.

From the main square, the road to the right curves around past the cinema to the bus stop for buses to Temacine. The road straight ahead leads past the old hotel on the left to the Hôtel Oasis and Temacine.

If you have a day to spare you could do worse than spend it here, but don't lose any sleep if you miss it.

### Places to Stay – bottom end

**Hostel** There is a hostel well signposted right in the centre of town – very well located. A bed is US$2.

**Hotels** The *Hôtel Marhaba* is right by the taxi station and costs US$8 for a double, although this is negotiable. The best idea is to follow the local custom and sleep on the roof in summer, as the rooms become intolerably hot.

Between the market and the main street is the *Hôtel de la Paix*, but it is no different from the Marhaba.

### Places to Stay – top end

The only improvement on these places is the expensive *Hôtel Oasis*, one km south of town on the road to Temacine, where rooms cost US$23 for a double with breakfast. The swimming pool may be usable. The most useful thing in the hotel is the map of the town on the wall in the lobby.

### Places to Eat

There are a few very basic restaurants between the taxi station and the market.

ALGERIA

## Getting There & Away

**Air** There is an Air Algérie (☎ 09-726096) office in the town centre. The airport is five km east of town along the El-Oued road. There are flights to Algiers.

**Bus** The bus station is right on the western edge of town, a couple of km from the centre; you'll need a taxi if you can't face the walk.

There are daily buses to Algiers, Biskra, Constantine, El-Oued, Ghardaia, Hassi Messaoud and Ouargla.

**Train** The railway station is close to the centre of town. There are trains to and from Constantine (eight hours) and Biskra (4½ hours).

**Taxi** The taxi station is just off the main El-Oued road, five minutes' walk from the centre, past the marketplace.

There are departures for Biskra, El-Oued and Ouargla, but very little happens after about 1 pm.

## Getting Around

**Bus** Local buses for Tamelhat and Temacine leave from a stop along the road that curves around to the right at the end of the main street – just ask around.

## AROUND TOUGGOURT
### Tamelhat

On the edge of the palmeraie 12 km south of Touggourt is Tamelhat, a traditional mud-brick village which, although inhabited, has the air of a place that has been abandoned. There are large open spaces where buildings have collapsed completely.

The narrow lanes wind between high walls, and in places the houses actually span the lanes. The occasional open door reveals a small courtyard where the family donkey is kept and where the women spread chillies out to dry.

In the centre of the town is the mosque and mausoleum of Sidi el-Hadj Ali; the cupola above the mausoleum is decorated with coloured tiles and stucco.

Chances are one of the local kids will latch onto you as a guide, although what they ca actually show you is limited. One thing the might try to drag you along to is the 'sea This is a small brackish lake betwee Tamelhat and Temacine – forget it.

**Getting There & Away** There are local buse from close to the centre of Touggourt an these drop you at an intersection a couple o km from the main road. Tamelhat is directl on the right; Temacine a few km to the lef Taxis run back to Touggourt via Temacin and the Hôtel Oasis.

### Temacine

Temacine is rather more picturesque tha Tamelhat, with its houses built around a ksa on top of a small hill. Palm tree trunks hav been used extensively in the construction o the fortifications. The mosque here date from 1431; all the building materials used i its construction were imported from Tunisia

## OUARGLA

The town of Ouargla has even fewer attrac tions than Touggourt, although if you fin yourself stuck here there are a couple o hotels (neither of them cheap), a hostel an a camp site.

Ouargla is very much a modern oil town if you are driving in the area at night th horizon is bright orange with the glow of th oil burn-off flames.

### Places to Stay

**Camping** The camp site is called the Kame Camping Rouissat (☎ 09-705776); it' signposted 4.5 km from the town centre o the Touggourt road.

**Hotels** The Hôtel de Tassili (☎ 09-700154 and the Hôtel el-Mehri (☎ 09-702066) ar both two-star and cost about US$14/18 for single/double with breakfast.

### Getting There & Away

**Bus** The bus station is at the eastern end o town on the Ghardaia road, about 1.5 km from the centre. There are buses to Algiers

Top: Sabratha, Libya (AJ)
Middle: Dunes encroaching on In Salah, Algeria (HF)
Bottom: Ras al-Ghoul, near Ghadhames, Libya (AJ)

Top Left: Oued Ouarzazate from Taourirt kasbah, Ouarzazate, Morocco (DS)
Top Right: Mausoleum of Moulay Ismail through gate, Meknès, Morocco (DS)
Bottom Left: Place el-Hedim, Meknès, Morocco (DS)
Bottom Right: Ghardaia medina, the M'Zab, Algeria (HF)

Annaba, Constantine, El-Oued, Hassi Messaoud, In Amenas and Oran.

**Taxi** The taxis congregate about 300 metres before the bus station on the Ghardaia road. They leave regularly for Biskra, Ghardaia (US$7, two hours), Touggourt and El-Oued (at least 2½ hours).

## HASSI MESSAOUD

Situated 85 km south-east of Ouargla, this is solely a service town for surrounding oil operations. There is absolutely nothing of interest, but you will find yourself coming through on the way south on the Route du Tassili N'Ajjer.

### Places to Stay

The only hotel is three km from the centre at the northern end of town, and it's expensive at US$15 for a single.

### Getting There & Away

There are regular buses between here and Ouargla, and a daily service to In Amenas, although you'll need luck to get a seat on it as it comes from Ouargla and is likely to be full.

# Route du Tassili N'Ajjer

This route heads south from Hassi Messaoud along the Gassi Touil, a large oued between two sections of the Great Eastern Erg, to In Amenas, 730 km to the south-east and very close to the Libyan border.

The road is bitumen as far as In Amenas but turns to piste between there and Djanet and Tamanrasset.

There is a weekly bus along here between Biskra and In Amenas but very little other traffic – just the occasional truck. If you are heading for Tamanrasset, the easiest and quickest way is to hitch to Ghardaia and then head down the N1. If you have the time and don't mind running the risk of getting stuck for a few days in some tiny backwater, it is possible to get to Djanet and then on to

Tamanrasset, but it's not a trip which should be undertaken lightly.

If you get really stuck there are flights from In Amenas and Illizi to Ouargla and Djanet.

## IN AMENAS

This is another modern, characterless town built to service the oil industry. There is a post office, service station and SNTR truck depot, where it may be possible to get lifts.

On arrival you must check in at the *daira* (municipal headquarters) and give them the details of your trip to Djanet.

### Places to Stay

The only formal accommodation is the *Hôtel Cash*, which charges US$14 for a double.

### Getting There & Away

**Air** The airport is 14 km south-east of town. There are flights to Algiers, Djanet, Oran and Ouargla.

**Bus** The bus station is south-west of the centre of the town, but there is just the one bus per week to Biskra.

## ILLIZI

Nearly 300 km south of In Amenas, Illizi is the main settlement between there and Djanet.

The town boasts a fuel station, hospital, basic shop, customs post (where you have to check in) and a hotel.

If you really get stranded here there are flights to Algiers, Djanet and Ouargla. The 'airport' is five km north of town and there's not a building at the place – just a graded runway.

## DJANET

The main town of the Tassili, Djanet is a pretty place built on the edge of a palmeraie. It has all the facilities, including post office, bank, basic restaurants and shops.

The main attraction is the collection of rock paintings in the nearby Tassili National Park, around Tamrit. Without a vehicle the only way to get out to these places is on a tour (expensive) or by hitching with other tourists. Even if you do have a vehicle, it is not possible to go into the park unless accompanied by an official guide.

### Places to Stay

The only place to stay is the *Camping Zeribas* in the centre of town, which has a restaurant attached. Camping in the palmeraie is prohibited.

### Getting There & Away

**Air** There is an Air Algérie (☎ 09-735032) office in the town centre. The airstrip is at Ilasadadi, 40 km from town.

There are flights to Algiers, Ghardaia, Illizi, In Amenas, Ouargla and Tamanrasset.

**Hitching** There is no public transport into Djanet other than plane. It's a matter of hitching with trucks or other travellers.

# Route du Hoggar

From El-Goléa, Route N1 continues south across the amazingly flat Tademait Plateau, where the largest thing in sight might be a rock the size of a tennis ball. After 410 km of good bitumen road you hit In Salah, the last town of any size before Tamanrasset. The latter is another 710 km farther south, along a road which is now nearly all bitumen. Tamanrasset is a good place to rest up for a while and a base from which to explore the Hoggar Mountains, which shouldn't be missed.

From Tamanrasset, the piste continues for another 410 km to In Guezzam, 10 km before the border crossing into Niger. The road is fairly punishing on vehicles but 4WD is not necessary.

Right along this route there's a fair amount of traffic, mostly trucks, and hitching is possible; however, it is a lucky traveller who can get all the way to Tamanrasset without having to catch a bus.

## IN SALAH

Built in the red Sudanese style, In Salah would be a very pleasant place to stay were it not for the problem that gives the town its name: salty water. The water is disgusting, so bring as much water with you as you can from Tamanrasset or El-Goléa. Even the local soft drinks are made from it and bottled water is often unavailable.

The most interesting feature of the town is the presence of a creeping sand dune on the western edge by the Aoulef road. Behind the mosque you can see how the dune is gradually encroaching on the town. From the top of the dune it becomes apparent that In Salah has actually been cut in two.

The dunes move at the rate of about a metre every five years. The amount of sand on the move actually remains fairly constant, so while it is swallowing up a building on its leading edge, it is uncovering one behind it which may have been under the sand for a generation or two. Once the ruins of a house have been uncovered, it is established who it used to belong to and then that person's relatives rebuild the place and move in.

The view from the top of the dune is great at sunset. To the west of town along the Aoulef road is the palmeraie, with its 225,000 trees. Formerly a trading town dealing in gold, ivory and slaves from the south in exchange for European goods from the north, the town's major occupation is now date-growing.

### Information

There is a bank in the main street, and the post office is one block to the north.

There is a big hospital out in the east of town near the Hôtel Tidikelt.

### Places to Stay

**Camping** The *Camping Tidikelt* at the end of the main street in the centre of town is the better of the two camping alternatives. There is a reasonable amount of shade and you can sleep in the tiny *zeribas* (palm-frond huts) if you want some privacy. It costs US$2.50 per person to sleep here.

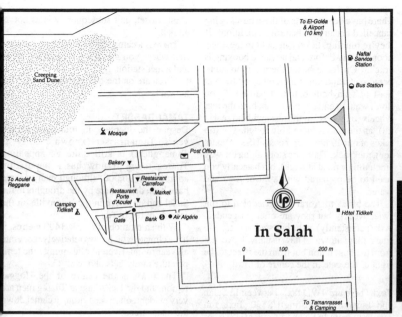

To El-Goléa
& Airport
(10 km)

Naftal
Service
Station

Bus Station

Creeping
Sand Dune

Mosque

Post Office

Bakery

To Aoulef &
Reggane

Restaurant
Carrefour

Restaurant
Porte
d'Aoulef

Market

Camping
Tidikelt

Gate

Bank

Air Algérie

**In Salah**

0   100   200 m

Hôtel Tidikelt

To Tamanrasset
& Camping

The other camp site is three km south of town on the Tamanrasset road. It is very desolate and has no shade, so there is really no incentive to stay here.

**Hotels** The only hotel is the three-star *Hôtel Tidikelt* (☎ 09-730393) on the outskirts of town, 30 minutes' walk from the centre. Rooms are air-conditioned and cost US$23 for a double with breakfast. You may be lucky and find water in the swimming pool.

**Places to Eat**

The *Restaurant Porte d'Aoulef*, just by the arched gate over the street, is no better than average, but it's as good as you'll get apart from the fancy restaurant at the *Hôtel Tidikelt*.

The sole bakery in town is just up from the Restaurant Carrefour. It bakes only in the morning and competition for its wares can be strong, so be there early.

**Getting There & Away**

**Air** The Air Algérie (☎ 09-730239) office is on the main street, next to a bank. The airport is 10 km to the north, to the right of the El-Goléa road.

There are flights to Adrar, Algiers, Borj Mokhtar, Ghardaia, Ouargla and Tamanrasset.

**Bus** The bus station is out in the east on the main Tamanrasset to El-Goléa road, about 20 minutes' walk from the centre. It is actually just a shopping centre (most of it unoccupied), and the bus office is inside towards the back.

There are buses to Adrar, Ghardaia and Tamanrasset. The Ghardaia buses leave at 4 pm every second day and it is essential that you book at 9 am on the day you plan to travel.

For Tamanrasset, in theory there are departures in Mercedes trucks/buses on Tuesday, Thursday and Sunday at 4 am.

There have been reports of these buses being cancelled because of bad road conditions. If they're running, tickets are sold in the afternoon the day before and advance booking is crucial. On these buses there are no numbered seats, and it is important to get there at least half an hour before departure if you don't want to end up in a seat behind the rear wheels (or, worse, in the aisle with no seat at all), as the ride is incredibly rough. The trip takes about 19 hours and costs US$12, extra for a rucksack. There are stops along the way (including a meal at Arak), but basically you need to be prepared with a bit of food and water.

The buses to Adrar are scheduled to run twice weekly but they are often suspended. Ask (persistently) at the bus station to try and track them down. They usually leave not from the bus station but from the street to the right of the gate in the centre of town.

**Taxi** There are 4WD taxis between In Salah and Tamanrasset costing US$30. Taxis run regularly from In Salah to Aoulef (US$6 per person), 170 km west along the road to Adrar, and from there you can catch a daily bus to Adrar. The road is surfaced, except for about 90 km of piste between In Salah and Aoulef.

**Hitching** From the main road you can hitch north from just by the Naftal service station, or south from past the Hôtel Tidikelt. Be prepared for a long wait.

There is very little traffic to Adrar, but you can stand on the road down near the Camping Tidikelt and try your luck.

There is an SNTR depot not far from the Hôtel Tidikelt and it may be possible to organise a lift with one of the drivers. They sometimes park overnight by the side of the road which runs from the centre of town to the bus station.

### ARAK

Although the gorges around Arak are quite spectacular, the little settlement itself is very humble. It doesn't have the altitude of Tamanrasset, and subsequently is as hot as all hell.

There is a camp site with zeribas, a restaurant where you can get a reasonable meal, and a fuel station.

If you are on the bus, it will stop here for a meal break.

### TAMANRASSET

Despite the increase in tourism over the years, Tamanrasset (known locally as Tamenghest) is still quite an appealing Tuareg town. It now has a population approaching 30,000, although many people have been driven here by the droughts in the Sahel and now live in the bidonville on the far side of the oued.

With an altitude of nearly 1400 metres, it has a climate which stays relatively moderate all year round. Even in midsummer the temperature rarely gets above 35°C.

The town is the centre of the Hoggar region, and the Kel Ahaggar Tuareg men are very evident, often seen riding a camel down the main street.

Tamanrasset is also the place from which to arrange trips up into the Hoggar Mountains to the east, something which should not be missed on any account. If you can't hook up with other travellers with vehicles in the camp site, it is possible to get a group together and hire a vehicle and driver from one of the travel agencies around town.

The town is one of those places where virtually all trans-Saharan travellers stop for a few days to rest up and make repairs to equipment, so at any time of the year there may be a dozen vehicles coming and going each day from the camp site. With such a high turnover you rarely have to wait longer than a few days for a lift.

If you are heading south, make sure you clear customs on the southern edge of town when you leave. They will scrutinise your currency form (which is handed in at In Guezzam) and check over your gear. Passport control is handled at the border post, 10 km south of In Guezzam.

If you have just arrived from Niger, check with the authorities at the daira (in the mili

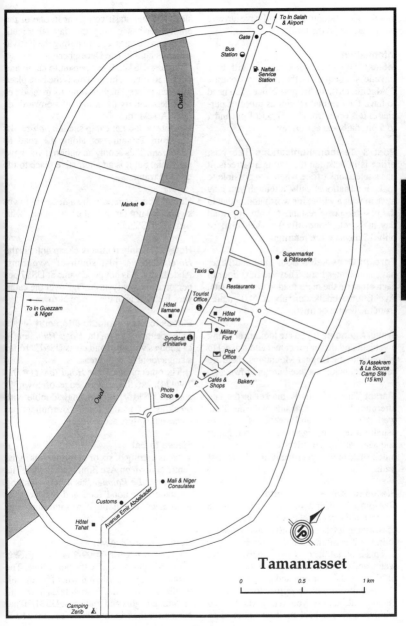

**ALGERIA**

## Tamanrasset

To In Salah
& Airport

Gate

Bus
Station

Naftal
Service
Station

Ouad

Market

Supermarket
& Pâtisserie

Taxis

Restaurants

Tourist
Office

Hôtel
Ilamane

Hôtel
Tinhinane

Military
Fort

Syndicat
d'Initiative

Post
Office

Cafés &
Shops

Bakery

Photo
Shop

To Assekrem
& La Source
Camp Site
(15 km)

To In Guezzam
& Niger

Ouad

Mali & Niger
Consulates

Customs

Avenue Emir Abdelkader

Hôtel
Tahat

Camping
Zerib

0        0.5        1 km

tary fort), even though you will have already been checked at the border.

## Information

**Money** The only bank which will take travellers' cheques is the Banque Centrale d'Algérie, close to the post office. You need to have the original receipt as proof of purchase. It is open from 8.30 am to 1 pm and 4 to 5 pm daily except Friday.

**Post & Telecommunications** The post office is in between the two main streets. It has a telephone office where it's possible to make international calls, although you may have to wait a while. It's worth noting that in the past the poste restante counter (open all day, in the telephone office) has held mail for only 15 days before returning it.

**Foreign Consulates** Both Mali and Niger have consulates here. They are next door to each other on the main road to the camp site, Ave Emir Abdelkader, about 500 metres from the centre of town.

**Travel Agencies** If you are looking at hiring a vehicle and driver (or camel and driver) to get out into the Hoggar Mountains, there are several agencies scattered around town.

**Market** There is a daily market in the late afternoon held on the far side of the oued. As well as limited fruit and vegetables, there are usually a few Tuaregs from Algeria, Niger and Mali selling jewellery and other items – much of it made specifically for the tourist trade.

## Places to Stay – bottom end

**Camping** The *Camping Zerib* is about three km east of the centre of town, near the village of Adriane. It takes about 40 minutes to walk to it, but it is often possible to hitch.

This is about the only place in town to get water, and even then it is only on for a couple of hours in the morning and evening.

There are very basic zeribas for US$5 per person but, unless you really can't sleep without a proper bed, the best option is to sleep out and stash your gear in one of the empty zeribas during the day (there are always spare ones, except during the festival which is held in late December).

It costs US$2.50 per person to camp and US$ 1.50 for a vehicle. This is the best place in town to stay if you want to meet other travellers and try to arrange lifts onwards or up to Assekrem.

There is another camp site, *La Source*, 15 km from Tamanrasset along the road to Assekrem. This is only an option if you have a vehicle, but it is an alternative place to fill up with water.

**Hostel** There is reportedly a hostel in town, signposted not far from the bus station, with beds for US$2.50.

**Hotels** The only remotely cheap hotel is the *Hôtel Ilamane*, just south of Ave Emir Abdelkader. It is not good value at US$7 per person and its only advantage over the camp sites is that it is in the centre of town.

## Places to Stay – middle & top end

In the centre of town, the *Hôtel Tinhinane* is as good as you need and costs US$12/16 for a single/double with breakfast.

The other choice is the *Hôtel Tahat* (☎ 09-734474), on the eastern edge of town. It charges US$15/18 for a single/double with breakfast. It is the usual government-run place and suffers accordingly.

## Places to Eat

There is a string of six or so restaurants in the centre of town on Ave Emir Abdelkader. The *Restaurant Le Palmier* has a long-standing reputation for good food and service. The other places are all much the same and serve the usual stuff.

## Getting There & Away

**Air** The Air Algérie (☎ 09-734174) office is in the group of shops by the post office. The airport is 12 km north of town, off to the left of the main road. Yellow taxis meet all incoming flights and seats cost US$1.50 per person for the trip into town. You may have to abandon your bags and grab hold of a door handle when a taxi rolls up, as demand for seats can be high.

There are flights from here to Adrar, Algiers, Constantine, Djanet, El-Goléa, Ghardaia, In Guezzam, In Salah, Oran and Ouargla.

**Bus** The bus station is in the northern part of town. It is a 20-minute walk from the centre of town and a solid hour from the camp site. If you arrive late at night, or are heading out early in the morning, it is standard practice to doss down at the station. It is a modern building but gets very little use. The bus schedule is displayed on a board inside the building.

Make sure you reserve your ticket the day before departure. They usually go on sale at 4 pm but it is worth checking earlier in the day, as things vary and demand is sometimes high.

Services to In Salah depend on the state of the road. The trip takes a gruelling 19 hours (barring breakdowns) and, for the privilege of having yourself tossed around inside a tin box on a truck chassis, you pay about US$12, plus US$2 for your bag.

There is a weekly departure to In Guezzam (Monday morning) but there is little point in catching this bus, as you still have to get across the border to Agadez. It's better to arrange a lift all the way from Taman-rasset.

Locally there are weekly buses to Idelès and Silet.

## AROUND TAMANRASSET
### Assekrem

Without your own transport, getting out into the Hoggar can be difficult. However, it's worth making the effort to get to Assekrem, 73 km north-east of Tamanrasset by the shorter of the two routes.

The scenery around here is absolutely incredible and a sunrise in these mountains is an experience you're likely never to forget. Words can't even come close to doing the place justice – get up there and see it for yourself.

Charles de Foucauld, a dedicated Christian who came to the Hoggar early this century, built a hermitage up here in 1910; this is still lived in and maintained by a religious order. The hermitage is on top of the Assekrem plateau and can only be reached on foot. It takes about 30 minutes to walk up from below and it is the place to come for the sunrise.

**Places to Stay & Eat** It is possible to stay at the refuge below the hermitage but you need to bring all your own food.

**Getting There & Away** The only way to get up to Assekrem is to get a lift. If you can't strike it lucky at the camp site in Tamanrasset, the only other alternative is to hire a 4WD and driver from one of the agencies. It is not possible to hire a vehicle without a driver.

This is only an option if you have five or six people, as it costs about US$150 per day for vehicle and driver. If you want extras such as food, the agency will charge an additional fee for this – typically about US$15 per person per day.

If you do manage to get out to Assekrem with someone who is going on to Djanet and you want to go back to Tamanrasset, you will probably have to spend a few days in Assekrem waiting for a lift back. You definitely can't walk there, although the agencies can organise trips with camels from Tamanrasset if you want to do it this way.

## IN GUEZZAM

The town is 416 km south of Tamanrasset and is the last place in Algeria before you cross into Niger. The Algerian border post is 10 km south of In Guezzam, so there is really no need to stop here for long.

Don't arrive at the border post between noon and 4 pm, as the border is closed during these hours and you have to sit it out in the heat without a scrap of shade. You're not even allowed to go back to In Guezzam.

### Places to Stay & Eat

The only place in town is *Le Restaurant des Dunes chez Omar*. Apart from a good collection of Western music, you can get OK food and stay overnight.

### Getting There & Away

**Air** There is a weekly flight between In Guezzam and Tamanrasset.

**Bus** There is a truck between Tamanrasset and In Guezzam every Saturday morning at 6 am (US$2), but you are far better off arranging a lift at least as far as Arlit or Agadez from Tamanrasset.

# Tunisia

# Facts about the Country

### HISTORY SINCE 1830

Tunisia has emerged from the struggle against French colonialism in much better shape than neighbouring Algeria. The Husseinid ruler Ahmed Bey, who governed from 1837 to 1855, took pains to give the French no pretext to invade. He outlawed piracy, encouraged Westernisation and brought in foreign advisers. In 1861, during the reign of Mohammed Sadiq, a constitution – the first in the Arab world – was proclaimed.

These Western reforms, however, exacted a heavy toll on the country's limited finances, necessitating heavy borrowing in the form of high-interest loans from European banks. Proposed higher taxes led to internal revolt, and by 1869 the country was in such a financial shambles that control of its finances was given to an international commission.

A final attempt to hold off European control was made by the short-lived ministry led by the reformer Khaireddin (1873-77), but he was forced from office and his plans were scuttled. At the Congress of Berlin in 1878, the major European powers divided up the southern Mediterranean region, and the only challenge to French dominance in Tunisia came from the Italians.

### French Occupation

In 1881, in order to consolidate their position, the French sent 30,000 troops into Tunisia on the pretext of countering border raids made by Tunisian tribesmen into French Algeria. They soon occupied the capital, Tunis. In 1883 the bey signed the Convention of La Marsa, which gave the French control over Tunisian affairs. The bey was answerable to a French resident general who presided over both domestic and foreign affairs.

The protectorate prospered under French rule until the coming of WW I, although it was at the expense of local interests. The best

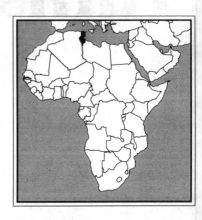

of the fertile land (in the Medjerda Valley and Cap Bon peninsula) passed into European hands, although it was not sequestered on quite the same massive scale as in Algeria. Mineral and phosphate reserves were tapped and a railway network was constructed to service them.

In 1920 the first nationalist political party, the Destour Party, was formed (named after the short-lived constitution of 1861). Its demands for democratic government, despite being supported by the bey, were ignored by the French, and the nationalist movement lost its way for some years.

In 1934 a young, charismatic Sorbonne-educated Tunisian lawyer, Habib Bourguiba, led a breakaway movement from the Destour Party. He founded the Neo-Destour Party, which soon totally replaced the old guard of the Destour. Support for the party soon spread, and the French, keen to put down any potential threat, outlawed the party and jailed Bourguiba.

### Wartime Tunisia

With the fall of France during WW II, the Neo-Destour leaders, who had been

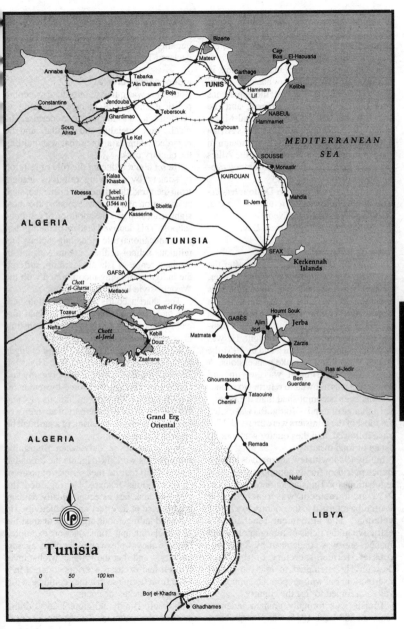

Tunisia

imprisoned there, were handed over to the Italians by the occupying Germans. Although they were well treated in Rome, they refused to support Italy.

In 1942 the Germans landed in Tunis in the hope that they could turn back the Allied advances from east and west: the Americans were on the way from Algeria, and the British forces, led by Field Marshal Montgomery, were driving back Rommel's Afrika Korps in Egypt and Libya. The campaign in Tunisia raged for six months, and the Allies lost more than 15,000 men before they captured Bizerte on 7 May 1943.

In the same year, the Neo-Destour leaders were finally allowed to return to Tunisia, where a government with Neo-Destour sympathies was formed by Moncef Bey.

### Towards Independence

When the French resumed control after the war, they were as uncompromising as ever; the bey was deposed and Bourguiba was forced to flee to Cairo to avoid capture. In the next few years he organised a propaganda campaign aimed at bringing Tunisia's position into the international limelight. He was extremely successful in this, and by 1951 the French were ready to make concessions. A nationalist government was set up and Bourguiba was allowed to return. No sooner had this been accomplished than the French had a change of mind – Bourguiba was exiled and most of the ministers were arrested. Violence followed, and the country was soon in a state of total disarray.

In July 1954, with few alternatives left, the French president finally announced plans for negotiations for Tunisian autonomy. In June 1955 an agreement was reached, and Bourguiba returned to the country to a hero's welcome. The agreement reached was restrictive in the fields of foreign policy and finance, and was condemned by Salah ben Youssef, former secretary of the Neo-Destour. He attempted to lead an armed insurrection, but without popular support he was soon forced to flee the country.

Tunisia was formally granted independence on 20 March 1956, with Bourguiba as prime minister. In the course of the following year, the last bey was deposed, the country became a republic and Bourguiba was declared Tunisia's first president.

### Independent Tunisia

Bourguiba was quick to introduce sweeping political and social changes, looking to Westernisation as the way to modernise. His ideals were socialist and secular, and he regarded Islam as a force that was holding the country back.

He set about reducing the role of religion in society by removing religious leaders from their traditional areas of influence, such as education and the law. Probably the most significant step was the abolition of religious schools. This deprived leaders of their grassroots educational role in shaping society. The religious school at the Zitouna Mosque in Tunis, a centre of Islamic learning, suffered the indignity of being incorporated with the Western-style University of Tunis.

The shari'a courts were also abolished, and more than 60,000 hectares of land that had financed mosques and religious institutions was confiscated.

Bourguiba also introduced major changes to the role of women in society. His 1956 Personal Status Code banned polygamy and ended the practice of divorce by renunciation. He called the hijab an 'odious rag' and banned it from schools as part of an intensive campaign to end the wearing of a garment he regarded as demeaning.

It was, however, only when Bourguiba began urging workers to ignore the Ramadan fast in 1960 that he met serious opposition from religious leaders. He regarded the dawn-to-dusk fast as economically damaging because of its effect on productivity. He mounted an ingenious argument against the fast, declaring that Tunisians were exempted because they were waging a jihad against poverty – and that the Prophet Mohammed himself had excused warriors engaged in a jihad from fasting so that they could be at full strength to tackle the enemy.

Not surprisingly, religious leaders didn't swallow the argument. Trouble broke out in

Kairouan following the transfer of a senior religious figure who had denounced the government, and the fighting took 24 hours to subdue.

## Opposition

Despite his autocratic style – and frequent prolonged absences through ill health – Bourguiba managed to keep the bulk of the population on side, and in 1974 the National Assembly made him president for life.

The 1970s were significant, however, for the gradual emergence of an Islamic opposition in the form of the Islamic Association, led by popular preacher Rashid Ghannouchi. Disillusionment with Bourguiba and his Parti Socialiste Destourien (PSD) – as the Neo-Destour Party became known in 1964 – increased dramatically following the use of the military to crush a general strike called by the UGTT (Tunisia's first trade union federation) in January 1978.

After promising more political freedoms, the government persuaded Bourguiba to call the first multiparty elections in 1981. The Islamic Association became the Islamic Tendency Movement (MTI), advocating a return to Islamic values. Bourguiba, who didn't have much time for opposition of any sort, was certainly not prepared to tolerate an Islamic party and refused to license the MTI.

The elections were a total letdown for the new opposition parties. The National Front (an alliance formed between the PSD and the UGTT) took all 136 seats on offer, bringing cries of foul play.

After the elections, Bourguiba cracked down hard on the MTI. Ghannouchi and its other leaders were jailed and remained so until 1984, when riots were sparked by the withdrawal of a bread subsidy. The rioting lasted six days and stopped only when Bourguiba resumed the subsidy. The riots were notable for the shouting of slogans such as 'God is Great' and 'Down with America', and the MTI leaders were freed to ease the tensions.

## Bourguiba's Final Years

As the 1980s progressed, Bourguiba was seen to be more and more out of touch with both the people at home and with Tunisia's position in the Arab world. An example of his erratic behaviour was his sudden decision in 1986 to sack Prime Minister Mohammed Mzali, just weeks after naming Mzali as his successor. Mzali's replacement, Rachid Sfar, lasted only a year before making way for the tough minister for the interior and former army general, Zine el-Abidine ben Ali, who eventually orchestrated the ousting of Bourguiba.

As minister for the interior, Ben Ali had only recently presided over yet another crackdown on the Islamic opposition, which produced more than 1000 arrests. In September 1987, 90 of those held, including Ghannouchi, were put on trial on charges ranging from planting bombs to conspiring to overthrow the regime. The bombings were a curious affair. Twelve tourists had been injured in hotel blasts at Sousse and Monastir, and responsibility had been claimed by the pro-Iranian Islamic Jihad organisation. The government, however, held the MTI to blame, even though most of those charged had been in jail at the time.

The trial produced seven death sentences, while Ghannouchi was given hard labour for life. Bourguiba had demanded the death sentence for all the accused and was furious at the outcome, insisting on retrials and that Ghannouchi and 15 others be executed by 16 November 1987.

It was against this backdrop that Ben Ali made his move. The arrest of Ghannouchi had sparked street battles, and there were fears that executions could lead to a popular uprising. On 7 November, a group of doctors assembled by Ben Ali were asked to examine the 83-year-old president, who was, predictably, declared unfit to carry out his duties. It seems that, despite a heart condition, his physical health was not too bad for a man of his age; it was his mental health that was causing the concern.

Bourguiba was held for some time in detention in his palace in Carthage before being shunted off to 'retirement' in another palace outside Sfax, where he remains today.

TUNISIA

Bourguiba's greatest achievements were the fostering of a strong national identity and the development of a standard of living which puts the country at the top of the pile in the developing world.

### President Ben Ali

Ben Ali moved quickly to appease the Islamic opposition. He headed off on a heavily publicised pilgrimage to Mecca to establish his own credentials as a good Muslim, and ordered that the Ramadan fast be observed. He also promised a multiparty political system, although he baulked at legalising the MTI – which by now had changed its name to Hizb al-Nahda (Renaissance Party).

Political prisoners were released, the State Security Court was abolished and police powers of detention were limited. Political exiles were invited to return, and many decided that it was safe to return to Tunisia.

However, the general elections held in April 1989 didn't exactly reflect a new liberalism. Ben Ali's Rassemblement Constitutionel Democratique (RCD), as the PSD had become, won all the seats amid charges of vote rigging. The presidential elections saw Ben Ali re-elected with 99.27% of the vote.

Al-Nahda was not allowed to contest the poll, but many of its candidates stood as independents. Estimates of their share of the vote varied from 13% up to 40% in some urban areas.

This result, coupled with the successes of the Islamic Salvation Front (FIS) in municipal elections in neighbouring Algeria, prompted Ben Ali to rule out official recognition of the Hizb al-Nahda.

However, no major move was made against the party until after the 1991 Gulf War. Tunisia officially supported the US-led alliance, but popular sentiment was very much behind Iraq's Saddam Hussein. In May 1991, the government announced that it had uncovered a Hizb al-Nahda plot to establish an Islamic state by force. A sizable number of those arrested were members of the military.

### Opposition Today

Officially, there is no opposition. The ruling party won all 144 seats at elections held in March 1994, and Ben Ali again won more than 99% of the presidential vote.

The official opposition in Tunisia is the Mouvement des Democratiques Socialites (MDS). It holds no parliamentary seats and supports the outlawing of Islamic parties.

In spite of his election victory, the Ben Ali government's main concern continues to be the Islamic opposition, especially in light of events next door in Algeria.

There is no suggestion that the government is anything other than in complete control. Politics is not a popular (or advisable) topic of conversation, but many Tunisians appear to have a genuine admiration for the present leadership.

### Foreign Policy

Much of the esteem in which Ben Ali is held stems from Tunisia's high standing in the Arab world. The country has developed a reputation for stability in a volatile region. Tunisia was home to the Arab League for most of the 1980s, but it returned to Cairo in the late 1980s as Egypt re-entered the Arab fold after years on the outer for having made peace with Israel in 1979.

The PLO was based just outside Tunis after it was forced out of Lebanon by the Israelis in the early 1980s. The headquarters were badly damaged by an Israeli bombing raid in 1985 in retaliation for the killing of three Israelis in Cyprus. In mid-1994, Yasser Arafat and the PLO returned to the Israeli-controlled occupied territories to set up a local autonomous government.

Tunisia also has been an important opening to the outside world for Libya since an international air embargo was imposed over alleged Libyan involvement in the Lockerbie jumbo-jet bombing.

Relations with France have been generally good since independence, despite a few major hiccups in the late 1950s and early 1960s. In 1958, France bombed the Tunisian border village of Sakiet Sidi Youssef, claiming that Algerian rebels had crossed into Tunisia and that France had the right to pursue them. The enraged Tunisians demanded that the French evacuate their military base in Bizerte, but it wasn't until 1961 (when the Tunisian army saw its first action) that the French began to withdraw. The withdrawal wasn't completed until 1963, by which time 1000 Tunisian soldiers had been killed.

Another incident flared up in 1964, when Tunisia suddenly nationalised land owned by foreigners. France responded by cutting off all aid, a situation that was not remedied until 1966.

Today, the Americans are the major supplier of equipment to the Tunisian army.

## GEOGRAPHY

With an area of 164,000 sq km, Tunisia is by far the smallest of the Maghreb countries; it's about half as big as Italy, or about the same size as Washington State in the USA or Victoria in Australia.

The country borders on Algeria to the west and Libya to the south-east. The ragged and

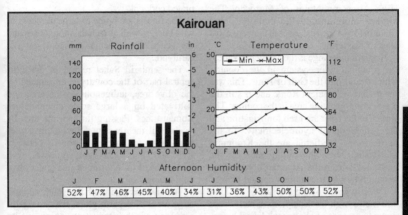

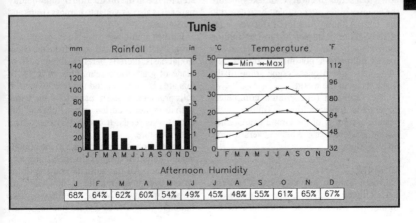

TUNISIA

irregular 1400-km Mediterranean coastline forms the eastern and northern boundaries. Tunisia measures 750 km from north to south but only 150 km from east to west.

Topographically, the country divides fairly neatly into the mountainous northern third and the flat southern two-thirds.

The main topographical feature in the north of the country is the Tunisian Dorsale, a range of mountains which runs from Kasserine near the Algerian border to Zaghouan, just south of Tunis. The mountains then taper off to form the Cap Bon peninsula. These mountains are actually a continuation of both the Algerian Saharan Atlas and the High Atlas mountains of Morocco. The highest mountain in the country, Jebel Chambi (1544 metres), rises in this range just west of Kasserine.

North of this range is the Medjerda Valley, the principal river system in the country, which drains into the Gulf of Tunis. This was the granary of ancient Rome and is still the major grain-growing area in the country. The waters of the river are used for irrigation and the generation of hydroelectricity. To the north of the Medjerda are the Kroumirie Mountains, stretching along most of the north coast from the Algerian border. This range gives way to a narrow coastal plain.

Directly south of the Dorsale is a 200 to 400-metre-high treeless plain, which drops down to a series of chotts (salt lakes) before the country gives out completely to desert in the south. Although this is only the very edge of the Sahara, it attracts up to two million tourists each year. Abundant artesian water makes cultivation possible in places, and from these green oases come some of the finest dates in the world.

The sand sea (erg) which completely covers the southern tip of Tunisia is the eastern extremity of the Grand Erg Oriental (Great Eastern Erg), which covers a large area of Algeria.

## CLIMATE

Northern Tunisia has a typical Mediterranean climate, with hot, dry summers and mild, wet winters. The mountains of the north-west occasionally get snow. The farther south you go, the hotter and drier it gets. Annual rainfall ranges from 1000 mm in the north down to 150 mm in the south, although some Saharan areas go for years without rain.

## FLORA & FAUNA

The climate dictates which plants and animals exist in Tunisia's different regions. Most of the large mammals live in the dense forests of the Kroumirie range, which receives the lion's share of the country's rainfall. The main trees are two oak species, the handsome Mirbecks oak and the celebrated cork oak.

The forests are home to large numbers of wild boar, as well as jackals, mongooses and the genet, a spectacular arboreal, cat-like carnivore.

The semiarid Sahel region in the east-central part of the country is dominated by the olive tree, indigenous to the area and cultivated on a large scale since before Roman times. Passing through the area by road or rail, the rows upon rows of olive trees seem to stretch forever. If you fly between Jerba and Tunis in daylight, you get an even better idea of the enormous area under olive cultivation.

The treeless plains of the south support large areas of esparto grass, which is gathered for use in the production of high-quality paper. It is also woven into harness straps and reed mats.

Farther south, the vegetation gives way altogether to desert, and, apart from the occasional oasis, there is barely a single bush or blade of grass to be seen. One curiosity of this area is a plant called the Jericho rose. It rolls around the desert, carried by the wind, with its branches curled up in a tight ball that encloses its seeds. It opens only on contact with moisture.

The desert regions are home to the famous camel, although there is no such thing as a wild camel. All the animals you see in the desert, even in the middle of 'nowhere', are owned by somebody. The gazelle was once hounded (literally, by Saluki hunting dogs) to the verge of extinction, but fortunately numbers are recovering since hunting was banned.

It may be too late for the fennec, the nocturnal desert fox. This delicate creature, with its enormous, radar-like ears, may exist only in Tunisia's zoos. There's more chance of meeting some of the reptiles, including the desert varanid – a smaller member of the family that includes Australia's goanna and Indonesia's Komodo dragon.

It's a good idea to play it safe and wear solid shoes when walking in rocky areas in case you meet a horned viper or one of the many species of scorpion.

## GOVERNMENT

The 1959 constitution of the Republic of Tunisia gives legislative power to the chamber of deputies, which consists of 144 members elected directly by universal suffrage to a five-year term.

The president, who is elected separately, has executive power and is the head of both the state and the government. The constitution states that the president must be a Muslim and can serve for no more than three consecutive terms; however, the first president of independent Tunisia, Habib Bourguiba, was elected president for life in 1974 before being ousted in 1987.

## ECONOMY

The mixed Tunisian economy, in which both the public and private sectors participate, relies heavily on tourism and, up until the Gulf crisis in 1990, on remittances from nationals working in the Gulf States.

Petrol and petroleum products account for about 25% of exports, but the lack of refining capacity within Tunisia means that most of the country's heavy petroleum needs have to be met with imports. Other important exports include textiles and leather (30%), fertilisers and chemicals, with the main destinations being France, the USA, Italy and Germany. Imports chiefly consist of food, raw materials and capital goods.

The agricultural sector has become smaller in the last 20 years and now provides

work for less than 30% of the workforce; almost 40% of food required has to be imported. Despite the fact that large areas of the south of the country are desert, over 55% of the land is cultivated. The main crops are wheat, barley, maize, sorghum, olives and dates.

Major industries are concentrated in the processing of agricultural produce and minerals, including textiles, foodstuffs, cement, steel and phosphate. The importance of Tunisia's mining industry is reflected in the fact that Tunisia is the world's sixth-largest producer of phosphate.

Unemployment is widespread and the situation is exacerbated by the fact that most manufacturing is small scale and most businesses employ no more than five people.

### Social Conditions

Unemployment is the main social issue, as it seems to be almost everywhere in the world. As a visitor, the unemployment rate in your country is one of the first questions you will be asked – closely followed by one about the chances of finding a job.

While the social-security system provides old-age and disability pensions, and compensation for sickness and injury, the unemployed get nothing. They survive thanks to the closeness of the family network; often one working adult will be supporting four or five other adult family members.

In spite of this, living standards are generally good and are considered high by developing-world standards. Per capita GDP is around US$1300.

Health care is also free, and low-income earners are eligible for extra benefits such as free milk for newborn babies and free school lunches. Although there are still shortages of trained personnel and modern facilities, general health conditions have improved dramatically in the last 20 years. The government claims a 96% coverage for its compulsory immunisation program, the most comprehensive in the developing world.

## POPULATION & PEOPLE

The people of Tunisia, who number around 8.5 million, are basically Arab Berber. The vast majority are Muslim, and the non-Muslim population numbers fewer than 40,000 (down from over 300,000 in the 1950s).

The country has a fairly high growth rate of about 2.5%. Almost half the population is under the age of 15, which places a great strain on social services. Another problem is the population distribution, which varies from over 2000 per sq km in Tunis to less than 10 per sq km in the south.

The Berbers were the original inhabitants of the area, but waves of immigration over the centuries have brought Phoenicians, Jews, Romans, Vandals and Arabs. There was a major influx of Spanish Muslims in the 17th century. The Ottoman Turks have also added their bit to the great ethnic mix.

## EDUCATION

Education is free and, thanks to the high government spending (typically 25% of total expenditure), the number of schools has increased rapidly since independence. Literacy is fairly high, at about 60% in males and 40% in females.

## ARTS

Arts lovers aren't in for a feast, unless they are visiting specifically for an event like the biennial Carthage International Film Festival (October, odd-numbered years) or the El-Jem International Symphonic Music Festival (every July). Most cultural events laid on for tourists take the form of fairly tacky 'folk nights'. Tunis has a number of art galleries and the inside back page of the English-language weekly *Tunisia News* has a list of exhibitions. The Galérie Yahia, next to the ONAT building on Ave Mohammed V, is a good place to look.

## SOCIETY & CONDUCT
### Traditional Lifestyle

**Cafés** Cafés are another integral part of Tunisian life. They are much more than a place to stop for a coffee. It is here that the menfolk gather in the evening to smoke their *chichas* (water pipes), exchange gossip and play cards. The main card games are rummy and *quarante*, a game with no Western equivalent that is played with such speed and enthusiasm that it's impossible to figure out the rules. Watching the animated participants is entertainment enough.

**Smoking** It is rare to find a male who doesn't smoke. Many women, too, are enthusiastic puffers of tobacco – although it is rare to find a woman smoking in public.

It has been estimated that 60% of the male population smoke the traditional chicha. Cafés provide the chicha free, charging only for a plug of tobacco.

Mars International are the most popular cigarettes among Westerners. They cost TD 1.150 from a tabac, 100 mills more from street stalls. Most Tunisians scorn Mars as being far too mild, and prefer Cristal. They cost 700 mills and are strong enough to make your head spin.

### Avoiding Offence

Some visitors get overly anxious about doing the right thing. There's no danger of being assaulted by some fanatic for inadvertently eating a chip with the left hand (which is reserved for ablutions). Locals make allowances for foreigners, and the surest way to avoid causing offence is by trying to be polite. What *will* cause offence outside the main tourist areas is immodest dress – and that goes for men too. The response to a man wearing shorts is more likely to be standoffish rather than hostile, but scantily clad women can expect more unwelcome attention.

### Sport

**Soccer** When Tunisians say football, it's soccer they're referring to. It's the country's most popular sport. After school, every side street and patch of wasteland is taken over by kids kicking a ball around. Although overshadowed by the exploits of the Moroccan team on the world stage, Tunisia fields one of the strongest teams in Africa. Its club teams are among the best on the continent, with both CA Bizertin (Bizerte) and Club Africain (Tunis) winning African cup competitions in recent years.

**Handball** While something of a curiosity to many Westerners, handball is taken very seriously in Tunisia. The national men's team is ranked among the best in the world, and the national competition gets a lot of press coverage.

**Volleyball** While I never saw a woman playing any form of sport, the papers indicate that this is the most popular women's sport. There are national competitions for both men and women.

## RELIGION

Islam is the state religion in Tunisia. While there has been a definite resurgence of religious adherence, particularly among the young and unemployed, Tunisia remains a fairly liberal society. For more on Islam, see the Religion section in the Facts about the Region chapter.

There is a small Jewish community, living mainly in Tunis and on the island of Jerba, as well as about 20,000 Roman Catholics.

## LANGUAGE

Tunisia is virtually bilingual. Arabic is the language of government, but almost everybody speaks some French. French was the language of education in the early Bourguiba years, and it is still taught from the age of six.

English and German are also taught at school, but it's rare to encounter either language outside main tourist areas.

The Berber language Chelha is heard only in isolated villages.

# Facts for the Visitor

## VISAS & EMBASSIES

Nationals of most countries in the EU need no visa for a stay of up to three months; you just roll up at immigration and get a stamp in your passport. Citizens of Canada, the USA, Japan and Germany can stay for up to four months without a visa.

Tunisia is not in the business of turning tourist dollars away. Most other nationalities, including Australians and New Zealanders, are technically allowed to stay for one month without a visa – although this seems to depend on which embassy you approach. They can also apply for a three-month visa, costing TD 6, before arrival. Visas can be obtained wherever Tunisia has diplomatic representation abroad.

Nationals of Israel are not allowed to enter the country. South Africans were barred at the time of writing, but this can be expected to change.

### Tunisian Embassies

Visas can be obtained from the following Tunisian diplomatic representatives abroad:

Algeria
  7 Rue Ammar Rahmani, El-Biar, 16000 Algiers (☎ 781480)
  23 Rue Gouasmi Ammar, Annaba (☎ 820666)
  Route de Morsot (PO Box 280), Tébessa (☎ 974855)
Australia
  Honorary Tunisian Consulate, GPO Box 510, Sydney 2000 (☎ 363 5588)
Austria
  Chegastr 3, 1030 Vienna (☎ 78 65 51/3)
Belgium
  Ave du Brésil 12, 1050 Brussels (☎ 734 56 78)
Canada
  515 O'Connor St, Ottawa, Ontario K1S 3P8 (☎ 237 0330/2)
Egypt
  26 Rue el-Jazirah, Zamalek, Cairo (☎ 340 4940)
France
  17-19 Rue de Lubeck, 75016 Paris (☎ 45.53.50.94)

14 Ave du Maréchal Foch, 96006 Lyon (☎ 93.42.87)
  18 Ave des Fleurs, 66000 Nice (☎ 96.81.81)
  8 Blvd d'Athènes, 13001 Marseilles (☎ 50.28.68)
Germany
  Godesbergerallee 103, 5300 Bonn 2 (☎ 37 69 81)
  110 Esplanade 12, 1100 Berlin (☎ 4 72 20 64)
  Overbeckstrasse 19, 2000 Hamburg 76 (☎ 2 20 17 56/7)
  Adimstrage 4, 8000 Munich 19 (☎ 18 00 12/3)
Greece
  Ethnikis Antistasseos 91, 15231 Halandri, Athens (☎ 671 7590)
India
  23 Olaf Palam Marg, Vavant Vihar, 110057 New Delhi (☎ 688 5346)
Italy
  Via Asmara 5, 00199 Rome (☎ 860 42 82/3)
  Via XX Settembre 2/13, 16100 Genoa (☎ 570 20 91)
  Centro Derizionale Isola F10, 80140 Naples (☎ 734 51 61)
Libya
  Ave Jehara, Sharia Bin 'Ashur, 3160 Tripoli (☎ 607161)
  2 Sharia Habib Norani, 85 Benghazi (☎ 86367/8)
Malta
  Quormi Rd, Attard, Valetta (☎ 49 88 53)
Morocco
  6 Ave de Fès, Rabat (☎ 730576, 730636/7; fax 727866)
Netherlands
  Gentestraat 98, 2587 HX The Hague (☎ 351 22 51)
Spain
  Plaza Alonzo Martinez 3, 28004 Madrid (☎ 447 3508)
Sudan
  55 Baladia St, BP 8270, 3533 Khartoum (☎ 76538)
Switzerland
  Kirchenfeldstrasse 63, 3005 Bern (☎ 44 82 26)
Turkey
  Cumhuriyet Cad 169/1, El-Madaq, 80230 Istanbul (☎ 152 8618/9)
  Cayhane Sokak 40, Gazi Osmane Paza, 06700 Ankara (☎ 37 77 20)
UK
  29 Prince's Gate, London SW7 1QG (☎ 0171-584 8117)
USA
  1515 Massachusetts Ave NW, Washington DC 20005 (☎ 862 1850)

## Visa Extensions

There's little likelihood of needing a visa extension, as a month is plenty of time for most people. In any case, from all accounts, the process involved is one to be avoided. Applications can be made only at the Interior Ministry on Ave Habib Bourguiba in Tunis. They cost TD 3 (payable only in revenue stamps), take up to 10 days to issue and require bank receipts, two photos and a *facture* (receipt) from your hotel for starters.

## Foreign Embassies in Tunisia

Most countries represented in Tunisia have their embassies and consulates in Tunis. See that chapter for contact details.

## DOCUMENTS

Visitors planning to hire a car or motorbike of more than 50 cc will need to bring their national driving licence, which must have been held for one year. There are no advertised discounts for student cards – although it never hurts to ask.

## CUSTOMS

The duty-free allowance is 400 cigarettes, two litres of wine, a litre of spirits and 250 ml of perfume. It is advisable to declare valuable items (such as cameras) on arrival to ensure a smooth passage on your departure.

## MONEY

The Tunisian dinar is a non-convertible currency, and its import or export is prohibited. Most major currencies are readily exchanged inside the country, although Australian travellers should be aware that Australian dollars are not accepted.

There is no black market and it is not necessary to declare your foreign currency on arrival.

When leaving the country, you can reconvert only up to 30% of the amount you have changed to dinar (up to a limit of TD 100), so hang on to exchange receipts and don't change too much towards the end of your stay. If you don't have any receipts to show, you won't be able to reconvert *any* dinar.

## Currency

The Tunisian currency is the dinar, which is divided into 1000 millimes. Coins in circulation are 5, 10, 20, 50, 100, 500 millimes and one dinar. Notes in use are 5, 10 and 20 dinars. Changing notes is no problem.

## Exchange Rates

| Algeria | AD 1 | = | TD 0.02 |
|---|---|---|---|
| Australia | A$1 | = | TD 0.74 |
| Canada | C$1 | = | TD 0.71 |
| France | FFr1 | = | TD 0.18 |
| Germany | DM1 | = | TD 0.63 |
| Japan | ¥100 | = | TD 0.99 |
| Libya | 1 LD | = | TD 2.75 |
| Morocco | Dr 1 | = | TD 0.11 |
| New Zealand | NZ$1 | = | TD 0.61 |
| Spain | 100 pta | = | TD 0.75 |
| UK | UK£1 | = | TD 1.53 |
| USA | US$1 | = | TD 0.98 |

Foreign currency can be changed at banks, flash hotels and major post offices. Exchange rates are regulated and so the same rate is given everywhere. Banks charge a standard 351 millimes commission per travellers' cheque, while the larger hotels take slightly more.

## Credit Cards

Major credit cards, such as Visa, American Express and MasterCard, are accepted widely throughout the country at large shops, tourist hotels, car-rental agencies and banks. If you want a cash advance, you can get only local currency.

## Costs

Tunisia is not a cheap place for visitors, unless you happen to be fortunate enough to be earning northern European wages. Its generally high standard of living and the fact that it is certainly not a Third World country are reflected in the cost of everyday items.

Accommodation costs about US$15 to US$20 for a double in a reasonable hotel and US$7 to US$10 for a single. By the time you add food and transport costs, you are looking at about US$30 per day all up.

Obviously you could spend a lot more

than this; you could also spend quite a bit less if you are prepared to rough it a bit, staying in hotels with cold showers (or no shower at all) or hostels, eating at cheap, local restaurants and travelling 2nd class or hitching.

## TOURIST OFFICES

The government doesn't put out a great deal of printed information, but it does issue some glossy handout stuff in various languages. Most tourist offices have lists of hotel prices in their region.

### Local Tourist Offices

The government-run Office National du Tourisme Tunisien (ONTT) has the following offices dotted around the country:

Bizerte
    1 Rue de Constantinople (☎ 02-432897)
Douz
    Place des Martyrs (☎ 05-495351)
Gabès
    Place de la Libération (☎ 05-270254)
Gafsa
    Place des Piscines Romaines (☎ 06-221664)
Hammamet
    Ave Habib Bourguiba (☎ 02-280423)
Jerba
    Rue Ulysse, Houmt Souq (☎ 05-650016)
Kairouan
    Ave de la République (☎ 07-221797)
Monastir
    Rue de l'Indépendance (☎ 03-461960)
Nabeul
    Ave Taieb Mehiri (☎ 02-286800)
Sousse
    1 Ave Habib Bourguiba (☎ 03-225157)
Tabarka
    32 Ave Habib Bourguiba (☎ 08-644491)
Tozeur
    Ave Abdulkacem Chebbi (☎ 06-450088)
Tunis
    1 Ave Mohammed V (☎ 01-341077)

Unfortunately, the standard of service in most of these offices leaves a lot to be desired – calling them information centres is a bit misleading. Most appear to be run by functionaries who have no idea about what's going on and even less of an idea of how to impart what information they do have.

There are some exceptions, such as the well-organised office at Sousse, which offer

a range of useful information on transport, accommodation and sightseeing. Some have lists (on request) of the region's hotels and tariffs. Most have nothing at all except a glossy brochure and a smile that says they'd love to help if only they knew how.

There are also quite a few local tourist offices, usually called syndicats d'initiative, which have a limited amount of information on a particular area.

### Overseas Reps

ONTT's overseas offices include:

Austria
    Landesgerichstr 22, 1010 Vienna (☎ 408 39 60)
Belgium
    Galerie Ravenstein 60, 100 Brussels (☎ 5111142)
Canada
    1125 Maisonneuve Ouest, Montreal, Quebec H3A 3B6 (☎ 985 2586)
France
    32 Ave de l'Opéra, 75002 Paris (☎ 47.42.72.67)
Germany
    Am Hauptbahnhof 6, 6000 Frankfurt (☎ 23 18 91/2)
Holland
    Muntplein 2111, 1012 WR Amsterdam (☎ 22 49 71/2)
Italy
    Via Baracchini 10, 20123 Milan (☎ 87 12 14)
Sweden
    Almlövsgatan 3, 11451 Stockholm (☎ 667 1765)
Switzerland
    Bahnhofstrasse 69, 8001 Zürich (☎ 211 48 30)
UK
    77a Wigmore St, London W1H GLJ (☎ 0171-224 5561)

## USEFUL ORGANISATIONS

The following organisations may prove to be useful:

Desert Club Tourism Services
    3 Place du Souq, Douz 4260
Touring Club de Tunisie
    15 Rue d' Allemagne, Tunis 1000 (☎ 01-243114)
Hostelling International
    25 Rue Saida Ajoula, Tunis medina (☎ 01-567850)

## BUSINESS HOURS
### Banks
Banking hours are a complicated business.

From July to September, opening times are 7.30 to 11 am Monday to Friday; for the rest of the year, the hours are from 8 to 11 am and 2 to 4.15 pm Monday to Thursday, and from 8 to 11 am and 1 to 3.15 pm on Friday. In tourist areas, one bank is rostered to open on Saturday morning. Ask at the local tourist office.

### Offices

These are open Monday to Thursday from 8.30 am to 1 pm and 3 to 5.45 pm, and on Friday and Saturday from 8.30 am to 1.30 pm. In summer, offices do not open in the afternoon at all.

### Shops & Souqs

Generally, shops are open Monday to Friday from 8 am to 12.30 pm and 2.30 to 6 pm, and from 8 am to noon on Saturday. Summer hours are usually 7.30 am to 1 pm. These hours vary slightly from place to place, especially in the south, where the weather is more extreme in summer.

### HOLIDAYS

Public holidays are primarily religious celebrations, or festivities which mark the anniversary of various events in the creation of the modern state.

As the Gregorian (Western) and Islamic calendars are of different lengths, the Islamic holidays fall 10 days earlier every Western calendar year. For the Islamic holidays see the relevant section in the Facts about the Region chapter. Ramadan is the main holiday to watch out for, because for an entire month the opening hours of everything are disrupted.

Other public holidays in Tunisia are:

*New Year's Day* – 1 January
*Independence Day* – 20 March
*Youth Day* – 21 March
*Martyrs' Day* – 9 April
*Labour Day* – 1 May
*Republic Day* – 25 July
Public Holiday – 3 August
*Women's Day* – 13 August
*Evacuation Day* – 15 October
*Anniversary of Ben Ali's Takeover* – 7 November

Some of these holidays, such as Women's Day and Evacuation Day, pass without notice. On others, everything comes to a halt and absolutely nothing happens (although transport still runs). On some long weekends, such as the 'Eid al-Fitr (celebrating the end of Ramadan), public transport gets strained to the limit as everyone tries to get home for the festival.

### CULTURAL EVENTS

Many of Tunisia's numerous festivals are staged with the tourist trade foremost in the minds of the organisers, although they are worth a look if you are in the area. The main ones are:

December/January
  *Sahara Festival*, Douz & Tozeur – everything from camel races to traditional marriages
April
  *Nefta Festival* – parades and folkloric events
May
  *Monastir Festival* – more parades etc
June
  *Dougga Festival* – performances of French classical theatre at the restored Roman theatre at Dougga
July-August
  *Carthage International Festival* – Tunisia's cultural event of the year, with music, poetry and theatre performances at the Roman theatre at Carthage
  *El-Jem International Symphonic Music Festival* – candle-lit performances of works by composers such as Mozart, Bach and Bizet at El-Jem's famous Colosseum
  *Siren Festival*, Kerkennah Islands – more folkloric favourites for the tourists
  *Hammamet Festival* – in spite of the location and timing, this is a serious arts festival with musical and cultural events
  *Tabarka Festival* – music and theatre, and a coral exhibition
  *Ulysses Festival*, Jerba – strictly for the tourists this one, right down to the Miss Ulysses competition
August
  *Baba Aoussou Festival*, Sousse – another event for the tourists
September
  *Grombalia Wine Festival* – sounds more promising than the month's other candidate, the *Wheat Festival* at Beja
October
  *Carthage International Film Festival* (biennial;

TUNISIA

every other year it is held in Ouagadougou!) – two weeks of films from around the world, with an emphasis on Arab and African cinema

## SUGGESTED ITINERARIES

The following are three suggested one-week itineraries, based on arrival at the country's three major international airports:

Arrive Tunis
Visit Tunis (medina and Bardo Museum), Carthage, Sidi Bou Said, Tabarka, 'Ain Draham, Bulla Regia and Dougga

Arrive Monastir
Visit Sousse, Kairouan, Mahdia and El-Jem

Arrive Jerba
Visit Houmt Souq (Jerba), Matmata, Tozeur and the ksour (fortified strongholds) around Tataouine

## POST & TELECOMMUNICATIONS
## Post

The Tunisian postal service is a little slow, but you will find that your things do arrive eventually.

Letters from overseas generally take about a week to arrive from Europe, and two weeks from farther afield. Times are very similar in the other direction, although up to three weeks to a destination like Australia is nothing unusual.

If you want to ensure that your mail gets through quickly, try the Rapide Poste service available at all post offices, or PTTs as they are always called.

**Postal Rates** Airmail letters to Europe cost 500 mills; to the Americas, Asia and Oceania they cost 550 mills. Postcards cost 100 mills less.

Parcels are not particularly cheap. To the Americas, Asia and Oceania, the rate is TD 8 for up to two kg; for parcels between two kg and five kg, you pay TD 11.605 plus 950 mills per kg; up to 10 kg, the rate is TD 15.150 plus 950 mills per kg. The rate to Europe is slightly lower.

In addition to post offices, stamps are available from major hotels and from some general stores and newsstands.

**Sending Mail** Post office hours differ between summer and winter, and also between city and country areas. Most places you are likely to visit will be keeping city hours. Post offices are open from Monday to Saturday from 8 am to 6 pm in winter and from 7.30 am to 1.30 pm in summer, and on Sunday throughout the year from 9 to 11 am. Summer hours are kept from 1 July until 30 September.

During Ramadan, the hours are 8 am to 3 pm Monday to Saturday. The main post office in Tunis is open seven days a week.

**Parcel Post** The best place to mail parcels is the parcel post office in Tunis on Ave de la République. You have to take the parcel there *unwrapped* so that it can be inspected; if you want to send something surface mail, make sure you stress the fact or you may find yourself getting charged for airmail.

**Receiving Mail** Mail can be received poste restante at any post office in the country. It should be addressed clearly with the family name in block capitals. Ask the clerks to check under your given name as well if you think you are missing mail.

There is a collection fee of 180 mills per letter.

### Telephone

The phone system is modern and efficient. Public phones can be found just about everywhere – look for the *taxiphone* signs, or try at the PTT.

**Local Calls** Local calls cost 100 mills from public phones, which can be found in many hotels and cafés. Hotels normally charge about 300 mills for local calls made from your hotel room.

Getting hold of telephone numbers is rather difficult. There are only two phone books, one for Tunis and one for the rest of the country. Both are hopelessly out of date – the country book was put out in 1989 and the Tunis book in 1991. They are published in both Arabic and English.

A complicating factor is that the numbering system for areas outside greater Tunis (the Governorates of Tunis, Ariana and Ben Arous) was changed in October 1993, by the addition of an extra digit before the existing number. All telephone numbers in Tunisia now have six digits, although most publicity material still carries the old five-digit numbers. Hopefully, the necessary adjustments will have been made by the time you get there.

If you have any problems, the number for directory information is ☎ 1818.

**Area Codes** Tunisia's major area codes are:

| Code | Region |
|------|--------|
| 01 | Tunis region |
| 02 | Bizerte, Hammamet & Nabeul |
| 03 | Sousse & Monastir |
| 04 | Sfax |
| 05 | Gabès & Jerba |
| 06 | Tozeur & Gafsa |
| 07 | Kairouan |
| 08 | Tabarka & Le Kef |

**International Calls** Making international phone calls is also no problem. In Tunis, the international telephone office is open 24 hours and you can dial direct to most countries. The digital payphones for international calls take only 500-millime and TD 1 coins. The phones that take 100-millime coins can be used only for local calls.

Outside Tunis, most towns have international telephone facilities at or around the PTT. Many taxiphone offices are equipped for international direct dialling. Calls can also be made from major hotels, but these are considerably more expensive. Phonecards are of no use at all.

**Codes & Charges** International codes and charges per minute are as follows:

| Country | Code | Cost |
|---------|------|------|
| Algeria | 00213 | 600 mills |
| Australia | 0061 | TD 3 |
| France | 0033 | 840 mills |
| Germany | 0049 | 960 mills |
| Italy | 0039 | 840 mills |
| New Zealand | 0064 | TD 3 |
| UK | 0044 | 960 mills |
| USA/Canada | 001 | TD 2 |

### Fax, Telex & Telegraph

Faxes are all the rage in Tunisia, and almost every classified hotel has a fax machine. Most major hotels also offer telex facilities. It will cost you less to use the public facilities available at the telephone offices in major towns. Telegrams can be sent from any post office.

### TIME

Tunisia is one hour ahead of GMT/UTC from October to April, and two hours ahead of GMT from May to September.

### ELECTRICITY

Most of the country is on 220 V, but the occasional hotel in Tunis and some of the smaller towns in the south are still on 110 V. Check before plugging in any appliance. The supply is reliable and uninterrupted. As in Europe, wall plugs have two round pins.

### LAUNDRY

Laundrettes don't exist in the Western sense, and they barely exist in any other sense. There are a couple of places in Tunis filled with washing machines and driers where you can pay for washing to be done by the kg. You just drop off the load and collect it later.

The only other solution is to ask about laundry at your hotel, although this can prove expensive. Washing and ironing of a shirt will cost about 500 mills at a rated hotel.

Tourist areas and most larger towns have dry-cleaning shops. Typical prices include shirt TD 1, silk shirt TD 1.300, slacks TD 1.200, jeans TD 1.700, cloth jacket TD 1.800 and women's skirt and jacket TD 2.800.

### BOOKS

The following are a few books which may help give you a better understanding of the country and its people. Books that deal solely with Tunisia are about as scarce as hen's teeth. If your French is up to book standard you have a far better chance of finding something. For more general reading on the region, see Books in the introductory Facts for the Visitor chapter.

*Katy in Tunisia* by Katy Hounsell-Robert

**TUNISIA**

(Nigel Day, 1991) tells of Katy's time spent sharing a house in Tunisia with a woman artist friend.

*Salammbô* by Gustave Flaubert (Penguin Classics) is really a pretty dreadful book. A 19th-century novel set in 3rd-century Carthage, it has a more than adequate quota of sex and violence.

*Fountains in the Sand* by Norman Douglas (Oxford University Press, 1986) is an entertaining account of Douglas's trip through south-western Tunisia early this century, so long as you can ignore his intolerance of Arabs and everything Tunisian.

### Bookshops

Unless you want your literary diet to consist of nothing but expensive English newspapers, bring enough books to keep yourself busy. Bookshops, although common, do not stock anything in English. There are a couple of exceptions to this rule, but they're not worth hanging out for. Again, French is the go.

The best solution is to look out for fellow travellers with books to swap.

### MAPS

ONTT offices, both in Tunisia and abroad, have a good free road map of Tunisia. It includes a fair amount of information, in English and in French, about places of interest. A second road map, *Tunisien Strassenkarte*, can be found at some tourist outlets for 250 mills. It includes basic street maps of Hammamet, Nabeul, Monastir and Sousse, as well as an information section in German. These are the only road maps available inside the country.

If you want to buy a map before you travel, Freytag & Berndt's map of Tunisia is very comprehensive. The offering from Hildebrand includes information on places of interest, but is a bit weak on place names.

If you want a map that covers Algeria as well as Tunisia, there is little to choose between the Michelin and the Hallwag. Michelin No 958, *Algeria & Tunisia*, is the most recent edition, published in 1992. It was No 972 in the previous series, which is still widely on sale.

### MEDIA

Understandably, the media in Tunisia is dominated by the French and Arabic languages. English-language offerings are restricted to a weekly newspaper and an hour of radio broadcasting time per day.

### Newspapers & Magazines

In the main centres you can buy two-day-old English, German, Italian and French newspapers. International current affairs magazines such as *Time* and *Newsweek* are also readily available.

The weekly *Tunisian News* (TD 1) is the only publication in English. It usually includes a few interesting feature articles about Tunisia alongside some very unexciting local news stories that read like ministerial press releases.

*La Presse* and *Le Temps* are the main French-language papers. They offer very similar fare. Both are published daily, and both include a couple of pages of international news and local service information such as train, bus and aircraft times – and both cost 300 mills.

Arabic daily newspapers include *Es-Sabah* and *Al-Houria*.

### Radio & TV

The French-language TV station has half an hour of news, with lots of foreign news and sport, at 8 pm every night. Most of the regular TV programs are mindless game shows (which you wind up watching in cheap restaurants), although they do sometimes have decent movies on Friday night.

Some of the more up-market hotels offer satellite TV, allowing guests to stuff themselves all day on CNN news.

There is a French-language radio station broadcasting on (or around) FM 98. It broadcasts in English from 2 to 3 pm, in German from 3 to 4 pm and in Italian from 4 to 5 pm.

A much better source of English-language radio is the BBC World Service, which can be picked up on 15.070 and 12.095 MHz. If you twiddle the dial a bit, you come up with all sorts of oddities – such as Radio Albania.

## FILM & PHOTOGRAPHY

Name-brand film such as Kodak and Fuji is widely available, but don't expect any bargains: it will cost you at least as much as it does at home. The Monoprix supermarket chain sells 24-print 100 ASA Fuji film for TD 3.575 and 36-print film for TD 4.550. It is harder to find slides and film of other speeds outside the main tourist areas. There are quick processing labs which can develop any type of print film in all the main towns.

## ACTIVITIES

### Sport

**Golf** Tunisia has six golf courses, none built with local players in mind. They are at Hammamet (☎ 02-282722), Monastir (☎ 03-461120), Skanes (☎ 03-461833), Tabarka (☎ 08-644321) and Tunis (☎ 01-765919). The Tunis course is at La Soukhra, north of the airport.

**Yachting** The tourist authorities have taken to promoting the country as a destination for yachting people. The main attraction seems to be the price of winter berthing compared with the trendy northern Mediterranean. The largest yachting marinas are at Monastir, Port el-Kantaoui, Sidi Bou Said, Tabarka and Zarzis.

**Hunting** Unfortunately, there seems to be plenty of people around who get a kick out of blasting to bits anything that moves. In Tunis, the Fédération Tunisienne de Chasse (☎ 01-296910) exists to let these people know what they can kill, where, when and how.

### Gambling

If you like a flutter, Tunisia has its version of the soccer pools in Promosport. It involves selecting the results (home win, away win or draw) of 14 games. You need to get at least 12 correct to win. Tickets are available from all cafés and cost 500 mills for four goes or

TD 1 for eight, plus 50 mills commission. The cut-off day is Thursday.

### Hammams

Hammams (public bathhouses) are one of the focal points of life in every Tunisian town – in fact, just about everywhere in the Middle East and North Africa.

They are much more than just a place to go and clean up. In the Roman fashion, they are a place to unwind and socialise. Every town has at least one, with separate times for men and women, while the bigger towns have separate ones for each sex. Some resort towns have unisex hammams for the benefit of the tourists.

You don't need to take anything. The TD 1 charge includes a *fouta* (cotton bath towel) and a rubdown with a *kassa*, a coarse mitten that is used to remove the grime and dead skin after your stint in the steam room. It is usually possible to have a massage as well. Hammams are recommended as a easy way to get a glimpse of real Tunisian life.

## ACCOMMODATION

Tunisia is well geared for tourism, and the accommodation available runs the gamut from basic Tunisian hotels to five-star luxury resorts. Such resorts are totally isolated from the local communities; they cater to tourists who want to spend time on the beach and not trouble themselves with what the local culture might have to offer.

### Camping

At the bottom of the scale there are a few official camp sites around the country. Most of them have only basic facilities and charge about TD 2 per person. Camp sites apart, it should be possible to camp anywhere as long as you get the permission of the landowner. Nobody has reported any problems camping.

On the beaches in the north at Raf Raf and Ghar el-Melh, sleeping out on the beach is the accepted thing. The same applies to the remote beaches of the north coast. However, in the resort areas of the Cap Bon peninsula and Sousse this would definitely be frowned on.

TUNISIA

The official sites are at Nabeul, Hammamet, Hammam Lif, Tozeur and Degache (near Tozeur). The hostels at Bizerte, Douz, Jerba and Tozeur also have camping facilities. Two resort hotels, the *Hotel Sidi Slim* on Jerba and the *Hotel Samaris* south of Hammamet, have camping grounds attached.

## Hostels

Hostels fall into two categories. There are the Auberges de Jeunesse, affiliated to HI, and there are the government-run Maisons des Jeunes. They couldn't be more different.

The Auberges de Jeunesse are thoroughly recommended. Most have prime locations, such as a converted palace in the Tunis medina and a fascinating old funduq (caravanserai) at Houmt Souq on Jerba. Others are located at Remel Plage outside Bizerte, at the beach in Nabeul and in Gabès.

They generally charge about TD 3.500 per night, with breakfast available for TD 1 and other meals for TD 3 each. Their popularity means that they impose a three-night limit during the high season.

There's no reason for anyone to introduce any time limits at the Maison des Jeunes. Almost without exception (see the one at 'Ain Draham), they are characterless concrete boxes with all the charm of an army barracks. They are run along the same lines.

Almost every town has one, normally stuck way out in the middle of nowhere. They are used mainly for holiday camps for school kids. The only reason to mention them is that sometimes they represent the only budget accommodation alternative.

They all charge TD 4 for a dormitory bed. Breakfast is served only for groups of 10 or more people.

There are a couple of places where the Maisons des Jeunes concept has evolved into a grander scheme called Centres des Stages et Vacances, holiday camps which combine hostel and camp site. These exist right on the beach at Aghir on Jerba, and in the oasis at Gabès. Camping charges are TD 2 per person and 500 mills per tent. Power and hot showers are available.

## Hotels

Tunisian hotels are generally clean, if a little shabby. Most come under the government's rating system and so have a maximum price that they can charge.

These hotels, rated from one star through to five star, must display the tariff by the reception desk, so you can always see what the top price should be. Out of season, they are often open to negotiation. Sometimes the ratings make no sense at all; you can find a well-kept one-star place that is far more comfortable than a run-down two-star hotel.

Using a popular tourist destination like Hammamet as an example, average high-season charges for each classification (and they do vary a bit from town to town) are: one star – TD 17/25 for singles/doubles, including breakfast (often compulsory); two star – TD 25/40; three star – TD 33/50; four star – TD 60/100; and five star – TD 80/130.

Looking at these prices, you may think it's going to be impossible to find a cheap bed, but below the one-star rating there are many unclassified hotels which are more than adequate and often better value than the rated places.

Medina hotels are usually unclassified; they are basic, often with no showers, and you pay for a bed in a shared room. These cost between TD 3.500 and TD 5 per person and vary from quite good, cheap hotels to filthy flophouses.

In most places, you can find a good, clean double room for around TD 15, although in summer places tend to fill up early and you may have little choice.

A hotel breakfast nearly always comprises coffee, French bread, butter and jam. Occasionally, a croissant makes an appearance.

## FOOD
### Restaurants

Restaurants nationwide can be divided into three broad categories: *gargottes*, rotisseries and tourist restaurants. Gargottes are cheap local restaurants, found everywhere, that serve traditional dishes such as couscous and stews. They vary from very basic to slightly up-market (ie, they have tablecloths). Generally, a main dish and salad won't cost much over TD 3.500. Many serve fish, lamb cutlets and kebabs.

Rotisseries are easy to spot as they normally have a rotisserie loaded up with rotating roast chickens outside. That's about all they serve, alongside chips and salad. Prices start at TD 1.600 for a quarter chicken.

Tourist restaurants, many of which serve what they call Franco-Tunisienne cuisine, range, as elsewhere, from the excellent to the pretentious to the ordinary. Larger tourist areas, like Sousse and Hammamet, have places which cater especially for visitors from Germany and the UK. Seafood is nearly always prominent on the menu, including lobster – for which you will pay up to TD 60 per kg. If you can resist such luxuries, most meals will cost under TD 10. Unlike other eateries, tourist restaurants normally sell alcohol.

## ENTERTAINMENT
### Cinemas
Cinemas are everywhere in Tunisia and are a popular form of entertainment. The movie posters point to lots of Rambo-style action, all in French or Arabic. A ticket costs between TD 1.200 and TD 2.

### Discos
Discos exist basically for the benefit of tourists and are virtually always associated with big hotels in the main tourist areas.

### Bars
Bars can be found in all the major towns. They are generally hard-drinking, smoke-filled, male preserves. Many bars sell plates of nibblies such as tajine (the Tunisian version is like a cold quiche), *lubia* (boiled broad beans) and nuts. It is possible for accompanied foreign females to stop for a beer at these places, but don't be surprised by the attention levels. This type of bar closes at 8 pm. In smaller towns, the hotel often doubles as the bar.

Most foreigners, particularly women, feel more comfortable enjoying their favourite tipple in the bars of the resort hotels.

### Spectator Sport
**Soccer** First-division soccer matches attract big crowds. Games between Tunis arch rivals Club Africain and Espérance Sportif draw capacity 80,000 crowds. Local first-division matches are played on Sunday afternoon at 2 pm; entry costs 400 mills. Match details can be found in the newspapers.

## THINGS TO BUY
### Rugs & Carpets
These are amongst the most readily available souvenirs and, although they are not cheap, there are some really beautiful ones for sale. The main carpet-selling centres are Tunis, Kairouan, Tozeur and Jerba.

There are two basic types of carpet: knotted and woven. The traditional (pre-Islamic conquest) carpet industry was based on the weaving of *mergoums* and kilims. Mergoums feature very bright, geometric designs, featuring bold use of reds, purples, blues and other vivid colours. Kilims use traditional Berber motifs on a woven background. Both are reasonably cheap to buy – you can reckon on paying about TD 50 per sq metre.

The best known of the knotted carpets are the classical (Persian-style) Kairouan carpets. This style of carpet-making was introduced to Tunisia by the Turks. Legend has it that the first carpet to be made in Tunisia with knotted stitches was the work of the daughter of the Turkish governor of Kairouan. Whatever the truth might be, today Kairouan is the carpet capital of the country.

Knotted carpets are priced according to the number of knots per sq metre. A carpet with a mere 40,000 knots per sq metre costs around TD 130 per sq metre, while you can pay TD 1500 for fine carpet with as many as 250,000 knots per sq metre.

The Berber *guetiffa* is another type of knotted carpet. This is a thick-pile carpet,

TUNISIA

normally cream-coloured, with Berber motifs.

All these types of carpets are on sale at ONAT (Office National de l'Artisanat Tunisien) emporiums in all major tourist centres. They will all have been inspected by ONAT and classified according to type and number of knots. They come with a label affixed giving this information.

The different qualities are Ordinary (*Deuxième Choix* – with up to 40,000 knots per sq metre), Fine (*Premier Choix* – with up to 90,000 knots per sq metre) and Superfine (*Qualité Supérieure* – with up to 250,000 knots per sq metre).

Prices are fixed at ONAT shops, and are slightly higher than those elsewhere – although you'll have to do some serious haggling to get below the ONAT price.

Many of the carpets on sale elsewhere have also been inspected by ONAT and come with a label of authenticity attached. There are also a great many carpets that have not been classified by ONAT, and in these cases you are on your own as far as authenticity and value for money are concerned. The prices will be cheaper, but the quality may be suspect – the only safeguard is to know your product.

### Pottery
Tunisia has a long connection with the art of pottery. The main centre is Nabeul, partly because of the number of tourists that pass through there; Guellala (on Jerba) is another.

### Leather
There is plenty of leatherwork for sale in the souq in Tunis, and some of it is really fine work. Much of it comes from Morocco, however, and is not all that cheap.

Leatherwork that originates in Tunisia often comes from Kairouan. Articles for sale include traditional pieces such as camel and donkey saddles, water skins and cartridge pouches, as well as more mundane objects like wallets and belts.

### Copper & Brass
Beaten copper and brass items are also popular and are widely available. Beaten plates, ranging in size from a saucer to a coffee table, make good souvenirs, although transporting the larger ones can be a problem.

### Jewellery
Arabic jewellery (and particularly gold jewellery) is often too gaudy and ornate for Western tastes.

The Hand of Fatima (daughter of the Prophet) is a traditional Arabic design; it can be found in varying sizes, from small earrings to large neck pendants, and is usually made of silver. In pre-Islamic times this same design represented Baal, the protector of the Carthaginians, and is also known today as the *khomsa*.

Other traditional pieces of jewellery include the *hedeyed*, which are finely engraved, wide bracelets made of gold or silver, and the *kholkal*, which are similar, but worn around the ankle. In Carthaginian times the kholkal were a sign of chastity; today they are still a symbol of fidelity and are often part of a bride's dowry.

The quality of pure silver and gold jewellery can be established by the official stamps used to grade all work. The quality of unstamped items is immediately suspect. The stamps in use are: the horse's head – used to mark all 18-carat gold jewellery (the horse's head was the Carthaginian symbol for money); the scorpion – used on all nine-carat gold jewellery; grape clusters– used on silver graded at 900 mills per gram; and the Negro head – used on poorer-quality silver graded at 800 mills per gram.

### Miscellaneous
**Chechias** *Chechias* are the small, red felt hats worn by Tunisian men, although it is unusual to see young men wearing them these days. The chechia souq in Tunis is the obvious place to look for them. Quality varies, but an average price is around TD 5.

**Straw Goods** The rectangular, woven straw baskets are practical and cheap. Some are pretty awful, with pictures of camels and typical desert scenes' woven into them, but there are plenty of other more simple designs.

Hats and fans are other popular goods. Most of the straw items come from Gabès and Jerba in the south of the country.

**Perfume** Cheap scented oils are sold everywhere. Bottle sizes range from a tiny five ml (TD 1.500) up to whopping half-litres.

**Sand Roses** You'll find these for sale all over the country, and in fact all over the Maghreb. They are formed of gypsum, which is present in the sand and has been dissolved and then dehydrated many times. When it crystallises, beautiful patterns are formed.

They are most prominent in the area from Ghardaia in Algeria through to southern Tunisia, and range from about five cm in diameter up to the size of a large watermelon.

They do make good cheap souvenirs, but, unless you have a vehicle, carting around a great load of gypsum for days or weeks on end won't be much fun.

**Chichas** The ubiquitous water pipes come in all shapes and sizes and are readily available from souqs and tourist shops, ranging in price from TD 4 for a small cheapie up to TD 70 for a good-quality, full-size version.

**Stuffed Camels** Well, much as I hate them, I have to mention them. It seems that in Arabic desert countries you can tell how well developed the tourist industry is by the number of stuffed camels for sale – Tunisia is way out in front in this field. Every souvenir shop has a selection, ranging from pocket size right up to about one-third full size! Prices start at TD 3.500.

## Presents for Children

**Books** A company called Editions Alif does an excellent series of pop-up books about Tunisian and regional life. The series includes only one title in English, *A walk through an Arab City: the Tunis medina,* which is also published in German and French. The other books in the series are in French, and they look at oasis life, ancient Carthage and Mediterranean life in 1492 AD. The books have two levels of appeal: children like them for their pop-up features, and adults will find a wealth of information that is hard to find elsewhere.

Unfortunately, they are not easy to find and at TD 15 they are not cheap. Editions Alif plans to open a retail outlet in Tunis on the corner of Rue de Hollande and Rue d'Allemagne. If it is not yet open, try the Librairie Diwan on Rue Sidi ben Arous, near the Great Mosque in the medina. The Dar Charait Museum in Tozeur stocks the full range.

Both of the latter two outlets also stock a series of books about Tunisian crafts by author/illustrator May Angeli. The titles are *Attia Chouraqi: jeweller in Mahdia, Marcus Magonius: mosaicist at Carthage, Ali al-Andaloussi: ceramist in Tunis* and *Saliha Karoui: weaver in Kairwan.* They all cost TD 3.500, and are published in English, French and German. They are aimed at seven to 10-year-olds. If you can't track them down, publishers Sérès Productions can be contacted in Tunis on ☎ 01-787 516.

**Jigsaws** Editions Alif also produces a range of jigsaws for various age groups. There are 100-piece maps of both Tunis and the Tunis medina (TD 6), a 50-piece mosaic of two fighting cocks (TD 4.800) and several mini-puzzles for TD 1.500. They are available from the bookshops mentioned above.

More widely on sale are 200-piece jigsaws of Sidi Bou Said, Carthage, Jerba and the Kerkennah Islands. Monoprix supermarkets stock the full range for TD 10.400. They cost a couple of TD less from tourist stalls such as those in the middle of Ave Habib Bourguiba in Tunis.

## Markets

Town and village life often revolves around the weekly markets. Market day is a good day to be in a town, as it will be far more lively than usual and, apart from the itinerant merchants selling fairly mundane household goods, there will be other local people who have travelled in from the outlying districts.

Some markets have become real tourist traps, and for that reason are crowded and worth avoiding; nevertheless, it is on market days that there is the best selection of stuff for sale. Nabeul is one that fits into this category.

Market days throughout the country are as follows:

| | |
|---|---|
| Monday | 'Ain Draham, Houmt Souq, Kairouan and Tataouine |
| Tuesday | Beja, Ghardimao and Kasserine |
| Wednesday | Jendouba, Nefta and Sbeitla |
| Thursday | Douz, Gafsa and Tebersouk |
| Friday | Mahdia, Mateur, Midoun, Nabeul, Sfax, Tabarka, Zaghouan and Zarzis |
| Saturday | Ben Guerdane, El-Fahs and Monastir |
| Sunday | El-Jem, Hammam Lif and Sousse |

Top: Troglodyte dwelling, Matmata, Tunisia (PP)
Middle: Tourist shops, Medenine, Tunisia (HF)
Bottom: Le Kef, Tunisia (PP)

Top Left: Arched colonnade inside the Ribat, Sousse, Tunisia (DW)
Top Right: Old granary, Medenine, Tunisia (HF)
Bottom Left: Looking into the Hôtel Sidi Driss, Matmata, Tunisia (DW)
Bottom Right: The Mosque of the Seven Sleepers, Chenini, Tunisia (DW)

# Getting There & Away

## AIR

Tunisia has three main international airports, at Tunis, Monastir and Jerba, to cater for the two million tourists who arrive each year. Tozeur also has scheduled international flights, and the new airport at Tabarka has occasional international charter flights.

### To/From Europe

A large percentage of the flights using the Jerba and Monastir airports are charter flights from Europe. These can be incredibly cheap if you don't mind the restrictions on the tickets, which usually affect the minimum and maximum permitted lengths of stay. Most tickets must be bought well in advance, although you can often buy them heavily discounted at the last minute.

The best sources of information are the overseas branches of the Tunisian National Tourist Office, which have lists of all holiday operators.

Two of the biggest British charter operators are Horizon Holidays (☎ 0181-200 8733) and Thomson Holidays (same phone number). Sometimes, tickets are available for as little as UK£49, although between UK£79 and UK£100 is more normal.

There are no cheap tickets for sale in Tunisia. You will have to take a scheduled flight. If money is your main consideration, take the ferry to Italy and go overland from there. The cheapest scheduled flight out of the country is with Tuninter from Tunis and Monastir to Malta. Tickets can be bought from Tunis Air offices.

The British operator to Gibraltar, GB Airways, has tickets to London for TD 380 return, or from London for UK£250. These must be purchased 14 days in advance.

Other airlines which serve Tunis include Aeroflot, Air Algérie, Air France, Alitalia, Czekoslovinski Aerolinee, EgyptAir, Iberia, KLM, Lufthansa, Middle East Airlines, Royal Air Maroc, Sabena and Swissair.

### To/From Morocco

Royal Air Maroc and Tunis Air fly regularly between the two countries. The standard economy fare is about US$500 return.

### To/From North America

There are no direct flights between Tunisia and the USA or Canada. The cheapest option is a cheap fare to London and then a charter flight or bucket-shop deal from there.

### To/From Australasia

As with the USA, there are no direct flights to or from Australia and New Zealand, so London is a good transit point.

It's worth asking about special deals. During the European winter of 1993/4, KLM offered a special which got you to Tunis from just about anywhere on the east coast of Australia for A$1670 return. The deal involved buying a return ticket from Sydney or Melbourne to Amsterdam, to which KLM added a free flight anywhere within Europe and the Mediterranean – good value!

## LAND
### To/From Algeria

There are numerous crossing points between Algeria and Tunisia, but not all of them are always open. The most popular points are at Babouch (connecting Annaba and 'Ain Draham), Ghardimao (Jendouba and Souq Ahras), Sakiet Sidi Youssef (Le Kef and Souq Ahras), Bou Chebka (Kasserine and Tébessa) and the desert post at Hazoua between Nefta and El-Oued.

**Bus** There is a direct, air-conditioned SNTRI bus daily at 6 am from Tunis to Annaba which goes via the border at Babouch. The return bus leaves Annaba at 6 am also. You need to book 24 hours in advance at the south bus station in Tunis or at the Annaba bus station. The fare is TD 17.250. This is the easiest way to cross between the two countries. The only drawback is that you have to get on at the point of origin, as they don't stop en route to collect passengers.

**Train** The advantage of crossing by train is that, unlike crossing by bus, you can board en route (in Ghardimao in Tunisia, or Souq Ahras in Algeria) instead of at the point of origin. In summer it can be hellishly hot on the train, and it takes a good deal of time to process everyone through customs. Women get preferential treatment.

The daily train is commonly known as the Trans Maghreb Express (more officially the Al-Maghreb al-Arabi). It links Tunisia with Morocco via Algeria. The trip all the way to Casablanca takes about 44 hours all up and involves a change of trains at Algiers and again on the Algerian border with Morocco.

The best bet is to take the train from Jendouba to Annaba (or vice versa), as there is not much in between. It leaves from Tunis daily at 10.20 am and gets to Annaba at 8.25 pm (Algerian time).

The fare from Tunis to Annaba is TD 19.100 in 2nd class and TD 25.530 1st class.

For more information on the Trans Maghreb Express, see the Morocco Getting There & Away chapter.

**Taxi** There are frequent Algerian louages (shared taxis) which run between Tunis and various towns in north-eastern Algeria, including Constantine, Annaba, Algiers and Sétif.

Of the local crossing points, the one in the desert between Nefta and El-Oued is the most popular. There are a few louages daily from Nefta to the border at Hazoua; alternatively, there's a daily bus at 10 am. Hazoua has a cheap café/restaurant where you can stay for the night.

From Hazoua it's a four-km walk to the Algerian post known as Bou Aroua, although there are occasional Algerian louages shuttling back and forth between the two posts.

From the Algerian side, there are irregular louages to El-Oued, 90 km away. In the north, there are regular louages from Le Kef to the border at Sakiet Sidi Youssef.

### To/From Libya
The border crossing between the two countries on the coast at Ras al-Jedir is once again open. Now the only obstacle to entering Libya by land is obtaining a tourist visa, which requires considerable advance planning (see Libya's Facts for the Visitor chapter).

Another border post is at Dehiba in the south, but Libyan immigration officials at Wazin have a habit of sending people back up to Ras al-Jedir.

The most straightforward way of getting into Libya is to take one of the regular louages which travel from the southern Tunisian city of Sfax to Tripoli. The journey takes about six hours and costs TD 20.

### SEA
### To/From Italy
There are frequent crossings throughout the year between Tunis and the Italian ports of Trapani (in Sicily), Naples, Livorno and Genoa.

The boats are heavily booked in summer, and if you are taking a vehicle at that time it is essential that you book well in advance. If you are on foot you may get on without a booking, but it can be torrid.

The Sicilian and Sardinian services are operated by the Tirrenia Line (see Operators' Addresses later in this chapter).

**Trapani-Tunis** Two Italian companies, Tirrenia Navigazione and Alimar Lines, run weekly services between Trapani and La Goulette (Tunis). Alimar's ferries leave Trapani at noon on Wednesday and La Goulette at 2 pm on Saturday. The trip takes six hours and the cheapest ticket costs about US$40.

Tirrenia's schedules from Trapani actually start from Cagliari in Sardinia.

**Genoa-Tunis** The Compagnie Tunisienne

de Navigation (CTN) operates regular boats between Tunis and Genoa. The number of services varies between four per month in winter to 11 per month at the height of summer. The one-way fare is about US$80 and the trip takes about 24 hours.

**Catania-Tunis** CTN operates a weekly car-ferry service between Tunis and Catania on the southern coast of Sicily. It leaves Catania at 9 pm on Saturday and arrives in Tunis at 3 pm on Sunday.

Departure from Tunis is at 6 pm on Thursday, arriving back in Catania at 6 am on Saturday. This service goes via Valletta in Malta on the way back to Italy.

**Trapani-Kelibia** From June until September, there is a ferry service three times weekly between Trapani and Kelibia.

**To/From France**
**Marseilles-Tunis** This service is also operated by CTN, and is packed in summer; vehicle owners will need to book ahead. There are up to five services per week in summer, and two a week in winter.

### Operators' Addresses
The four major ferry operators have the following offices:

### CTN
Tunisia
> 122 Rue de Yougoslavie, Tunis (☎ 01-242999)
> c/- Navitour, 8 Rue d'Alger, Tunis (☎ 01-249500)

Italy
> c/- Tirrenia Line, Ufficio Passeggeri, Ponte Colombo, 16100 Genoa (☎ 25 80 41)
> Stazione Marittima, Molo Angiono, 80100 Naples (☎ 31 21 81)

France
> SNCM, 61 Blvd des Dames, 13002 Marseilles (☎ 91.56.32.00)

Germany
> Karl Geuther GmbH, Heinrichstr 9, 6000 Frankfurt (☎ 7 30 47 11)

UK
> Continental Shipping, 179 Piccadilly, London W1V 9DB (☎ 0171-491 4968)

### Tirrenia
Tunisia
> 122 Rue de Yougoslavie, Tunis (☎ 01-242775)

Italy
> Via Roma 385, Palermo (☎ 58 57 33)
> Corso Italia 52, Trapani
> Ufficio Passeggeri, Ponte Colombo, 16100 Genoa (☎ 25 80 41)
> Stazione Marittima, Molo Angiono, 80100 Naples (☎ 31 21 81)
> Agenave, Via Campidano 1, Cagliari, Sardinia (☎ 66 60 65)

France
> SNCM, 12 Rue Godot de Mauroy, 75009 Paris (☎ 42.66.60.19)

Germany
> Karl Geuther GmbH, Heinrichstr 9, 6000 Frankfurt (☎ 7 30 47 11)

Switzerland
> Voyages Melia, 17 Rue de Chantepoulet, 1201 Geneva (☎ 31 71 74)

### Alimar Lines
Tunisia
> c/- Tourafric, 52 Ave Habib Bourguiba, Tunis (☎ 01-341480/8)

Italy
> Stazione Marittima, Livorno (☎ 88 07 33)
> Via F Caracciolo 10, 80122 Naples (☎ 761 23 48)
> Via Torre Arsa 1, Trapani (☎ 2 71 01)

### SNCM
Tunisia
> Tunis SNCM, 47 Ave Farhat Hached (☎ 01-336536)

Denmark
> Benn's Rejser, Norregade 51, 7500 Hostebro (☎ 97 42 50 00)

France
> 61 Blvd des Dames, 13002 Marseilles (☎ 91.56.32.00)

Sweden
> Benns Resor, Kastellgatan 17 (Box 7124), 40233 Gothenburg (☎ 74 00 25)

UK
> Southern Ferries, 179 Piccadilly, London W1V 9DB (☎ 0171-491 4968)

### TOURS
Nearly every European country has travel companies offering hotel and airfare packages to Tunisia. British operators have some of the cheapest deals, starting from UK£159 per week. The Tunisian Travel Bureau (☎ 0171-373 4411), at 305 Old Brompton Rd, London, has the biggest range of desti-

nations. They include Bizerte, Kerkennah, Mahdia, Nefta, Tabarka and Tozeur, as well as the standard beach resorts such as Hammamet-Nabeul and Sousse-Monastir. Prices start at UK£205.

## LEAVING TUNISIA

There is no departure tax to be paid when leaving the country.

# Getting Around

Tunisia's transport network is fairly well developed and, with the short distances, just about every town in the country has daily connections of some sort with Tunis.

For most of the year there is ample public transport to meet the demand. However, during public holidays and in the summer months, particularly August and September, there are many more people travelling, both locals and tourists, and competition for seats is high. At these times booking in advance where possible is highly recommended.

## AIR

Being such a small country, the domestic air network is fairly limited. The domestic airline Tuninter operates the following services: Tunis to Jerba (five flights per day); Tunis to Tozeur (Monday, Thursday, Friday, Saturday and Sunday); Tunis to Sfax (Monday to Thursday); Monastir to Jerba (Tuesday and Saturday); and Tozeur to Jerba (Monday and Tuesday). Domestic flights between Tunis and Tabarka are planned.

## BUS
### SNTRI Bus

The national bus company, SNTRI, operates daily air-conditioned buses to just about every town in the country. To the smaller places there is only one departure per day, while to major places there are three or four. The green-and-yellow buses run pretty much to schedule, and they're fast, comfortable and not too expensive. For long-distance travel, they are the way to go.

In summer, many of the long-distance departures are at night to avoid the heat of the day, so if you want to see something of the country you are travelling through, you will either have to hitch, or go by train, louage or local bus.

Booking in advance, especially when leaving from Tunis, is advisable, particularly in the summer months.

All buses originating or terminating in Tunis stop en route to pick up and set down passengers, so you don't have to be going all the way to or from Tunis to use them. If you want to pick one up en route, however, there is no guarantee that seats will be available.

For intercity bus timetables, see the Getting There & Away sections for individual towns and cities in Tunisia.

### Regional Buses

In addition to the national company, there are regional bus companies which operate services within a particular region and to nearby cities just outside the region. They often also operate services to Tunis.

The buses are reliable enough, but often they are getting on a bit, and are slow and never air-conditioned. Coverage of routes is good, and frequent enough to meet the demand most of the time. Booking in advance is both impossible and unnecessary. The only way to be sure of bus schedules is to go to the bus station and ask. Most depots do not have timetables displayed; those that do, have them in Arabic only – with the exception of Houmt Souq on Jerba. The bulk of departures tend to be early in the day. If seeking directions to the bus station, ask for the gare routière. One catch to be aware of is that some towns are served by two or three regional companies. Generally they share depots, but in some cases (Tabarka is one) each has its own. Officials from one company never know about the schedules of another, so always ask if there is more than one company in town.

## TRAIN

Trains are run by the Sociètè Nationale des Chemins de Fer Tunisiens (SNCFT). The rail network is a long way short of comprehensive. What there is, however, is modern and efficient – and the trains do run on time. (I'm sure there's a connection between a country's system of government and the punctuality of its trains!)

The main line runs north-south between Tunis and Gabès, via Sousse and Sfax. There are at least eight trains a day as far as Sousse, six to Sfax and three to Gabès. One train per day branches off at Mahres, south of Sfax, to Gafsa and Metlaoui. There also are lines to Bizerte, via Mateur; Ghardimao (near the Algerian border), via Jendouba; and Kalaa Khasba (halfway between Le Kef and Kasserine). Branch lines run between Bir Bou Rekba and Nabeul, and from Sousse to Monastir and Mahdia. Both these lines are linked to the main north-south line and offer at least one direct train to Tunis every day. Other rail lines shown on maps are for freight only.

Passenger trains offer three classes: 2nd, 1st and *confort*. Second class costs about the same as a bus, and is normally packed – with everything from people and produce to livestock. It's a circus that can be fun to experience for a short journey. Unless you get on at the point of origin, there's little chance of finding a seat.

There are no chickens in 1st class, which costs about 40% more than 2nd class. It's the most convenient way to travel. There are reclining, upholstered seats, and every chance of getting to sit in one. Confort costs a bit more again, but doesn't offer much extra. Most main-line trains have a restaurant car, which sends out a regular supply of sandwiches, soft drinks and coffee.

Train schedules are listed under the Getting There & Away sections for individual towns.

## TAXI

Tunisia's shared, long-distance taxis are called louages. Most of them are old, white Peugeot 404 station wagons with an extra seat in the back. The newer ones are Peugeot 504 or 505 wagons, usually with a distinctive red stripe. They all take five passengers and leave when full. They are the fastest way to get around, as it never takes long for them to fill up, and they are generally quite comfortable because the five-person limit is always adhered to. Fares are only slighter higher than for a bus.

The louage 'station' in most towns is usually just a convenient gathering point – a vacant lot or other open space – close to the town centre.

The louages themselves are instantly recognisable by their roof racks with white identification signs on the front and back. These have a town name on them (in Arabic or English or both) but, unfortunately, this sign does not tell you where the vehicle is going – just where it's licensed. There's always someone calling out destinations and directing people to louages. A foreigner is sure to be asked their destination and given assistance. It's a good idea to ask the fare before you get in. If you think you are being ripped off, ask to see the list of tariffs (set by the government) that all drivers are required to carry.

At certain times, particularly during the summer, public transport is in high demand and competition for seats in louages can be fierce. You may find it necessary to be fairly ruthless when it comes to the battle for a seat or you will simply not get a ride. The tactic is to grab onto a door handle as the louage arrives. Fortunately, this situation does not arise very often.

## CAR & MOTORBIKE

Tunisia's roads are mostly excellent and are tar surfaced. The minor roads in the north are usually just a single narrow strip of bitumen.

In the south there are more unsurfaced roads but these are usually easily negotiated. The worst road you are likely to encounter is the one from Matmata direct to Medenine; though people will tell you it's for 4WDs only, it can be negotiated with caution in even the small Fiats and Citroens that are for hire.

Tunisian drivers are generally well behaved, and drive fairly safely and predictably. For someone used to driving in Europe, the worst thing is not the cars but the thousands of moped riders, who weave suicidally in and out of the traffic, and the pedestrians, who think that it is their inalienable right to walk on the road regardless of traffic conditions.

## Car Rental

Hire cars can be a great way to see the country in a bit more detail, but they are so expensive that unless you have a fat wallet or are part of a small group they're not a realistic option in Tunisia.

Typical rental charges for the smallest cars (Renault Esp or Citroen 15) are about TD 22 per day plus 220 mills per km. It is cheaper to take one of the unlimited-km deals, which start at about TD 380 per week. On top of these rates you'll have to pay 17% tax, insurance at about TD 10 per day, contract fees, etc, etc. By the time you've filled up at the petrol tank at 570 mills per litre, your wallet will be a lot lighter.

All the major international operators have offices in the larger towns. Rental conditions are fairly straightforward. If you are paying by cash, a deposit of roughly the equivalent of the rental is required. Credit cards don't have the same restriction.

In summer, particularly on Jerba and in Tunis, it's almost impossible to get a car straight away. You may have to wait up to a week unless you are prepared to take a larger and more expensive model. Book as early as possible and check with the company every day to make sure that they don't forget your booking, as this does happen. Out of season, when things are much quieter, you can easily get a small car and it is even sometimes possible to bargain a bit on the rates, especially if you are paying cash.

When you hire the car, make sure that an accident report form has been included with the car's papers. If you have an accident while driving a hire car, both parties involved must complete the form. If the form is not completed, you may be liable for the costs, regardless of whether you have paid for insurance or not.

Rental companies require that drivers be aged over 21 and hold a driving licence which has been valid for at least a year.

There are military checkpoints all over the country; although officials are not too bothered with checking foreigners, it's best to make sure you have your passport handy at all times.

## Motorbike Rental

The short distances and fair road conditions make motorbikes an ideal way of making the most of Tunisia. Unfortunately, there is only one motorbike-rental agency in the country – Holiday Bikes on Jerba. It has a range of bikes, from 50-cc mopeds for TD 23 per day up to 600-cc Yamahas for TD 600 per week, fully inclusive. Another company in Houmt Souq, Rais Rentals, hires mopeds but no larger machines. No licence or insurance is required for a moped.

If you are bringing your own motorbike make sure you are carrying some basic spare parts. These are virtually impossible to find within the country, as people just don't own motorbikes in Tunisia.

## BICYCLE

At certain times of the year, cycling is also an excellent way to see the country. In the height of summer it is uncomfortably hot and winter is bleak, especially in the north, but for the rest of the year conditions are ideal. It's also possible to put a bike on the train if you want to skip a long stretch or get yourself back to Tunis.

There are a few places where bicycle rental is possible and you pay about TD 7 per day. A lot of the bikes are horrible old rattlers that leave you tired and sore at the end of the day. Where possible, check the bikes available to find the best one and to make sure that the brakes work. Hire places seem to be concerned only about whether the bike goes or not and aren't too bothered about how to stop it. Maintenance is done on a very casual basis – when something stuffs up it gets patched up, but nothing is done that might prevent the thing from failing in the first place.

Where there is no setup for renting bikes, it is worth asking at one of the many bike-repair shops in each town to see if they will rent you one for a few hours – they often will.

## HITCHING

The following information is intended solely as an explanation of how hitching works in Tunisia, not as a recommendation. Although many people do hitch, it is not an entirely safe method of transport and you do so at your own risk. It is strongly recommended that women do not attempt to hitch without a male companion.

Conditions for hitching vary throughout the country. The south is easiest as there is a great deal more tourist traffic – either people who hire cars on Jerba or overlanders heading for Tozeur and the Sahara. You shouldn't have to wait more than a couple of hours for a lift. In the north, people seem less inclined to pick up hitchers, particularly in the summer when there are so many tourists in the country.

Between small towns, louage pick-ups are the usual means of transport and hitching on these is a standard way of getting around, although you will normally be expected to pay the equivalent of the bus fare. If in doubt, check before you get in as to whether the driver expects payment or not, and try to establish what the locals are paying before you set out to hitch.

## WALKING

Most visitors confine their walking to what is required to get around town and check out the sights. In summer, it is too hot for walking to be a viable option except in the early morning and evening.

## BOAT

There are two regular scheduled ferry services in the country. The first connects Sfax with the Kerkennah Islands, which lie about 25 km off the coast. In summer, there are up to eight crossings daily, dropping to four in winter. The trip takes 1 ½ hours and costs 500 mills for passengers without vehicles. It costs TD 3.500 to take a car across, and you need to get in the queue well before the first departure at 7.30 am to be assured of getting across that morning.

The second service runs from Jorf on the mainland to Ajim on the island of Jerba. The crossing takes only a few minutes and the ferries run throughout the day and night.

## LOCAL TRANSPORT

Most towns are compact enough to get around on foot. The problem comes in summer, when it is too hot to walk very far during the day. Taxis are the best alternative. They can be found in all major towns and are reasonably cheap. Towns without taxis will normally have a *camionette* (utility truck) available for charter, or working a specific route. Some towns, including Gabès, Houmt Souq, Nabeul and Tozeur, have calèches (horse-drawn carriages) for hire. Prices start at about TD 5 per hour.

## TOURS

Unless you are very short of time and don't mind being herded around like sheep, organised tours are not an attractive option. It is, however, possible to get just about anywhere in Tunisia by tour bus or 4WD. Expect to pay about TD 25 for a half-day tour, TD 40 to TD 45 for a full day and about TD 70 per day for tours including accommodation.

The biggest operator in the north is Carthage Tours, with offerings ranging from half-day tours of Carthage to week-long nationwide extravaganzas. One tour that might appeal is the package that includes the Roman sites of Dougga and Bulla Regia, which require quite an effort to reach independently.

Saharan 4WD safaris are the name of the game in the south, and the main players are Douz Voyages and Abdelmoula Voyages. They can take you into the Sahara for any length of time between eight hours and a week. Many of the tours include camel riding and camping in the desert.

These tours take you to some spectacular and otherwise inaccessible (except to about a hundred other 4WDs) places, but they generally involve too many hours bouncing around in the desert crammed in a vehicle with 10 other tourists.

The half-day tours from Tozeur to the impressive mountain oases at Chebika, Mides and Tamerza are worth considering, again because of the difficulty in getting there independently.

# Tunis

Despite the claims made in the tourist literature, Tunis is not a wildly exciting city. The medina is only mildly interesting, while the French ville nouvelle is plain and functional in the extreme, with few redeeming features apart from some fine 1920s colonial architecture. It is the places surrounding the city, rather than Tunis itself, which are interesting.

As far as capital cities go, however, Tunis has an easy-going, unhurried air about it. It is quite easy to spend a few pleasant days here wandering in the medina, exploring the nearby ruins of Carthage or sitting on the beaches.

Tunis is a very liberal city by Islamic standards, and it is an easy place to make the adjustment from West to East. In fact, wandering around the new city, it is hard to tell that you are in a Muslim country, let alone in Africa.

## History

With Carthage as a neighbour, Tunis remained in the background for centuries. It wasn't until the 9th century, when Aghlabid ruler Ibrahim Ahmed I made Tunis his residence and built the Zitouna Mosque, that it took on any significance.

Its glory was short-lived, for the Fatimids chose Mahdia as their capital in the 10th century. However, the ravages of the Beni Hillal invasion in the 11th century left Tunis untouched and saw it once again become the capital.

The period of Hafsid rule and the following two centuries were the golden age of Tunis: souqs and medersas were built, trade with Europe flourished and one of the great Islamic universities was established in the heart of the medina at the Zitouna Mosque.

Until the time of the French protectorate, the medina remained very much the centre of things. However, when the French arrived they wasted no time in stamping their influence on the place by building a ville nouvelle

directly to the east of the medina on land reclaimed from Lake Tunis.

This new city, laid out on a grid, is today very much the heart of Tunis; it has a distinctly European feel, with its wide main boulevard, street cafés and balconied buildings.

## Orientation

The city lies at the western end of the shallow and often smelly Lake Tunis, which opens to the sea at La Goulette (the gullet). This is the first of a string of beach suburbs which stretch away to the north and it's here that the city's port is located. This coastal area includes the ruins of Carthage and the picturesque suburb of Sidi Bou Said (both dealt with in the Around Tunis section).

The lake itself is certainly not a thing of beauty, and pollution is an increasing problem. However, in November there are often small flocks of pink flamingos on the edge of the causeway which intersects the lake. This causeway carries both motor vehicles and the light-rail TGM line. It connects the beach suburbs, Carthage and the port with the centre of the ville nouvelle, the focus of which is the wide, tree-lined Ave Habib Bourguiba with its shady, paved central strip.

The ville nouvelle contains all the major banks, department stores and administrative services. Virtually all the mid-range hotels are concentrated in the streets to the south of Ave Habib Bourguiba, and it's also here that you'll find the railway station, southern bus station and the main louage station. Most of these streets are one way only, and it can be very frustrating getting to where you want to go if you are driving.

At its western end, Ave Habib Bourguiba becomes Ave de France, terminating in the Place de la Victoire and the entrance to the medina, where you'll find the cheap hotels, souvenir shops and most of the city's points

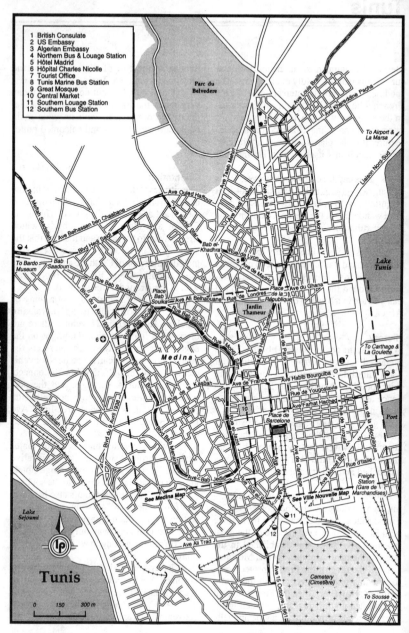

1  British Consulate
2  US Embassy
3  Algerian Embassy
4  Northern Bus & Louage Station
5  Hôtel Madrid
6  Hôpital Charles Nicolle
7  Tourist Office
8  Tunis Marine Bus Station
9  Great Mosque
10 Central Market
11 Southern Louage Station
12 Southern Bus Station

Tunis

of interest. The airport is only eight km to the north-east.

## Information

**Tourist Office** The tourist office (☎ 01-341077) is on Ave Habib Bourguiba, at Place du 7 Novembre 1987 with its large roundabout and clock tower. This is the head office of the tourist authority, but the service is largely restricted to handing out glossy brochures full of flowery descriptions of places of interest. Getting more information out of them can be like pulling teeth – slow and painful. The office does, however, have a good handout map of Tunis and a road map of Tunisia. The staff speak English, French and German.

The office is open from 8 am to 1.30 pm Monday to Saturday in summer, and from 8 am to noon and 3 to 6 pm in winter. It's closed on Sunday and public holidays.

There is another branch of the tourist office at the railway station, which hands out train timetables among other things; yet another branch can be found on the mezzanine level at the airport.

**Money** There are branches of the major banks along Ave Habib Bourguiba, most of which are open longer than normal hours. The branch of the STB next to the Africa Hôtel is one such bank.

There is another branch of the STB at the airport inside the arrivals hall, before you clear customs, which is open to meet incoming flights; however, if you arrive late at night you will probably have to wait for someone to come and open it up.

American Express is represented by Carthage Tours (☎ 01-254304) at 59 Ave Habib Bourguiba. Thomas Cook is represented by Tunisienne de Tourisme (☎ 01-342710) at 45 Ave Habib Bourguiba.

**Post & Telecommunications** The main post office is the cavernous old building on Rue Charles de Gaulle, between Rue d'Espagne and Rue d'Angleterre. The poste restante counter is efficient and well organised.

The post office is open in summer from 7.30 am to 12.30 pm and 5 to 7 pm Monday to Thursday, 7.30 am to 1.30 pm on Friday and Saturday, and from 9 to 11 am on Sunday.

The telecommunications office is in the same building as the post office, but the entrance is around the other side on Rue Jamel Abdelnasser. It is open 24 hours and, although it can be crowded at times, making international calls is straightforward. You can dial direct to most countries.

The area code for Tunis is 01.

**Foreign Embassies & Consulates** Tunis is a good place to pick up visas, as most countries in West Africa are represented here. Many of the embassies are up around the northern end of Ave de la Liberté. Bus Nos 5 and 35 go along the parallel Rue de Palestine, or a taxi costs about 500 mills from Ave Habib Bourguiba.

There have been reports that the Algerian Consulate is now issuing tourist visas to all-comers, instead of to residents of Tunisia only – as was the case for many years. Don't rely on it. The consulate is open from 8.30 to 11.30 am Monday to Saturday.

Countries which have diplomatic representation in Tunis include:

Algeria
18 Rue du Niger (☎ 01-283166)
Consulate: 136 Ave de la Liberté (☎ 01-280055)
Australia
Australian affairs are handled by the Canadian Embassy in Tunis
Austria
6 Rue Ibn Hamdiss (☎ 01-751091)
Belgium
47 Rue du 1 Juin (☎ 01-781655)
Canada
3 Rue du Sénégal (☎ 01-796577)
Denmark
5 Rue de Mauritanie (☎ 01-792600)
France
Place de l'Indépendance, Ave Habib Bourguiba (☎ 01-245700)
Consulate: 1 Rue de Hollande (☎ 01-333027)
Germany
1 Rue el-Hamra (☎ 01-786455)

Greece
3 Rue el-Biroumi (☎ 01-288411)
Consulate: 9 Impasse Antelas (☎ 01-288890)
India
4 Place Didon (☎ 01-891006)
Italy
37 Rue Jamel Abdelnasser (☎ 01-247486)
Consulate: 9 Rue Ibn Bassam (☎ 01-238455)
Libya
48 Rue du 1er Juin (☎ 01-780866)
Consulate: 74 Ave Mohammed V (☎ 01-285402)
Morocco
39 Rue du 1er Juin, Mutuelleville, Tunis (☎ 01-782775)
Consulate: 26 Rue Ibn Mandhour, Notre Dame, Mutuelleville, Tunis (☎ 01-283492)
Netherlands
8 Rue Meycen (☎ 01-799442)
Spain
22 Rue Dr Ernest Conseil (☎ 01-280613)
Consulate: 11 Rue Tertulien (☎ 01-793947)
Sweden
87 Ave Taieb Mehlri (☎ 01-795433)
Switzerland
10 Rue Ech-Chenkiti (☎ 01-280132)
UK
5 Place de la Victoire (☎ 01-340239)
Consulate: 141-143 Ave de la Liberté (☎ 01-793322)
USA
144 Ave de la Liberté (☎ 01-782566)

**Cultural Centres** The British Council, next to the British Embassy on Place de la Victoire, has a good library but it doesn't welcome tourists with open arms. It costs TD 8 to become a temporary member.

The US Cultural Centre, at 1 Ave de France, also requires visitors to become a member before they can come in and browse through the US papers etc. You'll need your passport and a couple of passport photos.

**Travel Agencies** There are a lot of travel agencies along Ave Habib Bourguiba offering tickets, tours and hotel bookings. The biggest is Carthage Tours at 59 Ave Habib Bourguiba (☎ 01-254304). It offers everything from one-day tours of Tunis's attractions to week-long coach jaunts to the farthest corners of the land.

**Bookshops** There are very few books available in English. The only place worth

visiting in search of English-language novels is the second-hand bookstall on Rue d'Angleterre, diagonally opposite the main post office. Novels in French are readily available from the many bookshops in central Tunis.

The lobby of the Africa Hôtel has a selection of glossy coffee-table books on the country. If that's what you are interested in, check the stalls in the centre of Ave Habib Bourguiba, as they often have the same books for much less.

Editions Alif, on the corner of Rue d'Allemagne and Rue de Hollande, is worth checking out for its range of publications about Tunisia (see the Facts for the Visitor chapter). The best selection of local publications, including a good many in English, is at the Librairie Diwan, near the Great Mosque on Rue Sidi ben Arous.

**Newspapers** The stalls in the middle of Ave Habib Bourguiba stock day-old English daily newspapers (such as the *Times*, the *Guardian*, the *Sun* and the *Sunday Times*) as well as *Time* and *Newsweek*. They also sell Italian, German and French newspapers.

**Emergency** Emergency phone numbers include: ambulance and doctor (☎ 01-341250 or 01-341280); Hôpital Charles Nicolle casualty department (☎ 01-664211); poisons centre (☎ 01-245075); and police and fire brigade (☎ 01-197). The inside back pages of *La Presse, Le Temps* and *Tunisia News* all have the addresses and phone numbers of late-night chemists.

Lost passports and travellers' cheques, etc should be reported to the police as soon as possible. The nearest police station to the central hotel district is just south of the PTT building on Rue Jamel Abdelnasser. A couple of the officers speak English. Be sure to ask for a copy of the police report. The loss of a passport should then be reported to your embassy (see above), while lost travellers' cheques should be reported to the company concerned. See this chapter's Money section for American Express and Thomas Cook details.

**Film & Photography** There are numerous shops in the city centre which sell and process print film. The one on the corner of Ave Habib Bourguiba and Rue de Rome also does cheap B&W passport photos on the spot.

### Walking Tours

The following walks are indicated on the Tunis Medina map.

**Walk 1** This walk covers the main points of interest in the northern medina. It starts at the main northern entrance to the medina and follows Rue Sidi Mahres past the Mosque of Sidi Mahres – the building opposite is the Zawiyya of Sidi Mahres. It then takes Rue el-Monastiri and crosses into Rue Sidi Ibrahim, turning south into Rue du Tribunal opposite the Zawiyya of Sidi Ibrahim Riahi. Rue du Tribunal is home to the Dar Lasram, a former palace that now houses the Association de Sauvegarde de la Medina (ASM) – the group responsible for preserving the medina's heritage. At the southern end of Rue du Tribunal, a right turn into Rue de la Hafsia (named after the medina's old Jewish quarter) leads to Rue du Pacha – the main street of the Turkish elite in Ottoman times. The walk is completed by following Rue du Pacha north to Rue Bab Souika.

**Walk 2** This walk follows the signposted 'Circuit Touristique' route devised by the ASM – look out for the faded orange signs. It begins at Place de la Victoire and continues down Rue Jemaa Zitouna, taking in almost all the major attractions: the Souq el-Attarine (the perfume souq), the Great Mosque, the Dar el-Bey, the Mosque of Youssef Bey, the Tourbet el-Bey, the Dar Ben Abdallah Museum and the Dar Othman.

**Walk 3** This walk takes in some of the quieter areas of the southern medina, as well as some of the major attractions. It starts at the medina's south-eastern gate, the Bab el-Jazira, and follows Rue des Teinturiers to the Dar Othman. A left turn here into Rue Sidi Kacem takes you past the Dar Ben Abdallah

Museum and the Tourbet el-Bey. Other points of note on the walk are the Dar Hussein, which houses the National Museum of Archaeology & Art, and the El-Ksar Mosque. A short detour also takes in the Dar el-Haddad, one of the medina's oldest dwellings. The walk back to Bab el-Jazira along Blvd Bab Menara and Ave Bab Jedid takes you through the bustling local market around Bab Jedid. The huge mosque at Bab el-Jazira is the 14th-century Mosque of Sidi el-Bechir.

### Medina

The medina in Tunis certainly doesn't compare with those in Cairo or Fès, but then again it is a great deal more manageable and hassle free. If you have just come from Europe it is the ideal place to get a feel for the North African way of life, as the medina, with its mosques, cafés and hammams, is the focal point of any Arab city.

The medina was founded around the end of the 7th century (shortly after the Arab conquest) on what was then a narrow strip of land between Lake Tunis and Lake Sejoumi, a salt lake just to the west of the city. It is the historical and cultural heart of the modern city of Tunis.

When the ville nouvelle was built by the French on reclaimed land by the east gate early this century, the medina lost its importance as the commercial centre of the city. These days, souvenir shops are the main commercial activity, catering for the thousands of tourists who pour through here each summer.

The most usual entry is through (or around) the old Bab Bhar, often known as the Porte de France, at the end of Ave de France. The paved square here, Place de la Victoire, has a small signboard with a detailed map of the medina.

Place de la Victoire is also something of an assembly point in the evenings; there are two roads which lead off in a 'V' to the heart of the medina and the Great Mosque. The one to the right, Rue de la Kasbah, cuts straight through the medina to emerge at the Place du Gouvernement. It is lined fairly solidly with tourist shops – as is the street to

# Tunis Medina

0     100     200 m

- - - Walk No 1
— — Walk No 2
····· Walk No 3

**PLACES TO STAY**

4 Hôtel Riadh
5 Hôtel de Tunis
6 Hôtel Milano
7 Hôtel Medina
10 Hôtel de Bonheur
11 Hostel
17 Hôtel Marhaba

**PLACES TO EAT**

12 Restaurant
   Dar el-Jeld

**OTHER**

1 Mosque of
   Sidi Mahres
2 Zawiyya of Sidi
   Ibrahim Riahi
3 Dar Lasram
8 British Embassy
   & British Council

9 Bab Bhar
   (Porte de France)
13 Museum 9 April
14 Kasbah Mosque
15 Dar el-Bey
16 National Library
18 Taxis to Algeria
19 Great Mosque
20 Mosque of
   Youssef Bey
21 Dar el-Haddad
22 El-Ksar Mosque
23 Dar Hussein
24 M'sed el-Kobba
25 Mosque of
   the Dyers
26 Dar Othman
27 Dar Ben
   Abdallah Museum
28 Tourbet el-Bey
29 Mosque of
   Sidi el-Bechir

TUNISIA

the left, Rue Jemaa Zitouna. It leads to the Great Mosque and is the most popular route into the medina for tourists. Some of the storekeepers are very persistent, although low-key by Moroccan standards. You can buy the same stuff for quite a bit less in other parts of the country.

When visiting the places of interest within the medina, it's possible to buy a multiple ticket for TD 2 at either the Great Mosque or the Dar Ben Abdallah Museum. This ticket gives entry to these two sites as well as Dar Othman (an old palace in the process of restoration and slated to become another museum) and the Medersa Mouradia (an old Islamic college).

**Great Mosque** Rue Jemaa Zitouna eventually comes out at the entrance to the Zitouna Mosque (the Mosque of the Olive Tree), also known as the Great Mosque. Built by the Aghlabids in the 9th century, its theological faculty was an important centre of Islamic learning until it was closed down by Bourguiba shortly after independence. The faculty, known as Zitouna University, was reopened in 1987. Non-Muslims are allowed in as far as the courtyard of the mosque between 8 am and noon daily, except Friday; modest dress is compulsory.

**Souqs** Surrounding the Great Mosque are the souqs of the so-called 'noble trades', such as perfume makers, booksellers, silk merchants, jewellers and spice sellers.

Although most souqs have long ceased to operate in their former capacity, one where little has changed over the centuries is the **Souq des Chechias**, where you can still see the traditional red felt hats being made. They are now also produced in a range of lurid colours for the tourist trade. The Petit and Grand souqs des chechias run between Rue Sidi ben Arous and Souq el-Bey, just to the north-west of the Great Mosque.

Traditional lines are certainly no longer stocked at the **Souq el-Berka**, the old marketplace for a much less noble business, slavery. The Souq el-Berka was part of the Turkish souq system around the Mosque of

Youssef Bey, built in 1616 and named after the ruling bey. Other names from this period include the Souq el-Bechamkia (where Turkish *bishmak* slippers were made) and the Souq el-Trouk (the Turkish sailors' souq).

The Souq des Etoffes (the fabric souq), to the south-west of the Great Mosque, houses the **Medersa Mouradia** behind the ornately studded door of No 37. The former Islamic college was built in 1673 on the ruins of a Turkish barracks destroyed during a rebellion. Today, it is used to train apprentices in traditional crafts and is open from 9 am to 4.30 pm; closed on Sunday.

**Dar el-Bey & Kasbah Mosque** The prime minister's office is now housed in the Dar el-Bey, a former palace guesthouse on Place du Gouvernement. The guards are a real sight in their fancy red uniforms.

On the edge of the medina to the west of the Dar el-Bey is the **Place de la Kasbah**. Now an enormous open square, beautifully paved with local granite, it was formerly overlooked by the old kasbah. The Kasbah Mosque dates from the 13th century. The call to prayer is signalled by a white flag hung from the pole on the minaret. You have to be quick to spot it as it is only displayed for a minute or two.

**Museum 9 April** Just beyond the Kasbah Mosque is the Museum 9 April, which is housed in an old prison where Bourguiba was once interned. It is full of photos and other memorabilia related to the fight for independence. Unfortunately, what could be an interesting display is rendered virtually meaningless to non-Arabic speaking (and reading) people, although the tiny cells speak for themselves.

**Dar Othman** The old palace of the dey, Dar Othman, is signposted through an archway off Rue des Teinturiers. ('Dey' was the title given to the commanders of Turkish janissaries.) Built by Othman Dey at the beginning of the 17th century, the palace is an excellent example of period architecture, distinguished by its magnificent façade. There are plans to house a museum of traditional handicrafts in the palace, presently under restoration after years of neglect under Bourguiba.

Rue des Teinturiers is one of the main thoroughfares of the southern medina. It runs from the southern gate, Bab el-Jazira, to the heart of the medina near the Great Mosque, and is named after the dyers who used to carry on their business here. Opposite the Dar Othman is the **Mosque of the Dyers**.

**Dar Ben Abdallah Museum** One of the finest sights in the old city, the Dar Ben Abdallah Museum, is signposted off the Rue des Teinturiers along Rue Sidi Kacem. Once an old palace, it now houses a collection of traditional costumes and everyday items. One room has a very detailed map of the old medina with all the hammams, mosques, souqs and other points of interest shown on it.

The building itself is probably of more interest: it has an usual, highly ornate entrance leading to a marble courtyard complete with fountains and sculptures. The museum is open Monday to Saturday from 9.30 am to 4.30 pm; entry is TD 1.

**Tourbet el-Bey** This mausoleum of the Turkish Husseinid princes was another victim of neglect during the Bourguiba years. The caretaker is keen to show visitors around the various funerary chambers and point out the salient features of the ornate marble sarcophagi. It's close to the Dar Ben Abdallah Museum at the junction of Rue Tourbet el-Bey and Rue Sidi Kacem. It is open from 9.30 am to 4.30 pm, Monday to Saturday.

**Mosque of Sidi Mahres** Because few tourists make it into the northern reaches of the medina, it is a good place for a stroll to get an idea of medina life. The main point of interest is the Mosque of Sidi Mahres, named after the city's patron saint, with its spectacular white domes.

**Ville Nouvelle**
There are very few points of interest in the ville nouvelle. The only unusual building is the **cathedral** on Ave Habib Bourguiba, and that is remarkable only for its ugliness. It was built by the French in 1882. The statue opposite is of Ibn Khaldoun, the great Islamic teacher and philosopher who was born in Tunis.

The streets are lined with French buildings complete with louvre windows and balconies with wrought-iron railings. This gives the whole place a very European air, which is heightened by the pavement cafés and the numerous pâtisseries selling all manner of both sweet and savoury pastries.

**Bardo Museum**
The best museum in the country, the Bardo is in an outer suburb to the west of the medina and is housed in an old palace set in a large garden. Even if you are normally bored silly by museums, you'll be missing out badly if you don't pay at least a brief visit to the Bardo. It is organised in sections which cover the Carthaginian, Roman, Palaeo-Christian and Arab-Islamic eras.

By far the most impressive display is that of **mosaics** from the Roman era. It is no exaggeration to say that the Bardo has one of the finest collections anywhere in the world – just when you think you have seen the best, another room reveals something bigger and better. There are so many mosaics, in fact, that they are overwhelming, and excellent pieces that would stand out on their own elsewhere get lost in the floor-to-ceiling displays. It is worth making a couple of half-day trips to the museum if you are keen, rather than trying to do it all in one hit and becoming so saturated that it is hard to appreciate yet another mosaic.

The best mosaics include the depiction of the poet Virgil flanked by the muses of literature and drama in room 15 and the monumental Triumph of Neptune in room 10. Room 15 is quite something in its own right. It was formerly the palace harem, and the four smaller corner rooms were occupied by the favourite wives. The statues in room 6 from Bulla Regia are also worth a look.

Not to be missed is the haul from the wreck of a boat which came to grief off the coast at Mahdia in the 1st century BC. It was carrying a load of marble and bronze statuary, and this adds some welcome variety to the museum. The exhibits are displayed in rooms 17 to 22.

The Islamic section is somewhat overshadowed by the other exhibits.

The Bardo is open from 8.30 am to 5.30 pm in summer, and from 9.30 am to 4.30 pm in winter; it is closed on Monday. The only public holiday on which it is not open is the 'Eid al-Fitr festival at the end of Ramadan. Entry is TD 2 and there is a further charge of TD 1 if you want to take photos.

Ceramic panels

Getting there is a bit of hassle. It's well worth spending a couple of TD on a taxi from Ave Habib Bourguiba if you don't want to do battle with public transport. No 3 buses, which leave from opposite the Africa Hôtel, terminate just around the corner from the museum entrance. Métro Léger (tram) line No 4 shows a Bardo station, but this was not scheduled to open until the completion of the Bardo tunnel. Presently, it's a 10-minute walk from 20 Mars station.

### Activities
**Hammams** If you are staying in a hotel without washing facilities, or if you just feel like a hot sauna and massage, there are numerous hammams in the medina. One of the best (for men) is the Hammam Kachachine at 30 Souq des Librairies; enter through the barber shop.

There's another at 11 Rue el-Methira, not far from the Rue des Teinturiers, but you'll have to ask for directions. It's open all day, but is reserved for women between 1 and 3 pm.

The hammam at 64 Rue des Teinturiers is for men only; a visit here costs 800 mills.

The Dar Ben Abdallah Museum has a very detailed map of the medina with all the hammams shown on it. It can be handy to know the location of the hammam nearest to your hotel if you are staying in a medina cheapie without showers.

**Beaches** The beaches of Tunis are all accessible by TGM. La Marsa, at the end of the line, is the best of them and is less crowded than those at Amilcar and La Goulette.

### Festivals
The main event on the Tunis cultural calendar is the Carthage International Festival in July and August – two months of music, dance and theatre held at Carthage's heavily restored Roman theatre.

The biennial Carthage International Film Festival is next due in October 1995. The two-week festival concentrates on Middle Eastern and African cinema.

TUNISIA

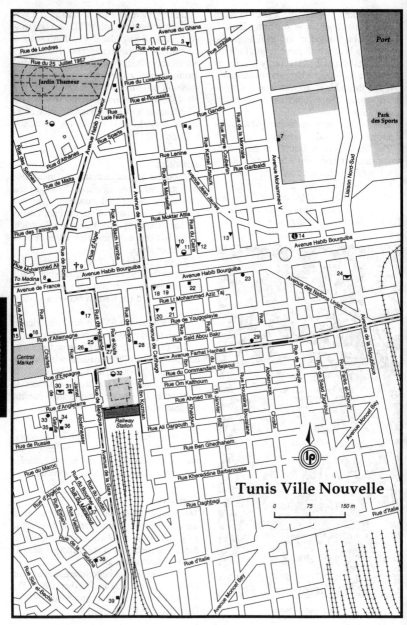

Tunis Ville Nouvelle

## PLACES TO STAY

4   Hôtel Ritza
6   Oriental Palace Hôtel
15  Grand Hôtel de France
19  Capitole Hôtel
22  Africa Hôtel
26  Hôtels de Suisse and Central
27  Hôtel Maison Doree
28  Hôtel Salammbô
35  Hôtel de l'Agriculture
36  Hôtel Cirta
37  Hôtel Savoie
38  Hôtel el-Mouna
39  Hôtel de la Gare

## PLACES TO EAT

2   Mac-Doly
3   Café Chicha
10  Restaurant Chez Nous
12  Restaurant Neptune
13  Restaurant Istanbul
18  Café de Paris
20  Restaurant Carcassonne
21  Restaurant Le Cosmos
34  Restaurant Saidouna

## OTHER

1   République Tram Station
5   Jardin Thameur Bus Station
7   ONAT
8   Carthage Tours (American Express)
9   Cathedral
11  Buses to Airport (No 35) & Bardo
    Museum (No 3)
14  Tourist Office
16  Laundry
17  French Embassy
23  Interior Ministry
24  Parcels Office
25  Editions Alif
29  Tunis Air
30  Main Post Office
31  International Phones
32  Place de Barcelone, Bus & Tram
    Stations
33  Second-hand Bookstall

### Places to Stay – bottom end

**Camping** The nearest site is more than 20 km to the south at Hammam Plage, near Hammam Lif.

**Hostels** The HI-affiliated *Auberge de Jeunesse* (☎ 01-567850) is a great place to stay. It occupies the 150-year-old Dar Saida Ajoula palace right in the heart of the medina on Rue Saida Ajoula, north-west of the Great Mosque. The dorms are quite good, if a little crowded, but you can't beat the price of TD 4 for a bed and free hot shower. Breakfast costs TD 1. Half-board is available for TD 7 and full board for TD 10. The place even has a washing machine (500 mills). You have to be an HI member to stay, but it's possible to join on the spot for TD 12. The hostel imposes a three-night limit if the demand for places is high.

**Hotels** All hotels display a chart, both at reception and in the rooms, listing the maximum price they can charge. In the off season the prices are definitely negotiable, but in summer, just finding an empty room can be a major job if you are searching late in the day.

Tunisia has literally dozens of cheap hotels. The real cheapies are either in the medina or very close to it. They are not set up with Western visitors in mind, and generally charge by the bed in a shared room. (If you want your own room, you will have to pay for all the beds in it.) Most of these places are extremely basic and often have no shower. This isn't really a problem, as there are a number of hammams dotted around. What is a problem is the rarity of clean places.

An example in this category is the *Hôtel de Bonheur*, about 50 metres along Rue de la Kasbah, which enters the medina near the British Embassy at Place de la Victoire. At TD 2.500 per person, the Bonheur is undeniably cheap, but it's impossible to recommend. Women travellers should stay well clear. The same goes for the cluster of cheapies on the eastern edge of the medina along Rue Mongi Slim. They include the *Hôtel de Tunis* and *Hôtel Riadh*.

You'll be much more comfortable at the next level up, generally charging about TD 5 per person. Most of the hotels in this bracket are to be found in the area

TUNISIA

immediately south of Ave Habib Bourguiba, although there are three medina hotels worth a mention. The *Hôtel Medina* (☎ 01-255056), on Place de la Victoire at the entrance to the medina, is basic but clean enough with doubles for TD 10. A trip to a nearby hammam is much better value than paying TD 1 for a hot shower. Unlike a lot of the cheapies, it has a few windows and doesn't get quite as stuffy in summer, although it is fairly noisy. The *Hôtel Marhaba* (☎ 01-343118), on the opposite side of the square at 5 Rue de la Commission, is slightly cheaper at TD 7.500 for doubles and 500 mills for a hot shower. The *Hôtel Milano* (☎ 01-246703), close to the Place de la Victoire on Rue de l'Ancienne Douane, charges TD 3.500/6 for singles/doubles and 500 mills for a shower.

Two of the most popular travellers' hotels are the *Hôtel Cirta* (☎ 01-241582) and *Hôtel de l'Agriculture* (☎ 01-246394), on opposite sides of Rue Charles de Gaulle just south of the main post office. They are both five minutes' walk from the railway station and 15 minutes from the southern bus and louage stations. The Cirta, with singles/doubles for TD 6/10, is the better of the two. The rooms have a bidet and washbasin, and the whole place is cleaned daily and is spotless, although shabby. The only drawback is that not only do they charge TD 1 for a hot shower, they also want the same for a cold one. The Agriculture offers much the same with singles/doubles for TD 4.500/8.

Cheap and quiet is a combination that's hard to find at the budget end of the market, but the two hotels on Rue de Suisse (between Rue de Hollande and Rue Jamel Abdelnasser) go closer than most. The *Hôtel de Suisse* (☎ 01-243821) has upped its rates and lowered its standards from the days when it was strongly recommended. These days it charges over the odds at TD 9.200/13.200 for singles/doubles, and TD 1.300 extra for a revolting bath. Its neighbour, the *Hôtel Central* (☎ 01-240433), is friendlier and cheaper at TD 7.500/11 for singles/doubles. It charges a hefty TD 1.500 for a shower.

If you have an early morning bus to catch, the closest hotel to the southern bus station is the *Hôtel de la Gare* (☎ 01-256754). It's a lot better inside than its shabby exterior indicates. Singles/doubles cost TD 5/9, plus TD 1 for a shower. A good alternative is the *Hôtel el-Mouna* (☎ 01-343375) in Rue de la Sebkha, which has large doubles with shower for TD 10.

There's very little budget accommodation north of Ave Habib Bourguiba. Some might like the sound of the *Hôtel Ritza* (☎ 01-245428), just south of Place de la République on Ave Habib Thameur. Singles/doubles cost TD 7/12, plus TD 1.500 for a shower, or TD 12/17 with en suite.

(You'll be better off in the Ritza than the *Hôtel Savoie*, a dilapidated dump off Ave de la Gare on Rue du Boucher! It charges a rock-bottom TD 2.500 per person.)

### Places to Stay – middle

There are plenty of hotels to choose from in this category, with some excellent places among them.

They don't come any better than the *Hôtel Maison Doree* (☎ 01-240632), an old-style French hotel on Rue el-Koufa, just north of Place de Barcelone off Rue de Hollande. It is immaculately clean and well kept, the staff are friendly and efficient, and it even has a lift. Singles/doubles cost TD 14.520/16.830 with washbasin, TD 17.930/19.800 with shower and TD 22.900/25.410 with shower and toilet. All prices include breakfast – which features chocolate croissants.

Two other good places nearby are the *Hôtel Salammbô* (☎ 01-337498), at 6 Rue de Grèce, and the *Hôtel Transatlantique* (☎ 01-240680), at 106 Rue de Yougoslavie. Despite its kitsch foyer décor and pink rooms, the Salammbô is quite good value at TD 10.500/16.500 for singles/doubles with breakfast. Showers cost TD 1. The Transatlantique is another fine old place, its name in mosaic on the corner of Ave de Carthage. Basic rooms cost TD 9/15 for singles/doubles.

Closer to the medina is the *Grand Hôtel de France* (☎ 01-245876) at 8 Rue Mustapha

Mbarek, not far from Place de la Victoire. It's another older-style place, and very reasonably priced with basic rooms from TD 12.100/16.200 for singles/doubles, including breakfast. Rooms with a bath cost an extra TD 1.600.

If you want to be right in the thick of things on Ave Habib Bourguiba, there's the noisy *Capitole Hôtel* (☎ 01-244997) at No 60, right by the cinema of the same name. Room rates are TD 19.200/26 for singles/doubles, which includes a good breakfast.

The *Hôtel Majestic* (☎ 01-242848), at the northern end of Ave de Paris, is a splendid piece of fading grandeur with one of the finest French colonial façades in town. Singles/doubles here are TD 25/35 with breakfast. Air-conditioning costs an extra TD 3.500 in summer.

## Places to Stay – top end

For those people with the money and the inclination, Tunis has a full quota of expensive places, including the city's leading architectural curiosity – the bizarre inverted pyramid behind the tourist office that calls itself the *Hôtel du Lac* (☎ 01-258322). Rooms here cost TD 41/61 with breakfast.

The five-star *Africa Hôtel* (☎ 01-347477), on Ave Habib Bourguiba, is a ghastly great blot on the landscape, especially as it's the only high-rise building in the whole street and practically the whole city. However, even if you are not staying here, the air-conditioned lobby with its luxurious armchairs is a welcome place to catch your breath for a few minutes on a hot and humid day. Expect to pay TD 116/132 for singles/doubles – without breakfast, unless you feel like lashing out TD 380 on the presidential suite!

Rather more discreet is the stylish *Oriental Palace Hôtel* (☎ 01-348846), at 29 Ave Jean Jaures, with its array of clocks showing the current time in a large number of the world's capital cities. Five-star treatment here costs TD 71/80 for singles/doubles with breakfast.

Hilton-hoppers will be happy to find their favourite here too, on Ave Salammbô in the northern suburb of Mutuelleville, 10 minutes by taxi from the centre of town and the airport. The *Tunis Hilton* (☎ 01-282000) prices its rooms according to what you can see. Rooms with a 'limited view' cost TD 112.500/135, while rooms with a 'panoramic view' go for TD 128/155.

## Places to Eat

Tunis has plenty of cheap and moderately priced restaurants but, although at first glance there appears to be plenty of variety, they have remarkably similar menus with about a dozen standard dishes. Service, prices and décor are the biggest variables.

**Markets** For fresh fruit, the stalls around Place de Barcelone, by the railway station, have a good selection of fresh fruit. Street vendors in and around the same area sell various things, including halva, bread, nuts, cigarettes and pretzel sticks – all very cheaply.

The central market on Rue Charles de Gaulle is always a busy place, with a good variety of produce and some excellent local cheeses and yoghurt available.

**Pâtisseries & Rotisseries** These are at the bottom of the cheap-eats scale and are found all over the new city.

The pâtisseries stock all manner of sweet cakes and croissants. They usually do other things like small pizzas, savoury pâtés (pastries) and crêpes, which are generally excellent and all you need for breakfast or lunch. At the back of these places there is nearly always a café, where you can stand while eating your croissant with a coffee. Some of the best cafés are on Rue Charles de Gaulle, between Ave Habib Bourguiba and Rue d'Espagne.

The rotisseries cook roast (or fried) chicken and chips, but they also have salads and, of course, bread. They are mostly stand-up joints where your food is served in a piece of paper; you either stand around and eat it with everyone else or take it away. You can find these places all over the ville nouvelle.

**Pizzerias** Pizza parlours are the most popular form of Western food outlet. As good a place as any is *La Mamma* (☎ 01-241256), at 11 Rue de Marseille, which does individual pizzas ranging from TD 3.800 to TD 4.200 and pasta from TD 2.800, as well as steaks and seafood.

Most pizza places serve takeaway pizza by the kg, starting at about TD 6 for the most basic.

**Hamburger Restaurants** Burgers haven't achieved anything like the popularity of the pizza, but they can be found. Addicts can be sure of getting a fix at the quaintly named Mac-Doly, on Ave du Ghana just off Place de la République. Offerings include a basic burger for 950 mills, Big Dolys for TD 1.500 and a Mac Senior for TD 1.900.

**Tunisian Restaurants** There's no shortage of reasonable places serving local cuisine. The best of these is still the long-time travellers' favourite, the *Restaurant Carcassonne*, at 8 Ave de Carthage, just off Ave Habib Bourguiba and down from the Café de Paris. The value offered by its TD 2.900 four-course menu is little short of remarkable, even if the meat dishes are not exactly enormous. The crème au caramels are a nice touch. The place also has welcome ceiling fans and fast, friendly service. It's not hard to understand why it's popular with tourists and locals alike.

The *Istanbul*, just north of Ave Habib Bourguiba on Rue Pierre Coubertin, does an even cheaper four-courser to exactly the same format for TD 2.300. The food is not as good, and the place is closed on Friday.

The *Restaurant Neptune*, 50 metres off Ave Habib Bourguiba at 3 Rue du Caire (almost opposite the Africa Hôtel), is a popular place that sticks to the simple things and does them well. A big bowl of spicy beans with chicken costs TD 1.800.

The *Restaurant Saidouna*, on Rue Charles de Gaulle next to the Hôtel Cirta, does pretty standard local food.

If you want to go a bit up-market, try the *Restaurant Baghdad*, opposite the Africa Hôtel at 29 Ave Habib Bourguiba. A meal here will set you back about TD 8.

Top of the range for Tunisian food is the *Restaurant Dar el-Jeld* (☎ 01-260916), on the western side of the medina in Rue Dar el-Jeld. It's probably the best restaurant in town, and it certainly has the best setting. The Dar el-Jeld is the palatial former home of a wealthy bourgeois family, and the dining room and table settings are quite magnificent. There's a tourist menu for TD 15; otherwise you can reckon on about TD 25 per person. The wine menu includes a cheeky little French champagne at TD 170 per bottle. Bookings are essential.

**Tourist Restaurants** There are stacks of restaurants around the ville nouvelle serving what many like to call Franco-Tunisienne cuisine. The main areas are Rue de Yougoslavie between Ave de Carthage and Rue Ibn Khaldoun, and the southern reaches of Ave de Paris and Rue de Marseille. You'll be lucky to get out of any of them for under TD 10 plus wine.

The *Restaurant Le Cosmos* (☎ 01-241610), at 7 Rue Ibn Khaldoun, is one place that has built up a solid reputation for good food and reasonable prices. You can amuse yourself by studying the pretty awful paint job of the universe on the ceiling, and the eclectic mix of kitsch wall decorations.

*Gaston's* (☎ 01-340417), at 73 Rue de Yougoslavie, has a different three-course menu for every day of the week (normally finishing with chocolate mousse), and has live music on Tuesday, Friday and Saturday. The menu looks much the same at *Le Strasbourg* (☎ 01-241139), on the opposite side of Rue de Yougoslavie – or Rue de Serbie, as it lists its address.

At 5 Rue de Marseille, *Chez Nous* (☎ 01-243043) makes a meal of all the celebrities who have graced its tables. There's lots of photos of the likes of Michael York having a good time. It doesn't say what they thought of the food. It does a three-course menu for TD 9.

At all these restaurants you need to arrive by about 8.30 pm at the latest or you miss out. They all serve alcohol – mostly local beer and red wine. Also, surprisingly, many of them close for their annual holidays for at least a couple of weeks right at the height of the season.

## Entertainment

**Cafés & Bars** Cafés are an essential part of life in Tunis, as they are in the rest of the country, and there are numerous places with tables and chairs out on the footpath. The *Café de Paris*, on the corner of Ave Habib Bourguiba and Ave de Carthage, is very popular. It can be a good place to pass some time, although you pay a little over the odds for coffee, the croissants are very mediocre and the service is, at best, surly. It must be just about the only café in the country that serves beer.

The bars in Tunis are serious drinking dens. Typical of them is the *Bar Coquille*, next to the Restaurant Carcassonne on Ave de Carthage.

**Cabaret** For nightlife with a local flavour, try one of the small cabaret places in the ville nouvelle. Typical is the *Cabaret Protiniére*, at the Place Barcelone end of Rue de Hollande. It's here that you'll find such exotica as belly dancers and singers, albeit barely visible through the dense cigarette haze. The decidedly sleazy atmosphere may not appeal to some, and it's definitely not recommended for single women looking for a quiet night out. The Protiniére is open from 10 pm to 4 am. The entry fee of TD 5 includes your first drink.

*Gaston's*, at 73 Rue de Yougoslavie, has Tunisian folk music on Tuesday, Friday and Saturday nights.

**Spectator Sports** There's horse racing every Sunday afternoon at L'Hippodrome de Kassar Said, about 10 km west of the city centre. The six-race card normally starts at about 1 pm, and includes events for Arab horses as well as for imported thoroughbreds. There is computerised betting, both on local races and on racing from France. Entry is 500 mills. Buses to Kassar Said (490 mills)

leave from the Jardin Thameur bus station. A taxi from the city centre will cost about TD 3.500.

During the soccer season, a first-division game is played every Sunday afternoon at 2 pm at the Cité Olympique, a short walk from the station of the same name on Métro Léger line No 2. Entry is 400 mills.

## Things to Buy

**Handicrafts** While Tunis is not known for its handicraft production, the shops of the Tunis medina offer everything the souvenir hunter could desire. Prices along Rue de la Kasbah and Rue Jemaa Zitouna tend to start fairly high, so get set to hustle. To get an idea of the quality and price of the best stuff available, visit the excellent ONAT showroom on Ave Mohammed V, 100 metres north of the tourist office. There is a huge selection of crafts from all over the country. It's a good place to pick up last-minute souvenirs without running the gauntlet of the shop owners in the medina.

## Getting There & Away

**Air** The domestic airline Tuninter flies at least five times daily to Jerba and less frequently to Tozeur and Sfax. It can be difficult to get a booking in the middle of summer. One-way and return prices are as follows: Tunis-Jerba, TD 43.800/85.600; Tunis-Sfax, TD 36.300/70.600; Tunis-Tozeur, TD 41.800/81.400.

Tickets can be bought at Tunis Air. The main Tunis Air office has been temporarily moved to 47 Ave Farhat Hached (☎ 01-330100) while the premises at 48 Ave Habib Bourguiba are being renovated. It looks as if the work will take some time. Tuninter also has a special reservations service on ☎ 01-701111.

The main airline offices in Tunis include:

Aeroflot
    24 Ave Habib Thameur (☎ 01-341888)
Air Algérie
    26 Ave de Paris (☎ 01-341590)
Air France
    1 Rue d'Athènes (☎ 01-341577)

TUNISIA

EgyptAir
    International Tunis Hôtel, 49 Ave Habib
    Bourguiba (☎ 01-341182)
GB Airways
    17 Ave Habib Bourguiba (☎ 01-244261)
KLM
    50 Rue Lucie Faure (☎ 01-341309)
Lufthansa
    Ave Habib Thameur (☎ 01-341049)
Royal Air Maroc
    45 Ave Habib Bourguiba (☎ 01-249016)
Tunis Air
    48 Ave Habib Bourguiba (☎ 01-259189)
    113 Ave de la Liberté (☎ 01-288100)

**Bus** Tunis has two bus stations. The Gare
Routière Nord de Bab Saadoun (☎ 01-
562299) is for services to the northern part
of the country, including 'Ain Draham, Beja,
Bizerte, Jendouba, Le Kef, Mateur, Menzel
Bourguiba and Tabarka. This bus station is
200 metres from Bab Saadoun, in the north-
west of the city, next to the louage station
servicing the same destinations.

The easiest way to get there is by Métro
Léger line No 3 or 4 to Bab Saadoun station,
310 mills from Place Barcelone or
République stations. Alternatively, take a No
3 bus from Tunis Marine bus station or Ave
Habib Bourguiba opposite the Africa Hôtel,
and get off at the first stop after Bab Saadoun
(which you can't miss, as it's a massive,
triple-arched gate in the middle of a roundabout); the bus station is 100 metres over to
the right.

The other bus station is the Gare Routière
Sud de Bab el-Fellah (☎ 01-495255). It is 10
minutes' walk south of Place de Barcelone,
to the left of the flyover at the end of Ave de
la Gare. You can't get there on the city's bus
and tram network. This bus station is the
departure point for all places in the country
other than those already mentioned, as well
as all the international services (see the
Tunisia Getting There & Away section).
Some of the regional bus companies also run
buses to and from Tunis and have their own
ticket windows at the station.

Times change, and so do timetables – frequently. The French-language papers carry
details of SNTRI departures from both Tunis
bus stations every day. The information
booths at both stations have booklets listing
prices and times of services. It should be
noted that these schedules list only final destinations and not the places passed en route.
Thus Sousse and Kairouan seldom get a
mention, even though all the southern buses
pass through one of them.

**Train** The railway station is close to the
centre of town on Place de Barcelone and is
the most convenient place to arrive, as there
are plenty of hotels within five minutes'
walk. It's a modern and efficient station, with
all scheduled departures and arrivals displayed on an electronic board in the terminal
building. There is a small information kiosk
in the foyer which is staffed irregularly.

Although the services are crowded in
summer, there is no need to reserve a seat,
although you can do this the day before or on
the air-conditioned services to Sfax.

There are daily services from Tunis to
Beja (six services daily, two hours travelling
time), Bizerte (four, 1½ hours), El-Jem
(four, three hours), Gabès (two, 6½ hours),
Ghardimao (five, one continuing on to
Algeria, three hours), Kalaa Khasba (one -
two from June to September, five hours),
Mahdia (two – one on Sunday, four hours),
Metlaoui (one daily via Sfax, nine hours),
Monastir (two, three hours), Nabeul (six, one
direct and the others involving a change at
Bir Bou Rekba, 1½ hours), Sfax (four, four
hours) and Sousse (eight, two hours).

Fares from Tunis are as follows:

| Destination | Confort | 1st Class | 2nd Class |
| --- | --- | --- | --- |
| Bizerte | 3.950 | 3.300 | 2.300 |
| El-Jem | 9.750 | 8.500 | 6.550 |
| Gabès | 17.500 | 15.200 | 10.600 |
| Hammamet | 4 | 3.500 | 2.500 |
| Jendouba | 6.900 | 5.850 | 4.300 |
| Nabeul | 4 | 3.500 | 2.500 |
| Sfax | 11.750 | 10.250 | 7.200 |
| Sousse | 7.150 | 6.250 | 4.450 |

**Taxi** Louages are a good alternative to the
buses. Although they are a bit more expensive, the services are more flexible: if there
are heaps of people trying to travel, the

ouages keep running. They operate mainly in the mornings, so if you are planning on catching one you will have a shorter wait then. Things slow down considerably in the afternoon and you may have to wait a while for one to fill up.

Tunis has two main louage stations, and these are right opposite the northern and southern bus stations. From the south station there are louages to Gabès, Gafsa, Jerba, Kairouan, Kasserine, Medenine, Nabeul, Sfax, Sousse, Tataouine and Tozeur. From the northern station they run to Beja, Bizerte, Jendouba, Le Kef and Tabarka.

**Car Rental** All the major companies have offices at the airport and in town, including:

Avis
  90 Ave de la Liberté (☎ 01-782017)
  Africa Hôtel lobby (☎ 01-347477)
  Hilton Hôtel lobby (☎ 01-282000)
Cartha-Rent
  59 Ave Habib Bourguiba (☎ 01-254605)
Europcar
  17 Ave Habib Bourguiba (☎ 01-340303)
Garage Lafayette
  84 Ave de la Liberté (☎ 01-280284)
Hertz
  29 Ave Habib Bourguiba (☎ 01-248559)
Topcar
  7 Rue de Mahdia (☎ 01-285003)

**Sea** The ferries from Europe arrive at the port at La Goulette, at the end of the causeway across Lake Tunis. To get there, take a TGM train to La Goulette Vieille, and walk back along the line towards Tunis until you get to the railway crossing; turn left and walk for 200 metres, past the kasbah, and there is a sign to the port off to the right. The whole walk takes about 20 minutes.

When arriving at Tunis, come straight out of the port, turn left at the first main intersection (by the kasbah) and walk to the railway crossing; the station is away to the right. A taxi from the port to Ave Habib Bourguiba shouldn't cost more than TD 2.500.

Getting a booking on a ferry out of Tunis at the height of summer can take days – they are often booked out for up to 10 days in advance. This especially applies if you are taking a vehicle. Make your reservations as early as possible.

The Tirrenia Line (☎ 01-242775) office is at 122 Rue de Yougoslavie. It can be a real bun fight here, with people doing battle for tickets. Turn up first thing in the morning when things are marginally less frantic.

There are regular departures to France (Marseilles) and Italy (Cagliari, Genoa, Palermo and Trapani). See the Tunisia Getting There & Away chapter for full details of services.

### Getting Around

**To/From the Airport** The Tunis-Carthage Airport is eight km north-east of the city. Yellow city bus No 35 runs there from the Tunis Marine terminus every 30 minutes or so between about 6 am and 9 pm. You can pick it up at the stop opposite the Africa Hôtel. The trip takes about 20 minutes and costs 550 mills. A taxi to the Africa Hôtel from the airport costs about TD 2.500.

From the airport, the bus leaves from just outside the terminal building, to the right of the exit.

**Bus** The yellow buses operate to all parts of the city, but you should have little cause to use them other than getting to the airport, the Bardo Museum or the northern bus station. The destination, point of origin and route number are all displayed on a board by the entry door near the rear of the vehicle. Routes of interest to tourists have the destinations in Latin script as well. The number is also displayed in the front window. The basic fare for a ride is 310 mills on most routes.

There are three main terminuses for the buses: Tunis Marine, which is right by the TGM station at the causeway end of Ave Habib Bourguiba; Place de Barcelone, in front of the railway station; and Jardin Thameur, just off Ave de France. The No 3 bus to the Bardo Museum and the No 35 to the airport both leave from Tunis Marine.

TUNISIA

**TGM** This is the light-rail system that connects central Tunis with the beachside suburbs of La Goulette, Carthage, Sidi Bou Said and La Marsa.

It is fast, cheap and convenient, although a little crowded at times. The first train leaves Tunis Marine at 3.42 am, and the last train at 12.30 am. The last train back from La Marsa leaves at midnight. Departures range from every 12 minutes during peak hours to every 40 minutes. There are 1st and 2nd-class compartments. There seems to be little point in forking out the extra for 1st class, although it is less crowded.

The 2nd-class fare from Tunis to La Goulette is 310 mills, to Carthage it's 500 mills and to Sidi Bou Said and La Marsa it's 600 mills.

**Tram** The fancy and relatively new tram service, Métro Léger, has four routes running to various parts of the city. The free map from the tourist office has the lines, but not the route numbers, marked on it. Line Nos 3 and 4 will get you to the northern bus and louage stations, and No 4 is scheduled to include a station for the Bardo Museum. Palestine station on line No 2 is the place to get off for the US Embassy and the British Consulate. Each of these journeys costs 310 mills.

**Taxi** Taxis are a fairly cheap way of getting around. They're especially good if you are visiting embassies, as the drivers always know where they are and can save you a good deal of foot slogging. They always use the meter and fares work out at about 350 mills per km.

The only problem with the taxis is that there aren't enough of them. During peak hours this is a real problem; you just have to be patient and lucky. One of the best places to pick one up is by the railway station on Ave de la Gare, while Ave Habib Bourguiba is one of the worst places. Taxis can also be booked by phone – very handy when you're trying to get to the airport with a mountain of baggage. Ask at your hotel reception.

# Around Tunis

There are quite a few places within day-trip distance of Tunis. Strictly speaking, the beach suburbs of Carthage, Sidi Bou Said and La Marsa are part of Tunis, but it takes a day trip to visit any or all of them.

Farther away to the south are the excellent ruins of the Roman town of Thuburbo Majus. A visit to these ruins can be combined with the nearby town of Zaghouan to make a good day trip.

## CARTHAGE

Despite its fascinating history and the position of dominance which Carthage held in the ancient world, the Romans did such a thorough demolition job on it that the ruins today are a major disappointment. For a full account of the city's history, see the Facts about the Region chapter.

Most of what there is to see is of Roman origin and there's not that much of it. However, as Carthage is so accessible, it's worth wandering around for at least a couple of hours. This could be combined with a visit to Sidi Bou Said or the beach at La Marsa.

If you have only a few hours, the best bet is to limit yourself to the museum and the ruins of Byrsa right outside it. With half a day you could also see the Antonine Baths, the Punic ports and the theatre, and in a whole day you would be able to see the lot.

The real hassle is that the sites are quite spread out. Although you can overcome this to a certain extent by making use of the TGM line which runs bang through the middle of the area, seeing everything requires a good deal of walking. In the heat and humidity of summer, this is more hassle than it's worth.

If you are intent on seeing the whole lot, the best way to tackle it is as follows. First take the TGM to Carthage Salammbô and then walk down towards the sea to visit Tophet, the Punic ports and the Oceanographic Museum. Next, take the TGM from Carthage Byrsa to Carthage Hannibal and head away from the sea to visit the museum and Byrsa Hill, and then continue down the other side of the hill to the amphitheatre and cisterns. Next, follow the back road to the US war cemetery, from where you can then cut across country to the basilica. From there, walk to the sea and the Antonine Baths via the theatre and Roman villas. To finish the walk, take the street just back from the sea, Rue Septime Sévère, to visit the Magon Quarter, from where it's a short walk back to Carthage Hannibal TGM station. Covering this whole route would take the best part of a day.

As is the case with the sites in the Tunis medina, it is possible to get a multiple ticket for all the sites at Carthage. It costs TD 2, plus TD 1 to take photos, but is available only at the museum, the Antonine Baths and the Roman villas. All sites are open daily from 7 am to 7 pm from June to September and from 8.30 am to 5.30 pm for the rest of the year.

### Tophet

When it was first excavated in 1921 this site near the Punic ports created a good deal of excitement, as it revealed evidence of child sacrifice. The area contained urns, each marked with a stele and full of burnt child remains. However, just how these children died is still open to debate. The Romans were keen to condemn anything Carthaginian and got plenty of mileage out of the child sacrifice issue. Just how widely it was carried on is not known, although it certainly did exist and probably only died out after contact with the Greeks and Romans. Animal sacrifice played a far bigger part in the local religion.

The word 'tophet' is in fact Hebrew and refers to a place near Jerusalem where human sacrifice was carried out. The other name for Tophet in Carthage is the Sanctuary of Tanit.

Today, the small site, which covers half an acre or so, is basically a patch of overgrown weeds with a few excavated pits. There are also some vaults here, which are the remains of 4th-century Roman warehouses. If you don't have a multiple ticket, it's not worth paying to get in – you can see almost as much from outside.

### Punic Ports

Although they don't look too impressive today, these two ports were the basis of Carthage's power and prosperity. The northern basin was the navy base and was originally circular with a diameter of about 300 metres. It is said that it could hold as many as 220 warships, although it's hard to work out how. The harbour was surrounded by a high wall on the landward sides, and the island in the centre held the naval headquarters. The southern harbour was for commercial shipping.

### Oceanographic Museum

On the island which separates the ports, this sorry display of fish and things nautical is a total waste of time. Entry is only 600 mills, however, so it won't break you if you feel like a wander around. It is open from 4.30 to 7.30 pm Tuesday to Sunday, and on Sunday morning from 10 am to noon; it's closed on Monday.

### Byrsa Hill

This hill dominates the area. To get to the top, head uphill from Carthage Hannibal TGM through the area of plush diplomats' residences, and then go up the stairs to the left at the top of the hill, just near the sign for the Reine Elyssa Didon (a fancy hotel). Although the museum building is just on the left, the entrance is around to the right, on the other side of the cathedral.

On the top of the hill is the **Cathedral of St Louis**, which is visible for miles around. Built by the French in 1890, and an eyesore of truly massive proportions, it was dedicated to the 13th-century French king. It has now been deconsecrated and is closed to the public.

The **National Museum** is the large white building at the back of the cathedral. Its displays have recently been revamped, with Canadian and US assistance, and they are well worth a look. The Punic displays upstairs are especially good.

The Byrsa Quarter (in the museum grounds) has the only Carthaginian ruins of any consequence. The Romans levelled off

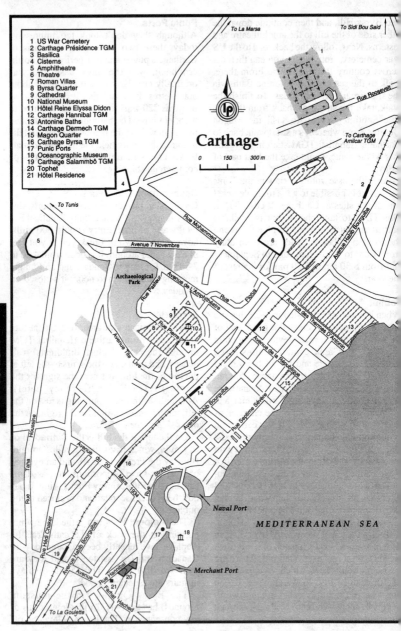

1  US War Cemetery
2  Carthage Présidence TGM
3  Basilica
4  Cisterns
5  Amphitheatre
6  Theatre
7  Roman Villas
8  Byrsa Quarter
9  Cathedral
10 National Museum
11 Hôtel Reine Elyssa Didon
12 Carthage Hannibal TGM
13 Antonine Baths
14 Carthage Dermech TGM
15 Magon Quarter
16 Carthage Byrsa TGM
17 Punic Ports
18 Oceanographic Museum
19 Carthage Salammbô TGM
20 Tophet
21 Hôtel Residence

# Carthage

0       150       300 m

To La Marsa

To Sidi Bou Said

Rue Roosevelt

To Carthage
Amilcar TGM

To Tunis

Rue Mohammed Ali

Avenue 7 Novembre

Archaeological
Park

Rue Pasteur

Avenue de L'Amphithéâtre

Rue Ptolée

Avenue des Thermes D'Antonin

Avenue Habib Bourguiba

Rue Pierre

Avenue Ille Live

Avenue de la République

Rue Septime Sévère

Avenue Habib Bourguiba

Avenue du 20 Mars 1934

Rue Strabon

Naval Port

MEDITERRANEAN   SEA

Rue Houssine

Rue Taha

Rue Hédi Chaker

Avenue Habib Bourguiba

Avenue

Rue Hannibal

Rue Farhat Hached

Merchant Port

To La Goulette

TUNISIA

the top of the hill, burying the Carthaginian houses under the rubble. The area has been well excavated and the finds are described in full (in French) in the museum.

## Amphitheatre

The Roman amphitheatre is on the western side of the Byrsa hill, about 15 minutes' walk from the museum. It was supposedly one of the largest in the empire, but not much remains today. Most of its stones were pinched for other building projects in later centuries. The outer circle is hard to distinguish, and the limited excavations and reconstructions date from 1919.

Across the road from the amphitheatre are some old cisterns, which used to hold the city's water supply. They are now ruined and not worth the scramble through the prickly pears to inspect.

## US War Cemetery & Basilica

The detour out to the war cemetery and basilica is only for the dedicated. The cemetery is extremely well kept, but the basilica across the field amounts to nothing much more than a few piles of stones.

## Theatre & Villas

The theatre has been completely covered in concrete and obscured with lighting towers and equipment for the annual Carthage International Festival. It really has very little going for it.

The same applies to the Roman Villas Archaeological Park (called the Villa de la Volière on the ticket), just downhill from the theatre – it is a largely decorative site which has been over-restored.

## Antonine Baths

The Antonine Baths are right down on the waterfront and are impressive more for their size and location than anything else. At the top of the steps just inland from the baths is a marble slab with a diagram which helps to give some idea of just how big they used to be.

The entrance is about 100 metres before the sea. From Carthage Hannibal TGM, take the main road (Ave Habib Bourguiba) and turn right at the intersection which features an enormous capital (headstone of a pillar) from the baths.

## Magon Quarter

The Magon Quarter is another archaeological park, this time down by the water, a few blocks south of the Antonine Baths. It has recently been excavated by a team of German archaeologists whose work has revealed a residential area. It is mildly interesting and the multiple ticket gets you in. If you don't have this ticket, don't bother.

## Places to Stay & Eat

There are a couple of hotels, both at the more expensive end of the market. The three-star *Hôtel Reine Elyssa Didon* (☎ 01-275344), named after the Phoenician queen who founded Carthage, has a magnificent location on top of the Byrsa Hill, right next to the museum grounds. It's worth visiting for the view alone. Singles/doubles cost TD 50/66 in summer, dropping to TD 40/50 in winter.

TUNISIA

It's popular at lunchtime for its TD 7.500 tourist menu.

The other place is the *Hôtel Residence* (☎ 01-731072), 100 metres from the Tophet site at 16 Rue Hannibal. Singles/doubles cost TD 24.500/39 in summer, and TD 6 per person less in winter.

### Getting There & Away

There is no need to consider any options other than the train. The journey from Tunis Marine to any of the six Carthage TGM stations costs 500 mills and takes about 20 minutes.

### SIDI BOU SAID

Sidi Bou Said is a small, whitewashed village set high on a cliff above the Mediterranean Sea just north of Tunis, and it's on every tour-group itinerary. Despite this it is still a remarkably laid-back town, especially outside the main tourist season.

The centre of activity is a small, cobbled square with outdoor cafés and sweet stalls, which can be an agreeable place to sit for a while with a cold drink. In fact, other than this, there is very little to see in Sidi Bou Said; after a half-hour wander you will have exhausted the possibilities.

Just past the sweet stalls on the right is a steep path and stairway which lead down to a small and relatively uncrowded beach, where there are a few fairly up-market restaurants. From here it is possible to follow the road around and back up the hill to bring you out at Carthage Amilcar TGM station. The walk from Sidi Bou Said takes about an hour.

### Places to Stay & Eat

There are two good places to stay in Sidi Bou Said. The *Hôtel Dar Said* (☎ 01-740215) is something special, occupying a beautiful old palace just beyond the northern end of the square. It charges TD 16/22 for singles/doubles with breakfast. For an extra TD 2 you can get a room with views over the Gulf of Tunis.

The *Hôtel Sidi Bou Fares* (☎ 01-740091) is signposted up some cobbled stairs to the west of the square. The rooms are small but clean and pleasant, encircling a traditional courtyard full of flowering shrubs and vines, although sadly minus the shady, old fig tree which fell down in early 1993. Singles/doubles with breakfast cost TD 10.500/17.

Down by the marina, the *Residence Africa* (☎ 01-740600) has doubles for TD 20 in winter. It's expensive in summer, and invariably fully booked.

For a meal, the *Restaurant Le Chargui*, at the northern end of the square, has a pleasant open-air courtyard and reasonable prices. You'll pay a lot more for a bit more style at the *Restaurant Dar Zarouk*, opposite the Hôtel Dar Said. It's closed in winter.

Better than either of these, and much more friendly, is the *Restaurant La Bagatelle* (☎ 01-741116). Coming down from Sidi Bou Said square to the TGM station, turn left at the roundabout at the foot of the hill and La Bagatelle is 100 metres along on the right. It has a three-course menu for TD 6 and excellent Tunisian food and fish. It's run by a colourful character with an impressive waxed moustache.

### Getting There & Away

Sidi Bou Said is on the TGM line and it takes about 30 minutes to get there from Tunis (600 mills). From the station it's about a 15-minute walk up to the top of the hill and the centre of the old part of the village.

### LA MARSA

La Marsa is another of the beachside suburbs and is at the end of the TGM line from Tunis. Because of this, it is one of the least crowded on hot summer days, although weekends are a bad time on any beach.

Along with the area around Byrsa Hill, La Marsa is one of the most exclusive residential suburbs of Tunis. There are a couple of good cafés and restaurants around the TGM station.

### THUBURBO MAJUS

This old provincial Roman city, some 55 km south-west of Tunis, is easily accessible by both bus and louage from Tunis and, along with the nearby town of Zaghouan, makes an interesting day trip. If time is short, however, you could easily miss these places without losing any sleep.

If you are travelling from Tunis to Kairouan or vice versa it would also be possible to fit in Thuburbo Majus on the way. If you are making a day trip from Tunis to Thuburbo Majus and Zaghouan, it is easiest to go first to Thuburbo Majus and then head for Zaghouan, as the transport connections are better this way.

Thuburbo Majus thrived as a town serving the agricultural hinterland from well before Roman times, but it wasn't until the 2nd century, when the emperor Hadrian visited and declared it a municipality, that the town really prospered.

## The Ruins

Ruins of the major monuments and various other remains are scattered around the edge of this site.

**Forum** As usual, the forum was the focal point of the city, where political and economic affairs were discussed. It is colonnaded on three sides; the columns were erected in 182 BC.

**Capitol** On the north-western side of the forum lies the capitol. It's in the required position of dominance, built on an artificial platform raised some two metres above the level of the forum. Built in 168 AD, it is reached by a wide flight of stairs which leads to the entrance and its six grooved pillars of pink limestone. The capitol was dedicated to two emperors, Marcus Aurelius and Commodus, and was under the protection of the ancient trinity of Jupiter, Juno and Minerva. Fragments of a statue of Jupiter were found here (now in the Bardo Museum in Tunis); the size of the pieces indicates that the statue was some 7.5 metres high.

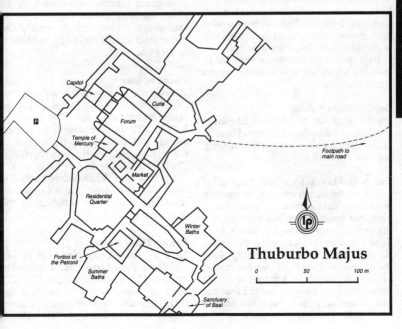

Thuburbo Majus

0        50        100 m

**Temple of Mercury & Market** The Temple of Mercury, on the south-western side of the forum, abuts the market, naturally enough, as Mercury was the god of trade. The stalls of the market can be discerned on three sides of the courtyard below the temple. Directly behind the market is a very un-Roman tangle of residential streets, which were obviously in existence before the Romans arrived.

**Portico of the Petronii** The Portico of the Petronii is named after the family of Petronius Felix, who paid for the construction of this gymnasium complex in 225 AD. The columns are unusual in that they are built of a yellow-veined black marble.

**Baths** Another unusual feature of the town is the two baths within 150 metres of each other. The Summer Baths are on the lower level, while the Winter Baths are higher up and contain some interesting veined marble columns. The most plausible explanation which has been put forward for having two baths so close to each other is that the well supplying the Winter Baths with water dried up in summer, necessitating the construction of the other baths lower down the hill.

Both these bath complexes were full of mosaics, which are now exhibited in the Bardo Museum.

### Getting There & Away

The totally dreary rural town of El-Fahs is the closest settlement to Thuburbo Majus. It is over three km away, so it can be a stinking hot walk in summer.

**Bus & Taxi** Louages run from Tunis to El-Fahs from the station opposite the southern bus station. Tell the driver you want to go to Thuburbo Majus and get him to drop you at the second turn-off to it (coming from Tunis), as from here it is only a short walk. At this intersection is a sign pointing along the side road to Thuburbo Majus but, instead of following the road, cut straight up the hill behind the sign; the ruins are just over the rise. If coming from El-Fahs, you have to either walk or hitch to the turn-off.

From El-Fahs there are regular louages (TD 1.050) and buses (870 mills) to Zaghouan. Buses and louages to Tunis and Kairouan are sometimes full, so you may have to wait a while or make a dive for a door handle when a louage arrives.

## ZAGHOUAN

This sleepy town, tucked in at the foot of the rugged 1295-metre Mt Zaghouan, is the place that used to supply ancient Carthage with fresh water. In those days a 70-km-long aqueduct was built to carry the water, and parts of it (in remarkably good condition) can still be seen alongside the Tunis-Zaghouan road, about 20 km from Tunis. The springs are still in use today; there are a couple of gushing outlets on strategic corners in the town, and the local residents still draw some of their water from them.

There are some fairly unremarkable Roman ruins in the form of the rather clumsily renovated Temple des Eaux, a once-grand fountain surrounded by 12 niches that used to hold statues depicting each month. It's not worth the walk unless you're stuck at the Hôtel les Nymphes with nothing else to do.

### Places to Stay

The only hotel in town is the two-star *Hôtel Les Nymphes* (☎ 02-675094), right up behind the town at the foot of the mountain. It charges TD 21/34 in summer for singles/doubles with breakfast, and TD 18/28 in winter. Rates are most definitely negotiable. The hotel doubles as the only bar in town.

The only other accommodation option is the *Maison des Jeunes*, and it's singularly uninviting even by the standards of the organisation.

### Getting There & Away

There are regular louages and buses to both El-Fahs and Tunis. Louages take 40 minutes to cover the 55 km to Tunis and cost TD 2.250. To El-Fahs, a bus costs 870 mills and a louage is TD 1.050 mills. There are also daily buses to Nabeul (TD 2.700) and Sousse (TD 3.450).

# The Cap Bon Peninsula

This is Tunisia's number one destination for package tourists. More than a quarter of the country's tourism revenue is generated by the small stretch of beachfront between Hammamet and Nabeul, to the south-west of the peninsula.

It's an area well worth avoiding during the peak season of July and August. The beaches are packed and both towns, which are rapidly merging, are crawling with scantily clad package tourists, and the prices hike up.

During peak season, budget accommodation is very hard to come by, especially in Hammamet. Fortunately, Nabeul does not suffer from quite the excesses of Hammamet, and it has one of the best camp sites in the country.

Kelibia, 40 minutes to the north of Nabeul, offers a much more relaxed atmosphere – although this is set to change with the area earmarked for major development. The excellent beach a few km away at Mansourah is to be the site of a massive, 2000-bed resort complex, scheduled to start operations in 1996.

The area around the small town of El-Haouaria, right on the northern tip of the peninsula, also is worth exploring.

The west coast is far more rugged, and, as a result, it is much less developed. Transport connections and accommodation are limited, but if you have your own transport there are plenty of beaches without the crowds of Hammamet or Nabeul. The small town of Korbous is well known for its hot springs.

## HAMMAMET

Unless you have a burning desire to be among other foreigners, you'd do well to bypass Hammamet. This former small fishing village has been transformed into a giant package-holiday resort with almost 100 resort hotels. They include such monsters as the Hôtel Bousten and the Samira Club with more than 1000 beds.

A walk down the main street during summer is likely to turn up about 10 tourists to every local – and the pace barely slackens except in the middle of winter.

The reason for Hammamet's popularity is its long stretch of beach, which is one of the better ones along this coastline.

### Information
**Tourist Office** The tourist office (☎ 02-280423) is in the centre of town on Ave Habib Bourguiba. It has a good handout map of Hammamet and Nabeul.

**Post** The main post office is on the Nabeul road, Ave de la République, close to the centre.

**Cultural Centre** Hammamet has a cultural centre, about two km south of the town on the beach road. Unless there's a special performance on (check with the tourist office), it's not worth the walk.

### Kasbah
Hammamet's over-restored kasbah is one of the least interesting around. The main reason to visit it is for the views from its ramparts. It's open daily from 8 am to 9 pm from May until September, and from 8 am to 6 pm for the rest of the year; entry is TD 1.

### Places to Stay – bottom end
**Camping** *Ideal Camping* (☎ 02-280302), on Ave de la République almost opposite the Hôtel Sahbi, doesn't really live up to its name. Although it's close to the centre, there is very little shade and the facilities are minimal. It charges TD 2.500 per person, TD 1.500 for power, TD 2 for a caravan and TD 1 for a hot shower. Cold showers are free.

**Hotels** The complete absence of budget hotels is as good a reason as any to stay clear of Hammamet. Most places slash prices in winter, but in summer everywhere charges an arm and a leg.

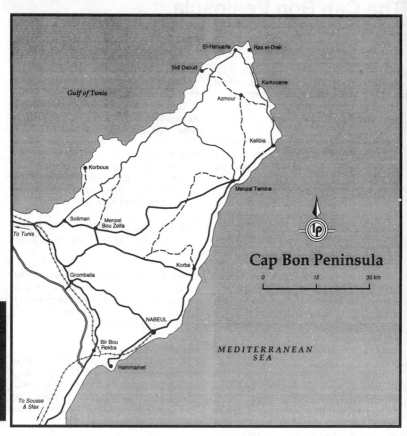

Cap Bon Peninsula

0    15    30 km

*MEDITERRANEAN SEA*

*Gulf of Tunis*

The Pension Hallous, formerly the only (comparative) cheapie in town, has closed, although the signs remain.

The best value for money is the *Hôtel Alya* (☎ 02-280218), right in the middle of town on Rue Ali Belhaouane. The rooms are large and airy with generous balconies, and those away from the road have good views of the kasbah. The low-season price of TD 10/18 for singles/doubles with breakfast rises to a hefty TD 31/38 in summer.

The *Hôtel Sahbi* (☎ 02-280807), on Ave de la République, is the cheapest place in town, at TD 10.500/15 in the low season and TD 18.500/28 in the high season for singles/doubles with breakfast, although it's hardly a backpackers' haunt.

**Places to Stay – middle & top end**

All the rest of the accommodation in Hammamet is of the resort-hotel type. These are nearly all located on the beach to the north or south of town. You're wasting your breath asking for a room in summer. In winter, you can take your pick for about TD 15/20 for singles/doubles with breakfast, plus such trimmings as swimming pools and tennis courts.

Two places worth checking are the *Hôtel Yasmina* (☎ 02-280222), 200 metres from the centre of town on Ave Habib Bourguiba, at TD 17/24 for singles/doubles with breakfast. On the other side of the road is *La Residence Hammamet* (☎ 02-280733) with apartments for between two and four people, starting at TD 17 for two.

### Places to Eat

The seafront along Ave Habib Bourguiba is just about a solid wall of tourist restaurants, hamburger joints, pizza parlours, pâtisseries and ice-cream shops.

For a cheap meal, try the *Restaurant Jasmine* in Rue des Jasmins. It does fish for TD 3.500, plus salads and casse-croûtes.

Another good place is the *Restaurant Sidi Abdelkader*, opposite the Hôtel Alya. It specialises in seafood and couscous. Expect to pay about TD 7 for a meal.

### Getting There & Away

**Bus** All buses leave from a small vacant lot about 100 metres uphill from the kasbah on Ave de la République. There are regular departures for Tunis and Nabeul.

**Train** The railway station is about one km from the centre at the end of Ave Habib Bourguiba, 15 minutes' walk past the tourist office. See the Nabeul section for details of train services. The direct train for Tunis leaves at 5.53 am.

**Taxi** Louages leave from the same place as the buses. The fare from Tunis is TD 2.700. Yellow taxis do the 18-km run to Nabeul for 700 mills per person; they leave from outside the kasbah. If you don't want to hire the whole cab, make sure that the driver understands you're only paying for one seat (*une place*).

### Car Rental

The agencies with offices in Hammamet include: Avis (☎ 02-280303), Rue de la Gare; Europcar (☎ 02-280146), Ave des Hôtels; Hertz (☎ 02-280187), Ave des Hôtels; and Topcar (☎ 02-280767), Ave de Koweit.

## NABEUL

After Hammamet, Nabeul seems pretty laid back. The biggest difference between it and Hammamet is its good range of budget accommodation, which means that even in summer it is possible to find a room that won't break the bank.

The town used to be an important service centre for the agricultural interior of the peninsula, but these days it has turned its back on the land and opened its arms to the visitors, mostly from sun-starved northern Europe.

The Friday market in Nabeul has become one of the major tourist events in the country. It is here that you'll find the widest range of pottery in Tunisia – Nabeul has long been associated with the craft. Many of the pieces on sale bear little relation to anything remotely Tunisian and owe more to the questionable tastes of the town's visitors. Because of the large number of tourists and the fact that most of them are only on short package tours, prices in Nabeul are high and bargaining is difficult. You stand a better chance on any day other than Friday, but even then it is difficult.

### Information

**Tourist Office** The office of the ONTT (☎ 02-286800) is on Ave Taieb Mehiri between the beach and the centre of town. It has a good brochure with maps of Nabeul and Hammamet and other information. Even when it's closed, bus, train and accommodation information is posted outside the office.

**Money** There are plenty of banks ready to take your money, mostly along Ave Farhat Hached and Ave Habib Bourguiba.

**Post** The main post office is on Ave Habib Bourguiba, north of the main intersection with Ave Farhat Hached.

### Museum

There is a small archaeological museum on Ave Habib Bourguiba opposite the railway station. It has a few pieces on display, but it's hardly worth the bother.

TUNISIA

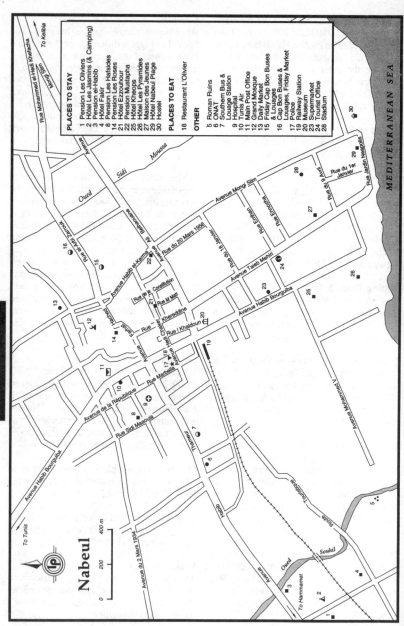

**Nabeul**

PLACES TO STAY

1 Pension Les Oliviers
3 Hôtel Les Jasmins (& Camping)
4 Pension el-Habib
8 Pension Fakir
14 Pension Les Hatsides
21 Pension Les Roses
22 Hôtel Ezzouhour
25 Pension Mustapha
26 Hôtel Kheops
27 Hôtel Les Pyramides
29 Maison des Jeunes
30 Hôtel Nabeul Plage
    Hostel

PLACES TO EAT

18 Restaurant L'Olivier

OTHER

5 Roman Ruins
6 ONAT
7 Southern Bus &
  Louage Station
9 Hospital
10 Tunis Air
11 Main Post Office
12 Grand Mosque
13 Daily Market
15 Friday Market
16 Cap Bon Buses &
  Louages, Friday Market
17 Police
19 Railway Station
20 Museum
24 Supermarket
28 Tourist Office
   Stadium

MEDITERRANEAN SEA

TUNISIA

## Market

The market is on Friday, mainly in the morning. Things have pretty much died down by 2 pm. When it's on, Ave Farhat Hached is closed to traffic between Ave Habib Bourguiba and Ave Habib el-Karma, and the whole stretch is packed with tourists and traders.

## Beaches

Most of Nabeul's beaches are in a disgraceful state, littered with all sorts of detritus (mainly plastic bottles). They are kept clean just in front of the resort hotels. It makes sense to take advantage of this and make discreet use of the beach umbrellas etc.

The beach at the Hôtel Les Pyramides is something to behold in summer. It's ridiculously crowded and claustrophobic – and such is its isolation from the real Tunisia that topless bathing is common.

## Places to Stay – bottom end

**Camping** The *Hôtel Les Jasmins* (☎ 02-285343) has a congenial camp site in the shady olive garden attached to the hotel, which is signposted off to the left, one km along the road towards Hammamet. The camp site is private and secure, and it costs TD 1.900 per person, TD 1.300 for a tent, TD 1.500 for caravans and camper vans, TD 1.700 for power and a hefty TD 2 for a hot shower.

The hotel is well situated, just five minutes' walk from the beach; the extra bit of distance between it and Nabeul means that the beach is relatively uncrowded. On the beach is a small café, which has some welcome umbrellas and serves tea, cold drinks and sandwiches.

If you've got a heavy pack when you arrive in Nabeul, it's worth taking a taxi (about 500 mills) to the site.

**Hostels** Nabeul has both a Maison des Jeunes and an HI-affiliated Auberge de Jeunesse. The only things they have in common is that they are both cheap and they are both likely to be fully booked in summer.

The no-frills *Maison des Jeunes*, towards the beach on Ave Taieb Mehiri, could easily be mistaken for a detention centre. It charges the standard TD 4.

The *Auberge de Jeunesse* (☎ 02-286689), right on the beach at the end of Ave Mongi Slim, is a bit on the primitive side, but the location is great and the manager is friendly and enthusiastic. Accommodation is in dormitories. Charges are TD 6 for half-board and TD 8 for full board.

**Hotels** The best place is the friendly, family-run *Pension Les Oliviers* (☎ 02-286865). It's the only cheap place where you can be assured of a quiet night's sleep. The only drawback is that it is a fair hike out of town. It's about a km from the town centre on the road to Hammamet, taking the turn-off 200 metres west of the oued (river). It's signposted down a small lane opposite the entrance of the Hôtel Les Jasmins. It charges TD 10/14 in the low season and TD 16.500/25 in the high season for rooms with shower, toilet and washbasin, plus breakfast. Both husband and wife speak excellent English.

Right in the middle of town, the *Pension Les Roses* (☎ 02-285570) on Ave Farhat Hached is friendly and comfortable, although its proximity to one of the mosques might give light sleepers a hard time. Prices range from TD 4 to TD 6, depending on the season. Cold showers are free and hot showers cost 500 mills. It is right on the corner of the small open square where Ave Farhat Hached makes a dogleg in the centre of the town.

Another good place is the *Pension Mustapha* (☎ 02-222262), on the corner of Rue Habib el-Karma and Ave Ali Belhaouane. It charges TD 7.500/12 for bed and breakfast in winter, rising to TD 10/17 in summer. The rooms have showers and hot water.

The *Pension el-Habib* (☎ 02-287190), on the noisy Ave Habib Thameur just over the Oued Souhil, would be a good place to stay were it not for the location. The view of a dry riverbed full of rubbish leaves a lot to be desired. Rooms are TD 6.500/10 in the low season and TD 11/18 in the high season, with breakfast. Some rooms have baths for an extra TD 1 per person. Showers are free.

Other cheap possibilities are the *Pension Les Hafsides* (☎ 02-285823), behind the hospital on Rue Sidi Maaouia, and the *Hôtel Ezzouhour* (☎ 02-224702) on Ave Hedi Chaker. Neither can be recommended. The Hafsides is open only between June and September.

### Places to Stay – middle
The *Hôtel Les Jasmins* (☎ 02-285343) was once a beautiful villa in an orchard. It's now a beautiful hotel in an orchard, with a swimming pool and good restaurant thrown in for good measure. It is likely to be fully booked in summer, but if you chance on a room it will cost TD 23/36 for singles/doubles with breakfast. In winter, the price drops to TD 14.500/22. Rooms come with shower or bath and toilet.

Between the Hôtel Les Jasmins and the beach is another possibility, the *Hôtel Fakir* (☎ 02-285477) with its grand, spiral staircase and big, airy rooms. It charges TD 17/21 for singles/doubles in the low season and TD 32.500/48 in the high season.

Don't bother with the grubby *Pension Monia Club* (☎ 02-285713) next door.

In winter, prices at most of the dozen or so resorts fall most definitely into the mid-range at about TD 15/20 for singles/doubles. They charge like a wounded bull in summer, when they are invariably fully booked by charter groups from Europe. They all have swimming pools and other sporting facilities.

### Places to Stay – top end
The only seriously up-market joint in town is the four-star *Hôtel Kheops* (☎ 02-285902), towards the beach on Ave Habib Bourguiba. It summer, it charges a whopping TD 85/114 for bed and breakfast, dropping to TD 42/54 in winter.

### Places to Eat
For self-caterers, there is a large supermarket on Ave Habib Bourguiba next to the Hôtel Imeme, halfway between the town and the beach. The wine shop next door has a good range of wine, beer and spirits.

There are a few restaurants around the square on Ave Farhat Hached. The two on either side of the entrance to the Pension Les Roses are both reasonable. A better choice is the restaurant attached to the *Pension Mustapha*, with most meals between TD 2 and TD 3. The self-service rotisserie on Rue Habib el-Karma by the minaret does chicken and chips for TD 1.600.

Both the *Hôtel Les Jasmins* and *Hôtel Fakir* do set menus for TD 5.

If money is no object, Nabeul's top restaurant is the *Restaurant L'Olivier* (☎ 02-286613), at the junction of Aves Hedi Chaker and Habib Bourguiba. It'll set you back TD 15 to TD 20, plus wine.

### Things to Buy
There is an ONAT emporium on Ave Habib Thameur not far from the bus station. It has the same good-quality stuff as the other branches in the country and gives you an idea of the maximum prices you should be paying for things.

### Getting There & Away
**Air** The Tunis Air (☎ 02-285193) office is at 145 Ave Habib Bourguiba, opposite the main post office.

**Bus** The station for buses and louages to Tunis and Hammamet is close to the centre of town on Ave Habib Thameur.

The regional bus service No 40 runs regularly from the southern bus station in Tunis (TD 2.380). Buses to Hammamet run every half-hour from 5.30 am to 7 pm (470 mills). There are also departures for Zaghouan (three daily, TD 2.100), Kairouan (three daily between 6 am and 12.15 pm, TD 4.200), Sousse, Monastir and Mahdia.

Buses for Kelibia and the rest of Cap Bon leave from the site of the Friday market on Rue el-Arbi Zarrouk on the other side of town. On Friday, the buses move to a vacant lot just opposite. There are 16 services a day to Kelibia between 7.15 am and 6.15 pm. The 10.30 am and 6.15 pm buses continue to

El-Haouaria. The last bus back from Kelibia is at 6.45 pm.

**Train** The station is close to the centre of town at the junction of Ave Ali Belhaouane and Ave Habib Bourguiba.

There are six trains a day from Tunis. Five of them (7.10 am and 12.05, 3.30, 5.30 and 6.05 pm) involve changing trains at Bir Bou Rekba. It's no hassle as the other train is there waiting. The journey takes 1½ hours and costs TD 2.500 in 2nd class and TD 3.500 in 1st class. There is one direct train from Tunis at 2.20 pm, but somehow it takes 10 minutes longer. Trains leave Nabeul for Tunis at 5.40 (direct), 6.25, 7.40 and 8.45 am and at 4.10 and 7 pm. The 7 pm trip involves a 30-minute wait at Bir Bou Rekba.

There are additional services to Hammamet and Bir Bou Rekba at 12.37 and 6 pm.

The 7.40 am train from Nabeul connects at Bir Bou Rekba for Sousse, Sfax and Gabès. The 12.37 pm and 4.10 pm connect for Sousse, Monastir and Mahdia and the 6 pm meets the train for Sousse and Sfax.

**Taxi** There are two louage stations. Louages to Tunis (TD 2.700), Sousse and Zaghouan leave from next to the Ave Habib Thameur bus station. Louages for Kelibia (TD 2.150) and other parts of Cap Bon leave from next to the bus station on Rue el-Arbi Zarrouk. The vacant lot opposite, which is used by the buses and louages on market day, is normally the departure point for share taxis to Hammamet. A seat costs 700 mills, although drivers often ask for far more if they spot a tourist.

**Car Rental** Half a dozen agencies are represented in Nabeul, including Hertz (☎ 02-285327) out towards Hammamet on Ave Habib Thameur. More convenient are Rent a Car (☎ 02-286679) and Mattei (☎ 02-285967) on Ave Habib Bourguiba.

### Getting Around
**Taxi** Nabeul is reasonably spread out, and in summer it's a major effort to walk the km or so from the main street to the beach. Taxis cost only a few hundred mills and can be a life-saver; otherwise you can take one of the many horse-drawn calèches, but bargain hard and agree on a price before setting off.

## KELIBIA
Suddenly you've left the commercialism behind, and what you have is a small, dusty town which still survives mainly on its fishing fleet. The town itself is not of great interest, but down by the small beach, two km away, are a couple of fairly low-key resort hotels. The port is dominated by a picturesque fort.

Despite the backwater feeling, Kelibia has international hydrofoil connections with Trapani in Italy from June to September.

There are plans to build a massive tourist complex at Mansourah beach, reached along the road that runs out to the east of the fort. There's likely to be more on the way, with Nabeul and Hammamet already at tourist-saturation point.

### Information
The town has services such as banks and a post office. If you don't take your meals at the hotels or are staying at the hostel, you'll need to stock up with food before heading for the beach.

### Things to See & Do
**Fort** The Romans were the first to occupy this area but the Byzantines built the first fort here. Today, the fort has been largely restored and dates from the Spanish invasions of the 16th century.

A dirt track leads up to it from opposite the hostel on the Mansourah road, just past the port, and it's only a short hike up to the top.

The fort is open most of the time – the caretaker and his extended family live there. The whole area is something of a farmyard, with chickens and cows. It's still a restricted area of some sort, so it's advisable to ask permission before taking photos and to heed the *accès interdit* signs. The views over the coastline from the ramparts are magnificent to both the north and south.

**Beaches** The best beach is at Mansourah, two km to the north along the road past the fort. The beach at Kelibia itself is very small and not that flash.

### Places to Stay & Eat

**Hostel** The *Maison des Jeunes* (☎ 02-296105), down past the harbour on the Mansourah road, is the usual masterpiece of architectural innovation and excellence for the usual TD 4 a night. The staff usually let people camp in the grounds.

**Hotels** Kelibia has a limited choice of hotels, and most are out at the beach by the harbour. The best of them is the fading *Hôtel Florida* (☎ 02-296248), which has a nice shaded terrace by the water's edge. Room rates range from TD 10 per person with breakfast in winter to TD 12 in summer. The restaurant does a good three-course meal for TD 5.

Next door to the Florida, a new *Hôtel Ennassim* is rising next to the shell of the old. It should be open by the time you read this.

Location is the only black mark against the friendly *Pension Anis* (☎ 02-295777), halfway between the beach and the town. It charges TD 14/22 for spotless rooms plus breakfast. Hot showers are free. The restaurant is well worth a visit whether you stay there or not. Leave room for dessert!

The *Hôtel Mamounia* (☎ 02-296088) is a big beach resort with the works to the south-west of the port.

Out past the fort, the road continues for a couple of km to Mansourah Beach. The *Restaurant el-Mansourah* has one of the best settings in the country. It's worth the trip for the view alone. Prices reflect this, with meals from TD 12.

### Getting There & Away

**Bus & Taxi** The bus station is a fair three km from the harbour and beach. There are regular louages doing the run between the two for 500 mills per person.

There are 10 bus departures daily along the coast to El-Haouaria between 6 am and 2.45 pm. Louages leave regularly from the bus station for the 30-minute, 850-mill journey.

**Hydrofoil** As unlikely as it may seem, from June to September Kelibia becomes an international port, with hydrofoil departures three times a week to Trapani in Sicily (Italy). The trip takes only two hours. The agency that handles the operation is Tourafric (☎ 01-341481) at 52 Ave Habib Bourguiba in Tunis. There are no services during the remainder of the year.

## EL-HAOUARIA

This small town is tucked right in under the mountainous tip of Cap Bon.

It's a quiet spot with a couple of good beaches, especially **Ras el-Drek** on the southern side of the point. There are also some interesting **Roman caves** just along from the tip of the cape, three km beyond the village. The caves are a 45-minute walk out along the road which runs straight through town; don't be surprised if a couple of locals latch onto you to guide you (unnecessary). The road curves around to the left, and although you can take a short cut straight ahead, this cuts right through the middle of the town garbage heap – and an unsavoury smelling place it is too!

The road ends at the small Café Les Grottes, and the caves are to the right. In some you can see where the Romans cut out and removed building blocks for their projects in Carthage. The official guide, complete with brass nameplate, is keen to show people around.

There are some good walks from the town up to the nearby mountain, where other caves are home to thousands of small bats.

El-Haouaria has a long tradition of falconry, and it stages an annual festival in mid-June. It is also one of the few places in Tunisia where bananas are grown. The El-Haouaria fruit is smaller and sweeter than its imported rivals, but hardly cheap at TD 3 per kg.

The town now has a choice of two hotels, and there are a couple of banks on the main street.

## Places to Stay & Eat

The *Pension Dar Toubib* (☎ 02-297163) promises much with its blue-tiled entrance. In fact, it's no more than adequate with singles/doubles ranging in price from TD 6.500/9 in the low season to TD 11.500/17 in the high season. Breakfast will set you back an additional TD 2.300. To get there, follow the 'hotel' signs from the main square out towards the mountain. It's a 10-minute walk.

In the middle of town, the two-star *Hôtel L'Epervier* (French for sparrowhawk) (☎ 02-297017), has finally opened after being under construction for many years. In winter, singles/doubles with breakfast cost TD 11.500/18, rising to a hefty TD 28/46 in summer. The restaurant does a three-course menu for TD 7.500. Try the owner's sweet Muscat d'Epervier, served chilled with a slice of lemon.

## Getting There & Away

**Bus & Taxi** There are regular buses (830 mills) and louages (950 mills) to Kelibia, and occasional buses and louages to Tunis. The bus to Tunis crawls along the north coast of Cap Bon, stopping at every little village along the way, and so takes 2½ hours. Louages are much faster.

Hitching between El-Haouaria and Kelibia is very easy.

## AROUND EL-HAOUARIA
### Kerkouane

Halfway between Kelibia and El-Haouaria is the relatively unheralded Carthaginian coastal site of Kerkouane. Its location makes it a bit of an effort to get to unless you have your own transport, but it's well worth a visit. The town is thought to have been a centre of

production of a purple dye made from shellfish that was highly prized by the Romans. It was abandoned in the years after the fall of Carthage. The place is notable for being in much better nick than most Punic ruins, having escaped the wrath of Rome. There's a museum as well as the site itself to explore. Opening hours are from 8 am to 6 pm in summer, and from 8.30 am to 5.30 pm in winter; closed on Monday. Entry is TD 1, plus another TD 1 to take photos.

**Getting There & Away** The site is easy to find if you're driving your own vehicle, being clearly signposted off the road between Kelibia and El-Haouaria. It's also possible to catch a bus or louage (or hitch) to the turn-off and walk the remaining 1.5 km to the site. Another option is to lash out about TD 10 for a return taxi fare from Kelibia, plus waiting time while you explore.

### Sidi Daoud

Much of the ubiquitous canned tuna served up in the nation's restaurants and casse-croûte shops originates from this small and otherwise unremarkable fishing village. The place used to be famous – or infamous – for the spectacular 'harvest' carried out in May, when the fish congregate off the coast to breed. These days the Tunisian authorities are a bit sensitive about the image created by the sight of blood-splattered fishermen slaughtering vast numbers of the giant fish.

**Getting There & Away** Irregular buses and louages servicing the north coast between El-Haouaria and Soliman represent the only public transport possibilities. Another alternative is to put your thumb out and hope – there's not a lot of traffic.

# Northern Tunisia

Since most visitors to Tunisia head for the Sahara and the beach resorts south of Tunis, the areas to the north are far less crowded.

The beaches at Raf Raf and Sidi Ali el-Mekki, between Tunis and Bizerte, are some of the best in the country. They are a favourite summer destination for Tunisian holiday-makers and scores of weekend trippers from Tunis, but foreign tourists are relatively rare. The town of Bizerte itself is worth a quick look, and from there the road stretches west to Tabarka. The coastline along here is isolated and, if you have your own transport, there are some excellent beaches and small settlements to explore.

Tabarka remains an attractive small town, but big changes are on the way. The region is earmarked as the country's next great package-tourist attraction, following the opening of an international airport in 1992.

Inland from here, perched high among the cork forests of the Kroumirie Mountains, the town of 'Ain Draham is high enough to get snow in winter and to remain pleasantly cool in summer while the rest of the country swelters.

Dougga, six km from Tebersouk, and Bulla Regia, just south of 'Ain Draham, are two of the best Roman sites in the country.

## BIZERTE

Bizerte is probably best known for being the strategic port city which the French refused to leave after granting independence to Tunisia. More than 1000 Tunisian lives were lost in the attempt to oust them before the French finally withdrew on 15 October 1963. The day is no longer a public holiday, but it is still marked with speech-making and the laying of wreaths.

Located just a few km south of Cap Blanc (the northernmost tip of the African continent), Bizerte has some quite reasonable town beaches away to the north, and it is the best launching pad for getting to the even

better beaches of Raf Raf and Sidi Ali el-Mekki to the south-east.

The French ville nouvelle follows the usual unimaginative grid; the medina and adjoining kasbah are also true to form – a tangle of lanes and narrow streets, notable mainly for being totally untouristy. The old and new towns meet around the old port.

The shipping canal, first built by the Carthaginians, connects the large Lake Bizerte with the Mediterranean Sea. It has formed a natural buffer that allows the town centre to breathe without getting hemmed in by housing and development. The canal is spanned by a modern bridge with a central span which can be raised to allow larger ships to pass through.

### Information

**Tourist Offices** The office of the national tourist body (☎ 02-432897) is on the corner of Quai Tarak ibn Ziad and Ave Taieb Mehiri. It has a reasonable handout map if you ask, and a useful sheet detailing accommodation prices for selected places in the whole northern region. Although it is not an exhaustive list, it will give you an idea of prices.

The regional syndicat d'initiative office is next to the service station on Ave Habib Bourguiba, not on the corner of Place du 7 Novembre 1987 as indicated by the old signposts that no-one has bothered to remove. It's open from April to September only, from Monday to Saturday from 9 am to 1 pm and 4 to 7 pm and on Sunday from 9 am to noon and 4 to 7 pm.

**Money** The banks are mostly grouped around Place du 7 Novembre 1987. Normal hours are 9 am to noon and 4 to 7 pm in summer, but one bank is always rostered to be open late; to find out which one, check the window of the syndicat d'initiative on Ave Habib Bourguiba.

**Post & Telecommunications** The main

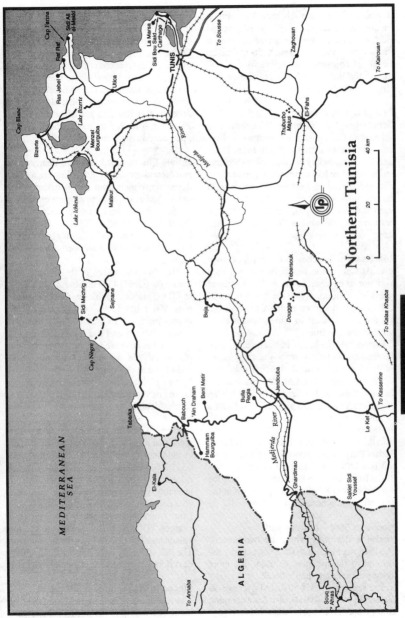

Northern Tunisia

post office is on Ave d'Algérie. Confusingly, the post boxes are in the otherwise deserted old service area. Everything else happens in a new office with its entrance 50 metres up the street towards Ave Habib Bourguiba; around the back is the telecommunications office, which is open late.

### Things to See & Do
**Oceanographic Museum** 'Museum' is a rather grand description for this small collection of sea beasties, which includes a mean-looking moray eel, a couple of lobsters and assorted fish. The museum is housed in Fort Sidi Henni at the southern entrance to the old harbour. It's open from 10 am until noon and 3 to 6.30 pm; closed on Monday. Entrance is 400 mills (200 mills for children).

**Beaches** The beaches to the north of town towards Cap Blanc would be better if they were not so exposed to the winds. A strip of hotels has a monopoly on the first few km of sand, a stretch known as the Corniche, but it's not too difficult to slip in and use the beaches and facilities.

Farther on, the beach backs directly onto the road and is very narrow – not that great. Farther on still, around the first cape and along a few more km, **Les Grottes** beach is the best of the lot. It's right at the foot of Cap Blanc. Access can be a bit tedious without a car, however, as you have to hitch or walk the last couple of km.

In the other direction, back towards Tunis, **Remel Plage** has a good strip of white sand and is a little easier to get to on your own. Buses from the main bus station heading for Raf Raf or Ras Jebel will drop you off at the turn-off, from where it's a one-km walk.

### Places to Stay – bottom end
**Hostel & Camping** There are two hostels. The first, the *Maison des Jeunes*, is up by the top end of the medina. As usual, it's more like a prison block than a hotel.

The second, the HI-affiliated *Auberge de Jeunesse* (☎ 02-440804), also has a camping ground and is a much better alternative –

especially if you have your own vehicle. It is three km back towards Tunis, signposted down a dirt track at the turn-off to Remel Plage. The hostel facilities are basic but adequate, and the relaxed atmosphere and beach location make it a good place. The cost is TD 4 for a bed, and meals can be ordered. To get there, take a bus going to Ghar el-Melh, Ras Jebel or Raf Raf and get off at the Remel Plage turn-off. Phone first to check that it's open outside the summer months.

**Hotels** The budget hotels are nearly all in and around the city centre. They are a pretty depressing bunch, with no concessions made to the tourist. It's hard to recommend any of them. Probably the best of the bunch is the *Hôtel Saadi* (☎ 02-437528) on Rue Salah ben Ali, at TD 6.500/10 for singles/doubles, plus 500 mills for a shower. At least it's clean.

The cheapest option is the *Hôtel Continental* (☎ 02-431437) on Rue 2 Mars 1934, at TD 4/5 singles/doubles without breakfast, plus 500 mills for a cold shower. Don't expect much in the way of frills: the door handles fall off and the toilet door doesn't close, but at least the staff are friendly. Other places include the hotels *Zitouna* (☎ 02-431447) and *Africain* (☎ 02-434412), side by side on Place Bouchoucha. The Africain is more up-market at TD 7/10 for singles/doubles, but neither is for light sleepers.

There is one budget option on the Corniche that requires a mention: the word is not to bother with the *Hôtel el-Khayem* (☎ 02-432120) – unless you like staying up drinking beer till all hours, in which case you probably won't notice the filthy rooms. It also happens to be the furthest beach hotel from town and the beach isn't great. It charges TD 7/10 with breakfast in the low season and TD 12.500/19 in the high season. The indescribably ugly Restaurant Zoubaida next door has to be seen to be believed.

### Places to Stay – middle & top end
The rest of the places are out along the Corniche beach strip to the north of the town.

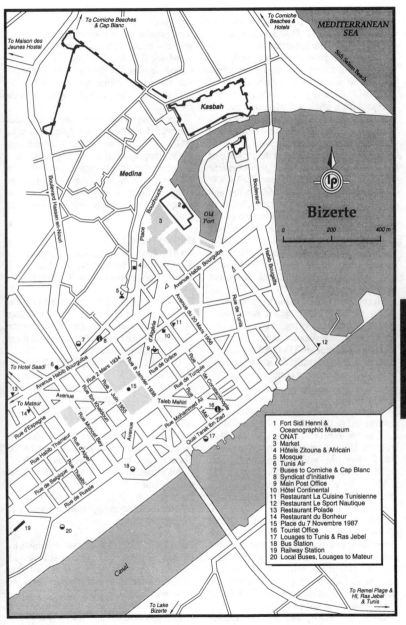

MEDITERRANEAN SEA

*Kasbah*

*Medina*

*Old Port*

**Bizerte**

0    200    400 m

1   Fort Sidi Henni &
    Oceanographic Museum
2   ONAT
3   Market
4   Hôtels Zitouna & Africain
5   Mosque
6   Tunis Air
7   Buses to Corniche & Cap Blanc
8   Syndicat d'Initiative
9   Main Post Office
10  Hôtel Continental
11  Restaurant La Cuisine Tunisienne
12  Restaurant Le Sport Nautique
13  Restaurant Polade
14  Restaurant du Bonheur
15  Place du 7 Novembre 1987
16  Tourist Office
17  Louages to Tunis & Ras Jebel
18  Bus Station
19  Railway Station
20  Local Buses, Louages to Mateur

TUNISIA

The best place to stay is the *Hôtel Petit Mousse* (☎ 02-432185). Singles/doubles cost TD 20/30 with breakfast. The owner is a serious Francophile and runs one of the best restaurants in the country. If you can afford it, it's well worth taking full board at TD 28.500/47. Even if you don't stay here it's nice to have a drink at the bar or a meal in the garden in the evening. Its only drawback is that the beach is extremely narrow and right next to the road at this point.

The best patch of beach is the preserve of the most expensive hotel, the *Corniche* (☎ 02-431844), where rates are TD 19.500/28 in the low season and TD 56/93 in the high season. It may be three-star inside, but from the street it makes the architecture of the average Maison des Jeunes look positively inspired. During summer you're unlikely to have the option of testing this delight, or any of the other resort-type hotels, because they're all booked out with package tourists from Europe.

The cheapest of these places is the *Hôtel Nador* (☎ 02-431848), which has a good stretch of beach, a swimming pool, tennis court, poolside restaurant and all the other trappings. Charges are TD 15/23 for singles/doubles with breakfast in the low season and TD 35/57 in the high season.

### Places to Eat

The restaurants in the city centre offer nothing out of the ordinary. The *Restaurant La Cuisine Tunisienne*, just over the road from the Hôtel Continental on the corner of Rue 2 Mars 1934 and Rue de Constantinople, does a perfectly serviceable meal for TD 2.500. The *Restaurant Erriadh*, a little farther along Rue 2 Mars 1934 towards Place des Martyrs, has similar fare.

The *Restaurant du Bonheur* (☎ 02-431047), on Rue Thaalbi just off Ave Habib Bourguiba, is a popular spot that does the simple things well – such as a spicy chorba for TD 1.500. It also sells alcohol. The *Restaurant Polade*, on Ave Habib Bourguiba opposite the junction with Rue Thaalbi, is another option in this price bracket.

Easily the best of the up-market restau-rants is *Le Petit Mousse* (☎ 02-432185), on the Corniche at the hotel of the same name, where an excellent three-course meal will set you back TD 15. Bookings are essential during summer. The *Restaurant Eden*, opposite the Hôtel Corniche, specialises in seafood and also comes highly recommended.

The setting is the star feature at the rather overpriced *Restaurant Le Sport Nautique* (☎ 02-431495), situated right at the entrance of the shipping canal on the edge of town.

For coffee, cakes and ice creams the *Pâtisserie de la Paix*, right opposite the Hôtel Continental, is something of a local hang-out; it's open long hours and has good products.

### Getting There & Away

**Air** The Tunis Air (☎ 02-432201) office is at 76 Ave Habib Bourguiba, but there is no airport. The nearest is Tunis-Carthage.

**Bus** The main bus station is down near the canal at the end of Ave d'Algérie, less than 10 minutes' walk from the cheap hotels. There are SNTRI departures as well as more frequent regional services.

There are buses to Tunis (TD 2.250) every half-hour from 5 am, and regular buses to Ras Jebel – the connecting point to Raf Raf. There is a 6 am departure to 'Ain Draham (TD 5.700) via Tabarka (TD 5). SNTRI runs buses to Jerba (TD 20.650) at 6 am and 6.30 pm. The morning bus goes via Kairouan and the evening bus travels via Sousse and Sfax. There are also buses to Jendouba and Beja.

All departures for Raf Raf and Ras Jebel will get you to the Remel Plage turn-off for the hostel and camp site. These buses leave from the bus station opposite the entrance to the railway station.

**Train** The modern railway station is down by the port, near the end of Rue de Russie.

Train is the most convenient way of trav-elling between Tunis and Bizerte. There are departures from Tunis at 5.50 and 11.30 am and 4 and 6.30 pm. From Bizerte they leave at 5.35 and 8.10 am and 1.45 and 6.40 pm.

The journey takes one hour and 40 minutes and costs TD 2.300 in 2nd class and TD 3.300 in 1st class.

**Taxi** Louages for Tunis (TD 2.600), Raf Raf, Ras Jebel and Ghar el-Melh leave from close to the bridge. For Menzel Bourguiba and Mateur, they depart from opposite the entrance to the railway station. There are no louages to Tabarka.

**Car Rental** The following major agencies have offices in Bizerte: Avis (☎ 02-433076), 7 Rue d'Alger; Hertz (☎ 02-433679), Place des Martyrs; and Europcar (☎ 02-431455), 19 Rue Rejiba, Place des Martyrs.

**Sea** The office of Compagnie Tunisienne de Navigation (☎ 02-431257) is in Place Tarak ibn Said, near the main bus station. It can arrange ferry bookings for departures from Tunis.

### Getting Around

Everything in the town centre is within easy walking distance. Getting out to the Corniche hotels and beaches requires catching either a taxi (about TD 2) or a local bus. Local buses leave from outside the railway station, but the best place to pick them up is from the bus stop at the corner of Blvd Hassen en-Nouri and Ave Habib Bourguiba. The bus numbers to look out for are Nos 29 and 2. If you want to get to the beaches right by Cap Blanc, the No 2 can drop you at the T-junction where the road leads off to the right to the beach. From there it's a two-km walk to Les Grottes beach, but hitching is usually possible.

### AROUND BIZERTE
### Ras Jebel

This is the main town on the large promontory south-east of Bizerte, which ends in Raf Raf beach and Cap Farina. It is a service town for the rich surrounding farming land and there's not much in the way of facilities.

The beach here is signposted from the main street but it is a three-km walk. The beaches at Raf Raf and Sidi Ali el-Mekki are a better bet.

**Places to Stay & Eat** The only place to stay in town is the *Hôtel Okba*, signposted down towards the market from the bus stop. From there the signs peter out, but all the locals know the hotel and can direct you. It charges about TD 15 for a double.

There are no restaurants to speak of in the town. There is a small sandwich shop which sells casse-croûtes and chips, on the road out of town towards the Lee Cooper factory and Raf Raf.

**Getting There & Away** Buses leave Bizerte regularly for Ras Jebel, and there are local buses between Ras Jebel and Raf Raf. The stop in Ras Jebel is at the main intersection.

There are also louages running infrequently to both Raf Raf and Bizerte. Share taxis also ply the route between Raf Raf and Ras Jebel.

### Raf Raf

Raf Raf has a reputation as one of the best beaches in the country. Unfortunately, the long stretches of white sand have more than their fair share of both garbage and people. You can escape the people by walking a bit, but not the rubbish.

Raf Raf beach is sheltered in a small bay, and the approach from Bizerte is spectacular: as you come over the hill from Raf Raf town (itself of no interest), the beach and bay are spread out below.

The scarred, pine-clad ridge at the far end of the beach is **Cap Farina**, and it's usually deserted here because it is a km or so along from the main part of the beach. You can walk to Cap Farina along the beach or, if you have a car, you can follow the tracks around behind the town, past the mosque, to the car park at the end of the track (complete with parking attendant on weekends!). From there a footpath leads down to the beach.

Although foreigners are rare in Raf Raf, it is a favourite summer spot with holidaying Tunisians, particularly at weekends, and there are numerous up-market restaurants as

**TUNISIA**

well as a hotel. As most people come on day trips only, things really calm down in the evenings.

**Places to Stay & Eat** The grass beach huts that used to offer a cheap accommodation alternative are in tatters and no longer for hire. Until the huts are rebuilt, the only place to stay is the *Hôtel Dalia* (☎ 02-447077) at the end of the road. It's quite a good place, charging TD 13/18 for singles/doubles with breakfast in the low season and TD 17/24 in summer. The restaurant on the ground floor does run-of-the-mill meals, but, in keeping with the area's tourist status, at rather inflated prices.

The unbelievably kitsch *Café Restaurant Andalous*, closer towards the water, has better prices and does excellent fish.

There are quite a few other restaurants, all signposted, but these are costly and aimed at day-trippers.

**Getting There & Away** There is a bus stop 50 metres before the beach for buses to Ras Jebel and the occasional direct service to Bizerte. There are regular share taxis to Ras Jebel, but no louages to Bizerte. In summer the transport gets pretty crowded, particularly around 7 pm when everyone is heading back to Tunis or Bizerte.

Hitching is possible, but you need to be patient because most cars are already full.

### Sidi Ali el-Mekki

On the other side of Cap Farina from Raf Raf, Sidi Ali el-Mekki is the best beach in northern Tunisia. The problem is getting there without your own transport. It's a walk of almost six km from the town of Ghar el-Melh – and hitching is reliable only on summer weekends. The dirt road out to the beach skirts the lagoon of Ghar el-Melh, the port and the old Turkish harbour.

Although there's little reminder of it, the town has quite a history. In the 17th century it was a pirate hang-out, which the famous English admiral Sir Francis Drake attacked and destroyed. In the 18th and 19th centuries the Ottoman beys fortified the town and

turned it into an arsenal in the hope of making the lagoon, connected to the sea by just a small channel, into a large naval base. Their schemes were thwarted by the Medjerda River, which silted up the lagoon. Today, the ruins of the forts and port are still visible, and the only boats able to use the lagoon are small fishing vessels.

**Places to Stay & Eat** The only place to stay is in one of the 30 or so grass shelters on the beach. They consist of one room and a shade area in front – welcome in summer. They are normally rented for the day by day-trippers, but you can stay overnight if you have something to sleep on. The custodian lives in one of them and keeps a careful eye on things, so your stuff is safe. The cost is TD 7, plus a TD 1 surcharge on Sunday. In summer, there is a small shop here which sells very basic provisions such as bread, eggs, drinks and a few canned goods. It also makes good casse-croûtes.

**Getting There & Away** Buses run infrequently from the Bizerte bus station to Ghar el-Melh, and from there it's a matter of walking or hitching to the beach.

### Utica

At one stage after the fall of Carthage this port city was the capital of the Roman province of Africa. It was originally situated on the banks of the Medjerda River, but when the river silted up it was reduced from being a fine city into an insignificant farming village.

The **ruins** today are unimpressive. They are signposted to the east from the small settlement of Zana on the main Bizerte-Tunis road. A visit is not really worth the effort unless you have your own vehicle.

Two km from the road on the left is the museum, which houses an extensive collection of bits and pieces found on the site. Some mosaics are displayed outside.

The site itself is a farther 500 metres along the road at the bottom of the slope. The only significant ruin is the **House of the Cascade**, named after the fountains which used to decorate this mansion. The best mosaics, of men fishing from boats with nets and rods, are small; they're protected from the elements by wooden covers which can be lifted.

Both the museum and site are open daily from 9 am to 7 pm in summer, and from 8.30 am to 5.30 pm in winter. Entry costs TD 1, plus TD 1 to take photos.

**Getting There & Away** The only way to get to the ruins by public transport is to catch a bus or louage travelling between Tunis and Bizerte and ask to be dropped at the turn-off to the ruins. After seeing the site, you will have to walk back to the road and either hitch or wait for a bus – a lot of work for very little reward.

### Menzel Bourguiba
On the southern side of Lake Bizerte, Menzel Bourguiba is a large and uninteresting provincial town. It is a service centre for a sizable military base and the site of a major metallurgical complex.

**Places to Stay** There is absolutely no reason to stop here, but, if you get stuck, the *Hôtel Younes* (☎ 02-460057) is the best bet with a double for TD 18. It is, however, a couple of km out of the town centre on the shore of Lake Bizerte, and the only way to get there is by taxi. The hotel is also the main drinking establishment in Menzel Bourguiba and is quite pleasant in the evenings with its outdoor terrace by the water, although in summer the mosquitoes also find it a good hunting ground.

### North Coast
Heading west from Bizerte towards Tabarka along the north coast are a couple of secluded seasonal settlements. These places are hard to get to, however, unless you have a vehicle.

**Sidi Mechrig** The coast around Sidi Mechrig can make an interesting diversion if you have your own transport. There are a few permanent residents, as well as families who camp here for the summer. You will need to bring your own supplies if you are contemplating

coming here. There is plenty of water, but there are no provisions of any sort for sale.

The people who stay in Sidi Mechrig buy their provisions in Sejnane, 17 km inland on the Bizerte-Tabarka road. If you don't have your own vehicle, the best way of getting out to Sidi Mechrig is to ask around in Sejnane for a lift.

**Cap Nègre** The track to Cap Nègre branches off the Sidi Mechrig track about one km after leaving the main road. Once a small village living off the trade in coral, it is now deserted.

### TABARKA
The last town along the coast before the Algerian border, Tabarka is small, scenic and friendly. It is becoming increasingly popular: people have discovered the beautiful little bay and beach, watched over by an impressive-looking Genoese fort. There is a rapidly expanding Zone Touristique some 10 km to the east of town, complete with its own golf course, and an international airport opened in July 1992. In spite of all this, the town remains a relaxing place to spend a few days.

The Carthaginians were the first to use the port, called Thabraca in those days. It really came into its own under the Romans, who built the causeway connecting the small island with the mainland. The volume of the famous Chemtou yellow marble shipped through the port was sufficient to justify the construction of a special road, over five metres wide, from the quarry some 60 km away. It was also the exit point for many of the African big cats en route to the colosseums of Rome and elsewhere.

Tabarka was also one of the string of pirate haunts along the Barbary Coast in the 1700s. In 1741 it was annexed by the Bey of Tunis. Its most recent claim to fame, however, is the fact that Bourguiba was forced to spend a short time here in exile in 1952.

Today, the port is the main shipment point for the tonnes of cork taken from the forests of the Kroumirie Mountains, which rise sharply behind the town. The red coral which

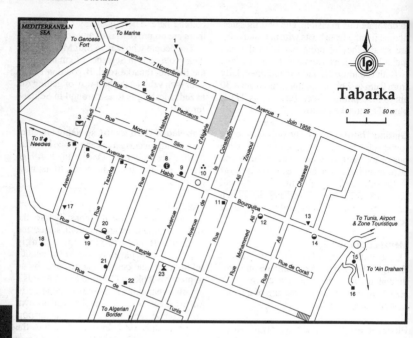

**Tabarka**

0    25    50 m

## PLACES TO STAY

2  Hôtel de la Plage
5  Hôtel Les Aiguilles
6  Hôtel de France
7  Hôtel de Corail
11  Hôtel Novelty
16  Hôtel Les Mimosas
22  Pension Mamia

## PLACES TO EAT

1  Porto Corallo Complex
4  Restaurant Khemir
13  Restaurant Les Pins
17  Café Andalous

## OTHER

3  Main Post Office
8  Tourist Office
9  Supermarket
10  Archaeological Site
12  SRN Jendouba Buses
14  Louages to 'Ain
    Draham & Jendouba
15  Abou Nawas Travel
18  Basilica
19  SNTRI Buses
20  Louages to Tunis
21  Hammam
23  Mosque

is found just offshore is exploited for the jewellery business.

Apart from climbing up to the fort, or walking around the bay to the unusual rock formations known as Les Aiguilles ('the needles'), there's little to do except wander along the tree-lined main street (called Ave Habib Bourguiba, just to be original), checking out the coral jewellery in the shops, or lie on the beach.

## Information
**Tourist Office** The tourist office (☎ 08-644491), centrally located on Ave Habib Bourguiba, is open from 9 am to noon and 4 to 7 pm. The opening hours are pretty erratic outside the main summer season. If you're desperate to find out what they've got, and it's not much, you can try the administration office opposite the Hôtel Novelty in Rue Ali Zouaoui.

**Money** Most of the banks are on Ave Habib Bourguiba in the centre of town.

**Post** The main post office is on Ave Hedi Chaker, diagonally opposite the Hôtel de France.

## Things to See & Do
**Cork Museum** A cork museum should be open by the time you read this, situated two km out of town on the 'Ain Draham road.

**Organised Tours** Abou Nawas Travel (☎ 08-644444), just off the roundabout on the 'Ain Draham road, has a half-day tour to 'Ain Draham and Bulla Regia on Tuesday for TD 15, and full-day tours to 'Ain Draham, Bulla Regia, Dougga and Thibar on Saturdays for TD 45. It also has half-day tours of Tabarka on Friday and Sunday (TD 7) which include a trip to the Algerian border and a visit to a cork factory.

Carthage Tours, based at the Hôtel Les Mimosas, offers much the same but at higher prices.

## Places to Stay – bottom end
Accommodation is at a premium, especially in summer when you'll be lucky to find a room after noon.

The cheapest place in town is the *Pension Mamia* (☎ 08-644058) in Rue de Tunis, and it's a hard place to go past. The rooms are basic but spotlessly clean, and the guy at reception speaks good English – something of a novelty at cheaper hotels. Facilities include hot showers or bath, a kitchen and a TV room. It's good value at TD 7 per person

with breakfast, rising to TD 13 in peak season.

Next best is the *Hôtel de la Plage* (☎ 08-644039), in Rue des Pecheurs, where singles/doubles cost TD 10/16 throughout the year, without breakfast. Some of the new rooms have shower and toilet. The *Hôtel Corail* (☎ 08-644455), on Ave Habib Bourguiba, is no great bargain at TD 9.500/15 for singles and doubles without breakfast.

## Places to Stay – middle & top end
Up on the hill by the roundabout on the way into town, the three-star *Hôtel Les Mimosas* (☎ 08-644376) has a commanding position and is the place to stay if you can afford TD 18.500/28 (low season) and TD 37.500/55 (high season) for singles/doubles with bath and breakfast.

The best deal is the new *Hôtel Les Aiguilles* (☎ 08-644183) at the beach end of Ave Habib Bourguiba. It's an old colonial building that spent its first life as a bank. The place is very well run and all rooms have en suite bath or shower and toilet. Some have satellite TV. It's not bad value at TD 16/24 in the low season for singles/doubles with breakfast and TD 22/34 in the high season.

On the other side of Ave Hedi Chaker is the crumbling *Hôtel de France* (☎ 08-644577). It's no great shakes at TD 12.500/19 with breakfast in winter and TD 17/26 in the high season, especially without hot water. The hotel's moment of glory came in 1952 when Bourguiba spent a couple of nights there, an event celebrated with a plaque at the head of the stairs.

The other choice in town is the *Hôtel Novelty* (☎ 08-643008), about halfway along the main street, Ave Habib Bourguiba, which offers a similar deal to the Les Aiguilles.

The hotels on the Zone Touristique strip are some 10 km east of town (TD 2 by taxi). It's the usual story – lots of stars and lots of money. They are normally fully booked with charter tourists and have little of interest for the independent traveller.

## Places to Eat
There are several gargottes around the junc-

tion of Rue Farhat Hached and Rue du Peuple, as well as on Ave de la Constitution, which serve excellent, fresh grilled fish for TD 1.500 to TD 2. The *Restaurant Les Pins*, towards the roundabout on Ave Habib Bourguiba, has a wider choice than many, with most meals under TD 3.

The restaurant at the *Hôtel de France* does a popular three-course meal for TD 5. The famous stuffed boar that used to greet diners has been moved out ('alas, monsieur, he was too old') as have all the other porcine odds and ends. The boar can, however, still be viewed on request at his new home in a storage room out the back. The waiter is all too happy to provide a graphic, animated account of precisely how to stuff a boar while you stuff yourself.

Opposite the Hôtel de France is the *Restaurant Khemir*, with a good range of seafood at prices that won't break the bank. There's a cluster of more up-market tourist restaurants in the Porto Corallo complex by the marina. The *Restaurant Pizzeria Les Arcades*, the *Restaurant Le Pirate* and the *Restaurant Touta* all do meals for TD 12 to TD 15.

Better value, but minus the marina, is the tourist menu at the *Hôtel Les Aiguilles* for TD 6.500.

### Getting There & Away

**Air** Tabarka now has its own shining, new international airport, but it has very little in the way of action apart from the occasional charter flight from Europe. At the time of writing there were no domestic flights, although a fare of TD 28 one way to Tunis had been set.

**Bus** The SNTRI (☎ 08-644404) office is on Rue du Peuple, one block behind the Hôtel de Corail. The company provides the only scheduled services between Tabarka and Tunis, with six buses daily via Mateur and three via Beja. For those who like to spend the shortest possible time on board, it's 15 minutes quicker via Mateur at 3¼ hours – and fractionally cheaper at TD 6.120.

SNTRI also has buses to 'Ain Draham at 9.30 am (830 mills) and to Bizerte at 12.45 pm (TD 5).

SRN Jendouba is the other major player, with an office on Ave Habib Bourguiba at the junction with Rue Mohammed Ali. It runs buses to 'Ain Draham at 8.30 and 10 am and 2, 3.30 and 5.30 pm. Buses to Jendouba leave at 7.30 am and 4.30 pm, and they also leave for Le Kef at 6 am and for Bizerte at 7 am.

SRN Beja buses can also be seen flashing through town, but it's a job to find out where they're heading – presumably Beja. They stop briefly opposite the SRN Jendouba office.

**Train** There are no passenger services to Tabarka at present, and little likelihood of them resuming.

**Taxi** Louages for 'Ain Draham and Jendouba leave from the main street, near the turn-off to the Hôtel Les Mimosas. For some strange reason, louages for Tunis leave from Rue du Peuple between Rue Tazerka and Rue Farhat Hached.

**To/From Algeria** In theory, it's possible to hitch to the border and, once across it, to the town of El-Kala, where there are hotels, a hostel and transport connections on to Annaba. From Annaba you can get a direct bus to Algiers, El-Oued or Constantine.

### 'AIN DRAHAM

Heading inland from Tabarka, the road almost immediately starts to wind upwards, and there are some spectacular views back towards the coast. Even in late summer, the fields around here are remarkably green and lush.

At Babouch there is a turn-off to the Algerian border. This is 13 km away and can be reached by taxi, but there is the problem of crossing the 10 km or so of neutral territory before the Algerian post. It may be possible, if time-consuming, to hitch. The turn-off also leads to Hammam Bourguiba – a three-star thermal-springs resort tucked in a small valley. Charges here are TD 28/36 for singles/doubles with breakfast.

The town of 'Ain Draham itself clings to the side of a hill almost 1000 metres above sea level. The elevation makes it quite a bit cooler than the plains or the coast, although in winter it means that deep snow is quite common.

The town was popular with hunters in the days of the French administration. Today, leisure activities are a lot more peaceful, and Tunisians come here to relax and escape the summer heat.

The architecture here, and at nearby Beni Metir, is quite unlike anything else in Tunisia. Locals are sure that their village looks just like a Swiss Alpine village. Interesting and different, yes; Swiss, no.

## Information

There is a syndicat d'initiative office halfway up the main street on the left – and yes, the main street is again called Ave Habib Bourguiba. The office has nothing other than a couple of brochures, although the woman who runs the place is very welcoming. There are also a couple of banks and a post office on the main street.

## Places to Stay & Eat

Accommodation is very limited, as most local tourists stay here for a week or more and rent out entire villas. The *Maison des Jeunes* is at the top of the hill on the road to Jendouba. At the usual TD 4, it is the only cheap option.

The only other place in town is the scenic *Hôtel Beauséjour* (☎ 08-647005) but it will very likely be full in summer. Rooms, if you can get them, cost TD 16.500/24 for singles/doubles with breakfast. The full board is much better value, with two three-course meals for TD 2 each. Its continuing association with game hunting is very evident thanks to all the boar skins and other 'trophies' hanging on the walls. The lack of hot water is a bit hard to handle outside summer.

A km or so out of town on the Jendouba road is the two-star *Hôtel Rihana* (☎ 08-647391). It offers magnificent views and a superior level of comfort (hot water) for TD

21.500/32 in the low season and TD 26/42 in the high season, with breakfast. The trouble is that it has all the atmosphere of a morgue outside the main season.

Seven km along the road to Jendouba is the *Hôtel Les Chênes* (☎ 08-647211), which is in the middle of a cork forest. It's an old hunting lodge and, again, there are stuffed 'trophies' in abundance. Singles/doubles with bath and breakfast cost TD 16.500/26 in the low season and TD 23/36 in the high season; however, unless you've got your own transport, you'll have to take full board, as there is nowhere else to eat. The hotel allows people to camp in the grounds and use the hotel facilities for a couple of dinar per person.

In 'Ain Draham itself there are several basic restaurants in the main street, the best of which is the *Restaurant du Grand Maghreb*. You can get casse-croûte and plates of assorted fried food (egg, chips, chillies) – there are certainly no gourmet delights here.

## Things to Buy

Carpets and kilims are produced by a small women's cooperative called Les Tapis de Kroumirie. Run with the assistance of the 'Ain Draham Centre d'Action Sociale, its joint aims are to provide employment for local women and to revive local carpet-making traditions. The project was launched in the early 1980s by two French doctors working in 'Ain Draham.

It's an interesting place to visit. The produce is sold directly from the workshop, where about a dozen looms are in operation. The appearance of a foreigner is likely to create a fair amount of interest. If you decide to buy, there's a good chance that you will get to meet the maker.

The carpets are the thick-pile Berber type. The kilims are more interesting, featuring simple, traditional Berber motifs. The wool is all spun by hand. Prices are fixed and clearly marked. They're not expensive – a kilim measuring 120 x 70 cm costs TD 25.

To get there, turn right at the bottom of the steps opposite the syndicat d'initiative. The

TUNISIA

cooperative is above the Ministère des Affaires Sociales, about 50 metres along on the right.

### Getting There & Away

**Bus** Buses leave from the station at the intersection at the bottom of town near the service station, 300 metres down from the hotel and hostel.

SRN Jendouba runs buses to Jendouba (TD 1.450) at 7, 8.15 and 9 am and 1.15, 3, 4 and 5.15 pm. The 8.15 and 9 am services continue to Le Kef. Buses to Tabarka (830 mills) leave at 6, 7.30, 8.30, 10 and 11.15 am, noon and 2.30, 4.30 and 6 pm.

SNTRI has three services a day between Tunis and 'Ain Draham (TD 6.820), leaving Tunis at 5.30 and 7 am and 2.30 pm, and leaving 'Ain Draham at 7 am, noon and 1.30 pm.

**Taxi** Louages leave from the top of the hill, opposite the Maison des Jeunes. They run only to Tabarka (900 mills) and Jendouba (TD 1.600). You'll need to be quick off the mark as demand normally exceeds supply.

### BENI METIR

A much-touted beauty spot, the village of Beni Metir was built by the French in the 1950s to house the workers who constructed the dam that is the reason for the place's existence. Once the work was completed, the village was handed over to the locals.

The setting is magnificent. It's interesting to observe the old French church and the new mosque standing almost side by side. The shores of the dam are a popular picnic spot, but it helps if there is some water. In late 1993, the dam was reduced to a tiny puddle by a year-long drought.

### Places to Stay

The only possibility is the *Maison des Jeunes* in the middle of the village. It charges the usual TD 4.

### Getting There & Away

Your own transport is the best option. That way you can enjoy the 20-minute drive from 'Ain Draham through the cork and European oak forests at your leisure. Otherwise, the 404 pick-ups opposite the Maison des Jeunes or hitching are the only options.

### BULLA REGIA

This Roman site is famous for being the place where the Romans went underground to escape the heat – they built their villas with one storey above ground and another below. The site was inhabited before Roman times: 'regia' refers to the royal Numidian kingdoms.

After the Romans moved in, the town's residents became wealthy, living off the revenue generated by the rich grain country of the Medjerda Valley.

Bulla Regia lies three km east of the 'Ain Draham-Jendouba road, and is six km north of Jendouba. Making your way from Jendouba out to the site and back takes at least half a day. Unfortunately, the management of the site is little short of disgraceful. It's hard to work out who the site is being run for – it's certainly not for tourists. There is no information available on the site, either locally or in Tunis, and the yellow signs that previously directed visitors around the site have been painted over. All this leaves those not travelling with a guided tour at the mercy of the local touts. They know next to nothing about the site, other than the obvious (it's Roman, sir), and are poorly equipped to impart what they do know.

For all that, the site is well worth a visit. It's open from 8.30 am to 5.30 pm every day, and entry costs TD 1, plus TD 1 to take photos.

### The Ruins

The entrance to the site is just to the left of the Memmian Baths, the most extensive of the remaining above-ground buildings.

The **Memmian Baths** are impressive in size, and some of its mosaics have remained intact. The street in front of the baths leads to the **theatre**, which has loads of atmosphere; it still has a mosaic of a bear in the centre of the stage.

Following the street along to the left of the

theatre brings you to the **forum**, which has the Temple of Apollo on the northern side and the capitol to the east.

A path along an overgrown water channel takes you to a spring which is fenced off; this has a pump house which supplies Jendouba with water. From here it's a matter of scrambling over a bank to the left until you come to another excavated street. The **House of Fishing**, to the right, has a basement with a fountain. Adjacent is the residence known as the **House of the Hunt**. Its colonnaded basement makes it the most impressive of the site's houses. To the north-east, the **House of Amphitrite** has a famous and beautifully preserved mosaic of Poseidon and Amphitrite surrounded by cupids.

A visit to the small **museum** outside the site, across the road from the entrance, is included in the entry fee. There are a couple of mosaics from the site, a collection of chipped Roman busts, sundry old things and an interesting layout of the area in Numidian times.

The hill behind the museum is covered with Neolithic tombs and is worth a stroll if time permits.

### Getting There & Away

From Jendouba, the simplest solution is to take a taxi to the site. It shouldn't cost more than TD 2, or about 600 mills in a share taxi. Buses between Jendouba and 'Ain Draham can drop you at the Bulla Regia turn-off bus stop, six km north of Jendouba, from where it's a three-km walk to the site. Hitching along this stretch is easy enough, as there is quite a bit of local traffic. Share taxis charge about 300 mills for this leg.

## JENDOUBA

Jendouba is dull in the extreme. Its only redeeming feature is that it's a handy base from which to visit Bulla Regia. Perhaps the most remarkable thing about the whole place is the collection of storks' nests on the roof of the police station.

If you are heading for Algeria, it is possible to pick up the Al-Maghreb al-Arabi train on its daily run to Algiers.

Fortunately, everything revolves around the central square, 100 metres north of the old main road through town. (The new road actually skirts the town to the south.) Around the square, complete with garden and fountain, you'll find the post office, banks, a supermarket, the police station and the railway station. All the hotels are nearby.

Being an important provincial town, Jendouba has branches of all the major Tunisian banks.

### Places to Stay – bottom end
The *Pension Saha en-Noum* is the best bet at TD 3.500 per person. It is on Blvd Khemais el-Hajiri, not far from the square.

### Places to Stay – middle
The town's premier establishment is the two-star *Hôtel Smitthu* (☎ 08-631695), right by the bus station. It charges TD 21.500/31 for singles/doubles with breakfast. A little bit down the two-star scale is the *Hôtel Atlas* (☎ 08-630566), a minute's walk from the railway station. It's right behind the police station with all the storks' nests. Despite the austere air, it is quite comfortable; for a room with washbasin and bidet you pay TD 14/20, which includes breakfast.

### Places to Eat
There are a couple of restaurants about 100 metres east of the main square. The *Restaurant Le Golfe* has a reasonable selection, and the nearby *Restaurant Carthage* is also not bad.

The nightlife is limited to the pleasant outdoor beer garden of the *Atlas Hôtel* – not a bad place to be on a hot summer evening.

### Getting There & Away
**Bus** The bus station is over the railway line on the western edge of town.

There are five buses a day from Tunis – at 9, 10 and 11 am and 4 and 5 pm, returning at 5, 7.30 and 10 am and 12.30 and 4 pm. The fare is TD 4.930.

There are also connections with 'Ain Draham, Beja, Bizerte, Ghardimao, Le Kef and Tabarka.

**TUNISIA**

**Train** The railway station is just off the main square, near the police station. There are five trains daily to Tunis (5.56 and 10.25 am and 12.31, 2.05 and 5.25 pm), and five to Ghardimao (9.23 am and 1.08, 3.47, 7.10 and 8.39 pm). It's well worth paying the extra for 1st class because there's little chance of getting a seat in 2nd class. You'll be up for TD 6.150.

The 1.08 pm train to Ghardimao continues to Algiers via Annaba and Constantine.

**Taxi** Louages for Ghardimao, 'Ain Draham and Le Kef leave from a dusty plot next to the railway line on the road to 'Ain Draham. For Tunis, they leave from Rue 1 Juin 1955, 50 metres along from the Pension es-Saada.

### GHARDIMAO

If anything, Ghardimao is even more deadly boring than Jendouba – it really is the end of the line. It's certainly not worth a special trip, but you may find yourself coming through here on the way to Algeria.

### Places to Stay & Eat

Just like the rest of the town, the *Thubernic Hôtel* (☎ 08-645043) is totally lacking in atmosphere, but there is no alternative. It's the two-storey building opposite the railway station (it has no sign). Rooms cost TD 10 for a double with breakfast. There's also a rather depressing bar and restaurant. The place is named after the nearby Roman site of Thubernica.

### Getting There & Away

The buses and louages leave from next to the railway line, about 200 metres towards Jendouba from the station.

There are frequent louages to Jendouba, and there is one direct bus daily to Tunis.

**To/From Algeria** The daily Al-Maghreb al-Arabi train crawls through here at around 1.30 pm every day. Don't be fooled by the name: although it conjures up romantic images of a great railway journey clear across the top of the African continent, it is in fact something of an endurance test – a slow and crowded trip requiring numerous changes.

The best bet, if you are heading for Algeria this way, is to take the train as far as Annaba, the first town of any note on the Algerian side. You could go just as far as Souq Ahras, but, apart from the interesting countryside (which you see from the train anyway), there is nothing to do there; if you do stop at Souq Ahras, there are buses to Constantine, Annaba and El-Oued, as well as hotels if you get caught overnight.

### DOUGGA

Another of Tunisia's excellent Roman sites, Dougga has a commanding position on the edge of the Tebersouk Mountains. It is six km along a bitumen road from the small town of Tebersouk and three km up a dirt track from the even smaller town of Nouvelle Dougga, which now houses the residents who were moved from the ancient site to protect the ruins from further decay.

If you haven't yet overdosed on Roman ruins, this one is well worth visiting. Most of the excellent mosaics from this site are in the Bardo Museum in Tunis.

### History

The town of Thugga was already well established in the Punic era, and the unusual monument just below the Roman ruins (known as the Libyco-Punic Mausoleum) dates back to the 2nd century BC.

In early Roman times, Thugga became one of the capitals of one of Rome's allies, a Numidian king by the name of Massinissa. Its fortunes followed the familiar pattern of Roman towns in North Africa: great prosperity in the 2nd to 4th centuries, followed by a steady decline during the Byzantine and Vandal occupation. Its prosperity was aided by its ample supplies of fresh water, its nearby, rich agricultural land and its marble quarries.

### The Ruins

The site is open daily from 8.30 am to 5.30 pm; entry is TD 1.

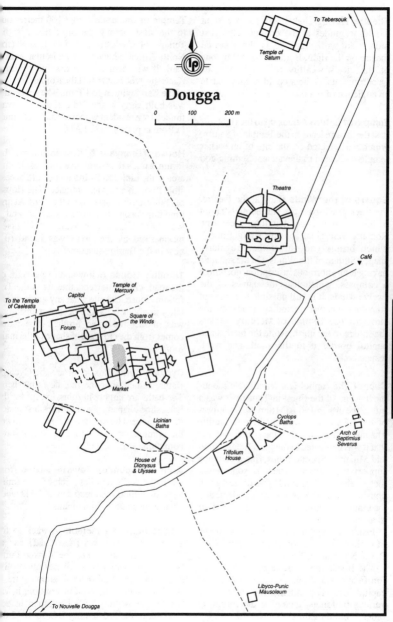

**Theatre** Having shaken off the persistent would-be guides at the entrance, the first monument you come to is the restored theatre on the right. Built in 188 AD by one of the city's wealthy residents, Marcus Quadrutus, its 19 tiers could accommodate an audience of 3500.

**Temple of Saturn** A track up to the right just past the theatre leads to the Temple of Saturn, which was erected on the site of an earlier temple dedicated to the ancient Semitic god Baal.

**Square of the Winds** Back at the theatre, the track leads past the site administration office to an unusual winding street (the Romans were great ones for straight lines), which brings you out at the irregularly shaped Square of the Winds. On the square's paving is an enormous inscription, not unlike a compass, which lists the names of the twelve winds. It is still possible to make out some of the names, including Africanus (the sirocco). The **Temple of Mercury** borders the square to the north, while the market and capitol border it to the south and west, respectively.

**Capitol** The capitol is a remarkable monument – one of the finest in Tunisia. It was a gift to the city in 166 AD from two members of the (obviously) wealthy Marcia family. The inscription carved on the portico records that it was dedicated to the gods Jupiter, Juno and Minerva. Six enormous, fluted columns support the portico, which is some eight metres above the ground. The frieze has an unusually unweathered carving depicting the emperor Antonius Pius being carried off in an eagle's claws.

Inside the capitol was an enormous statue of Jupiter, fragments of which are now in the Bardo Museum in Tunis.

The Byzantines were responsible for the fortifications that intrude on the forum and capitol here. They filched the stones from various buildings, including the forum, in order to build them.

**Temple of Caelestis** About 100 metres ou to the west, among the olive trees, is th Temple of Caelestis with its unusual (fc North Africa, anyway) semicircular court yard. It was dedicated to the cult of Jun Caelestis, who was in fact the Roman versio of the Carthaginian god Tanit. The sanctuar was built early in the 3rd century and wa funded by a resident who was made a flame (a Roman priest) in 222 AD.

**House of Dionysus & Ulysses** South of th forum, a track runs through an old residenti area to the **Licinian Baths** on the left, acces sible through a service entrance. The Hous of Dionysus & Ulysses is on the right. At on time this was a sumptuous residence, and was here that the mosaic of Ulysse mesmerised by the sirens was found (it now in the Bardo Museum).

**Trifolium House** Below and to the right the road which intersects the site is the Tr folium House. Despite what any guide migl tell you about it having been a mansion, was in fact the town brothel. The nam comes from the clover-leaf shape of the ma room.

**Cyclops Baths** Next door are the Cyclop Baths, named after the mosaic found her The baths are largely in ruins, except for th horseshoe-shaped row of latrines just insic the entrance. The Romans were obviously the opinion that having a crap should be communal experience!

**Arch of Septimius Severus** Across fro the baths is the derelict Arch of Septimi Severus, which was erected in 205 AD whe Thugga became a municipality.

**Libyco-Punic Mausoleum** A track to th south-east leads down from the House Dionysus & Ulysses to the Libyco-Pun Mausoleum, which is one of the only survi ing examples of pre-Roman architecture Tunisia. According to an inscription, it w erected in memory of a Numidian leade Ateban, in the 3rd century BC. In 1842 th

British consul removed the important inscription from it and the whole bloody thing collapsed. The inscribed stone was taken to England (where it is now the property of the British Museum) and the funerary tower was rebuilt.

## Getting There & Away
The simplest solution is to catch a bus or louage to Tebersouk (see following Tebersouk section) and then take a taxi for the remaining six km to the site. It's possible to stay the night in Tebersouk and make an early start.

If a delight in adversity, or the need to find the cheapest possible option, prevents you from travelling via Tebersouk, you can walk to the ruins from the village of Nouvelle Dougga on the main Tunis-Le Kef road.

The three-km track up to the site is signposted by the Mobil station at the far end of the village. You can save yourself a bit of the walk by cutting through the middle of the village and asking the locals for directions. It's a solid hour's walk but, as long as the weather is not stinking hot (as it invariably is in summer), it is an easy uphill grade and you will often have local people for company.

## TEBERSOUK
This small town sees its fair share of tourists, but no-one actually seems to stop; they are all in a hurry to get to Dougga and on to the next place. Not a bad plan really, as there is nothing else to do here.

## Places to Stay
The only reason you might want to stop here is to have a base for visiting the ruins at Dougga. The place to stay is the two-star Hôtel Thugga (☎ 08-465713), down by the main road, with singles/doubles for TD 20/30 with breakfast, as well as the option of half or full board. It's a popular spot with tour groups at lunchtime.

## Getting There & Away
**Bus** SNTRI has buses from Tunis at 8.30 am and 4.30 pm, returning at 5.35 am and 12.05 pm. The 2½-hour journey costs TD 3.490. There are also bus connections with Beja and Le Kef.

**Taxi** Louages run frequently to the villages of Nouvelle Dougga (not the ruins) and Thibar, and less often to Beja and Tunis.

## LE KEF
This is a picturesque village perched up on the side of a hill overlooking some fine agricultural land. Although it has little in the way of conventional attractions, it's a very pleasant place to spend a day or two. In summer its 800-metre elevation means it is significantly cooler than the plains, although it also means that it gets snow in winter.

Most of the essentials are to be found within a couple of minutes' walk of Place de l'Indépendance in the centre of town. There is a small tourist information centre on Rue Hedi Chaker, just off the Place l'Indépendance, and the main post office and international phones are 150 metres farther along. There are banks aplenty around the town centre.

### Kasbah
The kasbah dominates the town from the top of the hill. Although it is in a very bad state of repair it is still worth a wander around, and there are some excellent views over the town and surrounding countryside. Until quite recently it was inhabited by the army. There is usually someone hanging around to show you the various points of interest (Turkish mosque, prison cells, gates and walls of various vintages) if your French is up to it.

### Museums
Immediately below the kasbah is a small museum housed in what was originally a basilica and later a mosque. Its exhibits are not exactly riveting but entrance is free.

There is another regional museum, which is in a building which previously housed a zawiyya (a religious fraternity), in a small square not far from the presidential palace. The emphasis is on the culture of the Bedouin nomads and the well-displayed exhibits include a tent, some crude utensils, jewellery, weaving looms showing their unusual weaving technique, and agricultural implements. The museum is open from 9 am to noon and 3 to 7 pm Tuesday to Saturday, and 9 am to 2.30 pm Sunday; it's closed on Monday. Entry is TD 1 – worth a look.

### Places to Stay

The lack of both local and foreign tourists in Le Kef is reflected in the somewhat slender choice of accommodation.

At the budget end of the scale, the modern *Hôtel Medina* (☎ 08-220214), at 18 Rue Farhat Hached, is in the centre of town, about 20 minutes' walk uphill from the bus station. Rooms cost TD 8 for a double with shower (cold).

Although it looks mildly promising from the outside, the *Hôtel Auberge* (☎ 08-220036) is hard to recommend. The dark and gloomy entrance on Rue de la Source leads to an equally dark and gloomy bar, and the hotel rooms are not much better. Cheap, but only for the desperate.

The supposedly three-star *Hôtel Sicca Veneria* (☎ 08-221561), on Place de l'Indépendance, is one of those places that makes you wonder how the stars are awarded. Still, it's the best joint in town – and it does have hot water if you're prepared to wait. Singles/doubles cost TD 15.500/25 with breakfast. Half and full board are also available at TD 3.500 per meal.

### Places to Eat

As with the hotels, there's little choice. The best place is the small, popular *Restaurant el-Hanaa*, 200 metres along Ave Habib Bourguiba, opposite the white, ugly, multi storey Banque du Sud building. The top end of the market is represented by the restaurant at the *Sicca Veneria*, with a tourist menu for TD 6.

### Getting There & Away

**Bus** The town's transport centres around the bus station, 20 minutes' walk downhill from the centre. Shared taxis shuttle between the town centre and the main intersection at the bottom of the hill, passing the bus station on the way.

Buses leave regularly for Jendouba, Kasserine, Tebersouk and Tunis (three hours, TD 5.230). There are also services to 'Ain Draham, Beja, Bizerte, Gafsa, Nabeul, Sfax and Sousse.

**Train** There are no passenger services to Le Kef at present. There are trains from Dahmani, on the Tunis-Kalaa Khasba line, 20 km south of town.

**Taxi** There are louages to Tunis, Kasserine, Jendouba and Sakiet Sidi Youssef on the Algerian border, from where there are taxis to the town of Souq Ahras.

# Central Tunisia

The central coast of Tunisia has some excellent beaches and, consequently, a lot of tourist development. A constant flow of charter flights from northern Europe to the modern international airport at Monastir keeps the hotels topped up with package tourists.

Sousse and Monastir are the major attractions, along with the delightful old town of Mahdia a bit farther south. Farther south again is Sfax, an interesting regional centre and the country's second-largest city. The Kerkennah Islands just offshore are easily accessible, and offer a welcome opportunity to escape the crowds and slow down a bit.

Once you leave the coast and head inland, you are among the olive trees – millions of them! Olive growing has been big business

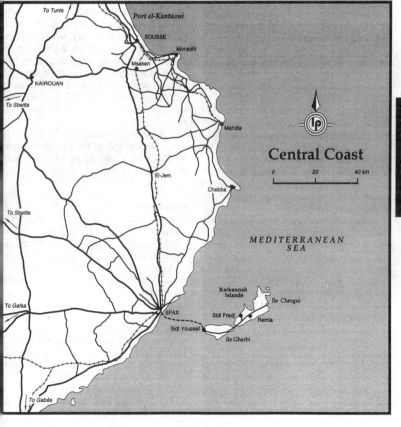

since Roman times and olives and their oil remain major exports.

Kairouan, the fourth holiest city in Islam, lies on the plains only a couple of hours from Sousse.

Other attractions of the area are the massive and remarkably well-preserved Roman amphitheatre at El-Jem in the olive country, and the ruins of yet another Roman city, Sufetula (modern Sbeitla), out on the hot plains near the dull provincial capital of Kasserine.

## SOUSSE

The major industrial centre of Sousse is the country's third-largest city and a major port. The huge medina and impressive fortifications are the main pointers to its long history as a commercial centre.

For today's visitors, and in particular the thousands of package tourists, it is the long beachfront that stretches north to the purpose-built tourist enclave of Port el-Kantaoui that is the main drawcard.

The coastline is virtually one hotel after another, with more under construction to fill any gaps that remain. Each new hotel seems to boast more stars and bigger and better facilities than its neighbours.

Fortunately, there is no need to join the packaged masses. The medina and town centre offer a good range of budget and mid-range accommodation.

One of the most unusual features of the town is the way the main Tunis-Sfax railway line runs right through the busy main square. There is constant talk of rerouting the line, but it remains in the too-hard basket. The sight of a giant locomotive, lights flashing and bells ringing, edging through the traffic will be around for a while to come. Don't become a decoration on the front of the 4.08 to Sfax!

### History

Founded in the 9th century BC, Sousse has been a popular spot for centuries. It was an important Phoenician town, called Hadrumète, long before Carthage was settled. Hannibal, as leader of the Carthagin-

ian forces, used it as his base in the fight against the Romans in the Second Punic War in 202 BC.

The town was saved from the fate that befell Carthage because it allied itself with Rome during the third and final Punic War. It prospered under Roman rule, and under the emperor Diocletian, Hadrumètum (as it was known under the Romans) was the capital of the Byzacèe Province which covered the whole of central Tunisia.

When the Vandals hacked their way across North Africa in the 5th century, it was a city of sufficient stature to be renamed Hunerico polis in honour of the son of the Vandal chief. Later, under the Byzantines, the name was changed to Justinianopolis.

It fared badly during the Arab conquest at the end of the 7th century, but hung on to become the main port of the 9th-century Aghlabid dynasty based in Kairouan; by then it was known by the Arab name of Susa, still commonly in use today. It was captured again in later years – first by the Normans in the 12th century, and then by the Spanish in the 16th.

Its most recent problems were in WW II when German use of the port drew heavy bombing from the Allies. All has been restored since then.

### Information

**Tourist Offices** A branch of the national tourist office (☎ 03-225157) is at 1 Ave Habib Bourguiba, right on the central square Place Farhat Hached. It is easily the best of its kind in the whole country. There is a notice board inside the office with comprehensive information on bus and train times, as well as details of other items of local interest. The women staffing the office speak excellent English, French and German and can be very helpful (if pushed a bit). It is open from Monday to Thursday from 8.30 am to 1 pm and 3 to 5.45 pm, and on Friday and Saturday in the morning only.

The local syndicat d'initiative (☎ 03 220431) is across on the other side of the street, in the small, white-domed building.

**PLACES TO STAY**

6 Hôtel Claridge
14 Hôtel de Paris
20 Hôtel Gabès
21 Hôtel Medina
22 Residence Fatma
23 Hôtel Amira
24 Hôtel Ezzouhour

**PLACES TO EAT**

1 Restaurant Atlantik
2 Restaurant Le Marmite
11 Restaurant Le Bonheur
12 Restaurant Tunisienne
17 Restaurant Populaire
25 Restaurant Hannibal

**OTHER**

3 Bookshop
4 Tunis Air
5 Tourist Office
7 Monoprix Supermarket
8 International Phones
9 Main Post Office
10 Syndicat d'Initiative
13 Local Buses
15 Ribat
16 Northbound Buses &
   Buses to Monastir & Mahdia
18 Louages to Tunis & Monastir
19 Great Mosque
26 Bab el-Gharbi
27 Markets
28 Bab el-Jedid
29 SNTRI Office
30 Buses & Louages to Kairouan,
   El-Jem & Sfax
31 Trains to Monastir & Mahdia
32 Museum
33 Bab el-Khabli

MEDITERRANEAN
SEA

To
Beaches

Rue Sadi Carnot

Avenue Habib Bourguiba

Rue de

Rue de l'Indépendance

Ave Hassen Ayachi

Railway
Station

Rue Ali Belhaouane

Avenue de la République

Place
Farhat
Hached

Boulevard Yahia Ibn Omar

Port

Boulevard Taïeb Slar

To Tunis

Rue Aghalbas

Rue d'Angleterre

Avenue Mohammed Ali

Avenue Mohammed V

Rue el-Mar

Ave du Commandant Bejaoui

Avenue Maréchal Tito

Rue el-Hadj Ira

Rue el-Ghazali

Ave 25 Juillet 1967

Rue de Sakka

Ave du 18 Janvier 1952

To Catacombs
(500 m)

To Kairouan

**Sousse**

0    100    200 m

TUNISIA

**Money** There are plenty of banks along Ave Habib Bourguiba and up by the beach. One branch of the STB on Ave Habib Bourguiba has long opening hours in the summer.

**Post & Telecommunications** The main post office is also right in the thick of things, on Ave de la République just off Place Farhat Hached.

There's a telephone office in Rue du Caire, signposted off Rue Ali Belhaouane near the Hôtel Claridge. It is possible to dial direct, or through the operator, between 8 am and 11 pm daily.

### Medina

The main monuments in the medina are the ribat (a sort of fortified Islamic college) and the Great Mosque, both in the north-eastern corner of the medina, not far from Place Farhat Hached.

The area surrounding the Great Mosque and ribat is thick with tourist stalls (complete with the obligatory stuffed camels), and the number of tourists that pass through here is reflected in the prices.

**Ribat** The ribat was built in the 9th century, and its primary role was as a fort to protect the local Muslim population. When its inhabitants weren't involved in hostilities they would pursue Islamic study. It's a structure of impressive architectural simplicity. Living conditions were extremely spartan, no doubt so as to be conducive to religious study. Small cells surround the arcaded courtyard and steps lead up to the roof, where it's possible to walk right around the ribat.

A narrow, winding staircase leads to the top of the watchtower, from where there are excellent views over the city and into the courtyard of the Great Mosque just below. It's open from 8 am to 7 pm every day in summer, and from 8.30 am to 5.30 pm in winter. Entry costs TD 1, with a further charge of TD 1 for photography.

**Great Mosque** The Great Mosque is also a fairly simple affair. Built in the 9th century, it has undergone 17th-century modifications and 20th-century restoration. The courtyard is open to visitors from 9 am to 1 pm every day, entry TD 1. Modest dress is essential, but if your garb fails to meet the required standard it is possible to rent a gown for a few hundred mills from one of the shops opposite the entrance.

**Dar Jellouli** The museum occupies the old kasbah on the south-western corner of the medina. The entrance is from Ave Maréchal Tito. It's impossible to enter from inside the medina; you'll need to exit the medina by either the southern gate, Bab el-Khabli, or the western gate, Bab el-Gharbi.

Exhibits are laid out in the rooms around the kasbah's courtyard. There are some excellent, well-presented mosaics, including some from the Christian catacombs in Sousse. There are also funerary objects and stelae from these catacombs. The catacombs themselves have been closed for a couple of years for restoration, with no reopening date in sight. The museum is open from 8 am to noon and 3 to 7 pm in summer, and 9 am to noon and 2 to 6 pm in winter; closed on Monday. Entry is TD 1.

### Other Attractions

The main **beach** is known as Boujaffar Beach (named after a local marabout), and is at the northern end of Ave Habib Bourguiba only a short walk from the centre. It is quite a decent strip of white sand but it's backed by high-rise hotels and apartments. At the height of summer it can get ridiculously crowded.

Farther north is the much-vaunted **Port el-Kantaoui**, a large tourist development touted as 'the garden and pleasure port of the Mediterranean with typically Tunisian architecture', etc, etc. It's about as Tunisian as bacon and eggs. It would be more appropriate to promote the place as the stuffed-camel capital of the country – the critters are in plague proportions. Steer well clear of Port el-Kantaoui unless your wallet/purse is crying out to be bled dry.

If the place turns out to have a fatal attraction, there's a 'Noddy' train which runs every hour on the hour (9 am to 11 pm in summer and 9 am to 6 pm in winter) from the beachfront at the northern end of Ave Habib Bourguiba, returning on the half-hour. The fare is TD 2.500 return, or TD 1.500 one way.

## Places to Stay – bottom end

As usual, the rock-bottom cheapies are in the medina. The pick of them – and that's not saying much – is the *Hôtel Gabès*, at 12 Rue de Paris. It is clean and surprisingly quiet, has free hot showers and costs TD 5 per person.

Farther along the same street, at No 48, is the *Hôtel Ezzouhour*. The entrance looks most unpromising, but it's considerably better inside, with stairways and passageways leading in all directions. The best rooms are at the top, as these have windows which open onto the outside world rather than onto the courtyard, but they are a bit on the small side. The two feet protruding from a sheet behind the reception desk were a bit of a worry!

There are several other cheapies nearby, such as the *Mestiri*, should these be full.

## Places to Stay – middle

If you're prepared to spend a little bit more, things improve rapidly. There are many who sing the praises of the *Hôtel de Paris* (☎ 03-220564), on the northern side of the medina at 15 Rue du Rempart Nord. It charges TD 11/18 for singles/doubles in summer and TD 8/14 in winter.

The *Hôtel Medina* (☎ 03-221722), right by the Great Mosque, has a nice, airy and cool lounge room in the centre and is popular with younger tour groups. Locals are attracted to the rather sleazy air-conditioned bar at the back. The place is well maintained, and costs TD 10 per person in summer for a bed and a breakfast that includes a croissant. The winter rate is TD 9/14 for singles/doubles.

The *Hôtel Amira* (☎ 03-226325), near Bab el-Jedid on the eastern edge of the medina, is a bit more up-market. In summer, it costs TD 18/25 for singles/doubles with breakfast, dropping to TD 11/14.500 in

winter. Rooms come with bath or shower, and some have little private courtyards with a table and chairs. You can opt to have your breakfast served outside on the upstairs terrace.

Just around the corner from the Amira, the *Residence Fatma*, with its beautiful, ornate green doors, is closed temporarily for repairs. It used to have a very good reputation, so it's worth checking to see if it's open again.

The *Hôtel Claridge* (☎ 03-224759), just off the main square on Ave Habib Bourguiba, has more than its name going for it. The Sousse version is a very good one-star hotel in the old style. Charges range from TD 11 to TD 17, according to the season, for a large room with shower, and breakfast served in the café next door.

Lastly, for those who want to be close to the beach, there is the friendly and comfortable *Hôtel Sousse Azur* (☎ 03-227760) at 5 Rue Amilcar, opposite the four-star Abou Nawas Boujaffar. Bed and breakfast here will set you back TD 22/34 for singles/doubles in summer, or TD 13/18 in winter.

## Places to Stay – top end

The top-end resort hotels are all along the two main streets in the north of town, Blvd Hedi Chaker and Blvd de la Corniche, and stretch all the way to Port el-Kantaoui. Most are geared to the package-tour industry and are fully booked for the season.

They range from such nightmares as the massive, sprawling, grey-concrete *El-Hana Beach*, a monster of truly gargantuan proportions, to the five-star luxury of such resorts as the *Hannibal Palace* and the *Dar Andalous*.

## Places to Eat

The medina is the place to go for a cheap feed. The best of the gargottes is the *Restaurant Populaire*. It's at the entrance to the medina near the Great Mosque. There is no indication in English above the restaurant, but there is a sign pointing to it a few buildings away – just to let you know you're getting warm. It's one of the places where you have to pay for your meal before sitting down.

Just inside the main western gate of the medina, Bab el-Gharbi, is the *Restaurant Hannibal*, which serves good couscous and fresh orange juice in season.

There are a couple of cheap local places in a small side street just opposite the Hôtel Claridge.

As you'd expect, given the number of tourists, there are plenty of smarter restaurants, although none offer anything out of the ordinary. Menus are often written in three or four languages and the waiters can speak any or all of them. They include the *Restaurant Atlantik* (☎ 03-224424), which does a roaring trade aimed chiefly at German visitors.

In the street parallel and to the west of Ave Habib Bourguiba is the *Restaurant Le Marmite*, named after the deep pot found in every Tunisian kitchen. It's a good, quiet spot, with main meals from TD 5.

For something a bit different, the *Restaurant Tunisienne* has a range of excellent curries from TD 4 as well as standard Tunisian fare. It's behind the Hôtel Hadruméte at 4 Rue Ali Belhaouane. The place has just been taken over by a very jolly fellow who spent years working in Indian restaurants in London. Expect a name change that reflects a more international outlook.

*King Food*, just off Ave Habib Bourguiba on Rue Amilcar, has various burgers from 750 mills, pasta from TD 1.500, pizzas from TD 1.900 and salads.

If Chinese food is the thing you can't go without, you can try the *Hong Kong*, on Blvd de Rabat, opposite the El-Hana Beach Hôtel. Bring plenty of cash, as they'll slug you to the tune of between TD 15 and TD 20 per person for your addiction.

### Getting There & Away

Sousse is very well served by public transport, with everything from an international airport at nearby Monastir to a comprehensive local bus network.

The most comfortable way to travel is by train, with regular services on the main line between Tunis and the south. There are, however, no trains to Kairouan, so the choice rests between bus or louage.

**Air** You'll find Tunis Air (☎ 03-225232) at 5 Ave Habib Bourguiba. The airport is on the road to Monastir, TD 5 by taxi from the town centre. Trains running on the Sousse-Monastir line stop at a special airport station, 200 metres from the terminal.

**Bus** Sousse has a host of bus stations. The SNTRI office is on Ave Mohammed Ali, not far from Bab el-Jedid, which is the main departure point for the south and inland. Services from here include:

| Destination | Time | Fare | Frequency |
| --- | --- | --- | --- |
| Douz | 8 hours | 14.040 | 2 daily |
| Gabès | 5 hours | 9.370 | 5 daily |
| Jerba | 7 hours | 12.840 | 2 daily |
| Kairouan | 1½ hours | 2.490 | 4 daily |
| Matmata | 7 hours | 10.740 | daily |
| Medenine | 7 hours | 11.760 | 5 daily |
| Sfax | 2½ hours | 5.060 | 5 daily |
| Tataouine | 9 hours | 13.110 | 2 daily |
| Zarzis | 8½ hours | 13.700 | 3 daily |

Northbound intercity services leave from the Place du Port, on the harbour side. There are regular buses making the 2½-hour trip to Tunis (TD 5.600), three buses to Hammamet (TD 2.990) and Nabeul (TD 3.450) and a daily connection to Bizerte (TD 7.640) at 3 pm. This is also the departure point for hourly buses to Monastir (830 mills) and Mahdia (TD 2.300).

Most local buses leave from Blvd Yahia ibn Omar, off Place Farhat Hached on the northern side of the medina. This is also the place to catch buses to Port el-Kantaoui (450 mills), which leave every half-hour.

Other buses, including those to Le Kef, Zaghouan and Enfidaville, leave from the gare routière at the end of Ave de la République.

**Train** The railway station is right in the middle of town, so train is a very convenient way to arrive. The medina and hotels are only five minutes' walk from here.

There are eight trains daily for the 2¼-hour journey between Sousse and Tunis. The fare is TD 4.450 in 2nd class and TD 6.250 in 1st class. For Sfax, there are five departures per day (two hours, TD 4.050/5.700). The 9.25 am southbound train continues to Gabès (4½ hours, TD 7.200/10.250).

For Nabeul and Hammamet, take any northbound train and change at Bir Bou Rekba.

There are also regular local trains on a branch line to Monastir and Mahdia. They leave from the station near Bab el-Jedid. For Monastir (680 mills), there are 15 trains a day – leaving almost hourly between 6.05 am and 7.10 pm. Seven trains continue to Mahdia (TD 1.830), the most convenient of which is the 10 am departure. It takes 30 minutes to reach Monastir, and another hour to Mahdia.

**Taxi** Louages for Kairouan (TD 2.800), El-Jem (TD 2.700), Mahdia, Sfax and Kasserine leave from next to the bus station at Bab el-Jedid. Other destinations, including Tunis (TD 5.400) and Monastir (950 mills) are served by the louage station at the northern end of Ave Mohammed Ali.

**Car Rental** There are 13 rental companies with branches in town, including Avis (☎ 03-225901), Blvd de la Corniche; Europcar (☎ 03-226252), Blvd de la Corniche; and Hertz (☎ 03-225428), Ave Habib Bourguiba. Port el-Kantaoui is served by Kantaoui Rent (☎ 03-242318).

## MONASTIR

Situated on a headland some 15 km south of Sousse, Monastir must have at one stage been a pleasant little village. Today it has become a national showpiece, mainly because it was Bourguiba's birthplace and because it is here that he has chosen to be buried when his time comes.

The monuments in the centre include the Bourguiba family mausoleum with its twin cupolas, the 8th-century ribat and the 9th-century Great Mosque.

Place du Gouvernorate, in the middle of town, sports a bronze statue of a chechia-clad Bourguiba as a young man. The square is quite a sight at night with its spotlights and large fountain.

Saturday is market day in Monastir and the area around the bus station is jam-packed with stalls and people.

While the Zone Touristique north of Monastir is a major package-tourist hangout, the town itself is not well endowed on the accommodation front – particularly at the budget end of the scale. It does have one of the best beach hotels in the country, but you'll need to have the gods on your side to get a room in summer. Still, there's enough to see to make it a pleasant day trip from Sousse.

### Information
**Tourist Offices** The ONTT office is at the airport, open (in theory) 24 hours a day, seven days a week – a remarkable waste of effort since it has nothing to offer except a fairly useless map.

More convenient, but not much more useful, is the tourist office at the syndicat d'initiative (☎ 03-461960), inside the medina and set back off Rue de l'Indépendance. There's a reasonable chance of getting answers to your questions here. It's open from 9 am to 1 pm and 3 pm to 5.30 pm; closed on Sunday.

**Money** There are two banks in Place du 3 Septembre 1934 in the middle of the medina, and others near the post office on Ave Habib Bourguiba.

**Post & Telecommunications** The somewhat chaotic main post office is on Ave Habib Bourguiba, just south of the medina. The best bet for international calls is the office at the northern end of the Habib Complex on the Corniche.

### Ribat
Monastir's ribat has been almost totally rebuilt, but it still has an interesting atmosphere. It has been used as a film set on more

TUNISIA

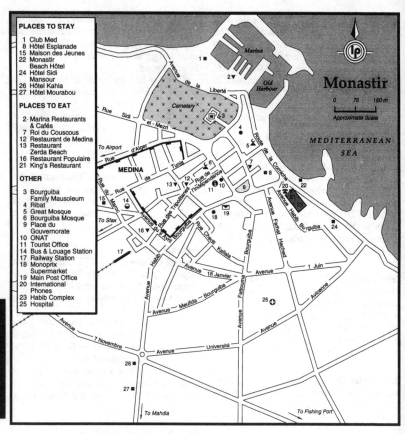

TUNISIA

than a couple of occasions. Two films that have had scenes shot here are *Life of Brian* and *Life of Christ*. There are excellent views of the town and coastline all the way back to Sousse from the top of the tower. The ribat also houses a fairly uninspiring museum. It's open from 9.30 am to 5.30 pm; closed Monday. Entry is TD 1, plus TD 1 to take photographs.

### Costume Museum

This small museum is right next to the tourist office in the medina, and is worth a quick wander through. It's open from 9 am to noon and 2 to 5.30 pm; closed on Sunday. Entrance is 400 mills.

### Marina

The new marina, a short walk from the ribat at the northern end of the beach, is a pleasant spot to enjoy a coffee and ponder the fortunes that have been spent on some of the luxury cruisers. The colourful marina is surrounded by a host of restaurants and cafés.

### Places to Stay – bottom end

The only cheap accommodation in Monastir is the *Maison des Jeunes*, which is opposite the bus station and set in the corner of the public gardens off Ave de la République. As usual, it offers all the comforts of an army barracks. A bed costs TD 4. Platoons of 10 or more can apply for breakfast at 700 mills per person.

### Places to Stay – middle

The choice of hotels in this range includes one of the most unusual hotels in the country. It took me a while to find the *Monastir Beach Hôtel* (☎ 03-464766), until I realised that I was standing on it! It runs virtually the length of the main beach, set beneath the massive sidewalk of the Route de la Corniche, and is invisible from the street. The rooms are basic but clean, and come complete with en suite hot shower and toilet. Every room has huge French doors opening to the beach. The views are great, although it doesn't do much for your privacy. Singles/doubles plus breakfast cost TD 18.500/26 in summer, falling to TD 9.500/14 in winter. Top value.

The other two options are a fair hike from both the town and the beach, on the road out towards Mahdia. The better of the two is the *Hôtel Kahla* (☎ 03-464570), right on busy Place du 7 Novembre. It has very comfortable singles/doubles with breakfast for TD 17/24 in the high season and TD 13/18 in the low season. It offers a money changing service.

A farther 100 metres out of town is the drab, modern *Hôtel Mourabou* (☎ 03-461585) with very similar prices.

Don't waste your time getting to the *Hôtel Yasmin*, a couple of km north of town on the coast road. It's closed – although it is still being touted in the tourist information brochure.

### Places to Stay – top end

Most of the three and four-star resort hotels are a fair way north of town in the Zone Touristique at Skanes. Places like the *Hôtel Ruspina*, the name of the town in Roman times, are aimed at the charter groups, not casual drop-ins.

A better bet is the three-star *Hôtel Sidi Mansour* (☎ 03-461311), past the main beach at the southern end of the Corniche. It charges TD 45/68 for singles/doubles in summer and TD 21/30 in winter.

*Club Med* (☎ 03-460033) is here in a big way, with a complex next to the marina.

### Places to Eat

Monastir is not the best place in the country to go looking for a cheap meal. Places like the *Restaurant de Medina*, in the centre of the medina, lead the way in charging over the odds for some ordinary offerings.

You're better off walking around the corner to the *Restaurant Zerda Beach*, which has similar stuff for a couple of dinar less.

Better still, try the *Roi du Couscous* on the beach side of the Gouvernorate. It has couscous of the day for TD 2.500 and a good general selection. The small *Restaurant Ridha* by the bus station is also good.

There's no shortage of tourist restaurants. The *King's Restaurant* (☎ 03-463394), in the Habib Complex, has a promising but pricey blackboard menu for TD 9. The best restaurant in town is *Le Grill* (☎ 03-462136) out at the marina, which has a range of other cafés and restaurants.

### Getting There & Away

**Air** The Tunis Air (☎ 03-462550) office is in the Habib Complex near the foreshore. The Air France (☎ 03-461316) office is at the airport.

Monastir's international airport is at Skanes, eight km north towards Sousse. It has its own station, 200 metres from the terminal, on the Monastir-Sousse line.

Although most of the international flights are direct charters from Europe, Tunis Air has scheduled flights to a dozen European cities, including Amsterdam, Brussels, Frankfurt, Marseilles, Paris and Rome.

On the domestic network, there is a return service to Jerba on Tuesday and Saturday (TD 29.800 one way, TD 59.600 return). The flight takes 35 minutes.

**Bus** The bus station is at the western edge of the medina. There are regular departures for Sousse, Mahdia and other towns in the area.

**Train** The railway station is also on the western edge of the medina. There are almost hourly departures for the 30-minute trip to Sousse (680 mills). There is a direct train to Tunis (three hours) daily at 5.58 pm. The direct service from Tunis leaves at 12.05 pm. There are additional services on Sunday.

There are also regular trains making the one-hour trip to Mahdia.

**Taxi** The louages leave from the bus station. Demand often exceeds supply so it is a matter of making a dive for a door handle to secure a place.

## MAHDIA

Mahdia is one of the few towns on this section of coast that has managed to escape being turned into a total tourist trap. It's a beautifully relaxed place, set on a small promontory 60 km or so south of Sousse.

### History

The town's history can be traced back to 916 AD, when the first Fatimid ruler, Obeid Allah, made it his capital. He was a self-declared Mahdi ('one who is guided' to convert the world to Islam). He belonged to the Shiite sect, considered heretical by the Sunni majority, and therefore needed a place that was easily defended. Mahdia fitted the bill neatly, as it is on a high promontory. A massive wall, in places up to 10 metres thick, was built right across the neck of the spit, with just one entrance through a heavily fortified gate.

However, in 969 the Fatimids realised their dream of becoming caliphs in Cairo and from that time on the town decreased in importance. It was still important enough for the Christians to invade in the 11th century, followed by the Normans in the 12th and the Spanish in the 16th. The Spanish destroyed the city's walls as they departed, and the walls were later partially reconstructed by the Ottoman Turks.

Today's tourist activity is largely confined to a string of resort hotels – with more under construction – on the beaches to the north.

The town remains a relative backwater with hardly a souvenir shop in sight.

### Information

There is a small tourist office (☎ 03-681098) just inside the main entrance to the medina, Skifa el-Kahla. The post office is near the Hôtel Panorama in the new part of town, 500 metres' walk along Ave Habib Bourguiba from the Skifa el-Kahla.

There are a few banks, mostly along the foreshore road on the harbour side of the promontory.

The Friday market and the daily fish market are held in the large white building opposite the fishing harbour.

### Medina

The main entrance to the medina is through the imposing **Skifa el-Kahla** gate, which at one time was part of the 10-metre-thick wall that blocked off this narrow part of the promontory. 'Gate' is a bit of a misnomer; it's a narrow, vaulted passageway almost 50 metres long that was once protected by a series of massive iron gates.

Once inside the medina, the tourist office is straight ahead on the right. On the inside of the wall here there are steps leading up to the top of the gate, from which you can get a good perspective of the town.

The narrow, cobbled main street opens eventually onto **Place du Caire**, an immaculate, small square, complete with shady trees, vines and cafés. By day, the old men sit around in the shade drinking coffee; later on, the square livens up considerably, with all the men coming out for their evening coffee and game of dominoes.

The main street then continues and comes out at a larger square dominated by the **Great Mosque**. This is a 20th-century recreation of the original mosque built by the Mahdi in the 10th century and it is a very simple construction. Its only major feature is the unadorned entrance, a characteristic of Fatimid design.

On the highest point of the headland is the **Borj el-Kebir**, a fortress which was built in the 16th century and has been heavily restored. It is not worth the 600 mills entry, as there is nothing to see inside and the views from the ramparts are not that much better than from on the ground.

The road past the fort leads through an enormous cemetery to the lighthouse on the end of the headland; down to the right is the old Fatimid port, with the crumbling remains of its fortifications on either side of the entrance.

Weaving (of cotton sheets and wedding cloth) on hand looms is widespread throughout the old city, and the click-clack of the shuttles is often the only sound disturbing the torpor which sets in on hot summer afternoons. Many of these small workshops have a definite air of the Dickensian workhouse about them, with poor lighting, cramped conditions and no ventilation. The weavers are usually more than willing to take a break to explain the finer points of their craft. Wedding material is full of gold thread and has to be ordered at least 12 months in advance.

The water here is a clear blue and swimming is definitely possible, either from the rocks outside the Hôtel el-Jazira or from the beach along the tourist strip north of town.

### Places to Stay – bottom end
The family-run *Hôtel el-Jazira* (☎ 03-681629), at 36 Rue Ibn Fourat, is the only hotel inside the medina. It's right on the water on the northern side of the headland. To get there, turn left as soon as you enter the medina and aim for the seafront. Rue Ibn Fourat is a small alleyway on the right just before you reach the sea. Some of the rooms look straight out over the water. It's good value at TD 8.500/14 for singles/doubles in summer and TD 6/9 in winter, including hot showers. There's a table and chairs on the roof.

The cheapest place is the *Hôtel Rand* (☎ 03-680525) at 20 Ave Taieb Mehiri in the middle of the new town. It's friendly enough, but a long way from anything of interest. For the grimly determined, follow Ave Habib Bourguiba (the Sousse road) away from the medina and fork left at the Hôtel Panorama after 500 metres, then turn left after another

500 metres at the first major intersection; the hotel is on the right. It charges TD 7 per person in the high season and TD 4.500 in the low season, including breakfast.

### Places to Stay – middle
You may wish that you'd stopped walking at the *Hôtel Panorama* (☎ 03-680039). It has a nice shaded garden, with pergolas covered in bougainvillea and even cute little cubicles where you can sit in privacy. Unfortunately, it is rumoured to be closing, but when I visited it was charging TD 18 in the high season for a double with bath and breakfast.

Another good choice is the friendly *Hôtel Corniche* (☎ 03-694201), a stone's throw from the beach on Route de la Corniche. It charges TD 13/20 in summer for singles/doubles and TD 10.500/15 in winter, including breakfast and hot shower.

### Places to Stay – top end
The Zone Touristique is home to a growing band of resorts aimed at the package market. As usual, they are packed in summer and dead in winter.

The best of them is the three-star *Hôtel el-Mehdi* (☎ 03-681300). Its facilities – tennis courts, indoor and outdoor pools, etc – are available for TD 16/26 for singles/doubles in winter. Don't bother asking in summer.

A bit closer to town, the one-star *Sables d'Or* (☎ 03-681137) charges fractionally less, but offers a hell of a lot less.

There are blue-and-white service taxis which run out to the Zone Touristique from the corner near the market for 300 mills per person.

### Places to Eat
Beware of thin chefs, or so the saying goes. Well, there's nothing to be afraid of at the excellent *Restaurant el-Moez*, easily the best gargotte I came across in the whole country. It's run by a big man with a big heart who welcomes you at the door with open arms. The choice is limited to the day's three blackboard selections, one of which will be fish. A plate of mloukhia, meat in thick sauce

made from ground herbs, costs TD 1.700, and there is nothing over TD 2. Other visitors have been equally enthusiastic about the skakshuka (vegetable stew) and the kammounia (a spicy meat dish made with lots of cummin). The El-Moez, named after a Fatimid princess, is on a small street between the Skifa el-Kahla and the market. Lunch is the best time to visit.

If this is not your style, there are a number of small restaurants facing the port along Ave Farhat Hached. The best of them, reportedly, is *Le Lido*.

### Getting There & Away
**Bus** Buses leave from the kiosk opposite near the markets, just to the south of the medina. There are regular departures to Sousse and Monastir, and less frequent departures to Kairouan and Tunis.

**Train** The relatively new railway station is by the port, just off Ave Farhat Hached. It's only about 300 metres from the medina. The line from Monastir was opened in 1987, so the station is very modern and comes complete with marble floors and potted plants.

There are seven departures daily for the 90-minute journey to Sousse (TD 1.830), via Monastir, but there's nothing between 7.50 am and 1.15 pm. The 4.50 pm train continues to Tunis (four hours).

**Taxi** The louage station is just in front of the railway station. There are departures for El-Jem, Kairouan, Monastir, Sfax and Sousse.

### EL-JEM
If it wasn't for the fact that El-Jem has one of the most impressive Roman monuments in Africa, this otherwise hot, dusty and unremarkable town would be low on the list of priorities for any visitor to Tunisia.

### Colosseum
The very well preserved colosseum is not much smaller than its world-famous counterpart in Rome. It rises spectacularly from the flat surrounding plains and completely dominates the town.

It was the crowning glory of the Roman town of Thysdrus, which prospered at the centre of a rich olive-growing region. It was a town of sumptuous villas adorned with some brilliant mosaics.

The vital statistics of the amphitheatre are impressive – 138 metres long by 114 metres wide, with three tiers of seating rising 30 metres. Its capacity has been estimated at 30,000, considerably greater than the population of the town itself. Under the arena run two long passageways which were used to hold the animals, gladiators and other unfortunates before they were thrust into the arena to provide entertainment for the masses.

The structure is believed to have been built between 230 and 238 AD, and is generally attributed to the African pro-consul Gordian, a local landowner and patron. In 238 AD, at the age of 80, Gordian was declared emperor of Rome here during an ill-fated rebellion against oppressive taxes imposed by Emperor Maximus. Gordian reportedly committed suicide in the amphitheatre when it became obvious that the rebellion was doomed, and the town was virtually wiped out in the ensuing retribution.

The amphitheatre itself suffered badly in the 17th century when the guts were blown out of one side of it in order to flush out some dissidents who had taken refuge within the walls. Not only did this completely demolish a large section, it also destabilised the rest of it; some fairly hasty and none-too-professional repairs were done to stop the whole thing collapsing.

The colosseum is open daily from 7 am to 7 pm in summer, and from 7.30 am to 5.30 pm in winter. Entry is TD 2, plus TD 1 to take photographs.

It plays host to an annual international symphonic music festival in July and August.

### Museum
Located about 500 metres south of the amphitheatre, along the road to Sfax, the museum houses the most spectacular collec-

tion of mosaics to be found outside of the Bardo Museum in Tunis. All the mosaics were found on the site right behind the museum building, which was an area of particularly luxurious villas. Some of the mosaics have been left *in situ* while the best have been moved into the museum. Particularly impressive is the huge and intricate depiction of the nine Muses.

Opening times and admission prices are the same as for the colosseum.

## Other Sites

On the opposite side of the railway line is a second, smaller **amphitheatre**, built on the ruins of a primitive fort.

There is a second area of Roman **villas** to the north of the colosseum, only some of which have been excavated.

Other sites wait to be uncovered. Aerial photographs have indicated the remains of another, even larger amphitheatre, barely visible from the ground.

## Places to Stay & Eat

Although there is a hotel in town, it takes only half a day to explore the various sites, so it's best to carry on to another destination later in the day. The railway station won't look after baggage but the guy at the entrance to the amphitheatre will keep an eye on it for a while.

The only accommodation in El-Jem is the *Hôtel Julius* (☎ 03-690044), right on the main road by the railway station. Rooms are arranged around a pleasant courtyard and cost TD 7.500/13 for a single/double; it fills up early in summer. The hotel also has the only bar in town, and a restaurant with a set menu for TD 5.

There are a couple of small restaurants along the main street between the hotel and the museum, but don't expect anything more exotic than brochettes.

For coffee and tea, there are a few cafés around the square directly opposite the railway station.

## Getting There & Away

**Bus** The SNTRI bus office is on the right just before the museum. The only departures are buses in transit, so it can be difficult to get a seat. The train is a better bet.

**Train** The railway station is right in the centre of the town and only about five minutes' walk from the amphitheatre.

For trains south, there are four daily to Sfax (one hour, TD 3.500 1st class) between 10.20 am and midnight. The 10.20 am train continues to Gabès (3½ hours), while the midnight service goes all the way to Gafsa and Metlaoui (six hours).

For Sousse (TD 3.500) and Tunis (TD 8.500) there are trains at 2.40 and 6.56 am and 1.24, 2.24 and 7.24 pm. The trip takes a bit over three hours.

**Taxi** The louages leave from near the railway station. Demand often exceeds supply here and it can be a bit of a scramble to get a seat. There are frequent departures to Sousse (TD 2.700), Sfax, Kairouan and Mahdia, although things dry up a bit in the afternoon.

## KAIROUAN

Historically, this is the most important town in the country. It ranks behind only Mecca, Medina and Jerusalem among Islam's holy places. The medina is compact and interesting and there are other sights around the town.

With a population of more than 100,000, Kairouan is the fifth-largest city in the country. It's the centre of a major fruit-growing region and is also well known for its carpet-making.

Because of its importance, however, Kairouan sees more than its fair share of tourists. Visiting the sites is best done either early in the morning or in the evening. You can set your clock by the wave of tourist buses that rolls up outside the medina at 9 am every day.

As a result, the medina is overflowing with tourist shops and some of the merchants have started resorting to a bit of good old Moroccan-style aggression to get business.

The place is plagued by 'guides', touts whose sole purpose is to get you into the carpet shops. You will be told constantly that where you are going is closed, has moved, no longer exists, etc. Practise saying 'no, thank you' firmly but politely – your politeness may be tested by the end of day – and treat everything you are told with a fair measure of scepticism.

If you want a genuine guide, they can be hired from the tourist office. These guys carry accreditation, with photo, and they know their stuff. They charge TD 7 for a tour of all the major sites in town – much less than any of the schemes the touts have in mind.

### History
Founded in the second half of the 7th century by Uqba bin Nafi al-Fihri, Kairouan is where Islam first took hold in the Maghreb. It became the capital of the Aghlabid dynasty in 800 AD, and it was under these rulers that the Great Mosque and other buildings of religious significance were constructed.

The Fatimids conquered the city in 909. When they moved their capital to Mahdia, Kairouan went through a period of decline, reaching a low point in 1057 when the Beni Hillal Bedouin tribe destroyed the city at the behest of the Fatimid ruler Mustansir.

Although Kairouan was largely rebuilt in the 13th century, it was never to regain its position of political pre-eminence. However, as a religious centre it was and still is the most important place in the country.

### Information
**Tourist Offices** The ONTT (☎ 07-221797) office is next to the Aghlabid Basins to the north of town, at the junction of Rue des Aghlabites and Ave de la République. Don't expect to come away from here much the wiser. The only offerings are a glossy brochure (available anywhere) and a list of hotels. The staff don't appear to know a whole lot about the town, which is a shame because the big smiles and welcome greetings indicate that they would love to help if only they could.

The ONTT does, however, know the way to the local syndicat d'initiative office, which is just across the corridor. This is a

useful place, because it is only here that tickets to the main sites can be bought. For TD 2 you get a combined ticket, valid for two days, that gives you access to the six major monuments around the city and the Islamic Art Museum at Raqqada, on the road to Sfax. The office is open daily from 8 am to 6 pm in summer and from 8 am to 5.30 pm in winter.

**Money** There are plenty of banks for changing money, including one just inside Bab ech Chouhada and a couple more opposite on Blvd Habib Bourguiba.

**Post & Telecommunications** The main post office is 100 metres or so south of Bab ech Chouhada, at the roundabout on the corner of Ave de la République and Ave Farhat Hached. It is open from 8 am to 6 pm from Monday to Saturday in winter, and from 7.30 am to 12.30 pm from Monday to Saturday in summer.

International telephone calls can be made from the Complexe Telephonique on the Sfax road, just south of Place du 7 Novembre 1987. It is open from 8 am to 10 pm daily. Calls can also be made from the Taxiphone office on the pedestrian precinct section of Blvd Habib Bourguiba, opposite the Bab ech Chouhada.

**Hammam** There's a hammam for men next to the Hôtel Sabra which is open daily until 3 pm. A bath costs 500 mills, or TD 1.500 with massage.

**Street Names** Street names seem to change so often in Kairouan that the street signs can't keep up. It's hard to find two people who agree on a name. The names of the monuments and hotels don't change, however, so ask for them rather than for the street they're in.

### Medina
The walled medina is the central part of the city; the new French section spreads away to the south and follows the usual orderly plan. The wall itself is pierced by a number of

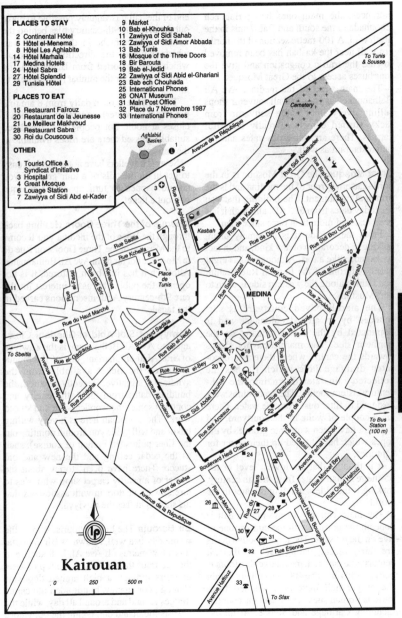

**PLACES TO STAY**

2 Continental Hôtel
5 Hôtel el-Menema
8 Hôtel Les Aghlabite
14 Hôtel Marhala
17 Medina Hotels
24 Hôtel Sabra
27 Hôtel Splendid
29 Tunisia Hôtel

**PLACES TO EAT**

15 Restaurant Faïrouz
20 Restaurant de la Jeunesse
21 Le Meilleur Makhroud
28 Restaurant Sabra
30 Roi du Couscous

**OTHER**

1 Tourist Office &
  Syndicat d'Initiative
3 Hospital
4 Great Mosque
6 Louage Station
7 Zawiyya of Sidi Abd el-Kader

9 Market
10 Bab el-Khoukha
11 Zawiyya of Sidi Sahab
12 Zawiyya of Sidi Amor Abbada
13 Bab Tunis
16 Mosque of the Three Doors
18 Bir Barouta
19 Bab el-Jedid
22 Zawiyya of Sidi Abid el-Ghariani
23 Bab ech Chouhada
25 International Phones
26 ONAT Museum
31 Main Post Office
32 Place du 7 Novembre 1987
33 International Phones

**Kairouan**

0      250      500 m

entrances, the main ones being Bab ech Chouhada to the south and Bab Tunis in the north wall. A 100-metre section of the northern wall near the kasbah has been removed to ease the traffic congestion and give the tour buses access to the Great Mosque.

The main street of the medina, Ave Ali Belhaouane has wall-to-wall souvenir shops selling every imaginable souvenir from tacky stuffed camels to really beautiful carpets. There are numerous cafés and the odd restaurant as well.

**Great Mosque** The Great Mosque is in the north-eastern corner of the medina and is the principal monument. The building that you see today dates from 670 AD, although it has been restored more than once since then.

From the outside it is extremely plain, lacking in decoration of any kind, and in fact looks more like a fort. Although it has eight gates, only one of the four on Rue Brahim ben Lagleb along the western side is open to non-Muslims.

The marble-paved courtyard is surrounded by an arched colonnade and is dominated by the square minaret on the northern side. The marble paving slopes towards the centre, where there is a decorated drainage hole which flushes the collected rainwater down into the 9th-century cisterns below. The decorations are designed to filter dust from the water. There are a couple of wells in the courtyard, and their lips have been worn into grooves by the ropes which have hauled up their water for centuries.

It is thought that the lowest level of the 35-metre minaret dates from the 8th century, making it the oldest standing minaret in the world.

The main entrance to the prayer hall is beneath the portico with the cupola, one of five on the mosque. The large wooden doors are fairly recent, dating back to the last century; the carved panel above the doors is particularly fine. The 400 or so pillars within the prayer hall have been filched from various Roman sites throughout the country, including Carthage and Sousse. At the far

end of the hall it is vaguely possible to make out the precious 9th-century tiles behind the mihrab (prayer niche in the mosque wall which indicates the direction of Mecca), which were imported from Baghdad along with the wood for the minbar (pulpit) next to it.

The mosque is open daily from 8 am to 3 pm (2 pm in winter), except Friday when it closes at noon. For people not considered suitably dressed there are robes available at the entrance.

Several travellers have noted that it is easy to get in on the tails of a tour group if you should happen to turn up at the mosque without a ticket.

**Mosque of the Three Doors** Heading back through the lanes of the medina you'll come to the Mosque of the Three Doors, on Rue de la Mosquée not far from Ave Ali Belhaouane. Although it has just been restored, it is not open to the public, but is of interest for the rare 9th-century Arab inscriptions carved in the façade.

**Zawiyya of Sidi Abid el-Ghariani** Closer again to Ave Ali Belhaouane is the Zawiyya of Sidi Abid el-Ghariani, one of the monuments on the ticket available from the syndicat d'initiative. Recently restored, the building dates from the 14th century and contains some fine woodcarving and stucco work. The custodian here is a very willing talker and will guide you around pointing out the finer points (in French of course), such as the cedar ceiling and the new and old stucco. There have been stories about the owner of a nearby carpet shop who tries to lure unwary visitors in with assurances that his shop is in fact the zawiyya.

**Bir Barouta** The biggest tourist trap in the whole city is a well, known as Bir Barouta. It is a few metres off Ave Ali Belhaouane in the centre of the medina, at the top of a set of stairs through a high arched doorway. Here, a poor, mangy, blindfolded old camel trudges around and around all day, while the tourists file in and out, taking the obligatory photo and leaving the obligatory tip. The well's popularity stems from the belief that it is connected to Mecca, so to drink the water will supposedly do wonders for you.

### Aghlabid Basins

These two cisterns are remarkable largely for the amount of garbage that has collected in their shallow waters. They were built in the 9th century and were filled by an aqueduct from a spring some 30 km away; they are relics of the water system which once supplied the town with water. The larger of the two pools is over 130 metres in diameter and the perimeter wall has curious buttressing. In the centre are pillars which used to hold a pavilion where the rulers could come to relax in the cool on summer evenings.

The basins were heavily restored about 20 years ago and are now mostly concrete, but they are still worth a quick look. The entrance is on the western side, which is the far side from the tourist office.

### Zawiyya of Sidi Sahab

Getting to this zawiyya takes a bit of effort. It's about 1.5 km from the Aghlabid Basins, heading west along Ave de la République.

It was built in honour of Abu Zama el-Belaoui, a saint and friend of the Prophet who was renowned for always carrying three hairs from the Prophet's beard around with him. For this reason he became known as the Prophet's barber, which explains the other name of this zawiyya – the Mosque of the Barber.

A very highly decorated passageway leads off the white courtyard into the main courtyard of the zawiyya, which is also highly decorated with tiles and stucco work. In a room off to the left is the tomb of the designer of the Great Mosque, while the saint's tomb is in the room on the far side of the courtyard. Non-Muslims are allowed to enter as far as the courtyard only.

As at the Great Mosque, robes are available at the entrance. This is the third of the monuments on the ticket.

### Raqqada Islamic Art Museum

The museum takes a bit of getting to, but it's well worth a visit. Raqqada is nine km south of Kairouan and is where the Aghlabid princes built their palaces. The museum occupies an old Aghlabid presidential palace. It can be reached by taking a bus from near the post office to the university, and then walking the remaining couple of km. There are buses at 8, 9, 10 and 11 am, and at noon. It's much easier to negotiate a taxi. The museum is open daily, except Monday, from 9 am to 2.30 pm.

### ONAT Museum

The ONAT museum (free entry) on Rue el-Mouiz has a good display of old rugs. There is no ONAT shop; the nearest one is in Sousse.

### Places to Stay – bottom end

The best place in town is just outside the medina, opposite Bab ech Chouhada. This is the big, clean *Hôtel Sabra* (☎ 07-220260), which is popular and conveniently located; it charges TD 6/10 for singles/doubles, including breakfast and free hot showers – a good place.

There are a couple of places in the medina. The *Hôtel Barouta*, just around the corner from the Bir Barouta, is one to avoid. A much better bet is the *Hôtel Marhala* (☎ 07-220736) at 35 Souq el-Belaghija, one of the covered souqs off Ave Ali Belhaouane right in the heart of the medina. This place is an old medersa (Islamic college) and offers something a little different from the average medina hotel. The rooms are tiny, however, and those on the roof get unbearably hot in summer. It charges TD 5.500 per person, plus TD 1.500 for breakfast.

The main drawback to the place is that the owner has hit on the brilliant idea of putting a carpet shop inside the hotel, cutting off all chance of an escape from the ubiquitous carpet salesmen.

To find the hotel, head through the big arch with the crenellated top, on the right of Ave Ali Belhaouane coming from Bab ech Chouhada. It's easy to miss during business hours because it is obscured by all sorts of offerings from the souvenir shops. The hotel is about 50 metres along on the left.

Another interesting place is the *Hôtel Les Aghlabite* (☎ 07-220880), a converted caravanserai off Place de Tunis to the north of the medina. Singles/doubles are TD 5/10 with free hot showers.

### Places to Stay – middle

The *Hôtel el-Menema* (☎ 07-220182) is a fairly new place a couple of blocks north of Place de Tunis. The rooms are all arranged around a covered courtyard but some also have windows to the outside. Charges are TD 13/20 in single/double rooms with bath, TD 1 less without bath; these prices include breakfast.

There are also a couple of good places just south of the medina. The two-star *Tunisia Hôtel* (☎ 07-221855) on Ave Farhat Hached has big rooms, centrally heated in winter, which cost TD 14/22 for singles/doubles with bath and breakfast. Close by is the characterless, three-star *Hôtel Splendid* (☎ 07-227522), where a room with bath and breakfast will set you back TD 18/26. This place is popular with tour parties.

### Places to Stay – top end

The *Continental Hôtel* (☎ 07-221135) is on Ave de la République, right opposite the Aghlabid Basins. It has definitely seen better days, but is air-conditioned and charges TD 27/41 for singles/doubles with breakfast in the low season, rising to TD 32/46 in summer.

### Places to Eat

The *Restaurant de la Jeunesse*, on Ave Ali Belhaouane near the Bir Barouta, is the best of the medina restaurants. Its couscous is as good as any in the country. A big bowl of couscous and chicken goes for TD 2.500.

Nearby on Rue des Tailleurs, signposted off Ave Ali Belhaouane, is the *Restaurant Faïrouz*. It has a good selection, but the prices are a bit over the odds. You can get a cold beer, served with a conspiratorial grin, with your meal for TD 1.500.

Much better value is the friendly *Restaurant Sabra*, next to the Tunisia Hôtel on Ave Farhat Hached. A huge portion of couscous, meat and vegetables will set you back a mere TD 1.700.

More up-market than any of these is the *Roi du Couscous*, on the southern side of town on Place du 7 Novembre. It has divan seating and main courses for about TD 5.

Kairouan is famous for its sticky sweets, especially a date-filled semolina cake soaked in honey called makhroud which can be found everywhere. A good place to sample this and other specialities is *Le Meilleur Makhroud*, in the middle of the medina on Ave Ali Belhaouane.

For a breakfast with a difference, the small gargotte right next to the Hôtel Sabra serves dragh, a kind of porridge made from sorghum, until 10 am. Dragh starts life as a rather disconcerting looking grey slop, into which the owner piles sugar, halva and various other powders. It's not as bad as it looks or sounds, and costs 500 mills a bowl.

As usual, there are numerous cafés in the medina, but one with a little more atmosphere than usual is the *Café Errachid*, housed in an old part of the medina near the Hôtel Marhala.

### Things to Buy

Kairouan is one of the country's major carpet centres, producing classical knotted carpets as well the woven mergoum. If you are in the market for a carpet, this is as good a place as any to do your shopping.

It is important, however, to do your homework first. Initial prices can be ridiculously high, often three times the true price.

Remember that all carpets which have been inspected and classified by ONAT carry a label and seal on the back. Ones without this label may be of dubious quality, so don't buy indiscriminately.

### Getting There & Away

**Bus** The bus station is about 10 minutes' walk to the south-east of Bab ech Chouhada. Both SNTRI and regional buses leave from here.

There are regular departures to Sousse, Sfax, Kasserine, Nabeul, Gafsa and Tunis.

**Taxi** Louages to all points north, south, east and west leave from the vacant lot next to the kasbah, north of the medina on Rue des Aghlabites. There are departures for Tunis (two hours, TD 5.600), Gafsa, Kasserine and Sousse (TD 2.800). There are no louages to Sfax.

## SBEITLA

Stuck right out in the middle of nowhere, the nothing town of Sbeitla merits a mention only because it is the site of the Roman town of Sufetula. It's worth a detour if you have your own vehicle; if you don't, it's not worth a special trip. Other sites are better value.

The ruins are only 500 metres or so out of Sbeitla, 38 km east of Kasserine and 108 km south-west of Kairouan.

The history of Roman Sufetula is not well documented. It is thought to have been founded at the end of the first century AD, although the site was occupied long before that.

If you're visiting in winter, make sure you bring warm clothing. Snow is quite common.

### The Ruins

From the town, the first monument you come across is the restored **Triumphal Arch of Diocletian**, among the eucalypt trees to the right of the road. The site entrance, however, is a farther couple of 100 metres along, between a couple of Byzantine forts.

Once inside, the ruins of interest are off to the left – there is a well-trodden path which is easy to follow. The walled **forum** is still easy to identify, but the dominant structures are the three **temples** on the northern side. Although they have been largely reconstructed, they provide one of the best examples of how the centres of towns were dominated by temple buildings.

Out behind the temples are the ruins of a couple of **churches**. The first is a basilica with three aisles and the second a Byzantine cathedral with five aisles. Just on the forum side of the latter is a beautifully restored

baptistry, complete with mosaics which include colourful floral and cross motifs.

Back towards the oued, the theatre is in a bad way; at one time it must have been fantastic, with its position right above the bank of the oued.

Opposite the entrance to the site is a small museum which even the custodian says is not worth visiting – sound advice!

The site is open every day, from 8.30 am to 5.30 pm in winter and from 6 am to 8 pm in summer. Entry costs TD 1, and the same again if you want to take photographs.

### Places to Stay

If bad luck or management finds you looking for a bed here, you do at least have a choice. The *Hôtel Bakini*, on Rue 2 Mars, has singles/doubles at TD 18/26 with breakfast.

There's also the fancy *Hôtel Sufetula*, 500 metres beyond the site on the Kasserine road. It's a bit more expensive at TD 25.500/36 with breakfast, but there is a swimming pool – and the hotel overlooks the Roman site.

### Getting There & Away

Transport centres around the dusty bus station, 200 metres south of the main intersection. You can't miss it; this is only a small town.

There are bus and louage connections with Tunis, Kasserine, Tozeur, Kairouan, Dahmani and Le Kef.

## SFAX

With a population of over 375,000, Sfax is the second-largest city in the country, and is a major port. Exports which are shipped from here include phosphate from the Gafsa region and olive oil from the thousands of groves near the coast. Sfax is the departure point for ferries to the nearby Kerkennah Islands.

Attractions are a bit thin on the ground in Sfax, but its walled medina is well worth a wander around, if only to see what a medina looks like before it gets filled with souvenir shops. It's a good place to buy things because the lack of tourists makes for more reasonable prices. The Dar Jellouli Museum of

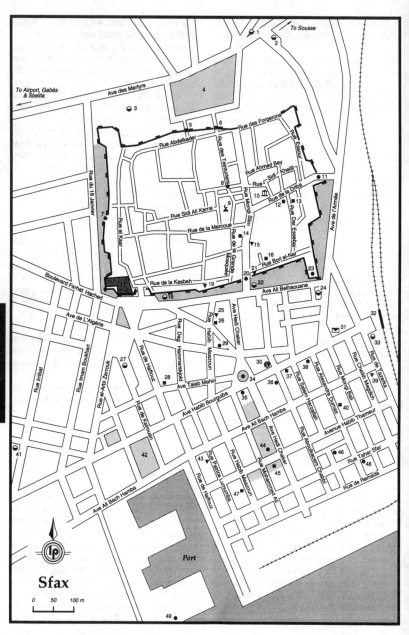

To Sousse

To Airport, Gabès
& Sbeitla

Ave des Martyrs

Rue des Forgerons

Rue Abdelkader

Rue Ahmed Bey

Rue Sidi Ali Karral

Rue de la Mercoue

Rue de la Kasbah

Ave Ali Belhaouane

Ave de l'Algérie

Ave de L'Algérie

Ave Taïeb Mehiri

Ave Habib Bourguiba

Ave Ali Bach Hamba

Avenue Habib Thameur

Rue de Remada

Port

**Sfax**

0    50    100 m

TUNISIA

## PLACES TO STAY

13  Hôtel du Sud
14  Hôtel Medina
16  Hôtel el-Habib
26  Hôtel Thyna
28  Hôtel Colisée
37  Hôtel Sfax Centre
40  Hôtels De la Paix and Alexandre
45  Hôtel Les Oliviers
47  Hôtel Mondial

## PLACES TO EAT

15  Restaurant Saada
19  Café Diwan
21  Restaurant Tunisien
25  Restaurant Le Corail
39  Restaurant Le Pecheur
43  Restaurant Chez Nous

## OTHER

1   Louages to Mahdia
2   Northern Bus Station
3   Local Buses
4   Markets
5   Bab Jedid
6   Bab Jebli
7   Bab Gharbi
8   Souqs
9   Great Mosque
10  Dar Jellouli Museum
11  Bab Chergui
12  Hammam
17  Kasbah
18  Louages to Mahres
20  Bab Diwan
22  Louage Station
23  Borj Ennar
24  Louage Station
27  Local Buses
29  International Newspapers
30  Syndicat d'Initiative
31  Post Office & International Phones
32  Railway Station
33  SNTRI Buses
34  Place Hedi Chaker
35  Town Hall
36  Supermarket
38  French Consulate
41  Southern Bus Station
42  Harbour Markets
44  Children's Playground
46  ONAT
48  Libyan Consulate
49  Ferries to Kerkennah Islands

Popular Arts & Traditions, set in a typical 17th-century house, is much better than the average small museum.

### Information

**Tourist Office** The syndicat d'initiative (☎ 04-224606) is in the small, green-roofed pavilion in a small square on Ave Habib Bourguiba. There is more information here than is first apparent, including ferry times and bus and train timetables, all kept in the ringbound folder on the desk. The office is open from 9 am to 1 pm and 3 to 5.30 pm Monday to Thursday, and 9 am to 1.30 pm on Friday and Saturday; closed on Sunday.

**Money** There are plenty of banks for changing money along Ave Habib Bourguiba and Ave Hedi Chaker. The post office has a separate foreign exchange counter, but it will not change travellers' cheques.

**Post & Telecommunications** The post office is the enormous edifice on Ave Habib Bourguiba which occupies the entire first block from the railway station. It is open Monday to Saturday from 8 am to 6 pm and Sunday from 9 to 11 am. There is an international telephone counter inside the post office, and it's possible to dial either direct or through the operator.

**Consulates** France, Italy and Libya have consulates in Sfax, all in the new town.

The Libyan Consulate is at 35 Rue Alexandre Dumas, and it is open from 9 am to 2 pm Monday to Friday. There's no sign in English – look for the eagle motif. Getting a visa is not easy. Requirements change, but in late 1993 they involved an invitation channelled through the Ministry of Immigration in Tripoli. That hurdle passed, they then wanted an Arabic translation of your passport details, two passport photos and TD 68.

The French Consulate (☎ 04-220788), at the northern end of Rue Alexandre Dumas, is open for visa business on weekdays between 8.30 and 11.30 am. The Italian Consulate (☎ 04-298973) is on the 3rd floor of the new office building on the corner of Rue

Salem Harzallah and Ave Habib Thameur. It's open from 9 am until noon on weekdays.

**Shopping** There is a Monoprix supermarket on Rue Abdulkacem Chabbi, near Ave Habib Bourguiba. It's open daily from 8.30 am to 7 pm. Monoprix has another branch on Ave des Martyrs, west of the Mahdia louage station.

ONAT has a crafts shop on the southern part of Rue Salem Harzallah, open from 9.30 am to noon and 3 to 7 pm; closed on Sunday.

**Newspapers** Foreign newspapers are available from the kiosks on Place Marburg and on the northern side of Place Hedi Chaker.

**Hammam** The Hammam Sultan is close to the Dar Jellouli Museum on Rue de la Driba in the heart of the medina. It is open for women from noon to 4 pm, and for men from 4 pm to midnight.

### Medina

The walls of the medina date from the 9th century, but what you see today is a mixture of many periods.

It is a good example of a working medina, although the population has declined dramatically over the last decade because residents can't match the rents that merchants are prepared to pay.

The main access to the medina from the new city is through Bab Diwan in the middle of the southern wall. The main street through the medina, Rue Mongi Slim, is incredibly narrow and is little more than a footpath.

About halfway into the medina, Rue de la Driba leads off to the right to the well laid-out **Dar Jellouli Museum of Popular Arts & Traditions**. The museum occupies a fine old 17th-century mansion, Dar Jellouli, at the junction with Rue Sidi Ali Ennouri. The house alone is worth a visit, with its beautiful carved wood and stucco work. The exhibits help give a better grasp of everyday life in the times of the beys, and include costumes, jewellery and household implements. The display of calligraphy is especially interesting. The museum is open daily, except Monday, from 9.30 am to 4.30 pm; entry is

600 mills and there's a TD 1 charge if you want to take photos.

The most interesting part of the medina is the area of old **souqs** just north of the Great Mosque (closed to non-Muslims). The souqs worth checking out are around the covered Souq des Etoffes. You can browse at your leisure without anyone trying to flog you anything – a refreshing change.

Just outside the northern gate, Bab Jebli, are the central vegetable, meat and fish markets. The meat market is not for the squeamish. As elsewhere, the butchers hang up the heads of the day's victims to show what they've got.

At the south-eastern corner of the medina, the **Borj Ennar** fort is the headquarters of the Association de Sauvegard de la Medina. It has a good map of the medina, showing all 69 of the mosques, as well as souqs and points of historical interest.

An essential stop during your tour is coffee at the Café Diwan, built into the medina's southern wall off Rue de la Kasbah.

### Ville Nouvelle

The focal points of the ville nouvelle are the very formal main square, Place Hedi Chaker, with its statue of Bourguiba, and the town hall with its dome and clock tower.

In the town hall itself is the Museum of Antiquities, which has a few mosaics and other bits and pieces of only passing interest – you can easily pass this one up.

### Places to Stay – bottom end

Once again, the cheapies are in the medina. Most are very basic and charge around TD 5 per person. There are five close together on Rue Mongi Slim, with the *Hôtel Medina* a cut (and a couple of dinar) above the rest. The best of the gang of four just inside the Bab Diwan on Rue Borj el-Nar is the *Hôtel el-Habib*. Quieter than any of these is the *Hôtel du Sud*, a bit harder to locate on Rue Dar Essebai near the junction with Rue de la Driba.

### Places to Stay – middle

The best place in this category is the *Hôtel*

*Alexandre* (☎ 04-221911), at 21 Rue Alexandre Dumas. It is good value at TD 10.500/16 for single/double rooms, with bath and breakfast included. There's ample hot water.

Almost next door to the Alexandre is the somewhat run-down *Hôtel de la Paix* (☎ 04-221436). It claims to have single rooms for TD 4.500, but you'll do well to actually get one for that price. You'll more likely be up for TD 9/11 a single/double. There's hot water, but the shower only delivers when held at knee height – which makes washing your hair a challenge. Breakfast here is an extra TD 1.

The two-star *Hôtel Colisée* (☎ 04-227800), on Ave Taieb Mehiri, has singles/doubles for TD 18.500/27 with breakfast, and TD 1.500 extra with bath. There's not much between it and the *Hôtel Thyna* (☎ 04-225317), on the corner of Rue Habib Maazoun and Place Marburg.

The *Hôtel Mondial* (☎ 04-226620), at the harbour end of Rue Habib Maazoun, is an outstandingly dull example of functional concrete architecture. Singles/doubles are TD 18/27.

### Places to Stay – top end

If you can afford it, the place to stay is the classy *Hôtel Les Oliviers* (☎ 04-225188), on Ave Habib Thameur, two blocks south of the town hall. It is a grand old building which still has an air of elegance. Rooms cost TD 22/34 for singles/doubles with bath and breakfast, and TD 3 more with air-conditioning. The hotel has a good bar and also a swimming pool.

Sfax's newest monster is the four-star *Hôtel Sfax Centre* (☎ 04-225700), on Ave Habib Bourguiba. Rooms cost TD 65/75 with air-conditioning; there's a swimming pool and all the other frills.

### Places to Eat

For cheap Tunisian food, there are a few good places just inside Bab Diwan. To the right as you enter is the clean *Restaurant Tunisien*, where a main meal costs around

TD 1.700. There are a couple of others up to the left of the Bab Diwan.

The small and cosy *Restaurant Saada* on Rue Mongi Slim also has quite reasonable food and friendly service.

The *Restaurant Colombia*, opposite the SNTRI bus station on Rue de Tazerka, is a good spot to grab a bite while you wait for your bus. You have to pay first – the owners got fed up with people running for their buses without paying!

There's good seafood from TD 4 at the *Restaurant Le Pecheur* near the Colombia on the corner of Ave Ali Bach Hamba. There's also large helpings of techno-pop played at high volume.

For a minor splurge, the *Restaurant Chez Nous*, towards the port on Rue Patrice Lumumba, is worth a try. It has a fairly extensive menu and also serves alcohol. Expect to pay around TD 8 per person, plus drinks. Top of the range is the *Le Corail* seafood restaurant at 39 Rue Habib Maazoun, near the Hôtel Thyna. A meal here will lighten your wallet of upwards of TD 12, plus wine.

If you're after a cold beer, the nicest surroundings are at the *Hôtel Les Oliviers*. It'll set you back TD 1.800 though. If you're after several cold beers, the spit-and-sawdust style small bar opposite the harbour on Ave Ali Bach Hamba is perfectly adequate and charges TD 1.

### Getting There & Away

**Air** The Tunis Air (☎ 04-228628) office is at 4 Ave de l'Armée. Air France (☎ 04-224847) has an office at 15 Rue Taieb Mehiri. There is at least one flight to Tunis (TD 36.300 one way, TD 70.600 return) every day except Sunday, as well as two flights a week to Paris.

The airport (☎ 04-242500) is six km from town on the Gafsa road at Tyna.

**Bus** The SNTRI office is almost opposite the railway station, at the eastern end of Ave Habib Bourguiba. There are departures for Gabès (five daily), Jerba (two daily), Medenine (three daily) and Tunis (four daily).

Booking in advance is advisable, although this is not always possible, as most buses are in transit.

There are two stations for buses run by the local transport authority, Soretras. Services to the north, including Sousse, Kairouan and Mahdia, leave from the station north of the medina on Ave de Martyrs.

Services to Gafsa, Gabès, Jerba, Medenine and other points south leave from the bus station at the western end of Ave Habib Bourguiba.

Local buses leave from the vacant lot to the north of the medina near the junction of Ave des Martyrs and Ave du 18 Janvier.

**Train** The railway station is at the eastern end of Ave Habib Bourguiba, and is a grand affair. Southbound, there are trains to Gabès (2½ hours, TD 6.250 1st class) at 2.15 and 11.28 am, and to Gafsa (five hours) and Metlaoui at 1.43 am. Northbound, there are five departures daily to Sousse (two hours, TD 5.700 1st class) and Tunis (four hours, TD 10.250 1st class).

**Taxi** The louage situation is even more complicated than the buses, with no fewer than five departure points. The division of destinations between stations is not based on anything straightforward, like north and south. They appear to have been drawn from a hat. Fortunately, the stations are not far apart.

Most leave from a shady square just north of the post office at the junction of Ave de l'Armée and Ave Ali Belhaouane. Destinations include Tunis (TD 9.050), Sousse (TD 5.050), Gabès (TD 5.650), Douz (TD 9) and Tozeur (TD 11).

Services for the Libyan capital of Tripoli (TD 20) leave from just to the west of Bab Diwan on Ave Ali Belhaouane. These vehicles are a distinctive yellow and white, many with Libyan markings.

On the other side of Ave Ali Belhaouane is the louage station to Gafsa (TD 9.100), Tataouine (TD 8.900), Jerba (TD 10.850), Kasserine (TD 6.900) and Sbeitla (TD 5.950).

Mahres (TD 1.200) has its own station 200 metres farther west along Ave Ali Belhaouane, opposite the junction with Rue Dag Hammarskjold.

Mahdia, too, has its own station, north of the medina on Ave des Martyrs, opposite the northern Soretras bus station. The trip to Mahdia costs TD 3.650.

**Car Rental** The following agencies have offices in Sfax: Avis (☎ 04-224605), Rue Tahar Sfar; Europcar (☎ 04-226680), 16 Ave Habib Bourguiba; and Hertz (☎ 04-223553), 47 Ave Habib Bourguiba.

**Sea** Ferries for the Kerkennah Islands leave from the port, a 10-minute walk from town hall. Timetables change seasonally, the frequency ranging from eight crossings a day in summer to four a day in winter. Current timetables are displayed at the port and at the syndicat d'initiative office. In summer, if you are taking a vehicle across and want to get on the first or second ferry, it is necessary to join the queue around 6 am to be assured of a place. The trip costs 500 mills for passengers, and TD 3.500 for a car. The crossing takes about 1¼ hours in good weather.

## KERKENNAH ISLANDS

This group of islands lies only 25 km off the coast from Sfax, but the pace of life is definitely a gear or two lower than on the mainland. If you want a place to do nothing for a couple of days, this isn't a bad choice. However, if it's a tropical-island paradise you're after, this definitely isn't it: the palm trees are all very shabby, the islands are extremely dry and the highest point is about three metres above sea level. The sea gets deep very slowly, which makes swimming pretty hopeless.

The two main islands, **Ile Gharbi** and **Ile Chergui**, are connected by a small causeway dating back to Roman times. Ile Gharbi has little more than the ferry port at Sidi Youssef, from where it's a 16-km drive to the causeway. Chergui has a bit more to offer – a few tourist resorts on the north coast at **Sidi Fredj** and the small village of **Remla**, the 'capital' of the islands. There is not a lot of tourist development, although the place is popular with British charter tourists in summer. In winter, the tourist hotels are virtually deserted.

Fishing is the islanders' main activity, and they still use traditional fish traps made from palm fronds. Lines of palm fronds are stuck in the sea bed in a 'V' shape, and the fish are then driven into this large funnel and into a small trap at the end.

**El-Attaya** is a small village right at the far tip of Ile Chergui, 12 km from Remla. If the weather is not too scorchingly hot, it is a pleasant walk (catch a bus there or back) or bike ride.

## Information

**Money** Remla has a branch of the UIB bank 50 metres from the Hôtel el-Jazira, down towards the sea. It's open from Monday to Thursday from 8 to 11.30 am and 2 to 5 pm and on Friday from 8 to 11 am and 1.30 to 4 pm. In July and August, it's open only from 7.30 am till noon from Monday to Friday.

It's much easier to change money at one of the hotels. The Cercina, Farhat and Grand all offer facilities, but only at certain times. Check at reception.

## Things to See & Do

**Borj el-Hissar** This is generally described as a Turkish fort, which is a bit misleading. The most interesting aspect of the site is the Roman ruins that surround the fort. It is well worth the 40-minute walk, clearly signposted from near the Hôtel Le Grand. You get the feeling that you are stumbling across something previously undiscovered, with mosaics covered by sand and ruins disappearing into the sea. There is a janitor who is very happy to talk about the site – for a small consideration.

**Fishing Trips** The Farhat and Le Grand hotels offer half-day outings for TD 18 complete with fish lunch, half-bottle of wine and all the gear.

Alternatively, ask the fishing enthusiasts who moor their boats near the Hôtel Cercina.

Guys like Jaber Khemis will take you out for a few hours for TD 5.

## Places to Stay

The only hotel in Remla is the very basic *Hôtel el-Jazira* (☎ 04-281058). It is quite clean and friendly, has showers and is next to the bus stop. It charges TD 6 per person, with breakfast. The hotel is also the main social point on the islands, as it has the only bar (900 mills for a beer) and one of the few restaurants.

The Zone Touristique resort strip is on the other side of the island at Sidi Fredj, eight km from Remla. There's nothing else at Sidi Fredj, so you're pretty much committed to staying and eating there unless you have transport.

The *Hôtel Cercina* (☎ 04-281228) is both the cheapest and by far the most convenient place to stay if you are on foot. It is only 200 metres from the bus stop. The only problem is that most of the 'rooms' are horrible, claustrophobic concrete shacks which are let out in summer for a ridiculous TD 18/26 for singles/doubles with breakfast. In winter, the rate drops to TD 6 per person. The best bet is to ask for one of the pleasant rooms that overlook the sea.

The *Hôtel el-Kastil* (☎ 04-281212) next door doesn't have a lot to offer, especially in winter when the restaurant is closed and the place goes into hibernation. Accommodation is in bizarre, square, whitewashed huts that look like foreign legion punishment cells.

The up-market options are at the eastern end of the resort strip: the two-star *Hôtel Farhat* (☎ 04-228555) and *Le Grand* (☎ 04-281266). Both are fully booked by the charter trade in summer. In the low season, you can enjoy their facilities (tennis, swimming pool) for TD 30 a double with breakfast.

There is no indication that the enormous *Residence Club* is about to reopen. The place is falling down, the swimming pool is full of rubble and the sheep droppings in the rooms are the only sign of life.

## Places to Eat

There's not a lot to choose from. At Remla,

the friendly *Restaurant Wafa* has good grilled fish and chips for TD 3.500, and chicken and chips for TD 1.600. The *Restaurant La Sirène* has a prime location on the waterfront at the end of the road next to the Hôtel el-Jazira. It has a shady terrace and meals for around TD 7, as well as beers for 900 mills.

The best restaurant out at the resort strip is at the *Cercina*. The drawback is the length of time it takes to deliver the goods.

Wherever you end up, look out for the local speciality, a thick, spicy octopus soup called tchich.

### Getting There & Away
See the Getting There & Away section for Sfax for details of ferries travelling between Sfax and Sidi Youssef.

### Getting Around
**Bus** There is a small bus network which connects the towns of the islands, and there are always at least two or three to meet each

ferry. One has a 'hotel' sign in the window and goes via Sidi Fredj (750 mills), from where it's a one-km walk to the Farhat and Grand hotels. All the buses go to Remla.

The Remla bus station is right next to the Hôtel el-Jazira. There are a couple of buses daily to El-Attaya. Be careful that you don't get stranded there, because there's no return buses after about 3 pm. If you do get stuck, there is a bit of local traffic and hitching is possible.

Leaving Kerkennah, there are buses from Remla and the Sidi Fredj junction about an hour before the ferry. Times are posted in the bus-station window.

There are also share taxis charging TD 1.200.

**Bicycle** The lack of hills makes bicycling the ideal way of getting around. It's a pity that the bicycles themselves are far from ideal. The resort hotels ask an exorbitant TD 1.500 (negotiable) for some horrendous old boneshakers that leave you sore for days.

# Southern Tunisia

The attractions in the south of the country are many – the Saharan oasis towns of Douz and Tozeur, the shimmering chotts, the troglodyte dwellings of Matmata, the ksour (fortified strongholds) around Tataouine, and the resort island of Jerba, reputedly the land of the legendary Lotus-Eaters.

Summer is not the time to visit. It's so hot, especially inland, that it can be a real effort to move. If you are here at this time of year, it makes a lot of sense to adopt the local habit of disappearing indoors during the heat of the day. The flip side of the coin is that while you might be shivering your butt off in Europe in winter, the temperature in southern Tunisia will still be a very bearable 15°C or so.

## Chott el-Jerid

The Chott el-Jerid is an immense salt lake covering almost 5000 sq km. It is dry for the greater part of the year, when the surface becomes incredibly blistered and cracked, and shimmers in the heat. A road on a two-metre-high causeway has been built right across the middle of it, and there are regular buses making the crossing between Kebili and Tozeur – a worthwhile trip. It is quite weird to drive across and see the water that has collected on either side of the road: because of the chemicals present, it may be pink on one side and green on the other. It is even more weird to come across small cafés

### Dates

Until very recent times, life in the Sahara desert was almost entirely dependent on one remarkable plant: the date palm (Phoenix dactylifera).

So important was the date to desert life that the traditional way of assessing the size of an oasis was in terms of the number of palms it could support, rather than the number of people. The largest of the Tunisian oases is Douz, with more than 300,000 palms.

The palm is much more than a source of food. The date palm provides all the essentials for existence in the harsh desert environment.

The trunk is used for building, and it can also be hollowed out to channel water. Its leaves are used for thatching, and the fibre can be woven into mats and rope. The woody fruiting stems are used to make a variety of goods ranging from brooms to birdcages. Nothing goes to waste. Even date pits are used: in the old days they were roasted and ground to make an ersatz coffee; these days they are more likely to be ground up as an animal fodder.

The very presence of the date palm is an indicator of the desert's most precious resource – water. The date palm is very specific in its climatic requirements. There is an old Arab saying that it likes 'its feet in heaven and its head in hell' – a reference to the tree's need for both very high summer temperatures and lots of water (about 500 litres a day in summer). The critical requirement, however, is that minimum temperatures never fall below 18°C during the March/April flowering season.

The palms require intense management. Male and female flowers are produced on separate trees, and the female flowers need to be pollinated by hand to bear fruit successfully. The busiest time of year, however, is harvest season in November – just in time for the Christmas tables of Europe.

There are more than a hundred varieties. The most prized is the deglat nour (finger of light), which comprises more than 50% of all plantings. Dates can be propagated from seeds, but these do not produce true to type. They are normally grown from suckers, which sprout profusely from the base of mature palms and are clones of the parent. They start bearing fruit at 10 years and reach full production of about 40 kg per palm at about 20 years. They can live for as long as 150 years. ■

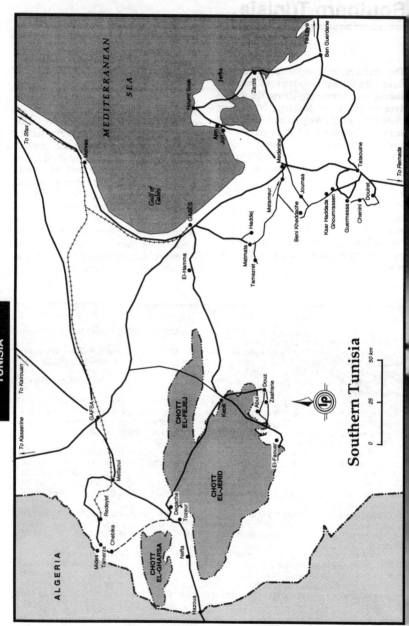

Southern Tunisia

and souvenir stalls by the side of the road at regular intervals! Mirages are also a common occurrence, and if you have picked a sunny day to cross you're bound to see some stunning optical effects.

The oasis towns of Tozeur and Nefta are right on the edge of the chott, and are welcome patches of green in an area that is otherwise totally barren. The oases rely wholly on fresh spring water, and there is fortunately enough to make quite intensive agriculture possible. The main crop is the famous and incredibly succulent deglat nour date, which is harvested in November – a good time to visit the area, as the weather is moderate and there is plenty of activity. Many villagers work in other parts of the country but return home every year for the date harvest.

## GAFSA

Gafsa is the major regional service town of the area, catering mainly for the phosphate mines which are in the surrounding hills. It holds very little of interest for the average visitor, although the hills – especially the Seldja Gorge, to the south-west on the Tozeur road – are well worth a visit.

### Information

There is a small tourist office (☎ 06-221644) in the small, dusty square by the Roman pools. It opens during standard syndicat d'initiative hours.

There are branches of all the major banks in and around the centre, and the post office is on Ave Habib Bourguiba, 300 metres north of the kasbah. For international phone calls, try the taxiphone offices next to the Mosque of Sidi Bou Yacoub and on Rue Houcine

Bouzaiane, off Ave Taieb Mehiri. The offices are open daily from 7 am to 10 pm.

### Roman Pools

These twin pools are easily located at the southern end of Ave Habib Bourguiba. There is little to see, but there is a pleasant café next to one, and it's easy to while away an hour or so watching the young boys jumping off the nearby roofs into the pool.

Right by the entrance to the pools is a small **museum** which houses, among other things, a couple of large mosaics from ancient Capsa. It is worth a quick look and is open from 8 am to noon and 2 to 6 pm; it's closed on Monday. Entry is free.

### Places to Stay – bottom end

The cheap accommodation is concentrated in the area around the bus station. The pick of the bunch is the *Hôtel de la République* (☎ 06-221807), on Rue Ali Belhaouane around the corner from the bus station. The place is clean and friendly and asks TD 6/9.500 for singles/doubles with breakfast, although this is definitely negotiable. Hot showers are 500 mills.

The *Hôtel el-Bechir* (☎ 06-223239), right next door, charges only TD 3/4 with free hot showers. It would be great if the toilets weren't so seriously on the nose.

It's a good idea to stay well away from the dilapidated *Hôtel de l'Oasis*. It appears to be on the point of collapse.

The *Hôtel Moussa* (☎ 06-223333) is good value at TD 7.500/10 for singles/doubles with breakfast. The trouble is that it's a fair way from the centre on Ave de la Liberté (the Tozeur road).

Other budget possibilities include the

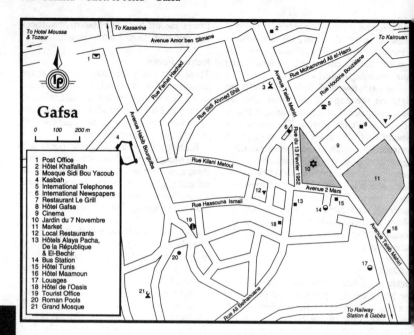

## Gafsa

0    100    200 m

1  Post Office
2  Hôtel Khalfallah
3  Mosque Sidi Bou Yacoub
4  Kasbah
5  International Telephones
6  International Newspapers
7  Restaurant Le Grill
8  Hôtel Gafsa
9  Cinema
10 Jardin du 7 Novembre
11 Market
12 Local Restaurants
13 Hôtels Alaya Pacha,
   De la République
   & El-Bechir
14 Bus Station
15 Hôtel Tunis
16 Hôtel Maamoun
17 Louages
18 Hôtel de l'Oasis
19 Tourist Office
20 Roman Pools
21 Grand Mosque

To Hotel Moussa & Tozeur
To Kasserine
Avenue Amor ben Slimane
To Kairouan
Rue Ferhat Hached
Rue Sidi Ahmed Shili
Avenue Taieb Mehiri
Rue Mohammed Ali el-Hami
Rue Houcine Bouzaiane
Avenue Habib Bourguiba
Rue Kilani Metoui
Rue du 13 Février 1952
Avenue 2 Mars
Rue Hassouna Ismail
Rue Ali Belhaouane
Avenue Taieb Mehiri
To Railway Station & Gabès

TUNISIA

rather spartan *Hôtel Tunis* (☎ 06-221660), off Ave 2 Mars, at TD 3 per person with free cold shower. The *Hôtel Khalfallah* (☎ 06-221468), off Ave Taieb Mehiri, charges TD 5 per person with breakfast. It used to be quite a reasonable joint, but these days it's heading for skid row. It claims to have hot water; maybe it does sometimes.

### Places to Stay – middle

The best hotel in town is the three-star *Hôtel Maamoun* (☎ 06-222433), just south of the main market square on Ave Taieb Mehiri. Large, comfortable rooms with en suite bathrooms cost TD 28/40 for singles/doubles. Full board, available for TD 33/50, is not a bad idea given the lack of reasonable restaurants in town. The hotel also has a swimming pool.

It's hard to miss the *Hôtel Gafsa* (☎ 06-224000), the only multistorey building in the middle of town. It charges TD 27.500/40 for singles/doubles with breakfast.

### Places to Eat

Gafsa is not a place to visit for its restaurants, and if you're here on a Friday the pickings are especially thin. There are a few basic places around the central square outside the bus station, the best of these being the *Restaurant Carthage* (closed Fridays).

The *Restaurant du Peuple* is one of three gargottes in the first street on the left through the arch opposite the Hôtel Alaya Pacha.

For something a bit better, the basement restaurant in the *Hôtel Gafsa* is very popular, probably because it serves alcohol, although the food is also pretty good. The *Restaurant Le Grill* behind the market also looks promising, but it too is closed on Friday.

The *Hôtel Maamoun* does a three-course menu for TD 7.500.

### Getting There & Away

**Bus** The bus station is right in the centre of town, next to the Hôtel Tunis. There are ticket windows for prebooking, and even boarding announcements.

SNTRI runs eight buses a day to Tunis (six hours, TD 12.530). There are four between 9.30 am and 2.30 pm, then four more between 11.30 pm and 1.30 am.

The buses run by the local company, Sotregafsa, are an amazing collection of wrecks that somehow are kept running – minus the odd panel etc.

Eight buses a day attempt the run to Tozeur and Nefta, with departures from 7.15 am to 6.15 pm. There are also buses to Sousse (6 am), Sfax, Gabès, Kasserine and Le Kef. There are regular buses to Metlaoui, some of which continue to Redeyef and the mountain oasis town of Tamerza.

**Train** Train services from Gafsa are of little more than academic interest. The station itself is three km to the south of town, and about 800 mills by taxi. There is just one train a day to Metlaoui, at 5.53 am, and a train to Sfax at 8.38 pm. It's much more convenient to take a bus or louage.

**Taxi** The louage station is five minutes' walk from the centre of town. Take the road to the railway station at the intersection opposite the Hôtel Maamoun, and it's next to the Esso service station. There are regular departures for Metlaoui (TD 1.400) and Tozeur (TD 3.500) and other departures to Tunis (TD 13), Sfax (TD 8.100), Kasserine and Gabès.

## AROUND GAFSA
### Metlaoui & the Seldja Gorge
There is little of interest in the drab town of Metlaoui, 42 km south-west of Gafsa, but it is the place to come for a visit to the spectacular Seldja Gorge west of the town.

The best way to see the gorge is to catch the Lizard Rouge, a restored, 19th-century train with red upholstery, formerly used by the Bey of Tunis, which is now laid on purely for the tourists. It doesn't run every day – only if it has been booked by a tour group – so you'll need to check with the booking agent, Transtours Tunisie (☎ 240634), in Metlaoui. If the train is running it costs TD

10 for the 1½-hour return journey. Thursdays and Fridays are the best bet. If you want to do it independently, you can try to hitch a ride on one of the phosphate trains which run regularly from Metlaoui through the gorge to Redeyef.

**Places to Stay** Metlaoui has just one hotel, the *Hôtel Ennacim* (☎ 06-240271), a km or so from the centre of town on the road to Tozeur. Singles/doubles are TD 9/13. There is a restaurant attached to the hotel and full or half-board is available.

**Getting There & Away** There are regular buses and louages between Tozeur and Gafsa, and these all pass through Metlaoui. There are also regular buses between Gafsa and Metlaoui, some of which continue on to Redeyef and Tamerza.

## TOZEUR
As it is the major town of the chott area, Tozeur has developed into something of a tourist centre – the number of Land Rovers and buses that comes through has to be seen to be believed. This is 'accessible Sahara' and, although you really have to get into Algeria to appreciate the enormous extent of this desert, there are enough dunes and picture-postcard oases in this area to make it a compulsory stop for any package tour – a fact reflected in the number of souvenir shops which have sprung up.

These shops are colourful affairs, mainly because of the displays of the rugs for which the area is well known. It's not a bad place to buy rugs, but quality and price vary enormously, so do a bit of comparing before buying.

Despite the pressures and prosperity which tourism brings, the town maintains a laid-back atmosphere and is indeed a pleasant place to pass a few days.

### Information
**Tourist Offices** There are two tourist offices in Tozeur. The local syndicat d'initiative (☎ 06-450034) is on Place Ibn Châabat, right near the corner of Ave Farhat Hached. There is also a branch of the national tourist

office (☎ 06-450088) on Ave Abdulkacem Chebbi, next door to the Hôtel el-Jerid, about 10 minutes' walk from the post office. This is by far the more useful of the two offices.

**Money** There are a couple of banks by the main intersection on the Nefta road.

**Post & Telecommunications** The post office is on the main square by the market (which is busiest on Thursday).

There's a small telephone office near the post office, open daily from 8 am to 9.30 pm. It has payphones only.

### Dar Charait Museum

Other than the Bardo in Tunis, this is the only museum in the country that's worth going out of your way to see. It's expensive by museum standards at TD 2.500, plus TD 1.500 to take photos, but it's a class act.

It has an extensive collection of pottery

and antiques, as well as an art gallery, but the star features are the rooms set up as replicas of scenes from Tunisian life, past and present. They include the bedroom of the last bey, a palace scene, a typical kitchen, a hammam, wedding scenes and a Bedouin tent. The museum attendants set the tone, dressed as servants of the bey.

The museum is open from 8 am until midnight every day.

The latest addition to the Dar Charait complex is a sound and light show titled '1001 Nights', open every night from 6 to 11 pm for TD 5.

There's also a bookshop selling a good range of the Editions Alif publications, including their pop-up Tunis medina and oasis books, jigsaws and other books that are hard to find elsewhere.

### Oasis

The huge oasis (palmeraie) is a fascinating

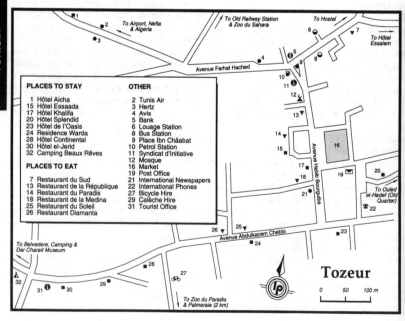

**PLACES TO STAY**
1 Hôtel Aicha
15 Hôtel Essaada
17 Hôtel Khalifa
20 Hôtel Splendid
23 Hôtel de l'Oasis
24 Residence Warda
28 Hôtel Continental
30 Hôtel el-Jerid
32 Camping Beaux Rêves

**PLACES TO EAT**
7 Restaurant du Sud
13 Restaurant de la République
14 Restaurant du Paradis
18 Restaurant de la Medina
25 Restaurant du Soleil
26 Restaurant Diamanta

**OTHER**
2 Tunis Air
3 Hertz
4 Avis
5 Bank
6 Louage Station
8 Bus Station
9 Place Ibn Châabat
10 Petrol Station
11 Syndicat d'Initiative
12 Mosque
16 Market
19 Post Office
21 International Newspapers
22 International Phones
27 Bicycle Hire
29 Calèche Hire
31 Tourist Office

**Tozeur**

place to explore. Covering an area of more than 10 sq km, it is too big to explore successfully on foot. The best bet is to hire a bicycle – TD 1 per hour or TD 4 for half a day – and set forth. If that sounds too energetic, horse-drawn calèches can be hired from the hotels Continental and El-Jerid for TD 5 per hour.

On the southern side of the oasis is the Zoo du Paradis, entry TD 1, where the exhibits include a Coca-Cola-drinking camel. As usual, the exhibits are kept in depressingly small cages.

### Belvedere Rocks
A sandy track off the extension of Ave Abdulkacem Chebbi, near the Dar Charait Museum, leads to a group of rocks known as the Belvedere. Steps have been cut into the highest rock, giving access to a spectacular view over the oasis and the chott. It's a pleasant 20-minute walk, with the best views in the early morning.

Near the rocks is a small pool fed by a hot spring – a popular local bathing spot. The Belvedere also has a dismal little camp site (see Places to Stay).

### Ouled el-Hadef
The town's old quarter, with its maze of narrow alleys and intricate, geometric brickwork, is a good place for a wander. It's home to the small Museum Archeologique et Traditionnel, signposted from near the Hôtel Splendid; entry is TD 1. The museum is interesting enough, but it is totally overshadowed by the Dar Charait. It's open from 8.30 am to noon and 3 to 5 pm every day except Sunday.

### Zoo du Sahara
This place is worth a mention only as somewhere to avoid like the plague. The place is a disgrace, complete with live scorpions housed in cigarette packets – 'just the thing for the mother-in-law' touts the attendant.

### Places to Stay – bottom end
**Camping** The better of Tozeur's two camp sites is *Camping Beaux Rêves* (☎ 06-451242), just past the tourist office on the way to the Dar Charait. There's plenty of shade, a café and hot showers for TD 3.500 per person.

*Camping Belvedere*, out by the rocks of the same name, has no shade, disgusting toilets and nothing to eat or drink. They want TD 2 for your company.

**Hostel** Tozeur's hostel (☎ 06-450514) is

**TUNISIA**

---

### The Welcome Oasis
'Oasis' is a Greek word thought to be derived from the Egyptian *wah*, meaning a fertile place in the desert. This carries the assumption that it is a place where the ample artesian water that lies beneath the Sahara comes to the surface.

There can be few more remarkable contrasts in nature than that between the harsh yellows and browns of the desert and the vivid green splash of an oasis. The oases are full of surprises. What from a distance appears to be no more than a large patch of palms turns out to be a veritable Garden of Eden.

An ingenious three-tiered system of agriculture has been devised to get the most out of the available resources. The towering date palm – normally the prized deglat nour variety – represents the top tier. Its giant fronds provide the shelter for an amazing range of fruit trees, grown as the middle tier. The unique oasis conditions allow plants that normally have quite different requirements, such as bananas and olives, to be grown right next to each other. Other fruits include pomegranates, figs and a range of citrus. These fruit trees in turn offer sufficient protection from the harsh sun for the growing of vegetable and vine crops. Again, the range is remarkable – from juicy carrots to beans, cucumbers, melons and tomatoes.

The irrigation systems that distribute the lifeblood of the oasis, water, can be sophisticated affairs. The system at Tozeur, where the waters rise from more than 200 springs, was originally devised hundreds of years ago by the noted mathematician Ibn Chabbat. ∎

only for the dedicated. It is in the usual inconvenient location – at least 1.5 km out of the centre on the Tunis road. A bed in a dorm costs TD 4.

**Hotels** The *Hôtel Khalifa* (☎ 06-450068) is right in the middle of town, opposite the market on Ave Habib Bourguiba. Although the place is fairly new, it's not very well built. However, it's a reasonably clean and friendly place. Rooms cost TD 6 per person, including breakfast. Hot showers are TD 1. Unfortunately, the only rooms with windows overlook busy Ave Habib Bourguiba.

Nearby is the *Hôtel Essaada* (☎ 06-450097), which offers no more than you would expect for TD 2.500 per person, and cold showers for 500 mills.

Inconvenient, but much better than either of these, is the *Hôtel Essalem* (☎ 06-450981), 150 metres past the roundabout at the western end of Ave Farhat Hached. It's quiet and friendly and has singles/doubles for TD 6/12 with breakfast and hot showers or bath.

### Places to Stay – middle

The best place in this category is the *Residence Warda* (☎ 06-452597), not far from the centre of town on Ave Abdulkacem Chebbi. The carpet is long overdue for replacement, but the rooms are clean and comfortable. It boasts the hottest hot water around and showers that deliver it at a great rate – a welcome change from the usual dribble. Singles/doubles cost TD 8.500/13, with a good breakfast included.

The *Hôtel Splendid* (☎ 06-450053) is behind the post office on the edge of the old town. 'Once Splendid' would be a more appropriate name for this French colonial relic that charges TD 12.500/18 for singles/doubles with breakfast. The owner does, however, have a splendid collection of notes and coins from all over the world.

The hotel's noisy and smoke-filled back bar has beers for TD 1.

### Places to Stay – top end

Three and four-star hotels are popping up like mushrooms on the northern edge of the palmeraie along Ave Abdulkacem Chebbi.

The three-star *Hôtel Continental* (☎ 06-450526) is as good as any. It's set back from the road among the palm trees and has a shaded swimming pool. It charges TD 22.500/34 in winter for singles/doubles with breakfast, and 25.200/37.400 in summer. Full board costs only TD 2.500 extra per person.

The *Hôtel de l'Oasis* (☎ 06-450522), on Ave Abdulkacem Chebbi and opposite the southern end of Ave Habib Bourguiba, is quite a sight at night with its illuminated, traditionally styled brick façade. It has a bit of class and is more central than any of its more up-market rivals. It charges TD 33/46 in the low season, and TD 37/52 in the high season.

### Places to Eat

For cheap food and friendly service you can't beat the *Restaurant du Paradis*, just a couple of doors along from the Hôtel Essaada. They have good soups and salad as well as all the other usual things, and the tables outside are a pleasant place to sit on a warm evening.

Just around the corner from the Hôtel Khalifa is the *Restaurant de la Medina*. There's not a lot to choose from, but the food is good. A generous serving of couscous and turkey costs TD 2.300.

The *Restaurant du Sud*, 100 metres east of the bus station on Ave Farhat Hached, specialises in the cuisine typical of the Sfax region. The place is spotless and most dishes cost less than TD 2.

Both the restaurants opposite the Residence Warda, the *Restaurant du Soleil* and *Restaurant Diamanta*, do local food of a pretty good standard.

The only other budget option is the *Restaurant de la République*, in an arcade off Ave Habib Bourguiba near the mosque. It has similar fare but is more expensive.

For a real lash out, try the TD 18 menu at the Dar Charait's *Restaurant Shehrezad*. The setting is positively palatial. The museum's café, with its divan seating and elaborate tilework, has performances by local musicians in the evening. It overlooks the palmeraie, which is illuminated at night.

A local breakfast speciality is a kind of deep-fried doughnut which is very filling and guaranteed to be devoid of any flavour or nourishment.

There are plenty of cafés and a couple of pâtisseries along Ave Habib Bourguiba. For fresh juices, try the pâtisserie right opposite the main mosque.

### Getting There & Away
**Air** The new Tunis Air (☎ 06-452127) office is a good 15 minutes' walk from the centre of town, out towards the airport along the Nefta road. It's the unmarked white building opposite the Hertz car-rental agency.

The airport is four km from town, TD 1 by taxi. Tuninter runs four flights a week to Tunis (TD 40.100 one way, TD 79.400 return), and a flight to Jerba on Thursday afternoon at 2.30 pm (TD 28.200 one way). There's also a weekly connection to Paris.

**Bus** The bus station for both regional and SNTRI buses is on Ave Farhat Hached near the intersection with Ave Habib Bourguiba. There are two air-conditioned SNTRI buses to Tunis daily, at 11 am and 11 pm. It's advisable to buy tickets the day before. The trip takes seven hours and costs TD 14.120.

Regional buses operate regularly to Gafsa (six daily, TD 3.450) and Nefta (six daily, 850 mills), as well as to Redeyef (three daily, TD 3.700), Douz (2.30 pm, TD 4.100) and Gabès (3 pm, 6.600).

The 9.30 am bus to Nefta goes all the way to Hazoua at the Tunisian border post. See the Nefta section for full details about tackling this border crossing into Algeria.

**Train** Tozeur has a railway station to the north of town but passenger services have been discontinued. Trains from Sfax now run only as far as Metlaoui, 50 km to the north.

**Taxi** The louage station is almost opposite the bus station, in a small yard just off the street. There are regular departures to Nefta (950 mills), Gafsa (TD 3.500) and Kebili

(TD 3.750). There are also occasional louages to Tunis (TD 15.850) and Redeyef (TD 4.050).

**Car Rental** There is an Avis (☎ 06-450547) office on Ave Farhat Hached, and a Hertz (☎ 06-450214) office is on the Nefta road.

## AROUND TOZEUR
### Mountain Oases
These oases, in the rugged ranges to the north-west of Tozeur, offer some of the most spectacular settings in the country – rich pockets of green among the barren surrounding hills.

While there are numerous small oases, it is the settlements at Tamerza, Mides and Chebika that draw most of the visitors. They are three very different sites with one thing in common – the original towns were all destroyed when the region was hit by 22 days of torrential rain in 1969. The freak rains turned the earthen houses into mud, and the towns were abandoned in favour of new settlements nearby.

**Tamerza** is the largest of the oases, nestled in a fairly broad valley, and the only one accessible by public transport. The shell of the old walled town is to the north of the palmeraie, opposite the flash Hôtel Tamerza Palace. The new town is a typical, characterless modern sprawl. There's a bank and a few small shops.

The setting at **Mides** is little short of spectacular, with the site cut in half by a deep gorge that was previously employed strategically as the town's southern fortification. Mides is the least accessible of the three sites. It's just one km from the Algerian border.

The oasis at **Chebika** has striking views out over the Chott el-Gharsa.

**Places to Stay & Eat** Accommodation and eating possibilities in this area are pretty limited and, apart from camping, are confined to Tamerza.

*Camping* There are two places at Mides calling themselves camping grounds. Neither have any set fees or facilities – just a patch of ground to pitch a tent. You will need to take your own food, or buy meals from local families for whatever price you can negotiate.

**Hostel** Tamerza has a *Maison des Jeunes*, on the southern edge of town towards Chebika. It charges the standard TD 4.

**Hotels** The *Hôtel Les Cascades* (☎ 06-448520), next to a small waterfall on the edge of the palmeraie, charges over the odds at TD 13/18 for singles/doubles with breakfast. The rooms are uninviting palm-thatched boxes with concrete floors. It's a pity, because the setting is great. The place is signposted in the middle of new Tamerza.

The well-heeled will probably prefer the four-star luxury of the *Hôtel Tamerza Palace* (☎ 06-445214), an unusual example of a big hotel attempting to blend in with its surroundings. Bed and breakfast here will set you back TD 58/78. It's worth visiting to take in the views of old Tamerza from the swimming pool terrace.

Tamerza has one restaurant outside the hotels – a small, nameless affair on the road leading down to the Hôtel Les Cascades.

**Getting There & Away** The only town in the region served by public transport is Tamerza.

**Bus** There are regular buses from Gafsa (2½ hours) and Metlaoui (two hours). From Tozeur and Nefta, take a bus to Redeyef and pick up the Tamerza bus there. Redeyef can also be reached by occasional louages from Gafsa and Metlaoui.

**Hitching** The low volume of traffic makes hitching a fairly unattractive option. The best bet would be to start from Tamerza, where there's a chance of meeting up with other people who might be going the same way. Chebika is 16 km south of Tamerza, while Mides is 11 km to the north. It's possible to take the Redeyef bus and ask to be dropped off at the Mides turn-off. From here, it's another four km along a road that is a challenge for conventional vehicles.

**Organised Tours** There are plenty of tour companies in Tozeur offering day trips that take in all three towns. They charge about TD 25 per person.

## NEFTA

Twenty-three km west of Tozeur is Nefta, the last town before the Algerian border at Hazoua. In many ways, it is a smaller version of Tozeur. The architecture is the same, with some very good examples of the highly distinctive ornamental brickwork in the old sections of town. The oasis is of equal size and importance.

Nefta is also the home of Sufism in Tunisia and there are a couple of important sites here.

---

### Sufism

The mystical Islamic sect of Sufism was formed by ascetics who wished to achieve a mystical communion with God through spiritual development rather than through the study of the Qur'an. This brought them into conflict with the religious orthodoxy but, because they were prepared to make concessions to local rites and superstitions, they were able to attract large numbers of people who had not embraced Islam. The Sufis also believed in the miraculous powers of saints, and saints' tombs became places of worship. A particular aspect of Berber Sufism in North Africa is maraboutism – the worship of a holy man endowed with magical powers.

Literally hundreds of different Sufi orders sprang up throughout the Islamic world. The differences between them lay largely in the rituals they performed and how far they deviated from the Qur'an. They were regarded with a good deal of suspicion, which was exacerbated by some of their peculiar devotional practices such as eating glass and walking on coals (which they did in order to come closer to God).

The Sufis held positions of power in Tunisia, particularly in rural areas following the breakdown of Almohad rule in the 13th century. ∎

Top: Ubari Sand Sea, Libya (AJ)
Bottom: Tuaregs, Acacus, Libya (AJ)

Gabraoun Lake, Libya (AJ)

## Information

Nefta has only one main street, Ave Habib Bourguiba (just for a change), which is the main Tozeur-Algeria road. The bank, post office, tourist office and bus station are all on the eastern side of the *corbeille* (gully).

There is a rapidly expanding cluster of hotels on the edge of the palmeraie at the western (Algerian) end of Ave Habib Bourguiba, and a ring road around the north of the town gives access to a couple of flash hotels overlooking the corbeille.

The small tourist office is set by the ring-road junction, on the right as you enter the town from Tozeur. The guy who staffs the office is quite helpful but he is there primarily to promote his services as a guide – which is fairly unnecessary as not a lot of assistance is required.

The post office is on the left, just where the road descends to cross the corbeille.

## Things to See & Do

Despite the town's attractive setting there is not much to do except explore the old town and the palmeraie.

The most obvious attraction is the spectacular **corbeille** that cuts the town in two. There's a hot spring at the northern end, hidden away in the palms below the Café de la Corbeille, with bathing pools for both men and women.

At the head of the corbeille is the **Zawiyya of Sidi Brahim**, where the Sufi saint and some of his followers are buried.

The corbeille leads to the **oasis** proper on the southern side of town. The palmeraie here is every bit as fascinating as its counterpart at Tozeur. The workers are generally happy to let you wander around, and to explain what's going on.

If you have your own transport, the guy at the tourist office insists that there is a spot 10 km out of town towards the Algerian border when he can guarantee a mirage on a sunny day. It was raining when I visited.

## Places to Stay

Nefta's cheapest hotel is the *Hôtel de la Liberté*, off Place de la Libération in the heart of the old quarter to the south of town. The best way to find it is to follow the signs to the Hôtel Habib, which is right on Place de la Libération. You then take Rue Chaffai Cherif, next to Restaurant des Amis on the north-western corner of the square, and look for the sign. If you need to ask directions, locals commonly call it the Hôtel Mahmoud – the owner is a bit of a character. What awaits you is a basic but friendly old hotel built around a vine-filled central courtyard. Beds are TD 3 per person, with free cold shower.

It's a better deal than the characterless *Hôtel Habib* (☎ 06-457497), which charges TD 7 per person with breakfast.

The best value in town is the *Hôtel Marhala* (☎ 06-457027), one of the four excellent places run by the Touring Club de Tunisie (the others are at Gammarth, Matmata and Jerba). It is on the western side of town, about 20 minutes' walk from the bus station, and is actually an old brick factory – it's better than it sounds. The rooms are a bit on the small side but they are spotless and comfortable. Singles/doubles cost TD 9.500/16 with breakfast, or TD 11/18 for rooms with shower. It's worth considering half or full board at TD 2.500 per meal because the town isn't exactly brimming with good restaurants.

By now, the Marhala should also be operating a second, rather more up-market, hotel right next door, charging TD 20/40 with breakfast. The new version has a large swimming pool, available to residents of both hotels.

The Marhala is surrounded by a growing band of three-star hotels, but if you want the best the place to go is the four-star *Sahara Palace*, spectacularly situated overlooking the town on the north-western side of the corbeille.

If it isn't open, the next best is the three-star *Hôtel Bel Horizon* (☎ 06-457088), equally well situated on the corbeille's north-eastern edge. The pool setting is great. Singles/doubles cost TD 43/60, rising to TD 53/80 for full board.

The *Hôtel Mirage* has been closed for so long now that no-one expects it to reopen.

TUNISIA

## Places to Eat

The sum total of Nefta's eateries is a few basic restaurants on Ave Habib Bourguiba near the bus station and around Place de la Libération, plus the hotel restaurants. The best of the cheapies is the *Restaurant Jemel*, next to the tourist office, which has a blackboard menu with meals for TD 2. The range isn't exactly riveting. Opposite the bus station, the *Restaurant du Sud* has a choice of couscous – take it or leave it – for TD 1.800. The *Café de la Corbeille* is a good spot to enjoy a cold drink and the views over the corbeille.

## Getting There & Away

**Bus** The bus station is on the northern side of Ave Habib Bourguiba, about 100 metres past the tourist office. SNTRI has buses to Tunis (7½ hours, TD 14.820) at 10.30 am and midnight.

There are frequent regional services to Tozeur (850 mills), buses at 9 am and 2.30 pm to Redeyef (TD 4.600) and a bus to Hazoua at 10 am (TD 1.300).

**Taxi** The louages leave fairly regularly from outside the bus station for the 20-minute ride to Tozeur (950 mills). There are also occasional departures for Hazoua (TD 1.450).

**To/From Algeria** The Algerian border is at Hazoua, 36 km south-west of Nefta. There is one bus daily from Tozeur at 9.30 am, stopping at Nefta at 10 am. Infrequent louages to Hazoua leave each day. There is no bank on the Tunisian side of the border.

Between the two border posts is a four-km stretch of neutral territory which you may have to walk across – be prepared with a hat and some water. There are occasional Algerian shared taxis and tourist vehicles but you can't rely on them.

At the Algerian post you have to declare your money and fill in a currency form. To save hassles later, read the information on money in the Algeria Facts for the Visitor chapter *carefully* before you reach this border. It is a very easygoing crossing and the officials are friendly. There is a bank on

the Algerian side at Bou Aroua but it is closed more often than it is open. If that's the case and you need to change money, you can change small amounts of cash (officially) at the customs office.

From the Algerian border post there are shared taxis to the town of El-Oued, a farther 80 km along a good bitumen road. The drivers accept either Tunisian dinar (TD 5) or Algerian dinar (AD 50). It is also possible to hitch along this stretch, but traffic is very light along the first 27 km until the road joins the road from Tébessa to El-Oued.

## KEBILI

This small regional town at the eastern edge of the Chott el-Jerid really has nothing to recommend it apart from its hot-spring baths on the road to Douz.

Facilities include a post office and bank (open for changing money from 9 am to noon only).

The baths are about a km from the centre of town. The men's pool is right by the roadside and has a couple of cafés around it. The pool for women is about 150 metres upstream and is screened by palm fronds stuck in the ground. The slightly sulphurous water gushes out of the ground at a high temperature, a couple of hundred metres from the women's pool.

## Places to Stay

There is no reason to stay overnight in Kebili. If you do get stuck, now might be the time to cast in your lot with the *Maison des Jeunes* (the standard TD 4) at the Douz turnoff. It's better maintained than the very basic *Hôtel Sahara*, about 10 minutes' walk from the centre of town on the Tozeur road.

The *Hôtel des Autriches* (☎ 05-490233) is the veteran of the resort hotels in the palmeraie. It's signposted 'to Fort des Autriches', off to the left near the military base on the Douz road and about 30 minutes' walk – or a short taxi ride – from the bus station. It's a pleasant spot with a swimming pool and terrace. Rooms are TD 28.500/42 for singles/doubles with breakfast.

## Places to Eat

There are quite a number of restaurants, but nothing to get excited about. The *Restaurant Les Palmiers*, right in the centre by the bus station, does fairly good meals. There are a few more places opposite the louage station.

## Getting There & Away

**Bus** The bus station is no more than an office on the main street, near the junction with the Gabès-Tozeur road.

There are frequent buses (either minibuses or regular-sized ones) to Douz, as well as regular departures for Tozeur and Gabès.

The SNTRI office, normally closed, is 100 metres away on the opposite side of the dusty square. There is one bus a day to Tunis, leaving at 11 am (TD 15.970).

**Taxi** It's only a short walk from the bus station to the louages, which leave throughout the day for Gabès (TD 4.350), Douz (TD 1.250) and occasionally Tozeur (TD 3.750). You can relax over a coffee at the café opposite while you wait for your louage to fill up.

## DOUZ

Although it promotes itself as 'the Gateway to the Sahara', Douz doesn't suffer from the tourist masses anywhere near as badly as Tozeur.

There is a new bank for changing money near the main intersection on the Kebili road, and opposite it there is a map showing a rough outline of the town.

The souq, the traditional centre of activity in any oasis town, is right in the middle of town. For most of the week, it is little more than a sleepy square with a scattering of souvenir shops selling local rugs. It comes alive for the popular Thursday markets, and you need to get there early before the tour groups arrive. The livestock market is signposted off Ave des Martyrs, close to the square.

Peak season in Douz is during the Sahara Festival in December and January, when the place is packed with tourists coming to watch such activities as camel racing and hunting with the famous Saluki desert dog,

an animal constructed along the same lines as the greyhound. In spite of the crush, it is generally possible to find a place to sleep – even if it's only on a mattress in a corridor.

## Things to See & Do

**Palmeraie** The palmeraie is deceptively large, the largest in fact of all the Tunisian desert oases, with more than 300,000 palm trees. The best way to explore is to walk out along the road to the Hôtel Saharien and strike off on one of the paths. The road past the Saharien continues to the Place du Festival, set on the edge of the dunes with all the flash hotels nearby.

Here you will find the much-touted Great Dune, a phenomenon that some (cynics) have suggested is not entirely natural. There is no doubt, however, about the credentials of the erg (sand sea) that surrounds the dune. It's a great spot for those all-important 'been there, done that' Sahara photos.

It takes about 30 minutes to walk to the Place du Festival from the town centre.

**Camel Rides & Safaris** It will be something of a minor miracle if you last more than 30 minutes in Douz without being asked if you want to hire a camel.

If no-one offers, the place to go looking is the café beside the tourist office. Expect to pay about TD 5 per hour – quite long enough for the average backside.

A more adventurous alternative is to go camping by camel, sleeping under the stars around a campfire. This can be organised through Kamel at the Hôtel Splendide. Douz is the base for some of the seminomadic tribes of the Nefzaoua, the name given to this south-eastern region of the country, and one family has set up a small business taking tourists out into the desert for TD 25 per night.

The trips start after the heat of the day has dispersed, with a three-hour ride out into the desert before pitching camp. Your guides prepare a fire and food, including a delicious damper-style bread cooked in the ashes. After dinner, they entertain you with desert songs before you bed down under the stars.

Fire and food are repeated in the morning before the ride home.

My trip was made more memorable by waking up in the middle of a fierce sandstorm. By morning I had become a sand dune – and the fine sand had penetrated everything, including the alarm clock inside my bag!

The two travel agencies in town, Douz Voyages (☎ 05-495315) and Abdelmoula Voyages (☎ 05-495484), both offer a range of excursions of up to eight days with accommodation in traditional, black goat-hair tents.

### Places to Stay – bottom end

**Camping** The *Desert Club* (☎ 05-495595) camping ground is set among the palm trees to the right at the end of Ave du 7 Novembre 1987. It is friendly and has plenty of shade as well as hot water. It charges TD 3 per person in tents, or TD 8 per person with breakfast to stay in their 'Bedouin' tents. The camping ground has its own restaurant and bar, and there is an international phone.

The Desert Club office in town, at 3 Place du Souq, hires out tents and other camping equipment. It offers all sorts of support services for those wanting to travel the Sahara by 4WD.

**Hotels** All the cheapies are in the town centre, around the souq and the bus station.

Management doesn't come any friendlier than at the *Hôtel 20 Mars* (☎ 05-495495), just north of the souq on the street of the same name. It is great value at TD 3 per person, with free hot showers and breakfast at 900 mills. The place is in the middle of a major facelift.

Just around the corner, on Rue Ghara Jawal, the *Hôtel Essada* (☎ 05-495019) has been completely gutted by its new owners; it should be open again by the time you read this.

The *Hôtel de la Tente* (☎ 05-495468), right by the louage station on the delightfully named Rue des Affections, is another good place. It also charges TD 3 and has free hot showers.

The management style at the *Hôtel Splendide* can best be described as eccentric. It charges TD 4 for a bed.

The squalid *Hôtel du Calme* is by the post office and should be avoided if at all possible.

### Places to Stay – middle

There are a couple of reasonable mid-range alternatives in the palmeraie, about 20 minutes' walk from the centre of town off Ave des Martyrs. Offering similar facilities are the huge *Hôtel Saharien* (☎ 05-495339), turn left at the Maison de Culture, and the *Roses de Sable* (☎ 05-495366), to the left opposite the tourist office. Both have swimming pools and restaurants. The Saharien is considerably more expensive at TD 22/34 for singles/doubles.

The road out to the Roses de Sable goes past a hammam fed by its own hot spring; it costs 500 mills a bathe.

### Places to Stay – top end

All the up-market hotels are in the Zone Touristique on the southern side of the palmeraie, facing the sand hills of the desert. The latest addition is the giant *Hôtel Tuareg* (☎ 05-495057), built in the image of an old-style kasbah, complete with crenellations. The swimming pool comes complete with a palm-covered island in the middle. Singles/doubles are TD 45/60 with breakfast. Prices are very similar at the neighbouring *Hôtel*

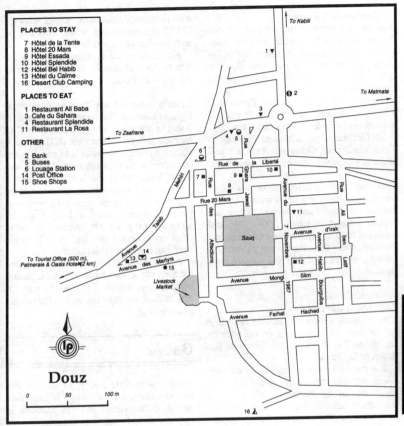

**PLACES TO STAY**
7 Hôtel de la Tente
8 Hôtel 20 Mars
9 Hôtel Essada
10 Hôtel Splendide
12 Hôtel Bel Habib
13 Hôtel du Calme
16 Desert Club Camping

**PLACES TO EAT**
1 Restaurant Ali Baba
3 Cafe du Sahara
4 Restaurant Splendide
11 Restaurant La Rosa

**OTHER**
2 Bank
5 Buses
6 Louage Station
14 Post Office
15 Shoe Shops

Douz

0     50     100 m

TUNISIA

*Sahara* (☎ 05-495246) and the *Mehari* (☎ 05-495149). The Mehari allows visitors to use the pool for TD 2.500 per day.

**Places to Eat**

For a town with such ambitions as a tourist destination, the pickings are remarkably slim.

The *Restaurant Splendide*, next to the bus station on Ave Taieb Mehiri, is one place that has set its sights on the tourist trade. It does a good chorba for TD 1.500, and Western-style dishes such as turkey schnitzel, chips and salad for TD 2.600.

The staff of the *Restaurant Ali Baba*, 100 metres north of the roundabout on the road to Kebili, are very welcoming and have a good choice, mainly under TD 2.

The *Restaurant La Rosa*, near the souq on Ave du 7 Novembre 1987, is a third possibility.

**Things to Buy**

There are three shops along Ave des Martyrs, just west of the souq, selling Saharan sandals (slip-on shoes made from camel skin). The tourist versions normally come decorated with palm motifs etc. The shops ask TD 10 to TD 15, depending on the level of decoration and quality.

## Getting There & Away

**Bus** Buses leave from the area next to the Restaurant Splendide, just by the main intersection in the centre of town. There are usually one or two buses parked nearby. The office of the regional bus company is also located here.

There are regular buses to Kebili (TD 1.050), as well as buses south to Tozeur at 8 am and to Gabès at 6.45 am and 9 pm.

SNTRI has air-conditioned services to Tunis via Tozeur, Gafsa and Kairouan at 6 am, and via Gabès, Sfax and Sousse at 9 pm.

**Taxi** The louage station, the only covered one in the country, is a block west of the bus station on Ave Taieb Mehiri. There are regular louages to Kebili (TD 1.250) and Zaafrane (600 mills). Services to Gabès and Tozeur are very infrequent – you're better off taking a louage to Kebili and another from there.

## AROUND DOUZ
### Zaafrane & Beyond

The small oasis town of Zaafrane lies some 12 km south of Douz, right on the edge of the Grand Erg Oriental. This is where the desert really starts.

It is one of the few villages in the country where you can still see the traditional goat-hair tents of the Nefzaoua. Most of the inhabitants actually live in houses like concrete blocks and have the tents set up outside, often to give shade to the families' mules, camels or goats.

Zaafrane is busiest during the date harvest in November; for the rest of the year, many of the people migrate to the east and the town slips back into the torpor that grips any desert settlement for much of the time.

The road continues on past Zaafrane to other small oases as far as El-Faouar, home to yet another nomadic tribe.

**Places to Stay** There is a hotel in Zaafrane. Singles/doubles with breakfast cost TD 13.500/21. The small oasis of Nouil, set on a small promontory into the chott due west of Douz, offers a different sort of experience

with accommodation in traditional tents for TD 12 per person full board. This can be arranged through the *Hôtel Nouil*.

According to the advertising signs by the side of the road near Zaafrane, there is also a hotel in El-Faouar.

**Getting There & Away** There are buses from Douz to Zaafrane, Sabria and El-Faouar at 7, 9 and 11 am and 1 and 2.30 pm, as well as frequent louages to Zaafrane (600 mills). A common practice in Douz is to stand on the corner of the road to Zaafrane and El-Faouar, which heads off to the south from almost opposite the louage station, and wave down any passing vehicles. Generally you will have to pay the louage fare, but you may be lucky and get a free lift. The flow of traffic dries up around 4 pm and there is never anything much on Friday afternoons.

Fridays aside, it is quite a busy road and hitching out to the end to El-Faouar should present no problems. The place to wait for lifts in Zaafrane is by the well in the middle of the village.

# Gabès

There's very little reason to stay in this modern town on the coast. It has been heavily industrialised and the pollution in both the air and water is noticeable.

The town has two supposed attractions: the beach and the oasis. The beach is raved about because it stretches so far, but it's smelly and unattractive; the oasis is nothing special either, even though it's a rare example of a maritime oasis. Despite this, dozens of tour buses disgorge their daily loads on the edge of the palmeraie, the waiting calèches take the tourists through it and the buses pick them up at the other end by the depressing zoo and crocodile farm. Calèches charge TD 10 for the experience.

## Information

**Tourist Office** The tourist office (☎ 05-270254) is in the small building in the middle of the intersection of Ave Habib Thameur and Ave Hedi Chaker, down towards the waterfront. The guy running it is reasonably helpful and there is a complete list of bus departures posted on the door.

**Money** There are a couple of banks along Ave Habib Bourguiba.

**Post & Telecommunications** The enormous new post office is on Ave Habib Bourguiba. International telephone calls can be made from the office on the corner of Ave Farhat Hached and Ave Bechir Dzir, open Monday to Saturday from 8 am to 6 pm.

**Newspapers** English, German and French newspapers are available year-round from the Librairie Jemai on Ave Habib Bourguiba, opposite Rue Bonté. In summer, the kiosk at the junction of Ave Habib Bourguiba and Ave Farhat Hached is another option.

### Things to See & Do

To get to the **palmeraie**, head west along Ave Habib Bourguiba to the oued, and then turn left and then right to cross it. The road twists and turns through the oasis until you finally come out at El-Aouadid, a small outlying town.

The crocodile farm and zoo are another km or so to the south; they are built at the site of a small Roman dam which has been reconstructed. As this is where the tour buses come to pick up their passengers after the carriage ride through the palmeraie, it is not surprising that a few entrepreneurs have set up stalls selling all sorts of junk at inflated prices. Don't waste your money on the zoo.

A path (negotiable by bicycle) heads off around the back of the dam and winds around through the palmeraie to the Chellah Club, a hotel tucked away in the palms. It's about a 20-minute walk and you can continue on along the creek to the end of the valley. Climb up the small escarpment out of the valley for a view of the surrounding area.

From the Chellah Club, the road leads back to the village of Chenini and the main Gabès-Jerba road. To do the circuit on a bicycle takes an easy half-day.

### Places to Stay – bottom end

**Hostels & Camping** Gabès has both a Maison des Jeunes and an HI-affiliated hostel. The *Maison des Jeunes* doubles as the camping ground. Dormitory beds cost the usual TD 4, while camping charges are TD 2 for a tent and 500 mills per person. Power and hot showers cost extra. There's plenty of shade, but the place has all the sense of fun of a military camp. It's 100 metres north of the oued, off Rue de l'Oasis.

There have been favourable reports about the HI *hostel* in its new site on Rue Sadok Lassoued. It charges TD 3.500 per person, with breakfast and hot showers available. The old site, on Ave Farhat Hached east of Rue Sadok Lassoued, is now a dry-cleaning shop.

**Hotels** Most of the budget places are at the western end of Ave Farhat Hached, not far from the bus and louage stations. The best of them is the *Hôtel Ben Nejima* (☎ 05-221062), at the junction with Rue Haj Djilani Lahbib. It's very clean and charges TD 6 per person, with free hot shower.

The *Hôtel Medina* (☎ 05-274271), 100 metres south on Rue Haj Djilani Lahbib, is a bit on the dingy side. It charges TD 5 per person, plus 500 mills for a shower.

The *Hôtel Lagha*, 50 metres from Ave Farhat Hached on Rue Sadok Lassoued, is basic but friendly and charges TD 4 per person, plus 800 mills for a shower. Rooms are built around a small courtyard.

### Places to Stay – middle

There are two hotels virtually side by side near the post office on Ave Habib Bourguiba. The *Hôtel Regina* (☎ 05-272095) is the better – and cheaper – of the two; the rooms are arranged around a pleasant courtyard and cost TD 8/13 for singles/doubles with shower and toilet. Breakfast is served at the tables around the courtyard. Two doors along is the *Hôtel Keilani* (☎ 05-270320). The large rooms cost TD 9.500 per person, but could do with a good airing.

TUNISIA

TUNISIA

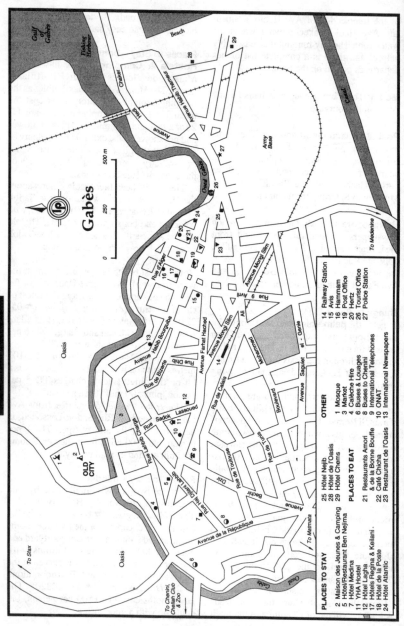

# Gabès

Gulf of Gabès

Fishing Harbour

Beach

Oued Gabès

Army Base

To Medenine

To Sfax

Oasis

To Chenini, Chelah Club & Zoo

Oasis

To Matmata

Avenue Habib Thameur

Avenue Habib Bourguiba

Rue d'Alger

Rue de Bizerte

Rue Dhib

Avenue Farhat Hached

Avenue Mong Slim

Rue 9 Avril

Avenue Mong Slim Ali

Avenue Seguiet el - Genie

Boulevard Mohamed

Rue de Cairos

Rue Sadok Lassoued

Rue Larbi Chaya

Rue Haj Djilani Lahbib

Rue de Toulouse

Rue de Tunis

Avenue Bechir

Avenue Dzir

Avenue de la République

OLD CITY

0    250    500 m

## PLACES TO STAY

2   Maison des Jeunes & Camping
5   Hôtel/Restaurant Ben Nejima
7   Hôtel Medina
11  YHA Hostel
12  Hôtel Lagha
17  Hôtels Regina & Keilani
18  Hôtel de la Poste
24  Hôtel Atlantic
25  Hôtel Nejib
28  Hôtel de l'Oasis
29  Hôtel Chems

## PLACES TO EAT

21  Restaurants Amori
    & de la Bonne Bouffe
22  Café Chicha
23  Restaurant de l'Oasis

## OTHER

1   Mosque
3   Market
4   Calèche Hire
6   Buses & Louages
8   Buses to Chenini
9   International Telephones
10  ONAT
13  International Newspapers
14  Railway Station
15  Avis
16  Hammam
19  Post Office
20  Hertz
26  Tourist Office
27  Police Station

The one-star *Hôtel Atlantic*, with its fine, old French façade, is a touch better than either of these, with singles/doubles with breakfast for TD 11.500/23. It's at the beach end of Ave Habib Bourguiba.

If you want to stay in the oasis, the *Chellah Club* (☎ 05-244446) is about five km from the centre of town in the middle of the palmeraie. The setting is pleasant, but there is little to see or do and it's a pain to get to. A taxi from the centre of town costs about TD 2.500. In the high season, bungalows cost TD 25/39 with full board, falling to TD 18.500/28 in winter.

### Places to Stay – top end

Right on the beach are two resorts, the *Hôtel Chems* (☎ 05-270547) and the *Hôtel de l'Oasis* (☎ 05-270381). Why anyone would choose this beach for a holiday is hard to comprehend, but die-hard beach fans can try the Chems. Its high-season rates for singles/doubles in air-conditioned bungalows are TD 35/52.

The best joint in town is the big, modern two-star *Hôtel Nejib* (☎ 05-271686), on the corner of Ave Farhat Hached and Ave Mohammed Ali, with singles/doubles with breakfast for TD 27/40 in the high season.

### Places to Eat

One of the few pleasant surprises in Gabès is the two tiny restaurants virtually next door to each other on Ave Habib Bourguiba, on the beach side of the post office.

The *Restaurant de la Bonne Bouffe* (literally, a good feed or pig out) lives up to its name. Nothing costs more than TD 3. Its neighbour, the *Restaurant Amori*, has a series of set menus for TD 2 to TD 3.

The *Restaurant Ben Nejima*, beneath the hotel of the same name, is the best of the cluster of restaurants at the other end of town. Most meals cost less than TD 2.

The top place in town is the *Restaurant de l'Oasis* (☎ 05-270098), at the beach end of Ave Farhat Hached. A meal here will set you back TD 12 or more, plus wine.

For a coffee, try the *Café Chicha* on Place de la Liberté, which is the junction of Ave

Habib Bourguiba and Ave Farhat Hached. It's up the stairs next to the Hertz office. The setting, with its intricate tiling, is a cut above the rest – although so are the prices.

### Things to Buy

There is a large government-run ONAT showroom opposite the post office on Ave Farhat Hached. It has the usual range of quality carpets and other handicrafts.

Gabès is a major centre for the production of straw goods – baskets, hats, fans and mats – and the souqs here are a good place to buy things.

### Getting There & Away

**Air** The Tunis Air (☎ 05-271250) office is at the beach end of Ave Habib Bourguiba.

**Bus** The huge new bus station and louage complex is next to the oued at the western end of Ave Farhat Hached, a solid 15 minutes' walk from the hotels on Ave Habib Bourguiba.

All three companies operating from Gabès are based here. The various booking counters are upstairs in the building behind the louages. You have to pay 50 mills for a platform ticket to descend to the buses, whether you've got a ticket or not.

There are nine buses a day to Matmata (one hour, TD 1.640) between 6.15 am and 6.30 pm. There are also seven buses a day to Jerba (3½ hours, TD 5.180) and regular services to Medenine, Sfax, Gafsa and Kairouan.

Kebili (2½ hours, TD 3.950) is linked by three buses a day, all in the morning. The noon service continues to Douz (three hours, TD 4.950).

There is one bus a day to Tozeur and Nefta, leaving at 8 am.

SNTRI has at least five buses daily to Tunis, but most of them come from points farther south and are often full in the summer; in winter getting a seat is not a problem.

**Train** The railway station is just off Ave 1 Juin, about five minutes' walk from Ave Habib Bourguiba. There are two trains daily to Tunis (at 3.42 and 11 pm). The journey takes seven hours and costs TD 15.200. Gabès is the southernmost point that can be reached by rail.

Die-hard rail fans can get from Gabès to Metlaoui by train by catching the 11 pm train north, changing at Mahres and waiting 1¼ hours for the Metlaoui service!

**Taxi** The louage station adjoins the bus station, with departures for Kebili, Jerba, Medenine, Sfax and Tunis. Things quieten down considerably as the afternoon wears on.

Surprisingly, there are no louages operating between Gabès and Matmata.

**Car Rental** The major agencies here are Avis (☎ 05-270210), on Rue 9 Avril, and Hertz (☎ 05-270525), at 30 Rue Ibn el-Jazzar.

### Getting Around
**Bicycle Hire** The small cycle and moped shop a couple of doors along from the Hôtel de la Poste towards the souq will usually rent out bikes for TD 7 for half a day. It's the best way to see the palmeraie, but make sure you aren't given an old, broken-down clunker with minor defects such as no brakes and a swivelling seat.

# Matmata

The Berbers of the Matmata area went underground some centuries ago to escape the extreme heat of summer. It was such a successful move that they have stayed there ever since.

Their homes are all built along the same lines: a central (usually circular) courtyard is dug about six metres deep into the very irregular terrain, and the rooms are then dug out from the sides. The main entrance is usually through a narrow tunnel leading from the courtyard to ground level. The larger houses have two or three connected courtyards, and some have now been turned into hotels.

There is something almost surreal about Matmata. The landscape is like something

from the moon – doubtlessly the reason it was selected as a location for the movie *Star Wars*. Because there are only a few buildings above ground, there doesn't appear to be much to the town. The TV aerials and parked cars, however, are a give away that there is more here than first meets the eye. A quick walk around soon reveals literally dozens of these craters.

It's hardly surprising that Matmata is probably the most visited site in the country. Unfortunately, the town is simply not big enough to cope with the tidal wave of tourist coaches that descends on the town every day. The barbed wire that rings some of the craters is an indication that many of the residents are sick and tired of being perved at like goldfish in a bowl every day of the year. On the whole, the 5000-odd locals are not all that friendly, which is understandable. Some of the children are very upfront about suggesting where tourists should go. They have picked up some very colourful language!

Fortunately, none of the bus groups choose to stay overnight, so in the early morning and late afternoon it's possible to wander around and have the place fairly much to yourself. Because of the exposure to tourism, you will no doubt be invited into the houses – which you may think is a nice gesture until you get pressured to buy handicrafts.

The best villages are in the surrounding area and Matmata makes a good base for visiting them.

There is no bank or post office in Matmata; these facilities are all at Nouvelle Matmata, five km or so back along the road to Gabès.

### Places to Stay
Three of the town's hotels are traditional troglodyte dwellings. They're well signposted and are within a few minutes' walk of the bus stop.

The best of them is the *Hôtel Sidi Driss* (☎ 05-230005), at TD 5.300 per person with breakfast and hot shower. It's the cheapest and the most interesting of the three – and it's only 100 metres from the bus station. The only real problem is that there are only a couple of double rooms – some rooms have as many as eight beds. It was in the bar here that the disco scene from *Star Wars* was filmed. A better recommendation might be that the place wins a mention as one of the 'world's loopiest hotels' by one airline's in-flight magazine.

The *Hôtel Marhala* (☎ 05-230015) is another in the chain run by the Touring Club de Tunisie. The rooms are clean and pleasant, but the 'friendly' service is way short of normal Marhala standards. The staff seem to share the town's general lack of enthusiasm for tourists. They are a miserable lot who appear to view guests as an unavoidable nuisance. Rooms cost TD 7.700/12.400 for singles/doubles with breakfast.

The final troglodyte option is the *Hôtel Les Berbères* (☎ 05-230024). The sleeping quarters here are recent additions and are not of traditional construction; the walls are so thin that you can hear a mosquito buzzing next door. It charges TD 6.500 per person with breakfast.

There's not much to recommend at the modern *Hôtel Matmata* (☎ 05-230066) except for a swimming pool. Bizarre is the only way to describe the paint job in the rooms – the vaulted, brick ceilings are a cooling pillar-box red with the mortar picked out in white. Singles/doubles cost TD 20/30 with breakfast. Regular folk nights are laid on for the tour groups that use the hotel.

If you don't mind paying for your comforts, the three-star *Hôtel Les Troglodytes* is one km out of town on the Tamezret road. It charges TD 34.500/49 for singles/doubles with breakfast. It also has a pool. The setting is well worth the walk, even if you're not staying.

### Places to Eat

The nameless restaurant next to the *Café de la Victoire* by the bus station does a perfectly adequate omelette, chips and salad for TD 1.800. The only other choice is the restaurant adjoining the *Café Ouled Azaiz*, which does three courses for TD 4. The stuffed peppers are worth trying.

Otherwise, visitors are better off taking a room with full or half-board – available at all five hotels.

### Getting There & Away

The buses terminate at the marketplace in the centre of town. There are eight services a day to Gabès (TD 1.620) between 5.30 am and 5.30 pm. Tamezret is serviced by buses at 1.30 and 5 pm, and Technine by buses at 12.30 and 5.30 pm. Both fares are 700 mills.

There is one SNTRI bus daily for Tunis at 8.30 pm (5½ hours, TD 13.820).

When coming from Gabès, make sure the bus you are catching is actually going all the way to Matmata, as some terminate at Nouvelle Matmata.

## AROUND MATMATA
### Haddej

This is a smaller village three km off to the east of the Matmata-Gabès road. It is much less developed than Matmata (with no electricity or restaurants) and the most substantial building in town is the school.

The people here are more friendly than in Matmata. Ask for someone to show you the underground olive press, where big millstones are turned by a camel in an impossibly small space. There is also a press operated by weights and levers which is used to extract the oil from the olives once they have been crushed. The guy who runs the small shop and post office can arrange for someone to take you there.

**Getting There & Away**  There are occasional buses and share taxis running between Nouvelle Matmata and Haddej. The Matmata tourist office should be able to help with bus times. Otherwise, the only way to get to Haddej is to catch a Gabès bus from Matmata for the four km to the village of Tijma, which is nothing more than the turn-off to Haddej. From there it's a three-km walk to Haddej; there is the occasional vehicle.

If the weather is favourable, it is an excellent walk back to Matmata along the mule track which cuts directly through the hills. It'll take you about 1¼ hours at a steady pace. Just ask the locals in Haddej to point it out to you, as it's not obvious where it starts. Once you are on it, it's well trodden and easy to follow.

### Tamezret

This is an above-ground village which sees very few tourists. It's an interesting place, but the bus schedule makes it difficult to spend more than a couple of hours there unless you can get a lift or are invited to stay.

**Getting There & Away** There are buses from Matmata at 1.30 and 5 pm, returning an hour later.

### Toujane

Toujane is built right on the edge of the range of hills on the rough track which runs from Matmata to Medenine. Although it is an isolated place it still sees its fair share of 'safari' tourists, rumbling through in Land Rovers on their way to Matmata.

The road is of more interest than the village itself, as it runs through some pretty wild country, much of it covered by esparto grass which the locals gather and use for making all sorts of things, from mats to mule harnesses.

**Getting There & Away** There is no scheduled transport along this route but you may be able to organise a lift from the Marhala or Matmata hotels, which is where most of the groups stay in Matmata.

Despite what you may be told, the Matmata-Medenine road *is* negotiable *with care* by even the smallest of the rented cars, although the rental companies would no doubt have a fit if you told them where you intended to go.

# The Ksour

Medenine and Tataouine are both fairly dull, modern administrative centres, but they're the centre of the fascinating ksour area of the south.

A ksar is a fortified Berber stronghold consisting of many *ghorfas* (arched structures built to store grain, often three or more storeys high). The Berbers originally built the ghorfas just for storage but, when the Arabs invaded, the structures were expanded to form formidable defensive positions. As they were usually strategically sited, they occupy some spectacular hill-top sites.

Today, most of the ksour are falling into ruin, but some are being put to good use – the one at Medenine has been restored and is now a tourist market, while at Metameur a three-storey ghorfa has been restored and converted into a cheap hotel.

The best of the ksour are to be found around Tataouine, a bit out of the way but well worth the effort. Some of the best sites take a lot of getting to. Your own transport is the ideal solution. With your own vehicle you can make an interesting loop from Medenine to Tataouine via Beni Kheddache, Ksar Haddada, Ghoumrassen, Guermessa, Chenini and Douiret, stopping for the night at Ksar Haddada where a ksar has been turned into a hotel.

The roads around here are usually not in fantastic condition and are poorly signposted. Getting lost is not difficult, but there are small villages and houses dotted around where you can ask directions. It doesn't rain very often, but when it does many of the roads become impassable.

The villages around here are among the last places where the local Berber language, Chelha, can be heard. The language is dying out, along with its elderly speakers.

## MEDENINE

Medenine is unexciting in the extreme. There is nothing that cannot be seen while waiting for a bus. If you get stuck overnight, there is a choice of hotels – all equally unappealing.

The skyline is dominated by the gigantic regional hospital, which seems totally out of proportion to the rest of the town. In the days when the Libyan border was closed it was a real backwater, but these days it is much busier, and seemingly every second car has Libyan licence plates.

There is a ghorfa fairly close to the centre of town, just before the Hôtel Les Palmiers. It has been done up and now houses a dozen or so souvenir shops. Although it is very colourful, with rugs hanging up on display, it is something of a tourist trap, as the tourist buses which don't make it any farther south all call in here.

The fruit and vegetable market is held in the streets up the hill behind the ghorfa and is also colourful.

There are a couple of banks along Ave Habib Bourguiba (a very original name for a Tunisian main street), which is basically the Gabès-Zarzis road. The Tataouine road leads off to the south by the bridge, and on it are the post office and the town's two-star hotel.

### Places to Stay – bottom end

The *Hôtel Essalema* (☎ 05-640509) is not exactly deluxe, but it does have the great virtue of overlooking the only point of interest in town – the ghorfas. It charges TD 3.500 per person. To get there from the bus or louage stations, walk downhill to the roundabout and turn left along busy Ave des Palmiers. The hotel is 150 metres along on the right, opposite the ghorfas.

You will probably get a better night's sleep at the *Hôtel Essaada* on Ave Habib Bourguiba, uphill from the bus station and opposite the Esso station. The rooms are around a courtyard set back from the street. Singles/doubles cost TD 3.500/6.

A bit farther up the hill on Ave Habib Bourguiba is the *Hôtel el-Hana* (☎ 05-646190), charging TD 3.500 per person. The only showers here are in the triple rooms, and you will have to pay full whack (TD 10.500) for the privilege.

### Places to Stay – middle

The *Hôtel Sahara* (☎ 05-640007), next to the post office on the Tataouine road, is supposedly the poshest place in town. It is, in fact, a dump – a characterless concrete monolith from which fresh air and daylight have been excluded. The rate is TD 9/12 for rooms with bath en suite and breakfast.

### Places to Eat

The food is OK at *Restaurant Carthage*, opposite the bus station, although the level of friendliness is about what you'd expect from a place that knows that its customers will be leaving town in 10 minutes.

A better bet is the nameless restaurant next to the Hôtel Essalema, which has a reasonable selection of dishes, including a big bowl of spicy beans for TD 1.

The restaurant in the *Hôtel Sahara* does a three-course meal for TD 5.500, but the general standard of cleanliness at the hotel does not inspire much confidence. It is, however, the only place in town that serves beer.

### Getting There & Away

**Bus** The bus station is in the centre of town on Rue 18 Janvier, halfway up the hill. Both regional and SNTRI buses leave from here.

There are six buses daily to Tataouine between 7.30 am and 4.30 pm (one hour, TD 1.580). For Jerba, there are regular buses and a choice of routes. The services via the ferries at Jorf are faster and cheaper than those via Zarzis and the causeway.

There are also regular buses to Gabès (1¼ hours, TD 2.530), and to the interesting Berber village of Metameur (15 minutes, 450 mills).

SNTRI has six air-conditioned services a day between Medenine and Tunis (6¾ hours, TD 13.650), but only the 9.15 pm service originates here. Getting a seat on the others is a matter of chance.

**Taxi** Louages leave from the small side street directly opposite the bus station. There are departures for Ben Guerdane, Gabès (TD 2.800), Tataouine (TD 1.750), Jerba (TD 2.500) and Zarzis (TD 2.100).

### AROUND MEDENINE
### Metameur

The attraction of this small village, six km from Medenine and one km off the main Medenine-Gabès road, is the old ghorfa on the high point of the village. The town itself dates back to the 15th century, but the ghorfa is obviously an earlier construction.

**Places to Stay & Eat** In one of the court-yards near the mosque, a ghorfa has been restored and turned into the *Hôtel Les Ghorfas* (☎ 05-640294), a budget hotel that offers a lot more than you normally get for TD 6.500 per person.

The place goes into a sort of semihiberna-tion when tourist numbers drop away in winter, so it's a good idea to phone before heading out with all your gear.

Meals are available, otherwise it's a matter of bringing food from Medenine because there is nothing much in the village.

**Getting There & Away** The easiest way to get to Metameur is on one of the regular buses from Medenine. If you face a wait, hitching the six km from Medenine to the turn-off on the Gabès road is pretty simple. The turn-off to Metameur is well signposted off to the left and you can see the village not far off.

There are local shared taxis which run to the neighbourhood villages; these are Peugeot 404 pick-ups with a red licence plate on the tailgate. A lift in one from the Metameur turn-off into Medenine costs 300 mills.

The back road to Matmata through Toujane runs through here, so it may be possible to hitch. Practically the only people using this road, however, are other tourists in rental cars.

### Joumaa

This is a magnificent hill-top site, 36 km south-west of Medenine. The village, visible from the road where the bus stops, is built on a spur and appears to be just a blank wall. Inside, however, there are a couple of streets, a mosque, a courtyard and some water tanks.

**Getting There & Away** There are a couple of buses every day from Medenine (TD 1.250).

### Beni Kheddache

From Joumaa you can continue on to Beni Kheddache, a market and administrative village in the hills with a low-lying ksar. It has been largely demolished but what remains is still in use.

There is no accommodation here but there are a couple of restaurants. There are regular minibuses back to Medenine.

## TATAOUINE

The other major centre of the ksour region, Tataouine is largely an administrative town with little to interest visitors. It's a friendly place, however, and the best time to be here is on Monday or Thursday for the markets.

The post office is at the southern end of the main street, Ave Habib Bourguiba, tucked in beneath the jebel – just look for the radio tower. There are a couple of banks in the streets nearby.

### Ksar Megabla

The ksar is within walking distance; it's a couple of km from the centre, signposted to the right off the Remada road. It takes about an hour to walk up to it, and there are good views of the town and surrounding area. The ksar itself is not in the best condition – in fact you need to be a bit careful when poking about in the courtyard. The villagers still keep their livestock in the cells.

### Places to Stay

Accommodation is a bit thin on the ground in Tataouine, but at least there are a couple of reasonable options. The best budget place is the *Hôtel Medina* (☎ 05-860999), very close to the centre of town on Rue Habib Mestaoui. It charges TD 4 a night, plus TD 1 for breakfast. Hot showers or baths are free.

Right opposite is the very basic, but very friendly, *Hôtel Nour* (☎ 05-860104), for-merly known as the Belmeharem. It's hard to miss the place with its colourful cartoon mural. A bed here costs TD 3, the same as at the uninspiring *Hôtel Ennour* at the junction of Ave Habib Bourguiba and Ave Ahmed Tlili.

If you're after a bit more comfort, the only two-star place in town is the *Hôtel La Gazelle* (☎ 05-860009), 150 metres from the post office on Ave Hedi Chaker. Rooms with en suite bath, hot water and breakfast cost TD 18/25.

A new resort complex, the three-star *Hôtel Le Sanghlo*, should be open by the time you read this. The place is a couple of km out of town on the road to Chenini, surrounded by a huge wall to keep undesirables out – or in. The hotel name is emblazoned in white on a hill behind.

## Places to Eat

The restaurant at the *Hôtel Medina* is a cut above its budget rivals with its smart red tablecloths and neat table settings. A plate of couscous and chicken plus a side salad costs TD 2.800.

The *Restaurant Essendabad*, on Rue 1 Juin 1955 opposite the Sotregames regional bus station, does a good fish chorba for 600 mills.

The tiny *Restaurant Chez Nous*, with its cheery window painting of a chef giving a thumbs-up sign, does basic stuff such as tajine or omelette, chips and salad. The fair-skinned chef in the painting couldn't look less like the huge African fellow who runs the place. Only the big smile is the same.

The up-market option is the restaurant at the *Hôtel La Gazelle*, which does a three-course meal for TD 5.500. The hotel also has the only bar in town, with cold beers for TD 1.450.

All Tataouine's many pâtisseries sell the local speciality, corne de gazelle (200 mills) – a pastry case, shaped like a gazelle's horn, filled with chopped nuts and soaked in honey.

## Getting There & Away

**Bus** The Sotregames bus station is on Rue 1 Juin 1955, pretty much at the centre of things.

There are buses to Medenine (TD 1.750) at 6.30, 8 and 10 am and 2.30 pm. The 10 am bus continues on to Zarzis and Houmt Souq.

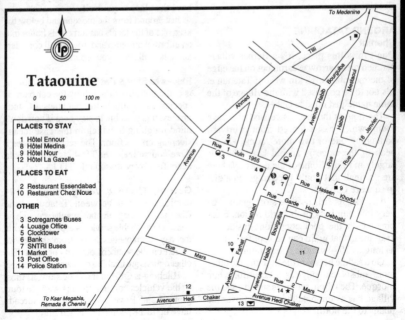

**Tataouine**

0    50    100 m

**PLACES TO STAY**
1 Hôtel Ennour
8 Hôtel Medina
9 Hôtel Nour
12 Hôtel La Gazelle

**PLACES TO EAT**
2 Restaurant Essendabad
10 Restaurant Chez Nous

**OTHER**
3 Sotregames Buses
4 Louage Office
5 Clocktower
6 Bank
7 SNTRI Buses
11 Market
13 Post Office
14 Police Station

To Medenine

To Ksar Megabla,
Remada & Chenini

TUNISIA

For Ghoumrassen (700 mills) and Ksar Haddada (TD 1), there are departures at 9 and 10.30 am.

Remada, the southernmost point in the country served by the bus network, can be reached by a daily bus at 3 pm (TD 2.850).

SNTRI runs air-conditioned buses to Tunis (TD 18.080) at 7.30 am and 7.45 pm. These buses travel via Gabès (TD 5.420), Sfax (TD 9.640) and Sousse (TD 13.640). They leave from the SNTRI office on Ave Habib Bourguiba, just around the corner from the clock tower.

**Taxi** The louages leave from the clock tower square, around the junction of Ave Farhat Hached and Rue 1 Juin 1955. Things are much busier in the mornings. There are departures for Ghoumrassen, Medenine, Remada, Zarzis and Tunis. Seats to Tunis can be reserved at the small louage office on Rue 1 Juin 1955.

Peugeot 404 pick-ups, or camionettes, run between Tataouine and the small villages of Chenini and Douiret.

## AROUND TATAOUINE
### Chenini

Don't miss this place. It's a Berber village perched on a narrow escarpment on the edge of the mountains, 18 km west of Tataouine. It's not to be confused with the village of the same name just outside Gabès.

The houses themselves consist of a cave room, which has a fenced front courtyard containing one or two more rooms. On the peak of the ridge is an old ksar which is largely in ruins. Some of the doorways here are so small that you'd need to go on a diet to squeeze through.

The ksar is still used to store grain. The very low humidity of this arid region, combined with the cool conditions inside the ksar, mean that grain can be kept for years – as long as 10 – without deteriorating.

On a saddle between the ksar and the other more substantial ridge is a beautiful white mosque. The whole setting is superb, and the village has a commanding position over the plains to the north.

On the far side of this saddle, a 20-minute walk leads to a mosque and the graves of the **Seven Sleepers**. A local legend has evolved to explain the existence of these strange five-metre-long grave mounds. The legend has it that seven Christians (and a dog) went into hiding in a cave to escape persecution by the Romans. When they awoke 400 years later, they found that their bodies had continued to grow until they were 12 feet tall – whereupon they all promptly died. There are as many versions of this tale, plus various embellishments, as there are tellers! The cave in question has been closed off and can be viewed only on postcards.

One thing that this story does not explain is the presence of no less than 11 extended graves in the relevant section, as well as others in adjoining parts of the cemetery.

There is a marabout's cave next to the cemetery.

Chenini is very much on the Land Rover trail, but if you can get out here in the early morning the light is excellent and you should have the place to yourself.

Just around from the mosque and below the ksar, one of the locals has turned his house into an informal museum and, for a small consideration, he will show you around.

**Places to Stay & Eat** The *Relais Restaurant* is at the bottom of the hill by the car park. It specialises in lunchtime banquets for tour groups. It is possible to stay here if you don't mind roughing it, which in this case means sleeping on the floor. The restaurant does a three-course meal for TD 4, as well as cold beers for a very reasonable TD 1.

**Getting There & Away** Peugeot 404 camionettes run between Tataouine and Chenini, but they are not regular enough to constitute a reliable service – especially later in the day. Camionettes leave from the service station on the southern outskirts of town. The other options are hitching or chartering a louage.

Hitching is OK but it can be slow, as most of the vehicles coming out this way are tour-group Land Rovers which usually already have up to 11 people crammed in!

To charter a louage, ask around the drivers in Tataouine. It shouldn't cost more than TD 15 for the round trip and it's quite possible that the driver will act as guide when you get there. An hour is the minimum time necessary for a leisurely scramble around, two hours if you want to visit the graves of the Seven Sleepers as well, so make sure the driver knows that you want to stay at least that long.

### Douiret

This is really something, perched as it is on a hill with its dazzling whitewashed mosque. The village is inhabited in parts and is a fascinating place to wander around.

The site is very well preserved, and from above you can get a good view of the layout of the houses. There are several camel-powered olive presses – just look for the telltale black streaks down the hillsides.

**Getting There & Away** As usual in this neck of the woods, transport is a bit of a hit-and-miss affair. If you don't want to hire a driver/guide in Tataouine (TD 12 return), there is a village camionette which makes the run, but it can be hard to track it down – ask around the camionettes at Tataouine.

Failing that, you can catch a louage to Dabbab and hitch from there. You may be in for a long wait, as there is very little traffic along this road, but you will get there in the end.

### Ksar Ouled Soultane

This is the best preserved of the ksour, and also the most difficult to get to. Buses and camionettes from Tataouine run as far as Maztouria, passing the ksour of Beni Barka and Kedim on the way.

From Maztouria the road to Remada turns to dirt; after eight km there's a signpost for Ksar Ouled Soultane and from here it's a farther three km.

Although not built on a particularly big rise, the ksar is visible for miles around and was obviously easily defendable. The ghorfas rise to four levels in two courtyards and the climb to the top of the stairs can be dizzying.

This is the best place to visualise the ksar as a storage place and not just as a ruin. There

are a couple of small shops and a café in this town, which sees only a handful of tourists.

### Ghoumrassen

This is the largest of the southern Berber villages and is the only one regularly accessible by public transport. It is surrounded by rocky cliffs on all sides and there are cave dwellings dotted all over the place.

There is a bank and a couple of restaurants but no place to stay, so it is necessary to return to Tataouine.

**Getting There & Away** There are regular morning buses to Tataouine (700 mills) as well as infrequent louages. Camionettes make the short run to Guermessa (300 mills).

## Jerba

If the locals are to be believed, Jerba is the Land of the Lotus-Eaters, where Ulysses paused in the course of Homer's *Odyssey* and had a lot of trouble persuading his crew to come back on board. If that's the case, then the island today is populated by the descendants of these people, who lived 'in indolent forgetfulness, drugged by the legendary honeyed-fruit'. The lotus is variously thought to have been hashish, jujuba or the lotus. The legend makes a good exotic story to draw the tourists, and it is capitalised upon by hotels with names like the Lotos and Ulysses.

The low-lying island is in the Gulf of Gabès. Its southerly location gives it a climate much envied by the people of Europe – so envied in fact that it has become a major tourist destination, complete with international airport and resort hotels. In the summer months, the place is crawling with tourists – you're better off visiting out of season, when it's cheaper and facilities are less in demand.

The architecture of Jerba is very distinctive. The island is dotted with square whitewashed houses (known as *menzels*) which, from the outside, look more like small fortresses. It is unlikely that you will be invited inside at any stage, unless you are lucky enough to befriend a local resident – there have been too many foreigners here for the locals to get any thrill out of inviting someone in for tea. This is not to say they are unfriendly – just reserved.

Jerba has an area of about 500 sq km. A causeway on the south-eastern corner links the island with the mainland town of Zarzis, another place which is cashing in on the tourist dollar (or yen, or kroner, or whatever). Ferries dock on the island's south-western tip at Ajim, and there are daily flights from the airport, just west of Houmt Souq, to Tunis and direct charter flights to points all over Europe.

Since the highest point on the island is less than 30 metres above sea level, Jerba lends itself to exploration by bicycle or, better still, moped. Both can be hired in the main town of Houmt Souq.

The bulk of the local people belong to the Kharijite secessionist sect of Islam. Known for their fanaticism, the Kharijites broke away from the mainstream Sunna (the body of traditional Islamic law) in disgust in AD 657 because they believed that the caliph Ali had violated the will of God by accepting human arbitration to resolve a rebellion.

They went on to become a major thorn in the side of subsequent Islamic rulers, resulting in constant persecution. The Kharijite sect was popular among the Berbers in the 7th century; when the Fatimids wiped them out in the early 8th century, Jerba was one of the few pockets to survive. It is the Kharijites who are largely responsible for the huge number of mosques on the island – 213 in all.

In the past, Jerba had a sizable Jewish community but, following the formation of the state of Israel, this has now shrunk to about 700. The Ghriba synagogue, one of 14 on the island, is the oldest in North Africa.

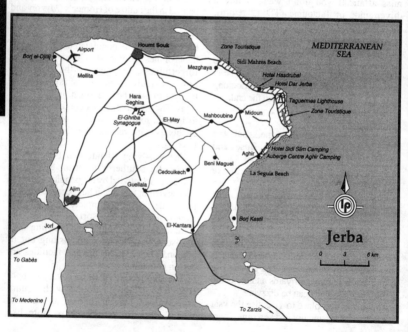

## History

The Phoenicians were the first to realise the potential of a virtually land-locked gulf and were the first of many invaders to occupy the island over the next 2500 years.

In Roman times it became an important commercial centre and the causeway connecting it to the mainland was built during this period. When the Romans left, the island was successively occupied by Spaniards, Barbarossa pirates, Italians and, in the 1500s, the Turks.

## HOUMT SOUQ

The island's main town, Houmt Souq, is on the north coast. Its 6500 residents depend fairly heavily on tourism for their livelihood; the other, more traditional, source of income is the fishing industry.

Out of season it's an easy-going place; the few hotels and restaurants are virtually deserted and the shop keepers don't even bother hassling for a sale.

## Information

**Tourist Offices**  The local syndicat d'initiative (☎ 05-650915) is set back from the main street (Ave Habib Bourguiba would you believe?), behind the two large maps of the island opposite Place Mongi Bali. The staff have a free map of the island and are also quite helpful with enquiries. It is open from 9 am to 1 pm and 3.30 to 6 pm from Monday to Saturday.

The office of the national tourist body (☎ 05-650016) is out on the beach road, Rue Ulysse, about 15 minutes' walk from the centre. It's not really worth the effort. It is open from 8.30 am to 1 pm and 3 to 5.45 pm from Monday to Thursday, and from 8.30 am to 1.30 pm on Friday and Saturday.

**Money**  There are a number of banks on Ave Habib Bourguiba and around the squares just off it. There is always one bank rostered to be open on Saturday and Sunday. The syndicat d'initiative can tell you where to look.

**Post & Telecommunications**  The main post office is also on Ave Habib Bourguiba.

There is a fairly useless international telephone office next door. It's open from 7 am to 7 pm Monday to Saturday, and from 8 am until noon on Sundays. There are very few phones and the place gets very crowded.

A much better bet is the telephone office on the other side of town, just north of the Mosque of the Strangers on Ave Abdelhamid el-Cadhi. It's open every day from 7.30 am to 10 pm or later.

## Souq

Houmt Souq is compact enough to make seeing everything on foot quite practical. The old souq is the centre of things and consists of a tangle of narrow alleys and a few open squares with cafés. The place is full of souvenir shops and, although the prices are high, there is some excellent-quality stuff for sale.

There are a few old **funduqs** or caravanserais, former lodging houses for pilgrims and the merchants of the camel caravans; some of these have been turned into excellent cheap hotels. The rooms are on two floors around a central courtyard, in the middle of which is a large cistern which previously provided water for the guests and animals. One of the hotels, the Arischa, has converted the cistern into a very small swimming pool.

## Islamic Monuments

There are a few interesting Islamic monuments around the town but they are all closed to non-Muslims. Just on the edge of the souq is the **Zawiyya of Sidi Brahim**, which contains the tomb of the 17th-century saint. On the other side of the road is the multidomed **Mosque of the Strangers**. The 18th-century Mosque of the Turks is north of the souq; it has a distinctly Turkish minaret.

## Museum of Popular Arts & Traditions

About 200 metres out along the eastern arm of Ave Abdelhamid el-Cadhi is the Zawiyya of Sidi Zitouni, which now houses the Museum of Popular Arts & Traditions. This has quite a good range of local costumes as well as other bits and pieces. One room still has the original terracotta-tile ceiling. The

TUNISIA

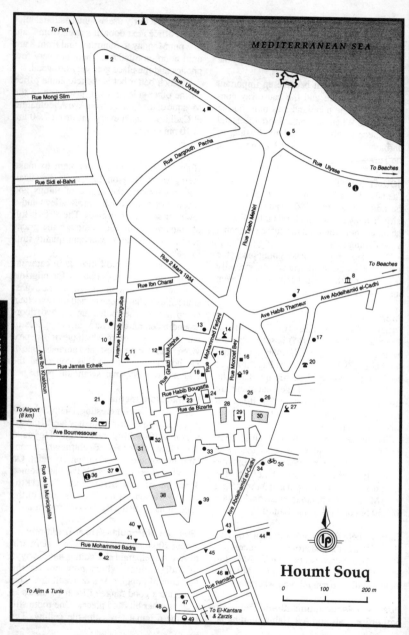

To Port

MEDITERRANEAN SEA

Rue Ulysse

Rue Mongi Slim

Rue Dargouth Pacha

Rue Ulysse

To Beaches

Rue Sidi el-Bahri

Rue Taleb Mehiri

To Beaches

Rue 2 Mars 1934

Rue Ibn Charaf

Ave Habib Thameur

Ave Abdelhamid el-Cadhi

Avenue Habib Bourguiba

Ave Ibn Khaldoun

Rue Jamaa Echeik

Rue Ghazi Mustapha

Rue Mohammed Ferjani

Rue Moncef Bey

Rue Habib Bougatfa

Rue de Bizerte

Ave Boumessouer

Rue de la Municipalité

Ave Abdelhamid el-Cadhi

To Airport
(8 km)

To Ajim & Tunis

Rue Mohammed Badra

Rue Remada

To El-Kantara
& Zarzis

Houmt Souq

0    100    200 m

museum is open daily, except Friday, from 9.30 am to 4.30 pm; entry is TD 1, plus an extra TD 1 if you want to take photos. The ticket office is the small traditional weaver's hut near the main entrance.

### Borj Ghazi Mustapha & Around

From the Mosque of the Turks, the main street (Rue Taieb Mehiri)is lined with beautiful, shady casuarina trees and heads north to the fort on the water's edge. Known as the Borj Ghazi Mustapha (and occasionally as the Borj el-Kebir), the fort was originally built by the Aragonese (members of an independent kingdom in north-eastern Spain) in the 13th century, and was extended in the 16th century under the Spanish. Later in the same century, a Turkish fleet under Dargouth Pacha captured the fort and massacred the Spanish garrison.

The skulls of the victims were stacked in a pile a couple of 100 metres along from the fort, a reminder to others not to try any funny business. This macabre tower of skulls stood for almost 300 years until it was dismantled on the order of the Bey of Tunis in 1848.

The fort itself is in the middle of a complete rebuild, but it's good for a quick wander around and there are good views along the coast. Look for the mounds of cannonballs, both stone and rusting iron, that have been found while excavating the rubble. The fort has the same opening hours as the museum. Entry is 600 mills, plus TD 1 to take photos.

The fishing harbour is 250 metres west of the fort.

### Places to Stay – bottom end

**Camping** The island's two camp sites are situated within a few hundred metres of each other on the east coast, near Aghir. The *Auberge Centre Aghir* (☎ 05-657366), at the junction of the Midoun road, is run by the Centre des Stages et Vacations organisation – the resort version of the Maison des Jeunes. It charges TD 2 per person, plus 500 mills for each tent.

You'll pay twice that at the site attached to the *Hôtel Sidi Slim* (☎ 05-657023), a resort hotel just to the north. It is on a decent beach, so if you just want to spend a few days doing nothing it's not a bad place to be; otherwise, it can be a bit isolated.

Both sites can be reached on regular buses from Houmt Souq. Catch the service to Club Med via Midoun.

**Hostel** Jerba's hostel (☎ 05-650619) is in a former funduq right next to the Hôtel Marhala. It's as good as hostels get. The staff are friendly, and the hostel is open throughout the day until at least 10 pm. In summer this may be the only place with a vacancy. Beds cost TD 3. Breakfast is available for TD 1, and lunch and dinner for TD 3.

**Hotels** The best places are the old converted funduqs.

The pick of the bunch is the *Hôtel Marhala* (☎ 05-650146), on Rue Moncef Bey, another in the chain of four run by the Touring Club de Tunisie. As usual, the standard is excellent, and it is good value for TD 9.500/14 for singles/doubles with breakfast. In winter, the price drops to TD 8.500/12. Hot showers are free.

The rooms are all arranged around the traditional colonnaded courtyard. They are small, but interesting enough to overcome any doubts. The management is planning to build a swimming pool in the courtyard.

Let's hope the pool is not allowed to develop into an uninviting, green algal bath like the one at the *Hôtel Arischa* (☎ 05-650384), another converted funduq just north of the souq on Rue Ghazi Mustapha. It costs much the same as the Marhala at TD 8/14 for singles/doubles with breakfast, and TD 6/10 in winter. Rooms with a bath cost an extra TD 2.

A third good option is the *Hôtel Sables d'Or* (☎ 05-650423), which occupies a fine old house on Rue Mohammed Ferjani. It charges TD 9/16.500 for singles/doubles with hot showers.

The *Lokanda Hôtel* (☎ 05-651513), on a small street running east off Place du 7 Novembre 1987, is the cheapest place in town, at TD 3.500 per person. It is hard to recommend. The nearby *Hôtel Essalem*

(☎ 05-651029) on Rue Remada, two streets south of Place du 7 Novembre, is gloomy but cheap at TD 5.500 per person, slightly less in winter.

It is equally hard to get excited about the final budget option, the *Hôtel Sindbad* (☎ 05-650047), despite the price tag of TD 5 per person, with free hot shower. It is right in the centre of town on Place Mongi Bali.

**Places to Stay – middle**
The *Hôtel Erriadh* (☎ 05-650756) is the most up-market of the old funduqs, featuring elaborate tilework and large rooms with baths around a pleasant vine-covered courtyard. It's just to the north of the souq on Rue Mohammed Ferjani, and charges TD 16.500/23 for singles/doubles with breakfast. This falls to TD 11.500/17 in winter.

There are two other good places facing the beach on Rue Ulysse to the west of the fort, both with the same management. The *Hôtel Dar Faiza* (☎ 05-650083) is much better than the average one-star hotel – and a fair bit more expensive. It's very private, with accommodation in bungalows spread through gardens at the rear of the hotel. It also has a small pool, heated in winter, and a tennis court. It charges TD 24.500/40 for singles/doubles with breakfast, dropping to TD 14.500/21.500 in winter.

Its stable-mate, the *Hôtel Lotos* (☎ 05-650026), represents much better value with singles/doubles for TD 19/29. This is the original tourist hotel on the island. The rooms are huge, with correspondingly large balconies, and most offer excellent views of the coast. Guests here can use the facilities at the Dar Faiza free of charge. In winter, the Lotos is a bargain at TD 11.250/16.500. The hotel is 200 metres west of the Dar Faiza, opposite the Tower of Skulls monument.

**Places to Stay – top end**
The island's tourist strip covers the entire north-eastern corner of the island, about 20 km of uninterrupted hotels that monopolise the beaches of Sidi Mahres and La Seguia.

They cater for those who come from northern Europe in search of sun and sand, not for the challenge of discovering a different culture. There is nothing here for the independent traveller.

The hotels include such monsters as the *Dar Jerba*, a conglomeration of four hotels catering for German tourists of various wallet sizes. More than 2700 sun seekers can enjoy the umpteen restaurants, bars, Bavarian folk nights, etc.

Top of the range is the five-star *Hôtel Hasdrubal* (☎ 05-657650), which has singles/doubles for TD 94/148, falling to TD 40.500/57 in winter.

### Places to Eat

If it's local food that you're after, there are a couple of good gargottes around town.

The good news is that the best of them also happens to be the cheapest. The small, nameless restaurant on Rue Habib Bougatfa, just north of the main souq area, is about as basic as gargottes get. It does a roaring local trade at lunchtime, with workers tucking into such staples as lablabi (chickpea soup) and the ubiquitous chorba (both 700 mills). It also has beans for TD 1 and spicy, Tunisian-style macaroni for TD 1.300.

The *Restaurant des Palmiers*, on the small square at the northern end of Rue Mohammed Ferjani, does a good couscous for TD 2.700.

The food is nothing to get excited about at the *Restaurant du Sportif*, but it's popular enough nonetheless because of its central location on Ave Habib Bourguiba.

You pay a bit more for the luxury of a tablecloth at the *Restaurant Aladin*, on Ave Mohammed Badra. The menu includes some interesting seafood dishes such as octopus in sauce for TD 3.500.

Most of the tourist restaurants are grouped around Place Sidi Brahim. The menus are posted outside, usually in four languages, and there is not a great deal between them.

Beware of the owners who try to persuade you to have a 'special meal', as the price will be pretty bloody special as well unless you clarify beforehand just how much you are prepared to pay.

The prices at the *Restaurant du Sud* are rather more reasonable than elsewhere, with three courses for about TD 7 plus wine. It's just off Rue Moncef Bey.

### Getting There & Away

**Air** The Tunis Air (☎ 05-650159) office is at the southern end of Ave Habib Bourguiba, a block in front of the bus station.

The domestic airline, Tuninter, has up to five flights a day to Tunis, depending on the season. The one-hour flight costs TD 43.800 one way and TD 85.600 return. Other internal flights go to Tozeur on Thursday (TD 28 one way) and Monastir on Tuesday and Saturday (TD 29.800 one way)

Jerba is also an international airport and in the summer months there is a constant stream of charter flights coming and going from Europe. You may be lucky and score a seat on one of these, but you would have to do the rounds of the resort hotels and get in touch with the company reps.

There are also scheduled Tunis Air flights to cities in Europe, although some of these operate only from April to October. They include Frankfurt (Tuesday), Geneva (Saturday), Paris (Thursday, Saturday and Sunday), Rome (Monday), Vienna (Tuesday) and Zürich (Saturday).

**Bus** The uncharacteristically well-organised bus station is at the southern end of Ave Habib Bourguiba. All the scheduled departures are listed on a board above the ticket windows.

SNTRI runs air-conditioned services to Tunis (6¼ hours, TD 15.220) at 6 am and 7 and 8 pm. The earlier two buses continue to Bizerte, but it is hard to fathom the fare of TD 20.650 and the journey time of 11 hours. It is cheaper and faster to buy separate tickets for the two legs of the journey!

The national line also runs a bus to Sfax at 12.45 pm (TD 8). The 6 am Tunis bus travels via Sousse (TD 12.280).

The regional company, Sotregames, runs buses to Gabès at 5.30 am, Zarzis at 10.30 am and noon, Medenine at noon and Tataouine at 8 am and 2.30 pm.

**Taxi** The louages leave from just opposite the bus station. There are departures for Zarzis, Gabès and Tunis.

Many of the mainland louage services go only as far as Jorf. From there you need to catch the ferry across, and then a bus or louage to Houmt Souq. Some services do go all the way but they usually do so via Zarzis, which makes the trip a good deal longer.

Louages to Tunis leave at 6 am and 6 pm and can be booked at the small office (☎ 05-650475) at the side of the bus station. The fare is TD 16.

**Car Rental** Jerba is a popular place to hire cars for trips around the island and to sights around the south of the country. All the major companies have offices both in town and out at the airport, where the phone number for them all is ☎ 05-650233.

The offices in town include: Avis (☎ 05-650151) on Ave Mohammed Badra; Europcar (☎ 05-650357) on Ave Abdelhamid el-Cadhi; Hertz (☎ 05-650196) on Rue Habib Thameur; and Topcar (☎ 05-650536) on Rue 20 Mars 1934.

### Getting Around the Island

**To/From the Airport** The airport is eight km to the east of the centre of Houmt Souq, signposted out past the village of Mellita. There are buses (700 mills) from the central bus station at 7.15 am and 12.30, 5.15 and 6.15 pm.

If the buses don't suit, you'll have to catch a taxi. It'll cost about TD 2.300 from Houmt Souq, or TD 6 from the Hôtel Dar Jerba.

**Bus** There is a fairly comprehensive local bus network connecting the larger towns of the island.

There is a timetable and a colour-coded route map of the services around the island above the ticket windows in the bus station.

**Taxi** There are two taxi ranks in Houmt Souq – on Ave Habib Bourguiba in the centre of town and at Place Sidi Brahim. Sample fares include Houmt Souq to Midoun for TD 3.600 and Houmt Souq to Aghir for TD 5. Fares are 50% higher after 9 pm.

The taxis are forever cruising the hotel strip for fares into Houmt Souq. The big hotels, such as the Dar Jerba, have their own ranks.

In summer, demand for taxis far exceeds supply and it can be difficult to get hold of one in Houmt Souq, especially in the early afternoon when things close up for a couple of hours.

The taxis can also be hired for the day for trips around the island. A daily charter costs between TD 35 and TD 40, depending on your bargaining skills.

**Bicycle & Moped** Bikes are available for hire from any of the hotels in Houmt Souq. In fact they just act as agents and take a small cut. Some of the bikes are in pretty poor shape, so make sure you get a decent one.

The amount you can see by bicycle in a day is very limited, as the island is too large to see the lot. If there were places to stay in the other towns you could make a great three or four-day circuit, but unfortunately this is not possible at the moment unless you sleep out somewhere. Another factor conspiring against cyclists is the strong winds which often prevail; trying to ride into them is no joke.

Rental costs are TD 1 per hour, TD 4 per half-day and TD 7 for a full day.

Mopeds are a much better bet for seeing the whole island. Rais Rentals (☎ 05-650303), north of the Mosque of the Strangers on Ave Abdelhamid el-Cadhi, rents them for TD 24 per day. It also has new mountain bikes for TD 14 per day as well as standard bikes. It charges five days for a week's rental.

Out on the tourist strip, Holiday Bikes (☎ 05-657169) has mopeds for the same price. It also has 80-cc scooters for TD 41 per day and 125-cc Yamaha trail bikes for TD 56.

When riding a moped you are not covered by any insurance. Be extremely careful, especially out in the smaller inland villages where young children, wayward cyclists and suicidal dogs can be a real hazard. No licence is needed for machines under 50 cc.

# AROUND THE ISLAND

## Midoun

This is the island's second major town and is best known for its busy Friday market. Most of the items on sale are really just tourist rubbish, with only a few stalls set up to sell fruit and vegetables.

While Friday is the day on which the markets are promoted, in reality every day is market day in Midoun.

There's not much else to do, apart from eat at a couple of the town's reasonable tourist restaurants.

**Places to Stay & Eat** If you want to stay the night, Midoun has the *Hôtel Jawhara* (☎ 05-657363) on Rue Echabi, a small street off the main market square. It's clean but basic, with singles/doubles for TD 10/16. It does have hot showers.

The *Restaurant el-Guestile*, on Rue Marsa Ettefah, has a pleasant outdoor setting and meals for about TD 10 plus wine, and the *Restaurant Khalife*, on Ave Salah ben Youssef, specialises in fish dishes at similar prices.

For local food, try the *Restaurant de l'Orient* with couscous for TD 2. It's next to the post office right in the centre of town.

**Getting There & Away** There are eight bus services a day between Midoun and Houmt Souq (700 mills).

## Hara Seghira

Once exclusively a Jewish settlement, Hara Seghira (or Erriadh) lies just off the main Houmt Souq-Zarzis road. With the mass migration of Jews to Israel, the population is now predominantly Muslim, but a number of synagogues still remain.

The most important Jewish synagogue is El-Ghriba (the Stranger), signposted a km south of the town. It is a major place of pilgrimage during the Passover Festival, when Jews come to pay tribute to the grand master of the Talmud, Shimon Bar Yashai, who died more than 400 years ago.

The site dates back to 586 BC, although the present building was constructed early this century. The inner sanctuary is said to contain one of the oldest Torahs (book of Mosaic law) in the world.

The site was apparently chosen after a stone fell from heaven; it is also said that an unknown woman turned up and performed a miracle or two to assist the builders.

It is open to the public but you need to be modestly dressed, and men have to don yarmulkes (skullcaps) on entering. Donations are compulsory but you don't have to leave much.

Buses from Houmt Souq to Guellala go right past the synagogue (450 mills).

## Guellala

This tiny village on the south coast is known for its pottery. In the past the pottery was sold on the mainland but these days almost all of it is sold on site.

The dozen or so workshops and galleries line the main road. They all sell much the same stuff, which unfortunately falls into the 'tacky souvenir' category with ease.

From Guellala there is a dirt track which skirts around a bay, where the local fishing people paddle around in waist-deep water. The track continues to the village of Ajim, where the ferries connect with the mainland.

There are seven buses a day between Guellala and Houmt Souq (700 mills).

## Ajim

There are no attractions in Ajim, but if your transport goes only as far as Jorf on the mainland you'll have to catch a louage from here to Houmt Souq.

The ferry dock is about 500 metres from the centre and the ferries run 24 hours a day, although the frequency drops in the middle of the night to about once an hour.

## West Coast

There is very little along the whole western coastline. There's just one dirt track, which hugs the swampy coast all the way.

The ruins of the 18th-century Turkish fort Borj el-Djillij are out past the airport, but you needn't waste your time trying to get out here

TUNISIA

unless you have a moped and an overpowering passion for ruined Turkish forts.

## ZARZIS

It's no use pretending otherwise, Zarzis is one of the less exciting towns in the country. The coast to the north of town is home to Tunisia's newest tourist strip, cashing in on the long stretch of decent beach.

### Information

**Banks** There are a couple of banks in the centre of town around Place de la Jeunesse.

**Post Office** The PTT building is on Ave Habib Bourguiba, close to the junction with Rue d'Algérie.

### Places to Stay – bottom end

There is not much reason to stay the night in town but, if you do, the best of a fairly motley bunch is the *Hôtel de la Station* (☎ 05-680661). It's on Rue Abdulkacem Echabbi, which runs off Ave Farhat Hached behind the Hôtel Olivier. A bed and hot shower here costs TD 4 per person.

The *Hôtel Olivier* (☎ 05-680637) itself, opposite the Sotregames bus station on Ave Farhat Hached, charges the same, but it looks as if the cleaners have been away for a while.

A better choice is the *Hôtel Afif* (☎ 05-681639) on Ave Mohammed V – the Jerba road. The place is clean and charges TD 6.500/10 for singles/doubles with hot showers. Breakfast is available for 600 mills.

There are reports of a good cheapie at the beach, called the *Amira* (☎ 05-680188), which charges TD 9/16 in summer for singles/doubles with breakfast. The rate drops to TD 7/12 in winter. The hotel is on the coast road, not far from the end of Ave Tahar Sfar. The walk from the bus station takes about 15 minutes.

### Places to Stay – middle & top end

The only faintly up-market place in town is the *Hôtel de Ville* (☎ 05-682388), on a side road off Ave Farhat Hached next to the Restaurant Tunisien. It charges TD 11/14 for singles/doubles with breakfast.

If giant resorts are what you're looking for, there are three that fit the bill perfectly. They all have names beginning with 'Z' – the *Zephyr* (☎ 05-681027), the *Zita* (☎ 05-680246) and the *Zarzis* (☎ 05-680160). All are packaged out in summer, but have plenty of room in winter and charge the same TD 20/33 for singles/doubles with breakfast, plus you get to use their pools etc.

### Places to Eat

If the locals are any sort of guide, the place to be is the imaginatively named *Restaurant Zarzis*, opposite the regional bus station on Ave Farhat Hached. It does a roaring lunchtime trade, which is no surprise because the place is good value. A bowl of chorba followed by couscous with chicken costs TD 2.500.

Another good place is the equally imaginatively named *Restaurant Tunisien*. Meals here are served on a tablecloth. It has a good selection, with pasta for TD 1.800 and grilled fish for TD 4.

Beachside tourist restaurants include the *République*, opposite the Hôtel Zephir, and *Le Pacha*, opposite the Hôtel Zarzis.

### Getting There & Away

**Bus** Local buses leave from the bus station on Ave Farhat Hached, near the junction with Ave du 20 Mars. There are regular buses to Ben Guerdane (TD 1.600), Jerba (TD 2) and Medenine (TD 2.200), as well as services to Tataouine (TD 3.850) at 3.30 pm and to Gabés at 6 and 9.30 am.

SNTRI has an air-conditioned service to Tunis every evening at 9 pm, costing TD 16.200 for the 8½-hour journey. The office is a couple of doors from the Hôtel de la Station, just off Rue Abdulkacem Echabbi.

**Louage** The louage station is 150 metres past the bus station towards Medenine on Ave Farhat Hached. Destinations include Gabés (TD 5.650), Jerba (TD 2.050) and Medenine (TD 2.350).

# Libya

# Facts about the Country

## HISTORY SINCE 1830
### The Turks

Following the Napoleonic wars, the Ottoman Turks hastened to regain control of Libya, which had been in the hands of semi-autonomous rulers for several centuries, with only nominal allegiance to the Sublime Porte. Libya had prospered through the illicit activities of the corsairs, who were the scourge of the Mediterranean and who had found protection under a rapid succession of deys and, eventually, under the powerful Karamanli dynasty (1711-1835). The state of virtual war which resulted between Tripoli and Europe did little to dampen trade, which continued to thrive. Even huge sets of marble columns from Leptis Magna were shipped to France during the building of Versailles.

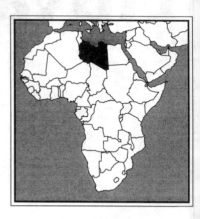

Confrontations between European and US fleets and the corsairs had become more and more frequent and by the 1830s piracy had all but ceased and the slave trade had been abolished by the European powers. Yusuf Karamanli was still nominally in charge of Tripoli, but he had lost the support of his people, who grew increasingly rebellious. Libya was heavily in debt and, in a desperate bid to raise money, he even tried to pawn Tripoli's defensive guns and levied such punitive taxes on the people that riots broke out in the city itself. In 1832 Yusuf was forced to abdicate, and his son Ali took over.

The sultan proclaimed Ali as pasha in 1834 but his rule was to be short lived. In 1835, taking advantage of the state of rebellion still raging in the country, the sultan dispatched a fleet ostensibly to support Ali. The sultan's troops occupied the town, and when Ali went on board the flagship to meet the sultan's representative he was promptly arrested, and Tripoli entered once more into the domain of the sultan of Turkey.

Occupation of Tripoli was one thing, but the interior of the country was still under the control of local tribal leaders who, while they were prepared to pay lip service to the sultan, were unwilling to pay taxes to the Ottoman administration. Libya's vast interior was still largely unexplored and extremely difficult to administer in the face of stiff local opposition. After a period of rebellion, the Turks finally settled into a period of unremarkable administration.

Libya at this time was poor. Having been deprived of its income from corsairing and slave trading, the country was thrown back onto its own modest resources, producing just about enough food to keep itself going. The Turks did not develop the agricultural potential of Libya and invested virtually nothing in developing the education and skills of the people. There was little cultural input from the Turks either, at least for the ordinary citizen, and they remained throughout their rule an alien influence. The Young Turk movement in the early years of the 20th century caused further alienation among the conservative Libyans. The friction caused by the movement's modern social and religious reforms caused its members to be recalled to Constantinople.

Meanwhile, in the eastern province of Cyrenaica a new religious movement, the

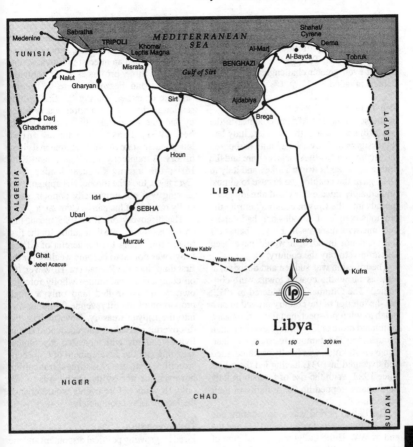

Libya

0    150    300 km

Senussi, had swept through the region and established itself as the de facto ruling element, providing much of the social infrastructure that the Turks had failed to contribute. The Turks appeared to be content with this arrangement as long as the taxes continued to be paid to the official Turkish administration.

The Senussi movement had originated in Algeria in 1837, founded by Mohammed ibn Ali al-Senussi, the Grand Senussi. He had studied at Fès and had then embarked upon a tour of the Sahara through Tunisia, Tripolitania and Cyrenaica, accompanied by his disciples. He finally chose Cyrenaica as the seat of the movement in 1843.

The teaching of the Senussis was one of Islamic revival in the Sufi mould. It has been described by one writer as 'Dervishes without the whirling', and it aimed to restore a pure form of Islam; an attempt to re-create the society of 7th-century Arabia. The idea had tremendous appeal for the rural population of Libya who were, in effect, already living in such a society, and the Senussi influence was significant throughout the country. It was the grandson of the Grand

Senussi who would eventually be proclaimed king of Libya after independence.

After 77 years of uneventful, but not entirely peaceful, Turkish rule Libya was to face an even greater challenge: in 1911 the Italians invaded.

## The Italians

In the scramble for African colonies in the late 19th and early 20th centuries, Italy had set its sights on Libya. It had long harboured the dream of a North African empire and the outbreak of war between Turkey and Italy in 1911 gave the country the excuse to almost immediately invade. Italy had already made inroads into the Libyan economy during the previous couple of decades and had deposited massive reserves in Libyan banks. If Italy had not invaded, it would have been determined to buy the country.

The invasion was sudden and decisive, at least as far as the coastal towns were concerned. The Ottomans surrendered in 1912, but the interior of the country proved to be a much tougher prospect, and fierce resistance continued more or less throughout the Italian occupation. The famous resistance fighter, Omar al-Mukhtar, was finally captured, tried and executed in 1931, having led the rebels since 1923. With the rise of fascism in Italy the Italians stepped up the brutality of their mission.

The Italian period was a devastating one for the Libyan people. Between 1911 and the end of WW II the indigenous population of about one million was halved by either forced exile or extermination. The Italians viewed Libya as Italy's 'fourth shore' and they embarked upon a complete 'Italianisation' program, sending huge numbers of immigrant farmers, mainly from Sicily, to develop the valuable agricultural land.

Libya suffered the crowning misfortune of being a theatre of war during WW II and the desert campaign left behind huge minefields, many of which still remain today.

## Independent Libya

In the postwar years, Italy was forced to give up Libya, which was placed under a United Nations trusteeship until the Allied powers could decide what was to be done with the country. The British, French, Americans and Russians all had an interest in Libya. At one point the three provinces – Tripolitania, Cyrenaica and Fezzan – were to become separate countries. During the final voting session at the UN the motion was defeated by one vote – that of Haiti – and, in December 1951, Libya became a united independent state for the first time in its long history. A monarchy was chosen, and King Idris, the ageing Senussi leader from Cyrenaica, took the throne. His appointment as king was not universally popular, especially outside of his native Cyrenaica.

The discovery of oil in 1959 meant that cash was flowing into the country for the first time. From being the Cinderella of Africa, Libya was poised to become wealthy for the first time since the Roman era. However, the oil companies were almost wholly foreign-owned and controlled, and only a small proportion of the oil revenue found its way into the Libyan treasury. Nevertheless, the discoveries caused an unprecedented rise in living standards, with increased government spending and the development of huge construction projects. As things transpired, however, the uneasy monarchy was to last only 18 years before events would change the face of Libya completely.

## The Revolution

Fired by growing political discontent and the mood of Pan-Arabism which was sweeping the Arab world, a small group of army officers, led by the 27-year-old Colonel Muammar Gaddafi, deposed the old king on 1 September 1969 in a virtually bloodless coup. The radical new regime swept away the old establishment at a stroke and drastically changed Libya's former status as a client state of the UK and USA.

Gaddafi's regime was pledged to the equitable distribution of Libya's enormous oil income, spending thousands of millions of dollars on roads, schools, housing, hospitals and agriculture. Soon after Gaddafi came to power, the British and Americans were ordered to leave the bases they had occupied since WW II, and the 25,000 descendants of the Italian colonists were also forced to promptly pack their bags and leave.

During the mid-1970s Gaddafi withdrew to his desert home to write the *Green Book* – a three-part political work he has described as the Third Universal Theory, a radical alternative to both capitalism and communism involving the devolution and sharing of political power. Launching his new revolution on the people of Libya and renaming the country the Socialist People's Libyan Arab Jamahiriya (the latter word loosely translates as State of the Masses), he set about dismantling the state apparatus and replacing them with People's Committees.

The *Green Book* describes the parliamentary system practised in the West as undemocratic because it is used by politicians to take power away from the people. Another of its tenets is that a multiparty system is detrimental to political progress, as it encourages sterile opposition for opposition's sake. Therefore, all political parties are banned in Libya, the only permitted outlet for political activity being within the arena of the People's Committees.

Although the book contains some refreshing insights and promising new directions which have revolutionised Libyan society, a fair amount of it is contentious, to say the least. It would be true to say that without a vast oil income at his disposal many of Gaddafi's high-flown theories would never have got off the ground.

Almost wholly foreign-owned and controlled at the time of King Idris's overthrow, Libya's oil deposits have gradually been taken over by a government determined to return control of the country's natural resources to its people. Despite an attempt to form a cartel to resist such a development, by 1973 all of the foreign oil companies had been forced to accept a minimum 51% Libyan participation.

The National Oil Corporation began independent operations in 1971 and by 1973, with its own operations and the participation agreements it had wrung from the oil com-

panies, it controlled 70% of oil production. Soon after, it embarked on its own refining, distribution of refined products and direct export of crude.

Throughout the 1970s and '80s Libya adopted a high international profile based on Pan-Arabism, its virulent condemnation of Western imperialism, its support of liberation movements around the world and a program of military adventurism in neighbouring African countries. As a result of this outward emphasis, by 1989 Gaddafi had abandoned his socialist program of centralised economic management.

## Foreign Adventures

At one time or another, Gaddafi has announced the formation of unions with Tunisia, the Sudan, Syria, Egypt, Chad and Morocco, but the attempts have all come to grief. Indeed, when the attempted union with Egypt fell apart as a result of the treatment of Egyptian workers in Libya (all of whom were subsequently expelled), the two countries drifted dangerously close to war. They did so a second time following the Camp David peace treaty between Egypt and Israel. A similar hiatus was reached with Tunisia following the expulsion of Tunisian workers from Libya. The announced attempt at union with Morocco, while it considerably angered the USA at the time, was little short of fantasy as the political differences between the monarchist Moroccans and the revolutionary Libyans were so great that the whole idea verged on the absurd, and soon foundered.

The closest approximation of real unity achieved so far has been the formation of the Arab Mahgreb Union between Morocco, Algeria, Tunisia, Libya and Mauritania, but this union is based more on economic than political cooperation.

What has angered Western countries most, however, has been Gaddafi's support of real and so-called liberation movements and, particularly, his alleged support of terrorist organisations. These have included various extremist Palestinian groups, the Irish Republican Army, Baader-Meinhof and the

LIBYA

Red Army Faction. He has even been accused of attempting to support terrorism in the South Pacific. It is hard to see any ideological connection between Libya and some of these groups beyond a common anti-imperialist stance.

While there probably has been some truth to these Western accusations, an equal if not greater amount of support has been provided by Syria, but the politics of the Middle East has demanded that Syria's favour be curried in the search for a peace treaty between Israel and its hostile neighbours.

What Gaddafi certainly did do was to unleash death squads on certain Western countries in order to eliminate exiles opposed to his regime. Such actions led to the breaking of diplomatic relations with many Western countries, including the UK when a policewoman was shot and killed during a demonstration by Gaddafi opponents outside the Libyan People's Bureau in London. These activities only served to isolate Libya further from the international community.

The most violent reaction, however, came from former US President Ronald Reagan, who had long harboured a grudge against Gaddafi for his uncompromisingly anti-US stance. He ordered the US fleet to assert its rights to sail in international waters in the Gulf of Sirt – claimed by Gaddafi as Libyan territorial waters. The Libyans saw this as a provocative act, the fleet being within shelling distance of Libya, and dispatched fighter planes to confront the fleet. During a skirmish several Libyan planes were shot down. This was followed in April 1986 by a US air attack on Libyan mainland targets, during which dozens of Libyan citizens were killed, including Gaddafi's adopted baby daughter who died when his house in the Azzizya barracks was targeted during a bombing run.

Gaddafi himself escaped unhurt but the experience was a sobering one for him. He retreated to his desert home and was rarely seen in public. Observers have noted a more cynical note in Colonel Gaddafi since the bombing raid and a more world-weary approach in his political thinking.

## Invasion of Chad

Libya's military adventurism in neighbouring countries has included Gaddafi's notorious support of Idi Amin's brutal regime in Uganda (although he claimed after it was toppled to have been duped by Amin, who he 'thought was a good Muslim'), involvement in attempted coups in both Egypt and the Sudan, and the invasion of Chad.

The invasion of Chad, ostensibly in support of ex-President Goukouni Oueddei who had been ousted by the French-supported Hissene Habré, brought Libya and France almost to the brink of war in September 1984. With the northern half of the country occupied by regular Libyan troops, Gaddafi and his Chadian protégés announced their intention to merge the two countries, but the idea was lost in the fighting which subsequently engulfed the country. A stalemate ensued for many years until the Libyans and their protégés were finally defeated and pushed back across the border in 1990.

The Libyan defeat also coincided with the ousting of Hissene Habré, whose regime had become increasingly unpopular. It's no secret that Chad has important deposits of uranium, gold, cassiterite and bauxite, especially in the north of the country. Their control by Gaddafi would have considerably boosted Libya's economic and political status.

While Gaddafi's political stance has earned him admirers in certain circles it has also undoubtedly made him many enemies. Even radical Arab regimes prefer to keep him at arm's length and are understandably lukewarm about his proposals for Arab unity. The Organisation of African Unity (OAU) also expressed concern about his involvement in Chad.

It's possible, however, that his radicalism may be on the wane. Though aligned with Iraq's Saddam Hussein during the Gulf War in 1991, Gaddafi maintained an almost deafening silence during the conflict and has retained a low profile ever since. One possible reason for this is disaffection within the

Top: Siesta in Casablanca medina, Morocco (DS)
Middle: Roman statue, Tripoli Museum, Libya (AJ)
Bottom: Tripoli, Libya (AJ)

Top: Leptis Magna, Libya (AJ)
Middle: Entrance to the Acacus, near Ghat, Libya (AJ)
Bottom: Tripoli Castle, Libya (AJ)

military as a result of his attempts to erode their influence by creating a 'people's army' under the authority of revolutionary committees and phasing out the regular army altogether. There have been rumours of several coup attempts, though news of them is generally suppressed.

## Lockerbie & the Embargo

The latest and most serious crisis to hit Libya came following the bombing and destruction of a US airliner over Lockerbie in Scotland. Libya was accused of planting the bomb and two Libyans were named as suspects. The investigators from Scotland and the USA demanded that Libya hand over the two for trial, a request refused by Libya, which denied the charges and argued that the suspects would not receive a fair trial in Britain or the USA. Infuriated by their lack of compliance, the UN security council (under strong pressure from the USA) ordered an embargo on any flights in or out of Libya and also a ban on military sales and related spare parts. Despite negotiations, the Libyans have stood firm in their refusal to hand over the two men unless the trial takes place in a neutral country. In the face of this standoff the embargo looks set to continue indefinitely.

Despite the isolation Libya now finds itself in, most Libyans would agree that Gaddafi has, on the whole, been a beneficial influence on the country and he still enjoys considerable support from within Libya, especially among the young. His control of the political scene will probably remain undisputed for the immediate future. Libya, however, is a country in rapid transition from a largely nomadic to a modern consumer society, with a rapid population growth (half of the population is aged under 15), and this has resulted in many problems. Not least of these is a high inflation rate and the need to import about 80% of its food. There are also about a million expatriate workers, who Libya relies on for both skilled and unskilled labour. This number is set to increase with the current influx of Egyptian workers. The use of imported labour has caused problems

in the past, and the recurrence of such friction could threaten large-scale disruption. Unless he can maintain his initiative, Gaddafi could become a casualty of such disruption.

Libya's political future depends now on breaking the deadlock over the sanctions issue. Although the official line is that Libya can survive indefinitely in the face of the air and arms embargo, in reality the deterioration of the domestic air fleet and the increasing scarcity of spare parts for industry and automobiles are causing domestic problems that will only get worse.

## GEOGRAPHY

Libya is the fourth-largest country in Africa, with 1,760,000 sq km of mostly desert terrain. It is bordered to the west by Tunisia and Algeria, to the east by Egypt and to the south by the Sudan, Chad and Niger. Only the narrow coastal strip receives sufficient rainfall to be suitable for agriculture and it's here that 90% of the population resides and where the capital, Tripoli, is situated. South of Tripoli is the Jefara Plain, which provides most of the agriculture for the country. The north-eastern part of the country, the Jebel Akhdar area (also known as the Green Mountains), is the most verdant region and also one of the most beautiful. The interior of the country is largely uninhabited desert dotted with small oasis communities, the largest being Kufra, in the south-east, and Sebha, capital of the Fezzan, in the centre.

In the extreme south are the Tibesti and Tassilimountains of the central Sahara, which rise to heights of 3000 and 1000 metres, respectively. Libya's sand seas include the Calanscio Sand Sea in the east near the Egyptian border and the Murzuk and Ubari sand seas in the south-west. These formations are vast areas of shifting sand dunes, some several hundred metres high.

There are no permanent rivers in Libya, only wadis (or watercourses) which catch the infrequent run-off from rainfall. In the Fezzan, years sometimes go by without rain and agriculture is sustained from subsurface aquifers. The existence of vast fossil aquifers

LIBYA

## Great Man-Made River Project

Imagine an enormous pipeline four metres in diameter that stretched from London to Zürich, and you would have some idea of the scale of Libya's Great Man-Made River project. In terms of cost, this project is so large it's twice the size of the Channel Tunnel. For a country such as Libya, with a small population and vast land area, the scale of the task is staggering.

It has long been known that the southern Sahara holds large reserves of subterranean fossil water, but the technical and financial means to extract and transport it have only recently been made available. The rapid development of the coastal areas and the increased population have placed a severe strain on the coastal water supply, consumption occurring at four times the rate of renewal. Some aquifers have been running so low that seawater has seeped through into the reservoirs, contaminating the fresh water supply. Tripoli's drinking water is noticeably salty!

The solution to the problem is to bring the water from the south to the populated coastal regions in the north. The fossil water supplies are so large, although not renewable, that they will guarantee water for at least the next 50 years. The decision to build the pipeline was taken in the 1970s, no doubt influenced by the very high price of oil at the time. During the 1970s Libya was spending money freely on all manner of development projects, and even the estimated cost of US$27 billion did not deter the authorities.

The country's commitment to the project should also be viewed in the light of the political ideology held by Colonel Gaddafi. One of the recurrent themes of the Colonel's thinking concerns self-sufficiency in food production. He has strongly argued that a country that relies on imported food can never be truly independent and free. As a consequence of this argument, enormous sums were spent on subsidising agriculture. Without a solution to the problem of water shortage, however, all attempts to increase agricultural production were ultimately doomed to failure.

The project was pushed ahead and strongly backed by Colonel Gaddafi, who has appeared on technicolour posters as 'The Great Man-Made River Builder'. Cynics claim that by creating a monument to the revolution that will stand long after he has gone, this support can be viewed as a bid for immortality. Alternatively, it could simply be indicative of a desert Bedouin's high regard for the value of water in an arid land. Whatever his reasons, Gaddafi has continued to nurture the project and has protected it from the savage realities of an economic slump.

There is a long way to go before all the phases are finally completed, but phase one is now on line. The most visible signs of the project can be seen at Suluq near Benghazi and at Sirt, where huge circular reservoirs have been built. Perhaps the most significant effect of the project will be in the field of industry, as Libya needs to diversify its economy in order to ensure a viable future. The roller-coaster ride of oil prices during the last two decades has reinforced this message. By the end of the century, the estimated 3 billion cubic metres of water provided by the project will hopefully liberate the natural flow of development in the country. In the future, water could prove to be as important to Libya's prospects as oil is today. ■

in the south and south-east has prompted the building of a huge pipeline to bring water to the coastal areas for use in agriculture and industry. The Great Man-Made River project is the largest engineering scheme currently being carried out in the world, and at an estimated US$27 billion it's probably the most expensive.

Libya has large, high-quality oil reserves, most of which are in the desert areas south of the Gulf of Sirt. The gulf area is dotted with oil terminals, mostly around Ras Lanuf and Brega, which does nothing for the landscape but a whole lot for the economy of the country.

## CLIMATE

Due to the lack of natural barriers, Libya's climate is affected by the Sahara desert on the one hand and the Mediterranean on the other. Summer is generally very hot, with temperatures on the coast around 30°C, often accompanied by high humidity, while in the south they can reach a sweltering 50°C. In the winter, the weather can be cool and rainy on the coast, even snowing occasionally in the jebels, while the desert temperatures can drop to subfreezing at night. Periodically during the spring, you may encounter the ghibli, a hot, dry, sand-laden wind which can raise the temperature in a matter of hours to

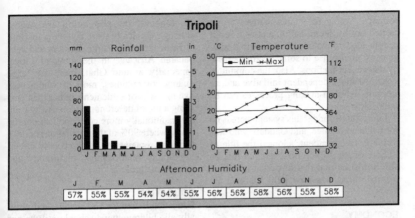

**Tripoli**

Rainfall | Temperature

| | J | F | M | A | M | J | J | A | S | O | N | D |
|---|---|---|---|---|---|---|---|---|---|---|---|---|
| Afternoon Humidity | 57% | 55% | 55% | 54% | 54% | 55% | 56% | 56% | 58% | 56% | 55% | 58% |

between 40° and 50°C. The winds can last from just a few hours to several days.

## FLORA & FAUNA

Inland, the only vegetation is largely confined to the oases, where the date palm reigns supreme, along with figs and oleander. Outside of the oases, the acacia tree can sometimes be found providing the only shade in the middle of a wilderness.

On the coast, the usual array of Mediterranean flora thrives. There are large areas given over to the cultivation of olives and citrus fruit.

A wonderful variety of bird life can be seen all over Libya, as it is on the migratory route of many species.

In the desert regions, the camel is the most common animal that visitors will come

Fennec

across (not surprisingly), but there are still a few herds of gazelle in remote areas and the nocturnal fennec (a small fox) can be glimpsed from time to time. Lizards, snakes and scorpions are also quite common; some of the snakes are poisonous, so great care should be exercised when travelling in the desert.

## GOVERNMENT

The government of Libya is the unique system of People's Committees introduced by Colonel Gaddafi in his *Green Book*. The system swept away all the previous administrative structures and replaced them with a pyramidical committee system. The lowest of these are the Basic People's Committees, to which every citizen over the age of 16 belongs. They act as sounding boards and organs of power for local issues and decisions. Committee representatives form other committees for the purpose of administering government. Once or twice a year a General People's Congress meets, which is roughly the equivalent of a parliament, but with ministries having been replaced by General People's Committees to carry out the affairs of state. The system outlaws political parties or activity outside the committees.

On paper the system sounds perfectly fair and democratic but it has some major short-

LIBYA

comings. Voting for representatives is not carried out by secret ballot, and as a result people tend to vote with their tribal allegiances, giving rise to some disgruntlement by the weaker factions. Also, the committee system stifles independent initiative and, as a result, decision-making processes can be rather slow.

Interestingly, under this system there is no formal head of state, and Gaddafi, who was formerly the president, adopted the title of Leader of the Revolution; despite this he still holds the real seat of power in Libya, a position he has now held for over 25 years.

## ECONOMY
Libya's economy is almost totally based on oil production, giving it the highest per capita income in Africa. It is estimated that some 90% of the country's income comes from this one resource. After the boom years of the mid-1970s oil income dropped dramatically, which, together with political pressures, put a large strain on the economy. Large and expensive development projects begun during the 1970s were struggling towards completion in the 1980s.

The lessons learned during this turbulent period have caused Libya to look more seriously at diversifying its economy. Industry, agriculture and even tourism are now being encouraged. During even the leanest times the hugely expensive Great Man-Made River project was given priority in order to provide necessary water for the coastal areas. It seems likely that the water will be used not only for agriculture and domestic use but also to develop more industry, such as the steel plant at Misrata.

Recent years have seen an emphasis on developing the agricultural sector, with large areas of the Jefara Plain and Jebel Akhdar given over to fruit and grain production. In the south the oases concentrate on date production.

## POPULATION & PEOPLE
Libya has a population of around four million, half of whom are under the age of 15. Most of the population are Arabs, although ethnically there is quite a mixture of races including Turks, Berbers and sub-Saharan Africans. In the south of Libya, especially around Ghat, there are large Tuareg communities, most of whom now live in towns or settlements rather than pursuing a life of desert nomadism. Away from the traditionally more cosmopolitan coastal cities (where 90% of the population resides), tribalism remains strong, especially affecting family relationships, matrimony and social structures.

## EDUCATION
Education is free for all Libyans, and virtually all children attend school until the age of 16, many continuing their education to college and university level. University students often study abroad on state-paid grants. Medicine, engineering and agriculture are the most popular fields of study. Women are being encouraged to continue their education to university level, although few study abroad.

## ARTS
There has recently been something of a revival of the arts in Libya, especially in the field of painting. Private galleries are springing up to provide a showcase for new talent. For many years there have been no public theatres and only a few cinemas showing foreign films, and therefore there has been no real activity in the fields of theatre and film production.

The traditional folk culture is still alive and well, with troupes performing music and dance at frequent festivals, both in Libya and abroad. A great deal of the TV schedule is taken up with various styles of traditional Libyan music. In Ghadhames and the south, Tuareg music and dance is still regularly performed.

## SOCIETY & CONDUCT
Modern Libyans adhere to the traditions of Muslim society which revolve around family life. A visitor's overall impression of Libya is one of a modest amount of material

comfort but with none of the flashy wealth of some oil-rich countries. As a result there is none of the general hassle towards tourists that you find in other North African countries, for example locals begging for baksheesh or hustling you to buy something. In fact, an offer of payment for a small (or even large) kindness would probably cause offence to a Libyan. It's also worth mentioning that haggling over prices in the souq is a no no.

Libyans are very friendly to visitors but it is important to bear in mind that they are not yet used to tourists and it is best to dress conservatively. This is especially important for women. Short skirts and tight tops should be avoided, as should shorts for either sex. Trousers are OK for women but they should not be too tight. Women travelling alone or without a male companion should double their efforts to cover up.

## RELIGION

The religion of the country is almost 100% Sunni Muslim, and Libyans are conservative, though not fundamentalist, in their outlook. For more details on Islam, see the Facts about the Region chapter at the beginning of this book.

## LANGUAGE

Arabic is the official language in Libya and knowledge of it is a great help, as you'll find few people who speak English outside the main centres. For details about Arabic, see the Facts about the Region chapter at the beginning of this book. English is often spoken by those in business and some older Libyans speak Italian. Some Berber groups, notably in the Jebel Nafusa, still speak their own language and Tuaregs in the south, in addition to Arabic, also speak Tifinagh (also known as Tamashek).

# Facts for the Visitor

## VISAS & EMBASSIES

Visas are required for all visitors except those from Arab countries and Malta. Nationals of Israel and South Africa are not admitted nor are those with an entry visa to either of those countries. Before applying for a visa you must have your passport details translated into Arabic, as otherwise the Libyan embassies will not accept your visa application. You can obtain a stamp in Arabic from most Western embassies or passport offices, and the details will then have to be written in by hand. Some embassies offer a translation service, or you can pay for a translator (or get a friendly Arab speaker to do this for you).

A few years ago the Libyan government declared that the country was to develop its tourism potential and that all nationalities (except Israeli and South African citizens) were welcome to visit Libya as tourists. In theory this means that it should be straightforward to obtain a tourist visa. In practice this new visa rule is unevenly applied from embassy to embassy. From all accounts the best place to apply for a visa is in Tunis or Malta, but expect to wait a week for the visa to be processed. It is still difficult (though not impossible) to persuade the authorities to issue a visa to single women travelling unaccompanied. Married couples should be able to supply a copy of their marriage certificate.

Visa charges vary from country to country but the average cost is US$28. Visas are normally valid for one month. Canada, the USA, Australia, New Zealand and Britain do not currently have diplomatic relations with Libya.

One way around the visa problem is to arrange your visit through one of the new privately owned tourism companies in Libya. These companies are authorised to arrange tourist visas for their clients and will fax your details to the relevant Libyan embassy for processing. The snag is that you will have to book a tour of some sort with the company concerned. This is not such a bad idea if your time is limited or if you wish to visit out of the way places. See the Tourist Offices section below for details of recommended agencies.

Because of the current UN air embargo, the only access to Libya is through the land borders. Clearing customs can be a lengthy process due to long queues at the border posts and thorough searches of baggage and vehicles. All pork and alcohol products are prohibited, as are goods manufactured in Israel or by companies listed in the Arab boycott (ie, those who trade with Israel). Books, magazines and videos may be confiscated. Immigration forms are in Arabic and if you do not read the language you will have to engage the help of an Arabic-speaking passer-by. Take great care of your immigration card as you will need it on departure.

Foreigners have to register at the *jawwazat* (permit office) within 48 hours. Usually your hotel will do this for you, but it is important to check. In Tripoli this building is not far from the Al-Kabir Hotel, close to the Gazelle Fountain on the far side of a small park. Once again, the forms are in Arabic.

### Libyan People's Bureaux

Visas and related information can be obtained from the following diplomatic missions:

Algeria
> 15 Rue Cheikh Bachir Ibrahimi, Algiers (☎ 783193, 781512)

Austria
> Gustav Tscharmak-Gasse 27, Vienna (☎ 266 245 36 11)

Belgium
> Ave Victoria 28, 1050 Brussels (☎ 649 15 03, 649 16 56)

Denmark
> Rosenvaengets Hovedvej 4, 2100 Ø Copenhagen (☎ 26 36 11)

France
2 Rue Charles Lamoureux, 75116 Paris
(☎ 55.34.070, 70.47.160)

Germany
Beethovenalle 12a, 5300 Bonn 2 (☎ 36 20 41)

Greece
Vironoz 13, 152-154 Psychikon, Athens (☎ 647 2120, 647 2122)

India
22 Golf Links Rd, New Delhi 10003 (☎ 69 7717)

Italy
Via Nomentana 365, Rome (☎ 83 09 51, 831 01 57)

Malta
Dar Tarek, Tower Rd, Sliema (☎ 356 34947)

Morocco
1 Rue Chouaib Doukkali, Rabat (☎ 731888)

Spain
Alphonso Rodriguez Santamaria 6, Madrid (☎ 548 0500, 548 0458)

Sudan
50 Africa Rd (PO Box 2091), Khartoum (☎ 40570 or 45388)

Switzerland
Travelveg 2, Bern (☎ 43 30 76)

Tunisia
48 Rue du 1er Juin, Tunis (☎ 780866)
Consulate: 74 Ave Mohammed V, Tunis (☎ 285402)

Turkey
Ebuzyia Tevfik Sokak 5, Çankaya, Ankara (☎ 27 40 92)

UK
c/- Royal Embassy of Saudi Arabia, Libyan Interests Section, 119 Harley St, London W1 (☎ 0171-486 8387)

### Visa Extensions

Tourist visas are usually valid for one month. If you wish to extend your visa you will need to apply to the jawwazat in Tripoli for permission. You can expect the process to take several days, and you will need to provide two passport photos.

### Foreign Embassies in Libya

Apart from Egypt, Italy and France, which have consulates in Benghazi, all foreign embassies are in Tripoli – for their addresses see the appropriate chapters.

All Libya's neighbouring countries have embassies in Tripoli, but not all land routes are open to Western tourists. The situation is constantly changing and travellers are advised to consult one of the local travel agencies for advice before applying for visas.

Travellers with Australian or New Zealand passports intending to travel to Tunisia should be aware of the lengthy delays in issuing visas; three weeks is quite normal. Tunisian immigration authorities at the border are extremely reluctant to issue transit visas, even for those with onward air tickets, and reports of travellers being sent back to Tripoli are not uncommon. Those travelling from Tunisia to Libya and intending to return the same way should ensure that they have a re-entry visa or else be prepared for a long stay in Libya.

## DOCUMENTS

Travellers intending to visit certain remote areas such as the Acacus mountain area will need a permit, which requires two passport photos.

If you intend to drive, you require an International Driving Permit. If you are bringing in your own car, you need to have documentary proof that the car you are driving is your own. You can buy insurance at the border. For the latest requirements, it's best to check with the embassy when you purchase your visa, as rules and regulations change frequently.

## CUSTOMS

Customs inspections can be very thorough, so bear in mind that the following are prohibited: alcohol, drugs, any pork products and any goods from Israel or from companies in the Arab boycott. Although things have relaxed slightly in recent years, books, magazines and video tapes are likely to be confiscated if they are judged to be 'suspect' in any way. It may be tempting to try to smuggle in alcohol, but you risk deportation and possible prosecution. Don't even consider smuggling drugs unless you relish the thought of a Libyan jail.

## MONEY

### Currency

The unit of currency is the Libyan dinar (LD), which equals 1000 dirhams. Dinars are

LIBYA

issued in 10, 5, 1, 0.50 and 0.25 notes. Coins, which are rarely used these days, are available in 250, 100 and 10 dirham denominations.

Libya does not accept credit cards, and travellers' cheques are all but impossible to change. Cash is the only practical option when travelling in Libya and the favoured currency is the US dollar, although sterling, Italian lira and Deutschmarks are also acceptable. The main banks and large hotels have money-changing facilities. There is virtually no difference in the rate offered.

### Exchange Rates

| Algeria | AD 1 | = | 0.01 LD |
|---|---|---|---|
| Australia | A$1 | = | 0.27 LD |
| Canada | C$1 | = | 0.26 LD |
| France | FFr1 | = | 0.07 LD |
| Germany | DM1 | = | 0.23 LD |
| Japan | ¥100 | = | 0.36 LD |
| Morocco | Dr 1 | = | 0.04 LD |
| New Zealand | NZ$1 | = | 0.22 LD |
| Spain | 100 pta | = | 0.27 LD |
| Tunisia | TD 1 | = | 0.36 LD |
| UK | UK£1 | = | 0.55 LD |
| USA | US$1 | = | 0.35 LD |

### The Black Market

A black market exists within Libya but great discretion should be exercised when changing money this way. Some shopkeepers in the souq are prepared to change money, but don't ask in front of other people. The current black-market rate is 3 LD to the US dollar.

The better hotels, Libyan Arab Airlines and the ferry companies insist on foreigners paying in hard currency at the punitive official exchange rate or producing a bank receipt proving that money has been changed officially.

### Costs

Depending on whether you change your money at the official or unofficial rate, Libya is either very expensive or very cheap (about six times the difference). If you stay at business-class hotels and change your money at the bank it is very expensive indeed, beating Geneva and Tokyo on a recent 'most expensive cities' survey.

For an average hotel room with a bathroom you can expect to pay about 20 LD. The prices tend to stay around this price bracket regardless of the quality of the establishment. Meals cost 3 to 4 LD from fast-food places and about 8 LD in restaurants. Buses and shared taxis are cheap (eg a nine-hour bus trip costs 9 LD). Private taxis, on the other hand, are expensive, especially in Tripoli and Benghazi. If you are taking your own car, petrol is very cheap indeed.

### TOURIST OFFICES

Libya does not have any regional government tourist offices but a number of small, private tourism companies have sprung up in recent years. They can be extremely useful for arranging visas, permits and travel around the country, particularly if you plan to visit the remote southern parts of the country where 4WD vehicles need to be arranged. Winzrik Travel & Tourism Services (☎ 021-36194; fax 021-45959), PO Box 12794, Tripoli, is highly recommended, as it has offices in all the key regions and is an efficient operator, particularly in the desert areas. There is also the government-owned Libyan Travel & Tourism Company (☎ 021-48011; fax 021-43455), PO Box 15371, Tripoli.

The government body in charge of tourism is the General Board of Tourism (☎ 021-503041), PO Box 91781, Tripoli.

### USEFUL ORGANISATIONS

Two organisations worth mentioning are Hostelling International (☎ 021-45171), 69 Sharia Ibn al-As, Tripoli, and Winzrik Travel & Tourism Services (☎ 021-36194; fax 021-45959), PO Box 12794, Tripoli, which can organise tours and permits and provide general assistance.

### BUSINESS HOURS

Libya operates an Islamic working week, with Friday as the day off. Summer business hours are from 7 am to 2 pm and in winter 8 am to 1 pm and 4 to 6.30 pm. Government offices are open from 8 am to 2 pm.

## HOLIDAYS

Libya observes all the Islamic holidays (see the Facts about the Region chapter at the beginning of this book), in addition to which there are several national holidays:

2 March
  *Declaration of the Jamahiriya* (the People's Authority)
11 June
  *Evacuation of Foreign Military Bases*
1 September
  *Revolution Day*
26 October
  *Day of Mourning.* Commemorating the Libyans killed or exiled by the Italians; on this day everything closes, including the borders, and there are no international telephones, telexes or ferries.

## CULTURAL EVENTS

The main secular holiday of the Libyan calendar is 1 September – Revolution Day. This is usually marked with a week of public parades, rallies and events. Folk troupes and musicians as well as horsemen and various military groups are bussed into Tripoli for the occasion. At this time all the top and middle-range hotels are full to bursting with invited official guests. Quite often there is a large rally in Green Square, during which Gaddafi gives a speech to the people.

Slightly lower in key is the date-harvest festival held in various parts of the country during October.

## SUGGESTED ITINERARIES
### Classical Tour

The main Roman and Greek sites are all situated on the coast. Coming from Tunisia, the best route would be Sabratha, Tripoli, Leptis Magna, Benghazi, Tocra, Tolmeita, Cyrene and Apollonia.

### Desert Tour

An on-the-road desert tour could take in Tripoli, Ghadhames, Nalut, Gharyan via the Jebel Nafusa, Sebha, Gabraoun, Ghat and the Acacus. An off-the-road route could take in Tripoli, Ghadhames, south across the sand sea to Aweinat, Ghat and the Acacus, Gabraoun and Sebha.

## POST & TELECOMMUNICATIONS
### Post

Libya's postal system, erratic at the best of times, has suffered since the UN embargo as there is now no airmail service. There is a high incidence of mail failing to be delivered both to and from Libya. A letter to Europe costs 350 dirhams. Poste restante services are available in the main cities.

### Telephone

The main post offices also offer public telephone services for both local and international calls. The system involves filling in a slip of paper, handing it in at the counter and waiting until you are directed to a booth to make your call; you can omit the 00 for international calls. You then pay at the counter when you have finished. You may be asked for ID, so take your passport or hotel registration card along. The main post office in Tripoli is open 24 hours.

**Area Codes** Area codes within Libya include:

| Code | Region |
|------|--------|
| 021 | Tripoli |
| 024 | Sabratha |
| 061 | Benghazi |
| 071 | Sebha |
| 081 | Derna |

## TIME

Libya is GMT/UTC plus two hours.

## ELECTRICITY

Libya uses standard 240 V power but various types of plugs are in use: two and three pin, both round and square.

## BOOKS

Few books of interest to the traveller have been written about Libya since the revolution in 1969, and most of those that have been written are now out of print. Some old travel and exploration books have been reprinted in hardback in recent years by Darf Publishers of London, which specialises in Libya. You can

LIBYA

write requesting a book list to 227 West End Lane, London NW6 1QS (☎ 0171-431 7009).

Fergiani's Bookshop in Tripoli has a limited selection of English-language books, most published by Darf (see the Tripoli section for details). One of the best books is *Desert Encounter* by Knud Holmboe, written in 1931, which tells of his adventures in Italian Libya.

If you are interested in Libya's political scene, David Blundy and Andrew Lycett's book Qaddafi & the Libyan Revolution (Weidenfeld & Nicolson, 1987) makes riveting reading.

For general reading on Islam and North Africa, see the Facts for the Visitor chapter at the beginning of this book.

## MAPS

The best map of Libya is published by Malt International of Beirut, and is available from Fergiani's Bookshop in Tripoli (see the Tripoli section for details).

## MEDIA
### Newspapers & Magazines

Libyan media is all state controlled. While the air embargo is in force there are no foreign publications on sale, other than those in Arabic, but in normal circumstances *Time* and *Newsweek* can sometimes be found, albeit usually out of date.

### Radio & TV

The TV station broadcasts a few hours a day in English and French. English news is at 9 pm each evening. Many Libyans now use satellite dishes and watch foreign stations in preference to the home-grown variety (which it has to be said is pretty dire).

The BBC World Service can be picked up on the following frequencies:

| MHz | Times |
| --- | --- |
| 21.470 | 4.30 am – 4.15 pm |
| 17.640 | 8.00 am – 3.15 pm |
| 15.070 | 6.00 am – 8.30 pm |
| 12.095 | 4.00 am – 7.30 am & |
| | 4.00 pm – 10.15 pm |

## FILM & PHOTOGRAPHY

Colour negative film is easily available in Libya, mostly Agfa brand. Transparency film is much harder to find and expensive. In Tripoli and Benghazi there are a number of new processing shops springing up. There is an E6 lab, DP Express, in Tripoli on Sharia 1st September, two blocks down from Green Square. This is one of the few places where you can buy fresh transparency film – at 10 LD a throw.

## HEALTH

Libya poses few health risks to travellers. For general advice see the Health entry in the introductory Facts for the Visitor chapter.

There is a tiny risk of malaria in the south-west of the country but it is recommended to use a good repellent rather than take prophylactics.

Travellers should bear in mind that there are no emergency airlift facilities while the air embargo is in force, but in the case of an accident foreigners can receive free treatment in Libyan hospitals.

## WOMEN TRAVELLERS

It is important for women travellers who are coming from Tunisia or Egypt to remember that Libya is much more conservative and unused to tourists than either of those countries and you should dress accordingly. See Society & Conduct in the introductory Facts about the Region chapter for more on dress codes.

## DANGERS & ANNOYANCES

One hassle that has recently come to light is the question of entry and exit at minor border posts, other than the main points of entry at the coastal borders with Tunisia and Egypt. Technically, if your visa is in order, it is legal to cross at any official border post. In practice, however, this is not the case. There have been several reports of people being turned back at other borders, causing massive inconvenience.

## ACTIVITIES
### Desert Safaris

An increasingly popular tourist activity is desert safaris. Libya has no shortage of desert and some of it is particularly stunning. Travellers either bring their own 4WD vehicles or hire them locally with a driver and guide (see the Fezzan chapter). There are some restrictions in certain areas about travelling without a guide, and travel in the Acacus region requires a permit, which is easily obtained for a small fee.

### Diving

Tripoli's Winzrik Travel & Tourism Services is in the process of installing diving facilities. The areas offshore near Leptis Magna and Apollonia have underwater ruins which offer especially interesting dives.

### HIGHLIGHTS
### Classical Sites

Libya's most obvious highlight is its archaeological ruins. Sabratha, Leptis Magna and the Greek city of Cyrene are all world-class sites which are now, fortunately, accessible to Western visitors. If you only have time to visit one of these sites, choose Leptis Magna. It really is one of the most vivid and spectacular Roman cities, rated by many as the best in the Mediterranean.

### Jebel Akhdar

The Jebel Akhdar area in general is very beautiful (the name means Green Mountains) and is well worth a visit. In some ways it is reminiscent of Crete, and is quite a contrast from the rest of Libya.

### Ghadhames

South of Tripoli, the desert oasis town of Ghadhames should not be missed. Its unique vernacular architecture is well preserved in the old town, with a strange beauty all its own. In the 1950s Ghadhames was known as 'the pearl of the desert' and was a popular weekend excursion from Tripoli.

### Rock Art of the Fezzan

In the Fezzan there are several places which should not be missed. In the Wadi al-Hayat there are the ruins of Garama, capital of the Garamantian kingdom, a mysterious people who ruled over vast areas of the Sahara for

more than a thousand years. In the same area there are some of the best concentrations of prehistoric rock art in Africa, some depicting the Garamantes riding their four-horse chariots.

Some of the most interesting paintings are in the Acacus, which even without the art would be one of the country's highlights because of its fabulous, mountainous terrain. The art vividly depicts a wide range of subjects: hunting scenes, dancing, ceremonies and wild animals.

### ACCOMMODATION
### Camping

There are no restrictions on camping in the wild open spaces. In fact there are very few official camp sites to be found anyway. If you are intending to camp anywhere near a town or village it would be prudent to let your presence be known to someone local and get their OK, as otherwise you may attract unwelcome attention from passing authorities.

In the Fezzan there is an attractive camp site at the lake at Gabraoun (see the Fezzan section), with showers and food available. The lakeside accommodation has been built from palm fronds, creating a most romantic setting.

### Hostels

There is an abundance of HI hostels in Libya, mostly well kept and clean, if somewhat basic. For those on a budget they offer a good alternative to hotels (in some far-flung places they may be the only accommodation). The charge for staying in a hostel is 2.50 LD with a card and 5 LD without. Facilities vary enormously from hostel to hostel both in terms of comfort and meals available. Some of them are so under-utilised that, although they are well equipped, many facilities have been shut down. Others are brand new with quite luxurious accommodation.

### Hotels

Accommodation tends to polarise into overpriced business-class hotels (expect to pay 40 to 50 LD) and cheap, but not very cheer-

**LIBYA**

ful, budget-class hotels (about 8 LD). In Tripoli even the cheapies tend to cost about 20 LD. If you stay in the better hotels you will be expected to pay in hard currency at the official rate (often in advance!). In the smaller, cheaper hotels you can pay in local currency. There is often little or no difference between single and double prices.

## ENTERTAINMENT

Well, this is going to be a short section. Libya has many things going for it but entertainment, in the conventional sense, is not one of them. Since the revolution, all nightclubs have been closed, alcohol banned and pretty well all public entertainment discouraged. Restaurants close early, in fact by 10 pm everything is closed. Just to make things worse, satellite TV has recently been banned from the bigger hotels in a petulant bid to force visitors to watch Libyan TV, a dire prospect even for the Libyans (and, inciden-

tally, another good reason to stay at a cheaper hotel). All I can recommend is that you take a good book; in fact, take several.

## THINGS TO BUY

The souq in Tripoli has a good jewellery section where old silver is a good buy. Most of the designs are traditional, heavy, Bedouin-style pieces, which are very popular at the moment. There are also textiles to be found – rugs, wraps and Bedouin seat covers, mostly in red and black. At Gharian in the Jebel Nafusa there is a lot of pottery, often sold by the roadside.

A unique purchase is the multicoloured slippers from Ghadhames, *belgas Gadamsi*, which have a highly decorated design. Unfortunately, it is becoming very hard to find any old Tuareg crafts for sale, but traditional baskets are still being made and are quite cheap.

# Getting There & Away

Access to Libya has been limited since the UN air embargo was introduced in April 1992, forbidding any international flights entering or leaving Libya. At the time of writing, the embargo was still in force and looked set to continue for some time. The following Air section describes travel to and from Libya under normal circumstances.

## AIR

Prior to the embargo, Tripoli had good connections with most of the Arab capitals and with Africa, Europe and the Far East.

Almost all international flights went to Tripoli, with a few going to Benghazi and Sebha. Even before the embargo there were no charter flights to Libya and so it was incredibly hard to get a discounted fare. The cheapest way was to buy a cheap Apex ticket to Europe and then the short, expensive hop to Libya. Airlines which offered the best deals included Swissair via Geneva or Zürich, Air Malta via Malta, or Alitalia via Rome. Even under normal circumstances there were no direct flights from the UK, the USA or Canada.

### To/From Europe

There were direct flights to Libya from Amsterdam, Athens, Belgrade, Brussels, Frankfurt, Geneva, Larnaca, Madrid, Malta, Paris, Prague, Rome, Vienna and Zürich, either with the national carriers or Libyan Arab Airlines.

During the embargo, the cheapest way to travel to Libya is by charter or scheduled flight to Jerba in Tunisia. There are frequent flights from Frankfurt, Brussels, Paris, Lyons and Rome, and one flight a week from London (contact Thomas Cook outlets). An even cheaper way is to fly on one of the many charters to Monastir in Tunisia. These flights run from many European destinations throughout the summer holiday season and are often heavily discounted. The snag is that there's a rather long bus or taxi ride at the other end.

### To/From the Middle East & North Africa

There were regular connections with Alexandria, Algiers, Amman, Cairo (to Tripoli, Benghazi and Sebha), Casablanca, Damascus, Dubai, Jeddah and Tunis.

### To/From Africa

There were direct air connections with the rest of Africa from Accra, Khartoum, N'Djamena, Nouakchott and Niamey.

### To/From North America

With or without the embargo, there are no direct flights to or from the USA or Canada. Probably the cheapest option would be to fly to Rome and connect from there.

### To/From Australasia

Apart from travelling via Europe, there were a few routing options for those coming from Australia or New Zealand, with direct flights to Tripoli from Delhi, Karachi, Istanbul and Seoul, as well as from the Middle East.

## LAND
### To/From Egypt

The only official border post is near the Egyptian coastal town of Sallum. Immigration procedures at Sallum can take ages in either direction so be prepared for a long queue. There are plenty of money changers on the Egyptian side of the border, and a bank in Sallum itself.

**Bus** Services with the Fast Transport Company (see the Tripoli section for details) run from Tripoli via Benghazi to Alexandria and Cairo on Monday and Tuesday at 7 am and on Thursday at 9 am. The one-way fare from Tripoli to Cairo is 50 LD. The journey takes 35 hours and the buses are air-conditioned. There is a more luxurious bus operated by the United Arab Company for

Transportation, which has video, on-board loo, etc, and runs daily to Alexandria and Cairo from Tripoli at 9 am. This costs 65 LD one way and includes a hotel room in Benghazi en route. The whole trip takes two days.

If you are travelling from Benghazi there are buses to Cairo daily at 7.30 and 8 am. The one-way fare is 40 LD. All the buses serving the main routes are air-conditioned.

Coming from Egypt, you can try the East Delta Bus Co on Midan Ulali in Cairo. Buses for Benghazi leave daily at 9 am and cost E£125. Some go on to Tripoli and cost E£230. The Hebton bus company runs buses right across North Africa, but departures are erratic. The company has offices behind the car park east of Midan Opera and at 305 Sharia Shubra, Midan al-Khalifawi. The West Delta and Arab Union bus companies run daily services to Benghazi and Tripoli from Alexandria.

**Taxi** There are also collect taxis running between Benghazi and Alexandria and Cairo which leave throughout the day. Some taxis just go to the border but you can easily pick up another on the other side. The fares vary but are cheap – not much more than the bus fare. Local taxis run between the border point of Amsaad and the town of Al-Burdi. On the Egyptian side, service taxis ply the 12 km between Amsaad and Sallum (about E£3), from where you can get several buses east to Marsa Matruh or on to Alexandria.

### To/From Tunisia

The main crossing point is on the main coast road at Ras al-Jedir and the queues can be horrendous (allow several hours to cross both border checks). The other border post from Tunisia to Libya is at Dehiba in the south of Tunisia. If your visa is in order, there is nothing in the rules to stop you from entering Libya here; however, in practice, people are being sent back to Ras al-Jedir by the Libyan immigration authorities at Wazin.

**Bus** Buses leave from the central Tripoli bus station and serve Sfax, Gabès and Tunis.

They leave daily (except Saturday) at 4 pm and the one-way fare is 10 LD. The fare coming from Tunis is TD 20.

**Taxi** Collect taxis leave Tripoli or the border at Ras al-Jedir for Jerba and Tunis at frequent intervals throughout the day. The fares are very low (not much more than the bus) but the driving can be erratic.

### To/From Other Neighbouring Countries

Libya also shares land borders with Algeria, Niger, Chad and the Sudan. For the time being the borders with Algeria are closed, at least as far as tourists are concerned. The situation with the southern borders is more confused. The tourism authorities and security department are still unclear about whether they will allow tourists to cross these borders. Suffice to say that it has been a long time since anyone tried it, let alone succeeded. Anyone planning a trans-African trip involving travel into Libya from Niger, the Sudan or Chad would be strongly advised to contact one of the tourist agencies (see Tourist Offices in the previous Facts for the Visitor section), which may be able to arrange a passage.

### SEA

For information about all the following services contact the General National Maritime Transport Company (☎ 021-34865 or 602694), Sharia Magarief, Tripoli.

### To/From Malta

Ferries for Malta depart a few days a week from the port in front of the Mehari Hotel on Sharia al-Fatah. The timetables are subject to frequent changes and cancellations due to season, weather and general chaos. The fares are extremely high – a one-way trip costs 61.50 LD, and this fare converts very badly into about Lm 60 if you are travelling the other way.

In Malta, contact Sea Malta (☎ 23 22 30/9), Valletta.

### To/From Morocco

There are erratic services to and from Casablanca. The trip takes four days and costs 105.50 LD one way.

## To/From Egypt

Again the service is erratic. The journey from Tripoli to Alexandria takes two days and costs 105.50 LD one way.

## TOURS

A few Western operators are now starting to run tours to Libya. Given the difficulty of the terrain and the great distances involved, these tours guarantee that you see the best sights with the least possible hassle, although they are quite expensive. On balance they are recommended if you can afford them, as, apart from anything else, the local agents can arrange access to places (such as closed museums or private houses) which would be difficult for an individual traveller.

Tours of Libya can be booked in the UK through Arab Tours (☎ 0171-935 3273; fax 0171-486 4237), 78 Marylebone Lane, London W1M 5FF, which specialises in desert tours. In Germany, 4WD tours using your own vehicle can be booked through GURI Tours (☎ 089-85 62 468; fax 089-85 62 268), Heimstrasse 12, 82131 Stockdorf.

## LEAVING LIBYA

Leaving Libya by the main land borders to Tunisia or Egypt is straightforward, if time consuming. There is another form in Arabic to fill out, similar to the entry form. Prior to the air embargo, a departure tax of 3 LD was levied if you were flying out of the country.

# Getting Around

Libya's road system is excellent on the whole, and frequent buses connect the main centres. The distances can be very great and the trips long but the buses are for the most part comfortable and air-conditioned. They are also cheap.

The domestic air service has suffered badly during the air embargo because spare parts are unavailable and many aircraft are grounded. The service is bound to continue to dwindle as time goes by and already many routes are cancelled or operating only a skeleton service. The schedules are updated every few weeks and it is wise to check whether a published flight is in fact running.

## AIR

The domestic air service has connecting routes between Tripoli, Benghazi and Sebha, and between smaller places such as Ghadhames, Ghat, Sirt, Houn, Tobruk and Kufra. There are several flights a day between Tripoli and Benghazi and frequent connections to Sebha from both Tripoli and Benghazi. All flights in Libya tend to be full so it is advised that you book well in advance. Schedules can be delayed or cancelled without warning, but fares are reasonable; eg Tripoli to Benghazi costs 17.50 LD.

Security is very tight on Libyan flights and items such as batteries are likely to be removed from cameras and tape recorders. Last-minute security checks are common and it is advisable to keep your passport handy at all times. You often have to identify your luggage on the tarmac before it is loaded. A word of warning – there are no seat allocations on Libyan Arab Airlines so you have to fight for a seat once you board.

## BUS

Air-conditioned buses serve all of the main towns and there are departures from Tripoli and Benghazi to almost all destinations at least once a day. Fares are low and, as buses tend to get fully booked, you are advised to buy your ticket a day in advance and turn up early (buses have been known to leave earlier than scheduled if they are full). For details of schedules see the Getting There & Away sections for each town.

## TAXI

There are many long-distance shared taxis covering almost every route possible. These are usually bright yellow converted Peugeots with three rows of seats, and they can be rather cramped on long journeys. Needless to say they also have no air-conditioning but on some routes they are the only practical option. In most towns they all depart from the one place, usually next to the bus station. They don't have any destination signs on them – it's just a question of asking.

## CAR & MOTORBIKE

Almost all the roads in Libya are surfaced and in good condition. The major problem for Western visitors is that none of the road signs are in Latin script. As if that were not enough of a problem, many road signs on the main coastal highway have been painted out, presumably as a security measure. If you do not read Arabic you will have to resign yourself to asking directions at every step of the journey. There are periodic checkpoints on all the main roads, so keep your passport and car papers to hand.

Another hazard to be aware of is the poor condition of many cars on the road. This is particularly a hazard at night when it is not uncommon to encounter cars with one or no lights.

As access to many of Libya's most interesting places requires an off-the-road vehicle, it is well worth the effort to bring one in yourself, as they are not available for self-drive hire.

### Car Rental

Saloon (sedan) cars are available, but the

prices are quite high and they can only be picked up in Tripoli and Benghazi. Car-hire offices can usually be found in the lobbies of the better hotels in the two cities (see the relevant getting There & Away sections). For a small saloon you can expect to pay about 30 LD per day, plus mileage and a deposit of 200 to 300 LD.

## Motorbikes

There are not that many motorbikes on the road in Libya but foreign riders are beginning to visit the country, attracted by the off-the-road possibilities. It is important if you are planning a motorbike tour to bring spare parts with you and to have a sound mechanical knowledge of your machine. The long distances across unpopulated stretches mean you may find yourself stranded. The need to carry sufficient fuel on long desert journeys is also a problem. On such trips it is strongly advised that you travel with another vehicle which can carry extra fuel and water.

There have been a number of accidents involving riders who have been dune riding and this is causing some concern to the Libyan authorities. The dangers of riding across dunes are considerable and if you don't know the route it is recommended that you take a local guide along if possible.

The Tripoli Motorcycle Federation (☎ 021-41274), PO Box 12794, Tripoli, can offer advice on riding in Libya.

## HITCHING

Hitching is never entirely safe in any country in the world, and we don't recommend it. Travellers who decide to hitch should understand that they are taking a small but potentially serious risk. However, many people do choose to hitch, and the advice that follows should help to make their journeys as fast and safe as possible.

It is not difficult to get a lift in Libya. Drivers will pick up foreign tourists out of curiosity, if nothing else. Locals will not expect payment but if the driver is not Libyan you may be expected to pay something for the ride. Although Libya is generally safe to travel around, it should be borne in mind that hitching anywhere involves a risk to your personal safety and, considering the remoteness of many areas in Libya, if you get into difficulties it could be very serious indeed. Under no circumstances should women unaccompanied by males hitch, not even if they are in pairs.

## LOCAL TRANSPORT
### Bus

Only Tripoli and Benghazi have a city bus service worth speaking of. In Tripoli the large coaches have been replaced by minibuses for all routes. The fares are 0.25 LD per single journey and routes cover all central areas and suburbs. Most buses terminate and depart from the central city bus stations in both cities.

### Taxi

City taxis run in Tripoli and Benghazi, but are hideously expensive and should be avoided where possible.

## TOURS

For details of local operators, refer to the Tourist Offices section in the previous Facts for the Visitor chapter.

LIBYA

# Tripoli

Tripoli, known as Tarabulus in Arabic, is the de facto capital of Libya, although there have been attempts in recent years to move some government departments to other areas of the country. Nonetheless, Tripoli remains Libya's main business and cultural centre and principal port. It has a population of approximately 1.5 million.

Known in the past as 'the white bride of the Mediterranean', Tripoli has lost most of its pristine allure, but it still retains a good deal of character. There are many colonial buildings, historic mosques and a lively medina. The city is unlike other large cities in North Africa. The Turkish and Italian colonial periods left a distinctive mark on the architecture, and the revolutionary period has ensured that the usual hallmarks of a modern commercial city, such as advertising hoardings, are completely absent.

## History

Called Oea in antiquity, Tripoli was founded by the Phoenicians in about 500 BC, as part of their colonisation of the North African coast. Tripoli is Libya's only ancient city to have been continuously occupied, and very few relics of the early settlements survive.

Following the fall of Carthage in 146 BC, Tripoli came briefly under the jurisdiction of the Nubian kingdom, before becoming a Roman protectorate. Following a period of civil war between Roman factions, Julius Caesar annexed Tripoli as part of the province of Africa Nova. Under the Romans, Oea grew very prosperous and, together with Sabratha and Leptis Magna (the other cities of the 'tripolis'), provided the Roman empire with grain, wild animals and slaves.

After the golden age of the 2nd century AD, Tripoli gradually fell into decline, along with the rest of the empire. When the Vandals overran North Africa in the 5th century, the damage to the city was devastating and it could easily have fallen into permanent ruin. The conquest by emperor Justinian's general, Belisarius, in 533 and the establishment of Byzantine rule stopped the total decay. Despite the efforts of the Byzantines to restore the city, however, Tripoli would spend the following centuries in a much reduced state.

When the first Arab invasion came in the 7th century, a new town was built amongst the ruins of the old. The Roman street plan can still be seen in the old city today, although only one Roman monument still stands – the Arch of Marcus Aurelius. It was after the second Arab invasion in 1046 that the old city walls were rebuilt, using the Roman remains as foundations.

Despite a very temporary Norman occupation, from 1146 to 1158, the Arab town flourished in the 14th and 15th centuries. Many of the Islamic buildings come from this age, as well as some fine civic buildings and merchants' houses. During the 16th century the city was occupied in quick succession by the Spanish and the Knights of Malta. The most visible result of their occupation is the extensive work they carried out on Tripoli Castle, the Assai al-Hamra, which has been fortified and extended throughout its history.

The most lasting architectural monuments in the old city were built by the Turks, who constructed most of the mosques, hammams and souqs which are still standing today. Under the Karamanlis, who ruled Tripoli virtually independently of the Sublime Porte during the 18th and 19th centuries, the boundaries of the old town became final and the city's characteristic winding lanes and houses were built. Most of today's old town dates from this era, including most of the buildings within the Assai al-Hamra.

It was not until the Italians invaded and conquered Libya that the city burst out of the confines of the city walls. The area which now composes central Tripoli used to be farms and gardens. The Italians built colonnaded streets radiating from the castle, thousands of houses and apartments and many public buildings. When Libya became independent many families left the old city to live in the newly vacated Italian apartments and houses. The old city suffered a decline and its buildings were poorly maintained, a process of decay which is only just starting to be halted today by the actions of environmentalists, and some of the more important buildings are now beginning to be restored.

## Orientation

Easily the most dominant feature of Tripoli is the castle, which sits on the northern promontory overlooking what used to be the sea. A recent development has reclaimed about 500 metres of land and a motorway now runs between the old corniche (coastal roadway) and the sea. Next to the castle is Green Square, a vast open area cleared after the revolution as a venue for mass rallies. All the main shopping and business streets radiate out from this square.

The city is divided into western and eastern halves by the castle and the tangle of lanes comprising the old city (medina). On the western half you will find the town bathing beaches and some seaside hotels, but very little else of interest. On the eastern side there is the old tree-lined corniche which leads past a line of Ottoman buildings. This is where most of the business-class hotels are situated, and there are also some small green spaces with cafés which are popular with the locals. Farther along to the east is the ferry port, almost opposite the Mehari Hotel. From Green Square everything of interest is within walking distance.

The medina itself has the most interesting shops for souvenirs, and just south-west of the old city are the bus and taxi stations. Some of the city's cheap hotels can be found in this area.

Most of the embassies are either along the corniche, about one km from Green Square, or set back behind the corniche in an area called Garden City.

## Information

**Tourist Office** The government's General Board of Tourism (☎ 021-503041), PO Box 91781, Tripoli, is currently preparing brochures and maps in English, German and

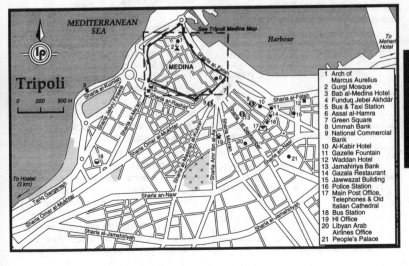

Italian. It may be worth writing in advance for information. If you telephone, some of the staff speak English. A good map is available from Fergiani's Bookshop (see the Bookshop section below).

**Money** The city's half-dozen main banks are to be found on or near Green Square, on Sharia 1st September, Sharia al-Magarief and Sharia Omar al-Mukhtar. They are open from 8 am to 2 pm, Saturday to Thursday. Outside banking hours, most of the main hotels have an exchange facility and the rates are often the same as the banks. The Al-Kabir Hotel is convenient as it is situated on Sharia al-Fatah near Green Square.

**Post & Telecommunications** The main post office is on Maidan al-Jazayir, near the former cathedral (you can't miss it) at the end of Sharia al-Magarief. Apart from the usual services there is also a collectors' counter for special-edition stamps. The public telephone office is in the same building and is open 24 hours a day. The area code for Tripoli is 021.

**Foreign Embassies** All the foreign embassies in Libya are in Tripoli. Countries with diplomatic representation include:

Algeria
    12 Sharia al-Qayrawan (☎ 021-34631, 40025)
Belgium
    1 Sharia Abu Ubaydah ibn al-Jarrah, PO Box 663 (☎ 021-37797)
France
    Sharia Ahmad Lotfi Said, PO Box 312 (☎ 021-33526, 37759)
Germany
    Sharia Hasan al-Mashay, PO Box 302 (☎ 021-30554)
Italy
    1 Sharia Wahran, PO Box 219 (☎ 021-31191)
Malta
    13 Sharia Ubay ibn Ka'ab, PO Box 2534 (☎ 021-38081/4)
Morocco
    Embassy: Blvd Ben Achour, BP 908 (☎ 021-600110, 601102)
    Consulate: Madinat al-Hadaiq, Sharia Bashir al-Ibrahimi (☎ 021-34239, 41346)

Netherlands
    20 Sharia Jalal Bayer, PO Box 3801 (☎ 021-41549, 41550)
Spain
    Sharia al-Jazayir, PO Box 2302 (☎ 021-35463, 36797)
Switzerland
    Sharia al-Wahshi, PO Box 439 (☎ 021-607365, 367366)
Tunisia
    Sharia Bin 'Ashur (☎ 021-607161)
UK
    British Interests Section, c/- Italian Embassy, 1 Sharia Wahran (☎ 021-31191)
USA
    US Interests Section, c/- Belgian Embassy, 1 Sharia Abu Ubaydah ibn al-Jarrah, PO Box 663 (☎ 021-37797)

**Travel Agencies** Winzrik Travel & Tourism Services (☎ 021-36194; fax 021-45959), PO Box 12794, is very helpful and the staff speak English. The central office (☎ & fax 021-38364) is not far from the bus and taxi station at the south-western end of the medina, in the large car park which faces the five large towers. Winzrik can arrange tours within Libya and book bus tickets etc.

The Libyan Travel & Tourism Company (☎ 021-48005 or 48011; fax 021-43455), Sharia 1st September, also runs tours throughout Libya.

**Bookshops** Fergiani's Bookshop on Sharia 1st September has a selection of English-language books available. Most of these describe historic travels through Libya and North Africa, and are published by Darf of London. It also sells maps and postcards. The shop is about two blocks down from Green Square, and there is another branch on Sharia Jamahiriya, which has a smaller selection of English-language books.

**Walking Tour**
Walking around central Tripoli is the most agreeable way of seeing the city, and, judging from the traffic jams, by far the quickest. Starting at Green Square and heading east along the old corniche (which, sadly, no longer has a sea view except through a pair of binoculars), the first build-

LIBYA

ing you come to is a highly decorated, wedding-cake confection constructed by the Turks. This is now a government office. Continuing east along the tree-lined street you pass what used to be the most important seafront buildings, mostly dating from the late 19th and early 20th centuries. Past the Al-Kabir Hotel there are several pleasant small squares shaded by palm trees and dotted with open-air cafés.

Soon you come to the **Gazelle Fountain**, which dates from the 1920s. Turn right and you come out in the Maidan al-Jazayir, and the **old cathedral** is in front of you. This was built in 1928 by the Italians in the neo-Romanesque style, but since the revolution it has become a mosque. If you continue a short way farther east you come to the **People's Palace**, which was previously the royal palace in the days of the monarchy. Beyond the palace is Garden City, an area of large villas, where most of the embassies are to be found.

Backtracking to Maidan al-Jazayir and walking straight ahead down Sharia al-Magarief takes you past some of the best **colonial architecture** in the city. Two streets across to the left is Sharia Mizran where the old **Arts & Crafts School**, built by the Turks, still stands. It has some interesting decorative tilework in the entrance and courtyard. This circuit takes in the best parts of the modern city. For the old city see the Medina section.

## Citadel

Tripoli Castle, the Assai al-Hamra, has evolved over the centuries into a vast citadel containing a labyrinth of courtyards, alleyways and houses, which represented the seat of power in Tripolitania until this century. Although the site itself dates from Roman times, much of the castle's existing interior was built during the 17th and 18th centuries. The total area of the castle is about 13,000 sq metres, with high defensive walls all around. Plans from the 17th century reveal that the castle was at that time totally surrounded by water. The landside moat has long since been filled in.

When the Turks occupied the castle in 1551, they carried out extensive works and the governors used it as their official residence. This practice was continued by the Karamanlis, who built the harems and a large reception room *(selamlik)* in which to receive official visitors. The castle also had a mint, courthouse, shops, jails and mills. Under the Spaniards and the Knights of Malta, the defences were built up with the addition of defensive towers in the southwest and south-east of the citadel.

After the Italian conquest the governor used the castle as official offices and parts were turned into a museum. The Italians also cut a road through the citadel in order to connect the two halves of the city. It is in this space that the new museum has been built, in excellent taste, to house the national collection of antiquities. Entrance to the castle is through the museum or there is a large gate on the landward side near the Souq al-Mushir. Most of the buildings inside the

Punic stele

LIBYA

castle are now used by the Department of Antiquities and there is also a library.

## Jamahiriya Museum

The entrance to the museum is in Green Square through a large wooden door. The new museum was built in consultation with UNESCO at enormous cost and is extremely well designed. The exhibits are laid out chronologically, starting with prehistory and early Libyan tribal history and working up

through the marble galleries to one devoted to the revolution.

The most impressive parts of the collection are the mosaics, statues and artefacts from classical antiquity. The Roman finds from Leptis Magna are particularly stunning. Overall, this is one of the finest collections of classical art in the Mediterranean.

For those interested in early Islamic architecture there is a gallery devoted to the various styles and periods of building in Libya. It is very useful for those planning to

---

### Tales of the Assai al-Hamra: the Red Castle

'I'm a great reader of Shakespeare... But a thousand Shakespeares, with all their tragic genius, could never describe the passions that have worked, and the horrors that have been perpetrated, in this place.'

**Colonel Hanmer Warrington, British Consul General, 21 May 1845**

When Colonel Warrington visited the castle with explorer James Richardson, on their way to an audience with the pasha, it was a gloomy place resonant with centuries of turbulent history. Today the gloom has vanished. The internal walls glow in the clear Tripoli light, vivid terracotta-red against the intense blue of the sky. Not all the courtyards have been restored; some still retain an air of genteel decay, and they are all still filled with the plants, fountains and statues which were added over the centuries.

Today the castle has an air of tranquillity, providing a welcome escape from the city without. This ironically defies the awful realities of its historical past, when the citadel was the seat of power, the object of invasion and the scene of much intrigue and violence.

Evidence from the period prior to the occupation by the Knights of Malta in 1530 is very meagre. Excavations have revealed that the castle was built on the site of the Roman *castrum*, but the fortress proper was not likely to have been built before the Arab invasion of 644 AD. There were presumably defensive walls in place by the 9th century, when the Aglabite prince, Abdullah bin Brahim, was besieged by his own troops and forced to quit the city in return for his life.

In 1146 the Norman king, Roger of Sicily, took possession of the castle. It was from there that he attempted to quell a revolt in the city by sending out his cavalry into the streets to crush the mob. The wily citizens strung ropes across the narrow streets and dismounted the troops, who were overpowered and imprisoned. Thus ended the brief rule of King Roger.

In 1510 the Spaniards refortified the dilapidated fortress, followed by the Knights of Malta, who constructed yet another bastion to defend the castle in preparation for an imminent Turkish attack. After a couple of assaults in 1531 and 1536 this decisive blow came in August 1551. Suleyman the Magnificent, sultan of Turkey, dispatched Sinan Pasha at the head of a large army to drive the Christians from Tripoli. The newly built St James bastion stood up to fire but, due to the treachery of one of the soldiers in the Knights' service, the Turks discovered the one weak spot in the walls and smashed their cannon fire into this defensive Achilles heel. The knights' morale crumbled as fast as the breach in the wall. Without water or hope, the governor emerged waving a flag of truce. The Turks, in no mood for observing the niceties of war, clapped him in irons and when his troops surrendered they were stripped and cast into ignominious slavery. Thus ended Christendom's 'stronghold' in Africa.

It becomes clear from the events which followed that the misfortunes which had befallen the castle so far were merely a 'warming up' for worse to come. There followed a succession of rulers whose eventful and tragic reigns encompassed just about every human misfortune and misdeed imaginable. The crusaders' ideological and religious zeal had given way to the ruthless politics of

visit the sites later on. There are also various folklore exhibits demonstrating traditional life, both in the cities and in rural areas. Perhaps the most startling exhibit is in the natural history section, which, for those tired of looking at classical artefacts, has a bizarre collection of deformed animals.

The museum is open from 8.30 am to noon and from 2 to 5 pm daily except Wednesday. The entrance charge is 250 dirhams. Photography is forbidden inside the museum but outside in the castle grounds it's OK.

## Medina

The medina is the heart of Tripoli, providing the most visually exciting and certainly the best shopping in the city, if not the whole country. As there are still only a handful of tourists visiting Libya, the souq has an authentic air and the goods on display cater to local tastes, although a few items of tourist tat have been spotted recently. The good news is that there is absolutely none of the hassle usually associated with a trip to a souq. Shopkeepers are friendly

---

the Renaissance, and Tripoli remained undisputably Ottoman for the next three and a half centuries.

Tripoli's Muslims elected their own leaders, called deys, who enjoyed a precarious relationship with the sultans back in Turkey, sometimes being recognised and elevated to pasha, sometimes not. Suleyman Dey, after a particularly brutal skirmish with the locals, found himself on the receiving end of a punitive mission from the sultan himself, who dispatched a fleet to Tripoli. Suleyman Dey was tricked out of the castle, taken on board one of the sultan's fleet and promptly crucified on the poop deck.

The next ruler, Sharif Pasha, met his fate at the hands of his own people. Unlike Suleyman Dey, his downfall came from being too mild with the local people. The janisseries plotted to overthrow him and, in a now familiar scenario, he barricaded himself in the castle. Like his predecessor, he too was tricked out of the castle, this time by a soldier disguised as one of his trusted friends, asking to be let into the castle. He was cut to pieces by those lying in wait for him.

Ramadan Dey, who succeeded him, cultivated the favour of the Bedouins with gifts 'donated' forcibly from the citizens of Tripoli, an act not guaranteed to secure his popularity. His mediocre rule was interrupted by the appearance of a dynamic corsair, Mohammed Saqisli, who came from the Greek island of Chios, and offered his services to the dey. So impressed was the dey with the booty he brought into Tripoli that he offered his daughter in marriage to Saqisli. He soon became the power behind the throne and Ramadan Dey agreed privately to hand over the reigns of government to him by means of a crudely stage-managed coup d'état, as a result of which Saqisli took control of the treasury.

He was probably disappointed with what he found there though, as the treasury had been badly depleted under the administration of so many poor rulers. One of his first moves was to impose a house tax on the city, a customs tax on the port and even a tree tax on all palms and olive trees. He also engaged the services of a fellow Greek convert from Chios, Otman Saqisli, who was put in command of the armed forces. Soon this pair of renegades had the area under control, although not without using some very dubious methods.

One mettlesome adversary was a woman called Miryam bint-Fawz, wife of a tribal chief, who had held considerable sway over Ramadan Dey. Mohammed Saqisli visited her while her husband was ill and took the opportunity to administer to him some poisoned medicine. He then invited the widow to come to the castle in Tripoli and marry him. Bringing her wealth with her, she arrived at the castle only to be turned over to the executioner as soon as the wedding ceremony had taken place. But poetic justice prevailed: Mohammed Saqisli died at the hands of his Christian doctor who fittingly poisoned him with an apple, leaving the uncomfortable throne to Otman Saqisli.

Elevated to Pasha, Otman's power soon developed into tyranny and, despite the astute political acumen he had acquired over 24 years, a mutiny broke out. A number of his loyal palace officials were slaughtered and thrown to the dogs. Seeing this he took his own life with poison, leaving a power vacuum in the castle which was to last until the Karamanlis took power in 1711. In the interim a bewildering number of rulers came and went. One died from plague, several were killed and the rest were deposed and exiled; only one managed to die of old age. ∎

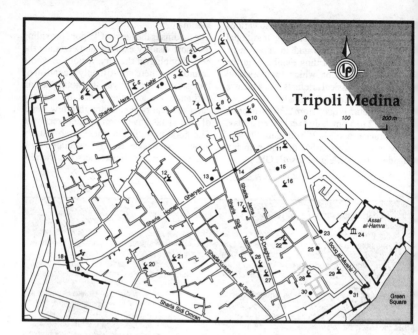

**Tripoli Medina**

1  Sidi Abdul Wahab Mosque
2  Arch of Marcus Aurelius
3  Gurgi Mosque
4  Former British Consulate
5  Ben Saber Mosque
6  Sidi Soliman Mosque
7  Church
8  Otman Pasha Mosque & School
9  Draghut Mosque
10  Hammam Draghut
11  Al-Kateis Mosque & School
12  Sidi Katab Mosque
13  Hammam al-Khabira
14  Roman Column Crossroad
15  Old Theatre
16  Mohammed Pasha Mosque
17  Huria Mosque
18  Bab al-Jedid
19  Bab Znata
20  Ben Latif Mosque
21  Charush Mosque
22  Kuaruba Mosque
23  Clock Tower
24  Jamahiriya Museum
25  Souq al-Turk
26  Ben Tabun Mosque
27  Khenara Mosque
28  Al-Naqah Mosque
29  Ahmed Pasha Karamanli Mosque
30  Hammam al-Heyga
31  Souq al-Attara

and often curious but there is no pressure to buy.

The old walled city contains virtually all of Tripoli's historic buildings. Many families who had lived in the medina for generations moved out following the expulsion of the Italians to take up residence in the modern housing vacated by them. As a result many of the old buildings fell into disrepair and the old city generally suffered as a result.

Recently moves have been made to halt the rot and carry out sympathetic restorations on the most important buildings. Also many of the families who left the old city now wish to return and open up their old houses. The medina in Tripoli is one of the largest in North Africa and contains a wealth of historic mosques, khans (inns), hammams and houses.

Starting from the castle, the first road into the medina leads past the old Bank of Libya and passes a decorative Ottoman clock tower, built in the 19th century. The road then follows what used to be the coast for a few hundred metres, bringing you out at one of the old city gates – a huge decorated door called the Bab Draghut. Behind this is the **Draghut Mosque**, named after the famous corsair admiral. The mosque has an Islamic school and a cemetery where the admiral is buried.

Continuing back along the coast road for another hundred metres, you come to the Sidi Abdul Wahab Mosque. Behind the mosque is the only Roman artefact of any significance in Tripoli – the **Arch of Marcus Aurelius**, which, although in some need of restoration, is an impressive, decorated triumphal arch.

Immediately behind the arch towards the city is the **Gurgi Mosque**, one of the most beautiful in the city. The courtyard has some lovely tilework and inlaid marble decorations. The prayer hall alone has 16 domes and the minaret is the tallest in the city. Next door to the Gurgi

Mosque on Zenkat Spania is Ahmed Pasha's house, formerly the British consulate. This fine old house has now been restored and is to be used as a library and gallery which will be open to the public.

Another important old house which has been restored is the **House of Karamanli**, near an ancient crossroad in the centre of the city called Al-Arba Asaht. The crossroad is marked by four Roman columns set into the corners of the buildings. Note that the name of the old house in Arabic is 'Hosn al-Harem', as you will almost certainly need to ask directions.

Back at the south-eastern end of the medina, near the castle, is the **Souq al-Mushir**. The entrance from Green Square is through an archway. Immediately to the left is the Souq al-Attara in which the jewellery shops congregate. At the end of this street is an old khan in which the jewellers have their workshops, which is worth a visit. If, instead of turning left into Souq al-Attara, you continue straight on, you will see on your left the splendid **Ahmed Pasha Karamanli Mosque**, the largest mosque in the old city. Turn left after the mosque and follow the road round to the right and you are in the **Souq al-Turk**, which is partly covered and sells clothes and all manner of general goods. The Mohammed Pasha Mosque is about 200 metres along on the right, marked by an elaborately carved door.

The oldest mosque in Tripoli is the **Al-Naqah Mosque**, which is close to the Ahmed Pasha Karamanli Mosque and well worth a look. In all there are 38 mosques within the walls of the old city, although some of them are tiny and of interest only to those with a serious interest in Islamic architecture. If you only want to see one or two, go for the Ahmed Pasha Karamanli and Gurgi mosques, as their decoration is particularly fine.

### Hammams

There are two hammams in the old city: Hammam Draghut is next door to the Draghut Mosque, and Hammam al-Heygha is near the Souq al-Attara. They both operate a rota for men and women. Hammam Draghut is open to women on Monday, Tuesday and Thursday, and to men on Wednesday, Friday and Saturday. The reverse days apply to Hammam al-Heygha. Charges are 1 LD for a steam bath, 2 LD for a massage and 5 LD for the works.

### Art Gallery

An interesting contemporary art gallery, featuring the work of Libyan artists, has recently opened on Sharia Taliq Assekker. It is a private gallery, and the work is for sale and well worth a look. It is also worth noting that in the same building, on the 1st floor, there is a well-stocked professional artists' supply shop, probably the only one in Tripoli. The gallery and shop are open from 9 am to 2 pm daily except Friday.

### San Francisco Church

There is one functioning Catholic church in Tripoli, the San Francisco Church at Dahra, which is worth visiting for its decoratively painted 1930s interior. The services are conducted in a number of languages:

| Day | Time | Language |
| --- | --- | --- |
| Friday | 9 am | Korean |
| | 10.30 am | English |
| | 4.30 pm | English |
| | 6.30 pm | Italian |
| Saturday | 6 pm | French |
| Sunday | 8.30 am | Italian |
| | 10 am | English |
| | noon | English |
| | 5 pm | Polish |
| | 6.30 pm | Italian |
| Monday | 4.30 pm | Arabic |

### Zoo

A trip to the zoo makes a peaceful break from the noise of the city. It is situated three km south of central Tripoli in a suburb called Abu Salim, and is set in a large wooded area which makes a good spot for a picnic even if you don't want to visit the zoo. The zoo is open from 10 am to 5 pm daily except Monday and Tuesday, and entrance costs 0.50 LD for adults and 0.25 LD for children. It has a pleasant café and a restaurant where lunch costs about 12 to 14 LD. To get to the zoo you can take a collect taxi from the main taxi station to Abu Salim, from where it is a short walk (about half a km). Ask for 'Hadikat al-Haywan' (Arabic for 'zoo').

### Beaches

There is a beach on the western side of town with changing facilities and cafés. The entrance is a little way south of the two beach hotels on the western corniche, and it costs 2 LD to enter. The water is reasonably clean by the standards of town beaches, but the beach itself suffers from a litter problem. A farther km south, in the Hay al-Andalous area, there is a private beach attached to a hotel, the Massif Garnata, which has safe bathing within a natural breakwater. There are some water sports available there.

### Language Courses

There are Arabic language courses for foreigners run by the Islamic Call Society in the building attached to the Central Mosque (the former cathedral). There is a sign in English by the doorway to the right of the mosque.

## Places to Stay – bottom end

**Hostel** The central hostel (☎ 021-45171) on Sharia Amr ibn al-As, as listed in the HI handbook, has recently closed, although the address and telephone number are still good for general enquiries about hostels throughout Libya. The new hostel (☎ 021-74755) is in Gagaresh, on the coast about three km from the centre of Tripoli. If you follow the main Gagaresh road south, take the second turning on the right after the big post office. This road leads to the sea, and the hostel is a large, new building close to a small fishing harbour. There are frequent buses and taxis serving this route. There are no family rooms, only dormitories, but it is clean and modern. There is a large restaurant, which sometimes has musical entertainment, and meals cost around 5 LD. Beds cost 2.50 LD for members and 5 LD for non-members, or you can have full board for 15 LD per day.

**Hotels** There is a shortage of good, cheap accommodation in Tripoli: hotels tend to either cater for international business people or, at the other end of the scale, are unspeakably awful. More or less anything under 20 LD per night falls into the latter category.

The best of the cheap hotels on the eastern side of town is the *Libya Palace Hotel* (☎ 021-31180/9) on Sharia Sidi Issa behind the Egyptian Embassy. This is a large 1960s hotel, formerly in the luxury class but fallen on hard times. There has been some attempt to renovate the hotel recently and so it is quite a bargain at only 13/18 LD for singles/doubles with bathroom. The hotel has two restaurants, where lunch or dinner costs 7 LD, and a rooftop coffee bar with a good view of the city.

If large hotels are not your cup of tea, the small and friendly *Funduq Ayyussar* (☎ 021-30911 or 37287) is a good bet. It is tucked away in a nameless back street in Dahra, directly opposite the San Francisco Church. Singles/doubles cost 20 LD for a room with a bath, including a simple breakfast. The rooms are by no means luxurious but they are tolerably clean and the showers are piping hot. In the same small street there are two other hotels: a couple of doors along there's the *Cleopatra Hotel* (☎ 021-22445), which is the same price as the former, and the *Marhaba Hotel*, which is on the corner opposite the church and is slightly more expensive.

Closer to the old city there are a few cheap hotels. The *Funduq al-Mamoun* (☎ 021-37919) on Sharia al-Ma'mun is quite good, but basic, and very close to the bus and taxi station. Singles/doubles with bathroom cost 13/20 LD, including breakfast. There is a small restaurant where meals cost 4 LD for a 'normal' and 8 LD for a 'special'. Farther down the road and down-market from the Mamoun is the *Funduq Jebel Akhdar*, overlooking the taxi station. This hotel is pretty awful and definitely not recommended unless you are on a seriously tight budget. Singles/doubles cost 5/10 LD. The only reason for staying here, apart from an extremely tight budget, is if you are catching a bus or taxi at the crack of dawn, in which case it is very handy.

## Places to Stay – middle

Mid-range hotels include the *Bab al-Medina Hotel* (☎ 021-608051/8) on Sharia al-Kurnish overlooking the town beach. The hotel has a pool and is quite comfortable. Rooms here cost 25 LD with private bathroom and air-con.

Farther down the coast at Hay al-Andalous there is a new private beach resort called *Massif Garnata*, which has apartment accommodation of various sizes. This is very much a family-oriented resort, with a pleasant setting. It can get very full in summer, when there are some water-sports facilities available. Prices for apartments range from 13 to 30 LD per night.

There is also the *Waddan Hotel* (☎ 021-30042/6) on Sharia al-Fatah, where singles/doubles cost 30/40 LD with bathroom and air-con. This is a very popular place with friendly staff and, because it is conveniently situated near the centre, it can get very booked up.

## Places to Stay – top end

The swankiest place in town is undoubtedly the *Mehari Hotel* (☎ 021-34091) on Sharia al-Fatah, with swanky prices to match. It is large and very comfortable, but still somewhat lacking in the services that would justify the price in any other part of the world. Single/double rooms here cost 65/75 LD, including breakfast, and the staff have a nasty habit of making you pay in advance in hard currency. There are three restaurants to choose from, including a sort of nightclub on the roof with live music. Lunch or dinner will probably set you back 25 LD.

Somewhat cheaper, but still in the luxury class, is the *Al-Kabir Hotel* (☎ 021-45945/9) which is wonderfully situated on Sharia al-Fatah, a couple of hundred metres from Green Square, close to the shopping district and within an easy walk of the castle and medina. The hotel has a pool, terrace coffee shop and two restaurants. Double rooms cost 40 LD.

On the western corniche, next door to the Bab al-Medina, is the *Bab al-Bahr Hotel* (☎ 021-608051/8), which manages to attain a reasonable level of comfort. It is part of the same development as the Bab al-Medina but with more luxurious rooms and better facilities. Singles/doubles cost 25/35 LD.

## Places to Eat

There is a shortage of restaurants in Tripoli, although the situation is getting better all the time with new places seeming to spring up overnight. The few good cheap ones can get very full. The *Bedouin Restaurant*, on Sharia al-Baladiya almost directly behind the Al-Kabir Hotel, is recommended. The food is Lebanese and lunch or dinner costs about 8 LD, which includes mixed starters, well-cooked grills and delicious, stuffed flat bread plus salads and pudding. The measure of the quality here is that you almost always have to queue for a table, but it is worth the wait. There is a popular felafel restaurant on Sharia al-Magarief, a couple of hundred metres from Green Square, which costs only a dinar or two for lunch.

There is a good fish restaurant called the *Gazala* (☎ 021-41079) near the Gazelle Fountain, facing the park. It always has a good selection of freshly caught fish and seafood. As with fish restaurants everywhere, the prices are a bit on the high side expect to pay 20 LD per head. In the same area, directly behind the Al-Kabir Hotel or Sharia al-Baladiya, is a new Moroccan place the *Safir Restaurant* (☎ 021-47064), which has good food and a lovely interior of Moroccan tile and stucco. Lunch and dinner cost about 15 LD.

There are many cafés serving soft drinks and light snacks around Green Square and along Sharia al-Fatah, tucked in amongst the parks and gardens. The new tea garden 100 metres east of the Waddan Hotel is a good one. It's a popular gathering place in the evening and the nearest thing to lively nightlife Tripoli has to offer. In the old city there are numerous small cafés and cubbyhole snack shops which are all very cheap.

All the restaurants in Tripoli seem to close early, about 10 or 10.30 pm, and if you want a table at the more popular places it is best to arrive no later than 8.30 pm. A few of the fast-food places stay open a bit later, but after 10.30 pm your choice is rather limited.

## Entertainment

Public entertainment is a bit thin on the ground in Tripoli. Occasionally there will be some kind of folklore festival or equestrian event. These events are listed in the local press but if you cannot read Arabic the only thing to do is ask around. Hotel reception staff are usually good at knowing what is going on. If your visit coincides with a national holiday there may well be some parades or other public festivities, which often centre around Green Square.

**Cinemas**   There are about half a dozen cinemas in Tripoli, most of which show Arabic or Asian films exclusively. There is a cinema next door to the Waddan Hotel which shows foreign films regularly, but check whether the film is dubbed first! Entrance to cinemas is about 1 LD.

**Spectator Sports** Football is a regular favourite with Libyans. There are a large number of local teams and there is often a game in Tripoli in either the main stadium in the south of the city or in one of the local sports centres. There is also a horse race-course about three km west of Green Square, just off Sharia al-Fatah, where there are periodic fixtures.

## Things to Buy

Tripoli offers the best shopping anywhere in Libya and the old city is the place to go. Old Bedouin silver is a good buy and gold is relatively cheap, although the large pieces made for traditional weddings would be hard to wear. Carpets and textiles are interesting and tend to be either very bright, African colours or very sober neutrals. There are many different styles of Arab clothes on sale. Lengths of hand-woven striped silk, as worn by women for festivals, are attractive. In the kitchen-supply shops there are simple, attractive utensils made from olive wood which are a bargain.

## Getting There & Away

**Air** Libyan Arab Airlines flies a regular service to and from Benghazi and Sebha, and a less frequent service to Sirt, Ghadhames, Ghat, Kufra and Tobruk. At the time of writing, all the domestic services were in a state of upheaval due to the UN sanctions.

Libyan Arab Airlines has the following offices in Tripoli:

Head Office, Sharia Haiti, PO Box 2555 (☎ 021-20333, 20193)
Sales Office, Sharia Omar al-Mukhtar (☎ 021-602091)
Airport Sales Office (☎ 021-605041/9)
Al-Kabir Hotel Sales Office, Sharia al-Fatah (☎ 021-37500, 35686)

**Bus** There are frequent, cheap bus services to and from Tunisia and Egypt as well as regional towns around Libya. It is a good idea to buy tickets the day before you intend to travel and turn up well ahead of the scheduled departure time. Buses leave from the main bus station at the western end of Sharia

al-Ma'mun. The green-and-white buses of the Fast Transport Company have a ticket office round the corner on Sharia al-Ma'ari. The ticket office for the super-luxury buses which serve international routes is on the eastern side of the square overlooking the bus station.

## Domestic Timetable – Fast Transport Company

| Destination | Day | Time | Fare |
|---|---|---|---|
| Ajdabiya | daily | 6.45 am | 9.25 LD |
| Benghazi | daily | 7 am, 10 am | 10 LD |
| Brak | daily | 7.30 am | 10 LD |
| Ghadhames | daily | 7 am, 10 am | 7.50 LD |
| Gharyan & Jadu | daily | 1 pm | 2.75 LD |
| Khoms | daily | 7 am, 1.30 pm | 1.50 LD |
| Kufrah | Mon & Thurs | 9 am | 20.50 LD |
| Nalut | daily | 7.30 am, 2 pm | 3.50 LD |
| Ras al-Jedir | daily | 8 am, 2 pm, 5 pm | 2.75 LD |
| Sebha | daily | 7 am | 10 LD |
| Yefren | daily | 2 pm | 2.75 LD |

**Taxi** The yellow-and-white shared taxis are frequent, efficient and cheap. They serve most destinations and leave from the same central station as the buses. The square is packed with taxis waiting to fill up, and the only way to find one going to your destination is simply to ask.

**Car Rental** There are car-rental agencies in the lobbies of the main hotels. Tripoli Office Car Rentals has offices in both the Al-Kabir (☎ 021-47208; fax 021-45959) and Mehari (☎ 021-34091/6, ext 404) hotels. You will need an International Driving Permit and a deposit of 300 LD. Rental charges are between 25 and 45 LD per day plus mileage. Unlimited-mileage deals work out at around 200 to 280 LD for three days.

## Getting Around

**To/From the Airport** There is a regular shuttle bus service to and from the airport which leaves from the city bus station in Maidan Asswayhli or from Green Square. The fare to the airport is 1 LD.

**Bus** Buses serving the city and the suburbs leave from the city bus station at Maidan Asswayhli, off Sharia Omar al-Mukhtar. Recently the large buses have been taken out of service and white minibuses are being used instead. Bus stops on the routes are easily recognisable by their concrete shelters. There is a flat fare of 0.25 LD.

**Taxis** Avoid the private black-and-white taxis as they are hideously expensive, even for short rides. For example, a taxi from the Al-Kabir Hotel to the Waddan Hotel (a two-minute journey) costs 10 LD – about the cost of a meal in an average restaurant. From Green Square to the Al-Kabir Hotel (about 500 yards) costs about 6 LD.

If you do need to use these taxis, they tend to congregate by the entrance to the medina on Green Square, outside the Al-Kabir Hotel and in the Maidan al-Jazayir, next to the large post office. Otherwise it is just a question of flagging one down.

# Tripolitania

Tripolitania covers the whole of the north-western part of the country. The area surrounding Tripoli as far south as the Jebel Nafusa is mostly farm land, with vast groves of fruit and olive trees and date palms. Most of Libya's fresh food comes from this area. Beyond the Jebel Nafusa is the start of the desert, with some spectacular scenery on the way. South-west of the mountains lies the oasis town of Ghadhames, which has its own unique attractions and should not be missed.

Sabratha and Leptis Magna, two of Libya's most famous tourist attractions and amongst the finest Roman cities in the Mediterranean, are on the coast of Tripolitania, within easy reach of the capital. As the coast dips down towards Sirt the desert comes up to meet the coast, forming the desolate natural boundary which historically divided the provinces of Tripolitania and Cyrenaica.

# West of Tripoli

## JANZUR
Janzur is the first town west of Tripoli and the nearest beach resort to the city, only 15 km down the old coast road. There are extensive palm groves here and it has the air of a prosperous suburb. There is an 18th-century mosque called **Sidi Amara** in the town but apart from that everything is modern. Right on the beach is a new tourist village with a restaurant and facilities for sports such as sailing and tennis. Needless to say, this place becomes packed at weekends.

### Places to Stay & Eat
The only choice is the *Janzur Tourist Village* (in Arabic, 'Medina Seahia Janzur'), which has a range of accommodation but averages out at 30 LD for a double room. Lunch and dinner at the restaurant cost about 15 LD. This resort is only open to 'families'. The overall quality of accommodation and food is very substandard. The main road through the village has a couple of small cafés and shops but there are no proper restaurants.

### Getting There & Away
There are very frequent buses to Janzur from central Tripoli which stop on the main road in the centre of town. There also appear to be nonstop collect taxis plying the route. Be warned though, the road between Janzur and Tripoli can be one long traffic jam during rush hours.

## ZAWIA
Zawia, 44 km west of Tripoli, is a small, pleasant town consisting mainly of farms, many dating from the Italian occupation. There is little to see here but there is a beach which can be reached by taking more or less any turning to the north from the highway. There are no facilities at the beach, but it is a pleasant place to stop for a picnic.

### Getting There & Away
Once again, this town is on a well-worn route, and most buses and collect taxis serving the coastal route pass through Zawia. The fare is 1.5 LD from Tripoli.

## SABRATHA
One of the 'must see' sights in Libya, Sabratha is a well-preserved Roman city, about 67 km from Tripoli. It has one of the loveliest theatres you could wish to see. Although the ruins overall are less spectacular than those at Leptis Magna, the site is very attractively situated overlooking the sea and there are nearby beaches. The modern town of Sabratha has grown up around the ruins.

Although it is possible to visit the site as a day trip from Tripoli or as a short stopover on the way to or from Tunisia, it is well worth it to allow at least a whole day to explore the ruins and view the museum, which would also leave time for a leisurely swim and sunbathe.

## History

The city, as seen today, dates from the Roman occupation of Tripolitania and was built during the 1st and 2nd centuries AD. It was destroyed by the Vandals, rebuilt during the Arab occupation and then neglected by the Turks. It was finally excavated during the Italian occupation and partly restored in the 1930s.

Sabratha was first settled by the Phoenicians as a trading post. The exact date of its foundation is largely a question of speculation, while Greek pottery has been found on the site which dates from the 6th century BC. The first literary reference to the settlement dates from the late 4th century BC. Excavations have revealed an early walled village of mud huts near the area of the Temple of Liber Pater. After the fall of Carthage, the Romans superimposed their ordered town plan over the original, more haphazard settlement. The transformation was slower than that at Leptis Magna. The early Roman city was concentrated around the forum with the Liber Pater and Serapis temples, after which it spread inland on the familiar grid pattern culminating in the theatre, which is Sabratha's crowning feature.

Sabratha did not enjoy such lavish imperial favour as Leptis and so its decline was not as dramatic. The city did not collapse until the Vandals wrought their usual destruction, although its downward fortunes had already begun, due to an earthquake in 365 AD rather than the usual economic decline. When the Byzantine armies reclaimed North Africa from the Vandals, Sabratha was in a weakened state and new defensive walls were built, plus a fine church which featured a mosaic floor.

After the Arabs arrived in Tripolitania and laid siege to Tripoli, the Sabrathans prepared for their own siege behind their Byzantine walls. Hearing that the Arabs had been repelled, they relaxed their vigilance, even to the point of leaving their gates open. When the Arabs finally took Tripoli, the inevitable happened. Riding through the night they took Sabratha completely by surprise and the city surrendered. Once established, the Arabs moved the market to Tripoli, depriving Sabratha of its means of economic survival, and thereafter the city declined into obscurity and ruin.

## Information

**Money** There is a bank in Sabratha on the road approaching the entrance to the ruins on the right-hand side.

**Post & Telecommunications** The post office is in the same street as the bank, and it also has public telephones.

## The Ruins

The earliest parts of the city are in the western area, which corresponds roughly to the original Punic city. When the Byzantines rebuilt the city walls they enclosed only this part, leaving the later Roman parts of the city farther to the east exposed and abandoned. The extent of this later, somewhat reduced, city can be clearly seen on the map. The entrance to the site is directly on the city's main road, and the museum is just to the south. Straight ahead lies the Byzantine gate to the city.

The site is open daily except Tuesday from 8 am to 5.30 pm and costs 0.25 LD to enter; keep your ticket for entry to the museum. There are some publications on sale in English and German.

**Mausoleum of Bes** There is a residential quarter to the left of the Byzantine gate. In this area is the Mausoleum of Bes, a rather repugnant deity whose image was often attached to the prow of Phoenician ships. The mausoleum has some rare Aeolic capitals, and it was originally covered in painted stucco.

**South Forum Temple** Passing the Byzantine gate, the first major building on the left is the South Forum Temple. It is not known to which deity it was dedicated but the temple is an impressive size. A rectangular courtyard with a marble-paved portico leads to the temple, which stands on a high platform with wide marble steps.

**Basilica of Apuleius** The building we see today dates from around 440 AD, in its final incarnation as a church. Before that it was a law court, where the famous trial of the writer Apuleius of Madaura took place. He was tried on a charge of witchcraft in 157 AD and delivered his apologia to great effect: he was acquitted of the charge. The baptistry, which was added in the 5th century, incorporates fragments of earlier buildings, such as a highly decorated pillar which is similar to the ones in the Severan Basilica in Leptis Magna.

**Forum & Nearby Monuments** The remains of the great forum visible today date from the 4th century restoration, perhaps carried out to repair earthquake damage. The siting of the forum away from the centre of the city

indicates that its builders expected Sabratha to expand. Before the Antonine period, the forum was closed to traffic and accessible by only a single entrance. Over time the shops and offices became grander and more permanent, and a portico was built with grey columns of Egyptian granite. Surrounding the forum are a number of important buildings. The **Antonine Temple** stands on the other side of the site's main thoroughfare, and the **Temple of Liber Pater**, or Dionysus, is next to it to the north.

Also north of the forum is the curia, marked by its restored archway at the entrance. The curia was the meeting place of the city's magistrates and senators. Columns of marble and granite held up the once impressive portico. There are steps on which the dignitaries sat on bronze or wooden seats.

Opposite the curia is the **Temple of Serapis**, a cult which originally came from Memphis in Egypt. Serapis was a healer and

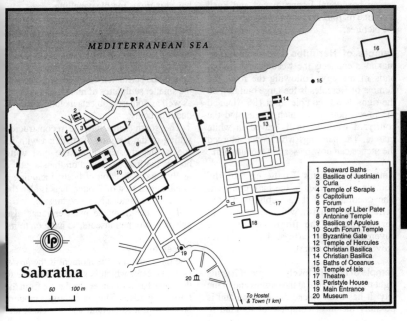

MEDITERRANEAN SEA

**Sabratha**

0    50    100 m

To Hostel
& Town (1 km)

1  Seaward Baths
2  Basilica of Justinian
3  Curia
4  Temple of Serapis
5  Capitolium
6  Forum
7  Temple of Liber Pater
8  Antonine Temple
9  Basilica of Apuleius
10  South Forum Temple
11  Byzantine Gate
12  Temple of Hercules
13  Christian Basilica
14  Christian Basilica
15  Baths of Oceanus
16  Temple of Isis
17  Theatre
18  Peristyle House
19  Main Entrance
20  Museum

LIBYA

miracle worker, and at Sabratha the cult was often associated with that of Isis. During the reign of Tiberius, Egyptian cults were outlawed throughout the Roman empire.

The **Capitolium**, or Temple of Jupiter, is the last of the important buildings around the forum. It is the principal temple of the city. The huge bust of Jupiter, now in the museum, and of the goddess Concordia were found here.

**Basilica of Justinian** North-west of the forum area and near the coast is the Basilica of Justinian. The magnificent mosaic which is now housed in a facsimile setting in the site museum was discovered here. Seeing the splendour of the mosaic it is easy to imagine the overall grandeur of the church, which has three naves, a raised presbytery, a pulpit and an altar. The pulpit originally formed a part of the cornice on the Capitolium.

**Seaward Baths** These are famous for their lovely mosaics and the wonderfully preserved hexagonal latrine, paved and lined with fine marble. A favourite spot for posing for pictures.

**Temple of Hercules** The decumanus maximus connects the western and eastern parts of the city. Following the road, the Temple of Hercules is the large building on the right. It was completed in 186 AD, and the raised porticoes which run around the courtyard were originally paved in white marble. The paintings which once adorned the niches can now be seen in the museum.

**Baths of Oceanus** To the east of the Temple of Hercules is the bath complex. The decoration of these public baths was extraordinarily lavish, with marble on every surface except the floors, which were covered in mosaics (these have been removed to the museum).

**Temple of Isis** The lovely Temple of Isis sits right by the seashore at the eastern end of the city. It has been splendidly restored and is possibly the most complete of its kind in Africa. The colonnaded courtyard has a row of eight Corinthian columns. The sanctuary is set on a podium reached by a broad flight of steps.

**Theatre** The most outstanding monument at Sabratha is the theatre. Built in the late 2nd century, it has been beautifully restored, with the imposing three-tiered *scaenae frons* dominating the view. This unusual backdrop is composed of 108 Corinthian columns. The design is reputed to be a replica of the palace built by Septimius Severus in Rome, and some visitors feel that it bears a passing resemblance, in terms of style, to Petra in Jordan.

The front of the stage is decorated with a series of marble reliefs in recesses showing various mythological and dramatic scenes. In the semicircular arena below the stage there are carved dolphins at either side. The backstage rooms are also very interesting: the dressing rooms and, in particular, the 'green room' on the western side of the stage have luxurious marble panelling.

**Sabratha Museum**
The collection at Sabratha Museum is well worth seeing and of high quality. The courtyard has a fine selection of statues displayed around the perimeter. The west wing houses the smaller sculptures of marble and bronze, as well as domestic objects including a large hoard of coins.

The south wing has the reconstructed setting of the Basilica of Justinian with its spectacular mosaic floor. The east wing houses the frescoes found on the site and a really good collection of busts, including a monumental bust of Jupiter. This is also the home of the famous Neptune mosaic.

The ticket from the main entrance also gets you into the museum, so hang on to it.

**Places to Stay**
The only option at the moment is the *hostel* (☎ 024-2215), which is situated so close to the ruins that you can see the theatre from the hostel's garden. This is a large, modern hostel with a restaurant, and it's clean and

comfortable. From the modern highway coming from Tripoli, take the turning on the right after the *baladiya* (town hall) and the mosque. The hostel is about one km straight ahead of you on a bend in the road.

On the same road, before you reach the hostel, a new hotel is being built on the right-hand side of the road. It may well be up and running by the time you read this.

### Places to Eat

Apart from ordering your meals at the hostel, there are a few small restaurants in the modern town of Sabratha. There is one just next to the baladiya on the main road. There is also a restaurant at the ruins which is only open for lunch, but has a pleasant outside eating area. You could do worse than take your meals outside in the garden at the hostel.

### Getting There & Away

Sabratha is situated on the very busy highway between Tripoli and the Tunisian border, and there is no shortage of buses and collect taxis passing through. Buses stop on the main road in the centre of town, from where it is a one-km walk to the ruins. For a small extra fee taxis will make the detour from the centre of town to the ruins or the hostel.

### ZUARA & RAS AL-JEDIR

Zuara is the last town before the border. If you are heading for the border, this is the last chance for a decent meal and a rest before the lengthy, hot process of customs and passport control. On the main road on the western side of town there is a small fairground with a good air-conditioned restaurant and terrace where you can get a meal for about 8 LD.

Ras al-Jedir, the border post, is not a town as such, more of a traffic jam with roadside shacks. The queues to cross the border can be horrific. The main customs building was bulldozed by Colonel Gaddafi a few years ago in a mood of 'openness' with neighbouring Tunisia. The various official processes are now carried out from a series of portable cabins set up in the middle of the road.

Depending on the time of day, the clearance of the border can take between one and several hours. Fifty metres ahead you have to go through the whole thing again on the Tunisian side. If you have a plane to catch at Jerba allow three hours on top of your journey time.

# East of Tripoli

### TAJURA

The popular weekend beach resort of Tajura is 32 km east of Tripoli. There are two tourist villages on the coast here, one pretty old and a bit run-down, the other brand new. Both have the usual beach and water-sports facilities. The beaches themselves, it has to be said, are nothing special and if you have your own car you would be better off driving farther along the coast where the beaches are much more attractive.

Tajura village itself used to be a quiet rural area before the suburban sprawl from Tripoli caught up with it. The settlement goes back to medieval times and its outstanding historical monument is the large **Murad Agha Mosque**, which dates from the middle of the 16th century. It is very plain from the outside and features a large square minaret. Inside it has a large arcaded prayer hall with 48 columns, which were brought from Leptis Magna.

### Places to Stay

The new beach complex, *Sidi al-Andalous Tourism Village* (☎ 021-690034), is open throughout the year but it can get very full in summer. Given that the beach is rather small, it would be best to avoid the place during the high season. There are 126 rooms, two restaurants and basketball and volleyball courts; a swimming pool is currently being built. Singles/doubles cost 10/15 LD.

The older beach complex, *Medinah Seahia Tajura*, is a couple of km farther east. It is set on a wider stretch of beach but the building is a bit shabby. It has the same basic facilities and is a bit cheaper.

## Places to Eat

Apart from the restaurants at the beach complexes there is little other choice for eating out. Meals at the complexes cost an average 8 LD. There are a few grocery shops in the village if you want to kit yourself up for a picnic.

## Getting There & Away

Buses from Tripoli stop in the village, but it is two km from the central roundabout to the nearest of the tourist villages. If you are heading for the beach, rather than Tajura, there is little option but to take a taxi.

## GARABULLI

This small coastal village is 60 km from Tripoli on the old coast road. Set in rural farmland, Garabulli has a few small cafés and shops and there's a pleasant beach just north of the village. Garabulli has a tourist village, but it is being used to house Bosnian refugee children and so is closed to the public. There are no facilities at the beach so it is important to take your own water and supplies with you.

## Getting There & Away

Most of the buses travelling along the coastal route use the new highway and bypass Garabulli (it is about three km to the coast from the highway). Collect taxis go from Tripoli to Garabulli and cost about 2 LD.

## KHOMS

Khoms is a small coastal town 120 km east of Tripoli, with a population of 25,000. It has low-built modern architecture and little of historical interest for the sightseer apart from a rather nice old mosque, the Ali Pasha. The real reason for visiting Khoms is its proximity to Leptis Magna, three km along the road to the east, which is one of the largest and most impressive Roman cities in the Mediterranean. As Khoms is also situated on a particularly fine stretch of sandy beach, it makes a good base to explore the ruins, swim and relax for a few days.

## Information

**Money** The Jamahiriya Bank is situated in a turning just off the main street, close to the baladiya, and is open from 8 am to 2 pm.

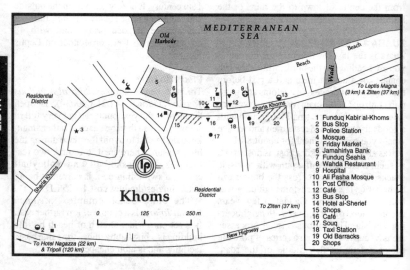

**Khoms**

1 Funduq Kabir al-Khoms
2 Bus Stop
3 Police Station
4 Mosque
5 Friday Market
6 Jamahiriya Bank
7 Funduq Seahia
8 Wahda Restaurant
9 Hospital
10 Ali Pasha Mosque
11 Post Office
12 Café
13 Bus Stop
14 Hotel al-Sherief
15 Shops
16 Café
17 Souq
18 Taxi Station
19 Old Barracks
20 Shops

To Leptis Magna (3 km) & Zliten (37 km)

To Zliten (37 km)

To Hotel Nagazza (22 km) & Tripoli (120 km)

There is also another bank on the northern side of the main street.

**Post & Telecommunications** The post office is on the main street, Sharia Khoms, and is open from 8 am to 2 pm for counter services. There are also public telephones in the same building.

**Shopping** There are small shops selling groceries and general supplies on Sharia Khoms and there is a souq in the area behind the taxi station. There is also a weekly Friday market in the area towards the old harbour where local produce and household goods are sold. It's worth a visit to catch a bit of local atmosphere.

**Places to Stay – bottom end**
The cheapest place in town is the *Hotel al-Sherief* (☎ 031-22816), on Sharia Khoms in the centre of town. There are 11 rooms, clean and simply furnished, but without private bathrooms. The shared bathrooms are rather basic, and there is no separate bathroom for females. For that reason the hotel is not really suitable for women. Singles/doubles cost 3/5 LD and breakfast is available for an extra 2 LD.

The *Funduq Seahia* (☎ 031-22130) is off Sharia Khoms towards the seafront, down a turning opposite the taxi station. This is an older hotel, built in the 1940s, and it has sea views. It is a bit basic at present but there are plans afoot to renovate and add more facilities. The rooms have TV and telephones, and they're clean and simple. Some rooms have private bathrooms. Singles/doubles cost 4/7 LD and breakfast is 2 to 3 LD. Full board can be arranged for 12 LD per day. After the improvements, the prices will increase a little, but not a lot, according to the management.

**Places to Stay – middle**
The *Funduq Kabir al-Khoms* (☎ 031-23333 or 26944) is on the main highway, close to the turn-off for Khoms. With 47 rooms, it has a coffee lounge, dining room and laundry facilities. Rooms cost 11 LD for a single or a double, and a small apartment is 20 LD, including breakfast. Lunch at the hotel costs between 4 and 10 LD and dinner is 15 LD.

The best hotel in the area, *Hotel Nagazza* (☎ 031-26691), is 22 km west of Khoms, two km north of the main highway (a signpost in Arabic indicates the turning). It is a charming, modern hotel set in wooded hills close to the sea. It has six rooms, two suites and 11 chalets. Single/double rooms with bath cost 20 LD, a suite costs 35 LD and chalets cost 10 LD; prices include breakfast. Lunch and dinner cost 6 LD. There are three good beaches four km north of the hotel. If you follow the road, you come to a three-way fork. The left-hand road is a bumpy track to a sandy beach; the middle track leads to a rocky beach, good for snorkelling; and the right-hand surfaced road leads to a long, sandy beach.

**Places to Eat**
Dining out in Khoms is a pretty limited experience. Outside of the hotels, the only options are the simple hole-in-the-wall restaurants in the centre of town. There are a few along Sharia Khoms and there is quite a good one on the same street as Funduq Seahia called the *Wahda*. These places have a limited, but tasty, selection of meals. Most offer Libyan variations of the soup, kebab, couscous and salad theme, which together with a soft drink usually cost around 5 LD. A slightly better bet is the restaurant directly opposite the entrance to Leptis Magna. It is more spacious and has outdoor seating in the summer. It serves the usual selection of salads and grills and costs about 8 LD for lunch or dinner.

**Getting There & Away**
There is an air-conditioned bus which leaves Tripoli daily at 9 am and returns from Khoms at noon, leaving from the bus stop on Sharia Khoms; it also stops outside the Funduq Kabir al-Khoms. There are more frequent buses which serve destinations farther east and stop on request on the highway. If you are going to Leptis Magna ask to be dropped at the turning for 'Lebda'. It is only about

LIBYA

500 metres from the highway to the entrance to the ruins. The fare to and from Tripoli is 1.50 LD.

A better way to travel is by shared taxi. There are plenty running between Tripoli and Khoms and the fare is only 2.50 LD. You can find them in the square off Sharia Khoms next to the old barracks. There are private taxis which are the only way, apart from walking, to take you the three km from Khoms to Leptis Magna. The fare is 4 LD, and you can arrange for the driver to pick you up again at an agreed time.

## LEPTIS MAGNA

If you only visit one archaeological site in Libya, this is the one to choose. It is widely regarded as the best Roman site in the Mediterranean. The spectacular architecture and the sheer scale of the city are impressive even if your appetite for ruins is somewhat jaded.

As the site is so large and there is only a small shop selling cold drinks just inside the entrance, it is advised to take some water with you, especially in the summer when temperatures can get very high indeed.

### History

Leptis Magna was originally a Phoenician port, settled during the 1st millennium BC. The growth of Leptis Magna into one of the most important Roman cities began in these preceding centuries, firstly through the lucrative trade with the Sudan and tropical Africa. Slaves, gold, ivory and precious metals soon brought in wealth, supplemented by the rich agricultural land which then surrounded Leptis. By around the 6th or 7th century BC, Leptis was a permanent colony under the domination of Carthage.

In the 4th century BC, Tripolitania came into conflict with the Greek colonies in Cyrenaica in the east. According to legend, the boundary dispute was settled in a unique way. After a period of indecisive battles, it was agreed that each side should dispatch its fastest runners – Cyrenaica's from Cyrene in the east and Tripolitania's from Leptis in the west. The point where the two teams met would decide the boundary. The Car-

thaginians sent two runners, the Philaeni brothers, who had covered about two-thirds of the distance before they met their rivals. Displeased with the result, the Greeks accused them of cheating. Offered to choose between being buried alive at the point they had reached or moving the boundary closer to Leptis Magna, the Philaeni brothers chose death. The point on the boundary where they were buried was once marked with a gaudy monument built by the Italians but it has been demolished since the revolution.

Although the Greeks were trounced, it was the Romans who finally ousted the Carthaginians from Leptis and the whole of North Africa. Following the third Punic War, during which Carthage was razed, Leptis Magna came under Roman domination. During the reign of Emperor Trajan (98-117 AD), Leptis Magna and Tripolitania became part of the Roman empire and its inhabitants Roman citizens.

Leptis Magna flourished during the rule of Septimius Severus (193-211), and many of the fine buildings seen today on the site date from this period. Septimius Severus was born in Leptis and favoured his home town above all others. Marble from the eastern Mediterranean was brought to Leptis for the construction of majestic public buildings. The public baths are the largest outside of Rome itself and the huge scale of the forum and basilica rival any in the Roman empire. At the height of its wealth, Leptis had a population of between 60,000 and 80,000 people.

Leptis fell into decline when the Severan dynasty ended. The harbour began to silt up and the Saharan trade route suffered. Tribal insurrections in Tripolitania added to the city's problems. The Vandals' occupation of Leptis in 455 finally signalled the end of the great city.

The Byzantine general, Belisarius, reoccupied Leptis in 533 and restored Roman rule for a short time. However, the city was under frequent attack from the Berber Lenata tribe. This turbulent period saw extensive repairs carried out on the city, especially the important public buildings. The city itself

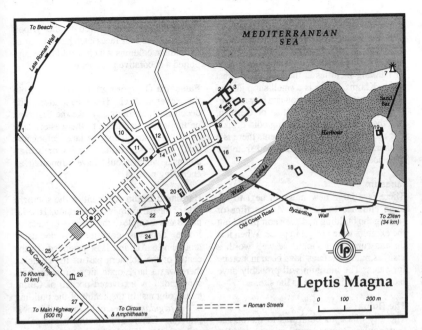

Leptis Magna

= = = = = = = Roman Streets

| | | | |
|---|---|---|---|
| 1 | Western Gate | 10 | Theatre |
| 2 | Temple of Liber Pater | 11 | Chalcidicum |
| 3 | Temple of Rome & Augustus | 12 | Market |
| 4 | Old Forum Church | 13 | Arch of Trajan |
| 5 | Old Forum | 14 | Arch of Tiberius |
| 6 | Curia | 15 | Severan Forum |
| 7 | Lighthouse | 16 | Severan Basilica |
| 8 | Old Basilica | 17 | Colonnaded Street |
| 9 | Byzantine Gate | 18 | Temple |
| | | 19 | Doric Temple |
| 20 | Church | | |
| 21 | Severan Arch | | |
| 22 | Palaestra | | |
| 23 | Nymphaeum | | |
| 24 | Hadrianic Baths | | |
| 25 | Entrance | | |
| 26 | Museum | | |
| 27 | Restaurant | | |

LIBYA

had shrunk, as can be seen by the extent of the new city walls which encompass only a fraction of the old city. Despite the efforts of the Byzantine administration, the tribes continued to revolt and eventually Tripolitania reverted to pastoral nomadism dominated by the Berber tribes of Nefusa and Houara.

The Arab invasions of 644 swept away the final traces of Roman and Byzantine life from the city. By medieval times the city was used for grazing sheep and in the 11th century it was finally abandoned to the encroaching sand dunes. It was not until the 20th century that any serious excavations were carried out. Most of the monuments were well preserved under their blanket of sand, and it is the fine condition of the ruins as well as the architecture which make Leptis Magna so outstanding.

## Information

The site is open from 8 am to 5.30 pm daily. The entrance charges are 0.25 LD for adults and 0.10 LD for children. There are no postal or banking facilities at the site; the nearest are in Khoms. There is a small shop just by the entrance gate where you can buy a selection of guidebooks in English or German, and there is also a shop selling cold drinks. For more substantial refreshments there is a restaurant directly across the road from the entrance to the site.

## Museum

There is a large new museum next to the main entrance to the site. At the time of writing the building had been completed but the exhibits were not yet in place. When it is up and running it should be well worth a visit, as many artefacts have been in storage for years. The museum will probably have the same opening hours as the site.

## The Ruins

The city of Leptis conforms to the classic rectangular Roman street plan, with the blocks grouped more or less symmetrically on either side of the cardo maximus, or main axial street. This 'Triumphal Street' runs south-west from the old forum, which was the nucleus of the old city. Over the first few centuries AD the city expanded in both directions and many of the monuments visible today date from this period of prolific building activity.

**Severan Arch** From the entrance, a path leads down to the excavations and a modern flight of stairs. At the bottom of the stairs stands the Severan Arch, which has recently been restored and is now free of scaffolding. It is thought that the arch was erected in honour of a visit from Emperor Septimius Severus to his birthplace in 203 AD. The arch is quite a grand affair, four-sided and straddling the intersection with the main transverse street, the decumanus maximus. Decorative carvings adorn the upper levels of the arch, but most of the carved marble friezes which formerly decorated the top of

the arch have been moved to the Tripoli museum. The four faces each have a pair of Corinthian columns which would have supported a decorative pediment.

**Palaestra** The sports ground is not far from the Severan Arch. Head east along the decumanus maximus and take the first road on the left, which leads to the western side of the palaestra. This is a large, elongated oval space surrounded by Corinthian columns which would have supported an encircling portico.

**Hadrianic Baths** Adjacent to the southern side of the palaestra is the enormous Hadrianic Baths complex, the largest outside of Rome. This vast complex was dedicated around 126 AD and later extended. In the centre of the northern part of the complex there was a large open-air swimming pool surrounded by a covered portico of Corinthian columns. In the centre of the building is the *frigidarium*, or cold room, the most important feature of the baths. It was paved and panelled with marble and the roof was supported by eight massive columns.

To the east and west of the frigidarium are two further decorated pools faced with black granite. South of the frigidarium is the *tepidarium*, or warm room, which contains one main bath and two small lateral baths. The next room south, through a small vestibule, leads to the hot room, the *caldarium*, which was a large barrel-vaulted chamber. Finally, there is a series of smaller rooms which were sweat baths, the *laconica*. From there the bather could return directly to the cold pool for a plunge.

There are several other rooms in the complex, notably the open-plan latrines in the north-eastern and north-western corners of the building. They consist of rows of marble lavatory benches with a deep flushing channel running beneath them.

**Nymphaeum** On the eastern side of the palaestra there is an open piazza. On the eastern side of this space sits the partially covered *nymphaeum*, a shrine dedicated to the worship of nymphs. It is a large, semicircular, open-fronted building containing a fountain basin. The flanking walls have niches for statues, now sadly removed, between the columns.

**Colonnaded Street** This runs straight to the harbour, north-east from the piazza. It has a broad, central roadway lined with colonnaded porticoes. The columns are raised on square bases and their capitals are decorated with lotus and acanthus designs. The arches formerly sprang directly from these capitals, and the design bears a resemblance to the colonnaded streets at Jerash in Jordan and those in Roman Syria.

**Severan Forum** About a third of the way along the colonnaded street there is a huge building on the left, the Severan Forum. Halfway along this wall there is a doorway which leads inside. There is a distinct similarity to the imperial forum in Rome and the scale of the place is similarly immense. The internal space of the forum is 100 x 60 metres and it is surrounded by colonnaded porticoes. At the south-eastern end of the forum a temple is raised against the wall. Around the portico of the forum were giant Medusa and Nereid heads, many of which are still in place or lying around the fallen columns. The sheer scale of the forum makes an impressive sight and, together with the basilica and theatre, it is one of the highlights of Leptis.

**Severan Basilica** A connecting doorway on the north-eastern side of the forum leads to the Severan Basilica. This large building has a half-domed apse at either end. Flanking the apses is a set of the most fantastic carved columns, solidly worked with acanthus scrolls, animals and figures. The extraordinary style of the carving is more reminiscent of medieval architecture than Roman, and their high relief creates a high-contrast effect. Originally, the building was faced and floored with marble and three lines of columns ran down its length.

**Harbour** If you continue along the colonnaded street, you come to the harbour (now silted up). In front of you are the western quays. Originally, the harbour was the Wadi Lebda's estuary, but later the banks of the estuary were built up into harbour walls and breakwaters were built around the northern and eastern sides to almost enclose it. The ruined structure on the northern breakwater was once a lighthouse. There isn't much left, most of it having fallen into the sea long ago; only the south-western corner of the foot of the tower remains.

Unless the wadi is in full flood you can walk across the sand bar, which now blocks the harbour mouth, to reach the eastern breakwater, where there are the remains of a small Doric temple. The buildings on the quay were warehouses and harbour offices, and on the southern edge of the harbour there is a large temple which has not yet been fully excavated.

**Circus & Amphitheatre** If you continue west along the seashore from the harbour you come to the circus and amphitheatre. They are about 700 metres from the harbour and it's worth driving to them if you have a car. To get there by road, follow the road east when you leave the main entrance and take the turning on the left just after you cross the wadi.

This is the only circus which survives in Libya, as the others at Oea and Sabratha were constructed of wood. It was used for chariot races and the like, and at 450 x 100 metres is one of the largest in the Roman world. The amphitheatre just to the south of it dates from 56 AD, during the reign of Nero, and is connected to the circus by way of covered passageways.

**Old Forum** Returning back to the harbour and heading west you come to the old forum. There are several important monuments clustered in this area. The forum itself is at the end of the cardo maximus between the sea and the wadi mouth. It is an open court with porticoes on three sides. Leading from this are the main temples of the city and public buildings. The **curia**, or senate house,

LIBYA

stands in a rectangular courtyard. Next to this is the **old basilica**, which was reconstructed during the reign of Constantine after a fire had destroyed the original.

Behind the portico of the forum is the **Temple of Magna Mater**, the Great Mother, and next to that another temple, built in the time of Trajan, contains the **old forum church**, which was built over the original temple. There are a number of other temples in the immediate area, including the **Temple of Liber Pater**, the **Temple of Jupiter-Serapis & Isis** and the **Temple of Rome & Augustus**. These temples are in various states of repair but are nonetheless interesting for their rich diversity.

**Market** Leaving the forum area and heading south-west along the cardo maximus, the market is on the right. It consists of a rectangular open space with two attractive circular pavilions in the centre. The market originally had covered porticoes around the sides. Along the external south-western side there was a row of shops, built during a later period. The pavilions have tall, arched windows and deep sills for the display of goods.

**Chalcidicum** Farther along the cardo maximus there are two arches, the **Arch of Tiberius** and the **Arch of Trajan**. The former is a plain arch with little decoration, and the latter is a tetrapylon with two carriageways intersecting it. The Arch of Trajan abuts onto the corner of a monumental building, the Chalcidicium, the exact function of which is unknown. The name comes from an inscription on a statue base nearby, 'Venus Chalcidica'. From the layout of the building it is probable that it was another market, perhaps for wild animals used in the amphitheatres, as marble statues of elephants have been found in the building.

**Theatre** The number one monument at Leptis is the theatre, which is situated just behind the Chalcidicium. From the upper tiers there is a fabulous view over the city and across to the sea. This showpiece was donated to the city by a wealthy citizen, Annobal Rufus, in the year 1 AD; the same patron built the market.

The auditorium is a semicircular structure rising to the same height as the stage building. The orchestra is also semicircular and is surrounded by a series of low steps which would have seated notable citizens. The stage itself has an ornamental wall of many columns arranged in three tiers at the rear and the front of the stage is decorated with niches which held statues of divinities. At the sides of the stage are two stone parapets ending in the heads of Dionysus and Hercules. There are several statues still *in situ* in the theatre, the rest having been removed to the museum.

Behind the stage is a separate quadrilateral portico surrounded by an abundance of impressive marble and granite columns. The portico contains a small temple dedicated to the *Di Augusti*, the deified emperors.

### Getting There & Away
For details on getting to and from Leptis, see the Khoms Getting There & Away information.

### ZLITEN
Leaving Khoms and Leptis there are two roads which you can take to Zliten, 34 km to the east – the new highway or the old coast road. If you are driving your own car, or have a private taxi, the old road is by far the more interesting drive. Past the ruins, the old single-lane surfaced road runs through attractive palm oases, villages and farms. Eighteen km from Khoms there is a village called **Souq al-Khamis**, where there is reputedly a good bathing beach. Farther along you cross the **Wadi Ka'm**, billed as Libya's only flowing river, although when I was there it was barely a trickle.

Zliten is an oasis town famous for a number of marabout tombs, also known as *turba*, which are dotted around the countryside and are often visited by pilgrims seeking their powers of increasing fertility. You haven't a hope of finding them without some help from a local person and, bearing in mind that these are not tourist sites, it is a good idea to have a local with you anyway.

The one holy site that you can't miss, however, is right in the centre of town and it towers above everything else. The tomb of Sidi Abdusalam, a famous scholar born in 1455, is the most venerated in Libya, and a gigantic new mosque and Qur'anic school bearing his name have just been erected at the site. This is no ordinary building. The artisans who built the Hassan Mosque in Casablanca have worked on it and the **Sidi Abdusalam Mosque** has wall to wall elaborate tilework with marvellous carved stucco ceilings. The high level of traditional craftwork makes this mosque a must-see if you are interested in Islamic architecture, even if modern mosques usually leave you cold.

### Places to Stay & Eat
The centre of Zliten is fairly compact and clustered around the mosque, about two km off the highway. At the time of writing there was nowhere to stay in Zliten, but a smart-looking hotel was under construction about a block away from the mosque. There are a few small, simple restaurants dotted around the central area, close to the mosque, but they are nothing special.

### Getting There & Away
You can pick up a collect taxi quite easily from Khoms, or from Sirt if you are coming from the east. Express buses doing the coastal run in either direction will drop you off on the highway, but it's a bit of a walk.

### MISRATA
Misrata is a fairly large town 51 km east of Zliten, whose inhabitants have a reputation for being very good at business. The prosperous air is due in part to its newish steel mill which has created something of a boom in the town. The whole area is surrounded by extensive palm and olive groves. Misrata has quite a different atmosphere from other towns in Libya. The first thing you notice is that the place has a sense of order: the streets are cleaner, and the buildings smarter.

### Information
The banks, baladiya, post office, hotels and shops are all within a 500-metre radius of Maidan an-Nasser, the main square in the centre of town.

### Things to See & Do
There is not very much of interest for the tourist, although there is a good beach five km north of the centre of town, but it is a good place to stop if you are touring along the coast. The town's main claim to fame is an enormous sand dune just to the west of the town. They say that it is the tallest dune in the world but I can't vouch for it.

On Sharia Daralry, next door to the Koztik Hotel, there is a tall observation tower called the **Koztik Tower**, built on a sand dune (now concreted over) as a memorial to Libyan resistance to the Italians. You can go up it for an eagle's eye view of the city. There is also a small memorial museum at its base, which is open daily; entrance is free.

The town also has a carpet industry which is still thriving. You can find the traditional designs of the region, which are mainly in fairly bright colours, in the souqs of the town.

### Places to Stay – bottom end
There is a small *hostel* (☎ 051-24880), but it is very inconveniently located outside town in a municipal housing estate. To find it, you need to take the turning on the left from the highway (coming from the west) just before the flyover, which is the main turn-off for Misrata. If you are coming from the centre of town, having arrived by bus, the only practical way to get there is by taxi.

A more pleasant option is to head for *Al-Jazera* on the beach, five km north of the Maidan an-Nasser. There are beach chalets here for 2 LD per night and they're open throughout the year. You can find a taxi easily around the Maidan an-Nasser or from the bus station.

### Places to Stay – middle & top end
The best place in town for the price is the *Funduq Misrata Seahi* (☎ 051-20323 or

LIBYA

20037), which is an old hotel recently refurbished with traditional furniture, and has some character. It is very conveniently located close to Maidan an-Nasser on Sharia Ramadan Asswayhli. Rooms with TV, aircon and bathroom cost 10 LD per person, including breakfast. It has a coffee bar and restaurant where meals cost 10 to 15 LD.

The poshest place in town is the *Koztik Hotel* (☎ 051-26999; fax 051-26013) on Sharia Daralry, in the southern part of town. Just look for the tall observation tower and the hotel is next door. This place has the works: swimming pool, shops, cinema, two restaurants – you name it. Singles/doubles cost 25/32 LD.

### Places to Eat

Most of the restaurants are on Sharia Ramadan Asswayhli or in the souq area just to the north. Most of these places serve the usual Arabic cuisine for 5 to 10 LD. If you crave something different there is a good pizza and burger place called *Bayt Fitayer* on Sharia Tarabulus, about 800 metres from Maidan an-Nasser. The owner, Nasser Darwish, told us he is planning to open a drive-in takeaway in Tripoli. You heard it here first! There are also three fish restaurants on the beach which by all accounts are rather good.

### Getting There & Away

**Air** Misrata has air connections to Benghazi on Tuesday, Thursday, Friday and Sunday. The flight takes 55 minutes, but schedules are liable to change at short notice. The Libyan Arab Airlines (☎ 051-23190 or 23554) office in Misrata is a couple of hundred metres north-west of Maidan an-Nasser along the road to the beach. The airport is about 12 km south of town. You can pick up a bus or taxi in Maidan an-Nasser.

**Bus & Taxi** There are daily buses to and from Tripoli and Benghazi and collect taxis leaving throughout the day.

### SIRT

Heading east, the highway from Misrata to Sirt dips inland and the landscape quickly becomes rather barren and dull after leaving the agricultural area. There are a number of small villages along the old coast road but nothing of outstanding interest. Forty km south of Misrata is **Tauorga**, a small community where many of the traditional palm-leaf mats are made.

Sitting in the dip of the gulf, Sirt was historically an important land communication point with the south and an embarkation point for many caravans. Under the Italians it was an administrative centre, and since the revolution it has increased in importance. The General People's Congress meets in Sirt and there are plans to move the main ministries here from Tripoli. There may be sound political motives for this move, but commiserations go out to the civil servants because Sirt, when all is said and done, has nothing whatsoever going for it. The only reason for spending any time here is to rest during the long coastal trip. If you do stay here there is a well-kept promenade complete with grazing sheep and goats, a boat-building yard and a small, but not very picturesque, fishing harbour.

### Information

The layout of Sirt is very simple. There is one main street running through the town and all the services are to be found either on or close to it. The Wahda Bank is down a turning to the left of the Medina Hotel. The post office is in the next road back from the main street, and can't be missed as it has a huge radio tower. The public telephones are in the same building.

### Places to Stay & Eat

There is a rather austere *hostel* (☎ 054-61825) just off the western end of the corniche, recognisable by its large green-and-white exterior. The rates are cheap at 2.50 LD a night, but residents are not allowed on the premises between 9 am and 3 pm and must be in by 10.30 pm. There is a maximum-stay rule of three days but I imagine one day would be more than enough.

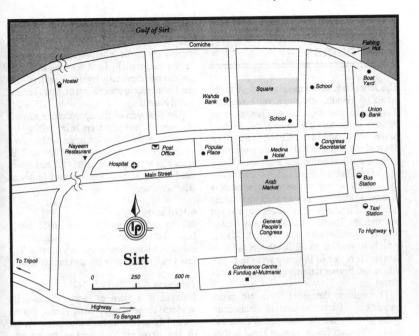

The *Medina Hotel* (☎ 054-60160/3; fax 054-4407) is right in the centre of the main street (which has no name) and is very comfortable and friendly. There is a café and restaurant, and all rooms have bathrooms and satellite TV. Singles/doubles cost 25/30 LD and lunch or dinner costs 16 LD. The hotel has its own minibus if you need collecting from the airport or bus station.

There is a five-star hotel in town next to the People's Congress complex called *Funduq al-Mutmarat*, which has all the facilities you would expect from such a place, and prices to match. Still, if you want croissants for breakfast in Sirt you can expect to have to pay for it. Rooms start at 35 LD and climb steeply upwards. If the congress is in session you will probably not get past the gate; the place is like Fort Knox.

The *Nayeem Restaurant* is just off the main street, at the western end of town.

## Getting There & Away

**Air** The airport is about 10 km east of town on the coast and is signposted from the highway. The Libyan Arab Airlines (☎ 054-2167 or 4472) office is at the airport. There are regular connections with Tripoli and Benghazi, and less frequent flights to Sebha. The one-way fare to and from Tripoli and Benghazi is 10 LD.

**Bus** There is one bus a day from Tripoli, which departs at 2 pm and costs 5.75 LD. There is also a bus which goes from Khoms to Benghazi and stops at Sirt on the way. The bus station is just off the main street, almost opposite the Congress Secretariat building.

**Taxi** There is a taxi station across the road from the bus station where you can easily pick up a collect taxi for most destinations. The fares are often not much more than the bus fares.

LIBYA

# The Jebel Nafusa & Ghadhames

The Jebel Nafusa is a mountain range to the south of Tripoli, stretching from southern Tunisia in the west to Al-Qusbat, near Khoms, in the east. The main area of interest to the visitor is between Gharyan, the major town of the jebel, to Nalut in the west, close to the Tunisian border. The jebel soars above the Jefara Plain to heights of 900 metres and the scenery is very dramatic. The weather is also quite different from the plain; in summer it is much fresher and in winter snow is not uncommon. The area is traditionally Berber and the inhabitants often speak Mazir, which is similar to Tifinagh, as well as Arabic. It is one of the only areas in Libya where the Berber language and culture still thrives.

Throughout the jebel there are many examples of Berber troglodyte architecture (which builds into the surrounding earth and rock), although few, if any, of these houses are still occupied, except perhaps by goats. Some of the villages feature fortified grain stores, which are impressive structures of mud-brick storage chambers stacked one on top of the other.

The road system in the jebel is like a horizontal ladder. The fast northern road runs from Bir Ayyad to Nalut, and the slower but more picturesque southern road runs from Gharyan to Nalut. Frequent turnings run between the northern and southern roads to serve the mountain villages. All of these roads offer spectacular views across the jebel, but the villages themselves offer varying degrees of interest. There are two main roads to the Jebel Nafusa: from Tripoli via Azzizya, and west along the coast from Tripoli to Surman, from where the road runs straight to Yefren in the mountains.

Ghadhames lies out on its own to the south-west of the Jebel Nafusa via Nalut and Darj. The road to Ghadhames crosses rather flat semidesert for a few hundred km before the desert proper starts.

## GHARYAN

The road to Gharyan from Tripoli soars steeply up to the jebel, offering fine views across the Jefara Plain. A warning to motorists though, especially motorbike riders – the road is subject to rock falls which can present a real hazard.

The first sign of the approaching town is the huge amount of pottery being sold by the roadside. Small kilns are often operated out of troglodyte workshops carved into the hillside. The style is quite colourful and funky but I suspect some of the wares are imported from Tunisia.

### Information

All the facilities such as post office, bank, buses and taxis are close to the Hotel Rabta, either on Sharia Jamahiriya or just off it. The few small restaurants are also in this area.

### Things to See

Gharyan is a town of mostly small-scale modern architecture, with farms dotted around the area. The most interesting things to see here are the Berber **troglodyte houses**. Few of these have been restored and many are sitting next to modern farmhouses owned by the original families and used only for keeping animals. One which has been restored belongs to the Rabta Hotel (although it lies a few km away) and the staff will take you there, free of charge if you are a guest and for a small charge if you are not. They will also arrange to take you to the springs which are near the town.

### Places to Stay – bottom

There is a cheap hotel in town, the *Funduq Gharyan Seahia* (☎ 041-30105), but it was closed for renovation at the time of writing and no-one was sure when it would reopen. It's worth a try, but by all accounts it was formerly an unappetising place.

### Places to Stay – middle

The good news is that the only up and running hotel in town is very good indeed. The *Hotel Rabta* (☎ 041-21971/4) on Sharia Jamahiriya is a brand-new place with clean,

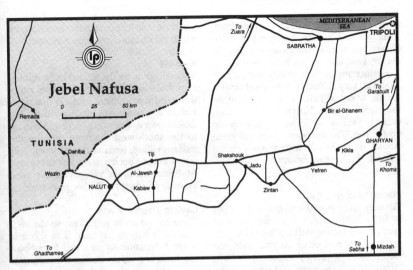

comfortable rooms and all mod cons. The staff are friendly and will arrange free trips around town. The rooms are also quite a bargain at 15/20 LD for singles/doubles. The restaurant serves Libyan and continental meals for 7 to 15 LD. Downstairs there is also a supermarket and a luxury cinema showing imported films twice a night at 7.30 and 9.30 pm. Tickets are 1 LD.

### Places to Eat
Outside of the hotel's restaurant, eating out is rather limited. There are a few small restaurants, one just up the road from the hotel, on the left towards the bus station. All of these places are within walking distance of the hotel.

### Getting There & Away
There is a daily bus from Tripoli at 2 pm; the fare is 2.75 LD. There are also frequent collect taxis coming and going between Tripoli and Gharyan. The bus station is about 500 metres from the Rabta Hotel. The taxis also leave from there.

### YEFREN
Yefren is perched on the top of a series of hill crests set in an attractive wooded area. The twisting mountain roads lead out in several directions and there are various monuments and places of interest in the surrounding areas, including several springs and a small lake. The deserted, old part of Yefren is 500 years old and is situated on the hilltop overlooking the town. The old grain store and traditional houses can be explored.

Heading out from town on the northern road there is an early mosque on a hill, on the left of the one-km mark, called **Nana T'gurjilt**. There is another called **Tewatirwin** a farther km along the road. At the four-km mark you come to a beautiful, ruined village called **Al-Ghala**, which is perched on a hillside and shows the traditional arrangement of upper and lower villages. Eighteen km north of the town there is a **Roman monumental tomb** at a place called Safit. This monument really stands out from its surroundings and can be seen from the road. Nearby is 'Ain Kujat, a small spring.

Other nearby places of interest include **Gasr Bir Niran**, where there are some impressive ruins. In the same area is a large cave called Umm Abdurabik, near 'Ain Fassat, where a wedding party is rumoured

**LIBYA**

to have completely disappeared. **Tasmirayt**, a village set in a valley between three hills, is very picturesque with an upper village on the crest and a lower one in the deep valley.

Finding any of these places without help would be very difficult but the good news is that the hostel will kindly take people to see the sights around Yefren free of charge, either in your car or the staff will rustle one up for you. The manager, Yusef Suleyman Aboud, is very helpful and has many photos and lots of information about the various places.

### Places to Stay & Eat

The only place to stay in Yefren is the *hostel* (☎ 0421-2585), which is in the centre of town. If you are approaching from Gharyan, you pass the post office on your right and then come to a service station on the left. Turn right and you come to a small square, and the hostel is on the right, opposite a park. It is a very comfortable and friendly place in an old Italian building. The coffee bar has music and, by Libyan standards, is a pretty lively place. There is a restaurant which does full lunch or dinner for 6.50 LD, or members can use the kitchen themselves.

### Getting There & Away

If you are coming straight from Tripoli there is a direct bus to Yefren and Jadu at 1 pm daily. The fare is 2.75 LD. There is also a bus which goes from Tripoli via Gharyan at 2 pm daily.

### JADU

Following the southern road, Jadu is the fourth main turning on the right, about 50 km from Yefren. Jadu is an old Berber cliff-top village, with ruins on the summit and spectacular views over the valley beneath to the west. If you follow the winding mountain road, you come out onto the fast northern road at Shakshouk. There is a service station on the main road just before the village.

### Getting There & Away

There is a bus to Jadu from Tripoli via Yefren leaving Tripoli once a day at 1 pm, but given

that there is no accommodation here it is only worth your while if you have a vehicle.

### KABAW

This village is on the second main turning from Nalut and can be reached from either the northern or southern road. On first sight, Kabaw is a rather dull modern village, but the old town is well worth visiting. A turning to the south-west, halfway through the modern village, leads to the old town. This is now in ruins but it's interesting to explore. At the summit of the village is a very good example of a fortified Berber grain store.

### Getting There & Away

There are no buses to Kabaw, so the only reasonable way to get there is to drive. It would be possible to get a taxi from Nalut and back, but, unless Berber architecture is your passion in life, the hassle and expense would not be worth it.

### NALUT

Nalut is perched high on an escarpment overlooking the plains below. It is the last town on the Jebel Nafusa before the Tunisian border, 35 km away to the west. Today, Nalut is a small modern town but the real interest for the visitor is a large old town overlooking the new. There is a gigantic qasr, which was the grain store rather than a castle, and is probably the best of its type still standing. There are also some old vernacular mosques which are worth seeing.

The qasr is reckoned to be at least 300 years old and the D'jmaa Alal'a Mosque could be even older. The storage chambers of the qasr were used to store oil as well as grain, and each keeper knew exactly how much each family had in storage at any one time, even though there were 400 chambers. There are so few visitors that there are no set opening times. If the door of the qasr is locked you should enquire at the baladiya, which is set back from the road near the bus stand.

If you have your own car, there is an interesting place called **Al-Ghazayeh** on the road to the border at about the 26-km mark

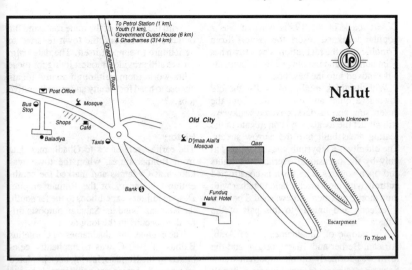

**Nalut**

Scale Unknown

from Nalut. You need to turn west down a small road to the right which runs steeply down into the valley. At the bottom is an abandoned village and palm oasis with a spring running through it. It is an attractive, shaded picnic spot and would make a good place to camp.

### Places to Stay

There is a new *hostel* about one km from the central roundabout in the direction of Ghadhames and the border. It is a brown building on the right before you get to the service station.

The *Funduq Nalut* (☎ 0470-2204) is the only hotel in town. It is superbly situated overlooking the ruined old town and was built in 1933 by the Italians. Despite its rather pleasant, solid architecture it has been allowed to become badly run-down. In fact it is quite filthy. There is talk of it being taken over and done up, but for now you just have to grin and bear it. There are 18 rooms and they cost 9 LD with a 'bathroom'. Dinner costs 4.50 LD.

### Places to Eat

There are a few simple restaurants around the centre of town, and there is a cheap place near the roundabout along the Ghadhames road which is quite good. You can expect to pay about 3 LD in these places for lunch or dinner. Apart from these, the only other place is the hotel dining room. The hotel also has a terrace café which is a good place for a pit stop – worth it just for the view.

### Getting There & Away

There are two buses a day from Tripoli to Nalut at 7.30 am and 2 pm, and two Ghadhames buses pass through Nalut around lunchtime. The fare is 3.50 LD, and the buses stop in the main street west of the main roundabout. There are also taxis which run between Tripoli and Nalut and stop by the roundabout.

### GHADHAMES

The oasis town of Ghadhames (population 9000) lies 650 km south-west of Tripoli and 314 km from Nalut, close to the borders with Algeria and Tunisia. If your time in Libya is limited and you want to see one traditional desert place, this is the one. Famed for its traditional desert architecture, Ghadhames earned itself the sobriquet 'Pearl of the

Desert' back in the 1950s when it was a popular weekend resort for visitors from Tripoli. Since the revolution, a new town has been built around the old and the inhabitants have moved into the new houses.

With its thick mud-brick walls, the old town is a quiet and cool retreat from the desert sun, and its dark, covered walkways still attract the locals, who congregate in the seating areas built into the narrow streets. The old city is a labyrinth, the dark streets lit only by the occasional overhead skylights and open squares. The town is constructed entirely with mud-bricks, held together with mud mortar and then whitewashed. The style is eclectic and unique to this part of the Sahara.

The people of Ghadhames are of Arab, African, Berber and Tuareg origin, and the town was formerly on an important trans-Saharan trading route stretching from Tripoli to Lake Chad and beyond. Apart from gold, ivory and wild animals destined for the Roman arena, slaves formed an important part of the trade in Ghadhames, and many of the people living in Ghadhames today are the descendants of former slaves.

With the decline of the trade route and the outlawing of slavery, the town reverted to agriculture to support itself. The date-palm groves still provide a modest living for those who work them, although many locals choose to head for the city and more lucrative jobs.

### History

The earliest references to Ghadhames date from Roman times, when the town was known as Cydamus and marked the southernmost boundary of the Roman empire. Despite military expeditions to the far south, the Romans found the Saharan outposts difficult to occupy in the long term.

The conquest of Ghadhames by Cornelius Balbus in 19 BC was triumphantly celebrated by the Romans, having been hindered by a period of raids and counter raids by the local Libyan tribes. The remoteness of the area combined with the presence of these tribes meant that the Romans had to grant almost complete autonomy to the region, sending out the occasional punitive raid if things got out of hand.

After the fall of the Roman empire, the history of Ghadhames becomes obscure. The few clues provided by archaeology attest to the importance of Ghadhames during the Byzantine occupation. It is known that four bishops of Tripolitania lived at Ghadhames during this period, and some Byzantine remains have been found near the town. The town's subsequent history until the early 19th century is largely hearsay. The first European to set foot in Ghadhames was the explorer Alexander Gordon Laing, who stopped there on his way to Timbuctoo in 1824. He commented that its people 'vie with each other in the continual performance of kind and hospitable acts'.

The Italians took the town in 1913 facing fierce resistance, and they did not bring it under control until 1924. During WW II Ghadhames came under French military control and was administered from Tunisia until independence. The old town suffered considerable damage during WW II.

## Information

**Tourist Offices** Although there are few facilities for tourists at present, there are a couple of tourist agencies in town which can offer advice and information. They can also arrange Saharan excursions and 4WD vehicles to visit places outside town. They include Ghadhames Travel & Tourism (☎ 0484-2307), PO Box 878, or Winzrik Tourism Services (☎ 0484-2533). As English is rarely spoken, some Arabic or French would be useful.

**Money** There is a small bank in the modern town, just north of the main square in an arcade of shops. It is open from 8 am to 2 pm daily except Friday.

**Post & Telecommunications** The post office is also just off the main square. International calls can be made, but with some difficulty due to the shortage of lines.

## Things to See & Do

The town is small enough to be entirely explored on foot. Its main attraction is the architecture of the old town (take a torch with you). Close to the 'Ain al-Faras Hotel near the western entrance to the old town, the **House Museum** is an old merchant's house with its original furnishings and decorations kept intact. It serves as a museum of local culture and is well worth seeing, but there are no fixed opening times. Enquire at one of the travel agencies to arrange for it to be unlocked.

The old town is an experience in itself. The square of the Mulberry is the old slave market. Periodically, the local people stage a musical evening open to all in the old town square, near the old **D'jmaa al-Kabir Mosque**. The minaret of the mosque can be climbed for an excellent view over the old town. The domes seen on the rooftops are family tombs or small prayer rooms.

Fifteen km outside Ghadhames there are (unspectacular) Roman ruins on the hill at **Ras al-Ghoul** (the Haunted Hill), which are worth visiting for the views over the desert. There is also a nearby lake which is popular for picnics and swimming. For both of these places you will need off-the-road transport. If you don't have your own you can arrange to hire transportation through one of the tourist agencies listed above.

## Places to Stay – bottom end

**Camping** As the town is surrounded by open desert, camping is a possibility. However, bear in mind that this is a border area, and that straying across could result in an unpleasant experience with the authorities. Independent tourists are virtually unheard of here, so it would be wise to seek the advice of one of the tourist agencies if you plan to camp.

**Hostel** There is a clean, modern hostel (☎ 0484-858) on the eastern outskirts of town, overlooking the desert and the old cemetery. Most of the 120 beds are in dormitories but there are a couple of family rooms with private bathrooms. There are seldom many guests but it is used by the young locals as a coffee house. Charges are 2.50 LD per night and meals can be arranged.

## Places to Stay – middle

The 'Ain al-Faras Hotel is an old and run-down place, but with a considerable amount of charm. It is conveniently situated next to the western gate to the old town, close to the House Museum. Rooms with air-con and bathroom cost 20 LD.

At the time of writing, a new hotel called the Hotel Waha was about to open on the outskirts of town. The rooms are expected to cost 20 to 25 LD, with bathroom. Enquire at one of the tourist agencies for information.

## Places to Eat

Bad news. Outside of the hotels, there is really nowhere to eat in Ghadhames. Dinner at the 'Ain al-Faras Hotel costs about 7 LD and there is a coffee bar. There are a few cafés in the new town around the main square serving snacks and soft drinks, but at night there's nothing at all. Those staying at the hostel can prepare their own food if they

**LIBYA**

wish. Hopefully, the situation will improve with the arrival of tourists.

## Things to Buy

The main square in the new town and the streets around it have a market selling food and general goods. The main market day is Tuesday. Ghadhames produces some interesting traditional goods. Brightly coloured palm-weave food baskets are a good buy, as are the area's unique slippers, belgas Gadamsi, which are multicoloured and highly decorated. There are sometimes old textiles and rugs but these are becoming rare.

## Getting There & Away

**Air** Normally, Libyan Arab Airlines (☎ 0484-2411, airport office) operates a service twice a week from Tripoli on Tuesday and Thursday, and once a week from Sebha on Wednesday. At the time of writing, the service had been suspended. The airport is about 10 km to the west of town and taxis are usually available for the trip to and from the airport. They can usually be found around the main square in the new town, or you can ask your accommodation to phone one for you.

**Bus** There are two buses a day running between Tripoli and Ghadhames. They leave Tripoli at 7 am and 10 am and from Ghadhames at 6 am and 8 am. The trip takes seven hours and the buses have air-conditioning. They park overnight and depart from outside the 'Ain al-Faras Hotel, which is handy if you are staying there. The one-way fare is 7.50 LD.

# Cyrenaica

The eastern part of Libya is quite different, both geographically and culturally, from the rest of the country. Egypt's proximity has influenced the region's cuisine, and parts of Cyrenaica are reputed to have populations with pure Arabian ancestry inherited from the time of the original Arab conquest.

The area's landscape is extremely attractive and, if you have spent any amount of time in the desert, a refreshing change. The Jebel Akhdar (the Green Mountains) lives up to its name and is reminiscent of Crete, which lies just 100 km or so to the north.

Geography aside, the main reason for visiting the region is to visit the wonderful Greek cities of antiquity. Five sites comprise the old 'pentapolis'. The most glorious of these is Cyrene, followed by Apollonia nearby on the coast. In isolation, the other sites would also command great interest but, in such a concentration of world-class ruins, they tend to play second fiddle.

This area also has the best coastline in the country and offers opportunities for divers to explore sunken ruins off the coast. The potential for diving holidays is one that is being seriously investigated by the tourist authorities. Even for nondivers, the beaches are very attractive and often empty.

# Benghazi

Benghazi is the second-largest city in Libya, with a population of about 600,000, and is situated on the eastern side of the Gulf of Sirt. It is a major commercial centre and port built around a large double harbour. The modern city displays little of its ancient heritage and is mostly a postwar development. But Benghazi make a good base for touring the Green Mountain area and there are good bathing beaches nearby.

## History

Founded by Greek settlers who were moving westward, the settlement was originally called Euserides, thought to be the site of the legendary Garden of Hesperides of Golden Apples fame. This site is slightly south of the city on the road to the airport at Benina.

By 249 BC, Benghazi was called Berenice, named after the wife of Ptolemy III of Egypt who subjected Cyrenaica to Egyptian rule and married Berenice, a Cyrenaican princess. The site of this later city corresponds to the modern city of Benghazi. The city became a part of the Roman empire, but little is known of its history throughout this period. Like many Roman cities in Africa, it suffered enormous damage during the Vandal invasion and, after a brief period of repair by the Byzantines, fell into obscurity.

Even after the Arab invasion, Benghazi was neglected in favour of other cities of more strategic importance, such as Ajdabiya. It was only in the 15th century that Benghazi was rediscovered by Tripolitanian merchants, taking the city into a new and prosperous phase. The name Benghazi came about in the 16th century when the city was renamed after Ibn Ghazi, a local holy man.

The Turks took Benghazi in the 17th century and built a fort there. Their attempts to make it a centre for tax collection drove traders to other towns and Benghazi suffered as a result. Under the Karamanlis, Benghazi once again suffered from neglect. It was only during the second Ottoman occupation, in the mid-19th century, that the city recovered its fortunes.

In 1911 the Italians laid siege to the city from the sea and it effectively became an Italian fortress in the face of fierce resistance by tribes from the surrounding areas. The resistance took 20 years to subdue and it was only in the 1930s that the city was built up into what was virtually an Italian city in North Africa. Quite a few of the buildings in

MEDITERRANEAN
SEA

1  Central Souq
2  Bus & Taxi Station
3  Funduq Market
4  Libyan Arab Airlines
   Office
5  Tomb of Omar al-Mukhtar
6  National Commercial Bank
7  Post Office
8  Omar Khayyam Hotel
9  Libyan Arab Airlines
   Office
10 Gar Younis University
   Building
11 Police Station
12 Municipal Hospital
13 Jazeer Hotel
14 Tibesti Hotel
15 Hostel
16 Uzu Hotel

New
Marina

Sharia Ahmad Rafiq al-Mahdawi

Sharia 7th October

Sharia Algeria

Sharia Abu Ghulah

Sharia Amir Ibn al-As

Sharia Bin Ghashir

Sharia Sherit

Ash

SIDI
HSAYN

Sharia Omar al-Mukhtar

Sharia al-Mahdawi

MEDINA

Sharia al-Maqariaf

Sharia Ahmad Rafiq al-Mahdawi

Sharia Omar Ibn al-Khatteb

Sharia al-Aqeeb

Sharia Qasr Ahmed

Sharia Amir Ibn al-As

Sharia Algeria

To People's
Garden

Corniche

Sharia Gama

Abdul Nasser

Sharia Aesh Shuhada

Sharia 1st September

RAS
ABAYDAH

Benghazi
Harbour

Sharia Gamal Abdul Nasser

Sharia 23rd July

Sharia Algeria

23rd July
Lake

Benghazi

0    250    500 m

To Garian
Tourist Village

Bathing Beach

Sports
City

e city today date from that era and have a
stinctly 1930s feel.

After a history of very mixed fortunes, the
orst was still to come. During WW II the
ty constantly changed hands and was under
ombardment from both the Allies and the
xis powers. By the time the war ended there
as very little left. The British administra-
on did little to restore the city, because of
ie uncertain future of Cyrenaica.

After independence, and more par-
cularly after oil was discovered, the
evelopment of the city began again and the
arbour was enlarged to accommodate more
ommercial shipping following the revolu-
on.

## Orientation

'he older part of the city is to the north near
ie harbour area. It is in this quarter that most
f the shopping and banking facilities can be
ound. There is a new marina jutting out from
ie western corner of the city, and along the
orthern shore there's a promenade, which at
ight comes alive with street vendors and
amilies out for a stroll. South of the prome-
ade are the souqs and a number of older
nosques. The farther south you go, the more
nodern the city becomes. Along the shores
f the inner harbour are some of the more
xpensive hotels and large commercial
uildings. The inner harbour is crossed by a
ridge which links the older part of the city
vith the new suburbs to the south.

## Information

**Tourist Office** Tourist information can be
obtained from the office of the Libyan Travel
& Tourism Company (☎ 061-93009) on
Sharia Gamal Abdul Nasser. As a private
company it can also provide tours.

**Money** There are plenty of banks in the
central area. They are concentrated around
Sharia Gamal Abdul Nasser and Sharia
Omar al-Mukhtar. There are also money-
changing facilities in the lobbies of the
Tibesti and Uzu hotels.

**Post & Telecommunications** The main
post office is on Sharia Omar al-Mukhtar,
and there are public telephones in the same
building. There is another post office close
to the Tibesti Hotel on Sharia Gamal Abdul
Nasser.

**Foreign Embassies** There are a few consulates in Benghazi. The Egyptian consulate is
right on the northern corniche, almost next
to the old Italian church. Italy has a consulate
on Sharia Amir ibn al-As (☎ 061-92331),
and the details for the French consulate are
PO Box 247 (☎ 061-27556).

## Things to See & Do

You can walk around the whole of Benghazi,
apart from the suburbs, quite easily on foot.
Walking around the older parts of the city is
especially rewarding, even though there are
no outstanding historical monuments in
Benghazi. The covered souqs are open daily
but they really come alive on Friday morning
when the whole city seems to congregate for
a shopping spree. The main covered market
is called **Souq al-Jreed** off Sharia Omar
al-Mukhtar, and it sells all manner of clothes
and household goods. Farther along Sharia
Omar al-Mukhtar, the street becomes a
pedestrian precinct and is lined with small
shops and cafés. At the end of the street is an
attractive small square with a mosque.

There is a lively wholesale fruit and veg
market in the old funduq next to the bus
station on Sharia Amir ibn al-As. This is well
worth a look for its atmosphere and for the
lively market cafés dotted around the
funduq, which are good places for a cheap
and delicious lunch.

Nearby is the **tomb of Omar al-Mukhtar**,
the freedom fighter of the resistance. This is
in the middle of a roundabout but, nonetheless, it seems to attract a fair number of
people who sit around the monument watching the world go by.

There are several **beaches** within easy
reach of the city centre. Most of these are
beach clubs or tourist villages with varying
facilities. The most popular and accessible
are to the south of the city. A good one is the
Garian Tourist Village, six km south of the

**LIBYA**

city centre, which has tennis courts and other sports facilities. There is also a **war cemetery** six km south-east of the city on the ring road.

### Places to Stay – bottom end
There is a *hostel* (☎ 061-95961) at the Sports City on the south-western side of the inner harbour. This is a very popular place in summer and, although there are 160 beds, it can get very full. The hostel is modern and has a garden café and views of the harbour. To find it, follow the road along the harbour until you come to the stadium complex, turn right down a small turning just past the stadium and it is the large building facing the water. Men and women's accommodation are in different parts of the building but there are a few family rooms. Meals are very cheap at 2.25 LD.

There are only a few cheap hotels in Benghazi, the best reputedly being the *Atlas Hotel* (☎ 061-92314) on Sharia Gamal Abdul Nasser. Singles/doubles cost 8/10 LD. A real cheapie is the *Medina Hotel* (☎ 061-98046), which is just behind the former Italian church on Sharia Munem Riyadh. It is extremely basic and none too clean, but rooms cost 5.50 LD without bath and 7.70 LD with. It should only be considered if the hostel is full, and even then I would take a sleeping bag as the sheets have led a rather active life.

### Places to Stay – middle
The *Jazeer Hotel* (☎ 061-96001/7), on the north-western end of the corniche, is a former luxury hotel in sadly reduced circumstances. The outside and lobby look very promising but the rooms tell another story. Formerly the showpiece hotel Berenice, this place has been badly neglected. The rooms could do with a good cleaning and the bathroom ceilings leak. However, the place is cheap and conveniently situated, with views over the harbour. Singles/doubles cost 10/15 LD, including breakfast. There is a restaurant and café with a terrace.

Moving a bit more up-market is the *Omar Khayyam Hotel* (☎ 061-95101/9), with entrances on the Corniche and Sharia Gamal Abdul Nasser. The hotel dates from the 1960s, but it has been recently done up a bit. There are 142 rooms, all with private bathrooms. Singles/doubles cost 21/26 LD including breakfast. The rooms on the 1st floor have terraces large enough to hold an embassy reception.

If you fancy a place on the beach, the *Garian Tourist Village* (☎ 061-96350) is about six km south of the city, and rooms here are pretty cheap. Be warned though, this place is very popular at weekends.

### Places to Stay – top end
The two hotels at the top end are both extremely comfortable and well appointed. They are also very expensive. The *Uzu Hotel* (☎ 061-95160/5), on the eastern side of the inner harbour on Sharia Juliana, is very popular. It has all the facilities you would expect from a hotel of this class: two restaurants, a café, shops, laundry, etc. Singles/doubles cost 32/45 LD.

The number one hotel in Benghazi is the *Tibesti Hotel* (☎ 061-92034), on the eastern side of the inner harbour on Sharia Gamal Abdul Nasser. Singles/doubles cost 30/40 LD. It is all marble lobbies and high-speed lifts. Even if you are not staying there, the rooftop Italian restaurant offers a rare change from Arab cuisine if you fancy pizza or pasta.

### Getting There & Away
**Air** There are regular flights from Tripoli usually several a day. The one-hour flight costs 17.50 LD. The airport is at Benina which is south-east of the city. Buses and taxis serve the airport from the central bus station. The Libyan Arab Airlines (☎ 061-92011/3) office in town is on Sharia Gamal Abdul Nasser. There is also a sales office on Sharia Gamal Abdul Nasser, close to the Tibesti Hotel.

**Bus** The main bus station is next to the funduq market area. Benghazi is well served by buses, both to and from other Libyan towns and to Cairo, Alexandria and Damascus. There are two buses a day to and from

ipoli, leaving in both directions at 7 and 10
n. The fare is 10 LD. It is best to buy tickets
ie day before as this route tends to fill up.
here is also a luxury bus which leaves
ripoli daily at 7.30 am in winter and at 6.30
n in summer, and costs 15 LD. For this
:rvice contact the United Arab Company
or Transport (☎ 021-41758).

There is a bus which serves the Green
Mountain area which leaves at 7 am daily.
There are connections to Kufra three times a
eek and connections to Sebha on Monday,
Wednesday and Saturday. The fare is 15 LD.

# South of Benghazi

he coastline south of Benghazi runs past a
arge area of salt flats, and the small towns
n the way to Ajdabiya have little or nothing
f interest. In fact, almost the entire length
of the coastal road between Benghazi and
Sirt has little to offer in the way of either
cenery or historical interest. The gulf
egion, known as Al-Khalij and now an
dministrative province in its own right,
vas historically the buffer between the two
ndependent regions of Tripolitania and
Cyrenaica until independence united the
ountry.

The most significant feature of the road
hrough the gulf are the oil towns of Brega
nd Ras Lanuf, which, unfortunately, are not
open to visitors; there are security checks
ven to enter the towns.

The most interesting place to stop on the
vhole trip is Sultan, 30 km from Sirt. It was
n early Islamic site, and has a small museum
vhich includes some unusual artefacts from
he Italian era.

## AJDABIYA

Ajdabiya was traditionally the end of the
rade route which came up from the central
Sahara to the coast. The town was important
during the Fatimid period and the most significant historical remains date from this
ime. There are also a few Roman inscrip-
ions. These days it is a large residential

district for oil workers and the central administrative centre for the region. It is a place of
little charm and not really the ideal place to
stop. The only reason to consider it would be
to break the long drive between the east and
west of the country. There are all the usual
shopping and refuelling facilities available
in the town, but there are no hotels.

### Places to Stay
There is a *hostel* (☎ 22726) in Ajdabiya on
the coast road near the police station. It is a
small place with 60 beds and very basic
facilities.

### Getting There & Away
Regular air-conditioned buses run from
Ajdabiya to Tripoli and Benghazi and also
down to Kufra in the south.

### BREGA, RAS LANUF & SIDRA
These towns along the dip in the gulf are oil
terminals and almost exclusively occupied
by industry personnel. They are not places
open to the casual visitor and often the access
roads are closed except to official visitors
and staff. Don't plan to drop in and have a
look around unless you happen to have an
invitation from an official source.

### SULTAN
Sultan was formerly an important Fatimid
site. There is only a small modern settlement
here today, but just off the main highway is
the ancient site, which is currently being
excavated. The entrance to the site, which
also has a museum, is through an arch and a
pair of green iron gates on the northern side
of the highway, visible from the road. The
place is not very well signposted and you
could easily miss it. There are no exact
opening times but there is an on-site keeper
who will open up for you. The entrance
charge for the site (including the museum
and mosque) is 0.25 LD.

The museum has a small collection of
early Islamic pottery and other artefacts, as
well as some Byzantine ceramics. Also near
the museum building are two enormous
bronze statues of the Philaeni brothers,

LIBYA

rescued from a 1930s Italian arch when it was demolished in 1973. The Fatimid Sultan Mosque is a couple of km from the gate and unfortunately you can only visit on foot.

# Jebel Akhdar

North of Benghazi is the Jebel Akhdar, an extremely scenic and refreshing mountain area, particularly after experiencing the desert. Also known as the Green Mountains, this part of Libya is indeed green and a great deal wetter than other parts of the country. Geographically it rather resembles Crete and much of the high jebel is given over to agriculture. It was a key area for food production during the period of Italian colonisation and the simple, low-built farmhouses from the 1930s still stand tòday amidst fruit and cereal farms. The whole area has a charming, rustic feel to it and the towns have hung on to their character rather more successfully than in other parts of Libya.

### TOCRA
The Greek city of Tocra (known in ancient times as Teuchira) is 70 km north-east of Benghazi on the coast road. Founded around 510 BC, Tocra was one of the first ports settled from Cyrene. It was renamed Arsinoe, after the wife of Ptolemy II, and later it was known as Cleopatris after the daughter of Cleopatra and Mark Antony. From the time of the Ptolemies, the city shared a similar history with its sister city Ptolemais, 37 km farther along the coast and known today as Tolmeita.

The new village is of no interest and has no facilities for visitors, but the old village square and surrounding area are quite charming. The old village is off the main road down a turning with a large pigeon house on the corner. The old village square is about one km down the road.

The entrance to the ruins of the original city is through the gates of the old Turkish fort, down a turning to the north-east of the square. The fort appears to have been built on the foundations of a much earlier church or temple, and there are some tombs carved into the side of a sunken pit nearby. The walls of the city have been partially excavated and within their circumference can be seen the remains of two Christian churches and

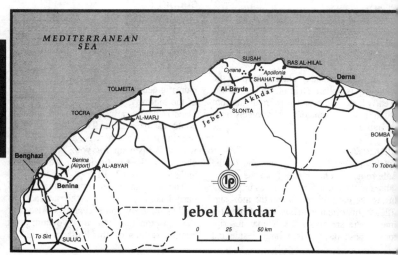

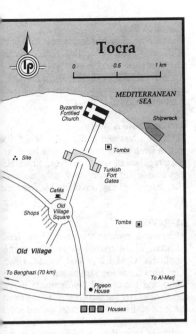

**Tocra**

partially excavated and it is spread over quite a large area. From the main road, you pass through the modern village and then along the streets of the old, which now has an air of abandonment, although a few houses still appear to be occupied.

### Information

**Money** There is a bank on the old harbour, close to the museum, which looks disused but is nonetheless open for business.

**Post & Telecommunications** The post office is just 100 metres from the museum along the main street of the old village. You can also make telephone calls from here.

### Things to See

The museum is on the right at the end of the road through the old village. Both the museum and the site are open from 8 am to 5 pm daily except Friday. The museum has

large, Hellenistic colonnaded courtyard and portico.

The site is open daily except Friday, from 8 am to 5 pm, and the entrance fee is 0.25 LD.

### Getting There & Away

Local buses and shared taxis serve Tocra from Benghazi. If you take a taxi, the driver will take you to the ruins for a small extra charge, but be sure to arrange your return or onward journey as there is nowhere to stay at Tocra unless you are camping.

## TOLMEITA

Farther east along the coast from Tocra is Tolmeita (formerly known as Ptolemais), probably the more rewarding site of the two. It is situated on an attractive stretch of coast fringed by palm trees. The beach here is open and often deserted, with good bathing and soft sand.

As for the site, again it has been only

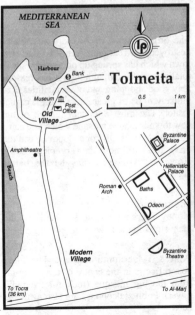

**Tolmeita**

LIBYA

a good collection of statues and carvings, mostly dating from the Greek period, and some mosaics.

From the museum, the entrance to the site is around to the right if you follow the road. Several notable buildings at the site have been excavated, including a Hellenistic palace, the forum and a monumental street with statues, inscriptions and fountains along its way.

Some of the other important monuments are not yet excavated, and the site, as a whole, can present a challenge to the imagination. It is worth persevering to see the excavated buildings listed above, even though it is quite a hike round the site.

### Getting There & Away

The local bus service will take you as far as the new village centre, and services from Benghazi are quite frequent. If you take a shared taxi you will have to pay a bit extra to be taken as far as the ruins, or otherwise expect a walk of two km.

### AL-MARJ

The original town of Al-Marj was totally destroyed by an earthquake in 1963. The new town which has sprung up on a nearby site is totally modern and, although it has reasonably good shopping and other facilities, it is unlikely to be of great interest to the casual visitor. The most dominant feature of the new town is a huge mosque which you can't miss. Al-Marj is OK for a stopover, and the drive from Tolmeita is very picturesque. However, Al-Bayda may be the better choice.

### Information

**Money** There are a couple of banks on the main street in the new town.

**Post & Telecommunications** The main post office is in the centre of town, not far from the big mosque (look for the radio tower). Public telephones are also available here.

### Places to Stay

The only hotel in Al-Marj is near the centre of the new town. It is called, rather predict ably, the *Al-Marj Hotel* (☎ 067-2700) Rooms cost 15 LD. There is also a restauran and café on the premises but the whole place is a bit run-down.

### Getting There & Away

There is a bus and taxi station about 500 metres from the big mosque. The buses are quite regular but run to no fixed timetable they tend to leave quite early in the morning The taxis run all day, travelling both east and west.

### AL-BAYDA

Al-Bayda is right in the heart of the Jebel Akhdar, close to the sites of Cyrene, Apollonia, Gasr Libya and Slonta. Under King Idris it was the administrative centre of Libya and the seat of his Sennussi movement. After the Italians controlled the town, the local resistance movement moved south to Kufra and Jaghboub. There are still many buildings from the colonial period in Al-Bayda, including the town's only hotel. The place still has strong religious connections and an Islamic university is based here.

The town is reasonably well supplied with facilities and there are definitely more restaurants and shops than at Al-Marj. Altogether, it has a more pleasant feel to it than Al-Marj.

### Information

**Money** The two banks in Al-Bayda are on the main street, Sharia Al-Aruba, both about 200 metres from the hotel. The Jamahiriya Bank is to the east of the hotel and the Atijani Bank is to the west.

**Post & Telecommunications** The post office is 500 metres to the west of the hotel, and, as usual, is easily spotted by the communications tower. The public telephones are in the same building.

### Places to Stay & Eat

The only hotel is the *Funduq Gasr Al-Bayda*

☎ 084-23455/9) on the main street. It is a large Art Deco building from the Italian period. It still has a lot of the original fixtures and fittings but the beds are a bit on the saggy side. Rooms cost 12/17 LD for singles/doubles; they are all air-conditioned and some have TV. There is a restaurant where the fixed-price menu for lunch or dinner costs 12 LD and, for a blowout, the à la carte menu costs up to 30 LD.

There are half a dozen restaurants within walking distance of the hotel. Almost opposite it is the *Riyadh Assalem Restaurant*, which serves standard fare. Past the bus and taxi stand is the *Babel Restaurant*, which seems to be very popular but closes quite early at around 10 pm, as do most of the other places. The only one open late is the recommended *Azzayad Restaurant* on Sharia Omar al-Mukhtar. This is a small Egyptian café serving delicious, spicy wrapped pizzas for a very modest sum. Another cheap place is the *Beirut Restaurant*, where you can get a substantial meal for about 3 LD. In all of these places a can of soft drink costs as much as the meal itself, so you can halve your bill by drinking water.

### Getting There & Away
The bus stand is on the main street near the big post office tower. There are two buses a day from Benghazi, both departing at 11.30 am and returning at 3.30 pm. Collect taxis leave from the same place and serve all the main destinations in the region. Buses for Shahat (Cyrene) depart hourly throughout the day until about 5 pm. In addition, through buses going east and west usually stop at Al-Bayda but they have no fixed timetables.

### GASR LIBYA
Gasr Libya, 25 km west of Al-Bayda, is well worth a visit. There is a Turkish fort, visible from the road, and a Byzantine church with a mosaic floor *in situ*. The main reason for visiting the site, however, is to see the wonderful collection of 42 square **mosaic panels** which were discovered nearby and are now mounted in a museum on the site. They originally came from the floor of a basilica and depict a wide and interesting range of subjects. The panels are in beautiful condition, and one depicts the only known representation of the Pharos Lighthouse at Alexandria, one of the wonders of the ancient world. The mosaics date from the early 6th century and they indicate the presence of a wealthy and prominent Christian community at that time, although little is known of the specific history of the place.

The site is open daily from 7.30 am to 5.30 pm (Friday from 9 am to 2 pm). The entrance is 0.25 LD. Unhappily, no photography is allowed.

### Getting There & Away
The best way is to take a taxi from Al-Bayda, as buses are few and far between. If you are coming from either direction by bus get the driver to drop you on the main road, not in the village. Don't take the turning into the village but continue west, branch off to the right at a line of houses and then take the right-hand turning. The fort is about one km to the left at a road sign. It is quite a long walk from the main road. There are no shops or refreshments available at the site, so take what you need with you.

### RAS AL-HAMMAMAH & AL-HANIYA
These are both excellent beaches, little used except on Fridays when local families drive up from the towns. Ras al-Hammamah is a tiny village 22 km from Al-Bayda. There is one shop selling only the most basic provisions quite close to the beach, but there are no shops or other facilities in the village apart from a clinic. There is no shade on the beach, which is a mixture of soft sand and rock pools. The swimming is excellent and clean, but you need to be self-sufficient.

Farther along the coast, 15 km south-west from Ras al-Hammamah, there is an even more wonderful beach at Al-Haniya. A sandy track running off the road leads to the beach. At the time of writing there was some construction going on at the beach, and clearly plans are afoot to turn it into a beach resort with accommodation and facilities. At the moment it is a large, sandy bay with clean

LIBYA

bathing, but without shade or refreshments. The road beyond Al-Haniya is currently under construction and will eventually link up with Tolmeita to the west and Susah (Apollonia) to the east. There are a number of unnamed and deserted sandy bays on this stretch of coast, some of which are visible from the road. You obviously need your own vehicle to visit these.

### Getting There & Away
Visiting these places without your own car would be a hassle but not impossible. If you are going for a day excursion it is possible to take a taxi from Al-Bayda and then arrange for the driver to pick you up at an arranged time, but you would need to negotiate the price beforehand. These beaches are not on any regular bus route, but once the resort of Al-Haniya is up and running the situation could change. Because of the remoteness of these locations, it is vital to take water and food with you and to bear in mind that there is no natural shade.

### SLONTA
South of Al-Bayda, about 24 km away on the south jebel road, is the small village of Slonta. The village itself is uninteresting, but its tiny archaeological site is of great importance, as it contains the only significant pre-Islamic Libyan artefact yet discovered – an exquisitely carved temple.

The site is at the top of the village (just follow the road up as far as you can go). Look out for an iron gate and an enclosure of chicken wire. The gate appears to be locked, but in fact it isn't – just push it open. Inside there is an abundance of huddled, carved figures, of both humans and animals, which are quite unique and rather lovely. The site was obviously a place of worship, but little is known about its cult. There are probably other sites nearby but none have yet been excavated. A facsimile of the carvings can be seen in the Tripoli Museum.

### Getting There & Away
There are taxis, either shared or private, serving the smaller villages in the jebel, and

this is the only practical way to get there. Al-Bayda is the nearest point from which you can pick up a taxi. As the site is small and can be viewed in a short time, it is better to get the driver to wait for you, otherwise you may find yourself stuck.

## CYRENE
Generally considered the second most important site in Libya after Leptis Magna, Cyrene is a must see. It is the most splendidly preserved of the Greek cities of Cyrenaica, known as the pentapolis, and its buildings were originally modelled on those at Delphi. Apart from the delicious Greek ruins, its location high on a bluff overlooking a plateau across to the sea is quite stunning. The city covers a huge area and is still only partly excavated. Not many world-heritage sites are still in this rather romantic condition; mosaics can still be discovered underfoot and priceless statues are often covered with creepers. Enough of the city has been resurrected to give the visitor an impression of how it originally appeared but without the over-restored air that detracts from many classical sites. Cyrene still has very few visitors and correspondingly few facilities. It is nonetheless a site which deserves at least a whole day, if not a few.

The modern village of **Shahat** has few, if any, diversions. The old houses near the ruins have been abandoned for the modern comforts of the new town, which is a pretty characterless place. But with Cyrene and all its magic nearby, who can complain?

### History
The city owes its name to the nymph Cyrene, known in Greek as Kurana. It was founded by a group of Greek immigrants who had fled from the island of Thera (Santorini). The date generally agreed upon for this event is 631 BC, but the historical facts are somewhat shrouded in legend. It is known that Thera at that time was suffering from a severe drought and emigration seemed to be the only solution.

Legend states that before setting out, the leaders of Thera consulted the Oracle of

Delphi and were advised to head for Libya. The leader of this expedition was Battus, who became the first king of Cyrene. The original party of about 200 set sail from Thera and landed at a small island called Platea in the Gulf of Bomba. This first settlement was not a success, as there was no water and very little land. They then moved to the mainland and again set up in a rather arid area. Finally, the local Libyan tribes pointed them in the right direction and helped them to settle in the favourable location which became Cyrene.

King Battus I ruled over the tiny community for 40 years, and during that time the nucleus of the future great city took shape. Battus was buried in what was to become the agora, and the Temple of Apollo was dedicated close to the spring which was named after the nymph Cyrene. The city flourished, and was soon attracting large numbers of Greek settlers. The dynasty of Battus lasted until 331 BC, encompassing a golden age of considerable power and prosperity for the city. At its height, it was a seat of culture and learning which rivalled Athens and Rome.

One of the city's most important exports was the silphium plant (now extinct), which was highly prized for its medicinal properties. Descriptions of these properties are rather extravagant but they indicate that it was used as a purgative and antiseptic. The plant was so highly regarded that its image appeared on the city's coinage.

With Barka, Berenice, Tocra and Apollonia, Cyrene was a member of the pentapolis, a federation of five cities which traded together and shared a common coinage.

When Alexander the Great took Egypt in 331 BC, he travelled to the Cyrenaican border and was met by ambassadors bearing gifts. Satisfied with this show of friendship he never set foot in Cyrene and headed south to consult the oracle of Zeus Ammon at Siwa, where he was promised world domination by Thursday.

Following Alexander's death, the Greek world fragmented and Cyrene came under attack from Egypt and fell under the rule of the Ptolemies. It was not until 75 BC, follow-ing the battle of Actium, that the pentapolis became part of the Roman empire. The period following the Roman takeover was generally marked by reconstruction and peace. This peace was shattered by the Jewish revolt in 115 AD, the effects of which were devastating. There was a large Jewish community in Cyrenaica at the time and, following the destruction of the Temple in Jerusalem, there was widespread disruption throughout the Middle East. Many of Cyrene's public buildings suffered significant damage during the revolt, and the number of civilian casualties was huge.

The city never fully recovered, despite efforts by the emperor Hadrian to reconstruct the buildings and repopulate the city. By the 4th century, Cyrene and the other cities of the pentapolis were virtually deserted. The city lay unexcavated until the Italians began work during the 1920s and '30s.

## Information

Downtown Shahat can be explored in about five minutes flat. The main road through the modern village passes a bank, a post office and a couple of shops, and there's not much else to say about the place. The only reason for visiting Shahat is to see the ruins and enjoy the pleasant setting.

The site itself is open from 7.30 am to 5.30 pm daily except Monday, and is closed on Friday from 12.30 to 2 pm. The entrance fee is 0.25 LD.

## The Ruins

The site is large and set out on several levels. There are many monuments to see and the following is a brief guide to the most interesting of them, although the list is by no means exhaustive. A more detailed guidebook can be bought from the ticket office at the site.

The best route is to start from the top of the hill, near the modern village of Shahat, and work your way down. Those with only a very short amount of time can enter by the northern gate to explore the lower ruins and enjoy the spectacular view from the escarpment.

LIBYA

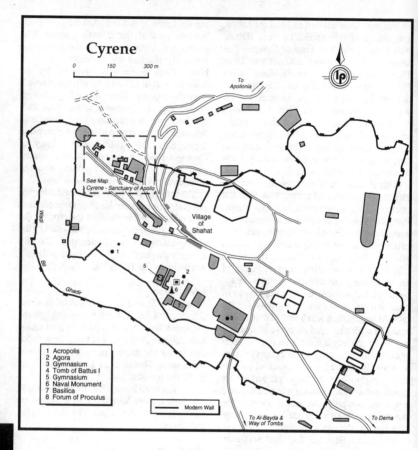

**Cyrene**

0    150    300 m

To
Apollonia

See Map
Cyrene - Sanctuary of Apollo

Village
of
Shahat

1  Acropolis
2  Agora
3  Gymnasium
4  Tomb of Battus I
5  Gymnasium
6  Naval Monument
7  Basilica
8  Forum of Proculus

—— Modern Wall

To Al-Bayda &
Way of Tombs

To Derna

LIBYA

**Agora** This was the principal square of a Greek city, corresponding to the Roman forum. Around this area were most of the important civic buildings and the space would probably also have been used as a market. The remains of many temples can be seen, along with fragments of statues and mosaics.

**Tomb of Battus I** The founder of the colony has the rare honour of being buried not only within the city walls, but in the middle of the principal square. His burial chamber can be reached by descending some steps. In the

chamber is an altar which would have been used for the sacrifice of animals.

**Gymnasium** This Greek building was used, not surprisingly, for exercise. Built around a courtyard, it would have been used by the city's elite youth for training programs, rather like an up-market health club.

**Naval Monument** Also in the agora area is this stylised ship of war dating from the 3rd century BC. A winged victory figure was previously affixed to its prow.

**Acropolis** Standing on the highest peak of the hill, probably selected early on as a point of defence, these remains date from the earliest Greek times, with later additions by the Ptolemies who kept a garrison there. On the northern side there are the remains of a Temple of Isis.

**Forum of Proculus** This large building is heavily colonnaded with Doric columns supporting a frieze. The building is large and impressive but it lacks the grace of the earlier buildings. Nearby is the **Street of Caryatids**, which is unfortunately very damaged with most of the figures lying face down on the ground.

**Temple of Apollo** On the lower levels of the city is the Sanctuary of Apollo with its Sacred Fountain. This is the earliest temple at Cyrene; the foundations date from around the 7th century BC, and it was rebuilt during

the 4th century BC. It was destroyed during the Jewish revolt and what you see now is essentially a later Roman building in the Greek Doric style.

**Greek Propylaea** This is a Greek gateway to the sanctuary area, with four Doric columns supporting an architrave and cornice.

**Temple of the Three Generals** Close to the Greek Propylaea is this temple which was initially dedicated to the victory of three generals in the 4th century, and was later dedicated to the emperor Tiberius. The names of the generals can be deciphered on the frieze, and the temple has some fine carving around the doorway.

**Theatre** This Roman theatre in the Greek style was probably erected on the site of an earlier Greek structure. Poised on the edge of the hill, with a sheer drop behind the stage,

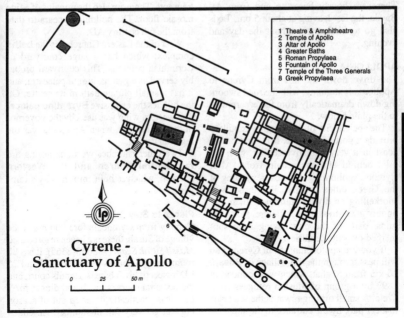

1 Theatre & Amphitheatre
2 Temple of Apollo
3 Altar of Apollo
4 Greater Baths
5 Roman Propylaea
6 Fountain of Apollo
7 Temple of the Three Generals
8 Greek Propylaea

**Cyrene -
Sanctuary of Apollo**

0    25    50 m

this monument provides good views down the hill and across towards the sea.

**Necropolis** Tombs from Cyrene cover a vast area around the site. A concentration of carved rock tombs can be seen going down the hill towards Apollonia. These tombs were later used by nomads for habitation, some of them being quite spacious.

### Places to Stay

The only place to stay in Shahat is the *hostel* (☎ 2102), which is very close to the ruins. To find it, follow the road to the entrance to the site and you will see two columns straight ahead of you. Take the turning on your left and then turn left again. The hostel is the grey building on the left. It is very badly signposted, but the entrance is marked by a picture of three copies of the *Green Book*. It is advisable to phone ahead in summer as it can get very full.

### Getting There & Away

There are hourly buses to and from Al-Bayda, the last leaving at about 5 pm. Taxis also go to Shahat throughout the day and evening.

### APOLLONIA

The drive down the hill from Cyrene to Apollonia is stunning, with the road swooping down dramatically from the escarpment to the plain below.

The ancient city of Apollonia was built to provide a port for Cyrene. It is right on the coast in a very attractive setting, with the hills behind and the sea in front. After Cyrene, Apollonia is the most rewarding of the Greek cities to visit. For those with snorkelling or diving equipment there are underwater ruins just offshore from the ruins, parts of the city having been submerged over the centuries.

If you are approaching from Cyrene you will pass through the tiny village of **Susah**, 20 km from Shahat, which was founded in 1897 by a group of Muslim refugees from Crete. A small turning towards the sea leads to a car park by the entrance to the site.

There is a small **museum** in the centre of the old section of Susah. It has a small but interesting collection of Greek funerary statues and some mosaics from Apollonia and nearby Ras al-Hilal. There is also a charming collection of miniature offering figures.

The Apollonia site is open daily except Monday, and there are several important monuments. The first is the **Extramural Church**, which is on the Derna road opposite the ruins. Crossing the road to the site, you can see that the mighty walls of the city are quite well preserved.

At the far eastern end of the site and also outside the walls is the **theatre**, carved into the rock abutting the ramparts of the city. Returning back along the coast there is an unexcavated **acropolis**, some large vaulted cisterns and the remains of Byzantine houses. The main street of the city passes an impressive structure, the **Eastern Church**, which has huge columns of cipolin marble dividing the nave and aisles and forming transepts. There are also the remains of a fine mosaic floor. The building appears to date from the 6th century AD.

West of the Eastern Church lies the **baths** complex, which has a large courtyard of Corinthian columns. This courtyard probably served as a gymnasium or palaestra, and it has a small plunge bath in its centre. On the hill lies the extensive **Byzantine palace**. The western wing was used by the governor in the 6th century, when Apollonia was the regional capital.

Two other churches worth exploring are the **Central Church** and the **Western Church**, which is built into the city's ramparts.

### Places to Stay & Eat

Coming from Cyrene, before you reach the village of Susah, there is a beach resort called *Massif Susah Seahi* (☎ 0853-2365). It has 80 rooms and 23 chalets which cost 20 and 25 LD, respectively. There is a tennis court, and the restaurant serves lunch and dinner for 7 LD. It is practically deserted out of season but can get very full in summer. An added attraction is that the resort has its own boat, which allows guests to have a look at the underwater ruins, only one km away.

### Getting There & Away

There are collect taxis (although not too many of them) running between Shahat and Susah fairly regularly. Otherwise you would probably have to get a private taxi from Al-Bayda. The collect taxis will also drop you at the beach resort.

## DERNA

Derna is situated around the outlet of an extremely attractive wadi, the steep sides of which are filled with lush vegetation; even bananas are grown here. Eight km from town at the top of the wadi is a waterfall, a rare sight in Libya, and the wadi is in flow almost all year round. The town itself is attractive enough, especially around the older quarter. The main square in the old town is surrounded by cafés and small restaurants. There is also a covered souq, which is well worth a look around for its local colour.

The town is on the coast and there are beaches on the western side and a small harbour. To get to the wadi, take the road south called the Bab Shelal which winds up the hillside behind the town. The wadi is crossed by a bridge which has the interesting nearby feature of what looks like the largest sinkhole in the world. Its height indicates just how high the wadi can get when in full flood. Normally the water is just a trickle and it is a popular walk from the bridge, along the floor of the wadi up to the waterfall. The walk takes about one hour and you need good sturdy boots, or at least be prepared to get your feet wet. The road continues past the bridge up to the waterfall, a farther four km south.

### Information

The banks, post office and airline office are all on the main beach road which runs east-west through town, within a short distance of each other. The hospital and service station are also along the same stretch of road.

### Places to Stay – bottom end

Unfortunately, the *hostel* listed in the HI handbook is now closed. The best of the few cheap places is the *Funduq al-Bahr* (☎ 081-26506), which is on Sharia Shati (the beach road). Although it is a bit run-down and dull, it's clean and reasonably comfortable. It is a bit hard to spot, being set back slightly from the road and not looking very much like a hotel. There is a brightly lit café next door which serves as a landmark. The rooms cost 4.50/6.60 LD for singles/doubles, but this does not include breakfast and there is no restaurant, just a coffee shop. There is also no air-conditioning.

### Places to Stay – middle

The best place in town is the *Hotel Jebel al-Akhdar* (☎ 081-22303 or 25857; fax 081-25858), which is right on the old town square. It is a lovely, solid 1930s building with green marble and a domed lobby. Its claim to fame is that Mussolini stayed there when he was in town. There is a café next door where all the locals gather to smoke hookahs and watch the world go by. Singles/doubles cost 10/15 LD and the large restaurant serves lunch and dinner for 6 to 12 LD.

### Getting There & Away

The bus and taxi station is next to the mosque on the main beach road. Like all the other jebel towns, the buses doing the east-west route stop here to pick up and set down a couple of times a day. The collect taxis leave throughout the day for local and long-distance destinations.

## TOBRUK

Tobruk is the last town of any size before the Egyptian border and, although there is nothing much to interest the visitor, you may find yourself making an overnight stop there.

Tobruk became a household name during WW II, when it became a key player in the power struggle between the Allied and Axis powers. The town sustained a lengthy siege, during which time it was virtually reduced to rubble. It has been rebuilt since the war and is now an ugly modern development with little charm. The key items of interest are the **war cemeteries**. There are two Commonwealth cemeteries: one is to the east of Tobruk, about six km outside town, and the other, the Knightsbridge Cemetery, is 24 km west of Tobruk. The German cemetery is close to the town at Al-Adem.

The town has some shops and banks and a small market, and since the air sanctions it has attracted a lot of through traffic, with vast numbers of people coming to and from Egypt.

### Places to Stay

Tobruk's one hotel is on the seafront, but, unfortunately, it's of the large and expensive variety. Given the unexpected influx of people passing through, there are reports of small 'hotels' springing up in Tobruk, but these are undoubtedly of the fleapit variety. Nonetheless, it would be worth asking around before checking into the expensive hotel.

### Getting There & Away

There are plenty of buses serving Tobruk. Some of the long-distance express buses call there on the way between Tripoli and Alexandria or Cairo. In addition, there are many collect taxis plying the route to Benghazi or to Egypt. The fares are very low. If you are crossing the border, bear in mind that there are long delays due to the slow customs formalities. The large air-conditioned buses may be a much more comfortable option than the crowded, hot taxis.

# Fezzan & the South-East

The Fezzan in south-western Libya covers a vast area of uninhabited but varied desert terrain, with a small population concentrated in wadi systems such as the Wadi al-Hayat and Wadi ash-Shatti. The wadi areas feature agricultural projects fed by underground water. Many parts of the Fezzan are covered with large areas of sand sea and there are some extraordinary lakes in the dune system north of the Wadi al-Hayat.

For lovers of the desert, the Fezzan area offers some of the best experiences to be found anywhere in the Sahara. There are beautiful landscapes with unworldly rock formations, virtually unvisited by tourists, and some of the best prehistoric rock art to be found in Africa. The tourism potential of this part of the world is tremendous and likely to be developed during the coming years, especially as Algeria has become a no-go area for tourists. However, at the moment the tourism infrastructure is minimal, and there are very few hotels and restaurants in the area. Even so, the traveller can experience the traditional hospitality of the region and the few companies offering tours and other facilities are enthusiastic and helpful.

It is worth bearing in mind that guides, 4WD vehicles and accommodation in this remote area do not come cheap. However, the safety and security obtained by using these services are well worth the cost involved. Even if you bring your own 4WD there will be occasions when, to get to the most interesting areas, you will be obliged to hire a guide. The Acacus and Waw Namus are two examples where the authorities have recently ruled that tourists must be accompanied by a local guide.

## History

In prehistory, the area which is now total desert was a much more temperate zone supporting a wide range of wildlife now only found in sub-Saharan Africa. The local human population of these early settlements left a vivid record over the millennia in the form of cave paintings. These extraordinary paintings and carvings cover a large time-scale of early human history, the earliest being thought to be 10,000 years old.

Looking at the arid area today, it is hard to imagine that this was once the homeland of the great Garamantian empire, which held sway in the Sahara for over a thousand years. The scale of their community can be appreciated by observing the vast system of water tunnels to be found all along the Wadi al-Hayat, where their capital city, Garama, was located. These underground canals, called fouggaras, run from the base of the escarpment to the centre of the wadi at frequent intervals. The scale of the construction is staggering, indicating a large population and extensive agricultural cultivation.

Despite this evidence of the extent of the Garamantian civilisation, there are few really concrete facts known about them or their origins. It is generally thought that they originally came from Egypt, bringing with them a religion similar to the Ra cult. There are some sketchy accounts by classical historians, such as Herodotus and Pliny the Elder, in which their famous four-horse chariots and long-horned, backward-grazing cattle are described. By about the 4th century AD the civilisation had slipped into obscurity, where it remained until archaeologists began to excavate the area during this century.

For centuries, beginning in the Roman era, the Fezzan was a key area on the trans-

## European Exploration in the Fezzan

From the end of the Roman era to the beginning of the 19th century, virtually no European travellers penetrated Libya's interior. In these intervening, dark centuries images of the southern Sahara had taken on the lustre of a mythical kingdom peopled by strange beings, created in the Western mind long before the age of reason and the new spirit of scientific exploration. It was thus into a truly *terra incognita* that the earliest European exploration took place. These early explorations were fired up by the rumours of fabulous cities south of the Sahara, kingdoms of unimaginable exoticism worthy of a Rider Haggard novel.

The dangers which accompanied desert travel in these early days were by no means exaggerated. The perils were twofold; firstly, the agonisingly slow and dangerous crossing of desert terrain, and, secondly, the unpredictable hostility of the local tribes. Many early explorers met a tragic end in the pursuit of their goals.

The first British explorer to attempt to cross the Fezzan was William Lucas, a member of the Association for the Discovery of the Interior Parts of Africa, whose expedition in 1799 came to grief at Misrata when he faced hostility from the local people. He nonetheless went on to publish an account of his travels in his *Historical Accounts of Discoveries and Travels in Africa*.

Almost at the same time as Lucas, a different route was travelled by Friederich Hornemann, who left Cairo in September 1798 and arrived in Murzuq on 17 November of that year. He was the first European to enter the town since the Romans.

During the next 50 years a great many expeditions from Britain, Germany, Italy and France set out to explore the unknown regions of Libya. Expeditions at this time were largely for the purpose of academic exploration and many returning explorers published valuable accounts of their findings. Not all of the early explorers returned to tell their stories, as many of the inhabitants of the interior were hostile to strangers.

One of the earliest journeys was carried out by the two-man team of Dr Joseph Ritchie and Captain George Francis Lyon, who set out from Tripoli in 1819 and headed south to look for a route through to the Sudan. They travelled to Gharyan, Beni Walid, Sokhna, Sebha and Murzuq, where problems set in. They had to abandon their journey due to ill health, and in November 1819 Dr Ritchie died. Lyon continued on alone, despite constant bouts of dysentery, malaria and infections, and he managed to reach Gatroon (probably Ghat).

A few years later one of the most extensive expeditions embarked from England, under the

---

Saharan trade routes, providing stopping places and trading centres for the large caravans which plied their trade between Tripoli and the African interior. Towns such as Ghat and Murzuk owed their wealth to these caravans. Throughout most of this time the Sahara was hidden from the eyes of Europeans. Until the 19th century, when the early explorers managed to penetrate the great desert, the Saharan interior was as alien as the outer planets are today. Legends of great wealth attracted explorers and adventurers alike, but sadly the 'cities of gold' were a mere fantasy.

The decline of the caravan trade, particularly after the abolition of slavery, meant that alternatives had to be found. During this century the oasis towns of the Fezzan have gradually returned to agriculture as a means of making a living. Following the discovery of oil in the 1950s, and the subsequent industrial development of the cities, many people gradually left the Fezzan for jobs in the main cities.

# Sebha

Sebha is the capital of the Fezzan and the main transport centre for the region. Most visitors use Sebha as a jumping-off point for their desert trips, arriving either by bus or by air. The town itself is mostly modern and architecturally rather dull, but it is quite well endowed with services and provides a good place to recharge the batteries after the rigours of the desert.

The town has some historical interest as the place where Colonel Gaddafi was edu-

patronage of the London African Society, to reach central Africa via Tripoli and the Fezzan. The three explorers – Denham, Oudney and Clapperton – left Tripoli in 1822 and travelled south to reach Kooka, the capital of Bornoo, a kingdom in the southern Sahara. Oudney died while attempting to reach the Niger with Clapperton, while Denham explored the course of the Shiati river. Denham and Clapperton were later reunited and returned to Tripoli in 1825. The two explorers published extensive and vivid descriptions of their travels. One such encounter describes what must have been the Dawada, an isolated tribe which existed on the tiny shrimps found in one of the Fezzan's saline lakes. One of the lakes is still known locally as Oudney.

Even more hazardous adventures were encountered by a German expedition. Heinrich Barth, who had joined up with two other explorers, Richardson and Overweg, wandered off to explore a high cliff and became lost for 24 hours in the desert. His thirst became so agonising that he was reduced to drinking his own blood in order to survive. By an extraordinary piece of luck he was found by a passing Tuareg who carried him back to camp.

However, their problems were only just beginning. After leaving Ghat, Tuaregs robbed them of all their belongings. The explorers then decided to separate for a while, Barth and Overweg meeting up again at Lake Chad. Richardson was not so lucky; he fell ill and died at Zindar in 1851. Overweg was also not destined to return home, succumbing to illness and dying in 1852. Barth, the only survivor, wrote up his prolific expedition notes when he returned home in 1855.

However, the doomed expedition led to yet more tragedy. Another explorer, Vogel, had been sent in 1854 to search for the expedition. In one of those extraordinary coincidences, which are too strange even for fiction, Vogel passed Barth on the road quite by chance. Vogel was later murdered by the Sultan of the Wadai, and, in what could have been a never-ending stream of casualties, another explorer, this time searching for Vogel, was murdered by the same sultan.

An even more romantically tragic figure was that of Alexine Tinne, a beautiful, young heiress from Holland, who had embarked upon extensive travels in the Sahara. Her beauty and wealth (she travelled in style) attracted too much attention for her own good. She met her grisly fate near Murzuq in 1863, when she was hacked to death by Tuaregs from another tribe to the one she was travelling with, while trying to intervene in an argument.

All in all some 150 Europeans lost their lives in one way or another exploring what was then one of the world's most hostile regions. After the great century of exploration had come to a close, academic travels gave way to the European powers' unseemly scramble for territory in Africa. ■

cated and where he began his political activities. The leader and his *Green Book* are fêted everywhere in Sebha, with public monuments and paintings prominently displayed. Gaddafi's school, around the corner from the Kalha Hotel, is still in use and has been rather poetically renamed the 'Point of Light School'. His old schoolroom is decorated with oil paintings depicting scenes from his life, although not the occasion of his expulsion from this very same school! As it's a fully functioning school, it is not usually open to casual visitors, but if you really want a look around you could ask at the baladiya to arrange a visit for you.

The only other building in town of any historical or architectural interest is the old fort. If you are arriving by air you can't miss it as it is right next to the airport. Unfortunately, you can't go inside as it is still in use

by the military. There is a small museum on Sharia Gamal Abdul Nasser displaying local artefacts, but it seems to have irregular opening hours.

### Information
**Tourist Offices** Once again there are no government tourist offices as such, but the person in charge of tourism at the Administration of Information Office (☎ 071-20251 or 26050) is Ali Aghil. There are a couple of private companies with offices here and they can also offer you advice and information. The main one is the government-owned Libyan Travel & Tourism Company (☎ 071-25834) on Sharia Gamal Abdul Nasser.

**Money** There are several banks on Sharia Mohammed Megharief, close to the bus station. These are the only banks in the whole

LIBYA

of the Fezzan with foreign-currency exchange facilities.

**Post & Telecommunications** There is a large post office and public telephone office on Sharia Mohammed Megharief, almost opposite the baladiya. The public telephones are open late.

### Places to Stay – bottom end

If you are desperate for a really cheap place to stay there is a *hostel* (☎ 071-21178) off Sharia Tarabulus. Its facilities are clean and modern, but the kitchens and laundry are only opened if there is a large group booked in. It is worth checking to see if any other groups are staying, as otherwise you will have to bring your own food or eat out. To find the hostel, turn off Sharia Gamal Abdul Nasser into Sharia Tarabulus and take the small turning just past the service station. You will see a large water tower looming

ahead and the gates to the hostel are in front of you.

A much better bet is the *Nakhil Hotel* (☎ 071-25049 or 26049) on Sharia Mohammed Megharief. It is a small place with only 16 rooms set around a courtyard. It has recently been taken over as a private business and has a café, a fountain in the courtyard and satellite TV. There is even a small barber shop. What more could you ask for? It is also very convenient for catching the bus as it stops right outside. Singles/doubles cost 10/15 LD. There is a restaurant next door which has an arrangement with the hotel and serves cheap meals.

### Places to Stay – middle

The *Kalha Hotel* (☎ 071-23104, 26650 or 27670) is a large and quite comfortable hotel bang in the centre of town on Sharia Gamal Abdul Nasser. It has all the usual facilities for a hotel this size, including lobby shops

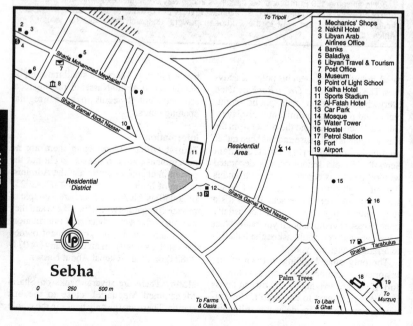

1  Mechanics' Shops
2  Nakhil Hotel
3  Libyan Arab Airlines Office
4  Banks
5  Baladiya
6  Libyan Travel & Tourism
7  Post Office
8  Museum
9  Point of Light School
10  Kalha Hotel
11  Sports Stadium
12  Al-Fatah Hotel
13  Car Park
14  Mosque
15  Water Tower
16  Hostel
17  Petrol Station
18  Fort
19  Airport

To Tripoli

Sharia Mohammed Megharief

Sharia Gamal Abdul Nasser

Residential Area

Residential District

Sharia Gamal Abdul Nasser

Sharia Tarabulus

**Sebha**

0    250    500 m

To Farms & Oasis

Palm Trees

To Ubari & Ghat

To Murzuq

LIBYA

and a swimming pool, which sadly has never been filled whenever I've been there. The rooms all have private bath and air-con. Singles/doubles cost 20/25 LD, including breakfast. Lunch and dinner cost 10 LD, or 20 LD for a 'special'.

Slightly more up-market is the *Al-Fatah Hotel* (☎ 071-23952/5) on the same street, near the hospital. Rooms here cost 20/25 LD and have satellite TV and air-con. There is a pool with a café and a rooftop restaurant with views over the city. Lunch or dinner costs about 10 LD.

The *Funduq Jebel* was closed for refurbishment when I visited, but it's worth a mention. When it's up and running this will definitely be the place to stay. It is outside town, five km down a turning off the Ubari road (there is a signpost). It is wonderfully situated on top of a small mountain, with panoramic views out across the desert – great at sunset.

### Places to Eat

The Fezzan does not have a restaurant culture at all. The only places to eat are in the hotels or the few places which are geared to the small number of travellers passing through. The few restaurants that exist are mainly along Sharia Mohammed Megharief. There are also a few cafés in the vicinity of the bus station.

Once you leave Sebha, your choices are limited to roadside shacks which often seem to exist in the middle of nowhere. The larger villages may have a café, but they are few and far between until you reach Ubari.

### Getting There & Away

**Air** Normally, there are good air connections with Tripoli and Benghazi, but during the sanctions the air service has been drastically reduced to just about zero. If flights are operating the fares are 17.50 LD one way, and the journeys take one hour. The airport is just four km outside town near the old fort. There are no buses to and from the airport but there are plenty of taxis just across the road from the terminal. The Libyan Arab Airlines (☎ 071-29120) office is on Sharia

Mohammed Megharief, close to the Nakhil Hotel.

**Bus** Sebha is well served with buses travelling to and from Tripoli. An express air-conditioned bus leaves Tripoli daily at 7 am, returning at 6 am, and the fare is 10 LD. There is also a bus which goes via Gharyan and leaves Tripoli at 7.30 am on Sunday and Wednesday. The trip takes 10 or 11 hours. There is a daily service along the Wadi al-Hayat to Ubari and Ghat which leaves early in the morning.

The bus station in Sebha is on Sharia Mohammed Megharief.

**Taxi** There are collect taxis serving the routes around the region. The taxis going to Ubari and Ghat leave from the taxi rank close to the bus station. Those going north and serving the Wadi ash-Shatti are on the next block along down a turning by the Libyan Arab Airlines office.

# North of Sebha

## WADI ASH-SHATTI

Taking the road north from Sebha in the direction of Tripoli, the left-hand fork follows the wadi to Brak about 100 km away, while the right-hand road is the new highway to Sirt.

A string of villages along the wadi leads to Idri at its western end. Needless to say, these villages are pretty remote and without any tourist facilities or indeed any action of any kind. However, they are nonetheless worth exploring for their traditional mud-brick architecture (mostly abandoned these days in favour of new housing built nearby) and for the surrounding areas of natural beauty and sand sea. There is a surfaced road as far as Qattah and beyond that it is rough track as far as Idri.

**Brak** is the first oasis town in the Wadi ash-Shatti, and its principal village. It is seven km off the main highway; the turning is by a service station. On the left as you enter

LIBYA

the town, there is a small 19th-century Turkish fort which has a small museum. There are some prehistoric carvings on display, along with some Ottoman pottery and local agricultural artefacts. The fort is open daily, except Friday, from 8 am to 2 pm. Beyond the fort there is a palm oasis and the old village, all of which can be explored on foot. In the centre of the modern village is an Italian fort, now the police station, which houses a collection of old firearms.

### Places to Stay & Eat
The only place to stay in the whole of the Wadi ash-Shatti is for men only. It is in Brak at the *student hostel*, on the south-eastern edge of the village, and it is not really geared up for foreign tourists. The accommodation is pretty basic and you would need to take your own supplies. The hostel which is listed in the HI handbook is now closed. The tourists who do come here almost always camp, which is the most pleasant option. The wide, open spaces offer limitless opportunities for a desert camping trip.

There are no restaurants in Brak, only a couple of cafés selling soft drinks and coffee, so if you are planning to visit this area you will need to bring supplies with you.

### Getting There & Away
There is a daily bus service to Brak from Tripoli, leaving Tripoli at 7 am and costing 10 LD. The return bus also leaves in the early morning. A bus travels from Gharyan on Saturday and Tuesday. There are collect taxis from Sebha to Brak. The only really practical way to explore the wadi and surrounding area is to bring your own vehicle (preferably a 4WD) and to be totally self-sufficient. Petrol is available at Brak, Birqin and Idri.

### AL-JUFRA
Halfway between Sebha and the coast in an area called Al-Jufra are the three adjacent oases of Sokna, Houn and Waddan. The road north from Sebha to Sirt is a fast highway which passes through the **Jebel Soda** – a wild, rocky landscape of black basalt with marvellous formations. If you have a 4WD

there are tracks off the main highway which you can take to explore this alien landscape.

### Houn
Houn, 340 km from Sebha, is the main town in the Al-Jufra area. It's the only town for hundreds of km in any direction with a hotel and facilities. The modern town in use today is the fourth settlement in an area which has been occupied for the last seven or more centuries.

The original town, called Sakanbinmiskan, is buried under the dunes four km to the north-west of the modern town and is still being excavated. The ruins of the second town, about 500 years old, can be seen in the same area, displaying the familiar mud-brick architecture found all over the Sahara. The third city is the medina of the current town and is 150 years old. It is now disused, its people having moved out into new houses during the 1950s and '60s. There are efforts being made to restore some of the architectural heritage of the medina, including a large merchant's house built in 1842.

The Al-Jufra area has been well known since time immemorial for its date production and this still provides the principal income for its towns. If you happen to be in Houn on the 15th of Ramadan you will happen upon one of the highlights of the social calendar – the annual sweet-making contest, in which the town's best cooks vie with each other to make the most outlandish sweets, to be consumed by all and sundry after sunset.

**Information** There is a bank on Houn's central main street. The post office is also on the main street, as are the airline office and museum. There are public telephones in the post office.

**Museum** There is a sweet little museum in Houn called Thakirat al-Medina, which has a collection of local artefacts and memorabilia. It is on the main street, close to the post office and almost opposite the turning for the old medina. As it is not signposted and doesn't look at all like a museum, more like a warehouse, you will probably need to ask someone for directions.

**Places to Stay – bottom end** There is a *hostel* (☎ 075-2040) in Houn, next door to the school and run by one of the teachers. It is about 500 metres from the highway and has 50 beds. The place is simple and friendly, if a bit noisy during term time. Look for a small HI sign painted on the wall outside. It has satellite TV and the staff can arrange for you to play tennis in the town's courts.

**Places to Stay – middle** The *Haruj Hotel* (☎ 075-3067 or 3381) is an oasis of comfort and the only hotel for hundreds of km. It is on the main highway near the Houn hospital. It is only three years old, with enormous rooms and excellent bathrooms, which are very welcome if you have been trekking across the desert. Rooms cost 25/40 LD for singles/doubles, including breakfast. Lunch and dinner cost 12 to 15 LD.

### Sokna & Waddan

Sokna is a few km south of Houn and is a smaller version of that main town. The landscape all around is very attractive – a picture-postcard version of the desert, with palm trees and sand dunes. There are no hotels or restaurants in Sokna, but a few shops can provide basic supplies.

Waddan is north of Houn at the crossroads where the highway splits to Misrata and Sirt. There are the usual palm groves and dunes around the town. Waddan is a small and quite charming town with a picturesque ruined castle on the hill in its centre, providing a panoramic view over the town and oasis. Close to the castle are some old vernacular-style mosques.

# Wadi al-Hayat

The Wadi al-Hayat (Valley of Life; formerly called the Wadi al-Agiel – the Valley of Death) is about 400 km long, running west from Sebha to Aweinat. A fast road runs

through the wadi, which is flanked by a rocky escarpment on the south and by the Ubari Sand Sea on the north. The wadi has various villages, farms and one main town, Ubari, dotted along its length. Much of the wadi floor has been developed for agriculture, and so you have three completely different topographies within view at any one time.

Historically, the wadi was important as the capital and seat of power of the Garamantes tribe. Their capital, Garama, near the modern village of Germa, is mostly unexcavated and the enigmatic ruins now on view date from a much later occupation. Throughout the region there are distinctive tombs (some dramatically large), water tunnels and other monuments left by the Garamantes, the most notable being the cemetery at Hatya.

North of the wadi there is a system of lakes set in the middle of the sand dunes. Some of these are permanent, some seasonal, but the larger these are well worth a visit for their beauty and the peacefulness of their setting.

The wadi proper starts at Al-Abyad, 66 km west of Sebha, and then passes through the villages of Al-Hamra, Qasr Kulaif and Bint Bayah. These tiny settlements are mainly clusters of farmhouses set in small agricultural holdings. There are frequent examples of Fezzan architecture visible from the road, although few of these mud-brick dwellings are still occupied.

At about the 106-km mark from Sebha there is a turning on the left near the village of Bint Bayah. This is one of the routes to Murzuk and Waw Namus.

### FJEAJ

There are a few more villages before you come to Fjeaj, which is easy to recognise because of its brand-new hostel, right on the main highway and well signposted with the HI logo. Fjeaj and Ubari are the only places in the whole of the Wadi al-Hayat with accommodation.

The village of Fjeaj is off to the north of the highway. It has a few shops and a post office. A few km east is **Terkirkiba**, which is

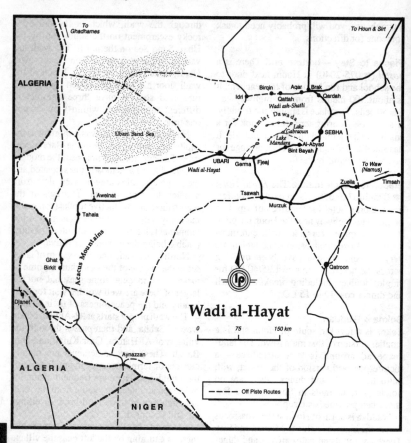

## Wadi al-Hayat

the point of entry into the sand sea for those heading for the lakes.

### Places to Stay

Fjeaj's *hostel* is large with good rooms, some with bathrooms. At the time of writing the hostel had no telephone but you could call the post office (☎ 071-28323) and speak to Ibrahim Abdusalam who speaks a little English.

### RAMLAT DAWADA

This area of the Ubari Sand Sea contains 11 lakes, the origins and extraordinary qualities of which have baffled geographers and explorers alike. To get there, you definitely need a 4WD vehicle and a guide is recommended. Contact Winzrik Travel & Tourism Services (☎ 0728-2726) in New Gabraoun to organise a vehicle and guide.

**Mavo Lake** is known as the lake which changes colour. Sometimes the water is red, sometimes blue or green. It is thought that the colour changes are caused by algae in the water. Whatever the cause it is a surreal sight, especially when the water is red. Another permanent lake is **Mandara**, which is very pretty and surrounded by palm trees, although the water level can sometimes drop to that of a muddy pool.

The lakes lie in two lines on a north-east to south-west axis. The other lakes of interest are Gabraoun, Umm al-Miah near Mandara, Fredrhrah, Umm al-Hassan, Tademka, At-Trouna (where the saline mineral natron is collected), Bera and Umm Hassas. To make life confusing, these lakes sometimes appear on maps under different names. These are the locally used names.

A couple of these remote lakes were occupied until quite recently by the Dawada tribe, whose history also remains the subject of speculation. Their name means 'worm-eater', arising from the fact that their diet was composed mainly from the small creatures fished from the main lake at Gabraoun. They were not worms at all, of course, but a species of tiny, red shrimp called *Artemia salina*, which thrived in the lake's high salinity. The shrimps are still valued locally, and are collected when in season by the women of the tribe to be pounded and dried into cakes.

### Gabraoun

Since the revolution, the authorities have found it difficult to maintain any kind of modern facilities at the lake and they have persuaded the Dawada to move to New Gabraoun – a new village on the wadi.

The lake itself is in a lovely setting, fringed on one side with palm trees and the ruined old village nestling on the other. The scene is topped off by the magnificent, high sand dune which is reflected in the lake.

One of the mysterious features of the lake is the fact that although it's as salty as the Dead Sea, if you dig a pit, even only a few feet from the lake's edge, it fills with fresh water. Very handy if you have been swimming!

### Places to Stay

The opportunities for camping in and around the wadi are limitless, but you need to be well equipped – the desert is unforgiving of carelessness. The most popular places to camp are out in the dunes of the Ramlat Dawada, around one of the lakes.

The lake at Gabraoun is the only one with facilities. You can rent a charming zeriba (palm-frond hut) for the night for about 20 LD. The huts are furnished with locally made Fezzan-style furniture and there are showers on the site. Cooks and facilities, such as laundering, can be arranged if you are travelling as a group. The site is owned by Winzrik Travel & Tourism Services (☎ 0728-2726), which has an office at New Gabraoun. Winzrik can also rent you a simple room for the night at its office camp at the lake for 5 LD a night.

### GARAMA & ZINCHECRA

The Garamantian ruins of Garama and Zinchecra are both near the modern village of **Germa**. The earlier capital, Zinchecra, is built high on a bluff overlooking the wadi to the south. Excavations have indicated that the earliest occupation was Neolithic, dating from at least the 1st millennium BC. The reasons for the move down into the wadi are not clear, but it is likely that an increase of population and the need to have easier access to water caused the move.

The ruins on the bluff consist of a fort, which covers the flat top of the promontory, and numerous houses and other buildings, which spill down the slopes to the north and south. The city was only rediscovered in the 1960s and there is still much excavation work to be done on the site. The earliest houses were merely scooped out shelters on the hillside, later giving way to dry-stone wall constructions and asphodel huts. These in turn were replaced by mud-brick houses. The promontory continued to be occupied until the 1st century AD.

After the move down to the wadi, Zinchecra continued to be used as a burial site, both within the walls of the fortress and in the surrounding areas, gradually becoming a city of the dead. The site is officially open from 8 am to 5 pm but it is often unattended and is not enclosed.

The site of Garama is situated behind the village of Germa, about two km north of the main road. Its ruins are very atmospheric, although much of what you see is not Gar-

LIBYA

amantian at all but the mud-brick city of a much later period. Some excavation work has been carried out in the centre of the city, and discoveries indicate that the site was occupied as early as the 5th century BC, long before Garama became the capital. The site was chosen no doubt because of its spring. There are legends also of a large lake at Garama, and this may well be true judging from the salt flats to the south of the city.

## UBARI

West of Germa is Ubari, after Sebha the second-largest town of the Fezzan. The town functions as both administration centre and marketplace for the region, and it is the only place for miles around with any shops or facilities. It is a convenient halfway stop if you are on your way to Ghat.

About 15 km before the town, you pass the ancient 'royal' Garamantian cemetery at **Hatya**. It is visible from the highway but you need to look out for it. Heading west, the distinctive mud-brick mausoleums are set about 200 metres back from the road on the left. They have a unique shape, like two pyramids stacked on top of one another, and

are grouped in a cluster in the sand. It is not known whether they really are royal tombs, but they are more elaborate than many of the other Garamantian graves in the wadi.

### Orientation & Information

The town of Ubari itself is small and quiet. The highway runs through the centre of town and it is along this main drag that most of the facilities can be found and the buses and taxis stop. There are grocery shops and small cafés in the centre of town and a traditional souq near the roundabout as you enter the town. This is open daily, except Friday, and sells all manner of household goods and food. At the far end of town, near the post office, is an old fort which is now used by the police.

**Money** The bank in Ubari is just past the taxi and bus stop, on the right-hand side if you are heading west. It is open from 8 am to 2 pm, except on Friday.

**Post & Telecommunications** The post office and baladiya are at the western end of Ubari, around the corner from the old fort

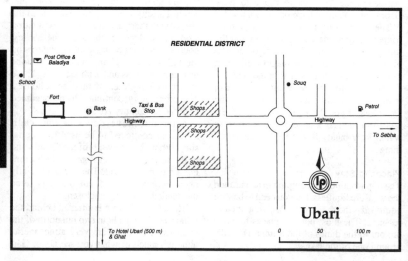

Ubari

and opposite the school. There are public telephones there with international lines.

## Places to Stay

The *Hotel Ubari* is the only 'real' hotel in the wadi. It is situated just around the turning which heads in the direction of Ghat. There are 29 rooms, but it is very run-down and has an abandoned air about it. There is no telephone but it is unlikely to be full, or even half-full. Singles/doubles cost 13/15 LD.

## Places to Eat

There are a couple of 'no-name' restaurants along the main street, which serve simple dishes such as kebabs, chicken and couscous. Meals in these places tend to cost about 3 or 4 LD.

## Getting There & Away

**Bus** There are two buses a day travelling between Sebha and Ubari. You can hail them or be dropped off at any of the points en route. The bus and taxi stand in Ubari is right on the main street.

**Taxi** There are frequent collect taxis doing the Sebha to Ubari run. The fare from Sebha to Ubari is 5 LD.

Between Ubari and **Aweinat**, 220 km away to the west, there are no towns or service stations. There is a service station just before Aweinat and a new roadside restaurant with a 'welcome' sign in English, one of the few in Libya, clearly laid on for the future tourists. Apart from that it is wilderness until Ghat, although the scenery for the last 100 km is stunning.

# Ghat & the Acacus

The Acacus mountain area is one of the highlights of Libya. Even without its cave paintings it would be one of the most stunning parts of the Sahara because of the wild beauty of the terrain. The cave art is generally very well preserved and is regarded as some of the finest in Africa. To get the most out of a trip to the Acacus you should allow a couple of nights camping, as the terrain is large and the sites are spread out. Expeditions can be arranged in Ghat, the only town in the area and a useful base for hiring vehicles and guides.

## GHAT

Ghat is a small Tuareg town set in a dip between two mountain ranges, the Acacus to the east and the Tassili to the west. The town, known as Rhapsa in Roman times, was a key trading post for the trans-Saharan caravans and until recently there were still occasional caravans going south to Mali. However, the old route up to Ghadhames and Tripoli hasn't been used for years.

Today, the town consists mostly of modern, low-built houses and shops, the old mud-brick medina having been abandoned since the revolution. Situated in an area with very little rain, old Ghat had the misfortune to be partially liquefied during a freak downpour in the 1960s. There are still many buildings intact in the old town though, and it sprawls on a hillside surmounted by an old Italian fort.

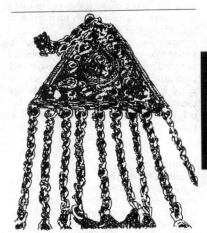

Berber jewellery

LIBYA

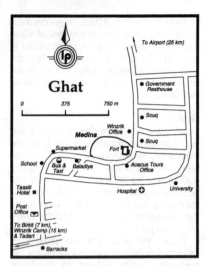

In 1916 the Tuaregs of Ghat launched ferocious raids on the French Saharan outposts across the border in Algeria, the first of many skirmishes. The fort was captured by the French during WW II and not handed back to Libya until 1956, when the French theoretically gave up their interests in the area. This is one of the few places in Libya where French is quite widely understood, at least among the older people.

Nowadays, the Tuaregs are almost all settled into urban or agricultural existences and the Toyota Land Cruiser has taken over from the camel, which is now kept only for sport. It is still just about possible to hire camels for an excursion into the Acacus, but only at great expense and with much persuasion.

### Information

**Tourist Offices** There are no government tourist offices in Ghat but a couple of private companies have offices in town and are helpful if you want information. Acacus Tours (☎ 0724-2804) and Winzrik Travel & Tourism Services (☎ 0724-2600) are both in the centre of town on the main road.

**Post & Telecommunications** The small post office is just past the hotel on the main road. You can make telephone calls from there, although connections are often slow.

### Things to See

There is not a great deal to do in Ghat apart from exploring the old medina on foot. It has some interesting architecture, including a lovely, old vernacular-style mosque, which is still in use. There are a couple of small souqs along the main road of the town and you can buy Tuareg robes and lengths of material. If you are lucky, you may find some genuine Tuareg leatherwork or jewellery but this is becoming rare.

About seven km south of Ghat is the village of **Birkit**. Its attractive old town has some good examples of local architecture, and one of the old houses has been done up in traditional style as a tourist exhibit. It is kept locked but if you want to see it ask at one the tourist agency offices.

Another site worth a visit is on the way to Tadart, near the entrance to the Acacus and next to the new camp site. It is a ruined city of stone of indeterminate age (the local I asked said it was 9000 years old, but that is stretching credibility a bit). It is called **Aghrim Mazarif**, meaning the 'city of the shaving stone'.

### Places to Stay

**Camping** The great outdoors beckons all around Ghat, and, bearing in mind that this is most likely the reason you are here, camping is a logical choice. If you want some facilities there is a purpose-built camp of zeriba huts about 15 km from the town in the direction of Tadart. The accommodation is very traditional and the site is sometimes used for Tuareg entertainments. The camp is owned by Winzrik Travel & Tourism Services, which can arrange your stay there. The setting is stupendous, especially at sunset.

**Hotels** There is only one place to stay in Ghat – the *Tassili Hotel* (☎ 0724-2570 or 2560). It is set back slightly from the main road, between the school and the post office.

The place has been undergoing some refurbishment and is under new private management. Singles/doubles cost 15/20 LD and meals cost about 15 LD.

## Places to Eat

The heady decision about which restaurant to eat in doesn't arise in Ghat – there aren't any. Only the hotel has any meals on offer, and the only other alternatives are to bring your own food or buy it locally from shops with a very limited choice. The situation is bound to improve with the arrival of tourists, but for now the dining experience in Ghat is a very limited one.

## Getting There & Away

**Air** There is an airport 25 km to the north of Ghat, just off the main highway. During normal operations there is a flight once a week, on Sunday, to and from Tripoli, which takes two hours 50 minutes. This service has been suspended due to the sanctions. When there are flights there is a bus from town to the airport.

**Bus** There are air-conditioned buses running to and from Sebha twice a day and to and from Ubari daily. The fare from Sebha is 10 LD and from Ubari it's 5 LD.

**Taxi** Collect taxis do the run to Ghat from Sebha for a similar fare to the buses. The journey time for both is about six or seven hours.

**Car & Motorbike** If you are crossing the Sahara with your own vehicle from west to east, you should be warned that at the moment the border crossing from Djanet in Algeria is closed to tourists in both directions. An alternative would be to cross farther north from Tunisia and travel south along the Ghadhames to Ghat route. This is a wonderful trip in its own right. However, the road is entirely unsurfaced between Ghadhames and Aweinat, with no fuel stops and very few wells. It is definitely not recommended for solo vehicles.

## THE ACACUS

There are only two ways to see this area: either you bring your own 4WD and hire a guide in Ghat or you book an all-inclusive excursion from one of the agencies, either locally or in Tripoli. The new government rules forbid anyone to travel unaccompanied by a guide into the area. This is for two reasons: firstly, to prevent people from getting lost, which has happened in the past and necessitates an expensive rescue operation; and, secondly, to protect the cave paintings from damage. A possible third reason could also be to make money, but that's another story.

The entrance to the Acacus is only 30 km from Ghat, but you cannot return the same way because of a staggeringly steep dune which is a one-way trip down in a vehicle. The return route takes you 190 km to the north and comes out near Aweinat, from where you can return to Ghat by road. Depending on how much time you have, an interesting route continues through the Acacus via Mathandous and comes out near Germa in the Wadi al-Hayat. This trip takes about two days, allowing for frequent stops to look at places of interest. There are **rock carvings** throughout the Mathandous area which are well worth seeing.

There are no roads in the Acacus area and some of the going is pretty rough. It is absolutely essential that you have a good vehicle and carry enough supplies and spares to see you through any delays or breakdowns. Wells are few and far between and it is not a good idea to depend on them for replenishing your water supplies. If you do use them, however, the water is perfectly safe to drink.

The area was previously occupied by Tuaregs but now only about 20 people live in the Acacus and the chance of bumping into anyone is slight. You occasionally see lean-to huts built against the side of the rock cliffs which are seasonally occupied by camel herders.

To get the most out of a trip to this area you should allow at least a couple of days to see all the principal sites. Most of them are tucked away in side valleys amidst fascinating rock formations. Few people have discovered this part of the Sahara. A battered visitors' book wrapped in oilcloth, shown to me by a Tuareg who appeared from nowhere, revealed that only a few hundred names had been entered since the mid-1960s. Needless to say, with increased tourism in Libya, the number of visitors will grow and the authorities are concerned about possible damage to the rock paintings. When you visit the sites it is important to avoid touching the painted surfaces and to keep camping debris to a minimum.

## Information

**Permits** To visit the Acacus you need a permit. This is really just a formality, and you can get one from the tour agencies in Ghat. You need two passport photos and 5 LD. The agencies usually charge a few dinars for doing the work for you, but it saves you the hassle of locating the desert patrol office, which is in the middle of nowhere south of Ghat. Allow half a day for the permits to be processed (the next day if you apply in the afternoon).

## Dangers & Annoyances

There are a couple of things to watch out for

---

### Rock Art

Libya has one of the finest concentrations of prehistoric rock art in Africa. Hidden in the wrinkled folds of the Acacus range and the area south of the Wadi al-Hayat are some extraordinary galleries, with paintings depicting life from as long as 10,000 years ago.

Libya's earliest human settlers lived in a very different climate to the desert environment of today. Cycles of wet and dry periods came and went, and along with them came the human settlements. Even as recently as 4000 BC there was a Mediterranean climate over the region, although the cycle was by that time swinging back to the dry phase which continues today.

Most of the paintings in the Libyan Sahara date from around 4000 years ago, although some are much earlier. The French archaeologist Henri Lhote made a comprehensive study of the paintings in Algeria and Libya in the 1950s and his classifications break the paintings and carvings down into four distinct periods.

The first period, from 8000 to 5000 BC, is called the 'round head' period. The human figures from this period resemble Martians from 1950s science fiction, with highly stylised bodies and large, round heads. They are often accompanied by incomprehensible objects or symbols. This style, which can be seen in many sites across Africa, has given rise to many high-blown theories such as those of Erich von Daniken, who speculated that the figures were in fact from outer space.

The second period, up to 2000 BC, shows a much more naturalistic style of painting. There are many vivid scenes of daily life executed in bright colours. The variety of animals which lived in the region at this time is also portrayed: antelope, elephant, ostrich, giraffe, crocodiles and hippopotami as well as domestic long-horned cattle and horses. The artistic skills of these painters was considerable and Lhote comments that they are 'worthy of the best schools of painting'.

The third period shows the change in climate; cows disappear from the paintings, as do, eventually, horses. The painting becomes less sophisticated. Much later, in the 1st century AD, camels were reintroduced into North Africa and they began to appear in the paintings. A number of sites have interesting depictions of the Garamantes tribes in their famous four-horse chariots.

The fourth period sees the introduction of writing around 500 BC in the Tifinagh script still used by the Tuaregs. This 24-character script can still be read by the few Tuaregs who still use the dialect. However, they cannot understand the earliest messages, which suggests that they were written in an even earlier Berber dialect. ∎

when travelling in the Acacus. The first is scorpions and the second is snakes. Although you can come across both of these hazards anywhere in the desert, they are particularly fond of the cool caves and rocks which you will no doubt be exploring. Do not put your hand into dark rocky crevices. This may sound obvious but I have seen people doing exactly that (presumably in the hope of finding some hidden Neolithic treasure). The best you can hope for is a scorpion bite, which is very painful, but some snakes here are fatally poisonous.

### Places to Stay & Eat

Apart from the camp at Tadart at the 'gateway' to the Acacus there are no permanent camps. There are no restrictions about where you can camp, just take your pick. If you are lucky, your guide will cook you a splendid local dish over a wood fire. Tuaregs are very adept at baking bread under the sand in the heat of the embers. Be warned – your meat may accompany you on the hoof. Squeamish travellers may find this a good time to go vegetarian.

### Getting There & Away

Most people start their trip from Ghat and pick up their guides there. It is possible to come in from the other direction, from Germa via Mathandous for instance, but you would have to prearrange your permits and guide from one of the tourist agencies' branch offices.

If you have your own vehicle, a guide will cost you 50 LD a day and of course you can set your own itinerary. If you need a vehicle as well it will cost 150 LD a day with everything included.

The easiest, most hassle-free way to explore the region is to book a trip with one of the agencies. This way you get everything arranged, camping equipment supplied, meals cooked for you – the works. It is a bit expensive, but, bearing in mind the difficulty of the terrain, well worth the expense for a couple of days. It is probably a good idea to book your trip before turning up in Ghat. Both Winzrik Travel & Tourism Services

and the Libyan Travel & Tourism Company have offices in Tripoli. Winzrik has offices in Ghadhames and New Gabraoun as well, and the Libyan Travel & Tourism Company also has an office in Sebha.

# South & East of Sebha

The southern and eastern parts of Libya are virtually uninhabited wilderness, punctuated only by the very occasional oasis, Kufra being the main one. For true wilderness freaks the Tibesti area in the extreme south is about as wild as it gets. Few people visit this remote part of the country, perhaps only a handful of geologists. The area as a whole is not really tourist-friendly and you need to obtain permission to visit it. The tourist agencies could advise you on this, although at the moment the more remote parts of the south are not really on their agendas.

## MURZUK

Lying to the south of Sebha is Murzuk, one of the great Saharan towns in history. Nowadays it is much reduced in stature and wealth, because of the decline of the trade route. When Friederich Hornemann first explored the Fezzan in 1798, he wrote:

The kingdom contains 101 towns and villages, of which Mourzouk is the capital. The principal towns next in order to the imperial residence are Sockna, Sibha, Hun and Wadon to the north; Gatron to the south; Yerma to the west; and Zuila to the east.

He visited the sultan, reporting that he lived in a castle with only eunuchs to serve him, a harem and about 40 female slaves.

Historically, Murzuk had a reputation for danger, and an alarming number of early explorers met their end in or around the town, including the heiress Alexine Tinne who was murdered by Tuaregs outside the town (see European Exploration in the Fezzan earlier in this chapter).

Today the town is a lot less dramatic. The castle is still there and it is open to the public

LIBYA

as a museum. Given the lack of visitors, however, its opening times can be a bit unreliable. Next to the castle is one of the most charming vernacular-style mosques in Libya. The prayer hall is vividly painted in Fezzan colours and the mud-brick minaret curves like a banana. The guardian of the mosque is not adverse to letting you see inside the prayer hall or even allowing you to climb the minaret (providing, of course, it is not prayer time).

The modern town which has grown up around the old, abandoned one is rather dull to look at, like most modern Saharan towns. There is a souq which has some local colour, but the goods on sale are mostly imported tat, with no concession to the tourists' search for authentic, indigenous wares.

### Places to Stay & Eat

Despite its listing in the HI handbook, the hostel in Murzuk is closed and there are no hotels. Camping is the only option if you want to stay overnight. There are a few simple restaurants in the centre of town where you can get a couscous or some chicken. There is a supermarket of sorts on the road to Zueila, near the baladiya.

### Getting There & Away

There are collect taxis from Sebha which go to Murzuk and Zueila, but they are not very frequent. The fare from Sebha is about 3 LD for the 120-km ride.

### ZUEILA

Zueila's claim to fame is its early Islamic ruins, and in the centre of the town is a site which is currently being excavated. Apart from the remains of a palace, it is thought that there may be an early mosque lying beneath the site. Just outside the town is an interesting set of seven early Islamic tombs where some followers of Mohammed were buried. Hornemann wrote in his journal: 'At some little distance farther from the city appear ancient and lofty edifices, which are the tombs of shereefs who fell in battle, at the time the country was attacked by Infidels'.

These have now been restored to something like their original appearance.

Today, the life of the town still revolves around agriculture, mainly date palms, but there is not much to detain the traveller for very long. The town is a bit short of facilities of any kind. For the adventurous there is an area 160 km south of Zueila called **Jebel Bin Ghanimah** where there are some prehistoric carvings.

### Places to Stay

The only accommodation of any kind in the area is a small hotel called *Funduq Hamera* in the village of Hamera, 30 km west of Zueila. Why there is a hotel here of all places is anybody's guess. However, it is not a bad place and it's friendly. The occasional tourists use it as a stopover on the way to Waw Namus. It has 10 triple rooms with shared bathrooms, and it costs 10 LD per person. Meals are available for 8 LD. If you are lucky, someone at the hotel will take you to the lake, three km to the south, where you can swim.

### Getting There & Away

There are collect taxis from Sebha to Zueila and from Murzuk, but they are not very frequent and you may have to hang around for some time. Unless you are planning to camp, it would be prudent to enquire about the return journey or you may find yourself stuck. If you do get stuck, however, it should be quite easy to pick up a lift on the road.

The road south to Qatroon is about 20 km west of Zueila. Qatroon marks the end of the tarmac road, and beyond it is the track to Tumu on the border with Niger. In the event that the authorities decide to let foreign tourists use this border, it is worth knowing that the formalities should be completed in Qatroon.

### WAW KABIR & WAW NAMUS

The road east from Zueila goes for another 76 km as far as Timsah, and then it is unsurfaced for about another 100 km to Waw Kabir. This tiny place has a spectacular desert setting but it has no accommodation and very little of anything else. It is a convenient pit stop on the way to the volcanic mountain at Waw Namus.

The authorities have recently decided that tourists must be accompanied by a guide if visiting Waw Namus. This is because visitors who had previously gone unescorted had apparently driven up the slopes on virgin pistes, leaving unsightly tracks all over the mountainside. If you do travel there alone be sure to use the existing track up the mountain, and be prepared to be turned back by desert patrols. You can hire a guide in Zueila, but the situation is not very well organised. Currently, guides are asking about 300 LD for the two-day trip there and back.

You may be thinking that this is a lot of trouble and expense just to see a mountain, but many people think it well worth the effort. The mountain area is like a moonscape and at the top is a water-filled crater, which is pretty unusual in the middle of the Sahara.

South-west of Waw Namus is the Tibesti mountain area. The route crosses 300 km of open desert to Aouzou, an area on the border which is under dispute with Chad. Unaccompanied travel to this region is not recommended, and if you run into a desert patrol they will probably turn you back because of the area's isolation, difficult climate and lack of policing authorities. If you want to travel there, you would be well advised to talk to the authorities at the baladiya in Sebha, and seek permission before setting out.

### Getting There & Away

The only way to see Waw Kabir and Waw Namus is to take your own vehicle or book the trip through one of the tour companies. You may get lucky and find some people prepared to give you a lift. The best place to try would probably be in Murzuk or at the Funduq Hamera.

### TAZERBO

Most people turn back from Waw Kabir, but if you continue east across the open desert for another 450 km you come out at Tazerbo.

The road marked on some maps does not yet exist, but apparently there are some vehicle tracks which you can follow.

Tazerbo is a small place, significant mainly because it is a source of water for the Great Man-Made River project. South of the town are the well fields which are now on-line supplying water to the coastal areas. Any travellers to Tazerbo would have to be self-sufficient and willing to camp, as there are no hotels or hostels in the area, although you can buy supplies here. The area surrounding the town has extensive palm cultivation which stretches for 30 km. There are the remains of an old Tibu fort in the town.

There is a road heading east which leads to the main north-south highway. The highway leads to Kufra in the south and to the north it heads back to Ajdabiya on the coast via Jalu Oasis.

### KUFRA

Kufra is the principal settlement in Libya's south-east. Rather than being just one town, it is more a group of oases clustered together in a remote island of habitation in the Sahara. Considerable efforts have been made during the last few decades to develop large-scale agriculture in the area, because of the abundant subsurface water available. This has proved to be expensive and difficult to justify economically. Now that the Great Man-Made River is carrying water to the coast it does not seem likely that investment in Kufra's agriculture will expand any further.

Kufra's trade links with Saharan and sub-Saharan Africa were well established early on, as it lay on a trade route. Textiles and trade goods were carried south and ostrich feathers, ivory and slaves were sent north from Kufra to be sold throughout the Ottoman empire. As early as 1895 the Senussi sect had moved the seat of its order to Kufra, reflecting the importance of the sect in the southern parts of the Sahara.

After the Italian invasion in 1911, Kufra became a stronghold of resistance. The famous fighter Omar al-Mukhtar operated from the Jebel al-Akhdar and later from Kufra during the 1920s and early '30s. Kufra became their last stronghold in a war of resistance which they were ultimately doomed to lose. Kufra was finally taken by the Italians in January 1931 and, in an act which characterised the Italian occupation, the fleeing refugees were bombed and attacked from the air. The Italians used Kufra as a link between the coast and their East African possessions, building a road to the coast and establishing a military base and an airstrip there. During WW II the oasis became a base for the Long Range Desert Group under the British. Following the war, Kufra declined into a sleepy backwater until oil money revived the town in the 1970s.

Today, Kufra is not in any way geared up for tourists. There is no hotel accommodation, few places to eat and a general sense that this is not a place to holiday. There is nothing of such great interest that would warrant a special visit, but if you are on a desert safari you may find yourself pitching up here.

### Getting There & Away

**Air** During normal services there are weekly flights to Benghazi on Monday. At the moment the service is suspended and is due to remain so for the foreseeable future.

**Bus** There are frequent air-conditioned express buses serving Kufra from Benghazi and Ajdabiya. From Tripoli they run on Monday and Thursday, leaving Tripoli at 9 am. The fare is 20.50 LD and the journey takes 30 to 32 hours. The return buses to Tripoli leave on Wednesday and Saturday and go via Ajdabiya, Sirt and Misrata.

# Glossary

This glossary is a list of Arabic (a), Berber (b), French (f), Spanish (s) and Turkish (t) terms you may come across.

A capital letter in brackets indicates that the word is used principally in one particular country – Algeria (A), Libya (L), Morocco (M) and Tunisia (T).

**Abbasids** – Baghdad-based caliphate dynasty (749-1258) claiming descent from Abbas, the uncle of Mohammed

**agadir** (b) – fortified granary

**Aghlabids** – dynasty (800-909) appointed by the caliph of Baghdad to promote religious orthodoxy in the Maghreb

**'ain** (a) – water source, spring

**aït** (b) – 'family (of)', often precedes tribal and town names

**akbar** (a) – great

**Al-Andalus** – Muslim Spain and Portugal

**Allah** (a) – God

**Almohads** – puritanical Muslim group (1130-1269), originally Berber, which arose in response to the corrupt ruling Almoravid dynasty

**Almoravids** – fanatical Muslim group (1054-1160) which ruled Spain and the Maghreb

**bab** (a) – city gate

**baksheesh** (a) – tip

**baladiyah** (L) – municipal town hall

**bali** (a) – old

**Barbary** – European term used to describe the North African coast from the 16th to 19th centuries

**basilica** – type of Roman administrative building; later used to describe churches

**Bedouin** (a) – member of nomadic Arab desert tribe

**beni** (a) – 'sons of', often precedes tribal name (also *banu*)

**Berbers** – indigenous inhabitants of North Africa

**bey** (t) – provincial governor in the Ottoman empire

**bidonville** (f) – shanty town

**borj** (a) – fort (literally 'tower')

**brochette** (f) – kebab

**burnous** (a) – traditional full-length cape with a hood, worn by men throughout the Maghreb

**calèche** (f) – horse-drawn carriage

**caliph** (a) – 'successor of Mohammed'; ruler of the Islamic world, the title was later appropriated by the sultans of Turkey

**calle** (s) – street

**camionette** (f) – utility taxi truck

**capitol** – main temple of Roman town, usually situated in the forum

**caravanserai** (t) – courtyard inn

**cardo maximus** – major Roman thoroughfare

**casse-croûte** (f)(T) – stuffed French bread

**chechia** (T) – red felt hat worn by men

**chergui** (a) – desert wind

**chicha** (T) – water pipe

**chorba** (A) – soup

**chott** (a) – salt lake

**corbeille** (f)(T) – gully

**corniche** (f) – coastal road

**couscous** (a) – semolina, staple food of North Africa

**daira** (A) – municipal headquarters

**dar** (a) – house

**decumanus maximus** – Roman thoroughfare

**deglat nour** (T) – 'finger of light' date

**dey** (t) – commander of Turkish janissaries

**douar** (a) – word generally used for village in the High Atlas

**douche** (f) – public showers (see also *hammam*)

**'eid** (a) – feast (also *'aid*)

**emir** (a) – military commander or governor

**erg** – region of sand

**Fatimids** – Muslim dynasty (909-1171) which defeated the Aghlabid dynasty;

descendants of the Prophet's daughter Fatima and her husband Ali (see Shiites)

**forum** – open space at the centre of Roman towns

**fouggara** (A/L) – system of underground water channels used to supply an oasis

**foum** (a) – usually mouth of a river or valley (from Arabic for 'mouth')

**funduq** (a) – caravanserai (often used to mean hotel)

**gare routière** (f) – bus station

**gargotte** – (f)(T) cheap restaurant for basic food

**ghar** (a) – cave

**ghorfa** (T) – arched granary

**grand taxi** (f) – (long-distance) shared taxi

**Hafsids** (T) – Tunisian dynasty (1400s-1500s)

**hajj** (a) – pilgrimage to Mecca; hence *hajji*, one who has made the pilgrimage

**hammada** (M) – stony desert

**Hammadids** (A) – Algerian dynasty conquered by the Almohads in 1152

**hammam** (a) – Turkish-style bathhouse with sauna and massage; also known by the French *bain* (bath) or *bain maure* (Moorish bath)

**harira** (M) – soup or broth with lentils and other vegetables

**harissa** (T) – spicy chilli sauce

**hijab** (a) – veil and women's headscarf

**hôtel de ville** (f) – town hall

**ibn** (a) – 'son of' (also *bin*, *ben*)

**Idrissids** (M) – Moroccan dynasty (800-1080)

**imam** (a) – Islamic prayer leader

**jamal** (a) – camel

**jami'** (a) – Friday mosque (also *djemaa* or *jemaa*)

**janissaries** (t) – the elite of the Turkish army

**jawwazat** (L) – permit office

**jebel** (a) – hill, mountain (also *djebel*)

**jedid** (a) – new (also *jdid*)

**jellaba** (a) – flowing men's garment, usually made of cotton

**jezira** (a) – island

**kasbah** (a) – fort or citadel; often also the administrative centre (also *qasba*)

**khutba** (a) – Friday sermon preached by the sheikh of a mosque

**kilim** (t) – woven rug with traditional Berber motifs

**koubba** (a) – sanctuary, marabout (literally 'cupola'; also *qubba*)

**ksar** (a) – (pl: *ksour*) fortified stronghold (also *qasr*)

**louage** (f) – shared taxi

**Maghreb** (a) – west (literally 'where the sun sets'); used to describe the area covered by Morocco, Algeria, Tunisia and, sometimes, Libya

**marabout** (a) – holy man or saint; often used to describe the mausolea of these men, which are places of worship in themselves (also *turba* (L))

**masjid** (a) – mosque

**mechouar** (a) – royal assembly place

**medersa** (a) – religious college for teaching theology, law, Arabic literature and grammar; widespread throughout the Maghreb from the 13th century (also *madrassa*)

**medina** (a) – city; used these days to describe the old Arab part of modern towns and cities

**mellah** (M) – Jewish quarter of medina

**menzel** (a) – square, whitewashed house

**Merenids** (M) – Moroccan dynasty which fell to the Wattasid dynasty in 1459

**mergoum** (T) – woven carpet with geometric designs

**mihrab** (a) – prayer niche in wall of mosque indicating direction of Mecca (the *qibla*)

**minbar** (a) – pulpit in mosque; the imam delivers the sermon from one of the lower steps because the Prophet preached from the top step

**moulay** (a) – ruler

**moussem** (M) – pilgrimage to marabout tomb

**Mozabites** (A) – Berber inhabitants of Algeria's M'Zab region

**muezzin** (a) – mosque official who intones the call to prayer from the top of the minaret

**Ottomans** – Turkish empire (13th to early 20th century)
**oued** (a) – river (also *wad* or *wadi*)
**oulad** (a) – 'sons (of)', often precedes tribal or town name

**palmeraie** (f) – oasis-like area around a town where date palms, vegetables and fruit are grown
**pasha** (t) – high official in Ottoman empire (also *pacha*)
**petit taxi** (f) – local taxi
**piste** (f) – poor, unsealed tracks, often requiring 4WD vehicles

**qaid** (a) – local chief, loose equivalent of mayor in some parts of Morocco (also *caid*)
**qissaria** (a) – covered market, sometimes forming commercial centre of a medina
**Qur'an** (a) – sacred book of Islam

**Ramadan** (a) – ninth month of the Muslim year, a period of fasting
**ras** (a) – headland
**reg** (b) – stony desert
**ribat** (a) – fortified monastery

**Saadians** (M) – Moroccan dynasty (1500s)
**saha(t)** (a) – square (or French *place*)
**sebkha** (a) – saltpan
**shari'a** (a) – Islamic law
**sharia** (a) – street
**sheikh** (a) – Islamic leader or religious person
**sherif** (a) – descendant of the Prophet
**Shiites** – one of two main Islamic sects, formed by those who believed the true imams were descended from Ali (compare *Sunnis*)
**sidi** (a) – honorific title (like Mr; also *si*)

**souq** (a) – market
**Sufism** (a) – mystical strand of Islam; adherents concentrate on their inner attitude in order to attain communion with God
**Sunnis** – main Islamic sect, derived from followers of the Umayyad caliphate (compare *Shiites*)
**syndicat d'initiative** (f) – government-run tourist office

**tajine** (M) – stew, usually with meat as the main ingredient
**tariq** (a) – road, avenue
**tizi** (b) – mountain pass (French *col*)
**Tuaregs** – nomadic Berbers of the Sahara, sometimes known by romantics as the 'blue people' because of their indigo-dyed robes, which give their skin a bluish tinge

**Umayyads** – Damascus-based caliphate dynasty (661-750)

**ville nouvelle** (f) – 'new city', towns built by the French, generally alongside existing towns and cities of the Maghreb
**vizier** (t) – another term for a provincial governor, usually in the Ottoman empire, or adviser to the sultan in Morocco

**wali** (M) – holy man or saint
**Wattasids** (M) – Moroccan dynasty (1400s)
**wilaya** (a) – province

**zankat** (a) – lane, alley (also *zanqat*)
**zawiyya** (a) – religious fraternity based around a marabout (also *zaouia*)
**zeitouna** (a) – olive tree or grove
**zellij** (M) – decorative tiles
**zeriba** (A/L) – palm-frond hut

# Index

---

## TEXT

Map references are in **bold** type